ENCYCLOPEDIA OF
Walt Disney's
ANIMATED
CHARACTERS

JOHN GRANT

FOREWORD BY DAVID R. SMITH
FOREWORD TO THE REVISED EDITION BY
ROY E. DISNEY

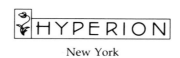 HYPERION
New York

Library of Congress Cataloging-in-Publication Data

Grant, John, 1949-
    Encyclopedia of Walt Disney's Animated Charcters: from Mickey Mouse to Hercules/John Grant; foreword by David R. Smith; foreword to the revised edition by Roy E. Disney.—3rd ed.
        p.   cm.
    Includes bibliographical references and index.
    ISBN 0-7868-6336-6
    1. Cartoon characters—United States.   2. Walt Disney Company.
I. Title.
NC1766.U52D52   1997b
741.5'09794'93—dc21   97-36101
                                                                           CIP

THIRD EDITION

10 9 8 7 6 5 4 3 2 1

CONTENTS

FOREWORD TO THE SECOND EDITION

When I was a little kid growing up around Walt and Roy Disney, and the many gifted artists at Walt Disney Productions, the constant proliferation of animated characters in the cartoons (which they used to test on me with some frequency) seemed like a perfectly normal progression of life.

In fact, it was only after I was out of college and working in the "real world" that I began to realize what a strange and magical place the Disney Studio was . . . and, as a matter of fact, still is.

This marvelous book brings back to me a whole flood of memories, as I'm sure it will to many people. They include things like seeing Snow White's flight through the enchanted forest in rough pencil sketches . . . to the time Walt sat on the edge of my bed and told me the whole story of Pinocchio . . . clear up to just recently when we saw the first rough animation of the beast.

More than anything, it brings back memories of the people behind the art, starting when the "nine old men" were nine very young men, and up through the many years since, it has always been the people . . . and their incredible talents . . . who have made it all work.

The best thing of all, though, is the knowledge that this is a book that will never stop growing. Even as I write these words I know of dozens of new characters that can't be added here yet until they mature through the next few years of production and their films are released.

So please, enjoy this gallimaufry of characters. We'll keep busy dreaming up the next group.

ROY E. DISNEY

4

FOREWORD

When we started the Walt Disney Archives in 1970, we knew that our purpose was to collect and preserve the history of Disney. But more importantly we had to make that history available for use. As an outsider joining the Disney company for the first time, I knew something of archival techniques, but I could only guess at what type of requests the Archives would receive from its clientele.

Like most business archives, the primary use of the Disney Archives comes from within the company itself. If you think of the major companies in the world, how many of them utilize their history more than Disney? The Disney films are classics. They can be brought back every 5-7 years to delight a whole new generation of children. Parents who enjoyed the films as children like to give their children the same experiences they had when they were young. If you ask most people what is the first film they recall seeing as a child, it is usually a Disney film. But Disney does not use its classic films only for reissue in theatres. The stories, the songs, the characters can be used in books, in educational materials, in computer software, on merchandise items, in attractions at Disneyland and the other Disney parks, on The Disney Channel, on commercial network television and in syndication, in literally dozens of different ways.

Soon after the Archives was established, we noticed that many of the questions that came to us were about the Disney characters. When is Mickey Mouse's birthday? How many films did Donald Duck appear in? When did Peg Leg Pete lose his peg leg? What is the name of the bulldog who was always chasing Pluto? As we started receiving these questions, we realized that existing sources of information were inadequate.

One question that really stumped us was: How many Disney characters are there? That question was frequently asked, and is still asked today, and we still do not have a single answer. How do you count the Disney characters? To do so you need to come up with some definitions first. Are you considering only named characters? Are you including only those with speaking roles in the cartoons? Where do you stop when it comes to the thousands of supporting roles, bit players, and "extras"? Do you consider the feature films but not the short cartoons? Do you include characters who have never appeared in a film, but were created for comic strip or comic book stories, for record albums, for books, or for Disneyland, Walt Disney World, or Tokyo Disneyland attractions? Because of the difficulty in answering all these questions, we have had to reply that it is next to impossible to say how many Disney characters there are.

We realized that most of the questions we were receiving could be answered by a basic list, so in 1973 we created our first list of Disney characters. We set some parameters, deciding on four major categories – (a) continuing characters from the short cartoons (this included Mickey Mouse and most of our well known characters), (b) other named characters in the shorts (omitting thousands of unnamed characters), (c) characters from the feature films, and (d) characters from books and comics, and at Disneyland or Walt Disney World. This list consisted of about 900 characters, listed only under their first appearance. Revisions in 1982 and 1985 brought the list up to date.

At the same time that we were coming up with lists of characters, we were trying to pin down other facts, such as birthdays. For example, in Disney publicity throughout the years, it had been written that Mickey Mouse's birthdate was when his film *Steamboat Willie* had first been seen by the public at the Colony Theater in New York City. But, when I checked the files, I found that Mickey's birthday had been celebrated on various dates in September and October, evidently on convenient Saturdays in the Fall when children could be invited to the theatres for a special birthday party. I realized that no one had taken the time to actually check and see when *Steamboat Willie* opened at the Colony Theater. By consulting old records in the Archives, I established that that date was November 18, 1928. For over a decade now, we have been promoting the November 18th date and by now it is readily accepted and appears regularly in press releases, books, and articles.

Our lists of characters were useful in some ways, but they were lacking in several important respects. These included compilations of all appearances of each character, physical descriptions of the characters, and discussions of their personalities. When we were first approached about an encyclopedia of animated characters, my first thought was that it could not be done. Intense research would be needed, research that we in the Archives had never had the opportunity or time to do.

As we met with Justin Knowles, whose company prepared the book you are holding, and came to agreements on necessary limitations to the project, we excitedly realized that such an encyclopedia might indeed be possible. Perhaps an extensively illustrated volume could be produced which would describe each significant character through discussions of his or her film appearances. Such a volume would supersede our barebones lists and become a useful tool to us in answering questions about our characters.

To accomplish the project, an author would have to be selected who could devote many weeks to intensive research. No authoritative text could be written without a survey of all published and unpublished material on the Disney characters and a systematic screening of the library of Disney films, and that could only be accomplished at the Disney studio. When author John Grant was selected to write the encyclopedia, he packed his bags and hopped on a plane from England in order to spend five weeks researching in the Archives. During this time, he watched films, read magazine articles, delved into dusty binders of newspaper clippings, studied stenographic notes of story meetings, and, in short, consulted every source on the Disney characters which we were able to dig up for him. Then he returned to England and began putting the knowledge he had gained into usable form for the encyclopedia. For months the air over the Atlantic was thick with movie synopses, cutting continuities (scripts), recorded highlights of the feature films, photocopies of articles, questions asked, questions answered . . .

Soon, section by section, his rough draft was airmailed to the Archives for checking. It was a monumental manuscript, but we started reading it and we were delighted with what we found. Here was a reference book on the Disney animated characters which not only would be fascinating for readers everywhere, but which could also serve as a useful tool for Disney personnel working on many different projects. There were added benefits in the book which even we had not envisioned when the project was begun.

For the first time in a single comprehensive volume can be found an exhaustive compilation of information about the Disney characters, made all the more useful by numerous illustrations and comprehensive indexes. Nowhere else can one find published so many accurate and entertaining synopses of our short cartoons, and nowhere else can one find the lists of film appearances for the minor characters as well as for Mickey Mouse, Donald Duck and Goofy.

We have been pleased to have been associated with the production of this encyclopedia and hope that it will prove as useful and entertaining to others as it will to us.

David R. Smith
Archivist
The Walt Disney Company

NOTES TO THE READER

How to Use This Book

This book is divided into two main sections, one dealing with the characters who appeared in the shorts and the other with the characters from the animated features. In both cases the arrangement is chronological, for reasons that will become apparent as soon as you start to use this book. First, the art of animation and the creation of animated characters have advanced over the decades since Walt Disney started work, and it is impossible fully to understand and evaluate the characters without seeing them in their proper historical context. Second, any approach other than the chronological would require an unacceptable level of tiresome repetition.

In Part I the chronological order is determined by the date of the character's first screen appearance. For some of the early years there are no accurate records of the release dates of the various shorts, and so the ordering of entries has had to be a matter of informed guesswork; however, in almost all cases the ordering is precise. (Where possible, the exact date of a character's first appearance is given in that character's filmography, alongside the first movie listed.)

Some characters have been grouped together, either where they have co-starred in only one or two shorts (such as the Three Orphan Kittens) or where they are essentially a sort of "group character" (such as Chip an' Dale or Donald's Nephews). When characters do not have an entry devoted to them, but are discussed within the article concerning another character or in a group article, their names appear within the text in **bold** at the site of their major discussion.

Part II, covering the characters in the features, is again arranged chronologically, although this time the major headings are not character-by-character but feature-by-feature. This approach has once more eliminated unnecessary repetition while also permitting the reader to see the characters in their historical context.

Some characters have appeared in both features and shorts, and the approach taken to them has been pragmatic. Mickey Mouse, for example, who appeared in the 1940 feature *Fantasia*, is nevertheless discussed primarily in Part I, although there is a brief description in Part II of his role in the feature. Jiminy Cricket, on the other hand, although he has made a number of appearances on television, is discussed almost exclusively in the article on *Pinocchio* (1940), since this has been his major starring role (he appeared also in the feature *Fun and Fancy Free* [1947], in the entry for which there is a minor discussion).

In order to help you find your way around this book there are copious cross-references: these take the form of "(➤**000**)", where the "**000**" indicates a page number. However, if you wish to find something quickly, you should go directly to one of the indexes. If you want to find the main entry on a particular character, use the General Index (➤**444**). It will give you page numbers for all the lesser references to that character, in addition, it provides a wealth of other information – so that you can find, for example, all the references to cats, mice, ducks, etc., the names of animators, technical staff and critics, and so on and so forth. The Index Animated Disney Films (➤**441**) is exactly that. In both of the latter indexes major discussions are indicated by page numbers in **bold** and pages on which relevant captions appear are indicated by numbers in *italics*.

Terminology

The name *Walt* is used not to imply any cosy familiarity but to avoid confusion with the name *Disney*, here used in a general way as shorthand to refer to the Disney company, the Disney studio, etc. The term *animated feature* refers to a full-length movie consisting partly or wholly of animation; where need be, to distinguish those movies that are entirely animated and that consist of a single story, the term *full-length animated feature* is used. Thus *Fantasia* (1940), which is

made up of a collection of sections, and *Song of the South* (1946), which is to a great extent made in live action, are described as animated features but not as full-length animated features.

Films are described either as *features* or as *shorts*. Disney has, however, produced what might be described as long shorts, or *featurettes*, lasting 25-40 minutes. In this book these are generally classified as shorts, but on occasion the distinction is made.

The naming of the characters is worth discussion. In some cases there is no dispute: Snow White is very definitely Snow White, for example. In other instances there has been no public mention of a particular name: it was simply the name used by the animators and, usually, in the cutting continuity (script). This applies to so many characters that to choose an example would be pointless. Elsewhere the name used by the animators was used also in Disney publicity material – *Fantasia*'s Hop Low is a notable example. I have adopted the system employed by the Disney Archives, which is to use names wherever possible, whatever their source. Thanks to this book's many illustrations, it should be possible to relate screen persona to character-name with little delay. If you wish to find out the name of, for example, that tough bluish dog with which Pluto so often does battle, look in the General Index under dogs and you will find cross-references that will eventually lead you to the name "Butch".

Mention is occasionally made of the *Nine Old Men*. The term was one of Walt's to describe those veteran animators whom he regarded as, as it were, his "Supreme Court". For the record, the Nine Old Men were Les Clark, Wolfgang (Woolie) Reitherman, Eric Larson, Ward Kimball, Milt Kahl, Frank Thomas, Ollie Johnston, John Lounsbery and Marc Davis. (Thomas and Johnston have between them produced *the* book on animation at Disney, *Disney Animation: The Illusion of Life*, Abbeville Press, 1981.)

INTRODUCTION TO THE SECOND EDITION

The revision of a book which one wrote some years ago is both a humbling and an exhilarating experience—humbling because the passage of time has exposed one's errors and hasty judgments, exhilarating because one has the opportunity to correct those flaws. One feels rather like a heart surgeon being given a second chance.

The task can also be, in prospect, quite daunting. I know that it was so in this case. The first edition of this book, published in 1987, was the result of a two-year jaunt I'd been lucky enough to spend in a magical kingdom. Memories of my travels there were fond ones: the journeys had often been long and arduous, over bumpy roads and with only the most rudimentary of wayside accommodations, but nevertheless I had spent the time infected by the place's magic. My reluctance to return to that kingdom was understandable. In the interim I had explored many different worlds through the fifteen or more subsequent books that I had written. If I were to return to the kingdom where I had enjoyed myself so much years earlier, might I not find myself facing the sort of crushing disappointment that so often awaits the person who tries to repeat the experience of a lifetime?

I swallowed my doubt. It was the best thing I ever swallowed. The kingdom was still as magical as ever.

During the past five years or more there has been a tremendous output of animated work from the Disney studio, and a new, expanded edition of this book would have been essential for that reason alone. There have been six new animated features, including at least one of Disney's finest ever, with a seventh, *Aladdin*, due for release at about the same time as this book is published. In addition there has been a vast surge in Disney's production of animation for television; whereas in the previous edition television work was touched on only lightly, now it has become necessary to expand the coverage to the point that Disney's animated TV series have been given a section of their own. Moreover, since 1987 a number of readers have been good enough to write to me pointing out errors in or omissions from the first edition, and these have been accommodated; my thanks to those readers. New books or articles have appeared that have added to my knowledge or altered my perceptions; two of these have not yet been published, so special thanks to Alberto Becattini, John Clute and Peter Nicholls for permitting me to make reference to their manuscripts-in-preparation. And, finally, those tireless people at the Walt Disney Archives have kept me posted with details of their own further discoveries.

So, although you will find much in this book that you will recognize from the first edition, you will also find a very great deal that is new. Above all, what I hope I have been able to communicate to you is the great pleasure I have had during my second excursion into the magical kingdom that is Disney animation.

JOHN GRANT, 1992

INTRODUCTION TO THE FIRST EDITION

Until a character becomes a personality it cannot be believed. Without personality, the character may do funny or interesting things, but unless people are able to identify themselves with the character, its actions will seem unreal. And without personality, a story cannot ring true to the audience.

In these words Walt Disney encapsulated the reasons why the Disney characters are *different* from those of any other studio; why watching a Disney animated movie as opposed to anyone else's is such a radically different experience; why Disney is the most successful animation company of all time; and even, indeed, why a book such as the one you are holding should come into existence. Disney characters have depth; they have consistency; we regard them as being almost real people, with real personalities, and we experience with them not only life's ups but also its downs. Other studios have produced very funny cartoons – it cannot be denied that a good Bugs Bunny or Tom and Jerry short is at least as funny as a good Donald Duck short – and some have been able to produce the effect of pathos or the thrill of true adventure, but no other studio has been able consistently to mix all three, as Disney has done in its full-length animated features, without the three elements jarring with each other. In such a potentially tragic story as *Bambi* (1942), for example, we can be laughing uncontrollably at Thumper's antics one moment, blinking away the tears on the death of Bambi's mother the next, and then thrilling as the animals flee the forest fire the next. Yet one feels no incongruity in having these three so-different emotions in such a short space of time – because that is what real life itself is like: it has times of mirth and rejoicing, times of sorrow and times of excitement.

It is because of the "reality" of the Disney characters that we *remember* so many of them: Mickey, Minnie, Donald, Daisy, Goofy, Pluto from the shorts, Dumbo, Pinocchio, Sleeping Beauty, Cinderella, Cruella De Vil, the Horned King, Peter Pan from the features; everyone could make extensive additions to those lists. Some of them are our friends and some our enemies, but we "know" them – and no other studio could make this claim for more than a few characters at best. It is like the difference between recognizing or remembering the members of one's own circle of acquaintances and recalling people about whom one has only read in the newspapers.

To carry this analogy slightly further: if a good friend does something unpredictable we are astonished, we say that they are "acting out of character", but if we read in the newspaper that the local mayor has done something unexpected we are usually only mildly surprised. In the latter case there may indeed be an inconsistency of character but we do not *know* this because we have only the sketchiest of notions as to what the mayor's personality is really like. But if a Disney creation "acts out of character" we are dumbfounded (Disney has sometimes deliberately used this for effect), whereas other studios' characters – even the most popular ones – can change their personalities from movie to movie and we hardly bat an eyelid. (*The*

Flintstones's Barney Rubble is the first example that springs to mind, but there are plenty of others.)

Achieving this effect, maintaining this consistency of personality, is not easy: everything must ring true, and if necessary large amounts of unsuccessful material must be jettisoned until the creators have painstakingly picked their way through to the version that is just *right*. Doing this is time-consuming and expensive, but Disney has since very early days been prepared to accept such burdens in order to produce something better than the opposition can even dream of, in the firm belief that, in the end, quality will out. In this it has been proved correct: movies such as *Pinocchio* (1940) and *Bambi* (1942), financially unsuccessful on first release, have over the decades earned their makers many, many millions of dollars. (Interestingly, on the rare occasions when Disney has tried to cut corners in hopes of a quick profit, as in the case of *The Reluctant Dragon* [1941], the results have been a financial disaster.) This attitude – that it is worth paying more to produce something better – can be traced right back to the aspirations of one man: Walt Disney himself. It has become almost fashionable these days to write hostilely about Walt Disney the man – to concentrate on nothing but the warts as an overreaction to the wartless image projected for so many decades by the Disney company – and critics state that Walt was feckless with money, that had it not been for the financial restraint exercised upon him by his brother Roy the company would have failed early on. This is a partial truth – more pernicious even than a direct falsehood. Roy O. Disney was indeed an essential factor in the company's survival through his strict control of the financial reins, but it was Walt's genius that ensured the company's success, rather than mere survival, and Roy knew this. He harnessed rather than shackled his brother's creative genius. Walt needed his guidance, but this does not mean that Walt was a financial fool: he was, instead, a perfectionist – and he realized that his perfectionism was, in the long run, good business.

As indeed did Roy, although this did not stop him speaking ruefully on occasion about his brother's belief that quality was a first priority, immediate financial concerns a secondary one. After the difficulties following the release of *Pinocchio* (1940) and the company's consequent need to sell additional preferred stock – the export markets, so important to Disney, had collapsed because of the war – Roy is reported to have remarked wryly: "I really believe that Walt is beginning to know the value of the dollar." An assistant promptly responded: "Yeah, now he thinks it's only worth about $1.50."

One cannot view Disney's success in creating "real" characters solely in terms of money, however. Another aspect, again traceable directly to Walt, has been continuity in terms of the animation team. Walt always regarded his animators as the most important people on the premises: for example, when the studio was going through difficulties in its early days Ub Iwerks, as chief animator, would often be receiving a higher wage than Walt himself. But Walt did not rely on cash incentives alone: he could be a shrewd manipulator of people when he needed to be, and he realized that job satisfaction and excitement could win over a person where a pay-rise could not. At least until the strike of 1941 he ensured that the company was more like a family than an orthodox studio (even today the most junior employee addresses the most senior by first name, titles like "Mr." or "Ms." being something of a taboo): everyone, from top to bottom, was an important element of a joint operation. And there is more than one tale of an animator going to see Walt to hand in his notice, finding the boss excited over some new idea, and charging away all fired with enthusiasm to work on it, the intended resignation forgotten.

Because the animators felt that Walt trusted them and because they respected him they were prepared to put up with quite a lot: in some ways he must simultaneously have been the best person and the worst person in the world to work for. His criticisms could be ruthless and tactless, and he had the habit – loathed by most creative artists, of whatever type - of pottering around the studio in the evenings looking at everyone's "work in progress". Yet, when people were genuinely upset about something, Walt almost always gave them a sympathetic ear – and they were safe in the knowledge, too, that in his view genuine talent was more important than administrative status. And he was adept at spotting such talent.

What he wanted his animators to do above all else was to create strong, true characters; that, he felt, was the key to success. (It is of note that, when *Alice in Wonderland* [1951] was received with only lukewarm enthusiasm, Walt blamed this on the character of Alice herself, rather than on the fact that the movie was a mismatch of two quite different creative geniuses, himself and the very British Lewis Carroll.) By the 1950s, for example, it was Disney practice that the animators rather than the storymen were responsible for controlling the recording of any movie's soundtrack. The reason? It helped them in the development of the *characters*. Projects might lie for years on the shelf before finally going into full production. The reason? Walt was not yet satisfied with the *characters*. And, once those characters had been successfully created, Walt as much as any member of his audience regarded them as entities in their own right: when he once heard an employee describe Mickey as an [expletive deleted] he sacked the man on the spot … although of course the employee concerned had chosen exactly *the* wrong character about whom to be offensive!

The creation of a new Disney character has always been an elusive business to describe. Although frequently one comes across references to animator X.Y. having created character A.B., such statements are in fact rarely true. Although often one can, as occasionally noted in this book, identify the foremost among a character's creators (and even here controversy can arise), because Disney has always had a team spirit, in truth what has happened is that all sorts of people have contributed ideas during the genesis of a new character: animators, gagmen, storymen, office boys, messengers, voice-actors – you name it – and for many years, of course, Walt himself. In some of the more recent features Disney has controversially based various leading characters on the personalities of their voices; often

they have used live-action movies as reference for the animators; but, even when one can point to a particular technique, one cannot say that this was *how* the character was created.

The story is never that simple – and never has been, even in the earliest days when the Disney company was little more than a few men united in a common enthusiasm. To take the most obvious example, although it is commonly repeated that Walt created Mickey Mouse's personality and Ub Iwerks his appearance, this is not the whole truth. Obviously Mickey's personality affected his appearance; equally obviously his appearance and especially his movements affected his screen personality. As always, the boundaries of responsibility were blurred. In later years, when tens or hundreds of artists might be involved in any one movie, those boundaries were so blurred as to be invisible.

The major Disney characters, notably Mickey and his gang, have of course developed and changed over the years, but Disney has been careful to ensure that this has come about through careful evolution rather than sudden revolution. The result is that, while comparison of the early Mickey (for example) with the star of *Fantasia* (1940) shows that the two look astonishingly different, *at the time* one hardly noticed the transition, because it had happened gradually. Moreover, Mickey's personality – while it too has developed – has had about it a remarkable consistency. This is hard to define, because Mickey has certainly mellowed over the years, from raucous rebel to good-natured little-guy-trying-to-make-good; perhaps the reason one can nevertheless describe his character as consistent is that this sort of mellowing is exactly what so many of us likewise experience as we mature. (All of these remarks, of course, could be applied to the other members of the gang.)

The Disney company, then, can owe a large part of its success to the characters it has created, for the reasons noted above. Its future success will depend quite probably on its creation of further characters with the same integrity and care as before. However, the company's attitude has always been one of extending its horizons, constantly striving to improve. So it is legitimate to wonder what the future holds.

The modern Disney company has inherited a great deal from Walt, not the least of which has been his vision. He was a man who seems always to have been impatient with the present, ever to be looking towards the future. In 1934 he wrote:

> The artistic development of the cartoon, in my estimation, is remarkable. We make our characters go through emotions which a few years ago would have seemed impossible to secure with a cartoon character. Their facial expressions and actions are worked out very carefully to be certain that they will not be overdone to the point of being silly. There is kept just enough exaggeration to take them out of the real and into the imaginary, yet it must all appear natural to be effective. It has been said that some of the action produced in the cartoon of today is more graceful than anything possible for a human to do.

Clearly, he implied, in a few years' time his cartoon

characters would be doing things *twice* as gracefully as any human being!

As an intriguing insight into Walt's eagerness to "get to the future", we can note that in 1934 R. C. Fleming wrote in what he clearly regarded as a mood of adventurous speculation that "it is quite within the range of possibility that full length feature cartoons may some day be made"; Walt had already started work on *Snow White and the Seven Dwarfs* (1937). Others might make cautious predictions about possible future developments; Walt was eager instead to make the actual developments (a trait he exhibited throughout his life). He was confident that the future would hold something new and exciting, that there were no limits to humanity's arts and sciences.

This powerful vision of the potentialities of tomorrow has remained with Disney – most of the time, anyway – since Walt's death, and never more so than today; for example, although in the end it proved impossible, there were plans to incorporate holographic effects in 1985's *The Black Cauldron* (and you can bet your boots there will be some in a Disney movie soon). Although new shorts characters are not being created for the very simple reason that neither are new shorts (except for children's television, but that is at a different level of animation), the list of Disney characters is still growing, thanks to the company's commitment to the animated feature as an artform. Moreover, the growth in popularity of the animated featurette – the "long short", lasting 25-40 minutes – means there will be a further crop of Disney friends to meet.

Ex-Disney artist Fred Calvert was addressing non-Disney animators when he wrote angrily in 1971:

> Because Sherwood Anderson was a great writer, should Hemingway have chosen dreck? Because Lincoln was a great president should all subsequent chief executives strive for mediocrity? And because Disney made *Fantasia*, should all animation producers now confine themselves to cheap comic strips, commercials, or pornography?

The point he was making was that animators had become resigned to the false idea that, since they could never do anything as good as Disney, it was not worth trying even to be as good. Walt himself would have regarded their attitude with contempt: the classic Disney movies unsurpassable? – what nonsense! They are *there* to be surpassed. This approach of Walt's is now very prevalent in Disney, so we can expect some exciting developments in the years to come as the company breaks new ground, and more new ground after that.

And inevitably there will come more new characters, some of them as good as if not better than the old.

But that is to talk of the future. In the mean time, welcome to the company of a glorious array of several hundred of the most fabulous characters ever created. Some will be old friends; some will be unfamiliar to you. But making or remaking their acquaintance will be a rewarding experience.

Promise.

John Grant, 1987

I
THE
SHORTS

INTRODUCTION

In 1983 something happened to Disney that had not happened for decades: a Mickey Mouse short received top billing in cinemas all over the world. The short in question was *Mickey's Christmas Carol*, and in it appeared a galaxy of Disney stars from both the features and the shorts: Mickey, Minnie, Donald, Daisy, Jiminy Cricket, Goofy, Pete, Willie the Giant, Mole, Rat . . .

Disney owes a lot to its shorts stars, even though the company is making very few animated shorts these days (except for television). Had it not been for the colossal successes of characters such as Mickey, Pluto and the gang, Disney would never have been able to raise the huge sums of money required to experiment in such fields as the animated feature; and, in turn, without the animated features Disney would not be in the position it is today.

Before the emergence of Mickey Mouse there was not much to distinguish Walt's cartoons – commercially or artistically – from those of his competitors. They were, after a somewhat primitive start, good of their kind, but there was nothing "special" about them. But with Mickey the animated cartoon for the first time had a series star with a distinct *personality*, and it is precisely this that even today distinguishes Disney animated movies from the rest.

The other notable characteristic about *Steamboat Willie* (1928), the first-released Mickey Mouse short, was that it had a soundtrack. To be sure, this soundtrack was far from sophisticated – music, plus a few squeaks and yelps – but it had one important quality: it synchronized well. It was really possible to believe that the noises were being produced by the activities on screen. (Later the animators discovered that the effect worked even better if the soundtrack lagged a few frames behind the visual images.) There had been experiments in providing cartoons with sound before, but the problem of accurate synchronization had proved insurmountable and the results had been appalling.

As they took their seats, the audience at the Colony Theater in New York on November 18, 1928, cannot have expected much more than an intriguing curio. Instead, as they loudly applauded the flickering antics of a cheeky little fellow on the cinema screen, they were witnessing the start of what would become the most important single empire in screen history.

And it would all happen thanks to that Mouse.

THE LAUGH-O-GRAMS

During his time in Kansas City Walt was busy producing the "Newman Laugh-O-grams" for a local cinema. These were very short subjects, lasting less than a minute, and dealt with topical local issues. Few of these "Lafflets" survive, and a viewing of those that do suggests that this is probably a good thing.

More substantial were the six Laugh-O-grams, which followed in 1922. These can really be regarded as Walt's first incursions into the realm of the animated short. They were *The Four Musicians of Bremen, Little Red Riding Hood, Puss in Boots, Jack and the Beanstalk, Goldie Locks and the Three Bears* and *Cinderella*. All of them were radical retellings of the original stories, updated and drastically changed. They cannot be described as good cartoons, but they can certainly be said to "show promise": there is an unusual attention to detail in them, as for example in *Puss in Boots* where the individual members of the crowd at a bullfight are animated. They are marred, however, by repetitiveness: every good gag is repeated several times over, so that it stops being a good gag. Critics claimed this was laziness on the part of the Laugh-O-gram company (and later the Disney company) – that they were using the same animation several times over in order to bump the shorts up to length – but Walt explained that the repetitions were for humorous effect. Significantly, the practice ceased.

Of the characters in three of these shorts we know nothing except that there was a Jack with a beanstalk, a Goldie Locks with three bears, and a girl with a red riding hood: if there are any prints still extant they are not known to the Disney Archives. Of **Cinderella** we know a little more. Her only friend is a cat. The role of the **Fairy Godmother** is not to turn a pumpkin into a coach but a garbage can into a Tin Lizzie: the cat drives Cinderella in this to the Prince's ball. Walt was to return to the subject more seriously decades later (➤234).

Viewing *The Four Musicians of Bremen* and *Puss in Boots*, however, gives us a fair impression of the way the characters were treated in the other four Laugh-O-grams.

In *The Four Musicians of Bremen* the central character is a little black cat – one is tempted to think of him as Julius (➤13) in an earlier incarnation, especially when he displays the ability to pull off his tail and use it as a baseball bat. (This cat uses the tail to knock away incoming cannonballs.) The other three musicians are a dog, a donkey and a chicken. The four are blamed for everything that goes wrong in town and are chased out. They pause for a rest by a pond and realize that they are hungry (hunger is personified as a demon with a pitchfork which he stabs at the relevant stomach). The cat has an idea: if they play their instruments they might charm a fish from the pond to dance to the music. This plan is successful – to an extent: a fish does indeed emerge from the water but, in his attempts to catch it, the cat falls into the pond, where he is pursued by a swordfish. In fact, he is pursued right back out of the water and, with his companions, up a tree ... which the swordfish proceeds to saw down. The four musicians fall down through a chimney into a house full of robbers, who dash out and start attacking the house with cannons. This is where the cat uses his tail as a baseball bat; later, having hitched a lift aboard a flying cannonball, he uses the tail also to belabour the robbers. He falls off his cannonball in due course and loses all nine of his lives; however, he manages to catch hold of the last one just in the nick of time and survives – as do the other three musicians, so that all four of them can live happily ever after.

Clearly the tale has little by way of coherent plot: it is essentially a good excuse for a series of visual gags. The same can be said of *Puss in Boots*, the third of the Laugh-O-gram shorts to be released. Just as the rest, *Puss in Boots* depends for its gags on extensive digressions from the main plot and the frequent use of repeated segments of action. It has little in common with the traditional tale.

We start in the grounds of the King's palace. A little boy (the male lead) is going with his trusty cat to give a bunch of flowers to the Princess, who is idling away the time in a swing-seat. She accepts the flowers and some shy kisses, and seems to be on the verge of accepting also his proposal of marriage (never has a courtship been so rapidly successful) when the King appears and wrathfully kicks the boy right out of the picture. A chase ensues, until finally the King fells the boy with a well aimed piece of stone statuary. With a cry of "And don't let me catch you here again!" he throws the boy out of the palace. Soon afterwards the cat, too, is hurled down the palace's long flight of stone steps; as he lands at the bottom with a crash he promptly loses four of his lives. Fortunately, though, the boy catches the fifth one and jams it back into his pet's inert form; the cat – soon to be **Puss in Boots** – wakes.

Sarcastically the boy asks: "What's the matter? Miss your step?"

The cat replies: "No – I hit 'em all!"

Once both have recovered they wander off through the town, the boy sorrowful over his loss of the Princess. They pass a "booterie", where the cat tries to persuade the boy to buy him a posh pair of boots on special offer in the window – reduced from $5 to the staggeringly low price of $4.99! But the boy refuses.

Later they find themselves outside a cinema, where the movie showing is to be Rodolf Vaselino in *Throwing the Bull*, a torrid tale of love and heroism among the matadors. They watch the movie (in whose opening credits, incidentally, the star's name is given as "Rodol*ph* Vaselino"), and the cat has a sudden inspiration as to how the boy might win back his lady-love and get into the King's good books. But he won't tell the boy what it is unless the boy buys him "those flapper boots" from the "booterie".

Over the next few days excitement in the town reaches fever pitch as announcements appear everywhere that "The Masked Toreador" will boldly battle the bulls. The cat is working hard putting up posters – he now, of course, is quite literally Puss in Boots. The King, whose eyes are doubtless too regal to share the posters with his subjects, instead reads about the forthcoming event in his newspaper, and determines to attend with his daughter.

The great day comes, and the cat shows the apprehensive boy a stunning new technological gadget, the Radio Hypnotizer, by means of which he will be able to hypnotize the crowd into believing that they are watching the boy fight bulls, when of course he won't be doing any such dangerous thing. However, by one of those astonishing coincidences that make fiction so much stranger than fact, a *real* bull escapes from somewhere nearby and charges into the ring to confront the terrified "Masked Toreador". A long and, in truth, somewhat tedious series of chases follows, until in desperation the boy yells for help. Puss in Boots responds by activating the Radio Hypnotizer and zapping the bull with what one can only assume must be mesmeric rays.

After the stunned bull has been thoroughly knocked around by the "Masked Toreador", whom the crowd cheers ringingly to the skies, the boy is called before the King and offered the Princess's hand in marriage. But, when the boy strips off his mask, the King is horrified to see who he is, and furiously demands the Princess's hand back again, thank you very much. Love conquers all, however, and the boy, the Princess and Puss in Boots jump into a car that has appeared out of a crack in the plot construction. They drive off into the distance, no doubt to live happily ever after, leaving behind them one lord a-leaping.

At any level, *Puss in Boots* is a fairly primitive piece of work – as were the other Disney shorts of the Laugh-O-gram years (and, in fairness, the shorts being produced by everyone else at the time). The animation is somewhat rudimentary and the characterization nonexistent, the plot is as rickety as a perpetual-motion machine and rather less convincing, and as we have noted any gag that looks as if it might have some remote chance of being funny is forthwith repeated several times in order to hammer that chance into oblivion. In terms of plot and gags, in fact, the overall feeling one gets from the movie is that it is the work of immature minds – *which of course it is*. As in any other sphere of the creative arts, it is unfair to criticize a great artist on the grounds of the work produced in his adolescence – and Walt, at the age of 20, was at the time of this film's production still barely more than an adolescent.

However, the movie is of some importance in the development of the Disney *oeuvre* for one reason: the character of Puss in Boots himself. Like the cat in *The Four Musicians of Bremen* he forms an essential stage in the evolution of what would prove to be Disney's first major cartoon-character creation: that of Julius. The big difference between the two is not so much a physical one (the two are quite similar in appearance) as one of characterization, because at some stage in the years between 1922 and 1924 Walt learnt the art of giving his characters that most elusive quality of all: *personality*.

JULIUS

The character of Julius must be considered in historical context.

In late 1922 Walt's financial bacon was saved by a $500 commission from dentist Thomas McCrum for a live-action dental-health film called *Tommy Tucker's Tooth*. The commission required Disney to hire back some of the staff he had had to make redundant from his Laugh-O-gram company, and also meant that he had just sufficient funds – when reinforced by many loans from family and friends (notably Roy) – to try, at least in theory, a new venture: a series of shorts in which a human character acted among animated ones. Thus were born the series of Alice Comedies and, with them, Walt's first two major animated characters, Julius the Cat and Peg Leg Pete (►**15**). Walt wrote in 1923 to Margaret J. Winkler, distributor of the successful *Out of the Inkwell* series produced by Max Fleischer, telling her of his plans. He hired six-year-old Virginia Davis to play the part of Alice, and work began on *Alice's Wonderland*, the first of the proposed series. However, funds ran out again, and the short was barely finished.

There were other human "stars" in *Alice's Wonderland* (for reasons discussed below, the short was "released" only decades later as the introduction to various Disney home-video packs): they were Walt himself, Ub Iwerks, Hugh Harman, Rudolf Ising and several others of the Laugh-O-gram tribe. The plot of the short has a certain historical interest. Alice goes to an animation studio (guess whose?) and is shown some animation of a dog and a cat (later to be developed as Julius) chasing and playing on a drawing-board. That night she dreams that she climbs aboard the train to Cartoonland, where she is greeted by

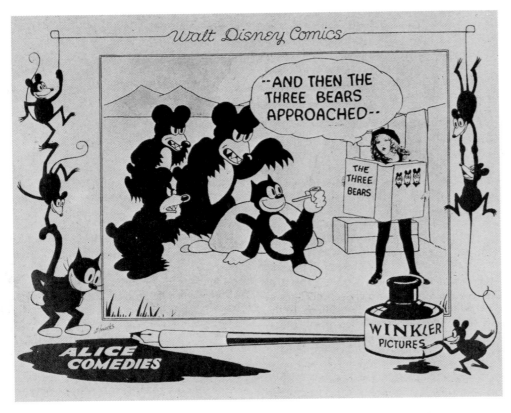

Julius the Cat enjoying some ill-timed relaxation as Alice (Virginia Davis) reads him a story. *Alice and the Three Bears* appeared in 1924.

various animated animals, takes part in a parade, dances, and is chased by some lions that have escaped from the zoo. All of this, although the Laugh-O-gram crew could not have realized it at the time, was excellent practice for the achievements they were to make in the years to come.

Still, Walt's company was nearing bankruptcy, and even the best of his friends told him that they would be doing him no kindness to lend him yet further money. The Laugh-O-gram Company had come to the end of the road. With difficulty Walt raised enough money for the fare – the first-class fare, mind you! – to Hollywood, his plan being to get right out of animation and become a movie director instead. Which, in a way, is exactly what was in due course to happen: he was to go on to become the best known name in cinematic history.

In Hollywood he tried unsuccessfully, like so many others, to break into the movies. In desperation he turned his attentions back to animation. He revived the idea of the Alice series, and distributor Margaret Winkler not only declared interest in a trial run of six, offering $1500 each, but generously agreed to pay for each of them immediately on delivery. Roy Disney was enlisted to seek finances for the new venture and, although the banks turned him away, Robert Disney, their uncle, eventually agreed to lend them $500.

Margaret Winkler was delighted with the series, and made good distribution deals for it. However, Walt's constant perfectionism meant that financial troubles still bedevilled

the Disney brothers: he kept spending more in trying to achieve a better result. To the same end, recognizing his own limitations as an animator, he imported Ub Iwerks from Kansas City. (Virginia Davis and her family had already come from there, since Winkler insisted that the child was just right for the role of Alice – Virginia, the best of the Alices, was eventually succeeded first by Dawn O'Day and then by Margie Gay.) After Iwerks' arrival, Disney ceased forever to animate cartoons himself.

Sadly, Walt could not use *Alice's Wonderland*, his prototype, as part of the newly released Alice series. His original distributors, Pictorial Clubs of Tennessee, had gone bankrupt, owing the Laugh-O-gram company a great deal of money. Pictorial Clubs of Tennessee's assets – although, disastrously from Walt's point of view, not its liabilities – had been passed to its sister-company, Pictorial Clubs of New York. Finally, in 1924, Pictorial Clubs of New York agreed to pay $12,000 by way of compensation, but for this it claimed all the rights in the six Laugh-O-gram cartoons, eight of the "Lafflets" and, miserably, *Alice's Wonderland*. At the time, to put it bluntly, Walt's company needed the money to pay off its creditors.

A further problem on the financial side was that Margaret Winkler had married and her husband, Charles Mintz, took over her company. He proved to be a devious business associate, sending only part-payments for the shorts the Disney company was supplying him. He claimed this was because he was in a difficult

cash-flow position himself; but by the end of 1924 he seemed to have seen sense, offering $1800 for each of a further 18 Alice shorts. On the strength of this Walt imported two more of his one-time Kansas City animators, Rudy Ising and Hugh Harman, and Roy married his long-time sweetheart, Edna Francis. Three months later Walt married Lillian Bounds, who had been working for him as an ink-and-painter; it was to prove an exceptionally fine and happy marriage. But the financial wrangles with Mintz went on, and on . . . and on. At the end of 1926, too, it was clear that the Alice series (the title role now being played by Margie Gay) had been carried as far as it could be. (Also, of the 56 Alice Comedies, all lost money after the first 16.) Mintz wanted a rabbit series instead, and Margaret Winkler suggested to him that this might be a good way of "losing" Alice while retaining the services of Disney. The result, of course, was Oswald, the Lucky Rabbit (►20).

The evolution of the character of Julius can be traced back to the cats that appeared in some of the Laugh-O-gram shorts – notably the eponymous star of *Puss in Boots* (►13). However, Julius' real *raison d'être* was that Charles Mintz wanted the shorts to be packed with as many visual gags as possible. Alice's was not a comic role – and anyway it would have been a bit much to expect seven-year-old children to take on the burden of being humorists. So, perforce, the shorts required a central comic character - and Julius provided this.

Not all of the Alice Comedies survive, and in some cases we have only the vaguest idea of their contents; it is therefore difficult to provide any sort of definitive account of Julius' career. However, we can look at a few representative performances of this cheery little cat.

Although a prototype had appeared in *Alice's Wonderland*, the first of the shorts in which we know that he featured was *Alice's Spooky Adventure* (1924). In the live-action preliminaries Alice climbs into a reputedly haunted house in order to retrieve a lost ball. After a few spooky creakings the short moves into animation, and we find ourselves, along with Alice, in "Spookville". Up runs a little ghost shouting: "Help! Take it off!" Alice obliges by removing his "dustsheet" and he is revealed as Julius – a mighty grateful Julius at that. "Fair one," he says, "you have saved me from the life of a spook!"

He takes her to an open-air concert in Spookville, and they dance enthusiastically together. However, such innocent jollification cannot last for long when Julius is around. Nearby some ghosts are sitting playing mah-jong when Julius lands on their table and wrecks the game. They react with perhaps excessive fury, and chase the cat and his new friend. But these two are not without their own resources: at one stage Julius pulls off his own tail and uses it as a club (the cat in *The Four Musicians of Bremen* was capable of the same trick [►12]); while Alice shows ingenuity by pulling down from above her head a cartoon exclamation mark and likewise using it as a club. After she has knocked out all the angry ghosts Julius swears his eternal love for her . . . and we return to live action. Alice wakens to find a pussy cat licking her hand – an experience that startles her. She drives it off, but soon afterwards is arrested by the police for housebreaking. We leave her sitting forlornly in jail: there's no Julius in real life to help her get out of this one!

Julius' tail is certainly a versatile implement, as he proves in *Alice's Fishy Story* (1924). We find him at the North Pole where, as he discovers from the newspaper ("GREAT FISH SHORTAGE," screams the headline), there is a crisis among the Eskimos because the fish have gone on strike and refuse to bite. Ever anxious to help, he uses his tail first as a corkscrew to cut through the ice and then as a fishing-line – but the fish are not as stupid as all that and refuse to bite. An aggressive swordfish takes the issue one stage further by cutting a circle in the ice around Julius' feet so that he plunges into the icy waters. After being chased by a huge and enthusiastically carnivorous fish, Julius is lucky enough to be hauled back out again through a hole in the ice by a friendly Eskimo. It is at this stage that he meets up with Alice, who suggests that they could raid the conveniently nearby wreck of the *Hesperus* to get some chewing tobacco. This done, Julius drops the tobacco in through a hole in the ice and the fish swallow it. As they leap up through the hole to spit the offending stuff out, Julius uses that versatile tail of his to club them unconscious. Millions of fish later, the problem of the starving Eskimos has been solved.

Interestingly, in a short released only two months later, *Alice the Peacemaker* (1924), Julius does battle with a mouse that looks almost exactly like Mickey – except that this mouse, called **Ike**, has a full complement of fingers. Julius (here called Mike) rivals Ike in raiding the icebox. After the two of them

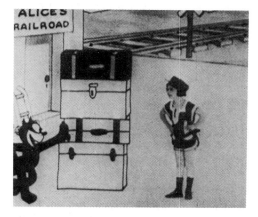

Julius took over the job of porter for *Alice's Tin Pony* (1925). Soon he was helping Alice fight the dastardly bandit Pete.

have been forcibly ejected from home because of their persistent crimes, Alice arrives on the scene and persuades them to become friends.

In the 1925 short *Alice Chops the Suey* Julius appears right at the beginning, in a scene reminiscent of a rival series (Fleischer's *Out of the Inkwell* cartoons): he is drawn in piecemeal by a live-action hand, and is joined on the screen shortly afterwards by Alice leaping out of a nearby ink-bottle. In this adventure Julius is promptly "skinned" by a demon who emerges from the ink-bottle; this demon, having flayed the cat, kidnaps Alice in a sack and runs off. Julius restores his dark coat by jumping into the ink and getting well and truly covered in it, and then chases off to rescue the little girl he loves. He saves Alice – still in the sack – from a pack of Chinese rats and, after a chase, indulges in a sword-throwing contest with them. In the end he catches three of their swords and uses them together as a propeller in order to fly off, bearing Alice with him.

Julius did not survive the demise of the Alice series – unlike Pete (►15), although Pete evolved into a character unrecognizably different from the one in these shorts. Another character of interest in the Alice Comedies made his first appearance in *Alice's Wonderland*: a little mouse drawn on an animator's drawing-board does some nifty fencing with a live-action cat. More than one critic has seen this mouse as a prototype of the most famous Mouse of all.

Filmography

(Cartoons in which it is known for certain that Julius appeared are indicated by *; it is possible that he appeared in others.)

Alice's Wonderland, 1923 (see text)
Alice's Day at Sea, March 1, 1924
**Alice's Spooky Adventure*, 1924
Alice's Wild West Show, 1924
**Alice's Fishy Story*, 1924
Alice and the Dog Catcher, 1924
**Alice the Peacemaker*, 1924
Alice Gets in Dutch, 1924
Alice Hunting in Africa, 1924
**Alice and the Three Bears*, 1924
Alice the Piper, 1924
**Alice Cans the Cannibals*, 1925
**Alice the Toreador*, 1925
*Alice Gets Stung, 1925
**Alice Solves the Puzzle*, 1925
**Alice's Egg Plant*, 1925
*Alice Loses Out, 1925
Alice Stage Struck, 1925
**Alice Wins the Derby*, 1925
**Alice Picks the Champ*, 1925
**Alice's Tin Pony*, 1925
**Alice Chops the Suey*, 1925
**Alice the Jail Bird*, 1925
**Alice Plays Cupid*, 1925
**Alice Rattled by Rats*, 1925
**Alice in the Jungle*, 1925
**Alice on the Farm*, 1926
**Alice's Balloon Race*, 1926

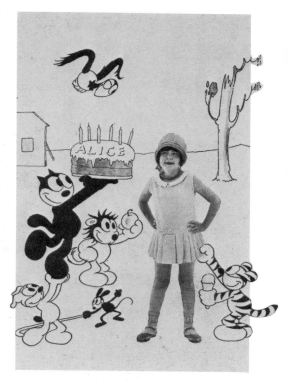

Alice, now played by Margie Gay, surrounded by some of her animal co-stars.

**Alice's Ornery Orphan*, 1926
**Alice's Little Parade*, 1926
**Alice's Mysterious Mystery*, 1926
**Alice Charms the Fish*, 1926
**Alice's Monkey Business*, 1926
**Alice in the Wooly West*, 1926
**Alice the Fire Fighter*, 1926
**Alice Cuts the Ice*, 1926
**Alice Helps the Romance*, 1926
**Alice's Spanish Guitar*, 1926
**Alice's Brown Derby*, 1926
**Alice the Lumber Jack*, 1926
**Alice the Golf Bug*, 1927
**Alice Foils the Pirates*, 1927
**Alice at the Carnival*, 1927
**Alice's Rodeo* (also titled *Alice at the Rodeo*), 1927
**Alice the Collegiate*, 1927
**Alice in the Alps*, 1927
**Alice's Auto Race*, 1927
**Alice's Circus Daze*, 1927
**Alice's Knaughty Knight*, 1927
**Alice's Three Bad Eggs*, 1927
Alice's Picnic, 1927
**Alice's Channel Swim*, 1927
**Alice in the Klondike*, 1927
**Alice's Medicine Show*, 1927
*Alice the Whaler, 1927
**Alice the Beach Nut*, 1927
Alice in the Big League, 1927

PETE

Time summed it up in 1954 when it described Pete as "a monstrous mingling of common house cat and Long John Silver". However, in his very earliest screen appearances – in the *Alice* Comedies – Pete could hardly be described as a cat. Exactly what animal he *was* is rather hard to guess: to take a wild stab at it, he was most probably a tail-less rat or an oversized mouse. Since his primary role was as an adversary for Julius (►13) to conquer, doubtless it was felt unsuitable that he be, like Julius, a cat; later, of course, things were different, because his main opponents were a certain Mouse and a certain Duck. However, he had the characteristic peg-leg and cigar in most of these appearances, so we know that he was definitely Pete.

In what was probably his first role (some of the Alice cartoons have been lost) he played the part of Bootleg Pete, an avid collector of crossword puzzles. This was in *Alice Solves the Puzzle* (1925), a short notable also for the fact that, in several places, the character of Alice herself is animated, rather than being live-action as elsewhere. The short starts with Alice trying to solve a crossword; Julius intervenes and takes her swimming instead. Enter Pete on water-skis. He does his bullying best to get Alice to surrender her crossword puzzle to him, but she refuses and a chase ensues. Alice takes refuge at the top of a lighthouse, and there Pete and Julius have a mighty fight – which, of course, Julius wins. Alice then realizes what the last word of the puzzle should be: "The." The solution enables her to complete the other remaining lights, which are "Alice", "Comedy", "Lafter" and "The End".

In *Alice's Tin Pony* (1925), his third appearance, he takes the part of the leader of a gang of mouse desperadoes. He is first

seen in a disreputable drinking dive fending off the attentions of a female mouse of purchasable virtue. Then he and his rotten crew set off to rob the train driven by Alice and Julius and containing a fat bank payroll. The gang's attempt to do so by placing a huge rock on the line fails because the train, an ancestor of Casey Jr. (►189), simply hops over the boulder. The obligatory chase follows, Julius coping with the difficulty this time by rolling up a bridge behind the train so that the pursuing gang falls into a canyon.

Another very early appearance of Pete's was in *Alice on the Farm* (1925), in which he miscegenistically falls in lust with Alice and expresses his romantic feelings by wrapping her up in a bag and galloping off with her. Julius, of course, comes to her rescue. The plucky little cat pulls off his tail, dips it in a bucket of starch, and uses it as a rapier with which to duel with Pete. Finally he finds that a more successful gambit is simply to throw the starch all over his adversary. Pete stiffens into immobility and, on being walloped by Julius, collapses into a heap of rubble. Julius finishes the argument by tossing the rubble into a stove – a rather drastic treatment. Despite this, of course, Pete lived to fight many another day.

His perennial role as evil antagonist was confirmed in at least a couple of Oswald (►20) shorts and then in the first Mickey Mouse short, *Steamboat Willie* (1928). Mickey

is the pilot of a paddlesteamer, Pete its skipper – and what a brutal skipper he is: William Bligh would have been proud of him. (He is also, now, very definitely a rogue cat, his appearance having been revised since the Alice days.) His final act of infamy is to throw Mickey into the galley to peel potatoes as a punishment for having enjoyed himself.

Pete featured more frequently during the 1930s than during any other stage of his career. Sometimes he changed his name: for example, in *The Cactus Kid* (1930) he was Peg Leg Pedro and in *The Klondike Kid* (1932) he was Pierre the Trapper – a persona he was to adopt again years later in 1941's *Timber*.

Other aspects of him changed, too. Although he always had the cigar, the animators had some difficulty in remembering which leg was the peg-leg, and in many movies they solved the problem by simply omitting it. (Another reason for the disappearance of Pete's peg-leg was that at times the animators exaggerated it to the point that it appeared painful. Walt felt that it was getting out of hand, and so after a while they "lost" it.) And in *Mickey's Service Station* (1935), although his voice is as usual deep, rough and coarse, it has also a slight Germanic touch to it, probably reflecting the fact that, even as early as 1935 when the short was released, the Disney studio was aware of the growing threat of Nazism.

At a less significant level this latter short warns of the dangers of taking your car to a service station run by Mickey, Donald and Goofy. Perhaps Pete would have fared better had he been rather less of an ugly customer! His snazzy roadster has developed a mysterious squeak but, in Flora O'Brien's words, "he's sure the trio can complete the task of fixing it without any need to invoke Pete's own brand of penalty clause – which seems to involve a degree of assault and battery". The roadster is attacked by the eager but inept mechanics and, during Pete's absence, systematically wrecked. As noon approaches, and with it Pete's terrifying return, the trio do their best to put all the pieces back together again, finding, as they do so, that the mysterious squeak has been caused by a cricket caught up in the machinery (Mickey rather brutally flattens it with a mallet). Pete finally arrives to find his car apparently mended; without offering payment other than a few vicious snarls, he climbs into the vehicle, foolishly ignoring the fact that the three mechanics are vanishing rather rapidly from the scene. Life seldom forgives Pete's bullying ways; on this occasion, as the car explodes back into fragments, he is hammered, beaten and thrashed by its tormented components.

Pete turned in a classic performance in *Moving Day* (1936) – a short that, incidentally, showed a startling degree of technical development over *Mickey's Service Station*, his immediately preceding movie, which had been released just a year earlier.

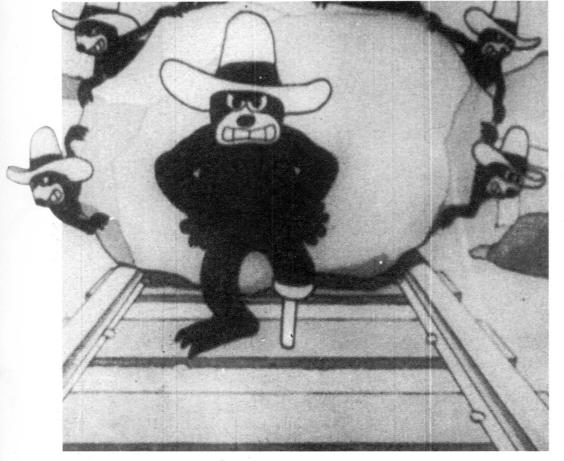

Pete's career goes all the way back to the Alice comedies. The appearance may have changed since then, but the character is still recognizably the same.

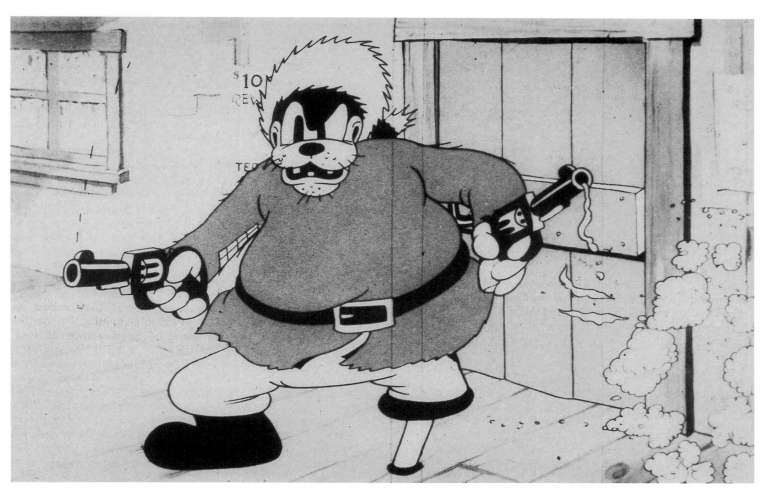

Pete in defiant mood in *The Klondike Kid* (1932). By now his foe was Mickey.

Here Pete – without his peg-leg – is the bullying sheriff who is going to evict Donald and Mickey and sell off all their furniture because they are seriously behind with their rent. He then departs – an error, because it gives the pair time to clear out, taking all their furniture with them in a truck generously lent by their friendly neighbourhood ice-man, the Goof. Or, at least, they would have plenty of time were it not for the classic incompetence of all three. Donald, after a prolonged and ill tempered battle with a bath-plunger, which persists in clinging to his behind with the tenacity of a half-starved leech, ends up by filling himself with gas from the mains. At this stage Pete returns, furious that "his" furniture has been extensively smashed up; moreover, his cigar has gone out. In his customary contemptuous fashion, he strikes a match on the Duck's chin. Poor Donald. Poor Pete. After the debris has settled we find Pete raging impotently from his precarious position: perched in a bath-tub high on a teetering water-pipe. The three pals drive off in glee, although Don's rejoicings are cut short when, with the unerring instinct of the malevolently inanimate, the bath-plunger falls from the skies to affix itself once more to his bottom.

Pete turned in another excellent performance in 1937 in *The Worm Turns*,

once again as an authority figure. Mickey has devised a concoction that will increase the strength and ferocity of any creature onto which it is sprayed. He experiments with it successfully first on a housefly, which proceeds to inflict severe damage on

a spider, and then on a little mouse, which cheerfully flattens a would-be predatory cat. Pluto, meanwhile, has entered into a slight contretemps with dogcatcher Pete; the plucky pup has gone so far as to release all the other dogs from Pete's van. Naturally

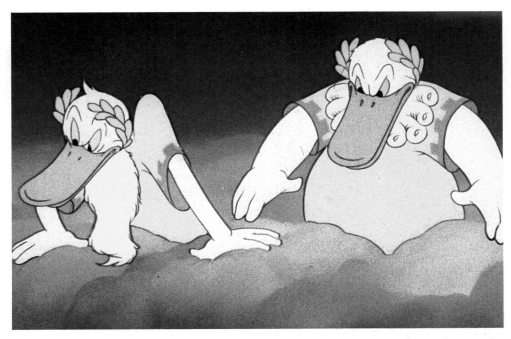

Jupiter and Vulcan took part in the action in the 1944 short *Trombone Trouble*. No prizes for spotting a certain family resemblance.

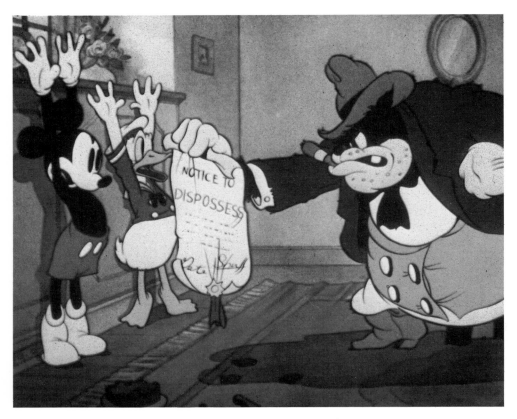

In *Moving Day* (1936) Pete officiously tries to evict Mickey and Donald for non-payment of rent.

enough, Pete's less than subtle approach to the problem is to go for Pluto with a double-barrelled shotgun. He is just about to shoot the hapless dog when Mickey appears on the scene with his wonderful spray-can of chemicals. Seconds later Pete has been violently disposed of by a dog with the strength of ten.

(Just afterwards, by the way, Pluto pauses to sniff at a fire hydrant preparatory to committing an indignity upon it. Mickey squirts the hydrant with his mixture and it blows apart to pin Pluto against a nearby wall with a forceful jet of water. It is not just living things that the miracle compound can transform!)

The authority figure played by Pete in *Mr. Mouse Takes a Trip* (1940) is that of a bullying train conductor and ticket-collector (he even punches the tickets with a big "OK" using his powerful front teeth). Mickey is travelling to Pomona by rail and wishes to take Pluto with him; Pete points out with considerable force that dogs are not allowed to travel on the train, and so Mickey folds Pluto up as tightly as possible and packs him into a small suitcase. A suspicious Pete puts an end to this subterfuge by convincingly miaowing like a kitten. Many gags later a great chase up and down the train is ended when Pluto is whipped off it by a mail-hook. Mickey tries to save him but falls off the end of the train. As they sit there sadly under a barrage of luggage hurled back at them by Pete they suddenly realize that Fate has landed them exactly where they were heading: a sign shows they are just outside Pomona.

Earlier in that same year Pete had done graphic battle with Donald in *The Riveter*. Here Pete (without his peg-leg) as foreman on a building site takes Don on as riveter and general slave: can Pete *never* learn? The short features an exquisite Harold Lloyd parody from the Duck, and Pete himself is involved in a classic visual gag. He forces Don to pepper his (Pete's) sandwich for him and the result is, as he should have predicted, a cloud of blinding pepper. Pete sneezes so hard that he quite literally blasts out the core of his sandwich so that he is left clutching only the crusts.

Of course, thanks to his new riveter, Pete eventually comes to even worse grief than the loss of his sandwich. After the statutory chase he plunges into some strategically placed quick-drying plaster. As he climbs furiously out, the stuff sets, leaving him as an elegant decorative statue in the new building's forecourt.

Pete was by this stage in his career a front-ranking Disney character – not in the same league as a Mickey or a Donald, of course, but nevertheless an instantly recognizable figure with a large *corpus* of work behind him. In the early years it was even intended that he have a starring role in a feature movie to be called *Morgan's Ghost*; this project was shelved when the Disney studio began producing wartime propaganda and training films. The plot was that Pete, in disguise, would captain a ship manned by his dastardly henchmen and take Mickey, Donald and the Goof to a treasure island, the entire party being led there by a parrot called Yellowbeak. The

movie never got beyond the story-sketch stage, although – in the typical Disney spirit of "waste not, want not" – Carl Barks and Jack Hannah used it as the basis of one of the comic books, *Donald Duck Finds Pirate Gold* (1942). In the book the parts that would have been played in the movie by Mickey and Goofy are instead played by the three Nephews (►85).

Although Pete has never entirely lost his bullying ways, his motives have not always been diametrically opposed to those of the rest of the pals. In *Symphony Hour* (1942) he plays the part of a musical entrepreneur called Mr. Sylvester Macaroni who is awestruck by the splendour of a rehearsal of Maestro Michel Mouse and his orchestra. "Tonight we make history!" he cries exuberantly in a carefully cultivated phoney Italian accent, puffing away on his omnipresent cigar (he is capable of blowing not only smoke-rings but a cloud shaped "$1,000,000"). He should know better than to permit himself such optimism when the orchestra, aside from being conducted by the Mouse, has Donald playing percussion and accordion, Clarabelle (►36) playing first violin, Horace (►37) playing French horn, trombone and trumpet, Goofy playing bassoon and trumpet and Clara Cluck playing double-bass and 'cello.

Oddly enough, though, Pete is right: that night's broadcast of the Macaroni Symphony Hour from the Wiz Theater does indeed make history – although not because of the high quality of the musical rendition. This is because, on his way to the stage, Goofy has flattened all of the instruments in an elevator shaft, and there is no time to seek out replacements: the musicians must simply do their best with the shattered remnants. Pete in the producer's box tears out his hair at the cacophony and vows bloodshed; Donald, for his part, gives up playing and reads the "Help Wanted" ads in the newspaper. But at the close of the performance – why, what is this? The audience is lustily roaring its approval of one of the funniest hours it has ever spent, and Pete – and the musicians – realize that their fortunes are indeed assured.

In a 1944 short called *Trombone Trouble* Pete shows that he himself is musically inclined – if not perhaps as talented as he might wish. In fact, his trombone-playing is so poor that he awakens the gods **Jupiter** and **Vulcan**, who in desperation send a bolt of lightning to (literally) electrify their fellow-sufferer Donald so that he has the strength to silence Pete. This he does, but then, to the gods' dismay, he discovers the trombone and simply cannot help giving it a try. Try, try and try again . . .

Pete shows a different facet of his character at the start of *The New Neighbor* (1953). Gone are his belligerent tones and his instinctive aggression, and in their place is a personality which, while coarse, slobbish and ever ready to rip off the unwary, is not actively malevolent – indeed, it could almost be described as genial. Certainly Don assumes the best when he moves into a new house and first meets his neighbour and his dog Muncey (➤119); he is very soon disillusioned.

When Pete asks if he can "borrow" a few ice-cubes Donald is only too glad to accede. But his neighbourliness wanes when Pete, in response, arrives with a supermarket trolley and empties into it the entire contents of Don's fridge. Things seem to improve, though, when Pete offers Don a bowl of food – except then, after he has tried it, Pete calmly admits that it has been declined by the dog! That is the last straw, and battle is joined. The whole neighbourhood gathers to watch the fun, and soon they are joined by television cameras and loudspeakers – the whole affray is treated like a championship boxing match. At the end the vast "spite fence" Pete and Don have built collapses on top of them and, bruised and battered, they *both* decide to move out of the area.

The New Neighbor was followed in the same year by *Canvas Back Duck*, in which Pete plays the part of Peewee Pete, a professional fighter. Donald and the Nephews (➤85) are at a carnival and Donald is showing off on the "try your strength" machines. The Nephews boast of their "Unca's" prowess to a nearby "sissy", who bets them that *his* uncle could whop theirs. The bet is taken. Donald, though, is less than happy about all this when he finds that his opponent in the ring is to be the hulking Peewee Pete. Nonetheless, by fair means or foul (well, primarily fowl!), he succeeds in knocking Pete cold.

After *Canvas Back Duck*, however, there was a three-decade hiatus in Pete's career. Yet his most recent role is also probably his finest. In *Mickey's Christmas Carol* (1983) he plays the part of the Ghost of Christmas Yet to Come. (In this featurette he was voiced, as was Willie the Giant, by Will Ryan. Ryan had the difficult task of matching the superb vocal characterization of Pete earlier given by Billy Bletcher.) Whereas, as we have seen, in most of his other appearances Pete is a thuggish bully, threatening only insofar as he possesses brute power and general malevolence, in this featurette his hooded figure conveys a genuinely *sinister* feeling. Yes, he is big and brash and gleefully malicious, but here he is something more

than that: he is truly *scaring*. Whereas in the earlier shorts you know that, sooner or later, he's going to get his come-uppance at the hands of Julius, Mickey or whoever, here the viewer *knows* that Pete represents a force that can never be defeated: in simplistic terms, that force is of course death itself. When Pete shows the quivering Scrooge (➤130) the miser's own neglected gravestone, and draws his attention to the callous small talk of the gravediggers, a shiver goes down the watcher's spine. Pete's performance is a triumph of animation. He is in fine form also as Captain of the Guard in the 1990 featurette *The Prince and the Pauper*.

Being typecast as a perpetual villain is not necessarily a good thing for one's career, as many other Hollywood actors will tell you: the pinnacles of stardom are for the (apparent) good guys. Pete, however, has borne his burden willingly, and unlike most of the other cartoon bad guys is fairly complex character – much more than just a monument of quivering rage. His most recent incarnation has been in the series *Goof Troop* (➤145) and its spinoff, *A Goofy Movie* (➤395).

In 1953's *The New Neighbor* Pete epitomized the person you don't want to live next door to – especially if you happen to be a mild-mannered duck.

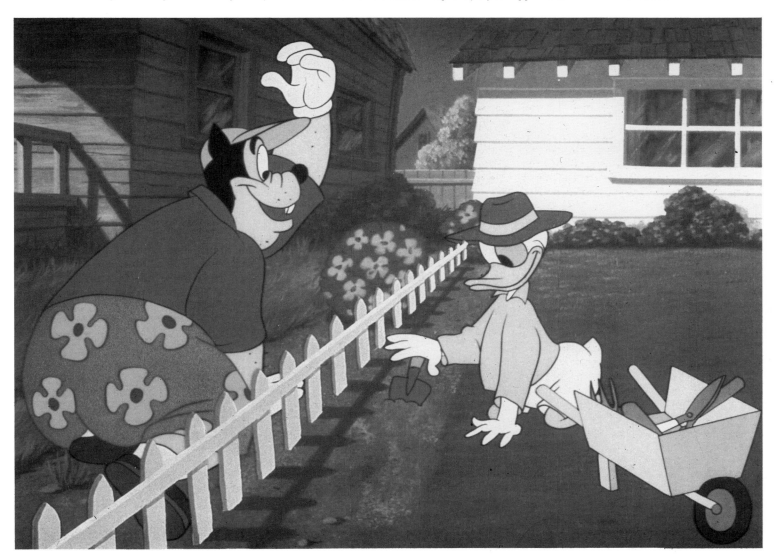

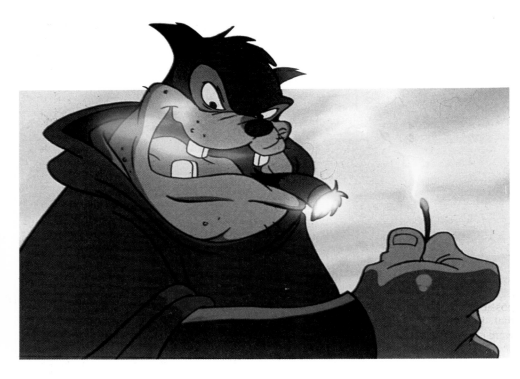

OSWALD THE LUCKY RABBIT

Oswald was born in 1927 as a replacement for the Alice comedies, which had run their course (➤**14**). The idea of having a cartoon series about a rabbit seems to have originated with the Disneys' by now regular distributor, Charles Mintz; that it should be produced by the Disneys was the suggestion of his wife, Margaret (*née* Winkler), who had distributed the Alice shorts before marrying Mintz and handing over her company to him.

The idea of Oswald himself, though, seems to have been entirely Walt's – and initially he fouled it up completely. The first short of the projected series, *Poor Papa*, produced in April 1927, had an Oswald who was old, gross, scruffy and improbably fecund – the kind of guy you don't want as a next-door neighbor. The response from Mintz and his colleagues was thunderingly negative. They thought the animation was poor (this was probably a no objection, introduced only as a way of trying to soften up the Disneys before embarking on a course of chiselling) but, more important, they didn't like the character of Oswald at all. What the public wanted were clean, young, respectable, and generally even romantically adorable comic cartoon characters–an astonishing reaction, in the light of subsequent history. Donald Duck respectable?–he would have been instantly forgotten if he had been. Goofy romantically adorable? Outside the Disney canon, what of the other classic cartoon characters like the distinctly seedy Popeye, the disreputable (albeit suavely so) Bugs Bunny, the mindless Road Runner and the evilly cunning nitwitted Coyote, the elderly Mr. Magoo, the anarchic Woody Woodpecker . . . the list could go on. In fact, the only clean-cut cartoon characters to "make it to the top" were Disney's own (later) Mickey and Minnie, and even they had (by design) their little failings.

Still, the Disneys did not have the benefit of hindsight and had little choice but to bow

Filmography

(Early records are scanty, and so Pete may appear in more Alice Comedies and Oswald shorts that are listed here. Pete's son, **Junior**, was in *Bellboy Donald* [1942].)

Alice Solves the Puzzle, February 15, 1925
Alice Wins the Derby, 1925
Alice's Tin Pony, 1925
Alice's Spanish Guitar, 1926
The Ocean Hop, 1927
Rickety Gin, 1927
Harem Scarem, 1928
Rival, Romeos, 1928
Oh, What a Knight, 1928
Sagebrush Sadie, 1928
Ozzie of the Mounted, 1928

Steamboat Willie, 1928
Gallopin' Gaucho, 1928
The Barn Dance, 1928
The Cactus Kid, 1930
The Mad Dog, 1932
The Klondike Kid, 1932
Building a Building, 1933
The Mail Pilot, 1933
Shanghaied, 1934
The Dognapper, 1934
Two-Gun Mickey, 1934
Mickey's Service Station, 1935
Moving Day, 1936
The Worm Turns, 1937
Donald's Lucky Day, 1939
Officer Duck, 1939
The Riveter, 1940

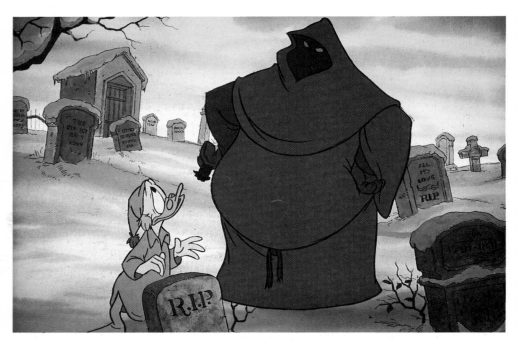

Pete, in his most effective role to date – as the Ghost of Christmas Yet to Come in the 1983 featurette, *Mickey's Christmas Carol.*

down before the judgement of their peers. Walt and Ub Iwerks set to work to revamp Oswald according to Mintz's dictates. He became younger and generally more cuddly, and the audiences of the day – both general and professional – loved the results. For the first time merchandising rights were sold in a Disney character (although the Disneys got nothing for them): Oswald was featured on candy bars and even a stencil set. And for the first time in a couple of years the Disneys were paid promptly by their distributor (Roy and Walt celebrated this by each building a house).

The differences between Oswald and Mickey Mouse (➤23) are few; aside from the lengths of their noses, the fact that Mickey had no top to his playsuit, Oswald's rabbit ears and Mickey's mouse tail, the two characters are basically identical. It has often been said that Mickey is composed entirely of circles, but of course this isn't quite true: his long tail is certainly not a circle. Oswald's little black scut, on the other hand, is; had Walt (or, to be precise, Ub Iwerks) simply put Mickey's ears onto Oswald's body then the all-circle cartoon character would have been born!

And the animation was not sophisticated. In their article "The Illusion of Life" (*Stanford Magazine*, Summer 1982) Frank Thomas and Ollie Johnston observed that

> . . . even [the Disney] studio's early characters were not very realistic. If Oswald the Lucky Rabbit had to put his arm around an object, he merely stretched the arm until it was long enough to do the job. There was no attempt at anatomy, no shoulders or spines or bones or muscles. Nor did characters or objects seem to have any weight.

The first of Oswald's movies to be released was *Trolley Troubles* (1927). It is a fast-moving and frenetic piece, suffering from a lack of overall cohesion – in other words, it is little more than a sequence of barely linked gags. Still, it was successful in its day.

Oswald is the driver of a trolley car. The track over which he has to drive is in poor repair and, curiously, seems to have been laid in a number of different gauges. With these the trolley car miraculously copes, expanding and contracting its base as necessary to accommodate the rails. In due course the car encounters a Clarabelle-like cow straddling the line; although it hits her at full pelt it simply bounces off, leaving her placidly unperturbed. The only way it can get past this obstacle is to demonstrate its shape-shifting abilities yet again: it shrinks to diminutive size and squeezes under her. Surprisingly, perhaps, there is hardly an udder joke in sight.

Oswald is set for further encounters with unfriendly animals. His trolley car fails to scale a steep hill, and slides back down to the bottom. When he gets out to try to sort matters out his own bottom is ruthlessly butted by a passing billy goat. But Oswald inventively enlists the goat to his own assistance, using a stick and a carrot to persuade it to push the trolley up and over the hill.

The trolley careers down the far side, losing passengers here and there as it rockets through a succession of tunnels. At last Oswald is the only one left aboard when a final tunnel emerges in the middle of a cliff-side. Trolley car and driver hurtle forth and drop into the waters below. Oswald and the base of the trolley eventually surface, and he rows off into the distance.

Like so many of the earliest (pre-Mickey) Disney cartoons, this one is not in the slightest funny – at least to modern eyes. It is a little hard to work out why it fails in this respect: it is competently animated, the pace is hectic and the story-line inventive. One possible reason for the movie's failure is that, in a curious way, the Disney people were *cheating*. It is one of the great strengths of animation that cartoon characters are able to perform the physically impossible. Nevertheless, in order for their exploits to succeed in entertaining the viewer, there must be a certain relationship between the animated impossibilities and the way things work in the real world. The audience must see the feats of the characters as a sort of idealization of the way in which human beings behave. For example, in a short like *Brave Little Tailor* (1938) Mickey, in thrashing the giant, on several occasions actually flies. Small people battling big bullies do not in fact fly, *but they idealize themselves as doing so.* (In much the same way, amateur athletes see themselves as performing with the same style as their professional counterparts, even though onlookers have a rather different impression.) In Oswald's case, however (as often with Julius and the very early Mickey), the animated impossibilities do not have much at all to do with reality: the gags are based almost exclusively on the ability of the animator to create situations that have *no* counterpart in real life – like the trolley car's ability to squeeze under the cow. In no way is this a caricature of reality: in reality, of course, the cow would by this time have been nothing more than hamburger on the line. The whole situation is reminiscent of those unfunny jokes that children tell – unfunny because their basic premises are at odds with real-life experience and hence the rest of the joke is unbelievable. A further quality shared by many of these very early Disney shorts and children's jokes is the matter of repetition: anything that looks like a passable gag is immediately repeated several times, as if the repetition alone will somehow make it even funnier.

Oh, What a Knight (1928) is a rather more successful Oswald cartoon so far as laughter is concerned, probably because, while it has little relation to reality, it accords with a perceived, if false, set of conventions regarding the actuality of medieval life – together with a witty admixture of just a whiff of anachronism. Oswald is a wandering troubadour – although his instrument is not a lute but an accordion. His horse stumbles and both of them fall into the moat of a castle . . . which happens to be infested by crocodiles. The pair escape unscathed (the horse loses its tail but is unconcerned: it simply yanks out a replacement from its rear). Oswald's attention is then attracted by a svelte cat-like female who blows him a kiss from a lofty balcony on the castle. He climbs swiftly up to join her and discovers that she is a prisoner, complete with ball and chain. Her captor, a vast rat-like creature, is Pete (➤15), and he and Oswald fight a duel. Oswald demonstrates the ability, on

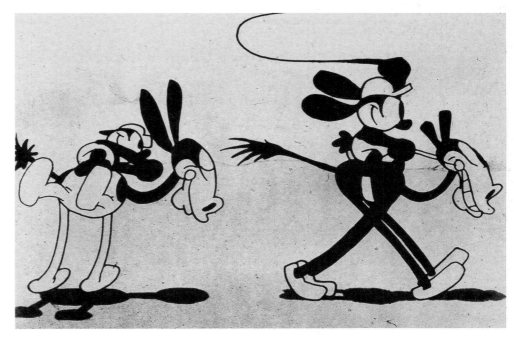

In this still we can see how close was the resemblance between Oswald and the early Mickey: change the ears and tail and the two would be indistinguishable.

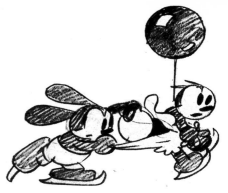

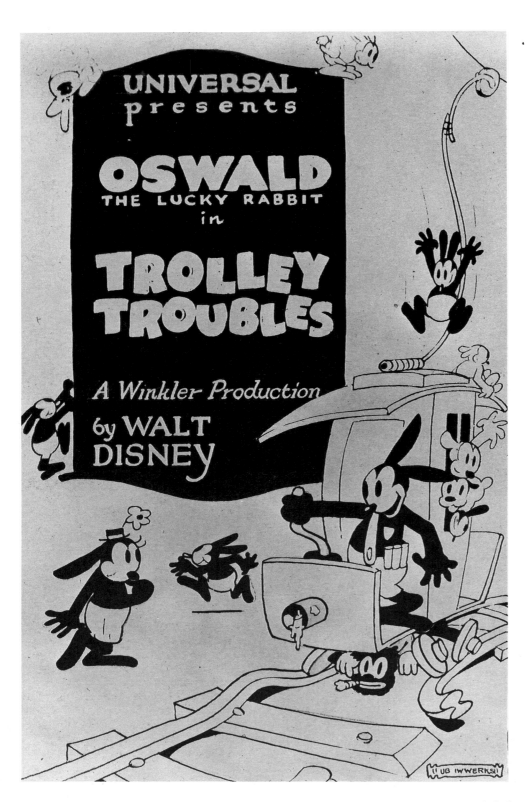

A poster for the first Oswald cartoon to be released, *Trolley Troubles* (1927). Notice Ub Iwerks' logo at the bottom right.

this is a cartoon rather than a live-action film.

The Disneys might have carried on creating Oswald cartoons in perpetuity, but what they did not realize was that Mintz was clandestinely working to take Oswald away from them. George Winkler, Mintz's brother-in-law, had been delivering the regular cheques for the Oswald cartoons to the studio, but at the same time he had apparently been recruiting Disney's animators (the notable *refusenik* was Ub Iwerks). In early 1928 Walt was given an option: either accept drastically reduced payments for future Oswald shorts or have the rights in the character taken away. In the end – very creditably – he chose the latter course. (Oswald was eventually taken over by Walter Lantz.)

He needed a new character, a new star for his cartoons. He began to wonder if he could do something with a mouse...

Above and below: Two of the animation roughs for Oswald's short *Sleigh Bells* (1928).

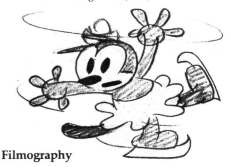

Filmography

Trolley Troubles, September 5, 1927
Oh, Teacher, 1927
The Mechanical Cow, 1927
Great Guns, 1927
All Wet, 1927
The Ocean Hop, 1927
The Banker's Daughter, 1927
Empty Socks, 1927
Rickety Gin, 1927
Harem Scarem, 1928
Neck 'n Neck, 1928
The Ol' Swimmin' 'Ole, 1928
Africa Before Dark, 1928
Rival Romeos, 1928
Bright Lights, 1928
Oh, What a Knight, 1928
Sagebrush Sadie, 1928
Ride 'Em Plow Boy, 1928
Sky Scrappers, 1928
Ozzie of the Mounted, 1928
Hungry Hoboes, 1928
Poor Papa, 1928 (first Oswald short made)
The Fox Chase, 1928
Tall Timber, 1928
Sleigh Bells, 1928
Hot Dog, 1928

occasion, to leave his shadow to do the fighting while he steals a kiss from the ladye fair – an act which infuses him with sufficient adrenaline to win the duel. He uses the ball of her ball and chain like a bowl to skittle over the villain and his equally repulsive henchmen, but is then confronted by a colossal cat – all teeth and claws – and decides with his new-found love that discretion is the better part of valour. The

two lovers leap from the window and drift slowly to earth using her skirt as a parachute. We are left in no doubt that they will live happily ever after.

In view of the events of this short it might seem strange to maintain that it is more "realistic" than *Trolley Troubles*, but in many ways it is. Here the animated impossibilities are *extensions* of reality – for example, Oswald being such an adept, adroit swordsman that even his shadow can take on the villain. The anachronisms – the accordion and the crocodiles – are successful gags rather than jarring *faux pas*. Hardly a single gag is based purely on the fact that

MICKEY MOUSE

> I love Mickey Mouse more than any woman I've ever known.
>
> Walt Disney

What can you say about Mickey Mouse? Perhaps Walt, in the single sentence quoted above, said it all – well, most of it (although years later he was to add that in real life he was actually frightened of mice!). But others have added their words of wisdom. Mary Pickford once said that the Mouse was her favourite actor of all ... including even her own husband of the time, Douglas Fairbanks. Walt himself, on the subject of his favourite rodent, said around 1933 that Mickey speaks to "that deathless, precious, ageless, absolutely primitive remnant of something in every world-racked human being"; and to the *New York Times* he said that the "best [reason for Mickey's popularity] any of us have been able to come up with is the fact that Mickey is so simple and uncomplicated, so easy to understand, that you can't help liking him". It has been widely reported that King George VI was a great fan, and had one of the Buckingham Palace nurseries done in Mickey wallpaper. Maurice Sendak planned to give Mickey an ultimate tribute by incorporating his image as the decoration of a cooking-pot in his classic children's book *In the Night Kitchen*, but permission was withheld by the Disney

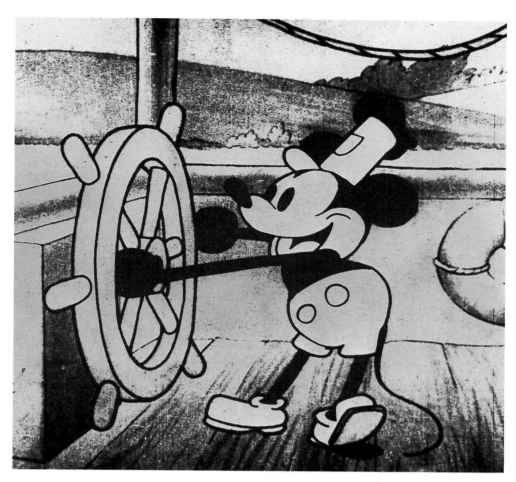

Steamboat Willie, released on November 18, 1928, represented more than just Mickey's first appearance, *Steamboat Willie* was the first animated movie with properly synchronized sound, and the illusion was so effective that it took the public by storm. The ensuing cinematic revolution soon made both Mickey Mouse and Walt Disney household names.

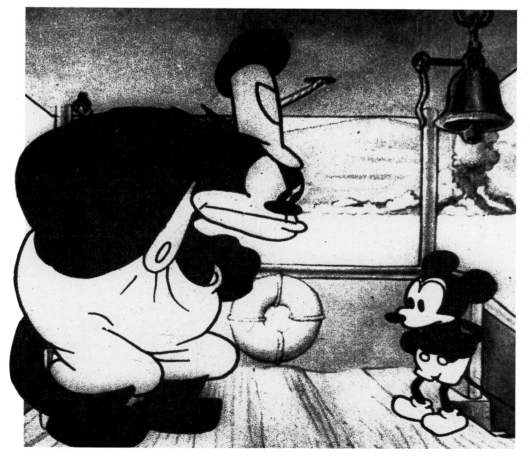

company. The sculptor Ernest Trova said that "For sheer power of the graphics, Mickey Mouse is rivaled only by the Coca-Cola trademark and the Swastika". Sergei Eisenstein described Mickey as "America's most original contribution to culture". New York's Metropolitan Museum of Art wrote of him that he was the "greatest historical figure in the development of American art". The cartoonist David Low called him "the most significant figure in graphic art since Leonardo da Vinci". Whoever wrote the catalogue for the 1935 exhibition devoted to Disney and its works at the Harris Museum and Art Gallery must have had something of the same in mind:

> Great lover, soldier, sailor, singer, toreador, jockey, prize-fighter, automobile racer, aviator, farmer, scholar, Mickey Mouse lives in a world in which space, time and the laws of physics are null.

The artist Roy Lichtenstein is said to have developed his comic-strip style of pop art as

Pete had appeared in a number of shorts with Julius and, later, Oswald. He survived to plague Mickey's existence too, appearing in the Mouse's first movie, *Steamboat Willie* (1928). Since Pete's career is far from over, he holds the record for the longest-lived Disney character.

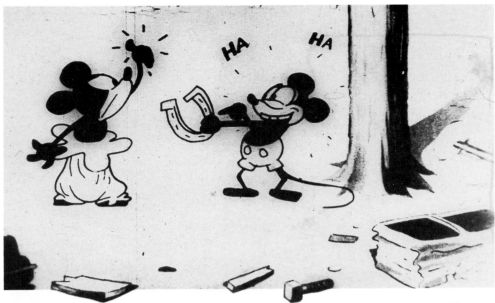

In 1928's *Plane Crazy*, Minnie rebuffs Mickey's jovial attempt to make the peace, having just forced her to make an emergency parachute jump and crashed the plane!

a direct result of his son having remarked to him that, if he were a *real* artist, he should be able to draw a decent version of Mickey Mouse. Mickey is even honoured by being featured, in wax, in London's world-famous Madame Tussaud's. Robert Sklar goes into the matter in more detail:

Like no other twentieth-century motion-picture character except Chaplin (on whom some say the mouse was modeled), Mickey possessed the world's imagination. He, too, was a creature of many masks, expressing what we all like to think are the best traits of our humanity: sweet sentiment, unfeigned pleasure, saucy impudence. Mickey was all heart, but in the beginning he did not wear it on his sleeve.

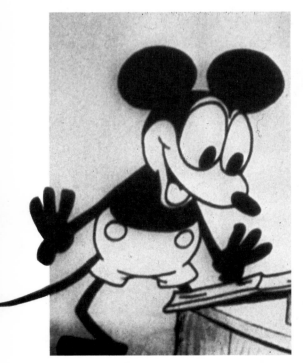

Mickey prepares for his nerveracking flight in *Plane Crazy* (1928).

At first he was very much a rodent. His limbs were thinner and his features smaller than the later, anthropomorphic version. In *Plane Crazy* (1928), his first [produced] film, made as a silent, then released with sound after *Steamboat Willie*, he went barefoot and barehanded, but by *Steamboat Willie* (1928) he wore shoes and soon acquired white four-fingered gloves. He was unselfconscious and egocentric, wearing the same confident, self-satisfied grin Edward G. Robinson was to flash a couple of years later as the immigrant gangster Rico in *Little Caesar* (1930). Unlike Rico, however, Mickey had no end. Success eroded him in other ways. "Mickey's our problem child," Disney said later. "He's so much of an institution that we're limited in what we can do with him." He became respectable, bland, gentle, responsible, moral. Donald Duck was added to the Disney cast to provide the old vinegar and bile.

The universality of both Mickey and Donald was something of which Walt himself was very well aware. In an article called "Humor – the World's Sixth Sense", which appeared in *Wisdom* in 1956, he discussed why it was that so much humour, like wine, doesn't "travel": what may make an American audience rock with laughter will leave a British or a French or an Australian audience cold. However, again as with wines, some forms of humour do "travel" successfully. He claimed that all of these were manifestations of a very basic type of humour common to all humanity, and that the commonest expression of it came in the form of pantomime – which is exactly the mode of humour employed by Mickey, Donald and the rest. "I cite Mickey," wrote Walt, "because he has been for over 26 years my guinea pig – if he'll pardon the expression – in this serious business of amusing people on the screen. And Donald – well I know him pretty well too, although he sometimes gets out of hand and turns on us in outraged dignity. Comedians are often very touchy that way." Although Walt

himself may not have been aware of it (he probably was), in the manner in which he writes about the Mouse and the Duck here he gives us a clue as to another secret of the phenomenal Disney success on the international level: *he writes about them as if they were real characters*, with their own individualities, quirks and idiosyncrasies – independent of their creators. It is as if he really *believes* in them as "people". This "belief" transmits itself through the medium of the cartoon to the audience, who likewise "believe" in the "reality" of Donald, Mickey and the gang. The characters behave with a certain consistency (even a consistent inconsistency!) that would be impossible to maintain if their creators did not treat them as if they were real, live actors – who may be "often very touchy that way", or whatever. This does *not* mean that the characters are static – Mickey has evolved dramatically over the years, the others rather less so – but that evolution has been like the growth of a child: the individual changes but is nevertheless quite obviously the same individual.

The naturalist Stephen Jay Gould pointed out in a 1979 essay, however, that Mickey's transformation over time has had the overall effect of making his features more juvenile. His cranial size has increased, as has his head-size relative to his body-size; his legs have become shorter and pudgier (although these days they are covered by long trousers); and his eyes have grown relatively larger, too. All of these developments are signs of increasing juvenility. This ties in interestingly with zoological/anthropological ideas that the bodily proportions of juvenility spark off an innate affectionate parental response in the adults of the species. Gould cites part of Konrad Lorenz's list of such juvenile attributes important as "releasers" of this response: "... a relatively large head, predominance of the brain capsule, large and low-lying eyes, bulging cheek region, short and thick extremities, a springy elastic consistency, and clumsy movements" – a fairly accurate description of the later Mickey! It's notable that Donald Duck (►61), although from the start more "adult" than Mickey (he could never have been Donald Duckling!), nevertheless has "become younger" in much the same fashion – albeit to a lesser extent.

Whether because of deliberate zoology-oriented plotting or not, Mickey has certainly altered over the years – indeed it seems barely credible that in 1948 Walt could have claimed that "he has changed little in behavior or appearance since that first rough drawing fixed his character and *Steamboat Willie* introduced him on the screen 20 years ago".

One thing in *Steamboat Willie* jarred at the time and does so even more today: the scene in which Mickey brutalizes a cat, then swings it around his head by its tail, and

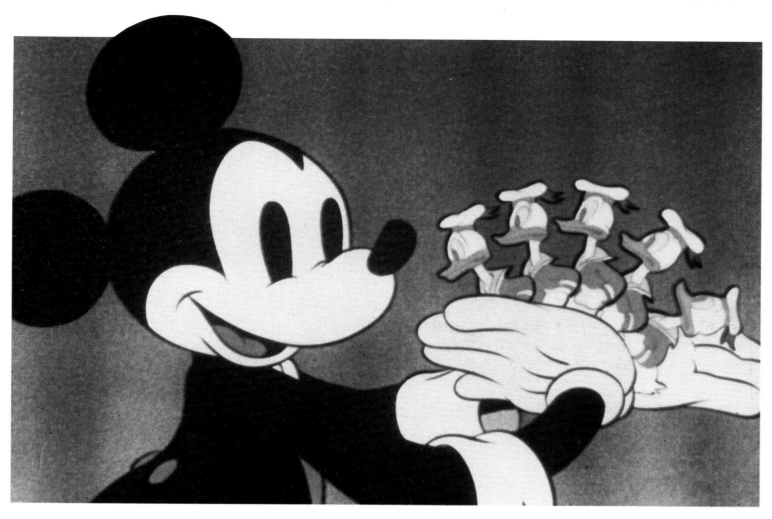

In *Magician Mickey* (1937) the world's most famous Mouse did something very foolish indeed: he created *more* Donald Ducks. Fortunately the spell wore off rapidly.

finally throws it out through the steamboat window into the river. The original version of the short, rarely seen now, had also a sequence in which Mickey separated a sow from several of her suckling piglets by shaking them off onto the deck: when one piglet holds on tight, Mickey removes it with a vicious kick, and then proceeds to squeeze the sow's teats so that her squeals of pain provide a rudimentary tune. Walt himself was shocked by such scenes, and vowed that never again would Mickey be seen wilfully to hurt another animal. It was a vow he kept.

The story of the genesis of Mickey Mouse is a fairly tangled one – and Walt himself did not help matters by cheerfully telling several different versions of it. One of these was that he and his wife Lillian dreamt up the character on their way home from New York after having lost Oswald the Lucky Rabbit (►20). It is, according to this version, thanks to Lillian Disney that this great cartoon creation was not called Mortimer Mouse; it is probably again thanks to her intervention that, for exactly the same reason, Mickey Mouse proved to be, indeed, a "great cartoon creation". She said that a character called Mortimer Mouse would never get anywhere, and she was probably right: much later, in 1936, a Disney short did indeed feature a Mortimer Mouse

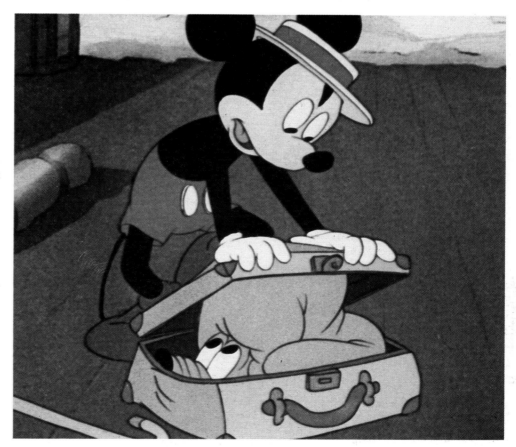

1940's *Mr. Mouse Takes a Trip* saw Mickey make the mistake of trying to take Pluto on a train journey with him. Little did he know that the guard was the bullying Pete.

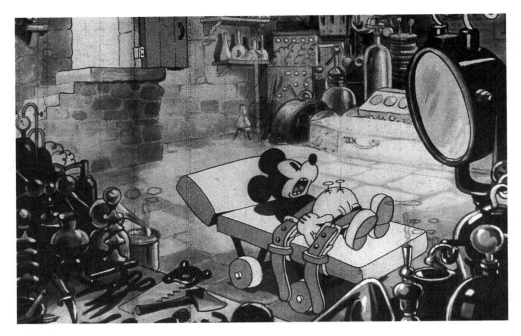

By 1933's *The Mad Doctor*, Mickey's appearance had changed considerably. Gone were the sly, rodent-like looks, and in their place was a much more cuddlable persona.

(►77), and his career was notably short. In one recounting of this tale Walt wrote:

> Out of the trouble and confusion stood a mocking, merry little figure. Vague and indefinite at first. But it grew and grew and grew, and finally arrived – a mouse. A romping, rollicking little mouse ... By the time my train had reached the Middle West, I had dressed my dream mouse in a pair of red velvet pants with two huge pearl buttons. I had composed the first scenario and was all set.

As far as one can gather from all the diverse accounts, however, Walt was responsible single-handedly for the creation of Mickey's *personality* while Ub Iwerks *designed* the physical appearance of the little fellow: this cannot have been a tremendously onerous task, since the early Mickey was virtually indistinguishable, except for the ears and tail, from Oswald the Lucky Rabbit (►20) – in fact, one can trace an early version of Mickey right back to *Alice's Wonderland*, the pilot for the Alice Comedies (►13). Iwerks was also responsible, almost entirely, for animating the first five Mickey cartoons (with Ben Sharpsteen first coming on the scene in *When the Cat's Away* [1929]).

Walt was exceptionally – if not excessively – fond of Mickey, possibly because he was Mickey's voice and, to a great extent, model. In the early days he once heard an animator describe Mickey as a four-letter word; exactly *which* four-letter word is not recorded, but what is known for certain is that Walt fired the man on the spot.

Walt described the form of the early Mickey in startlingly frank, businesslike terms:

> His head was a circle with an oblong circle for a snout. The ears were circles so they could be drawn the same no matter how he turned his head. His body was like a pear and he had a long tail. His legs were pipestems and we stuck

them in big shoes to give him the look of a kid wearing his father's shoes. We didn't want him to have mouse hands, because he was supposed to be more human. So we gave him gloves. Five fingers looked like too much on such a little figure, so we took one away. That was just one less finger to animate.

In other words, the design of Mickey was a pragmatic one: it depended to a large extent on what would be cheap and quick to animate (for a brief period around 1941 Mickey adopted three-dimensional ears – an experiment generally regarded as a disaster). This made a lot of sense

Brave Little Tailor (1938), based on the Grimm fairy-tale, saw Mickey rise from humble origins, defeat a giant, and win Princess Minnie's hand. A fairly normal day's work for the Mouse.

considering that Walt's company was at the time definitely ailing. In fact, in some shots in the earliest Mickey cartoons the hands seem not even to be four-fingered ones: they look more like table-tennis bats.

In 1952 Walt went further in his description of Mickey's origins:

> Quite consciously ... I had been preparing Mickey and his pals for the advent of sound. ... sound had a very considerable effect on our treatment of Mickey Mouse. It gave his character a new dimension. It rounded him into complete life-likeness. And it carried us into a new phase of his development.

This account fails, alas, to accord with the other versions of Mickey's genesis.

The matter of the sound for *Steamboat Willie* is important. It was not in fact the first ever sound cartoon – there had been a few experiments in this direction by the Fleischer brothers some years before, and Paul Terry's *Suppertime*, released shortly before *Steamboat Willie*, had had a soundtrack – but *Steamboat Willie* was the first with a properly synchronized track. It might have been a primitive piece of work by the standards of a few years later (Mickey first spoke in 1929 in *The Karnival Kid*), but the attention paid to the synchronism of actions with sounds marked the short as a milestone. On the subject of the sound, the great animator Wilfred Jackson recalled in 1973 in an interview with Mike Barrier (later reproduced in Barrier's superb piece, "Building a Better Mouse", in *Funnyworld* #20) that

> Walt didn't know if people would believe that the character on the screen was making the noise. Nobody had ever seen a drawing make a noise, and there was no reason to be sure that the people would believe it. It might just look like some kind of a fake thing, and Walt

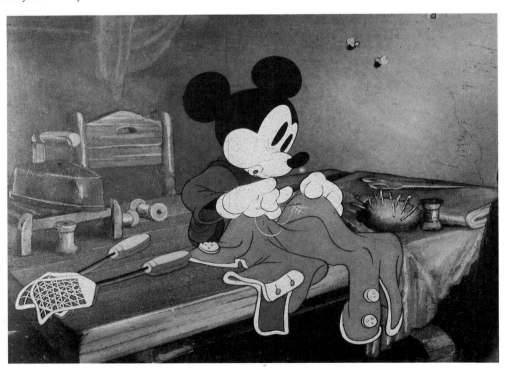

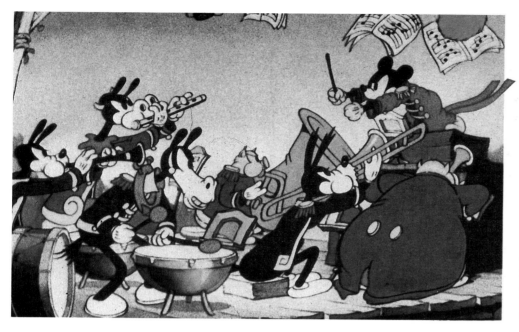

The Band Concert (1935) was Mickey's first Technicolor excursion – and he had to fight hard to try to stop Donald stealing the show. Noteworthy among the musicians are Clarabelle Cow and Horace Horsecollar.

wanted it to seem real, as if the noise was coming right from what the character was doing. So to find out whether the whole thing would be believable ... when a few scenes had been animated ... they set up this test. I was able to play a few simple tunes on a harmonica ... One of my favorite tunes was "Turkey in the Straw"; that's why it got used there. ...

We came back one night to try this thing out, and Ub Iwerks rigged up a little microphone and speaker out of something or other that he took apart and put back together. Walt's office had a glass window in the door, so we could close the door, and look through it, and see the back of the screen. ... Roy Disney got outside the building with the projector, and projected through a window, so the sound of the projector wouldn't be too loud.

When Roy started the projector up, I furnished the music, with my mouth organ ... and the other fellows hit things and made sound effects. We had spittoons everywhere then, and they made a wonderful gong if you hit them with a pencil. We practiced with it several times, and we got so we were hitting it off pretty well. We took turns going out there ourselves, and looking at the thing, and when I went out, there wasn't any music, but the noises and the voices seemed to come from it just fine. It was really pretty exciting, and it did prove to us that the sound coming from the drawing could be a convincing thing.

It would be a sorry soul indeed who failed to respond to the obvious excitement evinced by Jackson in this description of the genesis of *Steamboat Willie*'s soundtrack – perhaps the best such description extant from one of the participants in that history-making event.

People, of course, read into Mickey Mouse what they want to find. As an example of a somewhat odd reaction, here is Fritz Moellenhoff, writing in his essay "Remarks on the Popularity of Mickey Mouse" in 1940 in the psychoanalytical journal *American Imago* (as cited by Gregory A. Waller in *The American Animated Cartoon*):

... the symbolic meaning of Mickey's figure is obvious. Symbolically, we should have to call it a phallus but a desexualized one. Mickey's actions and adventures demonstrate his lack of genital interest. His audience feels that, and although he remains a mouse and a phallus, he does not stir up wishes which have to be suppressed and consequently he does not rouse anxiety.

We must leave Mr. Moellenhoff to his speculations.

In Mickey's early days Walt's most valued animator was still Ub Iwerks. In an article in

Mindrot in June 1977 Peter Adamakos points to a disparity in styles between the first three Mickey Mouse shorts and those that immediately succeeded them – a difference which he attributes to the fact that Walt himself was very closely involved with the first three but left the next few in the care of Iwerks, Walt being at the time rather more involved in commercial matters. In the earliest shorts Mickey and Minnie seem to be of roughly human size, but for some while after they were to be shown as small, mouse-sized characters – as in *The Barnyard Battle* (1929), in which Mickey is one of many similar mice involved in fighting the (relatively) huge cats. Also, in these next few shorts Mickey and Minnie *looked* different: they were more rat-like than mouse-like, less sympathetic in their appearance. Adamakos adds that Mickey "uses his tail like Felix the Cat, or, like the cat in *Alice in Cartoonland* [i.e., Julius]".

Sound, he suggests, is what saved these early Mickey Mouse shorts and the first Silly Symphonies from oblivion (a reasonable point, as anyone can attest who has tried the experiment of watching, say, *Steamboat Willie* without sound): the novelty of sound would, naturally, have worn off in due course, especially as other cartoonists developed or bought the technology.

John Canemaker in a 1979 article in *Millimeter* put this in another context:

As an "actor," the early Mickey's expressive range was as limited as his black and white coloring: there was a "happy" Mickey and a "not-so-happy" Mickey. He had personality because he could think and solve problems, but he was a character whose emotive reactions were of the broadest, most rudimentary sort and quite unconvincing.

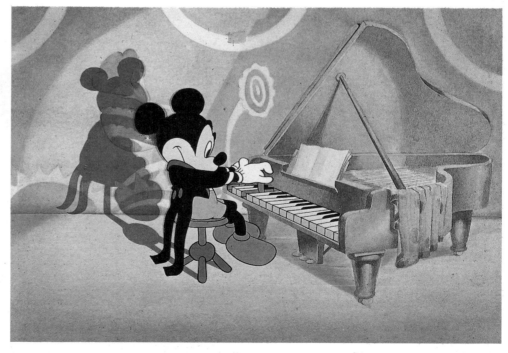

Mickey desperately tries to keep up with the singer (Clara Cluck) in the 1941 colour remake of 1934's original black-and-white *Orphan's Benefit*. The apostrophe in the movie's title was presumably misplaced by an artist in a hurry.

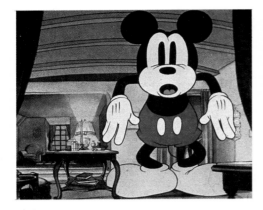

In *Thru the Mirror* (1936) Mickey emulated Alice in Wonderland.

With a few changes, this paragraph could equally apply to Oswald. It is difficult to resist the inference that, at the outset it was really just the sound that made the difference between Mickey and his rivals.

However, according to Adamakos, in 1931 there started a rapid improvement in the quality of the Disney output. The stories were better – not just a collection of gags that carried on until it was time for the short abruptly to end – and so was the drawing. He maintains that this was because of the departure of Iwerks to create cartoons in his own right. The younger animators were encouraged by Walt to experiment in a way that Iwerks would not have permitted when he was in charge of Disney animation. Moreover, from around this time Walt himself took the time to contribute more in the way of story to the shorts. As evidence of his claims, Adamakos looks at Iwerks'

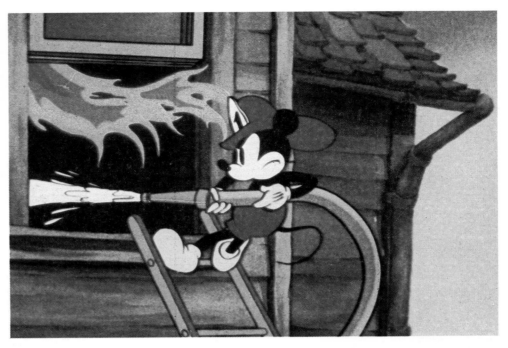

Ever in the forefront when there are dangerous deeds to be done, Mickey led the gang in its efforts to save Clarabelle Cow from the flames in *Mickey's Fire Brigade* (1935).

own independent cartoons and sees in them all the mistakes and crassnesses that are to be found in some of the early Mickey Mouse shorts – plus a few more.

Mickey's character was, for obvious reasons, not very strongly portrayed in his earliest shorts: the animation was too rudimentary and the dialogue nonexistent. However, it has remained true throughout his career that Mickey's character has a certain chameleon-like quality: there is only one Donald Duck, but there are many Mickey Mouses. Mike Barrier, in his excellent piece in the Summer 1979 issue of *Funnyworld*, has pointed out that this indefinite quality in Mickey's character was no disadvantage:

> ... Mickey's vagueness as a character became an asset – a source of his popularity. However difficult he might be to describe, he was undeniably an active, positive character, and this was very important at a time when the world was sliding into the worst days of the Great Depression. Audiences could read into him an optimistic affirmation of their own values.

Some of those early Mickey shorts, however, make good viewing even today. *Mickey's Orphans* (1931) is a case in point: by the standards that would be prevalent in the Disney studio two or three years later it is primitive stuff, but it is nonetheless a fine cartoon. Its essential plot is that on Christmas Eve someone dumps hordes of kittens on Mickey's doorstep and he, Minnie and Pluto must cope with these unexpected arrivals as best they can. The kittens are less than 100 per cent appreciative: Mickey as Santa gets his beard-elastic twanged; the hastily gathered stocking toys are used to demolish much of Mickey and Minnie's furniture; and when,

finally, the thousands of kittens are let loose on the Christmas tree, they reduce it within seconds to a skeleton. The short might not sound too promising from this summary, but it has many fine moments: it is much more than a fascinating museum piece.

It is hard for us now to realize fully the colossal impact that the early Mickey Mouse shorts and the Silly Symphonies had on the public: Walt Disney, the world seems to have thought, was creating magic (as, in a way, he was). The tale is still current in the Disney studio of a visitor who came around in a party and who was eager to see how the Mouse was made to move. Obligingly, one of the animators made a series of quick sketches in order to demonstrate. Astoundedly – and astoundingly – the visitor remarked: "Gee, if I could draw like that I'd never do another lick of work in my life!" The average Mickey Mouse short contained a total of over 12,000 drawings.

It is no easy matter to choose a representative Mickey Mouse short from the period after the first few years – the period in which most Mickey Mouses featured also Goofy and Donald, both contributing with Mickey and separately to the general chaos. Perhaps a typical example is *Mickey's Service Station* (1935 [►45]). Mickey's task is to get an inner tube back into its allotted tyre, but the inner tube, quite clearly, is less than enthusiastic about this. As soon as he gets one side of it in the other bounces out. He resorts to using feet as well as hands, and moments later he and the inner tube are in a tangled knot – inside the tyre.

It is classic Disney gaggery, of course, as is another of Mickey's exploits in the short. Mickey is struggling within the bowels of Pete's car when Goofy, exhausted from one

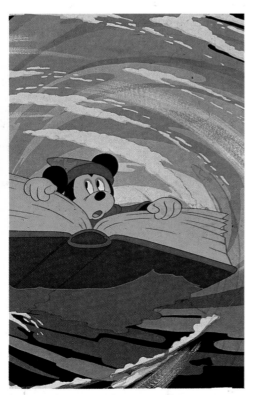

Mickey's first role in a Disney feature was as the apprentice in *The Sorcerer's Apprentice* in *Fantasia* (1940). His attempts to imitate his master led him to near-disaster.

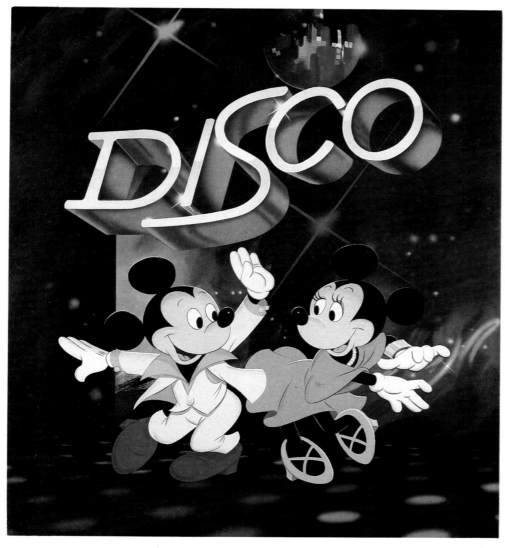

In 1979, keeping abreast of the times, Mickey recorded *Mickey Mouse Disco*. The result was far beyond anyone's expectations: the record went "multi-platinum".

course - many years later - the Disney company's own science-fiction movie *Tron* (1982). In addition, he made major appearances in the Disney features *Fantasia* (1940 [➤176]) and *Fun and Fancy Free* (1947 [➤222]).

One of the finest of Mickey's middle-period shorts was *Thru the Mirror* (1936). (Disney's fascination with the subject was manifested over many succeeding years until the release of the feature *Alice in Wonderland* [➤239]). Mickey falls asleep reading Lewis Carroll's *Through the Looking-Glass* and, sure enough, dreams: his dream-self climbs up onto the mantelpiece and through the mirror. There he discovers a land where inanimate objects have lives and personalities of their own: there is a lugubrious armchair, a footstool that has all the attributes of a yappy little lapdog, an umbrella that behaves like a prim maiden aunt, and so forth. Mickey comes across a bowl of nuts ("Aw, nuts," he says unhappily, as if he had expected something better) and eats one, whereupon he promptly shrinks – to about the size of a real mouse, in fact! The scene is set for some high-class tomfoolery.

Music plays a very important part in this short (as in so many other Disney classics), since almost all of its set-pieces are dances of one kind or another. The tiny Mickey dances with the cord of the telephone, with a pair of gloves, and so forth. But life really starts hotting up for him when he comes across a pack of cards, which he leads around like a column of soldiers. There follows a series of gags with the cards as they cut and shuffle themselves – at one

of his own battles with hostile machinery (➤46), collapses against the lever of the jack that is supporting the vehicle. Instantly the jack's cylinder rockets up, carrying the helpless Mickey with it. Anxious to help his pal, the Goof seizes the cylinder and staggers all over the yard with it, like a Scotsman with a too-heavy caber. In the end the Goof's scrabbling feet encounter a patch of spilled oil, and ...

Mickey was more than sufficiently famous by the mid-1930s to become a guest star in the movies produced by other studios. Of the several such movies in which he appeared the best known is almost certainly *The Hollywood Party* (1934). One reason for the movie's fame is that it is a mess. Virtually all of the current MGM stars were in it – Jimmy Durante, the Three Stooges, Laurel and Hardy, Robert Young, etc., etc. - and virtually all of the MGM directors did a section of the movie. At last the director Allan Dwan was called in to see if anything could be done to save it. His suggestion was that the entire movie be "framed" as if it were a dream of Durante's

while he was waiting for his wife to finish dressing – in this way the movie's disjointedness would, Dwan hoped, seem to be deliberate.

Mickey is found hiding behind the furniture by Durante; after various oddments of by-play, including an excellent impersonation by the Mouse of his human co-star, we leave Mickey playing the piano and move directly into another Disney contribution to the film. This is a colour short called *The Hot Chocolate Soldiers* which, one cannot help feeling, would normally have been released as a Silly Symphony had it only been good enough. Chocolate soldiers do battle with gingerbread men using candies and desserts as weapons; although the chocolate soldiers win the fight they are almost immediately themselves conquered by Nature when the sun comes out and they all melt. It is a short that is, like the feature in which it appears, best forgotten.

Other features in which Mickey made minor appearances include Fox's *My Lips Betray* (1933), starring Lillian Harvey, and of

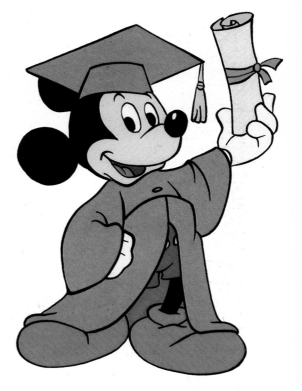

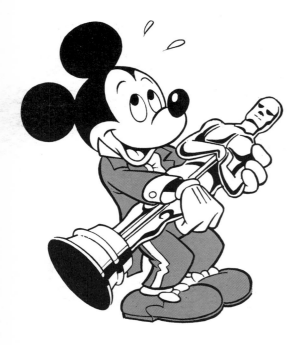

stage in the shuffling Mickey gets unwisely close and temporarily becomes a flat card himself, buffeted in the middle of the pack by the others.

In due course the cards begin to dance, and Mickey joins in enthusiastically – especially when dancing smoochily *à deux* with the beautiful **Queen of Hearts**. Word of this reaches the ears of the powerful **King of Hearts**, who not unnaturally objects and challenges our hero to a duel; the King has an advantage here, because both his top and bottom halves are capable of independent swordsmanship! Nevertheless, Mickey wins, the King ending up sploshing furiously in an inkwell.

The monarch may be down, but he is not out. Calling every card in the mirror-house to his aid, he sends out a huge army to chase the impertinent rodent. Mickey fights back, first squirting the cards with a fountain-pen and then employing the superweapon of an electric fan, which scatters them in all directions. Still, though, it looks as if force of numbers will win the day, and Mickey has to flee. After a superb chase sequence involving King Neptune (➤51) he finds himself back in the room into which he initially stepped after climbing through the mirror; he dashes past the ringing telephone, up onto the mantelpiece and back into the "real world", where he melds into his own restlessly sleeping form. Soon he wakes, finding that the ringing telephone of his dream is in fact his bedside alarm clock. Needless to say, he's a very relieved little mouse.

On occasion the use of music to reinforce the action in such shorts became too much, to the extent that eventually the term "Mickey Mousing" was used by musicians to describe the (sometimes less than subtle) use of music to accentuate every piece of action. It is interesting to note that, while in the Mickey Mouse shorts the music had to follow the trail blazed by the animation, in the Silly Symphonies the two facets of the short were very much more closely entwined, with the action if anything being subservient to the dictates of the music.

For pace and inventiveness *Thru the Mirror* took a lot of beating, but then, in 1938, along came *Brave Little Tailor*, a short based, like so many of Disney's, on a Grimm fairy-tale. In it Mickey succeeded – as ever! – in winning the hand of the fair Princess Minnie (➤33).

Mickey's most celebrated appearance of all is undoubtedly that in *Fantasia* (➤176), where he plays the eponymous role in the section *The Sorcerer's Apprentice*. It is interesting to notice here that the underlying moral of the story of *The Sorcerer's Apprentice* is rather different from that of so many other Mickey Mouse shorts. In many of these the Mouse plays the part of the humble underdog (undermouse?) who makes good in the face of seemingly impossible odds – think of his defeat of the giant in *Brave Little Tailor* or, at a more mundane level, his triumph over Mortimer (➤77) in *Mickey's Rival* (1936). The message would seem to be that the meek will inherit, if not the Earth, then at least the hand of a fair maiden or a certain degree of worldly respect (or both). In *The Sorcerer's Apprentice*, by contrast, the message (as in the original tale) is that the humble should not entertain ideas above their natural station in life.

Terry Ramsaye, in *Motion Picture Herald* in 1932 summed up the more general ethic of Mickey's roles:

> … the irrepressible Mickey in charmingly typical expression of his own psychology, which is based on the principle of the triumph of the boob, the cosmic victory of the underdog, the might of the meek, has in a very certain sense paid tribute to Mr. Chaplin by becoming his successor in certain considerable sectors of the world of the motion picture.

Even before *The Sorcerer's Apprentice*, however, Mickey had received something of an overhaul: his screen persona was capable of increased subtlety of mood; these greater powers of expression were present not only in his face but also in his much more flexible body (it is a staggering experience to watch a late 1930s Mickey short and then, immediately afterwards, *The Sorcerer's Apprentice*: the difference in the two versions of Mickey is profound). The transformation was executed by the great animator Fred Moore. John Canemaker, in his 1979 *Millimeter* piece, spells out how great a transformation this was:

> Mickey had traveled, it seemed, light years away from the crudely drawn, rat-like barnyard sadist he had been, to the tremendously appealing, versatile and subtle performer he became.

Ignoring the difference in message between *The Sorcerer's Apprentice* and the rest, the US literary critic and novelist, the late John Gardner, was moved by Mickey's performance as the Apprentice to write in 1973 that

> From *The Band Concert*, where neither bee nor tornado nor even Donald Duck can interrupt his conducting, to *The Sorcerer's Apprentice*, where he takes on the powers of the universe, Mickey is the Artist, the Ordering Intelligence that will not be abashed by its littleness, at least not for long.

The rise of Nazism in Germany provoked a number of anti-fascist propaganda shorts from the Disney stable, the effectiveness of which tends to be underestimated: a good joke shared by millions does more to damage a tyranny than any number of well reasoned political tracts. Certainly the Nazis took the Disney efforts seriously, banning Mickey Mouse as "the most miserable ideal ever conceived".

Mickey received the same sort of backhanded compliment many years later, in 1954, when the East German government banned him as "an anti-communist subversive". Doubtless the little fellow's chest swelled with pride on both occasions.

Even before the Nazis came to power Mickey had run into trouble in Germany. In 1930 *The Barnyard Battle* (1929 [➤27]) had been banned in that country because of the cats' wearing of German World War I military helmets. Said the authorities: "The wearing of German military helmets by an army of cats is offensive to national dignity." The implications of that statement are worth pondering for a moment!

That other great nation of censors, the Soviet Union, decided during the most frigid period of the Cold War that Mickey was nothing more than "a warmonger" – an opinion which is rather hard to substantiate (another time he was denounced by the Soviet Union as "a typical example of the meekness of the proletariat under capitalist rule"). Earlier, however, the Soviets had avidly pirated Mickey's cartoons. The system was that, immediately on the release of each, the Soviet embassy in the United States would telephone the Disney company and ask to borrow a print for "private screening within the embassy".

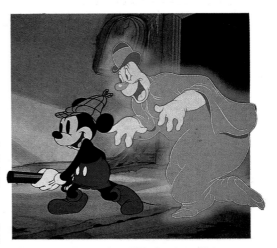

The pursuer pursued in 1937's *Lonesome Ghosts*.

The print would then be rushed by diplomatic bag to Czechoslovakia, copied and then returned to Washington – all within the space of 72 hours! It would finally be handed back to the Disney company with polite thanks for the loan. High flattery indeed.

Although the most important relationship in Mickey's career has obviously been that with Minnie (➤32), he has also for many years acted in – sometimes acerbic – partnership with Pluto. This partnership started with Pluto's third screen appearance, in 1931's The Moose Hunt (➤38). In due course, Pluto became generally independent of Mickey, starring in his own shorts with such characters as Fifi (➤59) and Dinah (➤93), but for his first six years or so he was very much Mickey's dog. And clearly Mickey was very fond of him: in 1939's Society Dog Show, for example, after the pair have been forcibly ejected from the exhibition hall, Mickey hugs the pup and says almost tearfully, "Don't worry, Pluto. You're a better dog than any of 'em." Nevertheless, this affection and mutual respect was often strained, primarily because of Pluto's difficulty in communicating with his master: a good example is Pluto's Christmas Tree (1952 [➤41]), in which Pluto signally fails to convey to Mickey that the Christmas tree they have obtained contains a pair of unwelcome "lodgers" in the form of Chip an' Dale (➤97).

From about 1940 each major Disney shorts character was ascribed its own production team – for both financial and artistic reasons. The team devoted to Mickey was headed by Bill Roberts and Riley Thomson. However, Mickey was by this time very far from the impudent little rebel he had once been – in fact, if anything he had become a little staid. In a retrospective piece published in The Marianist in 1949 James Conniff spelled this out:

He was holier than a horse opera hero, goody-goodier than any cartoon character has a right to be, he never dared to set a bad example by so much as flying off the handle in a situation where anybody but a saint would've blown his top. He turned into this paragon of virtue under pressure from the nearly 500,000,000 fans who, one year during the zenith of his fame, paid for their tickets and stampeded theater ushers to get seats to see their idol. It hasn't made Disney, or anybody else, for that matter, love Mickey any the less. But it has definitely put a limit to the number of situations you can get Mickey into in the course of a year without repeating yourself.

For exactly this reason, Donald Duck (➤61), rather than Mickey, became the front-line Disney star. But this is not to say that during the early 1940s Mickey's cartoons were either nonexistent or low in quality. Among the fine appearances one thinks of The Nifty Nineties (1941 [➤34]), Lend a Paw (1941 [➤39]), Mickey's Birthday Party (1942

[➤45]) and others – not to mention his great role in Fantasia (1940). However, it is significant to note that, while Mickey appeared in six cartoons in 1941 and three in 1942, he turned in only eight further performances in the whole of the rest of the 1940s (one of which was in Fun and Fancy Free [➤222]). Moreover, in most cases he was not so much a star as a co-star, or even a supporting actor. Clearly his theatrical career was starting to decline.

After his penultimate screen appearance (to date), in The Simple Things (1953), however, he made a name for himself in two different media. One was as a live host at Disneyland and Walt Disney World; the other was on television. The Mickey Mouse Club was a phenomenally successful Disney venture from the mid-1950s onward, and the more recently launched New Mickey Mouse Club succeeded in attracting the kids of the kids who watched the original. The album of Mickey Mouse Disco, released in 1979, went "multi-platinum".

As we have noted, Mickey's image is a very potent one; that much cannot be doubted – as advertisers over the years have been glad to note (as an aside, since 1973 many of the merchandizing images of Mickey have shown him in his earlier rather than his later forms). But the epitome of this is to be found in a tale from the late 1950s. A certain Dr Tom Dooley was running a hospital ship off the coast of south-east Asia, offering free medical care to anyone who would come and get it. Sadly, very few would. Clearly the symbol of the Red Cross wasn't a powerful enough attractant and so, as an experiment, he applied for and got permission to put a big picture of Mickey Mouse on the side of his ship. Sure enough, all the local kids came down to the beach for medical check-ups. The interesting point here is that those kids had never even heard of Mickey Mouse: it was the symbol of his face that attracted them.

A rather different south-east-Asian tribute to the power of Mickey's image came in 1970 with a non-Disney animated short called Mickey Mouse in Vietnam. In this cartoon Mickey is depicted as a US soldier who is ferried out to Vietnam. As soon as he gets there he is shot dead – and that is the end of the short. This might not have been quite the role for which the Disney company had been grooming Mickey, but it nevertheless shows the extent to which he was then taken as representing "boy next door" America.

After a 30-year absence from the cinema screens Mickey returned in 1983 playing the role of Bob Cratchit in the featurette Mickey's Christmas Carol, one of the most popular and successful short theatrical subjects of all time. However, it should be noted that here again, despite the title, Mickey (voiced here by Wayne Allwine) plays a supporting rather than a starring part: the real star of the movie is Scrooge McDuck (➤130).

And then, in 1990, came The Prince and

the Pauper, a featurette based on the 1882 Mark Twain novel. Mickey plays a dual role as the Prince whose father dies leaving him to the tender mercies of the treacherous Captain of the Guard (Pete), and as the pauper with whom the Prince – almost disastrously – elects to change places for a time.

And, to everyone's surprise, Mickey has made an even more recent appearance, in the 1995 short Runaway Brain (➤35).

Filmography

Steamboat Willie, November 18, 1928
Gallopin' Gaucho, 1928
Plane Crazy, 1928
The Barn Dance, 1928
The Opry House, 1929
When the Cat's Away, 1929
The Barnyard Battle, 1929
The Plow Boy, 1929
The Karnival Kid, 1929
Mickey's Follies, 1929
Mickey's Choo-Choo, 1929
The Jazz Fool, 1929
Jungle Rhythm, 1929
The Haunted House, 1929
Wild Waves, 1929
Just Mickey (copyrighted as Fiddlin' Around), 1930
The Barnyard Concert, 1930
The Cactus Kid, 1930
The Fire Fighters, 1930
The Shindig, 1930
The Chain Gang, 1930
The Gorilla Mystery, 1930
The Picnic, 1930
Pioneer Days, 1930
The Birthday Party, 1931
Traffic Troubles, 1931
The Castaway, 1931
The Moose Hunt, 1931
The Delivery Boy, 1931
Mickey Steps Out, 1931
Blue Rhythm, 1931
Fishin' Around, 1931
The Barnyard Broadcast, 1931
The Beach Party, 1931
Mickey Cuts Up, 1931
Mickey's Orphans, 1931
The Duck Hunt, 1932
The Grocery Boy, 1932
The Mad Dog, 1932
Barnyard Olympics, 1932
Mickey's Revue, 1932
Musical Farmer, 1932
Mickey in Arabia, 1932
Mickey's Nightmare, 1932
Trader Mickey, 1932
The Whoopee Party, 1932
Touchdown Mickey, 1932
The Wayward Canary, 1932
The Klondike Kid, 1932
Mickey's Good Deed, 1932
Building a Building, 1933
The Mad Doctor, 1933
Mickey's Pal Pluto, 1933 (remade as Lend a Paw, 1941)
Mickey's Mellerdrammer, 1933
Ye Olden Days, 1933
The Mail Pilot, 1933
Mickey's Mechanical Man, 1933
Mickey's Gala Premiere, 1933
Puppy Love, 1933
The Steeple Chase, 1933
The Pet Store, 1933

MINNIE MOUSE

Time, in 1954, called Minnie Mouse "a mousy young lady who looked as much like Mary Pickford as a rodent could". Critic Judith Martin encapsulated her character rather more kindly when she

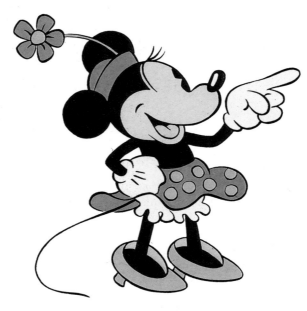

described her as "the shy giggler whose favorite posture is clasped hands, crossed-eyed toes and a face decorated with a bashful smile and a blush". Voiced during the 1930s by Marcellite Garner and later in her career by Ruth Clifford, Minnie Mouse has a special place in everybody's heart – most notably Mickey Mouse's.

In an article in *Scribner's Magazine* in 1934 Claude Bragdon points out that in cartoons, aside from heroes and villians (e.g., Mickey and Pete), a third standard character is the stooge, or feeder, whose task it is to allow the hero to shine by contrast. He elaborates:

> The first and second Little Pigs are feeders for the Third Little Pig. Minnie Mouse is Mickey Mouse's feeder – as when, in *Building a Building* Minnie's hat blows into the excavation, giving Mickey a chance deftly and gallantly to retrieve it in the great iron maw of the steam-shovel which he is operating.

Curiously, in her first screen appearance, in *Steamboat Willie* (1928), she has a rather more independent role – "curiously" because, although this was the first Mickey Mouse short to be released, it was in fact the third to be made, and she was very definitely a "feeder" in the earlier two.

Minnie is late to catch the paddle-steamer piloted by Mickey and skippered by Pete (➤16), and as it moves away from the dock she runs squeaking along the riverside after it, clutching her ukulele and her sheet music. Mickey takes pity on pilot and, hooking a crane into her voluminous bloomers, hauls her aboard. A goat devours her music and her instrument; however, she refuses to be downhearted, and in a famous scene cranks the goat's tail to produce beautiful music – well, a slighty imperfect rendering of "Turkey in the Straw." This starts the two mice off on an orgy of playing animals as

musical instruments – stretching a cat and a goose, pulling piglets' tails, playing a cow's teeth like a xylophone, and so forth. The cruelty implicit in all this later caused Walt some soul-searching (➤25).

But Minnie's role as Mickey's "feeder" is manifest in most of her other early appearances. The third of these, in *Plane Crazy* (1928), involved her playing the part of the archetypal useless hysterical female encountered so often in fiction but so rarely in real life. The short was created by Ub Iwerks – indeed, as in other early Mickey shorts, the credits carry the line "A Walt Disney Comic by Ub Iwerks".

It starts with various farmyard animals building a rickety aeroplane which Mickey plans to fly. He peers into a book on flying and studies carefully a picture of the great Lindbergh; then he ruffles up his hair so that it looks a little more like that of his hero. However, his plane – whose motive power is a dachshund wound up like an elastic band within – fails to perform as successfully as Lindbergh's crashing into a tree soon after take-off.

But Mickey is undaunted. He and his assistants wreck a car to adapt it as a second aircraft; a peacock involuntarily yields its tail for use as a tailplane. Minnie adoringly presents Mickey with a good-luck horseshoe, and he responds by inviting her aboard for the flight. However, just after they have taken off one of the plane's wheels strikes a rock and Mickey is thrown to the ground, leaving Minnie as sole passenger and far from the controls. She has hysterics while the aircraft criss-crosses the sky.

There follows a somewhat distasteful scene in which the aeroplane "chases" a cow – an early version of Clarabelle (➤36) – with a vast udder, the beast fleeing in panic from the prospect of her udder being sliced up by the propeller. The cow ends up hanging grimly onto the back of the plane while Mickey attempts to clamber up her. *De rigueur*, he receives several facefuls of milk before he succeeds (a gag virtually identical with one in *Steamboat Willie*).

With Mickey back in control all seems well, but he lecherously attempts to kiss Minnie; on her refusal he deliberately flies like a madman, hoping to terrify her into submission. However, when he does forcibly kiss her she slaps his face and leaps from the aircraft, using her bloomers as a parachute as she floats to the ground. Mickey, for his part, is now in trouble. The 'plane goes into a spin and crashes groundward. After the inevitable, the lucky horseshoe lands excruciatingly on the Mouse's head, and he shows it with a smile to the simmering Minnie. When she responds by simply stalking off, Mickey throws the artefact away . . . but, like a boomerang, it zooms back and makes a fair try at wringing his neck.

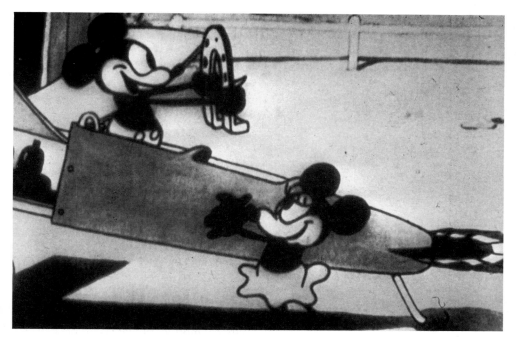

In 1928's *Plane Crazy* Minnie was at first just as keen on flying as Mickey.

Another early Minnie role was in *The Pet Store* (1933), a short which introduced a minor character, **Tony**, in his solitary appearance. Tony is a pet-shop owner who is foolish enough to hire Mickey as an assistant. Minnie arrives to keep Mickey company while Tony is out at lunch, and entertains the animals by singing to them. Alas, she has not reckoned on the presence of **Beppo**, the **Movie Gorilla**, whose hobby is imitating film stars. He comes across a reference to King Kong and decides to emulate him, with Minnie in the role of Fay Wray. The birds and monkeys in the shop help her out, and finally she is released – but not before the shop is wrecked. Mickey, for once displaying abject cowardice, grabs Minnie by the hand and rushes outside, putting Tony's ''Boy Wanted'' sign back in the window. As the pair hear Tony coming back from his lunch they flee.

What is interestingly different between Minnie's roles in many of these early shorts and those she was to play later is that, while in most of them she is very definitely a "feeder" for Mickey she nevertheless retains a sort of romantic independence. She may well be hysterical and useless when the 'plane goes out of control, but she is certainly not going to surrender herself to Mickey's attentions simply because he has rescued her (anyway, he was the one who got her into this mess). In later years she often played a much more passive part, being either Mickey's docile helpmeet or the beautiful lady whose hand he would win in marriage (whether she wished it or no) for some great feat of derring-do.

But this should not be taken to mean that she is a weakling – far from it, as she proves in *Boat Builders* (1938). Mickey, Donald and Goofy have received a boat-building kit and after many a false start they succeed in erecting the proud vessel *Queen Minnie*. The gracious Minnie herself is co-opted into launching this ramshackle construction. Sadly, she wields her champagne bottle with such exuberant zeal that she succeeds not only in launching the boat but also in causing it to break up into its constituent parts.

Nowhere was Minnie's role as the one "whose task it is to allow the hero to shine by contrast" more evident than in *Brave Little Tailor* (1938), in which she plays the fair princess whose hand Mickey would fain win.

The short starts with Mickey working away in his tailor-shop. Buzzing flies are annoying him, and so he goes for them with a swat, killing seven of them with a single swipe. Outside, and unknown to him, the people of the town are discussing a fearsome giant who is terrorizing the neighbourhood, and so naturally they misunderstand when Mickey proudly appears at his window to boast that he has just "killed seven with one blow!". Before he knows quite what is happening, he has been taken to see the King, to whom he is presented as a doughty giant-killer. He is offered six million gold pazoozas and the hand of the King's fair daughter (the curvaceous Minnie) if he will only deal with this one. He sees Minnie, his eyes boggle, and all of a sudden he discovers that he has been nominated Royal High Killer of the Giant.

Armed only with his tailor's shears, plenty of thread and several gallons of nervous adrenaline, he sets off to do battle. Despair overtakes him – just how *do* you do battle with a giant? Needless to say, he finds a (very long and complicated) way, and in due course the deed is done. Mickey returns home to claim the pazoozas and the hand of Minnie. The story could not be more traditional, and versions have often been used by Disney: against all odds the little guy wins the riches *and* the girl.

Minnie's role in *Brave Little Tailor* is, then, a small one in terms of screen-time, but it is absolutely fundamental to the plot of the film: the little tailor is barely tempted by the six million gold pazoozas – there are, after all, lots of other pazoozas in the world, and anyway who needs money? – but there is only the one Princess Minnie. His bravery is born not only out of circumstances – he must battle the giant or die ignominiously –

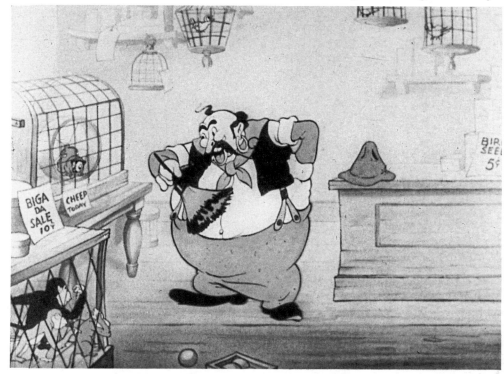

Tony co-starred with Minnie and Mickey in *The Pet Store* (1933). One experience of their little ways seems to have been enough; he never appeared again.

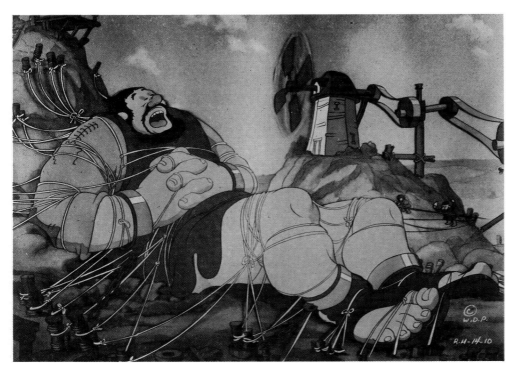

The giant in *Brave Little Tailor*, roundly vanquished by a Mickey spurred on by thoughts of the beautiful Princess Minnie, whose hand is one of the perks in the giant-felling biz.

but also from his instant love for the princess. This theme of a male going through incredible rigours in order to win the favour of a fair lady is prevalent throughout the Disney canon, but nowhere more so than in the shorts featuring Mickey and Minnie. At the other end of the dramatic scale there is, for example, Minnie's inspiring role in *Mickey's Rival* (1936 [➤77]).

In a famous article in *The Spectator* in 1934 the novelist E. M. Forster described his own feelings about this way in which Minnie inspires Mickey:

... I like him as a lover most ... Minnie is his all, his meinie, his moon. Perhaps even the introduction of Pluto was a mistake. ... Mickey's great moments are moments of heroism, and when he carries Minnie out of the harem as a pot-plant or rescues her as she falls in foam ... he reaches heights impossible for the *entrepreneur*. I would not even have the couple sing. The duets in which they increasingly indulge are distracting. Let them confine themselves to raptures appropriate to mice, and let them play their piano less. ...

About Minnie too little has been said ... Nor do we know anything about her family. When discovered alone, she appears to be of independent means, and to own a small house in the midst of unattractive scenery, where, with no servants and little furniture, she busies herself with trifles until Mickey comes. ... Without him, her character shines not. As he enters she expands, she becomes simple, tender, brave and strong, and her coquetterie is of the delightful type which never conceals its object. Ah, that squeak of greeting! As you will have guessed from it, her only fault is hysteria. Minnie does not always judge justly ... It is possible that, like most of us, she is deteriorating. To be approached so often by

Mickey, and always for the first time, must make any mouse mechanical. Perhaps sometimes she worries whether she has ever been married or not ... it seems likely that they have married one another, since it is unlikely that they have married any one else, since there is nobody else for them to marry.

Her role in *The Nifty Nineties* (1941), however, shows her in a quite different guise: rather than being largely the passive

object of Mickey's romantic approaches she is in this case herself the predator. For once she is clad in a full-length dress; in navy blue, it features a prominent inverse-heart-shaped bustle. Spotting Mickey in the park, she lures him using the classic handkerchief-dropping technique: love is instant and fervent, and off the two go to a variety show. After a magic-lantern display about the evils of drink (Minnie weeps over this) they see a pair of tap-dancers, described as "two clever boys from Illinois", **Fred** and **Ward**. (These two were based on the animators Fred Moore and Ward Kimball.)

Afterwards, on their way home in Mickey's car, the loving pair pass a succession of major Disney characters. Goofy (➤44) raises his hat to them and, as a result, falls off his penny-farthing (high-wheeler). Donald (➤61), Daisy (➤80) and the Nephews (➤85) go by on what would be a tandem except that it has five seats rather than two. Then a macho Mickey revs up the car until it is going at a devasting 15mph - although, unlike in *Plane Crazy* (➤32), he is not deliberately trying to scare her. As in *Plane Crazy*, however, the vehicle goes out of control and chases a large-uddered cow – in fact, the sequence involving the cow is so similar to the earlier one that we must wonder if the basic animation were reused. After the car crashes, leaving the terrified cow safe, Mickey and Minnie giggle lovingly together over their narrow brush with death.

While Minnie's relationship with Mickey lay at the heart of the vast majority of the shorts in which she appeared, we should not forget that in a number of them she

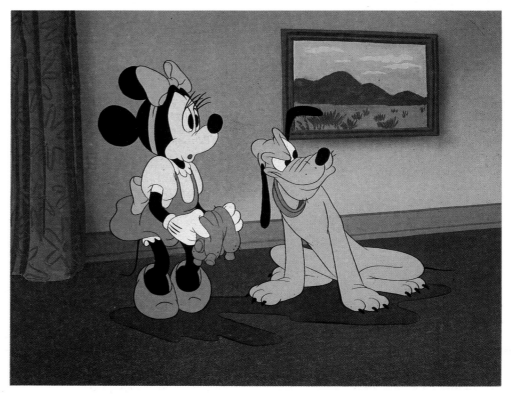

Minnie starred in a number of shorts alongside Pluto and Figaro. Here we see her in *Pluto's Sweater* (1949).

appeared without her true love, notably as the mistress of the house in the series of shorts in which Figaro (➤90) and Pluto (➤38) co-starred. Since Pluto is generally regarded as Mickey's dog rather than Minnie's, one can only assume that she is looking after Pluto while Mickey is out accomplishing some further great adventure.

More prosaically, perhaps Mickey is merely out at work, because a perennial question is: Why, over more than 50 years, has Mickey never done the decent thing and married Minnie? Several plausible reasons have been proposed. One is that Walt himself was positively jealous of her, wished that he'd never created her, and so on, because she had the potential of intruding into that "special relationship" which he had with Mickey. There is evidence outside that of the Figaro and Pluto shorts that this is untrue, for in 1933 Walt confounded the hypothesis by writing in *Film Pictorial* that

> In private life, Mickey is married to Minnie. A lot of people have written to him asking this question, because sometimes he appears to be married to her in his films and other times still courting her. What it really amounts to is that Minnie is, for screen purposes, his leading lady. If the story calls for a romantic courtship, then Minnie is the girl; but when the story requires a married couple, then they appear as man and wife. In the studio we have decided that they are married really.

Minnie has appeared in a total of 70 shorts (if one counts 1929's *The Opry House*, which shows her on a poster, and 1934's *The Dognapper*, in which her picture appears in a newspaper), and yet her starring parts have been few: shorts such as *Mickey's Rival* and *The Nifty Nineties* are among the rare exceptions. Neither has she appeared in any of the features. Her screen role has almost exclusively been a supporting one, whether the character being supported be Mickey himself or Pluto and Figaro. In a way she is rather like Pete (➤15) in this respect, for he too has appeared in a very large number of shorts and yet always as a foil for some one more prominent character. Again like Pete, Minnie may be on screen throughout most of a short and yet always be, as it were, off the centre of the stage; in other shorts she may (essentially) appear only at the beginning and end, acting an absolutely vital "framing" part in terms of the plot and yet not herself contributing a great deal to it.

Unlike Pete, however, she has proved herself over the years to be an immensely popular and enduring character – and children in their hundreds of thousands flock to her at Disneyland and Walt Disney World. It hardly came as any surprise when the Disney company declared that 1986 was to be Minnie's year. It was merely an overdue recognition of the astonishing contribution she has made to our popular culture over the last half-century and more.

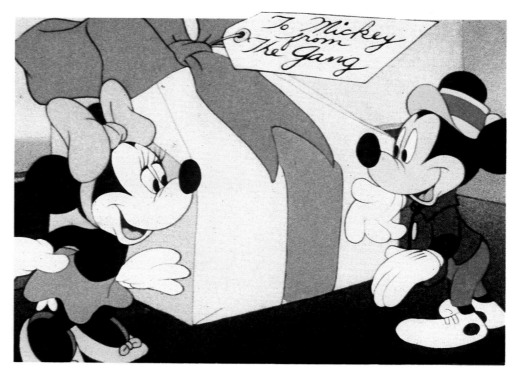

Minnie was delegated by the gang to give Mickey his present in *Mickey's Birthday Party* (1942).

Filmography

Steamboat Willie, November 18, 1928
Gallopin' Gaucho, 1928
Plane Crazy, 1928
The Barn Dance, 1928
The Opry House, 1929 (on a poster)
When the Cat's Away, 1929
The Plow Boy, 1929
The Karnival Kid, 1929
Mickey's Follies, 1929
Mickey's Choo-Choo, 1929
Wild Waves, 1929
The Cactus Kid, 1930
The Fire Fighters, 1930
The Shindig, 1930
The Gorilla Mystery, 1930
The Picnic, 1930
Pioneer Days, 1930
The Birthday Party, 1931
Traffic Troubles, 1931
The Delivery Boy, 1931
Mickey Steps Out, 1931
Blue Rythm, 1931
The Barnyard Broadcast, 1931
The Beach Party, 1931
Mickey Cuts Up, 1931
Mickey's Orphans, 1931
The Grocery Boy, 1932
Barnyard Olympics, 1932
Mickey's Revue, 1932
Musical Farmer, 1932
Mickey in Arabia, 1932
Mickey's Nightmare, 1932
The Whoopee Party, 1932
Touchdown Mickey, 1932
The Wayward Canary, 1932
The Klondike Kid, 1932
Building a Building, 1933
Mickey's Pal Pluto, 1933
Mickey's Mellerdrammer, 1933
Ye Olden Days, 1933
The Mail Pilot, 1933
Mickey's Mechanical Man, 1933
Mickey's Gala Premiere, 1933

Puppy Love, 1933
The Steeple Chase, 1933
The Pet Store, 1933
Shanghaied, 1934
Camping Out, 1934
Mickey's Steam Roller, 1934
The Dognapper, 1934 (appears in newspaper)
Two-Gun Mickey, 1934
On Ice, 1935
Mickey's Rival, 1936
Hawaiian Holiday, 1937
Boat Builders, 1938
The Fox Hunt, 1938 (cameo appearance)
Brave Little Tailor, 1938
Mickey's Surprise Party (commercial), 1939
The Little Whirlwind, 1941
The Nifty Nineties, 1941
Out of the Frying Pan Into the Firing Line, 1942
Mickey's Birthday Party, 1942
First Aiders, 1944
Bath Day, 1946
Figaro and Frankie, 1947
Mickey's Delayed Date, 1947
Pluto's Sweater, 1949
Pluto and the Gopher, 1950
Crazy Over Daisy, 1950 (cameo appearance)
Pluto's Christmas Tree, 1952
Mickey's Christmas Carol, 1983
Who Framed Roger Rabbit, 1988
Runaway Brain, 1995

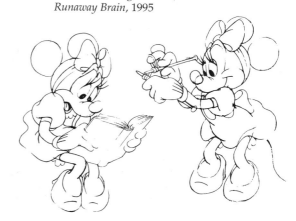

CLARABELLE COW

One of the earliest appearances, if not the earliest, of a Disney cow that bore all the hallmarks of Clarabelle was in *Alice on the Farm* (1926). The most prominent feature of this animal is her vast, multi-studded udder, which Julius the Cat (►13) tries with little success to milk in progressively more improbable ways: suffice it to say that the cow ends up inside a vacuum cleaner.

This business of the udder is important in terms of Clarabelle's career. In fact, one could suggest that Clarabelle has really had two quite distinct incarnations. The first was when Ub Iwerks was largely responsible for the output of Disney shorts, doing much of the animation and supervising everything. In this incarnation her role was hardly more than as a mobile udder – Iwerks was very fond of udder jokes (it is reported that Walt himself was not, but permitted them because he respected Iwerks' judgement and because audiences liked them – yet the udder jokes did not stop after Iwerks' departure). The wit of such jokes can be sampled by watching *Plane Crazy* (1928 [►32]) in which there is an extended sequence in which one is supposed to laugh as Clarabelle flees in panic from the prospect of having her udder sliced to ribbons by an aircraft propeller.

In an "interview" with Mickey Mouse published in *Funnyworld* in 1969 John Benson puts into Mickey's mouth a comment on the udder problem, suggesting that it was part of the reason for Clarabelle's demise:

> She was a very sensitive performer, and when I knew her, she was on her way to becoming a star. Then that vicious and completely baseless scandal [i.e., the udder business] ruined her career. It was a tragic waste; she never really completely recovered from it, personally, you know.

Interestingly, after Iwerks had left the Disney court, he seems to have been reluctant to relinquish some of the Disney characters. In his own short *Mary's Little Lamb*, for example, two of the characters, a cow and a horse, are virtually indistinguishable from Clarabelle and Horace Horsecollar (►37). Indeed, a number of the Disney characters made unauthorized and unacknowledged "guest appearances", in all but name, in the cartoons produced by Iwerks' studio.

Clarabelle has had, let us face it, the odd brush with the censor. One Mickey Mouse short in which she appeared was banned in Ohio because in it she was seen to be reading a copy of Elinor Glyn's *Three Weeks* (1907), described in *Chambers Biographical Dictionary* as "a book which gained a reputation for naughtiness". More serious, though, was this question of her udder. In the early shorts it was vast, elastic and the subject of many a ribald and not very funny

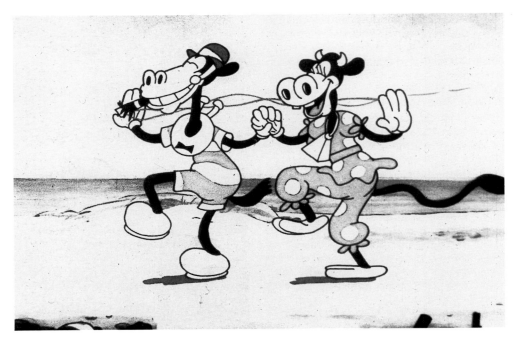

Clarabelle with Horace Horsecollar in the 1931 short *The Beach Party*. The two of them worked well together, but somehow never made it into the big time.

gag. After Iwerks went, as we have noted, the udder jokes were toned down a little, but it nevertheless took the pressure of several censorship boards to persuade Walt to drop them completely. Thereafter, Clarabelle always wore a modest skirt.

But Clarabelle's basic trouble has had nothing to do with censors: it is that she has never caught on. She is a perennial extra.

One of her few comparatively major roles was in *Mickey's Fire Brigade* (1935). The regular gang of Mickey, Donald and Goofy are in their usual incompetent way trying to save a blazing building; Clarabelle, bathing songfully on one of the upper storeys, is oblivious to all danger. When Fire Officer Goofy pops his head through the bathroom transom her response is to scream and wrap the shower curtain modestly about herself; when the Goof tries to explain she refuses to listen and beats him over the head with her back-scrubber, screaming again and again. She is, shall we say, a trifle nonplussed when Mickey and Donald use the Goof as a battering ram to break down the bathroom door and force her, the bath and themselves

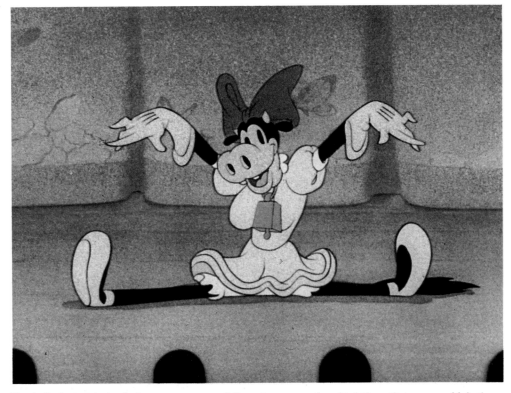

Clarabelle demonstrates that you were wrong all those times you refused to believe that cows could do the splits. The still is from the 1941 colour remake of *Orphan's Benefit*.

out through the window and slithering down their fire-ladder. She, still ensconced in her bath-tub, lands in the fire engine first, but is shortly joined among the suds by the intrepid trio. As their heads surface one by one from the churned waters she swats them with her back-scrubber.

Later appearances were in bit parts – for example, in *Pluto's Christmas Tree* (1952), in which she plays the role of a carol singer. She has a tiny part, too, in a party scene in *Mickey's Christmas Carol* (1983). In fact, Clarabelle's great trouble has been that she has never really developed beyond the stage of being a minor supporting actress: while other Disney characters started off in a small way and then surged to stardom, she could never quite manage it.

Filmography

Plane Crazy, 1928
The Plow Boy, 1929
The Beach Party, 1931
Mickey's Revue, 1932
Touchdown Mickey, 1932
Mickey's Gala Premiere, 1933
Camping Out, 1934
On Ice, 1935
Mickey's Fire Brigade, 1935
Mickey's Grand Opera, 1936
Mickey's Polo Team, 1936
Mickey's Amateurs, 1937
Orphan's [sic] *Benefit*, 1941 (colour remake of 1934 original)
Mickey's Birthday Party, 1942
Pluto's Christmas Tree, 1952
Mickey's Christmas Carol, 1983
Who Framed Roger Rabbit, 1988
The Prince and the Pauper, 1990

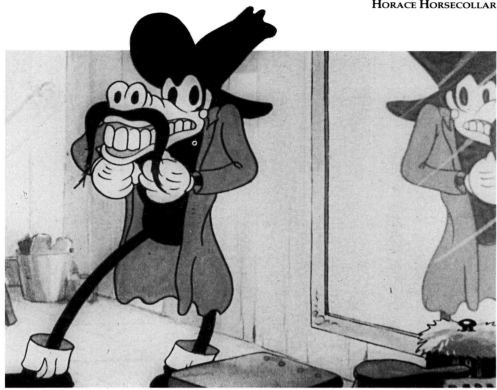

Horace, disguised as Simon Legree for *Mickey's Mellerdrammer* (1933), manages for once to look terrifying. Well, almost.

HORACE HORSECOLLAR

Like Clarabelle Cow (►36), Horace Horsecollar, the cheerfully goofy horse with the studded collar slung nonchalantly around his neck, has never succeeded in graduating from bit-part supporting actor to Disney star: he has appeared in no fewer than 14 shorts yet he has failed to make any real impact on the audience. This is probably because, in a way, he has no real personality: the great strength of the Disney characters has always been that they are *real*, with their share of "human" failings and strengths, yet both Horace and Clarabelle are simply recognizable faces brought in to swell the ranks. The only time that Horace influenced the course of a short – other than by serendipitous accident – was in *Mickey's Mellerdrammer* (1933), in which he played the part of Simon Legree in a play based on Harriet Beecher Stowe's 1852 novel *Uncle Tom's Cabin*. Here Horace attempts on stage to whip Uncle Tom, played by Mickey; the audience boo and throw decaying vegetables, and the whole show ends in disarray. It is interesting to note that Horace has to "borrow" a character in order to make any real impact.

A typical example of a late appearance by Horace came in *Pluto's Christmas Tree* (1952), in which, right at the end, Horace played the part of a carol singer. Also, he acted as an extra in *Mickey's Christmas Carol* (1983) – but then so did virtually every other classic Disney character (with the astonishing exception of Pluto).

Why did Disney make no attempt to develop Horace and Clarabelle? The question is unanswerable: we can no longer ask Walt. Perhaps he just felt that the two characters lacked what it takes to achieve stardom (which is true) and therefore simply lost interest in them.

After a very long hiatus, Horace had cameo roles in *Mickey's Christmas Carol* (1983) and *Who Framed Roger Rabbit* (1988), and then a much more significant role in 1990's *The Prince and the Pauper*, in which he played the part of the Prince's pompous tutor. Could this be the herald of an unprecedented screen comeback?

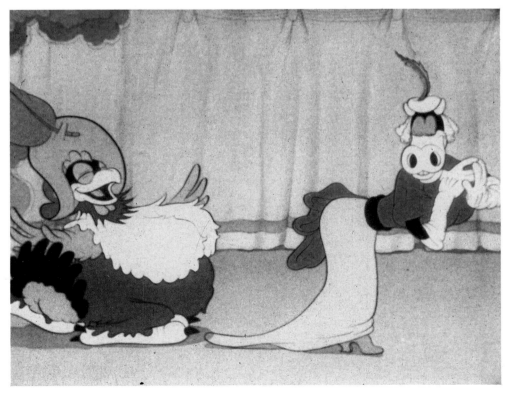

Clarabelle singing with bovine chic in *Mickey's Amateurs* (1937).

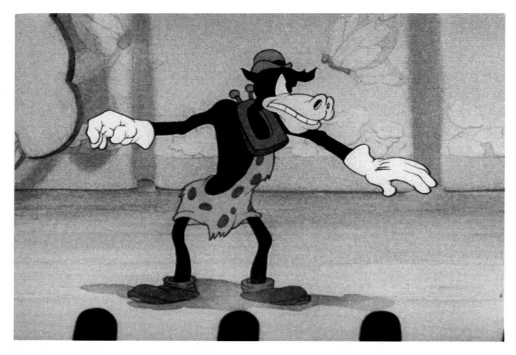

Horace shows that macho is as macho does in the 1941 colour remake of *Orphan's Benefit*.

Filmography

The Plow Boy, 1929
The Beach Party, 1931
Mickey's Revue, 1932
Mickey's Mellerdrammer, 1933
Mickey's Gala Premiere, 1933
All Together, 1942
Mickey's Birthday Party, 1942
Pluto's Christmas Tree, 1952
Mickey's Christmas Carol, 1983
Who Framed Roger Rabbit, 1988
The Prince and the Pauper, 1990

SATAN

Satan – the Devil himself – appeared in a 1930 Silly Symphony called *Hell's Bells*. The short's copyright synopsis is lost, and so we cannot establish Satan's exact role.

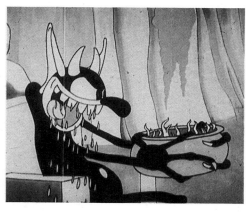

Satan, as seen in the 1929 Silly Symphony *Hell's Bells*. Seems they make their chilies *hot* down there . . .

Of course, in a different guise, Satan made a chilling apperance in the 1940 feature *Fantasia* (➤186). Rather confusingly, in *Fantasia* he is called Chernabog, which is more properly the name of a sort of demon-deity. Satan, as Satan, appeared also in the 1942 propaganda short *Stop That Tank! Pluto* (the god of the underworld, not the pup!) appeared in the 1934 short *The Goddess of Spring* (➤73).

PLUTO

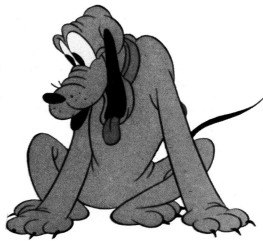

The first short in which Mickey Mouse and Pluto appeared together was *The Chain Gang* (1930); it was also Pluto's own first and second appearance. The reason for this cryptic comment is that *The Chain Gang* featured two identical and unnamed Plutos who, far from being Mickey's friendly pup,

were relentless bloodhounds. Since Mickey was playing the part of a prisoner escaped from a chain gang, the first encounter between Pluto and himself could hardly have been less propitious.

Pluto's second outing – in *The Picnic* (1930) – was but little more indicative of his future career. In this short he at least had a name, Rover, but he was very definitely Minnie's dog rather than Mickey's; indeed, he was a confounded hindrance to Mickey's amorous intentions during a picnic "the mouse" shared with his bashful little paramour. After a fight with some jack-rabbits that inexorably destroyed any prospect of romantic dalliance, he found himself eventually used by a frustrated Mickey – his tail made a perfect windshield wiper for Mickey's car.

Six months later all had changed, and one of the most famous friendships in cinematic history was forged. The short in question was *The Moose Hunt*, which saw Pluto pretending to have been accidentally shot by the Mouse. Sometime in the early 1940s the Disney company released a publicity document, ostensibly written by Mickey Mouse, which described how this transformation of roles had come about:

Well, along about this time, Walt decided that I should have a permanent pet. First we had to find a name for him. Everybody in the studio got to thinking. Names like Rover and Pal were dreamed up, but none seemed to fit. One day Walt came in and said, "How about Pluto the Pup?" – and Pluto it's been ever since.

Pluto's career has really had several strands. In one he is Mickey's boon companion, the faithful, loving dog of every little boy's dreams. In another he seems very definitely to be Minnie's dog, sharing the household with her and Figaro (➤90). Many of his screen appearances, on the other hand, show him as an independent agent, although often captivated by the sensual allure of either Fifi (➤59) or Dinah (➤93). Yet another strand sees him bedevilled by Chip an' Dale (➤96), although their major victim was of course the Duck. The transfer of their unwelcome attentions was well deserved, because during the 1930s Donald himself was not averse to persecuting Pluto. In *On Ice* (1935), for example, the mischievous Duck takes great pleasure in tormenting the poor foolish hound . . . only, as one might expect, to get his come-uppance in the end. The gang are enjoying (if that is the right word) a skating party on the frozen surface of the river. Mickey is doing his best to impress Minnie with his skating prowess, an effect rather spoilt when he falls through a gap in the ice and gets entangled in a NO SWIMMING sign. Goofy is trying to catch fish by throwing tobacco as bait down through a hole in the ice and then clubbing the creatures as they leap out of the water to spit the stuff out; alas, his club always misses by a fair margin.

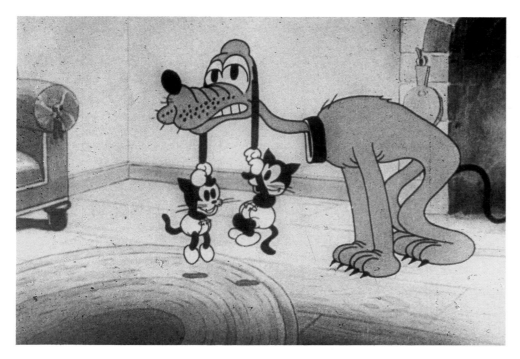

It's tough being a dog – especially Mickey's – as Pluto finds in *Mickey's Orphans* (1931).

Pluto, for his part, has dozed off beside a campfire on the shore by the time that Donald appears on the scene. A plot hatches visibly in the Duck's brain. Moments later he has tied skates onto the hound's feet. Don runs off to hide and then makes the sound of a vexatious cat. Instantly Pluto is awake. He chases the sound but, because of the skates, ends up in a tangled heap on the ice. While Donald makes a fair attempt literally to explode with laughter, the unfortunate dog does his best to learn how to stay standing on the skates. At last – success! But then he sneezes, blowing himself backwards across the ice to land bottom-first in the campfire. The howls are piteous to hear as the red-hot pup skates across the ice to find a hole through which he can prod his agonized rear into the frigid waters. This gambit cures the pain but creates new problems for Pluto: when his tail emerges frozen into a rapier-like stiffness he fails to recognize it, and has a frenzied skidding fight on the ice with this "stranger".

Donald, of course, finds all this the height of wit. In due course, however, he decides that all good things must come to an end, and goes off to do some serious skating. "Serious"? – you must be joking. After a dangerous contest of wills with a precipitous waterfall Donald is plunged into the river's icy waters, his only escape being a certain hole in the ice. Goofy, who is by now using a club the size of a smallish redwood tree in his attempts to stun the leaping fish, for once makes contact ... and now, at last, it is Pluto's turn to laugh.

However, Pluto and Donald shared the screen only rarely – in only seven shorts, in fact (if you count 1952's *Pluto's Christmas Tree*, in which the Duck has a fleeting part as a member of a band of carol-singers). The

experiment of pairing the two of them up was obviously tried quite seriously in 1936 with *Donald and Pluto*, but the blend was not really a successful one: the short is rather pedestrian by Disney standards, almost all of the gags centring on Pluto's having swallowed Don's powerful magnet, so that metal objects fly at him. The problem was probably that it was impossible to find a formula whereby the Duck's explosively violent humour could interact with Pluto's much gentler style, other than by having Don constantly tormenting the poor beast before inevitably getting his come-uppance. That worked once, in *On Ice*, but it wouldn't really have been funny time after time. The whole principle of the Disney "constant tormentors", such as the Nephews and Chip an' Dale, is that they are ostensibly smaller and weaker than the targets of their unwelcome attentions. Pluto, by contrast, would be very much the underdog (quite literally) in any confrontation with Don. Much easier to keep Pluto paired, for the most part, with the far gentler Mickey.

And of such shorts there are dozens. Many are based on Pluto's inability to communicate some important fact to his master; many others centre on his affection for Mickey and his consequent jealousy should he perceive that something is coming between him and the object of that affection.

Typical of this latter type is *Mickey's Pal Pluto* (1933), which Disney remade in colour in the form of the Academy Award-winning short *Lend a Paw* (1941). In the latter version Pluto sees, floating down the river, a bag from within which are coming pathetic whines; bravely he pulls the bag ashore and rescues its occupant – but when he discovers what he has rescued he is disgusted. It is a kitten – ugh! – and in true

canine fashion he tries to chase it away. But it follows him home through the snow, and Mickey showers a great deal of attention on it: he even feeds it milk from Pluto's very own bowl. Jealousy takes the visual form of a Devil-Pluto with a red-lined black cape, little black horns and a trident; the Devil-Pluto's message to the dog is unequivocal: "Don't let that mug muscle in. Who's it going to be? – You, or him?" However, the Devil-Pluto is not to have everything its own way, because down drifts a haloed Angel-Pluto to put the opposing point of view: "Don't take that Devil's bad advice. Be a good dog – treat him [the kitten] nice." Great poetry this may not be, but one approves the sentiment. (This dual nature was to characterize Pluto throughout his career: in one moment he is the genial pup, in the next he is ready to go for the throat of *anybody*.)

Pluto does not, though, pay too much attention to the Angel-Pluto: he has an ear only for the Devil-Pluto, and follows its instructions in attempts to land the kitten in trouble with Mickey. He puts the kitten up next to the bowl of Mickey's goldfish, Bianca (►88), with the result that kitten, dog and goldfish bowl end up in a heap on the floor. An irate Mickey, unfortunately for Pluto, discovers from Bianca, who has somehow survived all this, who the *real* culprit was, and Pluto is cast out of the house into the snow.

Inside, the kitten has great fun playing with a ball; but this bounces out through the front door and eventually into the bucket of the house's well. The kitten follows, and the bucket drops down the shaft into the murky cold waters beneath. A ferocious argument breaks out between the Angel-Pluto and the Devil-Pluto: should the dog rescue the kitten or leave it, heh heh, to drown? Verbal warfare descends into physical warfare, from which the Angel-Pluto emerges scathed but triumphant. Pluto saves the kitten but is himself trapped at the bottom of the well in the freezing water: all is not well that ends in a well.

But Mickey comes to the rescue. He hauls up a Pluto who is frozen solid, and soon has him thawed out. Scenes of mutual love and restored affection break out, and Pluto is positively delighted when the little black kitten goes so far as to kiss him on the nose. The moral of the tale is made piously clear by the Angel-Pluto: virtue will always be rewarded in the end.

Pluto has had, of course, many different feline adversaries: Figaro (►90) is the most notable "regular" among these but there have been plenty of others. In one short, *Pluto's Judgement Day* (1935), Pluto, having chased a kitten, is reprimanded by Mickey and then has the most appalling nightmare about being put on trial by a court of cats. Various of his crimes are recounted through flashbacks. (Interestingly, a cat called **Uncle Tom** displays a gag not used by Disney since the times of Julius (►13) – that of nine

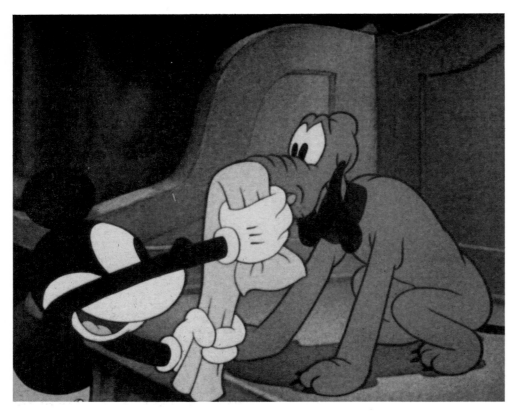

Mickey thinks Pluto is better than any other dog, but still a bit of last-minute spit-and-polish is called for in *Society Dog Show* (1939).

lives ghostishly leaving his body, the last being caught and returned just in the nick of time.) Needless to mention, Pluto, once he has awoken, makes up with the kitten.

In the following year, in *Mickey's Grand Opera* (1936), Pluto discovered the hard way that one of the virtues worth practising is obedience: had he obeyed when Mickey had told him to go home, rather than fool around behind-stage at the opera, various disgraceful scenes might not have ensued. On second thoughts, perhaps they might have anyway, because the high-point of the opera is a duet between Clara Cluck (➤72) and Donald Duck (➤61), two characters with a shared talent for wreaking accidental destruction. Still, in this case it is definitely Pluto's fault. He begins innocently enough by stalking the top-hat left lying around by the conjurer who is going to be performing in the theatre all next week. This is certainly a magic hat: as Pluto prowls after it, it spills out rabbits, pigeons and various other items of wildlife. After a chase it leads him slyly on-stage, where Donald and Clara are singing their hearts out. Here it shows the versatility of its magical abilities, for it leaps into the bell of a tuba in the orchestra; moments later the tuba sprouts a flower and from this leaps a cheeky green frog. And where might you expect a frog to seek refuge in these circumstances? Correct: inside Don's mouth at the moment that he is hitting a most imposing high note. The unfortunate Duck discovers in an explosion of frustration quite what it means to suffer from a frog in the throat.

1939 saw a rather special Pluto/Mickey short in the shape of *The Pointer*. Here Pluto shows himself to be the worst hunting-dog of all time; especially memorable is the scene in which Mickey is stalking along confidently imagining that the footsteps rustling behind him are Pluto's; of course, they're not – they belong to the biggest grizzly bear in the entire forest! The short

ends with Pluto self-assuredly doing some "pointing" amid the wreckage of their campsite: the target of his "pointing" proves to be a can of beans – their supper.

From about 1940 onwards the major Disney characters were each assigned their own production teams. The team devoted to Pluto shorts was led by Norm Ferguson and Nick Nichols. Other Pluto specialists were Bill Roberts and Shamus Culhane.

1942 was something of a bumper year for Pluto fans: the five shorts in which he featured, *Pluto, Junior*, *The Army Mascot*, *The Sleepwalker*, *T-Bone for Two* and *Pluto at the Zoo*, are all classics in one way or another; notably, *Pluto, Junior* saw the sole appearance of the character of that name (➤93), *T-Bone for Two* saw the second appearance of Butch (➤92), and *The Sleepwalker* introduced the sultry Dinah (➤93).

In *Pluto at the Zoo*, however, the world's favourite pup is very much the sole star of the show. Pluto is out walking with a tiny bone in his mouth when he spots, through the gate of the zoo, that the lion is sleeping in its cage beside a real monster of a bone. In the wink of an eye Pluto's own bone is in a litterbin and he is inside the lion's cage. Alas, he cannot get the vast bone out through the bars, and so he swiftly tunnels into the next cage. He returns for the bone and escapes narrowly with his life from a now wakeful and furious lion. Life is not so much easier for him in the next cage, however: its occupants are a mother and baby kangaroo and, after the baby has had some pleasure twitting the poor pup, the

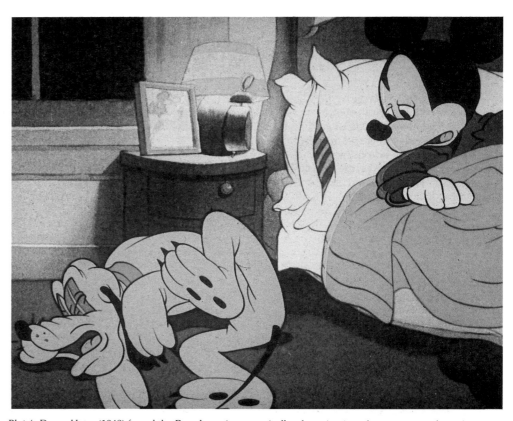

Pluto's Dream House (1940) found the Pup dreaming ecstatically of moving into the most magnificent kennel in the world.

mother awakens and painfully kicks him into the next enclosure. Things go from bad to worse: Pluto is confronted by a giant gorilla and, when this lineal descendant of King Kong grins at him, collapses in a faint. With a leer of innocent fascination on its face, the enormous creature "winds up" the unconscious Pluto's legs, so that he zooms all over the place like an overwound clockwork toy, finally ending up in the – oh no! – alligator pond.

Escaping from the snapping jaws, Pluto flees so swiftly that, for example, when he hurtles past a drowsy tiger he strips all the stripes off it. Sadly, however, at the end of the flight he finds himself right back in the lion's cage. It moves to gobble him up but, thinking swiftly for once, the resourceful pup props the creature's jaws open using the huge bone and makes his escape.

Rather touchingly, the final section of the short shows Pluto retrieving his original tiny bone from the litterbin and being quite delighted that, after his hectic adventure, he still at least has *it*.

The following year, 1943, saw the genesis of the two rascally chipmunks, Chip an' Dale, in a short called *Private Pluto* (➤96), where the hapless pup, on military service, experienced the sharp end of their unwelcome attentions. Although Donald was to be their main victim, Pluto was not entirely to escape their clutches, and they tormented him in such shorts as *Squatter's Rights* (1946 [➤96]) and *Pluto's Christmas Tree* (1952 [➤97]). Both of these shorts are of especial interest in the context of the relationship between Pluto and his master, because the plots of both are based on the dog's frustration at being unable to communicate with Mickey. In *Pluto's Christmas Tree*, for example, Mickey and Pluto have brought home a Christmas tree which contains, unknown to Mickey, two sitting tenants in the form of the wicked little chipmunks. Pluto, however, knows the truth, but everything he does to try to evict them has the sole result of landing him in hot water with his lord and master. In the end the spirit of Yuletide triumphs.

Another tormentor was the coyote Bent-Tail (➤104), who appeared in a series of shorts succeeding *The Legend of Coyote Rock* (1945). In fact, Pluto's very last cinema release – and then it was really a 1961 television featurette released in 1968 to cinemas outside the United States only – was a film called *The Coyote's Lament*. The coyotes in this latter were named not as Bent-Tail and his family but as Pappy Coyote, Junior Coyote and Grandpappy Coyote – but they are very closely related to Bent-Tail.

Plenty of other animals sought to bedevil Pluto's life – and usually succeeded. Figaro (➤90) was a notable adversary, and another (appearing in three shorts) was the **Gopher**. This creature first appears in the 1941 short *Canine Caddy*; he is not to be confused with the Gopher who appears in a couple of the Winnie the Pooh featurettes

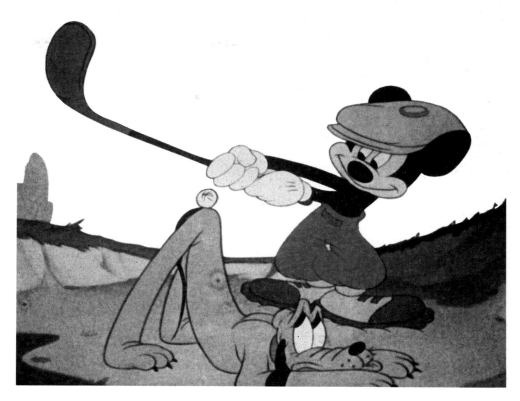

A still from *Canine Caddy* (1941).

(➤125) and *The New Adventures of Winnie the Pooh* (➤140). This one is yet another soldier in the animal kingdom's ruthless war against the unfortunate Pluto. He appears also in *Bone Bandit* (1948) and notably in *Pluto and the Gopher* (1950).

In the former, Pluto wakes from a snooze in the yard to find that his bowl is empty. However, no panic: he remembers where he has buried a large bone. He locates the spot but, as he sniffs around, he shakes pollen from the flowers and sneezes mightily. This alerts the attention of the Gopher, who appears on the surface to gather in some vegetation; as Pluto turns to investigate the Gopher grabs his tail, thinking it to be a plant, and pulls *hard*. Pluto is lucky to escape interment, but puts his paw down into the ground to investigate the Gopher's cavernous home. He finds his bone: it has been serving as a main prop for one of the Gopher's tunnels. A fight ensues over the ownership of the bone, with Pluto twice more encountering pollen which causes him to sneeze; his final sneeze, which occurs when he is actually inside the Gopher's subterranean home, blows up the entire backyard. Still, it reveals the bone which moments before was in the Gopher's possession. As Pluto looks up he sees the Gopher floating down from on high using a bunch of flowers as a parachute and surrounded by a cloud of pollen; for once it is the Gopher who is sneezing uncontrollably . . .

In his second short the Gopher is unwittingly scooped up by Minnie when she is potting a plant in the garden and so is brought into the house. In this short it is interesting to note that Pluto and the little animal are united in a single aim: to get the Gopher back out of the house again, an aim not assisted by the Gopher's lack of knowledge of such materials as window-glass – nor indeed by Pluto's desire to chase him rather than assist him back into the garden. Pluto, of course, gets the full blame from Minnie for the destruction caused.

Time was running out for Pluto. In 1951 he appeared in four shorts, in 1952 two, and in 1953 there was only a single short, his farewell (very surprisingly, he was not in the 1983 featurette *Mickey's Christmas Carol* – the only one of the central gang to be passed over in this way). This film, his last to receive full-scale cinema release, was *The Simple Things*. It is not one of Pluto's most distinguished shorts, consisting essentially

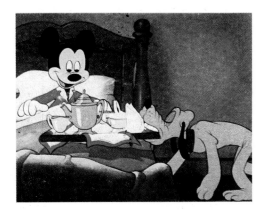

Keeping Mickey in luxury in *A Gentleman's Gentleman* (1941).

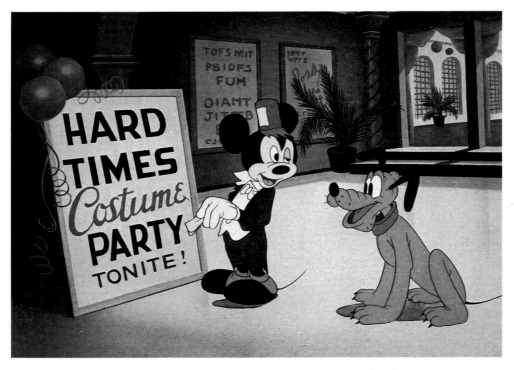

Pluto and Mickey in *Mickey's Delayed Date* (1947). Can *you* decode the posters behind?

himself should stop doing the part. Bill Farmer took the role in *The Prince and the Pauper* (1990), in which Pluto is the pauper Mickey's ever-loyal mutt.

Finally, a matter of urgent debate. The love-life of Pluto, "the arch-shaped dog with the vivid imagination kept busy constantly turning out schemes which don't work", as critic Judith Martin once described him, has had its complexities. For a number of years the target of his passionate yearnings was

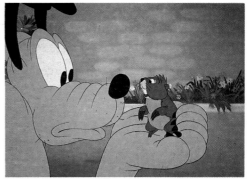

The Gopher in his second and final short, *Pluto and the Gopher* (1950).

of a string of gags centred on a trip taken by Mickey and his faithful pal to the seaside. One sequence deserves special mention, though. Pluto has more than his fair share of difficulties with a particularly obstinate clam, which heaps a final indignity upon him by becoming stuck in his mouth. When Pluto tries to get help from Mickey, the Mouse fails to understand, and assumes that he is simply hungry. Generously Mickey tosses a hot dog towards Pluto, and the clam opens inside the dog's mouth

eagerly to gobble the hot dog down. Mickey cannot, of course, believe Pluto's ill manners, ingratitude and greed. Only after the clam has inadvisedly swallowed a great mass of pepper does it finally sneeze itself out of the miserable pup's mouth.

Pluto's barks have been voiced variously during his long and respected career by the versatile Pinto Colvig, better known as the "voice of Goofy", by Lee Millar and by Jim Macdonald, who voiced many Mickey cartoons after Walt had decided that he

Fifi (►59), who starred with him in *Puppy Love* (1933), *Pluto's Quin-Puplets* (1937), *Society Dog Show* (1939) and the commercial *Mickey's Surprise Party* (1939); she bore him at least one litter during these years. In later life, however, his more mature tastes led him to a curvaceous dachshund and semi-professional heartbreaker called Dinah (►93), who rent his emotions in the shorts *The Sleepwalker* (1942), *Canine Casanova* (1945), *In Dutch* (1946), *Pluto's Heart Throb* (1950) and *Wonder Dog* (1950). Why Pluto shifted his attentions from the complaisant Fifi to the flirtatious but ultimately non-complying Dinah we may never know. Nor will we know why, as late as 1947 in *Pluto's Blue Note*, Fifi appears amid a crowd of other lady dogs who scream their romantic approval of Pluto's singing prowess. The mysteries of the heart are mysteries indeed.

Filmography

The Chain Gang, 1930 (unnamed)
The Picnic, 1930 (called Rover – Minnie's dog)
The Moose Hunt, 1931 (first named as Pluto)
Mickey Steps Out, 1931
Fishin' Around, 1931
The Beach Party, 1931
Mickey Cuts Up, 1931
Mickey's Orphans, 1931
The Duck Hunt, 1932
The Grocery Boy, 1932
The Mad Dog, 1932
Barnyard Olympics, 1932
Mickey's Revue, 1932
Just Dogs, 1932
Mickey's Nightmare, 1932
Trader Mickey, 1932
The Wayward Canary, 1932
The Klondike Kid, 1932
Mickey's Good Deed, 1932
The Mad Doctor, 1933

Pluto followed Mickey when the Mouse became more urbanized; a still from *Mickey and the Seal* (1948).

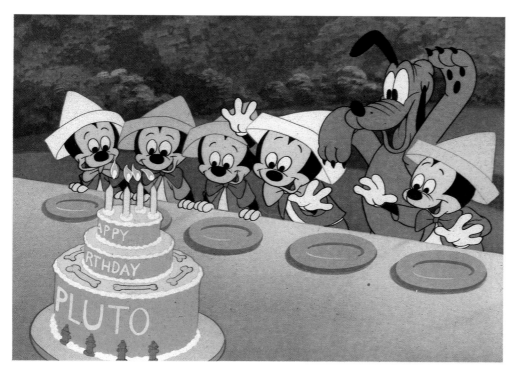

Pluto's Party (1952) saw Pluto prepare to wrap himself around the birthday cake. He reckoned without the guests ...

Mickey's Pal Pluto, 1933 (remade as *Lend a Paw*, 1941)
Puppy Love, 1933
Playful Pluto, 1934
Mickey Plays Papa, 1934
Mickey's Kangaroo, 1935
Mickey's Garden, 1935
Pluto's Judgement Day, 1935
On Ice, 1935
Mickey's Grand Opera, 1936
Alpine Climbers, 1936
Donald and Pluto, 1936
Mickey's Elephant, 1936
Mother Pluto, 1936
The Worm Turns, 1937
Hawaiian Holiday, 1937
Pluto's Quin-Puplets, 1937 (1st "Pluto" cartoon)
Mickey's Parrot, 1938
Society Dog Show, 1939
Mickey's Surprise Party, 1939 (commercial)
Beach Picnic, 1939
The Pointer, 1939
Donald's Dog Laundry, 1940
Bone Trouble, 1940
Put-Put Troubles, 1940
Pluto's Dream House, 1940
Window Cleaners, 1940
Mr. Mouse Takes a Trip, 1940
Pantry Pirate, 1940
Pluto's Playmate, 1941
A Gentleman's Gentleman, 1941
Canine Caddy, 1941
Lend a Paw, 1941 (remake of *Mickey's Pal Pluto*, 1933)
Pluto, Junior, 1942
The Army Mascot, 1942
The Sleepwalker, 1942
T-Bone for Two, 1942
Pluto at the Zoo, 1942
Pluto and the Armadillo, 1943
Private Pluto, 1943
Springtime for Pluto, 1944
First Aiders, 1944

Dog Watch, 1945
The Eyes Have It, 1945
Canine Casanova, 1945
The Legend of Coyote Rock, 1945
Canine Patrol, 1945
Pluto's Kid Brother, 1946

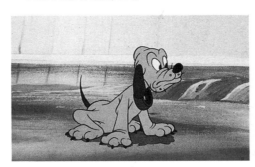

In *Pluto's Kid Brother* (1946) we find that the pup referred to is nothing but trouble. He disturbs Pluto's snooze, is chased by a cat, steals some wieners, gets himself and Pluto chased by Butch ... you name it. In the end Pluto feels entitled to forget his qualms about theft and tuck into his share of the wieners.

In Dutch, 1946
Squatter's Rights, 1946
The Purloined Pup, 1946
A Feather in His Collar, 1946 (commercial)
Pluto's Housewarming, 1947
Rescue Dog, 1947
Mickey's Delayed Date, 1947
Mail Dog, 1947
Pluto's Blue Note, 1947
Mickey Down Under, 1948
Bone Bandit, 1948
Pluto's Purchase, 1948
Cat Nap Pluto, 1948
Pluto's Fledgling, 1948
Mickey and the Seal, 1948
Pueblo Pluto, 1949
Pluto's Surprise Package, 1949
Pluto's Sweater, 1949
Bubble Bee, 1949
Sheep Dog, 1949
Pluto's Heart Throb, 1950

Pluto and the Gopher, 1950
Wonder Dog, 1950
Primitive Pluto, 1950
Puss-Café, 1950
Pests of the West, 1950
Food for Feudin', 1950
Camp Dog, 1950
Cold Storage, 1951
Plutopia, 1951
R'coon Dawg, 1951
Cold Turkey, 1951
Pluto's Party, 1952
Pluto's Christmas Tree, 1952
The Simple Things, 1953
The Coyote's Lament, 1961 (TV; theatrically released 1968)
Who Framed Roger Rabbit, 1988
The Prince and the Pauper, 1990
Runaway Brain, 1995

PAN

The god Pan appeared in the 1930 Silly Symphony *Playful Pan*. We first see him playing to the forest animals on his pipes – even the fish and the trees dance to the music. Unfortunately, so do the clouds, and when two of them bump into each other they create a flash of lightning which sets fire to the forest. Little realizing what is going on, Pan keeps playing until a little raccoon anxiously gives him the news. Immediately Pan rushes to the flames and, rather like the Pied Piper of Hamelin, leads them dancing to the waters' edge, where

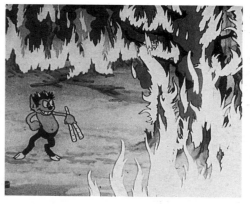

From the 1930 Silly Symphony *Playful Pan*, the god Pan himself.

they are extinguished. We leave Pan playing his pipes once more to the animals, flowers and trees.

We just hope the clouds do not start dancing again.

THE UGLY DUCKLING

Disney took two stabs at making a short of the Hans Andersen tale of the Ugly Duckling, one in 1931 and the other in 1939. Of the two, the second is by far the more faithful to the original story.

The 1931 short has a mother hen scorning a little duckling that has accidentally hatched out among her chicks (note that this is a *duckling* and not a cygnet, hatched out among chicks rather than among ducklings). A cyclone blows the entire family to the river and the Ugly Duckling, being able to swim, succeeds in rescuing the chicks from their inundated coop. He becomes the hero of the hour.

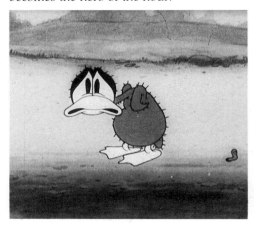

Every line etched in misery – the star of the 1931 version of *The Ugly Duckling*.

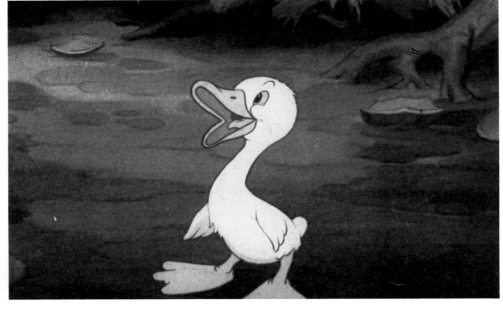

The Ugly Duckling, 1939 style – definitely a cuddlier character than his 1931 precursor.

The 1939 remake got a very friendly reception from the critics. *Pic*, for example, described it as "the best Silly Symphony Walt Disney has ever produced". Others agreed: the short won an Academy Award.

In a way, the movie is the epitome of the Silly Symphony style: it takes an existing fable (in this case by Hans Andersen) and expands it using a good helping of gags. This sort of treatment has drawn a good deal of criticism over the years: the claim is that Disney is essentially bastardizing existing tales so that modern children recognize the Disney version rather than the original. The very fact that people criticize such essays is a tribute to the overwhelming popular success of the "Disney treatment"; moreover, such new versions have the benefit of keeping alive classic tales that might otherwise die.

The Ugly Duckling, 1939 version, is a truly great short movie. It has fun, pathos, and just the right amount of bathos. It starts with the father doing the traditional expectant-father act of pacing up and down so much that he wears a trench in the ground: the whole scene is reminiscent of that at the start of 1933's *Birds in the Spring* (➤52). Four of the eggs hatch and the new parents are delighted; but when the fifth and final egg cracks open and the Ugly Duckling pops out the seeds are sown for domestic dissent: as the father correctly points out, this last chick looks nothing like him. Mother's response is rather more venomous than you might imagine ... the Ugly Duckling has had an inauspicious entry into this world.

And as time goes on it is clear that the bad start has been merely the preface to a bad continuation: he is really not wanted. White where the other chicks are yellow, bigger than they are with feet that are proportionally still bigger, and possessed

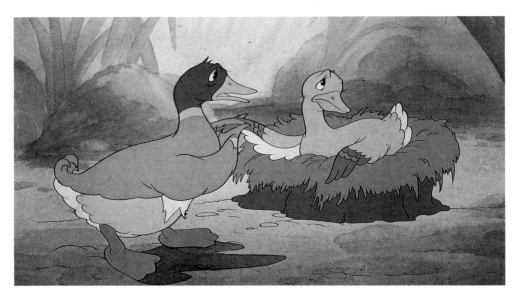

Mother and father duck awaiting a happy event in the 1939 remake of *The Ugly Duckling*.

of an appalling honk, he is hardly the answer to an anseriform's dream. In due course things come to a head and the mother and chicks drive him off; in anguish he gazes at his own reflection in the water and realizes his own "ugliness". He looks at the rest of his family at play and weeps piteously.

But his misery cannot last forever – or can it? He is welcomed into a nest by a group of crow chicks, but when the mother returns she drives him off; and as he flees he bumps into a decoy duck. Here at last, he thinks, is a waterbird that seems to love him, and he plays with it for a while before some rogue waves make it seem to attack him and he flees once more.

This time his sobbing is heard by a family of swans – and to his initial disbelief they adopt him – the mother giving him multitudinous cuddles of welcome and the cygnets (who are, curiously, white rather

than grey) playing with him fraternally. And, as he swims along proudly with his new family, his old one quacks admiringly at him: he responds by putting his beak in the air and ignoring them. No one calls him ugly now ...

Filmography

The Ugly Duckling, December 12, 1931
The Ugly Duckling, 1939

GOOFY

Goofy is unique among Disney's major characters – the central gang surrounding Mickey Mouse – in that, while like Donald and Pluto he appeared initially in only a bit part, he thereafter took several years to evolve into a major star. Moreover, he is the only one of that central gang not to have an alliterative full name (as in Pluto the Pup, Peg Leg Pete, Horace Horsecollar, etc.).

His first appearance was in May 1932 in a Mickey Mouse short called *Mickey's Revue*. Here he played the part of a member of the audience, laughing uproariously at the antics of the more established members of the Disney gang on stage. Curiously enough, he looked far older than he was to seem in later years when he was a star in his own right: he had venerable whiskers, a dilapidated-looking, square-lensed pince-nez, and a disreputable hat. Moreover, he made his appearance under a name other than the one he was to make famous: he was in those days known as Dippy Dawg. Already, however, he was recognizable as the Goof we have all come to love.

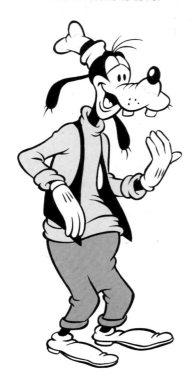

During 1932 and 1933 he made occasional appearances as an extra in Mickey Mouse shorts; probably he was considered as a sort of perennial extra for the simple reason that Mickey's gang already contained a much loved dog in the shape of Pluto (➤ 38). Other characters in the same sort of predicament never did graduate from that role of perennial extra – such as Clarabelle Cow (➤ 36) and Horace Horsecollar (➤ 37) – but the Goof was destined for greater things.

It is noticeable that in these early appearances Goofy had yet to develop his infinite capacity for chaos. Steve Hulett, a senior Disney storyman, has observed that in *The Whoopee Party* (1932) Goofy

helped Mickey prepare party eats in the kitchen, and he did it without a hitch. His characteristic klutziness and naiveté had not yet been fully discovered. In the later *Mickey's Birthday Party* [1942] he was able to destroy a kitchen, cake and party single-handed, all with perfect innocence and good humor.

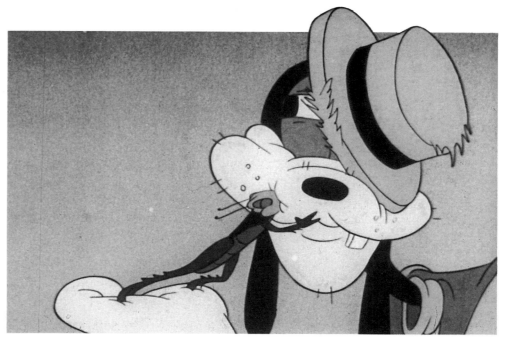

Goofy with his grasshopper chum Wilbur in the first movie in which Goofy starred alone, *Goofy and Wilbur* (1939).

However, Goofy was simultaneously rising to a position of some importance in the syndicated daily Mickey Mouse comic strips in the newspapers, where he became an integral member – along with Minnie, Donald and Pete – of the gang of characters involved in Mickey's adventures. He was still very rough around the edges, and what was to become his lovable bumblingness was in those days a rather rebarbative stupidity – both features which were for a short time to be reflected in his screen persona. His only real distinguishing feature in the movies of this era in which he appeared was his raucous laugh.

Art Babbitt, who was largely responsible for ushering Goofy into greatness, put his finger on another problem in Goofy's early screen career when he wrote in 1934 that ". . . the Goof hitherto has been a weak cartoon character because both his physical and mental make-up were indefinite and intangible . . . the only characteristic which . . . identified itself with him was his voice. No effort was made to endow him with appropriate business to do, a set of mannerisms or a mental attitude." Elsewhere he described him somewhat unflatteringly as a "barnyard schnook".

Babbitt changed all that – with a vengeance. He spotted that in a short called *Mickey's Service Station* (1935 [➤ 28]) there was to be a brief sequence in which Goofy, acting as a motor mechanic, ran into a little difficulty: ". . . Goofy was on top of an engine block and, as he reached down into it, his own hand came up behind him and goosed him. Then there was a bit of monkey business before he found out it was his own hand." Babbitt could see immense

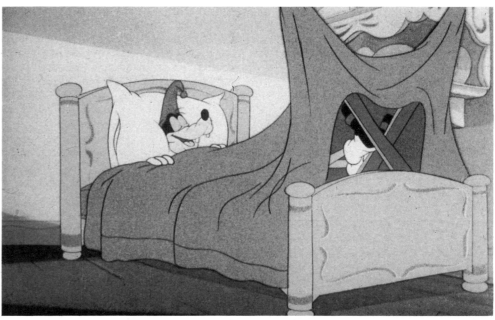

There's nothing like a good night's sleep after a long day out on the piste, as Goofy demonstrates in *The Art of Skiing* (1941).

possibilities in this scene, and begged to be allowed to work on it. "Finally, I made a deal with [Walt] Disney that I would work on a sequence for Peg Leg Pete, a character I detest. In return, I would have the Goofy thing to do."

The scene, originally planned to run for 7½-8ft, came out at a length of 57ft! The sequence shows Goofy reaching deep into the entrails of Pete's unfortunate car engine – so deep, in fact, that his hand emerges from behind him and gooses his own bottom; when he turns to see who is the offender, the hand has of course disappeared. Finally, after this has happened several times, the Goof is so irritated that he takes a hammer and wallops the impertinent offender. After a moment's stark agony, a slow smile appears as he realizes his own numbskulledness – a slow smile that was to become one of his trademarks over the years. Thanks to Babbitt, then, Goofy had finally discovered his glorious art of taking as long as possible to achieve as little as possible.

A supremely important part of Goofy's character was his voice, which was supplied by one-time circus barker Pinto Colvig (real first name Vance), who was responsible also for most of the purely vocal noises in the early Mickey Mouse shorts and Silly Symphonies; for *Moving Day* (1936 [►16]) Colvig actually acted out much of Goofy's role so that animator Art Babbitt could film him and use his actions for reference. During the years 1937-41, however, when Colvig was away from the studio, desperate measures had to be taken to give the Goof a voice. In some contexts it was feasible to use a voice-over narration (see below), but in others it was not. One technique of coping with the problem was to use cut-up versions of previous recordings of Colvig's voice (this was done extensively); a more satisfactory solution was the use of a new person to voice Goofy. This was Disney employee Stuart Buchanan, who was accustomed to voicing Goofy on the Disney radio show. (Colvig died in 1967, aged 75.) Others, such as Bob Jackman, also on occasion voiced Goofy.

By this time the Goof had long since dropped his old name of Dippy Dawg (his title both within the studio and in the comics) and become Goofy – a transition which he made in the 1934 black-and-white Mickey Mouse short *Orphan's Benefit* (remade in color in 1941; the apostrophe was misplaced in both versions); the name "Goofy" arose from Walt Disney's colloquial description of the sort of comedy that surrounded (and frequently overwhelmed) Mickey and the gang as "goofy". Our hero had, too, developed the bizarrely amiable Goofy walk – described by Flora O'Brien as one "in which every step represented a miniature encyclopedia of the humanly impossible". The result was a sort of shambling progress that expressed Goofy's character to a T.

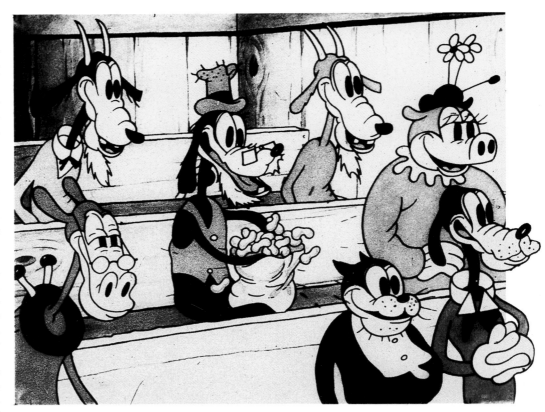

Goofy, with pince-nez and whiskers, in his first movie, *Mickey's Revue* (1932).

He also developed a habit of succeeding in his endeavours only at inopportune moments. In *On Ice* (1935) he is attempting to catch fish using the technique of throwing pieces of chewing tobacco as bait through a hole in the ice, so that he can club the fish as they leap from the water to spit out the offending stuff (Julius had used the same trick in *Alice's Fishy Story* many years earlier [►15]). The Goof has a zero success-rate, until finally his club connects dizzyingly with a solid object: unfortunately the solid object emerging from the water is not a fish but the head of Donald Duck.

In a report written in 1935 Babbitt described the character that Goofy had now become:

Think of the Goof as a composite of an everlasting optimist, a gullible Good Samaritan, a half-wit, and a shiftless, good-natured hick. ... He can move fast if he has to, but would rather avoid any overexertion, so he takes what seems the easiest way.

No matter what happens, he accepts it finally as being for the best, or at least amusing. He is willing to help anyone, and offers his assistance, even where he is not needed and just creates confusion. He very seldom, if ever, reaches his objective or completes what he has started ... Any little distraction can throw him off his train of thought. ...

His hands are very sensitive and expressive, and though his gestures are broad, they still reflect the gentleman. ...

He is very bashful, yet when something very stupid has befallen him, he mugs the camera like an amateur actor with relatives in the audience, trying to cover up his

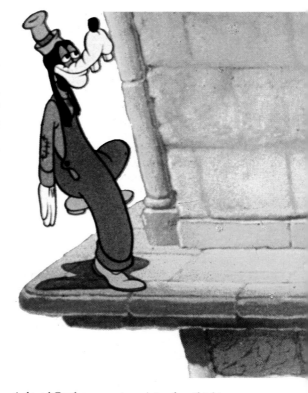

A dazed Goof prepares to go into a breathtaking Harold Lloyd act in 1937's *Clock Cleaners*.

embarrassment by making faces and signalling to them.

And with devastating accuracy and perception Babbitt added:

He is in close contact with sprites, goblins, fairies and other such fantasia. Each object or piece of mechanism, which to us is lifeless, has a soul and personality in the mind of the Goof. The improbable becomes real where the Goof is concerned.

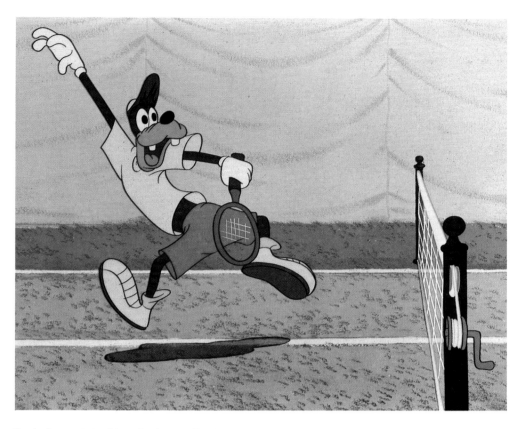

Goofy demonstrates his enthusiasm in *Tennis Racquet* (1949), one of many sporting shorts in which our hero shows that it's not the winning that's important.

augmented by the appearance of Pete at beginning and end as a foe.)

In this context it is interesting to view *Moose Hunters* (1937). Although Mickey's part in the story is quite separate, Donald and the Goof interact together – to devastating effect, of course – throughout the short. The two are playing the part of a decoy, to which end they have a moose costume of unequivocal femininity which they liberally splatter with lipstick, face-powder and "Deer Kiss" perfume. This latter is potent stuff: a huge bull moose is almost physically hauled through the forest towards them. But then – disaster! His lustful bellow blasts their costume from them, and they have to do a coquettish fan-dance, using snatched items of shrubbery, until they reach the shelter of a rock and can swiftly "get dressed" again.

In the same short their efforts are bedevilled – as so often! – by a determined bee. This buzzes eagerly into the back of the costume where Donald, acting the part of the hindquarters, goes even wilder than one might expect – to the delight of the bull moose. At last the bee lands instead on Goofy, delicately enacting the role of the forequarters, and Donald's vindictive swat tumbles the Goof forwards to kiss the bull moose. Romance is definitely as thick as "Deer Kiss" perfume in the air – to the Goof's manifest horror – but in the end the deception is revealed and the pals flee from the moose's wrath.

The Duck and the Goof worked extremely well together in this short, and so it is perhaps surprising that the experiment was repeated so rarely.

In fact, a couple of years later, in 1939, there came the first short in which Goofy starred in his own right: *Goofy and Wilbur*. The **Wilbur** of the title is Goofy's pet grasshopper, and the short follows the pair of them on a fishing expedition. The comedy centres on Wilbur's Goofy-like capacity for getting into dangerous predicaments – indeed, they would be fatal ones if Disney's cartoon world obeyed the normal rules of logic. Goofy himself has us

Babbitt was later to remark that "Goofy was the kind of character that thought very hard and very long about everything he did. And then he did it wrong."

Nowhere is there a better example of an inanimate object having "a soul and personality" of its own than in the 1936 short *Moving Day*. Goofy, as the neighbourhood ice-man, kindly lends his truck and his services to Donald and Mickey who are trying rapidly to move house before Pete (►16) returns to confiscate their furniture in lieu of the rent they owe. The Goof's Waterloo comes when he attempts to load their upright piano into the back of his truck. He should have known better than to take on a sentient piano. This one delights

in trundling back down the loading ramp at the rear of his truck. But it does so only when he is not looking. Soon a full-scale battle of wills develops, and there are no prizes for guessing who wins.

The Disney shorts in which Goofy was appearing around this time had a certain rigidity of structure that may have been a weakness. In essence, they would start off with a situation shared by Mickey, Donald and the Goof and then the story would split up into three quite distinct strands, following the individual antics of the three characters. The final moments of the short would see a resolution, with the three of them brought together again. (Often enough, this basic structure would be

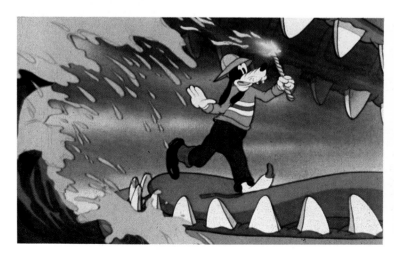

No, no, Goofy, When you go whaling it's *you* who is supposed to catch the *whale*...

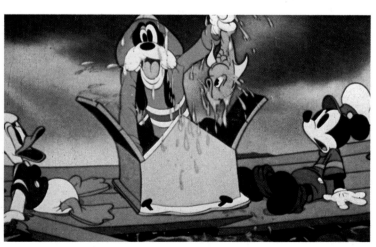

...but if you catch *anything*, celebrate! Both stills are from *The Whalers* (1938).

in one moment rocking with laughter at his complicated, hopeless attempts at rescue and, in the next, moist-eyed as we share his desolation at the apparent loss of his friend – although, if he was all *that* concerned, perhaps he should have thought twice before using his pet as live fishing-bait. When Wilbur is swallowed by a frog which is in turn swallowed by a stork, the end has surely come – and we see in Goofy's imagination the sad trudging of the little grasshopper up to the pearly gates. But then – deliverance! Joyfully, Wilbur pops out of an egg in the stork's nest, and the two chums are reunited.

From about 1940 separate units were set up within the Disney organization to deal with the shorts of each major character, the idea being to stop using them as a group in the same shorts. There were two motives behind this. First, when there were several major characters in a short a great many animators and other creative people had to be more or less simultaneously involved in its production, which was expensive – and it was difficult to recoup such expense from the proceeds of only a single short. Second, and perhaps more important in Walt's eyes, the new approach might result in a better-quality end-product – because each team could concentrate more effectively on "their" character. Donald (►61) was passed to Jack King and Jack Hannah, Pluto (►38) to Norm Ferguson and Nick Nichols, Mickey (►23) to Bill Roberts and Riley Thomson, and the Goof to Jack Kinney.

Kinney brought in Ralph Wright as a story-and-gag man, Jim Carmichael to assist on story and then follow through on production layout, Wolfgang Reitherman and John Sibley as chief animators, and Lou Debney as assistant director. Another important recruit was John McLeish as voice-over narrator. Colvig had by this time left the studio, so the voice-over approach

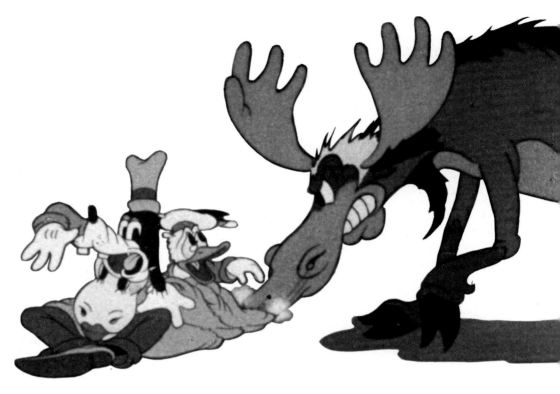

Goofy and Donald find their audience does not like their moose act in *Moose Hunters* (1937).

was important as a way of reducing Goofy's vocalizations to the minimum. In fact, McLeish was really a Disney artist, but his voice was excellent and he had a fondness for producing John Barrymore-like monologues for the entertainment of his colleagues. For the first few "how to" shorts (see below) McLeish actually believed that he was narrating an educational script, and Kinney wisely kept him in the dark about this. When McLeish discovered the use to which his honeyed measures were being put he was somewhat annoyed – he described the Goof as "that anthropomorphic nonentity"! More to the point,

from then on Kinney had the very difficult task of persuading McLeish to play it straight and *not* to ham up the narrations, since much of the humour of these "how to" shorts derives from the sobriety of the voice-over being in stark contrast with the chaos depicted on screen.

This is not to say that traditional-style Goofy shorts did not continue. Typical is *Foul Hunting* (1947), in which Goofy and his decoy duck Clementine do unsuccessful battle with the rest of the duck world (although one particular Duck and his relatives are noticeable by their absence). After various predictable vicissitudes, the Goof ends up sadly eating his decoy.

Goofy eventually starred in 50 shorts, two of which, *How to Ride a Horse* and *El Gaucho Goofy*, were extracted from the features *The Reluctant Dragon* (1941/1950 [►190]) and *Saludos Amigos* (1943/1955 [►204]), respectively. (He appeared also in a section, *Mickey and the Beanstalk*, in the feature *Fun and Fancy Free* [1947 (►223)].) He shared star billing with others of the gang on numerous occasions: one of the most entertaining was *Frank Duck Brings 'em Back Alive* (1946), a parody of the "Frank Buck" adventure series of the day. Here Goofy is the jungle Wild Man and Donald the intrepid explorer set on his capture.

Many of the shorts in which Goofy has starred have been concerned with some aspect of the public good. *Motor Mania* (1950), *Freewayphobia No. 1* (1965; Goofy plays the parts of *Driverius timidicus*, *Neglecterus maximus*, *Motoramus fidgitus* and *Stupidicus ultimus*) and *Goofy's Freeway Trouble* (1965), for example, deal with road safety – or the lack of it when motorists allow their aggression and recklessness to take over as soon as they get behind the wheel. Interestingly, *Motor Mania* was not originally intended to be an educational

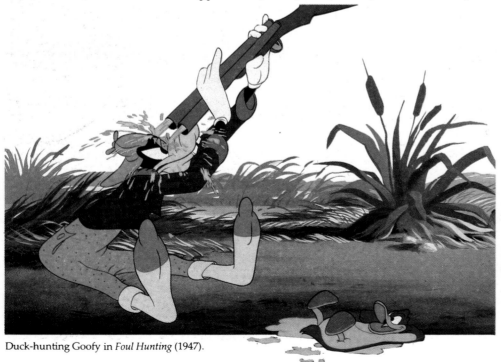

Duck-hunting Goofy in *Foul Hunting* (1947).

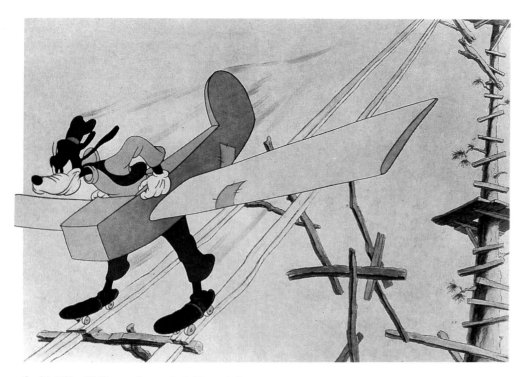

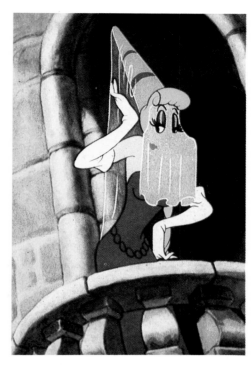

Goofy's Glider (1940) was director Jack Kinney's first outing with the Goof.

The Goof craftily disguised as Princess Penelope in 1946's A Knight for a Day.

movie – just another good short. However, soon after its release the studio was called by the Oakland Police Department who wanted a print to show in their Traffic Violator School; Disney made a 16mm copy, and soon other orders were pouring in.

Other "educational" movies from the Goof addressed the problem of children's perceptions of adults – Fathers Are People (1951) and Teachers Are People (1952) are examples of these. He helped boost public morale during the dour days of World War II with shorts such as Victory Vehicles (1943) and How to Be a Sailor (1944). He also acted as a subject in one of the fact-packed TV extravaganzas of the flamboyant Professor Ludwig von Drake (►124), Square Peg in a Round Hole (1965).

However, in terms of his more recent career, by far the most important of the Goof's "educational" shorts are those to do with sport. An interesting irony surrounds one of the early ones, How to Ride a Horse. This was originally intended to be a straightforward short release, but RKO, then Disney's distributor, felt it shouldn't be "wasted" as a short and insisted that instead it form a part of the feature The Reluctant Dragon. Nowadays, of course, while the short has its own fame as one of the great classics of the period, the feature is largely forgotten. Many years later director Jack Kinney remarked in Funnyworld (Fall, 1979) of our hero's role in this short: "Goofy blissfully demonstrated some of the most ridiculous horsemanship seen since man first bestrode a shaggy prehistoric nag."

There were plenty of others in the same vein as How to Ride a Horse: Goofy's Glider (1940), The Art of Skiing (1941), The Art of Self

Defense (1941), How to Play Baseball (1942), The Olympic Champ (1942), How to Swim (1942), How to Fish (1942), How to Play Golf (1944), How to Play Football (1944), How to Be a Sailor (1944), Hockey Homicide (1945), Goofy Gymnastics (1949), How to Dance (1953), and TV's Goofy Sports Story (1956) and Goofy Cavalcade of Sports (1956). Double Dribble (1946), which showed the art of basketball, featured not only Goofy as himself but also a plurality of other Goofies as the rest of the

players; these others were rendered without ears to show that they were not the "real" Goof. They were given names like Kinney, Hannah, Sibley, Lounsbery and Berg – in other words, the names of people who were then in the Disney story department (the "Kinney" being Dick Kinney, younger brother of Jack). As a variant form of

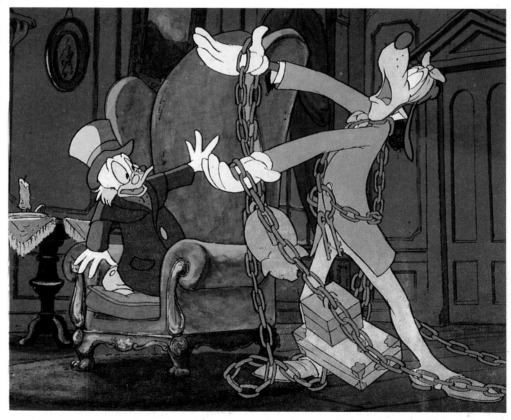

Goofy turned in a hair-raisingly incompetent performance as Marley's ghost in the 1983 featurette Mickey's Christmas Carol.

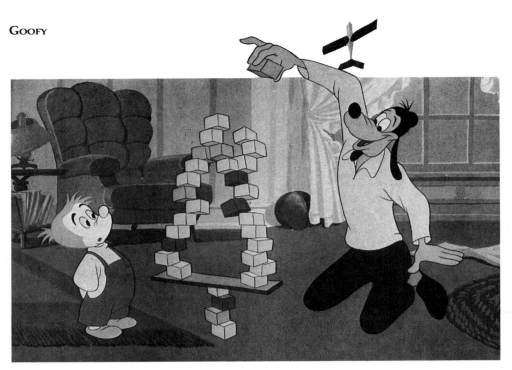

Goofy, Junior, makes Pop's life a misery in *Fathers Are People* (1951).

sporting cartoon, *A Knight for a Day* (1946) featured jousting, with the Goof playing all the main parts – including even that of the fair **Princess Penelope**, whose hand will go to the winner of the tourney (guess who). He appears also as various knights whose names display Disney punnery at its best/ worst, such as Sir Loinsteak and Sir Cumference (who is large and round).

Visual gags abound in these sporting cartoons: a couple that stick in the mind are from *Goofy Gymnastics* and *The Olympic Champ*. In the former (which features in *Who framed Roger Rabbit* [➤326]), as Goofy strains to lift the heavy bar, all the spots on his leopard-skin leotard abruptly pop off; in the latter, as he runs the hurdles, he picks up so many of them on his feet that he reaches the finish line in a heap of tangled, smashed wood.

Of course, in all of these Goofy demonstrated quite conclusively how *not* to ... Still, these shorts were excellent preparation for a much later development in Goofy's career. The Disney company had long been concerned with promoting sport as a way of achieving health and fitness. In 1980 a redesigned Goofy – "Sport Goofy" – was launched into the world. His chest was expanded and his original Goof-type clothes discarded in favour of an elegant sporting outfit, his hairstyle was subtly altered and his teeth shortened, but he remained much the same Goof as of old. His new role was as a sponsor of sports of all types – particularly tennis. He was adopted in that same year, 1980, by the French Olympic team as its official mascot; in 1981 West Germany named Sport Goofy the spokesman for the German Sportlife Fund; in 1983 the International Tennis Federation at Wimbledon announced its first Junior World Tennis Championship, the "Sport Goofy Trophy", to be held at Walt Disney World, and later in that year youngsters from 39 different countries participated in it

(in the following year there were 49 participant nations). In 1983 the television show *Mickey and Donald Present Sport Goofy* was launched in 36 countries.

In his later sporting incarnation, Goofy is just as prone to disaster as he was in his earlier "how to" days – but for a somewhat different reason: overenthusiasm rather than stark inability. His message is that the taking part is the important thing, the winning perhaps secondary – although it is nice to win a few.

Goofy, then, seems set to make a comeback, despite the long hiatus in his career between *Goofy's Freeway Trouble* (1965) and his thrillingly incompetent rendition of the part of Marley's Ghost in *Mickey's Christmas Carol* (1983 [➤130]). In this movie Hal Smith voiced the Goof superbly; Bill Farmer did likewise in *The Prince and the Pauper* (1990 [➤132]).

Goofy's family have made occasional appearances: his son **Goofy, Junior**, and his wife, **Mrs. Goofy**, appeared first in *Fathers Are People* (1951) and thereafter acted in several shorts. Mrs. Goofy (or Mrs. Geef – Goofy occasionally appears as Mr. Geef) appeared only fleetingly in any of these, but Goofy, Junior, played slightly more major roles. Somewhat less of a grotesque than his father, he has a red "parp" nose on the end of his snout and a mop of red hair on his head. His primary function is to allow his papa to boast on a Baron Munchhausen scale and then watch as father fails to live up to expectations – needless to say, the Goof fails with dramatic verve. Junior's best performance is probably that in *Father's Lion* (1952 [➤111]).

It is legitimate to ask why it is that the Goof has become such a popular member of the central Disney gang – arguably more so than even Mickey Mouse. Perhaps the answer to the question is that most of us can find something with which to identify in the character of Goofy: we are all from time to

time capable of demonstrating his distinctive brand of good-humored folly, of bumbling when we try to excel. Rather different versions of Goofy and of Goofy, Junior appear in the television series *Goof Troop* (➤**145**) and its spinoff, *A Goofy Movie* (➤**395**).

Filmography

Mickey's Revue, 1932
The Whoopee Party, 1932
Touchdown Mickey, 1932
The Klondike Kid, 1932
Mickey's Mellerdrammer, 1933
Ye Olden Days, 1933
Orphan's [sic] *Benefit*, 1934 (first appearance as Goofy)
The Band Concert, 1935
Mickey's Service Station, 1935
Mickey's Fire Brigade, 1935
On Ice, 1935
Mickey's Polo Team, 1936
Moving Day, 1936
Moose Hunters, 1937
Mickey's Amateurs, 1937
Hawaiian Holiday, 1937
Clock Cleaners, 1937
Lonesome Ghosts, 1937
Magician Mickey, 1937
Boat Builders, 1938
Mickey's Trailer, 1938
Polar Trappers, 1938
The Fox Hunt, 1938 (remake of a 1931 Silly Symphony)
The Whalers, 1938
The Standard Parade, 1939 (commercial)
Goofy and Wilbur, 1939 (1st cartoon starring Goofy)
Tugboat Mickey, 1940
Billposters, 1940
Goofy's Glider, 1940
Baggage Buster, 1941
The Nifty Nineties, 1941
Orphan's [sic] *Benefit*, 1941 (colour remake of 1934 original)
The Art of Skiing, 1941
The Art of Self Defense, 1941
The Reluctant Dragon, 1941 (section: *How to Ride a Horse*)
Mickey's Birthday Party, 1942
Symphony Hour, 1942
How to Play Baseball, 1942
The Olympic Champ, 1942
How to Swim, 1942
How to Fish, 1942
Saludos Amigos, 1943 (section: *El Gaucho Goofy*)
Victory Vehicles, 1943
How to be a Sailor, 1944
How to Play Golf, 1944
How to Play Football, 1944
Tiger Trouble, 1945
African Diary, 1945
Californyer Bust, 1945
No Sail, 1945
Hockey Homicide, 1945
A Knight for a Day, 1946
Frank Duck Brings 'em Back Alive, 1946
Double Dribble, 1946
Crazy with the Heat, 1947
Fun and Fancy Free, 1947 (section: *Mickey and the Beanstalk*)
Foul Hunting, 1947
They're Off, 1948
The Big Wash, 1948

Tennis Racquet, 1949
Goofy Gymnastics, 1949
Crazy Over Daisy, 1950 (cameo appearance)
Motor Mania, 1950
Hold That Pose, 1950
Lion Down, 1951
Home Made Home, 1951
Cola War, 1951
Tomorrow We Diet, 1951
Get Rich Quick, 1951
Fathers Are People, 1951
No Smoking, 1951
Father's Lion, 1952
Hello Aloha, 1952
Man's Best Friend, 1952
Two-Gun Goofy, 1952
Teachers Are People, 1952
Two Weeks' Vacation, 1952
How to Be a Detective, 1952
Pluto's Christmas Tree, 1952
Father's Day Off, 1953
For Whom the Bulls Toil, 1953
Father's Week End, 1953
How to Dance, 1953
How to Sleep, 1953
Aquamania, 1961
Freewayphobia No. 1, 1965
Goofy's Freeway Trouble, 1965
Mickey's Christmas Carol, 1983
Who Framed Roger Rabbit, 1988
The Prince and the Pauper, 1990
A Goofy Movie, 1995

Goofy, **Junior**, appeared in *Fathers Are People* (October 21, 1951), *Father's Lion* (1952), *Father's Day Off* (1953), *Father's Week End* (1953) and *Aquamania* (1961). **Mrs. Goofy** appeared in *Fathers Are People* (October 21, 1951), *Cold War* (1951), *Get Rich Quick* (1951) and *Father's Day Off* (1953). **Wilbur** appeared only in *Goofy and Wilbur* (March 17, 1939). A dog called **Bowser** appears in *Man's Best Friend*, 1952.

FLOWERS AND TREES

The unnamed protagonists of the 1932 Silly Symphony *Flowers and Trees* are mobile trees with many human characteristics.

The hero and heroine are a lithe young male sapling and a glamorous, Garbo-esque lady sycamore; of course, the two fall passionately in love with each other. Their romance is interrupted, however, by the intervention of the gnarled old oak, who wishes to have the young damsel for himself. The two males fight a duel, using whatever comes to hand(?) as weapons, and in due course the young sapling triumphs. However, in a fit of pique the old oak sets the forest on fire. The forest is saved, thanks to the valour of the young sapling, the only sentient victim being the old oak himself, who is reduced to a pile of ashes. The two lovers live happily ever after.

It is impossible adequately to describe the visual presentation of the characters in this movie. They are grotesques, yet in their caricatured forms they convey only too clearly the human models upon which they are based. The young sapling would give

one nightmares for the rest of one's life were one to meet him, yet for the purposes of the short one accepts him as a handsome young man. His true love is glamorous indeed, the animators having cleverly used her foliage and other extraneous pieces of wildlife to present an impression of sophisticated beauty. And there is villainy etched in every wrinkle of the old oak's trunk. The movie is something of an experience to watch, and is rightly well spoken of. It is quite unforgettable. The first Silly Symphony to be made in full colour (Technicolor) – indeed, the first colour cartoon of all time – it was also the recipient of Disney's first Academy Award.

Some of the flowers and trees are seen briefly in *Who Framed Roger Rabbit* (➤326).

NEPTUNE

The figure of Neptune, the god of the sea, has made two appearances in Disney shorts, once in a starring role in a 1932 Silly Symphony and the other in a subsidiary one in a 1936 Mickey Mouse short. In both he is burly and bulky, with a gold crown, a bulbous red nose and a long white beard.

King Neptune (1932) is a tale of derring-do at sea. A gang of pirates viciously kidnaps an innocent mermaid, and the other mermaids raise the alarm among the denizens of the deep. The pirates discover that they have made a foolish mistake when various big fish (and not so big ones) attack them, but even more so when the powerful King Neptune raises a mighty storm and a maelstrom to sink the pirate ship. The kidnapped mermaid is rescued and proves to have found untold quantities of jewels

with which she generously bedecks all the others. There is much rejoicing in King Neptune's court, and everyone lives happily ever after – except the pirates.

Neptune's other Disney-shorts appearance is a rather shorter one. It occurs during the dramatic chase sequence in *Thru the Mirror* (1936), when Mickey is fleeing from the wrathful King of Hearts and his army of cards (➤30). At one stage the Mouse runs pell-mell onto the surface of a household globe, which spins beneath his desperately scurrying feet. Of course, it's part of the gag that he has to leap the oceans, for fear of getting wet – until one time he falls short and plummets into the water. A somewhat harassed-looking Neptune emerges from the waves and, with a well placed jab of his trident, sends Mickey squealing on his way.

Neptune appeared also in *The Three Caballeros* (1945 [➤211]).

Filmography

King Neptune, 1932
Thru the Mirror, 1936
The Three Caballeros, 1945 (section: *The Cold-Blooded Penguin*)

SANTA CLAUS

In both 1932 and 1933 the Disney company released just before Christmas an animated short featuring Santa Claus.

The first of these was *Santa's Workshop*. Disney's Santa is big and jolly, with a nose that suggests he has a certain way of keeping out the cold during those long Artic months. When we are first introduced to him he is going through all the "Dear Santa" requests from the world's children, assisted by an elf who could certainly be described as Grumpy's (➤164)

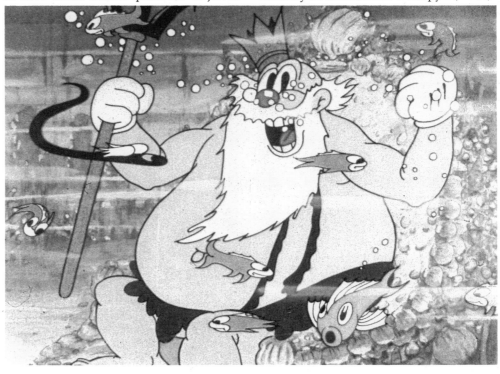
King Neptune, in a mood of regal austerity in the 1932 Silly Symphony *King Neptune*.

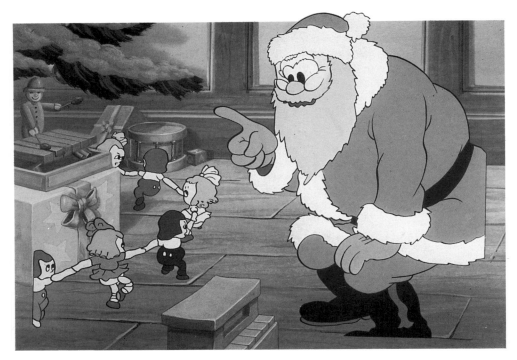

Santa Claus indulging in a little interaction with the toys in 1933's *The Night Before Christmas*.

However, the noise wakes the eight children of the house, and they prepare to creep downstairs from their bedroom to spy on Santa. Fortunately for him one of them sneezes: all the toys leap into their boxes while he shoots up the chimney. When the children reach the downstairs room they find that all is as it should be.

Or almost. The smallest of the eight children inquisitively looks up the chimney and receives for his curiosity a faceful of soot. He knows only too well what this means: Santa really *has* been here! Then all of the children hear the sound of sleighbells on the frosty wind and rush to the window: sure enough, there is jolly Santa riding off into the sky drawn by Prancer, Dancer and all the rest.

Both of these cartoons are successful: it is a little surprising that Disney did not continue the series into later years.

Filmography

Santa's Workshop, 1932
The Night Before Christmas, 1933

cousin. The task of this elf is to look in the polar reference books to find if the children sending the requests have been naughty – which, naturally, most of them have. However, Santa is very generous in his dispensations: even a little boy who has not washed behind his ears for *seven years* gets something. Whether the cake of soap will be well received is another matter.

The elves are responsible, according to tradition, for making the toys that Santa will deliver. In this short there are numerous gags about the way in which they do so. Highlights are the mode of producing chessboards – the elf responsible simply splashes on a few brushfuls of chequered paint! – and the use of a spider to make the dolls' hair stand on end so that the elfin machinery can more easily apply a permanent wave.

Santa, however, must check that all the toys the elves make are up to standard, and he registers his approval – at least in the case of the dolls – by rubber-stamping a large "OK" on their bottoms. One of the dolls is so confident of her degree of "OK-ness" that she does the stamping herself, and Santa laughs with such zeal at her feistiness that he half-swallows a model aeroplane. On escaping from his maw this toy proceeds to wreck as many other toys as possible.

But all is well in the end. The vast army of toys marches, wheels or bounces in military precision into Santa's sack, and he sets off with his reindeer to deliver those morsels of happiness.

Santa appeared again in the following year's Christmas offering, *The Night Before Christmas*; it could very well have been tacked straight onto the end of *Santa's Workshop* to form the second half of what would then have been a short featurette.

We join Santa as he arrives at a home and plunges down its chimney, burning his bottom on the blazing yuletide fire and roaring with laughter at his own clumsiness. Still, to business. He erects a Christmas tree and blows on a toy trumpet to summon all the other toys he has brought; these march in military formation out of his patchwork sack. (They include a number of little clockwork models of Mickey Mouse!) Troops of model soldiers embellish the tree by firing decorations onto it using their cannon, while Santa dashes around filling stockings, reading the children's notes to him and laughing "Ho ho ho" as often as possible. All these jobs done, he and the toys start to have a tremendous party.

OTTO THE BABY BIRD

Birds in the Spring (1933) was one of the most charming of the Silly Symphonies – although marred (from the standpoint of the 1980s) by a moment of dubious taste in the final frames. It introduced one of those Disney characters who are lovable simply because they are the *naughty* one in any given situation.

This naughty one in *Birds in the Spring* is Otto the Baby Bird. We join the short when Otto's father-to-be is pacing up and down anxiously waiting for his wife's three eggs to hatch (shades of *The Ugly Duckling* [➤ **44**]). Otto starts life the way he means to continue, by being the third of the three

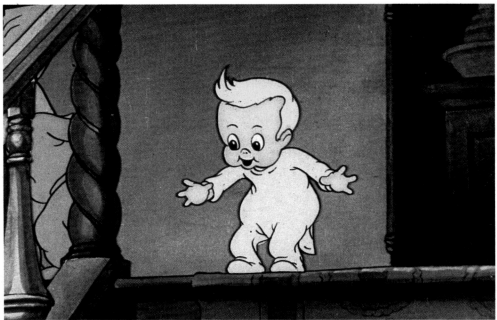

The smallest and cutest of the eight children in 1933's *The Night Before Christmas*.

chicks to arrive; moreover, he has rather different coloration from the rest – where they have green "waistcoats" his is red, where they have red "dickies" his is yellow, he has yellow marks on the head which they do not have, and so forth.

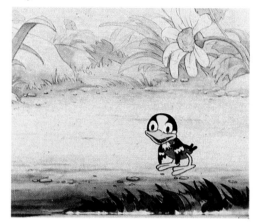

Otto the Baby Bird from 1933's *Birds in the Spring*.

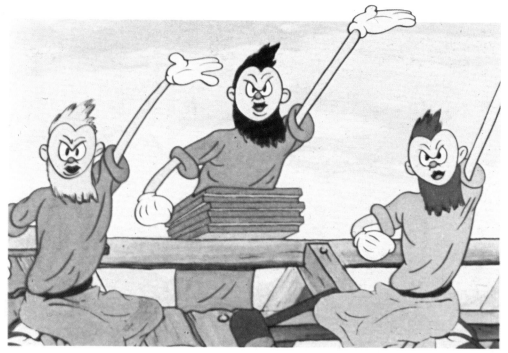

Noah's three sons, Ham, Shem and Japheth, from Disney's first short based on the Flood story, *Father Noah's Ark* (1933).

Father takes over the chicks' education. First he teaches them to sing in harmony, but Otto sneaks off and swallows a bee. When next he is called upon to sing a note all that emerges is a loud buzzing sound – followed in due course by a discontented bee. Father is not pleased.

Father becomes, if anything, even less pleased when he starts teaching the chicks how to fly for, while he is demonstrating the art with suave aplomb, he goes smack into a tree. After that slight hitch, the training continues. All three chicks start flying with confidence but are soon tumbling to the ground; their parents scoop up two of them in a net but the third – Otto, inevitably – they miss, and he tumbles all the rest of the way to the ground, breaking his fall on a toadstool. All this of course is not, strictly speaking, Otto's fault – but the same cannot be said for his hiding in a thistle-patch when Father comes looking for him.

Now his adventures begin in earnest. He swallows a grasshopper and for a while is bounced along by it before it escapes. He imitates a humming-bird but gets himself firmly stuck in a bellflower (the humming-bird, not realizing this, delivers him a painful jab). He is hypnotized by a rattlesnake but escapes when it accidentally ties itself in a knot. Worst of all, though, he flies into a hornets' nest. Exit, pursued by a swarm. The viciously humming hornets chase him wherever he goes, buzzing like a circular saw through everything that lies in their path; for example, they go through a field of corn like a Mach-3 combine-harvester, leaving neat bales in their wake. Finally Father happens upon the scene and saves Otto from the vindictive insects.

Instantly the little bird's attitude changes from stark terror to cheerful cockiness, and he blows a raspberry after the departing swarm. But his moment of triumph is not

longlived: Father descends upon him and gives him a thorough spanking.

It is this final scene which, while presumably hilarious when the short was first released, is no longer in accord with modern standards of good taste; for in order to spank his wayward son Father peels back Otto's outer feathers to reveal a miniature of the rear end of a chicken ready for roasting. It is a tribute to the general timelessness of the Disney humour that this stands out as a visual gag that has definitely dated, that has gone from general acceptability to tastelessness over a period of more than half a century. There are very few other examples of Disney gags having dated in this way (perhaps the *only* other is one in the original version of *Three Little Pigs*

[►55]). Considering the millions of gags produced by the Disney company that remain as fresh today as they were when first created, the record is not bad.

NOAH

The Disney studio had two bites at the story of Noah's Ark, once in 1933 with a Silly Symphony, *Father Noah's Ark*, and again in 1959 with *Noah's Ark*. Both tell the biblical story of Noah, **Ham**, **Shem**, **Japheth** and their wives, but they do so in very different ways.

The earlier short was very much part of the Silly Symphony series, telling the tale in a straightforwardly animated way (if

Mr. and Mrs. Noah celebrate the end of the Flood in 1959's *Noah's Ark*.

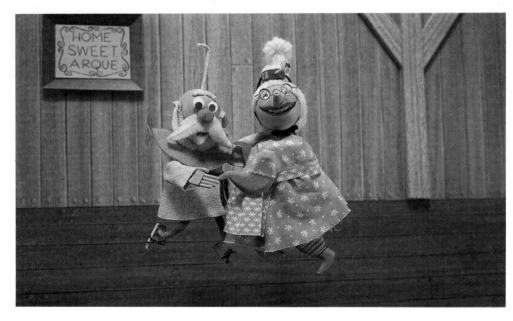

animation can ever be straightforward!), with plenty of visual gags. *Noah's Ark*, however, is very different. It was produced using the stop-motion technique on characters largely built out of household objects such as bottles, pipe-cleaners, pencils, corks, toothpicks and nuts. The effect is brilliant.

Moreover, the script is very well crafted. A representative sample:

Noah: Boys, we made the deadline and now we've got to name this ark.
Shem: Let's see ... how about "Shem's Ark"?
Ham: "Ham's Ark"?
Japheth: "Japheth's Ark"?
Noah (visibly inspired): Boys, I think I've got it! Why don't we call it "Noah's Ark"?
Sons (gloomily): I guess we call it "Noah's Ark" ...

The short was nominated for an Academy Award that year, and it is a disappointment that it failed to get it.

Filmography

Father Noah's Ark, 1933
Noah's Ark, 1959

THE BIG BAD WOLF

A certain degree of controversy surrounds many aspects of the Big Bad Wolf, the eternal foe of the Three Little Pigs (►55).

The character was originally, in the early stages of making *Three Little Pigs* (1933), called the "Big Old Wolf" – as in traditional versions of the story. However, this created a certain amount of confusion among the singers of the soundtrack, who kept coming out with "Big Bad Wolf", a phrase that skipped more easily off the tongue. In the end Walt told them to keep it that way because, on reflection, he thought that "Big Bad Wolf" was in fact better. It was one of the wisest decisions he ever made.

In Spanish the name-change worked even better: the Spanish version of the song "Who's Afraid of the Big Bad Wolf?" translates as "Who Has a Fear of the Wolf Grand and Ferocious?"!

Another oddity concerning the Wolf was that one of his words was censored not long before the short's release: this vile curse was the word "lousy". At an employees' pre-release screening of the short a woman queried it; and, on the basis that if she did so then thousands of members of the general public might follow suit, the word was excised. Surprisingly, in this context, the scene was allowed to remain in which the Wolf expends so much energy huffing and puffing at Practical Pig's stone house that his trousers fall down.

A further bone of contention was the scene in which the Wolf acted the part of a caricatured Jewish door-to-door salesman – a caricature which drew accusations of antisemitism. Later Disney admitted that the scene was a very serious lapse of taste (rare for Disney), and it was reworked. If you see the short today you will find that the disguised Wolf no longer has Hebraic tones or mannerisms, instead saying: "I'm the Fuller brush-man. I workin' me way through college." The syntax alone belies *that* statement! The excision removed from the film the only part of the Wolf's voice done by Pinto Colvig, the "voice of Goofy" (he also voiced Practical Pig); everywhere else the Wolf was voiced by Billy Bletcher (known also for voicing, *inter alia*, Peg Leg Pete [►15] and, in *The Wizard of Oz*, the Munchkins).

At the time, and occasionally since, there have been objections to the cruelty of the Wolf's punishment in *Three Little Pigs*. Walt defended himself against such criticisms vehemently. Robert White, in a 1950 piece in *Redbook*, cited one such defence: "The punishment of the big, bad wolf ... is not likely to give the youngster nightmares. Frustration, through lack of adequate punishment, might do just that." In fact, the punishment does not seem to be too terribly dire: when the Wolf forces himself down Practical Pig's chimney he lands bottom-first in a cauldron of hot oil that Practical Pig has put there in readiness. Exit one Wolf, at great speed, howling at the top of his voice.

The Wolf's next movie was *The Big Bad Wolf* (1934) in which once again he found himself up against the Three Little Pigs (or, at least, Practical Pig: the other two hardly count as adversaries). This is a second reworking by Disney of the Little Red Riding Hood legend (the other was a Laugh-O-gram [►12]), and has **Little Red Riding Hood** warned by the three pigs of the presence of the Big Bad Wolf in the region. Sure enough, there he is in Granny's cottage, disguised as the old lady, but in this version Little Red Riding Hood is

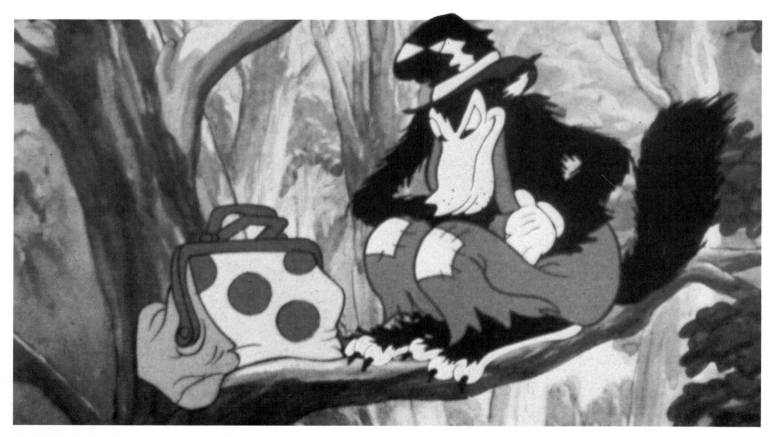

The Big Bad Wolf plotting how he can have Little Red Riding Hood for supper in *The Big Bad Wolf* (1934).

of course saved not by the woodcutter but by Practical Pig, who uses wildly popping corn to send the Wolf screaming off into the distance.

1936 saw the Big Bad Wolf's third appearance as well as the first performance by his rapscallion offspring, the **Three Little Wolves**. The short concerned, *Three Little Wolves*, suffers a little from a *deus ex machina* at the end. Because the two frivolous pigs have fooled around once too often with the "wolf warning horn" the Wolf dresses up as Bo-Peep and, accompanied by the Three Little Wolves disguised as sheep, has little difficulty in capturing the silly pigs. Luckily Practical Pig is still at large, and he comes to their rescue in the nick of time using the "wolf pacifier" which he has invented.

This inventiveness of Practical Pig is rather more satisfactorily incorporated into the plot of *The Practical Pig* (1939), which saw the second appearance of the Three Little Wolves. This time Practical Pig has drawn up plans for a lie-detector which he wants to build. However, the other two pigs want to play instead, and so off they go for a swim, ignoring Practical Pig's warnings that the Big Bad Wolf is somewhere in the neighbourhood. And, sure enough, here is our favourite villain, disguised as a mermaid in a long blonde wig, strumming a lyre and tossing a rose to lure the two foolish fellows. Catching them is not a particularly difficult exercise; but then the Wolf decides greedily that he would like to try to add the third pig to the supper-table. He leaves Fiddler and Fifer in the care of the Three Little Wolves with

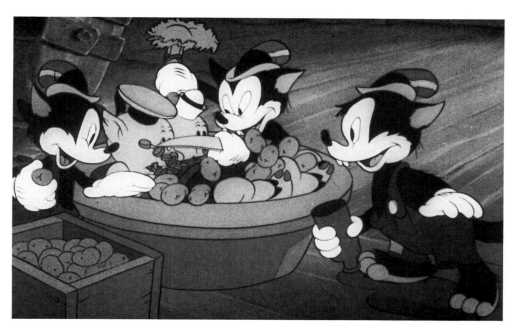

The Three Little Wolves, in *The Practical Pig* (1939).

stern instructions: "No eats 'til Pop comes back!" He should have known better. In his absence the hungry little wolf cubs decide to make their two captives into a vast pork pie. However, while they're adding the pepper the foolish pigs go into sneezing fits, blasting the rest of the pie into smithereens and making their escape under cover of the rain of pastry fragments.

Meanwhile, at home, Practical Pig has cunningly tempted the Wolf into his prototype lie-detector and extracted from him the location of Fiddler and Fifer. After

some obligatory scenes of suidine chivalry and courage, the two foolish pigs are home again – very glad to have survived the experience but, one somehow knows, none the wiser for it.

The Big Bad Wolf is more than just a stock adversary: he is a properly rounded character. Obviously he is a master of disguise, and equally obviously he is possessed of a fair degree of innate guile. The fact that he always fails to achieve his ends is due entirely to the Practical Pig's resourcefulness – perhaps assisted by the Wolf's own overpowering greed.

Filmography

Three Little Pigs, May 27, 1933
The Big Bad Wolf, 1934
Mickey's Polo Team, 1936
Three Little Wolves, 1936
The Practical Pig, 1939
Thrifty Pig, 1941 (commercial)
Mickey's Christmas Carol, 1983
Who Framed Roger Rabbit, 1988

The Three Little Wolves appeared in *Three Little Wolves* (April 18, 1936) and *The Practical Pig* (1939). **Little Red Riding Hood** appeared in *The Big Bad Wolf* (April 14, 1934) and *Who Framed Roger Rabbit* (1988).

THE THREE LITTLE PIGS

It took Walt six months to persuade his staff that his idea for a short called *Three Little Pigs*, based on the old tale, was a viable project. It was a good job that he did. In its first 15 months the film grossed $150,000 and proved to be most popular cartoon short ever up to that time (and possibly of all time). Figures from 1934 have it that the average Silly Symphony then grossed $80,000 in its first year and $40,000 in its

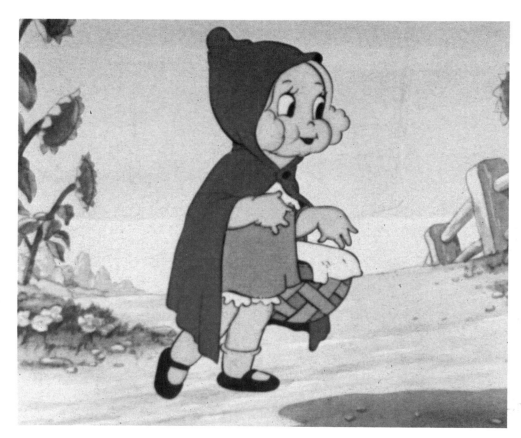

Little Red Riding Hood, in *The Big Bad Wolf* (1934).

second and that they costed, again on average, $50,000 to make (including the cost of making duplicate prints – $17,500); in fact, though, Disney got only $48,000 from the first year's takings (the rest went to United Artists, the distributor), thereby in general not quite covering costs until sometime during the second year of a short's release. The figures began to make sense, however, when it was taken into account that his profits by the end of the second year after a short's release could be expected to be of the order of $22,000 – and thereafter, of course, any income received (and it could be quite a *lot* of income) was straight profit. *Three Little Pigs*, by contrast, must have made something like a staggering $88,000 profit in its first two years.

But Walt didn't have things all his own way. His idea was that there should be only two little pigs – and he was dismayed when the movie's director, Bert (Burton) Gillett, stuck out obdurately for three. In the end Walt gave in, and Gillett (one of the very few people on the lot to get away with habitually calling Walt "Walter") performed an almost unique feat, that of countermanding one of Walt's "suggestions". In the light of hindsight we can see this as another very wise decision on Walt's part.

An internal memo circulated from Walt is revealing:

> These little pig characters look as if they would work up very cute and we should be able to develop quite a bit of personality in them. ... Might try to stress the angle of the little pig who worked the hardest, received the reward, or some little story that would teach a moral. Someone might have some angles on how we could bring this moral out in a direct way without having to go into too much detail. This angle might be given some careful consideration, for things of this sort woven into a story give it depth and feeling. ... These little pigs ... will be more like human characters.

The three little pigs are nowadays universally known as Fiddler Pig (voiced by Mary Moder), Fifer Pig (voiced by Dorothy Compton) and Practical Pig (voiced by the great Pinto Colvig); interestingly enough, though, no one knows exactly where those names came from. The characters were unnamed in the initial short; but by the time of *The Practical Pig* (1939) the names had "evolved". It is worth noting in this context that in the original *Three Little Pigs* Fifer Pig describes his instrument as a flute rather than as a fife.

One of the reasons for the cartoon's success was almost certainly its attention to detail. This aspect was pointed up by Claude Bragdon in an essay in *Scribner's Magazine* in July 1934:

> *Three Little Pigs* is one of the simplest pictures, yet how many persons, seeing it for the first time, notice that the Third Little Pig's house is laid up in "wolf proof cement", take in *all* the family portraits, or notice that not only the bedstead but the piano is solidly built of brick? If they do it is most likely at the expense of missing some detail of the action.

One way of really ruining a viewing of *Three Little Pigs* by paying attention to such minutiae is to watch the pigs' tails. From studies of real pigs the animators discovered that in a healthy pig the tail is tightly coiled while in a weak one it tends to be flaccid. They used this knowledge in the short, treating the pigs' tails according to their degree of tiredness or elation/strength. Despite the fact that pigs' tails, obviously, do not actually keep coiling and uncoiling in this way, the illusion conveys – subliminally – the required impression.

Another reason for the short's success was almost certainly the music – not just the hit song "Who's Afraid of the Big Bad

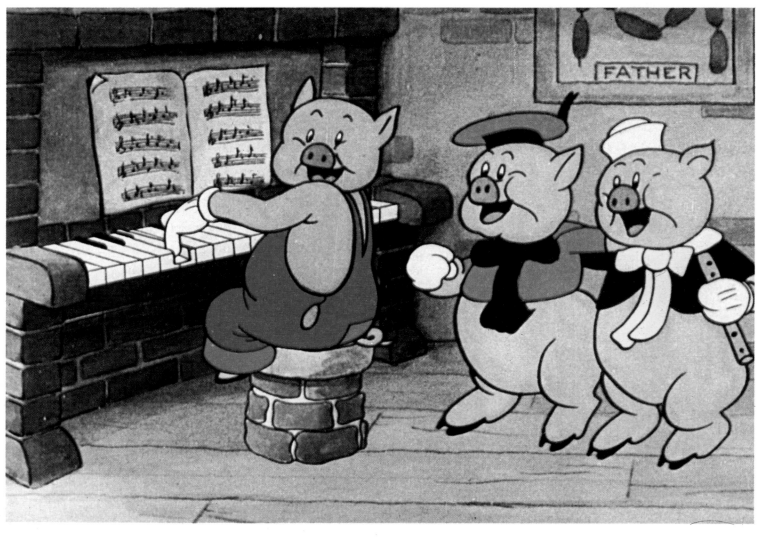

The Three Little Pigs in the 1933 movie named after them. Note the delicately tasteful "portrait" in the background.

Wolf?". Carl Stalling was composer-in-residence at the studio during the early years – in fact, his association with Walt went right back to the 1920s in Kansas City when he gave the live accompaniment to a short "song film" which contained the words of a song called "Martha" as well as complementary visuals. Later, it was with Stalling that Walt left prints in Kansas City of *Gallopin' Gaucho* (1928) and *Plane Crazy* (1928) for scoring. Stalling then went to New York to join Walt and record the two soundtracks. After going to Hollywood Stalling worked on about fifteen other shorts, both Mickey Mouses and Silly Symphonies. The latter were a concept for which Stalling himself was largely responsible: he suggested the idea of *Skeleton Dance*, for which he arranged the music (although based on the programme of Saint-Saëns' *Danse Macabre* the short used instead Grieg's *March of the Dwarfs*). He was also adept at taking works of music that were out of copyright and tailoring and arranging them for use in the Disney shorts. And, when Practical Pig in *Three Little Pigs* is at the keyboard, it is in fact Stalling who is playing. (After Stalling had left Disney with Ub Iwerks in 1930 – he returned for a short period as a freelance in 1932 – his position was taken over by Bert Lewis, who scored about 25 shorts between then and 1935.)

Although Stalling played on *Three Little Pigs*, the main musical honours on the short must go to Frank Churchill, who composed "Who's Afraid of the Big Bad Wolf?" (with the help of Pinto Colvig, who also, as noted, voiced Practical Pig and, in one later excised section, the Big Bad Wolf; lyrics were by Churchill, Ted Sears and Ann Ronell). In publicity releases of the time an almost certainly apocryphal tale was told. It seems that Churchill, as a child, had been given three piglets by his mother to look after. He was very proud and fond of them, and used to play them tunes on his harmonica. Then one day a real "Big Bad Wolf" did indeed descend from the mountains and deprive young Frank of one of his three little pigs. Decades later, when he was asked to work on the short, it is said that he threw his mind back to his childhood tragedy and composed "Who's Afraid of the Big Bad Wolf?" in about five minutes.

The plot of *Three Little Pigs* is familiar. Fifer Pig builds his house of straw, Fiddler Pig builds his of sticks, and only Practical Pig has the sense to build his of brick. The Wolf huffs and puffs and blows the first two houses down. There is a lovely moment when, after he has blown the stick house down, only the front door is left standing. In typical animated pseudo-logic, Fiddler and Fifer Pig have to open the door to check that the Wolf is still there; when they see that he is they slam the door in his face and he bursts it open with a shoulder-charge. He could have gone round it but . . .

A rather sick gag, although a very funny one, concerns one of the pictures hanging

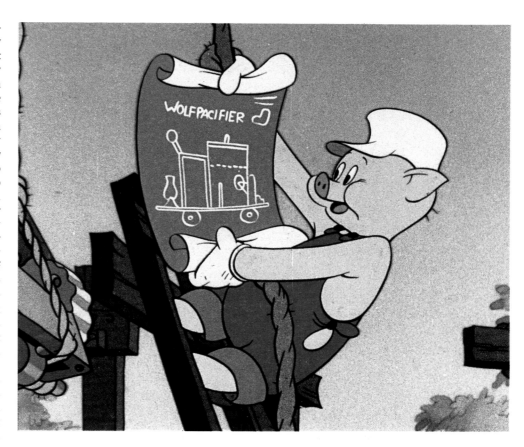

Practical Pig has always been the only sensible one of the three – and the only inventive one as well.

on Practical Pig's wall. It is a painting of a string of sausages, and it bears the caption "Father".

Whatever the furore it created in and around the Disney studio because of its great commercial success, *Three Little Pigs* was probably responsible for a far greater revolution in cinematic art. It is reasonable to maintain that the Silly Symphonies were primarily responsible for the revival of interest in Technicolor. There had been an earlier flurry of interest in 1928 when the process had been used by Warner Brothers and others; however, it was then only a two-colour (rather than a three-colour) process and the results were not very convincing: the interest soon died. However, Herbert Thomas Kalmus, managing director of Technicolor Inc., approached Walt suggesting that the Silly Symphonies would be ideal for the new three-colour version, and Walt had sufficient vision to pick up the exclusive rights in the process. It must have looked at first as if he had bought a pup, because the new Technicolor Silly Symphonies created little stir; but then along came *Three Little Pigs*, which was so popular that it proved a greater "draw" in the cinemas than the feature films it was supposed to be "supporting". Thanks to this short, Technicolor became an essential for every new movie.

The Three Little Pigs featured in three other theatrical shorts, their adversary being in all cases the Big Bad Wolf (►54 for further discussion of these shorts), and

also had small parts in *Mickey's Polo Team* (1936), *Toby Tortoise Returns* (1936), *Mickey's Christmas Carol* (1983) and three commercials, notably *All Together* (1942).

Filmography

The Big Bad Wolf, 1934
Three Little Wolves, 1936
Mickey's Polo Team, 1936
Toby Tortoise Returns, 1936
The Practical Pig, 1939
Thrifty Pig, 1941 (commercial)
Mickey's Christmas Carol, 1983
Who Framed Roger Rabbit, 1988

THE PIED PIPER

The figure of the Pied Piper appeared in two Disney shorts during 1933: he made a brief entrance in July's *Old King Cole* and starred in his own right in September's *The Pied Piper*.

The story of *The Pied Piper* follows the Browning version approximately except for the grafting onto it of a happy ending: perhaps Walt felt that dooming scores of children was hardly a satisfactorily up-beat finale for a Silly Symphony! The Pied Piper himself is not in fact dressed in a pied outfit, just costumed in red and yellow with a red Robin Hood hat. His pipe looks like an oboe but when played sounds more like a pair of tenor recorders.

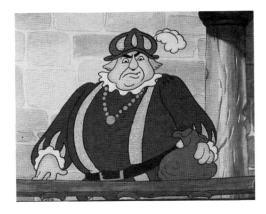

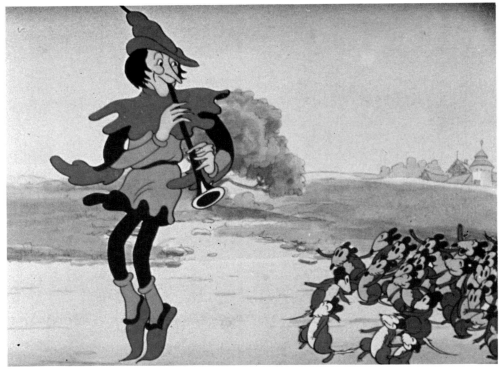

The **Mayor of Hamelin**, a plump and venerable figure, has offered a bag of gold to anyone who can rid his town of rats. This the Pied Piper succeeds in doing by hypnotizing the rats so that they have a mass hallucination of a colossal round of cheese; once they have all cheerfully jumped into the holes in the cheese the Pied Piper makes it disappear – and the rats with it. However, the Mayor reneges on his promise, giving the Piper not a bag of gold but only a single coin. The Piper berates the people of Hamelin for their meanness and dishonesty and says that it would be a shame if the town's children grew up to be like their parents; he has therefore decided to spirit the youngsters away.

Off they all go to a mass grave in the mountains – but this opens to admit the children to the Garden of Happiness (a sort of high-blown Toyland), where they stay playing in immortally youthful happiness for the rest of eternity.

Filmography

Old King Cole, 1933
The Pied Piper, 1933

In *The Pied Piper* (September 1933) the Piper *(above)* took revenge when the Mayor of Hamelin *(left)* tried to swindle him.

MR. SANDMAN

This famous nursery character makes a single Disney appearance – in a 1933 short called *Lullaby Land*.

The plot of the short is that a toddler, after a day of being told "Don't!", drops off to sleep in his cradle and then falls with his dog into the land of "real dreams". They have a number of adventures involving portmanteau creatures – such as a pacifier-bush – before coming across a cache of items with which toddlers are generally Not Allowed To Play. One of these is a box of matches, which catches fire quicker than you can lose your wallet in New York. The smoke forms into a troop of bogeymen, who chase the pals. The chase ends when Mr. Sandman steps from behind a tree to sprinkle sand over the child and dog. The sand takes its effect and the pair obediently lie down. Moments later, they are back in the cradle – and in the real world.

The Sandman starred in the 1933 Silly Symphony *Lullaby Land*.

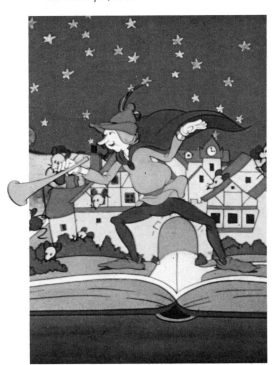

The Pied Piper in *Old King Cole* (July 1933).

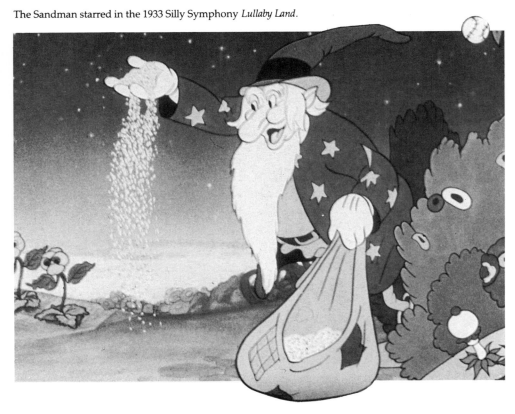

This short has some similarities with the 1938 Silly Symphony *Wynken, Blynken and Nod* (➤88).

FIFI

Fifi, a mischievous little brown dog with black ears, was to be Pluto's first great love. However, where she came from and where she rather abruptly vanished to are questions that remain unanswered. Of her four appearances in the shorts (plus one commercial), only one can be said to show her as a star.

She first appeared in 1933 in a comparatively minor role in *Puppy Love*, which has her primarily as an excuse for Pluto inadvertently to disrupt the course of the romance between Mickey and Minnie. Pluto, much enamoured of Fifi, switches the gifts given to the two ladies, so that Minnie apparently receives from Mickey a bone and Fifi receives some candy. Minnie is quite naturally enraged with Mickey until she sees what has been going on, and there is a happy ending with a joyous reunion between both pairs of lovers.

There was to be a long gap between this first appearance of Fifi's and her second, in *Pluto's Quin-Puplets* (1937). But the wait was worth it: the resulting cartoon was a classic.

Fifi and Pluto are evidently married – a fact which calls into question his later relationship with Dinah (➤93)! – and they have five little puppies. They are very much in love, too, as we see in the short's opening shot when they nuzzle romantically against each other. But then the spooning has to stop: on the other side of the fence the butcher goes by with a string of sausages dangling tantalizingly from his basket. The two dogs instinctively pursue the siren

scent ... but then Fifi, realizing that the quin-puplets are being left on their own, with some difficulty sends Pluto back to look after them.

Looking after the mischievous pups is no easy task, especially for a dog as deep-thinking as Pluto. Whatever he tries to do, sooner or later one or more of them escapes from the safe haven of the kennel and, while he goes off in search of the fugitive(s), the others seize their own chance of escape. Even the use of his hypersensitive bloodhound-like nose is of little avail: the pups, following their own noses, trail a goofy caterpillar right through the arch of his legs while he is still trying to pick up their elusive scent.

Pursuing the caterpillar, the pups fall into the house's cellar where they encounter a compressed-air bottle and its attendant length of rubber hose; this, they assume with their finely honed puppy-dog instincts, is a snake, and one of them goes for it with his needle-sharp teeth. As the air escapes the hose lashes around, reinforcing their suspicion that it is indeed a snake. All join in the glorious fracas.

Enter Pluto the magnificent, having heard the furore. In no time at all he too is bravely doing battle with the "snake", with the result that he is grievously inflated. When the pressure becomes too great, he zooms off like a punctured balloon, bouncing off the walls and floor and creating havoc wherever he impacts. Finally he crashes into the wall under a shelf which bears a bottle of brandy; as he lies there dazed there is a dripping on his head and he half-unconsciously slobbers up this heaven-sent nectar ...

The pups, now that Dad has quietened down a bit, decide to enter battle with a stack of paint-cans: the short was made in Technicolor.

A little later Fifi reappears in high spirits with the string of sausages – but only to find that the kennel is empty. Her apprehension is short-lived, though, because up to her bound merrily a collection of five exceptionally Technicolor pups. Her fury knows no bounds, merry or otherwise, when Pluto with a leery belch emerges, or tries to, from the cellar's hatch: as he stands there covered in paint and paint cans, lurching on his rubbery legs, Fifi seems to search within her heart for some excuse to continue loving him. The search ends abruptly when one of his miscellaneous paint cans topples off him to land on her head.

In the final sequence of the short we see the result of Pluto's day with the quin-puplets. Fifi sleeps – or, rather, does not sleep – in the kennel with her teeth furiously and coldly a-chatter while Pluto suffers all the pains of the outer darkness. Well, not quite. The camera pans across to find him and the pups sleeping the sleep of the virtuous, warm and snug, in a battered and broken old rain-barrel.

Society Dog Show (1939), another classic, shows an earlier episode in the two dogs' romance. Fifi very definitely belongs in such a high-class gathering, but Pluto has been dragged along by Mickey, who touchingly believes that his dog is as good as if not better than all the others – and who could argue with that? Despite their differing social status, Pluto and Fifi fall instantly for each other and when Pluto – dog number 13, of course – is called to the judge's stand he is found to be canoodling with the little debutante. As Mickey remarks crossly: "This is no time for women!"

It is also no time to become furious at the judge and to go for him with many a snarl and growl, as Pluto begins to realize when he and Mickey are thrust unceremoniously from the building. Mickey, though, is not too cross with him and still has faith. With a catch in his throat he says: "Don't worry, Pluto. You're a better dog than any of 'em."

Just before they slink away, though, pandemonium breaks out. A photographer's flash-powder has set fire to the building and all the people and dogs flee in panic. All but one – poor Fifi is trapped in the flames. It is time for Pluto to show that he is indeed "a better dog than any of 'em". With a courageous disregard for both his own personal safety and the laws of gravity, he struggles through many dangers at last to save the beautiful damsel. As the hero of the day he receives a special award, but of course this means nothing to him in the context of the greatest prize of all, the love of Fifi.

But it was not to last. Although Fifi played a minor part in a commercial in that same year, *Mickey's Surprise Party*, and years later had a tiny role in a crowd scene in *Pluto's Blue Note* (1947), and although as we saw in the earlier *Pluto's Quin-Puplets* the two lovers settled down and had a family

Fifi played a cameo part in the 1939 commercial *Mickey's Surprise Party*.

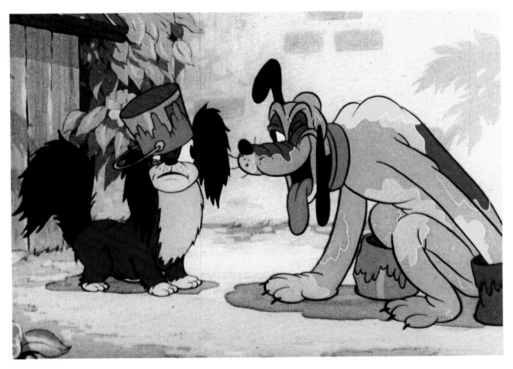

The end of a beautiful relationship: *Pluto's Quin-Puplets* (1937) saw Fifi's last major appearance.

together, Fifi vanished from the scene and a couple of years later Pluto was laying siege to the heart of Dinah (►93). Perhaps that drunken binge of Pluto's was too much for Fifi and she expelled him from her life forever. Who knows?

Filmography

Puppy Love, September 2, 1933
The Dognapper, 1934
Pluto's Quin-Puplets, 1937
Society Dog Show, 1939
Mickey's Surprise Party, 1939 (commercial)

THE COLONEL

The Colonel made his solitary appearance in a 1933 Mickey Mouse short called *The Steeple-Chase*. He is the owner of a racehorse called **Thunderbolt**, which Mickey has agreed to ride in the grand steeplechase.

Unfortunately, just before the start,

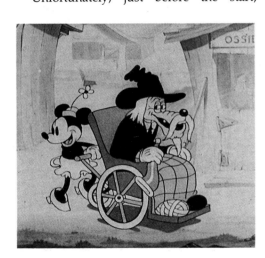

The Colonel, from 1933's *The Steeple-Chase*.

Thunderbolt finds a hidden gin bottle and downs it; it is no coincidence that the horse collapses just before the race. The Colonel is desperate – he has bet his last dollar on Thunderbolt winning. But Mickey has an idea: he takes two stable lads to a theatrical costumier and dresses them up as a pantomime horse. However, they get left far behind in the race – until, that is, they knock over a hornets' nest. Moments later, the Colonel's financial problems are solved.

GRASSHOPPER

Two of the most enduring characters, in terms of the popular memory, to have appeared in the Silly Symphonies did so in 1934. One was the immortal Donald Duck (►61), who went on to star in countless movies. The other appeared in only a single short yet is still widely remembered.

The lesser light was the Grasshopper; he featured in *Grasshopper and the Ants* (1934) and his memorability is probably in large part due to his catchy song, "The World Owes Me a Living", composed by Frank Churchill, which had a fair degree of commercial success at the time (it fell just short of being a hit) and has remained in the fringes of the public consciousness ever since. It was a song that was right for its time – just like the Three Little Pigs' "Who's Afraid of the Big Bad Wolf?" a year earlier (►54). (In the 1935 short *On Ice* Goofy first appears singing "The World Owes Me a Living". In fact, the Grasshopper, like Goofy, was voiced by Pinto Colvig, so it was only to be expected that Goofy would pick up the song.)

The Grasshopper has a red waistcoat, an impertinent green top hat, green shoes with eye-wrenchingly red bows on them, a tailed jacket (also in green) and a black-green bowtie. We first encounter him skipping through the shrubbery, playing his fiddle and singing "Oh, the World Owes Me a Living". This is all very well during the balmy days of Summer but, as we see, Autumn soon comes and, in its wake,

The Grasshopper, in 1934's *Grasshopper and the Ants*, voiced by Pinto Colvig, who sang the catchy "The World Owes Me a Living".

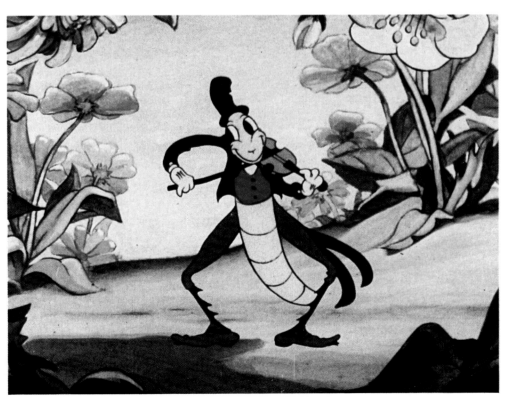

Winter. Stumbling along in starvation, the Grasshopper finds the very last leaf still available for him to eat; but just as he grabs at it with a piteous cry of "Food! Food!" the fickle wind carries it away into infinity. Blue with cold in the snow, he collapses from exhaustion outside the ants' nest. They drag him in, and on his recovery he finds himself confronted by a wrathful **Queen Ant**. As tears form in his eyes she says imperiously: "Only those who work can stay, so take your fiddle ..." He turns for the doorway leading to the cruel blizzard. But then the Queen finishes her couplet with the words: "... and *play!*"

The Grasshopper joyfully complies, boisterous in the relief of his reprieve, but now he has a rather different song to sing: "Oh, I Owe the World a Living...".

Of the ants in the short Richard Plant wrote rather politically in 1941 that

These hordes of busy ants recall the masses of human workers, compelled to do the same thing, at the same time, day in and day out in eternal monotony. Disney industrializes the world of animals, he rationalizes the animal kingdom.

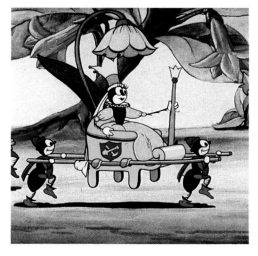

The Queen Ant, from *Grasshopper and the Ants* (1934).

In fact, one doesn't need to agree with Plant's political analysis to recognize that he is approaching the cartoon on its own territory, for it is indeed an intensely *political* movie. And, refreshingly, its message – or, rather, twin messages – is one that can be agreed with by both ends of the political spectrum (yet again Disney managed to hit upon a truth that unites, rather than a contentious issue that divides!): first, the parasites upon society will eventually come to grief (and quite right too, the short suggests), and, second, when that comes about, society should treat those parasites with mercy. In this light, the short can be seen as a plea for political tolerance. Twenty or so years later, of course, both the American people and Walt himself were to have rather different ideas on this score.

DONALD DUCK

Whenever the corners of Donald Duck's eyebrows begin to meet and his webbed foot begins to stamp, most audiences squirm in pleasant anticipation of Donald's forthcoming anger. Never in motion pictures has there been such a funny fury as Donald's.

Richard Tobin, 1935

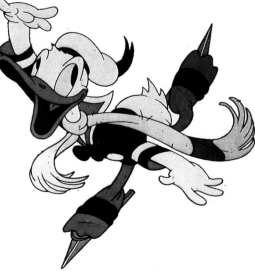

"Who? Me? Oh, no, I've got a bellyache."

Who could have guessed that these eight words, uttered in a 1934 short called *The Wise Little Hen*, would herald the arrival of one of the world's most popular and durable movie stars? Animated in this first short by Art Babbitt and Dick Huemer, Donald Fauntleroy Duck was here to stay. In 1970 the Republic of San Marino issued a postage stamp in Donald Duck's honour. In 1984 Bhutan, the Maldives and Grenada (among others) followed suit. Donald is a worldwide "personality". His only close rival in the Disney canon is Mickey Mouse himself (►23), but Donald has appeared in far more movies (128) and has occupied far more hours of screen-time; moreover, he appeared in colour from the outset; i.e., about a year before Mickey made that particular breakthrough (in *The Band Concert* in 1935 – a movie in which Donald stole the show). Helen G. Thompson, writing in 1935 in *Stage* of his second appearance, summed it up in a nutshell:

... at the opening of *The Orphan's Benefit* [sic], he brought down the house, along with bricks, potted palms and other available impedimenta. ... He was hailed as the bad penny de luxe. He was called the greatest pest since ... chain letters. It was said that no one had been as beguilingly cross-eyed since Ben Turpin. No one had been flattened out with such finality since the steam roller ran over little Fido. His persistence was comparable to Jean Valjean's in *Les Misérables*.

Much later, a Disney publicity release was likewise to encapsulate Don's abilities: "Although he takes many a blow on the chin, he always dusts off his feathers and rises to take it on the chin again."

Today Donald's movies are seen in 76 countries; his daily comic strips appear in 100 newspapers around the world; his comic books are published in 47 countries, and he is seen on television in 29. He has his own television series, *Donald Duck Presents*, on The Disney Channel in the USA; and he acts as host at both Disneyland and Walt Disney World. Yet as Jack Hannah, who played a supremely important part in the Duck's later career, has remarked: "Donald was an accident. Just like in real life, someone comes on as an extra and then BOOM! Most of the popular animated characters were accidents. They just seemed to work for an audience."

Walt himself (in the Manila *Sunday Times Magazine* in 1948) gave an account of Donald's precipitate rise to stardom:

Donald Duck came into being in 1934 to fit a voice which had interested me a couple of years before. He first appeared in a bit in our *The Wise Little Hen*, and proceeded to steal the picture. He squawked and strutted his way into the production until he was practically the star of the film. He was a character we simply couldn't keep down. And the public took him to heart completely after his second picture appearance in *Orphan's Benefit*. His towering rages, his impotence in the face of obstacles, his protests in the face of injustice, as he sees it, even though he brings disaster upon himself – have kept him an audience favorite from that day to this.

Hannah expanded on the theme:

We began to have an awful hard time finding stories for Mickey. Mickey began as a mischief-maker, but he developed right off the bat into a little hero type, and you couldn't knock him around too much. And Goofy – you couldn't knock the simpleton. The great thing with him was watching him thinking. The Duck was very versatile to work with – it was easy to find a situation for him. ... Donald could be anything. He had every emotion a human being has. He could be cute, mischievous, go from warm to cool at any moment. You could half kill him and he'd come right back. He instigated trouble. Not mean – but he always saw a chance to have fun at other people's expense. He'd set up a situation, let's say with the two chipmunks, and kill himself laughing behind a fence, and then he'd go too far and it would backfire. That was the essence of his personality – that and his temper. He'd start out looking like he'd just stepped out of Sunday School, and he'd try so hard to be good, but then he'd get tempted.

An anonymous Disney writer in the late 1940s put rather a different slant on this, stating things somewhat more bluntly:

Mickey is limited today because public idealization has turned him into a Boy Scout. Every time we put him into a trick, a temper, a joke, thousands of people would belabor us with nasty letters. That's what made Donald Duck so easy. He was our outlet. We could use all the ideas for him we couldn't use on Mickey. Donald became our ham, a mean,

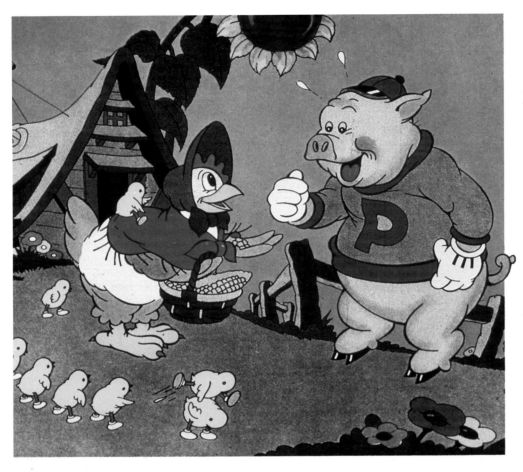

The Wise Little Hen and Peter Pig, two of the stars of 1934's *The Wise Little Hen*. The short's third star, Donald Duck, was to go on to greater things.

irascible little buzzard. Everyone knew he was bad and didn't give a damn. So we can whip out three Donald Duck stories in the time it takes us to work out one for the Mouse.

This certainly explains why Donald is the most prolific of all the Disney characters – in terms of number of appearances, total screen-time, comic-book career ... any way one cares to do the mathematics. But Donald's naughtiness and bad temper probably have another effect: he is significantly more popular among *adults* than Mickey is. Adults see in Donald a caricature of the characters of their own beloved offspring; also, he touches a chord in that part of the grown-up that will remain forever a child – we would all like, now and again, to behave like Donald, if only we thought we could get away with it! While Donald is, of course, also phenomenally popular among children, Mickey appeals to them just as strongly, if for rather different reasons: they see him as a figure worthy of their respect – in short, a hero – just like the Famous Five or the Hardy Boys. This difference in primary audience of the two characters is responsible for some interesting cultural phenomena – for example, Donald's colossal popularity (along with other naughty ducks such as Scrooge) in the strips and comics is almost certainly because these are read as widely – if not more so – by adults as by children.

Similarly, Mickey's popularity is higher in the United States, where there is a strong popular misconception that animated cartoons are only for kids, than in, say, the United Kingdom, where cartoons are generally regarded as fit and enjoyable viewing for people of all ages.

Still extant is a 1939 character analysis of the Duck produced by the Disney story department as a guide for use in creating scripts for new Donald Duck cartoons. It is a devastating critique of his many little failings.

The Duck is the most versatile of all Disney characters. Given almost any role, he will carry it off with honors. Exceptions are dumb roles and gentlemen parts – he is too smart and active to play the former, and, as for the latter, he just can't be bothered.

He is vain, cocky and boastful; loves to impose on other people and to heckle them, but if the tables are turned, he flies into a rage. He can dish it out, but he can't take it. It is his cockiness that gets him into most of his scrapes, because it is seasoned with a foolhardy recklessness.

His most likeable trait is determination. In most of his pictures, he has some goal to achieve, and he goes after it with a vim that brooks no interference. When an opposing factor rears its ugly head – and it always does – he loses his temper. The Duck never compromises. Regardless of the odds against him, he comes back again to the fray, each time

more determined than before, and rants and kicks and punches and yanks until either he or the opposition is in ruins.

When attacking a problem, he may be either cocky, cautious, or cunning – or all three by turns. Some of his best stuff is done when he attempts to be cunning. On these occasions, he frequently enjoys temporary success (which goes to his head), but his craftiness always backfires sooner or later with disastrous results.

He seldom flies into a rage at his first rebuffs; usually these defeats serve to bring out his cleverness. For instance, if he attacks a problem with an oversupply of confidence, and meets unexpected resistance, he will change his tactics. His stock remark for these occasions is: "This requires strategy."

His well-known quick temper arises in most instances from frustration of his desires, but ridicule, petty annoyances, impatience, or ruthless destruction of some valued possession can make him turn the air blue. He doesn't stay angry for long periods; even in his wildest rages, he can be completely and instantly mollified by a little gratification.

When opposed by living characters, his rage seldom goes beyond the bluffing point, but, occasionally, he comes in with his dukes flying and gives a very good account of himself. Always, however, the characters that he beats up are menaces much larger than himself.

He is easily amused, and laughs especially heartily when he thinks he has caused some person or thing discomfort. The reason that he has few opportunities to laugh in his pictures is because audiences prefer to see him taking it, not dishing it out.

He isn't funny in situations that do not offer a considerable amount of action, or that require a great deal of dialog. The Duck's dialog should be used sparingly, because it is funny only in sound; *few* people understand his words.

That voice of Don's was, throughout his career (to date), supplied by Clarence "Ducky" Nash (who died of leukemia on February 20, 1985). In a number of interviews Nash recalled how he had first come to Walt's attention. Although Nash's accounts of it all tend to be inconsistent, we can get a pretty clear idea of what happened.

Nash had put his talents as a vocal impressionist to good use on a Radio KHJ (Los Angeles) show called *The Merrymakers*, and as a result had been employed by the Adohr Milk Company to drive around a team of miniature horses and give little goodies to the children; he was "Whistling Clarence, the Adohr Bird Man". Coincidence began to play a part in events. In 1932 Nash did a reprise performance on *The Merrymakers* and Walt accidentally picked it up: "Hey, that man sounds like a duck!" Walt is reported to have said: "Let's hear the rest of that." A couple of days later Nash was passing the studio with his team of horses and impulsively popped in to give the receptionist a copy of his publicity sheet as "Whistling Clarence, the Adohr Bird Man". And a few days after *that* Wilfred Jackson 'phoned Nash up to ask him to come in for an informal audition.

As Nash was in the middle of imitating a precociously shy child reciting "Mary Had a Little Lamb" Jackson suddenly switched over his intercom so that Walt could hear what was going on. And when Nash moved on to impersonate a family of ducks Walt cried excitedly: "There's our talking duck!" In due course Walt worked with Nash to develop the voice; as Nash commented once: "Before Walt I never thought of being mad or laughing in the Duck voice, but when he suggested it, I found that I could do it. After that, the more I used it, the more I developed it."

Although the Duck's first animators were Art Babbitt and Dick Huemer, the person responsible for developing Donald's appearance and general style in the first few shorts (when, incidentally, he was only about half as tall as the Mouse – later he became more nearly the same height) was Fred Spencer. When they were trying to work up the cartoon character of Donald to match Nash's voice Walt is reported to have said to Spencer: "Make this duck kinda cocky. And since he's a duck and likes water, how about giving him a little middy blouse and a sailor hat?" And, sure enough, that is the way he has been – aside from the occasional "fancy-dress" performance – ever since his first short.

Don had been mentioned in 1931 in a book called *The Adventures of Mickey Mouse*, but his first screen appearance did not come until 1934; it was a quite small part in the short *The Wise Little Hen*. He shared the billing with **The Wise Little Hen** herself and **Peter Pig**. Peter Pig was voiced, like Donald, by Nash; it was lucky for Nash, in terms of his nickname, that it was Donald rather than Peter who became a major star. Nash declared in later years that the reason for Peter's abrupt demise (although years later he made a cameo appearance in *Who Framed Roger Rabbit* [➤**326**]) was that nobody could understand his snorts *at all* – at least people could work out *bits* of Donald's dialogue! In fact it is reasonably easy, if potentially painful, to imitate Peter's voice: all you have to do is try to speak through your nose. To complete the impersonation, you should be large and round and wear a white sweatshirt with trimming at neck, waist and wrists as well as a ridiculously small red-and-blue-panelled schoolboy cap.

The Wise Little Hen has a "cluckety" sort of voice. Her face is quite similar to that of Clara Cluck (➤**71**) and her voice was in fact supplied by Florence Gill, who voiced Clara, but otherwise she could hardly be more different: she is a frail, busy little figure in a red shawl, a blue bucket hat and grey bloomers. She is also surrounded by countless chattering chicks – something one could never imagine Clara being!

With her chicks the Wise Little Hen calls on Peter Pig to ask him if he will help her plant her corn, but with a graphic demonstration of abruptly assumed agony

he responds: "Who? Me? Oh, no, I've got a bellyache." Then she goes to the home of Donald Duck, but he, like Peter, is anxious to dodge anything as exhausting as work and so clutches his stomach, rolls his eyes in badly acted torment, and repeats those famous first words: "Who? Me? Oh, no, I've got a bellyache." The Wise Little Hen sniffs disbelievingly at the pair of them, but without further demur she and the chicks plant the corn themselves.

Harvest time comes and the Wise Little Hen drops round to the Idle Hour Club – President, Peter Pig; Vice President, Donald Duck – and again asks the lazy pair if they will help her, but alas, by a strange coincidence, they have these pesky bellyaches again. But this time the Wise Little Hen spots them surreptitiously shaking hands to congratulate each other on having got rid of her, and her wrath knows few bounds. However, she and the chicks have little choice but to harvest the corn for themselves.

And now it is baking day, and from her oven pour hosts of different corn goodies. She casts her eye over to the Idle Hour Club, and as soon as Don and Peter spot her watching they clutch their tummies again. But no, this time the Wise Little Hen does not want them to do a job: instead she asks if they will help her eat the delights she has baked – and sure they will, bellyaches or no! However, the bowl she passes them contains not some rich delicacy: instead they find a bottle of castor oil – to help with those bellyaches. As she and the chicks happily tuck into the freshly baked cakes and scones we see Don and Peter taking turns in kicking each other. The moral is obvious.

An interesting coincidence concerning this short is that, while Disney was planning it, Nash was approached by Ub Iwerks' studio to see if he would be interested in working as a duck on a short for them. With Walt's consent (Nash was anyway not yet under contract) Nash went along to explore the idea; but when he reported back to Walt the latter was horrified: it turned out that the Iwerks short in question was also to be called *The Wise Little Hen*!

Although Don's part in *The Wise Little Hen* is a good one it is very much a supporting role to that of the eponymous heroine, and so it is perhaps surprising that both public and Disney people alike spotted that here was a future star. However it came to pass, Donald was back later in the year in a more important part in *Orphan's Benefit* (1934). This was Donald's big break. Mickey gives a vaudeville show for an opera house full of orphans and Donald comes along to give his celebrated rendition of "Mary Had a Little Lamb". (Walt had clearly not forgotten hearing Nash recite the poem.) If that were not painful enough, Don insists on giving an encore – his version of "Little Boy Blue". Every time he comes to the line "Little Boy

Blue, come blow ..." the myriad orphans blow their noses. This heckling does not go down well with a nascent star, but conscientiously he tries to carry through and complete his performance. It is not to be. The final scene sees him flattened beneath several gross of eggs.

One feature is missing from Donald's personality in *The Wise Little Hen*: his highly inflammable temper. This emerged with a vengeance in *Orphan's Benefit* and has remained with him ever since (except in the 1983 featurette *Mickey's Christmas Carol*). This type-casting of the Duck as a hot-tempered, almost bullying personality proved a distinct limitation to the efforts of the animators and story-men for a number of years – a limitation felt as much in the comic strips as in the animated shorts. John Hubley in 1944 expressed this forcibly:

The Duck ... became set in his characteristics, his cockiness, quick temper, carelessness, and exhibitionism. Result was a limitation both on writers, in their attempts to broaden the story content, and on the animators in expressing the character's actions and reactions.

And not all of the animators liked him: in 1940 Paul Hollister quoted the great Bill Tytla as saying: "Ducks I don't like, I do not. Ducks I got no patience with." Other animators, too, had their rather more technical problems with Don. The reason he had, in the early days, such an exaggerated waddle was that the animators found it difficult, on paper, to distinguish between a duck and a goose (they were at the time basing a lot of their work on observations of live animals); in the end they compromised by giving Don a goose-like waddle. However, whatever the creative people might have thought, the public loved him.

Wilfred Jackson directed *The Band Concert* (1935), a short that saw one of the Duck's supreme performances (astonishingly, it was only his fourth screen appearance). Arturo Toscanini was so enamoured of Don's performance in this movie that he admitted to having seen it at least ten times. Even as early as this Don's career was seen to be in the ascendant over Mickey's. In 1981 Steven Schneider wrote (perhaps a little unfairly to the Mouse) that in *The Band Concert* "Mickey functions essentially as a passive agent, an almost noninteractive character that serves primarily to fill out the demands of the graphic presentation".

Donald, an itinerant ice-cream vendor, wrecks the concert by playing "Turkey in the Straw" on a succession of fifes, which he produces with bewildering speed in response to the efforts of the rest to smash or otherwise render the instruments unavailable to him. (It might seem that Walt had a "thing" about the song "Turkey in the Straw", because it is also the tune used in *Steamboat Willie* [1928], his very first sound cartoon [➤**23**], but in fact the choice for the earlier cartoon had been made by ... Wilfred Jackson.) Every time Mickey has

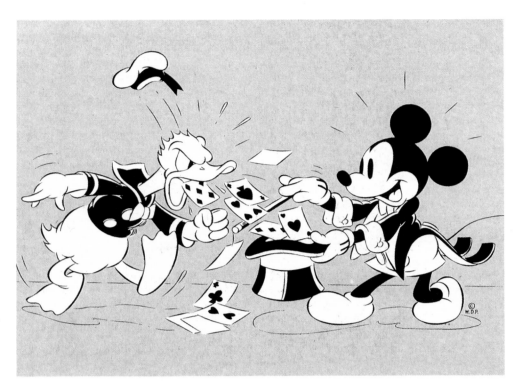

Mickey calls the shots in *Magician Mickey* (1937), and in due course the ubiquitous heckler gets his come-uppance.

things under control for his band's rendition of the William Tell Overture, Don literally pipes up again with "Turkey in the Straw" and the musicians unerringly begin to follow him. It was a triumph of scoring that the two pieces of music could be so elaborately combined: the honours go to Leigh Harline and Frank Churchill.

Interestingly, the original outline for *The Band Concert* had Donald listed as playing the part merely of a saxophonist in Mickey's band. However, Walt, because of the Duck's growing popularity, decreed that Don's role should be expanded: the rest is history. Another significant point about this short is that a devastating influence on the proceedings is played by a bee – Don's first encounter with the species, and one often to be reprised with Buzz-Buzz (➤110).

Movies featuring Donald were coming thick and fast: notable ones are *Mickey's Service Station* (➤28), *Mickey's Fire Brigade* (➤36), *On Ice* (➤39), *Moving Day* (➤16), *Donald and Pluto* (➤39), *Don Donald* (featuring the first appearance of Donna Duck, who was immediately transmuted into Daisy Duck [➤80]), *Moose Hunters* (➤47) and above all 1937's *Modern Inventions*. At the end of *Modern Inventions*, the first short in which he was the solo star, the unfortunate Duck finds himself pinned upside-down in a barber's chair with the robots rubbing shoe-polish all over his head while the feathers of his tail are being assiduously combed and trimmed. His furious protests are blandly ignored by the mechanical barber, which happily continues with its prerecorded "natural" prattle. This particular gag is of some considerable significance in Donald's history – and,

indeed, in the history of Disney. It was dreamt up by Carl Barks, then a trainee animator but later one of the major gagmen for Disney shorts – and later still, of course, *the* artist for Donald Duck and Scrooge McDuck comic strips and books. For this first significant gag he received $50 from Walt, who decided that Barks might be better moving from animation to the story department. This promptly came about and, with director Jack King, Barks eventually worked up the entire story-line of *Modern Inventions*. The result was so funny that, many years later, "Ducky" Nash recalled: "I think that was the picture where the man in Canada laughed so hard he left his crutches behind in... the theater."

And still the great Donald Duck shorts kept coming, often with him working along with Mickey and Goofy, of course. *Clock Cleaners* (1937), *Boat Builders* (1938 [➤33]), *Donald's Nephews* (1938 [➤85]) ... The list is almost endless. Daisy began to play a more important part in Don's life, as did the Nephews. He battled with most of the genera of the plant and animal kingdoms; then life became a little more serious as he took on Hitler's Nazis.

On the eve of the outbreak of World War II the Duck came out with a short called *Donald's Lucky Day* (1939); his co-stars are Pete (➤15) and a black alley-cat. Pete, seen only in silhouette, is a gangster boss who hires messenger-boy Don to carry a time-bomb to the home of an enemy. Don's lucky day is of course the 13th of the month, and his destination is 1313 13th Street – nothing to worry about there! Someone less debonaire than our Don might have been upset about breaking a mirror early on, or

by a black cat not so much crossing his path as leaping into his package, but the Duck is not worried by such superstitious hogwash. Moments later, as he and the alley-cat (and the bomb) perform a complicated seesaw balancing act on a plank over the murky depths of the river, Don begins perhaps to wonder; but he eventually wins this contest and the bomb falls safely into the river. The resulting explosion covers Don in dead fish, and the alley-cat and all his chums arrive like wolves on the fold to devour this unexpected feast.

Soon after this short Donald started doing his bit to encourage the Allied effort against the Nazis. Various shorts were released – the most important being *The New Spirit* and *Der Fuehrer's Face* – but sometimes, for reasons of economy or deadline, shortcuts had to be taken in their production. For example, in *Donald's Decision* (1942), a movie designed to persuade people to buy Canadian War Bonds, footage was reused from the 1938 short *Donald's Better Self*: an original conflict between the Duck's saintly and not-so-saintly *alter egos* (and who would have believed that Don had a saintly *alter ego*?) is transmuted into an argument between the two over whether or not to buy the War Bonds.

The New Spirit (1942), commissioned by the US Government and distributed by the War Activities Committee of the Motion Picture Industry, has Donald being moved by the "new spirit" – i.e., the anti-Nazi urge – willingly and promptly to send in his income tax when he realizes how necessary the money is for the purchase of guns, aircraft and warships to counter Hitler's threat. It is impossible to quantify precisely the effect of this short on otherwise recalcitrant US tax-payers, but it is believed that it had a very significant influence.

Getting this short out on time was something of a triumph for all concerned: from conception to finish the entire production took only a month. Wilfred Jackson was responsible for directing the parts featuring the Duck; Ben Sharpsteen the end sections demonstrating military might. The fee for the film was $80,000, but there was some little difficulty in getting it: Congress refused to grant the money and so the Treasury had, perforce, to seek funds elsewhere with which to pay Disney. The film's motto was "Taxes – to sink the Axis".

Der Fuehrer's Face (1943) was probably an even more important contribution to the anti-Nazi propaganda – and in making it Donald made one of his very best shorts (it received an Academy Award for Best Cartoon Short Subject, the only one of Donald's cartoons to do so). Even today it has a powerful impact – on two levels: it is both a hilarious piece of work, combining excellent animation with an extremely witty set of gags and a catchy song, and an impressive satirical outburst.

It starts with a marching band of grotesquely caricatured German and

Japanese war leaders, including Goering, Mussolini and the Emperor Hirohito, singing the song "Der Fuehrer's Face" by Oliver Wallace. The record of the song, with its strategically if indelicately placed raspberries, went on to become a phenomenal bestseller. As the February 2 issue of *Pic* remarked laconically, "Donald's raspberries are not fruit". The raucous music wakes Don, who responds with a bleary-eyed salute and a weary "Heil Hitler" – as indeed do his alarm clock, his rooster, and virtually anything else capable of motion.

Don drags himself out of bed and proceeds to fetch himself breakfast. This is not a magnificent meal. His meagre ingredients have to be stored in a wall-safe to keep them out of sight of the authorities. With many a nervous glance over his shoulders he guiltily lowers his single coffee-bean for a moment into a cup of hot water and sprays the aroma of bacon and eggs into his mouth from an aerosol. Finally he produces a loaf of bread, but this proves to be made of solid wood; undeterred, he saws a slice from it which, with teeth-shattering eagerness, he desperately

devours. It would seem that times are a little tight in Der Fuehrer's Utopia.

Don's job is to screw on the tips of shells of all sizes, from great megaweapons to tiny bullets. These come past him on a conveyor belt at ever-increasing speed and, just to make his task that much more difficult, they are interspersed with framed photographs of Adolf Hitler – every one of which Don must salute! At one point his resolution breaks down and he snarls at Der Fuehrer's face, only to be instantly surrounded by a forest of rifles and bayonets. Exhaustion sets in – but at last comes the announcement that, thanks to the generosity of the Fuehrer, Donald is due a holiday in the Alps. Relief floods his face. But the holiday, like everything else in the Fatherland, proves to be somewhat less than expected. A backdrop of snowy mountains descends and he is put through a series of rapid physical jerks. One minute later the "holiday" is over ... and Don learns that he is going to have to work overtime in order to make up the minute he has lost from his work!

Faster and faster come the shells along the conveyor belt; greater and greater grows

Don's exhaustion – until finally, inevitably, something cracks and his mind flies off into a surreal nightmare of flying shells, barked orders, stabbing weapons ... even a vision of himself as Adolf Hitler, complete with toothbrush moustache.

At the crescendo of the nightmare Don wakes in a tangle of sheets. He instinctively starts up to give the fascist salute, and then realizes to his slow, heartfelt delight that the entire experience has itself been a nightmare: he is safe at home in the Land of the Free. One can almost hear his thoughts of thankfulness as he looks over towards his bedroom windowsill, where stands a model of the Statue of Liberty.

Der Fuehrer's Face was directed by Jack Kinney, later Goofy's premier director. But, for a number of years before, during and after World War II, the Duck was directed almost to exclusion by Jack King, and several critics have suggested that Donald's career suffered as a result of this. Mike Barrier, writing in *Funnyworld* in Fall 1979, is typical of such critics:

> Jack King was a stodgy director, who sacrificed every other consideration in order to stage the gags in his cartoons clearly; watching them is

Donald and Mickey, *alias* nephew Fred and Bob Cratchit, cower in the face of Scrooge's fury in *Mickey's Christmas Carol* (1983).

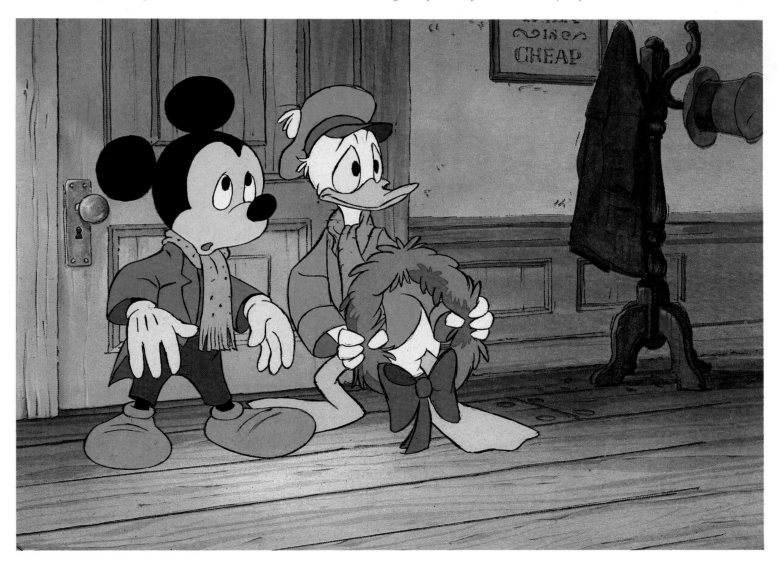

like listening to a comedian enunciate the words very slowly and precisely as he tells a joke. King's direction usually made the gags in his cartoons seem worse than they were – quite an accomplishment, since many of the gags were terrible.

Jack Hannah echoed that King "knew how to put a gag over but paid little attention to personality in Donald. Jack would very seldom add 'touches' that would enhance personality in the characters."

King certainly did pack in the gags, but the critics are possibly being just a little unfair, castigating him for failing to achieve a sophistication to which, with hindsight, they feel he ought to have aspired: it probably never crossed his mind to do so (although he did direct one of the most sophisticated – and brilliant - Duck cartoons, *Donald's Dilemma* [1947], which parodies psychoanalysis and gives Daisy a chance to excel [➤82]). Often enough, however, his quasi-logical progression of events, married to the fact that some of those events could be quite surreal, means that many of his Donald shorts still have audiences rolling in the aisles. Moreover, there are contexts in which, the worse a joke is, the funnier it also is (as with puns).

One sees King's virtues in all their glory in *Chef Donald* (1941), one of the simplest and yet at the same time one of the most hilarious of all Donald shorts. It is impossible to do this movie justice in words. The essential plot is that Don, slavering at the mouth with greed, follows a radio recipe for the making of delicious

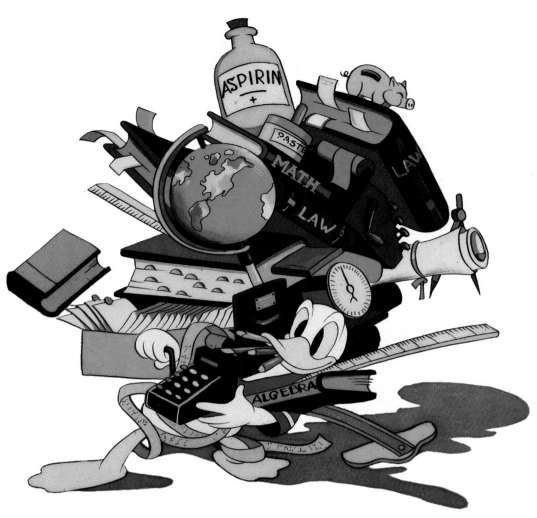

Above: Don brings with him a few helpful items to enable him to fill out his tax form in *The New Spirit* (1942). This pro-taxes commercial was vastly successful. *Lower left:* Donald in *Mickey's Amateurs* (1937). Butter wouldn't melt in his mouth . . . yet.

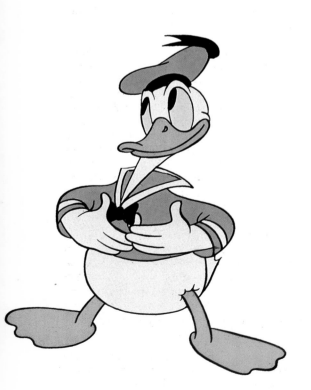

waffles. Unfortunately he is concentrating so much upon the glories that are to be that he fails to notice that he is tipping into the mixture not baking powder but rubber cement. The resultant goo has a mind of its own, and Don, while trying to beat it or separate it, is subjected to some of the funniest indignities in his long career. At the end of the short, with Donald having come out definitely second in his contest with the mixture, the radio chef declares in a honeyed voice that she would love to hear from listeners just how much they enjoyed cooking the waffles. Lucifer himself lights up Donald's eyes. Moments later he is gone from the house; and moments after that we hear through the radio the impassioned screams of the radio chef as she discovers quite how much a certain Duck enjoyed her recipe.

A couple of years later King was again the director of another Donald classic, *Spirit of '43* (1943). A highlight of this short occurs when a kilted Don is seen against the background of a brick wall in which is set a window starred by bullet-holes. The whole arrangement, brilliantly set up and lasting for only a few moments, gives the visual impression of the Stars and Stripes – the Disney patriotism was never in doubt during those dark years.

There were other great moments for Donald during the 1940s – his appearances in the features *The Reluctant Dragon* (1941), *Saludos Amigos* (1943), *The Three Caballeros* (1945), *Fun and Fancy Free* (1947) and *Melody Time* (1948) are noteworthy examples, but there were plenty of excellent Duck shorts pouring out of the Disney studio, too. It is no wonder that *Trombone Trouble* (1944) had earlier been given the provisional title *Superman Duck*! Also of note is *The Plastics Inventor* (1944), generally said to have been the first Disney short to bear full credits (it depends how full you mean by "full"). Another well worth watching is *Donald's Crime* (1945), in which a penurious Donald steals the contents of the Nephews' piggy-bank in order to take Daisy, in her Southern Belle mode (➤80), out on a date. On the way home from his ecstatic experience he is so consumed by guilt over his crime that he suffers a series of hallucinations about being a gangster on the run, and finally he realizes that, if he works the rest of the night as a café dishwasher he will have enough money to replace what he has stolen. After he has done so, though, the voice-over narration tells him that he has put a nickel too much into the piggy-bank. He is trying to extract that extra nickel when the Nephews, all bright-eyed after a good

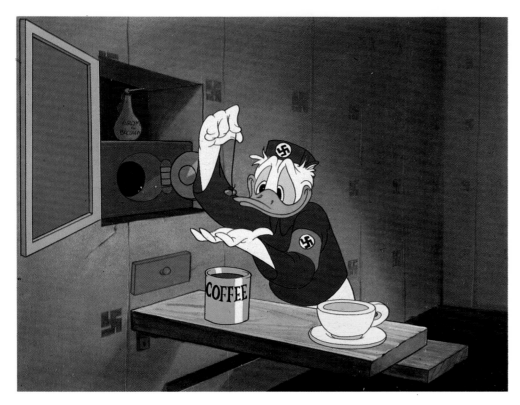

Donald's powerful performance in *Der Fuehrer's Face* (1943) represents the highpoint of the Disney wartime propaganda movies.

night's sleep, come bounding down and catch him apparently robbing their piggy-bank. Despite his eventually good intentions "Unca Donald" is treated to a full measure of high-pitched opprobrium for his "crime". Some ducks can never win.

In *Duck Pimples* (1945) Donald introduced a whole string of minor one-off characters. The short – whose title is given in the opening moments as *Goose Pimples* with the "*Goose*" crossed out and replaced by "*Duck*" – has Don initially listening to the radio and,

whatever station he turns to, discovering that his ears are being subjected to a diet of nonstop violence and horror. He hallucinates, one of his hallucinations being a door-to-door horror-novel salesman, who vanishes leaving Don covered in grisly books.

One of these he begins fascinatedly to read, and all of a sudden up out of its pages leaps a big city cop called **Paddy**; hard as it might be to credit, this cop has a thick Irish brogue.

Paddy commences to interrogate the world's most famous Duck, demanding that Don tell him where the pearls are; when Don says that he does not know, Paddy calls for his torturer, **Leslie J. Clark**, a specialist in the use of hot irons. At the same moment arrives **Pauline**, the sweet lady whose pearls have been stolen: she believes that Paddy has them and spends much of her time searching him. He, for his part, does his best to persuade her of Donald's guilt until finally **J. Harold King**, the author of the relevant book, pops into real life to declare the Duck innocent. It proves that the real villain is one Hugh Hennesy, better known as Paddy the cop, and Don is exonerated. After a suitably 1940s "you'll never take me!" scene, all the book characters vanish, leaving Donald no more than half-persuaded that the entire incident was a product of his imagination.

We have already quoted Jack Hannah's remark that "he'd try so hard to be good, but then he'd get tempted". Nowhere is this more true than in *Tea for Two Hundred* (1948). The Duck, fascinated by a troop of ants and their individual ability to carry loads far larger than themselves, "experiments" by piling huger and huger loads onto the back of one unfortunate ant. Since the load is made up of much of Don's picnic food, this is a silly mistake, because obviously the little ant tells the good news to all the rest back at the nest. Using mushrooms as tomtoms, the ants recruit millions of others to rob Don of the rest of his picnic grub. Despite retaliation with a mixture of venom and dynamite, the Duck is finally robbed of everything he possesses – notably his dignity. In a moment of poetic justice, while the myriad ants are scoffing his cake, the long-suffering ant with which Don had "experimented" is allowed to eat the cherry on top.

A chore which Donald had to take on from the mid-1950s was working on television with Walt. This was not an easy task for a Duck, especially one with a – shall we say? – shortish temper. In an interview in *Mindrot* Jack Hannah remembered some of the problems – and they were certainly not all of Don's making:

The stand-in would come in and we'd get the scene lighted and Walt would come on and work with an idiot card, especially on the longer speeches. However, when he was playing with the Duck, he had it all worked out, even his mannerisms. He knew ahead of

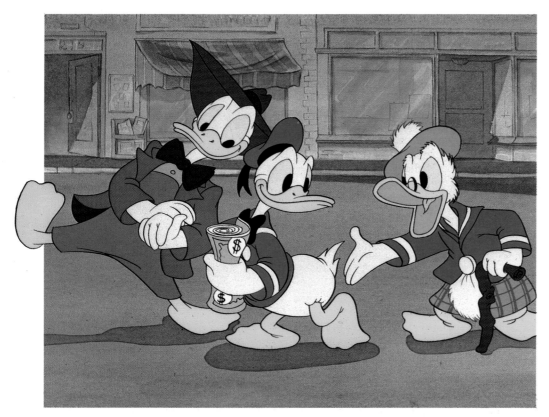

The Spirit of '43 (1943) was a reworking of *The New Spirit* (1942). Here Don resists the blandishments of a canny Scot and a zoot-suited spendthrift.

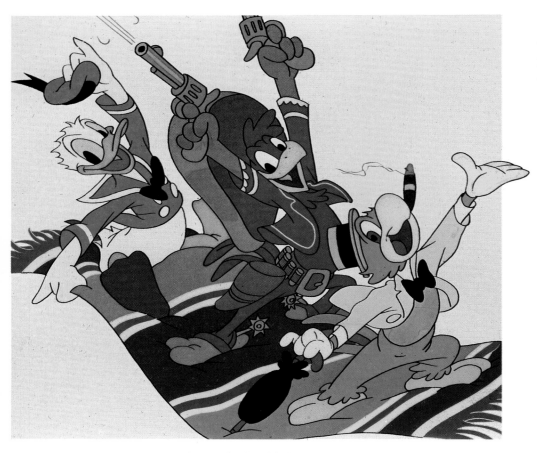

Donald, Panchito and José in the feature *The Three Caballeros* (1945).

Other comparatively late performances by Donald included two in the role of **J. J. Fate**—sort of gremlin duck to be blamed for all mishaps. The function of these two shorts – *How to Have an Accident in the Home* (1956) and *How to Have an Accident at Work* (1959) – was of course to propagandize domestic and industrial safety, respectively. As with movies like *The New Spirit* it is impossible to assess their effectiveness in terms of lives saved, but certainly they are examples of the Duck using his fame for worthwhile social ends. After another socially conscious educational film, *Donald's Fire Survival Plan* (1966 – not released theatrically), the Duck was absent from the screen until 1983, when he played the part of nephew Fred in the featurette *Mickey's Christmas Carol* (➤130). In a way, while it was good to see him there, it was a disappointing appearance because *not once* did he look even remotely as if he were about to lose his temper. He was the only character in the featurette to have his original voice: Clarence "Ducky" Nash. In *Who Framed Roger Rabbit* he loses his temper, all right, in a raucous piano duel with Daffy Duck (➤333), and as Mickey's valet in *The Prince and the Pauper* (➤132) he is delightfully waspish.

Donald, as a worldwide phenomenon, is known under different names in different countries. For example, in Italy he is "Paperino", in Finland "Aku Ankka", in most South American countries "Pato Donald", in Denmark "Anders And", in Saudi Arabia "Batut", in Sweden "Kalle Anka" and in Indonesia "Donal Bebek". Just to add to the confusion over his name,

time what he wanted to do. Many times in the lighter situations he would ad-lib with Donald and that would surprise us and we'd have to go back and revise the storyboard.

But their problems were not only with Walt: the television cameramen (unlike the Disney workers, who were used to such things) had very great difficulty visualizing the existence of an invisible – i.e., an animated – character, and so they generally tended to frame up all the shots wrongly, with Walt dead centre, as opposed to off to one side so that he and the Duck would share centre stage. In the end Hannah and his fellow-directors had to get around the problem by putting cardboard cutouts where Don was going to be in order to give the cameramen a guide.

Donald's list of awards from many lands is impressive. While his cartoons have received only a single Academy Award (for *Der Fuehrer's Face* [➤64]), they have been nominated for no fewer than 14 others: *Good Scouts* was nominated for the 1938 award as Best Cartoon Short Subject, and the same award was proposed for *Truant Officer Donald* for 1941, *Donald's Crime* for 1945, *Chip an' Dale* for 1947, *Tea for Two Hundred* for 1948, *Toy Tinkers* for 1949 and *Rugged Bear* for 1953. *Saludos Amigos* received nominations in the fields of scoring, song and sound for 1943, and *The Three Caballeros* for scoring and sound for 1945. *The New Spirit* was nominated Best Short Documentary for 1942, and the same nomination was made for 1959 for *Donald in Mathmagic Land*.

This latter piece of work was a triumph. Written by Milt Banta, Bill Berg and Heinz Haber (technical advisor), it was a year and a half in production – the time-consuming part of it all being the task of making it simple! The movie begins with Donald among the ancients, starting his mathematical education with the musical scale and, of course, Pythagoras. Here he also encounters the concepts of the Golden Rectangle and the Golden Section, and finds that these proportions have featured not only in classical Greek architecture but also in some of New York's modern skyscrapers. A review of the short in *Chemical and Engineering News* in the year of its release says:

The Mona Lisa, who is proportioned in the "golden" manner, provides a bridge to carry the designs from architecture to the fine arts. But when Donald tries to fit his squat features into the golden rectangle, this classic form slowly dissolves. With much squirming and wiggling, though, Donald finally finds his own pattern – many-sided but still mathematical.

But maths really comes home to the Duck when he uses it to make a perfect billiards shot – Don is ecstatic that this can be achieved by use of merely a simple preliminary calculation. At the end of the movie Don is confronted by a long corridor lined by locked doors. "Who has the keys?" he asks crossly, and the Spirit of Adventure (narrating) replies: "These are the doors of the future. Perhaps you may find one."

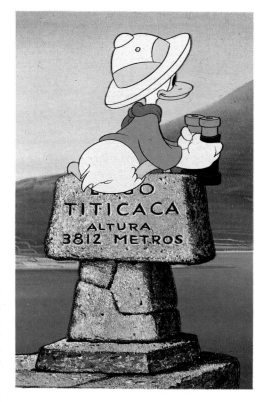

Donald was one of the stars of the first of Disney's Latin American features, *Saludos Amigos* (1943).

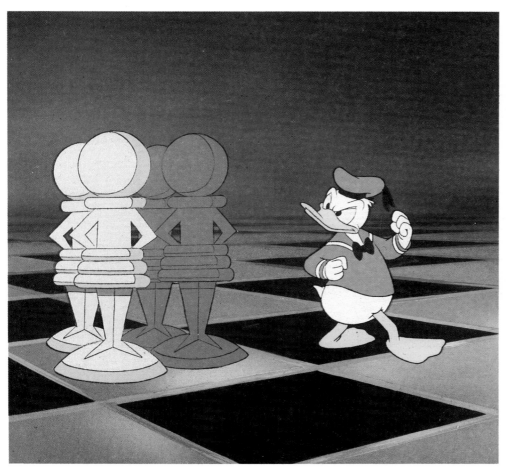

Don proves he can be as educational as the next duck, in *Donald in Mathmagic Land* (1959).

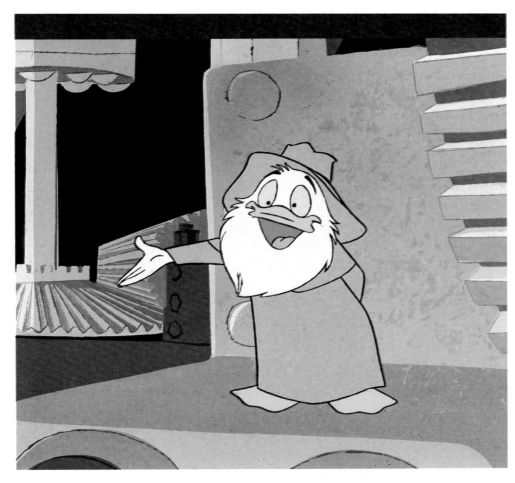

J. J. Fate, Donald's *alter ego*, in *How to Have an Accident at Work*. (1959).

in the Latin editions of the comics he is "Donaldus Anas"!

Whatever the name, Donald most certainly lives on, not only in terms of popular culture but also in more serious realms of the public consciousness. Although he had been castigated in a foreign land as long ago as 1950, when a leading Swedish home journal condemned him as unfit viewing for children, this was in no way a full preparation for the onslaught directed against him (or, conversely, the honor accorded him) in 1971: a Chilean Book, *How to Read Donald Duck*, appeared which virtually accused the Duck of being an agent of the CIA and condemned him, Mickey, Pluto, Goofy and the rest as "cultural imperialists". (The censure is, of course, made less ridiculous in light of events in Chile a couple of years later.) At a lighter level, the Duck's "footprints" are preserved in cement in front of Mann's Chinese Theater. One can predict with some confidence that he will still be well remembered in a century's time when many of today's live actors have been forgotten. And why? Well, probably because he is the perfect epitome of so many human characteristics: pest or not, he is just right. Helen G. Thompson put it in her 1935 *Stage* article, "I wouldn't change him – not one little cross-eyed quack." She added a piece of fine poetry:

I'm stuck
On Donald Duck.

Donald has recently re-emerged as a star of television's *Quack Pack* (➤**151**).

Filmography

The Wise Little Hen, June 9, 1934
Orphan's [sic] *Benefit*, 1934
The Dognapper, 1934
The Band Concert, 1935
Mickey's Service Station, 1935
Mickey's Fire Brigade, 1935
On Ice, 1935
Mickey's Polo Team, 1935
Orphan's [sic] *Picnic*, 1936
Mickey's Grand Opera, 1936
Moving Day, 1936
Alpine Climbers, 1936
Mickey's Circus, 1936
Donald and Pluto, 1936
Don Donald, 1937
Magician Mickey, 1937
Moose Hunters, 1937
Mickey's Amateurs, 1937
Modern Inventions, 1937
Hawaiian Holiday, 1937
Clock Cleaners, 1937
Donald's Ostrich, 1937
Lonesome Ghosts, 1937
Self Control, 1938
Boat Builders, 1938
Donald's Better Self, 1938
Donald's Nephews, 1938
Mickey's Trailer, 1938

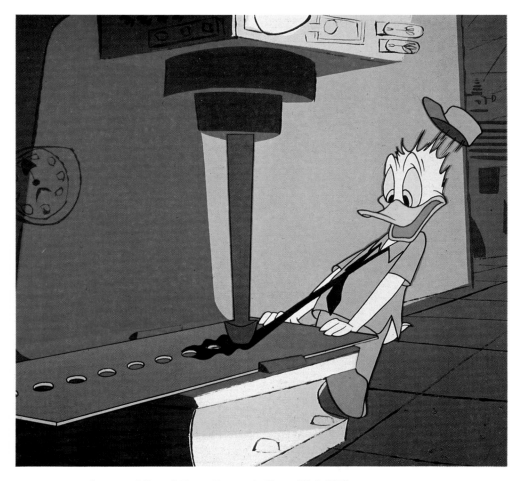

Demonstrating all too painfully well *How to Have an Accident at Work* (1959).

Polar Trappers, 1938
Good Scouts, 1938
The Fox Hunt, 1938
The Whalers, 1938
Donald's Golf Game, 1938
Donald's Lucky Day, 1939
Hockey Champ, 1939
Donald's Cousin Gus, 1939
Beach Picnic, 1939
Sea Scouts, 1939
Donald's Penguin, 1939
The Autograph Hound, 1939
Officer Duck, 1939
The Standard Parade, 1939 (commercial)
The Riveter, 1940
Donald's Dog Laundry, 1940
Tugboat Mickey, 1940
Billposters, 1940
Mr. Duck Steps Out, 1940
Put-Put Troubles, 1940
Donald's Vacation, 1940
Window Cleaners, 1940
Fire Chief, 1940
The Volunteer Worker, 1940 (commercial)
Timber, 1941
Golden Eggs, 1941
A Good Time for a Dime, 1941
The Nifty Nineties, 1941
Early to Bed, 1941
Truant Officer Donald, 1941
Old MacDonald Duck, 1941
Orphan's [sic] *Benefit*, 1941 (colour remake of 1934 original)
Donald's Camera, 1941

Chef Donald, 1941
Mickey's Birthday Party, 1941
The Reluctant Dragon, 1941 (section: *Old MacDonald Duck* [shortened, revised version])
The Village Smithy, 1942
Symphony Hour, 1942
Donald's Snow Fight, 1942
Donald Gets Drafted, 1942
Donald's Garden, 1942
Donald's Gold Mine, 1942
The Vanishing Private, 1942
Sky Trooper, 1942
Bellboy Donald, 1942
The New Spirit, 1942
Donald's Decision, 1942
All Together, 1942
Der Fuehrer's Face, 1943
Donald's Tire Trouble, 1943
Flying Jalopy, 1943
Fall Out – Fall In, 1943
The Old Army Game, 1943
Home Defense, 1943
Saludos Amigos, 1943 (section: *Lake Titicaca*)
The Spirit of '43, 1943
Trombone Trouble, 1944
Donald Duck and the Gorilla, 1944
Contrary Condor, 1944
Commando Duck, 1944
The Plastics Inventor, 1944
Donald's Off Day, 1944
The Clock Watcher, 1945
The Eyes Have It, 1945
Donald's Crime, 1945

Duck Pimples, 1945
No Sale, 1945
Cured Duck, 1945
Old Sequoia, 1945
The Three Caballeros (feature), 1945
Donald's Double Trouble, 1946
Wet Paint, 1946
Dumb Bell of the Yukon, 1946
Lighthouse Keeping, 1946
Frank Duck Brings 'em Back Alive, 1946
Straight Shooters, 1947
Sleepy Time Donald, 1947
Clown of the Jungle, 1947
Donald's Dilemma, 1947
Crazy with the Heat, 1947
Bootle Beetle, 1947
Wide Open Spaces, 1947
Chip an' Dale, 1947
Fun and Fancy Free, 1947 (section: *Mickey and the Beanstalk*)
Drip Dippy Donald, 1948
Daddy Duck, 1948
Donald's Dream Voice, 1948
The Trial of Donald Duck, 1948
Inferior Decorator, 1948
Soup's On, 1948
Three for Breakfast, 1948
Tea for Two Hundred, 1948
Melody Time, 1948 (section: *Blame it on the Samba*)
Donald's Happy Birthday, 1949
Sea Salts, 1949
Winter Storage, 1949
Honey Harvester, 1949
All in a Nutshell, 1949
The Greener Yard, 1949
Slide, Donald, Slide, 1949
Toy Tinkers, 1949
Lion Around, 1950
Crazy Over Daisy, 1950
Trailer Horn, 1950
Hook, Lion and Sinker, 1950
Bee at the Beach, 1950
Out on a Limb, 1950
Dude Duck, 1951
Corn Chips, 1951
Test Pilot Donald, 1951
Lucky Number, 1951
Out of Scale, 1951
Bee on Guard, 1951
Donald Applecore, 1952
Let's Stick Together, 1952
Uncle Donald's Ants, 1952
Trick or Treat, 1952
Pluto's Christmas Tree, 1952
Don's Fountain of Youth, 1953
The New Neighbor, 1953
Rugged Bear, 1953
Working for Peanuts, 1953
Canvas Back Duck, 1953
Spare the Rod, 1954
Donald's Diary, 1954
Dragon Around, 1954
Grin and Bear It, 1954
Grand Canyonscope, 1954
Flying Squirrel, 1954
No Hunting, 1955
Bearly Asleep, 1955
Beezy Bear, 1955
Up a Tree, 1955

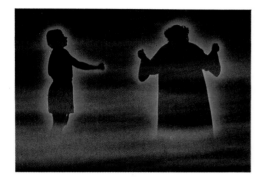

The **Spirit of Progress, Senior,** and the **Spirit of Progress, Junior** assisted Don's efforts in the 1961 educational short *Donald and the Wheel*. Donald, we discover in the movie, is the archetypal inventor – responsible for the wheel and all its many developments – and the two spirits help or hinder him as seems best at the time.

THE FLYING MOUSE

The Flying Mouse was the eponymous hero of a short released in 1934. Obviously, since he came from the Disney stable, one looks for resemblances between him and the most famous Mouse of all, but there are very few. In fact, the only two of note are that he has Mickey's white-gloved hands and that he wears clothing; otherwise he could hardly be more different – in fact, he is much more reminiscent of Chip or Dale (►96). His clothing consists of a red jacket, a blue bow-tie and red shoes; and his proportions are closer to those of a real mouse than to Mickey's.

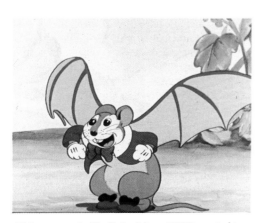

All the mouse in *The Flying Mouse* (1934) wanted to do was fly.

The aim of this mouse is to fly: nothing more. He ties leaves to his forelegs and tries to use them as wings, but all that happens is that he plummets to the ground and, on his second attempt, is rewarded by his mother with a spanking. Finally, though, thanks to the intervention of a fairy who magically gives him wings, he succeeds, only to find that he is rejected by the other flying creatures: the birds who were once his friends now abuse him and, when he flies into a bats' cave, he is told rudely that if he is not a bat then he is *nothing* – because it is a well known fact that mice cannot fly. After a tearful attempt to tear his now-loathed wings off he is confronted once again by the fairy, who tells him that it is folly to try to pretend to be something that you are not – "Do your best, be yourself, and life will smile on you." The morality of this conclusion is perhaps controversial.

A bit part in the short is played by a spider who bears a strong resemblance to W. C. Fields – with a disreputably battered top-hat, a "parp" nose and a red-and-black striped jersey. Whether the caricature is deliberate or not is debatable.

FERDY AND MORTY

Mickey's two mischievous nephews Ferdy (sometimes spelled Ferdie) and Morty have had a career of some note in the comics, but their sole screen appearance has been in a 1934 short called *Mickey's Steam-Roller*. A

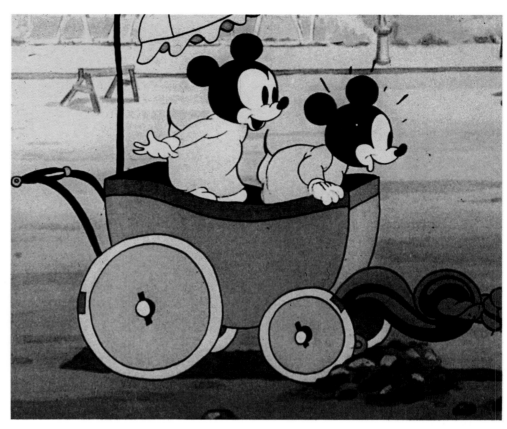

Ferdy and Morty, Mickey's mischievous nephews, made their sole screen appearance in *Mickey's Steam-Roller* (1934).

street is being repaired, Mickey driving the steamroller, when along comes Minnie pushing a baby buggy containing the terrible two. After Mickey has driven them around for a while he attempts to steal a kiss from Minnie and she flees, scandalized. Mickey, displaying more libido than in later years, gives chase; free from adult constraints, the nephews hijack the steamroller and go on the rampage. Finally they, the steamroller and Mickey crash into the front of a hotel, and as the dust clears we find the two nephews playing seesaw using a floorboard, Mickey's head being the unwilling fulcrum.

Mickey's nephews, unlike Donald's (►85), never reappeared on screen. The reasons for this abruptly terminated career are obscure – but see page 131.

CLARA CLUCK

There has never been a prima donna like Clara Cluck, and probably there never will be again: she was inimitable. Built on the grand scale, with a bosom of Brobdingnagian proportions that seems constantly to be struggling to escape from an elaborately frilled costume, with a plumed hat apparently designed to shield a surrounding family of chicks from the elements (although no one could ever imagine Clara permitting herself something as lowly as motherhood), she struts the boards with massive solidity and

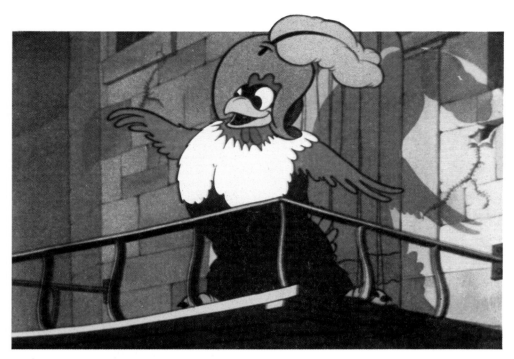

The Disney folk put on all their most uncomfortable gladrags to witness Clara's stunning (well, numbing) second performance: *Mickey's Grand Opera* (1936).

inexorability. Her voice (supplied by Florence Gill) is perhaps not of the very highest calibre, but what it lacks in gracious timbre it certainly makes up in sheer volume and venom. She is one of a kind.

Her first performance, in *Orphan's Benefit* (1934), was a riveting one and probably unique in operatic history: she performed the sextet from *Lucia* – but *on her own*. The audience of eager orphans raised the roof with their applause when she had finished. Unfortunately, waiting impatiently for her to leave the stage – no, to stride from it – was Donald Duck, jaws locked in determination to recite his piece yet again. After that things fell apart, rather (➤61).

Clara's second appearance was in *Mickey's Grand Opera* (1936), in which she sings a most impassioned duet from *Rigoletto* with a somewhat accident-prone chevalier in the shape of Donald Duck. Perched high on a balcony she is aloof from Don's many mishaps until, for reasons not unconnected with Pluto and an escaped frog, he leaps heavenward, sword rampant, to pierce her from beneath. Hitting notes undreamt-of by other opera singers, she collapses together with the scenery to land in a heap of board and timber with Don and Pluto. Like real pros, however, the three succeed in pushing their heads through the wreckage in order to sing the opera's final spine-curdling note.

As Helen G. Thompson put it in *Stage* in 1936, "Madame Cluck sings the quartet in two minutes, two and one half seconds – beating the Metropolitan record by several dull hours and the audience to a bowlful of jelly."

Her last major role – although she has had small parts in later movies, including *Mickey's Christmas Carol* (1983) – was in *Mickey's Amateurs* (1937). In this short, which is centred on an ill-fated radio broadcast organized by Mickey – who else? – she supplies one of the acts drafted in after Donald's recitation has been received noisily but with less than enthusiasm by the audience (much as in *Orphan's Benefit*). Clara meets with much more approval, as do Clarabelle Cow's piano-playing and Goofy's one-man-band act. In the end, however, thanks to some plot-manipulations effected by the malevolently sentient musical instruments, the audience has to settle for a repeat of Donald's recitation. It is not a pleasant moment.

The operatic world mourns the demise of this titanic luminary, but a close cousin of Clara's does, however, appear in 1973. This is Lady Kluck (➤294), Scottish startlet of the feature *Robin Hood*.

Filmography

Orphan's [sic] Benefit, 1934
Mickey's Grand Opera, 1936
Mickey's Amateurs, 1937
The Fox Hunt, 1938
Orphan's [sic] Benefit, 1941 (remake of 1934 original)
Symphony Hour, 1942
Mickey's Birthday Party, 1942
Mickey's Christmas Carol, 1983
Who Framed Roger Rabbit, 1988

PETER AND POLLY PENGUIN

Peculiar Penguins (1934) was the short in which these two amusing penguins made their appearance. The plot could easily have been one for a Mickey/Minnie film.

Peter gives Polly an ice-cream cone made up of an icicle and a snowball. For inscrutable sphenisciforme reasons, Polly regards him as her hero as a result of this gift, and rubs his bill with hers. Peter is wild with excitement over this, and sets off to catch her a fish. Unfortunately, the one he catches her proves to be a puffer fish, which inflates promptly after ingestion, so that a roly-poly Polly bounces around helplessly. At last the fish deflates and Peter extracts it from poor Polly by the simple if unsubtle technique of kicking her in an unladylike spot.

Polly is furious, and stalks off. A little later, however, she is out rowing when a shark chases her boat. Peter saves her from this peril and is thereby reinstated as her hero and number one true love.

Clara Cluck made her entrance – and golly what an *entrance*! – to the world of movies in 1934's *Orphan's Benefit*. Here we see her in the 1941 colour remake.

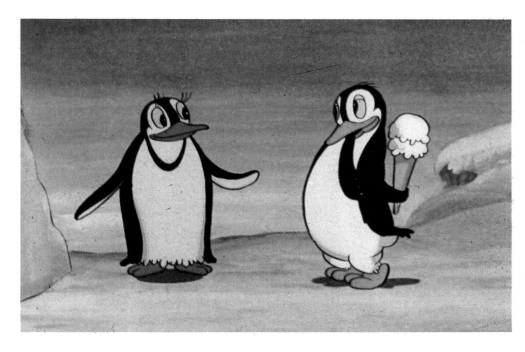

Polly (left) and Peter Penguin, the spheniaciform stars of *Peculiar Penguins* (1934).

PERSEPHONE

The Goddess of Spring (1934) was a Silly Symphony retelling the well known Greek legend about the deal struck between **Pluto**, god of the Underworld, and Persephone: if she will spend six months of each year as his bride in Hades she can spend the other six months in the upper world as the goddess of Spring. The tale symbolizes the growth of crops, which spend six months (or so) in the ground as seeds but then during the Spring grow up out of the soil.

Both characters are rather cypherish in the short, which is not one of Disney's more

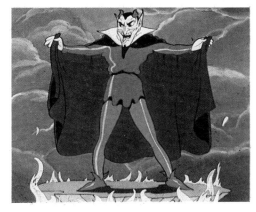

Pluto, King of the Underworld, in 1934's *The Goddess of Spring*.

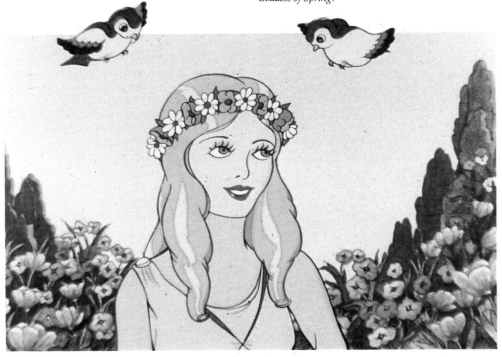

The figure of Persephone, in *The Goddess of Spring* (1934), was modelled on Mrs. Hamilton Luske.

inspired. In a piece in *Funnyworld* in 1979 Dick Huemer recalled that

> [Hamilton Luske] did a great job on Snow White (➤**157**); it was moreover a big advance on *The Goddess of Spring*. He told me that his wife acted the Goddess in that cartoon for him, but they didn't photograph and draw over it so it came out pretty terrible. But then none of us were very proud of our animation in that picture. I animated Pluto, the devil character, and I didn't do it over any live action either. I just kind of acted it out myself and then drew it. It wasn't very good either.

JUDGE EGG

Judge Egg is one of the few Disney animated characters to have been created exclusively for a non-Disney film. The movie in question was the 1934 Fox feature *Servants' Entrance*. Judge Egg – who reminds one insistently of Humpty Dumpty – presides over a midnight trial of a housemaid who, it is asserted, is guilty of long-term maltreatment of the house's cutlery. At the end of the hearing the assembled items of cutlery very decently call upon Judge Egg to give her a suspended sentence, which indeed he does. After all the others have left, the Judge falls off the end of the maid's bed, where he has been perched throughout, and shatters. From the shell hops a little chick, who crows like a cock in order to wake the maid. It has all, as you might expect, been a dream.

TOBY TORTOISE AND MAX HARE

Toby Tortoise and Max Hare appeared in two shorts, *The Tortoise and the Hare* (1935), a straightforward revamping in the Silly Symphonies style of the famous fable, and *Toby Tortoise Returns* (1936); the former won an Academy Award. Both characters had bit parts in the 1983 featurette, *Mickey's Christmas Carol*.

In an interview with Joe Adamson in 1977 Dick Huemer had some pertinent points to make about the characterization of both Toby and Max in this renowned first film:

> It was clearly laid out to have the hare act the way he did, bombastic and boastful, yet talented. That was good, clear characterization. The tortoise was definitely staged as a stupid guy who could good-naturedly be taken advantage of. Actually he won by default. This was the kind of strong characterization that Walt always insisted on. If anybody else had done *The Tortoise and the Hare* it would have been a series of assorted gags about running, one after another. Not all this clever, boastful stuff like stopping with the little girls and bragging, and being admired, and showing off how he could play tennis with himself.

But Max, while he is ostensibly a hare, is not all that he seems. In an article in 1938 George Kent spilled the beans:

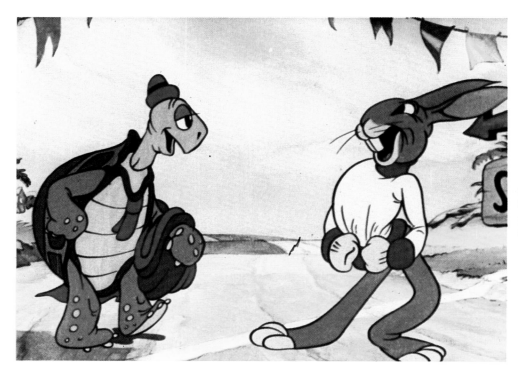

Max Hare seems to think Toby Tortoise might lose the race: *The Tortoise and the Hare* (1935).

Remember the rabbit [*sic*] in *The Tortoise and the Hare*? ... Well, that rabbit was half wallaby. A friend had presented Walt with a pair of them and for a long time they were the studio pets. From watching their antics, the artists got the idea for the lightning-speed rabbit which we saw in the cartoon.

Whatever his ancestry, Max Hare is, as you might expect, brash and super-confident – he has "winner" written all over him. More literally, he has written in gold all over the back of his bright blue robe: "Max Hare – The Blue Streak." He emerges at the start of the race to the cheers and huzzahs of the crowd, in distinct contrast to the reception accorded poor downtrodden-looking Toby Tortoise: the crowd greet him with jeers and catcalls, because he has "loser" written all over him. And *he* is certainly a very different type of racer from Max: on the back of his much patched and mended robe his character and technique are summarized by the slogan "Toby Tortoise – Slow but Sure".

Slow he certainly is: at an early stage in the race four little snails cheerfully gambol about his feet. Max, on the other hand, is off like a bullet and gets so far ahead that he is able to stop to natter and brag to four little girl bunnies (*not* bunny girls!) sitting on the wall outside the local school. It is for them that he does the tricks of being both archer and apple-support in a quick re-enactment of the William Tell scene, plays baseball with himself (he pitches, hits *and* catches!) and finally tennis with himself. But then he hears in the distance the cheers of the crowd as slow-but-sure Toby is approaching the finish line. Blowing the girls a kiss, Max speeds off, but Toby, putting on an unexpected last burst of speed, wins by a nose. With his wilting red tie and his horrendous red hat, the underdog conquers all physical obstacles to become winner of the race and a public hero.

The "message" of the movie was undoubtedly right for its time, with many Americans still suffering the psychological aftermath of the Depression years – not to mention other effects of that traumatic period. Roosevelt's "New Deal" had been announced only the year before and, while it was already beginning to have an effect, many ordinary working men and women must have been glad to have the reassurance that their own slowness and any concomitant sureness were not necessarily handicaps – that not only the fittest would survive. Of course, it is a fact of life that slowness is all too often accompanied not by sureness but by stark all-round incompetence, and that Toby would in real life have lost the race: speed

such as Max's does not necessarily imply mental sloppiness and hence eventual failure. However, what the short was trying to get across was roughly the same sort of moral as that of *Three Little Pigs*, released about a year and a half earlier in 1933 when the Depression was still at its worst (➤55): that doing a job properly, even if as in Toby's case slowly, will always be worthwhile in the end.

In the follow-up short to *The Tortoise and the Hare* (no short as successful as that one could go without a follow-up!), *Toby Tortoise Returns*, the two of them compete in a prize-fight. I. Klein, who did some of the animation for this short, recalled that

> [Wilfred] Jackson gave me as a starter, a busy scene laid in the fight ring; Max Hare seated in his corner puffing on a cigar while two manicurists work on each of his hands and a shoe-shine boy polishes his foot ...

In other words, Max is at his flashy best again. Aside from that, though, the short is a far inferior version of the earlier one (although beautifully animated). Toby, for obvious reasons finding himself in a losing position, retreats in panic into his shell, but some rather synthetic gaggery with fireworks enables him to win, with both Max and the referee being taken to hospital. The short lacked the integrity of plot of the earlier one, and is rarely seen today.

Characters very similar to Toby appeared in *Snow White and the Seven Dwarfs* (1937) and especially in *Robin Hood* (1973); the latter is actually called Toby Turtle (➤295), but is a child rather than an adult. Toby is also seen briefly in *Who Framed Roger Rabbit*.

Filmography

The Tortoise and the Hare, 1935
Toby Tortoise Returns, 1936
Mickey's Polo Team, 1936 (Max only)
Mickey's Christmas Carol, 1983
Who Framed Roger Rabbit, 1988 (Toby only)

In *Toby Tortoise Returns* (1936) the pair forsook running in favour of boxing.

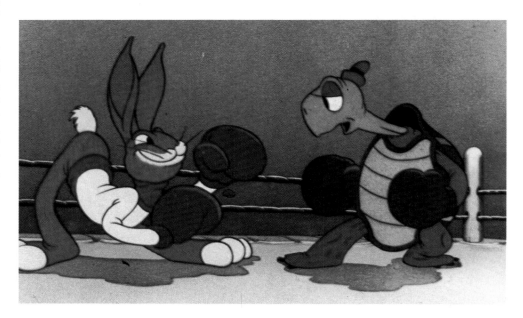

FRIDAY

Friday makes his solitary appearance in the 1935 short *Mickey's Man Friday*, which was based – surprise, surprise! – on Defoe's *Robinson Crusoe*.

Shipwrecked, Mickey finds his way to a desert island where he discovers almost immediately on the beach a footprint. Hearing a drumming sound, he creeps up to spy on a group of cannibals who are preparing supper in their traditional way: making some poor innocent walk the plank into a boiling cauldron. Mickey disguises himself as a hideous idol and chases off the cannibals, rescuing the entrée and christening him Friday. The two build a fort equipped with all sorts of trick gadgets – which they use to good effect when the tribe of cannibals attacks. We last see the pair escaping in a trick boat.

MIDAS

King Midas appeared in the 1935 Silly Symphony *The Golden Touch*, which was a reworking of the Greek legend. In this version it is a dwarf, **Goldie**, rather than the god Dionysus, who gives the cupiditous King the "gift" of turning everything he touches into gold. Of course, this creates

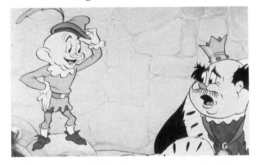

Goldie tries to get Midas to look on the bright side in *The Golden Touch* (1935).

difficulties because even the food the King tries to eat becomes metal; and eventually the King persuades the dwarf to take away the "gift". The dwarf agrees, but only if Midas forswears also all his worldly possessions. The King ends the short in rags, but overjoyed that he now has the gift of life. The moral is obvious: "For what shall it profit a man . . .?"

The character of Midas was animated by Norm Ferguson, the other characters by Fred Moore. Midas was voiced by the veteran actor Billy Bletcher, later a stalwart of the Disney voice team, working on such characters as Peg Leg Pete (►15) and the Big Bad Wolf (►54). Many years after he recalled in an interview with Mike Barrier, published in *Funnyworld* #18, that the Disney people had put white make-up on his lips and photographed him as he voiced the role, thereby giving Norm Ferguson reference from which to work.

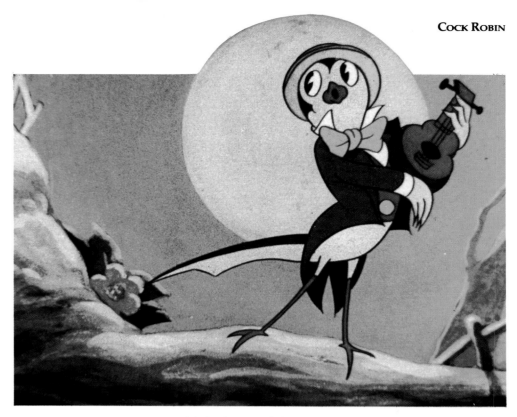

Cock Robin, victim in 1935's *Who Killed Cock Robin?* Or is he?

AMBROSE

Ambrose is a kitten who does not like being bathed: what kitten does? He made his sole appearance in the short *The Robber Kitten* (1935).

We first see him playing as a bandit: he handles a mean popgun. When his mother calls that it is bathtime he sneaks out of the house, leaps onto his trusty hobby-horse, and rides off to earn his living as an outlaw. In the underworld he meets a notorious hood called **Dirty Bill**, and the two swap tales of derring-do (fictitious in Ambrose's case, of course). Finally Dirty Bill, who knows a sucker when he sees one (hitmen are notoriously disrespectful towards kittens armed with popguns), threatens to kill Ambrose for his bag of gold. Ambrose flees and Dirty Bill discovers that the bag contains only cookies.

Back home, Ambrose – to his mother's astonishment – leaps voluntarily into his bath.

COCK ROBIN

The short *Who Killed Cock Robin?*, released in 1935, has many points of interest. For example, it was the first short ever to be featured in the National Board of Review's listing of the ten best films of the year. It featured importantly in Alfred Hitchcock's 1936 thriller *Sabotage*, starring Sylvia Sidney and John Loder (the movie was based on Conrad's novel *The Secret Agent* [1907]). As Cock Robin is failing to be killed in the background, in the foreground one of the film's human stars is being creepily bumped off. And most of the characters in the short are based on human stars. The Sparrow is a

direct descendant of Harpo Marx, while Stepin Fetchit inspired the character of the Blackbird. **Cock Robin** himself was based on Bing Crosby, whose voice he apparently shares. **Jenny Wren**, according to Otis Ferguson's "Extra Added Attractions", is "feathered, but by virtue of certain astonishing developments in the upper regions, forward, and by a routine of sundry bumflips, you-impress-me's, etc., turns out a dead ringer for Miss Mae West, complete with voice and picture hat". Other inspirations included John Barrymore Sr.

The story of the short has only a little to do with the original nursery rhyme. Cock Robin is shot with an arrow while serenading Jenny Wren in his best Bing Crosby style. Up rushes a wagonful of police, who leap savagely into the crowd, making much use of their truncheons, and haul everybody concerned off to court. Here the judge is an owl and the prosecuting attorney is a parrot which curiously seems to have hands under its coat-tails.

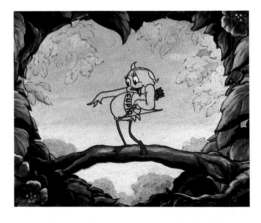

Dan Cupid, who has a lot to answer for in *Who Killed Cock Robin?* (1935).

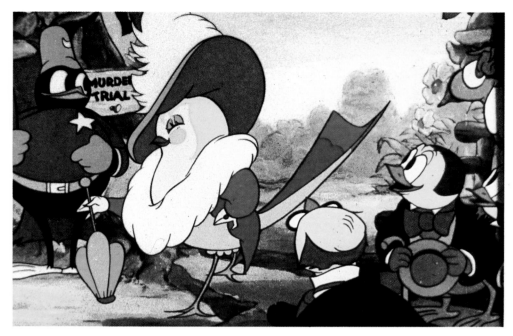

Jenny Wren, the sumptuous female protagonist of *Who Killed Cock Robin?* (1935).

1935 was a good year for Disney in terms of Academy Awards: they received in that year one for 1934, for *The Tortoise and the Hare* (►73), and would in 1936 receive another for 1935's *Three Orphan Kittens*. The curious thing is that the former cartoon is still widely watched today but the latter has never been rereleased.

The plot of *Three Orphan Kittens* is simplicity itself. The three little castaway kittens, Fluffy, Muffy and Tuffy, seek refuge in a house from a great blizzard. However, their various mischievous activities land them in hot water with **Mammy Twoshoes**, who runs the house, and they are saved from expulsion back into the snows only by the intervention of the young mistress of the house. What the movie lacks in storyline, however, it certainly makes up for, as Davenport pointed out, in terms of cuteness of the characters.

The three orphan kittens reappeared the following year in *More Kittens*, in which

All of the prisoners are suspects: prosecutor and judge make that perfectly plain. There is much debate, however, as to who should actually be the guilty party. Indeed, it is said to have taken the Disney team two full years to decide who it was who "killed" Cock Robin, and in the end they rather copped out. Cupid appears in a bower of flowers to say that Cock Robin is not dead but "fell for Jenny Wren and landed on his head". Jenny Wren revives the unconscious swain with a kiss, and all live happily ever after.

Jenny Wren has made cameo appearances in *Toby Tortoise Returns* (1936) and *Who Framed Roger Rabbit* (1988).

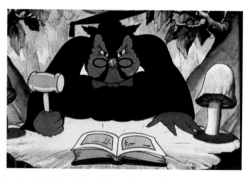

Judge Owl in *Who Killed Cock Robin?* (1935).

FLUFFY, MUFFY AND TUFFY

In 1936 Marcia Davenport wrote in *The Stage* of *Three Orphan Kittens* (1935) that

Reams have already been written about the profound psychology of [Disney's] characterizations, and of the extraordinarily diverse and appealing qualities of the animal actors. Any cat lover will have a conniption fit at the sight of Disney's kittens batting at piano keys or massaging their backs under a convenient piece of furniture.

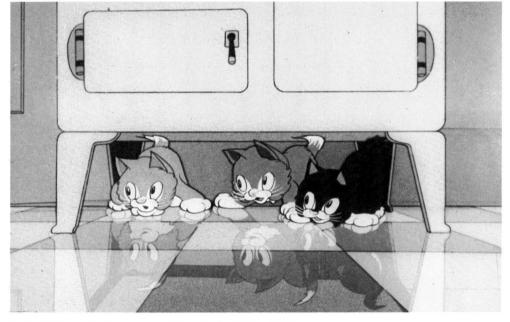

Fluffy, Muffy and Tuffy, the stars of *Three Orphan Kittens* (1935).

Toliver the dog befriends the kittens in *More Kittens* (1936).

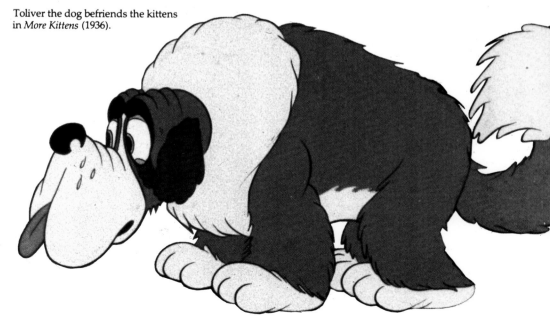

movie Mammy has succeeded in chasing them out into the yard. There they find sanctuary with a Saint Bernard dog, *Toliver*, who protects them from the consequences of their various adventures. In the end they succeed in covering the family wash with muddy pawprints, an act that would result in their early demise were it not for the fact that the Saint Bernard once more provides them with a haven.

Filmography

Three Orphan Kittens, 1935
More Kittens, 1936

COCK O' THE WALK

Three named characters make their appearance in the 1935 short *Cock o' the Walk*: they are the Cock o' the Walk himself (he is often called City Slicker in the literature), Hick Rooster and Prunella Pullet.

The world-champion boxer, Cock o' the Walk, has returned to his home town and is being given a hero's welcome. The hens and pullets are very admiring as he struts around being macho in all directions. Among the adoring is **Prunella Pullet**, who leaves the arms of her boyfriend, **Hick Rooster**, in order to dance in the ring with the musclebound Cock o' the Walk. Hick is not wildly pleased about this, and leaps into the ring to challenge the champ. It is a bruising experience for him, and he is in the process of becoming a shapeless pulp when some documents of Cock o' the Walk's leap out of the ring and into Prunella Pullet's lap. She examines these and discovers that her exciting new boyfriend is in fact well and truly married – at least once. Wrathful, she leaps into the ring to encourage an unconscious Hick – who is sufficiently galvanized by her revelations to (a) recover consciousness and (b) knock Cock o' the Walk right out of the ring. Prunella Pullet, whose morals are best left unexamined, is now of course madly in love with the brand new world-champion boxer, Hick Rooster.

MORTIMER MOUSE

The story has it that once upon a time Walt Disney had a pet mouse called Mortimer, and that it was of Mortimer that he thought when he had to develop a new character to succeed Oswald the Lucky Rabbit (►20). When he talked his idea over with Lillian, however, she told him that the character was all right but that "Mortimer" was a rotten name for him: "Mickey" would be better.

Quite how much truth there is in this tale is hard to assess, but it adds particular poignancy to the fact that the only rival for Minnie's affections whom Mickey has ever had to face was indeed called Mortimer Mouse.

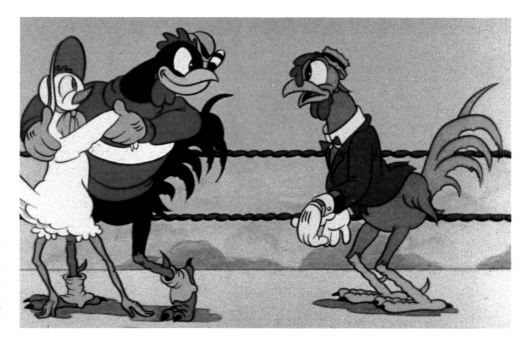

From left to right, Prunella Pullet, Cock o' the Walk and Hick Rooster in 1935's *Cock o' the Walk*.

Mortimer is, in physical terms, very much more "adult" than Mickey. Not only is he taller (by a long chalk), his bodily proportions are much more those of an adult mouse. His head is relatively smaller than Mickey's and his nose is much longer relative to his head (although the earliest version of Mickey had a similarly long nose); his ears are somewhat less stylized, and his dandified clothing – including the long trousers that Mickey would not affect for another couple of decades – is much more like that of an adult. His voice is deep and virile, unlike Mickey's falsetto. When you take into account his higher level of streetwise sophistication – he drives a snazzy yellow sports car, for example – well, it is obvious that Minnie was merely tempted for a while to fall for "the older mouse".

The short in question was *Mickey's Rival* (1936). It starts with Mickey and Minnie out on a country picnic. Suddenly a bright yellow car zooms past them at such speed that all their picnic things are blown away. The car stops and Mortimer, its driver, suavely says to himself: "Well, if it ain't my old sweetie, Minnie Mouse!" He reverses at such speed that he crushes Mickey's rather battered roadster against a tree, hops out of his car and is reunited with his old flame. She introduces him to Mickey, who is just

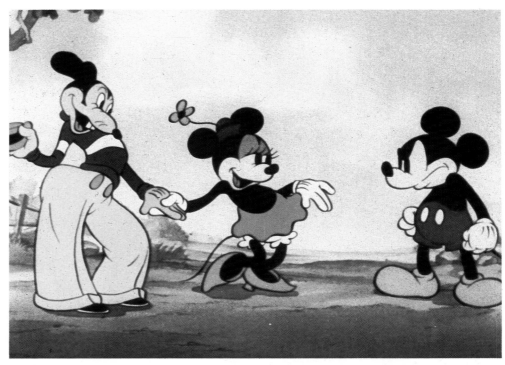

In *Mickey's Rival* (1936) Mortimer thought a wild bull was lethal, but perhaps the bull wasn't the most dangerous animal in the movie . . .

emerging from the picnic's stickier remnants, and a period of humiliation for the world's favourite Mouse begins.

After subjecting him to a fake-arm trick when Minnie encourages the two to shake hands, Mortimer indulges in a piece of playground foolery that surely *must* have been picked up from one of the gagmen's children.

"Do you want that button?" asks Mortimer, pointing at one of the famous pair of pearls.

"Yes," says Mickey, startled.

"Well, here it is," says Mortimer, pulling it off and planting it firmly in Mickey's hand.

But worse is to follow, because Mortimer than points at the other and says: "Do you want *that* button?"

"Eh . . ." says Mickey, thinking fast, "*no!*"

"Well, OK," says Mortimer with a raucous cackle. So he pulls the button off and carelessly kicks it away.

Mickey, whose trousers surprisingly do not fall down, gets madder and madder (even his car starts arguing with Mortimer's), but Minnie is captivated by the suave hilarity of this *quondam* sweetheart. She passes Mortimer the best bits of what is left of the picnic and giggles appreciatively when, using the red picnic cloth, he goes through a mock-toreador act with a ferocious bull that is safely on the other side of the fence. At this stage Mickey stalks off in a jealous sulk; clearly Minnie thinks he is being boring. When the bull escapes, however, Mortimer abruptly drops his toreador routine, leaps into his car and within seconds is over the horizon, leaving Minnie to fend for herself as best she may –

which is not very well, because she is all tangled up in the suddenly discarded red picnic cloth.

Luckily, though, Mickey hears her scream and rushes to the rescue. He pulls the bull bodily off her and then uses the cloth to perform a *real* toreador act while she scrambles up a tree. Just when it looks as if Mickey is about to lose the bullfight, his shabby old roadster intervenes, first battling the bull and then scooping up the two mice and carrying them out of danger.

"So you still think that guy's funny?" says Mickey as they coast away to safety.

"Who?" says Minnie, as if racking her brains to remember who he's talking about. Then: "*Mortimer!* No."

"Shake," says Mickey, and they do. This time there is no fake-arm trick.

ELMER ELEPHANT

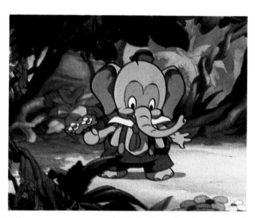

The eponymous star of 1936's *Elmer Elephant* sets off through the jungle, his heart filled with romance.

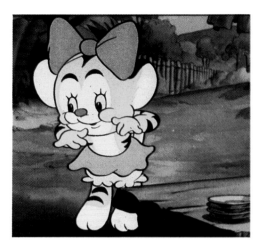

The object of Elmer's dreams, Tillie Tiger.

Elmer Elephant is the central character and eponymous hero in a 1936 Silly Symphony. The cuteness of the movie was fine for its time but rankles a little today.

Elmer, a smart little sailor hat perched on his head, skips along to the birthday party of **Tillie Tiger** (who features a really ferocious bow in her hair), where he manages to become covered in much of her cake. She, however, is sympathetic, kissing him and cleaning him up. Not so a group of monkeys, who taunt him over his trunk and generally make his life a misery. Just as he is wondering whether to End It All there is a cry of panic: Tillie's treetop home is on fire, and she is inside it. Using **Joe Giraffe** rather like a fireman's ladder, Elmer uses his much mocked trunk to put out the fire and becomes a jungle hero. (A hippo called **Joey** is also featured.) Much later, in 1988, Elmer and Joey made cameo appearances in *Who Framed Roger Rabbit* (➤**326**).

THE THREE BLIND MOUSEKETEERS

There may be three of them, and they may be mice, but there any resemblance to the Three Blind Mice ends, for the Three Blind Mouseketeers are perfectly capable of taking care of themselves – albeit their ways of doing so seem to rely more upon Providence than upon anything else.

Captain Katt anticipates three blind mouseketeers for breakfast, in the 1936 short.

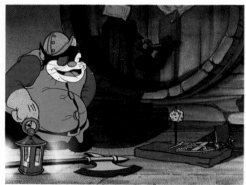

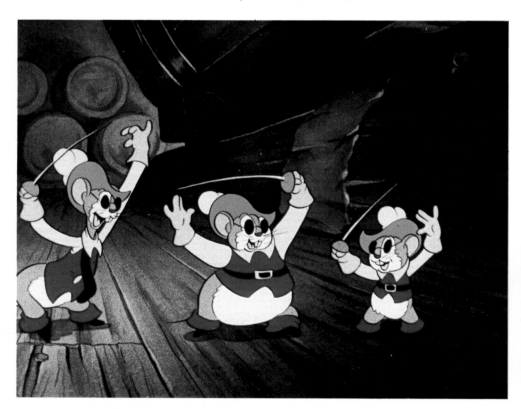

Three very daring and dashing mice starred in *Three Blind Mouseketeers* (1936).

Dressed in blue uniform as if from a 19th-century European army, they seem to be born survivors. As is common with Disney trios, one is tall and thin, one is of medium height and plump, and the third is a little feisty fellow.

It is interesting to note that in other hands the mice's disability and the gags based on it might have seemed extremely tasteless, but in *Three Blind Mouseketeers* (1936) the whole matter is treated in such a way that never for a moment is one invited to laugh *at* the disability: instead, one laughs almost in admiration of the way in which the Mouseketeers circumvent it.

Their adversary, the vile and vicious **Captain Katt**, clearly a close relative of Pete (►15), is little better off himself, having only one eye: for reasons presumably unintended his eyepatch switches from his right eye to his left and back again during the course of the short. He is dedicated, obviously, to the slaughter of our heroes, and will stop at nothing to achieve this end. He boobytraps lumps of cheese and sets traps all over the house; but, as he sleeps smugly satisfied that in the morning he will find a sad little collection of corpses, the Mouseketeers, blissfully unaware of all these dangers, stumblingly and trippingly succeed in emptying all the traps, oblivious to the hostile steel whistling close by their necks and bodies. When they accidentally start letting off the corks of a rack of Champagne bottles – like Napoleonic soldiers firing cannon – they naturally smite the sleeping Captain Katt who wakes in a rage and chases them furiously. Of course, in the end he is unsuccessful and gets himself caught swingeingly in all his own traps. We last see him fleeing, howling in abject fear and pain, away across the moonlit countryside. No doubt the Three Blind Mouseketeers live happily ever after.

BOBO

Bobo the baby elephant starred in the 1936 short *Mickey's Elephant*. Given as a new pet to the Mouse, he soon finds that Pluto (►38) has firm ideas on how many pets Mickey should have: one, and that one a

dog. Responding to the advice of his "Better Self" – normally more pacific (►39) – Pluto feeds Bobo some hot pepper. The little elephant's consequent sneezing fit causes him to bounce around all over the place. Ever resourceful, Mickey ties a knot in Bobo's trunk, but this makes matters even worse. After an orgy of destruction, both Pluto's kennel and the house Mickey has just finished building for Bobo lie flattened.

ABNER AND MONTY

Abner the country mouse and Monty the city mouse made their sole appearance in *The Country Cousin* in 1936 – a good year for Disney mice, in fact, because it saw also the appearances of Mortimer Mouse and the Three Blind Mouseketeers plus no fewer than nine Mickey Mouse shorts.

Abner, who lives in backwoods Podunk, is invited for a stay by his cousin Monty, who lives in 66⅛ Park Ritz Row in the big city. On his arrival Abner knocks at the door of No. 66 but is drawn aside by Monty, who has emerged from his own tiny nearby door, marked "66⅛".

Straw-hatted rural Abner, with his blue dungarees and his baggy old grey umbrella, is an innocent abroad. Top-hatted, tuxedo-toting Monty, with constant admonishments to "sssshhh!", saves him from a mousetrap and various other perils and leads him to a dinner-table covered with goodies. Monty's cries of "sssshhh!" become legion as Abner cheerfully munches at the celery – indeed, even his loud

swallowing of it brings a reprimand: "Sssshhh!" Life takes a turn for the worse when Abner experiments with a pot of mustard: he has to cool himself off by lying face-downwards in a glass of champagne. Several fluid ounces later he is in no condition for subtle poaching: the noise of his less than delicate progress around the table (he has a desperate struggle with a jelly) attracts a cat. Monty, streetwise and sober, prepares to flee but Abner is ready to – hic! – fight *anything*, and boots the cat firmly in its rear. This is not a popular move with the cat, and a vast chase follows.

Abner escapes down through a drainpipe and out onto the street – where Monty goes we do not know, but certainly he finds safety somewhere. Abner, however, has escaped only from the frying-pan: he finds himself in due course in the middle of the road, dodging apparently hostile speeding automobiles – one even has malevolent eyes and vicious teeth. He survives – just – and the last we see of him is as he runs as fast as his legs will carry him down the railway line towards the rural safety of Podunk. Not for him, ever again, the bright lights and sophistication of the city!

Many years later Art Babbitt was to recall of this short that

I had just finished [animating Goofy in] *Moving Day* and was picking up the assignment on *Country Cousin*, in which there is a drunken mouse. Walt Disney came in the room and said, "Now I'd like to see you get the same sort of a characterization that you got in Goofy in *Moving Day*." There was no relation at all between the two but this was typical of his

A publicity picture for *The Country Cousin* (1936). Note that the artist has got Monty's apartment number wrong.

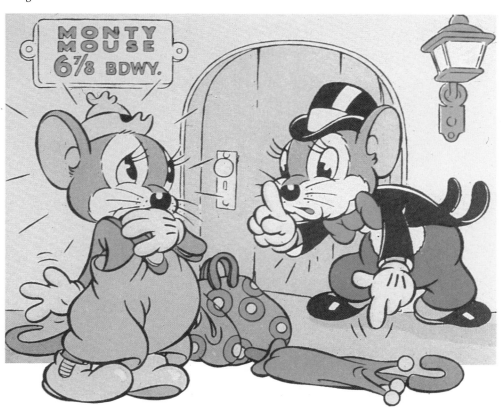

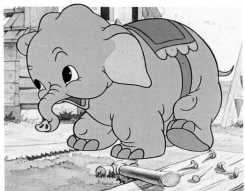

Bobo befriended the Mouse in the 1936 short *Mickey's Elephant*.

getting you steamed up on the next project. So I said, "Well, Walt, I'm going to need a research fund." "Whaddya mean, a research fund? The front office is complaining about costs already!" I said, "Well, if I'm going to do a drunken mouse I have to know what it feels like to have a drink inside me, some alcohol." One of Walt's eyebrows went down, the other went up, he looked at me and I'm sure he didn't figure it out for quite a while.

DAISY DUCK

How cruel was critic Judith Martin being when she described Daisy as being "the quarrelsome nag whose idea of heaven is the purchase of a new flowered hat"? The answer, sadly, has to be: not very.

And yet the description is only a partial one, for while there is only one Donald Duck there seem to be several Daisies. These facets of her character fall into two main classes, because a curious feature of her personality is that she has a schizophrenic voice, her two different voices apparently affecting her character and behaviour. One voice is much like Donald's – in other words, the familiar dulcet tones of "Nash-speak" – and is matched by eruptively irascible behaviour just as bad as Donald's, if not worse. The other is quite different: slow and langorous, it is more like the voice of a sensuous Southern Belle; and when speaking in this mode Daisy tends to act like such a Southern Belle, too. Her Southern Belle self is generally restrained and indeed civilized, although quite capable of exploding abruptly into violence for purposes of dramatic effect. Both of her characters are strongly delineated: her Southern Belle is extremely distinctive within the Disney canon, and her "Nash-speak" personality is much like Donald's and therefore by definition a powerful one. It is surprising, then, that either or both of her personalities did not go on to star in as many movies as, say, Minnie: Daisy featured in only 14 shorts, in some of which she had only a bit part and in one of which, *Dumb Bell of the Yukon* (1946), while she is mentioned and is Donald's guiding spirit, she does not actually appear (Don starts out on a hunting quest because he has received from Daisy a terse note that "In Spring a young girl's fancy turns to fur coats").

Her first role was as the rollicking Mexican Donna Duck in *Don Donald* (1937): hot-blooded, mercurial and passionate, she is capable of switching from warm tenderness to destructive wrath in less time than it takes to fracture a lover's heart. She has, of course, a mantilla and comb in place of the later customary bow, and she speaks with the inimitable voice of Clarence Nash.

As Donald discovers, it is foolhardy practice to collapse in laughter when your beloved falls off your burro: young ladies of fiery temperament have a habit of responding vigorously in such moments. Indeed, when Donald calls round to Donna's house a little later she is in the process of pulverizing her picture of him, and dissuades herself from smashing a heavy vase over his head only when she notices that he has traded in his burro for a flashy bright red sportscar. Off they drive into the desert and, at her fervent urging, he drives faster and faster (a nice touch is that when he pulls the "Choke" knob the car promptly does so). The drive turns into a nightmare: the car, which is definitely sentient and hostile, goes wild, runs Don over several times and finally crashes into a rock, in so doing neatly decanting Donna into a mudpit. As far as she is concerned her indignity is All Donald's Fault – especially since, as before, he finds the incident raucously amusing. With a deftness of touch not exhibited by every shy young maiden, she forcefully and quite comprehensively rearranges most of his features, not necessarily for the better, before taking a unicycle from her handbag and vanishing back towards town. It is going to be a long, lonely walk for Donald.

The short has many strengths, although the concluding unicycle gag is somewhat artificial, but it is not a classic and gives little indication of the character(s) that Daisy would later portray so impressively. She was still very raw at the edges. Probably for this reason, three years passed before her next appearance, the first in which she was to appear with the name Daisy. This was in *Mr. Duck Steps Out* (1940). In this short she and Donald shared star billing with the dreaded Nephews (►85); it is interesting to note that, while the Nephews appeared on the scene well over a year after Daisy, this is already their sixth short but only her second.

The role of the Nephews in *Mr. Duck Steps Out* is of course to disrupt the developing romance between Daisy and and a very hip, jitterbugging Donald, which they do with devastating effect. The two young lovers *manqué* are keen to have a *tête à tête*, but they should have known better: the tripartite menace is as easy to get rid of

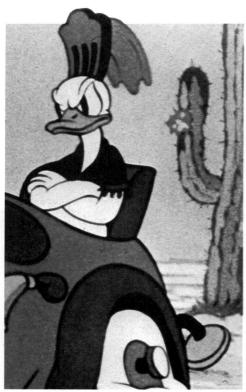

Daisy makes her first appearance as Donna Duck in 1937's *Don Donald*.

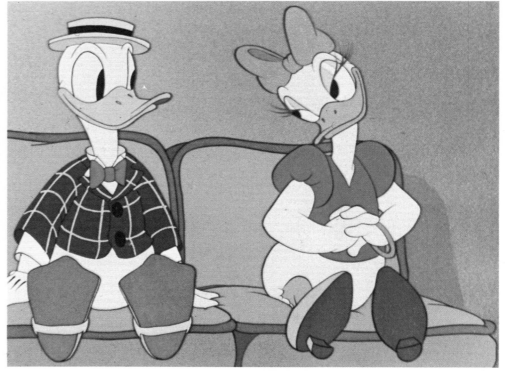

Romance seems to be blooming in *Mr. Duck Steps Out* (1940), but the two young lovers have reckoned without the dreaded Nephews.

as a limpet mine and only slightly less destructive. Bribery gives the lovers a moment's respite – no more than that – and so in desperation they switch on the radio, hoping to be able at least to dance together. The effect is not as planned: the Nephews want to dance too – with Daisy, and to the exclusion of Donald. When he banishes them to the kitchen with a dexterous flick of the rug on which they are standing the opportunities open up for further menacing. They seize upon a corncob and within moments have it at red heat; instants later they have it well and truly embedded in "Unca Donald", for whom things really start to get popping. Alas for the Nephews, their scheme backfires because Daisy is progressively more enamoured of Don's almost superduck ability at jitterbugging as he fizzes and pops all over the house. At the end of the dance she covers him in admiring bright red kisses. The romance appears to be sealed. Bad luck, Nephews!

Daisy's next appearance was a brief and anonymous one; it is also her sexiest. In *A Good Time for a Dime* (1941) Don is trying with difficulty to get good value out of an amusement arcade. In a happy mood of naughtiness he puts his cent into a flicker machine described as "The Dance of the Seven Veils", and to his delight he sees a somewhat orientalized Daisy doing the dance. His frustration when the machine cheats him of the odd veil here and there is, as one might imagine, devastatingly violent.

Daisy had subsidiary parts in *The Nifty Nineties* (1941) and *Donald's Crime* (1945), returning to the limelight only in 1945's short *Cured Duck*. In this movie, for reasons that will become evident, she is in her

Southern Belle mode: laid-back and calmly in control.

The short starts with Daisy asking Don to open one of the windows in her house. He has a little difficulty doing this, perhaps because he has failed to notice that the catch is on, and so responds in his conventional manner – by smashing the window and most of the other objects in the house. Daisy tells him sternly that, unless he can learn to control his temper, in future she will decline his dates. This is serious stuff, and Don promptly sends off to the Institute of Temperism for a mail-order cure. What arrives is a curious robot, which tells him that, if he can put up with its insults for a mere 10 minutes, he will be a cured duck. Don perseveres, despite the machine battering him with a variety of implements.

But he is cured! Daisy is delighted. Don suffers several misadventures in attempting to open her window for her, and does so with a smile. *Now* she can go out on a date with him without worries. She goes upstairs and changes, donning, *inter alia*, a hat that seems to feature the combined stocks of a fruiterer and a pawnbroker. Don's reaction is the obvious (if foolish) male response: he falls about laughing. In the succeeding violent seconds Daisy proves that, while Donald may indeed be a cured duck, there are other ducks who are still likely to dismantle the furniture if crossed.

Again in *Donald's Double Trouble* (1946) she was in her Southern Belle persona, and again for obvious reasons – only this time they were obvious in the opening seconds of the short, which see Don in a callbox listening to Daisy nagging him: "Your English is terrible!" and "Until you develop

a more pleasant personality I don't want to ever see you again!" (Despite Daisy's criticism of Don's English she is perfectly capable of producing an injudicious split infinitive.) She concludes by slamming down the phone at her end with such force that Don's callbox explodes.

But help is at hand for the miserable Duck. In the street he bumps into his double – only the other guy has a sophisticated, well modulated voice: he is quite a smoothie. Could he, asks Donald, for an agreed fee act as a stand-in with Daisy for a while? The double, who is little more than half a step away from Skid Row, gladly consents to the deal. The trouble of the title starts because, not only does Daisy go for the "new Donald" in a passionate way, he is equally captivated by her. Donald's fury finally erupts as his true love and the interloper enter a carnival tunnel of love on a boat together; the resulting fracas is, needless to say, dramatic and destructive - and poor Daisy ends up in the water. An

A swift titivation in *Donald's Diary* (1954).

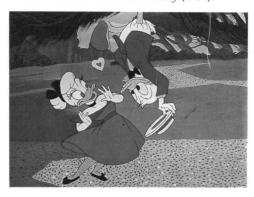

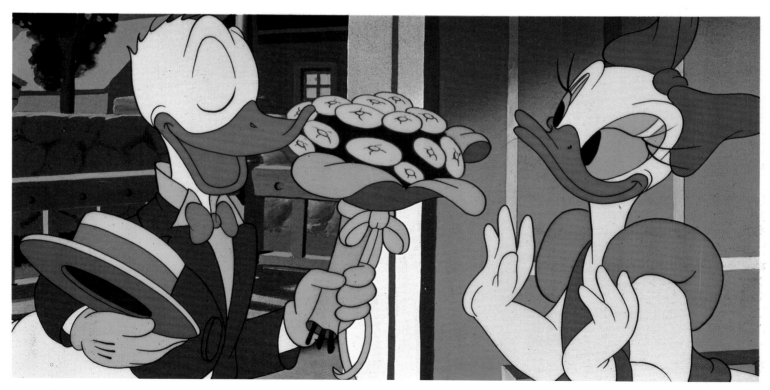

Donald's sophisticated double used all his oleaginous charm to win Daisy back for Donald in *Donald's Double Trouble* (1946). But then love struck...

even more dramatic and destructive fracas is averted only by the two versions of Donald Duck fleeing her spectacular wrath.

Despite the events of *Donald's Double Trouble*, in Daisy's next role she was once more to be selflessly in love with the Duck, whatever his voice and personality might be like. This was *Sleepy Time Donald* (1947), a short that reflected the cartoonist's endless fascination for somnambulism. (Another notable Disney somnambulist was Pluto [➤38].) Here Donald, with a galosh chirpily poised on his head, sleepwalks around to the home of his sweetheart (yet again in her Southern Belle mode). She knows better than to wake him, having heard that waking a sleepwalker can prove fatal, but determines to follow him on his nocturnal stroll to make sure that he stays out of danger. This proves easier thought than done. Don strays, in succession, into the zoo, the lion's cage and the lion's mouth, and there is little Daisy can do to stop him. Once away from that hazard, though, there is worse to follow – for the sleeping Donald has no fear at all of heights and also displays a disconcerting ability to walk, fly-like, up walls and across ceilings. Daisy, to her very considerable credit, follows him all over town, rescuing him from every danger. Finally she gets him home and back into bed, whereupon he wakes up and, seeing her there, accuses *her* of being a sleepwalker. Daisy's resulting storm of rage – well, with Daisy you always know it is going to come in the end – necessitates that she hits him over the head with his own galosh – an action that sends him cozily back to sleep again, only this time rather more peacefully.

For *Donald's Dilemma*, released later in the same year, Daisy retained her Southern Belle voice and her love for Donald – in fact, she is so self-abasing that one has to wonder seriously about Martin's criticism.

The dilemma of the short's title is really Daisy's rather than Donald's for, after a flowerpot has fallen from a great height to land on his head, he no longer recognizes her – yet she retains her passionate love for him. The impacting flowerpot has had another effect on the Duck: he has become the world's finest crooner. As she explains to her psychiatrist, Donald's career is progressing by leaps and bounds whereas her only role is to languish for him, waiting outside the stage door of Music City throughout the heat, rain and snow of a full twelvemonth. On the sole occasion on which she does manage to confront him with tearful implorations his only response is curtly to toss her a dime.

So what should she do? The psychiatrist tells her that she has a moral choice: either she should share Donald's marvellous voice with the whole world or she should have him all to herself. Daisy's response is obvious – vehemently so.

Acting according to the psychiatrist's advice, she replants the original flower in a new and even heavier pot and drops it from high up above the Music City stage on Donald's head. The effect is exactly as she had hoped: his wonderful crooning voice reverts to "Nash-speak" and he is thrown bodily out of Music City. Daisy, her love requited after her long and rather uncharacteristic period of stoic patience, is reunited with her darling in a lengthily passionate kiss.

A happy ending ... but one could not expect her self-abasing devotion to last. Nor, for that matter, could one expect her to put up very long with the incomprehensible voice of her mate. In fact, only a year or so later, by the time of *Donald's Dream Voice* (1948), her patience had run out completely – for Donald, sunk from superstardom to a job as a door-to-door salesman, is in dire straits because no one can understand what he is trying to sell them. His fiancé Daisy, though, in clear Southern Belle tones tells him that she – she alone – has faith in him.

Faith, however, does not sell brushes. Indeed, all seems lost until Don buys for 10¢ a box of Ajax Voice Pills. These transform his voice from the familiar "Nash-speak" to a suave gentlemanly enunciation – with the result that his door-to-door salesmanship booms. The only trouble is that the pills are fairly short-lasting, and so Don has to conserve them – in particular saving one for the moment when he will propose to Daisy, something he feels he can now do because his business has become so successful. But

keeping hold of that pill proves difficult: after many vicissitudes it vanishes into the gaping maw of a bellowing bull, and Don's chances of marital bliss with Daisy have vanished with it.

In Daisy's next short, *Crazy Over Daisy* (1950), there were two very definite reasons for the failure of the romance between her and Donald: those two reasons were Chip an' Dale (➤96). All four of the main protagonists seem to have been transported back in time a few decades – to about the time of *The Nifty Nineties*, in fact: Don, for once in his life, has romantically longish hair while Daisy's own hair is prolific and yellow.

Don sets off on his penny-farthing bicycle (high-wheeler) for a date with his beloved; the chips decide that the date will come to nothing and torment him with their usual determination. After the last straw, and the one after that (the wrecking of his bicycle), Don catches the two mischievous chips and builds from the wreckage a new vehicle that incorporates a novel source of motive power: it has chipmunks running treadmill-fashion in its wheels.

So far so good, but when Don gets to Daisy's house he discovers that she's an animal lover as much as a bird fancier: she slaps him with shoulder-wrenching strength, berates him for his cruelty, and takes the two chips into her house as pets. Donald is given his marching orders in no uncertain terms.

Donald was never to admit this reason for the end of his prominent screen romance. Although Daisy played a bit part in *Mickey's Christmas Carol* (1983) as Scrooge McDuck's youthful sweetheart (➤130), her last starring role was in 1954, in *Donald's Diary*. This short causes biographers of her and Donald some problems in that, while it explains (in a way) why she was never to star again, it also raises questions as to how she ever managed to become Donald's romantic partner in the first place. That

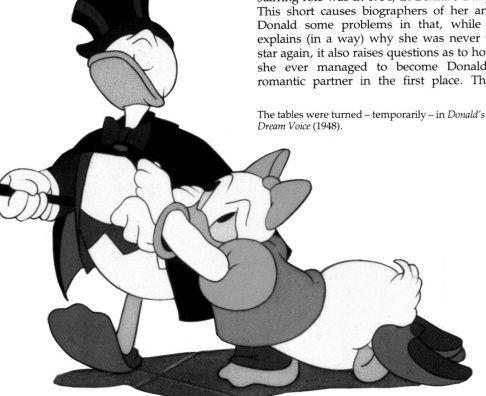

The tables were turned – temporarily – in *Donald's Dream Voice* (1948).

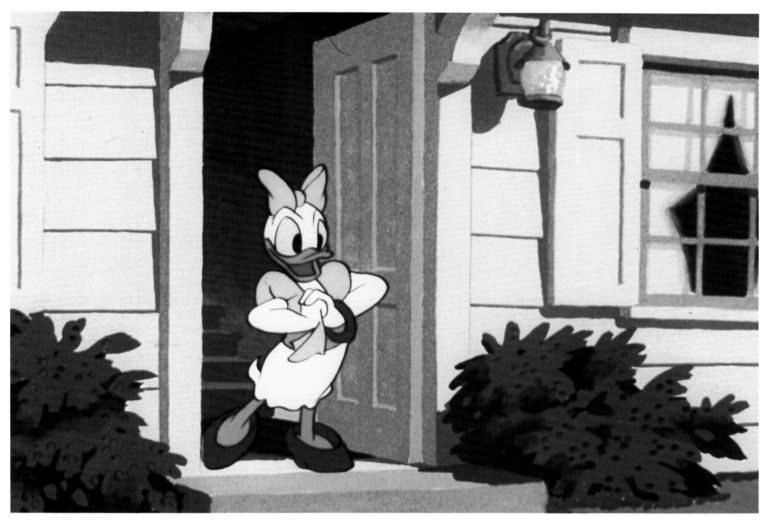

Daisy in all her elegant finery found herself grossly mismatched to down-at-heel door-to-door brush salesman Donald in *Donald's Dream Voice*.

said, it was one of her finest performances, and it is pleasing to record that she made her exit from showbiz when she was still at the peak of her achievement.

The short has several other curiosities. First, the narration, although ostensibly by Donald in a voice-over, is certainly not in his *real* voice: gone are the Nash vocal explosions and in their place are the suave, debonaire tones of a man-about-town. Daisy, for her part, is vocally in her Southern Belle mode. Moreover, Don displays none of the customary tantrums, and Daisy is more of a vamp than a nag. We can only assume that the two of them decided to celebrate Daisy's swansong – ducksong? – by showing the public how capable they were of acting completely out of character.

We first see Daisy reading a book called *How to Catch a Husband*, and immediately afterwards we get a glimpse of what the book must say. Daisy dresses up in her gladrags, sprays herself liberally with cloyingly sensuous perfume, and adopts a cigarette-holder that might be better employed by a pole-vaulter. Her initial gambits, once she has spotted Don as a natural "mark", are not too successful, though. She drops her handkerchief sultrily

in his path but he just walks over it; she "faints" in front of him but, well, he just walks over her, too; she pretends to be drowning but he simply walks by oblivious to her synthetic howls of distress. Finally she is reduced to using a noose as a trap to catch him by the feet, so that he finds himself all of a sudden hanging upside-down and at her tender mercy. As Don comments in his voice-over: "My technique was simple – I swept her off her feet. My search was over. I had found my dream girl."

The romance proceeds apace, although Daisy has trouble, having taken Don to her favourite spot, in making sure that he does not notice a nearby tree on which carved hearts link her name with those of countless other swains. A girl must preserve that sense of mystery, after all.

And so it is home to meet her family. The impression her folks create is not of the finest, but he is too besotted with love to care. Why should he worry that he is greeted at her home with a squirt of a waterpistol wielded by her three young brothers (the Nephews in disguise)? Why should he worry that her grumpy mother, wielding an ear-trumpet, welcomes him reluctantly and then proceeds to look him

up in *Dunn and Bradstreet*? Why should he worry that her father, an evident simpleton, is caught in the act of lecherously creating strings of naughty dancing girls using folded paper and scissors? Why should he worry? Well, he soon finds out why.

Having pawned his treasured possessions to buy an engagement ring he calls round to her home again to pop the question. When he gets there she is in the shower, titivating herself for an evening out with him. As he sits waiting for the statutory hours in an armchair he dozes off, and dreams of their future life of married bliss. But is this bliss? Will her three little brothers really insist on coming with them on the honeymoon, and will her mother really be waiting in their "dream cottage" when they return? Will Daisy really insist that he uses a machine and a time-card to clock in and out of home each day, and will she really extract all the money from his wallet at the end of each week's work? Will her culinary prowess really extend only to cooking a T-bone steak until nothing but the T is left? Will he really be expected to do *all* of the household chores? These are only some of the questions which the dreaming Don does not in fact want answered.

She wakes him with a loving kiss, and all

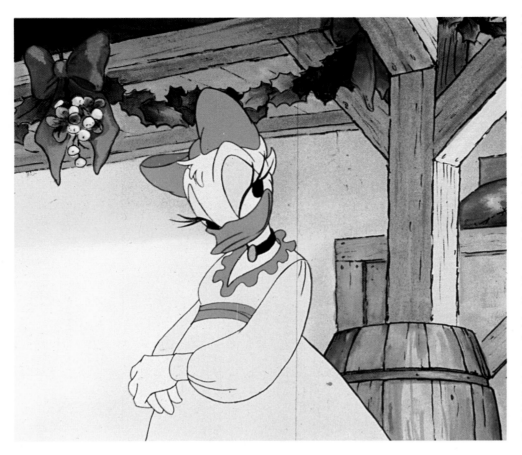

Daisy's most recent role, as Scrooge's youthful sweetheart in the featurette *Mickey's Christmas Carol* (1983).

of his dreams come crashing into his mind. With a yell of desperation he bursts from the confines of the house, smashing through all obstructions in his eagerness to be free, and vanishes over the horizon towards a land far away from his erstwhile darling. Quite how far he has had to travel we realize only in the short's closing shots, when we discover that Don has been writing up all these reminiscences while serving in the French Foreign Legion. Even so we are left to wonder if he is *still* safe . . .

Daisy, then, was one of the most complicated and inconsistent of all the Disney characters yet, out of all her starring performances, there is not a single one that could be regarded as a flop: she was brilliant, in either of her two principal guises. After 1954 Daisy's fans were starved of her presence except for her cameo roles in 1983's *Mickey's Christmas Carol* (➤130) and 1988's *Who Framed Roger Rabbit* (➤326). Then along came the television series *Quack Pack* (➤151), and we were reunited with her.

Filmography

Don Donald, 1937 (as Donna Duck)
Mr. Duck Steps Out, 1940 (first named as Daisy)
A Good Time for a Dime, 1941
The Nifty Nineties, 1941
Donald's Crime, 1945
Cured Duck, 1945
Donald's Double Trouble, 1946
Dumb Bell of the Yukon, 1946 (mentioned only)
Sleepy Time Donald, 1947
Donald's Dilemma, 1947

Donald's Dream Voice, 1948
Crazy Over Daisy, 1950
Donald's Diary, 1954
Mickey's Christmas Carol, 1983
Who Framed Roger Rabbit, 1988

LITTLE HIAWATHA

Little Hiawatha, although he has made only the one screen appearance, has lived on in comic strips and books.

His solitary screen appearance was in a 1937 Silly Symphony called, appropriately, *Little Hiawatha*. Here we see the young Indian determined to become a mighty

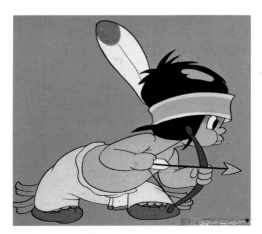

The star of the 1937 short *Little Hiawatha*.

hunter – a venture in which he is notably unsuccessful. In the course of it, however, he is kind to a little rabbit. Much later Little Hiawatha is chased by a grizzly bear and the rabbit whom he befriended returns the favour by raising the alarm so that all the animals of the forest take a part in rescuing Little Hiawatha from the grizzly's clutches.

Little Hiawatha, with his button nose, his sturdy boyish body and his single-feather head-dress, is an appealing character, if perhaps a little cute. Certainly one would have expected him to make further screen appearances, but this was not to be – although some work was done on a proposed feature starring him.

HORTENSE

Hortense the ostrich appeared in the 1937 short *Donald's Ostrich*.

Donald is a railway station announcer whose announcements are marred by interruptions from his radio; swiftly he switches it to a station other than the one featuring high-pitched opera singing. Just then he hears an approaching train and dashes out onto the platform to be crushed

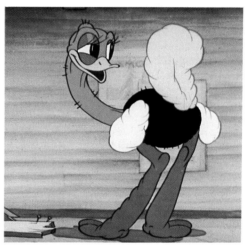

Hortense, one of the many animals to get on Donald's wrong side, appeared in *Donald's Ostrich* (1937).

by the heap of baggage it disgorges as it passes through. One of the items of baggage proves to be a crate containing Hortense, an ostrich with a curious passion for ducks. Donald escapes her amorous advances, but she proceeds to eat everything in sight, including Don's radio. Her mixed diet gives her a severe fit of hiccups, and at each hiccup the radio station changes within her, causing her to respond physically to the music of the moment. Donald's attempts to extract the radio from her are disastrous, and his life becomes endangered when a fresh hiccup from Hortense causes the radio to switch to the commentary to a motor-race. The Duck and

Hortense end up in a pile of baggage, where she, cured of her "condition", proceeds to caress a reluctant Donald.

Poor emotional Hortense: she never appeared on screen again.

DONALD'S NEPHEWS

Huey, Dewey and Louie: the very names are enough to make Donald Duck's spine convulse. For these three cheerful individuals have with deliberate malice made his life a misery over the years.

They first arrived on the scene in a short called, appropriately, *Donald's Nephews* (1938). Donald was unlucky enough to receive from his sister Dumbella a postcard telling him that her three sons – "angel" children, as she described them – would shortly be arriving to stay with him. Little did Donald realize, as he smiled in fond anticipation, that the three Nephews might never, never permanently go home.

Anticipation was to be tempered with pessimism on their arrival, though. They immediately played a vastly destructive polo game on their tricycles all over his house, and shortly were engaged in some really serious mayhem. After he finally got them out of the house – although not for long! – he glanced at his ever-ready child-raising instruction manual and spotted the sentence: "After all, little children are only angels without wings." Recalling Dumbella's expression he set to with a will, shredding the offending book.

This showed a lack of foresight. As Ludwig Von Drake would years later remark (➤125), if nothing else, child-raising handbooks are good and heavy for hitting the little monsters with.

Donald has had many foes over the years: there have been Humphrey the bear (➤113), Buzz-Buzz the bee (➤110) and of course the irrepressible Chip an' Dale (➤96); but none have been so actively malicious as his three Nephews, who have ever delighted in tormenting "Unca Donald".

Donald's Golf Game (1938), their third short, although it is perhaps not one of the Nephews' classics, certainly does show the depths to which their impish maliciousness will sink. Possibly Don brings the whole fiasco on himself by press-ganging the Nephews into service as a sort of multiplex caddy; even with all three of them carrying his golfing kit they buckle under the weight. It takes them but a moment to decide that they will do all in their power to wreck "Unca Donald's" game. They have two allies in this: one is an unwilling grasshopper, the other a set of "goofy" golf clubs. The grasshopper is firmly squeezed into a hollow golf ball, which Don pursues with ever-mounting fury as it hops and skips around the course. The "goofy" clubs are a less successful comic device, but they provide some moments of hilarity – notably

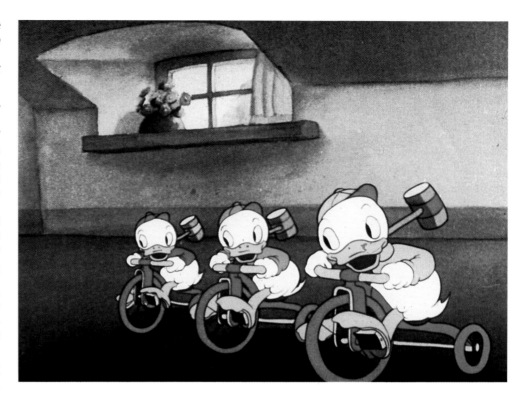

It doesn't take much to demolish "Unca Donald's" home – just a quick game of polo: *Donald's Nephews* (1938).

towards the end of the short when the Duck, little realizing that one of the clubs is designed to transform itself into a boomerang, throws it angrily at his Nephews. Needless to say, the club "returns to sender" at spine-chilling pace and wraps itself around Don's neck.

In *Straight Shooters* (1947), to take another example, Donald plays the part of a barker in a shooting gallery. Huey, Dewey and Louie appear and within moments have won for themselves some small boxes of candy. But this is not enough for them: moments later they have climbed on each other's shoulders and dressed up as an exotic princess, who bats "her" eyes at the gullible Donald. What else can the eager young Duck do but offer her some candy? Later the Nephews adopt a different disguise, that of a mummy straight out of a

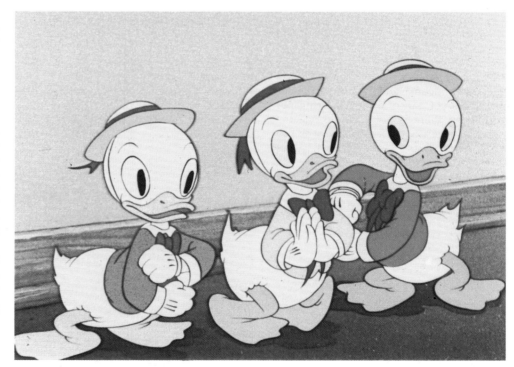

1938 was a dismal year for Donald Duck, for it saw the first appearance – in the short *Donald's Nephews* – of a trio more terminal than the Four Horsemen of the Apocalypse: Huey, Dewey and Louie. Life would never be the same again.

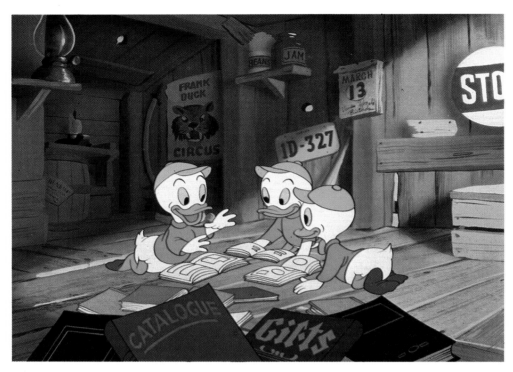

Even when the Nephews plan a pleasant surprise for Donald – as in *Donald's Happy Birthday* (1949) – somehow their uncle always ends up ruing the day.

horror movie, and extort yet further candy from their luckless uncle.

In other shorts Donald's misery was of his own making, born of his characteristic inability to stop and think before believing the worst of other people. Typical is *Donald's Happy Birthday* (1949), in which the Nephews club together to use the $2.98 they have earned by doing household chores to buy a box of cigars (La Smello Panatellas) for "Unca Donald's" birthday (the 13th of the month, as you might expect). When he comes across the box he assumes immediately that the kids have bought it for their own use and, to teach them a lesson, forces them to smoke all of the cigars, one after the other, until they're sick. Only then does Donald discover the greetings note in the bottom of the box. (Incidentally, Louie's name is spelled "Luey" on this note.)

Frequently Donald created his own bed of nails because of his instinctive urge towards cruel practical joking. *Donald's Snow Fight* (1942), for example, finds him out sledging when he comes across the Nephews building a snowman. What else should a naughty Duck do but direct his sledge straight through the middle of this lovingly crafted edifice, destroying it completely and smothering three innocent little ducklings in snow? Those three "innocents", of course, respond by erecting a snowman whose core is a huge rock, so that when "Unca Donald" repeats the jape ...

Don's urge for practical jokery lands him in trouble with Ajax (►101) in *Donald Duck and the Gorilla* (1944); but even when it is the Nephews rather than Donald who are the jokers the affair seems inevitably to backfire on the poor "Unca" – one thinks of *Lion*

Around (1950), when Don has an unhappy episode with the Mountain Lion (►111) after the Nephews have teased him by dressing up as a mountain lion.

In *Good Scouts* (1938) he tries to show them the glories of his own knowledge of woodcraft. He makes a bone-shattering attempt to fell a petrified tree, but still fails to learn his lesson. He next shows them how to erect an impromptu tent by pulling down the top of a young sapling so that it forms a ridgepole. Alas, when Don stands

proudly on top of his creation his knots come untied and he is launched into the middle distance.

The Nephews are not exactly downcast by this misfortune of his, and so he plots his revenge on them. While doing the cooking he spots a bottle of tomato ketchup and, quicker than thought, uses it to transform himself into an unconscious bloodstained uncle. This is a foolish move. In no time at all the Nephews have gleefully made use of the first-aid kit to truss him up like an Egyptian mummy. Along ambles a vast bear (a precursor of Humphrey perhaps?) to nuzzle this curious object and Donald, assuming that the Nephews are tormenting him yet further, lashes out ...

Sometimes the Nephews' revenge against "Unca Donald" can flirt pretty dangerously with the limits of good taste. In *Truant Officer Donald* (1941) – Donald is of course Truant Officer No. 13 – there is a section in which Don is trying to smoke the three errant Nephews out of their gang hut. They have been roasting chickens in there; and so they put three roast chickens on their bed, under the bedclothes, and sneak out through the skylight. When Donald finally breaks into the hut and discovers these cooked corpses he naturally thinks the worst.

The Nephews take matters further. Down from the skylight they lower one of their number, accoutred as an angel. With Don's permission this vision kicks his rump several times, allowing him to wallow in his own anguish of guilt. (Idly, one wonders *why* he is so grief-stricken. After all the things the Nephews have done to him ...) At last, though, he sees through the ruse and his wrath is – quite justifiably –

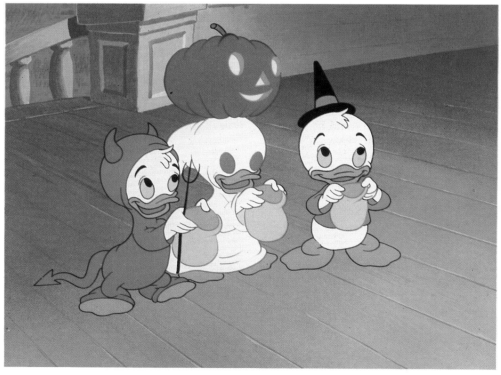

1952's *Trick or Treat* saw Donald doing exactly what every other adult in the world would love to have the courage to do: strike back at the trick-or-treaters. Unfortunately, he came off worst, as usual.

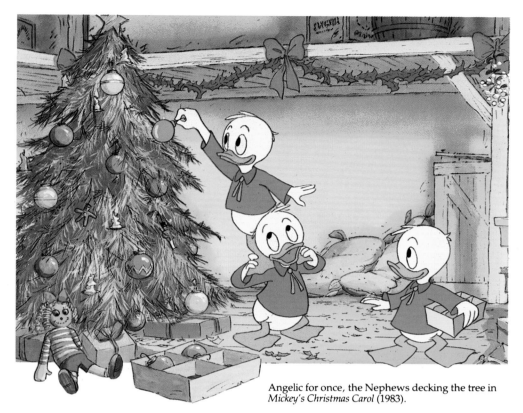

Angelic for once, the Nephews decking the tree in *Mickey's Christmas Carol* (1983).

awesome to behold. He ropes them round their necks and takes them to school – only to discover that they weren't really playing truant at all: school is closed for the first day of the summer holidays.

The roast-chicken gag earned the short a certain amount of flak at the time, and still induces some queasiness. As with the gag about the sausages in *Three Little Pigs* (1933 [►57]), there is something not quite *right*.

Even when Don resists any urge to play malicious practical jokes but instead merely indulges in a burst of showing off, the Nephews exact a terrible revenge: he should have learned the dangers of boasting from his experiences in *Good Scouts*, but no. In *Hockey Champ* (1939) he finds the three of them playing ice hockey and lectures them gloatingly on his own past achievements in the sport. After demonstrating a few skills he says patronizingly that he is prepared to take on all three of them – and he will wear a blindfold! After a dizzyingly rapid succession of visual gags the puck rockets down poor Don's throat, and the Nephews "reluctantly" conclude that their only way of scoring a goal now is to wallop both the puck and its unwilling container into the back of the net.

Sometimes, however, Donald is the totally innocent victim of the Nephews' practical jokes. In *Soup's On* (1948), one of the truly classic contests between the Duck and the kids, his only sin is to insist that they wash their filthy hands before sitting down to eat the great turkey feast that he has cooked for them all. Their response is as cooperative as you might expect, and at the climax of the resulting chase Don is knocked unconscious. Swiftly the Nephews dress him up in an angel costume while also

producing a fake of his corpse lying largely obscured under a huge fallen boulder. When Don comes to he naturally enough assumes that he has died, an inference assisted by the Nephews carefully hoisting him heavenwards using a conveniently nearby pulley. A sobbing and repentant "Unca Donald" tells them to go home and eat that turkey banquet that had started the whole sequence of events – and to remember their uncle fondly. It is a touching moment.

The bathos ends when Don tries to fly. In moments he is transformed from an angel into a devil, and the Nephews flee.

Huey, Dewey and Louie are indistinguishable: the three of them act with a single evil mind. In rather different guise, they have also revelled in plaguing the life of Scrooge McDuck (►130); while in *Donald's Diary* (1954) they play the part of Daisy's three obnoxious little brothers; *Mr. Duck Steps Out* (1940) is another short in which they demonstrate their ruthless enthusiasm for wrecking Don's burgeoning romance with the delicious Daisy. All three were generally voiced by Clarence "Ducky" Nash, who not only did Donald's voice in English but also all the foreign-language versions of the Duck. The fact that Nash did all of these voices contributed to the search for other adversaries for Donald: it was all very well having *one* major character whose dialogue was largely incomprehensible – but not all four!

Jack Hannah has recalled (in an interview with Jim Korkis in *Mindrot*) an experiment with the three Nephews that failed:

... somebody came up with the idea that it would be clever to have the three nephews say

one line of dialog with all three of them sharing in the sentence. One nephew would say the first two words, the next would say the middle of the sentence and the third would finish it up. I put a stop to this because it ruined all sense of timing and you couldn't go on and carry through a gag. You'd have to stop and wait for each nephew to carry through his lines and you couldn't incorporate the dialog in the action as well that way. We got each nephew saying an individual line all by himself.

It might well be wondered, in view of their evident character defects and their cruelty to their surrogate parent, if the three Nephews will ever attain more mature years: tormenting the Duck is not an activity designed to prolong one's life-expectancy. In one short, however, our minds are set at rest. This short is *Lucky Number* (1951), a variation on the theme of *Donald's Happy Birthday*, in which the three appear as teenagers. Don, working as a garage assistant, has entered a lottery, and we find him listening avidly to the radio announcement of the result. Duckish fury: the winning number is 341, while he has ticket 342. Moments later, after Donald has departed to fume in private, the Nephews hear over the radio the announcement that there was an error in the earlier report: in fact, the winning number is 342.

Donald is sceptical, to put it mildly, on hearing this news – as one might expect in light of past events. But the Nephews, for once eager to help, determine to go in their old jalopy to pick up their uncle's prize for him. The only trouble is that they have no petrol – and Donald is determined not to let them have any *gratis*. They use a succession of ruses – including dressing one of themselves up as a ravishingly vampish woman driver to arouse Don's baser instincts – before finally succeeding in extracting the necessary gas. Alas, when they return in the flashy sportscar that Donald has won in the lottery he assumes that this is yet another of their ruses to swindle free petrol out of him, and smashes the roadster to smithereens. Moments later, of course, he hears on the radio a repetition of the lottery's result and realizes to his horror and wrath that the heap of tangled metal in his forecourt is ...

Huey, Dewey and Louie represent mischievous children the world over – which is probably why they have so many staunch devotees today among kids who read of their exploits in the comic strips as well as seeing the revivals of their classic shorts on television or (very occasionally) in the cinema. Their external appearance is that of angels, belying their malevolent intent. And yet, over the years, they have mellowed a little: they have proved themselves intelligent, resourceful, loyal, brave and, on occasion, even affectionate. Better equipped than "Unca Donald" to cope with the pressures of the real world, they have often saved him from the consequences of his worst excesses.

In *The New Spirit* (1942) we see Donald entering the Nephews on his tax form as "adopted"; in fact, in recent years they have spent most of their time with his uncle, Scrooge McDuck (➤130). Then, however, they returned (in modified form) to infest Donald's life in the television series *Quack Pack* (➤151).

Filmography

Donald's Nephews, 1938
Good Scouts, 1938
Donald's Golf Game, 1938
Hockey Champ, 1939
Sea Scouts, 1939
Mr. Duck Steps Out, 1940
Fire Chief, 1940
Truant Officer Donald, 1941
All Together, 1942
Donald's Snow Fight, 1942
Home Defense, 1943
Donald Duck and the Gorilla, 1944
Donald's Off Day, 1944
Donald's Crime, 1945
Straight Shooters, 1947
Soup's On, 1948
Donald's Happy Birthday, 1949
Lion Around, 1950
Lucky Number, 1951
Trick or Treat, 1952
Don's Fountain of Youth, 1953
Canvas Back Duck, 1953
Spare the Rod, 1954
Donald's Diary, 1954
Scrooge McDuck and Money, 1967
Mickey's Christmas Carol, 1983
DuckTales: The Movie – Treasure of the Lost Lamp, 1990

WYNKEN, BLYNKEN AND NOD

The cartoon *Wynken, Blynken and Nod* (1938) represented one of the earliest uses of the multiplane camera (its first use was in the short *The Old Mill* [1937]). Many years later I. Klein recalled:

I ... knew how my work looked from the various stages of pencil tests including the cleanups. But when I sat in on the first screening of the finished picture I did not recognize my own work (at first) ... the depth of focus added a new and unexpected dimension and dream quality to the cartoon.

The short shows the three little boys sailing across the sky fishing for golden stars from their vessel, a wooden clog equipped with a sail. Wynken has brown hair and a pale green-blue sleepsuit; Blynken has orange-red hair and a blue sleepsuit; and Nod, who is much like the other two but seemingly younger, has blonde hair and a pink sleepsuit. As fishing hooks they use candy walking-sticks.

Their adventures in the night sky are not happy ones. In one sequence a big gold star links the hooks of Wynken and Nod together under their boat so that the two lads are straining against each other: the result is that Nod is pulled overboard, ending up hanging beneath the vessel with

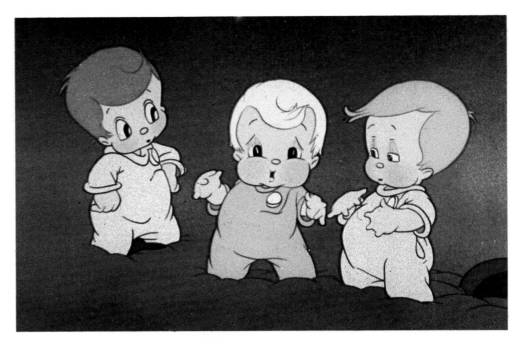

The three little boys of 1938's *Wynken, Blynken and Nod*.

his hook fortunately entangled in his sleepsuit. After he has been rescued the craft is "buzzed" several times by a rogue comet. This celestial object they catch in a net, but it drags them for a wild career across the sky and finally escapes, leaving the children in the midst of a brewing storm. Their mast is swept away and their craft is blown all over the sky before finally they tumble downward to earth and are absorbed into a single little boy lying sleeping – and of course dreaming – in his cradle.

Many of the gags in the short depend upon the children's bottoms: on several occasions a sleepsuit gratuitously pops open to reveal a cute little pink bottom within. Some critics have belaboured the Disney studio of this era for being preoccupied with children's bottoms, but in this instance it seems that, with a short which inherently lacked obvious gags, the story-men sought to insert a few – however artificially. Animated cartoons of the time, we should remember, were generally expected to be *funny*, not works of art. However, this is a very minor criticism of one of Disney's most eloquent and well drawn shorts.

BIANCA

In the 1938 short *Mickey's Parrot* we are introduced to Mickey's goldfish Bianca, who bears a strong physical resemblance to Cleo (➤172), although her coloration has rather less orange and rather more black; indeed, it is curious that Bianca was not given the role in *Pinocchio* (1940).

The plot of this first short of hers was quite simple. Mickey's parrot has become locked in a cupboard under Bianca's bowl and for reasons beyond human understanding is threatening a tin of fish-food. Pluto, hearing the voice, assumes that Bianca is viciously threatening him. The fierce fight that ensues is ended by Bianca leaping out of the water and biting him savagely on the nose.

Bianca's part in *Lend a Paw* (1941) is to land Pluto (➤39) once again in some well deserved trouble. Mickey has adopted a kitten, and a jealous Pluto is keen to make sure that this intruder is expelled from both Mickey's home and his affections. Pluto puts the kitten up near Bianca's bowl into which, according to plan, the cheerful little kitten attempts to clamber. Moments later the kitten, bowl – with Bianca still, fortunately, safe inside it – and Pluto are all in a chaotic heap on the floor. Mickey arrives to see what is going on and Pluto gleefully waits for the kitten to receive a roasting. But Mickey is not such a fool: he asks Bianca who is the culprit and she, with a gesture of an elegant fin and the gurgled enunciation of the name "Pluto", makes sure that justice is done.

As Pluto's Devil-self snarls in frustration: "How did I know that sardine was gonna turn stool-pigeon?"

Filmography

Mickey's Parrot, 1938
Lend a Paw, 1941

FERDINAND THE BULL

The character of Ferdinand the Bull was created by Munro Leaf in his bestselling book published in 1936 and illustrated by Robert Lawson. When the animated short *Ferdinand the Bull* came out in 1938 *Life* commented that

To Robert Lawson's celebrated drawings have been added Walt Disney's sly and cock-eyed genius and a hilariously purring sound track by Radio Announcer Don Wilson. What emerges from this combination is a completely charming creature with a benign white nose who threatens to supplant Mickey Mouse, Donald Duck and Lone Ranger's Silver as the most beloved animal of the movies.

So who is Ferdinand? He is a little bull who prefers sniffing the flowers under the trees to rushing around fighting all the other little bulls. One day five men come to the farm looking for fierce bulls for the bullfight. The other calves show off for them, but Ferdinand slinks away to sit under a tree in peace. Unfortunately, in so doing he sits on a bee, and the pain makes him dash around snorting and grunting in furiously bellicose fashion. The "talent scouts" see all this and assume that Ferdinand is ideal bull-ring material: they haul him off to Madrid.

The women cheer and throw bunches of flowers as the banderilleros, picadors and matador enter the ring (these characters are caricatures of various Disney personnel including, notably, Walt himself) – but when Ferdinand puts his head shyly into the arena all of these "heroes" flee with the exception of the matador. Ferdinand, to everyone's dismay, spots one of the bunches of flowers lying in the sand and sits down to sniff it quietly; despite the furious pleadings of the matador he refuses to fight. In the end he has to be dragged off, still with his treasured bouquet, and sent back home to the farm where he can live out his days in peace – although he was later to make a very brief appearance in *Who Framed Roger Rabbit* (1988) (➤326).

A point of interest is that among the animators on this short was Jack (John) Bradbury, who worked also on *Fantasia*, *Bambi* and *Pinocchio*. However, he went on to achieve his major recognition as an artist for the Disney comic strips.

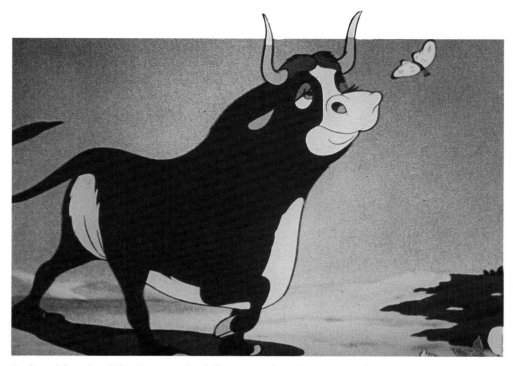

Ferdinand, based on Robert Lawson's book illustrations, from the acclaimed short *Ferdinand the Bull* (1938).

GUS GOOSE

Dear Nephew
This is your cousin Gus Goose. I'm sending him to visit you –
    Love,
        Aunt Fanny
PS: He don't eat much.

This was the message that Donald got – but Aunt Fanny (there must be a "goose" pun here) did not exactly tell the truth: in his one short, *Donald's Cousin Gus* (1939), Gus Goose proved that he was capable of eating a lot more than "much". Indeed, his watch did not have the usual hourly markings but instead the four divisions "tea", "supper", "lunch" and "dinner". Donald must have wondered if, as in the letter about the Nephews (➤85) from Dumbella, he was receiving a sentence to hard labour for life.

Gus is not very clever: even his best friend, on the shaky assumption that he has one, would admit that. He is pudgy (to put it kindly) and has a battered brolly and a little red hat. He has a red waistcoat with a blue shirt under it, and his sole means of communication is by use of finger and thumb to "parp" his ample rear end. His only skills are the ones he exercises in his relentless pursuit of appetizing food: with the greatest of ease he knits a plateful of spaghetti into a sock before devouring it, and with all the artistry of an experienced card-sharper he is able to shuffle slices of bread and cold cuts to produce a deck of sandwiches before the eye can blink. He also, in the process of eating Don out of house and home, manages to induce the Duck into coming out with one of his very few screen lines of understatement: as Don perches with his head stuffed into his own mailbox all he can find to say is "This is very, *very* ex-asp-er-ating".

Finally Don resorts to the use of "Barking Hot-Dogs – a sure way to get rid of hungry relatives", as they are described on the label. Gus gobbles the bait with a will, and his stomach starts to act like a dog – so much so that when Don throws a bone out the front door Gus's stomach drags him after it. The eager Duck slams and bars the door, but his relief is short-lived, for he turns to discover that Gus has darted in through the back door and is demolishing the contents of Don's fridge.

When Donald finally got rid of this gluttonous pest he was effectively ending Gus's film career (Gus's sole further appearance was as an extra in *Mickey's Christmas Carol* [1983], although he has guzzled his way through a number of comic strips). One has to speculate that Gus was being introduced as a new "regular" but that he proved not to be up to the mark so far as cinema audiences were concerned. Certainly his personality is almost unbearably rebarbative, and certainly his monomania means that it would have been very difficult to develop his character in any way. Other studios might have been prepared to endure an undevelopable character – think, for example, of the Roadrunner shorts – but not Disney.

Filmography

Donald's Cousin Gus, May 19, 1939
Mickey's Christmas Carol, 1983

TOOTSIE

When Tootsie the penguin shared star billing in *Donald's Penguin* (1939) he came within an inch of upstaging the world's most famous Duck. He arrives, neatly parcelled up, as a present to Donald from a certain Admiral Byrd: what Admiral Byrd has against Donald we shall never know! Tootsie proves to be quite a handful, immediately trying to eat Don's pet fish. When he sees the bowl apparently empty Don bawls the penguin out – only to have to apologize when it proves that the fish were merely hiding in the bowl's ornamental castle. Tootsie, however, refuses to accept his apologies and, while Don is out of the room fetching some conciliatory food, promptly gobbles the fish.

Don's rage on discovering this is, as we might expect, staggering to behold. A chase ensues, climaxing with Don having Tootsie cornered, a shotgun levelled at the penguin's breast. Several times he tries to pull the trigger, but each time, as the penguin weeps uncontrollably, compassion conquers the lust for vengeance. Finally he puts the gun aside, but it falls to the floor and goes off, blasting a huge hole in the wall where Tootsie has been standing. Donald is stricken with remorse – the penguin has apparently been so

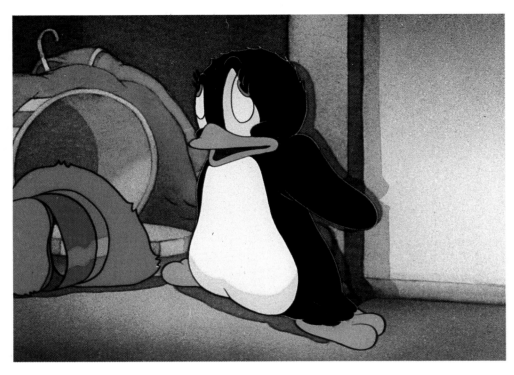

Tootsie, who plagued the Duck's existence in *Donald's Penguin* (1939).

comprehensively pulverized that not a feather remains – but then Tootsie appears from behind a door and there is a joyous reunion and reconciliation.

Like Gus (➤89), Tootsie's character is dominated by the desire for food – preferably Donald's. However, unlike Gus, Tootsie has a personality outside this. He is a very snobbish penguin, from the moment of his (or her? – it's so hard to tell with penguins) arrival indicating to Donald precisely which webbed foot the boot is on. He has his pride, too; after Donald's false accusation of him he becomes very aloof, refusing disdainfully to accept even the Duck's most abject beseechments for forgiveness. Despite this well thought-out personality, however, it is obvious why Tootsie never reappeared: there was essentially only a single joke to be derived from his relationship with Donald.

FIGARO

Figaro first appeared in a comparatively minor role in the feature *Pinocchio* (1940 [➤166]), so it is perhaps surprising that he appeared in the war-savings advertisement *All Together* (1942) as part of a double parade in which marched much more famous Disney stars: Donald and the Nephews, Mickey, Pluto, Goofy, Horace, Clarabelle, the Three Little Pigs and, like Figaro from *Pinocchio*, Geppetto and Pinocchio himself. Clearly Figaro was destined for more than a single role in a feature film.

And so it proved. The appealing little kitten appeared in six shorts, either in a starring part or stealing the show – usually from Pluto; in one instance he shared star billing with his fellow supporting actor in *Pinocchio*, Cleo (➤172). His character was changed a little for these later appearances: he became much more cat-like and less cuddly, with his hackles much more ready to rise and his voice readier to be a snarl than a plaintive "miaow". The Cleo of *Pinocchio* would have been promptly devoured by the later Figaro! Figaro's miaows were voiced by Clarence Nash, of Donald Duck fame (➤62), and by Kate-Ellen Murtagh.

His first short, *Figaro and Cleo* (1943), was a fairly routine matter centred on the eternal quest of cats to catch goldfish. In his second, *First Aiders* (1944), he is teamed up for the first of several appearances with Minnie and Pluto.

Minnie, amateur nurse extraordinary, asks if either Figaro or Pluto will act as her experimental subject. Both are eager to please, but in the ensuing scrap Pluto emerges victorious – especially since Figaro gets all the blame for the destruction caused by their affray. Pluto loves the gentle massage of Minnie's practice of artificial resuscitation – until, that is, a bottle of smelling salts rolls under his nose with an oblivious Minnie pinning him in place.

After further manipulations Pluto is left thoroughly splinted up – even his tongue is splinted! – while Minnie goes out to buy further bandages, and now it is Figaro's turn for a little revenge. He torments the much hampered dog until Pluto deservedly loses his temper and progressively more of his bindings. The fight is breathtaking in its destructiveness. On her return, Minnie horrifiedly surveys the chaos. Finally, though, she persuades the two antagonists to kiss and make up – although both are clearly prepared to fight another day.

Pluto, however, was not to feature in Figaro's next excursion, which was *Bath Day* (1946), one of the kitten's finest performances. Figaro is mortified at the prospect of a bath – especially when bubble-liquid is added to it – but eventually knuckles down and accepts the worst. The only problem is that that worst is even more dire than he had expected: Minnie ties around his newly washed neck a bright red bow and sprays him with a few generous squirts of perfume. With the same insensitivity that she was to show Pluto in *Pluto's Sweater* (➤91) Minnie shoves the little cat out to face his peers.

Poor Figaro! He follows a lovely fishy smell and finds at the end of it a gang of alley-cats whose leader would like nothing better than to beat up this smartypants. He chases the much smaller Figaro into an adjacent yard and props him up against a pile of dustbins, ready to hammer him into a shapeless pulp. But Figaro is trembling so much that he topples all the dustbins down on top of the alley-cat. The others of the gang, hearing all the kerfuffle, rush over to congratulate their leader who, they assume, must have added another scalp to his belt. Not so, because Figaro is unscathed and their leader lies unconscious. Not surprisingly they flee in terror the instant the little cat looks marginally annoyed.

But the day is not really to be his. On his proud return home Minnie hits the roof when she sees his bedraggled, disreputable-looking form and promptly insists that he has *another* bath. Back to square one for Figaro.

In the following year, 1947, the kitten turned in a first-rate performance in *Figaro and Frankie*, in which both he and Butch (➤91) had designs on a little pet bird called Frankie (➤107); at one point Figaro was close to being expelled from Minnie's home forever. However, the worst did not happen, and a year later he was back for *Cat Nap Pluto*.

The plot of *Cat Nap Pluto* (1948) is a simple one. Pluto arrives home in the early morning after a night on the tiles: he is in indescribably bad shape, and all he wants to do is grab a few hours' sleep. Figaro, by contrast, is in the mood for play, and does his best to rouse the sluggish pup. His efforts are countered by those of a Sandman-Pluto figure, who keeps turning up to decant vaster and vaster quantities of sand into the dog's eyes. Finally, in desperation, the dissolute Pluto crawls into Figaro's bed and the Sandman-Pluto hits him decisively over the head with a huge mallet. Figaro is none too pleased that his "chum" has been put out of action, but sensibly the Sandman-Pluto calls up a Sandman-Figaro, who applies a mallet likewise to the cat's head. Finally the two sandmen knock each other out and the short ends with all four of them snoozing peacefully. Lucky Pluto!

Figaro's final appearance was in *Pluto's Sweater* (1949), in which Minnie has knitted a bright red pullover of many strange proportions, all of them large. Despite Pluto's furious protests she stuffs him into this obnoxious garment and thrusts him from the house so that he can have a chance to show it off to all the other less fortunate dogs. Figaro watches with side-splitting delight, and in due course Butch (➤91) and the rest of the alley-dogs find it every bit as funny as Figaro did. Pluto, after many tussles with the sweater, finally falls into a pond so that the garment shrinks until it is only just large enough to cover his head.

When he returns home he finds Figaro curled up happily and Minnie engrossed in a horror novel, *The Hooded Monster*. All unawares, Pluto makes his presence known, and both Figaro and Minnie leap shrieking in terror at the sight of this "hooded monster". Once Minnie has realized what has happened she berates the poor pup in no uncertain terms for wrecking his "beautiful sweater" while Figaro cackles merrily at the dog's discomfort. But Pluto is not always so slow on the uptake as we might expect; he looks at the sweater and he looks at the kitten, and he indicates to Minnie that the former is now just about the right size for . . .

Never has smile vanished so abruptly from feline face. Alas, however, it was the signal for Figaro likewise to vanish from the Disney canon. Quite why this incredibly appealing character, who was certainly popular, should have fallen from grace is unknown. Perhaps it was simply that the story-men felt that they had exploited all the possibilities of the relationship between him, Pluto and Minnie. And, of course, there is no reason why Figaro should not return to the screen in the years to come.

Filmography

Pinocchio (feature), 1940
All Together, 1942
Figaro and Cleo, 1943
First Aiders, 1944
Bath Day, 1946
Figaro and Frankie, 1947
Cat Nap Pluto, 1948
Pluto's Sweater, 1949

BUTCH

Butch the bulldog: he is big, blue and macho, with dark blue jowls and a pale blue-gray body, black eyebrows that slant malevolently, a white underbody that reeks of raw power, a *very* studded collar and lower canine teeth that could hardly protrude more than they do. His favourite victim is Pluto (➤38), either as a subject of loutish derision or simply as somebody to beat up, but he is not particular: anyone else will do. Like most other male dogs he is passionately enamoured of Dinah (➤93), which brings him into rivalry with Pluto; however, while Pluto may be said to lack

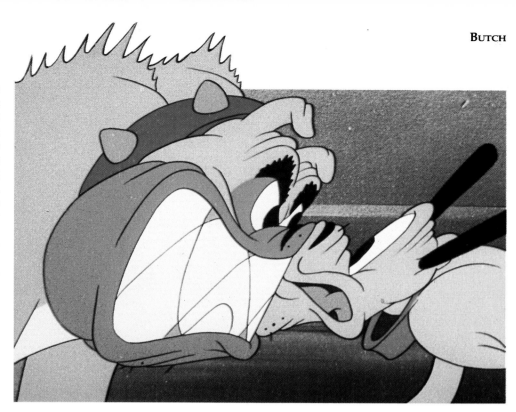

Butch and Pluto using body-language in their typical conversational posture: a still from *Pluto's Kid Brother* (1946).

subtlety in his courtship of the alluring little dachshund, Butch lacks even the slightest vestige of civilization. Butch battles with Pluto for Dinah's affections in *Canine Casanova* (1945) and *Pluto's Heart Throb* (1950), as well as doing his best to disrupt their romance in *Wonder Dog* (1950). Another animal with good cause to curse Butch is the little cat Figaro (➤90); and Frankie (➤107) likewise regrets his encounter with the big blue bulldog.

Butch's first outing was in 1940 in a short called *Bone Trouble*. In this film Pluto brings the wrath of Butch on himself, rather than

Pluto's bitterness knew no bounds when even his master seemed to favour Butch, as in *Pluto's Purchase* (1948).

merely being picked on as in so many others. The feud starts off when Butch catches Pluto stealing his bone: naturally there is a snarling hue and cry, and the world's favourite pup takes refuge in a carnival – more specifically, in its hall of mirrors. It takes Pluto a little while to realize what all the vaguely Pluto-ish monstrosities staring from the walls actually *are*, but once he does so he pauses to have some fascinated fun with his own distorted reflections, contorting himself so that the reflections imitate other animals – such as a croc, a kangaroo and a seal. His "imitation" of a vast, blue, many-toothed hulking bulldog, however, proves to have a life of its own – it is Butch, who has tracked him (and the bone) down at last. There is further

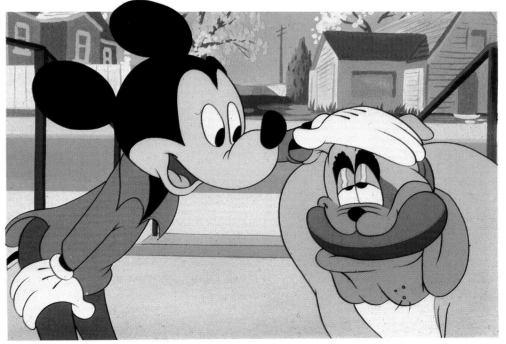

hilarious chasing through the hall of mirrors until Pluto cleverly uses a gallery of his own huge and hugely distorted growling reflections to scare off the unfortunate bulldog, leaving Pluto happily in possession of the bone. Crime, it would appear, does on occasion pay.

In fact, it would seem that Butch's perennial role was to lose out, whether his adversaries used fair means or foul. *T-Bone for Two* (1942) has Pluto yet again successfully stealing a bone from him. *Canine Casanova* (1945), *Pluto's Heart Throb* (1950) and *Wonder Dog* (1950) all have him losing out in the romantic stakes to Pluto, the target of their joint affections being Dinah. He played only bit parts in *Pluto's Kid Brother* (1946) and *Pluto's Sweater* (1949 [➤90]), but more major ones in *The Purloined Pup* (1946), where he was the evil kidnapper, and *Pluto's Purchase* (1948), in which he tries to steal the salami that Pluto "at Mickey's behest" has bought; the irony is that, after Pluto has outsmarted him and taken the stuff home to his master, Mickey gives it to Butch as a birthday present. Pluto is displeased by this.

An important appearance by Butch was in the 1947 short *Pluto's Housewarming*. Pluto has taken over a new luxury kennel, but discovers that a little turtle believes that the property belongs to it. After much fighting, during which we discover not only that the turtle can pop out of its shell at will, but also, under its shell, wears red underwear, Butch appears on the scene to chase both of them away from this desirable residence. While Pluto is all set to forget the issue, the turtle determines to fight back, biting Butch on the nose, foot and tail before eventually winning the day. In the end Pluto and the turtle make friends and settle down to share the kennel together.

Rather like Pete (➤15), Butch has to play the part of the eternal villain; again rather like Pete he is a character of just a little more complexity than other studios might have bothered with. Butch is a genuine personality rather than merely Pluto's brute oppressor.

Filmography

Bone Trouble, 1940
T-Bone for Two, 1942
Canine Casanova, 1945
Pluto's Kid Brother, 1946
The Purloined Pup, 1946
Pluto's Housewarming, 1947
Figaro and Frankie, 1947
Pluto's Purchase, 1948
Pluto's Sweater, 1949
Pluto's Heart Throb, 1950
Wonder Dog, 1950

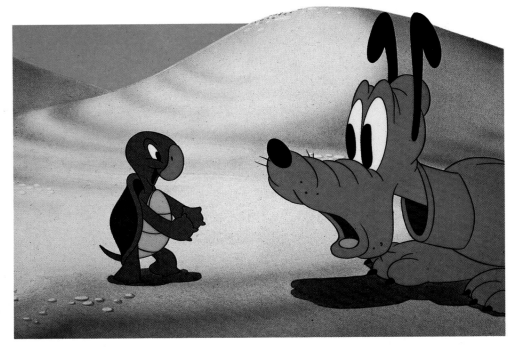

In *Pluto's Housewarming* (1947) a little turtle started off as Pluto's foe, but then became his ally in the struggle to prevent Butch from appropriating Pluto's luxury kennel.

LITTLE WHIRLWIND

Mickey has had many adversaries over the years, from giants to Mortimer Mouse (➤77) to perverse inanimate objects, but none can be so strange as the ones he encountered in a 1941 short called *The Little Whirlwind*.

Mickey is an itinerant. Passing a house one day his nose is captivated by the scent of recently baked cake, and he proposes to the householder (who proves to be Minnie, although in this short they act as if they do not know each other) that he will clean up her untidy yard for a share of the cake. The bargain struck, he sets to with a will; but soon afterwards a small tornado – the Little Whirlwind of the title – arrives and proceeds to take great delight in tormenting him by dispersing his neatly arranged piles of dead leaves, and so forth. After some

difficulty Mickey succeeds in catching Little Whirlwind in a sack; when the mischievous wind eventually breaks out of this Mickey chases it away and gets back to work.

But Little Whirlwind returns with **Mama Whirlwind**, who is quite a different proposition. Darkening the sky with her awesome presence she makes it clear that

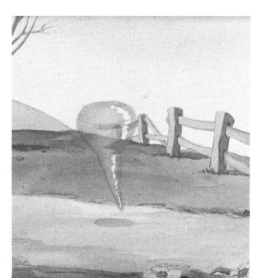

In 1941's *The Little Whirlwind*, Mickey found coping with the title-character bad enough – tackling Mama Whirlwind was another matter.

no one is going to be allowed to discipline her little darling and get away with it. Mickey chooses the better part of valour, and she chases him all over the countryside, spreading destruction wherever she goes, and finally sucking him up aloft and dumping him down again in the fountain in Minnie's yard. She vanishes just before Minnie reappears with the huge, glistening, wobbling sticky cake.

Mickey looks at the cake and he looks at Minnie's fury as she surveys the wreckage of what had once been her yard, and he turns with a shrug to depart. "Well," he says, "I guess I don't get the cake, huh?"

The pest itself in *The Little Whirlwind* (1941).

"Oh yes you do!" snaps Minnie.

And he does, with all the force that her good right arm can muster.

The interesting feature about the characters of Mama Whirlwind and her offspring is that they are just that – characters. It is impossible to put one's finger on exactly how the animators managed to give two tornados, of all things, genuine personalities, but somehow they managed it.

PLUTO, JUNIOR

Pluto, Junior made his solitary appearance in a short called, appropriately, *Pluto, Junior* in February 1942; since Dinah (➤93) did not make her entrance until July of that year, one must assume that this mischievous little pup was a son of Fifi (➤59). The father, very obviously, was Pluto himself (➤42); from physical evidence alone there was no way that Pluto could get out of that one!

Pluto is trying to sleep in his kennel. Pluto, Junior is making a similar attempt in his own kennel, but he is less determined about it than his father – little distractions keep wakening him. After fighting with a ball, which naturally enough ends up firmly lodged in Pluto's mouth, and then with a balloon which finally becomes a knotted mass of taut rubber enshrouding Pluto's head, the puppy decides that it would be much safer to pursue mischief further from home. In due course he finds himself locked in aerial combat with a bird; when he is finally dropped from the heavens he lands in a sock on a high washing-line and is unable to escape. Pluto bravely struggles to rescue him, tightrope-style, but finds himself in very much the same predicament. Finally both dogs plummet like stones – but fortunately land safely, although with a splash, in a wash-tub. Both are exuberantly happy that the adventure is over and that they are safe together.

Pluto, Junior never made another screen appearance. Possibly this was because, while the character himself is appealing, the short is not one of the stronger Disney cartoons. Perhaps the mischievous little puppy will return in years to come.

DINAH

True love, they say, comes only once in a lifetime, but nobody ever told Pluto that. After a relationship lasting several years with Fifi (➤59), with whom, we discover from *Pluto's Quin-Puplets* (1937), he shared at least one litter, he lost his heart to the sinuous Dinah, a red-nosed dachshund who like Pluto had, as we shall see, A Past.

In fact, he lost his heart to her several times. The first was in *The Sleepwalker* (1942), one of the best Pluto cartoons, containing an adroit and well balanced mixture of

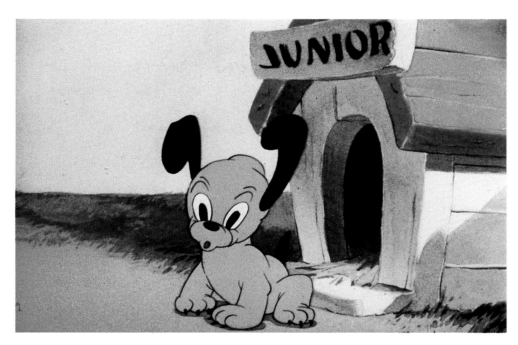

No doubt about Pluto, Junior's parentage! From *Pluto, Junior* (1942).

fast-moving visual gaggery and occasional moments of pathos that never quite descend into bathos, as might so easily have been the case.

Pluto is asleep in his kennel, dreaming the dreams of (we assume) the righteous and from time to time lolling out his sleeping tongue to lick lovingly the big bone that lies on his dish in front of him. Enter Dinah, who cautiously steals his bone – but not quite cautiously enough, because he awakes and gives spirited chase. After a bruising encounter with a croquet set Pluto finally retrieves his bone, largely because Dinah has difficulty in running at speed owing to her sheer length, which varies elastically up to staggering proportions:

somehow her hindquarters seem to get left behind, and have to struggle to catch up with her head and shoulders. Whatever the reason, Pluto returns bone-laden to his kennel to settle down for another period of wary dozing, leaving Dinah weeping as she looks at the significant emptiness of her own bowl.

Well, if at first you don't succeed ... She steals his bone again, and again he furiously retrieves it, in his rage shattering her bowl and kicking the shards into her kennel. On the way home to his own kennel, however, he falls asleep – and his canine subconscious (who would have guessed that Pluto's brain could encompass such a thing?) takes over. He turns around and

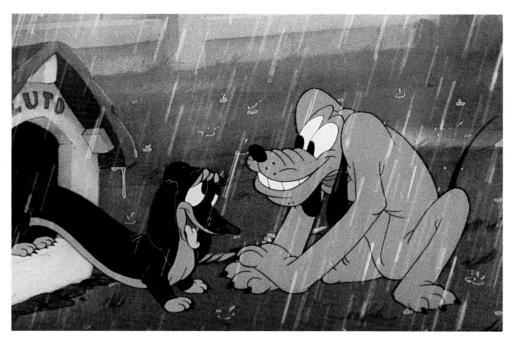

Delicious Dinah, the second love of Pluto's life, first appeared in *The Sleepwalker* (1942).

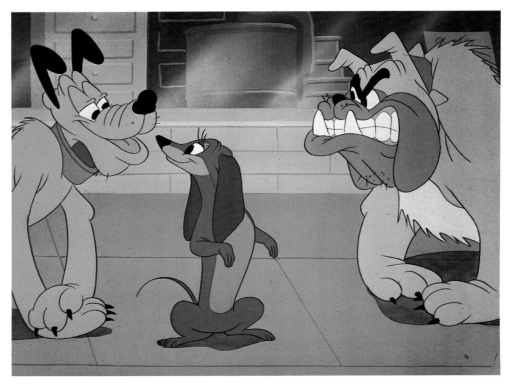

Although Dinah preferred Pluto *really*, she was not averse to playing him off against Butch: a still from *Pluto's Heart Throb* (1950).

eager for vengeance on this scurvy pup. Naturally he leads them to where Dinah is stopping the gap – indeed, she is now completely immersed in it. The hole is sealed up and she and Pluto are the heroes of the hour. Both live together in eternal bliss . . . well, at least until the next short.

In *Pluto's Heart Throb* (1950) we again see an unattached Dinah, although this time she is living once more in the USA. She and Pluto pass in the street and, thanks to the intervention of a canine Cupid, he falls madly in love with her. However, she responds to his subtly enunciated comment of "W-w-w-o-w!" by merely sticking out her tongue; clearly she thinks that Pluto needs a few lessons from a school of etiquette. The canine Cupid intervenes again, though, and this time it is she who pursues Pluto, luring him with a saucy look and a saucier gait.

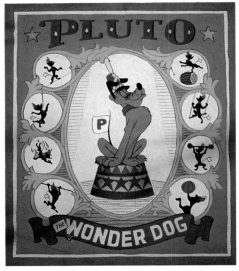

In 1950's *Wonder Dog*, a poster of Prince the Wonder Dog inspired Pluto, who saw himself in Prince's place.

brings the bone back to her. Not allowing her confusion over his schizophrenic behaviour to cause any delays in the more important business, she swiftly buries the bone – only to be startled when yet again he returns in a rage. Even though she meekly disinters the bone and offers it back to him, in his wrath he smashes her kennel to bits.

Out from the debris pop six eager, friendly little dachshund puppies, who swarm lovingly all over this big new friend. Their presence puts a different complexion on things – it was for them that Dinah was stealing the bone, and not just for herself – and Pluto's emotions are tortured still further when, moments later, a great thunderstorm breaks and he sees that the pups' only shelter from the beating rain is under their mother. Pluto looks at the sadly dripping little collection, and his heartstrings are well and truly wrung. He dashes off to fetch his own kennel, which he offers to Dinah and her brood along with a whole stack of his favourite bones. As reward she gives him a kiss and he is transported into ecstasy. In the final sequence we see Dinah and the pups sleeping warmly in the kennel while outside Pluto shelters as best he can under a newspaper . . . cold, wet, but happy.

Her second appearance was in *Canine Casanova* (1945); interestingly enough, during the three-year gap she seemed to have lost about 25 per cent of her prodigious length. Pluto spots the luscious Dinah and instantly seeks to make her his. However, his various stratagems are unsuccessful, and in due course she is captured by the dog-catcher and taken to the pound, whence Pluto stalks her bloodhound-

fashion (a sequence reminiscent of *Lady and the Tramp* [➤252]). There he finds that the two male bully-dogs in the pens on either side of her (one of whom is Butch [➤91] are trying to force their attentions upon her: Pluto's chivalrous instinct is obviously aroused. He sneaks into the pound, finds the back of the pen with the name "Dinah" on it (in fact, the artists rendered it as "Dina"!), releases her and, after a chase by the dog-catcher, escorts her home.

Back at her place she gives him a kiss. Maddened with romantic fervour he pursues her to the mouth of her kennel, only to find himself clambered over by five eagerly swarming puppies. In the short's closing sequence Pluto shrugs expressively; "Shucks," he seems to be thinking, "the gal's married!"

In later appearances, however, Dinah was to be conspicuously single. Indeed, in her next appearance she was also to be Dutch – but then so was Pluto.

In Dutch (1946) combines the themes of the tales of the boy who cried "Wolf!" and of the boy who put his finger in the dyke. Pluto is a Dutch milkman, Dinah Pluto's paramour and the mayor's daughter. As a result of a series of mishaps, they set off the dyke-breach alarm bell, and are expelled from the town for their apparent hoaxing. Far from the town, they discover that there is indeed a hole in the dyke, and Dinah plugs it while Pluto races back to sound the alarm. Of course, he is greeted with a hail of curses and unsavoury garbage: the fool dog is trying that same old stunt again. However, he goes into a series of naughty tricks – stealing a soldier's pikeshaft, and so forth – until a hostile crowd chases him,

But then Butch (➤92) arrives on the scene, just as love seems to be very much in the air. She introduces the two dogs to each other as her joint friends, and then strolls along cheekily as they vie with each other for the honour of courting her. Her tactics are not precisely designed to produce peace and harmony between the two.

After many a scrap Dinah falls into a pond while trying to evade Butch's unwelcome attentions. Butch, it proves, cannot swim, and so Pluto rescues her and they swear undying love. Once again, this lasts only until the next short . . .

That next short, just a few months later, was to be her last: it was *Wonder Dog* (1950). Since she and Pluto ended the short passionately in love with each other we can assume that they lived happily ever after – but we are getting ahead of ourselves.

The short starts with Dinah positively salivating over a poster announcing the forthcoming appearance of "Prince the Wonder Dog", who can walk the tightrope, juggle barrels on his feet, and do everything else you would expect a superdog to be able to do. Dinah finally tears herself away from this delicious sight, and Pluto approaches the poster: he can see it subtly changed so that *he* is the one performing all the stirring deeds. He looks at a nearby backyard full of junk and the junk magically transforms itself into circus equipment. Say – if *he* could do all the things Prince the Wonder Dog can, he might maybe win the heart of the fair Dinah.

The only trouble is, as he discovers, that he can't.

Enter Butch, who falls around with laughter at Pluto's efforts. Pluto's response to this is less than totally polite, and a chase ensues, with Butch emphatically playing the role of the aggressor. In his desperation to escape those cruelly gnashing fangs Pluto finds himself using all the junk in the yard to perform miraculous feats. Dinah, seeing his efforts from afar – but not the reason for them, Butch snapping angrily below – promptly falls in love with Pluto, who henceforth becomes in her heart her "Wonder Dog".

This short represented not only Dinah's final appearance but also Butch's. As noted above, we have to assume that Pluto eventually won his Dinah and that Butch was finally repudiated. In that case justice was probably done: Pluto had, after all, been the more *romantic* of the two dogs. And Dinah has always been a romantic – albeit a trifle saucier than the average Georgette Heyer heroine.

Filmography

The Sleepwalker, 1942
Canine Casanova, 1945
In Dutch, 1946
Pluto's Heart Throb, 1950
Wonder Dog, 1950

LITTLE HANS

The short *Education for Death* (1943) was one of the Disney contributions to the

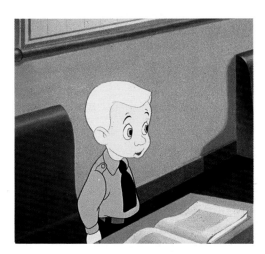

Little Hans, from the wartime propaganda short *Education for Death* (1943).

propaganda war against Nazism. Based on a book by Gregor Ziemer, it starts off in a documentary style, showing the way in which fascist bureaucracy takes over the lives of its victims from the moment of birth – the parents of the short's central character, Little Hans, are given strict instructions as to what they may or may not call their newborn child (naturally, the names

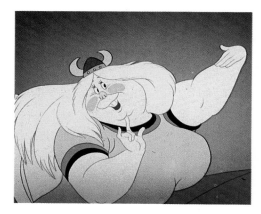

Germania, who took the title role in a hideous parody of the *Sleeping Beauty* story in 1943's *Education for Death*. Adolf Hitler was her "handsome prince".

Winston and Franklin are top of the *verboten* list!).

We are then introduced to a distorted version of the children's nursery tale *Sleeping Beauty*. But this is a very different rendition from the one that Disney filmed some years later (although the witch in it, styled "Democracy", is very like the witch in *Snow White and the Seven Dwarfs* [➤**157**]). The main action concerns the "beautiful" Princess **Germania**, depicted as a vast boozy blonde valkyrie surmounted by a horned Teutonic helmet, and her "handsome" prince, a caricature of Adolf Hitler. After a fair degree of clowning, done to the thundering background of Wagner's "Ride of the Valkyries", the diminutive prince succeeds in hauling the bulging princess onto his horse, which staggers off miserably under the colossal load.

We return to "real life" to find that Hans, now a little blond boy, is sick. His Mama knows that sick children are generally taken away and never heard from again, so she does her best to hide his condition from the world. However, in due course a Gestapo thug arrives and tells her to stop mollycoddling the child. Sickness, in Nazi Germany, is not a weakness that should be pandered to.

But soon enough Hans recovers and returns to school. Here we see one of his lessons – on natural history. The teacher, who is shown as a brainless bigot, is telling the class about a rabbit and a fox, the former playing the part of dinner for the latter. All the other kids except Hans join in a chorus of derision over the rabbit's fate – "The world belongs to the strong ... and to the brutal ... the rabbit is a coward and

deserves to die ... we spit on the rabbit." Hans protests about this, expressing sympathy for the victim, and so draws down upon himself the full wrath of his teacher. In a sequence described in the January 18, 1943, issue of *Time* as the "most pointed" in the movie, Little Hans, after his admonishment, realizes that the correct response – the one which will earn him credit among not only his contemporaries but also the grown-ups – is: "I hate the rabbit – the rabbit is a weakling – he is no Nazi rabbit."

There is a further moving moment later in the short. We see Little Hans, still a child, marching as a member of the Hitler Youth. The troop of marching children transmutes into a vast horde of strictly disciplined soldiers. As the young man Hans fills the centre of the screen the narrator tells us that "in him are planted no seeds of laughter, hope, tolerance or mercy". But this is not the only sense in which Hans is doomed, for right at the end of the short the company of soldiers, in its turn, transmutes – this time into a huge graveyard filled with featureless crosses.

Education for Death is an excellent cartoon – there can be no doubt about this. However, it was far more a straightforwardly propagandizing movie than, say, *Der Fuehrer's Face* (➤**64**), and consequently is much more "dated" when viewed today. Nevertheless, it has many strengths – one of which is that, contrary to all the normal rules of good story-telling, its central character, Little Hans, is nothing more than a cypher: he could be *any* of the other indoctrinated, brain-washed German children and soldiers we see in the short. The point is brilliantly made.

BEN BUZZARD

Ben Buzzard is both an avian and an aviationary crook, owner of a used-airplane establishment in the 1943 short *Flying Jalopy*. One knows what to expect when one sees that his billboard originally said "Wrecked Airplanes", but that the word "Wrecked" has been crossed out and replaced by "Used". Well, you or I would know what to expect, but Donald Duck, of course, being eternally gullible, does not. Ben persuades him to buy a jalopy at very favourable terms – and also to sign an insurance policy making Ben the sole beneficiary in the event of Donald having anything so unlikely as a fatal accident. The remainder of the short shows Ben doing his best to shorten the odds of such a thing happening, growing ever more desperate as Don has increasingly improbable escapes; oh what a carrion. Of course, virtue triumphs and the buzzard is humiliated.

Ben also makes a cameo appearance in 1988's *Who Framed Roger Rabbit* (➤**326**).

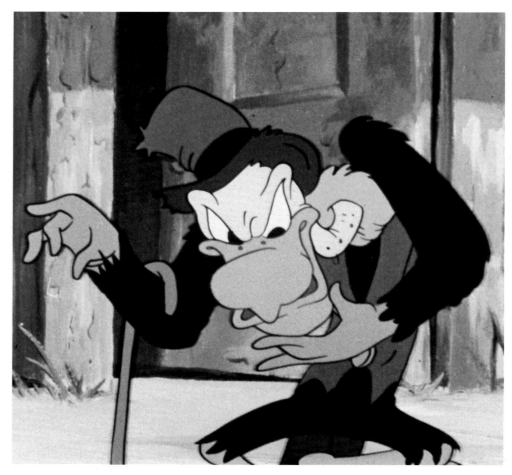

Ben Buzzard, seedy owner of a seedy used-airplane business in *Flying Jalopy* (1943). The standard of the goods on offer can be inferred from the fact that Donald is a customer.

CHIP AN' DALE

Jack Hannah, who succeeded Jack King as the principal director of Donald Duck's movies (➤61), has an interesting recollection about the way in which Chip an' Dale rose from the obscurity of their first supporting role in *Private Pluto* (1943) to such stardom that by the time of *Chips Ahoy* (1956) the two little kleptomaniacs were arguably a greater "draw" than Donald himself (certainly the Duck found himself forced to share star billing with them). Hannah recalls (in an interview in *Mindrot*):

We began looking for foils [for] the Duck. Naturally his three nephews [➤85] were always available. . . . While Donald and his nephews worked well together, we needed variety in our material so we tried a variety of characters. The Aracuan bird [➤212] who was introduced earlier in *Saludos Amigos* was one of our first attempts. There was a series with a beetle named Bootle Beetle [➤107]. . . . Working with these other characters led up to Chip 'n' Dale.

Dale gets a ride on Chip's shoulders in 1950's *Crazy Over Daisy*.

One interesting point about the two chips is that, unlike the three Nephews (➤85), for example, Chip an' Dale have quite distinct personalities. Dale – who has a red nose – is certainly the more capricious and flutter-witted of the two (although that is not saying a great deal!), and the slightly more logical Chip – who has a black nose – frequently has to bring him back into line by brute physical means. Hannah reminisces once more:

I believe Gerry Geronimi did a picture with two impish little chipmunks that just squeaked and chattered with a speeded-up soundtrack but no words. He used them with Pluto. . . . I wanted to use them with the Duck but with a little more personality put into them. So we decided to put words into their mouths but speed 'em up so you could just barely understand them [the voices were originally those of Jim Macdonald, veteran Disney voice actor, and Dessie Flynn]. . . . We gave them both the same personality – but something was missing. Bill Peet came up with the suggestion of making one of them a little goofball to give them two different personalities. Immediately I saw the advantage of that and took the suggestion.

But Chip's sturdy punches and Dale's scatter-brained habit of unnecessarily landing them both in scrapes never seem to create any ill-feeling between the two of them, nor to divert them from their main aim in life, to amass as vast a stockpile of food as possible – if not rather more than that. The fact that they delight in making the greatest possible nuisances of themselves in so doing is really secondary, if only just.

These two lovable (?) little creatures were of course to prove the most popular and enduring of Don's adversaries, but Donald was not the only unfortunate to suffer from their mischief – Pluto, too, had good reason to curse their existence. Indeed, he was their first adversary, in *Private Pluto* (1943).

In this short Private Pluto, dragooned into the army under who knows what emergency rule, is ordered to guard a pillbox which, unbeknown to him and his masters, the chips have been using as a haven and nut-store. The big gun they have pressed into service as a nut-cracker, but anything else will do! For example, a useful technique is to fill Pluto's helmet with nuts and then crunch the gun down on top of it to crack the nuts *en masse*; it is just a pity that Pluto is still wearing the helmet . . . Finally they use the gun to shoot the unfortunate dog miles into the air and fill his landing-site with nuts: the impact of his precipitate arrival cracks all of these, the chips retreat into the pillbox with their treasured kernels, and we leave Pluto beating against the pillbox's locked door, weeping with frustration.

Squatter's Rights (1946), their second venture, ranged them against Pluto once more – only this time Mickey was involved too. The two chips have been hibernating in

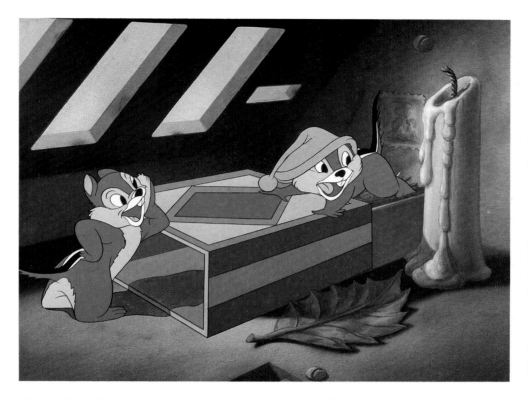

The two chips in *Squatter's Rights* (1946), in which their enemy was Pluto, Unusually, both have black noses. (Normally Dale's is red, Chip's black.)

the wood-stove of Mickey's country cabin, and when he arrives for a hunting trip they naturally resent his presence; the Mouse cannot understand why things seem to keep on going wrong, and Pluto, who has spotted the chips, is incapable of telling his master the reason. Various gags ensue, the final one involving Pluto narrowly escaping having his head blown off by a shotgun. However, the gun falls down on top of him and knocks him out; the chips decorate him artistically with tomato ketchup so that when Mickey returns from a hunting foray outside he assumes that his dog has been desperately injured. As Mickey rushes off with Pluto towards the nearest vet, the two chips happily shake hands: they have got rid of those invading pests and are now in sole occupation of the cabin once more.

In *Pluto's Christmas Tree* (1952) they take on the hapless dog yet again. This time Pluto and Mickey have obtained a little fir with two sitting tenants – the chips. Mickey is blissfully unaware of all this and, while Pluto does his best to drive out the unwanted guests, all he succeeds in doing is get into trouble with his master. The chips, meanwhile, are obviously keen to appropriate as many goodies as possible – although their efforts are not always successful. On one occasion Dale, using a twig, tries to "fish" a candy-stick which Mickey is putting on the tree and instead catches a bauble. When Dale sees his own distorted reflection in the bauble he is violently scared. However, even this commotion fails to alert Mickey to the presence of the chips ... and once again Pluto gets the blame.

But their main adversary was to be – gloriously – Donald. He first makes their acquaintance in *Chip an' Dale* (1947), and their adventures in that short set the pattern for most of their future shorts with him. Woken in the depths of winter by the cold he goes out to chop himself a log for burning. Little does he realize that the hollow log he selects contains the chips'

nut-store. They chase him back to his house and, after much gaggery, succeed in rescuing their supplies.

Their second outing against the Duck was in 1948, in *Three for Breakfast*. The story-line of this short is oddly contrived; its director was Jack Hannah and not, as one might be led to expect, Jack King (➤65); unlike *Chip an' Dale*, in this short the chips are gratuitously on the offensive, the raiders rather than the rescuers. They are out to steal Don's breakfast pancakes by harpooning them with a fork. When he cottons on to what's happening he "plants" a fake rubber pancake on them – begging the question of why he should happen to have a fake rubber pancake in the house. This fake stretches elastically as the chips haul their end of it up the inside of the chimney to the top, with Don clinging on like grim death at the other end; it stretches yet more when Don, in an attempt to moor his end, runs all over the house and garden and finally up onto the roof. A resourceful chip hops out of the chimney and puts butter under his feet so that he loses his footing and...

In 1950 *Trailer Horn* came along. Donald, little realizing what he is letting himself in for, has decided to go on a caravan holiday – probably glad to leave the Nephews behind. Sadly for him, he doesn't realize that he has parked his car and caravan near to the tree in which live a certain pair of creatures who adore tormenting ducks. The indignities heaped upon Don in this short are too many to list; but the high-point must be the sequence in which he does his best to show off his exquisite springboard diving. The second nastiest trick of the chips is to

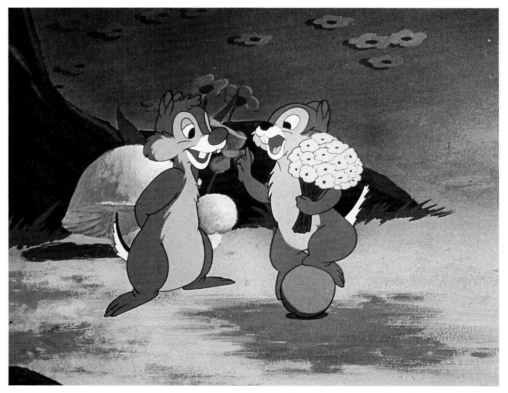

Chip an' Dale set out to prove that it's not just ducks that can show a romantic streak in *Crazy Over Daisy* (1950).

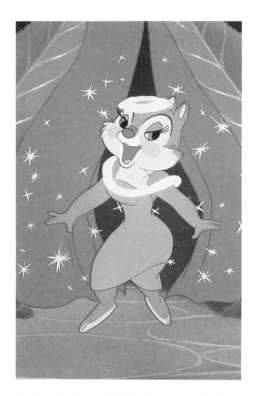

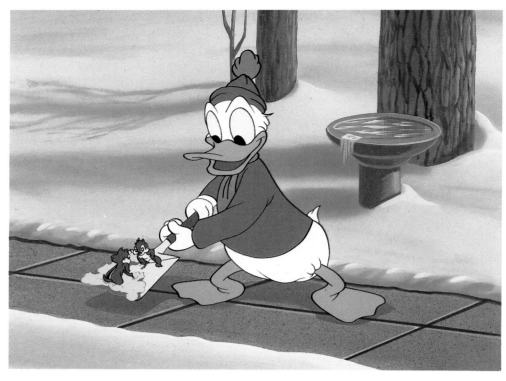

Clarice, a luscious nightclub singer, stole the hearts of both of the chips in the 1952 short *Two Chips and a Miss*.

The two chips – no doubt calling a spade a, well, shovel – find that Donald has, at least temporarily, the better of them in *Corn Chips* (1951).

push the board several extra feet out from shore while Don is elegantly pirouetting in midair ... so that he falls from on high onto it with a beak-shattering crash. And the *nastiest* trick they play is, on his second attempted dive, to swivel the board around so that instead of landing in the water he plummets into his own caravan, smashing rather more of the furniture than you might have thought possible.

Don does not take this lying down, of course. He uses his car to batter repeatedly at the base of the chips' tree, hoping to bring them tumbling down to his level. Instead all he succeeds in doing is to bend back the tree like a catapult, with his car in the crucial launch position. All is well, however, because the weight of Don, the car and the chips is just enough to hold the tree down in this tense position. The trouble is that then the chips step demurely off ...

1953 saw Donald supplied with an ally in the form of Dolores the elephant (►**102**). In *Working for Peanuts* Donald is a zoo attendant and Dolores one of the exhibits. The aim of the chips is to steal the peanuts with which the visitors liberally shower the zoo animals, and they try a number of ways of doing this. Not all are successful: when Dale climbs up onto a rock and imitates a seal, his expectantly gaping mouth receives not a shower of peanuts but a huge fish hurled at colossal velocity. One flattened chipmunk. In the end, of course, they succeed, by deceiving Donald into thinking that they are rare albino specimens, and his colleague Dolores is unable to tell him the awful truth.

Incidentally, there is a moment early in this short which seems to betray the

underlying motive for their eternal quest to amass food. On encountering a peanut for the very first time they prize open its shell and discover, nestling within, the two kernels. Thereafter they seek more and more peanuts because, delightfully, each shell *contains one kernel for each of them*. In other words, their motivation here is to do with fascination rather than with gourmandizing. Similarly, one suspects that

they stockpile all the other sorts of nuts in other shorts because it intellectually pleases them so to do and not just because they plan to eat the stuff.

Not all of the Chip an' Dale cartoons have been among the most inspired of the Disney output, but all have at least one moment of pure genius. In *Donald Applecore* (1952), for instance, in the midst of some fairly routine gags there is a piece of sheer surreal lunacy

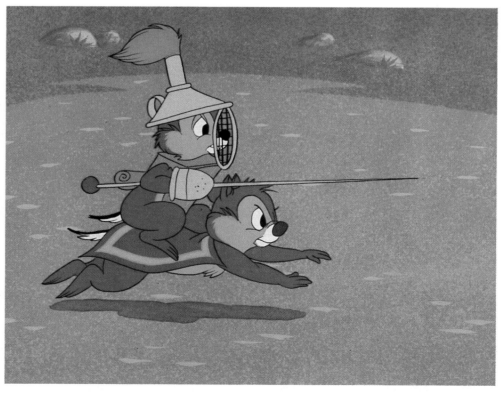

Sir Chip, on his trusty steed Dale, rides out to do battle with Donald's "dragon" in *Dragon Around* (1954).

that raises the rest of the short above the common herd. The chips are hiding in a haystack, which Don consequently blasts in no uncertain fashion. From the maelstrom of hay Dale emerges with a look of innocent delight on his face: in his paw he is clutching a needle!

As in the matter of hoarding food, the fascination of the experience dominates his mind – in this case banishing concerns about his immediate peril. It is this perfect consistency of personality which has made so many of the Disney characters stand out in contrast to the products of other studios.

Incarnations of the two chips have become popular in TV's *Chip 'n Dale Rescue Rangers* (➤141).

Filmography

Private Pluto, April 2, 1943
Squatter's Rights, 1946
Chip an' Dale, 1947 (chipmunks first named as such)
Three for Breakfast, 1948
Winter Storage, 1949
All in a Nutshell, 1949
Toy Tinkers, 1949
Crazy Over Daisy, 1950
Trailer Horn, 1950
Food for Feudin', 1950
Out on a Limb, 1950
Chicken in the Rough, 1951
Corn Chips, 1951
Test Pilot Donald, 1951
Out of Scale, 1951
Donald Applecore, 1952
Two Chips and a Miss, 1952
Pluto's Christmas Tree, 1952
Working for Peanuts, 1953
The Lone Chipmunks, 1954
Dragon Around, 1954
Up a Tree, 1955
Chips Ahoy, 1956
Mickey's Christmas Carol, 1983

REASON AND EMOTION

Reason and Emotion (1943) was, like *Education for Death* (1943 [➤95]) and various others, a contribution from Disney to the propaganda war, although its message was very considerably more muted.

The main action of the short occurs inside the heads of the two human protagonists, **John Doakes** and a pretty girl. We see his head in cross-section: the inside of his skull is fitted out like an automobile, with a steering-wheel, a front seat and a back seat. The back-seat driver, **Emotion**, has been described by James Algar (in *The Pacific Spectator*, Winter 1950) as "an uncouth little caveman", a description which perhaps rather flatters him. In the front seat, at the wheel, is **Reason**, a bookish bespectacled fellow. Reason is very much in charge.

But then the man sees the pretty girl – as, of course, do Reason and Emotion. Emotion, as you might expect from an uncouth little caveman, wants his "host" to whistle and leer, but Reason refuses to let

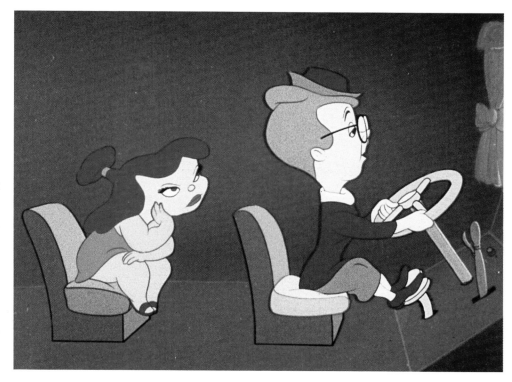

Miss Reason and Miss Emotion were equally as adept as their male counterparts in making a hash of decisions: a still from 1943's *Reason and Emotion*.

this happen – until, in frustration, Emotion simply kicks him out from behind the wheel and takes over, steering the man after the girl and making him shimmy suggestively and shout a macho "Hi Babe!". The girl's understandable response is to slap John Doakes's face and strut off indignantly. But inside her head we discover that she too has some passengers, **Miss Reason** and **Miss Emotion**. The former, firmly ensconced in the driving seat, has her prim nose firmly in the air; but the latter, a pouting woman with

a less than discreet touch of the floozy about her, reproaches: "Ya shouldn'ta slapped him! ... He was kinda cute! Ya wanta be an old maid all your life?"

There's a subtlety here which you do not expect to find in a "mere" animated short – even one by Disney – because both Reason (and Miss Reason) and Emotion (and especially Miss Emotion) are, in their own different ways, *right*. The point is, of course, that only by maintaining a balance between the two can humanity conduct its affairs in a

Inside John Doake's skull, the dapper Reason and the paleolithic Emotion, in *Reason and Emotion* (1943).

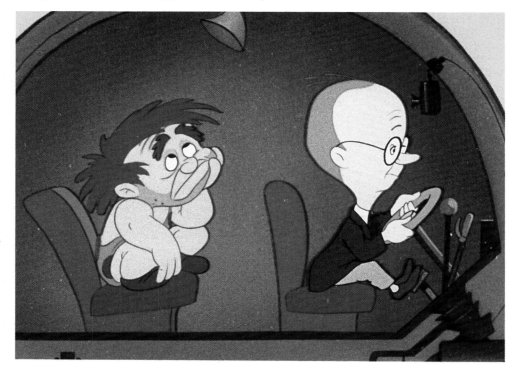

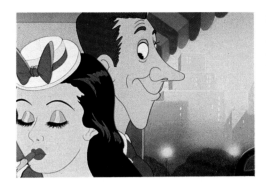

John Doakes spots the pretty girl: where should he go from here?

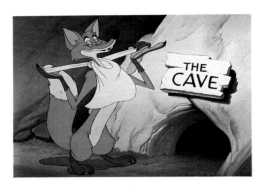

sane fashion. Brute Emotion will drive us to early destruction; but pure Reason, in its own way, will also – rather more insidiously but perhaps even more swiftly – destroy us. In Nazi Germany at the time, of course, there managed to be a simultaneous imbalance of both qualities – emotional witch-hunting anti-Semitism combined with the detached "reason" that was capable of ignoring the suffering of the human subjects of horrific "scientific" experiments – although these were un-known at the time to the Allies. The Dis-ney propaganda may well have been directed instead towards the United States public.

The character Emotion is briefly seen in 1988's *Who Framed Roger Rabbit* (➤326).

CHICKEN LITTLE

The 1943 short *Chicken Little* was a radical retelling of the popular story.

The tale is set in a poultry-run, protected by high wooden fences but only

insufficiently so from the cunning **Foxey Loxey**. This character has a streetwise New York voice reminiscent of that of Timothy Mouse (➤194) and an appearance that stirs memories of the Big Bald Wolf (➤54). Inside the run are various other characters. The big red cock **Cocky Locky** is definitely the boss of the region, the supervisor of egg-collection and the darling of the ladies. These ladies largely consist of **Henny Penny** and her cronies who, while definitely elderly, still have vocal cords in youthful condition: they can be relied upon to pass on a secret quicker than thought. (It is stressed that these gossips, while spilling the beans at the run's hair salon, always opt for the "popular red *hen*na rinse" – oh dear.) By contrast, **Turkey Lurkey** and *his* cronies are the local gentry, and they do not gossip at all: instead they, um, have serious political discussions about the other personalities in the run. There are also **The Jitterbirds** – "a pretty featherbrained crowd", according to the narration – and, in addition, the seedy clientele of the run's bar, **Goosey Poosey**, **Ducky Lucky**, and other inebriates.

But our "hero" is Chicken Little himself. We are told that he is "a good egg as chickens go" – a description that merits some careful thought when one sees Chicken Little himself: despite the fact that he is a famous yoyo champ and an infamous playboy, he has spiky yellow hair, a diminutive stature, a blue bow-tie clashing dramatically with his little yellow jacket, a straw boater and a facial expression astonishing in its insipid vacuity. How can this lacklustre hero save the hides of the assembled poultry? How indeed?

The fox, although outside the poultry-run, whispers through a chink in the fence

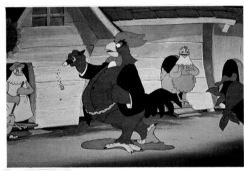

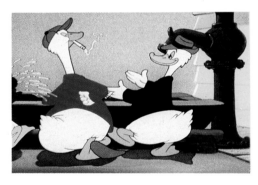

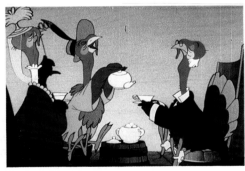

It wasn't just the fans who were to devour the star of 1943's *Chicken Little*.

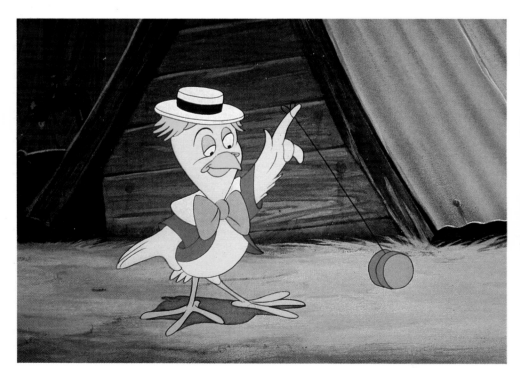

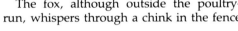

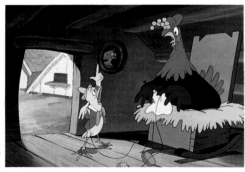

Some of the main characters in the 1943 short *Chicken Little*. Foxy Loxey (*top*) plotted to get himself a poultry supper and would have failed had the birds in the run listened to Cocky Locky (*second top*). Fortunately for the fox's schemes, Goosey Poosey and Ducky Lucky (*middle*), Turkey Lurkey (*on right of fourth picture above*) and Henny Penny (*above*) chose to listen to Chicken Little instead.

to Chicken Little that there is a grave danger that the sky might fall, killing all the fowl. Our "hero" swallows this hook, line and sinker, especially when Foxey Loxey adds "evidence" to support the rumour by dropping onto Chicken Little's head an appropriately celestial section stolen from the signboard of a conveniently nearby astrologer. The little fellow panics, spreading alarm and despond throughout the run.

But Cocky Locky is not as stupid as Chicken Little looks: he discounts out of hand the story of the falling sky. The fox then decides that a little propaganda is called for: again whispering through gaps in the fence, he persuades the milksop chicken that he is really a born leader, despite appearances to the contrary. Moreover, Foxey Loxey spreads a spiderweb of rumours around the run that Cocky Locky is past it, that his leadership shows signs of great folly, that he is endangering everybody's lives by refusing to credit that the sky could fall, that ... The net result is that the poultry vote with their feet, neglecting Cocky Locky's leadership and running with Chicken Little in a mass panic to shelter from the sky in a nearby cave . . . outside the poultry-run.

In the final scene we see Foxey Loxey standing in the cave amid a veritable forest of wishbones. The narrator of the short protests strongly: "Hey, wait a minute! This isn't the way it ends in *my* book."

Foxey Loxey replies: "Oh, yeah? Don't believe everything you read, brother."

Chicken Little makes a cameo appearance in 1988's *Who Framed Roger Rabbit* (➤326).

MONTE AND VIDI

Monte and Vidi appeared in a 1944 short called *The Pelican and the Snipe*, Monte being the pelican and Vidi the snipe.

The two engaging birds are pals based on a lighthouse near Montevideo. Monte, however, has a habit of sleepwalking – or, really, sleepflying – a practice that brings him into all sorts of dangers. His chum Vidi is running himself down trying to stay awake in order to save Monte. Amusingly, each morning Monte cannot understand why his friend is so lie-abed. In desperation, Vidi turns to various stratagems in order to pin Monte down during the night: he ties their legs together with disastrous results; he ties Monte to an anchor, again with disastrous results; and so forth. In fact, all his various efforts prove disastrous, but the use of the anchor is worst of all, because, while Vidi catches up on some much needed sleep, Monte walks to the edge of the lighthouse, steps off to try to fly, and ends up at the bottom of the ocean. Somehow he escapes.

The next morning a sleeping Vidi is roused to be told very firmly that he is no longer wanted in these parts: Monte has no

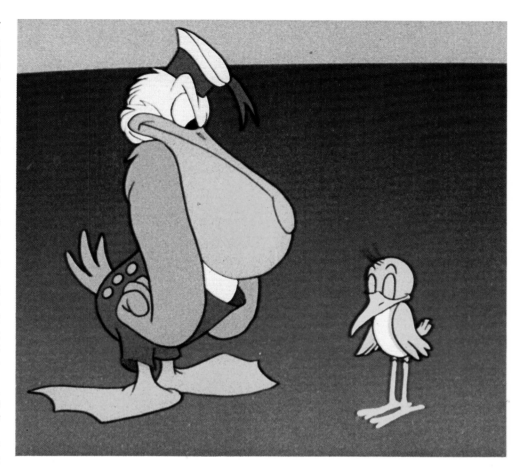

Monte *(left)* and Vidi in the 1944 short *The Pelican and the Snipe*.

need of friends who tie him to anchors during the night. Vidi flies off sadly, for he realizes the peril his pelican pal is now in.

He is right to worry. That night Monte, no longer encumbered, dreams that he is a Flying Fortress, and off he sets, still fast asleep, to fly around the sky. As it happens, however, there are some military aircraft on manoeuvres near the lighthouse that night, and Monte finds himself mixing it with them. He bumps into one of them, and this is enough to waken him from his dream: suddenly he recognizes the reason for Vidi's apparently odd behaviour over the last few weeks.

Even worse, he realizes that the bombers among which he is flying are aiming at a target in the dead centre of which sleeps ... Vidi! Plummeting from the sky, dodging and racing with the bombs, he saves his pal in the nick of time.

The last we see of the two is when Vidi is – hurrah! – catching up on his beauty sleep having solved Monte's problem once and for all: he has tied the pelican to the central pole of the lighthouse so that, even if he does go sleepflying, he cannot go far enough to get into any trouble.

Or so one hopes. Tomorrow Vidi is going to have one very dizzy pelican to deal with . . .

AJAX THE GORILLA

Once upon a time in 1944, as recorded in *Donald Duck and the Gorilla*, Donald Duck (➤61) and the Nephews (➤86) receive a newsflash that a gorilla – Ajax – has escaped from a nearby zoo and is on the rampage. The Nephews are terrified and Don teases them with various tricks using mock-gorilla hands; they respond, as he might have anticipated, by dressing up in a gorilla costume and terrifying him, in turn.

Then, however, the real Ajax is seen outside the window and very soon afterwards he is in the house. Don, of course, reckons that this big shambling figure is merely the Nephews in disguise – he starts to realize his appalling error when he spots the disguised Nephews simultaneously with Ajax, but he still cannot quite believe his evil luck: "Oh, *boys!*" he shouts despairingly down the gorilla's throat. There is no response from that gaping pink canyon. Oh, dear: poor Donald.

Just then the radio cheerily tells the world that the way to conquer wild animals is to stare them straight in the eyes. Don gives it a try, but all he sees in Ajax's eyes is the image of a gravestone inscribed: "Here Lies a Dead Duck." This vision fails to reassure him.

After various chases the Nephews hear a further radio bulletin, that the way of mastering gorillas is none of this subtle

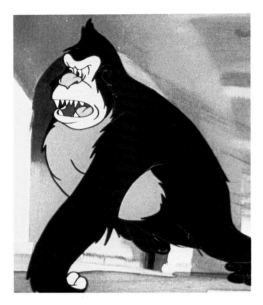

Ajax gave Donald and the Nephews a nasty time of it in *Donald Duck and the Gorilla* (1944).

stuff: use tear-gas. Seizing a handy nearby canister of tear-gas (well, you never know when a canister of tear-gas might come in useful around the home!) they throw it at the tussling duo of Ajax and the Duck. This ruse works ... too well. The last we see of the pair of them is that they are blubbing uncontrollably together, expressing mutual sympathy.

Ajax is a far from evil character: despite the fact that he is intent on crunching Donald and the Nephews, he has a certain genial good nature that suggests that in other circumstances they might all have been the best of friends. In this sense the character of Ajax accords with the reality of gorilla nature – which is interesting because, back in 1944, it was still popularly assumed that gorillas were violent, vicious creatures. Disney prescience or just the exigencies of plot? Who can tell?

THE SPIRIT OF SPRING

The Spirit of Spring makes his sole appearance in a 1944 Pluto short called *Springtime for Pluto*. The plot of the short is of little interest in our present context; it involves a narration about the joys of Spring contrasted with Pluto having on-screen a miserable time – much as in the Goofy "how to" shorts (►48).

The Spirit of Spring, in this short, is a flute-playing Pan-like figure, whose music causes the plants virtually to leap from the soil – for example, Pluto is awoken from his initial slumbers by a clump of mushrooms bursting forth from the ground to wallop him under the chin. The movie ends with the Spirit of Spring merrily piping on his flute as the narrator tells us how wonderful Spring is. Pluto, suffering from the effects of

multiple bee-stings and an excursion into a patch of poison ivy, quite naturally chases the cheery Spirit of Spring from the screen.

DOLORES

Dolores, the cheerful little elephant (well, she's little for an elephant), appeared three times between 1945 and 1953. Podgy and grey-green, with a smile never too far from her lips, she bears little resemblance to the average behemoth of the African plains. In two of her shorts she interacted with Goofy and in the third with Donald – obviously in both cases her role was a subsidiary one, but if there were an award for "best supporting actress" in the Disney canon she might well be worth considering.

Tiger Trouble (1945) saw her and the Goof far from the circus and zoo that she was later to occupy (perhaps he brought her into captivity – who knows?). With Goofy precariously perched on Dolores' howdah, the two of them set off on a tiger hunt – which is, of course, doomed to disaster. As they are eating their lunch a tiger approaches, and there are various "cat and mouse" gags of the type that Goofy often encountered in his experiences with the Mountain Lion (►111). Finally there is the inevitable chase, which ends with things in such confusion that Goofy is carrying Dolores – who has the tiger's stripes on her rear!

Three years later, by the time of *The Big Wash* (1948), Dolores had made the transition from Africa to a circus in the USA. But this is not to say that she has escaped from the Goof's clumsily tender mercies. No such luck: he is her attendant, and his job today is to give her a bath. Dolores, as you might expect, does not particularly want to

have a bath, and she does everything in her powers to dodge the experience. Her manoeuvres even include dressing up as one of the most unlikely clowns ever to be seen on screen. Goofy, soaked from head to foot because she naturally takes every opportunity to drench him, suffers his final indignity when the soap gets into her trunk and makes her sneeze. The force of this gargantuan blast is enough to rocket him off his feet and into a mud-puddle.

Clearly Goofy decided that enough was enough, because in Dolores' third and final outing (in the 1953 short *Working for Peanuts*) she acts as an all too rare ally of Donald Duck in his relentless war of attrition with Chip an' Dale (►96). This is almost certainly her funniest performance.

Donald is her keeper at the zoo; the chips are intent on poaching as many as possible of the peanuts thrown to the animals. Dolores, for her part, has something of an

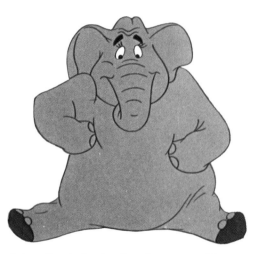

Dolores the elephant easily outmanoeuvred the Goof in *The Big Wash* (1948).

The playful Spirit of Spring in *Springtime for Pluto* (1944).

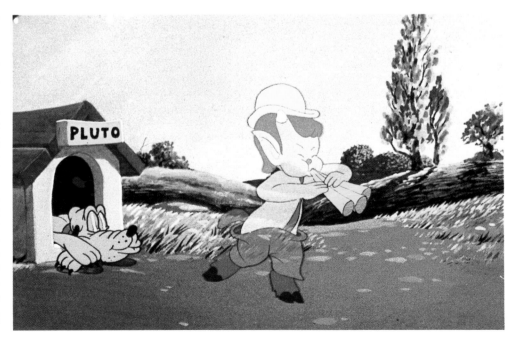

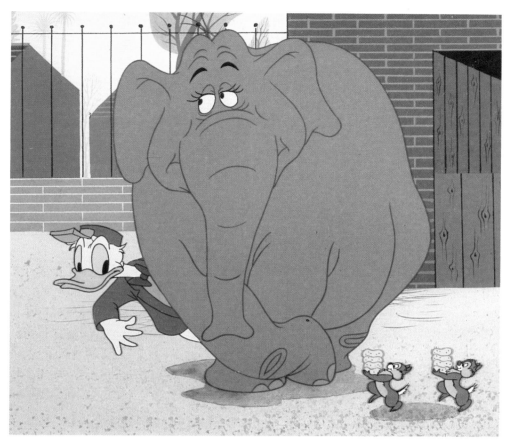

In *Working for Peanuts* (1953) Dolores became one of Donald's few allies in his long career.

advantage over the other zoo animals because she can use her trunk like a vacuum cleaner to hoover up peanuts in their millions. Her trunk, in fact, is a versatile organ, because she can screw it up into a helix for use as a corkscrew or, at Donald's instigation, fire through it volleys of peanuts with all the accuracy and rate of fire of a submachine-gun.

Dolores is an active assistant to Donald in his attempts to expel the two little scroungers from the zoo, using fair means or foul. Towards the end of the short, when the chips have hit upon the stratagem of dunking themselves in whitewash so that they appear to be rare albino chipmunks, and therefore acceptable as zoo exhibits in their own right, it is Dolores who summons the Duck on spotting that Dale has accidentally washed the white off his lower half. But for once Dale is quick-witted, claiming to be an albino wearing brown trousers and tracing with his fingers through the whitewash a couple of lines to resemble braces. This is enough to convince Don, although Dolores wants to take matters further. The issue is settled, though, when Dale snaps the "braces" against his chest – to Chip's incredulity. Now how on earth did he do *that*?

Dolores was a character of considerable appeal, although perhaps she was too bland ever to contemplate taking the step into the front line of the Disney personalities. Besides, by the time she appeared it was too late for such bids for stardom: the day of the

animated short – at least as a commercial enterprise – was drawing to its close.

Filmography

> *Tiger Trouble*, 1945
> *The Big Wash*, 1948
> *Working for Peanuts*, 1953

CARELESS CHARLIE

This character featured in a couple of the animated shorts that the Disney company made for the Coordinator of Inter-American Affairs.

The first was *Hookworm* (1945). Here Charlie suffers from the disease and infects the rest of his family because of his bad habit of defecating in the cornfields, so that the intestinal parasites are conveyed *via* the ground and his bare feet into the home. However, he has the good sense to go with his family to the clinic where they are treated with the appropriate pills. He builds a latrine, and his family take to wearing shoes. Now he is known as "Careful Charlie".

In *Planning for Good Eating* (1946) Charlie and his family go through much the same sort of ordeal. This time they have poor health, low resistance to disease, and general lassitude – because their diet is bad. However, Charlie sees the light and starts including fruit, vegetables and so forth in the family diet, and once again he becomes known as "Careful Charlie".

Filmography

> *Hookworm*, June 30, 1945
> *Planning for Good Eating*, 1946

JOHNNY CARELESS AND TOMMY CLEAN

Cleanliness Brings Health (1945) was one of the animated shorts the Disney company made for the Coordinator of Inter-American Affairs. Obviously aimed at Latin America, it was part of the attempt to persuade unsophisticated farming peoples to build and use latrines rather than to continue the old tradition of defecating in the fields. The plot is simple. The Careless Family are traditionalists, so that little **Johnny Careless'** attack of gastro-enteritis (or worse) is passed along to his father, who is consequently unable to work. Little **Tommy Clean**, on the other hand, makes enthusiastic use of the earth-latrine his father has built, and so his family stays healthy. "Always remember," we are told: "Cleanliness brings health and happiness."

JOE BURNS, JOHN SMITH, BILL JONES AND JOHNNY JONES

Burns, Smith and the Joneses feature in a member of the series of animated shorts made under the overall title "Health for the Americas" by Disney for the Coordinator of Inter-American Affairs. In *How Disease Travels* (1945), however, the real central character is "you" – in other words, the viewer to whom the narrator directs his argument.

Joe Burns, a farmer who lives some distance from you, is suffering from an intestinal infection. How does this infection reach you? Well, what happens is that Joe, as is his normal habit, defecates in his fields and then the rain washes his bugs into the river; further downstream, you drink the river-water. Moreover, flies breed on Joe's faeces and then walk all over your food. The situation can only be improved by Joe building a latrine – or, since his illness is a debilitating one, having a latrine built for him.

But disease lurks elsewhere. For example, **John Smith**, who runs the local store, has a lung infection. Every time he coughs he scatters the relevant bugs all over everything and everybody, with the result that your wife, while doing the shopping, catches the ailment and passes it on to you and your son. To judge from the other shorts in the series you might expect that John Smith would be urged to cough only into a latrine; but in fact the message is that he should use a handkerchief *and* isolate himself in bed until the illness has cleared up.

103

Bill Jones' son Johnny has spots and has been put to bed. Your son goes to visit him and foolishly handles his skin and his clothing, and consequently is responsible for spreading the disease all over town. What the Joneses should do is to isolate Johnny in bed, allowing him no visitors except his mother, who should wash herself thoroughly with soap and water every time she has been in with him.

The stated moral of the film is: "To keep disease from travelling, it must be stopped at its source."

BENT-TAIL AND BENT-TAIL, JUNIOR

Bent-Tail the coyote first appeared in a 1945 short called *The Legend of Coyote Rock*; the other three shorts in which he appeared featured also his son, Bent-Tail, Junior.

Bent-Tail's adversary is Pluto (➤41) – not the Pluto who is Mickey's or Minnie's house-dog but a Pluto who is, albeit incompetently, master of a flock of sheep. That the two should come into conflict is inevitable, because if Bent-Tail has a weakness it is, as he puts it, for lamb chops "on the hoof".

In *The Legend of Coyote Rock* the most notable member of Pluto's flock is **Blackie**, the little black lamb. The wily coyote lures Pluto away from the corral and disguises himself as a sheep in order to lead all the lambs to a cave where he will be able to devour them at his leisure. Blackie, however, escapes, and when Bent-Tail pursues him he is suddenly confronted by a wrathful Pluto. Naturally there is a colossally violent chase which ends when

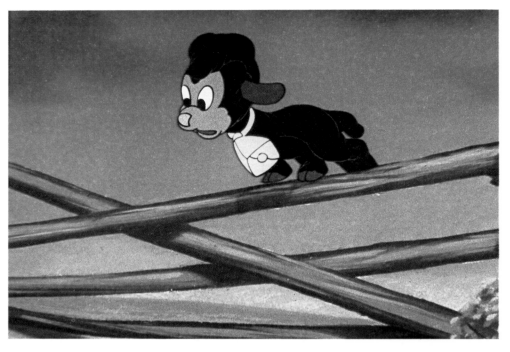

Blackie, the mischievous little lamb in *The Legend of Coyote Rock* (1945).

Bent-Tail falls off a rock pillar. The impact of his fall causes a landslide, and when the dust clears we find that the tumbling rocks have created a natural edifice that looks for all the world like a coyote squatting on its haunches.

Pluto herds all the lambs back into the corral except Blackie, who tells him tremulously that he has just seen the most enormous coyote. Pluto reassures him: it is only "Coyote Rock". Just then, though, Coyote Rock lets out a howl ...

Sheep Dog (1949), Bent-Tail's next movie, saw the introduction of his son, **Bent-Tail, Junior**. It is a reasonably routine comedy of

mistaken identities, with Pluto dressing up as a sheep and chasing Bent-Tail, Bent-Tail, Junior getting into the corral, and then Bent-Tail stealing what he thinks is a lamb but discovers to his chagrin is only Junior. *Pests of the West* (1950) has the two up to their thievery again, but this time Pluto is in charge of a hen-house; perhaps the gag-men felt they were running out of sheep jokes.

Bent-Tail's fourth and final short was *Camp Dog* (1950). This time Pluto has been left on guard by a group of campers, who have gone off to hunt, shoot and fish. Bent-Tail and Bent-Tail, Junior are drawn irresistibly by the ambient smell of food; unfortunately for their thieving aims, the younger coyote has got it into his head that the slumbering Pluto is a part of that food. His father, however, knows better: the food has been hung up over the branch of a tree. Various gags ensue with Bent-Tail being alternately raised and lowered in an impromptu pulley arrangement by his overenthusiastic son; but in due course the two of them have all the campers' food-supplies gathered together. Further gaggery follows as Bent-Tail, Junior tries to add Pluto to the heap of food and Bent-Tail himself tries to counter these moves.

At last the two coyotes have their picnic set out, but a now-wakened Pluto chases them off. The dog is tempted into taking a bite out of a ham himself; however, suddenly and ominously, he hears the tramping of the returning campers and realizes that it might just perhaps be a good idea if he, like the coyotes, were out of the picture. The short's last scene has Bent-Tail and his son howling on a rock: they are suddenly joined by a somewhat crestfallen Pluto, who produces a quite passable imitation of a coyote's howl.

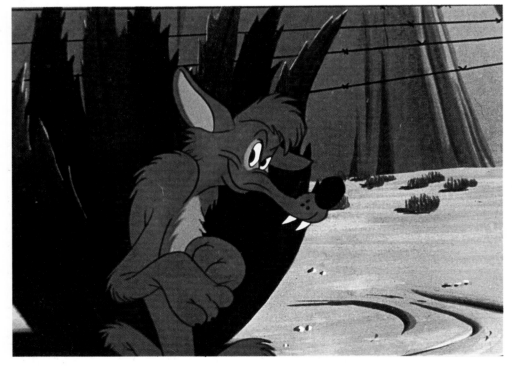

Bent-Tail, the coyote with a perpetual yearning for lamb chops "on the hoof", seen here in *Sheep Dog* (1949).

Some very close relatives of Bent-Tail and Bent-Tail, Junior appeared with Pluto in a television featurette (released theatrically outside the United States) called *The Coyote's Lament* (1968); these characters were **Pappy Coyote**, **Junior Coyote** and **Grandpappy Coyote**. Their role was much the same as those customarily adopted by Bent-Tail and his son.

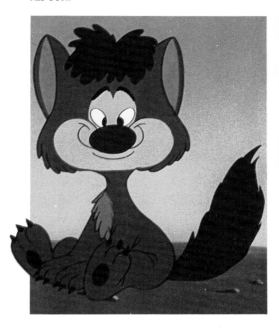

Bent-Tail, Junior, helped – or, rather, hindered – his papa in three shorts. Here he is in 1949's *Sheep Dog*.

Filmography

The Legend of Coyote Rock, August 24, 1945
Sheep Dog, 1949
Pests of the West, 1950
Camp Dog, 1950

Bent-Tail, Junior did not appear in *The Legend of Coyote Rock*. **Blackie** appeared only in *The Legend of Coyote Rock*.

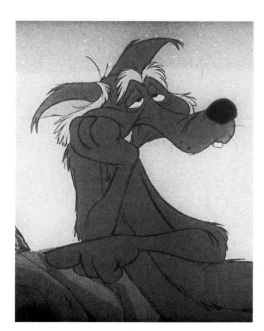

Grandpappy Coyote who ineptly assisted Pappy Coyote.

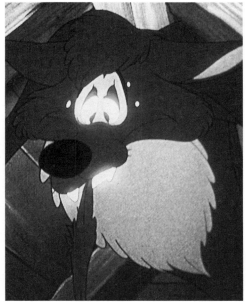

In the TV featurette *The Coyote's Lament* Pappy Coyote took on Bent-Tail's role in the theatrical shorts.

LUCIFER

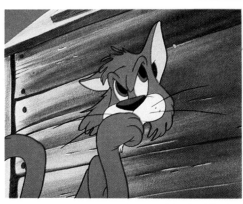

Tough guy Lucifer, from *Pluto's Kid Brother* (1946).

The tough alley-cat Lucifer made his appearance in *Pluto's Kid Brother* (1946), as did the eponymous **Pluto's Kid Brother** – who unsurprisingly strongly resembles Pluto, Junior (➤93). Lucifer was not to appear again, although of course there is a cat called Lucifer in the 1950 feature *Cinderella* (➤236).

Pluto (➤38) is doing his best to have a siesta, but his kid brother keeps causing trouble – even when Pluto ties him up he manages to escape. He picks a fight with Lucifer who chases him home and, when Pluto attempts to intercede, chases Pluto as well. However, as Lucifer triumphantly leaves he encounters Butch (➤91), who is too much for the cat to handle. Exit cat, rapidly. The kid brother, impressed by Butch's toughness, follows him into a life of crime – stealing wieners from a nearby butcher – and is extracted by Pluto from this and from the clutches of the dog-catcher only with the greatest of difficulty. In the end Pluto embarrassedly shares the purloined wieners with his brother.

RONNIE

A cuddly little Saint Bernard puppy, Ronnie made his first appearance in the 1946 Pluto short *The Purloined Pup*. As we see from a newspaper page, he is a kidnap victim, Butch (➤92) is the suspected culprit, and Pluto is the rookie cop sent to track them down. In this Pluto succeeds, locating Ronnie tied up in an old mansion, the grounds of which are being used as a pipe-storage yard. Butch is on guard, but Pluto sneaks by and after several attempts unties Ronnie. This so excites the puppy that he begins to bark, attracting Butch's attention: no prizes for guessing that a chase ensues, with many gags centred on the multitude of stacked pipes. Finally Butch is so well beaten that he is taken by Pluto and Ronnie off to the local jail.

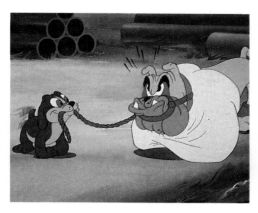

Ronnie and Butch in *The Purloined Pup* (1946).

Ronnie reappeared – albeit with somewhat different coloration – in 1949 in *Pueblo Pluto*, a short set in Latin America, in which Ronnie and Pluto are rivals for a bone given to Pluto by Mickey. After an extended chase Pluto recovers his bone but finds himself trapped in a thick clump of cacti. Ronnie helps him out of his predicament and the two dogs agree to share the bone.

Filmography

The Purloined Pup , July 19, 1946
Pueblo Pluto, 1949

SUSIE

In the 1946 Donald Duck short *Wet Paint* we encounter a determined mother bird called Susie. When a long piece of string she is carrying back to use in her nest snags onto the radiator of a parked car, she is not to know that it is Don's roadster, which he has just finished repainting, and that it is therefore an unwise ploy to swoop down and walk all over the car while untangling the string. Don takes this philosophically – the philosopher of his eventual choice being Genghis Khan. There follows a series of fine visual gags, each of which results in further damage to Don's paintwork and in due

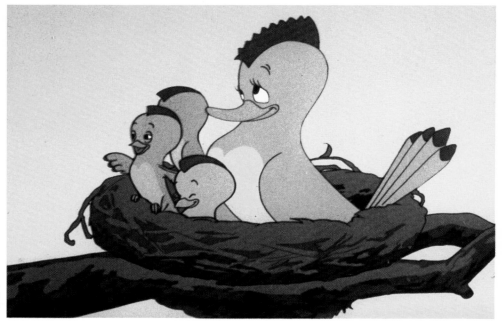

Susie, the mother bird, with three of her chicks in the 1946 short *Wet Paint*.

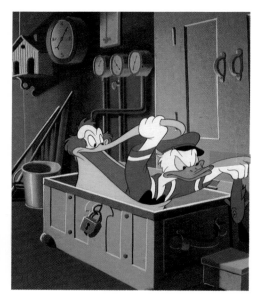

Marblehead the Pelican gave Don a few problems in *Lighthouse Keeping* (1946).

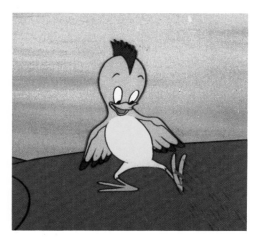

This little chick, Johnnie, successfully appealed to Donald's better nature in *Wet Paint* (1946).

course to the roadster itself. At one point Susie pulls a thread from his upholstery and, as she flies off, unleashes the filling, which covers the auto so that it looks like an Old English sheepdog; Donald has to produce a razor and shave the car back to some semblance of normalcy.

Finally, armed with an axe, Don has Susie trapped in a tree and is about to perform murder. Just then, however, her chicks – including a captivating little fellow called **Johnnie** – appear and Donald's heart for once melts.

MARBLEHEAD

Marblehead the pelican is one of the string of birds with which Donald Duck has had to contend; he appeared in the 1946 short *Lighthouse Keeping*.

Don is a lighthouse-keeper. We first see him attempting to read by the intermittent glare as his beacon swings around; he tries

to solve the problem by attaching his chair to the light's mechanism, so that he swings around with it, but this proves foolhardy. Deprived of reading as an occupation, Donald instinctively turns to practical joking instead, deliberately shining the light into the eyes of a pelican, Marblehead, sleeping on a nearby rock. The remainder of the short is taken up with Marblehead attempting to blow out the light and Don trying to keep it shining, and there are chases a-plenty all over the lighthouse. In a couple of instances Don even finds himself trapped in Marblehead's bill! The film ends

A surprise encounter. Pluto did battle with Salty the brandy-loving seal in the 1947 short *Rescue Dog*.

with the dawn, although Don and Marblehead, despite the fact that it no longer matters whether or not the light is blazing, continue their contest ... perhaps forever?

SALTY

By 1947 Pluto must have been threatening to go on strike. Short after short pitched him against a succession of other animals and, while happy endings were obligatory, Pluto generally received a fair deal of physical punishment before they came. In 1947's *Rescue Dog* his foe was a seal called Salty.

Pluto is working as a rescue dog, complete with keg of brandy slung around

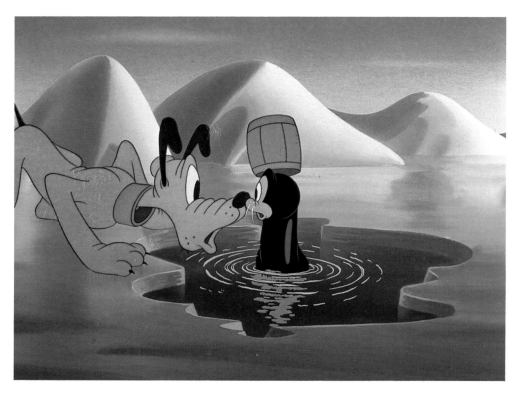

his neck, when he meets with Salty, who wants to play with him and especially with the keg. Pluto angrily snatches it back from him; Salty succeeds in recapturing it; Pluto reclaims it; and so on, several times over. In the end, Salty has it, and there is a great chase which culminates in Pluto falling off a cliff and through the frozen surface of a lake below. In his panic, he cannot find the hole through which to climb out, but luckily Salty has spotted his predicament and finally succeeds in hauling a lifeless Pluto out onto the ice. Thanks to the administration of draughts of brandy, the seal succeeds in reviving the dog and Pluto, realizing that his life has just been saved, gratefully clips the brandy keg around the seal's neck.

FRANKIE

Minnie's little cage-bird Frankie made only a single appearance, in the short *Figaro and Frankie* (1947). The wise money must be on the theory that it was Figaro's responsibility that Frankie never appeared again.

For in the short *Figaro* (➤90) is determined to have Frankie for supper. The first time he makes an assault on Frankie's high cage the little bird spits birdseed at him with machine-gun-like ferocity and accuracy; the second time he tries to scale the cage's pole Minnie catches him and threatens that, should he ever go near the cage again, she will beat him with the broomstick. To add injury to insult, as Figaro stalks off (if his movements could ever be described as stalking!) Frankie once more bombards him with birdseed.

His third attempt, inspired by this attack, results in his knocking the cage over and

stunning himself; indeed, when Minnie arrives on the scene she finds him lying half inside the cage and with a yellow feather guiltily protruding from his mouth. "Figaro – you *fiend!*" she cries, and as promised she goes for him with the broom, chasing him out of the house and telling him never to darken her door again.

Has Figaro indeed guzzled Frankie? No – as we soon discover when we are shown the little bird on the windowsill, hiding behind the curtain. But Frankie is not out of danger yet. He sees some distant gulls flying and decides that he would like to swoop and soar like them. Stepping off the sill he flaps his meagre wings enthusiastically, but all that happens is that he sinks slowly to the ground – which is a pity, because Figaro is waiting with lip-licking relish beneath.

Temporary help is at hand, though, in the unlikely form of Butch (➤91). When he arrives Figaro flees precipitately up the wall to seek the protection of the windowsill, passing Frankie, who is still on the way down. And down, down Frankie drifts, until he comes to rest on Butch's nose.

This is not the easiest of situations for the average cage-bird to be in, for Butch on the ground would like to gobble him and Figaro on the sill would be only too glad to do likewise. Flapping his wings with a new desperation Frankie goes up and down like a yoyo between his Scylla and Charybdis. This could go on forever – but then an Angel-Figaro appears and, on the third attempt (but *only* on the third attempt, mind you), succeeds in persuading the little cat to give him a hearing. Finally Figaro has pity on the bird, drops a flowerpot on Butch's head, is gushingly congratulated by Minnie for having saved the canary's life, is

readmitted to the home, and then, poor kitten, is forced to kiss Frankie and make up.

Figaro goes through with this touching reconciliation, but a certain gleam in his eyes tells you that Frankie is being a trifle premature in his exultant celebrations of the new friendship.

One point of interest is the profound difference between Frankie and virtually every other cage-bird playing a similar role in animated cartoons – Tweety Pie is the obvious example. Whereas Tweety Pie and the rest are almost always youthful in a rather goofily appealing way – i.e., they are chicks rather than adult birds – Frankie has white feathers around his mouth which give the definite impression of maturity. Yet, as with the others, his song is that of a shy young creature. Well, perhaps not so shy …

BOOTLE BEETLE

If they were small, and especially if they were insects, they inevitably became the foes of Donald Duck (➤61). Bootle Beetle, who first appeared in the short *Bootle Beetle* (1947), carried on the great tradition. Voiced by Dink Trout, the little coleopteran got his name thanks to Jack Hannah, who directed the original short *Bootle Beetle* (1947). Hannah's wife knew of a racehorse in Pomona called "Beetle Bootle", and so he merely switched the two names around.

Of the four shorts he made, the first, *Bootle Beetle*, is probably the best known. The elderly Bootle is telling the younger **Ezra Beetle** of the ills of running away and recalls the story of his own youth, which seems mainly to have been occupied by chases between himself and Don. Nowadays, although Bootle is an old man, so is Donald – and an elderly Duck is still chasing him. He is still reminiscing in *Sea Salts* (1949), this time about the time he and Donald were shipwrecked. Of their surviving provisions Donald always seems to get the best ration but somehow this does not disrupt the friendship of the two.

His third outing was in the short *The Greener Yard* (1949). Yet again he is reminiscing to Ezra. Once upon a time, he tells the little beetle as the two of them survey Donald's yard over the fence, he took the risk of plundering that yard for food. However, all that happened was that he was chased by Donald and nearly lost his life. He tells this story so dramatically (with flashbacks to the real action) that young Ezra is content to stick with the meal he has in front of him rather than trying for the delights on the other side of the fence.

Bootle Beetle's career never really got off the ground. Somehow he was not really enough of a personality to make it to the top – although, in contradiction to that, it should be pointed out that Buzz-Buzz

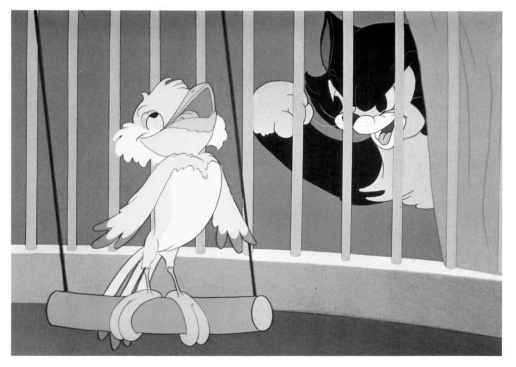

Frankie the cage-bird survived the attentions of Figaro and, later, Butch in *Figaro and Frankie* (1947).

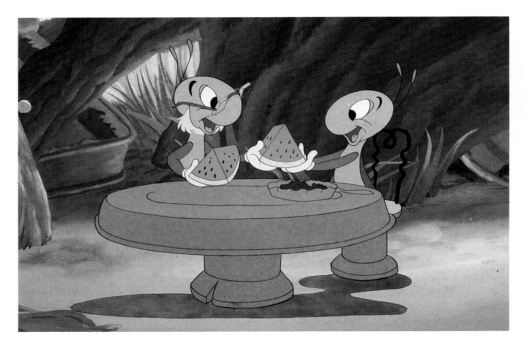

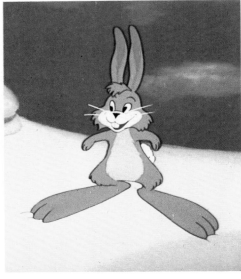

Flutter Foot the snowshoe rabbit wanted only warmth from Pluto in *Mail Dog* (1947).

Bootle Beetle *(left)* and Ezra Beetle in *The Greener Yard* (1949).

(►110), who has virtually no personality except a venomous desire to use his sting, did much better for himself.

Filmography

Bootle Beetle, August, 1947
Sea Salts, 1949
The Greener Yard, 1949
Morris, the Midget Moose, 1950
Ezra Beetle appeared only in *Bootle Beetle* (August, 1947) and *The Greener Yard* (1949).

FLUTTER FOOT

The snowshoe rabbit Flutter Foot has one aim in life: to keep warm. Pluto, unfortunately for himself, is the solitary source of warmth in the snowy wastes of the north as he battles through foul weather to take the mail by toboggan to Quagmire Airport in *Mail Dog* (1947). Flutter Foot locates Pluto and rushes up to snuggle against him – something which infuriates

the dog, who chases him off. They end up fighting and thereby launch the toboggan, with Pluto aboard, on a nightmare downhill helter-skelter. Flutter Foot, rather than dodge the rapidly moving toboggan, goes into a skiing action. Unwittingly the two arrive at Quagmire Airport, and Pluto is on time with the mail. As the mailplane departs with its cargo, he and Flutter Foot demonstrate their new-found affection.

SNAPSHOT III

Snapshot III is a racehorse who features in one of the Goofy shorts in which most of the parts are played by different versions of the versatile Goof himself (►49). The short in question is *They're Off* (1948), and it stars also an aging bag of bones of a racehorse called **Old Moe**. The two of them take the parts of Max and Toby, respectively, in what is in essence a reworking of *The Tortoise and the Hare* (1935 [►73]).

Goofy's enthusiasm this time around is for horse-racing, and we see a confident-looking clone of him studying the form of Snapshot III while the narrator tells us that "horses of this line have been noted for their burning speed, and also are noted as *camera muggers*". The confident Goof puts his wad on Snapshot III, while a milksop clone, who has operated on the eeny-meeny-minie-mo system, places his bet on Old Moe.

As in *The Tortoise and the Hare* the hot favourite is too confident of success: he does not bother to start until long after the others have gone; and, once he has rocketed into the lead, he loses it again because he pauses to have his photograph taken. However, once again he is easily able to burst through the pack and into the lead – except this time Old Moe (whose jockey stays boredly emotionless throughout all this!) comes with him. They cross the line in a photo finish – which, it is discovered, Old Moe

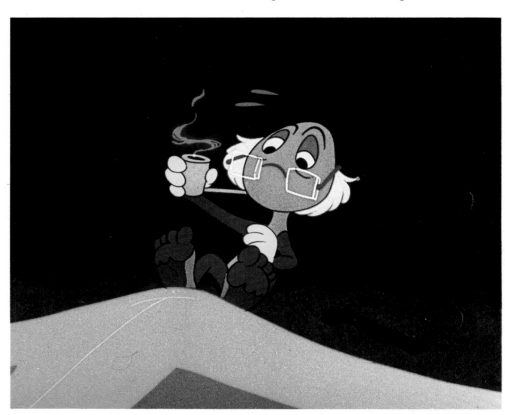

Bootle Beetle in *Sea Salts* (1949). Although Bootle was a constant rival of Donald Duck, there was also a certain curious affection between the two.

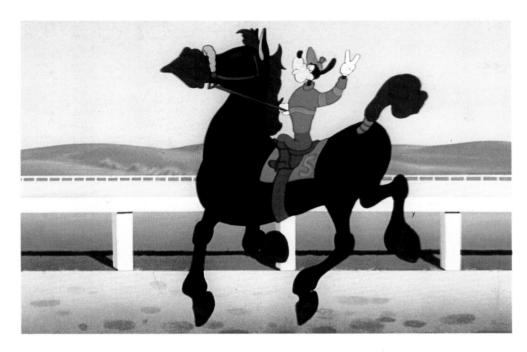

which he loathes because of Mickey's habit of playfully "buzzing" him with it; the dog ends up with the offending implement jammed immovably in his jaws. Mickey is hunting for the dog when he comes across a huge egg. He is just about to pick this up when the egg's mother, Esther, appears. Mickey flees and she gives chase, but fortuitously Pluto, still struggling with the boomerang, staggers into her path and she is left in a tangle. Pluto sails on to bump into Mickey, who falls on him and thereby shoots the boomerang forcibly from his mouth. We last see the two troublemakers running from the forest with the boomerang swooping in hot pursuit.

JOEY

Donald Duck's encounters with other members of the animal kingdom have rarely been happy ones, and his adoption of Joey, a baby kangaroo, in *Daddy Duck* (1948), provides no exception to the rule. Joey is trouble from the word "go", both because he is mischievous and because he is excitable: his initial act on reaching Don's home is to bounce uncontrollably all over the front room, in the process wrecking it. Not long after, Donald receives a phonecall from the orphanage reminding him that it is Joey's bath-time. However, bathing Joey proves easier said than done: inevitably, it is Donald who ends up in the bath. Just then, the phone goes again and, while Don is speaking into it, Joey explores. This time he is terrified when he comes face to face with a bear rug. Donald, to reassure him (and perhaps to show off a little, too), wrestles with the "bear" but goes a little too far when

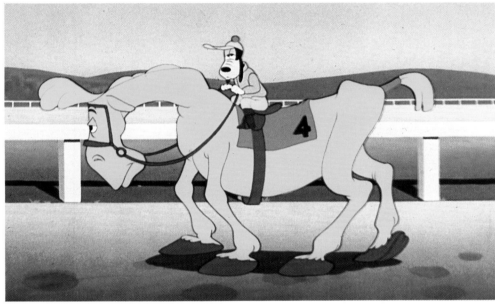

A little contretemps between Esther the emu and Mickey in *Mickey Down Under* (1948).

Snapshot III *(top)*, the proudest racehorse in cinematic history, loved to look good for the cameras: a still from *They're Off* (1948).

Old Moe *(above)*, the beat-up nag, won the race in *They're Off*.

has just won thanks to Snapshot III having been unable to resist turning so as to offer his best profile for the judges' camera.

We leave the confident Goofy tearing up his tickets and out his hair and the milquetoast version counting his cash.

ESTHER

Esther the emu gave her solitary performance in 1948's *Mickey Down Under*. Pluto and Mickey are unfortunate enough to encounter this big tough inhabitant of the Australian rain forest while, one assumes, they are on holiday. Pluto is fighting a losing battle with Mickey's boomerang,

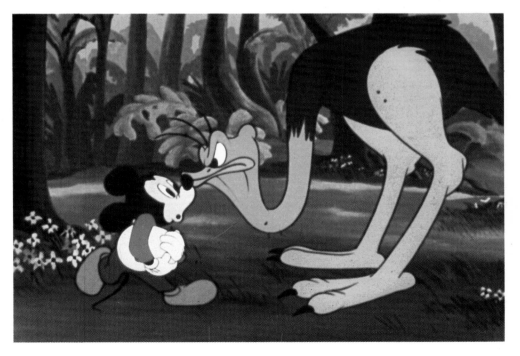

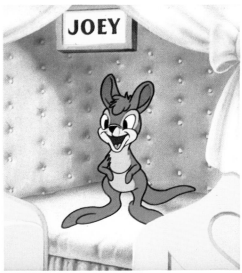

Donald Duck encountered Joey the baby kangaroo in *Daddy Duck* (1948).

he accidentally works himself inside it. Joey bounces up and down with all his might on the monster he assumes has swallowed his adoptive father. Don is finally hammered out of the rug and into a cradle, where we last see him and Joey grinning happily in the realization that their adventure is over.

BUZZ-BUZZ/SPIKE

There is some debate as to whether Donald has been plagued by two major bee characters or by only one with two names. It is certain that the bee who appeared in *Bee on Guard* (1951) was called Buzz-Buzz; a bee antagonized Donald in six other shorts, and this bee has often been called Spike. The two bees are, to this eye at least, hard to tell apart; it is possible that any perceived differences may be simply a result of different artists working at different times. In this discussion it will there-

> I know we did go to smaller characters with the Duck because it would make it funnier when the situation backfired on him. This was one of the reasons Chip 'n' Dale [►96] were created [in fact, it wasn't] ... we usually found a little person that could talk. For instance, there was a Bootle Beetle [►107] and we gave him a voice

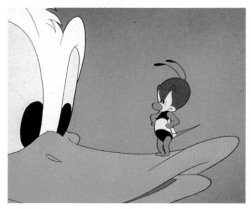

Buzz-Buzz/Spike the bee first met Donald in *Inferior Decorator* (1948).

fore be assumed for the sake of brevity that the two are one.

In an interview with Jim Korkis in *Mindrot* in 1978 Jack Hannah, the doyen of Duck directors, confessed that he did not know why the team had used bees so often as Donald Duck's adversaries. His personal hunch was that "the bee is a menace with that stinger as a weapon and is much smaller than the Duck so it would be funny having the little guy battling a big bully". This matter of littleness was very important;

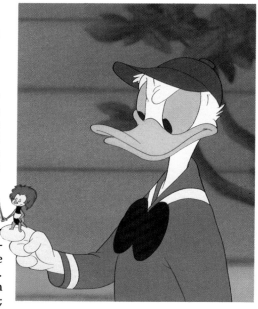

In *Slide, Donald, Slide* (1949) the Duck and Buzz-Buzz/Spike "debated" about the channel to which the radio should be tuned.

All's well at the hive, for the moment. A still from *Bee on Guard* (1951).

you could understand. You'll notice he was much smaller than Donald.

Hannah also remarked: "You can get a funny sound effect out of a bee. They can cuss you out with that little bee noise." Buzz-Buzz/Spike, however, was a "little person" who could *not* talk.

A predecessor of Buzz-Buzz/Spike had appeared as early as 1935 in *The Band Concert* (►63); in fact, this bee was responsible for much of the chaos that came to reign. Its opening gambit is to fly into Donald's flute. Once he has got it out of there, battle is inescapable. The concert is adversely affected when the bee hovers around conductor Mickey's head: an ice-cream hurled at about Mach 3 at the obnoxious insect by Donald sadly fails to hit it and instead impacts on the Mouse. The bee further complicates matters as Mickey vainly tries to swat it with his baton: the unfortunate band-members do their best to accord with their frenzied conductor's gesticulations, to dire effect.

Buzz-Buzz/Spike first appeared in an encounter with Donald called *Inferior Decorator* (1948). This is a reasonably standard Duck short of the time: hysterically funny and frenetically fast-moving, but perhaps a little "formula". Don is hanging wallpaper, and the bee, fooled by the flowers on it, tries to land on one of them. After getting well and truly stuck in the paste the bee does his best to sting Donald and, failing on his own, calls in the rest of the swarm to help him out.

Pluto was his adversary in his next movie, *Bubble Bee* (1949). Here Pluto spots a bubblegum machine and, naturally, wants some; however, also naturally, he lacks the wherewithal to put in the slot. But then he notices a bee – Buzz-Buzz/Spike – who is small enough to creep into the machine and steal a ball. Pluto follows the bee back to his hive and finds that it is bulgingly full of bubblegum balls. When Buzz-Buzz/Spike has zoomed back to the machine for

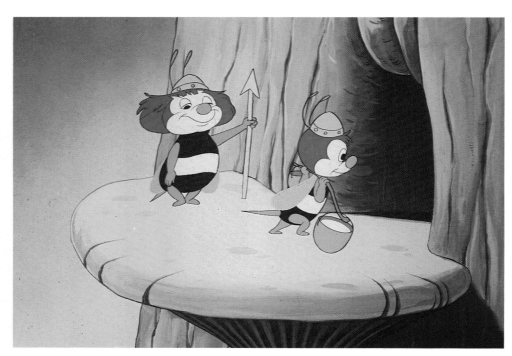

further supplies Pluto smashes open the hive and eats bubblegum balls by the billion. The irate bee tracks down the thief and, after various gags involving bubbles of gum floating around like helium-filled balloons with angry insects buzzing frustratedly inside them, succeeds in stinging Pluto in the predictable region.

The little bee was beginning to emerge as a definite character, despite the confusion concerning his name (among the others used were Claudius and Hector), and he spent a number of shorts making Donald's life a misery. In *Honey Harvester* (1949) he stores honey in a car radiator and stabs Don with a cactus spine when he tries to steal the honey. In *Slide, Donald, Slide* (1949) the bee and Donald have a dispute over which channel the radio should be turned to – music (the bee) or baseball (Donald); guess who wins. *Bee at the Beach* (1950) sees the pair of them at the seaside, with Donald happily abusing Buzz-Buzz/Spike; the bee wins in the end by unscrewing a valve on Donald's inflatable raft so that it goes jetting off into a crowd of sharks. *Bee on Guard* (1951) sees a fairly standard dispute between them over the rights of possession of the hive's honey; as always the bee wins the fight. Rather different is the final bee short, *Let's Stick Together* (1952), for it has the bee reminiscing with Donald about old times and the many scrapes they have got into together; it is very interesting that this obvious retrospective should appear so abruptly, and at a time when the bee's career looked to be highly successful – as if, indeed, he were all set to become a regular fixture in Duck movies in perpetuity. One can only assume that Disney had been overestimating his popularity.

Filmography

Inferior Decorator, August 27, 1948
Bubble Bee, 1949
Honey Harvester, 1949
Slide, Donald, Slide, 1949
Bee at the Beach, 1950
Bee on Guard, 1951
Let's Stick Together, 1952

ORVILLE

Orville the baby bird made a single appearance in a Pluto (►38) short called *Pluto's Fledgling* in 1948. A little red chick, he captures our hearts through his youthful goofy inability to do anything right: how well matched he is, in that respect, to Pluto!

The short starts with Orville trying to fly but instead landing in Pluto's drinking bowl; he returns to his nest with difficulty. His second attempt to conquer the air lands him on Pluto's nose, and he explains the dire problem to the initially dubious dog. But Pluto is nothing if not big-hearted: he takes it upon himself to teach the chick the art of flight. He tries various means – such as making Orville cling onto his tail while he

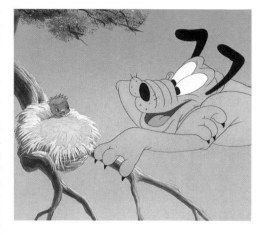

Orville and his chum Pluto in *Pluto's Fledgling* (1948).

runs along at great speed, trying to give him a glider-type launch – but the most successful is when Pluto stretches an old inner tube between the gateposts and launches Orville catapult-fashion. It is just a pity that Pluto launches himself at the same time . . .

After various improbable aerial encounters Pluto lands with a crunch in front of his own kennel. Orville, for his part, arrives to show Pluto that he now really truly has learned to genuinely fly: very impressive.

Pluto responds with a grin of happiness that his little pal has succeeded – or might it be that he is grinning purely because now he can hope for an undisturbed sleep?

MOUNTAIN LION

The Mountain Lion, sometimes known as Louie, appeared initially in the short *Lion Around* (1950), a film in which Donald and the Nephews (►85) interacted in usual violent fashion. He appeared in four other shorts, yet he was ever to remain a rather anonymous character: this, indeed, was his strength, for it was as a mysterious lurking presence that he had his greatest effect.

His finest performance – and yet his most humiliating – was probably in a Goofy short called *Father's Lion* (1952). Goofy, on this occasion acting under the pseudonym G. G. Geef, is as ever boasting to Goofy, Junior, as they head off on a hunting expedition; while they drive along Goofy tells his son exaggerated tales of his own past bravery, creating an effect which is only 100 per cent marred when, at a sudden noise, the Goof leaps into his son's lap: the car's back tyre has blown out.

In due course, though, they decide to set up camp and do a bit of practice shooting. Alas, they pitch their camp directly beneath the tree in which the Mountain Lion is sitting, and when Goofy unwittingly ties up their joint of meat on what he thinks is a dangling vine but which is in fact the Mountain Lion's tail the latter, unable to believe his luck, hoists up the generous joint and throws back down the stripped bone.

Junior, by no means such a fool as his father (well, who could be?), spots this and asks the Goof what he would do were there to be, er, ferocious wild animals hiding up that tree. Goofy, not really looking at what he is doing, seizes a nearby "dangling vine" and demonstrates enthusiastically how he would take any wild animal, pull it down, rough it up, jump up and down on top of it and give it "the old heave-ho". Junior is

Goofy gives the Mountain Lion "the old heave-ho" in *Father's Lion* (1952).

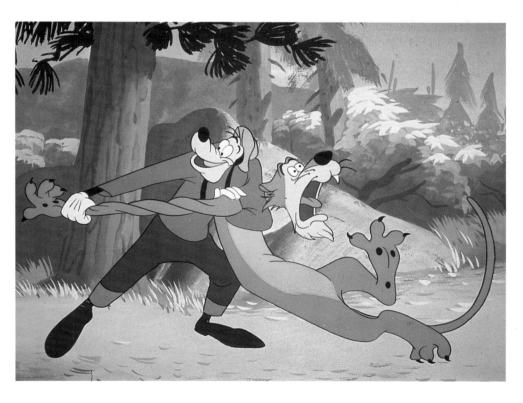

impressed; the Mountain Lion is bruisedly *de*pressed.

Various similar gags ensue, each time Goofy being quite unaware that he is thrashing the Mountain Lion. Junior demonstrates cheerfully that, in the absence of father's help, he can cope with the beast quite contentedly using his popgun. In the end, though, even the Goof realizes that they would be best to camp elsewhere, and they pack up their kit – including the Mountain Lion, now nestling in Goofy's sleeping bag. As it makes its bid for escape Goofy once again demonstrates what he'd do to any mountain lions that might be around, but this time the creature recovers from "the old heave-ho" and goes for the two. Junior's popgun slows it up just long enough for them to leap into the car and zoom off at top speed; and the Goof, who by this time should perhaps have known better, turns to Junior and says in a self-satisfied way: "Son, did I ever tell you about the time I was a race-driver? ..."

The Mountain Lion's other performances should not go unnoticed. In *Lion Around* (1950) the Nephews (➤86) dress up as a mountain lion in order to extract a pie from "Unca Donald"; he gets wise to their trick and chases them. Of course, when he catches them and starts spanking them he discovers that he has caught the wrong menace. In the same year's *Hook, Lion and Sinker* the Mountain Lion and his cub come off worse in their attempts to steal the fish Donald has caught. In his first short with the Goof, *Lion Down* (1951), the Mountain Lion competes with the amiable buffoon for a place in a hammock, and loses. And in *Grand Canyonscope* (1954) the Mountain Lion does battle with both Donald and the Ranger, J. Audubon Woodlore (➤120); after the three of them in a mad chase have succeeded in knocking over so many rock-pillars that the Grand Canyon is filled with rubble, the Ranger insists that the Mountain Lion and the Duck enter an uneasy working partnership in order to shovel out all the debris and restore the Canyon as a tourist site.

Grand Canyonscope might have signified the start of a great career for the Mountain Lion – it was the first time that he had really stepped out from behind his mask of anonymity – but for some reason it instead signified the end of the line. Nonetheless, there are echoes of him in various other Disney movies, notably in the form of Shere Khan, the tiger in *The Jungle Book* (1967 [➤280]), and in the beast which futilely stalks Wart and Merlin in *The Sword in the Stone* (1963 [➤270]).

Filmography

Lion Around, January 20, 1950
Hook, Lion and Sinker, 1950
Lion Down, 1951
Father's Lion, 1952
Grand Canyonscope, 1954

CASEY JONES

The tale of the 1950 short *The Brave Engineer* is one of determination to get the mail through on time, and thus has parallels with the story of Pedro (➤203). The brave messenger this time is not an airplane, however, but a railway engineer, Casey Jones. He leaves his station in hair-raising style and sets off for the West. Soon, alas, he encounters a flood, and this slows him up so much that he is eight hours behind schedule – an eight hours that he desperately tries to make up, despite obstacles such as bandits, a dynamited bridge and even a girl tied to the rails. These dealt with, he opens up the throttle to a terrifying extent: rivets pop and rails melt but Casey keeps pounding on ... until he crashes head-on into a slow-moving freight train.

At his destination station the station-master assumes that Casey is simply not coming, but just as he begins to erase Casey's name from the arrival board we hear a feeble toot, and around the corner comes Casey in the wreckage of his engine cab, clutching the mail bag and grinning broadly. He holds his watch up to the camera and we see written on its face: "On time ... almost."

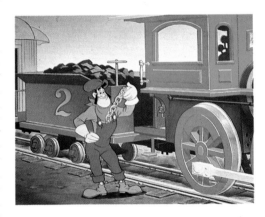

Casey Jones, aptly described in the title of 1950's *The Brave Engineer*.

PRIMO

Primo is the "primitive instinct" of Pluto (➤39); even so, he joins many other members of the animal kingdom in taking time out to make the poor pup's life a misery for a while – in 1950's *Primitive Pluto*. Primo is a little wolf who crawls out of Pluto's tail one night when the pup is sleeping in Mickey's hunting cabin. He tells Pluto he is his "primitive instinct" and exhorts him to go out into the wild and hunt for his food like a real dog. This Pluto does, accompanied by Primo, and they follow various animal tracks including – at Primo's unwise behest – a set of bear-tracks. On escaping from the bear which he has only-too-successfully tracked down, Pluto

scampers home – only to discover that Primo, declining to practise what he preaches, has snaffled all of the food Mickey left out for Pluto. The short ends with the enraged pup chasing Primo back into his tail: he has had enough of his vulpine heritage for one night.

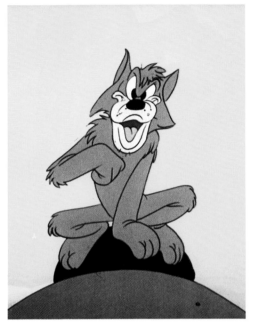

Primo, Pluto's vulpine "primitive instinct", appeared in *Primitive Pluto* (1950).

MILTON

Milton the cat first appears in the 1950 short *Puss-Café*, in which he and his pal **Richard** participate in a fairly standard Pluto story of the period. Pluto (➤38) is intent on having a peaceful siesta in his hammock; the cats are intent on relieving his yard of birds, milk and fishes from the fishpond. The fights and chases can be imagined, although for once Pluto is the outright winner of the contest.

Cold Turkey (1951), Milton's other movie, is more interesting. Now Milton is sharing the house with Pluto – it is surprising that Figaro (➤90) did not play this role – and the two are sleeping in front of the television. Milton is awakened by a commercial extolling the virtues of Lurkey's Turkeys, and he rouses Pluto to drool over the delicious turkey depicted on screen – they even reach into the back of the television set in an attempt to prise the luscious fowl out. When the advertiser tells them that there should be a Lurkey's Turkey in every kitchen, they rush into their own home's kitchen on the off-chance. And, indeed, there inside the freezer is a lovely frozen turkey. A fair amount of clowning follows, with the pair of them disputing ownership of the turkey and locking each other up inside the freezer. Finally Milton bolts with it into the back of the television set ... which Pluto sadistically switches back on. The heat is enough to send Milton racing back to the kitchen and into the sink to cool himself off.

Pluto thinks this is hilarious until he smells something burning. The turkey, left inside the television, is by now red-hot. At

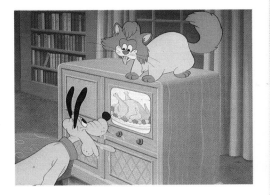
Milton the cat and Pluto demonstrate a Pavlovian response to a TV ad in *Cold Turkey* (1951).

last seeing the sense in acting in concert, the two drag it out and blow on it to cool it off. However, it has been reduced to a cinder. This, Pluto believes, is All Milton's Fault and, as the television commentator excitedly describes the action of a bloodthirsty wrestling match, we see Pluto and Milton furiously acting out the commentary.

Filmography

Puss-Café, 1950
Cold Turkey, 1951
Plutopia, 1951

HUMPHREY THE BEAR

Humphrey was to appear in a number of shorts as a friendly sort of grizzly, but in his debut role he was initially anything but. In fact, he was such a fierce (if eventually placable) beast that the archivists of the Disney company question whether he was the same character. However, he *looks* like Humphrey and, towards the end of the relevant short, he *acts* like Humphrey, too. For the sake of argument, the present writer has decided that indeed he is Humphrey. (Such problems are familiar to all students of the Disney characters!)

This first appearance was in *Hold That Pose* (1950), a Goofy "how to" cartoon (➤48) intended to show the joys of photography. After the Goof has been infected by the thrill of taking his own photographs we see him in the darkroom winding his film into his camera. In fact, we see exactly what happens as he keeps winding: various symbols of dubious nature appear on the orange background of the film and then – lo and behold! – the background colour shifts

to blue. How can this be? Easy enough: the Goof has unwittingly started winding his tie into the camera.

But his main objective is to get out there and photograph wildlife, and that is when he makes the acquaintance of a grizzly who has no real desire to be photographed: it is Humphrey, of course. Much of the short is taken up by a huge chase – Humphrey doing the chasing – until the pair end up not only in the Goof's apartment but actually in his darkroom. We hear all sorts of mayhem in progress behind that firmly locked door; but when it opens we find Goofy doing some earnest explaining to the bear. We discover what he has been talking about in the closing sequence of the short: there is Humphrey suavely selling signed photographs of himself to the eager tourists.

The bear could easily have been a one-off, but then he was taken up by the great Duck director Jack Hannah. Hannah recalled in a 1978 interview with Jim Korkis in *Mindrot* that

> For the sake of something new, we tried the Duck with a bear in *Rugged Bear* and it seemed like an immediate success for them to play against each other. At the time we had not named the bear. Later, when we started thinking of another picture for the bear, it seemed natural to be in a National Forest ... We again used the bear and now he got his name of Humphrey.

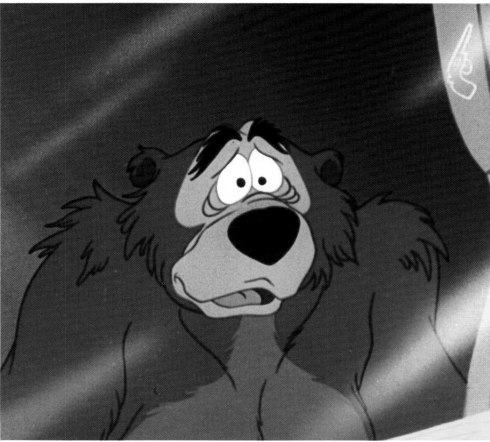
Humphrey the Bear was first given his name in the 1953 short *Rugged Bear*. It's hard to think of another animal that actually came off worst in an encounter with Donald Duck.

The pun in the title of Humphrey's second movie, *Rugged Bear* (1953), is exquisitely painful – not just for the viewer but for Humphrey himself, as will become evident. Three years had passed since his first appearance, and during that time his personality had changed: no longer was he the vicious if ultimately genial grizzly; he had become the slob of the bear population.

At the start of the hunting season all the bears flee instinctively to their caves, but Humphrey, happily slumbering, is a little slow on the uptake and finds that all the caves are barred when he tries to escape to them. He takes refuge in Donald Duck's (➤61) hunting lodge ... despite the fact that it is covered with weapons and stuffed bears' heads. When Donald the hunter returns to the cabin, Humphrey, in desperation, rolls up the bearskin rug on the floor, hides it, and takes its place. This proves to be a foolish move. Don submits his "rug" to various indignities – for example, using Humphrey's mouth as first a nutcracker and then a bottle-opener. Matters get worse when a spark from the log fire lands on the "rug": Humphrey's cry of agony wakens Don, who responds to the crisis by applying liberal doses of ashes and water ... so that his "rug" is now a mess. One session in the washing machine later, Humphrey's fur is like a porcupine's – and Don, after trying to use a rake to smooth it down, opts instead for a lawnmower.

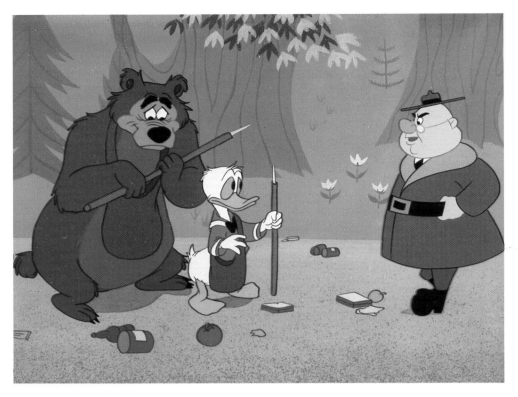

Humphrey, Donald and the Ranger (J. Audubon Woodlore) in the 1954 short *Grin and Bear It*. This was the Ranger's first outing.

But, as with all things, the hunting season must draw to a close, and as it does so Donald leaves for home. As Humphrey desperately pulls up his dishevelled form from the floor, that "bearskin rug" he so long ago rolled up and stuffed into a hiding place pops out cheerily: like Humphrey, this grizzly initially tried to use the trick of pretending to be a rug ... only he has had a rather more peaceful and less painful time of it. Thank you, Humphrey, the other grizzly says ... Humphrey's response is better not imagined.

From 1954 onwards Humphrey, voiced by veteran Disney voice artist Jim Macdonald, was joined in all of his shorts (except *Bearly Asleep* [1955]) by the Ranger, J. Audubon Woodlore (➤120). In the Ranger's first outing, *Grin and Bear It* (1954), we discover him at the opening of the tourist season telling the bears of Brownstone National Park that their duty is to entertain the tourists – and not to steal anything! Each of the bears selects a tourist to entertain: it is just bad luck that Humphrey's choice should be Donald. Bad luck for whom? Well, initially for Humphrey, because Donald refuses to hand out free grub to him: Humphrey has to use every trick in his bulging book to try to get food out of Don, and all to no avail. Eventually he deceives the Duck into believing that he has run him over, and is paid "hush money" in the form of – you guessed it – food. But when Don realizes that he has been hornswoggled a huge fight develops and food is scattered all over the surrounding area (and a few others). Enter the Ranger, to insist that they clear up all this mess. It is only as the two

foes finish doing so that they spot the Ranger himself succumbing to temptation: he is surreptitiously "borrowing" a ham from Donald's hamper. The resulting explosion is best measured in kilotons.

Bearly Asleep sees Donald, for some inexplicable reason, doing the Ranger's job. The tourist season is over and the Duck has packed off all the bears to their caves to hibernate. However, Humphrey snores so lustily that the other bears kick him out, and he tries to take refuge in Donald's cabin. If at first you don't succeed ... after Humphrey's second attempt Donald is so outraged that he throws out of the house *everything* that has anything to do with bears, including both Humphrey and Donald's own teddy-bear. The resourceful Humphrey steals the teddy-bear's bonnet and pretends to the other bears that he is a little lost baby. Needless to say, they fall for the ruse and take him back into the cave again for the winter.

After another couple of rather more "formula" shorts – *Beezy Bear* (1955) and *Hooked Bear* (1956 – this short has a marvellous moment with the Ranger, but is otherwise so run-of-the-mill that it actually reuses some footage from *Rugged Bear*), Humphrey – and, for that matter, the Ranger – danced their swansong in *In the Bag* (1956). It was a fine swansong.

The tourist season is over and the Ranger is doing his best to persuade the bears to pick up all the litter. At first he uses guile: he invents a game that involves the bears picking up bits of paper and putting them in sacks. Pretty cunning. Finally Humphrey guesses what is going on and the bears tip

out all their sacks and, for good measure, deposit the Ranger forcibly in a trash-basket. It is time for him to resort to crude blackmail: any bear that fails to clear its area of the park will go without supper. The result? – all the other bears sweep "their" rubbish into Humphrey's sector, and he is left doing his best to tidy up. He tries everything, but is beset by reverses: it would have to be *his* sack that burst, wouldn't it? Finally, in desperation, he jams all the rubbish into a convenient hole in the ground and dashes to claim his supper. Alas, that hole in the ground was "Old Fateful", the regular-as-clockwork geyser; and as the short concludes we see Humphrey hungrily and dolefully setting about his miserable task yet again ...

It is slightly surprising that Humphrey and the Ranger disappeared from view after this short (they did not even appear in *Mickey's Christmas Carol* [1983]): during the years 1953-56, out of the 22 Disney animated shorts released, Humphrey had featured in no fewer than six (and the Ranger had appeared without Humphrey in *Grand Canyonscope* [1954]) – an astonishingly high proportion of the Disney output. It would have seemed that they were heading for megastardom, but something intervened. That something may well have been fashion: ideas in the field of animation were changing, and Humphrey and the Ranger belonged to an earlier tradition. Unlike characters such as Donald Duck, they had not had the time to establish for themselves a huge following that gave not a fig for fashion, and so they were doomed. (Ironically, Hanna-Barbera's Yogi Bear enjoyed huge popularity on TV during the 1960s.) Several of the movies which Humphrey and the Ranger did make are, however, minor classics of the genre.

Filmography

Hold That Pose, November 11, 1950
Rugged Bear, 1953
Grin and Bear It, 1954
Bearly Asleep, 1955
Beezy Bear, 1955
Hooked Bear, 1956
In the Bag, 1956

MORRIS, THE MIDGET MOOSE

Several characters made their appearances in the 1950 short *Morris, the Midget Moose*, the major one being Morris himself.

The short starts with two little beetles desperately trying to get at a berry that is just out of reach. Then Bootle Beetle (➤107) calls them over and sets out to tell the story of another little fellow who, because of his size, had difficulties: he is referring, of course, to Morris.

Morris is the laughing-stock of the moose

tribe. He cannot keep up with the herd as it runs and, even worse, he has food difficulties: he is not tall enough to reach the succulent leaves on the trees, and when he tries to wade out into the lakes to eat water-grasses the waters come up over his head long before he reaches the grasses.

The day arrives for all the other buck mooses to challenge the current leader of the herd, the titanic **Thunderclap**. Morris, of course, is not really in contention … except that he suddenly realizes that he has a spread of antlers as big as any of them: he decides to give it a try. A not very good try. Because he is so small his charges at Thunderclap miss – by miles! – and the big moose goes away laughing, leaving Morris humiliated.

To Morris, this seems to be the end of the road, but then he encounters **Balsam**, a big moose endowed with only a tiny set of antlers, and the two "freaks" become great pals: mounted on top of Balsam Morris can reach the leaves and water-grasses. And suddenly he has an idea: when they are in such a configuration the two of them together resemble a single moose with a

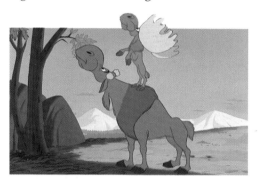

In *Morris, the Midget Moose* (1950), Morris teamed up with Balsam *(above)* after failing on his own to defeat Thunderclap *(below)*.

huge, bulky body and a vast spread of antlers: might they not be able jointly to challenge Thunderclap?

They might indeed. After a vast battle Thunderclap is revealed as a coward and a bully – a cad and a bounder, in fact – and the Morris/Balsam combination becomes the new leader of the herd.

We return from the scenes of jollification to Old Man Beetle, now happily munching the berry the kids have finally been able to fetch for him. He tells them: "The moral of this story is, two heads are better than one – or, might be, *three* heads are better than one."

Morris should be compared with characters such as Dumbo (➤192), Goliath II (➤123) and Lambert, the Sheepish Lion (➤116); Old Man Beetle with Bootle Beetle (➤107).

FRED STORK

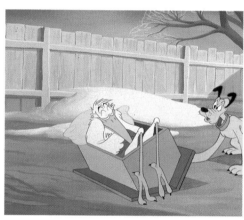

Fred Stork and Pluto feuded in 1951's *Cold Storage*.

Fred Stork made his solitary appearance in the 1951 Pluto (➤38) short *Cold Storage*. On a cold wintery night he is keen to find shelter – which he does: in the kennel of a certain famous dog. Alas, that certain famous dog, equally cold and wet, is quite keen on using it too. The short concentrates on their battle for possession of this minor piece of real estate. Towards the end of their fight Spring arrives, the thermometer explodes, and now the quarrel is over who is allowed *out* of the kennel! We leave them with Fred's legs strapped across the kennel door like the bars of a prison cage but with a resourceful Pluto, trapped inside, having "walked" the kennel so that he can sit in the glorious coolth of the fishpond.

ROVER BOY #6

There are few species of the animal kingdom that have not, at one time or another, done battle with Donald Duck (➤61), and *Equus caballus* is no exception. In particular, in a short called *Dude Duck* (1951) Donald met his equine nemesis in the shape of a horse called Rover Boy #6 – occasionally referred to in the literature as "Charlie Horse". *Dude Duck* also saw an innovation in Donald cartoons: the use of the rotoscope (although Disney had used the technique before). It was employed by Bill Justice to get an accurate version of various dude girls pouring onto the ranch where Don is foolishly seeking to have himself a good holiday. In fact, Justice used the live filming as a guide only. According to Jack Hannah, many safe years later, "We didn't really need to do it that way but it gave us a chance to look at girls in sweaters."

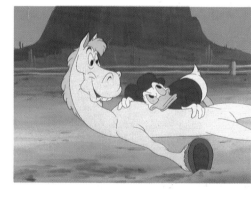

Rover Boy #6 was less than keen on the "Dude Duck" in the 1951 short of that name.

So here we have the Duck eager for healthy leisure, and here we have the horse Rover Boy #6 to whom our Donald is assigned – a ruling to which Rover Boy #6 (a close relative of many other Disney horses; e.g., Cyril (➤231) quite naturally objects. He pretends to be in rotten shape, to have a broken leg, to be wracked by

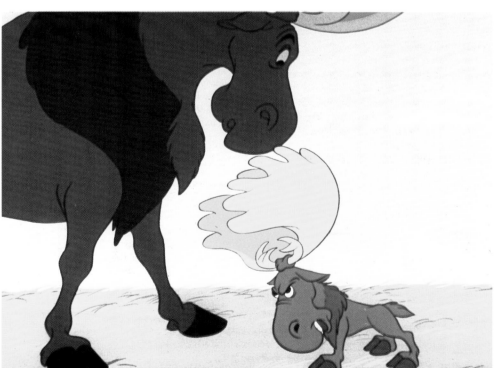

croup, etc., etc. and etc. Donald, in fact, has to hold him at gunpoint merely to put a saddle on him. Even so, the horse has second thoughts and shucks off his burden and bolts. Rover Boy #6, fleeing a lasso-swinging Duck, goes to every length to escape, even disguising himself as a cow; but all to no avail, because the Duck eventually catches him. Not for long, though: the horse gets out of the noose and slips it instead over the neck of a vast bull. Don, all unknowing, hauls in his uncooperative "horse" and discovers his unfortunate catch. At the end of the short we see Donald vanishing into the sunset, screaming and yelping, on the back of the bull: never was there a more unwitting or unwilling Brahma-bull wrestler.

Rover Boy #6, of course, finds himself instead left among the dude girls, leaning against a fence and getting the last laugh.

COMMON MAN AND COMMON SENSE

These two characters featured in an animated educational short, *How to Catch a Cold*, produced in 1951 for International Cellucotton (Kleenex). Common Man has caught a common cold. Luckily he has a sidekick called Common Sense – a little fellow with spectacles and a nightcap who is strongly reminiscent of Jiminy Cricket (➤169). Common Sense lectures Common Man on how not to get run down, catch colds and spread them. Paper tissues play an important part in all this.

LAMBERT, THE SHEEPISH LION

Lambert was introduced to the world in the short *Lambert, the Sheepish Lion* (1952). His story, in broadest outline, is very similar to that of Dumbo (➤192); it has parallels also with that of the Ugly Duckling (➤43). The short started with director Bill Peet, was handed over to Ralph Wright, and then finally came to fruition under the directorship of Jack Hannah.

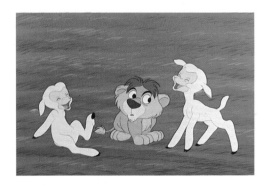

Lambert begins to suspect that he's not quite like all the other lambs in *Lambert, the Sheepish Lion* (1952).

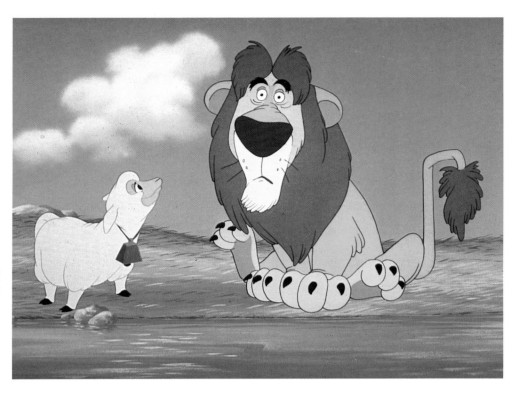

Even when he was grown up, the sheep didn't think much of Lambert until the night the hungry wolf came by.

It starts with a delivery stork – almost identical with that in *Dumbo* – seeking to deliver a new batch of lambs to the flock. Owing to an administrative error somewhere, one of the "lambs" proves to be a little lion cub; however, one of the expectant sheep is so keen to have a lamb of her own that she is happy to accept this new arrival – indeed, she insists upon it.

But cubhood is not all roses for young Lambert. He tries to act like the other lambs, but all he ever seems to succeed in doing is making them laugh at him; and when he picks a fight with one of the jeering crowd he is humiliated – he is incapable of fighting ram-fashion, by battering skulls together. Even when his generation has reached adulthood he is still the target of general derision – which he bears good-naturedly, with a "sheepish" grin. His mildness of nature and rather vacuous expression are in some contrast to his physical attributes because, as an adult, he is not just a big lion, he is a *vast* one.

One night, though, a hungry wolf comes by. (This beast, incidentally, is probably the most vicious-looking wolf the Disney animators have ever created. Even the one in *Peter in the Wolf* [➤215] pales beside this slavering monster.) The wolf drags off Lambert's adoptive mother while he lies there too terrified to move and the rest of the flock scatter in panic. But then, when he hears his mother's piteous cries for help, something snaps within Lambert and he is transformed from a genial buffoon into a beast of dignity and ferocity. With a roar fit to wake the forest he charges on the wolf and drives it away.

Having rescued his mother and elected himself protector of the flock his status has of course rather changed. No longer is he the butt of all the local humorists: he is definitely the flock's hero.

A somewhat similar lion appeared two years later, in 1954, in a short called *Social*

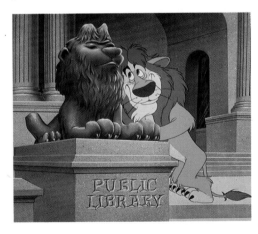

In 1954's *Social Lion* appeared a lion who may or may not have been Lambert – opinions differ.

Lion. Unlike Lambert, this one lives in Africa among the other wild animals; his big aim is to become a star attraction in the zoo, which in due course he does.

An interesting footnote is that the last original print of *Lambert, the Sheepish Lion* was presented by Roy Disney to the Emperor Hirohito of Japan because the Emperor had said that he enjoyed the movie so much. There is just a trace of Lambert in *The Lion King*'s Simba (➤387).

SUSIE, THE LITTLE BLUE COUPE

The story of Susie belongs in the realm of soap opera: she hits the heights, she plummets to the depths, and finally she attains salvation – and all thanks to her body. However, in this case Susie is an

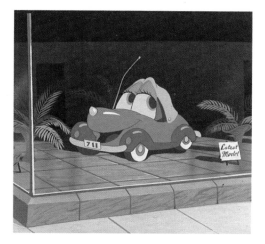

From riches to rags and, finally, happiness – that was the story of *Susie, the Little Blue Coupe* (1952).

automobile – the star of *Susie, the Little Blue Coupe* (1952).

We first see her gleaming and new in the showroom, attracting possible purchasers with a jaunty headlamp/eye. One day a neat little man is attracted by the brilliant smile on her radiator and love between them is instant. Susie mingles in high society – parked alongside all the upper-class limos – and she loves every moment of it. But this cannot last: age comes to us all, and a garage mechanic tells Susie's owner that she is so out of condition that he would be best to buy a new automobile. Susie is discarded onto the second-hand lot.

Her new owner is no social climber. She spends much of her time parked in dark alleys and back streets: she has descended to the automobile's Skid Row. Worse, one night she is stolen and hunted by the police all over town as if she were a criminal. She has been down so long it looks like up to her when they drag her off to a junkyard.

But there is still hope! A teenaged boy buys her for $12.50 and starts to work on her: new fenders, new bodywork, newly invigorated engine – she is a new woman! She feels 50,286 miles younger and overjoyed to be a cute "youngster" again.

THE LITTLE HOUSE

Probably no one but Disney could have created a sympathetic animated heroine out of a house, but this the studio did in a short called *The Little House* (1952), based on Virginia Lee Burton's book. The house in

question is, at the start of the short, "living" in the 19th century, situated on a little hill out in the country; she is delighted when an old-fashioned bride and groom arrive to live in her – even more so when her yard fills up with children. However, the nearby town is expanding, and soon she is surrounded by haughty Victorian houses who reject her as "common". A fire breaks out and they all burn down, leaving her once more on her own.

We switch to the early 20th century, and now the Little House is surrounded by raucous tenement buildings. Life is a torment for her, and the screws are tightened when the family to which she has been a home for so long moves out.

However, time passes and soon the tenements are demolished to make room for three pompous skyscrapers, which look down upon her disapprovingly: she is a relic of a past age. She is in a deep dark canyon between them, and fears she will never see the sun again, nor feel the gentle touch of the summer breeze.

Soon we are in the present (i.e., the 1950s), and workmen come to prise this anachronism of a Little House from her foundations. She feels that this is the end, and closes her eyes to thank the Lord that, at least, she has led a pretty full life for a house.

But all is not lost! She is hauled through the city streets on rollers and out into the countryside to be settled once more on top of a little hill. A new bride and groom arrive, and she knows that soon there will be children playing in her yard once more. As the narrator tells us: "The best place to

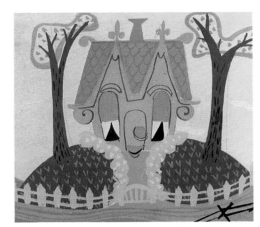

The star of 1952's *The Little House*.

find peace and happiness is in a little house, on a little hill, 'way out in the country."

The really interesting point about this movie is that the Little House really *is* a character: one feels for her when the wreckers threaten her; one is delighted when she reaches her happy ending. As noted at the outset, no one but Disney could have done it. Indeed, probably no one but Disney would even have tried.

WITCH HAZEL

Trick or Treat (1952) was a Donald *versus* the Nephews short (➤85), but it introduced a charming new character to the Disney canon, Witch Hazel – surely everybody's favourite witch. Well, certainly she is the Nephews', because she helps them notch up yet another triumph over their long-suffering "Unca Donald".

Her physical appearance is not that of a screen-goddess, to be true. Her mouse-blonde hair is tangled in a seedy fashion; her nose seems to owe something to regular infusions of port (or cheaper equivalent); and her attire, while traditional for a witch, looks as if it might have been worn for perhaps one century too many. But she has a cheery, practical nature that is infinitely appealing – and she has a broomstick, **Beelzebub**, which is really a character in itself (and which, during the course of the short, we discover can double as a banjo). She is also not without her own little human failings: early on in the short we see her scared silly by a glowing Hallowe'en pumpkin-head, borne upon the head of one of the Nephews, who are out on the prowl, trick-or-treating. Be glad that you don't live in that area.

Donald, as you might expect, starts the trouble. He plants firecrackers in the Nephews' collection bags – the noise causes Beelzebub to shy, which is why Witch Hazel enters the battle – and drenches them with a bucket of water. When Witch Hazel knocks on his door, ostensibly to trick-or-treat him, he pulls her nose with a savage glee, assuming it is a mask, and then dowses her, too, in floods of water. Even the best tempered of witches would take objection to this treatment, and Witch Hazel is the best tempered of witches.

She calls upon her magical knowledge (much like Eglantine in *Bedknobs and Broomsticks*, [➤287]) to conjure up a potion that can do things like bring pumpkin-masks to terrifying life and startle stolid fence-posts into becoming ghosts. Needless to say, all of these new-created haunts visit the Duck and cause him visibly to pale whiter than his normal white. But not for long is Don downcast. When Witch Hazel and the Nephews jointly come to trick-or-treat him he initially agrees to "treat" and even gets various goodies out of his heftily safeguarded store-cupboard, but then, when he overhears Witch Hazel describing him to the Nephews as a "pushover", he crossly slams shut the cupboard door and, to make sure of its security, swallows the key (millions of parents, worldwide, must have cheered at this point). However, Witch Hazel is not to be intimidated by this tactic: she casts a spell so that Donald's own feet quite literally kick the key back out of him. He tries the desperate remedy of kicking the key under the cupboard door but Witch Hazel casts another spell on his feet so that

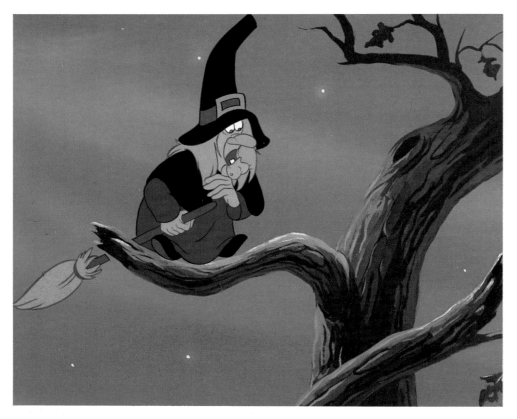

Witch Hazel with her broomstick Beelzebub in the 1952 short *Trick or Treat*. Between them they foiled Donald's attempts to resist the Nephews' seasonal blackmail.

they force him to batter the door down with his head. The Nephews, never slow on the uptake, snatch all his parsimoniously hoarded food and set to with a will. Meanwhile Witch Hazel, her task of goodwill done for the night, realizes that it is close to dawn and embarks into the sky upon the faithful Beelzebub.

The witch was voiced by June Foray, and director Jack Hannah recalled in a 1978 interview with Jim Korkis in *Mindrot* that she

... did such a great job as the voice of the witch [and] still mentions the film to me whenever I see her. The short got a very high [audience response] when the studio watched it in the sweat box. [Walt] Disney said he couldn't understand some of the words. That the dialog was too fast. That reminds me that my dad liked my cartoons but thought they were too fast as well. Maybe he was just old because now I agree with him. Then, I didn't.

Witch Hazel is certainly a popular character, and so it is rather surprising that she has yet to appear in a further Disney movie.

MULDOON

A tough cop called Muldoon – bearing a marked resemblance to Pete (➤ 16), right down to the cigar – appeared in one of the funniest of the Goofy "how to" shorts (➤ 48), *How to be a Detective* (1952).

The Goof is "Johnny Eyeball, Private Eye", and, as the narrator explains, what he needs first is "a classy dame with a

problem". Enter one classy dame with a problem – what an astonishing coincidence. She tells the Goof to "find Al" and leaves him clutching a $100 bill. Just after she has gone, Muldoon comes barging in crying: "Leave this 'Al' case to the police!" Classy dame, obstructive policeman: the vital third element, the narrator explains, is "a shady or suspicious character". Moments later a **Weasel** arrives, with the classic line: "You know too much about Al." Soon Goofy is recovering consciousness in a back alley.

Muldoon's attitude does not change, and on every available occasion he tells the Goof to lay off the case. At one point the Goof spots a mugging in process and intercedes. The mugger – the ubiquitous Weasel, who appears in several guises in this short – responds: "Beat it! I'm busy," which seems fair enough, but the reaction of the victim is

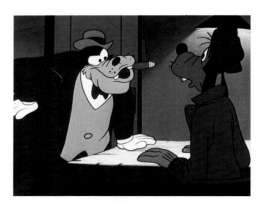

Al Muldoon intimidates Johnny Eyeball, Private Eye (*alias* the Goof), in the classic 1952 short *How to be a Detective*.

less predictable ... for he proves to be Muldoon. "I thought I told you to leave this case alone!" he snaps, and carries on being mugged.

In the end there is the statutory car chase, with the Goof following the Weasel, Muldoon following the Goof, and the classy dame following Muldoon. Finally all four cars crash into a Justice of the Peace's building and the girl grabs Muldoon and drags him inside. They are immediately married, with the Weasel performing the ceremony. As Muldoon roars at Goofy: "I *told* you to leave this case alone!"

Well, how was Goofy to know Muldoon's first name?

PROFESSOR OWL

Professor Owl, a zany character in blues and greys wearing big, circular thin-rimmed spectacles, appeared as narrator of two 1953 shorts, *Adventures in Music: Melody* (often listed as *Melody – Adventures in Music*) and *Toot, Whistle, Plunk, and Boom*. Both were rather significant.

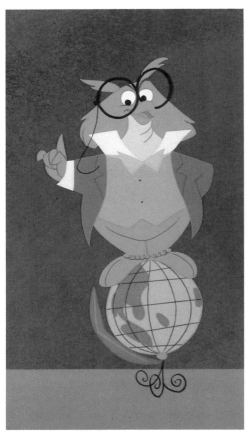

Professor Owl, the hyperactive educator, in *Toot, Whistle, Plunk, and Boom* (1953).

The former represented Disney's first venture into the field of 3-D animation. In it the Professor and his bird students explore the subject of melody, which they find all around them in nature and in human lives. The climax of their exploration is a symphonic presentation of *The Bird and the*

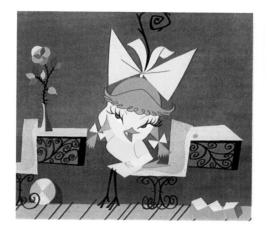

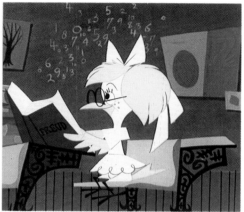

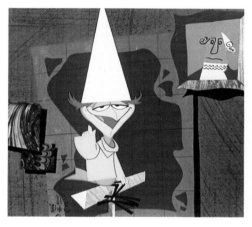

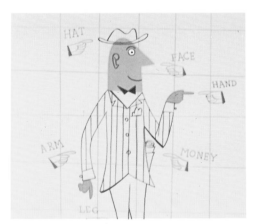

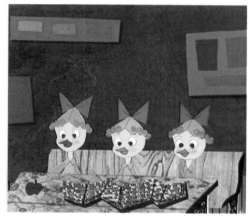

Cricket and the Willow Tree. Other (very minor) characters involved are the students **Bertie Birdbrain**, **The Canary Sisters**, **Penelope Pinfeather** and **Suzy Sparrow**, as well as our old friend *Homo sapiens*.

The second, made in CinemaScope, also represented a landmark: the use by the Disney studio of limited animation of stylized, rather than realistic, characters in most of the sequences. This technique had become popular at other studios over the preceding year or two, and the critics were castigating Disney for retaining a style that they considered *passé*. Whether or not the critics were right is a matter outside the scope of this book, but Disney responded to the comments in brilliant fashion with *Toot, Whistle, Plunk, and Boom*, carrying off the Academy Award for best animated short of 1953. In it Professor Owl draws the attention of his students to the four original

Some of Professor Owl's pupils in 1953's *Adventures in Music: Melody*: Suzy Sparrow *(top left),* Penelope Pinfeather *(top right),* Bertie Birdbrain *(above left)* and the Canary Sisters *(above).* On the *left* we see the plain bird's guide to *Homo sapiens*.

musical sounds used by our caveman ancestors and then traces the evolution of instruments capable of producing those sounds up to the present day. The short climaxes with a performance by a full symphony orchestra – whose output, the Professor explains, is based entirely on the four sounds "toot", "whistle", "plunk" and "boom".

After these two shorts Professor Owl never appeared again. Some years later, in 1961, his didactic role was taken over by an even zanier pedagogue, the irrepressible Ludwig Von Drake (►**124**).

Filmography

Adventures in Music: Melody, May 28, 1953
Toot, Whistle, Plunk, and Boom, 1953

MUNCEY

You do not expect a dog owned by Pete (►**16**) to be exactly Lassie, and so it is hardly surprising that Muncey, who appears in *The New Neighbor* (1953), is a great shambling English sheepdog with an orange tuft of hair coming down over his eyes. In this short his owner, Pete, plays the slobbish and theft-prone neighbour of Donald, who has just moved into the area.

At a late stage in the build-up to the confrontation between the two, Pete and Muncey arrive at Don's house with a bowl of food and Pete says: "Say, neighbour, try this."

Don, believing that perhaps his new neighbour is not quite so bad after all, takes a spoonful, savours it, and judges: "*Delicious!*"

The problem is that, as Pete and Muncey stroll away again, Don hears Pete saying to the dog: "See? *He* eats it. Trouble with you, Muncey, is that you're too finicky..."

Battle is joined very shortly thereafter.

FLANNERY

Flannery, the station-master of Westcote Railway Station, appeared in a short called *Pigs is Pigs* (1954), based on a book by Ellis Parker Butler. He has bright orange hair, balding on top, a thick Irish accent, a pear-shaped figure, navy blue dungarees and cap, a red spotted handkerchief perpetually dangling from his back pocket, an upside-down clay pipe and a nose that is forever buried in the railway company's imposing rule-book. Indeed, as the narration tells us,

> Flannery ran his station exactly by the rules. He tried to learn them all by heart, just like a kid in school.

One day in 1905 a train passes through and drops off a crate containing a pair of guinea-pigs. Flannery, going by the rules as ever, reads the label and declares that, even if they don't *look* like pigs, that's what they are and that's what he's going to treat them as. "Pigs," as he declares firmly, "is pigs."

The customer who turns up to collect the animals is **McMorehouse**, a tall rangy old Scot with a tammy on his head and raggedy yellow hair and beard. He proffers his 44¢ collection charge, but Flannery will have none of it: 44¢ is the charge for pets, he proclaims, but these are not pets, they are pigs, and the charge for pigs is 48¢. Until he is paid 48¢ the crate stays where it is.

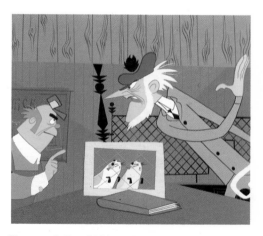

Flannery *(left)* and McMorehouse argue over what is and what is not a pig. Flannery's view is that pigs is pigs – hence the title of the 1954 short.

McMorehouse, of course, being a good Scot, says that in that case it can stay in Flannery's station until the end of time as far as he is concerned.

Flannery wires to head office for clarification of the situation. There his telegram hits the bureaucratic fan: thousands of copies are made for every conceivable department, files bulge with further thousands of copies, the copies are recopied, and so on – in short, the copies of Flannery's telegram multiply like rabbits … or, come to that, like guinea-pigs.

For out at Westcote Station Flannery has a problem on his hands. Initially he named the two guinea-pigs Pat and Mike but now he has had to rechristen Mike as Marie, for obvious reasons. His next telegram, informing head office that he now has nine "pigs" rather than the original two, suffers the same fate as his earlier one, and again goes unanswered.

Finally expert advice is sought by the company's board of directors: the zoologist they interrogate explains that guinea-pigs really are *not* pigs, and that the 44¢ rate should therefore apply. The directors grab their golfbags as one man and depart to celebrate, which is perhaps why there is still further delay in getting the message to Flannery, who by now has completely lost count of the millions of guinea-pigs that have taken over his station. And there is worse news for the poor Irishman: McMorehouse has moved house, and cannot be traced. What should Flannery do?

After due delay head office, which has yet to realize that the original problem has increased several millionfold, tells him to ship the guinea-pigs there, which he does with considerable relief and a great deal of difficulty. Still, at last he's got rid of all the little pests and can settle back and relax, mopping his brow and thanking the heavens that at least the animals were only guinea-pigs; after all, they could have been elephants. Just then, as you might expect, a circus train pauses at the station and he sees a brace of elephants standing there: his instant reaction is to pass out in horror.

After he has recovered, and just before the short ends, his blue cap is lifted and out grin at us impertinently a couple of cheeky little guinea-pigs. And Flannery thinks his problems are over, does he?

THE RANGER (J. AUDUBON WOODLORE)

The fussy little Ranger, J. Audubon Woodlore, voiced by Bill Thompson, has appeared in a number of shorts with Donald Duck (➤61) and Humphrey the Bear (➤113). Had he first come on the scene in 1944 or 1934 rather than 1954 there is little doubt but that he would have become a fairly major Disney character.

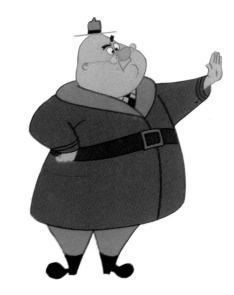
The Ranger in customarily bossy mood in *Hooked Bear* (1956).

One might say that the Ranger is shaped like a pear, except that one would then get letters from angry pears. Dressed in a dishevelled brown uniform and with a ridiculously small hat perched on top of his plump head, he sports funny little thin-rimmed spectacles and has a highish-pitched fusspot-type voice and a habit of saying "Heavens to Betsy!" when things are going wrong, or even when they are going right. Naturally, since his regular adversary is Humphrey the Bear the latter is very rarely the case.

He came into being, according to Jack Hannah in an interview with Jim Korkis in *Mindrot* in 1978, because the team, having used Humphrey once against Donald and now wanting to use him again, thought that "it seemed natural to be in a National Forest". Hannah goes on to recall a particular sequence from *Beezy Bear* (1955):

> One of the sequences I remember having a lot of fun with was when the Duck had a honey farm next to the Ranger's station. The Duck complained that the bears were stealing the honey so the Little Ranger had them stand up in a police line-up fashion. The Little Ranger always treated his bears like his own pets.

In *Hooked Bear* (1956) there is another glorious moment when the Ranger demonstrates the art of restocking the river with fish because the supplies are running low. It is easy enough – for the Ranger, at least. All he needs to do is grab a packet of "fish seeds" and sow them in a trough of water, smooth over the ripples and rush up and down sprinkling liberally with a watering-can. Moments later the new fish pop up like a row of vegetables, and the job is done!

And he can be quite cunning, too. In *In the Bag* (1956 [➤114]), his final movie, he has the chore of persuading the bears at the end of the tourist season to pick up all the litter that has been left scattered everywhere. Swift-wittedly he devises a musical game that involves the bears dashing around all over the park and –

surprise, surprise – putting bits of paper in sacks. Quite a while passes before one of the bears tumbles to the ruse – no prize for guessing the name of the bear – and the Ranger has to resort to crude blackmail: no supper for any bear which fails to clear up its quota of litter.

In only one short has the Ranger appeared without Humphrey. This is *Grand Canyonscope* (1954), in which he has been transferred, for the nonce, from the Brownstone National Park to the Grand Canyon; by a startling coincidence a certain Duck decides for once to visit the canyon rather than the park. Needless to say, Don proceeds to make as much of a nuisance of himself as possible – rather more, if anything. Finally Don loses his burro and asks the Ranger to find it for him. After a quick search the Ranger spots the burro's tail sticking out of a cave-mouth and starts to p-u-l-l. Bad luck, Ranger: wrong tail. The enraged Mountain Lion (➤111) chases both Donald and the Ranger all over the canyon ("nilly-willy"), as one Disney document expressively puts it), and in the process they break up many of the rock-pillars, filling the canyon with detritus. The short ends with the Ranger fussily insisting that Donald and the Mountain Lion shovel all of this debris out of the canyon so that it will be all pristine and ready for the next batch of tourists. Bad geology but good cartooning!

(For futher details of the Ranger's career see discussion of Humphrey the Bear [➤113]).

Filmography

Grin and Bear It, August 13, 1954
Grand Canyonscope, 1954
Beezy Bear, 1955
Hooked Bear, 1956
In the Bag, 1956

AMOS

One of a family of 26 mice living in a Pennsylvanian church, Amos, voiced by Sterling Holloway, was the star of the 1953 featurette *Ben and Me*.

Because the family is "as poor as church mice" Amos sets out to make his way in the world, finally finding a job in the shop of **Benjamin Franklin**, printer and bookbinder. The two become firm friends, Amos helping with the publication of the *Pennsylvania Gazette*, and many of his inventive ideas being picked up by Franklin – such as bifocal spectacles and the "Franklin" stove. However, Franklin – an inveterate joker – almost electrocutes the mouse during his famous kite-flying experience, and Amos retires in a huff to his church.

Franklin makes his second – 1764-65 – trip to England to argue the colonies' case before the new king, George III. As with his previous mission in 1757-62 to argue before

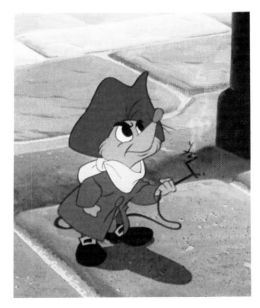

As we find in the 1953 movie *Ben and Me*, it was Amos the mouse who did all those things we thought Ben Franklin did.

George II, his representations are unsuccessful, and on his return he seeks out Amos's church and begs him to help. Amos eventually agrees to help him, but only on condition that Franklin sign an agreement which he, Amos, will sign the following day.

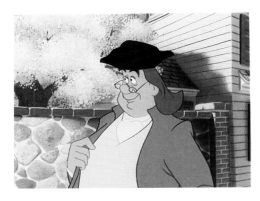

Benjamin Franklin in *Ben and Me* (1953), looking not remotely guilty about taking the credit for Amos's feats of genius.

Next morning Franklin is just about to sign the paper when **Thomas Jefferson**, who has been having difficulty getting the phrasing right for the opening lines of the Declaration of Independence, rushes in to see if Franklin, a professional journalist, could help him out. While the two men chew the matter over Amos becomes impatient, and threatens to leave unless his agreement is signed without delay. Franklin looks at it and discovers that its opening lines are exactly what are needed for the Declaration of Independence. Jefferson, having been given this start, is able to write the rest of the document without trouble.

Franklin flew his kite in 1752 and he helped frame the Declaration of Independence in 1776. Clearly, although

the movie does not tell us so, among Amos's inventions must have been some kind of longevity pill.

Thomas Jefferson asked Franklin's advice about the wording for the Declaration of Independence, and was glad to accept Amos's version.

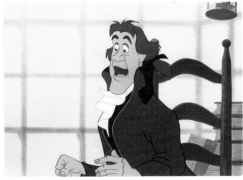

GRANDPA DUCK

Several of Donald's relatives have appeared on screen, usually to his regret – think of the Nephews (►85) – but none can have caused him more heartache than Grandpa Duck. Come to that, none can have starred with him in such a morally ambiguous short as *No Hunting* (1955), in which for once the ducks are the hunters rather than the hunted.

Donald is relaxing in his snug dining-room when the narrator points out that the soft life he enjoys was not shared by Grandpa Duck – whose portrait just happens to be hanging up there on the wall. We see the picture come to life, with old Grandpa bagging a buffalo – yes, he had to hunt for his food, unlike lucky 20th-century Donald.

But what is this? Don opens up his newspaper to find a headline saying: "HUNTING SEASON OPENS TOMORROW." Grandpa leaps out of his portrait and his spirit enters Don's body: as the narrator explains, it is because of the spirit of our forefathers within us that we have the urge to go out and hunt wild game. Well, some of us must just have had defective forefathers.

The hunt is, fortunately for the local wildlife, a fiasco, the only successful hunter being Grandpa, who has bagged a cow. He

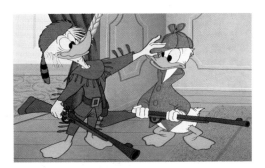

Grandpa Duck tells Donald what's what in *No Hunting* (1955).

is convinced that it is an item of game, despite the fact that the farmer who owned it had thoughtfully painted the letters "C", "O" and "W" on its side. Wanton slaughter of a domesticated animal? Theft? As noted, this is a morally ambiguous short. It is no surprise that Grandpa failed to appear again.

OLD MacDONALD

Old MacDonald made his appearance in a curious two-part short, directed by Bill Justice, called *Jack and Old Mac* (1956). In the first part of the short, based on the nursery rhyme "The House that Jack Built", animated letters distort themselves into the objects being described – a technique much used in television's *Sesame Street*. Old MacDonald himself appears, with his wife, in the second part of the movie. Here, joined enthusiastically by their children and several farm animals, they give a rendition of the song "Old MacDonald Had a Band" – based, of course, on the nursery song "Old MacDonald Had a Farm".

The movie was an interesting and worthwhile experiment, but can hardly be judged a success.

Old MacDonald and Mrs. MacDonald in *Jack and Old Mac* (1956).

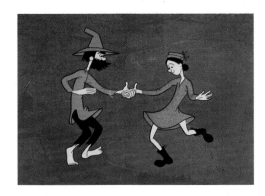

PAUL BUNYAN

The featurette *Paul Bunyan* (1958) is interesting in several ways, not least because of the stylized nature of its drawing: this is very much the use of animation to tell a story rather than a straightforward animated story – an effect enhanced by the use of three separate story-tellers to narrate the three different sections of the tale. The consequent integrity of drawing and narrational techniques gives the movie a cohesion which it might not otherwise have had.

The first section is introduced by **Cal McNab**, a tall thin lumberjack with a trim black beard and a long hooked nose; he tells us that he reckons he was the first to see the gigantic hero, the morning after a huge storm had hit town: Cal, going out to investigate at daybreak, finds that a vast

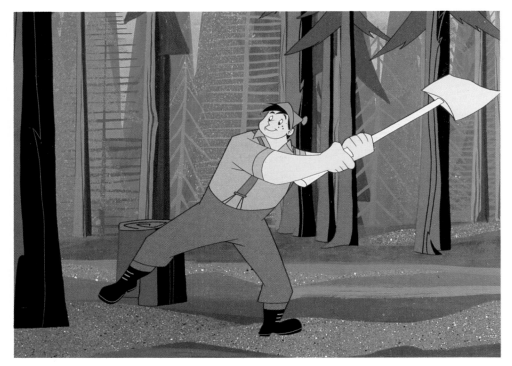

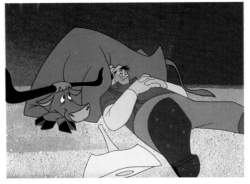

Babe, the Blue Ox, with her bosom companion in the 1958 featurette *Paul Bunyan,*

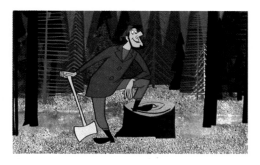

Cal McNab *(above)*, who found a huge baby on the shore in *Paul Bunyan* (1958). The baby became an even huger adult *(top)*.

wooden cradle has been washed ashore. Inside it is an equally vast baby boy, whom the people of the town promptly christen "Paul Bunyan".

They clothe and feed him and generally look after him – with some difficulty because he is so huge. In fact, he needs a *whole choir* – led by Cal McNab – to sing him to sleep at nights! He has to sit beside, rather than in, school, but nevertheless he is a good and willing pupil; and when he and his schoolfriends go swimming he happily takes on the role of diving-board.

The years tick by and he becomes a young man of colossal stature. With dark hair and a cleancut expression, he is genial almost to the point of lack-wittedness; later he becomes a little less clean-shaven and a lot less lack-witted.

Christmas comes and the townsfolk set up a tree in the central square so that Paul can join them gathered around it. Cal hands out the presents, and Paul discovers to his delight that the townsfolk have clubbed together to give him a vast double-bladed axe. In succeeding weeks he uses this to fell trees all over the area, with the result that there is a plethora of wood for the local sawmills as well as lots of new farmland

being opened up. The town grows and prospers until the day comes when it is too crowded for Paul, who departs one night leaving a note behind to say that he is going out West.

The next episode of the tale is introduced and narrated by **Chris Crosshaul**, a biggish beefy character with carrot-red hair who is strawboss (foreman) of a logging crew in the Middle West. He leads us into a song about the giant lumberjack in which we learn that Paul was so mighty that, having felled the trees, he hammered their stumps into the

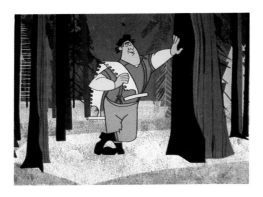

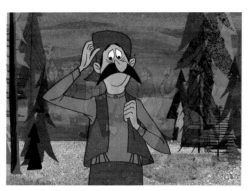

Two of the three narrators of the 1958 featurette *Paul Bunyan*: Chris Crosshaul *(above)* and Shot Gunderson *(below)*.

ground just to make everything neat and tidy again!

Once Paul has cleared Chris Crosshaul's locality of anything that looks remotely like a tree he decides to head out West again, but this time he runs into a blizzard so severe that "even the snow was blue". He builds a fire to warm himself but the flames freeze; just as he is about to light a second fire to melt the first he hears a throaty "moo" from the depths of the storm. Following the sound, he comes across an ox frozen as blue as the snow; even when thawed out, **Babe, the Blue Ox** will retain this colour.

The two are destined to become bosom pals. They plough on through the storm together and, the following Spring, rain fills in their gigantic footprints ... which is why North America now features a Land of Ten Thousand Lakes. In fact, between them they have a devastating effect on North American geography, carving out the Mississippi River and building Pike's Peak. These two jobs together make for a long day's work – so long that the following morning Paul sleeps in. When he finally does wake up he makes himself a shower-bath – which nowadays we know as the Yellowstone Falls. The spirit of Baron Munchhausen is certainly not dead.

The third section – the one concerning the fabled hero's nemesis – is introduced by **Shot Gunderson**, a timber foreman over near the Oregon trail who is depicted with a big black moustache and an outsized hat which has an irritating habit of falling down over his eyes. He tells us how, in the old days, his lumber camp was in grave difficulties because the river down which the logs had to be sent was full of twists and bends. That was before the arrival of Paul Bunyan: he and his trusty friend Babe sort out the problem by jamming an anchor into the riverhead and pulling on the other end so that the river becomes as straight as a die. As in other cases, this action immediately causes the surrounding countryside to prosper.

Paul is a local hero, but it cannot last. Enter **Joe Muffaw**, a salesman travelling in steam-powered saws. It would be hard to imagine a character more the antithesis of our vast rock-jawed hero: Joe is small and slight with a pointy black moustache, a blue suit, a white shirt, a black bowtie and a funny little hat. His philosophy is likewise directly opposed to Paul's: a power-saw, says Joe, is better than an axe for felling trees, no matter who the wielder, and a steam train is better even than Babe for hauling logs. Paul begs to disagree, and a big contest is set up with Shot Gunderson as the judge. After an hour's worth of frantic felling Shot has to confess that, while Paul's pile of logs has attained a height of 240ft, Joe's has achieved 240ft *plus a quarter of an inch!* Paul has finally failed.

Joe Muffaw, traveller in steam-powered saws, prepares to display his wares in *Paul Bunyan* (1958).

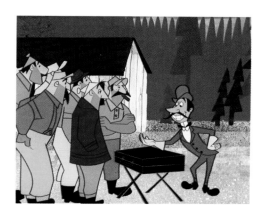

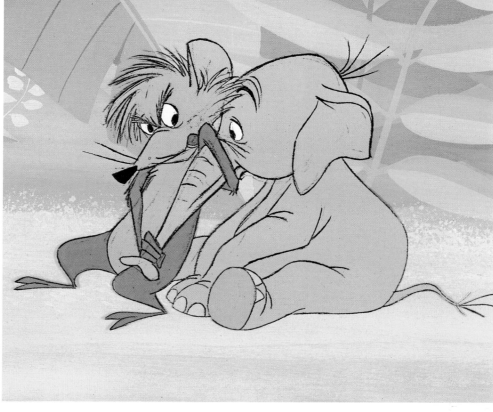

Goliath II found someone his own size to take on in the 1960 short *Goliath II*.

But don't worry, Shot tells us. Paul Bunyan and Babe have headed for yet another territory where there aren't too many people and where there is plenty of room for horsing (oxing?) around. Now they are up in Alaska, enjoying the physical rigours of life just as much as they used to when first they were forging a legend.

Babe also makes a cameo appearance in 1988's *Who Framed Roger Rabbit* (➤326).

GOLIATH II

Goliath II, who stars in a 1960 short of the same name, is rather small for an elephant: 5⅛ in. tall, to be precise. His father, the mighty **Goliath I**, the leader of and biggest tusker in the herd, is outraged by what he sees as a direct personal insult from Fate, but his mother, **Mrs. Goliath I**, is convinced that one day her little boy will come to something and proudly devotes her time to looking after him. This is not easy: the jungle is full of dangers, not the least of them **Raja**, a crafty old tiger – one of the few in the Disney canon, for reasons given elsewhere – who has always wanted to find out what elephant tastes like and at last sees his opportunity. To keep Goliath II out of Raja's clutches, his mother hides him in a bird's nest high in a tree at nights.

One night, however, when Goliath II is eight, he decides that he is tired of being

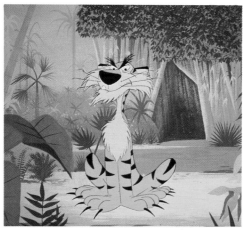

Raja, who had a yen for a little elephant – Goliath II would do nicely.

treated like a baby and sneaks off to explore the jungle on his own. This is Raja's big chance, and he stalks the bite-sized creature through the undergrowth. Just as he is about to pounce, however, he is seized by the tail and jerked high in the air: Mrs. Goliath has arrived on the scene in the nick of time. She hurls the tiger clean out of that part of the jungle, and he is never seen again.

But Goliath II's troubles have only just begun. As an attempted runaway he has broken one of the main rules of the herd, and so he is treated like a criminal.

One day, as Goliath I is leading the herd through the jungle, they encounter that

ultimate terror, a mouse. The elephants flee in terror – all except Goliath II, who at last has an adversary of his own size. A furious fight ensues, with the little elephant emerging as the victor. Goliath, who has achieved the "impossible" for an elephant, is made a great hero, and is thereafter given a position of honour perched high on his father's head at the front of the herd.

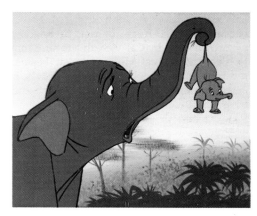

He might be small, but his mother loved him anyway. Mrs. Goliath I and offspring in *Goliath II* (1960).

A small part in the movie is played by an elephant called **Elloise**. She is rebuked by Mrs. Goliath for being insufficiently careful of Goliath II's wellbeing – she almost stands on him!

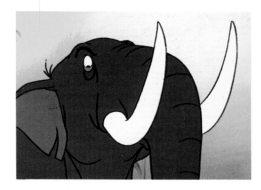

Goliath I, mightiest elephant of the herd, was mortified when his son and heir proved to be only 5⅛ inches tall.

Goliath II is one of a fairly extensive set of Disney movies featuring young animals who are initially despised for one reason or another but who in the end achieve glory – the most famous being another elephant, Dumbo (➤192). Other noteworthy members of the set include Lambert (➤116) and Morris (➤114).

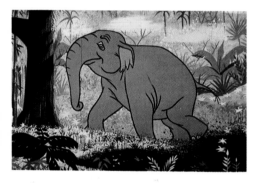

Elloise, whose careless step almost meant the end for Goliath II.

WINDWAGON SMITH

Windwagon Smith is a bold Disney lunk in the great tradition; he is also something of an eccentric. As we discover in *The Saga of Windwagon Smith* (1961), he has sailed the seven seas and has determined to put the knowledge he has gained at sea to use on the land: he has rigged up a Conestoga

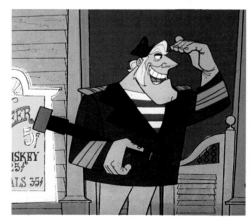

The hero and title-character of the 1961 featurette *The Saga of Windwagon Smith.*

prairie wagon like an old-fashioned sailing-ship.

One day he arrives in the town of Westport, Kansas, the starting point on the old Oregon and Santa Fe trails westward. He drops anchor in Main Street and bellows: "Ahoy, me hearties!" The locals are much impressed by him, clad as he is in full sailship-captain's rig, and the pudgy, bushy-moustached **Mayor Crum** welcomes him officially to Westport. Oh, and would he not like to partake of a few in the Star of the West Saloon?

He agrees, and while he talks of the possibilities of sail-powered journeys to the West – much easier than using oxen to

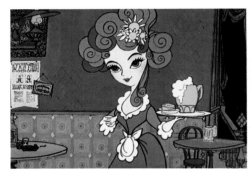

Molly Crum, the Mayor's Daughter, who captured Windwagon Smith's heart within nanoseconds of their meeting.

ploddingly draw one's wagon – they recognize the commercial possibilities. He, for his part, recognizes true love when it hits him between the eyes: the girl who is serving him is the luscious **Molly Crum**, daughter of the mayor and darling of the region. She, for that matter, sees all his hidden depths and falls in love too.

The inhabitants of Westport erect a vast windwagon, the prototype of a putative fleet, and the local dignitaries join Windwagon on the artefact's maiden voyage. (Among these dignitaries should be noted **Jake**, a member of the Board of Directors, who figures out how fast the windwagon will be able to go, and who persuades the mayor of how profitable it could be.) Unfortunately a hurricane blows up and the tiller gets stuck, and one by one the dignitaries leap off, back into safety.

Molly's father, the Mayor, backed Windwagon's scheme to open up the West using prairie schooners.

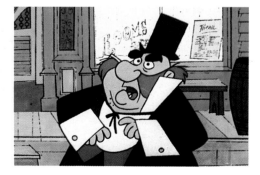

Windwagon Smith seems to be alone on the vessel when out from the underdecks appears Molly, whose love for Windwagon Smith has made her a stowaway. Just then a huge tornado strikes the vessel, which disappears into the skies.

Smith, Molly and the windwagon are never seen again – unless, of course, you look into the golden sunset, when you might just see the great windjammer circling in the clouds, with Windwagon and Molly singing happily together . . .

LUDWIG VON DRAKE

Ludwig Von Drake, described as Donald Duck's eccentric uncle from the European side of the family and Mother Goose's grandson, is almost exclusively a television personality, his sole theatrical appearance being in the 1962 featurette *A Symposium on Popular Songs.* Nevertheless he has become one of the most popular figures in the Disney canon.

Ludwig is a polymath, as he is not too modest to remind us – frequently. In fact, it is rather hard to think of a subject in which he is not a self-styled expert: history, science, child psychology, big-game hunting . . . His speech, unlike that of his even more famous nephew, is largely intelligible despite being cloaked in a thick Germanic accent. (This voice was supplied by a specialist voice-actor, Paul Frees, who made some 20,000 "appearances" on radio and as a television voice-over; he also voiced the narration to Disneyland's "Haunted Mansion".)

One of Ludwig's early TV appearances, *The Hunting Instinct* (1961), was not auspicious. He had the following dialogue with Walt himself:

Walt: How do you do, Professor? I'm Walt . . .
Ludwig: Don't tell me! I'm gonna tell you. Dat's Mr. Dilly – isn't that you? Willy? Nilly? Fisby?
Walt: Disney. D-I-S-N-E-Y.
Ludwig: Hah, hah, ha . . . oh! "Disney"! Of course, I knew it all the time. I never forget a face. You're the fellow who works for my nephew Donald Duck, isn't that right?
Walt: Yes, I guess you *could* put it that way . . .

Von Drake, however, went on to have a distinguished television career, hosting no fewer than 17 television featurettes, all of which mixed humour with a certain degree of educational material. Typical of these is *Kids is Kids* (1961), which is really just a good excuse for cobbling together a collection of old shorts in which Donald Duck (➤64) does battle with the dreaded Nephews (➤85). Ludwig, as link-duck, declares at the outset that his subject for the day is to be child psychology. He has a little difficulty in explaining what psychology actually *is*, but then that is a failing shared by many. What he has discovered from letters sent in by thousands of anxious parents is, though, that "their brats . . . er, children . . . are

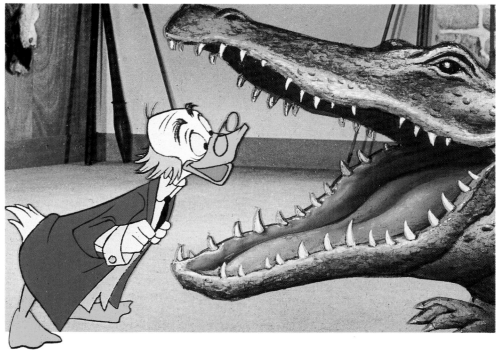

Ludwig Von Drake, Donald's uncle on the European side, displays his typical curiosity in the television featurette *The Hunting Instinct* (1961).

naughty ... in other words, perfectly normal"; to show what he means he holds up to the camera a typical parents' letter: "Dear Doctor: **HELP!**" Parents should not lose hope, though, he claims, because his vast forthcoming book on the subject will be jam-packed with useful hints on child-management, and will certainly be useful to all parents because "in case you get nothing useful from the *in*side, you'll find the *out*side useful – on their little *back*sides".

But how has he gathered all the information for this weighty tome? Of course, by studying a typical North American family. Well, perhaps not so typical: the one he has chosen to observe covertly consists of Donald and the Nephews. This is Ludwig's cue to introduce a succession of relevant shorts, each comprising a chapter of his book: they are *Donald's Happy Birthday* (1949), *Hockey Champ* (1939), *Good Scouts* (1938), *Don's Fountain of Youth* (1953), the classic *Soup's On* (1948) and *Lucky Number* (1951). (For discussion of these shorts please refer to Index of Film Titles.)

Von Drake's sole excursion on the big screen has been in *A Symposium on Popular Songs* (1962), a featurette much like the ones he has done on television. Stop-motion photography using paper cut-outs illustrates various popular musical styles (the songs were by the ubiquitous Sherman brothers) from ragtime to rock 'n' roll; the director was Bill Justice. What carries the featurette is the personality of Ludwig Von Drake himself: his zaniness is capable of making even this unpromising subject come to life. In fact, it is astonishing that his personality has not been exploited further by Disney, for in many of his featurettes viewers put up with the more didactic

sections of the movies in order to watch the interspersed Von Drake segments. Surely it is time that Ludwig was allowed genuinely to star in some movies of his own, rather than act merely as a link-duck?

Filmography

An Adventure in Color/Mathmagic Land, September 24, 1961 (TV)
The Hunting Instinct, 1961 (TV)
Inside Donald Duck, 1961 (TV)
Kids is Kids, 1961 (TV)
A Symposium on Popular Songs, 1962
Carnival Time, 1962 (TV)
Von Drake in Spain, 1962 (TV)
Man is His Own Worst Enemy, 1962 (TV)
Three Tall Tales, 1963 (TV)
Inside Outer Space, 1963 (TV)
Square Peg in a Round Hole, 1963 (TV)
Fly With Von Drake, 1963 (TV)
The Truth About Mother Goose, 1963 (TV)
Mediterranean Cruise, 1964 (TV)
In Shape With Von Drake, 1964 (TV)
A Rag, a Bone, a Box of Junk, 1964 (TV)
Music for Everybody, 1966 (TV)
DTV Valentine, 1986 (TV)

WINNIE THE POOH AND FRIENDS

Winnie the Pooh and his friends from the A. A. Milne classics have appeared so far in four Disney featurettes: *Winnie the Pooh and the Honey Tree* (1966), *Winnie the Pooh and the Blustery Day* (1968), *Winnie the Pooh and Tigger Too* (1974) and *Winnie the Pooh and a Day for Eeyore* (1983). (The first three have also been released together, in March 1977, as a composite feature called *The Many Adventures of Winnie the Pooh*. Although it is outside our discussion, it should be noted that Pooh has appeared also in an

educational short called *Winnie the Pooh Discovers the Seasons* [1981].) All four show considerable skill in matching the Disney art of animation with the original illustrative style of E. H. Shepard; generally the critics have declared that the fourth, released under the Disney name but in fact animated and made entirely by Rick Reinert Productions, is inferior to the other three, but this is a matter of taste.

Sterling Holloway, a Disney favourite, has supplied the voice of Winnie the Pooh, the "bear of little brain". This is a masterly piece of casting so far as US audiences are concerned, but the reaction has been, to put it politely, somewhat mixed in the United Kingdom, where perceptions of Pooh's character, based on the books, are rather different. The other voices in the featurettes have been generally well received in both countries: Christopher Robin has been voiced by Jon Walmsley, Bruce Reitherman (son of Woolie Reitherman, co-director with John Lounsbery) and Timothy Turner; Eeyore by Ralph Wright; Kanga by Barbara Luddy and Roo by Clint Howard (later by Dori Whitaker); Owl by Hal Smith; Piglet by John Fiedler; Gopher by Howard Morris; Rabbit by Junius Matthews; and, especially successfully, Tigger by Paul Winchell. (Narration is by Sebastian Cabot.) A further interesting point is that musical instruments are used on the soundtracks of the cartoons as a way of heralding the arrival of each of the major characters; this was the brainchild of Buddy Baker. The instruments used are as follows:

Pooh	baritone horn
Christopher Robin	trumpet and guitar
Rabbit	clarinet
Owl	ocarina and French horn
Kanga	flute
Roo	piccolo (obviously!)
Eeyore	bass clarinet
Piglet	oboe
Gopher	bass harmonica

The story of *Winnie the Pooh and the Honey Tree* is that Pooh follows a bee to find a hive high in a tree; on climbing up to get at the honey, though, he achieves little more than falling off to land in a gorse bush. At Christopher Robin's suggestion he rolls in some mud and uses a blue balloon to float up to the hive, thus disguised (as he persistently informs the bees) as "a little black rain-cloud – pay no attention to me". But even this cunning stratagem for some reason comes to naught, and he and Christopher Robin have to jump into the mud and shield themselves with the latter's umbrella in order to escape the wrath of the swarm.

Pooh, however, is still hungry, and so goes to Rabbit's home to beg a spot of lunch. It proves to be quite a big spot – indeed, on trying to leave, Pooh finds himself tightly wedged in Rabbit's hole. Christopher Robin, Rabbit and Eeyore attempt to drag him out, but all to no avail;

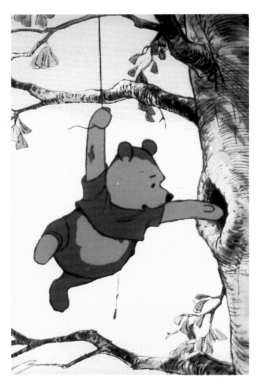

Winnie the Pooh and the Honey Tree, in the 1966 featurette of that name.

the only solution they can think of is to leave him there until he gets thinner by natural processes. Finally, days later, he has slimmed enough for them to haul him out – and out he shoots like a cork from a popgun to end up with his head firmly stuck in a hole in the honey tree. But this time, he assures his friends as the terrified bees flee, there is no need to be in too much of a hurry to rescue him: inside the tree he is feasting on the lashings of honey the bees have left behind.

The hilarious sequence in which Pooh's bottom becomes immovably fixed in Rabbit's rabbit-hole was born from Walt's own childhood musings as much as from the Milne text. When Walt was a child, he recalled years later, he wondered on reading the book not just what it would have been like for Pooh to be in this predicament but also what it must have been like for *Rabbit* to find that there was suddenly a new element added to the internal decor of his home – a point which Milne himself apparently ignored. What do you *do* with a teddy-bear's bottom in the middle of your wall? In the featurette Walt tried to solve the problem ... as does poor Rabbit. Firstly he tries to cover the intruding rear end with a stuffed moose-head; then he frames it with a picture-frame; then he drapes a sheet on it to make it look like an armchair; then ...

Walt was to comment: "I think it might be my funniest scene in the picture."

Winnie the Pooh and the Blustery Day has the friends in the Hundred Acre Wood suffering from storms and floods. The story starts with Pooh going to the "Thotful Spot", where Gopher pops up to tell him

that it is "windsday" – and so of course Pooh goes to wish his old pal Piglet a "happy windsday". "Windsday" is the right name for it – no sooner has Pooh greeted his friend than Piglet is swept off into the air by a particularly violent gust. Moments later Pooh is up in the air with him, and the two crash into Owl's house; Owl, politely, invites them in, but just as they are relaxing another gust throws Owl's house to the ground. Surveying the wreckage, Christopher Robin and the others decide that there is no hope of repair: Owl must have a new house. Eeyore volunteers to find one for him.

That blustery night Pooh is unnerved by ominous sounds outside, and in bounds Tigger. Tigger samples Pooh's honey, decides that honey is "not for tiggers", and departs as forcefully as he arrived, warning Pooh about mysterious honey-raiders called "heffalumps" and "woozles": Pooh tries to correct him but Tigger, characteristically, will not be corrected. And perhaps Tigger was right, for despite all his best intentions Pooh, standing (well, sitting) guard with a

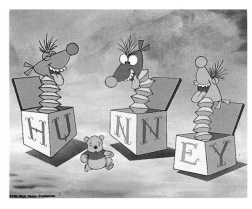

A gaggle of Woozles from *Winnie the Pooh and the Blustery Day* (1968).

ferocious-looking popgun, falls asleep and has a nightmare about those heffalumps and woozles. Frightening creatures they are, too. They come in all shapes, colours and sizes – one of the heffalumps even flies like a bee to steal (back) Pooh's treasured honey; others are like hot-air balloons, and for several terrifying moments Pooh finds himself floating through the sky suspended beneath one of them.

Pooh is woken by a thunderclap to find his house knee-deep in water. He takes refuge on a tree-limb, safely ensconced with ten reassuring jars of honey. Temptation strikes, and while he has his copiously licking head stuck in one of them he falls blindly into the floodwaters.

Piglet, too, has had his difficulties with the flood. Pausing only to put a message in a bottle reading "HELP! P-P-PIGLET (ME)", he sets sail on a chair, using a spoon as a paddle. Soon he and Pooh are united on the storm-tossed waters – but danger beckons. They are swept over a waterfall and all, to a distressedly observing Owl, seems lost;

then, though, Pooh pops up out of the water like a cork and Piglet is discovered to be safe inside Pooh's honey-pot.

After the floods have died down Christopher Robin organizes a "hero party" to celebrate Pooh for having saved Piglet's life, but just before the junketing gets under way Eeyore turns up to announce that he has found a new home for Owl. Excitedly the friends follow him – only to discover that the home in question is Piglet's. Despite Pooh's urgings, Piglet nobly refuses to tell Owl the truth, and so Pooh invites his little friend to come and live with him. Christopher Robin decrees that the feast become a "two-hero party" to commemorate Piglet's sterling self-sacrifice.

The star of *Winnie the Pooh and Tigger Too* is really Tigger rather than Pooh. The trouble is that the over-exuberant animal is getting on everyone's nerves by *bouncing* so much: it would be all right if he just bounced on his own, but he much prefers bouncing on other people. Rabbit organizes a protest meeting and suggests to the gathered friends that they take Tigger on an "Explore" and ... well ... sort of lose him. Surely, he adds, when Tigger finds his way home he will be so glad to see them that he will tone down all this bouncing.

Rabbit, Pooh and Piglet set off with Tigger on this venture, but after the three have succeeded in offloading the villain they find the journey home is not quite so simple as they had expected: indeed, they are lost, although Rabbit doggedly refuses to admit it. Pooh and Piglet try the cunning ruse of following the bear's hungry stomach, on the grounds that this will lead them to Pooh's stock of honey back home, but Rabbit will have none of it, and plunges deeper and deeper into the woods. All of a sudden he finds himself violently "bounced" by Tigger – who explains reassuringly that "Oh, tiggers do not get lost"!

Later Tigger bounces with little Roo to the top of a tree only to discover that tiggers do not like heights. How can he get himself and Roo down again? Not by bouncing, nor by climbing – and no one can suggest a solution. Eventually Tigger pleads with the narrator, saying that if only the narrator will narrate him out of the tree he will promise never to bounce again. And so the narrator tilts the picture to let Tigger slide safely to the ground. He is so excited at his salvation that he feels like having a good *bounce* – but Rabbit reminds him of his promise. Poor Tigger: he is quite lost and glum without his bounce! Finally, after a little moral blackmail from the others, Rabbit relents and lets Tigger start bouncing again: even he, he admits, prefers a happy bouncing Tigger to a gloomily bounceless one.

If Tigger is the star of *Winnie the Pooh and Tigger Too* then Eeyore is certainly the star of the fourth (and to date last) of the Pooh movies, *Winnie the Pooh and a Day for Eeyore*. It is, you see, his birthday.

The story starts with Pooh, Piglet, Rabbit and Roo playing a new game which the bear of little brain has accidentally invented: Pooh-sticks. (As any child will tell you, the game involves standing on a bridge over a river and all together dropping a stick each into the water. You then rush to the other side of the bridge, downstream, and the person whose stick first emerges beneath is the winner.) But suddenly a stick floats by below which no one can claim: it proves to be Eeyore's tail – with Eeyore attached to it. The doleful donkey has been "bounced" into the water by Tigger. Pooh's suggestion that they help Eeyore out by dropping rocks on one side of him, so that the waves will wash him to the riverbank, has the obvious result: Pooh's first huge boulder strikes Eeyore firmly amidships.

Eeyore, in due course, climbs out and explains to the friends why he is particularly depressed today – as if anyone would have noticed. It is his birthday, yet no one has given him a present or organized a party for him – *and* he has been bounced into the river. Pooh and Piglet determine to amend at least the gift part of this. Pooh sets off from home with a pot of honey for Eeyore, but unfortunately the contents get slightly eaten up along the way – still, at least Eeyore will have a useful pot to put things in. The balloon with which Piglet sets off sadly arrives as a tatter of punctured rubber, but Eeyore is consoled by the thought that he now has not only a useful pot but also something to put in it.

And the friends throw a birthday party for the little donkey, too. When Tigger arrives Rabbit is all for expelling him – after all, was it not he who "bounced" Eeyore into the river in the first place? – but Christopher Robin suggests, in order to cool things down, that they ought all to go and play a game of Pooh-sticks. And at last something nice happens for Eeyore: he wins consistently all the long afternoon – even though he has never played the game before!

Tigger, of course, is less successful – and is very grumpy, because tiggers are supposed to be good at Pooh-sticks. Eeyore takes pity on him and whisperingly tells him his "secret". Tigger is so utterly *delighted* to discover how to master the game that he ... well, poor old Eeyore gets "bounced" again.

Ironically, of all the characters in the Pooh shorts, **Winnie the Pooh** himself is probably the least successful in terms of capturing the spirit of the Milne original. Perhaps this has something to do with his voice, perhaps something to do with his physical appearance (on screen he comes across as fat rather than, as in the books, cuddlably pudgy); more likely, though, it is because his screen persona in a way falls between two stools. While he is not close enough to the "real" Pooh to be regarded as merely a faithful screen rendition of him, at the same time he is not *different* enough to be treated as a wholly new Disney creation – in the way that Tigger, for example, can.

However, he certainly does share many of the characteristics of his literary predecessor. He truly is a bear of little brain, although he possesses also a certain simple-minded, almost instinctive cleverness: in the search for adequate supplies of honey, his primary preoccupation, he is capable of lateral thinking almost to the point of genius. In *Winnie the Pooh and the Honey Tree*, for example, once he has begun to suspect that the bees are not 100 per cent convinced that he really is a little black rain-cloud, he asks Christopher Robin beneath to put up his umbrella and say: "Tut, tut – it looks like rain." In fact, this clever ruse fails to deceive the insects – but the *idea* was a good one! In the same short, when Gopher calls to visit Pooh, who is stuck in Rabbit's hole and being starved to slimness, it takes Pooh only a moment to discover that, yes, there is honey in Gopher's lunch-box and to ask for some of it. (Rabbit resourcefully scotches this wheeze by rushing out to put up a "Don't Feed the Bear" sign.) Pooh's suggestion for saving Eeyore from the river in *Winnie the Pooh and a Day for Eeyore* (in which he was voiced by Hal Smith) is again perfectly reasonable – it just happens not to work.

But cleverness does not very often visit Pooh. Again in *Winnie the Pooh and a Day for Eeyore* there is a moment when he comes across Piglet outside his (Pooh's) front door. Piglet, being very small, cannot reach the knocker, and so Pooh kindly helps him – by rat-a-tat-tatting a few times. Only when Pooh remarks conversationally, *inter alia*, that the person inside is taking a long time to answer can Piglet get the necessary word in edgeways to point out that ...

The screen character of Pooh profits also from reproducing some of the verbal lunacy of the literary original. In *Winnie the Pooh and the Honey Tree* there is a glorious moment, during his initial scrounging of a meal of honey from Rabbit, when he asks for just a "small helping". This Rabbit duly supplies. On seeing the bear's disappointment Rabbit queries: "Is there anything wrong?" Replies a saddened Pooh: "Well, I did mean a little *larger* small helping."

The other controversial character in the Pooh shorts is **Gopher**: one unkind remark from a critic was that Disney's first mistake was including Gopher in *Winnie the Pooh and the Honey Tree*, the second including him also in *Winnie the Pooh and the Blustery Day*. In fact, Gopher is the one character in the Pooh movies who cannot be found in the original books by A. A. Milne: he was included in the shorts at Walt's own insistence. Whenever he appears, he acknowledges his dubious origins by crying: "I'm not in the book, you know!" In 1966 the Hartford (Connecticut) *Times* produced an interesting article in this respect: the reporter claimed that Milne's niece Angela had said that Milne himself had originally planned to put a gopher in the books, because he and Christopher Robin had seen one near their home, but that his publisher had insisted that the character be removed. By an astonishing

Pooh correctly identifies the better part of valour in *Winnie the Pooh and the Blustery Day* (1968).

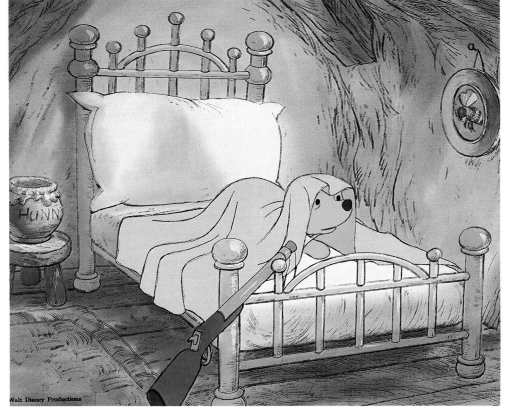

Walt Disney Productions

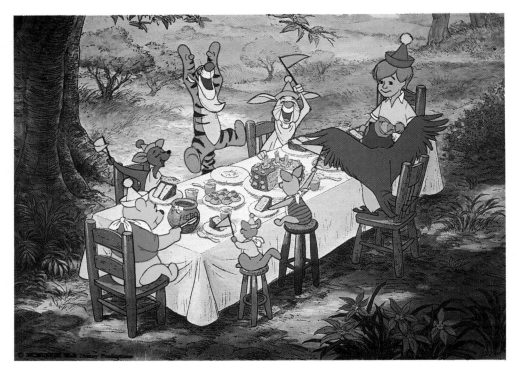

Christopher Robin and friends enjoy a "hero party" in *Winnie the Pooh and the Blustery Day* (1968). Clockwise from bottom left: Pooh, Kanga, Tigger, Rabbit, Christopher Robin, Owl, Piglet and Roo.

exasperated point, "Why did I *ever* invite that bear to lunch?"). He it is who plans the "cure" for Tigger in *Winnie the Pooh and Tigger Too*, and then resolutely refuses to believe in the possibility that he might have got the "Explore" party lost. And he it is, too, who quite rightly claims that Tigger ought to be expelled from Eeyore's birthday party in *Winnie the Pooh and a Day for Eeyore*. Rabbit is a major cartoon creation: it is perhaps too much to hope that he may feature in further "non-Pooh" movies.

Owl, by contrast with Rabbit, is not so much the intellectual as the pseudo-intellectual of the group. His erudition is certainly overrated by his friends. For example, when Pooh, in *Winnie the Pooh and a Day for Eeyore*, is hoping to enhance the "useful pot" which he is taking to the sad donkey and asks Owl to write "Happy Birthday" on it, the result is: "HIPY PAPY BTHUTHDTH THU HDA BTHUTHDY." Even the illiterate bear thinks that this does seem rather a lot of words for the simple message "Happy Birthday", but he takes

coincidence, Walt had unknowingly insisted that a gopher be put into the story because he felt it needed one. This is a very good tale, but it suffers from the embarrassing disadvantage that gophers do not exist in the United Kingdom, so Milne and his son certainly could not have seen one near their home. The whole report is probably an example of "modern mythology".

Gopher, purple-blue, whistling his "esses" and fronted by two outrageously buck teeth, is a caricature of the handyman you never want to pick out of the Yellow Pages – but inevitably do. When called in to help extract Pooh from Rabbit's hole (in *Winnie the Pooh and the Honey Tree*) he refuses to give an estimate for the job, except to promise that it will be expensive. Any time of the day or night seems to represent "unsocial hours" to him. After his brief appearance near the start of *Winnie the Pooh and the Blustery Day* he failed to feature again in the Pooh shorts, perhaps wisely.

Christopher Robin, as in the books, plays in the movies the important role of peacemaker. Whenever quarrels threaten to break out – notably between Rabbit and Tigger – Christopher Robin is there to calm things down. Aside from that, however, he is rather like Wart (➤270) and Taran (➤314) in being a sort of cypher of a character: attractive in a little-boy way, yet nowhere as strongly portrayed as those surrounding him. He seems almost extraneous to the action of the movies – which is exactly the way he is portrayed almost throughout the books. Christopher Robin may instigate projects, he may mediate between foes, but he rarely intrudes upon the story proper. And this is exactly as it should be.

As noted above, the voice of **Rabbit** was supplied by Junius Matthews (except in *Winnie the Pooh and a Day for Eeyore*, when Will Ryan did it), who had earlier voiced Archimedes (➤273). He had first come to Walt's attention when the latter had heard him on the radio playing the part of a potato. "Anyone who can personalize a potato," Walt is reported to have said, "should be good for Rabbit."

Rabbit is the radical, the labour-organizer, of the group of friends in Hundred Acre Wood; he is also, despite Owl's claims, probably the most intelligent of them – and he is certainly the most irascible and obstinate. He it is who has to put up with Pooh's rear end protruding immovably into his home (in *Winnie the Pooh and the Honey Tree*), who disguises it in various cleverly thought-out ways (as he comments at one

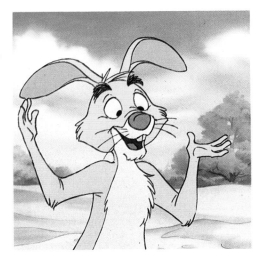

The irrepressible Rabbit, one of the best characters in the Pooh shorts.

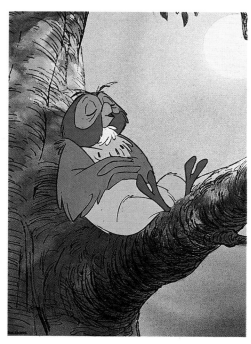

Owl takes a rest in *Winnie the Pooh and the Honey Tree* (1966).

Owl's word for it that all is well. This is foolish: Owl's erudition cannot be relied upon. Neither, for that matter, can his advice. In *Winnie the Pooh and the Honey Tree*'s great Rabbit-hole scene, he correctly judges that Pooh is "a wedged bear in a great tightness" but incorrectly decrees that the sole course of action is to call in an expert – in this case Gopher, who proves to be utterly useless. Still, it cannot be argued but that Owl's heart is in the right place – although one must wonder if he was being totally disingenuous in accepting the "new home" at the end of *Winnie the Pooh and the Blustery Day*.

Owl is the latest representative of a distinguished line of Disney owls: two earlier ones of note were Friend Owl in *Bambi* (➤200) and of course Archimedes in *The Sword in the Stone* (➤273).

Eeyore, the gloomy donkey, is very much a faithful version of Milne's original

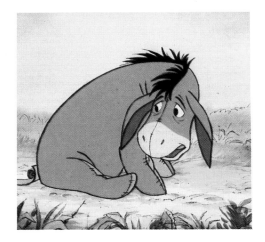

Eeyore gives us a glimpse of his cheerier side.

character, with a few touches added by Shepard. His prime characteristic, aside from his universally pessimistic mood, is his tail: constantly dropping off despite Christopher Robin determinedly nailing it on, it has a sort of sullen inertness that renders it almost a character in its own right. Deliciously, it sports a pink bow which is quite at odds with both its own and its owner's general depressingness. Voice and image combine in Eeyore to create a superb characterization of determined gloom – and his dialogue helps, too. In *Winnie the Pooh and the Honey Tree*, as Christopher Robin yet again hammers in a nail to affix the donkey's tail, Eeyore comments: "It's not much of a tail, but I'm sort of attached to it." And when, in the same short, Pooh wishes him a good morning, Eeyore responds with: "Good morning. If it *is* a good morning, which I doubt."

The donkey, however, is of good heart: consider his selfless quest for a new home for Owl in *Winnie the Pooh and the Blustery Day*. Only very occasionally can Eeyore burst out of his pervading depression – no, "burst" is the wrong word for a character so lethargic. But he does on occasion *seep* momentarily out of it, as in *Winnie the Pooh and a Day for Eeyore*, when Piglet tells him that he has brought him a balloon as a birthday present: Eeyore faints in sheer ecstasy. Mind you, Eeyore's bleak perception of the hostile universe is amply confirmed when he comes to his senses again and Piglet shows him all that is left of this once-beautiful balloon.

Piglet, although a major character in the Milne books, is a comparatively minor one in the Disney shorts: he does not even

appear in the first of them, *Winnie the Pooh and the Honey Tree*. Whether by popular request or not, he has a slightly more major role in the rest, although only in *Winnie the Pooh and the Blustery Day* could he be said to play a central part. In that movie he tells us forthrightly that his house was once owned by his grandfather, a character called Trespassers Will. Piglet proudly points to a sign bearing his grandfather's name. The fact that there is a corner missing from the sign might lead a sceptic to suggest that there are a couple of words missing, but never mind.

Piglet was always represented as curiously revolting in the Shepard illustrations – deliberately so, for children's favourite suckable toys often have this characteristic – and Disney reproduces this aspect faithfully: he has pink ears, a red-and-black striped jersey, a clammy-looking little scarf and an oddly penetrative high-pitched voice. In the Disney shorts he is given no memorable lines, and yet, in *Winnie the Pooh and the Blustery Day*, he

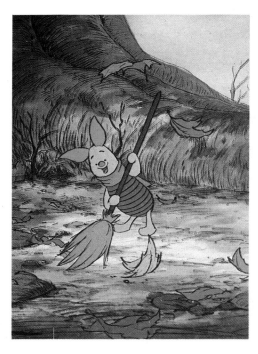

Busy, busy, busy – Piglet tackles the leaves in *Winnie the Pooh and the Blustery Day* (1968).

shows himself to be a truly noble character, with a generosity of spirit lacking from most of us. It is little wonder that children watching the Pooh movies have a great affection for Piglet.

Kanga and **Roo** are fairly minor characters in the books and remain so in the movies, but **Tigger** is a major cartoon creation by any standards: he succeeds because, unlike Pooh, he is almost completely dissimilar from the original Milne creation, being aggressively American rather than merely aggressively un-British. He leaps exuberantly into the Disney Pooh canon in *Winnie the Pooh and the Blustery Day* announcing to the world

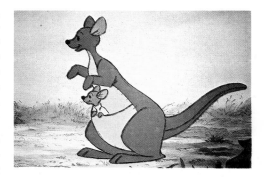

Kanga and Roo, from *Winnie the Pooh and the Honey Tree* (1966).

large and the befuddled bear in particular that "the most wonderful thing about tiggers is that I'm the only one". The other characters have good cause to be thankful that he is indeed the "only one", for his boisterousness, especially his less than considerate habit of "bouncing" people, is a little hard for them to tolerate (although audiences view it with delight). He has also a perennial habit of announcing that "tiggers do [something] best" and then later, ruefully, concluding that "tiggers don't do [something]" – like, in fact, a child confronted by a plate of unknown yet appetizing-seeming foodstuffs.

Tigger is not an utterly flawless fellow, though. Ignoring for the moment his bouncing (which is difficult!), in *Winnie the Pooh and a Day for Eeyore* we discover that he is a little less than totally honest, should the occasion demand disingenuousness. After Eeyore has told the friends that he has been "bounced" into the river by Tigger, the guilty party is questioned about the affair and claims that oh, no, it wasn't *really* that he "bounced" Eeyore, just that he explosively coughed at the wrong moment. A flashback proves that Tigger's version of events is, well, a little out of accord with the facts. Yet for all his faults Tigger is a difficult character to dislike: he has a hearty good nature which is very appealing.

After the hostile critical reaction to *Alice in Wonderland* Walt declared that he would never tackle, in animation, a classic fictional creation again: since then he and his successors have produced successful screen versions of *Peter Pan* (➤247), the Pooh stories and *The Little Mermaid* (➤342). While the Pooh featurettes are arguably the least engaging of these adaptations, they are far from poor, and the same can be said of the TV series *The New Adventures of Winnie the Pooh* (➤140), which features all the main characters in new stories.

For once, Walt's instinct was wrong.

Filmography

Winnie the Pooh and the Honey Tree, February 4, 1966
Winnie the Pooh and the Blustery Day, 1968
Winnie the Pooh and Tigger Too, 1974
Winnie the Pooh Discovers the Seasons, 1981
Winnie the Pooh and a Day for Eeyore, 1983

Eeyore did not appear in *Winnie the Pooh and Tigger Too*. **Gopher** did not appear in *Winnie the Pooh and Tigger Too*, *Winnie the Pooh Discovers the Seasons* and *Winnie the Pooh and a Day for Eeyore*. **Owl** did not appear in *Winnie the Pooh and Tigger Too*. **Piglet** did not appear in *Winnie the Pooh and the Honey Tree*. **Tigger** did not appear in *Winnie the Pooh and the Honey Tree* and *Winnie the Pooh Discovers the Seasons*.

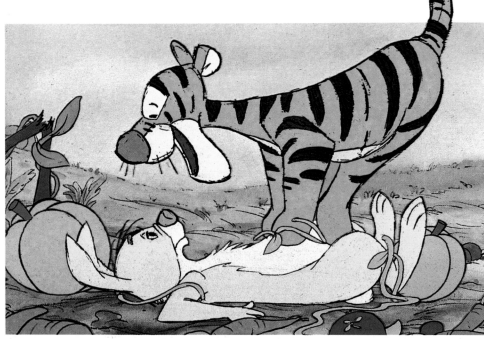

Rabbit experiences Tigger's favourite pastime – bouncing – in *Winnie the Pooh and Tigger Too* (1974).

SCROOGE McDUCK

Until 1987 and the advent of the Disney TV program *DuckTales* (➤**139**), Scrooge's career had been primarily off-screen: he had taken only two screen roles – and, although both of these had been memorable, he was much better known for his extensive appearances in the comics, especially when drawn by the prolific pen of the great Carl Barks. It is from the comics that we learn that he gathered his billions in various ways, not all of them 100 percent savoury, until by the late 1940s he had amassed a fortune unequaled by any other duck in history: no less than *three cubic acres* of money plus, almost by afterthought, an international financial empire. Of all this, though, his favourite piece of money is still the first dime he ever owned – a prize which is to this day the target of his old adversary, the sorceress Magica de Spell. His indefatigable allies in his encounters with her and with others who would like to help themselves to part of his fortune are none other than Donald Duck's three Nephews, Huey, Dewey and Louie (for whose career in the shorts p. 85; further discussion is in the context of *DuckTales*, p. 139).

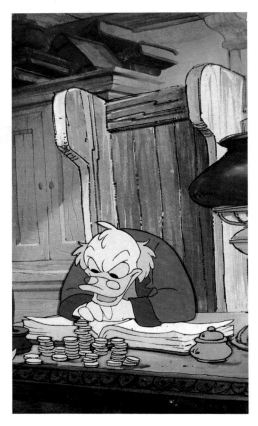

Scrooge McDuck's finest hour – typecast as the miser in *Mickey's Christmas Carol* (1983).

Scrooge's comic-book popularity may have derived from the fact that the flat artwork produced by Barks (who earned somewhat less than three cubic acres of money from his creation) shared many of the qualities of an animated cartoon. George Lucas has written of the strips that they are "very cinematic . . . They . . . don't just move from panel to panel, but flow in sequences, sometimes several pages long". In light of this, it is very curious indeed that it took so long for Scrooge's screen career to take off. In a 1978 interview with Jim Korkis in *Mindrot*, Jack Hannah explained that, so far as he could recall, the problem was that someone at the Disney studio felt that a character whose sole motivation was the lust for money was not genuinely funny – or, at least, had few comic possibilities in animated form. Moreover, the general feeling was that Scrooge, being a mono-maniacal personality, wasn't really strong enough to "carry" animated films. In any case, by this time – the mid-1950s – Disney's production of theatrical shorts was petering out, so there really wasn't much point in continuing the debate. When at last given the chance, Scrooge was to show how wrong that earlier decision had been.

His first screen performance was in the 1967 featurette *Scrooge McDuck and Money*, in which he was voiced with great zeal by Bill Thompson. This movie was in the prevalent Disney vein – a mixture of education and entertainment. The three Nephews (confusingly described as Scrooge's own, whereas in fact they are and have always been Donald's) visit him in order to find out how to become as wealthy as he is. He gives them an illustrated lecture, punctuated with songs, on the history of money and on the way both domestic and national budgeting works. Finally he charges them 3 cents for his advice, on the basis that "nothing good is ever free"– a dubious conclusion.

Scrooge's second screen appearance was in *Mickey's Christmas Carol* (1983), in which – naturally! – he plays the part of Ebenezer Scrooge, the misanthropic miser of Charles Dickens's popular 1843 short novel. The overall story is well enough known to need little by way of repetition here; what is of much more interest is the way in which this featurette became not only the first bill-topping animated short for many a long year but also featured so many of the classic Disney characters in Dickensian guise. Mickey Mouse plays Bob Cratchit, and Minnie his wife; Donald Duck plays Scrooge's jolly nephew Fred; Daisy Duck is there as Isabel, Scrooge's one-time fiancée and the sole true love of his life apart from money (the money won); Goofy turns in a memorable performance as Marley's ghost; the ghosts of Christmas Past, Present and Yet to Come are played respectively by Jiminy Cricket, Willie the Giant and Pete (probably Pete's best-ever performance); Toad appears as Fezzywig, Scrooge's first employer when he was just a slip of a penny-pincher; Rat and Mole are there as collectors for the poor, while Donald's horse is Cyril Proud-bottom and two of the weasels from Toad Hall act as gravediggers; even Skippy Bunny and Toby Turtle from *Robin Hood* appear in a street scene. And, to cap it all, when the Ghost of Christmas Past shows Scrooge a wild party in progress at old Mr. Fezzywig's, there we see among the celebrants a whole galaxy of old-time Disney stars: Clarabelle Cow, Horace Horsecollar, Clara Cluck, Gus Goose, Chip an' Dale, the Nephews . . .

A single new character threatens to steal the show: **Tiny Tim**, the crippled child of Bob and Mrs. Cratchit. This little fellow is probably one of Mickey's nephews Morty and Ferdy (➤**71**). However, Scrooge has never been a duck to be generous about anything, and the limelight is no exception: voiced in astringent Scots by Alan Young, he is very much the star of the featurette, and to him goes its best line. Speaking of Marley he fondly recalls: "In his will he left me enough for his tombstone. Ha! And I had him buried at sea!"

Scrooge's most major screen role to date has been as himself in *DuckTales: The Movie – Treasure of the Lost Lamp*. That performance is discussed in the section (➤**139**) on the TV series *DuckTales*.

Filmography

> *Scrooge McDuck and Money*, 1967
> *Mickey's Christmas Carol*, 1983
> *DuckTales: The Movie – Treasure of the Lost Lamp*, 1990

M. C. BIRD

It's Tough to be a Bird (1969), which won an Academy Award, was in part an educational short discussing the evolution and history of birds and the legends about them, in part an advertisement for the National Audubon Society – that is to say, it

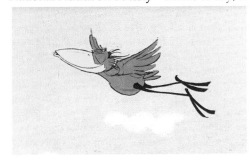

M.C. Bird, from 1969's *It's Tough to be a Bird.*

was a "conservation movie". Mostly animated, it included some live footage. Its narrator is a rather disreputable-looking red-orange bird – M. C. Bird – who sings the song "It's Tough to be a Bird" and has the immortal catchline: "We birds are born losers." In various ways M. C. Bird proves the apparent truth of this statement.

Christopher Columbus, Leif Ericsson and Edgar Allan Poe all make cameo appearances (the two former using birds as navigational aids, and the latter in connection with "The Raven"). A further brief appearance, right at the end of the short, is by none other than Mary Poppins!

SMALL ONE

The 25-minute *The Small One* was released in 1978; based on a book by Charles Tazewell, it had a story by Vance Gerry and Pete Young.

In the true Disney tradition, the story of Small One is a mixture of happy and sad. Small One is a donkey – a donkey with little going for him. He is grey, with lighter grey tufts of hair, and he has two goofy front teeth and floppity ears which droop when he is sad and perk up when he is happy; he is distinctly smaller and more incompetent than all the other donkeys in the stable – who despise him not only because of his weakness but also because he is much loved by the **Boy**, a funny little fellow with a ragged red tunic and a mop of black hair held back by a blue ribbon.

In this short we find ourselves in the Holy Land a little before the birth of Jesus. A poor farming family are ekeing out a living as best they can from the unwilling soil. The loving relationship between the Boy and Small One is established in the opening sequence when the two play a great chase game around the stable in the early morning, as the world is waking. Later they go out into the fields with the **Father** and the other asses to fetch in wood; but Small One is so feeble and undersized that he has great difficulty carrying his assigned load.

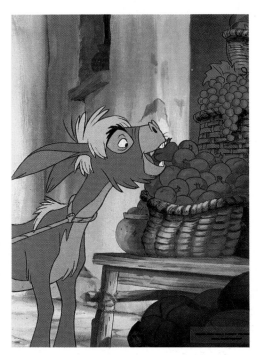

Small One, star of the 1978 movie *The Small One* which was seen as a testing ground for the "new breed" of Disney animators.

Nevertheless the Boy helps out until, tried beyond the limitations of patience, the Father says to him: "Don't you have enough work without doing Small One's, too?" And the Father goes on to explain that Small One is old, eats as much as the other donkeys, and cannot pull his weight. The family cannot afford to keep him on longer; he must be sold at market. Anyway, reasons the Father, Small One will be happier living in the city, where his tasks will be less onerous. The Boy, sadness filling his big blue eyes, asks to be allowed to be the one to take Small One to market, and the Father agrees.

On the next day the Boy and Small One go to the city. At the city gates they are stopped by a bullying Roman guardsman who, on hearing of their errand, directs them to the third shop inside the gates; there, he claims, they are bound to make a sale. In the cavernous shop they find a tall cadaverous figure sharpening a knife ominously; he offers the Boy a single piece of silver for Small One. The Boy is horrified by how low the price is – and even more horrified when he realizes that the would-be purchaser is a tanner, who wants Small One only for his hide.

Small One and the Boy flee with precipitate haste and, after they have recovered themselves, wander around the market watching the money change hands and seeing the vicious greed of the merchants. Three of these form a sort of song-and-dance act, doing a number in which they express the avaricious ethos of the market to perfection:

> Clink clink, clank clank,
> Get the money to the bank
> Telling little stories you can trust.
> We never ever fail
> If we go to make a sale . . .
> We simply cheat a little if we must.

But the three twisters, while declining themselves to purchase Small One (not even for one single silver piece), nevertheless display a modicum of kindness to the Boy, directing him towards an auctioneer.

The **Auctioneer**, whom we discover selling top-quality horses, is a big fat fellow dressed largely in red, with a black beard and moustache and a bright red turban. He announces to the eager crowd that the next animal on show will be "a fine steed of great breeding"; the raucous laughter of the audience persuades him to turn around to *look* at this "fine steed", and he finds that it is Small One. He tries to drive boy and donkey away, but the Boy insists that Small One is good enough to live in a king's stable; and so the Auctioneer mockingly pretends to try to sell the donkey – starting at a price of 1,000 pieces of silver (a top horse at his stand fetches, normally, only about 60). It is a great joke to the Auctioneer, and he milks it for all it is worth – leaping astride Small One, who buckles

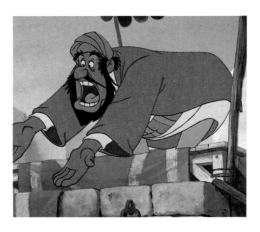

The Auctioneer clearly thinks the Boy has valued his donkey a little high in *The Small One* (1978).

under the weight. But Small One is tougher than the Auctioneer thinks, and throws him – to the delight of the crowd. The furious Auctioneer chases our friends away, but they escape. "I'm sorry, Small One," the Boy weeps, collapsing down beside the animal; but Small One stoically leads him off through the city. They end up trying to sleep in a back alley.

But then a man appears whom we instantly recognize as **Joseph**, father of the Christ; clad in a white robe with a bluish cowl, he is gentle-voiced and kindly of expression. He needs a quiet donkey to carry his wife to Bethlehem for the census; he cannot offer more than a single silver piece for the animal, but he promises to give Small One a good home. The Boy, by this time desperate, agrees, and the money changes hands. There is a happy-sad scene of parting between boy and donkey; the lad tells Small One to be strong, sure of foot and obedient.

In the closing scene we see, in the distance, Joseph walking alongside Small One, who is bearing on his suddenly strong back the pregnant **Mary**. The Boy waves his goodbye and, while we sympathize with his temporary grief, we know that both he and his donkey friend will in due course be happier in the new lives which Fate has apportioned them.

The Small One has been widely reported as being nothing more than a featurette designed to allow the "new breed" of Disney animators the chance to show what

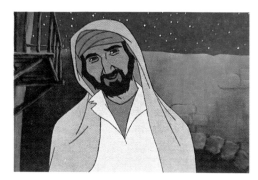

Joseph, father of Jesus, seeks a donkey to carry a pregnant Mary in 1978's *The Small One*.

they could do before being let loose on a full-length feature. One retired veteran animator described the movie uncompromisingly as "flat". John Canemaker, the doyen of animated-cartoon critics, was equally hostile in his article "Disney Without Walt" (*Print*, 1978): he said that

> it merely provided the new people with another chance to practise realistic, emotional animation in a vehicle that does not stretch their techniques or give them experience handling truly different stories, characters or designs. ... this by-the-numbers exercise aimed at the usual Disney audience.

The "usual Disney audience", of course, loved every moment of it!

OILSPOT AND LIPSTICK

Produced by David Inglish and directed by Michael Cedeno, *Oilspot and Lipstick* was a short premiered at the SIGGRAPH Convention in Anaheim on July 28, 1987. It uses computer-generated graphics animation to depict the adventures of two "junk dogs", made out of discarded metal pieces, in the junkyard that is their home. The junk in the yard is capable of producing quasi-living beings other than dogs: the villain of the piece is the **Junk Monster**, who threatens our hero, **Oilspot**, and his girlfriend, **Lipstick**. It hardly needs to be mentioned that Oilspot defeats the monster and wins the girl, just as in the old theatrical cartoons.

THE ARCHBISHOP

Almost without exception the characters in the 1990 featurette *The Prince and the Pauper* are old and tested favourites from the Disney stable: Mickey Mouse (voiced in both of his roles by Wayne Allwine), Donald Duck (voiced by Tony Anselmo), Pete (voiced by Arthur Burghardt) and Goofy, Pluto and Horace Horsecollar (these three voiced by Bill Farmer); Clarabelle Cow (voiced by Elvia Allman) also puts in an appearance.

The plot of the movie bears basic resemblances to the 1882 Mark Twain novel on which it was based. The king of England is dying. His son and heir, the Prince (played by Mickey), feels ensnared by the responsibilities he must soon assume: the awaiting adult world is personified in his droningly pompous tutor (Horace). When

a pauper (also Mickey) inadvertently comes into the palace in pursuit of his dog (Pluto) and proves to be the Prince's exact double, the Prince insists that the two exchange places for a single day. He reckons without the machinations of the evil Captain of the Guard (Pete); also, he has no idea of what life is like in the downtrodden city outside his palace walls. The net result is that both the real and the stand-in Prince (the latter aided by the valet, Donald) are soon entangled in problems – especially since the **King** (whom we never see) chooses this moment to die. Pete, discovering the substitution, plans to dispose of the real Prince and force the substitute to reign as his (Pete's) puppet. To this end, the Prince and Donald are cast into the dungeons, preparatory to summary execution, but Mickey's (the pauper's) old pal Goofy, with whom the Prince was staying, comes to the rescue – although not, it seems, in time to stop the coronation of the reluctant substitute.

It is at the coronation that the owl-headed Archbishop makes his appearance; he is voiced by Frank Welker, who also serves as the featurette's narrator and speaks the dusty words of the dying King. Although the Archbishop seems less than fully compos mentis, he is as determined to put the crown on Mickey's head as Mickey is to wriggle away from it:

> *Archbishop*: Ah, be seated, sire.
> *Mickey*: Ha – after you!
> *Archbishop*: Ha ha! No, no – beauty before age, sire.
> *Mickey*: Oh, oh no . . . huh-ah . . . age before beauty. . . .
> *Archbishop (his cool lost, his smile frozen)*: Your Highness, you're such a sport! Sit down!
> *Mickey*: Hee hee – got it!

Even once Mickey is on the throne, the Archbishop's tribulations are not over:

> *Archbishop*: It is both my duty and pleasure to crown you . . . (*Mickey squirming away*) er-uh . . . to . . . crown you . . . to . . . eh . . . I say, a rather wiry lad! Eh, to, eh . . . so slippery . . . (*angry*) would you hold still? Gee . . . eh . . .
> *Mickey*: Uh . . . hee hee . . . stop! . . . Look, I'm the Prince, right? And whatever I order must be done, right?
> *Archibishop*: Uh, uh, yes.
> *Mickey*: Hah! Well then, the Captain is an insolent scoundrel! Guards – seize him!

Of course, it doesn't work out as easily as all that, for the guards are loyal to their wicked master, Pete. However, the Prince, Goofy, Donald and Pluto burst onto the scene and, after an ostentatious brawl, Pete and his hench-weasels are vanquished.

Those weasels are among the minor characters worth noting. They owe a great deal to the ones in *The Adventures of Ichabod and Mr. Toad* (➤**230**), but they have certain oily brio that puts us as much in mind of the Toontown Patrol in *Who Framed Roger Rabbit* (➤**326**). Among the other minor characters there are a peasant, a pig driving a wagon and Clarabella's two children; we encounter the latter when two of Pete's hench-weasels are robbing her of food in the (misused) name of the King.

OFF HIS ROCKERS

In 1992 Disney released the animated short *Off His Rockers* alongside their live-action movie *Honey, I Blew Up the Kids*. Only five minutes long, this was an experimental piece, done entirely at Walt Disney Feature Animation Florida and apparently by animators who simply fell

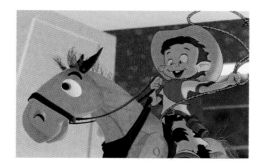

Rocking Horse and Boy playing in *Off His Rockers*.

in love with the subject and so worked on the project in their spare time. The basic plot is that a small boy abandons his trusty rocking horse in favor of video games; the rocking horse lures him back to the saddle, and off they go together to have further genuinely imaginative adventures.

There is some irony that, although the rocking horse loathes what the video games are doing to the boy, the character itself was animated using computers—as were many other parts of this short. Barry Cook, the short's director, has commented of this character:

The catalyst for the whole idea was the rocking horse itself. I was thinking: "What kind of character would contain geometric shapes and be suitable for the level of computer graphics that we wanted to experiment with?" The horse is made of carved wood and has flat surfaces on the sides and legs. He looks like he's cut out of boards.

By contrast, the boy was animated in the traditional fashion—in other words, by hand. The use of the two techniques alongside each other might have looked uneasy, but in fact, it merely added to the movie's interest.

II
THE TELEVISION SERIES

INTRODUCTION

In the first edition of this encyclopedia I wrote that "in recent years the Disney company has concentrated much of its creative attention on two animated children's series for television: *The Wuzzles* and *Disney's Adventures of the Gummi Bears*." Although the remark was in no way disparaging, it was nevertheless made rather sadly, for at the time (1986) it seemed to me that Disney was reducing the status of its production of animated features to "gesture" level; it was my impression that the commercial people at Disney were prepared to permit the creative people to make animated features only every few years, and then only as tokens intended to remind their rivals and the public at large that Disney could still do it best—a claim that was at the time looking increasingly dubious, because a number of those rivals were taking great strides into Disney's traditional territory.

In this light, two television children's series—however good of their kind they might be—seemed a poor swap. And news of plans to develop television output further brought nothing of the anticipatory tingle one experiences on discovering that a major new animated feature is on its way.

Unfortunately, no one loaned me a crystal ball. Since then, of course, there has been an outburst of feature movies from the Disney animators, not just in terms of quantity but also in terms of innovation and quality. It is fair to claim that the company's current standard of animated features is the finest it has ever been. Moreover, this enthusiastic flurry of activity hasn't been confined to the cinemas, for Disney has been developing its animated television output as well, setting standards of television animation that it is hard for any competitor to match.

It should be noted that it would be impossible to treat every Disney television animated character within the covers of this book. Television is a transient medium, and there are no records of many of the characters—especially the early ones. Moreover, some of the characters are of such fleeting interest (many appear in only one episode, and then only briefly) that to describe them would be nothing more than excessive pedantry.

THE WUZZLES

The Wuzzles premiered on September 14, 1985; there were thirteen episodes. From the series was drawn the featurette *Bulls of a Feather,* which was first released theatrically in the United Kingdom in March 1986; it was not released theatrically in the United States. The series was designed to appeal to kids aged two to ten and was probably most successful at the lower end of that age range.

Somewhere in the world there is (or was) the undiscovered land of Wuz, in which the adventures are set. The Wuzzles themselves are all winged creatures, their genetically suspect origins being inferable from their names:

Bumblelion	bumble bee/lion
Eleroo	elephant/kangaroo
Hoppopotamus	rabbit/hippopotamus
Moosel	moose/seal
Rhinokey	rhinoceros/monkey
Butterbear	butterfly/bear
Woolrus	lamb/walrus
Tycoon	tiger/raccoon
Pandeaver	panda/beaver
Piggypine	sow/porcupine
Koalakeet	koala/parakeet
Skowl	skunk/owl

Ranged against the happy-go-lucky Wuzzles there are three primary baddies, who are likewise of hybrid origin:

Croc	crocodile/bull
Flizard	frog/lizard
Brat	dragon/frog

The six main Wuzzles are Bumblelion, Eleroo, Hoppopotamus, Moosel, Rhinokey, and Butterbear. The voice of Bumblelion was supplied by Brian Cummings; that of Eleroo by Henry Gibson; that of Hoppopotamus by Joanne Worley; that of Moosel by Bill Scott; that of Rhinokey by Alan Oppenheimer; and that of Butterbear by Kathy Helpie. The series' narrator was Stan Freberg.

Bumblelion has strength and vivacity in his muscles but, sadly, not so much in his brain cells. Still, he is of good heart, even if he does have the unfortunate habit of leaping with both feet straight into new and unexpected—at least by him—scrapes. **Eleroo**, by contrast, is a rather coy character, constantly stocking up in his pouch things that might be useful—or, failing those, things that might not. His main problem is that he's very scatterbrained and disorganized and can't remember from one minute to the next just what it is that he's stowed away there. **Hoppopotamus**, it has to be admitted, is less dainty than a gazelle. However, this is not the way that she sees herself: as far as she is concerned she is a demurely alluring, sylphlike individual . . . unless, of course, circumstances cruelly conspire to transform her into the toughest Wuzzle of them all. So choose with care the gazelle with which you plan to compare her. **Moosel** is ever the optimist: he never gives up, no matter how bad things are looking. He is also a good team man—correction: team moose/seal. When the others flag he appeals to their team spirit, and this merry blitheness inspires them to keep on trying. **Rhinokey** is just as likely as Bumblelion to leap in where angels fear to tread; in addition he is something of an eccentric. His rhinoceros horn is striped like a barber's pole and sits incongruously in the middle of his face. **Butterbear** is the cutest of all the Wuzzles, as you can tell by the two flowers growing like antennae from her brow. For obvious reasons, bearing in mind her part-butterfly heritage, her wings are much more prominent than those of the other Wuzzles. She is a nature lover, always orderly and organized, and is ready to exhibit her emotions—joy or sorrow alike—at the drop of a hat. All told, she's the sort of girl your parents would like to see living next door.

As can be gathered from the above character descriptions, the Wuzzles were generally rather *too* lovable: the series as a whole lacked the occasional waspishness that Disney audiences of all ages look for. This oversweetness was accentuated when the Wuzzles made their excursion (in Europe) onto the big screen.

THE GUMMI BEARS

Like the Wuzzles (➤137), the Gummi Bears made their television debut on September 14, 1985; in September 1991 they left commercial television for the Disney cable channel. Aimed at a slightly higher age group, the series has been much more successful: after five seasons of morning appearances it moved to join the *The Disney Afternoon* in the fall of 1990. The featurettes *A New Beginning* and *Faster than a Speeding Tummi* premiered theatrically in the United Kingdom in 1986 and 1987, respectively.

The legend of the Gummi Bears begins long ago when this shy and kindly race, possessed of magical powers, lived in harmony with mankind. However, because of repeated human attempts to uncover the secrets of Gummi magic, the Gummies withdrew into secret subterranean warrens; eventually most of them sailed away to another land. As time passed, people grew to believe that the bears were nothing more than fairy – tales. Eventually, however, six of the remaining Gummies came out of hiding to help a young page called Cavin do battle with the evil Duke of Drekmore, one Igthorn by name. The television series and the theatrical featurettes center on this conflict, as the courageous six (sometimes assisted by a seventh, Gusto Gummi) make new discoveries after the centuries of their self-imposed isolation.

The action takes place in pseudomedieval times—that golden, nostalgia-tinted past that never in fact existed. Castles, knights, and ogres still hold sway in the world. Gummi Glen, the home of the Gummi Bears in the kingdom of Dunwyn, is a wonderland of tun-

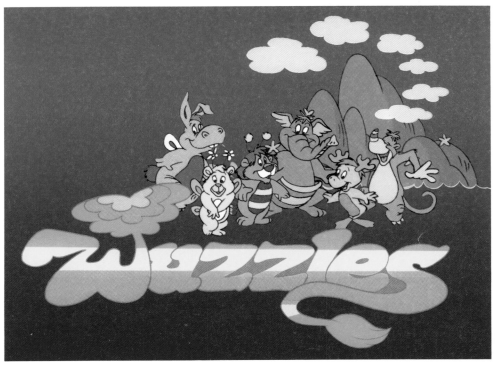

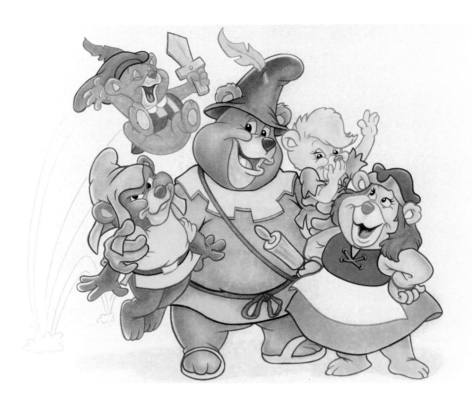

The Gummi Bears seem to have something to celebrate. From left: Gruffi, Cubbi, Tummi, Sunni and Grammi

nels and underground rooms; the former, known as "quicktunnels," run for miles and miles, and to traverse them the Gummi Bears often hop into their correspondingly named "quickcars."

In stark, gloomy contrast to the kingdom of Dunwyn is the dreary, drab dukedom of Drekmore, ruled over by the villainous **Duke Igthorn** (voiced by Michael Rye). The duke's modest ambition is to be omnipotent, and he is touchingly confused when no one else can see the sense in him fulfilling this desire. Notable among his cohorts is his oft-maltreated and abused sidekick **Toadie** or **Toadwort** (voiced originally by Bill Scott and then, after his death in 1985, by Corey Burton), a runtish ogre who occasionally displays unexpected good nature, and **Gad** and **Zook** (both voiced by Will Ryan, who also voices some of Igthorn's ogres as well as the character Unwin—see below). Also ranged against our heroes is **Lady Bane** (voiced by Tress MacNeille); this evil human sorceress is obsessively dedicated to unearthing the Gummi Bears' magical secrets. She entered the saga for the 1990–1991 season.

Turning to the good guys, we find Cavin, a humble page at Castle Dunwyn who was the first human ever to stumble across a way into Gummi Glen. His voice artist has changed regularly over the years (youthful actors grow up and their voices break): Christian Jacobs (1985 season), Brett Johnson (1986), David Faustino (1987), Jason Marsden (1988 until partway through 1990 when his voice

broke) and R. J. Williams (1990–1991). Cavin is in many ways the archetypal Disney boy hero: courageous, intelligent, resourceful, prone to mishaps at crucial moments, and just old enough to be attracted to his master's daughter. That master is the benevolent **King Gregor** (voiced like Igthorn by Michael Rye), whom Cavin idolizes. Gregor himself has a single overriding preoccupation: dissatisfied with the inherited glory of monarchy, he yearns to earn the right to become a knight in his own right. His other single preoccupation is his daughter, the beautiful **Princess Calla** (voiced by Noelle North): petite and delicate, Calla has the curious habit of being always in the thick of the fray. A further significant member of King Gregor's court is his most valiant knight, **Sir Tuxford** (voiced originally by Bill Scott, then by Roger C. Carmel for the 1986 season, and thereafter by Brian Cummings). Like Sir Giles, the foppish knight of *The Reluctant Dragon* (➤192), the stuffy Sir Tuxford is a decade or two past his prime and none too bright. His squire is **Unwin** (voiced by Will Ryan), a beanpole who attempts to bully Cavin much as Sir Kay bullied Wart in *The Sword in the Stone* (➤262). This generally ends in tears—and they're not Cavin's.

Of the Gummi Bears themselves, the most sophisticated is probably **Zummi Gummi**, the amateur Merlin of the group. He has charge of the *Great Book of Gummi,* a sort of cross between an encyclopedia and a home-repair manual, which holds full details of Gummi tradi-

tions, Gummi history, and Gummi magic. It contains the answer to almost any question you may care to ask; the difficulty is that you can't rely on Zummi Gummi to find that answer. Zummi Gummi was until 1989 voiced by Paul Winchell, then by Jim Cummings.

The self-appointed and occasionally acknowledged leader of the Gummies is **Gruffi Gummi** (like Toadie, voiced originally by Bill Scott but since 1986 by Corey Burton). Conservative to the very soles of his feet, Gruffi Gummi is never truly happy unless he has something to be unhappy about. Tough as nails on the outside, he does his best to obscure all traces of the many good and kindly deeds he performs.

Grammi Gummi is the mother-figure of the clan and the official tastemistress of Gummiberry Juice. Gummi Bears who drink this marvelous stuff are able to bounce—over high walls and/or across many leagues—and thereby to confuse and bewilder their foes. Played by veteran voice actress June Foray, Grammi Gummi seems to be a sweet, maternal old dear, but when roused she can be as ferocious as any other Gummi. Sadly, though, she has an Achilles' heel: her cooking.

The softest part of Grammi Gummi's heart is reserved for the two youthful Gummies: Cubbi Gummi and Sunni Gummi. The irrepressible **Cubbi Gummi**, the youngest of all the Gummies, is predictably full of unpredictable mischief—talkative, excitable, and prone to the taking of ill-advised shortcuts. He loves human beings, and often acts as the go-between/catalyst for the Gummies and their human friends. For his voice Cubbi shares Noelle North with Calla. **Sunni Gummi** is much more of a teenager than her brother, but has the same childlike ability to get into trouble. Irredeemably cute, pertly wholesome, with a proud plume of backswept blonde hair, she has a habit of letting her emotions override her not considerable intellect. Her voice is supplied by Katie Leigh.

The final member of the main Gummi clan is **Tummi Gummi**, a kindly, loyal, even-tempered giant of a Gummi; his motto is "Never Say Diet," so he's pretty tall even when lying down. In precise analogy with the Wuzzles' Hoppopotamus (➤137) he sees himself still as the sveltely slim young Gummi he was in the long ago. Tummi's voice is provided by Lorenzo Music.

Outside the central clan is **Gusto Gummi** (voiced by Rob Paulsen), a free-spirited, lateral-thinking artistic type who has chosen an existence independent of the rest. When he appears on the show his eccentric and mercurial mind galvanizes the others. He has as a sidekick a wry, sly toucan called **Arte Deco** (voiced by Brian Cummings). The ancient

Gummi kingdom of Ursalia features on occasion: it has as its caretaker a dithering and querulous character called **Sir Thornberry** (voiced by Walker Edmiston). This wrinkled old retainer has spent fifty years alone walking the halls of the capital discussing life's anomalies with the ancestral portraits.

The Gummi Bears may not be high art, but they can be a lot of fun. In judging them one has to keep in mind that they were designed for television: the animation, done largely in Japan under the direction of David Block, is good in terms of current television standards but inarguably elementary by Disney standards. What goes for the animation quality goes likewise for the characterization. In their own context, children's television, however, the Gummies work well.

DISNEY'S FLUPPY DOGS

Disney's Fluppy Dogs was a one-hour television special aired on November 27, 1986; it featured six magical talking dogs that came through an interdimensional doorway into the lives of a ten-year-old boy, **Jamie Bennett**, and his toffee-nosed neighbor, **Claire**; they were the intended prey of an animal collector called **Wagstaff**. Co-developed with the marketing and design group of Kenner Parker Toys, Inc., the Fluppy Dogs were matched with a supporting line of merchandise: a series of children's books, collect-the-set plush toys of the six characters, etc.; it seems clear the intention was that the television special should serve as pilot for a series.

The six Fluppy Dogs—**Lavender the Loving Fluppy, Blue the Loyal Fluppy, Pink the Pretty Fluppy** (also known offscreen as Fanci Flup), **Yellow the Playful Fluppy, Green the Cool Fluppy** and **Peach the Shy Fluppy** (smaller than the others)—were pastel-colored much according to their principal names and had characters inferable from their subsidiary names, although it is pleasing to discover from the merchandising litera-

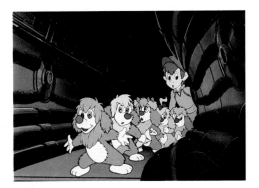

ture that Pink was also possessed of "savoir faire."

No more has been heard of the hypothetical series.

DUCKTALES

Perhaps surprisingly, it was not until the fall of 1987 that Disney began to exploit the medium of television in order to capitalize on one of the company's most enduringly popular characters, Scrooge McDuck (➤130). For *DuckTales* he was joined not only by the Nephews (➤85)—how could he escape them?—but also by some other characters who had led lives of stardom in the printed comics but not on screen. The most notable among these are Magica de Spell, Gyro Gearloose, and the Beagle Boys.

Scrooge McDuck himself was created by Carl Barks for a December 1947 Donald Duck comic book called Christmas on Bear Mountain. His career in the comic books and strips thereafter mirrors that of his illustrious nephew Donald (➤61) in the shorts: introduced initially as a supporting character, he was an immediate success and very soon came to outshine his erstwhile principal. The first of Scrooge's quarterly comic books was dated December/February 1953–1954, and from then until the appearance of issue #40 in 1963, Barks was solely responsible for writing and drawing these adventures of the miser and the Nephews; Barks's wife Garé (Margaret) did all the lettering and some of the background inking. Not until 1967, with book #71, did an issue appear that did not contain anything by Barks. Unfortunately for Barks, the terms of his employment meant that all copyright in this phenomenal body of work rested and still rests with Disney; as the comics historian Alberto Becattini has remarked, "Barks may have succeeded in creating the world's richest Duck, but clearly he did not succeed in creating the world's richest artist." Barks, in retirement, has earned an income from selling portraits of the Ducks, done in oils, watercolors, or pastels; most successful have been his various series of limited-edition lithographic prints.

In his *DuckTales* incarnation, Scrooge is voiced in a surprisingly convincing Scots accent by Alan Young, as in *Mickey's Christmas Carol* (➤130).

Scrooge's major obsession is accumulating money; his hobby is to wallow joyously in his Money Bin, a colossal vault that serves as both his cash repository and his swimming pool, complete with diving board. The equation of the money with water (liquid assets?) and swimming is a recurrent one, serving to under-

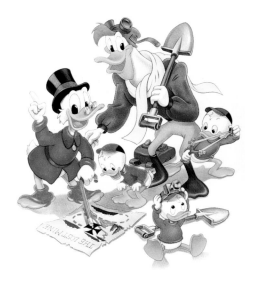

pin many of the *DuckTales* plots and also providing a basis for frequent scenes of dark fantasy that prove to be his nightmares. Though wealth is at the center of Scrooge's existence, he is surprisingly unostentatious about it: his *idée fixe* seems, often, to be less the acquisition of further cash than the dread of losing what he already has.

Yet, despite his stinginess, Scrooge is not without a soft heart—indeed for all his protestations it is not hard to make him quite gooily sentimental. For example, in *DuckTales: The Movie* the Genie (➤356) who emerges from the lost lamp of Collie Baba is soon able to pluck Scrooge's heart strings with his wistful desire to lose his magic and enjoy the "real-boy" life of the Nephews, and at the end of the movie Scrooge gladly uses his third and final wish not to increase his own store of material wealth but instead to grant the Genie that desire. There is sentimentality, too, in Scrooge's recollections of his youthful true love, Glittering Goldie (see below), as well as in many of his daily dealings with the three Nephews and especially Webbigail Vanderquack (again see below).

In most of his adventures his companions are of course **Donald's Nephews** and Webbigail Vanderquack. Left with him by Donald "temporarily" many years ago, the Nephews are here much less abrasive than in their shorts version (➤85): their characteristic overcuteness, which makes them so hilariously irritating in their dealings with Donald, is for *DuckTales* toned down, so that it is rendered merely as a slightly over-the-top charm, albeit with just enough of a whiff of mischief added to it that it never quite crosses the line to become stomach-turning preciousness. Nevertheless, sometimes we do feel the lack of the old quality.

Webbigail Vanderquack (voiced, like all three Nephews, by Russi Taylor) on rare occasion acts like just a fourth member of the trio, so that some critics have been moved to discount her as merely a token female chucked into the mixture to keep the feminists happy. This is a double misjudgment. In the vast majority of her roles she is quite distinct from the Nephews—distinct precisely because of her femininity, which is not usually portrayed as an asset. When she is not being a slightly cloying little girl, she is customarily a tag-along behind the other three. The contrast with the "token females" of *Chip 'n Dale Rescue Rangers, TaleSpin,* and *Darkwing Duck* could not be greater: Gadget (➤142), Rebecca Cunningham (➤143), and Gosalyn (➤144) are significantly brainier and frequently more resourceful than the male stars whom they support.

Scrooge's regular domestic staff are two in number. **Mrs. Beakley** is the Nephews' governess and seems also to act as the family housekeeper and cook—about whose culinary expertise there are the predictable jokes. Plump, matronly, and gray-haired, she is not overendowed with brains, yet mixed in with her querulously plum-voiced (by Joan Gerber) flightiness we find a rich strain of common sense and grit.

A much smaller part in the series is played by Scrooge's manservant, **Duckworth** (voiced by Chuck McCann), who is really little more than a caricature of the stereotyped uppercrust Amerenglish butler. Scrooge's pilot, **Launchpad McQuack** (voiced by Terence McGovern), a lumbering numbskull of a bird, took a much more major part in the earlier episodes than in the later ones, and then opted for a new career in *Darkwing Duck.* Launchpad is occasionally seen in company with his sidekick **Doofus.** Another member of Scrooge's entourage is **Bubba Duck**, an engaging (to the audience) little Neanderthal fellow with a mop of hair, a skin loincloth, a bad habit of, in games, using rocks in place of balls, and a propensity for trouble. He has a pet, a small dinosaur called **Tootsie**—the sixty-million-year disparity between their eras of origin counting for nothing.

Much more important is **Fenton Crackshell** (voiced by Hamilton Camp), Scrooge's accountant. A rather foppish duck in his normal guise—sometimes he seems like a milquetoast version of Donald (➤61)—he becomes somewhat more physically impressive when he dons a robot-style costume (invented by Gyro—see below), gives a mystical cry of "Blatherin' Blatherskite!," and shifts to become his superhero secret alter ego **Gizmoduck** (also voiced by Camp)—although, since Fenton himself is somewhat indecisive and ineffectual, Gizmoduck (who has a tenuous fan club called the Gizmo Guys) is not the most

dread-inspiring of superheroes. Scrooge's factory receptionist is the somewhat demurely sexy **Gandra Dee.** Fenton's mother, **Ma Crackshell**, is a scrawny, seedy woman with her hair habitually in curlers.

Magica de Spell is of course another perennially popular Barks creation from the comics; she dates from 1961, and soon became a comics star in her own right, teaming up with Madam Mim (➤272), from *The Sword in the Stone,* in many resourceful attempts to deprive Uncle Scrooge of his millions—but most especially of his treasured good-luck charm, the first dime he ever earned. Interestingly, although Disney has had to be careful about using witches as characters in some countries, there has never been any trouble with Magica de Spell. In the television series she is voiced in ringing Mittel-European tones by June Foray. She has thin features and long, straight, center-parted dark hair. Special fun for the audience is to identify the various pieces of music that accompany Magica in her various voyages across the sky.

One of Scrooge's most important allies is **Gyro Gearloose** (voiced quaveringly by Hal Smith). Gyro first appeared in the comics in 1952 as the self-proclaimed "Inventor of Everything." He's the classic cartoon inventor: the devices he creates are often fundamentally both very useful in principle and very ingeniously conceived, yet inevitably they go wrong—usually disastrously so.

It is hard to decide whether Scrooge's youthful sweetheart, **Glittering Goldie**, should be described as an adversary or an ally, for relations between the two of them are quite obviously affectionate—even romantic—while all the time they are eager enough to chisel each other. The episode "Back to the Klondike" tells the story of their amour in full. Goldie shows a rough-edged pseudosophistication in her manner and in her drawling voice (supplied by Joan Gerber); the overall effect reminds us of the "Southern Belle mode" displayed by Daisy Duck (➤80) on occasion. That episode also features **Dangerous Dan**, a greasy saloon owner who manages to fleece them both—a rare feat!

Flintheart Glomgold (voiced by Hal Smith) is the second richest duck in the world and consequently Scrooge's longtime rival; he is much weightier than Scrooge, although no taller, and he proclaims his Scottishness in a way that Scrooge would never do by habitually sporting a kilt and a tam o' shanter. He is also a rival for Glittering Goldie's affections.

And so to the **Beagle Boys.** This incompetent gang of crooks is responsible for most of Scrooge's worst nightmares, for they have thoughts for little

but parting him from as much of his fortune as possible. Their tactics are not subtle. Their disguise takes the form of highly distinctive little masks that are little more than dark rings around their eyes; as a way of avoiding attention this could be matched only by having BURGLAR in studs across the backs of their jackets. As an additional form of camouflage, they wear their prison numbers around their necks; these numbers are (although the combinations are not entirely consistent from episode to episode, a mixture of 1, 6, and 7). The "brains" of the quartet is by far the smallest, and so is called **Big Time Beagle.** The muscles of the organization is **Bouncer Beagle.** Fat and with a squeaky voice is the food-loving **Burger Beagle.** Finally there is the clumsy, oafish, rather pathetically friendly **Baggy Beagle**, who whines his lines as he struggles with a speech impediment. Big Time and Baggy are voiced by Frank Welker, Burger and Bouncer by Chuck McCann. Perhaps the most enjoyable of the bunch is **Ma Beagle** (voiced by June Foray). Related in some way to the main Beagles (cousins, perhaps?) is another gang. It is led by the small, bearded **Backwards Beagle.** Likewise bearded but hulkingly larger is **Binky Beagle. Bacon Beagle**, is . . . a pig. This bizarre anomaly of species is because Bacon suffered a bad dose of swine flu in his youth.

THE NEW ADVENTURES OF WINNIE THE POOH

The New Adventures of Winnie the Pooh, which began life on Saturday mornings on commercial television in the autumn of 1988, clearly constitutes an extension of the four Pooh featurettes released theatrically between 1966 and 1983, and all the main characters of the television series are discussed at length in the course of the general discussion of those featurettes (➤125). Naturally, as time has passed, the story lines have become progressively more Disney and less Milne, although this transition has not happened to quite the extent that one might have feared: story editor Bruce Talkington is proud that the spirit of Milne is still evident in the series, which he attributes to the writers' habit (enforced by him) of, when in doubt, going back to Milne's original texts in order to reinforce their understanding of the characters and the ways in which their minds—and the general skew-logic of the Hundred Acre Wood—work.

The series has been the recipient of a quite astonishing number of awards: two Emmy Awards in a row (1989 and 1990)

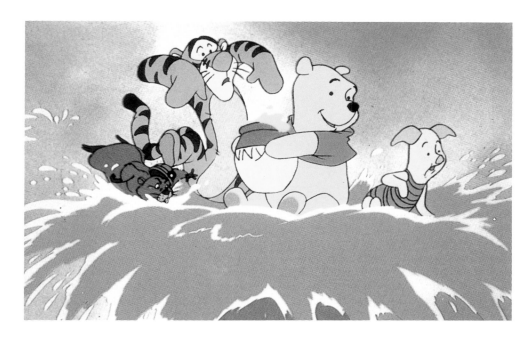

A group from *The New Adventures of Winnie the Pooh*. From left: Gopher, Tigger, Winnie the Pooh and Piglet.

as Best Daytime Animated Program; a Humanitas Award (1989), given annually by the Human Family Educational and Cultural Institute in recognition of "outstanding examples of communicating human values through the television medium" (*The New Adventures of Winnie the Pooh* was singled out among daytime animated series for "humanizing achievement in television writing"); an ACT (Action for Children's Television) Award (1989); and a Gold Seal from the Parents' Choice Awards (1989).

The voices for the characters in the series are provided as follows: Jim Cummings for **Winnie the Pooh,** John Fiedler for **Piglet,** Hal Smith for **Owl,** Ken Sansom for **Rabbit,** Patty Parris for **Kanga,** Nicholas Melody for **Roo,** Paul Winchell (1988–1989) and Jim Cummings (1990 onward) for **Tigger,** Michael Gough for **Gopher,** Peter Cullen for **Eeyore,** and Tim Hoskins for **Christopher Robin.**

CHIP 'N DALE RESCUE RANGERS

Chip 'n Dale Rescue Rangers premiered in 1989, and in the autumn of the following year moved into a regular slot in *The Disney Afternoon.*

It is worth noting here that each of the succeeding series had its original U.S. television appearance on the Disney Channel shortly before its "premiere" on *The Disney Afternoon.* The situation is now that the arrival of a new series on *The Disney Afternoon* displaces an earlier one, which then goes to the Disney Channel. Thus *Darkwing Duck* displaced

Disney's Adventures of the Gummi Bears, Goof Troop displaced *Chip 'n Dale Rescue Rangers,* and so forth.

The two central characters, **Chip and Dale**, are based on the Chip an' Dale (➤**96**; note punctuation) of the shorts and, more significantly, on their incarnations in the comics. The expression "based on" is used advisedly because, although the pair have similar appearances to their shorts precursors and certainly share with them broad similarities of personality, they are otherwise quite different. For a start, they're extremely loquacious, their voices being supplied

by Tress MacNeille (Chip) and Corey Burton (Dale); although, since both have been subjected to audio processing, it is hard to evaluate the contributions of the voice artists. The effect of the processing—notably via speeded-up recordings—is to give the voices both a high pitch (especially Dale's) and a lack of subtlety that is far from restful. Another overt difference from the chips who used to torment Donald in the shorts is that they are dressed—Chip rather flashily and Dale in an eye-numbing Hawaiian shirt. They thus come across to the audience less like animals, as of old, and more like human beings who, for the sake of fantasy, have adopted chipmunk form and size. This slightness of stature—although it varies a little depending upon the exigencies of plot and visual effect—is often put to good purpose.

In terms of personality, Chip is the dominant—even domineering—member of the partnership, while Dale is the flighty, candy-addicted, irresponsible one, as one might have guessed from their contrasting clothes styles—although on occasion Chip briefly lets his mask slip and joins Dale in some act of heedless frivolity, even when circumstances should dictate otherwise. In general, however, the two chips serve as two different aspects of the same persona. Nevertheless, Chip shows (albeit very rarely) a further adult trait that seems totally absent from Dale: he is cognizant that there is an opposite sex (it would be wrong to put it more strongly than that).

Very frequently featured in *Chip 'n Dale Rescue Rangers* is television, which seems to play a large part in all of the Good

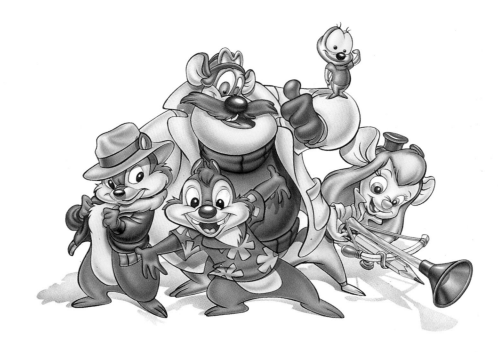

The stars of *Chip 'n Dale Rescue Rangers*. Clockwise from left: Chip, Monterey Jack, Zipper, Gadget and Dale.

Guys' lives. Dale is, of course, well nigh addicted to it, which plays an integral part in many of the episodes' plots. The series is also characterized by a willingness—perhaps an overwillingness—to venture into the realms of science-fiction cliché. These science fictional plot turns are not always successful: as too many sci-fi writers have demonstrated, there is a thin line between the exercise of the fantastic imagination, on the one hand, and gratuitous silliness, on the other, and *Chip 'n Dale Rescue Rangers* perhaps too often treads on the wrong side of that line.

The most important further member—and the most successful creation—of the series is undoubtedly **Gadget** (voiced like Chip by MacNeille), an inventive mouse responsible for most of the squad's technological accessories, most notably the curious flying vehicle that they use, which has wings like an airplane's except that they flap. The real source of lift seems to be the sausage-shaped balloon that is strapped above the craft's empty-detergent-bottle fuselage. Quick-moving, -thinking, and -talking, Gadget comes across as somehow very fresh and crisp, as if she always knows exactly what she's doing and why—even when exactly the reverse is the case. She is also easily the most intelligent of the characters and debatably the most personable. Because of the general resourcefulness of her character, there seems to be something of a clash on some occasions when her role has to be that of a captured blonde requiring macho rescuing; we can't help feeling that either she would have avoided the predicament or she would have already escaped by the time the rest of the squad appeared. Despite this dichotomy, Gadget is, with her trim overalls, her perceptiveness, her quick wit, and her playful smile, an intensely appealing figure.

Monterey Jack (voiced by Jim Cummings, as are Fat Cat, Wart, Professor Nimnul, and others) is the second of Chip and Dale's two important sidekicks. A bellicose mouse from Australia, he is considerably larger and beefier than any of the others. He has an overpowering passion for cheese, the scent of which can send him floating uncontrollably across the floor, his eyes lost in trance. He is also swift to anger whenever he feels that a slight has been cast on either his own honor or that of any of the gang members; a characteristic photograph would show him, moustaches a-bristle, rolling up his sleeves preparatory to doing battle (or attempting to—usually his colleagues succeed in quelling his ambitions) with a vastly larger and/or more powerful adversary. Monte—as the others generally call him—is also a fund of reminiscences about his experiences in exotic faraway

lands, anecdotes which his colleagues usually cut off with indecent haste as soon as he has begun; we sense that the stories are both improbable and well-worn. His language is peppered with marvelous pseudo-Australianisms: "Stripe me starkers!" is a personal favorite.

The final member of the squad—and the only one not able to join in with their habitual rallying call of "Rescue Rangers . . . Away!"—is Zipper, a housefly whose pluck is clearly intended to outweigh his diminutive size and, as an inevitable consequence of his lack of speech, his dearth of overt personality. His most prominent means of expression is through his eyes, which are so large that normally they are shown squashed together to form a single pinched-oval shape in which the two pupils swim. Although obviously much weaker than the others, he is on occasion capable of what are, bearing in mind his low body mass, quite astonishing feats of strength. Perhaps his physical limitations are more than compensated for by the strength of his loyalty to his fellow Rescue Rangers, which is unwavering.

And then there are the villains. Some adorn but a single episode, but two are recurrent. The lesser of these is **Professor Nimnul**, a madcap human scientist responsible for all sorts of crazy inventions (again the science fictional connection), whose main purpose seem to be the acquisition of wealth and power. By far the more significant is **Fat Cat**, a Moriarty of the urban animal world; despite the obvious difference of species, it is impossible not to note the similarities between him and *The Great Mouse Detective*'s Ratigan (➤**322**)—right down to the voice, supplied by Jim Cummings in a very passable adaptation of Vincent Price. Nevertheless, Fat Cat is quite a delightful

villain in his own right. He is inordinately proud of his appearance, fastidiously grooming his whiskers and his three oily locks of head-hair whenever the moment arises, and often enough even when it doesn't. He is sophisticatedly sadistic, a trait conveyed not only by his actions and voice but also by the joy with which he cavorts among the byways of the English language. Fat Cat's downfall is of course customarily brought about by the baroque overcomplexity of the felonious schemes he devises.

There are three major members of Fat Cat's gang. **Meps** (on occasion spelled Mepps) is a distinctly ropy-looking alley cat with a disreputable woollen ski cap, large eyes that are almost tragically expressive, and a whining voice that insinuates itself repulsively under our skins (it is much like Mad Dog's [➤**143**] in *TaleSpin*). No cigar for guessing **Mole**'s species: he's a cheerfully pudgy little thicko whose main function in the band seems to be as a punchbag for Fat Cat after each new setback caused by his bumbling clumsiness; he takes his punishment with seeming good humor. **Wart** is a lizard not unlike the anomalous thug in Ratigan's cutthroat crew (➤**323**), although perhaps with a somewhat more cogent screen personality. A fourth gang member is **Snout**, who is either a rat or something very like one; his appearances are generally brief.

TALESPIN

Introduced in the fall of 1990, *TaleSpin* is a quite significantly more mature series than its predecessors. Where *DuckTales* and *Chip 'n Dale Rescue Rangers* can often suffer from their own frenetic pace,

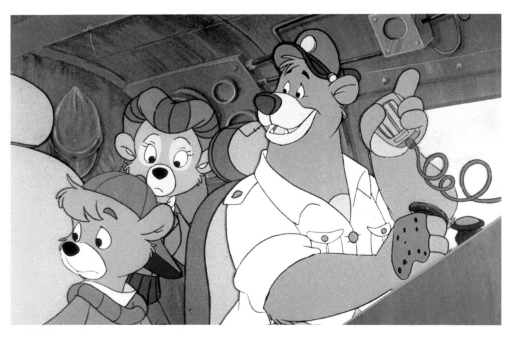

Baloo is cheerful enough, but Kit and Rebecca seem to be expecting a bumpy landing.

TaleSpin concentrates much more on solid storytelling and, in particular, on depth of portrayal of characters and relationships. It thus functions less as a straightforward comic-capers show and more as a sitcom-cum-soap-opera. This has the effect of making the jokes more long-lasting, and also permits the series to examine some quite serious issues—although this is not to imply that it is ever glum.

Three of the major figures are revamped versions of characters from the feature movie The Jungle Book; it would be misleading to say that the Baloo (➤278), King Louie (➤278), and Shere Khan (➤280) of *TaleSpin* are the same individuals as their cognates in the feature, although obviously there are strong similarities. The series' other leading characters are original to it.

The central character of the series is **Kit Cloudkicker** (voiced by R. J. Williams), a bear cub of about twelve. His passion is for "surfing" over the tops of the clouds, which he does—usually either as a joke when weather conditions are ridiculously unfavorable or in order to get his allies out of some predicament—on a collapsible board shaped rather like a boomerang. Stills of Kit can make him seem potentially overcute. In action, however, he is depicted as a sharp-witted and very appealing individual. Notably, although he is clearly a child, it is very rare that the series' makers show him as childish or exploit his youth for the sake of cheap gags: his youthful failings are used more sparingly than that, and quite often to sober purpose. Kit serves as the navigator on the *Sea Duck*, a seaplane "of a certain age" attached to the air-charter company Higher for Hire, which is based somewhere in the tropics at a port called Cape Suzette. The pilot of this craft is **Baloo** (voiced by Ed Gilbert), who is physically very much like his counterpart in *The Jungle Book* but mentally, while no more intellectually adroit, substantially less irresponsible.

Higher for Hire's owner is an elegant bear called **Ms. Rebecca Cunningham** (voiced by Sally Struthers). Although clearly intended to be of about the same age as Baloo, the contrast between them could not be greater: where he is shambling and slow-thinking, she is trim of form and sharp of wit. Although she is depicted as very definitely one of the Good Guys, many of her actions are dominated by her need for money—her ever more baroque schemes for earning, which frequently land her and her fellows in dire straits. In an argument with Baloo in an episode called "The Bigger They Are, the Louder They Oink," she proudly delineates her own nature:

> I'm an entrepreneur with good money-making sense. . . . I know business, Baloo—supply and demand, cause and effect. I'm tenacious and clear-headed.

Since her wizard money-making wheeze at the time is to buy a pig and go truffle hunting, it is not hard for us to match her self-assessment with the reality. Rebecca—Becky—was unique among regular Disney television animated characters to that date in that she was not just cast in an adult role: her personality was actually depicted as that of an adult.

Rebecca has a daughter, **Molly Cunningham** (voiced by Janna Michaels), who according to the Disney outlines is aged five but who looks and acts about three. Molly is slightly reminiscent of a much younger Sunni Gummi (➤138), and suffers from the same irremediable problem. She is, naturally, a mistress of the art of getting into trouble.

The final member of the Higher for Hire personnel is the mechanic, **Wildcat** (voiced by Pat Fraley), even more dunderheaded and very much less responsible than Baloo: he vaguely resembles a lunk-jawed Bagheera (➤278) played for laughs. One shudders to think too hard about the quality of his repairs.

Last among the regular Good Guys is **King Louie** (voiced by Jim Cummings), portrayed less exuberantly than in *The Jungle Book*—and sensibly so: the Louie of the feature was great as a zany, but could hardly have been expected to carry forward a plot. Louie owns the bar-and-gas-station nearest to the Higher for Hire HQ and uses slightly dated California-hip talk, such as "bodacious."

Ranged against the Good Guys are various villains, the most regular of whom are the air pirates led by the dashing **Don Karnage** (voiced, like Louie, by Cummings); his name rhymes with "raj" rather than "page." He is a fox and, when not recently disheveled by some new disaster, is presented as a spruce dresser. His accent is a curious mixture, with some Spanish, a trace of something Central European, and occasionally a hint of Puerto Rican. His depiction is pleasurably zestful, and clearly he is impressed by his own panache: "The feared pirate Don Karnage knows all a feared pirate needs to know, you know?" he remarks at one point, meanwhile strutting happily and strumming a glittering swordblade. He is totally in command of his sidekicks, who are dogs. The most notable is probably **Mad Dog**, a mangy cur whose whining voice is incredibly similar to that of *Chip 'n Dale Rescue Rangers*'s Meps (➤142), even though the two characters have different voice actors (Charlie Adler for Mad Dog, Peter Cullen for Meps); he has, however, nothing of Meps's woeful wistfulness, so the effect of his nasal drone is—deliberately—to irritate. The other prominent member of

the air pirates is **Dumptruck** (voiced in pseudo-Teutonic by Chuck McCann), a huge mastifflike beast whose skull seems to be made of solid bone. He is Don Karnage's heavy but, since he is so patently inept, his intervention rarely has any noteworthy consequence. A further canine air pirate, **Gibber**, makes far less frequent appearances.

A completely different set of baddies is the metronomically marching troop of fascistically uniformed soldiers led by **Colonel Spigot** (voiced by Michael Gough). Spigot—or, as he himself pronounces it, "Thpigot"—is a warthog of Germanic enunciation and diminutive stature; this latter characteristic makes him the butt of much unsubtle humor from Baloo. The pipsqueak fascist is very, very amusing both to listen to and to watch: he is in many ways much more like a Warner Bros. comic villain than a Disney one; his creation may have been affected by the experiences of some of the Disney team who had worked on *Who Framed Roger Rabbit* (➤326). His sidekick, **Dunder**, is in appearance a much larger version of the same, although he moves, speaks, and thinks much less energetically. Emanating from his weighty frame, his voice (supplied by Lorenzo Music) is surprisingly mild and can on occasion sound almost cultured. His fate is to be frequently and gratuitously slashed by the riding crop of his militaristic superior officer, to whom he is surprisingly devoted.

Playing a rather more remote role is **Shere Khan** (voiced by Tony Jay), cast as a felonious plutocrat in smart suits and ties, and frequently masterminding operations from a plush office with plenty of kowtowing staff in attendance. Other villains appear from time to time, including a grizzled and irascible doglike trader called **McNee** and a smooth-talking coyotelike conman, **Dan Dawson** of Daring Dan's Circus of the Air.

The depth of characterization in *TaleSpin* has been noted. Another attribute of the series is the relative sobriety of its scripts: it rarely falls into the trap of overinventiveness that can so often spoil episodes of the earlier Disney series. The two qualities, taken together, allow many of the stories to center on the relationships among the various regular characters, of which that between Baloo and Kit is undoubtedly the most important. It is a bond rooted in equality but difference: they have equal status (in essence, both are children) but, even so, Baloo possesses an adult viewpoint to which, obviously, Kit cannot as yet aspire, which is symbolized by their nicknames for each other, "Papa Bear" and "Li'l Britches."

Two less significant relationships can play their part in the stories, that between Baloo and his old friend Louie, and that between Baloo and Rebecca. Of the two, the latter is by far the more interesting, since it sets up also a curious triangle of affection between these two and Kit. When the slimy Dan Dawson assumes they are Kit's parents, Becky recoils in immediate revulsion at the thought that she might be married to Baloo; yet Dan's assumption is perfectly natural, and he is merely voicing our own minor puzzlement about why there seems to be no romantic hookup between them. Their everyday banter is likewise antagonistic in the way that banter can be between couples.

It is on the framework of these relationships (there are others) that most of the best *TaleSpin* stories are based—hence the assertion that there are elements of serious drama beneath the flights of fancy and the laughter. *TaleSpin* may not be the most flamboyant or orthodoxly comic of the Disney television series, but it is among the most interesting of them. Its episodes withstand repeated viewing.

DARKWING DUCK

Darkwing Duck premiered on *The Disney Afternoon* in September 1991 and rapidly achieved considerable popularity for both its humor and its inventiveness.

The main premise of the series may seem to scholarly readers just a trifle familiar. No one might look twice at the respectable duck-about-town **Drake Mallard**, a real Mr. Average Suburban Dweller, but when he dons a mask, hat, and cape he becomes the dashing crimebuster **Darkwing Duck**, a justice-seeking costumed adventurer who has devoted his life to righting wrongs and conquering evil—and doing so with *style*, as evidenced by his credo: "Look good while doing good." As he modestly admits, he is a duck of action, a masked phantom who operates with an air of mystery fueled by his own tenacity and raw courage; his movements are quick and his patience short—a characteristic that often lands him in trouble, especially when he is confronted by gadgetry, for which he has a natural affinity that would stand him in good stead were he ever to have the patience to pause long enough to figure out how to operate the various machines correctly. He frequently takes assignments from SHUSH, an international agency so secretive that it can never be named; it is headed by **J. Gander Hooter** and has **Gryzlikoff** as its chief agent. SHUSH's rival organization is FOWL, the Fiendish Organization of World Larceny, which is supported by some of the most dangerous criminals in the world, notably Steelbeak, Tuskerninni, Megavolt, and Bushroot (see below

for all four). In accordance with his sense of the melodramatic, Darkwing Duck approaches his foes with a bold attitude and the ominously enunciated words:

> I am the terror that flaps in the night. I am the winged scourge that pecks at your nightmares. I am Darkwing Duck!

In his duck-faced jet the *Thunderquack*, or roaring through the streets of his home city of St. Canard on his turbocharged motorcycle *Ratcatcher*, Darkwing Duck is implacable in his search for new crimes to bust.

His self-image is hardly helped by his assistants. One of these is **Launchpad McQuack** (voiced by Terry McGovern), imported from *DuckTales* (➤140) without any noticeable increase in brainpower. He likes to think of himself as a brave avenger cast from the same mold as his mentor—another duck of action, in fact—but in reality his primary function within the series is to complicate Darkwing Duck's adventures through adding his blunders to the crimebuster's own. Another of Darkwing Duck's sidekicks is **Gosalyn Mallard** (voiced by Christine Cavanaugh), the niece whom he has adopted as his daughter. Nine years old, she is an independent spirit, a tomboy, and an athletics fanatic: having little in common with our stereotyped images of other girl ducks her age, she excels in all types of sports and takes full advantage of her athletic abilities to make herself stand out from the crowd and to help Darkwing Duck at every turn, despite her unquenchable predilection for mischief.

Her best friend is **Honker Muddlefoot** (voiced by Katie Leigh), the bespectacled little boy duck who lives next door. He idolizes Darkwing Duck and is eager to help in any way he can—indeed, he is often the brains underlying the masked crusader's operation. However, he hides his brilliance behind a wall of shyness, and Gosalyn seems to be the only one who can make him break his silence. His father is **Herb Muddlefoot** (voiced by Jim Cummings), an overweight Quackerware salesman who is Drake Mallard's self-proclaimed best buddy. A gross and portly figure garbed in a Hawaiian shirt, which is if anything slightly louder than his voice, he has all the dynamism you might expect from a full-time couch potato. (Pete and Goofy share a similar relationship in *Goof Troop* [➤145]) His wife, **Binkie Muddlefoot** (voiced by Susan Tolsky), is a quintessential apron-clad 1950s-style mom, complete with a crazy scheme of logic that somehow contrives to make a specious form of sense. She is the neighborhood's number one do-gooder and is forever organizing block parties and other fun-filled events. The final member of Honker's family is

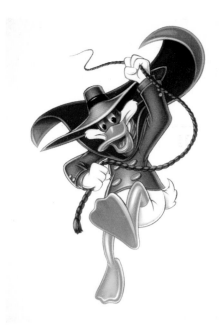

Darkwing Duck, the caped courge of crime.

his elder brother **Tank Muddlefoot**, an oversized bully who terrorizes the neighborhood kids. The height of his vocal abilities is an inarticulate grunt (supplied by Dana Hill).

Tank's delinquencies are as nothing alongside the menace of the various villains against whom Darkwing Duck must match his wits and his valor. **Dr. Reginald Bushroot** (voiced by Tino Insana) was once a government research scientist but then his funding was cut and so he was forced to begin experimenting on himself. The result is that he has become that most nightmare-inspiring of hybrids: half-plant and half-duck. He has the preternatural ability to command all members of the vegetable kingdom to obey his bidding. Fortunately he has a broad streak of cowardice and, as a villain, is distinctly accident-prone. **Tuskerninni** (voiced by Kenneth Mars), a broad-beamed walrus with a waxed and pointed moustache, is a flamboyant villain with a thespian background. He is characterized by his seemingly insatiable appetite for food. Though he has changed his vocation from the stage to crime, he still has a considerable fondness for histrionics; he frequently goes out of his way to be able to film his various nefarious deeds thus giving himself a starring role at last. **Megavolt** (voiced by Dan Castellanetta), a formidable adversary who conducts a personal vendetta against Darkwing Duck, is a living power battery who is a master of all things electrical: a touch of his glowing finger is sufficient to turn everyday household appliances into weapons of his vengeance. Luckily for the forces of good he has, over the years, zapped a few too many of his own brain cells.

Further villains to make their appearance have been **Quackerjack**, a demented toy maker, and **Steelbeak**, FOWL's principal agent. In addition there are the multifarious FOWL thugs known collectively as the **Egg Men**.

GOOF TROOP

After an airing on the Disney Channel in spring 1992, *Goof Troop* premiered on September 7 of the same year on *The Disney Afternoon*, then on ABC's *Saturday Morning Lineup* on September 12. It combines the elements of a domestic situation comedy with broad, slapstick humor.

The star of the show is of course our old friend **Goofy** (➤44), but a Goofy recast for the 1990s: voiced by Bill Farmer, he is living in suburbia and coping with the challenges of raising his eleven-year-old son **Goofy Jr.** or **Max** (voiced by Dana Hill), who should be distinguished from the **Goofy Junior** (➤50) who appeared in the shorts. Although in some ways they resemble each other physically, the television version has much more "boy" in his appearance. As we might expect, Max is forever getting himself and his father embroiled in neighborhood misadventures. There are two banes of Max's life. First, though he considers himself the last word on what's cool ("screamin'") and what's not ("frosty"), he has inherited Goofy's "Hyuck!" chuckle. Second, he has to live in constant dread of what his father will do next to mortify him. At the same time, Max learns that, however frightful his parent may be, he is the solid pillar in his life and will always be there to bail him out.

Max's best friend is the pudgy lad from next door, **P.J.** (voiced by Rob Paulsen), a genial youth who somehow manages to emit a certain avuncularity. P.J. has a devoted mother named **Peg** (voiced by April Winchell); she has a job as a real estate agent. His precocious five-year-old sister is called **Pistol** (voiced by Nancy Cartwright); she tags along behind the two boys, to their embarrassment, and tries to impress all and sundry by the size of her vocabulary. In our context the most interesting member of the family is undoubtedly P.J.'s father, **Pete**—a reincarnation of another of our old Disney friends (➤15). Pete (voiced by Jim Cummings) is, for the purposes of the series, everything that Goofy is not: he's a loud-mouthed manipulating used-car dealer obsessed with success, and having Goofy as a neighbor is the reification of his worst nightmare. He and Goofy stay on speaking terms purely because of the inseparable friendship of their sons. Pete's frequent attempts to fleece Goofy invariably backfire.

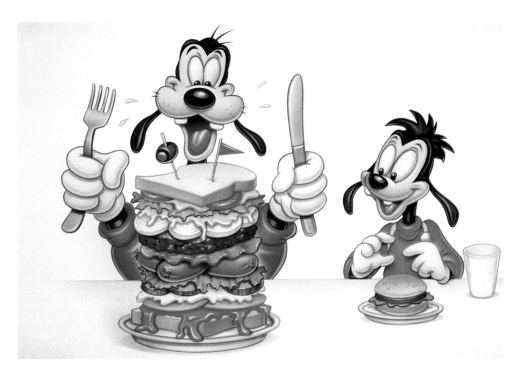

Goofy and son Max about to share a meal in *Goof Troop*.

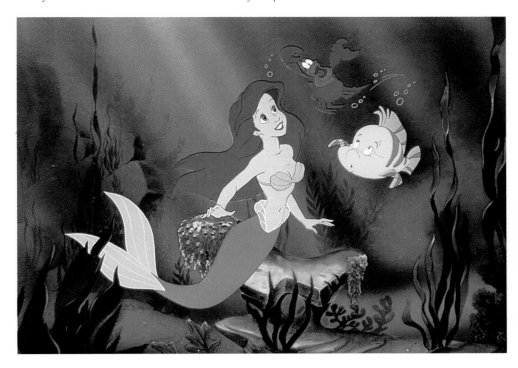

Ariel, under the sea with her two best friends, Sebastian and Flounder.

Animal associates are **Waffles**, the Goofy family cat, and **Chainsaw**, the Pete family dog; needless to say, they are sworn enemies. Both are voiced by the veteran vocal-effects man Frank Welker.

In 1995 the feature *A Goofy Movie* (➤395) was based on the series. Here the associations between the characters are somewhat different. Pistol, Peg, and the two pets seem to have vanished from the scene. Pete seems less inclined to dislike Goofy—in fact, they are partners in a photographic business—but is keen instead to mess up his relationship with Max and, possibly unintentionally, to make the Goof feel small by ostentatious displays of Pete's wealth. Goofy, of course, notices nothing of this.

THE LITTLE MERMAID

Derived from the popular movie *The Little Mermaid* (➤342) and premiered on CBS on September 12, 1992, this was the first ever television animated series to be based on a feature. The time of the action is before **Ariel** has encountered Eric, and so the concentration is on the movie's undersea characters. As in the movie, Jodie Benson voices Ariel, Samuel E. Wright reprises his brilliant role as **Sebastian**, Pat Carroll is again the sinister sea witch **Ursula**, and Kenneth Mars is Ariel's father **King Triton**. Edan Gross takes over as **Flounder** and Maurice La Marche as **Scuttle**. The only major new character is **Urchin**, a merboy who becomes friends with Ariel. He is voiced by Danny Cooksey, best known for his role in the hit comedy *Diff'rent Strokes*.

Many of the plots concern threats to the integrity of Atalantica. These may be launched by Ursula or by other villains, or they may be incurred through some misadventure of the central gang of friends. Naturally, all turns out well by the end of each half hour.

ALADDIN

Following the lead of *The Little Mermaid* (see above), this was based on the sensationally animated movie *Aladdin* (➤374); clearly the television animation cannot match that of the big screen, but on occasion it can generate the same sense of wonder. The series premiered on February 6, 1994, on The Disney Channel before syndication from September 5 of that year and appearance on CBS from September 17. Most of our old friends are here, the notable exception being Jafar—who can hardly be counted as a friend, anyway. Many of the voice actors from the movie reprise their roles: Scott Weinger is **Aladdin**, Linda Larkin is **Princess Jasmine**, Frank Welker is **Abu**, and Gilbert Gottfried is **Iago**. Other characters are played by new voices: Val Bettin takes over from Douglas Seale as the **Sultan** and Dan Castellanetta very courageously takes over from Robin Williams as the **Genie**—and makes a very good go of it. This version of the Genie is slightly different from the movie one. At the end of the movie he gained his freedom, but this has come at a cost: while he still possesses magical powers, they are nowhere near as powerful as before. There is also a shift in the relationship between Aladdin and Jasmine: it is often she who saves the day.

There are some new noteworthy characters as well—all villains. The bearded bandit **Abis Mal** (voiced by Jason Alexander) was shortly to plunge himself into an unholy alliance with Jafar in the direct-to-video movie *The Return of Jafar* (➤379); here, with the help of his Forty (predictably incompetent) Thieves and his enigmatic, dry-witted accomplice **Haroud** (voiced by James Avery), he frequently does his best to outwit Aladdin:

he fares no better than many another Disney comic baddie. **Saleen** (voiced by Julie Brown) is the sinuous Ruler of the Ocean and **Magma** (voiced in inimitable fashion by Tone Loc) splatters lava in his characterization as Ruler of the Forces of the Earth. Also of note are **Mirage** (voiced by Bebe Neuwirth), a feline demon who has the power of shapeshifting, and the scheming barbarian **Runtar** (voiced by Michael Jeter) and his equally barbarian wife **Brawnhilda** (voiced by Carol Kane). In one episode our heroes encounter the **Great Sand Shark**, who erupts from the desert in a feeding frenzy—shades of *Beetlejuice* (1988), whose heroes have to face a similar peril.

The general theme of the episodes is that, after Aladdin and Jasmine have been permitted by the Sultan to fly off from Agrabah on the Magic Carpet at the end of the feature movie, they must discover that it's a big, wide world out there. They must also discover themselves, and the nature of their affection toward each other. As so often in Disney features but more rarely in Disney's television series, this is less about mere adventure than about rite of passage (a rite of passage to be completed in the direct-to-video movie *Aladdin and the King of Thieves* [➤380]). They have to confront reality, which of course was in short supply in the feature movie's magical city of Agrabah and its environs—although there is plentiful magic in the series' seventy-eight episodes (sixty-five in the main series, plus thirteen for CBS).

The first of the direct-to-video movies can be regarded as adjuncts to the feature, the second movies as adjuncts to the series. The latter movie, in which Jasmine and Aladdin finally marry, is claimed to be the conclusion to the *Aladdin* saga . . . but one wonders.

GARGOYLES AND GARGOYLES: THE GOLIATH CHRONICLES

Long, long ago—in A.D. 994, to be precise—Castle Wyvern, a remote castle in Scotland, was guarded by a passel of gargoyles. These were no normal gargoyles, however, for their abilities were not restricted to staring fiercely but motion-

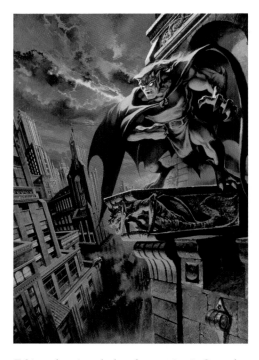

Taking place in a dark, urban setting is *Gargoyles* and *Gargoyles: The Goliath Chronicles*.

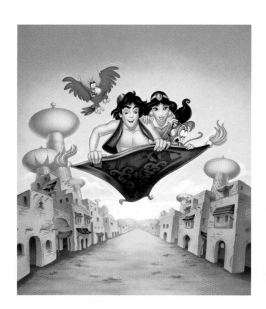

Enjoying a carpet ride are Aladdin, Jasmine, Abu, and Iago.

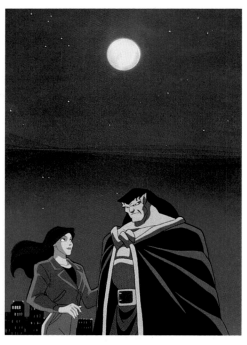

Beautiful detective Elisa Maza and a Gargoyle ally.

lessly from the tops of high walls. Though they were stone from sunrise to sunset, by night they were fierce warriors, able to defend their masters in battle. Wounds they received during warfare would cure themselves while the gargoyles were in stone form, although they could be killed when motile and any limbs lost during such a time were lost forever. There was—to talk in terms of this series' backstory—a rulebook, as is generally the case in such fantasy constructions: vampires cannot face sunlight, werewolves have no choice at the time of full moon but to transform, and so forth. One night, the leader of the gargoyles, Goliath, was lured away from the castle and a sneak attack was launched on it. The king's sorcerer, the **Archmage** (voiced by David Warner), cast a spell upon the gargoyles such that they would never again come alive "until the castle is above the clouds"—i.e., for eternity.

A thousand years pass. Technology advances. Shady U.S. financier David Xanatos decides for reasons of ego to buy the castle and fly it to New York City, there to rebuild it on top of his corporation's skyscraper. The castle therefore does indeed find itself above the clouds, and so the gargoyles come back to life, ready once more to defend the castle. Detective Elisa Maza of New York's Finest discovers the secret while at the same time finding that Xanatos is a bad egg, and so gives the gargoyles a new home in the clock tower above the police precinct house. From there they wage a neverending war against the forces of evil, which are just as prevalent in twentieth-century New York as they were in tenth-century Scotland, if not more so. Most of the gargoyles take on fresh names associated with New York.

Unlike so many others of the characters in Disney television animation, whom Bill Cotter in *The Wonderful World of Disney Television* (1997) has generically characterized as "warm and fuzzy," the gargoyles have a decidedly hard edge to both their designs and their personalities. This series is not particularly aimed at children, rather in the same way that Warner Bros.'s 1992–1994 *The Adventures of Batman and Robin* (originally syndicated as *Batman: The Animated Series*) recognized that, particularly with the rise of animé, there was a huge adult audience for animation. (This has been true since the earliest days, of course—it's a standard joke that parents drag their children along to the latest animated release—but it took animators a long time to recognize it.) Moreover, the series takes upon itself a moral role, promoting such causes as adult literacy and the conservation of the rain forests. Disney has made much of the cast, which comes from a variety of ethnic backgrounds.

As noted, the leader of the clan is **Goliath** (voiced by Keith David); he is much revered by **Brooklyn** (voiced by Jeff Bennett), the prime mover of a trio of ostensibly younger gargoyles, the other two of whom are **Lexington** (voiced by Thom Adcox-Hernandez) and **Broadway** (voiced by Bill Fagerbakke). Although all three are over a thousand years old, they have spent much of that time in stasis and are thus basically still teenagers. In the second season a further "young" gargoyle was introduced: **Angela** (voiced by Brigitte Bako), who slowly finds out that she is the offspring of Goliath and the villainess of the piece, **Demona** (voiced by Marina Sirtis). Demona, who was the one who originally betrayed Goliath all those centuries ago, is rather different from the other gargoyles in that she has been cursed to turn by day not into stone but into a human being: she becomes Dominique Destine, high-flying chief executive officer of a company called Nightstone. The irony is that, in combination with **David Xanatos** (voiced by Jonathan Frakes), she wants to destroy the entire human species.

Other gargoyles of note are **Hudson** (voiced by Ed Asner), the quondam leader of the clan, a veteran warrior and a loyal friend of Goliath's, and **Bronx** (voiced by Frank Welker), described as the "beast and ultimate watchdog," who has terrifying jaws and long claws. The main human ally of the gargoyles is of course Detective **Elisa Maza** (voiced by Salli Richardson), a sassy, attractive woman who comes from mixed Asian and Afro-Caribbean stock; she is a very appealing character. The second season gave Xanatos a hyperefficient executive assistant, **Owen** (voiced by Jeff Bennett).

Gargoyles premiered on October 24, 1994. The finale to the series' second season was a three-parter called *The Hunter's Moon*, in which we discovered how a medieval youth was attacked by Demona and determined to destroy her and all her kind. He failed, but all down through history his descendants have vowed to fulfill the vendetta. Some significant new characters appeared: **Robyn Canmore** (voiced by Sheena Easton), **Jason Canmore** (voiced by Scott Cleverdon), and **Jon Canmore** (Cleverdon again), who are the descendants; and **Dr. Anton Sevarius** (voiced by Tim Curry), an evil scientist who helps Demona in her quest to annihilate the human species by releasing toxic chemicals. The day is saved, oddly, by a suddenly benevolent Xanatos, who returns the gargoyles to their sanctuary in Castle Wyvern.

On September 7, 1996, a spinoff series started on ABC—*Gargoyles: The Goliath Chronicles*—which took as its starting point this fresh scenario. Now the existence of the gargoyles becomes known to many more of the denizens of New York beyond Maza and Xanatos, and a faction called the Quarrymen is set up among the citizenry with the aim of capturing our heroes. Perhaps the most significant extra character in this spinoff is **Jeffrey Robbins** (voiced by Paul Winfield), a blind man who, despite his own blindness, has been encouraging the gargoyles to learn to read. When Hudson begins to lose the last of his failing eyesight, Robbins persuades him that it doesn't matter: he is still valued by all his friends. The leader of the Quarrymen is a character called **John Castaway**.

This series may have sparked some of the inspiration for the mobile gargoyles in *The Hunchback of Notre Dame* (➤425), but those are straightforward comic characters—there's no real resemblance.

BONKERS

Once upon a time in Hollywood, the major star of Wacky Studios was the Toon (animated character) Bonkers D. Bobcat, but then his light faded and he was laid off. He could have gone in for a life of crime, like so many other discarded Toons before him, but instead he chose the opposite course: he joined the police force. He and the human partner with whom he was teamed trawled Hollywood, solving crimes committed by either Toons or humans. Down these mean streets a Toon must go . . .

And, in this series, a Toon still goes, although usually in the police car driven by his partner, Sergeant Lucky Piquel. The scenario may sound familiar: didn't Roger Rabbit, in *Who Framed Roger Rabbit* (➤318), team up with a Chandleresque human detective in order to solve a crime? Indeed he did, and the basic joke of this series is much the same: humans must live according to the way mundane reality works while Toons live by Toon rules, which allows them much greater flexibility while at the same time opening different pitfalls. The big difference between the series and the movie is that here the humans are, like the Toons, animated: there is no live action.

The big similarity, on the other hand, is between **Bonkers D. Bobcat** and Roger Rabbit (➤330). Although Bonkers is a bobcat and Roger is a rabbit, and although the facial features have been modified accordingly, there is very little to choose between them. Both are frenetic in their movement and their speech (Bonkers is voiced by Jim Cummings); both have a habit of landing their human companions in great trouble; both can be squashed and squeezed in the way that all Toons can and still emerge unscathed. Bonkers can be here one moment and

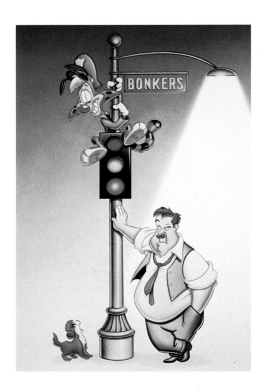

Toon police detective Bonkers D. Bobcat and his human partner Sergeant Lucky Piquel, with Jitters, the Toon dog.

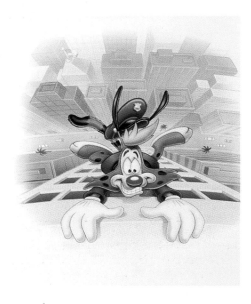

Bonkers, in trouble, as usual.

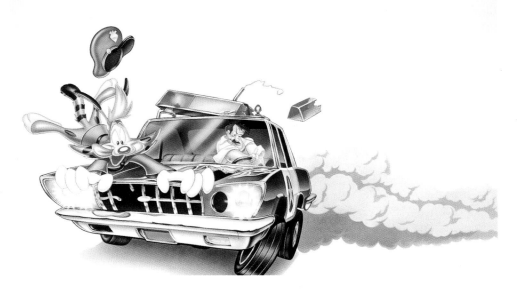

The detectives racing off in their police car to solve yet another crime.

there the next: there is no need for him to pass through the intervening space. And herein lies a weakness of the character, and of the series. Since Bonkers can do all this, he should be able to solve every crime immediately: he could zip from one end of Hollywood to the other in seconds and apprehend the criminal—for that matter, he could go straight through a wall or a door and stop the crime from being committed in the first place. While there were restraints placed upon Roger's activities in the human world—Toontown being a separate place where anything went—Bonkers can never be in

serious danger, because he can always use some Toon means of getting out of it . . . except at the whim of the scriptwriters. Nevertheless, he is a memorable Disney television zany, with a touch of Tex Avery in the character's surrealist capers.

His partner in crime detection is **Sergeant Lucky Piquel** (also voiced by Cummings). Piquel would dearly love to see the back of his partner. Unfortunately for him the two of them have been teamed and there are to be no arguments about that, according to Piquel's superiors. Large and bumbling, with a paunch that defies description—Piquel's waistline is perhaps a third of the way up his body, and perhaps even less—the sergeant consistently follows the wrong leads in the pair's attempts at detection, with Bonkers predictably saving the day. Even more unfortunately for him, any attempt he might make to shuck off Bonkers is going to be thwarted by his improbably lovely blond wife **Dyl(andra) Piquel** (voiced by April Winchell) and his thumb-suckingly cute eight-year-old daughter **Marilyn Piquel** (voiced by Sherry Lynn), both of whom are extremely fond of Bonkers. Lucky—the name is an obvious irony—has a major ambition: to be promoted. Although the Lucky/Bonkers partnership succeeds in solving crimes galore, the ways in which they do so inevitably mean that Lucky's chances of promotion are yet again dashed.

The person who does the dashing is **Police Chief Leonard Kanifky** (voiced by Earl Boen). It is clear to us that he is a mere chair-occupier; as with Lucky, he is of sufficient bulk that, when a chair is occupied by him, it *stays* occupied. He seems affable enough on the surface. The only times that he shows any sign of steel

are when, at the end of each successfully solved case, he denies Lucky any chance of promotion. His beautiful secretary is **Miranda C. Wright** (voiced by Karla DeVito), who aspires to become a police officer and in due course does so; naturally enough, she is very much smarter than her boss. Also involved in the 87th Precinct—sorry, the Hollywood Precinct—is **Sergeant Grating**, a mean, possibly corrupt, and certainly sexist cop who has a bitter dislike of Toons.

Bonkers and Lucky have the assistance of various informants, eyewitnesses, helpers and so forth. By far the most important and interesting of these is the **Fall Apart Rabbit** (voiced by Frank Welker). This is a Toon who is way past his sell-by date: whenever he is startled or excited, bits of his body drop off. He is conceptually a brilliant creation, and although he appears frequently throughout the series, he could perhaps have been used even more. Then there is **Jitters** (voiced by Jeff Bennett), a little Toon dog who was once Bonkers's co-star and who now is always able to supply Bonkers with exactly the right vehicle in which to pursue a fleeing criminal—Murch, from Donald E. Westlake's novels, might show an interest in Jitters, although the characterization is in all other ways utterly different: Murch has never worn the neat hat, vest, and tie, and of course works on the other side of the law. Jitters's girlfriend is **Tanya Trunk** (voiced by Rita Moreno). Odd that she should have set her heart on Jitters, because she is a large Toon elephant. **Snitch** is a Toon rat whose seeming omniscience derives from his habit of delving through trashcans: he describes this activity as "refuse archaeology." **Grumbles Grizzly** (voiced by Rodger Bumpass) is another Toon who once co-starred with Bonkers: a loudmouth in the Bluto style, he is now Bonkers's neighbor. **Roderick Lizzard** (voiced like Jitters by Bennett) is an effete Toon lizard who cannot understand why the world does not recognize his thespian genius; his valet is **Tuttle Turtle** (voiced by Maurice LaMarche), despite the name in fact a tortoise. Uniformly outfitted in their leather jackets and supposedly smooth shades are **Bull Dog, Bull Frog** and **Bull Finch,** who together make up the Toon blues band known as The Bully Boys (voiced respectively by Cummings, Bennett, and Jon Bauman). The Moriarty of Bonkers's Hollywood is **Al Vermin** (voiced by Bob Ridgely), a huge Toon cockroach dressed in a crook-style three-piece suit. No listing of such ancillary characters would be complete without mention of the beautiful **Fawn Deer** (voiced by Nancy Cartwright), who once worked with Bonkers and has no realization that he is still impassioned over her. **Mickey Mouse** makes a quasi-appearance—we only see his silhouette and hear his voice—in one episode.

Various supposedly inanimate objects have Toon personalities of their own. Among these is the **Toon Siren** (voiced by Charlie Adler), which pops out of the glove compartment of the cop car when required: it wears a Maurice Chevalier outfit and spouts bad vaudeville jokes. **Toots**, a small bulbhorn, is the Hollywood Toon Division mascot. The **Toon Radio** (voiced by Welker) in the cop car has the ability, if required by the exigencies of the plot, to follow Lucky and Bonkers around.

The show was prequelled by the theatrical short *Petal to the Metal* (released summer 1992 as a backup to Touchstone's feature *Three Ninjas*) and by segments of CBS's compilation television series *Raw Toonage*, and was introduced by a syndicated two-hour special, *Going Bonkers*. It premiered on February 28, 1993, on the Disney Channel, with syndication running from September 6 in that same year.

THE SHNOOKUMS AND MEAT FUNNY CARTOON SHOW

This syndicated compilation series premiered on January 2, 1995. Each airing consisted of three fast-moving shorts: *Shnookums and Meat, Pith Possum: Super Dynamic Possum of Tomorrow,* and *Tex Tinstar: The Best in the West.*

Shnookums (voiced by Jason Marsden) is a pampered cat unlucky enough to find himself in the same home as **Meat** (voiced by Frank Welker), a

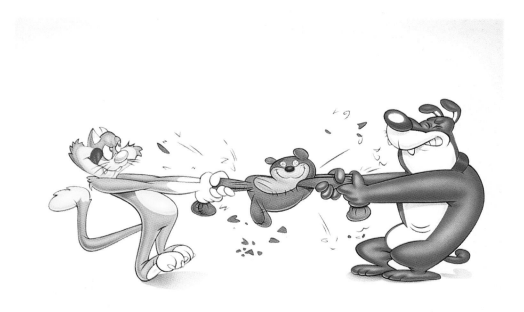

Shnookums the cat and Meat the dog, at each other's throats, again.

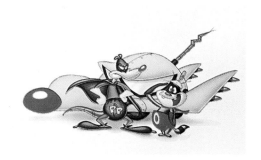

Caped superhero Pith Possum and his raccoon sidekick Obediah in front of their Possummobile.

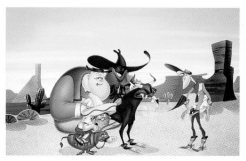

Sheriff Tex Tinstar with bad guy Wrongo and his Wrong Riders.

macho dog. The two are constantly either at each other's throats or cooperating as best buddies against a common threat. Also featuring in this strand are the two animals' owners, voiced by Steve Mackall (husband) and Tress MacNeille (wife).

Humble cowboy **Peter Possum**, when crime is ahoof, becomes caped and masked superhero **Pith Possum** (both versions are voiced by Jeff Bennett) and, assisted by his raccoon sidekick **Obediah**, rushes around in his Possummobile until the villains are brought to justice. Officers of the local law are **Commissioner Stress** (voiced by Brad Garrett) and **Lieutenant Tension** (voiced by Jess Harnell). Love interest is provided by **Doris Deer** (voiced by April Winchell).

Third in the weekly trio of shorts, and the shortest of the three, Tex has the running gag that doughty sheriff **Tex Tinstar** (voiced by Bennett) faces certain death at the end of each episode—usually through the dastardly activities of **Wrongo** (voiced by Garrett) and his gang of Wrong Riders— but is reincarnated, or

has somehow escaped, for the beginning of each new episode.

The Shnookums and Meat Funny Cartoon Show is distinctly wackier than most of Disney's television output, filled with bad puns and general zaniness and owing more to Tex Avery and Chuck Jones than to the Disney tradition.

THE LION KING'S TIMON AND PUMBAA

This weekly series premiered on September 8, 1995; twelve different episodes ran on CBS from September 16. This series is more of a compilation: each alternate episode has two short Timon and Pumbaa adventures; the others have a Timon and Pumbaa adventure for their first half and then a cartoon in one or other of two sets, "Rafiki's Fables" and "The Laughing Hyenas." The main characters involved are of course from *The Lion King* (➤387): **Timon** (voiced by both

149

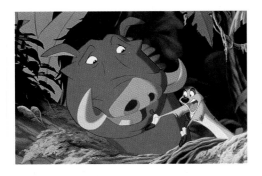

Timon and Pumbaa star in their very own show.

Nathan Lane and Quinton Flynn), **Pumbaa** (voiced by Ernie Sabella), and **Rafiki** (voiced by Robert Guillaume), plus, of course, the hyenas. The *Timon and Pumbaa* cartoons take the characters to various distant parts of the globe; the other cartoons are always set in Africa. The "Rafiki's Fables" cartoons involve the wise old baboon telling a tale that has some moral principle at its heart. The cartoons featuring the hyenas are much more straightforwardly slapstick.

There are a few extra recurring characters, possibly the most significant of which is **Quint** (voiced by Corey Burton), a human being who is really several characters bundled up into one, because wherever he appears it is in a different role: he may be Culinary Quint or Criminal Quint or Congo Quint . . . Others are **Fred**, a practical-joker meerkat distantly related to and somewhat smaller than Timon; **Speedy**, a cute little snail who might have been eaten by our heroes had he not struck up a conversation with them; a pompously arrogant elephant friend of Pumbaa's called **Ned**, whom Timon and the other animals find insufferable (Pumbaa, who has a secret wish

that he had been an elephant rather than a warthog, almost worships Ned); and **The Vultures,** two deadpan individuals who act like a pair of cops in a late-night television drama series, finishing each other's sentences and reading jungle animals their rights.

The hilarious theatrical short *Disney's Timon and Pumbaa in "Stand by Me"* (1995) can be regarded as either a spinoff from or an advertisement for the series.

MIGHTY DUCKS

This series is, apart from the name, not related to the 1992 Disney live-action feature *The Mighty Ducks* and its sequels, nor, one hopes, to the ice-hockey team The Mighty Ducks, which Disney founded in 1992 and which first played in 1993. It concerns a team of benevolent ducks who, like Steve Gerber's Howard the Duck, come from an alternate universe to Earth, where they right wrongs.

The story really starts on Puckworld, an icy planet in that alternate universe, where hockey was a sacred art. When Puckworld was invaded by the Saurian Overlords, long years of warfare ensued. The resistance movement was headed by a brave warrior called **Drake DuCaine**, who created The Mask, a biomechanical, cybernetic, interface device, programmed with all the noble qualities this heroic duck had learned from a lifetime of practicing the sacred art of hockey. At last, there was only one surviving Overlord, Dragaunus. However, accompanied by various sidekicks, he escaped through a dimensional gateway into our universe, arriving on Earth. A duck called **Canard** rediscovered The Mask and sent a team

of six—the Mighty Ducks—through that same dimensional gateway to protect the inhabitants of Earth from the Overlord. There, by way of disguise, the ducks formed an ice hockey team, the Mighty Ducks, whose home ground is Anaheim Pond (the real Mighty Ducks team plays at Arrowhead Pond, in Anaheim). Under Anaheim Pond the ducks constructed a headquarters containing a supercomputer called Drake One, which was linked to a surveillance satellite that could locate trouble spots anywhere on Earth.

So much for the backstory. The six Mighty Ducks are Wildwing, Nosedive, Tanya, Grin, Duke L'Orange, and Mallory. **Wildwing**, leader of the virtuous team, is the Mighty Ducks' goalie—and also proud guardian of The Mask, which functions also as a normal hockey mask. Rather larger than the rest of the team (aside from Grin), he is never quite certain if his leadership qualities come from The Mask or from within himself. He is voiced by Ian Ziering, who has been quoted as saying: "It's not often that I get to play an intergalactic freedom-fighting duck." His younger brother is **Nosedive** (voiced by Steve Mackall), the joker in the Mighty Ducks pack. He's not as clever as he thinks he is, either with words or on the rink; some of his sarcasms backfire disastrously. Like several of the others he is armed with a device called a puck launcher—something like a *Star Wars* (1977) laser gun but firing pucks rather than inaccurately directed coruscations of sizzling light.

Mallory and Tanya are the female members of this doughty band. **Mallory** (voiced by Jennifer Hale) may seem to be the boy next door's dream but in fact she is a martial arts expert who practices her skills with such fluency that she rarely needs to draw upon any other weaponry. Substantially more flippant than Tanya, she is nevertheless on occasion glad of Tanya's ability to deal with technical devices, which to Mallory are a mystery. **Tanya** (voiced by April Winchell) is the cool-headed brain behind the team— probably too cool-headed for her own good, because the exercise of reason and logic can lead one into sticky situations. If there is ever a piece of tech that needs to be interpreted, used, or defused, Tanya is the one the Mighty Ducks call upon. She carries with her a gadget called the Omnitool, which is rather like the Swiss Army knife your parents refused to buy you when you were a kid: use the right control and it can produce a laser beam, a chainsaw, and so forth.

Duke L'Orange (voiced by Jeff Bennett) was once upon a time a member of the notorious crime ring called The Brotherhood of the Sword, but now has been converted to the cause of good. Somewhat dandyish, in the manner of

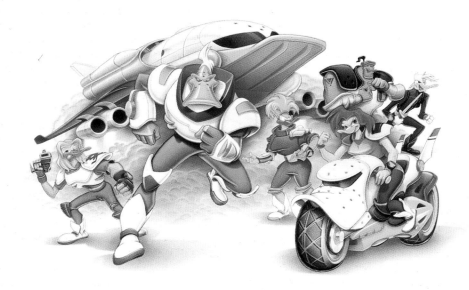

The Mighty Ducks are Wildwing, Nosedive, Tanya, Grin, Duke L' Orange, and Mallery.

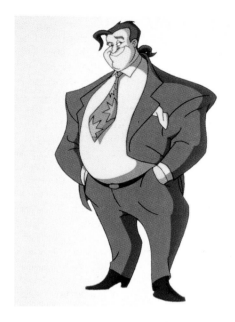

Phil, the Mighty Ducks' team Manager.

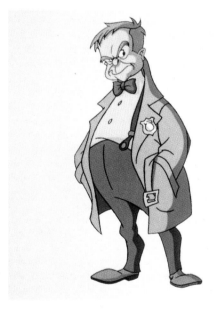

Captain Klegghorn.

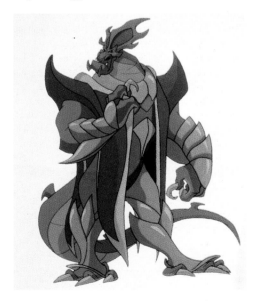

The evil Lord Dragaunus.

Don Karnage (➤143)—although, obviously, ducklike rather than wolflike—he brandishes his sword with panache, using it to cut through various materials (concrete, metal—you name it) but not human flesh, for he is too much of a chivalrous knight to take advantage of the weapon's abilities. Last among the Mighty Ducks is Grin (voiced by Brad Garrett). He is the muscles of the team, yet also a devotee of what might be called Zen: there is nothing worse for his foes than to be flattened by not so much the sound, as the actuality, of one hand clapping. Tanya, devoted as she is to the rigor of the Scientific Method, finds him intolerable. Grin doesn't speak much, but when he does it is to utter a profound statement such as: "Karma always gets you in the end."

The Mighty Ducks' team manager is **Phil** (voiced by Jim Belushi). There was a time when he managed a successful ice hockey team in California, but then the team moved to Piscataway, New Jersey, leaving Phil behind. Desolated, he is ripe for the picking when the Mighty Ducks arrive on Earth; having witnessed their amazing ability on the ice, Phil signed them up as the new residents of Anaheim Pond. He is the sole human to know that they are alien creatures from an alternate universe, and he sort of supports their efforts to clean up all the evil on Earth . . . but at the same time he wishes they'd pay more attention to the efforts he makes on their (or, more likely, his own) behalf to exploit their phenomenal success on the rink. He is rarely to be seen without a mobile phone at his ear.

An ancillary member of the Good Guys is **Captain Klegghorn** (voiced by Dennis Franz). He is generally pretty suspicious of the Mighty Ducks whenever things go wrong, but on the other hand he'd rather see the back of them than press a charge, so they always escape scrutiny.

Ranged against the Mighty Ducks is the usual gamut of villains, foremost among them being **Lord Dragaunus,** voiced by Tim Curry, who played to such fine effect Frank N. Furter in the original London production of *The Rocky Horror Show* (1973) and reprised the role in the movie version, *The Rocky Horror Picture Show* (1975); notable other roles have been the Devil analogue in Ridley Scott's *Legend* (1985) and the part of Mozart in the 1981 Broadway production of *Amadeus*, not to mention the know-it-all Butler in 1985's *Cluedo?* (known in the United States as *Clue*). Curry is a man of many parts, and in certain of his performances most of them are visible. Dragaunus in his natural form represents a *Triceratops*, but here on Earth he has taken on a humanoid appearance. When it comes to battle with the Mighty Ducks or anyone else, however, he transforms

into something which, if you met it up a dark alley in one of your worst nightmares, the moment would be the bit that woke you up: he has a beaklike mouth whose edges are razor-sharp, an armored head encircled by gnarled horns (a direct link to *Legend*, because in both places the reference is to Cernunnos, the Horned God), and hands that are a forest of claws.

Among Dragaunus's sidekicks is **Chameleon** (voiced by Frank Welker) who, as one might expect from the name, is a shapeshifter: he can adopt human appearance with ease, and then become many different humans, notably Hollywood actors of times long gone. Not only does his shape shift: his personality does likewise. The strongest and nastiest of Dragaunus's henchmen is **Siege** (voiced by Clancy Brown), who has largely retained his Saurian form: he is the thug whom the Mighty Ducks fear most when engaged in head-on dinosaur-to-duck confrontation, for with his weighty tail he can cause massive destruction to animate and inanimate targets alike. Much less physical—and he wishes it were otherwise—is the spectral **Wraith** (voiced by Tony Jay), a morose saurian revenant whose depression stems from his inability to scare anyone to death. If only Dragaunus, his Master, would allow him to call up "the black arts of our ancestors" . . . but Dragaunus has more sense.

Mighty Ducks is an enjoyable series, and its voice cast is of course distinguished, but it fails to stay in one's memory for long.

QUACK PACK

Premiering on September 3, 1996, *Quack Pack* is in effect an attempt to repeat the success of *Goof Troop* (➤145), only this time using not Goofy but a thoroughly modern Donald Duck. As with *Goof Troop*, the characters have been updated and put into an urban setting, so they cannot really be considered to be the same characters of old. What next? Mickey as a masked avenger?

Donald Duck (➤61) is a cameraman for the television news show *What in the World?*, and, as such, he is sent all over the globe (and sometimes beyond it) in company with his "significant other," Daisy Duck (➤80), here incarnated as a career-driven news reporter. There are adventures, sometimes comic, sometimes exciting. Donald's Nephews (➤85) tag along "helping."

The most obvious difference between the revised **Donald Duck** (here voiced by Tony Anselmo) and the real one is that it is quite often possible to understand

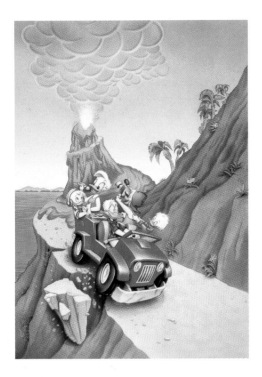

Having another adventure.

what he is saying; only when he encounters one of his famous temper tantrums (which is fairly frequently) does he become *totally* incomprehensible . . . except that such "quack attacks" have always been totally comprehensible, even if one cannot make out the individual words, if words they be. The modernized **Daisy Duck** (voiced by Kath Soucie) is a hard-bitten news seeker, always in search of the big story, and a thoroughly independent female. She lives on her own

houseboat and is possibly in love with Donald—although it's hard to tell. She has a pet iguana called **Knuckles,** who is as protective of her as any dog could be.

The Nephews are given, for the first time, individual personalities: they are Kool Kids, which clearly makes them intolerable to Donald. **Huey** (voiced by Jeanne Elias) is the leader of the pack: he can be picked out because he is dressed entirely in red. He has charisma and style but is essentially useless. **Dewey** (voiced by Pam Segall), wearing blue, has now become a computer nerd and the most knowledgeable of the trio—he is also the most likely to indulge in a prank. **Louie** (voiced by E. G. Dailey) is appropriately dressed in green because he is environmentally conscious; he is also very much into the martial arts and their opaque underlying philosophy, as in: "The toenail of success often gets snagged on the athletic sock of defeat."

There are other recurring characters. **Kent Powers** (voiced by Roger Rose) is the egomaniacal anchorman of *What in the World?*: he regards himself, rather than the newshounds, as the *raison d'être* of the show. The villainous **Moltoc** (voiced by Tim Curry) crops up frequently in order to be thwarted by the Quack Pack; power mad, he has dreams of world domination but for the moment will settle for booty. **Professor Ludwig Von Drake** (➤124) makes a new television incarnation as the zany presenter of a line of self-help inserts in which he demonstrates how to do something—and himself proceeds to make a public hash of that something. Finally there is

Gwumpki, Donald's Mittel-European immigré next-door neighbor, a hunky guy who treats the Nephews as if they were family—as well he might, for their favorite hangout is his diner, Gwumpki Burgers.

BRAND SPANKING NEW DOUG

Disney seems to have decided that there must be gold in them thar pubertal crises because, as with Max in *Goof Troop* (➤145), **Doug Funnie** is hitting the time of life which we all remember with the most loathing—when the prospect of living to the grand old age of twenty-seven seems a grossly obnoxious idea. The original character Doug debuted in 1991 on Nickelodeon and remained 11½ years old on that channel for several years. Jumbo Pictures, in conjunction with Disney, brought *Brand Spanking New Doug,* the revamp, to ABC on September 7, 1996. Now Doug is a few months older and just about to hit That Age.

Knobby-kneed and skinny, prone to dreaminess in class—where he often doodles in order to escape from the hell of education—Doug Funnie (voiced by Thomas McHugh) is the archetype of the immediately prepubertal boy. He knows

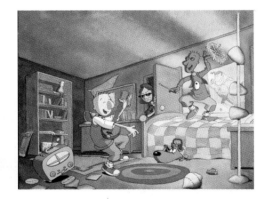

Doug Funnie, pal Skeeter Valentine, and Doug's dog, Porkchop, making trouble.

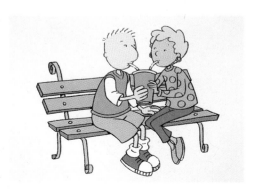

Doug with the love of his life, Patti Mayonnaise.

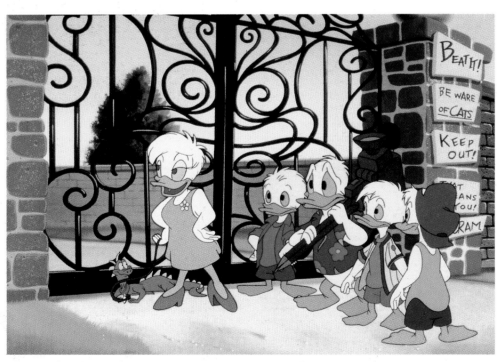

The modernized Daisy Duck, Donald Duck (with his camera), and Nephews Huey, Dewey, and Louie. Daisy's pet iguana is Knuckles.

that desires wrestle strongly within him, but identifying those desires is a trickier matter. His glamorous and somewhat precocious classmate **Patti Mayonnaise** (voiced by Connie Shulman) is the major obsession of his life—he doesn't like to admit it to himself, but he might very well be in full, proper, mature, love with her, and anyway he sure wants to kiss her—except that he also has a deeply loving relationship with his dog **Porkchop** (voiced by Fred Newman), who is his fiercely faithful ally. Tough stuff, this divided-loyalty business. And then there is Doug's allegiance to his best pal, **Skeeter Valentine** (voiced by Fred Newman), who is a bit of a misfit, like Doug himself, but otherwise a fairly typical schoolkid, except that he happens to be colored blue—not, in this instance, to indicate that he's "cool." The friends who gather around Doug and Skeeter to make up the rest of their gang are **Beebe Bluff** (voiced by Alice Playten)—whose father, **Bill Bluff** (voiced by Doug Preis), is the bigshot of Bluffington, the town where the series is set; **Chalky Studebaker** (voiced by Doug Preis); and **Connie Benge** (voiced by Becca Lish). Possibly also to be counted as part of Doug's circle of friends is **Quail Man,** a cartoon character he has created who can help him out by telling him what to do when things look threatening on the playground.

Doug's family circle is made up of mother and father **Theda Funnie** (voiced by Becca Lish) and **Phil Funnie** (voiced by Doug Preis) but, most important—although Doug would wish it other-

wise—elder sister **Judy Funnie** (voiced by Becca Lish). Judy is an entertaining comic creation, a would-be neogoth of the thespianic persuasion, she is one of the greatest embarrassments of Doug's life—although, since he is at That Age, it's a bit hard for him to pick out which embarrassment is actually the greatest.

Next door live the Dinks. **Mr. Dink** (voiced by Fred Newman) is slow-witted but good-natured—he has a certain amiable wisdom that on occasion stands Doug in good stead. **Tippy Dink** (voiced by Doris Belack), Mr. Dink's improbable wife, is a much more get-up-and-go character: she gets elected as Mayor of Bluffington, thereby creating a difference in status that Mr. Dink in no way resents.

Doug's existence has several banes, as might be expected. A minor one is **Lamar Bone** (voiced by Doug Preis), the prissy vice-principal of Doug's school. **Coach Spitz** (voiced by Jeff Bergman) is the school's sports coach: As tender to the touch as a sheet of sandpaper, he has the habit of making the kids squeeze vegetables to a soggy pulp between their fingers in order to demonstrate what it takes to become a winner.

Roger Klotz (voiced by Chris Phillips) is the biggest blight on Doug's horizon. Swaggering around in his black leather jacket, Roger is the school bully and takes particular delight in picking on Doug. Of course, Doug—with the mental assistance of Quail Man—usually comes off better in these encounters, even if sometimes with a loss to his own self-esteem. Roger has a vile cat called, suitably,

Stinky (voiced by Fred Newman), which makes Porkchop's life a misery at every available opportunity.

One notable feature of this series is the small number of voice actors involved in the portrayal of the main characters: Lish, Preis, and especially Newman do the bulk of the work. In addition, Newman provides some of the music for the show; he hosted The Disney Channel's *The Mickey Mouse Club* for six seasons.

NIGHTMARE NED

The primary conceit of *Nightmare Ned* is more or less that of the classic comic strip *Little Nemo in Slumberland,* created by Winsor McCay (1867–1934)—a pioneer not just in the field of comics but also in animation. McCay himself produced a short based on the idea, *Little Nemo* (1911), and much more recently there has been a full-length Hemdale/TMS animated feature based on it, *Little Nemo: Adventures in Slumberland* (1993), a guiding spirit behind which was the prolific and highly imaginative artist Moebius.

In the *Nightmare Ned* incarnation of the concept, young **Ned Needlemeyer** (voiced by Courtland Mead) is a bespectacled and somewhat dreamy schoolboy, isolated from his peers; his dreams are unduly affected by his daytime experi-

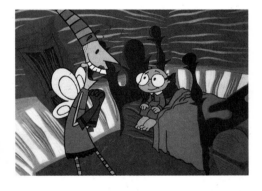

Poor Ned Needlemeyer's nightmares are so real that they're worse than reality. Here he must negotiate with the Tooth Fairy so he can keep the rest of his teeth.

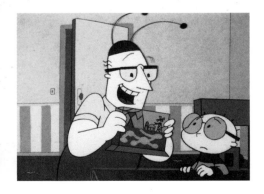

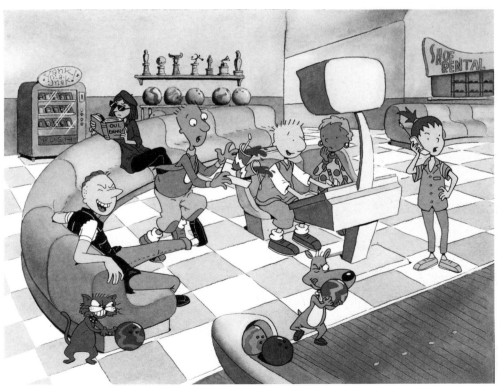

The gang bowling.

Ned and his father.

ences—in fact, those experiences are transmuted into the stuff of nightmares. The nightmares become more real to him than living reality. As an example, in one episode Ned during the daytime loses the last of his baby teeth and then dreams that the **Tooth Fairy** (voiced by Judy Tenuda) takes him to her realm and proposes to yank out all the rest of his teeth. Only by winning a game of checkers against **Old Man Wisdom Tooth** can Ned retain his set of fangs—Ingmar Bergman's *The Seventh Seal* (1956) is the obvious precursor of this latter strand of the plot, with *Bill & Ted's Bogus Journey* (1991) offering a hilarious reprise.

Based on a CD-ROM interactive game project created by Sue Shakespeare, Terry Shakespeare, and David Molina, and produced by Donovan Cook, the series by its very nature has few running characters apart from Ned himself; exceptions are **Dad Needlemeyer** (voiced by Brad Garrett), an oafish hulk who loves his son but doesn't really understand him, and **Mom Needlemeyer** (voiced by Victoria Jackson), who understands her son only too well and has a wicked sense of humor. Of the one-time appearances, the character **Florence Henderson** is of interest because she is voiced by Florence Henderson herself (of *The Brady Bunch*). The series premiered on April 19, 1997.

DISNEY'S PEPPER ANN

Two new shows created for Disney's Saturday-morning lineup on ABC, premiereing fall 1997, deserve brief mention.

Disney's Pepper Ann features a young girl named Pepper Ann Pearson, who is on an eternal quest for coolness. In her first few episodes Pepper Ann deals with such adolescent plights as pimples, an after-school job, and best-friend rivalry.

DISNEY'S RECESS

From the co-creator of *Rugrats* comes *Disney's Recess,* an ensemble show featuring fourth-grade friends P.J., Vince, Spinelli, Mikey, Gretchen, and Gus. As these pals steer clear of scary sixth-graders and annoying kindergartners, they maneuver for the best position in an unwritten but well-understood pecking order on the playground.

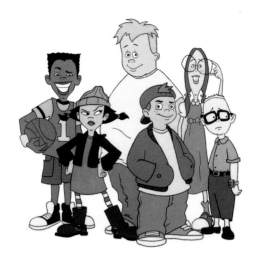

Disney's new ensemble show, *Recess.*

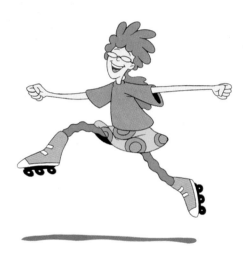

Pepper Ann skipping along on her usual quest for coolness.

III
THE
FEATURES

INTRODUCTION

Snow White and the Seven Dwarfs premiered on December 21, 1937, at the Carthay Circle Theater in Hollywood; at the end of the showing the audience, packed out with celebrities, rose to its feet and cheered. The movie which, during its making, had been widely described as "Disney's Folly" was on course to be the biggest news in cinema history.

It succeeded because of its artistry, because of its blend of action and humour, because of its songs, because it was the first of its kind ... but most of all because of its characters.

Press and public were agreed as to who was the star of the show. Not Snow White or her Prince, not even the wicked Queen who transforms herself into a hideous hag, but Dopey – who does not even have a speaking part. (Another character who did not have a speaking part had received a similar reception nine years earlier: he was of course Mickey Mouse.) In succeeding weeks and months Walt was bombarded from all sides by appeals to make Dopey a series star in the shorts, but these he wisely ignored: the cute little dumb dwarf had been created specifically for *Snow White*, and that was the way he should stay. The same attitude has prevailed, almost without exception – the main one being Figaro, from *Pinocchio* (1940) – in Disney ever since.

Walt was right. The creation of a character for a full-length feature is an altogether different art from developing one for a series of shorts; this is why Mickey and Donald have yet to star in a full-length feature. What is demanded of a shorts character is that it should hold an audience for five or ten minutes and preferably make that audience want to come back to watch it perform for another five or ten minutes. Although it is a joy to watch ten of Mickey's or Donald's shorts one after the other, each individual short tells a (usually) quite simple story and is (again usually) packed with gags. Features, by contrast, must have much more complex plots and *cannot* be so intensely packed with gags: as any comedian knows, in order to make an audience stay with you for more than a few minutes, you have to have "arid" patches in between the punchlines – a laugh a minute means that after a while there are no more laughs. Thus major characters in the animated features – aside from the villains, who must be starkly evil – must be capable of both rousing an audience to hilarity and making that same audience, moments later, start to gulp back the tears.

Of all the Disney characters Dopey is, debatably, the one most capable of doing this. (Mickey has something of the same ability; Donald and Goofy have not.) Dopey is a tragicomic character: we weep for him because, even while we laugh at his antics, we love him deeply – just as we love

our children even more because sometimes we laugh at them. But this ability is of no use in shorts. In five or ten minutes there simply is not the time to firmly establish the character, make us empathize with him or her, and then to rack our heartstrings. If Donald strikes disaster at the end of one of his shorts we laugh at him; we may reach for a handkerchief to dry our eyes, but not because of sorrow. Of course, it would have been possible to transform Dopey into a straightforwardly comic character for use in the shorts, but it would have been a travesty: apart from the fact that it would be a very different Dopey from the one we know and love, sooner or later, willy-nilly, we would find ourselves being asked to laugh at his affliction. (This is one of the reasons why Pete lost his peg-leg.)

So, as noted, Walt was right to refuse all incentives to turn Dopey into a shorts star.

Features characters are, then, a very different breed from shorts ones. This applies not only to the comic characters but also to the villains. Although Vladimir (Bill) Tytla succeeded in capturing the true smell of evil in the form of Chernabog in one of the sections of 1940's *Fantasia* (i.e., in a short), this was something of a one-off: almost every other shorts villain in the history of animation has been essentially a comic character. In the features, by contrast, villains must be unmitigatedly evil, like Maleficent, or Cruella De Vil, or the abstraction of "Man" in *Bambi* (1942), or Madame Medusa, or ... It is interesting to note that a Disney feature frequently panned (rightly or wrongly) by the critics as being too milquetoast, *The Aristocats* (1970), has a villain with whom one has certain reluctant sympathies. Once again, transferring the typical features villain to the sphere of the shorts would be madness: not only would it simply not work, it would diminish the villain's screen presence in the original feature.

The characters in this part of the book, therefore, have almost all made only the one screen appearance. This does not mean that they are in any way less significant creations than characters who have made many appearances in the shorts – far from it, because the major characters in the features are portrayed in greater depth than any shorts character could be. Or, at least, in Disney features. That represents a big difference between the Disney features and all but a handful of offerings from elsewhere. The depth and definition of characters in the Disney animated features distinguish them from most others. That is why people go to Disney features, often several times over, and enjoy themselves; all too often they find themselves simply bored by the products of other studios. Disney creates "real" characters; very few other studios have discovered the trick.

SNOW WHITE AND THE SEVEN DWARFS

Characters:

Snow White; Prince; Queen/Witch; Seven Dwarfs: Bashful; Doc; Dopey; Grumpy; Happy; Sleepy; Sneezy.
Spirit of the Magic Mirror; Huntsman; Raven; Miscellaneous animals.

Credits:

Based on the tale as told by the Brothers Grimm in *Kinder- und Hausmärchen* (1812-15)

Voices: Adriana Caselotti (Snow White); Harry Stockwell (Prince); Lucille LaVerne (Queen/Witch); Scotty Mattraw (Bashful); Roy Atwell (Doc); Pinto Colvig (Grumpy, Sleepy); Otis Harlan (Happy); Billy Gilbert (Sneezy); Moroni Olsen (Spirit of the Magic Mirror); Stuart Buchanan (Huntsman)

Music: Frank Churchill; Leigh Harline; Paul Smith

Story Adaptation: Ted Sears; Otto Englander; Earl Hurd; Dorothy Ann Blank; Richard Creedon; Merrill De Maris; Dick Rickard; Webb Smith

Art Directors: Charles Philippi; Hugh Hennesy; Terrell Stapp; McLaren Stewart; Harold Miles; Tom Codrick; Gustaf Tenggren; Ken Anderson; Kendall O'Connor; Hazel Sewell

Backgrounds: Mique Nelson; Merle Cox; Claude Coats; Phil Dike; Ray Lockrem; Maurice Noble; Samuel Armstrong

Character Designers: Albert Hurter; Joe Grant

Supervising Animators: Hamilton Luske; Vladimir Tytla; Fred Moore; Norman Ferguson

Animators: Frank Thomas; Dick Lundy; Arthur Babbitt; Eric Larson; Milton Kahl; Robert Stokes; James Algar; Al Eugster; Cy Young; Joshua Meador; Ugo D'Orsi; George Rowley; Les Clark; Fred Spencer; Bill Roberts; Bernard Garbutt; Grim Natwick; Jack Campbell; Marvin Woodward; James Culhane; Stan Quackenbush; Ward Kimball; Wolfgang Reitherman; Robert Martsch

Sequence Directors: Perce Pearce; William Cottrell; Wilfred Jackson; Larry Morey; Ben Sharpsteen

Supervising Director: David Hand

Release Date: December 21, 1937

Running Time: 83 minutes

THE MOVIE

In November 1933 Ted Sears wrote to I. Klein that "having just completed *The Pied Piper*, we [Disney] have come to the conclusion that our best screen values are in small cute animal characters, we haven't advanced far enough to handle humans properly and make them perform well enough to compete with real actors". The following year, Walt Disney initiated work on a new project, *Snow White and the Seven Dwarfs*, whose central characters are convincingly animated human beings. The art of animation was advancing rapidly.

There were a number of good reasons for the Disney company to tackle an animated feature film. The costs of the shorts were rising inexorably, but the returns from them were not rising in tandem. Moreover, it seemed important that the studio should make the transition as soon as possible – and certainly before any of its competitors got around to it. Nevertheless, the sums of money involved were staggering for the times: Walt originally planned to spend as much as half a million dollars on the project (in the end he spent $1,480,000 on it). A further worry was that, while the animated cartoons being produced by the studio were capable of entertaining an audience for a few minutes at a time, it was by no means generally believed that viewers could tolerate an hour and half of animation – people might simply get bored. But, despite the qualms of Roy and Lillian, Walt was determined to push ahead.

Having decided to produce a feature, the next task was to determine what it should be. Walt himself was never quite sure how he came to settle on the Grimms' fairy tale *Snow White and the Seven Dwarfs*, although in 1938 he was to offer a reminiscence by way of tentative explanation:

I saw Marguerite Clark in [a movie of] *Snow White and the Seven Dwarfs* when I was delivering papers in Kansas City, and the film made such an impression on me I'm sure it influenced my decision to use the Grimm fairy tale when I decided to make an animated feature.

So keen was he that, when he discovered that there was a stage-play version of the story still in copyright, he bought the movie rights just in case. In fact, not one word of the play appeared in the feature.

Work on the project really started for the studio one night late in 1934 when Walt took a group of the animators to the sound stage and began to talk about his idea for *Snow White and the Seven Dwarfs* as it might be in an animated feature. By all accounts the performance was electric. Walt acted out all the roles as he told the story, and the animators were rapt. One later said: "That one performance lasted us three years. Whenever we'd get stuck, we'd remember how Walt did it that night." Ken Anderson has been reported as saying that, even though the movie was good, Walt's rendition had been even better!

From 1934 750 artists were employed, at one time or another, on *Snow White*. Some two million sketches were made for the movie, the final version of which contained over 250,000 separate pictures. The amount of loving care devoted to the film by all concerned – especially Walt – can be deduced from two rather different items of information. First, there was so much by way of revision, rehashing, scrapping and so on in order to get things just *right* that the animators exhaustedly used to advise Walt at every stage that the screen-time of the characters *they* were animating should be cut! (This especially applied with the Dwarfs.) Second, *Snow White* cost roughly $200 per foot of completed film to make: on average the shorts were costing only $50-$75 per foot at that time. (The old Laugh-O-grams had cost 30¢ per foot.)

In addition to the technical bravura involved, a considerable deal of psychological subtlety was employed. For example, the colours used are comparatively restrained for cartoons of the period – except in the case of the principal characters, who were deliberately depicted in much bolder colours in order to bolster their "stage presence". This matter of the colours went further – to an almost incredible level of sophistication. Take the example of the Dwarfs' clothing: Doc has a russet jerkin to mark his cheery character, Grumpy a dull magenta one to reflect his wet-blanket personality, and Dopey is clad in a saffron robe and a lavender-grey cap to denote his comic irresponsibility (the other four Dwarfs have grey and tan clothing). The Queen has a heavy black cape and is normally associated with unhealthy greens and blues – the colours of decay – in stark contrast to the healthy, fertile colours associated with Snow White, reds and browns. Snow White has brown eyes as have all the Dwarfs except Dopey, who has innocent blue ones, and Grumpy, who has unsympathetic black ones; by contrast both the Queen and the Huntsman have green eyes. All of these different colour effects, while not consciously noticed by the audience (they would be useless if they were), immediately make one form an opinion of the various characters' personalities, before they so much as open their mouths.

The subtlety went yet further: not just the colours were carefully deployed but also the *textures*. Walt was determined that the clothing of the various participants would not be represented by straightforward flat colour. At considerable expense, therefore, the Disney laboratories developed new paints to give different effects: for example, a satin effect for the Queen's collar and a velvet effect for her robe, the appearance of a linen texture for Snow White's skirt, and a "homespun" effect for the Dwarfs' clothing.

Further expense was involved in providing the animators with good reference material. For the animals they could work with a menagerie Walt had installed on the lot as well as with live-action films. One member of the menagerie was a tortoise who was used as the basis for the unfortunate little fellow who several times during the movie suffers for his slowness (see below). After the movie had been completed this animal remained as a studio pet, but his shell was now adorned with the words "Traffic Department" – a cruel comment on the lot's messenger service.

For the humans the animators used their own skills and imaginations as well as, for Snow White, the Dwarfs and the Prince, live-action films. In these films the part of Snow White was played by Marjorie Belcher (who shortly married Art Babbitt, and later became the movie actress Marge Champion); aged 18, she was the daughter of a Los Angeles dancing teacher. Later she recalled that the scene she found most difficult to mime was the one where Snow White is fleeing in terror through the forest. The model for Prince Charming was Louis Hightower, one of her father's pupils and a frequent dancing partner of herself. He was chosen not only because he had worked with her before but also, according to a *Life* report, because "Disney also liked his sturdy legs". A troop of dwarfs was imported to the lot for the animators to study.

The amount of care taken to get the animation just right was amazing. While working on the scene in which the Huntsman threatens Snow White the animators actually set up an experiment to map out exactly how his shadow would fall at three o'clock in the afternoon! They felt that, while no one watching the movie would know how the shadow *ought* to fall, lots of people would unconsciously "feel" that there was something wrong if the shadow were out of place and incorrectly shaped.

Still, it was all worth it. On December 21, 1937, *Snow White and the Seven Dwarfs* was premiered at the Carthay Circle Theater in Hollywood before an audience composed almost entirely of movie-business people; 30,000 onlookers who could not get in gathered around the theatre. The guest list reads like a directory to the Hollywood of the time: Chaplin, Dietrich, Temple, Fairbanks (Junior), Berle, Benny, Rogers, Pickford, Grant, Burns ... Years later Steve Hulett cited a reminiscence of Ken O'Connor's of that night:

> The audience was wildly enthusiastic. They even applauded the background and layouts when no animation was on the screen. I was sitting near John Barrymore when the shot of the Queen's castle above the mist came on, with the Queen poling [punting] across the marsh in a little boat. He was bouncing up and down in his seat he was so excited. Barrymore

was an artist as well as an actor, and he knew the kind of work that went into something like that.

In general, the critics were ecstatic. Westbrook Pegler in the *New York World-Telegram* called it "the greatest moving picture ever made", which was not hyperbole. "If you miss *Snow White and the Seven Dwarfs*, you'll be missing the ten best pictures of 1938," said Frank S. Nugent in the *New York Times*. In the *Los Angeles Times* Edwin Schallert called it a "motion picture miracle". Munro Leaf in *Stage* probably summed it up best of all: "He's just put all your dreams and my childhood fancies into life, where we can almost – not quite – touch them. For that we thank him with all our hearts."

Walt himself knew to whom the thanks should be directed. Right at the opening of the film's credits appears the following paragraph:

> My sincere appreciation to the members of my staff whose loyalty and creative endeavor made possible this production.
>
> Walt Disney

Walt Disney received a well deserved special Academy Award for *Snow White and the Seven Dwarfs*, but it was an award with a difference. On the night, Shirley Temple handed to him not just a single Oscar figure but eight: one big one and seven little ones, all on the same stand.

THE STORY

Since *Snow White* is one of the most watched movies of all time, and since it is based on one of the best loved fairy tales of all time, its plot is well known.

The film opens with the turning pages of a book, a gambit that was to become familiar in many other Disney movies. We read that

> Once upon a time there lived a lovely little Princess named Snow White. Her vain and wicked Stepmother the Queen feared that one day Snow White's beauty would surpass her own. So she dressed the little Princess in rags and forced her to work as a Scullery Maid.

Shortly afterwards, we are transported into "magicland". We see the wicked Queen asking her Magic Mirror who is the fairest of them all, and her fury when it replies, honestly, that there is one fairer in the land. Then we find Snow White in rags in the courtyard, playing with white doves beside a wishing-well and singing the song "I'm Wishing". A passing Prince hears her song and hops over the castle wall to join her: in a particularly splendid piece of animation we see Snow White's singing face reflected in the water of the well, traversed by ripples; then, still in the rippled reflection, we see the face of the Prince suddenly appear beside hers. He obviously has fallen in love at first sight, but she modestly panics and

flees from him into the castle. As he continues to sing to her she looks down adoringly from one of the balconies ... but the scene is observed also by the Queen, and her jealous fury is awesome to behold.

Vengeance will be hers, and she calls upon her Huntsman. She instructs him to take Snow White off into the forest and there slaughter her. At first he is unwilling, and she has to threaten him with dire retribution before he will obey: even then, in order to check that he obeys her command, she gives him a casket and instructs him to bring Snow White's heart back to her in it. Quakingly, he promises to do her bidding.

However, he finds it easier to make the promise than to keep it. Out in the forest he watches Snow White's gentleness and grace as she helps a baby bird that is in difficulties. Still, he steels himself to the task – but as he lowers over her stooping form she suddenly turns and, seeing him, screams. He cannot force himself to do the deed; instead he tells her to flee, flee, flee away through the forest.

And flee she does, as night falls and she stumbles through blackness, the finger-like branches of the trees catching at her as she blindly runs on. She falls into a river and is instantly surrounded by logs that look like hungry alligators (this is a bad piece of ecogeography, although it is only afterwards that one thinks: how could this medieval European princess have known about alligators?). Once she escapes from that she finds that the night is full of a thousand eyes. She throws herself to the ground in terror ... but then day breaks and she finds that the owners of those eyes are cute, cuddlesome rabbits, deer, raccoons, skunks and other innocuous forest animals. These are no enemies: they are her friends.

And so she comes to the Dwarfs' cottage, and a delapidated and visibly foul-smelling heap it is. In a superbly crafted moment the tragedy of the Dwarfs' orphanhood and neglect is expressed by way of a contrast. As Snow White is looking at the house we see a mother and baby deer together: the fawn rubs affectionately against its mother, and she turns her head to give it a loving lick.

Snow White sets with a will to cleaning the cottage, helped by her new-found animal friends. Squirrels use their bushy tails as brooms, a raccoon helps dry the dishes, and so forth. The animal occupants of the cottage are less than delighted about this: a feisty little mouse blasts out all the dust which the squirrels have somewhat covertly brushed into its hole, and an equally feisty little spider responds with some vigour when her web is "tidily" rolled up into a ball of twine.

Still, at length the task is done and Snow White, exhausted but confident that the seven children whom she assumes occupy the cottage will welcome her presence because of her hard labours, staggers upstairs to bed.

We first encounter the Dwarfs working in their diamond mine – and it is one of the great triumphs of the movie that we are instantly aware of their different characters. Work over, home they go, singing the great song "Heigh Ho". As they march along they cast giant shadows – another masterpiece of animation. When they arrive home they instantly realize that someone has been there – as Doc puts it, characteristically murdering the English language, "The lit's light." They creep up to the house and in through the door and discover to their horror that the whole place has been tidied and scrubbed.

Doc: Why, the whole place is clean!
Grumpy: There's dirty work afoot.

Their initial hypothesis is that the intruder might be a ghost, a theory strengthened when Dopey, deputed by the others to go up to the bedroom and check, and too foolish to resist their urging, discovers Snow White stretching her arms under the sheet as she wakes up. However, after a long series of misunderstandings the Dwarfs happily welcome her to their home – although Grumpy resists to the last. Grumpy is especially infuriated by the suggestion that he – along with the other Dwarfs – should wash thoroughly before supper; in the end the others, enamoured of this new-fangled notion, forcibly scrub him.

An interesting point here is the matter of role-reversal. Snow White is depicted as a child, and the Dwarfs (with the exception of Dopey) are not only adults but elderly adults, with white hair and flowing beards. Yet it is Snow White who adopts the maternal role in the household and the Dwarfs who are – much as she suspected when first she entered the cottage – the "children". They act as adults when she is not there, but very definitely they are youngsters in her presence.

After supper and much singing and dancing, Snow White and the Dwarfs go to sleep – she occupying the bedroom and they making do as best they can in the livingroom.

We cut back to the Queen, who discovers from the Magic Mirror that

Snow White still lives, the fairest in the land;
'Tis the heart of a pig you hold in your hand.

What happened to the Huntsman as a result of his deception is not recorded, but the Queen's reaction most certainly is. In what is probably the most exciting and decidedly the most controversial sequence in *Snow White* she transforms herself from a beautiful (if evil) woman into a grotesque hag, and at the same time she imbues a fresh apple with poison.

The Dwarfs leave home for their work in their diamond mine; the Queen makes her way to the cottage. As she travels along, cackling and leering, two vultures watch her, and then turn to look at each other with a grin of eager anticipation. This grin will be repeated later, first when the Witch tempts Snow White with the poisoned apple and second when, in the moments before her death, she tries to tip a heavy rock down onto the pursuing Dwarfs and forest animals.

As Snow White is being tempted with the apple the Dwarfs are told by the animals that she is in danger. They start an amazing chase, accompanied by the forest animals, but although they succeed in ensuring the destruction of the Queen, they are too late to avert the death of Snow White . . . except that she can be rescued from death by "True Love's First Kiss". Sure enough, while the Dwarfs and the forest animals tearfully surround Snow White's funeral bier, the Prince rides to the rescue. A kiss later and there is a happy ending for all.

Walt made the occasional pertinent comment to criticisms produced in the wake of the movie. To the charge that he had distorted the original tale he responded that

It's just that people now don't want fairy stories the way they were written. They were too rough. In the end they'll probably remember the story the way we film it anyway. That's been our experience up to now.

THE CHARACTERS

Snow White

Snow White in the Disney version is, strangely, not in fact very beautiful – although extremely attractive. Presumably deliberately, Disney opted for girl-next-door prettiness rather than out-and-out beauty. Moreover, Snow White appears to be extremely youthful, aged perhaps between 12 and 14 (although modelled by 18-year-old Marjorie Belcher), and still with a trace of early adolescent plumpness. However, framed by her dark, shortish hair, her face has an infinitely appealing innocent charm and sweetness.

Snow White's voice reinforces this impression of youth. This voice was supplied by Adriana Caselotti, the daughter of a Hollywood singing teacher. Interestingly, among the many hundreds of young women who were auditioned for the part was Deanna Durbin; she was turned down on the grounds that her voice was too mature, too well honed. What is startling is that the Snow White we see and hear is in fact an older version of the original character with whom the Disney animators worked: quite early on Walt had to decree that their Snow White figure was really too young for the tempests of love (she must have looked about 8!), and that they should add a few years to her age.

Animated by Hamilton Luske and Grim Natwick, Snow White is herself in many ways something of a cypher: a character to whom things happen rather than a doer. This is a quality shared by many Disney heroes and heroines and, in terms of the resulting features, is in fact a strength rather than a weakness, since it allows all the other characters to shine by contrast. The only time during the movie that Snow White acts on her own initiative and exerts her personality is while she is cleaning up the cottage and then "adopting" the Dwarfs. Otherwise she is forced or led to do things: she is chased off into the forest by the Huntsman; she is led by the animals to the

To convey Snow White's purity, the animators showed her as little more than a child.

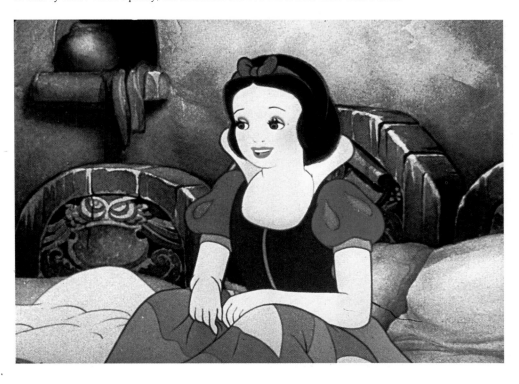

cottage; she is persuaded by the Witch to eat the apple; she is brought back to life by the kiss of the Prince.

In an interview with John Canemaker published in *Film Comment* in 1975, Grim Natwick makes several pertinent remarks on Snow White's character and appearance:

They didn't want her to look like a princess, really. They wanted her to look like a cute little girl who could be a princess. ... Snow White was a sweet and graceful little girl and we just tried not to clown her up. Betty Boop [whom Natwick created – a strong contrast!] gets quite wild at times, you know, but it's in her character. ... The best animation, generally, that I think I ever did was where [Snow White] runs down the stairs. It was too risky a thing to rotoscope so I had to animate that and it turned out to be one of the nicest [scenes] ... I think we could have animated a lot of [the film without rotoscope] probably. But we didn't know. Nobody had ever done a [human] character like this. It was a new problem for all of us.

(In fact, Disney had animated human characters before, but the results had not been deemed too successful.)

Reminiscing in *Funnyworld* in 1979 Dick Huemer had more to say on the animation:

[Hamilton Luske] was, I would say, directly responsible for the animation of Snow White herself. This was the first time that anything had been done that was beautiful in simple analysis of the action. It was done over live action, but if you could have seen what he did, taking the figure of Marjorie Belcher ... , making the head almost twice as large and cutting down the waist and reducing it to a cartoon format. This was a big job ... What he did was really a sensational advance in the history of animation for serious human characters. ... He changed the proportions so [Snow White] became a cartoon-proportioned figure. Study her if you get a chance some time and see if you can tell how many heads tall she is. Instead of a human being a normal eight heads tall, she is about five heads tall, so it all had to be in different proportion. He did a great job on it ...

The effect of such proportional changes, especially the relatively large head, was of course to emphasize the youthfulness of Snow White in contrast to the more mature and striking beauty of the Queen. At the same time, such changes of physical appearance underwrote her essential passivity.

However, even although Snow White is essentially a passive personality, it is not without its inner strengths. After her nightmare flight through the night-time forest she almost immediately wins the hearts of the timorous little animals, and in due course exactly the same happens with the Dwarfs. Moreover, or perhaps as a reason for this, she is very definitely portrayed as being in some way in communication with the simple things of

Nature – the Earth and the flowers and the air – and in that respect she is almost like an elemental. Her passivity is not a sign of a character-failing: it is a symptom of the strength of her goodness.

The Prince

If Snow White is, as it were, a "strong cypher", the Prince is a weak one. For an important central character he appears on the screen for an astonishingly short period of time – once early on when singing "One Song" with Snow White and the other time right at the end when his kiss wakes her from her otherwise endless sleep. Strangely enough, although he has only a few lines, his voice part proved the most difficult in the film to cast aside from that of Snow White, and indeed it was the last one to be finalized, the part eventually going to the established actor Harry Stockwell. The problem was that of finding a voice that captured the Prince's screen image as a robust, handsome young man (he had originally been envisaged as a Douglas Fairbanks type). In the event Stockwell achieved this to perfection.

We first see the Prince riding along on his pure-white steed outside the castle walls and hearing Snow White singing beguilingly. It is the work of a moment for him to shin over the wall and join her. His masculinity is impressive and yet not overcrowding; it contrasts interestingly with Snow White's much more youthful femininity – in terms of appearance he is at least ten years her senior. Like her he is depicted in "earth" colours: tall and slender, he has brown hair and his clothing is brown, white and clear blue. He shares with her the dramatic piece of animation

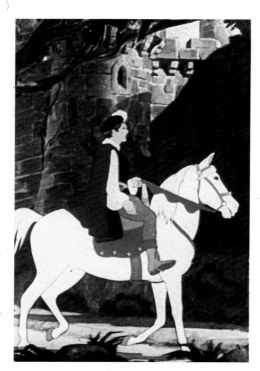

The Prince has only a tiny part on screen, yet his function in the plot is crucial.

when he joins her at the end of "I'm Wishing" while we see their faces reflected in the waters of the wishing-well.

Walt was obviously very sensitive to the criticism that the Prince's role was so small. Questioned on the subject by the *Christian Science Monitor*'s Frank Daugherty in 1938 he responded:

I suppose that's legitimate criticism, but it might help if people knew we were plain scared. None of us knew how those drawings of human figures on the screen were going to be taken. We were prepared for any sort of ridicule. We had an idea we could put them across, and if we could it meant the removal of our biggest limitation; we were willing to face the ridicule for that. Today, human characters don't scare us at all. We know we've licked 'em.

In fact, the depiction of the Prince is imperfect. As he climbs from his pristinely white horse to kiss the sleeping Snow White there is a moment when his image "shimmers", as a result of a fault in the accuracy of the drawing. This was discovered too late for the fault to be amended, and Walt had to allow the film to be released with this imperfection. Oddly enough, it is a flaw audiences hardly ever notice.

Queen/Witch

Aside from the Dwarfs, the Queen/Witch is easily the most powerful character in *Snow White*; Walt himself described her as "a mixture of Lady Macbeth and the Big Bad Wolf". In effect, she is really two characters, the icily beautiful evil Queen and the grotesquely evil Witch into which she transforms herself; both personas were magnificently voiced by Lucille LaVerne, an established star of the stage.

When we first see her as the wicked Queen she has an orange-gold crown, a blue-black robe with a high winged collar, a rich pendant, black eyes and black, thin high-arched eyebrows, red lips, and features that are aristocratically beautiful yet at the same time patently cruel. So obsessed is she with her own beauty that she has installed her Magic Mirror, which she constantly questions as to her rivals in fairness; it is also why she envies so bitterly the innocent beauty of the youthful Snow White, her stepdaughter. Her jealousy is superbly captured in the early scene where she watches from the castle balcony as Snow White and the Prince sing their loving duet: her face is contorted into a vicious mask of jealous evil. According to Kirtley Baskette in an essay in *Photoplay* in April 1938, the "experiments on her lovely cruel mouth and eyes alone represent drawings enough to paper a house".

Art Babbitt, who animated the Queen before but not after her transformation into the Witch (Norm Ferguson animated her in this latter role), said rather surprisingly that "I didn't find her especially difficult. It was a

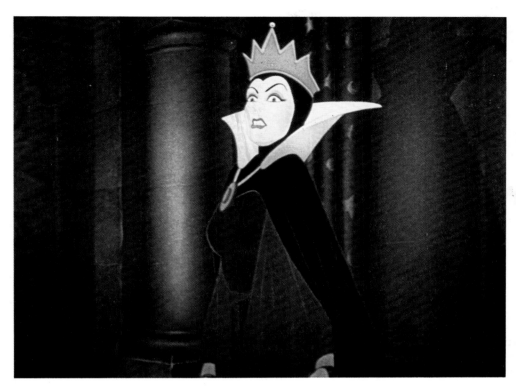

The Queen, animated mostly by Art Babbitt; Norm Ferguson took over for the Witch.

matter of drawing which was important there, simplifying, refining, things like that." However, the difficulty in animating the Queen concerned not either of her two distinct incarnations but her transmutation from one into the other: who could forget the fell sequence where she transforms herself from beautiful monarch to vile hag?

Now a formula to transform my beauty into ugliness – change my queenly raiment to a peddler's cloak.
    Mummy dust to make me old.
To shroud my clothes the black of night.
To age my voice an old hag's cackle.
To whiten my hair – a scream of fright.

After she has mixed all these bizarre ingredients together she holds the flask containing the evilly bubbling green mixture up to a storm-lit window and declares triumphantly:

A blast of wind – to fan my hate.
A thunderbolt to mix it well.
Now begin thy magic spell ...

This was a very difficult scene to animate, for reasons given by Baskette:

The hardest sequence in the whole film ... was where the wicked Queen changes into the Witch. Walt Disney insisted on not just showing her change (mere child's play in ordinary animation [hah!]) but how she felt as she changed! Every trick and effect developed for *Snow White* went into this scene. Whirling backgrounds, wind, highlights, animated color, glare, bubbles, and color mood. It is the real masterpiece of *Snow White* ... from a technical standpoint, and it represents the labor of years.

After her diabolic mixture has done its work we discover her transmuted into an ugly old hag. Her hands are long-taloned claws; her nose is long and decorated with a vast, off-centre, warty protuberance; her chin is pointed; her eyes are huge and hyperthyroidally bulbous; her voice is rasping and coarse; and she has only a single remaining tooth, sited just off-centre in her lower jaw. Before she had been beautiful, her cruelty and evil a matter of inference rather than overt: now the wickedness that has always been within her is fully demonstrated in her cackling, spitting face. (A similar figure appeared in a

similar role in the 1943 Disney propaganda short *Education for Death* [➤ 95].)

Thereafter the Witch is a caricature of evil – and yet, through her very loathsomeness, she has a certain beguiling quality. One cannot help but feel that she is successful in her attempts to seduce Snow White into eating the poisoned apple purely *because* she is so ugly – as if the young girl were thinking that surely somebody *that* ugly must have a heart of gold! Of course, any such thoughts are misleading, as the forest animals, who can see through the ugly exterior to the even uglier soul within, realize immediately and only too well. And in the climax of the great chase, as she prepares to cast a great boulder down upon the pursuing Dwarfs, even the evil elements seem to be coming out on her side until one of them – a bolt of lightning – destroys her. This is the nearest that the film gets to the old moral concept that the evil shall fittingly be destroyed by evil.

Over the years there have been occasional complaints that the Queen/Witch is simply too frightening a character for a movie intended to be watched by children, that she gives them nightmares and so on. Walt squashed this fairly effectively on numerous occasions when he asked: what made anyone think his movies were designed for children? However, children certainly do watch Disney cartoons: the only real way to judge the merit of such criticisms is to take a child to see *Snow White and the Seven Dwarfs* and observe the reactions. Children may find the Queen/Witch frightening, all right, but they love every moment that she is on screen.

The Witch's ugliness symbolizes the evil disguised by the Queen's customary beauty.

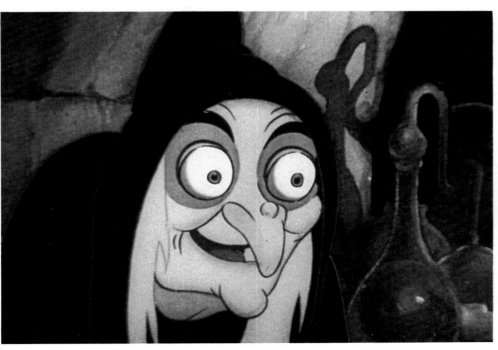

The Seven Dwarfs

The characters who stole the show were of course the Seven Dwarfs: Doc, Dopey, Grumpy, Happy, Sleepy, Bashful and Sneezy - especially Dopey. This line-up of names had had, however, a long and tortuous history. It would probably be impossible to construct a complete list of names and personalities considered by the Disney studio before it eventually settled for these (a long list is contained in the 1987 book *Snow White* by Brian Sibley and Richard Holliss). Wheezy, Puffy, Stuffy, Biggo-Ego and Burpy were considered; Sneezy was originally planned as Deefy, a deaf Dwarf, but Walt (wisely) decreed that this would not do because deaf people might justifiably take offence on seeing their disability the subject of laughter. Jumpy, Baldy, Nifty, Gabby and Stubby all failed to make the grade. In fact, there was a certain amount of academic argument as to whether Disney might not be betraying the folklore tradition by naming the dwarfs at all: surely, said the critics, the dwarfs in fairy tales are never named? Rumpelstiltskin springs to mind. In a 1980 paper Robert T. Sidwell sprang to Disney's defence, pointing out that among the very earliest traditions the dwarfs of myth and legend are indeed named. Moreover, he wrote, from the Eddas you can draw the following set of dwarf-names: Toki, Skavaerr, Varr, Duri, Orinn, Grerr and Radsvid – names that can be translated with reasonable accuracy as Dopey, Happy, Bashful, Sleepy, Grumpy, Sneezy (a little imagination is required for this translation) and Doc! In his book *The Folktale* (1977) Stith Thompson concurred with Sidwell's favourable judgement:

Heigh-ho, heigh-ho and it's home from work the Seven Dwarfs go.

In his production of *Snow White* Walt Disney was particularly successful in catching the traditional conception of the dwarf.

The Dwarfs have a number of things in common aside from their cottage and their diminutive size. All, like most nonhuman Disney creations, have only three fingers and a thumb; and all (except, obviously, Dopey), in times of stress are wont to use an exclamation that, in the light of hindsight, seems positively precognitive: "Jiminy Crickets!"

Producing the soundtrack for the Dwarfs was no easy matter, and some unusual measures had to be taken. In order to provide the noise of the Dwarfs washing themselves before supper, seven Disney sound-men actually stood around a huge water-tank, literally washing their faces, sticking them under the water, blowing bubbles and so on; they even sang with their faces submerged in order to get the right effect. All of this underwater cacophony was recorded using a specially made water-protected microphone. Even greater dedication was required by an anonymous sound-man to provide the effects when Grumpy, having been kissed by the young princess, furiously slips and falls into a stream: this unsung hero selflessly agreed to splash and slither around in a bath-tub filled with genuine mud – anything for authenticity! To achieve the sound of Grumpy's organ-playing in the party thrown by the Dwarfs to mark their acceptance of Snow White, the sound-men blew into bottles partly filled with water: this was all very well, but changes in the ambient temperature altered the pitch of the notes produced – as, too, did the slow but constant evaporation of the water. All in all, providing the sound for the Dwarfs was something of a nightmare.

Of the three principal Dwarfs – Doc, Grumpy and Dopey – there is no doubt at all as to who stole the show. **Dopey** is a vacuous-eyed little fellow, totally irresponsible, youthful where the other Dwarfs are elderly, dressed in oversized clothing, with ears like jug-handles and a mouth that almost drools with stupidity. Yet, and this is very curious, his caricature on screen is somehow by no means offensive – quite the opposite. Under normal circumstances one would expect this parody of imbecility – or at the very least mental retardation – to be utterly tasteless, yet for some reason Disney got away with it and created a character who was a runaway success (some reviewers even claimed that Disney had found a new Mickey Mouse).

Another point of interest concerning his appearance as it relates to his personality is the matter of his tooth. Like the Witch he has only one of these, but the effect created is utterly different. Her single fang merely adds to the overall malevolence of her vile mask, but in Dopey's case the single tooth, sited centrally in the upper jaw rather than off-centre in the lower, contributes instead to his childish lovableness – his is the first tooth of a baby rather than the last remaining tooth of an oldster.

Probably Dopey is such a successful character because his entire personality is imbued with a sense of fun (sincerity is his other major trait). We see this right at the beginning, when the Dwarfs are working in their diamond mine: Dopey, just for the heck of it, like any mischievous child pops a couple of huge diamonds in his eye-sockets to produce an apparition that initially scares Doc silly. Moments later, Dopey is again involved in a superb piece of gaggery when he tries to toss a heavy bag of diamonds into the store: he forgets to let go, and disappears with the bag. His finest piece of visual comedy is probably (it is very hard to choose) one that occurs during the washing scene: after a moment's thought he realizes that the best way of getting the pestilential soap out of his ears is to stick his finger in his mouth and blow against it very hard!

Dopey had not always been the merry little chap we see on the screen. Initially he was depicted as a big, broad grotesque clown with large eyes, a gaping mouth and a yet more imbecilic expression on his face: the mischief and simple-minded cunning were quite missing. He was also, like the rest of the Dwarfs, of advanced years. This image of him, however, simply did not work when Walt and the rest of the crew viewed him in the sweat-boxes, and so he was radically revised. His mouth was made much smaller and decades were taken off his age; the jug-ears were incorporated, as were his innocent blue eyes. He went from being a minor character to the star of the entire movie.

He is the only one of the Dwarfs not to speak – probably because it was quite impossible to find a suitable voice for him.

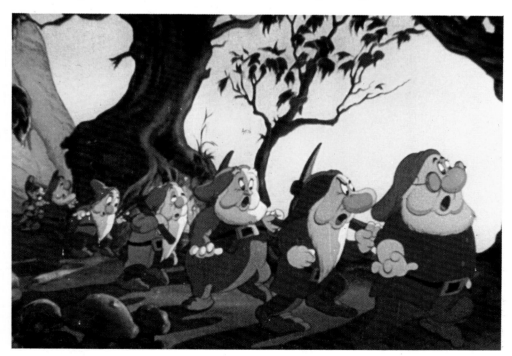

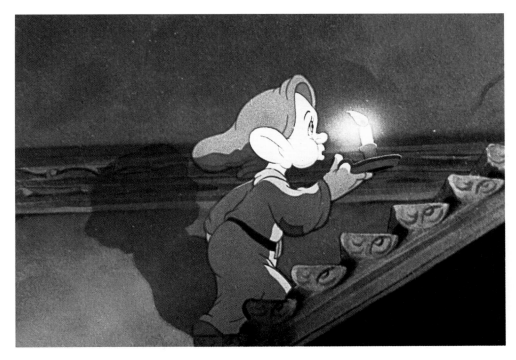

Walt received many requests to turn Dopey into a series star in the shorts.

he so strikingly resembled so many former French premiers.

If Dopey is the major figure in the line-up of Dwarfs their true leader is **Doc**. Before the ascendance of Dopey, in fact, he might have been the Dwarf to steal the show, but it was felt necessary to tone his personality down a little: waving his hands like a frenetic semaphore he was dominating all the scenes. In fact, his character is still a very strong one. He has a cheerily broad red face, seemingly redundant thin-rimmed spectacles, a ready smile and a mop of white hair; his beard is distinctly shorter than those of the other Dwarfs except Happy and, of course, Dopey. But his predominating characteristic is his habit of murdering the English language. Consider the dialogue when Doc confronts Snow White and attempts to be polite to this intruder – a politeness not shared by Grumpy:

Doc: Well, my dear Quincess ... uh, uh, uh, Princess ... we're a – we're a – honoured ... yes, we're a –
Grumpy (prompting): Mad as hornets.
Doc: "Mad as hornets" – uh – no we're not! We're bad as cornets – no – no – bad as a – uh – what was I sayin'?
Grumpy: Nuthin'. Just standin' there sputterin' like a doodlebug.
Doc: Who's butterin' like a spoodledug? Who's – wuh-huh, ruh, gutter-glove?
Grumpy: Aw, shut up an' tell her to git out!

Although, as with the other Dwarfs, much of Doc's animation was worked out using the troop of real dwarfs specially brought onto the Disney lot (comedian Eddie Collins

His style of humour is essentially non-verbal: to make his character more specific through the use of any particular voice would have been to shackle it and thereby destroy it. He does not in fact *need* to use words: his every thought or emotion is graphically displayed in the expressions on his face or the attitude of his body. He is, moreover, as we discover while Snow White sleeps in the bedroom and the Dwarfs camp in the livingroom, the only one of the Dwarfs not to snore: that would be discordant with his child-like image.

During the course of the movie Dopey gets knocked around quite frequently and violently, yet it never seems to bother him. For example, when the Dwarfs storm into their cottage to discover that there has been an intruder, Dopey, creeping fearfully, is trodden underfoot – yet seems to feel little or no pain and humiliation. Some while later, after Snow White stretching under her bedsheet has convinced him that the place has been infested by a ghost, he flees rather more slowly than the other Dwarfs, so that he finds the cottage door slammed in his face. It is useless for him to pull on the handle because the other six, convinced that he is the "nameless menace" and is striving to be at them, are equally determinedly clutching the handle on the other side. Finally the doorknob comes away in Dopey's hands and he shoots backwards to land in an avalanche of pots and pans. Dressed now like a surreal parody of a knight in armour he staggers blindly out into the forest, where his six erstwhile friends vigorously clobber this monstrously clanking apparition. In real life most of us would promptly succumb to concussion at this treatment, but not Dopey: he is momentarily discommoded, it is true, but

seconds later that infectious little vacant grin is back on his face.

Almost immediately after the release of *Snow White* Dopey had attained the status of a truly internationally popular star. We can theorize as to how this came about: his clothes, his eyes, his grin, his youthfulness, and so on. However, the front-running hypothesis must surely be one produced anonymously in France not long after the movie appeared: Dopey was so popular in that country, the argument went, because

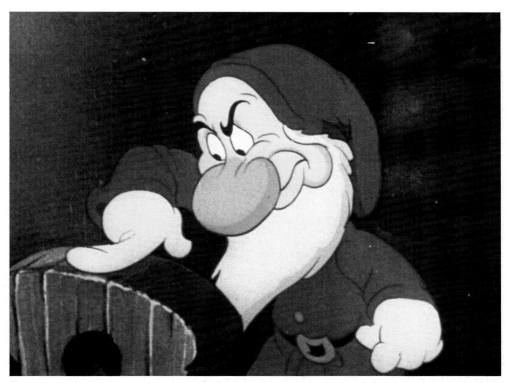

Grumpy was the only one of the dwarfs who did not almost immediately fall in love with the beautiful little interloper.

163

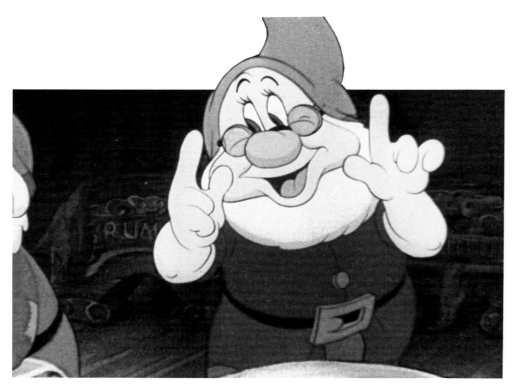

Doc was the acknowledged leader of the dwarfs.

helped the animators with some of the Dwarfs' funny walks), there is an extra element in his personality. The animators discovered that sequence director Perce Pearce did a very good impersonation of Doc, and so they used him for much of the live-action reference footage.

Doc is not nearly so powerfully caricatured a figure as the other Dwarfs – indeed, his near-normality provides a welcome oasis of calm in the midst of their high-spirited buffoonery – but this is not to say that he is not a well rounded, well portrayed personality. He is respected by the others (with the occasional exception of Grumpy) as their undisputed leader, and he shows the true sturdiness and solidity of character lurking behind that malapropistic exterior in such scenes as the "Bluddle-Uddle-Um-Dum" washing scene (animated almost exclusively by Bill Tytla – the "Michelangelo of animators" according to Chuck Jones) and especially in the mourning scene around Snow White's bier (animated largely by Frank Thomas).

The third of the main triumvirate of the Dwarfs is definitely **Grumpy**. Viewing the Universe as generally malevolent, the efforts of his fellows as largely folly, himself as the only sane person in sight, and women as sheer poison, this misogynistic little character ought to be one of the villains of the piece: instead he proves to be one of its heroes. In the initial draftings of his character, indeed, he was, according to Kirtley Baskette, "irritatingly tough and nasty at first. He had to be sweetened up." In fact this is something of a simplification: what Disney did was to turn Grumpy's into the most complex and three-dimensional of all the Dwarfs' characters. The other Dwarfs change little during the course of the movie

(aside from removing several inches of grime), but Grumpy (brilliantly voiced by Pinto Colvig) is transformed from a hostile and suspicious little paranoid – "give Grumpy a doughnut and he'll see the hole", as one Disney publicity release had it – into a creature of sweetness and light.

Early on Grumpy's opinion of Snow White is: "She's a female, and all females is poison! They're full of wicked wiles!" (The effect is rather spoilt when the other Dwarfs ask him what exactly "wicked wiles" are, and he has to resort to saying: "I don't know . . . but I'm agin 'em!") Sooner or later, however – although rather later than the others – even Grumpy learns to love the beautiful little Princess . . . although he will be the last to admit it. As the Dwarfs set off for work one morning they are all, except Grumpy, volubly eager to be given a goodbye kiss by Snow White – Dopey, with characteristic simple-minded cunning, comes around for seconds. Grumpy, however, is like a rebellious small boy being threatened with the embrace of a well cushioned great aunt, and only consents to the kiss after much persuasion. Yet, afterwards, as he stomps "angrily" off (having tellingly told Snow White to "take care"), it is clear that he too is in love with the girl: the movie's script (cutting continuity) describes it with more percipience than elegance when it gives the direction "sourpuss softens into grin – sneaks look back at Snow White". Indeed, Grumpy is so filled with love that he proceeds to get his nose stuck in a tree and, when he succeeds in pulling it out again, falls into a stream.

Still more significant, however, is the fact that, when the Dwarfs finally understand the message from the animals that Snow

White is in danger, it is *Grumpy*, of all people, who is the first to shout out: "The Queen! She'll kill her! We've got to save her!" His views of her have obviously turned completely around, from hostility to rapt loyalty.

Real people do change in this way: even the dourest person can, over time, become sunny. Grumpy is a very *real* personality because he is capable of doing this. While he might not hog the limelight like Dopey, he is almost certainly the best conceived and best executed character in the movie.

The other four Dwarfs, Happy, Sleepy, Sneezy and Bashful, are much more minor characters – although each of them is very definitely a personality rather than a cypher: one of the considerable strengths of the film is that all the Dwarfs are individuals, whereas many other studios might well have rendered them as carbon copies of each other.

The least of the four of them is **Happy**, voiced by Otis Harlan. Somehow Happy's character never really seems to make much of an impact on proceedings. This is probably because all the other Dwarfs – except Grumpy, of course – are likewise pretty happy individuals, so that Happy's primary characteristic has no way of distinguishing itself among the personalities of the other five. With an almost imbecilic grin of cheerfulness on his broad face (his face is much like Doc's, but without the spectacles), he plays what is no more than a supporting role.

Bashful, by contrast, is paradoxically a much more forcible character, and comes across far more strongly. He is – no prizes for guessing – excessively modest, a trait exaggerated in the presence of the lovely

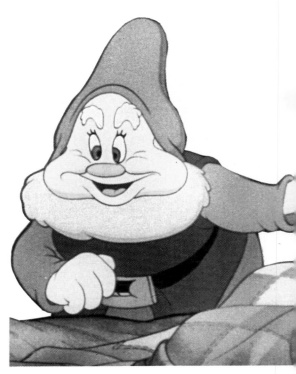

Happy's character was perhaps the least defined personality among the dwarfs.

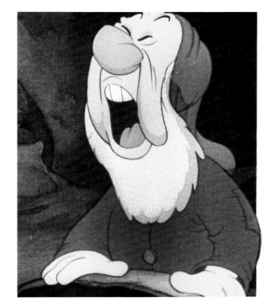

Sneezy (*above*) preparing for action. It isn't the dawn that's coming up like thunder.

Sleepy (*right*) – whose snoring dominated the dialogue during Snow White's first night at the cottage.

Snow White. When the Dwarfs and the Princess are singing "A Silly Song" in the cottage to celebrate their new-forged friendship, Bashful is the one who has difficulty in contributing his verse: over and over again he deliquesces into a puddle of shy giggles. (Grumpy, vamping on the organ, is very definitely Not Amused.) Again, in the scene where Snow White gives the Dwarfs their goodbye kiss, the ecstatic mortification of Bashful is almost painful to behold. Correction: it *is* painful.

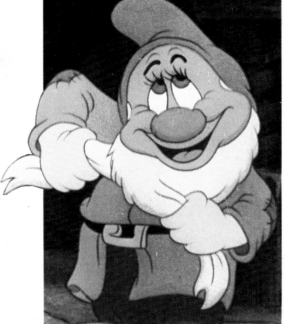

Bashful. One suspects he was shy of addressing his own reflection in the mirror.

Sleepy, voiced like Grumpy by Pinto Colvig, has of course the predilection for ... well ... dropping off for a little while whenever the time is appropriate, or even if it is not. His somnolent powers are quite striking, in fact: during the scene in which the seven Dwarfs are snoozing in the cottage's livingroom a fly comes buzzing through the air and finally settles on Sleepy's nose: within moments it, too, is snoring stertorously. Despite such delightful moments, however, Sleepy is, like the other "minor Dwarfs", a one-characteristic character.

Sneezy, too, is primarily distinguishable from the rest by his habit: he sneezes whenever and wherever possible; he has also a studiously adenoidal voice, supplied by veteran comedian Billy Gilbert. His sneezes are not the normal eruptions you or I might produce: they have the ferocity of a

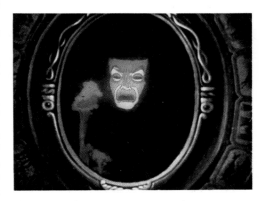

hurricane, and the other Dwarfs have had to learn to counter them. In one glorious sequence during the film he sneezes once to blast all his fellows across the room to land in a heap. Needless to say, they are less than thoroughly pleased by this. However, there is very obviously another sneeze eruptively on its way. His six friends, moved by a single impulse, leap on him and in violent desperation knot his beard very firmly around his nose.

The Dwarfs appeared also in some commercial shorts. One was *The Standard Parade* (1939), in which they took part with other front-line Disney characters in the parade; another was *All Together* (1942) in which they did much the same, except this time for the National Film Board of Canada and exhorting people to invest in war-savings bonds. A third, also for the Canadians, was *The Seven Wise Dwarfs*

(1941). Here the Dwarfs head into town singing an adapted version of "Heigh-Ho" and six of them – the exception being Dopey – take the diamonds they have brought from the mine to invest in war savings. Dopey, on the other hand, misses out and puts his funds into the bank – with the consequence that he makes a loss. The various propaganda messages are epitomized by one that flashes on the screen: INVEST IN VICTORY. They appear also in 1943's *The Winged Scourge*.

It is slightly surprising that Disney did not produce the much predicted series of shorts featuring the internationally loved Dwarfs. Possibly one reason was financial: in the average short the animators had to concentrate their attentions on one, two or at most four central characters, but had they worked with the Dwarfs that would have implied seven major characters to start with, not to mention any other "guest stars" that might have appeared. Those shorts would have been expensive.

Spirit of the Magic Mirror

The Spirit (or Slave) of the Magic Mirror was voiced by Moroni Olsen, an actor who frequently appeared in movies in supporting roles. The voice is sepulchral and sinister, reflecting the screen appearance of the face in the mirror, yet Olsen managed also to give it a sense of detachment: the Spirit is neither for nor against the Queen and her plans, merely a disinterested observer who answers her questions truthfully. In an interesting article in the January 1938 issue of *Popular Science Monthly* Andrew R. Boone had this to say on the subject of the Spirit's voice:

It was decided that should a mirror ever actually speak, there would emerge from its silvered surface a sepulchral, masculine voice. For weeks, voices were recorded in boxes, through sheets, before sounding boards. At last a sound technician hit upon the idea of building a square box with old drumheads stretched taut over five sides, leaving an opening in the sixth. Through that opening an actor placed his head, spoke the prescribed

The Spirit of the Magic Mirror – a superb piece of characterization bearing in mind the minimal potential of the role.

lines into a nearby mike, and became the talking mirror.

A green and blue mask, swirled about by cold smoke, the Spirit of the Mirror has only a few lines, yet the part is an effective and memorable one for all that.

Huntsman

The role of the Queen's Huntsman (occasionally referred to as Humbert) is another minor but interesting part. Although the Huntsman is an agent of the Queen's evil, he is not himself actively evil: he is most reluctant to accept her order to murder Snow White, and yet he is cold-blooded enough to promise, under threat, to carry it out – and very nearly does, failing only at the last minute, when even his stony heart is softened by Snow White's innocent gentleness. There is more than a trace of kindliness lurking within that tall, bulky peasant form, but one senses that he has grown used, over the years, to overriding it. As he stoops hugely over Snow White, his

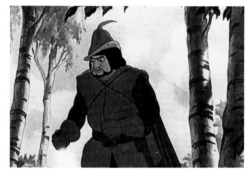

The Huntsman, steeling himself for a terrible task.

knife poised and his green eyes flashing, one knows that he has often in the past steeled himself similarly for the kill.

He is also, of course, prepared to deceive the Queen in order to save his own skin, by presenting her with a pig's heart and claiming it to be Snow White's. Or perhaps he did this more to protect the young Princess by making it seem as if she were dead, so that the Queen would not hunt her down.

Raven

In the later film *Sleeping Beauty* (1959) the Raven (➤263) who acted as familiar to the wicked fairy Maleficent was a fully rounded

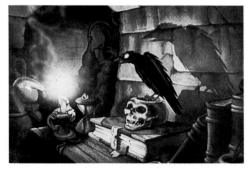

The Raven in this movie was a much more minor character than its analogue in the later *Sleeping Beauty*.

character acting in definite alliance with her evil. The Raven in *Snow White* may be regarded as a prototype of that later version and is a much more minor character, in terms of screen-time, effect on the plot and depth of personality. It responds to the Queen, but does little else.

It has some gorgeous moments, though, the best probably being on its first encounter with the Queen after she has transformed herself into the hag. Clearly terrified even more than any of the other characters will be, it swoops for protection into a nearby skull, part of the debris littering her occult laboratory. It peers nervously out through one of the skull's eye-sockets so that it appears as if the skull has a single staring eye. Which eye this is, left or right, changes agitatedly in response to the Witch's further cacklings and cries of anticipated triumph.

Minor Characters

Of the minor and unnamed characters in the movie, one of especial note is a little tortoise which is part of the regular band of Snow White's forest-animal friends. Wherever they lead, it follows – but usually a long way behind, and there is a running gag about this. For example, early on, when Snow White has retired to the bedroom after she and the animals have cleaned up the cottage, the animals tiptoe up the stairs to peep at her sleeping form. The tortoise follows laboriously behind but, just as he reaches the top of the stairs, the animals hear the Dwarfs returning and flee, trampling the tortoise underfoot in the rush. The gag is repeated elsewhere in the movie – as for example when the animals are rushing to fetch the Dwarfs to try to save Snow White. Similar little tortoises, under different guises and names (and sometimes as a turtle), make many minor appearances in Disney movies.

Pinocchio

Characters:

Pinocchio; Jiminy Cricket; Geppetto; Figaro; Cleo; J. Worthington Foulfellow; Gideon; Stromboli; The Coachman; Lampwick; Monstro the Whale; The Blue Fairy.

Credits:

Based on the tale by Collodi (Carlo Lorenzini), published in serial form from 1880 and in book form in 1883

Voices: Dickie Jones (Pinocchio); Cliff Edwards (Jiminy Cricket); Christian Rub (Geppetto); Walter Catlett (J. Worthington Foulfellow); Mel Blanc (Gideon); Charles Judels (Stromboli, Coachman); Frankie Darro (Lampwick); Evelyn Venable (Blue Fairy); Don Brodie (Barker on Pleasure Island)

Music and songs: Leigh Harline; Ned Washington; Paul J. Smith.

Story Adaptation: Ted Sears; Otto Englander; Webb Smith; William Cottrell; Joseph Sabo; Erdman Penner; Aurelius Battaglia

Backgrounds: Claude Coats; Merle Cox; Ed Starr; Ray Huffine

Art Directors: Charles Philippi; Hugh Hennesy; Kenneth Anderson; Dick Kelsey; Kendall O'Connor; Terrell Stapp; Thor Putnam; John Hubley; McLaren Stewart; Al Zinnen

Character Designers: Joe Grant; Al Hurter; John P. Miller; Campbell Grant; Martin Provensen; John Walbridge

Animation Direction: Fred Moore; Franklin Thomas; Milton Kahl; Vladimir Tytla; Ward Kimball; Arthur Babbitt; Eric Larson; Wolfgang Reitherman

Animators: Jack Campbell; Oliver M. Johnston; Berny Wolf; Don Towsley; Don Lusk; John Lounsbery; Norman Tate; John Bradbury; Lynn Karp; Charles Nichols; Art Palmer; Joshua Meador; Don Tobin; Robert Martsch; George Rowley; John McManus; Don Patterson; Preston Blair; Les Clark; Marvin Woodward; Hugh Fraser; John Elliotte

Sequence Directors: Bill Roberts; Norman Ferguson; Jack Kinney; Wilfred Jackson; T. Hee

Supervising Directors: Ben Sharpsteen; Hamilton Luske

Release Date: February 7, 1940

Running Time: 88 minutes

THE MOVIE

Pinocchio, Disney's second animated feature, is widely regarded as the best cartoon ever made; it was also, in real terms, one of the most expensive ($2,600,000), which put the Disney company into some difficulty, because the feature's release coincided almost exactly with the disappearance of the studio's overseas market thanks to World War II: since the overseas market had previously accounted for some 45 per cent of the company's income, this was bad news indeed, and Disney had to write off a loss of one million dollars on the film's initial release (since then, of course, it has earned back this sum many times over). One reason for the expense was the extensive use of the multiplane camera (or, at least, a horizontal version of it: the new camera could dolly into and out of a scene more successfully and had the advantage that the backgrounds could be twice as large as with the vertical multiplane camera): the opening scene, in which we are drawn down over the village rooftops to find Jiminy Cricket, lasts only seconds and yet cost about $25,000. Walt, after pressure from his accountants, thereafter restricted the use of such elaborate set-ups of the multiplane camera in the movie (the opening scene had used no fewer than 12 planes).

Generally speaking the critical reaction to *Pinocchio* was not merely favourable but enthusiastically so: the reasons for this can be all too easily deduced by viewing the movie today, for it is hard to think of any animated feature (or, for that matter, short) that has surpassed it during the last half century or so since its release. However, there were some harsh criticisms, primarily on the grounds that Disney had distorted the original Collodi story. In fact, any distortion of Collodi's original is likely to be a good thing: it is immensely long, morally dubious and exceptionally tedious. However, during the 1960s Frances Clark Sayers, a US authority on children's literature, became a leader of the anti-Disney faction when she attacked in no uncertain terms both the movie and particularly the Disney book-version of *Pinocchio*. Her *bête noire* was Jiminy Cricket. According to her Disney was

> always making it so obvious. In *Pinocchio*, which is one of the children's classics, he labels everything. He leaves nothing to the imagination of the child. In the initial story of *Pinocchio*, there is a character of a cricket. The cricket gives Pinocchio good advice, to which he pays no attention. In the Disney book [and movie], it's labeled that this cricket is the conscience of the child. That's sort of overworking the idea.

Whether or not this is valid criticism is a matter for debate, but it is certainly worth pointing out that, had it not been for the Disney version of the tale, Collodi's *Pinocchio* would almost certainly have been forgotten by now: have *you* read it? Moreover, Collodi's *Pinocchio*, written for serialization, was a long and frequently inconsistent work: the task of Disney was not to represent it in its entirety on screen (which would have anyway been impossible) but to distil from it a sufficiency of good adventures and to knit those together into a single, satisfying story. In a curious way, however, a comment by Wanda Burgan, quoted in *Punch* in 1962, creates rather greater unease than any of Sayers' castigations:

> Soft little faces turned stony when I dealt out books by such counterfeit authors as Barrie, Collodi and Salten. Was I really so dumb, their withering looks asked plainly, as not to know that Walt Disney had written *Peter Pan* and *Pinocchio* and *Bambi*?

That is fair criticism: the Disney versions have indeed tended, thanks to 20th-century communications, to squash the originals of some classics out of popular consciousness. However, in the case of a subject such as *Pinocchio*, which was never *in* 20th-century popular consciousness in the first place, the criticism does not hold. In a paper presented to the Annual Conference of the Children's Literature Association in 1981 Richard Wunderlich and Thomas J. Morrissey take up the point:

> ... the transformation [of *Pinocchio*] began prior to Disney ... the fundamental changes often attributed to him were created independently by others prior to or simultaneously with him, and ... most later adaptations do not in fact demonstrate his influence.

Their main burden is that *Pinocchio* as a story was altered because for a longish time, starting around the beginning of this century, adults refused to believe that children in any way experienced such emotions as sexuality, hatred, aggression, jealousy and so forth, and preferred instead to believe that such emotions were purely adult phenomena: Collodi's *Pinocchio*, which had the eponymous character subject to all of these emotions, was therefore generally unacceptable to the adult world. What the children thought of all this is of course not recorded.

Other critics, grounded rather in tne cinematographic arts than in children's literature, were usually far more friendly: they praised the movie as one of the finest of all time – surpassing even Disney's own *Snow White and the Seven Dwarfs*. They accepted that the plot was episodic rather than tightly controlled, but noted that the various episodes were knitted together so expertly that this structure was hardly a failing. And they were ecstatic about the animation – which has rarely been surpassed by Disney or anyone else. In *Art Digest* C. J. Bulliet summed up the art-critic's point of view when discussing the storm scene in the movie:

> Here was "abstract" art that was great. The difference between Disney's lines and volumes indicating the storm and the abstractions of our "peewee Picassos" is that Disney's "abstracts" definitely function – have something significant to do, and do it. Picasso's abstractions and the abstractions of Braque likewise are profoundly "functional", whereas our "peewee Picassos" and "midget Matisses" are trivial imitators of the surface features of the work of their betters.

For *Pinocchio* the various objects and artefacts were designed by Albert Hurter, who had worked also on *Snow White and the Seven Dwarfs*. For the earlier movie he had produced between 50 and 100 sketches *per day*, covering all aspects of the production. His job for Disney during these years was essentially to produce "idea" sketches, something he had been doing since the

heady days of *Three Little Pigs* (1933). In *Snow White* he was responsible for, among others, the nightmare forest, the Queen's castle and the Dwarfs' cottage. In *Pinocchio* he played a rather lesser part because Disney had drafted in the brilliant children's book illustrator Gustaf Tenggren (unmentioned in the movie's credits because he left Disney before *Pinocchio* was completed). Ken O'Connor, quoted in Steve Hulett's article "A Star is Drawn" in *Film Comment* in 1979, recalled that

> I tried hard to keep the feeling of his drawing in my layouts ... [but] I never did feel I caught as much of the flavor of Tenggren's sketches as I wanted to.

The animation for *Pinocchio* was even more sophisticated than had been that for *Snow White and the Seven Dwarfs*, and certainly in general better than that for 1940's other Disney release, *Fantasia*; it is almost impossible to think of any other film whose animation might better *Pinocchio*'s. The primary reason for this qualitative difference was financial: Walt was very buoyed up by the success of *Snow White* and so was quite happy to spend a dollar and a dollar and a dollar more to ensure that *Pinocchio* was just right. In later years the money has simply not been available. Even Disney animators would probably now dodge such scenes as that where Pinocchio, slung in a birdcage, is rocking about in the back of Stromboli's caravan. This scene is far from the most spectacular in the movie as *watched* yet it was one of the most complex to shoot. It was done with the multiplane camera. On the rearmost level is the Moon, shining in the night sky. Then, coming one level forwards, there is the light coming in through the caravan window. After that, still travelling forwards, we have (a) the rear bars of Pinocchio's cage, (b) Pinocchio himself, moving independently of the swinging cage, (c) the fore-bars of the cage, and (d) the racked puppets swinging in the foreground. All of these elements are moving both dependently and independently; for example, Pinocchio's motions are determined not just by the rocking of all the other elements but also according to the dictates of the laws of gravity. Finally, in addition to all these many layers of animation, the light-ray of the Blue Fairy is shown beaming in through the window and thereby interacting with *all* of the other levels. For reasons of economy it is unlikely that such a complex piece of animation will ever again be attempted.

A further reason for the movie's incredible expense was, as with *Snow White and the Seven Dwarfs*, Walt's perfectionism: this we can admire now, but at the time it must have been a severe problem not only for the animators but also for the accountants. Many years later Bill (Vladimir) Tytla was to recall in an interview with John Canemaker (published in 1976, years after Tytla's death) one of his many encounters with this perfectionism of Walt's:

> I had to animate one sequence in *Pinocchio* and I gave it everything I had. There were several scenes I showed to the other animators. They all said "great" or "nothing else needed" or "don't change a thing." I felt pretty good about it.
>
> Finally the time came for Walt to see it. He was subdued and even jolly in the "sweatbox". He said "That was a helluva scene, but" – there's always that cruel "but" in there – "if anyone else had animated it I would have passed it. But I expected something different from Bill!"
>
> Well, he sunk a ship with that remark. ... it took a couple of weeks before I could work again. I was crushed. But one day I took up my pencil and started to draw again, differently. It was as if something hit me and I started all over. This time I showed it to Walt, he said, "Great! Just what I was expecting!" He never did explain what was wrong. It was as if by some magical way you would know.

Had Walt been content with second-best during the making of *Pinocchio* it is probable that the movie would have done thunderingly good business on its first release and then rapidly faded from sight. In fact, because of his perfectionism and that of his dedicated team, the movie suffered a grievous loss on first release but has been earning progressively huger amounts of money on each rerelease. Quality always pays in the end.

THE STORY

We are introduced to the story of Pinocchio by the charismatic figure of Jiminy Cricket, a wanderer from many a door to many a door. He is a streetwise little fellow, far removed from the rustic wisdom of typical Disney characters such as Mickey. He takes us into the shop of Geppetto, carpenter and puppet-maker; Jiminy hopes to have the chance merely to settle down on the hearth but, just as he is doing so, Geppetto and his kitten Figaro appear. Jiminy watches as Geppetto puts the final touches to his best puppet to date. The question arises as to the puppet's name: Geppetto suggests "Pinocchio" but neither Figaro nor the goldfish Cleo like that, and eventually Geppetto has to resort to subterfuge – secretly nodding the puppet's head – in order to get his way. In a sequence animated by Frank Thomas, Geppetto "walks" the little puppet up and down – to the intense infuriation of Figaro.

But such things must come to an end: Geppetto goes to bed and so does Figaro. As they sleep Jiminy hears the old man somnolently wishing that the marionette he has just created will become a real boy; also, through the bedroom window, the Wishing Star hears Geppetto's words. It is a wish that will shortly be granted in one way and yet be a long time waiting in another. For the Blue Fairy descends from the skies to give life to the puppet, but tells him that he will remain for the while an animated marionette: in order to become a real boy he must prove himself brave, truthful and unselfish. When Jiminy jumps down beside the puppet to give him an unsolicited moral homily the Blue Fairy dubs him Pinocchio's conscience, and promises him a gold medallion if he fulfils the function satisfactorily.

After she has gone Jiminy and Pinocchio dance and sing together, and the noise wakes Geppetto, who is obviously delighted that his wish has at least in part come true. The puppet-maker, the kitten, the cricket, the puppet and even Cleo the goldfish celebrate the happy event – surrounded by countless moving clocks, toys, music-boxes and other automata in an incredible *tour de force* of animation.

Next morning Geppetto sends Pinocchio off to school, but the naive puppet is waylaid by the trickster J. Worthington Foulfellow and his equally unscrupulous (if inept) cohort, the cat Gideon. Despite Jiminy's ignored protests, they persuade Pinocchio to be engaged (in fact sold, although Pinocchio doesn't realize this) to the wicked puppeteer Stromboli: an independently walking puppet should be a great draw at the theatre. And so it proves: Pinocchio, dancing and singing with Dutch, Russian and French puppets of more orthodox abilities, brings the house down. Jiminy, realizing that a successful actor doesn't need a conscience, slopes off disconsolately, his job apparently at an end.

Afterwards, however, Stromboli reveals himself in his true colours to Pinocchio. Realizing what a money-spinner he has on his hands, he threatens the puppet with dismemberment if he fails to cooperate and, in case he should attempt to escape, locks him in a bird-cage. He sets off in his wagon for the next engagement. Jiminy, however, seeking simply to bid Pinocchio farewell, hops onto the wagon and, discovering his friend's incarceration, does his best to release him – but all to no avail. Help comes from the skies, though, for suddenly the Blue Fairy reappears in the wagon. She questions the puppet concerning his predicament but he tries grandiloquently to lie about it. Each time he does so, in this famous scene, his wooden nose grows longer – until finally it even has leaves and a birds' nest, complete with birds, on the end of it! At last he promises never to lie again, his nose shrinks back to normal proportions, and the cage is unlocked.

As Pinocchio and Jiminy flee for home, however, they become separated, and the puppet is once more intercepted by the fox J. Worthington Foulfellow. This time the fox is working on behalf of a genially sinister figure called the Coachman, who has promised to pay a good price for every boy delivered into his clutches. The gullible marionette is only too eager to believe the fox when he tells him that, after his awful adventure, what he really needs is a holiday at the Coachman's holiday camp for boys, Pleasure Island. Jiminy arrives just too late to stop Pinocchio setting out for this new peril, but succeeds in boarding the coach transporting the boys to Pleasure Island

This "haven" is in fact a place of general dissolution, and the boys are soon degrading themselves by loudly partaking in its easy pleasures. Pinocchio, with a new-found friend called Lampwick, indulges as much as the rest, learning, *inter alia*, the joys and the miseries of smoking cigars. But there is worse to follow: one by one the boys are being turned into donkeys for profitable sale, and the Coachman, all trace of his jovial mask now gone, whips the unfortunate animals unmercifully as he crates them up ready to be sent to market. By the time Jiminy realizes fully the evil at work Pinocchio has already sprouted asses' ears and tail. The two plunge into the sea and swim for the distant shore.

When they reach home, however, they discover that Geppetto, Figaro and Cleo are long gone. A note brought to them by a dove from the Blue Fairy floats down: their three friends have been swallowed by a giant whale, Monstro, who dwells at the bottom of the sea. Without hesitation Pinocchio dashes to throw himself from a clifftop into the sea, a rock tied to his foot to take him to the bottom; Jiminy goes with him. After a long submarine quest Pinocchio is finally swallowed by the huge whale, inside which he discovers Geppetto, Figaro and Cleo aboard an old wreck and rapidly running out of food.

Pinocchio realizes that escape is essential, and so he builds up a big fire. The internal irritation causes Monstro to puff and sneeze, and finally the friends are blasted out of the whale, clinging precariously to a raft Geppetto has constructed during his long confinement.

But the whale has not finished with them. Maddened, it shatters their raft with one blow of its tail, and a terrifying chase ensues. Pinocchio saves Geppetto, hauling him to shore, and the others too are saved – although for reasons less apparent. However, as they all pick themselves up they find that Pinocchio is still lying face down on the sand, apparently dead.

They take him home and, as they weep over his body, he is suddenly filled with a great radiance. He stirs. The outlines of his body subtly alter – and suddenly he sits up, his face covered in joy. "I'm alive!" he gasps. "And I'm – I'm *real*!" Sure enough, his self-abnegation in rescuing Geppetto has at last earned him from the Blue Fairy the right of being a genuine boy.

Jiminy, his task over, quietly slips away. As he does so he discovers on his chest a great, glowing, star-shaped gold medallion, inscribed "Official Conscience". Proudly he flashes it up at the Wishing Star, whence the Blue Fairy came ... and the Wishing Star flashes back.

THE CHARACTERS

Pinocchio

The critic Judith Martin was being perhaps deliberately unkind when she remarked of the movie's eponymous hero that "everyone agrees now on what Pinocchio looks like, because he's received the Disney treatment. He looks like a paler, blander Mickey Mouse." In fact, Pinocchio neither looks nor acts much like Mickey; he rather more falls into what would become the Disney tradition for the features' central characters: that of being someone to whom things happen rather than a prime mover. Later on in the movie, of course, Pinocchio does become a "doer" – and that is what leads to his salvation. But his earlier history can be seen as consisting of his submission or subjection to the control of a succession of increasingly authoritarian or dominant characters: Geppetto, Foulfellow, Stromboli and the Coachman – with even Lampwick and Monstro, in their different ways, falling into the list, and the Blue Fairy and Jiminy likewise exerting authority over him.

The character of Pinocchio was voiced by a boy called Dickie Jones, aged 12, who had been discovered by Hoot Gibson in a Dallas radio station strumming a ukulele under the billing of a "cowboy rambler". In fact, it is a little surprising that Disney had to go to such lengths to find the "right" voice, for the voice is as featureless as Pinocchio's personality initially is – in fact, the problem might have been finding a sufficiently featureless voice. It is claimed that the gurgling effect of Pinocchio speaking underwater had never been achieved in the movies before. Jones says that he almost

drowned during the early attempts to produce the effect!

Animating Pinocchio as a living puppet rather than as a real boy caused some problems: the difference in the bodily actions is a subtle one, but Walt and the rest felt that it had to be retained in order to add conviction to the part. A January 1940 article in *Popular Mechanics* told how the animators had coped with the problem:

... actual puppets were created by the model department for the use of the animators responsible for the live marionette hero ... These animators took lessons from the fellow worker who created the puppet. A well known puppeteer before joining the studio, he showed them how to make Pinocchio go through all sorts of antics. This was necessary because although, in the story, the puppet is alive, he is still wooden, and therefore cannot move as a real boy would move.

In fact, he can also move in ways in which a real boy could *not* move, as he proves when dancing with the Russian puppets in Stromboli's theatre. He can spin the lower part of his body while keeping his head motionless – a trick later to be displayed by, for example, the owl in *Bambi* (➤200).

Pinocchio is, then, a character seeking to "find himself". At first his quest is led dramatically astray, as he is led into worse and worse company, all the while ignoring the good advice of his faithful conscience, Jiminy Cricket. Finally, however, when he learns to think and act for himself (and it is interesting that Jiminy plays little or no part in this transition), Pinocchio finds his salvation: his return from the dead and his conversion into a real boy. The analogy between this progression and the process

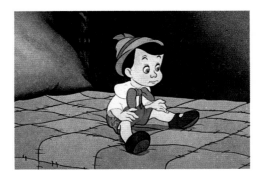

Right at the end of the movie, Pinocchio turns from a puppet into a real boy.

shared by all of us of simply growing up need not be laboured.

The most touching moment in the entire process of his transformation, however, must be the one right at the end, when he looks at his hands. Once they were the white gloves of a puppet: now they are the fingered hands of the real boy he has always wanted to be.

Jiminy Cricket

By far the most significant character in *Pinocchio* is Jiminy Cricket: he went on to make an important appearance in *Fun and Fancy Free* (1947), in which he played the part of link-cricket, as well as numerous appearances on television and a starring part in *Mickey's Christmas Carol* (➤130). In *Pinocchio* he is the "identification figure" – sceptical and cynical, ever eager to reduce marvels to mundane terms, a brilliant contrast to the high-fantasy main story-line of the movie. He is a compromise between Disney's general rural trend – as epitomized by the early Mickey Mouse – and the then-current general attraction in the USA to more urban styles. (Donald Duck had a roughly similar role in the shorts.) Indeed, Jiminy was probably the nearest Disney came to an urban "sophisticate" such as Bugs Bunny or Daffy Duck – a fast-talking, wise-cracking cynic – and yet Jiminy is full also of homespun rural wisdom.

He was voiced by Cliff Edwards, a radio singer from Missouri known also as "Ukulele Ike", and it might have been expected that Edwards would cruise, thanks to Jiminy, to some sort of stardom. In fact this never came about: Edwards died penniless and virtually unknown in 1971, aged 76. It seemed a sad reward for one of the finest voice characterizations of all time.

The cocky, streetwise little cricket is, at least initially, not an untarnished character. For one thing, he seems to be something of a womanizer. In the early scenes of the film, when he and Pinocchio (joined later by Geppetto and Figaro) are celebrating the puppet's acquisition of at least some sort of life, Jiminy has a great time flirting with the carved female figures among Geppetto's various moving toys. He leans impudently against the bustled bottom of one wooden

Every time Pinocchio lied to the Blue Fairy his nose grew longer – sometimes to a ridiculous extent!

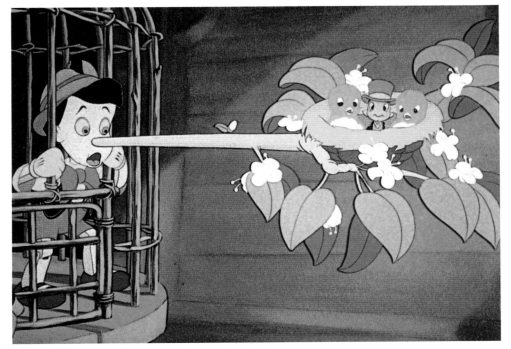

lady and later, while dancing with another, suggests with a lascivious flicker of the eyebrows that they might try "sitting out the next one". By the time of this later proposition, however, he has attained a certain degree of sartorial elegance and is a very much smarter cricket. When we initially met him he had a bent top hat with its top broken open like the lid of a can; now, however, since the Blue Fairy has dubbed him Pinocchio's conscience, his hat is a brand-new topper and his rags have become a smart suit. Nonetheless, the wooden lady ignores him.

Moreover, according to an article by William Paul in the Summer 1977 issue of *Movie*, Jiminy

> is a wanderer who is easily distracted from his set goals. He is late on the first day of his new job as Pinocchio's conscience and is always lagging a few steps behind Pinocchio through all the adventures. ... It is only after the all-knowing Blue Fairy has seductively batted her eyelashes at him that he agrees to become Pinocchio's conscience at all.

Jiminy also has resources unknown to most of us. Although he has to put on spectacles for reading, he is able, as we discover while he and Pinocchio are searching for Monstro, to breathe underwater (in the same situation the puppet, being pseudo-live rather than live, obviously does not have to breathe). Again while underwater, Jiminy shows that he is capable of riding a seahorse – although that animal, resentful of his invasion, promptly goes into a bucking-bronco act and finally succeeds in dislodging him. When he is trying to sleep in Geppetto's house and finds the racket of all the clocks and automata simply too much to bear, he responds by yelling "Quiet!", and even the clocks abruptly stop.

And he is only too willing to burst into song at the slightest provocation. On the scene, early on, where Jiminy is trying to tell Pinocchio the difference between right and wrong, William Paul has written (in *Movie*, Summer 1977):

> After a couple of failures at purely verbal communication, Jiminy thinks the lecture could be rendered better in song and says, quite simply: "C'mon, let's sing!" This is easily one of the lamest introductions to any song number in movie musicals, yet it doesn't *feel* that way.

Despite his pivotal importance to the movie *Pinocchio*, and despite the illustrious career which he was thereafter to pursue, in the original schema for the film Jiminy did not appear at all. He was brought in because it was felt that there was "something missing". The cricket that featured briefly in Collodi's original might not have seemed the ideal candidate for this filling-in role – in the book it is nameless and, after producing a few banally moralistic statements, is wisely crushed underfoot by the boy-

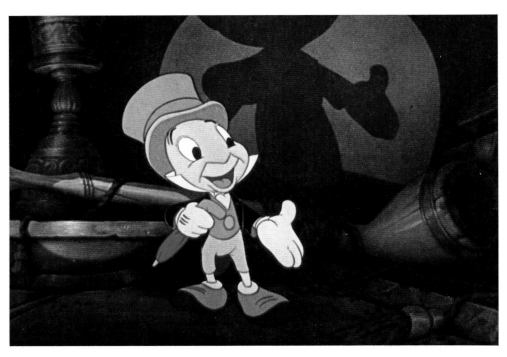

Jiminy Cricket, created by Ward Kimball, made his first appearance in *Pinocchio*; he was to become one of Disney's most popular characters.

puppet (later it appears as an equally tedious ghost) – but Walt knew his own mind and called in Ward Kimball to create the character. This was not an easy task, as Kimball much later recalled. The cricket

> started out as a pretty ugly-looking insect from which all the somewhat grotesque insect appendages and characteristics ultimately had to be eliminated.

Of course, as we now know, Kimball was brilliantly successful in creating this character. Moreover, he set a precedent for later Disney animated features: that of the small sidekick who directs activities when the theoretically central character is incapable of doing so. The most obvious example of this is Timothy Mouse in 1941's *Dumbo* (➤**194**).

Jiminy went on to star in the 1947 feature *Fun and Fancy Free*, which was really a compilation of two featurettes, *Bongo* and *Mickey and the Beanstalk* (➤**222**). Here he played the role of link-cricket. We first encounter him sailing along on a leaf and singing that he is "a happy-go-lucky fellow, full of fun and fancy free". After various gags he comes ashore and we realize that he has been performing in an artificial scene in a flowerbowl. He hops out of this onto a bookshelf and then uses his umbrella to parachute down to a lower level, narrowly missing a goldfish-bowl; through the glass he sings to the goldfish, who looks much like Cleo, that "You know, you worry too much. In fact, everybody worries too much ..."

He prances along merrily for a while before accidentally prodding the nose of a cat with his umbrella. After the predictable chase he escapes through a door and, sheltered by it, renders to the cat a

respectable imitation of an angry dog. The cat panics and Jiminy comments: "See, jumpy as a cat. Comes from rushing into things." He is clearly much more of a carefree wastrel in this movie than he was in *Pinocchio*. Finally, after some further gags, he puts on the record of *Bongo*, "a musical story sung by Dinah Shore".

After the end of the *Bongo* featurette we find Jiminy sleeping in the arms of a doll – "Who says dreams don't come true?" he wryly asks us. Soon he comes across a party invitation addressed to Luana Patten (the little-girl star of *Song of the South* [➤**211**]) from the house across the way – occupants Edgar Bergen and his ventriloquist dummies Mortimer Snerd and Charlie McCarthy. Eager to join in the fun, Jiminy Cricket is moments later an unnoticed guest at the party: some clever animation mixes him in with the live action. He, along with the rest of us, watches as Bergen relates the tale of *Mickey and the Beanstalk*. Afterwards, on the appearance of Willie the Giant, Jiminy scampers ahead of him down through Hollywood.

Jiminy is essentially the only Disney character – aside from those like Mickey and Donald whose genesis was in the shorts – to appear in more than a single feature: generally speaking, Disney wisely decided that the features characters, having been designed for one part, should not be grafted onto others. However, some of the features characters – Figaro is the prime example – did make a number of appearances in shorts, and it is a little surprising that Jiminy did not join this select crew. Instead, however, he was to follow a career in television, starring both on *Mickey Mouse Club* programmes and in several series of television shorts. Mind you, he was a much depleted Jiminy by this time. In a 1979 article in *Film Comment* Steve Hulett cites veteran Disney man Claude Coats:

> There were twenty-two different-color ink lines on Jiminy Cricket alone [in *Pinocchio*]. Later on, TV shows with the cricket had six or seven. And now, with Xerox, maybe one color change around the face would be about it.

A complete catalogue of Jiminy's television appearances would be impossible to compile, but here are the main ones:

"Encyclopedia" series
Cork and Wheelwright; Milk; Navajo Jewelry; Railroads; Steel; Tuna.
"I'm no Fool" series
I'm no Fool as a Pedestrian; I'm no Fool Having Fun; I'm no Fool in Water; I'm no Fool with a Bicycle; I'm no Fool with Fire; I'm no Fool with Electricity.
"Mickey Mouse Book Club" series
Cinderella; Lady and the Tramp; The Littlest Outlaw; Oregon Trail; Secrets of Life; Uncle Remus; Westward Ho!
"Nature of Things" series
The Camel; The Elephant; The Horse.
"You" series
You and Your Ears; You and Your Eyes; You and Your Five Senses; You and Your Food; You and Your Senses of Taste and Smell; The Human Animal; The Living Machine.

He has also hosted several TV shows, including the holiday-time *From All of Us to All of You*.

Jiminy Cricket, in short, was to become one of the most enduring of all the Disney characters.

Geppetto

The kindly figure of Geppetto, the old wood-carver, caused the studio some initial problems. As Frank Thomas and Ollie Johnston related in their *Stanford Magazine* article in 1982,

> ... a character actor named Spencer Charters seemed to have the perfect voice for ... Geppetto ... but after a hundred feet were animated (a little over one minute of screen time), we realized that the voice was too abrasive. A mellower voice was found in another character actor, Christian Rub, and the dialogue was changed to fit the new personality. The original Geppetto, who looked somewhat like Charters, began to take on the physical characteristics of Christian Rub.

This latter was hardly an accident, since Rub made extensive live-action films for the animators to use as reference. In the 1984 edition of his *The Disney Films* Leonard Maltin summed it up when he said that "Christian Rub *was* Geppetto". In March 1981's issue of *Cartoonist Profiles* Preston Blair concurred: "Geppetto ... was a caricature of the voice actor, Christian Rub. His gestures were noted and caricatured also in the animation." Rub, a 52-year-old from Vienna, had acted many character parts on Broadway. Much of Geppetto's

animation was executed by Art Babbitt, who felt it was one of the best things he ever did.

The character portrayed by Rub and hence by Babbitt and the other animators is infinitely kindly and almost as infinitely absent-minded. The latter characteristic was used to good effect in *Pinocchio* to provide some moments of light relief when things might otherwise have become either too gloomy or too maudlin. The prime example of this occurs at the end of the movie when Pinocchio is "wakening from the dead". The revived Pinocchio asks him: "What're you crying for, Father?" Geppetto's response is slightly patronizing, as if to a halfwit: "Because you're dead, Pinocchio – now lie down!"

But if Geppetto is absent-minded and gentle he is certainly not without a certain stoic courage. Inside the belly of Monstro he awaits his anticipated fate of starvation with resignation for his own part and sincere regret for Figaro and Cleo. When Pinocchio shows how they can escape, Geppetto ignores the potential dangers, which are many, and joins in the attempt with a will.

After the opening scenes, when Geppetto "walks" the puppet up and down, wishes it life, and then celebrates the granting of life to his wooden creation, the old wood-carver's role is a comparatively small one, yet his stability forms a sort of bedrock of sanity amid the high caricatures of the other characters. His is an oddly important role in the movie.

Figaro, unlike most Disney features' characters, went on to star in shorts.

Figaro

Geppetto's little kitten Figaro, largely created by Eric Larson, was to go on to star in a number of Disney shorts, although in those he was to develop a slightly more feline streak of violence. In *Pinocchio*, though, he is a cute little black-and-white ball of fur with tufty ears and a knack of kittenishly going for the wrong targets. In an early stage of the movie, just after Geppetto has completed the marionette and overruled Figaro and Cleo concerning the puppet's name, the old toymaker takes pleasure in "walking" his new creation up and down the floor, pretending that it is alive. This does not go down well with Figaro at all: he is patently jealous. He more or less puts up with it when Geppetto causes the puppet to stroke him, but when the puppet accidentally (we hope) kicks

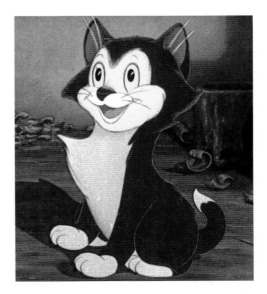

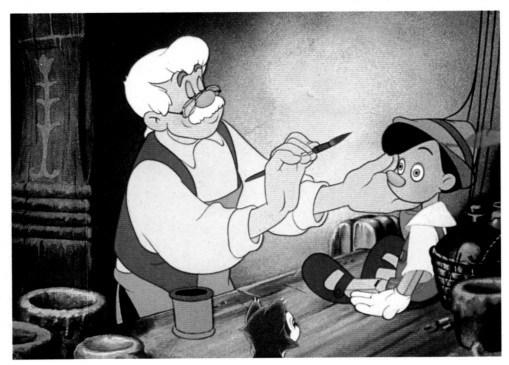

Geppetto, the kindly old toymaker, wanted a son – but instead he got a mobile puppet. The character of Geppetto was enacted for the animators by Christian Rub.

Figaro in the hindquarters the claws come out. Figaro thwacks the puppet's foot so that it kicks itself in the head. Honour might have been satisfied at this stage, but then Geppetto makes the puppet go down on all fours and stalk Figaro like a cat. As Figaro retreats, hackles high, one has to reflect that this is not an auspicious start to a friendship.

Figaro, however, is manifestly devoted to Geppetto. After the two of them have gone up to bed following the "walking" scene, Figaro raises only a token grumble when Geppetto insists that he (Figaro) climb out of his nice warm bed to open the window – good work by Figaro, because otherwise the Wishing Star might not have heard Geppetto's request and so the whole story might never have happened. Later, when they come downstairs again to find the source of the noise that has roused them and have the shock of discovering that Pinocchio is now mobile, Figaro displays his complete trust in his master: he leaps in terror right up Geppetto's nightgown, eventually coming to rest in his nightcap.

In fact, Figaro frightens easily, and not always for the most important of reasons. Confined with Geppetto and Cleo to Monstro's belly he faces the future with a fair degree of equanimity, fishing over the side of the rotting hulk with a line tied to his tail; yet he is terrified (as is Cleo) by Pinocchio's new long ears.

Figaro could hardly be more different from the other cat in the movie, Gideon. He is almost certainly – with the possible exception of Jiminy Cricket – the most instantly appealing of all the characters in the movie. (For discussion of his shorts ►90-91.)

Cleo

Geppetto's other pet is the goldfish Cleo. All fluttering eyelashes (on a goldfish?) and floating fins, she is the epitome of female affection. A few decades later Disney might have toned her down a little but this was, we must remember, 1940, when American women had yet to establish themselves as equal in all respects to American men. Nonetheless, although time has passed, Cleo's is an attractive character: although she has no spoken lines she conveys a genuine good will towards the other characters around her. Like Figaro – although the kitten would probably object to the comparison! – she is utterly devoted to Geppetto. Early on, as the toymaker prepares to go to bed, we see her reacting to his kindly "good night": she turns over on her back to have her tummy tickled. And she refuses to be cross with Figaro, who shows marked reluctance when Geppetto insists that the two of them exchange a goodnight kiss. Later, after she has had some sleep in the mock-castle in her bowl and after Geppetto and Figaro have discovered that Pinocchio is alive, she

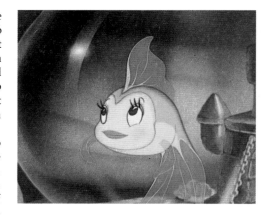

Cleo, Geppetto's goldfish, was much like Mickey's pet Bianca (► 88).

impulsively leaps out of her bowl to kiss both Pinocchio and Figaro full on the lips. This is all the more remarkable because, when Geppetto was "walking" his new puppet around, she was treated (as were we) to an almost nightmare vision of Pinocchio through the distorting lens of her bowl.

Once Pinocchio has come to life she has little cause to love him, and yet she does. One of his first actions is to attempt to pick up a candle-flame. Naturally this sets his hand on fire, and he quick-thinkingly dunks it into Cleo's bowl, fouling the water. We next see her rather sourly blowing underwater smoke-rings. Nevertheless, she it is who stops Figaro from callously eating his supper while Geppetto is out tearfully searching for his lost Pinocchio. (A curious point is that Figaro's supper consists largely of fish, yet Cleo is not apparently revolted.)

Thereafter Cleo plays a very minor part in the film. She was, however, to co-star with Figaro in a 1943 short called, aptly enough, *Figaro and Cleo*. In this short the little kitten has ideas that Cleo might form an appetizing dinner, and does everything in his powers to bring this about. He is scolded by his mistress, but then she falls asleep, face-down on the table, and the vibrations of her snores wobble Cleo's bowl to the edge and finally over. The bowl lands on Figaro's head, knocking him flat. His mistress, believing that he has almost drowned and that it is all her fault (which of course it is), pets him and gives him milk. Cleo is saved, and the three live happily together ever after ... except that the goldfish was never to appear again, which makes one wonder if Figaro was eventually successful.

A close relative of Cleo's, Bianca, appeared in the shorts as Mickey's goldfish (►88).

J. Worthington Foulfellow (Honest John) and Gideon

One can tell instantly from J. Worthington Foulfellow's sobriquet, "Honest John", that he is a crook; the fact that he is a fox, a notoriously wily and surreptitious creature, is further betraying evidence. And yet he has his devious charms – charms to which Pinocchio all too easily responds on two near-fatal occasions: first when the "newborn" puppet, on his first day out, is lured off by promises of bright lights and

J. Worthington Foulfellow (Honest John), anything but an honest fox, lured Pinocchio into temptation.

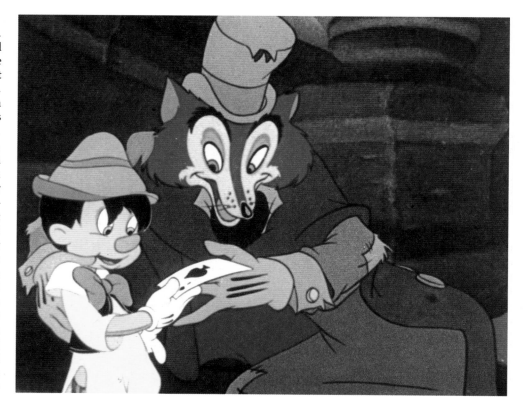

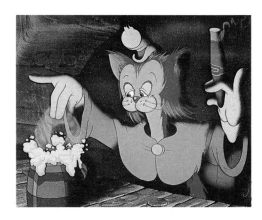

Gideon, the only truly comic character in the movie, seen here dunking a smoke-ring from his cigar in his beer!

stardom on Stromboli's stage, and second when he is tempted into opting for the easy delights of the Coachman's Pleasure Island. Tall and not quite elegant, clad in a royal blue cape and a green suit, his brush white-tipped, J. Worthington Foulfellow has a hoped-for plausibility that would not deceive the average purchaser of a second-hand car – but it is quite sufficient to deceive Pinocchio.

Foulfellow was voiced by Walter Catlett, who had already attained some recognition as an actor in live-action movies: often enough his roles were very similar to the part of the fox, as a flamboyant fraudster. For flamboyance is Foulfellow's other major characteristic. As he swirls his cape and his stick one knows that, whatever temporary reverses might affect his plans, he will ever be scheming anew.

His sidekick Gideon, the cat, is a much less subtle personality – indeed, his is the only out and out comic character in the movie. Dressed in a tiny top hat, scruffy trousers and a poncho, he is armed with a huge mallet, which he has a habit of applying at the wrong moment and/or to the wrong person: his attempt to mash Jiminy, for example, who is trying to counter Foulfellow's persuasive temptation of Pinocchio, results in a scenery-shaking impact on the fox's head. In appearance he is the exact opposite of Figaro, the other cat in the movie: he is much larger, and his colouring is pale brown with a dark-brown back and ruff; his mouth is invisible when his face is in repose, and his nose is tipped with a bright red bobble.

The animators were helped on Gideon by an old burlesque comedian who was brought to the studio to perform a comic dance for them, which was then rotoscoped. His voice was supplied by Mel Blanc, one of the great voice-actors of all time, who supplied the voices for virtually all of the major characters at the Warner Brothers' studio – Bugs Bunny and the rest. Gideon was his only role for Disney. But wait a moment: Gideon does not speak. Quite right. Disney decided that the cat should not be permitted to vocalize, and so

all that remains of the soundtrack that Blanc recorded is a solitary hiccup. He was Blanced out, in fact.

Gideon's finest moment in the movie comes when he and Foulfellow are in the inn, plotting to sell boys to the Coachman. Idly Gideon pulls a smoke-ring from the air, dunks it in his beer, and eats it.

Stromboli

Stromboli was animated by the great Vladimir (Bill) Tytla and voiced (as was the Coachman) by Charles Judels, a Dutch actor who played occasional screen parts. John Canemaker, in a 1976 essay in *Cinéfantastique*, described Stromboli in glowing terms:

> An overweight monster of mercurial moods, capable of wine-soaked, garlic-breathed Old World charm one second and knife-wielding, chop-you-up-for-firewood threats the next, the Stromboli character is larger than life, frightening and comic by turns. Stromboli, as Tytla captured him, is one of the most three-dimensional of all the Walt Disney cartoon villains.

Thomas A. Nelson, in a piece in the Spring 1978 issue of *Film Literature Quarterly*, has a further pertinent point to make: he sees Stromboli as a sort of complement to Geppetto.

> In such pure form, as with the motiveless malignity of Shakespeare's Iago, evil takes on an allegorical character and, in *Pinocchio*, Stromboli's urge to subjugate, whip, cage, and tyrannize stands in opposition to the sentimentalized Geppetto. Both symbolize fathers and creators, one fostering life and growth, the other a dehumanizing control. ... Even Monstro the Whale does not prove to be as terrifying as Stromboli and his whip ...

A similar point was made by William Paul in the Summer 1977 issue of *Movie*:

> If Geppetto is the good artist, selfless, obsessed, devoted to his art to the point of absent-mindedness about everything else, then Stromboli is the corrupt artist, selfish and devoted more to money than art. It's not too difficult to regard Stromboli as a burlesque of a Hollywood studio boss, complete with foreign accent. ... Geppetto is obsessed with his art, even to the point of ignoring his audience, naming his new puppet Pinocchio over the clear objections of Figaro and Cleo. Stromboli, on the other hand, like a successful Hollywood producer, is only interested in what will immediately please his audience; he is ready to give up on Pinocchio when success is not instant, and he survives only by exploiting the talent of others, turning his old marionettes into firewood when they are no longer of use to him.

Paul makes it clear, in his discussion of movie producers, that he thinks Walt Disney himself was very much in the Geppetto category.

The scene in which Stromboli threatens Pinocchio with dire punishment should he attempt to escape and warns him of the consequence should he perform poorly through age or any other reason, is widely regarded as the most terrifying in the movie. In a huge and roaring exhibition of brutal ferocity Stromboli demonstrates dramatically to Pinocchio what becomes of puppets who have served their purpose by hurling a cleaver to impale the chest of a broken-down marionette's body, lying like a murder victim in a bunker full of firewood. Pinocchio's gaze moves with the same speed as the cleaver towards this corpse, and the dread and horror of the sudden revelation are writ large across his face. (The music, scored by Paul Smith, plays a very important part here in conveying Pinocchio's terror.) Yet, oddly enough, there is an even greater horror involved here than simply Stromboli's venom or the macabre display: it is the betrayal of trust. Pinocchio had assumed that the apparently genial puppeteer was his friend, a new father taking the place of Geppetto; but his "friend" is not a friend at all, and *very evidently never has been*. The real shock for the puppet is this abrupt discovery. Overlying this is his sudden realization that he is completely helpless, that his friends are far away and have no idea where he is (he does not know that Jiminy will soon join him). The fear is the paralysing one of the solitary seaside stroller who suddenly discovers that he or she is in the midst of a quicksand: there seems no hope of escape, yet doom will be a long time in coming.

It is worth noting idly that it is pleasing to discover in the movies an example of a wicked stepfather (which is what Stromboli in effect is), rather than the usual wicked stepmother.

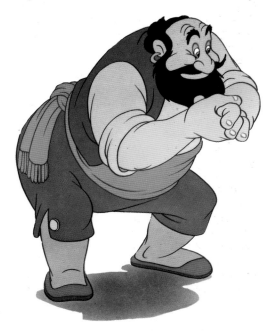

Stromboli seemed to be the little puppet's friend, but ...

Stromboli's great power as a villain is that he is a layered character rather than a straightforward thug; it is a quality he shares with the Coachman, who is probably even more frightening. The audience, like Pinocchio, starts out on a youthful fantasy adventure – running away with the circus, as it were – and yet the dream is violently shattered. The apparently friendly ringmaster proves to be a murderous abductor. He is mean, too – Pinocchio's share of the takings is a single washer – and this meanness is likewise shocking in that it is in such direct contrast with Stromboli's apparent generosity of nature.

Stromboli is a character from nightmare: such characters are often found in the real world, too, which makes Stromboli all the more terrifying.

The Coachman

If there is a character anywhere in the Disney canon who could create more stark fear than Stromboli it is the Coachman, the evil boss of Pleasure Island, the apparent benefactor of unhappy orphan boys. The horror of his personality has the same roots as that of Stromboli – the betrayal of trust by a seemingly benevolent father-figure – but for several reasons in the Coachman's case it is even worse. First, the Coachman's victims are not lifeless marionettes but real boys: where Stromboli was discarding firewood the Coachman is cynically and ruthlessly using living human flesh for his own profit. Second, he is condemning the boys not to sudden death but to a lifetime of

misery, drudgery and back-breaking work – to a slow death rather than a rapid one. He represents that human animal even more evil than the murderer: the torturer. Third, his outward persona is even more divorced from his true nature than with Stromboli: the latter, after all, represents himself as an employer, although a fair one, whereas the Coachman sets himself up as an open-hearted benefactor, seeking out of kindness to bring happiness to the neglected. He appears at first to have many of the same traits and motivations as the good Geppetto, and it is this that makes the betrayal so much worse.

The fourth and probably most important reason why the Coachman is so much more terrifying than Stromboli is that he *looks* so kindly: pudgy-faced and white-haired, a pipe protruding from his kindly smile, a sort of dumpling figure, he has the appearance of everybody's favourite grandfather. Stromboli, by contrast, has the face and hulking body of the born bully – although at first Pinocchio, as may we, believes that as with so many people Stromboli's appearance belies his true nature: it is less of a shock to discover that that optimistic belief has been misplaced. The Coachman is not only a brutal villain, he is a sinister one.

Lampwick

The Coachman and Stromboli represent the siren voices of true evil, luring the innocent deliberately to doom. Lampwick, on the other hand, the boy who befriends

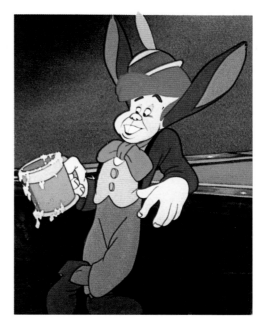

Lampwick was Pinocchio's pal on Pleasure Island . . . and also the first to start turning into a donkey.

Pinocchio on Pleasure Island, is a tempter of a different type. We have all met him at school: he is the essentially friendly kid who tells his friends that the grown-ups are being exaggerating old fuddy-duddies when they talk of the evils of cigarettes, alcohol and even, in more recent years, hard drugs. Life is for living is his apparent motto, so why not just enjoy all its available luxuries to the full *right now*? People who talk about gloomy consequences are just deceiving you because they cannot or do not know how to enjoy these things themselves. Of course, in many cases – as in Lampwick's – one suspects that the genial kid is really only too well aware of the self-inflicted destruction that must inevitably result from his dissolution, and is seeking to encourage others to partake so that, once "everybody else" is doing it, he can disguise from himself his own folly and slough off his own feeling of guilt.

Lampwick is the perfect caricature of such a child. He is bigger than Pinocchio, displays a paucity of front teeth (although the few he does have are large and protuberant), and has unruly red hair – all characteristics which, however unjustly, can be taken to represent assertiveness and a certain hedonistic lackwittedness (he was voiced by Frankie Darro, an actor who had made a career out of playing tough kids on screen). As if to underline this, he carries a catapult (slingshot) – a symbol of unthinking destructiveness – and, in a memorable moment, heedlessly strikes a match to light his cigar on the *Mona Lisa*. He is counter-culture, counter-civilization: everything must be subjugated to the pleasures of the moment. Not for him the strait and narrow: he chooses the wide gate and the broad way to destruction, and he is eager to encourage fellow-travellers. His is

Of all Pinocchio's foes, the Coachman was the most sinister.

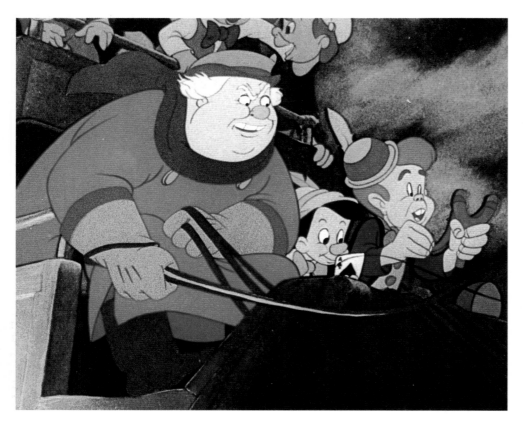

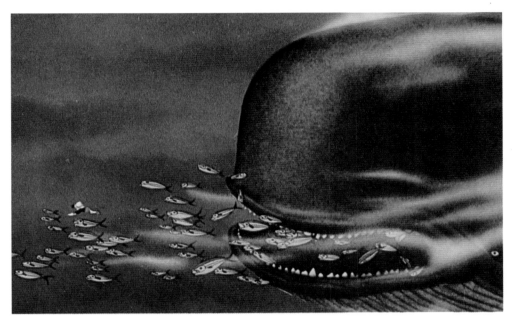

The sequence in which Monstro the Whale chases Pinocchio and his friends is one of the most terrifying in the movie.

the most insidious form of corruption, because it is not motivated by malevolence.

It is perhaps harsh to describe Lampwick as one of the movie's villains: he is in no wise malicious. Yet he is the only one of the "baddies" in *Pinocchio* to receive the come-uppance that we generally expect for cinema rogues. J. Worthington Foulfellow and Gideon presumably carry on their con-trickster lives, Stromboli rides off in his wagon to terrify and tyrannize any marionette that comes his way, the Coachman is left to convert more boys into donkeys and sell them into slavery; yet the consequence of Lampwick's much less malicious sin is that he, we must assume, lives out the rest of his short and unhappy life as one of those frequently beaten, overworked donkeys. It all seems very unjust and curiously immoral. But then Collodi's *Pinocchio*, despite its heavy moralistic overtones, was not in today's terms an especially moral work. Those who criticize Disney for failing accurately to reproduce the work on screen might care to ponder this point.

Monstro the Whale

The whale is Pinocchio's biggest foe and yet by far the least evil, and therefore in some ways the least terrifying. The very mention of its name is enough to cause panic among the fishes, as Pinocchio and Jiminy discover during their underwater quest, but this is because Monstro is a hungry creature, not an actively malevolent one. His vindictive rage against the fleeing party on the raft is not a truly spiteful one: it is merely that … well, how would *you* feel if somebody had just lit a fire inside you? A little hot under the collar, perhaps.

Monstro generates fear in Pinocchio and his friends (and hence in the audience) not because he is evil but simply because he is *big*. To support this assertion we can point out that Willie, the "whale who wanted to sing at the Met" in 1946's *Make Mine Music* (➤218) displays a quite distinct morphological similarity to Monstro and yet, while obviously a friendly and even lovable character, nevertheless inspires fear in a number of that movie's human characters: they are frightened of him solely because of his size.

Thomas A. Nelson, in his 1978 *Film Literature Quarterly* piece, is sensitive to this point:

> … although those scenes inside the giant whale are some of the finest moments in Disney, the *anxiety* [my italics] generated by Monstro's menacing enormity is greatly relieved by his Bunyanesque sneezes.

Those sneezes – Monstro sounds like a motorbike revving up as each new one approaches – do indeed relieve the tension. However, even without them, Monstro is far less than the terrifying monster of Collodi's original: this was in fact not a whale but a dogfish, *il pesce cane* as he was known to Italian folklore, a sort of bogey-fish which had the nasty habit of eating up children who swam too far out to sea. Quite why Disney should have opted to transform this much more frightening creature into a whale is uncertain.

Producing the noises for Monstro created some interesting technical problems for the soundmen. The noise of the whale churning up the sea in its fury was actually produced using a kind of double-paddle in a tank measuring a mere three feet by four feet by five feet. However, the technique was not quite as simple as it might seem: the soundmen discovered that plain water did not give quite the right "heavy" feeling to the sound and so experimented with soapy water. For some reason this was much more successful. To obtain other "massive" sound effects they stretched a screen across a frame and to it attached by a

The Blue Fairy, Pinocchio's benefactress, was modelled on Marjorie Babbitt (née Belcher); her voice was supplied by Evelyn Venable.

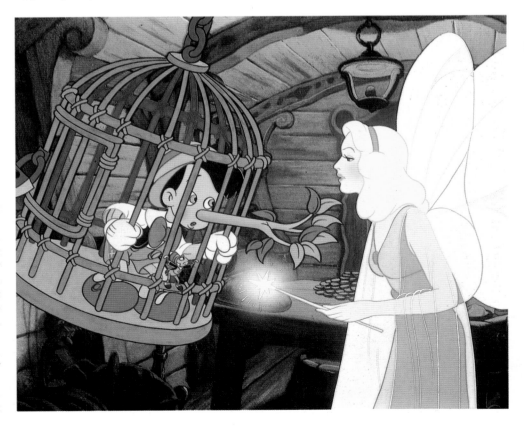

wire a phonographic pickup. They then thundered the screen with drumsticks and the like and played out the vibrations from the pickup through a large horn. The results were dramatically successful.

Monstro, of course, cannot really be said to be a character, a personality: the whale represents brute nature and overpowering voracity, no more. Yet the beast proves the greatest threat to Pinocchio's life of all – greater even than the sophisticated evil of the Coachman and the rest. Indeed, Monstro in his blind rage actually succeeds in taking Pinocchio's life ... only for it to be restored, with interest, by the Blue Fairy.

The Blue Fairy

The force of good might seem to be underrepresented in the movie when compared with the force of evil, incarnate in J. Worthington Foulfellow, the Coachman, Stromboli, Lampwick ... On the side of good are only Geppetto (a fairly passive ally), Jiminy Cricket, the Blue Fairy and eventually, towards the end, the late-discovered integrity of Pinocchio himself. Yet good, of course, eventually triumphs (although, as noted, it does not *destroy* the evil).

The Blue Fairy is a blonde of pristine beauty; she is so realistically depicted that it seems almost as if one were watching some kind of special-effects treatment of a live actress rather than an animation. Her voice enhances her purity of image: it was supplied by Evelyn Venable, a movie actress from Cincinnati, and was recorded in an unusual way. She spoke each of her lines several times over, using different inflections, and then the soundmen dubbed in the version they thought worked most effectively in the context of the other characters' vocalizations.

There is a definite resemblance between the Blue Fairy and Marilyn Monroe, and some writers have gone so far as to claim that Monroe served as the model for the character. This was only a fancy; Monroe was a 14-year-old schoolgirl at the time!

(Similar accusations have been made about Tinker Bell [➤**249**].) The model was Marjorie Babbitt (neé Belcher, and now calling herself Marjorie Bell), who had earlier enacted the part of Snow White for the animators (➤**159**). The difference between the two – it is not just a matter of hair-colour – can be accounted for by noting that the animators were artists rather than mere slavish copiers of the live-action films.

The Blue Fairy is the motive force behind the entire movie: she it is who grants Pinocchio life (twice!) and appoints Jiminy as his official conscience, and she acts as guardian angel to both of them. Yet her appearances on screen are few and brief, and her character is hardly a fully rounded one. We must assume that this was deliberate, that what Disney was trying to capture and convey was the fact that she is an ethereal being, the spirit of goodness – indeed, not so much a character or individual as what the mysticists might call a "principle".

FANTASIA

Characters:

The Nutcracker Suite section: Dewdrop Fairies; Hop Low; Mushroom Dancers; Blossom Ballet; Goldfish; Thistle Boys; Orchid Girls; Autumn Fairies; Milkweed Ballet; Frost Fairies; Snowflakes Fairies
The Sorcerer's Apprentice section: Mickey Mouse; Brooms; Yen Sid
Rite of Spring section: Dinosaurs
"Pastoral" Symphony section: Pegasus; Pegasus' family; Brudus; Melinda; Bacchus; Jacchus; Zeus; Vulcan; Iris; Apollo; Diana; Morpheus; Cupids; Centaurs; Centaurettes
Dance of the Hours section: Mlle. Upanova; Hyacinth Hippo; Elephanchine; Ben Ali Gator
Night on Bald Mountain section: Chernabog; Demons; Ghosts
Ave Maria section: Pilgrims.

Credits:

Narrator: Deems Taylor Conductor: Leopold Stokowski Orchestra: The Philadelphia Orchestra Production Supervision: Ben Sharpsteen Story Direction: Joe Grant Dick Huemer
Musical Direction: Edward H. Plumb
Musical Film Editor: Stephen Csillag
Recording: William E. Garity; C. O. Slyfield; J. N. A. Hawkins

Toccata and Fugue in D Minor section:
Music: J. S. Bach
Story Development: Lee Blair; Elmer Plummer; Phil Dike
Art Director: Robert Cormack
Backgrounds: Joe Stahley; John Hench; Nino Carbe
Animators: Cy Young; Art Palmer; Daniel MacManus; George Rowley; Edwin Aardal; Joshua Meador; Cornett Wood
Director: Samuel Armstrong

The Nutcracker Suite section:
Music: P. I. Tchaikowsky
Story Development: Sylvia Moberly-Holland; Norman Wright; Albert Heath; Bianca Majolie; Graham Heid
Character Designers: John Walbridge; Elmer Plummer; Ethel Kulsar
Art Directors: Robert Cormack; Al Zinnen; Curtiss D. Perkins; Arthur Byram; Bruce Bushman
Backgrounds: John Hench; Ethel Kulsar; Nino Carbe
Animators: Art Babbitt; Les Clark; Don Lusk; Cy Young; Robert Stokes
Director: Samuel Armstrong

The Sorcerer's Apprentice section:
Music: Paul Dukas
Story Development: Perce Pearce; Carl Fallberg
Art Directors: Tom Codrick; Charles Philippi; Zack Schwartz
Backgrounds: Claude Coats; Stan Spohn; Albert Dempster; Eric Hansen
Supervising Animators: Fred Moore; Vladimir Tytla
Animators: Les Clark; Riley Thomson; Marvin Woodward; Preston Blair; Edward Love; Ugo D'Orsi; George Rowley; Cornett Wood
Director: James Algar

Rite of Spring section:
Music: Igor Stravinsky
Special Camera Effects: Gail Papineau; Leonard Pickley
Story Development and Research: William Martin; Leo Thiele; Robert Sterner; John Fraser McLeish
Art Directors: McLaren Stewart; Dick Kelsey; John Hubley
Backgrounds: Ed Starr; Brice Mack; Edward Levitt
Supervising Animators: Wolfgang Reitherman; Joshua Meador

Animators: Philip Duncan; John McManus; Paul Busch; Art Palmer; Don Tobin; Edwin Aardal; Paul B. Kossoff
Directors: Bill Roberts; Paul Satterfield

"Pastoral" Symphony section:
Music: Ludwig van Beethoven
Story Development: Otto Englander; Webb Smith; Erdman Penner; Joseph Sabo; Bill Peet; George Stallings
Character Designers: James Bodrero; John P. Miller; Lorna S. Soderstrom
Art Directors: Hugh Hennesy; Ken Anderson; J. Gordon Legg; Herbert Ryman; Yale Gracey; Lance Nolley
Backgrounds: Claude Coats; Ray Huffine; W. Richard Anthony; Arthur Riley; Gerald Nevius; Roy Forkum
Supervising Animators: Fred Moore; Ward Kimball; Eric Larsen; Art Babbitt; Oliver M. Johnston, Jr.; Don Towsley
Animators: Berny Wolf; Jack Campbell; Jack Bradbury; James Moore; Milt Neil; Bill Justice; John Elliotte; Walt Kelly; Don Lusk; Lynn Karp; Murray McClellan; Robert W. Youngquist; Harry Hamsel
Directors: Hamilton Luske; Jim Handley; Ford Beebe

Dance of the Hours section:
Music: Amilcare Ponchielli
Character Designers: Martin Provensen; James Bodrero; Duke Russell; Earl Hurd
Art Directors: Ken O'Connor; Harold Doughty; Ernest Nordli
Backgrounds: Albert Dempster; Charles Conner
Supervising Animator: Norm Ferguson
Animators: John Lounsbery; Howard Swift; Preston Blair; Hugh Fraser; Harvey Toombs; Norman Tate; Hicks Lokey; Art Elliott; Grant Simmons; Ray Patterson; Franklin Grundeen
Directors: T. Hee; Norm Ferguson

Night on Bald Mountain and *Ave Maria* sections:
Music: Modeste Moussorgsky and Franz Schubert
Special Animation Effects: Joshua Meador; Miles E. Pike; John F. Reed; Daniel MacManus
Special Camera Effects: Gail Papineau; Leonard Pickley
Story Development: Campbell Grant; Arthur Heinemann; Phil Dike
Art Directors: Kay Nielsen; Terrell Stapp; Charles Payzant; Thor Putnam
Backgrounds: Merle Cox; Ray Lockrem; Robert Storms; W. Richard Anthony
Supervising Animator: Vladimir Tytla
Animators: John McManus; William N. Shull; Robert W. Carlson, Jr.; Lester Novros; Don Patterson
Director: Wilfred Jackson
Ave Maria Chorus: Charles Henderson (director); Julietta Novis (soloist)

Release Date: November 13, 1940

Running Time: 120 minutes

THE MOVIE

Having adapted Beethoven's Sixth Symphony for *Fantasia* Walt Disney commented, "Gee, this'll make Beethoven."
Marshall McLuhan, *Culture is Our Business*

Fantasia will amaze ya.
Disney publicity slogan for 1946 rerelease

These two quotations encapsulate and explain the views of the hostile critics concerning *Fantasia*, one of the most enduringly popular of the Disney classic features. Audiences initially voted with their feet, making the movie's first general release something of a disaster – although its first run on Broadway lasted a year, then the record for any "talking picture". Of course, the movie suffered the problem of having been released initially to only 14 theatres: *Fantasia*, in its first version, required some expensive technology in order to play the music on "Fantasound", a sort of proto-stereophonic sound system. Few theatres and high admission prices are not the way to launch a mass-audience movie. The suggestion at the time, however, was that potential audiences were frightened off by the apparent cultural overtones of the movie: they wanted light entertainment rather than Bach, Beethoven, Stravinsky, Dukas . . .

Of course, that theory was a nonsense. Aside from such issues as prices and lack of local venues, people were put off because the musicological purists insisted that Disney had committed not one but two travesties: first, Stokowski's score had heavily tampered with the original versions of the various pieces of music; second, the animation itself raped even these adulterated versions. Such views betrayed a narrowness of vision on the part of the purists: what was being attempted was not a screen enactment of various popular

classics but a melding of classical music with animation. As such, *Fantasia* was a brave experiment and, according to modern tastes, a fairly successful one. There are, of course, certain gaucheries in the movie, but these are far outweighed by its strengths. Apart from anything else, it awakened whole new generations to the joys of classical music; the educationist Martha W. D. Addams commented:

To my mind, *Fantasia* is the greatest contribution motion pictures have made within the ten years in which I have been actively engaged in community work for better films. It should be seen by every child and every adult, over and over again.

Other critics were, if anything, even more enthusiastic. "Terrific as anything that ever appeared on the screen," said the New York *Times*. "An earthquake in motion picture history," said the Los Angeles *Times*. "The screen's greatest departure since the introduction of sound," said the *Philadelphia Evening Bulletin*. "Nothing ever existed like *Fantasia*. To describe it is impossible. You must see it," said *Esquire*. "Like *Snow White*, *Fantasia* marks a milestone in the development of the cinema," said the New York *Herald-Tribune*. Emil Ludwig judged that Disney had created "a new kind of art, and that is the greatest praise one can give an artist".

In fact, one can make a good case for either set of viewpoints. Stokowski's musical arrangements are indeed butchery of the originals, especially the version of Beethoven's *Pastoral* – assuming, that is, that you are thinking in terms of sitting in a concert hall listening to them. But the whole point of *Fantasia* is that you are *not* sitting in a concert hall: you are watching a movie. The animation may be crass in places, but the overall effect is of a superb piece of entertainment, one that has, over the decades, introduced countless thousands to the joys of classical music. The worst criticism of the movie must be that, very often, it is the (superbly performed and recorded) music that carries the animation along, rather than the other way around.

Certainly there was some controversy over the arrangements. The one that caused the most unpleasantness was that of *The Rite of Spring*, Igor Stravinsky being the only one of the composers affected still to be alive. In *Expositions and Developments* (1962) Stravinsky recalled his quarrel with Disney – and especially Walt – over the section based on *The Rite of Spring*:

In 1938 I received a request from the Disney office in America for permission to use *Le Sacre* [*The Rite of Spring*] in a cartoon film. The request was accompanied by a gentle warning that if permission were withheld the music would be used anyway. (*Le Sacre*, being "Russian," was not copyrighted in the United States.) . . . I saw the film . . . at Christmas time 1939. I remember someone offering me a

score and, when I said I had my own, the someone saying, "But it is all changed." It was indeed. The instrumentation had been improved by such stunts as having the horns play their glissandi an octave higher in the *Danse de la terre*. The order of the pieces had been shuffled, too, and the most difficult of them eliminated – though this did not save the musical performance, which was execrable. [Stravinsky's spite shows a little here: the musical *performance* is excellent.] I will say nothing about the visual complement, as I do not wish to criticize an unresisting imbecility . . .

This account of events failed to accord with the standard Disney version, that Stravinsky had been overjoyed by the Disney treatment of his piece. In a 1960 letter to the *Saturday Review* Stravinsky had commented on the "official" version of events:

A letter printed in the *Saturday Review* for January 30th, 1960, quotes Mr. Walt Disney as follows: "When Stravinsky came to the studio . . . he was invited to conferences with [the] conductor . . . and [the] commentator . . . was shown the first roughed out drawings, said he was "excited" over the possibilities of the film . . . agreed to certain cuts and rearrangements and when shown the finished product emerged from the projection room visibly moved . . . and we paid him $10,000 not $5,000."

In fact, my contract . . . states that the Walt Disney Enterprises paid the sum of $6,000 for the use of *Le Sacre du printemps* and that $1,000 of this fee was to be paid to the publisher for the rental of the material. . . . This contract further states that the *Sacre* was to be recorded between March 25 and April 20, 1939. At this time I was in a tuberculosis sanitorium near Chamonix. I did not, indeed, could not have consulted with the musical director or commentator of the film . . . The allegation that I visited the Disney studios on two separate occasions, once to see preliminary sketches and later to see the final film, is also false. I appeared there a single time only . . . I was greeted by Mr. Disney, photographed with him, shown drawings and sketches of the already finished film, and, finally, the film itself. I recall seeing a negative film of the *Sorcerer's Apprentice*, and I recall that I was amused by this and said so. That I could have expressed approbation over the treatment of my own music seems to me highly improbable – though, of course, I should hope I was polite.

People's memories of the same event often differ: here there was clearly a clash in the two men's recollection of what had happened. Decades later, we can only speculate.

Fantasia was born from a chance meeting between Walt Disney and Leopold Stokowski. The latter said that he would love to work with Walt on something; the former responded that, right at this moment, his studio was working on a version of Dukas' *The Sorcerer's Apprentice*, featuring Mickey Mouse. Stokowski eagerly agreed to conduct the music for this projected short, and later suggested to Walt that there was no reason why he should not construct a full-length feature made up of a sequence of shorts matched to various pieces of popular classical music.

There was extended debate as to precisely which pieces of music should be used in *Fantasia* (during production the movie was generally referred to only as "The Concert Feature", but Stokowski referred to it in technical terms as a *fantasia*, and the name stuck). Originally planned as parts of the programme were Sibelius' *Swan of Tuonela*, Debussy's *Clair du Lune*, Wagner's *Ride of the Valkyries*, Prokofiev's *Peter and the Wolf* (later to be incorporated by Disney into *Make Mine Music* [➤215]) and Weber's *Invitation to the Dance*. Most of these were dropped early on, but the Debussy piece, for example, was still under active development in July 1939. Frank Daugherty, writing in *Christian Science Monitor Weekly* in 1938, reported that Walt "thinks Ravel's *Bolero* and Strauss's *Til Eulenspiegel* will be fair game for future productions". Even some of the final sequences were not quite what they seemed; for example, the section that became Beethoven's *Pastoral* had originally been intended to represent Gabriel Pierné's "The Entrance of the Little Fauns" from his operetta *Cydalise et Chévre-pied*. However, this selection ran for only some three minutes, and the animators felt they had too much good material for such a short time. Also, according to Dick Huemer, Pierné's music itself gave the animators a problem:

> ... it bounces along without stopping, never a pause or slowdown. So it didn't give us any kind of a handle or change of pace, or contrasting phraseology. You have to have accents and phrases to work with when you transpose something from music to animation. You've got to have resting points, in other words, and we found none. This music would just go playing straight ahead.

The result of the change was described by Ward Kimball in 1977 as the *Pastoral* being "made to look like a candy box" although, as he added, "the studio generally did not like the sequence". Stokowski is reported as having been from the start against using the Beethoven music: since this is the section of the movie that has come in for the most virulent castigation over the years, Stokowski may well have been right.

The only complete version of *Fantasia* to be shown theatrically in the early days was during the roadshow release: the distributors, RKO, insisted that at two hours it was far too long for general release, and so the version for general release lasted only 81 minutes – this reduction essentially being achieved by cutting out much of the narrator, Deems Taylor.

Walt had to face other unpleasant matters after the movie's roadshow release. One of the saddest was the necessity of jettisoning "Fantasound", the sound system whereby, using a plethora of specially installed loudspeakers in every selected cinema, the illusion of stereo was created. This proved too expensive. A further disappointment was RKO's insistence that the movie be cut. Walt declined to do the job himself – and was proven right in later years when fuller-length versions of the movie were released to general public delight. Yet another disappointment was the abandonment of a dream of his, the re-release from time to time of *Fantasia* with an altered programme, some pieces dropping out to make room for new ones, much as an orchestra on tour might retain the basic programme of its concerts but introduce new works between one hall and the next. The initial failure of *Fantasia* at the box office put an end to this grand plan. In this context it is interesting to note that around 1980 there was talk of Disney doing a new feature called *Musicana*, which like *Fantasia*, would consist of a series of top-quality shorts set to music. One impetus for the idea was that, with the much reduced animation output of the studio, it was hard to give the new generation of animators a sufficient diversity of styles in which to try out their skills. However, to date little more has been heard about this proposed project.

Fantasia has become a legend and, as with so many legends, some people love it and some people hate it. Nowadays most people love it, forgiving it its occasional crassnesses; perhaps this is a reflection of more (artistically) liberal times, when ersatz purism is rejected in favour of multi-media experimentation; to play Devil's advocate one might suggest that instead we are simply less critical than those who went before, that we are content to describe virtually anything as "Art" with a capital "A". Whatever the truth of the matter, Walt was certainly correct when he said:

> *Fantasia* is timeless. It may run ten, twenty, thirty years. *Fantasia* is an idea in itself. I can never build another *Fantasia*. I can improve. I can elaborate. That's all.

The statement is true in several senses. *Fantasia* has survived not 10, 20 or 30 years but, so far, nearly 50. And Walt would indeed never be able to "build another *Fantasia*": he would make pale attempts with *Make Mine Music* and *Melody Time*, but he would never again be able to create something that was on the one hand a collection, an anthology, yet on the other was a unified whole. *Fantasia* was one of those movies that, on its own terms, will never be surpassed.

As a footnote, one can reflect on the nature of fame and turn to a magazine (which shall be nameless) from the early 1940s where one sees a photograph cheerfully captioned: "Walt Disney with two of his studio artists." The two "studio artists" conferring with Walt in front of the *Rite of Spring* storyboard are Leopold Stokowski and Deems Taylor!

THE CHARACTERS

Toccata and Fugue in D Minor Section

Walt wanted in this section, he said, to create the sort of impression you might get were you attending a symphony concert with your eyes half-closed: your vision would be caught by the tips of the violinists' bows, the sheen on the fronts of the cellos, the bridges on all the string instruments ... This is exactly the impression created by the animation. Clearly there are no characters in this abstract piece of work.

The Nutcracker Suite Section

This section is itself segmented into six parts, each representing one of the dances from Tchaikowsky's original work, all of which have had, of necessity, to be curtailed.

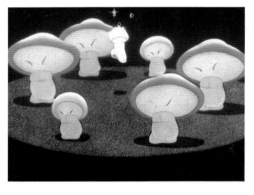

The Mushroom Dancers, the stars of *The Nutcracker Suite*.

The first dance, that of the Sugar Plum Fairy, is performed by the **Dewdrop Fairies**. They are tiny yet, on their own scale, tall and slender; they are semitranslucent and very delicate. Their task is to decorate the flowers and, as they touch each blossom, it bursts into a brilliant sparkling pattern of dewdrops. The first fairies that we see are all in gleaming blues, but in time they are

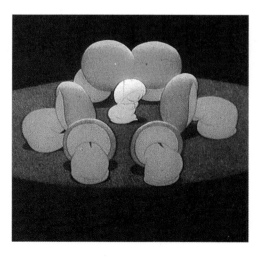

Hop Low was widely hailed as "*Fantasia*'s Dopey".

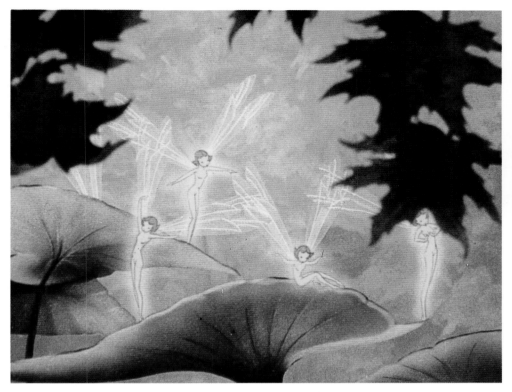

The Dewdrop Fairies, who performed the Dance of the Sugar Plum Fairy for *Fantasia*'s version of *The Nutcracker Suite*.

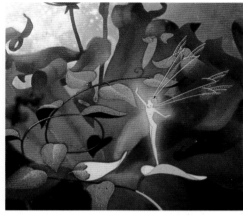

One of the Autumn Fairies, brilliantly illuminated.

Dance begins. This is performed by a troupe of pouting **Goldfish** with immensely long diaphanous fins and tails and intensely feminine eyes. They are very timid of the camera, but in due course become bolder as the slow dance continues. They are typically pink-orange, although they look black in some lights (and some are indeed black). Finally their tails form a flower from the heart of which emerges a brilliant white

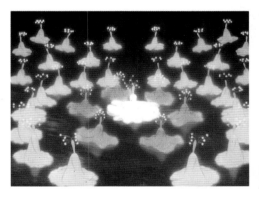

The Blossom Ballet in full flight at the end of the Dance of the Flutes.

never imagine that hectic trio being able to emulate the sincere gravity of the Mushroom Dancers.

The Dance of the Flutes is performed by the **Blossom Ballet**. These start off as separate blossoms in pink, blue and other colours drifting down onto the surface of a stream; there they come together to form a chorus of ballerinas. The principal ballerina,

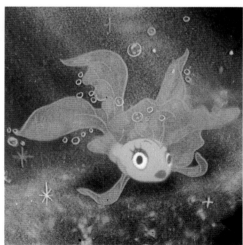

One of the shimmeringly elegant goldfish in the Arabian Dance.

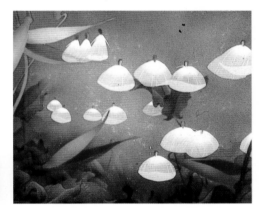

The Milkweed Ballet performing the Waltz of the Flowers.

fantail with a vast double tail. At the end of the dance we follow bubbles from the fish up to the surface to find ourselves close to the shore, where stands a group of thistles.

These are the **Thistle Boys**, and soon they are joined by many of their fellows to perform the Russian Dance. Topped in pink, red and orange they dance in vigorous, high-kicking cossack style. Now enter the **Orchid Girls** to join in the fun: in reds, purples and other colours they are dressed in the traditional costume of Russian matrons. The dance wildly continues until all the flowers and thistles come together in a whirling climax which resolves itself into a tableau of realistic-looking thistles.

We fade to find the **Autumn Fairies** and a scene of falling leaves in the typical browns and bronzes of that season. These gradually transmute into ballerinas and, as the fairies

joined by red, yellow, pink and orange companions. In one lovely scene we see an orange Dewdrop Fairy bathing in the upturned bell of a flower. Finally they collide to form a burst of shards of light which slowly settle towards the ground.

These shards coalesce to form the figures of the **Mushroom Dancers**, who strongly resemble stereotypes of Chinese rice-workers, with red coolie hats and blue robes. One, much smaller than the rest, is obviously the focus of attention: he is **Hop Low**, described by an anonymous reviewer as "the Dopey of *Fantasia*". The Mushroom Dancers perform a grave and stately little dance – the Chinese Dance – in what is one of the most charming sequences of the movie. Interestingly, Art Babbitt, who animated the dancers, studied a jump and the subsequent knee action of one of the Three Stooges; but somehow one could

a stately flower in white, is followed by the spotlight as she sways among the encircling chorus. Finally the ballet disappears over a waterfall, leaving behind a host of rising air-bubbles.

We find ourselves in the murky gloom of an exotic underwater scene as the Arabian

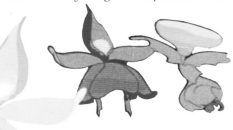

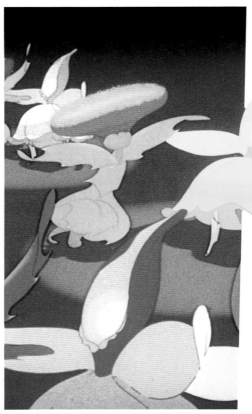

The Thistle Boys and the Orchid Girls, looking suitably Russian.

touch open milkweed pods, they are joined by the drifting **Milkweed Ballet**: the Waltz of the Flowers (which had been under consideration for Silly Symphony treatment as long before as May 1935) is in full swing. The pale brown Autumn Fairies are replaced as the focus of attention by the

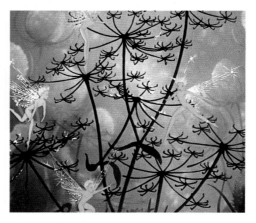

A group of *Fantasia*'s blue-green Frost Fairies.

blue **Frost Fairies**, who slide gaily down plant stems leaving trails of frost wherever they touch. Two of them dance like ice skaters on the surface of a pond, and in a dramatic piece of animation they leave frozen trails behind them. Snow starts to fall and the flakes, led by the **Snowflake Fairies**, eddy and swirl to perform a complicated dance down through the sky. The movement – and with it the suite – ends in a gorgeous abstract of crystalline beauty.

The Sorcerer's Apprentice Section

"In a recent interview," reported Mary Bancroft in *Psychological Perspectives* in Fall 1978, "Mickey said that he considered his most difficult role that of 'The Sorcerer's Apprentice' in *Fantasia*. 'There was no such thing as a stuntmouse in those days,' he pointed out. 'I had to do it all myself – without wires!'"

It was by no accident that this was one of the finest, if not *the* finest, of **Mickey Mouse**'s roles: Walt had intended it that way. When the project of making a two-reel Silly Symphony-type treatment of Dukas' *The Sorcerer's Apprentice* had first been mooted, someone suggested using Dopey

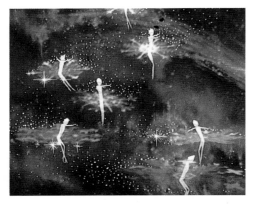

The Snowflake Fairies, whose dance provided the finale to *The Nutcracker Suite*.

as the Apprentice (a much more obvious characterization), but Walt turned the idea down flat. Later a rather more serious challenge came from Stokowski, who proposed that an entirely new character should be created for the role, a

> personality which could represent *you and me* – in other words, someone that would represent in the mind and heart of everyone seeing the film their own personality, so that they would enter into all the drama and emotional changes of the film in a most intense manner.

Of course, by this stage in his career Mickey was a character with whom most Americans *did* identify, but this was not the real reason why Walt refused to budge: he wanted his Mouse to have the part, to reach once again for the stardom he had once enjoyed (although David R. Smith, in a February, 1976, article in *Millimeter*, reported that Ben

Sharpsteen disagreed with this assessment: "... there was no thought to upgrade Mickey Mouse as a character ... it was simply a kind of progressive evolution"). Moreover, the part of the Apprentice was ideal for Mickey's comeback, since it was not a speaking role: Walt had a sneaking suspicion that one of the reasons for Mickey's demise was his shy falsetto voice. The argument was easily resolved: Walt was the boss. He was probably right, although in Mickey's mannerisms and actions one can definitely see traces of that earlier suggestion concerning Dopey.

Mickey's image in general was modified for the occasion. Under the overall guidance of Fred Moore, the Disney artists worked towards a shorter, chunkier and generally cuter version of the Mouse – which is what they achieved. As part of this work, the movie saw for the first time a Mickey who had pupils in his eyes (although a short called *The Pointer*, released just before, had Mickey with his "new eyes"). And he was to be less of a knockabout comedian. Perce Pearce summed up this aspect in a memo from November 1937:

> Please avoid slapstick gags in the ordinary sense; work instead toward fantasy and business with an imaginative touch, especially during the dream sequence. Our movie is designed to intrigue the audience, thrill them, entertain them, but not in the bellylaugh manner. ... What cute poses do you see for Mickey suggesting the inflation of ego typical of the little man suddenly blessed with great power?

The very first piece of animation in *The Sorcerer's Apprentice*, and thus for *Fantasia*, was executed by Preston Blair. It is well worth examining in some detail his account (published in *Cartoonist Profiles* in 1981) of his achieving what he described as his "later notoriety", because it tells us a lot about why this performance of Mickey's was such a triumph.

> It was well along, near the center, of "The Sorcerer's Apprentice". Mickey is asleep in the chair, directing the universe in his sleep. He slips into the rising water brought in by a hundred brooms with buckets. He comes up in a double take, floundering through the water, reaching out to stop the brooms. I can remember ... live-action research, especially made to help me with this floundering-through-water business. ... an athlete from UCLA had been hired to jump pell-mell over a bunch of barrels and boxes, with his arms floundering out in protest. To show you how you use this research, I remember the fellow had quite long hair, or hair that bounced all over the place. I studied the film for hours, made a lot of thumbnail sketches of the sequence ... Using the hair as a guide I transposed all the data into Mickey's robe, that flops around ... as he grabs for his hat and flounders ... and falls. ...
>
> After I had finished the scene with little revisions here and there, it was turned over to a master of effects animation, Ugo D'Orsi, who

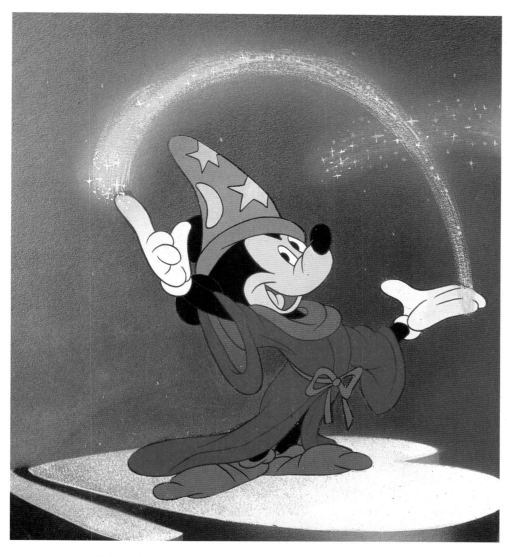

from the outset the importance of this contribution, writing in a memo in October 1937 that

> I am all steamed up over the idea of Stokowski working with us on *The Sorcerer's Apprentice*. I feel that the possibilities of such a combination are so great that we could stretch a point and use his hundred men, as well as work out an arrangement to compensate him, personally, for his time – and we could well afford to record the music in any manner Stokowski would want to do it.

The story of the section is well known. The Apprentice, in the absence of his master, borrows the magic hat and orders the broom to take over the tedious chore of bringing in water from the well to fill a great tub in the workshop. While it goes about this task he falls asleep and dreams of how his magical powers will enable him to command all the forces of the Universe. On his awakening he finds the workshop flooded, with the broom robotically fetching more and more bucketfuls of water – and the Apprentice does not know how to stop it. In desperation he attacks it with a hatchet, but his Alexandrine solution to this Gordian Knot is counterproductive: the splinters form countless little brooms, all of which commence fetching yet further water. The situation is saved only by the return of the Sorcerer, who magically clears the workshop of water and brooms alike, and then reproves his erring Apprentice.

The other character in *The Sorcerer's Apprentice* is the Sorcerer himself, **Yen Sid** (no prizes for spotting what that spells backwards); Nigel de Brulier, a star of the silents, was hired to do the live-action

then animated all those fantastic water effects in this scene and the others of my character animation where Mickey is finally thrown in the vat by a broom. Now, if there ever was a case in which live-action research has helped the animated film these great effects-animation feats in those Disney films are an example.

The most famous picture of all from *Fantasia* – Mickey Mouse in the role of the Sorcerer's Apprentice.

In other words, the section is a triumph for Mickey and for Disney because a fantastic amount of effort was put into making it one: responsible for that expenditure of effort was of course Walt himself.

This was not in fact the first use of *The Sorcerer's Apprentice* in the movies. There had been two earlier attempts. In about 1930 Hugo Reisenfeld and the Artcinema Association had made *The Wizard's Apprentice*, and a few years later a version of Goethe's *Der Zauberlehrling*, upon which Dukas had based his work, had been filmed by the Compagnie Française des Films. But it is the Disney version which has remained in the public consciousness – far more so, even, than the other sections of *Fantasia*. This is largely due to the brilliant animation and fast-moving, perfectly defined action, but it is also partly a result of a superb rendition of the music by Stokowski and, in this case, a "pick-up" orchestra in Hollywood. Walt himself realized right

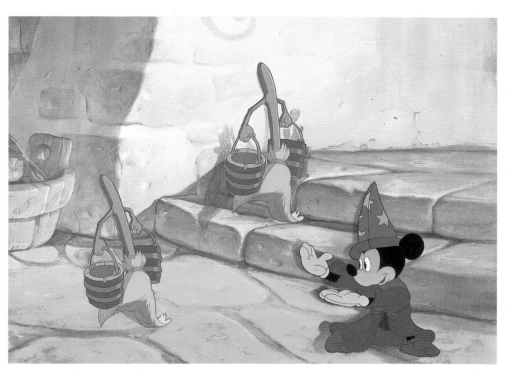

Mickey was able to control a single broom, more or less, but when the brooms multiplied he found himself in difficulties.

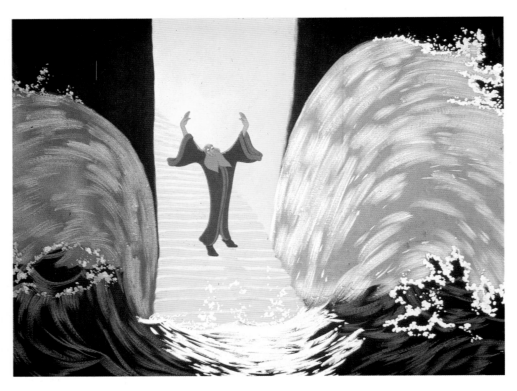

Yen Sid, the sorcerer of *The Sorcerer's Apprentice*. If spelled in reverse, his name is that of a rather different "sorcerer".

act-out of the part for the animators.

Clad in blue, Yen Sid is tall and balding with a long grey beard and long grey eyelashes. We first see him wearing the hat which Mickey will later appropriate: it is blue and conical, with a crescent Moon and various other astronomical symbols on it. Although he spends comparatively little time on screen and speaks not a word, it is enough for us to gain some impression of his character: he is stern and somewhat inscrutable, but we sense that all this is tempered by a deep understanding of, and compassion for, the failings of lesser mortals – such as his own Apprentice. His attitude towards Mickey on discovery of his "crime" is not so much vexation as wryly humorous reproof – the reaction more of a loving father than of a strict master.

After the close of *The Sorcerer's Apprentice* Mickey Mouse makes a further appearance in *Fantasia*: he climbs up beside Stokowski on the conductor's rostrum and shakes his hand. The voice of Mickey is supplied by Walt, which is as it should be:

Mickey: Mr. Stokowski. Mr. Stokowski. Ah ... my congratulations, sir.
Stokowski (laughing): Congratulations to you, Mickey.
Mickey: Gee, thanks. Well, so long. [Exits. Voice from offstage:] I'll be seein' ya.
Stokowski: Goodbye.

Rite of Spring Section

Disney used Stravinsky's music to accompany not the ballet of a prehistoric mystery cult, as performed on the stage, but a combined lesson in historical geology and palaeoecology. We see the birth of the Earth and then follow the history of the life (as it was understood at the time) up to the end of the Age of Reptiles. There are no true characters in this section (certainly no named ones): the nearest to it is a magnificently vicious and lumbering specimen of *Tyrannosaurus rex*, which does gory battle with a stegosaur. Other giant reptiles abound – brontosaurs, pterodactyls, plesiosaurs ... you name it. There is also a fleeting glimpse of an *Archaeopteryx*.

Josh Meador, who did the special effects for this section, was years later to do the

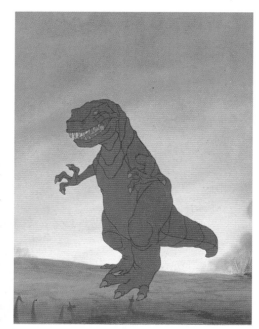

Scariest of all the dinosaurs in *The Rite of Spring* – *Tyrannosaurus rex*.

effects for the Monster from the Id in MGM's famous science-fiction movie, *Forbidden Planet* (1956).

Pastoral Symphony Section

The reduction of Beethoven's Sixth Symphony must have been a major chore for Stokowski, and even Beethoven might have found it tricky: five movements of orchestral Beethoven in twenty minutes or so seems like a contradiction in terms. It sounds like one, too, if one listens to a recording of the result; but curiously enough one does not really notice this while watching the movie, even though the images portrayed are certainly the least sophisticated in *Fantasia*. The version in the rerecorded 1982 version of the film (the first digitally recorded movie soundtrack) is even shorter, for reasons reported by Larry Blake in *Recording Engineer/Producer* in 1982:

One of the more unique problems [Irwin] Kostal was faced with concerned Beethoven's Sixth Symphony. In the original version of the film there was a scene where black centaurs could be seen shining the hooves of white centaurs. It was not until the Sixties that this scene was regarded as offensive, and at that point deleted; the accompanying music was also removed, resulting in an abrupt cut. This "across the board" cut ... was done for convenience's sake, since everything before and after the cut would remain in its original sync.

Kostal solved the problem, but in fact the scene in question hardly seems offensive now ... assuming the viewer bears in mind when the movie was made. After all, at the time, most of the shoeshine boys in the USA *were* black. Moreover, one of the stars of the first movement is the lovable little black child of (also black) Pegasus, whose colour is in stark contrast to the peach, pink, yellow and pale blue of his brothers and sisters. As Paula M. Sigman of the Disney Archives has pointed out, one can go too far in one's searches for racial comments!

The first movement opens with sunrise on Mount Olympus. Fauns and unicorns frolic happily in the lush countryside – there is a hilarious scene where a faun teases a unicorn by intermittently pretending to be a statuette. **Pegasus** glides in to land beside his wife (who is white); surrounded by their three offspring she is nurturing a fourth in her nest. This fourth, **Baby Pegasus**, eventually emerges and, seeing that the others are having such fun flying, decides to try to join them. After several false starts he succeeds and, fluttering and floundering, he follows the rest of the family as they fly over the clouds (or in his case generally through them) and soar to the outer edges of the atmosphere. Finally the family comes to rest on the surface of a lake, where they are joined by other flying horses. All are playing together happily and splashily in the water as the movement ends.

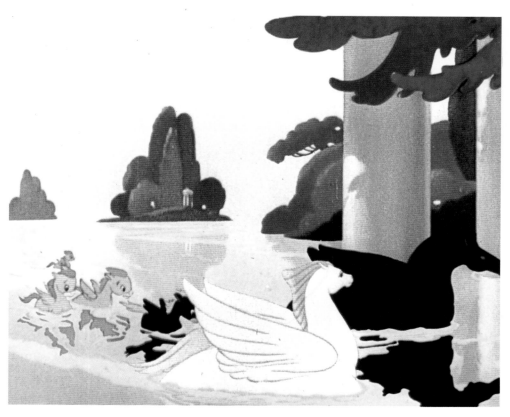

The family Pegasus, from the section of *Fantasia* based on Beethoven's "Pastoral" Symphony.

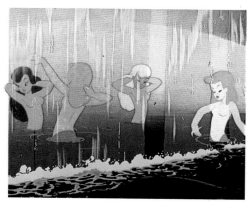

A group of nubile "centaurettes".

("broods", in other words): he has a purple body, a blue torso, black hair and a black tail. A third cupid joins them and shows them that one of the "centaurettes", **Melinda**, is doing much the same: she has a pale blue body with a torso in an even paler shade of blue, and her blonde hair is done in pigtails. This lack of love is intolerable to the cupids, who play their pipes in order to lure the two together. As the movement closes the cupids tactfully draw a floral curtain over the scene of the two new-found lovers reclining together: in the final moment the last remaining cupid's bottom transmutes into a throbbing heart. Richard Schickel, who can see two cupids where others see only one, comments acidly in his *The Disney Version* (1986 edition) that this is

the most explicit statement of anality ever made by the studio, which found in the human backside not only the height of humor but the height of sexuality as well. Two of the little

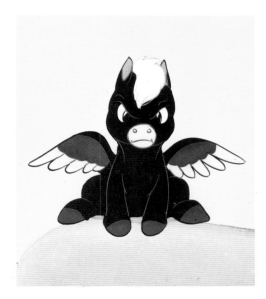

The audience's favourite member of the Pegasus family.

The second movement brings us to where a group of "centaurettes" (young female centaurs) are grooming their teenage hair and generally preening themselves; they are helped in this by little fat pink cupids who are in truth, as many critics have asserted, somewhat obnoxious. The "centaurettes" wear floral brassiéres: this was in deference to the Hays Committee, which was apparently incensed at Disney's original proposal to show them (the "centaurettes") bare-breasted (although it was, it seems, OK to have bare breasts in *Night on Bald Mountain*). The result of the Hays Committee's pressure was an artistic disaster, as a comparison of the initial character sketches and the final results attests.

A herd of centaurs passes nearby, and the cupids whisper various sweet nothings into the ears of the "centaurettes". Soon there is much pairing off. However, two of the cupids despair over sad **Brudus**, a young centaur who just sits alone and sighs

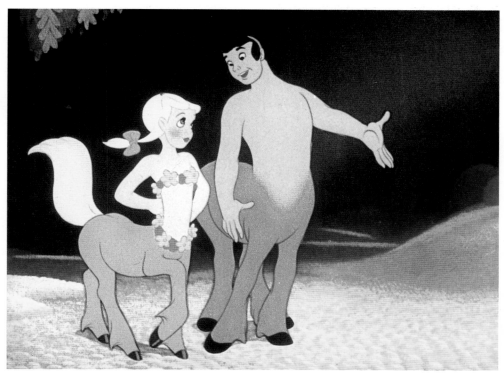

Melinda and Brudus, discovering the joys of love. Very 1940s!

cupids who scamper incessantly through the sequence finally – and blessedly – draw a curtain over the scene. When they come together their shiny little behinds form, for an instant, a heart.

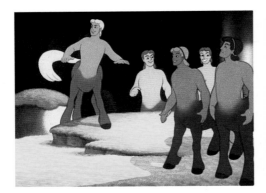

A group of centaurs, alert for signs of "centaurettes".

In fact, since only a single bottom is involved in this scene, Schickel's accusation of anal sexuality is rather pointless, but nevertheless the image does leave a somewhat nasty taste in the mouth.

The opening of the third movement finds the "centaurettes" and fauns making wine. Attracted doubtless by the smell, **Bacchus**, riding on his donkey-unicorn, Jacchus, is soon with them and eagerly partaking. Bacchus, dressed in a white robe and with a grapevine garland around his neck, is not especially large, but he is rotund and very obviously heavy: it is all that Jacchus can do to stagger along under the weight. Bacchus also has a startling habit of falling over, due no doubt to the wine with which the "centaurettes" constantly replenish his

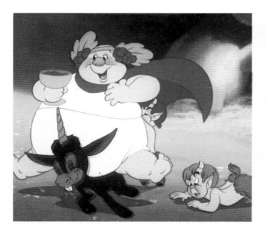

Bacchus and Jacchus, certainly *Fantasia*'s two most disreputable characters.

glass. He has bulbous cheeks and a squashy nose and looks as if it has been a long time since a logical thought chased its futile way through his head. His amorous pursuits of the "centaurettes" end in predictable failure: falling flat on your face is no way to win the heart of a fair lady. **Jacchus**, for his part, is small and black; like his master he is not averse to the occasional draught of wine,

although the effects on him are even swifter than they are on Bacchus. This dissolute pair end the movement when Bacchus, thinking blearily that he has at last caught a "centaurette", purses his lips to proffer a kiss to an equally drunken Jacchus.

The fourth movement starts with a rainstorm. Melinda and Brudus are seen fleeing for cover. Bacchus and Jacchus cringe as **Zeus** pulls apart the clouds to cast thunderbolts at them: the king of the gods finds this prank much funnier than does the

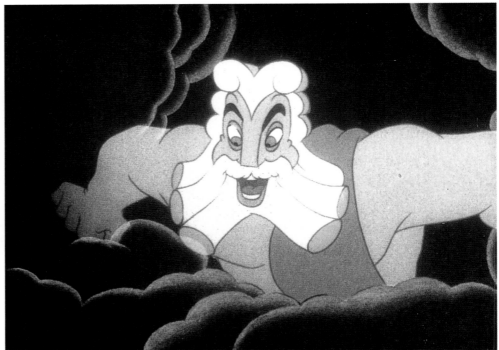

Zeus, king of the gods and cheerful tormentor of the mortals in the "Pastoral" section of *Fantasia*.

audience. Zeus has white hair and a white beard, black eyebrows, a blue off-the-shoulder cape and a sort of "big lunk" facial expression, but the dominant aspect of his personal appearance is that his head is drawn as if carved from stone: the ringlets of his hair and beard are stylized scrolls, and his facial colouring is as of white marble. **Vulcan** (animated like Zeus by Art Babbitt) is the god who is supplying the thunderbolts: with red hair and beard and dressed in a white loincloth and armbands,

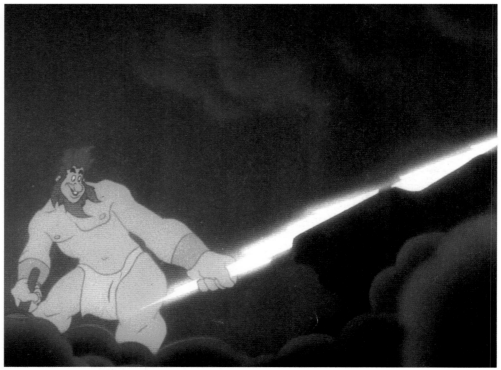

Vulcan, who like Zeus enjoyed pestering the mortals below. Both gods were animated by Art Babbitt.

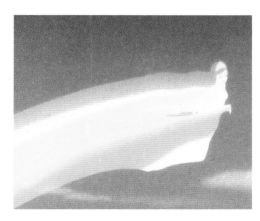

The goddess Iris, painting the rainbow across the sky.

he shares with Zeus that "lunk" expression: he moves in an exaggeratedly doltish, although rapid, fashion as he forges new thunderbolts. The bullying hilarity of the two gods is counterpointed by a brief scene in which Mrs. Pegasus bravely saves one of her children (the peach-coloured one) from being buffeted by strong winds.

Those are floods of water: Bacchus and Jacchus are delighted when Zeus shatters

The dazzling image of Apollo briefly graces the screen.

with a thunderbolt the wine-vat behind which they have been cowering to produce floods of gaudy red wine. Bacchus uses his happily drunk donkey as a boat to paddle around, and it is evident that they are both delighted to be literally swimming in wine.

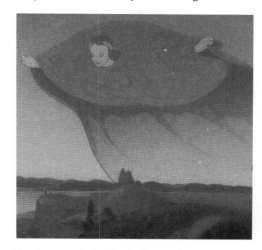

Morpheus, god of night, looks very female in *Fantasia*.

Having tormented the various inhabitants of Mount Olympus long enough, Zeus opts for bed: he tucks himself down on a cloud as the sun comes out. The movement ends.

The fifth movement is set in the calm after the storm. Melinda and Brudus emerge into

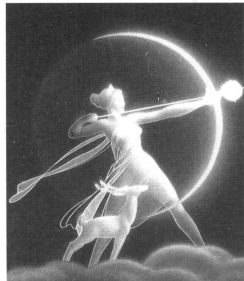

Diana, complete with attendant hart.

the damp sunlight, as do Pegasus and his family. **Iris**, the goddess of the rainbow, paints the sky and the land as well – even Bacchus' draught of wine turns rainbow-coloured. Iris is seen only briefly, as a fair damsel arcing across the sky, drawing the rainbow out behind her. **Apollo** makes an equally brief appearance, riding the chariot

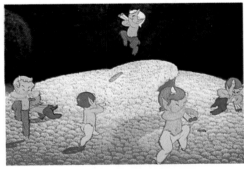

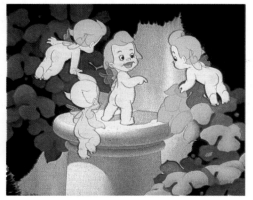

The section based on Beethoven's "Pastoral" Symphony has been the most widely criticized part of *Fantasia*, essentially because its characters are rather too cute. The little fauns (*above*) were cute enough for most stomachs, but the cupids (*below*) were devastatingly cuter.

which draws the sun to its evening rest: he waves to all and sundry as he goes, much as if he were an athlete doing a lap of honour. **Morpheus**, god of night, sleep and dreams, depicted as a rather androgynous figure, crosses the sky, his great billowing cloak of clouds forming the night. And finally we see **Diana** standing on a cloud: she is a tall, noble figure clad in long, wispy gauze-like coverings and has a hart by her side. Goddess not only of hunting but also of the Moon, she holds the crescent Moon as if it were a bow. Using it she shoots a comet, studding the sky with a spray of glittering stars.

Dance of the Hours Section

Ponchielli's *Dance of the Hours* is one of those pieces of classical music that has become something of a joke in itself, and so it seemed in no way unjustifiably irreverent for Disney to make its accompanying animation also something of a joke – and a

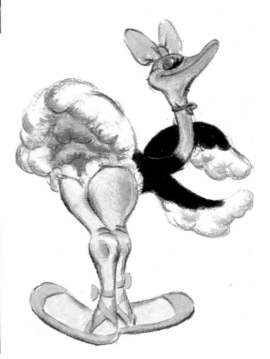

Mlle. Upanova – a reference painting produced for the artists.

very funny joke at that. By contrast with the other sections of the movie, there is no attempt to set the action in any kind of naturalistic background: this is very definitely a ballet performance, and the characters are dressed accordingly. The whole piece is an affectionate parody of the pretensions of classical ballet.

The first dancer we see is **Mlle. Upanova**, encountered as she sleeps at the top of a flight of stairs. She is an ostrich of less than sublimely elegant proportions dressed in a black tutu and pink shoes with a pink bow in her hair; the pinkness is continued for her beak, but her legs, neck and face are pale mauve. She has big eyes and long eyelashes. The most noticeable thing about her is the size of her thigh muscles: extra large. The members of her ostrich *corps de ballet* are similar except that their accoutrements are blue rather than pink. All of the ostriches were modelled by Irina Baranova of the Ballet Russe.

Mlle. Upanova awakens and stretches "gracefully"; soon she has awoken the other members of the ostrich chorus, and the ballet begins. From a stand in the background she fetches a cornucopia of fruit which she feeds to her fellows and, ultimately, herself. Then she indulges in prima donna vanity, for she admires her reflection preeningly in the surface of a pool.

However, the pool proves not to be empty: from it emerges a platform bearing the sleeping figure of **Hyacinth Hippo**; moreover, this lady of the ballet is in a state of undress – a state which she coyly tries to hide once she realizes that the cameras are upon her. It is the cue for the entry of the hippo *corps de ballet* (the ostriches have now departed): these dancers hastily clothe their leader in a gauzy pink tutu and yellow ballet shoes. Modelled, as were all of the hippos, by Tatiana Riabouchinska of the Ballet Russe (Marjorie Babbitt did live action), Hyacinth is big, bulky and brown with a pale brown tummy and a smug expression: astonishingly, Ms Riabouchinska is reported to have been delighted with the result. After a spinning dance with her chorus, Hyacinth drops in an exhausted sleep onto a divan; the others leave her.

Now there enters the elephant ballet led by **Elephanchine**; this collection was

modelled for the animators by Roman Jasinsky, again of the Ballet Russe. The six elephants use the pond-water to generate a cloud of bubbles in the air (one of the bubbles contains a startled-looking goldfish!). The elephants perform a dance with the bubbles, at the conclusion of which they are all blown away by a gust of wind, leaving Hyacinth Hippo still snoozing soundly on her divan. It is time for the villain to come onto the stage.

This villain is **Ben Ali Gator**, leader of a horde of twelve ballet-dancing alligators all

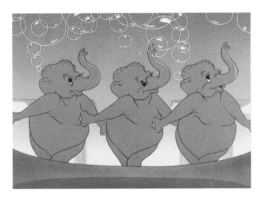

Question: how do you make dancing elephants look graceful? Answer: you can't.

of which look almost as seedy and disreputable as he does. All are basically green with yellow undersides, all have red cloaks, all have four canines at the front and four molars at the back but otherwise a total absence of teeth; Ben is distinguished

because he has a little red skullcap with a great blue plume. All of the alligators gaze longingly at Hyacinth's scantily clad sleeping form until Ben commands the others to go. With imperious confidence he throws off his red robe; one suspects that this is not because he has suddenly decided to take a bath. He approaches the sleeping beauty, but she awakens and flees in alarm. The two of them then perform a complicated *pas de deux* which is less of a partnership than a lustful chase by Ben Ali Gator. Fortunately he comes off much the worse in this unequal contest: when Hyacinth leaps joyously into his arms she flattens him; and, after he has been wound like a helix about her ample form, she leaves him spinning like a corkscrew on his tail before collapsing vertiginously to the ground.

Undeterred by the rotten hand which Fate has dealt their leader, the other alligators rush on stage and engage in a similarly lustful dance with the reappearing hippo dancers. By the end of the piece there are a lot of flat alligators.

Night on Bald Mountain and Ave Maria Section

James Morrow, writing in 1978 in *Media and Methods*, summed it up:

> In *Fantasia*, Bald Mountain erupts with more cacodemonic imagery than those of us equipped with only two eyes can ever hope to absorb.

The triumph of *Fantasia*'s concluding sequence was the animation by the great Bill Tytla of the monstrous demon figure, **Chernabog** (often incorrectly referred to as "the Devil"). It is hard to think of a better character in the entire Disney canon, and yet Chernabog does comparatively little and occupies only a few tens of seconds of screen-time. There is probably no other animator in history who could have brought off a triumph like this one. Tytla modestly ascribed this to his nationality in a quote cited by John Canemaker in an article in *Cinéfantastique* in 1976:

> ... for the devil on Bald Mountain ... I did some reading about Moussorgsky. Now I'm Ukrainian and Moussorgsky used terms I could understand. He talked about "Chorni-bok," the Black Art. Ukrainian folklore is based on "Chorni-bok" – I related to this and studied up.

The "story" element of *Fantasia*'s *Night on Bald Mountain* section is simplicity itself. Night-time over a sleeping village, and Chernabog appears. Drawn to him are numerous ghouls, imps, phantoms and ghostly skeletons, and all of them indulge in a mad aerial dance. The spectral characters have a taste of the torments of Hell before dawn comes and Chernabog banishes them back to the graves and vaults whence they came.

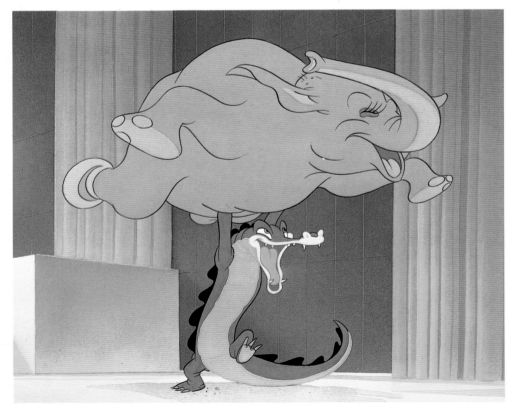

Ben Ali Gator being wicked with a dancing partner. The overt lechery of Ben and the other alligators raised surprisingly few eyebrows.

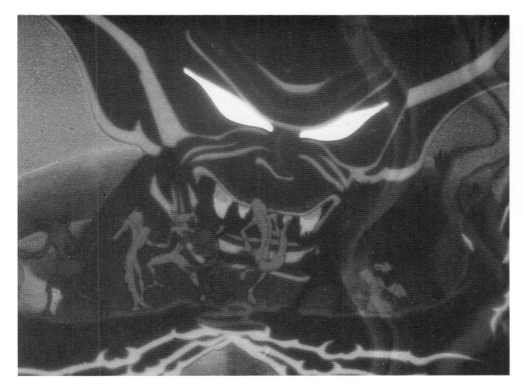

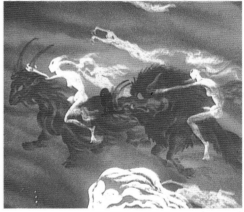

Ghosts, pulled across the night sky as if by a magnet towards Chernabog.

Chernabog, in *Fantasia*'s *Night on Bald Mountain* section, represented a brilliant piece of artistry by Bill Tytla.

It is the animation of Chernabog himself that turns the sequence into a masterpiece. When first we see the sleeping village surmounted by the gloomy hulk of the Bald Mountain it seems to be nothing more than a night-time scene, all in blues and blacks, with some dark greens on the mountainside. Then the very summit of the mountain stirs, and we realize that its apex has been formed by Chernabog's crouching form, his great black bat-wings shrouding his ivory-white body. As he snarls down towards the valley, his yellow eyes filled with malice, he sends a shiver through the collective spine of any audience. When he claps together the hands within his wings and two flames spring up in response from a chasm in the ground, we realize that we are in the presence of unadulterated evil.

Into the fiery chasm he throws handfuls of the wailing ghouls; this is mindlessly wicked torture. Then he picks up some of the flames in his huge hand and watches as these are transmuted into the figures of three dancing nude females; they in turn transform into vicious manifestations of a pig, a goat and a wolf. Even these figures do not last long, for Chernabog on a whim turns them into five bizarre, blue, shuffling monsters. These he watches for a while before crushing them by clenching his fist;

when he opens his hand again we see in his palm blue flames which almost immediately are transmogrified into the distorted forms of four blue male dancers with horns, tails and cloven hooves. These change into a kaleidoscope of colours as they leap from Chernabog's hand to join the ghouls in a saturnalia among the flames of the chasm. The screen is filled with clouds of erotic succubi. Chernabog's evil permeates all.

Disney was wading in deep waters here: the studio had successfully portrayed on the movie screen – decades before *The Exorcist* – the mixture of the evil and the erotic which lies at the heart of demonolatry. It has frequently been suggested that this is why, on the breaking of dawn, the sequence melds into a rendition of Schubert's *Ave Maria* (new lyrics by the US novelist and poet Rachel Field), with its overtly Christian symbols of torch-bearing pilgrims. A

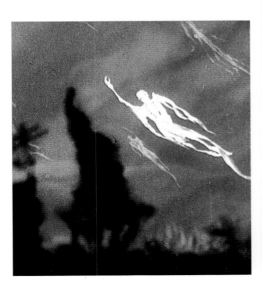

The demons of *Night on Bald Mountain* left a lasting impression on most audiences.

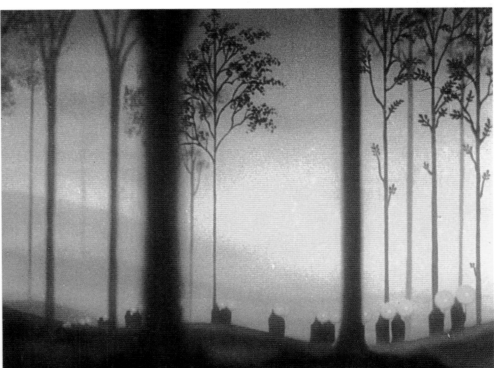

After the nightmare figures of *Night on Bald Mountain*, relief was provided by the massed pilgrims of the *Ave Maria* section.

number of critics have proposed that such a copping-out from the implications of this necromantic drama must be the only possible reason for what they regard as a monstrous mismatching of the two pieces of music. The average viewer, by contrast, sees the *Ave Maria* as a perfectly calming influence to conclude the demonic wildness of *Night on Bald Mountain*.

Whatever the truth of the matter, the sequence as a whole is "carried" by the figure of Chernabog. It is no wonder that the other animators – and not just the Disney ones – regarded Tytla as a genius.

THE RELUCTANT DRAGON

Characters:

Casey Jr. section: Casey Jr.

Old MacDonald Duck section: Donald Duck; Clementine (cow)

Baby Weems section: Baby Weems; Mr. John Weems; Mrs. Weems; Albert Einstein; George Bernard Shaw; President F. D. Roosevelt; Salvador Dali; Walter Winchell

How to Ride a Horse section: Goofy; Percy (horse)

The Reluctant Dragon section: The Boy; The Father; The Reluctant Dragon; Sir Giles; The Horse

Credits:

The Reluctant Dragon section based on Kenneth Grahame's short story of the same name first published in *Dream Days* (1898)

Live Characters: Robert Benchley; Frances Gifford; Buddy Pepper; Nana Bryant; Florence Gill; Clarence Nash; Norm Ferguson; Ward Kimball; Jimmy Luske; Alan Ladd; Truman Woodworth; Hamilton MacFadden; Maurice Murphy; Walt Disney; numerous Disney employees

Voices:
Baby Weems section: Gerald Mohr (narrator); Leone LeDoux (Baby Weems); Raymond Severn (also Baby Weems); Ernie Alexander (John Weems); Linda Marwood (Mrs. John Weems); Art Gilmore (F. D. Roosevelt); Edward Marr (Walter Winchell).
Old MacDonald Duck section: Clarence Nash (Donald Duck)
How to Ride a Horse section: John McLeish (narrator); Pinto Colvig (Goofy)
The Reluctant Dragon section: J. Donald Wilson (narrator); Barnett Parker (Dragon, father); Claud Allister (Sir Giles); Billy Lee (Boy)

Special Effects: Ub Iwerks; Joshua Meador

Sound Recording: Frank Maher

Film Editor: Paul Weatherwax

Music: Frank Churchill; Larry Morey

Story:
Baby Weems section: Joe Grant; Dick Huemer; John P. Miller
The Reluctant Dragon section: Erdman Penner; T. Hee

Screenplay: Ted Sears; Al Perkins; Larry Clemmons; Bill Cottrell; Harry Clork

Additional Dialogue: Robert Benchley

Art Director: Gordon Wiles

Cartoon Art Direction: Ken Anderson; Hugh Hennesy; Charles Philippi

Backgrounds: Ray Huffine; Arthur Riley

Set Decoration: Earl Woodin

Director of Photography: Bert Glennon

Technicolor Sequences:
 Director of Photography: Winton Hoch
 Color Director: Natalie Kalmus
 Special Sound Effects: Sonovox

Animators: Ward Kimball; Fred Moore; Milt Neil; Wolfgang Reitherman; Walt Kelly; Jack Campbell; Claude Smith; Harvey Toombs; Bud Swift

Production Manager: Earl Rettig

Director of Cartoon Sequences: Hamilton Luske

Assistant Directors of Cartoon Sequences: Ford Beebe; Jim Handley; Erwin Verity

Assistant Director: Jasper Blystone

Director: Alfred L. Werker

Release Date: June 20, 1941

Running Time: 72 minutes

THE MOVIE

The Reluctant Dragon is probably the least of the features discussed in this book, yet in a curious way it has some importance. For one thing, it was the first Disney release to incorporate large sections of live action since the long-ago days of the Alice Comedies (►13). For another, it was the first Disney feature to be an anthology of essentially unrelated sections (if we assume that *Fantasia* was knitted together by its aim of relating music to animation). Third, it contains two of the most important shorts ever produced by the studio – *Baby Weems* and *How to Ride a Horse* – as well as a perfectly competent one in the shape of *The Reluctant Dragon* itself.

For all that, it is a fairly unsatisfying viewing experience – especially in later versions, which omit *How to Ride a Horse*. It was conceived for two primary reasons: first, *Pinocchio* was bringing in much less than predicted, because World War II had virtually destroyed the foreign market , and *Fantasia* was doing badly in the box office, so Disney needed a quick, cheap and profitable feature; second, it served as an advertisement for the Disney product – an especially appealing advertisement, because

its targets would actually pay to come to see it. In both respects the making of *The Reluctant Dragon* was something of a cynical move, and audiences voted with their feet by staying away. By and large, the critics encouraged this attitude: they felt that the whole venture was something of a rip-off. And, curiously enough, they were not especially enamoured of the feature's showpiece, the 12-minute version of Kenneth Grahame's "The Reluctant Dragon" itself. Richard Plant, writing in *Decision* in 1941, summed up many critics:

> ... nothing more than a warmed over and blown up Ferdinand [►88]. For the first time Disney is guilty of repeating himself.

Nevertheless, the feature is still worth watching today. Its live-action "exposé" of the way the Disney studio worked is basically fallacious (there are numerous unhappy "simplications" concerning the way in which cartoons were and are made), but its three principal shorts are certainly of interest.

THE STORY

The overall story of the feature is comparatively simple. Mrs. Benchley, who has just read Kenneth Grahame's "The Reluctant Dragon", thinks that it would make an ideal Disney movie, and forces Benchley to take the book to the studio and put the idea to Walt. On his arrival he is greeted by an officious messenger boy, Humphrey (played with zeal by Buddy Pepper), who proposes to take him to Walt; however, Benchley "escapes" from this paragon of efficiency and starts wandering around the Burbank studio, meeting various Disney staff – some of whom really *are* Disney staff (e.g., Ward Kimball and the various other animators, Clarence Nash, Florence Gill) and some of whom are not (e.g., Frances Gifford, who plays a pretty young woman whose job seems astonishingly varied and ill defined). After meeting Nash and Gill and seeing some early workouts of Casey Jr. (to feature in *Dumbo* [►195]), of *Bambi* (►197) and of a proposed Donald Duck short, he stumbles into a story conference for *Baby Weems*. Using the sketches from the storyboard, an odd but brilliant rendition of the tale is given to both Benchley and the audience. After this he stumbles through several more wrong doors until he finds Ward Kimball working on a new creation, the next Goofy short, *How to Ride a Horse*, the first in what would prove to be an astonishingly successful series. After watching it Benchley is finally taken to meet Walt in the projection room, where the team is just about to screen an early version of ... *The Reluctant Dragon*, based on the Kenneth Grahame story. As she drives him home Mrs. Benchley pitches into him for having missed the opportunity of being the first to present this idea to Walt and he responds with a typical Donald Duck vocal explosion – a trick he had learned from Clarence Nash during his day of exploration.

THE CHARACTERS

Casey Jr. Section

The animation of this piece lasts only a few seconds and serves primarily to allow Frances Gifford to demonstrate to Benchley how sound effects are produced and then integrated into animated cartoons. The little, slow freight engine **Casey Jr.**, later to feature as the circus train in *Dumbo* [➤195], is shown as fearful of a big express locomotive. Nevertheless he battles intrepidly through a storm and then, on finding that a bridge across a ravine is out, solves the dilemma by jumping over the chasm (shades of Oswald's trolley car in *Trolley Troubles* [➤21]). Finally he crashes.

Old MacDonald Duck Section

If anything, this section is even shorter than the preceding one. Benchley is encouraged to peer into the animation camera, where he sees the image of **Donald Duck**. Donald himself demonstrates some of the simpler techniques of animation, and this merges into a very short extract from a putative

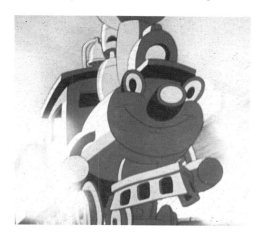

Casey Jr., later to make a more significant contribution in *Dumbo*, featured briefly in *The Reluctant Dragon*. His role in this movie had the basic purpose of allowing sound-effects techniques to be demonstrated to Robert Benchley.

Duck short called *Old MacDonald Duck*, which features a brief glimpse of a cow called **Clementine**. Obviously, the extract is accompanied by a few lines of "Old MacDonald Had a Farm".

Donald makes brief further appearances in the feature – in the form of "Old Master"

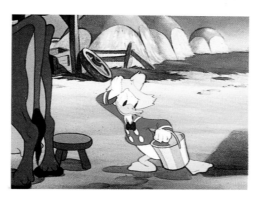

A brief clip from Donald's forthcoming short, *Old MacDonald Duck*, appeared in *The Reluctant Dragon*.

paintings of him on the office walls. The best is probably a portrait of the Duck accoutred like the Laughing Cavalier and with his face miraculously distorted into a close approximation of that worthy's grin. The marvels of the animator's art.

Baby Weems Section

Baby Weems is a delicious satire of the short-term fads and the destructiveness of the consumer society, but it is notable primarily for the way in which it is animated. Rather than the rich, full Disney animation to which audiences had become accustomed, it uses a form of partial animation which is incredibly effective. Essentially, what the viewer is shown are (at least in theory) the working drawings taken from the storyboard of a cartoon in preparation; fairly often, there is a degree of animation within what are otherwise still sketches. The strength of these sketches can be gathered from the fact that most audiences, after a moment or two of the short, "forget" that what they are watching is not full animation. The experience is a strange one, and difficult to explain to people who have not undergone it.

The story is not complex. Baby Herbert Weems is born an infant prodigy, and within months is regarded as some kind of guru by the greatest (and the least) in all the land. He advises scientists and artists and even President Franklin D. Roosevelt; but, on the eve of a worldwide broadcast during which he is scheduled to announce the solution to all mankind's problems, he is taken ill and has to be rushed to hospital. On his emergence he is a changed personality, as the world soon discovers:

Announcer: All right, Mr. Weems, you're on the air.
Baby Weems: Gloggle.

Yes, he has returned to his proper mental age again, and the fickle public promptly abandon him: even his carved head is rudely blasted from the side of Mount Rushmore. The only people who are happy about the change are Mr. and Mrs. Weems, who at last have their beloved baby back after his months-long sojourn through the halls of fame. And, because they are happy to have him back in the family fold, Baby Weems himself is equally happy to be there.

The character of **Baby Weems** is exquisitely created. It would have been too, too easy to have concentrated on his cuddly-infant aspects and thereby produced a character who was cloyingly cute; alternatively, by mixing in *too* much of the venerable-sage element an unconvincing character might have been generated. In fact, even as we laugh at the incongruity as (for example) little yellow-haired Baby Weems conducts his own orchestral composition at the Carnegie Hall perched on a high chair and waving his baby-spoon for a baton, we somehow *accept* him as a genuine personality.

The level of his precocity cannot be exaggerated. Moments after his birth he briefly stops crying to apologize for the din: "I'm awfully sorry, gentlemen, but it's rather necessary for our lung-development, you know." He is also a polymath: one minute he is conducting urgent researches into bacteriology, the next he is vamping away on his baby grand piano. It is no surprise when he is called to the White House to meet **President Franklin Delano Roosevelt** and given a tickertape welcome: if he can understand the arcane mysteries of microbiology then such concerns as politics and economics should be (literally) child's play to him.

John Weems is a fairly minor character, the more important parent being the baby's mother, the blonde and graceful **Mrs. Weems**: she, even more than her husband, is desperate to be with her child and desolated that he has been "taken over" by the great for the purposes of discussion and learning. The reactions of those in authority are totally unsympathetic towards her maternal emotions:

Mrs. Weems: But where's my baby? Can't I even see him?
Faceless Official: Sorry, Mrs. Weems, he can't be disturbed now. He's in conference.

Both of the adult Weemses are turned away from their baby's hugely successful Carnegie Hall concert (all the seats have been sold). They are thrown out of the cinema when they become overexcited on seeing him in a newsreel. Mr. Weems is barred from the baby's press conferences because, of course, he has no press-card. When Baby Weems is welcomed at the White House the nearest his parents can get to him is the roof of a nearby skyscraper.

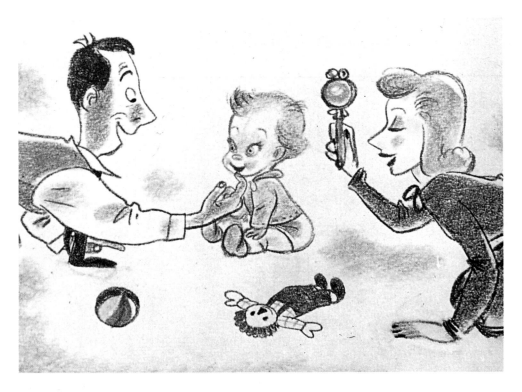

The family Weems, in happier days. Generally, Baby Weems was separated from his parents because of pressing affairs of state.

When he is ill in hospital they must keep their parental vigil not by his bedside but by the radio. All in all, it is not much fun being the parent of a prodigy. In the end, when he is restored to them, it is obvious that they are the only people in the world who really love him, who really care for him for who he is rather than for the things he can do for them.

The other named characters in the movie are very minor – at least in terms of the movie. **Albert Einstein** is shown in deep discussion with the drooling genius:

Baby Weems: I'm awfully, sorry, Dr. Einstein, This reverses your whole basic theory.
Einstein (finger to lips): Ssssh! Not so *loud!*

While the little child sits playing merrily in his baby-bath **George Bernard Shaw** perches at his feet, listening intently:

Baby Weems: It's not just the things you say, Mr. Shaw, it's the cute way you say them.
GBS (mopping brow with handkerchief): Ptash! Two thousand years ahead of its time!

A third cultural pillar makes an even briefer appearance: after Baby Weems has been featured on the cover of *Life*, and after his image has been carved into Mount Rushmore, we see yet another visual representation of him being made – by the painter **Salvador Dali**, who was himself to work with Disney on a proposed surrealist cartoon (➤217). **Walter Winchell** makes a brief appearance.

How to Ride a Horse Section

This was the first of the great series of the "how to" movies (➤48) featuring **Goofy** and narrated by John McLeish, and it set

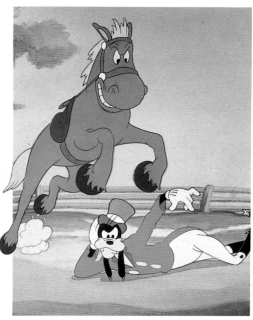

Percy, the horse who made Goofy's life such a misery in the *How to Ride a Horse* section of the movie.

the pattern for the others. Goofy is keen to demonstrate to us the fine art of horsemanship; his mount, **Percy**, has other ideas. The humour in the short arises

because of the utter disparity between what the cool-voiced narrator is telling us is happening and what we see Goofy doing on the screen; this effect is intensified when some of the faster and more visually confusing sequences are shown to us in the form of a slow-motion action replay: if we thought it was confusing at full speed we find it is *even more so* when we can see what was *really* happening!

Although Pinto Colvig is generally credited with voicing Goofy's various pained grunts and yelps in this short, it appears that he did so only at secondhand, as it were: the relevant noises were stitched together from the soundtracks of earlier Goofy cartoons, Colvig at this time being on one of his periodic absences from the Disney fold.

Ironically, although this section was originally intended for individual short release, the distributor, RKO, felt that it was so good that it deserved to be encased in a feature so that, in theory, more people would see it. Of course, what happened was that the short has had a very wide circulation while the feature as a whole has been virtually ignored.

The Reluctant Dragon Section

This short was intended to be the showpiece of the feature. In truth it is quite a good piece of work, but it seems pale by comparison with such outstanding shorts as *Baby Weems* and *How to Ride a Horse*. As noted above, critics have compared it with 1938's *Ferdinand the Bull*; there are also similarities with the later *Peter and the Wolf* (➤215), released as part of *Make Mine Music* (1946).

In its essence the plot is simple. We are back in the knights-in-armour age, and a dragon is reported to be scourging the countryside. A little boy sets off to hunt it down with his catapult (slingshot) but, when he encounters the beast, discovers that it is a friendly, shy aesthetic character with a predilection for writing pretentious poetry. Boy and Dragon strike up a friendship. But to the area comes the doughty dragon-slayer Sir Giles. The boy contacts this warrior and finds that he, too, is a writer of bad verse. The boy introduces knight to monster, and a mutual fan-club is set up. Still, for the sake of form, a battle must be joined. When this finally comes about the knight and the Dragon conspire to fake a contest, at the end of which the Dragon histrionically acts out its own death. But then Sir Giles magnanimously raises it from the dead, announces that he has "reformed" it from its assumed earlier habit of scourging the countryside and carrying off fair maidens, and watches as the Dragon is welcomed by the villagers as a new friend.

The Boy is small and cute, with carrot-red hair. Although he is the prime mover in the plot, his is not a strongly portrayed character: presumably Disney intended this as a way of helping the audience to identify with the little hero. He first hears of the Dragon while he is sitting under a tree reading a book about – would you believe it? – knights conquering dragons. Past him flee in alarm the sheep of which his **Father** is the shepherd; the Father has his son's carrot-red hair plus a moustache in the same color, and has what seems like an Italian accent, although his son's is American.

Others may be frightened of the Dragon but the little boy is not (exactly as in *Peter and the Wolf* [➤**216**]): off he sets with his catapult; but on finding and befriending the beast he forgoes slaying him and instead warns that the Father and the rest of the villagers are planning to form a posse to, as it were, terminate him with extreme prejudice. Thereafter the boy's role is essentially that of a "fixer". He is the one who contacts Sir Giles and brings about the fateful meeting between the two later "contestants". He is the one who sets up the staged battle between the two of them. He is the one who incites the Dragon into a display of suitable ferocity.

The Reluctant Dragon himself was described with cruel accuracy in the Disney pressbook for the movie as "a pink tea

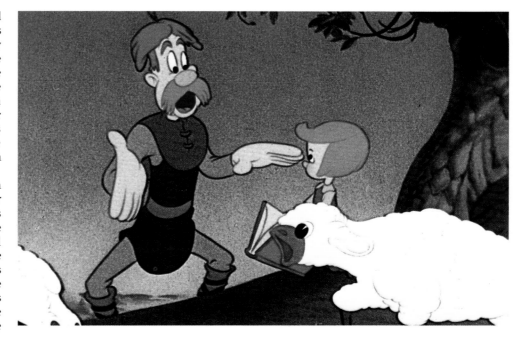

The Father explains to the Boy that there's this, um, dragon plaguing the land . . .

the Dragon admits that in fact he has yet to get started on this scourging the countryside bit: the worst he has done is to scourge it with his poetry, which, as we discover, is of sub-McGonagall standard – dragons have been slain for less! However, this poetry is important to the Dragon: it is, indeed, his *raison d'être*. This fact has an important effect on the later development of the plot, for it is thanks to their joint appreciation of the worst of verse that he and Sir Giles make their unique compact.

The "fight" between the two of them is the highlight of the short. Here we find a

bookmaker taking odds as if at a racecourse; here we find barkers selling souvenir "Dragon" balloons for the kids. It is all very much like the preliminaries to a boxing match. Despite the howling of the fans, though, the Dragon has decided that he has little interest in even a mock fight: he wants to stay safely sheltering in his cave. Finally the boy has to resort to drastic measures – he tells the Dragon that he is a "punk poet", and fire starts to roar from those great nostrils. As the Dragon comes charging out of his cave the villagers, gathered around to watch the fracas, wisely scatter for safer

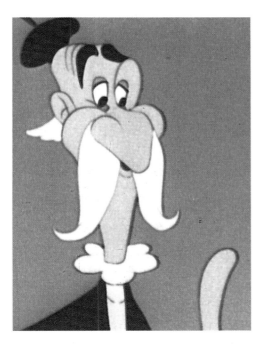

Sir Giles was the Dragon's foe – at least in theory.

character". He is blue with a white belly, has prominent nostrils, black ears, carefully groomed eyelashes and a normally cheerful expression on his face. His voice betrays him as, shall we say, an artistic type. When first found by the Boy he is showering in a waterfall; he is demonstratively shy of his nakedness. This is curious, because he fails to don any clothes during the ensuing moments when he invites the boy to tea and shares it with him. During the conversation

A picture of studied viciousness – the Dragon in the movie's *The Reluctant Dragon* section.

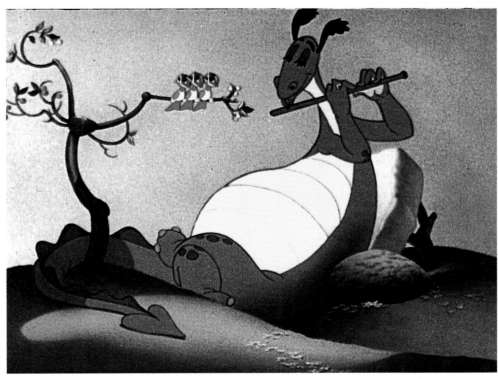

territory. But his fury is utter sham: he is an unwilling participant even in the mock fight, in case he might get hurt.

Sir Giles, first encountered by the Boy in his bath in the local hostelry, is much like a coloured version of Tenniel's drawing of the White Knight in *Through the Looking Glass*. Of medium height and skeleton slenderness, sporting a monocle, he has droopy white moustaches and a frosting of white hair surrounding his bald pate. Despite his awesome reputation as a slayer of monsters, he is, like the Dragon, definitely an artistic type. His voice is as uppercrust English as an American speaker can make it.

Unlike the Dragon, however, Sir Giles is in no wise a coward: he chooses to undergo the mock fight because he wishes to save the Dragon and preserve his own reputation, and not out of fear. In a way, he is rather like an also-ran Renaissance Man: imbued with culture and creativity, yet also a man of action – just not especially

distinguished in any sphere. Again like the Dragon, he is keen on cups of tea to the extent of being absentminded in their presence. There is one glorious moment in this respect during the sham combat. Knight and monster have retreated into the Dragon's cave, whence emerge great clouds of smoke and painful-sounding crashes. We are shown the inside of the cave, and find Sir Giles assiduously fanning a fire while the Dragon is beating a drum and various other suitable objects; as they do these things the two are sharing a pot of tea and discussing this and that. When they feel the time has come, the Dragon charges out into the open again with Sir Giles galloping in hot pursuit. However, the knight has had one of his absentminded moments again: instead of threatening the Dragon with his lance he is instead wielding nothing more ominous than a teacup. It is all he can do to get back to the cave and swap implements before the villagers notice what is going on.

Also worthy of mention in this short is Sir

Giles' **Horse**. It is orange-brown and seems to have seen better days. However, the most obvious key to its personality is the expression it bears throughout the mock battle: it is utterly fed up, disgusted, repelled and revolted by this charade. Clearly it would be much, much happier were Sir Giles doing his normal job and actually *killing* the Dragon, not just playing the fool with it.

No one could claim that *The Reluctant Dragon* is a great short, and one can say the same thing about the feature in which it appears; yet this is not to imply that either are in any way second rate. The short suffers by comparison with the other shorts in the feature; the feature likewise suffers by comparison with the other Disney features of the time. *Snow White and the Seven Dwarfs, Pinocchio, Dumbo* . . . it takes a fine movie to compare with those three, and *The Reluctant Dragon* is simply not of that standard.

DUMBO

Characters:

Dumbo
Timothy Mouse
Ringmaster
Casey Jr.
Messenger Stork
Mrs. Jumbo
Elephants: Prissy; Matriarch; Giggles; Catty.
Joe
Skinny
Crows: Fat Crow; Dandy (or Jim) Crow; Glasses Crow; Preacher Crow; Straw Hat Crow

Credits:

Based on *Dumbo, the Flying Elephant* by Helen Aberson and Harold Pearl

Voices: John McLeish (narrator); Ed Brophy (Timothy Mouse); Herman Bing (Ringmaster); Margaret Wright (Casey Jr.); Sterling Holloway (Messenger Stork); Verna Felton (elephant); Sarah Selby (elephant); Dorothy Scott (elephant); Noreen Gamill (elephant); Billy Sheets (Joe, clown); Billy Bletcher (clown); Malcolm Hutton (Skinny); Cliff Edwards (crows); Jim Carmichael (crows); Hall Johnson Choir (crows); Eddie Holden (clown); The King's Men (roustabouts); Harold Manley (boy); Tony Neil (boy); Charles Stubbs (boy)

Special Sound Effects: Sonovox

Music: Oliver Wallace; Frank Churchill

Lyrics: Ned Washington

Orchestration: Edward Plumb

Story: Joe Grant; Dick Huemer

Story Development: Bill Peet; Aurie Battaglia; Joe Rinaldi; George Stallings; Webb Smith

Story Direction: Otto Englander

Backgrounds: Claude Coats; Al Dempster; John Hench; Gerald Nevius; Ray Lockrem; Joe Stahley

Art Direction: Herb Ryman; Ken O'Connor; Terrell Stapp; Don Da Gradi; Al Zinnen; Ernest Nordli; Dick Kelsey; Charles Payzant

Character Designers: John P. Miller; Martin Provensen; John Walbridge; James Bodrero; Maurice Noble; Elmer Plummer

Directing Animators: Vladimir Tytla; Fred Moore; Ward Kimball; John Lounsbery; Art Babbitt; Wolfgang Reitherman

Animators: Hugh Fraser; Howard Swift; Harvey Toombs; Don Towsley; Milt Neil; Les Clark; Hicks Lokey; Claude Smith; Berny Wolf; Ray Patterson; Jack Campbell; Grant Simmons; Walt Kelly; Josh Meador; Don Patterson; Bill Shull; Cy Young; Art Palmer

Sequence Directors: Norman Ferguson; Wilfred Jackson; Bill Roberts; Jack Kinney; Sam Armstrong

Supervising Director: Ben Sharpsteen

Release Date: October 23, 1941

Running Time: 63½ minutes

THE MOVIE

In an interview in *Funnyworld* in Fall 1977 Joe Adamson cited Dick Huemer on the subject of the origin of the story of *Dumbo*:

I never saw it, but they say it was on a little strip that was given away on a cereal box. Or maybe it was even printed on the outside, I don't know. But it had the basic elements of

the story: the little elephant who had big ears, was made fun of, learned to fly, and was redeemed. All in just a few panels. Well, we took it from there, had a few story meetings, then Joe Grant and I wrote it up a chapter at a time and submitted it to Walt. He used to come down and say, "That's coming along good. We'll make it!"

Disney's two previous non-anthology features had been based on classic tales, one a traditional fairy-tale and the other a famous 19th-century book; currently being worked on was the Disney version of another "great", Felix Salten's 1929 masterpiece *Bambi. Dumbo* was different. Based loosely on a recent book of little pretension to literary fame, it nevertheless touched a chord that few other of the features were as successfully to strike: some of the shorts – such as 1952's *Lambert, the Sheepish Lion* and 1960's *Goliath II*, for example – were to reiterate the theme, but because of their brevity could not hope to do so as effectively. Dumbo is a freak who is initially taunted but eventually makes good: as we cheer for him we are indulging in the potent human activity of supporting the underdog. If the underdog is cute, as Dumbo most definitely is . . . well, so much the better.

The great thing about the movie was that it was short (63½ minutes) and cheap: it cost $812,000 – a huge sum in the early 1940s, but trivial in comparison with the cost of, say, *Pinocchio*. Walt desperately needed a cheap feature: not only were his main movies losing money hand over fist, for reasons beyond his control (there was a war, for example), but also he had had an expensive flop in *Fantasia*. Moreover, the strike at the studio inevitably eroded profits.

The Reluctant Dragon was cheap and basically tacky; *Dumbo* was cheap and brilliant. This was essentially because of its artistry. *Dumbo* might not have the richness of a *Snow White*, a *Pinocchio* or a *Bambi*, but what it did have was a simple and emotive story well told. One radical suggestion was that it was so successful, in terms of costs *vs* revenue, because Walt, shy after the strike, was unwilling to interfere too much, to demand endless workings and reworkings. This is probably unfair to him: what is more likely is that he realized the strength of the story and took the wise artistic decision to stand back a little and let things take their course. In his important book *The Disney Films* (1984 edition) Leonard Maltin cites Ward Kimball on the subject:

Sure, we've done things that have had a lot more finish, frosting, and tricky footwork, but basically, I think the Disney cartoon reached its zenith with *Dumbo*. To me, it is the one feature cartoon that has a foolproof plot. Every story element meshes into place, held together with the great fantasy of a flying elephant. The first time I heard Walt outline the plot I knew that the picture had great simplicity and cartoon heart.

Dumbo was also one of the cheapest films we ever made. It came in for around $950,000 [*sic*] which was damn reasonable, even for 1940, when our cartoon features like *Bambi* climbed into the $2 million or even $3 million bracket. The reason we brought it in for a low price was that it was done quickly and with a minimum amount of mistakes. The story was clear and airtight to everyone involved in the project. We didn't do a lot of stuff over due to story-point goofs. There were no sequences started and then shelved, like in *Pinocchio*. Walt was sure of what he wanted and this confidence was shared by the entire crew. *Dumbo*, from the opening drawing, went straight through to the finish with very few things changed or altered.

We may not agree with Kimball that "the Disney cartoon reached its zenith" with *Dumbo*, but we can certainly say that it was one of Disney's all-time greats. There are few children in the western world today who do not think with affection of the big-eared baby elephant; that is the measure of the movie's success.

THE STORY

Dumbo is a charming tale, and like so many other charming tales is simple. Lots of the circus animals are expecting "newcomers", including Mrs. Jumbo of the elephant herd; however, the messenger storks fail to deliver her baby. This is because the stork charged with the delivery has inefficiently lost his way; however, he eventually tracks down Mrs. Jumbo aboard a circus train hauled by the little engine Casey Jr., first encountered in *The Reluctant Dragon* (▶181). The stork delivers the eagerly awaited

bundle, and all the elephants cackle adoringly over what seems to be the cutest elephant on four legs – until, that is, he sneezes, and his huge ears flop down: then the elephants, except for his loving mother, turn from compliments to mockery.

The train stops and the circus hands pitch the Big Top in a thunderstorm. The following day Dumbo, as he is by now universally called, takes part in the circus parade, a child's doll in a makeshift palanquin on his back. However, he trips over his ears and falls into a puddle, to general derision. The day after that Dumbo is still the object of mockery – especially by a gang led by a particularly vicious bully, Skinny. When Skinny turns from verbal to physical abuse Mrs. Jumbo loses patience and spanks him with her trunk. The crowd goes wild with fear over this "rogue elephant", and Mrs. Jumbo is roped and imprisoned.

Dumbo seems totally alone – for the other elephants are interested in him only as a source of malicious gossip – but then he is befriended by a little mouse, Timothy. Dumbo, says Timothy, could be the star of the circus. But the first attempt at making Dumbo a star proves disastrous: instead of springboarding to the top of a pyramid of elephants he trips over his ears and sends all the teetering elephants flying. In the ensuing chaos the Big Top is wrecked.

In the next town Dumbo, now declared a non-elephant by the others, has been pressganged into being part of the clowns' routine. He must act the part of a baby high up in a burning building: the "joke" is that when he plunges in terror down into the safety net held by the "fire brigade" he goes straight through to land in a vat of plaster. Afterwards the clowns, ignoring a weeping Dumbo, agree that it is the funniest thing they have ever done; Timothy, to comfort the little elephant, takes him to see his imprisoned mother – an encounter which is hardly a bundle of laughs for all concerned.

Meanwhile, back at the circus, the clowns are getting steadily tipsy: they sing the famous song "We're Gonna Hit the Big Boss for a Raise". Michael Wilmington has claimed that

the clowns, incredibly, are malicious caricatures of striking Disney Studio cartoonists executed by the strikebreakers who worked on *Dumbo* [he means the drawings were executed, not the . . .]. Their mercenary mistreatment of Dumbo and their unsympathetic song "We're gonna hit the big boss for a raise," are conservative comments on the labor unrest sweeping through Hollywood at the time.

However, Art Babbitt, who was at the very heart of the strike and who, having little reason to side with Disney, is certainly to be believed, has gone on record as saying that such an accusation is utterly baseless. Nevertheless, the myth persists.

In the course of their drunken carousal the clowns accidentally tip a bottle of

champagne into a water bucket, and naturally it is precisely this water bucket from which Dumbo and Timothy refresh themselves. Soon both are very drunk, and Dumbo hallucinates a great pageant of dancing, trumpeting pink elephants – the most famous scene of the film, and regarded as one of the best feats of animation of all time.

When the two friends wake from their stupor the following morning they find themselves high up in a tree. How could they have got there? Timothy realizes that the only solution must be that Dumbo flew up there – a notion much derided by five passing crows. However, those crows befriend the pair and, seeing Dumbo's nervousness at the prospect of repeating the feat, give him a "magic feather" (in fact, one plucked painfully from the tail of the smallest of them) to bolster his confidence. Sure enough, Dumbo flies.

Back at the circus, Dumbo is now expected to plummet from an even higher burning building for the delight of the clowns and the crowd. Timothy is up there with him, as is the "magic feather", but as they fall the feather is wrenched from Dumbo's clutches, and he panics. Egged on by Timothy, though, at the last moment he pulls out of his dive and goes swooping around the Big Top, at last able to strike back at his many tormentors.

Dumbo is famous. Timothy becomes his much revered manager. Mrs. Jumbo is freed. The tormentors are humiliated. We last see all the circus animals back in the train except Dumbo, who is leading the crows as they fly behind it. Even Casey Jr.'s face is wreathed in smiles. It is definitely a happy ending.

THE CHARACTERS

Dumbo

The characterization in *Dumbo* depends to a far greater extent than is generally true of Disney on verbalization: we immediately identify Timothy, for example, as the type of person he is because of his accent and his use of words, while the gossipy, backbiting elephants are almost entirely depicted in terms of their voices and the unpleasant things those voices are saying. In this context it is curious that the eponymous star of the movie says not so much as a syllable. Curious, that is, until we speculate as to what sort of a voice Dumbo would have had: it is immediately clear that *any* voice for him would be wrong.

For Dumbo is a baby – everyone's baby – and babies do not speak. Thus our heartstrings are especially wrung because we unconsciously apprehend him as the weakest and most defenceless sort of *human being* there is. (Babies bawl their heads off, of course, but that would have been counterproductive!) In fact, the model for Dumbo was somewhat older than might be expected, as Bill Tytla, the animator responsible, explained in an interview with John Canemaker:

> I saw a chance to do a character without doing any cheap theatrics. Most of the expressions and mannerisms I got from my own kid [Peter]. There's nothing theatrical about a two-year-old kid. They're real and sincere. . . . I tried to put all these things in Dumbo.

And well he succeeded, which is why Dumbo is such a popular character.

Like a small child, and like many another Disney hero or heroine, Dumbo is not so much a doer as someone to whom things happen: even his great achievement, that of flight, is initially carried out when he is drunk and therefore a totally passive participant, and when he later repeats the feat it is thanks to Timothy and the Crows. Yet he strikes a chord in almost every watcher: there is hope, his story seems to say, for every one of us, no matter how disadvantaged, to make it to the top, to come good in the end. The message is even more powerful in *Dumbo* than in other similar Disney characterizations, such as the Ugly Duckling (➤43) and Lambert the Sheepish Lion (➤116), because those others only *appear* to be disadvantaged: in fact they are superior in either beauty or strength to their associates. Dumbo, by contrast, despite his ability to fly, will always be a freak elephant.

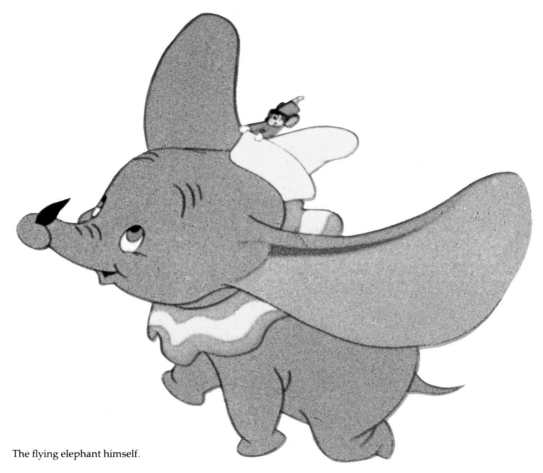

The flying elephant himself.

Timothy Mouse

Timothy Mouse is an illustrious member of a long line of Disney stars: the feisty little fellow who helps the main hero or heroine to succeed. Michael Wilmington has summed it up:

> Timothy, a brash Brooklynese rodent in a garish red-and-gold marching outfit, is a familiar Disney figure. Not only do we see traces of Mickey in his character (his indomitability and his resilient optimism), but he is also a distant cousin of Jiminy Cricket in *Pinocchio* (1940), Gus and Jaq in *Cinderella* (1950), the Seven Dwarfs, even, to an extent, Tinker Bell in *Peter Pan* (1953).

In fact, it is stretching matters a little to compare Timothy with the world's most famous Mouse: virtually everything about him is different. Brilliantly voiced by Ed Brophy, Timothy is very much his own mouse: streetwise yet soft-hearted, he is the single reason why the movie has a happy ending. We are introduced to his essential goodness almost immediately he appears on screen, when the elephants are maliciously gossiping about the incarceration of Mrs. Jumbo and blaming her misfortunes on the unfortunate Dumbo. Timothy steps in and says aggressively: "What's the matter wid his ears? I don't see nothin' wrong with 'em. I tink they're cute!" He then uses classic techniques to terrorize the huge backbiters (elephants are, of

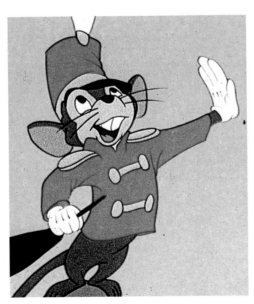

Timothy Mouse, streetwise long before the word had even been invented.

course, legendarily afraid of mice – a legend that seems to have little basis in reality) and to work very hard indeed to befriend an initially recalcitrant Dumbo.

And Timothy it is who has faith in Dumbo when no one else has. He seeks no reward for himself in all this, yet he is pleased enough, towards the end of the movie, to become Dumbo's manager, dressing now not in his mock-ringmaster's uniform but in tweeds and a bowler hat: virtually the last we see of him is a

newspaper photograph of him signing, with a flourish and a quill pen, a big Hollywood contract on Dumbo's behalf. (For completists, the signature is "Timothy Q. Mouse", although it is not on record what the "Q" stands for.)

Cliff Edwards, who had voiced the prototype for Timothy, Jiminy Cricket in *Pinocchio*, was in this movie relegated to the part of one of the crows – albeit the leader of them.

Ringmaster

Most of the characters in *Dumbo* serve as, as it were, backdrops against which Dumbo

The Ringmaster made a brief appearance in *Dumbo*. Interestingly, Disney did not make him into a villain, *à la* Stromboli.

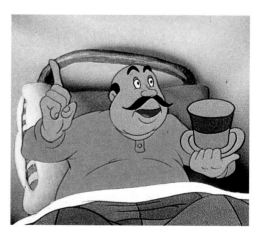

and Timothy perform: the Ringmaster is one such. He is not exactly against Dumbo and Mrs. Jumbo, but neither is he for them: he is the epitome of the person who simply does not understand what is going on. Fattish and habitually clad in a red uniform (like Timothy's) with a starched dickie and a bow-tie, he is simply a boss-figure. It is surprising that all of the commentators who saw in the clowns parodies of the striking animators did not see in the Ringmaster a caricature of Walt: both ideas would have been equally fanciful.

Casey Jr.

It is hard to give a railway engine a personality, yet the Disney people did their damnedest: the way they tried was to give Casey a voice. This voice is deliberately distorted to mix in with the normal sounds of a steam engine, as demonstrated in *The Reluctant Dragon* (➤189). Thus, when Casey puffs his way up a hill, we hear the chuffing transformed into "I think I can, I think I can", to be followed, as he successfully surmounts the summit and starts down the other side, by "I thought I could, I thought I could". Clearly someone in the Disney organization must have been musing during a rail journey!

Messenger Stork

Sterling Holloway, later to become one of the stalwarts of Disney voicing (as for Winnie the Pooh [➤125]), made his first feature appearance in a Disney movie as this character: it is probably his best performance.

the Messenger Stork has to be alert to catch it every time it shows signs of dropping.

Even when he identifies the train in which Mrs. Jumbo is travelling, he displays some difficulty in tracking her down: he even peeks optimistically into the tigers' cage. Finally the elephants beckon him to the right coach by waving their trunks through a hatch in the roof. Then, like any inefficient bureaucrat, he insists that the formalities be observed: Mrs. Jumbo must sign his delivery book, and she must name the newborn on the spot ("Jumbo Jr.," she pronounces, a name that was of course not to stick). As he sings a rousingly appalling version of "Happy Birthday", posing in the train window, a mail hook mercifully snatches him from our sight.

Mrs. Jumbo

Mrs. Jumbo inspires our tears and fears not because of her personality but because of what she represents: she is the mother whom every child dreads losing. Her love for Dumbo is pure and sincere – *she* does not mind that her new son has big ears – yet, thanks to the ignorance or foolishness of the humans of the circus, she is separated from him. Her imprisonment is a trial for Dumbo as much as it is for her.

It is interesting that Mrs. Jumbo is the least strongly characterized of all the elephants in the film. Perhaps the view was that a mother needs little by way of characterization: she is a *symbol* rather than a specific individual. Whether it is deliberate or not, the trick works: audiences weep during the piteous scene when Timothy

brings Dumbo to visit his mother and the song "Baby Mine" is sung.

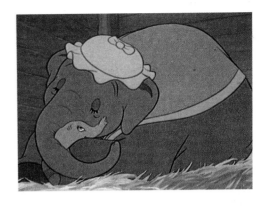

Mrs. Jumbo, initially the only one to offer Dumbo her love. Countless millions of moviegoers later followed suit.

Prissy, Matriarch, Giggles and Catty

We have all of us met these characters before: you can find one or other of them living in every street and, if you are unlucky, you can meet all four of them together. Their names (of which there are several versions extant – "Giddy" and "Fidgety" appear in some accounts) betray their natures: Prissy is exactly that; the Matriarch is the leader of this unholy crew and decidedly a pillar of the establishment; Giggles does, and frequently; Catty is. We first see Prissy in a red headdress and are struck by her gushing, rather twee, voice; the Matriarch, somewhat larger and greyer than the others and with a deeper voice,

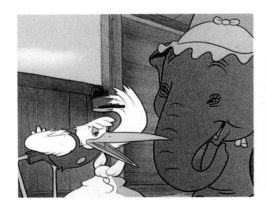

The Messenger Stork, delivering his package.

The Messenger Stork, one of a flight of colleagues, is dressed in a blue mailman's uniform: that is the nearest he gets to normal efficiency, for he is a very scatty bird. On having initial difficulty in locating Mrs. Jumbo in order to deliver her precious bundle, he indulges in some glorious clowning as he sits on a cloud to consult a map: the bundle by his side shows a disconcerting tendency to sink through the cloud and plummet to the ground, and thus

The elephants – each less appealing than the last – found Dumbo's ears hilarious.

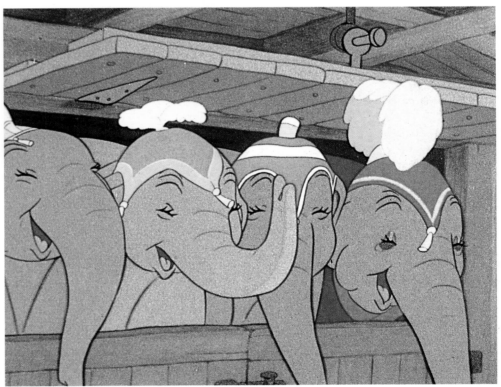

starts off with a pink-violet headpiece; Giggles, a viciously accurate portrayal of a spoilt, pretty but largely brainless individual, is initially seen in blue headgear; Catty, the worst of the lot of them, with her sly, behind-the-hand way of saying everything, starts the movie in a yellow headdress. (The colours of the elephants' accoutrements change during the movie, which makes the task of the keen elephant-spotter problematic.)

That the elephants are obnoxious is apparent from the moment that the newborn baby's ears pop spectacularly into view: seconds before the repulsive quartet had been mooning over the new arrival; now their tone changes, especially when Mrs. Jumbo objects to their derision:

> *Prissy*: After all, who cares about her precious little Jumbo?
> *Catty*: You mean "*Dumbo*"!

And they all chuckle at this *bon mot*. Catty, indeed, is ever keen to find something nasty to say about somebody: in the scene where the elephants are discussing Mrs. Jumbo's incarceration it is she who gleefully breaks the news.

> Girls, girls, listen! Have I got a trunkful of dirt! ... I heard today that they've put her – in solitary confinement!

And when the elephants weep crocodile tears (as it were) over Mrs. Jumbo's misfortunes, it is Catty who blames young Dumbo: "It's all the fault of that little F-R-E-A-K," she spells out within Dumbo's all too understanding earshot.

Joe

The part of Joe is extremely minor. Identified as the elephant trainer in most synopses of the movie, he is described merely as a "flunky" in the cutting continuity (script). He is seen solely in silhouette (his shadow on a tent wall) as the Ringmaster brags to him about his great idea for a pyramid of elephants as an audience-drawing stunt.

Skinny

Skinny is the leader of the band of small boys who tease and terrify the young Dumbo: he is the one who quite justly is spanked by Mrs. Jumbo, to the sound of fervently muttered hurrahs from the cinema audience. With red hair, freckles, buck teeth and an attitude you do not encourage in your own offspring, he is the arch-persecutor of the weak and unfavoured. Uttering the rallying cry of the stupid – "Nyah! Nyah!" – he initially taunts Dumbo by holding up his own coat in imitation of the little elephant's big ears. Later he drags Dumbo painfully around by his tail and then, most sadistically of all, finds humour among his peers when he stretches one of Dumbo's ears out as far as it will go before

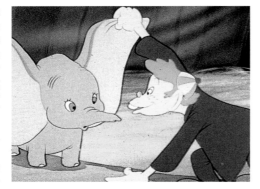

Skinny, the boy who tormented Dumbo and was promptly thrashed by Mrs. Jumbo.

letting it go suddenly – an agonizing trick.

Fortunately, many boys like Skinny grow out of it. Others, sadly, do not.

The Crows

People short of something to protest about often seize on the characters of the crows in *Dumbo*. Here is Richard Schickel:

> There was one distasteful moment in the film. The crows who teach Dumbo to fly are too obviously Negro caricatures.

Yes, the voices and appearances of the crows indicate that they are indeed black Americans but, since they are among the few goodies in a film well populated by baddies, it seems strange that racial offence should be discovered in their depiction: is it somehow all right to caricature whites but not blacks? That surely is a very deep racism, far deeper than anything in the friendly portrayal (by Ward Kimball) of the

crows ... although perhaps naming one of them Jim Crow was a little questionable.

There are five of these birds: **Fat Crow**, **Dandy (or Jim) Crow** (the acknowledged leader of the bunch), **Glasses Crow** (by far the smallest – almost another Dumbo figure in his size and apparent youth), **Preacher Crow** and **Straw Hat Crow**. (The names changed from time to time during the making of the movie.)

As with the elephants, the names largely describe the creatures, although in this case it is their physical appearances rather than their characters which are described. Dandy Crow is smart and hip and has a ubiquitous cigar from which he puffs appropriate smoke signals. Straw Hat Crow has not a full straw hat but merely the brim, which he wears with jaunty confidence. Little Glasses Crow is clearly shortsighted; Fat Crow is, shall we say, a trifle plump; Preacher Crow is a first-rate caricature of a trendy yet benevolent, if slightly disreputable, local minister. All of them are flip with the English language in a delightful way, as evidenced in the introduction to their great song "When I See an Elephant Fly":

> *Glasses Crow*: Did you ever see an elephant fly?
> *Preacher Crow*: Well, I've seen a horse fly.
> *Fat Crow*: Ha! I've seen a dragon fly.
> *Straw Hat Crow*: Aheh, I've seen a house fly.

They are initially sceptical of Timothy's claim that Dumbo might be capable of flight, as would be you or I, but soon they are converts – if not totally believing then at least eager to befriend the mismatched pair. They are among the most warmly delineated characters in the movie, and they are often enough the ones that audiences remember with the greatest fondness.

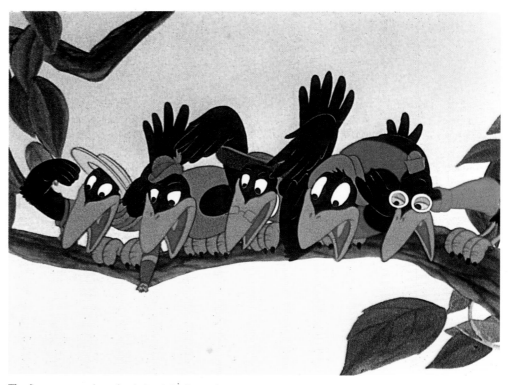

The five crows – who, after being initially scathing, proved to be true friends to Dumbo and Timothy.

BAMBI

Characters:

Bambi; Bambi's Mother; Faline; Aunt Ena; Great Prince of the Forest; Ronno; Friend Owl; Flower; Bambi (baby skunk); Thumper; Mrs. Rabbit; Miss Skunk; Miss Bunny; Mrs. Quail; Mrs. Possum; Mr. Mole; numerous forest animals.

Credits:

Based on Felix Salten's book *Bambi* (1929).

Voices: Bobby Stewart (Bambi); Donnie Dunagan (Bambi); Hardy Albright (Bambi); John Sutherland (Bambi); Paula Winslowe (Bambi's mother); Cammie King (Faline); Ann Gillis (Faline); Mary Lansing (Aunt Ena, Mrs. Possum); Fred Shields (Prince of the Forest); Bill Wright (Friend Owl); Stanley Alexander (Flower); Sterling Holloway (Flower); Peter Behn (Thumper); Tim Davis (Thumper, Flower); Thelma Boardman (Mrs. Quail); Marjorie Lee (Mrs. Rabbit); Marion Darlington; Thelma Hubbard; Otis Harlan; Jeanne Christy; Janet Chapman; Bobette Audrey; Jack Horner; Francesca Santoro; Babs Nelson; Sandra Lee Richards; Dolyn Bramston Cook; Elouise Wohlwend

Music: Frank Churchill; Edward Plumb

Orchestration: Charles Wolcott; Paul J. Smith

Choral Arrangements: Charles Henderson

Conductor: Alexander Steinert

Story Adaptation: Larry Morey

Story Development: George Stallings; Melvin Shaw; Carl Fallberg; Chuck Couch; Ralph Wright

Story Director: Perce Pearce

Art Directors: Thomas H. Codrick; Robert C. Cormack; Al Zinnen; McLaren Stewart; Lloyd Harting; David Hilberman; John Hubley; Dick Kelsey

Backgrounds: Merle T. Cox; Tyrus Wong; Art Riley; Robert McIntosh; Travis Johnson; W. Richard Anthony; Stan Spohn; Ray Huffine; Ed Levitt; Joe Stahley

Supervising Animators: Franklin Thomas; Milton Kahl; Eric Larson; Oliver M. Johnston, Jr.

Animators: Fraser Davis; Bill Justice; Bernard Garbutt; Don Lusk; Retta Scott; Kenneth Hultgren; Kenneth O'Brien; Louis Schmitt; John Bradbury; Joshua Meador; Phil Duncan; George Rowley; Art Palmer; Art Elliott

Sequence Directors: James Algar; Bill Roberts; Norman Wright; Sam Armstrong; Paul Satterfield; Graham Heid

Supervising Director: David D. Hand

Release Date: August 13, 1942

Running Time: 69½ minutes

THE MOVIE

Bambi, released in 1942, had been a long time in the making; in fact, work on it had started as early as 1935 when Walt read Salten's book and decided that it would be the ideal basis for a feature. There was one main problem: the movie rights had already been bought. However, after long negotiation, the director Sidney A. Franklin, who had the rights, agreed to allow Disney to proceed – and even acted on the movie as a sort of part-time advisor. Disney acknowledged this generosity of heart by incorporating prominently in the opening credits the message: "To Sidney A. Franklin, sincere appreciation for his inspiring collaboration."

Although work on *Bambi* was not continuous over its five-year gestation period – Walt had other preoccupations in the form of *Pinocchio* and the others – it rarely came to a complete halt, for four of the Nine Old Men were instructed to keep it ticking over. These four, Johnston, Larson, Kahl and Thomas, must have worked diligently on their part-time assignment, for *Bambi* was largely finished as early as 1941, when the completion of *Dumbo* allowed the *Bambi* project to receive more concentrated attention. Nevertheless, we can gain some appreciation of the timescale of the movie by learning that the composer Frank Churchill, who in collaboration with Larry Morey wrote all of its songs (and many others for Disney), was actually dead by the time of its release, having committed suicide in May 1942.

One of the first things that strikes one about *Bambi* is its incredible naturalistic detail. This had been attained with considerable difficulty and expense. Maine game wardens supplied a pair of four-month-old fawns for the animators to study, and these formed the nucleus of a little zoo created on the lot, but there were soon problems: the fawns became far too tame and well adapted to the luxuries of human civilization – in other words, they were no longer accurate models for deer performing in the wild, being far too pampered and docile. Walt's solution to the problem was to send a pair of cameramen off on a seven-month trip through the Katahdin country of Maine state, with instructions to shoot as much footage as possible of not only deer in the wild but also any other natural scene that might help the animators: fallen logs, pawprints, mountain streams – *anything* that might help the artists. The results of this dedication to accuracy are readily appreciable on screen.

Paradoxically, human models were also used, even though humans never actually appear in the film (although they have a profound effect on the plot). For the scene in which Thumper and Bambi go skating the skaters Donna Atwood and Jane Randolph performed for the cameras.

Not everyone liked the realism which Disney had created: in fact, many critics decreed that by creating a realistic rather than a fantasy world Walt was actually subverting the *raison d'être* of the animated film. *The New York Times* decreed that

> Mr. Disney has again revealed a discouraging tendency to trespass beyond the bounds of cartoon fantasy into the tight naturalism of magazine illustration. ... His central characters are as naturally drawn as possible. The free and whimsical cartoon caricatures have made way for a closer resemblance to life, which the camera can show better.

There is more in the same vein. It is always fascinating how critics tell creative artists what they *ought* to be doing rather than comment discerningly on what they *are* doing. The relevance of the strictures can be gathered from the fact that *Bambi* has so far grossed some $30 million: audiences, although initially deterred by the critics (the film was a financial disaster on first release, partly because of the war), have voted with their wallets.

Bambi has often been described as a very gentle film, which seems to ignore the fact that there are many scenes of accurately depicted natural violence in it: Bambi's fight with Ronno over Faline and the flight from the burning forest are the two obvious examples. Some critics saw fit to castigate Disney precisely because he (and for that matter Salten) gave such an accurate depiction of the unpleasant realities of life in the wild. Lloyd Morris was typical:

> Disney's animal world was one in which violence, conflict, ruthless physical force and utter desperation were normal, accepted elements of experience. It was a world in which kind-heartedness was associated with brutality, in which contempt for the weak prevailed, in which conscience had become a kind of stupidity ... This was a society in which aggression paid out, inhumanity was practical, and power, being right, was always admirable.

We may not *like* the fact that animals often fight others of their own species and kill members of other species, but surely it is the height of illogicality to complain because Disney portrayed animals as they are rather than as we might wish them to be.

Overall, when considering *Bambi*'s reception by the critics during the decades since 1942 rather than merely on the movie's first release, it has had a favourable press – and it is nowadays generally regarded as one of the Disney masterpieces.

THE STORY

The story of *Bambi* is one of the cycle of life.

As dawn breaks in the forest a young rabbit called Thumper brings the news to all and sundry, notably old Friend Owl: a new Prince has been born. This Prince proves to be a young deer called, as decreed by his mother, Bambi. The animals gather to admire the young heir.

A few days later a still rather wobbly Bambi is out with his mother when they reencounter Thumper, who takes it upon himself to teach the fawn various tricks, notably that of speech. Bambi learns a few words, one of which is "flower"; when he finds a little skunk in a bank of flowers and unwittingly calls him this, the skunk gleefully takes on the new name. They play together until a thunderstorm sends them to their separate shelters.

Some weeks later Bambi's mother leads him through the dawn to a meadow where, after initial hesitation, they play together. Thumper and Flower reappear to join in the games, but Bambi also encounters a pretty young girl fawn, Faline. He is startled and shy at first, but soon he and Faline are gambolling happily in the field. In the course of this Faline kisses him, to his immense chagrin. Many other deer come to frolic in the meadow, but then all fall silent with respect as the Great Prince of the Forest appears to inspect his new heir.

As the Great Prince moves off through the forest he detects that Man is near, and he rushes back to warn the rest. Soon all are in flight and, as shots begin to ring out, the Great Prince rescues Bambi, who has become separated from his mother. When later he asks her what that was all about she answers with the single devastating sentence of explanation: "Man was in the forest." The finality with which she says this casts a chill down the spine of any audience.

Winter comes and with it Bambi's first discovery of the joys and perils of snow. He has something else to learn: Thumper takes him out onto the lake in an attempt to demonstrate to him the pleasures of skating on "stiff water". Bambi, however, proves less than adept at this new sport, sliding and stumbling all over the ice. He seems half-convinced when Flower, woken by the two raucous friends, explains the benefits of hibernation.

However, Bambi learns to love the Winter, although as it draws to a close he and his mother become exceedingly hungry. Finally the great day arrives when there is enough grass showing through the snow in the meadow for them to eat. This outing, however, is not to have such a happy ending as their last: once again, Man is in the forest, and as the deer flee shots ring out. When Bambi finds his way home he looks around expectantly for his mother, whom he has assumed to be right behind

him: "We made it! We made it, Mother! We – *Mother*?" Out of the blizzard steps the Great Prince, who solemnly says: "Your mother can't be with you any more. Man has taken her away. Now you must learn to be brave, and learn to walk alone. Come, my son."

Now it is the next year, and Spring has come around once more. Love is very much in the air, a fact which disturbs Friend Owl to distraction, for he finds it difficult to sleep through all the loving birdsong and so forth. He becomes particularly irate when the whole branch on which he is perched begins to vibrate violently; but then he calms down when he discovers the cause: Bambi is rubbing his antlers against the tree to remove the velvet. Gesturing about him at the courting birds, Friend Owl addresses Bambi, Thumper and Flower on the perils of "twitterpation" – something that can happen to any unwitting young creature. The three, horrified, promise that they will never allow themselves to become twitterpated, but as they walk along together first of all the skunk and then the rabbit succumb to the lures of females of their respective species. Even Bambi, disgusted by the others, eventually bumps into a young doe – Faline, of course – and is in turn twitterpated.

On declaring their love for each other the two fall into a romantic dream-sequence. When they emerge from it, though, they discover that a tough young buck called Ronno wants Faline as his mate, and is prepared to fight Bambi over her. After early reverses, Bambi succeeds in defeating his adversary and he and Faline set off to spend their lives together.

One evening that Autumn Bambi detects that something is wrong in the forest. Leaving Faline asleep he goes off into the woods, where he meets the Great Prince. Together they see a distant campfire: "It's Man," explains the Prince. "He is here again. There are many this time. We must go deep into the forest. Hurry! Follow me!"

Bambi rushes back to where he left Faline, but she has gone. He hears her cries of terror in the distance, and dashes to find her: she is being threatened by a pack of brutal hunting dogs. Bambi leaps to her rescue and fights off the dogs so that she can escape. He hurries in pursuit, but as he leaps over a ravine shots ring out and he falls wounded to the ground.

Back at camp the fire is spreading out of control: soon the whole forest is ablaze. The Great Prince forces his way through the smoke and falling embers to find Bambi and make him flee, despite his painful wounds. Finally the two of them swim out to an island in the river, where they find other forest animals cowering for safety; among them is Faline.

The following Spring sees life renaissant in the forest. Both Thumper and Flower now have families of their own, and soon the news is rife that Faline and Bambi, too,

have been blessed with children: two fawns. As Bambi's friends watch mother and young, the Great Prince and Bambi himself survey the scene from a high crag. Soon the older stag nods to Bambi and turns to head off into the forest, leaving him behind as the new Great Prince of the Forest.

THE CHARACTERS

Bambi

As we can see from the summary above, *Bambi* is not a tightly plotted movie in the way that *Dumbo*, for example, is: it depends much more for its effect on the superb animation and the exquisitely executed backdrop of the forest. As with the story, most of the characterization is not profound – one does not find oneself rooting for Bambi in the same way that one does for, say, Dumbo (again) or Snow White. The only really strong characterizations are those of Friend Owl and Thumper. But this lack of depth in the characterization is not important; indeed, it would probably have been a mistake, for the point of the movie is that these are real animals – *any* animals – living in a real forest.

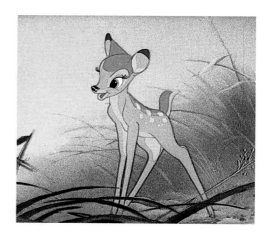

As Bambi grew a little older, he still retained for a while his spindleshanks appearance.

The character of Bambi himself fits in with this scheme. In his early youth he has a full measure of all the charm that a young mammal can display, with his spindly legs and his wide-eyed innocence. His voice, supplied by Bobby Stewart, is childishly cute; as he grows older his voice becomes progressively more mature, being supplied in these later stages of the movie by Donnie Dunagan, Hardy Albright and John Sutherland. Simultaneously he loses his spots and develops an array of antlers, yet throughout the ageing process he nevertheless always seems somehow a very young buck, much lighter than, for example, the Great Prince, even though latterly the two of them are depicted as being much the same in size.

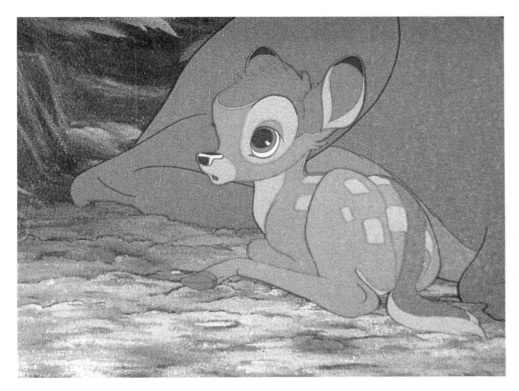

Bambi as a newborn fawn.

Faline

There can be no greater contrast in two such superficially similar characters as between Bambi's mother and the adult Faline. As a young fawn, Faline is a much more dashing and daring version of Bambi, but in many

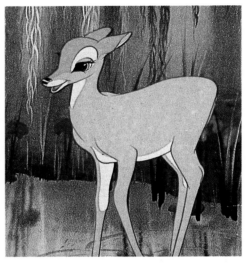

Faline. Bambi initially rejected this little fawn, but as they grew older he realized quite how attractive she was.

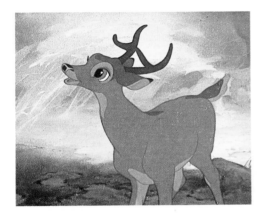

Bambi, approaching adulthood; later he will become a proud stag.

Bambi has no memorable lines to deliver, yet he has nevertheless won a vast band of loyal devotees over the decades.

Bambi's Mother

The clever trick of the portrayal of Bambi's mother in this movie is that we are led to appreciate her in the same way that the young Bambi does, yet Disney avoids the obvious means of doing this – i.e., showing her on screen as if through Bambi's eyes. The effect is a very subtle one, yet clearly it was essential that it be achieved if Disney were to be able to extract the full feeling of Bambi's anguish during the main emotional climax of the film, the mother's death; we should note that likewise her death is not a matter straightforwardly shown on screen, a fact which once again increases the emotional impact of the episode. Of the sequence James Morrow wrote in 1978 that

the ultimate childhood trauma of losing a parent is dramatized with honesty and power. It is these moments, not the occasional kitsch, that audiences actually take away with them. On their indisputable strength rests a sound defense against the charge of schmaltz.

Bambi's mother is, then, in a curious way not a character in herself: the *real* character

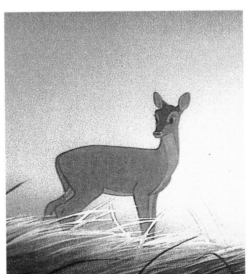

Bambi's mother, whose off-screen death made millions weep.

in the movie is Bambi's perception of her. She has an invariably loving maternal voice, supplied by Paula Winslow, and everything about her physical appearance speaks of gentleness and loving motherhood.

ways she is not an especially feminine figure. Later, when they are young adults and she cheerfully twitterpates him, she is most definitely a female, but while she may have changed in this respect she has retained her advantage over him in terms of quick thinking, daring, dashingness and general force of character; her voice and her mien are in a way still more mature than Bambi's. It is only after the young buck has fought off the challenge of Ronno that he can truly be said to join her in adulthood.

Where Bambi's mother is essentially a placid character – as is Faline's own mother, **Aunt Ena** – the same could never be said of Faline. She is intensely active, whether the activity be playing in the forest or in responding to her own hormones or in using her intelligent, inquisitive brain; she is, to put it bluntly, sexy. She does not share the (literally) doe-like eyes of Bambi's mother; instead, hers are brighter, harder and darker, always with a hint of mischievous laughter behind them: both as

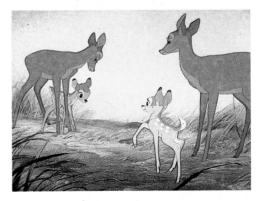

Reading from left to right, Bambi's mother, Bambi, Faline and Aunt Ena (Faline's mother).

a fawn and as a young adult she is giggling as she steals a kiss from Bambi. Yet she can be serious, too, as when she accepts his "proposal of marriage".

Interestingly, in the few seconds during which she is on screen after the birth of her own fawns, she is depicted very much more in accordance with the characterization of Bambi's mother. Clearly the animators felt that it was time that Faline grew out of her coquetry and took on the responsibilities of motherhood, and that this involved her adopting a greater degree of tranquillity, stoicism and pragmatism.

Faline, then, is a very subtly and complexly created character. Although our main focus of attention in the movie is

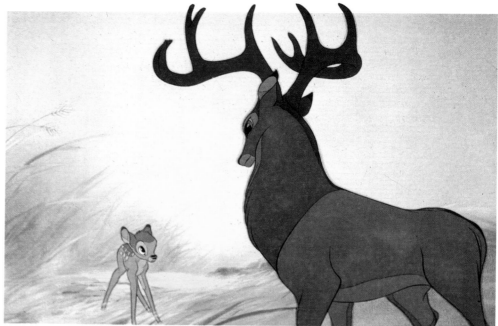

The Old Stag addresses his son.

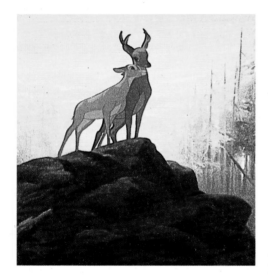

Bambi and Faline, as adult deer, proudly silhouetted against the skyline.

obviously the growth to maturity of Bambi, it is a joy to watch Faline undergoing the same process.

Great Prince of the Forest

The old stag, Bambi's father, serves two functions in the movie. First, he is a symbol of the maturity, wisdom and revered status to which Bambi will one day attain. Second, he performs rather like a Greek chorus, turning up opportunely when things are going wrong to provide Bambi with comment and counsel. Like various others of the ostensibly major characters in *Bambi*, he is not really a character at all. That this was a quite deliberate ploy is evidenced by the old stag's voice, supplied by Fred Shields: it is flat and cipher-like, containing a certain gravity but in truth no real emotion. One presumes that what the Disney people were trying to convey was the fact that in a herd of deer the dominant male, while taking responsibility for his own harem of females, is nonetheless essentially remote from them and even more so from any offspring he might sire upon them.

The importance of the depersonalized voice seems to have been evident to Walt

right from the beginning, for during one of the first story conferences on *Bambi* he said:

> I would like the Old Stag to say what he has to say in a direct way, and in such a voice that Bambi is unable to answer him. What he says will be sort of final. That can be put over through the voice.

It must have been an infernally difficult piece of work for the animators to achieve. As Disney artists they were accustomed to portraying characters in depth – it is the fact that even most of the minor characters are *real* that distinguishes the Disney creations from most of their rivals – and somehow to unlearn this art in order to create a cipher-figure cannot have been at all easy. The voice, obviously, helped, as did the fact that the Great Prince is depicted as aloof and is also almost always slower-moving than the other deer, as if he were somehow operating in a different time-rate. Nevertheless, despite these aids, it was a brilliant feat.

The irony, of course, is that other studios would have given their right arms to be able to create characters that were *not* ciphers!

Ronno

The part of Ronno, the buck whom Bambi fights over Faline, is small yet quite vivid, all the more so as the animators adopted a semi-abstract treatment for large sections of the fight. The striking thing about Ronno is that he is much more *solid* than Bambi: darker in colour and heavier of build, he seems to be definitely heavier and definitely older than our hero. Clearly it was important to portray him in this way, for thereby Disney ensured that our sympathies are doubly engaged on Bambi's side – he is the underdog, triumphing even although the odds are stacked against him.

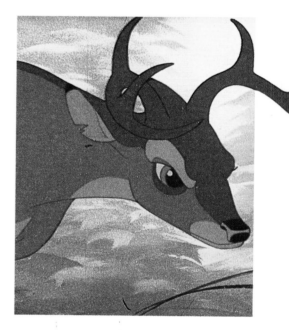

Ronno, who sought to win Faline from Bambi.

Friend Owl

Friend Owl is a straight caricature, but a glorious one. Zany and yet affectionate, he is a sort of kindly misanthrope (if that word may be used in the animal context). Although in some ways it is tempting to see in him a sort of father-figure to the young animals, this is really fallacious: his single attempt at paternal instruction – twitterpation and the necessity of avoiding it – is not only a disaster in practical terms but also, of course, exactly the wrong lesson to teach young animals in Spring, when it is their positive duty to seek mates. No, Friend Owl is not a father-figure: his inclusion in the cast-list is for humorous purposes. That he has a secondary function

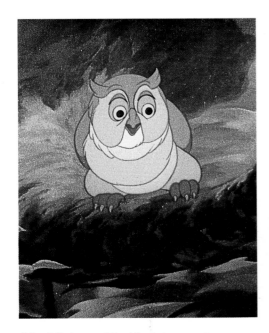

Friend Owl, one of *Bambi*'s glorious comic characters.

– to be a sort of "link" in the story, in the way that a narrator might have been – is almost accidental. He is often at the heart of the action, but he never really affects it in any way.

The depiction of Friend Owl seems to have been rooted in his voice: brilliantly enacted by Bill Wright, it is larger than life. Although in visual terms Friend Owl is not nearly so dramatically caricatured, his behaviour has a similar flamboyance, notably during the twitterpation lecture, when he paces up and down his branch, turning his body around as need be but keeping his head constantly pointing towards the agog figures of Bambi, Thumper and Flower. In fact, this zaniness of his is very important during this scene, which could easily have become too mockably coy about the whole matter of courtship and mating. All in all, though, Friend Owl is in the film simply because he is fun – and funny, as any cinema audience will loudly attest.

Flower

Although Flower is like Thumper intended to be one of the major figures in Bambi's life – he is a childhood pal and the friendship persists into adulthood – his part in the film is only a minor one. It is astonishing that Disney used no fewer than three voices for him (although one of these, the ubiquitous Sterling Holloway, spoke only a few lines).

Flower's role suffers from the fact that Thumper, Bambi's other childhood sidekick, steals the show: it would have been intolerable to have had Flower depicted with anything like the same strength. Indeed, Flower appears in only four short sequences. In the first of these he takes his name from Bambi's mistaken identification of him as a flower. In the second Thumper and Bambi ask him if he is

hibernating which, he tells them, he most certainly is. In the third, although he listens with the others to Friend Owl's twitterpation lecture, he is the first to vanish from our sight as he is adroitly twitterpated by a pretty young female skunk. It is in the fourth and final one that it is brought to us quite how strong the bond between him and Bambi actually is: shyly appearing with his wife and family he introduces one of his progeny, whom he has named **Bambi** in honour of his friend.

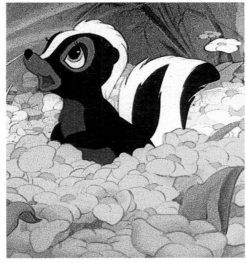

Flower, who took his name from a certain misunderstanding on Bambi's part.

Thumper

Thumper, animated by Ollie Johnston; Frank Thomas and others, is probably the star of the movie. To a great extent this is because of the unconsciously brilliant voicing of the part by young Peter Behn, said to have been discovered by two of the

animators when visiting a friend's house. (David R. Smith has checked with Johnston and Thomas, who say that Behn was instead discovered at an audition. As with so many matters concerning the early Disney movies, memories differ.) The voice is cute, but not in a nauseatingly affected way: it is ingenuous and clearly that of a real child rather than of an adult pretending to be one. Of course, Disney exploited its natural cuteness to the utmost, as in the classic piece of dialogue a few weeks after Bambi's birth:

> *Thumper*: He doesn't walk very good, does he?
> *Mrs. Rabbit*: Thumper!
> *Thumper* (shrugging sadly): Yes Mama.
> *Mrs. Rabbit*: What did your father tell you this morning?
> *Thumper* (as by rote): If you can't say something nice … [thinks hard and fast] … don't say anything at all.

Ironically, at one stage early in the production it was almost decided to drop Behn's voice altogether; fortunately one of the animators recognized how much of Thumper's characterization could be based on it.

"When it comes to the animation," Walt had said in one of the first story conferences, "we can do a lot with the rabbit. He [should have] a certain mannerism that can be drawn. We might get him to twitch his nose." Even Walt could hardly have realized quite how much they would eventually "do" with the rabbit. The mannerism to which Walt referred proved eventually to be Thumper's furious drumming of any available hollow log with his right rear foot – a trait inherited by his entire family, as we discover during the closing stages of the movie.

Thumper was the comic hit of the movie. Here he – typically – stands out in front of the rest of the family. Mrs. Rabbit, also seen here, was noticeable less on screen than in the soundtrack.

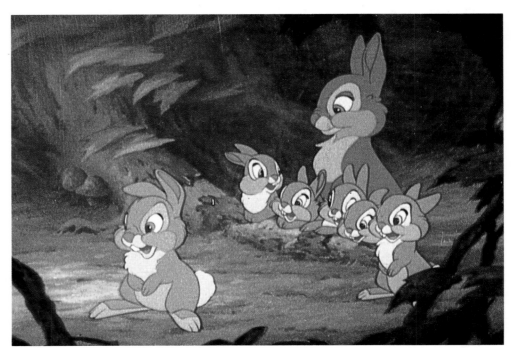

Blue-grey with pink-brown tummy and face, with a fluffy cottony "bib" and the most prominent buck teeth one could imagine, Thumper brings the house down. But it is not simply that we laugh at his antics: we *like* him, too.

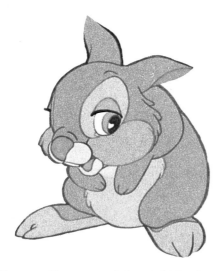

The young Thumper, ready for mischief and impertinence.

Forest Animals

A number of the forest animals are named, although their roles are very minor. There are of course **Miss Skunk** and **Miss Bunny**, who go on to become, respectively, Mrs. Flower and Mrs. Thumper. Also in evidence are **Mrs. Quail**, **Mrs. Possum** and

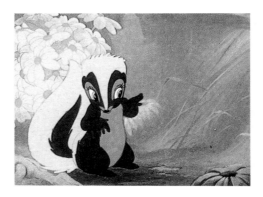

Miss Skunk, whose presence made poor Flower forget his vows of chastity.

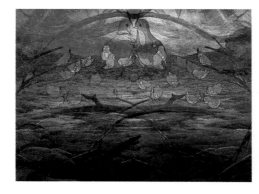

Mrs. Quail, with only a few of her many chicks.

Mr. Mole, Thumper's brothers and sisters (although his father is always merely an off-screen authority figure cited by **Mrs. Rabbit** for reasons of discipline), and countless deer, birds and other animals.

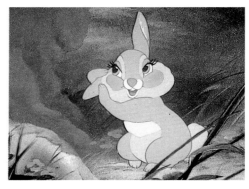

Miss Bunny. If Flower found Miss Skunk alluring, Thumper found Miss Bunny even more so.

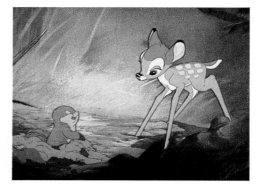

Bambi having a discussion with Mr. Mole.

That this cast of supporting actors should be so vast is a sign of the intricate and painstaking care that went into the making of *Bambi*, and one of the main reasons for the movie's success.

SALUDOS AMIGOS

Characters:

Lake Titicaca Section:
Donald Duck; Llama; Boy with Flute

Pedro Section:
Pedro; Papa Plane; Mama Plane; Signal Tower; Condor

El Gaucho Goofy Section:
Goofy; Horse; Ostrich

Aquarela do Brasil Section:
Donald Duck; José (Joe) Carioca

Credits:

Voices: Clarence Nash (Donald Duck); Fred Shields (narrator); Frank Graham (narrator); José Oliveira (Joe Carioca); Pinto Colvig (Goofy)

Musical Director: Charles Wolcott

Music: Ed Plumb; Paul Smith

Songs: Ned Washington; Charles Wolcott; Ary Barroso; Zequinta Abreu; Aloysio Oliveira; Ervin Drake

Story Research: Ted Sears; William Cottrell; Webb Smith

Story: Homer Brightman; Ralph Wright; Roy Williams; Harry Reeves; Dick Huemer; Joe Grant

Art Supervision: Mary Blair; Lee Blair; Herb Ryman; Jim Bodrero

Foreign Supervision: Jack Cutting

Backgrounds for *El Gaucho Goofy* inspired by F. Molina Campos

Backgrounds: Hugh Hennesy; Al Zinnen; Ken Anderson; McLaren Stewart; Al Dempster; Art Riley; Claude Coats; Dick Anthony; Yale Gracey; Merle Cox

Animators: Fred Moore; Ward Kimball; Milt Kahl; Milt Neil; Wolfgang Reitherman; Vladimir Tytla; Les Clark; Bill Justice; John Sibley; Hugh Fraser; Paul Allen; John McManus; Andrew Engman; Dan MacManus; Josh Meador

Sequence Directors: Bill Roberts; Jack Kinney; Hamilton Luske; Wilfred Jackson

Associates: Gilberto Souto; Alberto Soria; Edmundo Santos

Release Date: February 6, 1943

Running Time: 42 minutes

THE MOVIE

After *Bambi* Disney was not to make another full-length feature story until *Cinderella*, in 1950: his next nine movies comprised six anthologies of shorts or featurettes and three films that, while they contained sections of animation, are essentially live-action.

The first in the series of anthologies was *Saludos Amigos*, and it had a rather tangled genesis. In 1941 times were troubled for the Disney studio. Thanks to the initial unprofitability of most of its first four features the company was in some financial difficulties and, although the Bank of America was generously forbearing from turning the screws too tightly, one cannot rely on bankers' generosity forever. When Walt was approached by the office of the Coordinator of Inter-American Affairs in the US State Department and asked if he would go on a goodwill trip to South America, where many Italians and Germans had settled and where there was a fair amount of pro-Axis feeling, he was initially unkeen: he claimed not to be good at such social-political affairs. If he were going to research some movies, on the other hand ... The upshot was that the Government offered to provide a financial guarantee for the trip and the making of four or five shorts with South American themes. This was good news indeed.

There was another reason in favour of the excursion. The studio was in the thick of a bitter and extended strike, which had taken on a fair element of direct personal confrontation between Walt and the strikers, who he felt had betrayed his trust. It was widely believed within the company that if Walt were off the scene for a while this might provide a much needed cooling-off period, and indeed the strike was settled in his absence.

He and his party visited several South American countries, being lionized in all of them. The reason why the feature *Saludos Amigos* was released rather than simply its four constituent shorts is unclear – accounts vary – but it was certainly fortunate that Walt had with him a 16mm camera, which had been used to make some souvenir film of the trip. This film proved to be of sufficient quality to be used as a sort of live-action framework for the animated shorts.

Saludos Amigos broke all cinema records in the South American countries in which it was released. At home, the critics either liked it or loved it, but most of them loved it, and it performed respectably. Certainly Disney had no need to call on the Government's financial guarantees. It is rarely seen these days (although the shorts have been released individually), and this is probably both because it was a child of its time and because it is extremely short for a feature – a mere 42 minutes.

It is pleasing to record a notice that appears in the movie's credits:

With sincere appreciation for the courtesy and cooperation shown us by the artists, musicians and our many friends in Latin America.

Walt Disney

THE STORY

Saludos Amigos does not really have a story as such: the cartoons are linked only by their all being set in South America, and the intervening live footage is largely just a record of the trip. Also of note are the various watercolour sketches of scenes interspersed here and there among the travelogue.

THE CHARACTERS

Donald Duck

Donald Duck was chosen to play such a prominent part in this and the other Disney South American movie on the basis of his voice, which provided a way of getting around the language problem. Since his speech is virtually incomprehensible even in one's native tongue, the animators had to develop various techniques of pantomime and "body language" in order to convey his meaning. Yet Donald is not dumb: while one may not understand the words it is generally easy to identify the general tenor of his emotions; in order to understand a totally silent character, such as Dopey, one requires clues provided by the dialogue of the characters around him. All in all, then,

Donald was reckoned to be easily the most intelligible of the Disney gang to a non-English-speaking audience.

Donald features in two of the animated sections: *Lake Titicaca* and *Aquarela do Brasil*.

The gags in the former are almost exclusively visual as the Duck interacts (if one may put it thus politely) with both the environment and the native Peruvians. What happens to him is narrated much like a Goofy "how to" short: the narration consists of instructions on how to cope with being a tourist in Peru. In one memorable moment, as Don dangles from the wreckage of a high rope bridge the narrator soothingly says: "Above all, one should never lose one's temper." The response from Donald may be imagined – or, perhaps, should not be.

Two minor characters in this short are the **Boy with Flute** and, more notably, the **Llama**. As the Boy plays his instrument the Llama which Donald has hired to take him across the mountains dances; when Donald attempts to emulate it the Llama is visibly nauseated. It is with the Llama that Donald crosses the rope bridge mentioned above, and it is as a result of the competition between its obstinacy and Donald's hot temper that the bridge is largely demolished. Here is one tourist who, it seems, will not recall his South American trip with relish.

However, Donald has a better time of it in *Aquarela do Brasil*, perhaps because he prefers the other country but more probably because it is in this short that he first makes the acquaintance of José Carioca.

In many ways, just as *Saludos Amigos* can be seen as a warm-up for 1945's *The Three Caballeros* (➤208), so Donald's role in the former movie can be seen as a practice for his much more central role in the latter.

Pedro

Pedro introduced a wholly new cast of characters.

Once upon a time in Santiago there was a little airport from which the airplanes flew out to fetch the mail back over the Andes from Mendoza. The family of aircraft that lived there numbered three: Pedro, Papa Plane and Mama Plane. Also on the airfield is a **Signal Tower**, which is capable of pseudo-human vocalizations and certainly pseudo-human facial expressions.

Pedro we first see sucking petroleum from a nipple on a fuel line. He is very definitely a baby airplane: he has huge eyes and an expression of such trusting, innocuous naivety that even Goofy might have worried. His parents are rather larger versions of himself and endowed with symbolically male and female attributes.

One day **Papa Plane** cannot go out to fetch the mail – he has a "cold in his cylinder-head" – and neither can **Mama Plane** – she has "high oil-pressure" and so would not be able to stand the altitude. Clearly it is up to little Pedro, who unlike his

Pedro, the baby airplane, getting a little top-up before taking off to do battle with the elements.

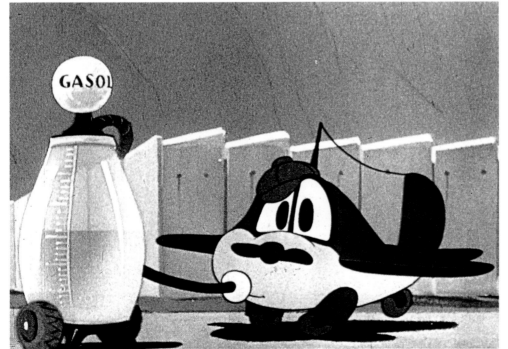

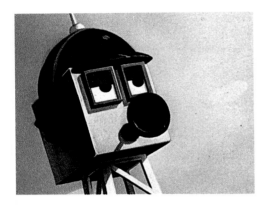

The Signal Tower in the *Pedro* section of *Saludos Amigos* appeared only briefly, but was nevertheless a forceful character.

parents does not speak during the short, to fulfil the family obligation. He is clearly terrified by the prospect, but metaphorically shrugs and girds up his loins to attempt the feat.

The trip out to Mendoza goes calmly, and he picks up the mail without a hitch. With a satchel of mail slung jauntily over his right

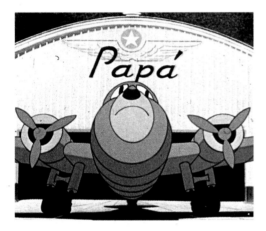

Papa Plane, all ready to take off – only he can't.

wing (although in one shot the animators forget to include the satchel!), Pedro sets off for home. *En route* he enters a physical argument with a fierce **Condor**, and as a result takes himself away off course, within

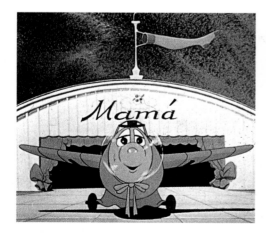

Mama Plane might have done the mail-run, but like Papa Plane she was incapacitated.

sight of the dreaded Aconcagua mountain which, according to the story, has "the face of a leering monster": it certainly looks that way on screen. Thunder and lightning fill the sky, and as Pedro battles pluckily onward the narrator advises him to drop his mail package and climb above the storm. Pedro declines to drop the mail, but he does attempt to soar upwards above the storm; sadly, however, he starts to run out of gas.

We leave him there, and find ourselves some while later back at the Santiago airfield, where Mama Plane and Papa Plane have been driven to the conclusion that Pedro is long dead – yet another victim of the cruel Aconcagua. However, for reasons which are not explained (magic, we must assume), he finally succeeds in making it home – although his upside-down landing is perhaps not as graceful as he might have hoped – to a tumultuous welcome from his parents and the Signal Tower. He is certainly Hero of the Day.

And now they come to examine the satchel of mail which he has brought through the valley of the shadow of death: it proves to contain but a single postcard, whose vital message is

Having wonderful time, wish you were here.

"Well," as the narrator sums up, "it *might* have been important."

Pedro is one of those Disney characters who, while in fact a nonsentient machine, yet succeeds in inspiring our sympathy and our support; another classic example is Little Toot (➤**227**). In his *Not So Long Ago* (1949) Lloyd Morris went rather over the top about this:

Disney made audiences roar with laughter by endowing such inanimate objects as steam-shovels and rocking chairs with human emotions. Was he not depicting a world in which scientists would speculate about the analogies between electronic "thinking machines" and the human brain? His pictures were pure fantasy, and almost pure fable, but what they reported about twentieth-century existence afforded little warrant for optimism or complacence. That they seemed so funny to so many Americans was, in itself, socially

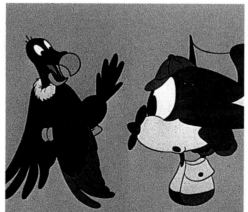

The Condor made it difficult for Pedro to take his mail across the Andes.

significant. It indicated the extent to which a mood of disillusion had overtaken the nation. It testified that an old faith was in temporary eclipse, and that a traditional dream had, for the time, ceased to be potent.

Perhaps more probably, the studio anthropomorphized airplanes and tugs and steam-shovels and rocking chairs with the same amount of profound metaphysical ponderings as when it was giving human characteristics to ducks and mice and trees and not-quite-certains like Goofy. In the Disney fantasy world *everything* is capable of being "humanized". In the process some charming machine-human characters were created, and Pedro is one of them.

Goofy

Thanks to magic, we are told, Goofy is drawn from Texas to be a gaucho in Uruguay. Still no doubt suffering from the bruises he incurred in *How to Ride a Horse* in 1941 (➤**190**), he is going to demonstrate to us the art of failing to survive on the pampas.

His **Horse** in this short, however, is even more of a doughty adversary than in the earlier movie: although it greets the Goof with a liquidly tender kiss, it proves thereafter not to be an easy customer. When it bolts he snares it, using a lasso, with what he clearly hopes is the calm grace of a superbly trained athlete, but unfortunately the beast just keeps on running. Goofy, dragged along behind, is firmly whammed into a tethering post and then, as the still-lassoed Horse runs around in circles, is pinioned there.

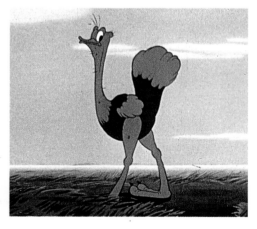

The Ostrich which Goofy had cause to curse in the *El Gaucho Goofy* section of *Saludos Amigos*.

It seems that Goofy, as usual, just cannot win. Later the narrator tells us that at night the gaucho can use his saddle as a bed, and we see Goofy practising just this, although unfortunately he has omitted to remove the saddle from the Horse. His mount, moreover, on hearing the word "bed" gives an eager repetition of it – "*Bed?*" – and promptly turns over so that it is comfortably couched on top of the saddle ... which in turn is on top of Goofy.

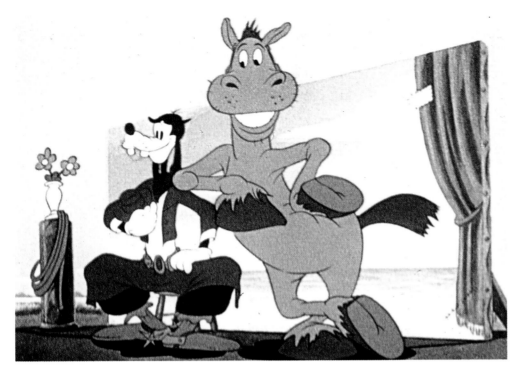

Goofy's horse in *Saludos Amigos* seemed almost less respectful than Percy in *The Reluctant Dragon*.

Of course, it is ridiculous to think of Donald being upstaged by *anyone*, but José Carioca comes as close as anybody could, being if anything an even more forceful character than Donald himself. In the sequence in which he appears, *Aquarela do Brasil*, we meet him first as he presents his card to the Duck; he is delighted to meet at last the famous "Donaldo Duck", but it is a little hard to work out what he is saying because his Portuguese is rapid to excess. He has a bow-tie, a yellow jacket, a big beaky nose (for obvious reasons), earth-coloured eyes, green plumage (brown lower down) and a tail formed from a single red feather set between two green ones. Of great importance to his general rig-out is his umbrella, which he impresses Donald by playing like a flute; when Don tries to repeat

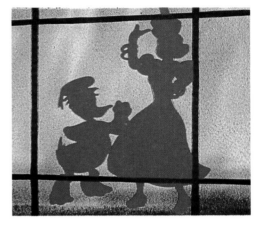

Donald tries his best to look *macho* as he dances with a samba-mad lady in *Saludos Amigos*. Well, some of us have tried more successfully . . .

Also featured in the short is an **Ostrich** (more formally, a rhea) which he chases, whirling his bolas, on his for once cooperative horse. At normal speed we see what appears to be a perfect capture, but then the narrator suggests that we watch the scene again in slow motion to observe the serene beauty of the gaucho's actions. Sadly, what we see in slow motion is the true chaos of the affair, with Goofy managing to get both himself and his steed completely entangled in the bolas.

Clearly this short is really a part of the great "how to" series. Goofy must have been attractive as a character for much the same reason as Donald – his dialogue consists largely of grunts and nonverbal mumblings, and those are much the same in any language.

One interesting technique employed in the short is the use of the wipe-over to change one scene to the next. Often enough, the edge of the wipe-over drags or pushes the characters into the next scene.

José (Joe) Carioca

Based on a traditonal Brazilian character – the central figure of many of the country's jokes – the parrot José Carioca appeared in this feature, in 1945's *The Three Caballeros* (where he is separately discussed [➤**211**]), and in 1948's *Melody Time*, although he has also had an extensive career in the comics. That his movie career should have been cut so short (only in *The Three Caballeros* does he have a central role) is astonishing, because at the time he was regarded by both critics and public alike as being a major new star in the Disney firmament. Some critics went even further, such as the reviewer in *Collier's Magazine* for December 19, 1942:

As an indication of the warmth of Disney's feeling for our Latin-American neighbours, he has allowed Joe Carioca to top Donald Duck, a pretty smart fellow himself. ... There is some doubt about using Donald Duck again [in a South American movie] because of his accent. Argentinians swore he was speaking Portuguese; the Brazilians were just as positive it was Hungarian; some keen-eared listeners even suspected it was profanity. Donald says nothing, being still too sore about [being upstaged by] Joe Carioca.

Donald with his new-found friend José Carioca, described as the "Brazilian Jitterbird" by Disney publicity. This South American character came close to upstaging the Duck.

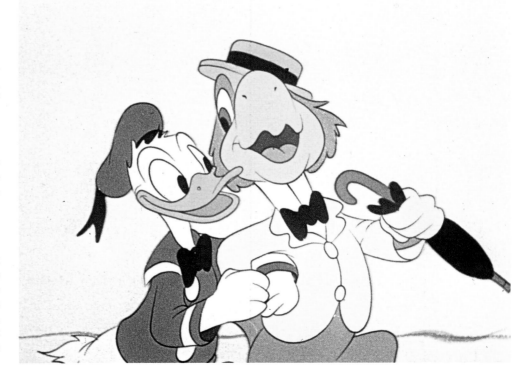

the manoeuvre all that happens is that the umbrella opens.

Important in the animation of this short is the use of a paintbrush, wielded by an off-screen character, to paint in backgrounds as the two newfound friends travel along. The most striking example of this occurs when the two are walking down a flight of stairs: the paintbrush fills in each next step just before the two arrive on it.

There are plenty of gags between Donald and this "Brazilian Jitterbird", as a Disney publicity document described him. Perhaps the best is when José sits down with the Duck at a café table and polishes off a glass of South American hooch in a single gulp; when Donald tries the same trick his breath is so alcohol-laden that he is able to ignite José's cigar with a single puff.

The short is set largely at the Rio *Carnaval*. José Oliveira (who also voices Carioca) sings the song "Aquarela do Brasil" ("A Watercolour of Brazil"), and the movie steadily travels towards its close.

VICTORY THROUGH AIR POWER

Characters:

Orville and Wilbur Wright; Alberto Santos-Dumont; Eugene Ely; Calbraith P. Rodgers; Sir John Alcock; Arthur Brown; Charles Lindbergh; Pierre and Fritz; The Eagle and the Octopus

Credits:

Based on the book *Victory Through Air Power* (1942) by Major Alexander de Seversky

Narrator: Art Baker

Starring: Alexander P. de Seversky

Sound Recording: C. O. Slyfield; Lodge Cunningham

Film Editor: Jack Dennis

Music: Edward Plumb; Paul J. Smith; Oliver Wallace

Story Direction: Perce Pearce

Story Adaptation: T. Hee; Erdman Penner; William Cottrell; Jim Bodrero; George Stallings; José Rodriguez

Art Direction (live action): Richard Irvine

Colour Direction (live action): Natalie Kalmus

Colour Associate (live action): Morgan Padelford

Interior Decoration (live action): William Kiernan

Art Directors (animation): Herbert Ryman; Don Griffith; Donald Da Gradi; Bill Herwig; Tom Codrick; Cliff Devirian; Charles Philippi; Glen Scott; Elmer Plummer; Karl Karpé

Backgrounds: Al Dempster; Dick Anthony; Claude Coats; Ray Huffine; Robert Blanchard; Joe Stahley; Nino Carbe

Animation Supervision: Dave Hand

Animators: Ward Kimball; Josh Meador; John Lounsbery; Carleton Boyd; Hugh Fraser; Bill Justice; George Rowley; Ed Aardal; John Sibley; John McManus; Norm Tate; Oliver M. Johnston, Jr.; Vladimir Tytla; Marvin Woodward; Harvey Toombs

Sequence Directors: Clyde Geronimi; Jack Kinney; James Algar

Director of Photography: Ray Rennahan

Scenes with de Seversky directed by: H. C. Potter

Production Manager: Dan Keefe

Release Date: July 17, 1943

Running Time: 65 minutes

THE MOVIE

Right at the outset we are told the *raison d'être* of *Victory Through Air Power*:

Our country in the past has struggled through many storms of anguish, difficulty and doubt. But we have always been saved by men of vision and courage, who opened our minds and showed us the way out of confusion. One of the men who foresaw the present mortal conflict, who tried desperately to awaken and prepare us for the issue, but who was ignored and ridiculed, was General Billy Mitchell. So to the memory of Billy Mitchell, pioneer and prophet of air power, and to the gallant airmen of America, this picture is dedicated.

This is a movie quite different from anything else produced by the Disney studio: it is simultaneously a documentary and a feature-length piece of propaganda. It was born from Walt's reading de Seversky's book and deciding that the man had something important to say about the way in which the Allies should conduct the war against the Axis; so eager was Walt to convey this cinematographically to the public that from start to release the project took a mere 14 months. The fact that de Seversky's hypothesis has since been shown to be wrong – strategic bombing, according to countless studies, is not an effective military technique – should not be taken as an excuse to belabour either Disney or de Seversky: the theory was on the face of it pretty good, and it was only after the practical experiments that its flaws could be detected. (What is curious is that the theory is still, decades later and despite all the evidence, accepted by many as what Richard Schickel calls "revealed truth".) There can be no doubt that Walt and his staff acted in the best of faith: they believed fervently that they were acting in the interests of democracy against fascism.

Although Disney by this stage had been commissioned by the US Government to make a fair number of propaganda films, *Victory Through Air Power* was not one of them; indeed, if anything it flew against the prejudices of some of the studio's most important contacts within the Government, who regarded "Sasha" de Seversky as something of a crank and believed firmly in the military supremacy of the battleship (they proved to be as wrong as he was). However, a copy of the movie was seen by British premier Winston Churchill, and he was apparently much impressed. However, efforts to let President Roosevelt view it were foiled by Admiral Leahy at the White House – one of those military top-dogs who believed that de Seversky was nothing more than a monomaniacal eccentric. In 1943, though, Churchill asked Roosevelt at the Quebec Conference if he had seen the movie; on it being discovered that FDR had not, a print was flown by rapid fighter plane up from New York to Quebec. The two men watched it several times, and it was shown also to the Joint Chiefs of Staff. The net result was, according to Bob Thomas and others, that the D-Day invasion was supplied with sufficient back-up bombers. This conclusion, alas, lacks something: de Seversky's preoccupation was *strategic* bombing, which the USA barely used in Europe, rather than *tactical* bombing, which they used a great deal and with great success, and *support* bombing, which was what they used for D-Day. It is legitimate to assume, however, that Churchill was much more impressed than Roosevelt, for Britain made extensive, if counterproductive, use of strategic bombing during World War II.

Discussion of *Victory Through Air Power* would be incomplete without mention of another proposed feature movie, *The Gremlins*, centred on World War II; it was to be based on a short story sent to the studio by a then little known writer, Roald Dahl. The gremlins of the title were of course the neomythological and invisible creatures said to bedevil the efforts of the RAF, and Walt seems to have leaped on them as an opportunity to combine fantasy (his great natural forte) with topical wartime relevance. After a while, however, the project foundered – perhaps because the prerelease publicity came far too early and was far too effective. The USA was saturated with the idea of these gremlins and they became a whimsical fad: there was even a fashion for women to wear "gremlin hats". Then, after a year, in 1943 everyone was sick of them. By that time the project was still hardly off the ground, essentially because no one could think of a gripping plot, and Walt had the good sense to pull the plug on the whole thing.

THE CHARACTERS

Almost all of the animated characters in this movie appear in an early section of it entitled *History of Aviation*; the only noteworthy exceptions are The Eagle and The Octopus. All of the animation is very simple – "minimal" – by Disney standards: Walt was more concerned to get the movie out than to present a great work of art.

Pioneering Aviators

The most important animated characters are, as one might expect, **Orville and Wilbur Wright**. We see them as they make several attempts to fly and then on that famous day, December 17, 1903, finally succeed. Orville, the pilot, has a droopy moustache and wears a cap; Wilbur, his brother, whose job is to steady the wing, is depicted as much more of a city slicker – clean-shaven and wearing a bowler hat and a black suit. Also of interest in this sequence are the various independent witnesses to the Wrights' several attempts at flight: at first these five worthies are manifestly bored to tears, but suddenly their ennui turns to amazement as the aircraft finally achieves its epoch-making journey: in the

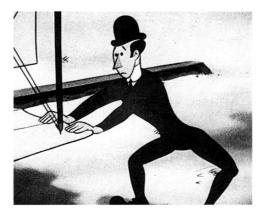

landing on the deck of a ship; **Calbraith P. Rodgers** making the first transcontinental flight; **Sir John Alcock** and **Arthur Brown**, and then **Charles Lindbergh**. In all cases aside from the Wrights all we see are fleeting moments on the screen.

Pierre and Fritz

These two doughty fighters appear in various incarnations; needless to say, one is French and the other German. They demonstrate to us the development of relations between airborne foes from the initial World War I stages, when they waved in comradely fashion at each other, to the latter World War II phases, when they used sophisticated gadgetry to blast each other out of the skies and burn each other alive. A high moment is probably that when Fritz first tries to fire a machine-gun through the blur of his propeller: he shears the blades off close to the axle and plummets in a cloud of smoke.

Some of the scenes between Fritz and Pierre would be genuinely funny were it to

be, say, Donald Duck dropping to the ground: we know that moments later Donald would be picking himself up, dusting off his charred feathers and his bruises, and going off on the rampage again. As it is, because Pierre and Fritz represent all the gallant young men who died in agony in aerial combat, any modern viewer must feel a deep sense of unease when viewing these scenes – as did a number of the critics (notably James Agee) when the movie was first released.

The Eagle and The Octopus

While there is a surprising amount of animation in *Victory Through Air Power* – much more than the standard texts might lead one to believe – there is long gap, right until the very end of the movie, before any further nameable characters appear. These two are the American **Eagle** and the Japanese **Octopus**: it was already clear to Disney and de Seversky that it was the Japanese, rather than the Germans, who were the real threat to the USA. These two beasts engage in a symbolic fight, the Eagle obviously being the victor – on the basis that the USA has followed de Seversky's advice. The Eagle then flies off to perch on the top of a flagpole from which depends the "Stars and Stripes".

If anything, the depiction of these two animals may have dulled the sharp edge of Disney's propaganda sword, for if anything one's sympathies tend to lie with the poor floundering Octopus rather than the cruelly predatory Eagle. But this is to take a modern view: in the 1940s Americans, for the best of reasons, wanted to see their side win over what were indeed truly evil enemies.

Orville (below) and Wilbur (above) – the Wright Brothers, not perhaps as they looked in history but as they appeared in Victory Through Air Power.

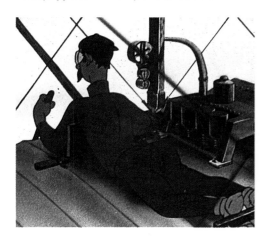

air for 12 seconds and flying a grand total of some 120 feet.

Other historical highlights are picked out, and sometimes we have brief glimpses of the aviators involved: **Alberto Santos-Dumont**, making the first European heavier-than-air flight in 1906; **Eugene Ely** in 1910 first making a take-off from the deck of a ship and then, a couple of months later, performing the "corollary" of this feat by

The American Eagle duels with the Japanese Octopus in the closing stages of Victory Through Air Power.

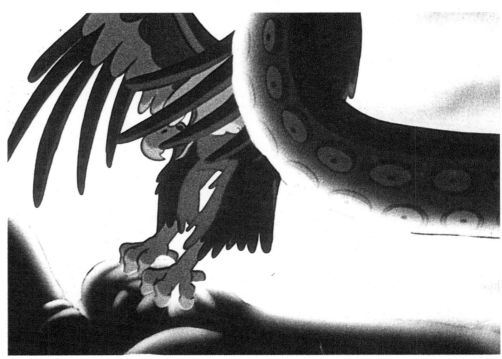

THE THREE CABALLEROS

Characters:

Donald Duck

The Cold-Blooded Penguin Section:
Pablo; Neptune

The Flying Gauchito Section:
The Gauchito; The Burrito

Baia and *La Piñata* Sections:
Panchito; José (Joe) Carioca; Aracuan Bird

Credits:

Live Characters: Aurora Miranda; Carmen Molina; Dora Luz

Voices: Clarence Nash (Donald Duck); José Oliveira (José Carioca, Aracuan Bird); Joaquin Garay (Panchito); Frank Graham (narrator); Fred Shields (narrator); Sterling Holloway (narrator)

Process Effects: Ub Iwerks

Process Technician: Richard Jones

Technical Adviser: Gail Papineau

Sound Recording: C. O. Slyfield

Film Editor: Don Halliday

Music Direction: Charles Wolcott; Paul J. Smith; Edward Plumb

Songs by: Manuel Esperon; Ary Barroso; Agustin Lara; Charles Wolcott; Ray Gilbert

Musical Performances: Nestor Amaral; Almirante; Trio Calaveras; Ascencio del Rio Trio; Padua Hills Players

Choreography: Billy Daniels; Aloysio Oliveira; Carmelita Maracci

Story: Homer Brightman; Ernest Terrazas; Ted Sears; Bill Peet; Ralph Wright; Elmer Plummer; Roy Williams; William Cottrell; Del Connell; James Bodrero

Layout: Donald Da Gradi; Yale Gracey; Hugh Hennesy; Herbert Ryman; McLaren Stewart; John Hench; Charles Philippi

Technicolor Colour Direction: Natalie Kalmus

Technicolor Colour Associate: Morgan Padelford

Colour Consultant: Phil Dike

Backgrounds: Albert Dempster; Art Riley; Ray Huffine; Don Douglass; Claude Coats

Art Direction: Richard F. Irvine

Art Supervision: Mary Blair; Ken Anderson; Robert Cormack

Photography: Ray Rennahan

Animators: Ward Kimball; Fred Moore; Eric Larson; John Lounsbery; Les Clark; Milt Kahl; Hal King; Bill Justice; Frank Thomas; Oliver M. Johnston, Jr.; Harvey Toombs; Milt Neil; Bob Carlson; Marvin Woodward; John Sibley; Don Patterson

Special Effects Animation: Josh Meador; George Rowley; Edwin Aardal; John McManus

Sequence Direction: Clyde Geronimi; Jack Kinney; Bill Roberts

Brazilian and Spanish Supervision: John Cutting

Associates: Gilberto Souto; Aloysio Oliveira; Sidney Field; Edmundo Santos

Director in South America: Harold Young

Production Manager: Dan Keefe

Assistant Production Supervision: Larry Lansburgh

Production Supervision and Direction: Norman Ferguson

Release Date: February 3, 1945

Running Time: 71 minutes

THE MOVIE

Walt seems to have decided that he had learned a number of lessons from 1943's *Saludos Amigos* (➤**202**), one of his few feature movies to have made any money by this stage. It had been profitable for a number of reasons including the fact that it was essentially an anthology of shorts: it was far cheaper to make a collection of shorts each with only a limited number of characters and with comparatively simple background detail than to animate a full-length feature such as *Bambi*, where virtually every scene is packed with birds, trees, animals, raindrops ... Another lesson to be learned was that there was money in South American movies: with much of Disney's traditional export market closed off by the war, it made sense to pander to the export market that still was available. Again, *Saludos Amigos* had interested Walt in the possibility of exploiting situations in which animated characters interacted directly with live actors. A further (and possibly false) lesson was that anthologies were popular – Disney was to experiment with them for some years. Finally, although it was generally believed around the studio that the character of Donald Duck could not sustain a full-length feature, it was obvious that his massive popularity did fill cinemas.

As a result of all these factors *The Three Caballeros* came into being. In it Disney pulled out all the technical stops, and it is a marvel of special-effects wizardry as well as a triumph of animation. Oddly, Walt himself disagreed: in a 1945 article Frank Daugherty cited Walt as declaring that he thought the movie suffered from "a severe lack of talent", blaming the draft and wartime economies for this. In fact, if anything *The Three Caballeros* suffers from a severe surfeit of talent: both soundtrack and screen are so packed with devastating, quick-fire action that one's head is pounding by the time the movie ends.

Perhaps the talent that Walt declared lacking was that of toning the whole thing down a little, thereby allowing the quieter moments to act more effectively as a showcase for the various moments of technical brilliance.

The interaction between live action and animation was something Walt had not really attempted since, years before, the Alice Comedies – and there was a slight difference. In the Alice Comedies a live actress is introduced into a cartoon world, whereas in *The Three Caballeros* animated characters are introduced into the real world. (Decades later, a critic who had best remain nameless claimed that this was first achieved in 1977's *Pete's Dragon* [➤**304**], but in fact Disney had done it a number of times before: 1947's *Fun and Fancy Free* is another example.) In *The Three Caballeros* it was decided that the best way of achieving the effect was to use rear projection of the animated characters onto a 14ft by 20ft screen, with the live actors performing on a stage in front of this. Various technical problems had to be solved to perfect this – there was a grave danger that the animated characters on such a scale and filmed twice might "fuzz up" – but these the Disney studio took in its stride. Primarily, the whole special-effects business was made possible because Ub Iwerks, Walt's first great animator, had returned to the fold: over the succeeding years he proved to be a special-effects genius, making possible things that had hitherto seemed impossible.

Many of the critics at the time hated the movie, and it is easy to understand why: the word "psychedelic" had yet to be coined, but it can certainly be applied to *The Three Caballeros*. It would be easy to compile an anthology of hostile reviews, but things had changed by the 1960s and 1970s, and a new generation of critics found itself able to appreciate the movie on its own terms rather than compare it unfavourably with the earlier Disney classic features.

Besides, in any age a full-length movie starring Donald Duck is *bound* to be worth watching ...

THE STORY

Unlike *Saludos Amigos* and the other anthologies, *The Three Caballeros* does have something of a continuous story in that Donald Duck features during most of the running time, with the two shorts *The Cold-Blooded Penguin* and *The Flying Gauchito* as interpolations.

It is Donald's birthday. The first package he opens contains home movie equipment – including movies to show on it. Donald, naturally enough, takes on every malevolent piece of hardware from the screen to the projector and loses, but finally he succeeds in getting the system in operation. The movie he shows proves to be *The Cold-Blooded Penguin*.

After it is over we are back with Donald and his movie outfit. This time the film gives him a nature-study lesson, concentrating on the bird-life of South America. These include *La Tijerata*, the Scissors bird, whose tail takes the form of a swiftly snipping pair of scissors with which it accidentally lops off the favourite tail-plumes of the narcissistic *Arapapa* bird. Then we first meet the Aracuan Bird (see below), which coolly strolls out of the screen and up the projector beam to shake Donald's hand. After it has returned to its rightful place and performed some crazy antics, we meet a nest-building bird called the *Marrequito*: it has nearly finished constructing its intricate nest, and foolishly accepts a final twig offered to it by the Aracuan Bird. The result of adding this last twig is, of course, that the entire edifice collapses. After Donald has engaged in a number of further gags (surprisingly, when he falls flat on his bottom trying to imitate the flamingoes he simply laughs rather than tearing the joint apart), we are drawn into the tale of *The Flying Gauchito*.

When we return once more to Donald we find him struggling with uncooperative rolls of film – but what is this? One of his other birthday packages is jumping and singing and smoking a cigar. He unwraps it to find a pop-up book, which opens to a scene of our old friend José Carioca from *Saludos Amigos* (➤205). The cheerful parrot sings the song "Baia" to Donald while dancing and juggling and, of course, playing his umbrella like a flute; meanwhile the background shows various scenes of the beauties of Brazil. On Donald telling José that indeed he has never been to Baia, the parrot goes into another number, at the end of which he and the Duck decide that a visit can no longer be delayed. They run back to the pop-up book, which flips to a different page to show a little train chugging along; the two pals leap aboard. After some vicissitudes – the Aracuan Bird is incapable of resisting a practical joke on the train and its occupants – they hop out of the book, turn to another page, and this time leap into a street scene.

Aurora Miranda appears carrying a tray of cookies and trilling musically; Donald's heart goes visibly gelled with love on sight of her, and it is all José can do to restrain him from an amorous embarrassment. They both pursue her eagerly along the street, but then up turn a group of (live) male dancers who perform with her a song-and-dance routine; Donald and José join in, each struggling to be in the forefront of her attention. However, when Ms. Miranda strolls off to parley with a handsome orange-seller, Donald's mood switches from gay optimism to jealous fury: he goes green, grows devil's horns, and storms towards

the couple preparing himself ferociously for a punch-up. José pulls him back, but this time not for purposes of pacific restraint but simply to give him a huge mallet. Sadly for Donald, the sole result of his trying to use this implement is that he smites himself mightily over the head.

All the others leave, and Donald with soapy humility and spurious nonchalance presents Ms. Miranda with some flowers. She scoops him up and gives him a kiss – and he is immediately transported into ecstasy. (It is fortunate that Daisy never saw this movie, or at least one promising career might have been cut brutally short!) Donald has various surreal hallucinations all to the sound of pounding percussion and thundering music – doubtless the noise of his own bloodstream.

We dissolve back to the live action and to an evocative dance: soon it is not just the people in the town who are gyrating to the pulsating rhythm but even the buildings themselves. We draw back to discover that the whole scene is still set in the pop-up book, which almost immediately slams shut. Out from the closed pages emerges José, who turns to drag Donald out too.

José reminds Donald that he still has some further presents to open. After much gaggery the rooster Panchito bounds out of a parcel and onto the screen: he gives the other two huge sombreros and announces that "now we're three gay caballeros!". After a big song-and-dance number we are left with a decorated Mexican jar (*piñata*), out of which Panchito leaps. He tells Donald that it is his birthday gift from Mexico and is full of presents – traditionally, the *piñata* is the "very spirit of Christmas". He describes Mexican Christmas customs (we see them enacted in limited animation) and explains that the climax of them all for the children is the shattering of the *piñata*.

After much clowning Donald succeeds in smashing his own *piñata* and thousands of presents come tumbling from the shards. One of these is the "book of Mexico", which Panchito uses as a vehicle for telling Donald the fable of the building of Mexico City. Then Panchito takes both José and Donald into one of the book's illustrations and off for a trip by magic *serape* to see the splendours of Mexico – these splendours, in live action behind their animated figures, resemble nothing more than a tourist movie. It is not long before they are joining in dancing the Lilongo with a group of Mexican dancers – and Donald has fallen in love again, this time with Carmen Molina: the other two have physically to wrench him away from the scene.

They might have taken him somewhere more suitable than the beach at Acapulco: it is packed with scantily clad bathing beauties, and Donald loses no time in joining them. However, after he has acted out an extended sequence of adolescent fantasy José hooks him up onto the magic *serape* and off they go to sample the nightlife

in Mexico City. Donald's heart, bruised and battered as it by now is, instantly falls for Dora Luz, whom we see singing "You Belong to My Heart" – certainly Donald's does to her. There is a further surreal dream-sequence, wrecked by Panchito with violent glee.

It is time for the movie's grand finale, and the animators pull out all the stops to present as many visual gags as humanly possible. These in fact need not concern us, since they add little to the existing story: presumably intended to be a further psychedelic addition to Don's earlier dream visions, their most important element is an exploding bull. In a cacaphony of sound, action and colour the movie ends.

THE CHARACTERS

Donald Duck

Several of the reviewers of *Saludos Amigos* made much of the fact that Donald had allowed José Carioca to upstage him for general flamboyance and exuberance. In fact, this was not really the case in that movie, but in this one it most certainly is – not just with José but also with Panchito. This is not to say that Donald's own performance is in any way inhibited: it is simply that his two South American friends burst noisily and with great audacity into any situation in which they appear.

It is difficult to add to the descriptions of Donald which appear elsewhere in this book: in general, in *The Three Caballeros* he is his same old vigorous self. However, there is one trait which he displays in this movie which is not noticeable in his others: eager lechery! He falls headfirst into a love we suspect is less than platonic with Aurora Miranda, Carmen Molina and Dora Luz in succession, and in between times shamelessly cavorts with innumerable underdressed women on the beach at Acapulco. As Panchito remarks acerbically, Donald is a "little wolf in duck's clothings". And he is not really too choosy about *which* woman should be the target of his affections: after José has hooked up the blindfolded Donald from the beach the Duck inadvertently kisses his "rescuer" with deep passion, assuming that *at last* he has been snared by one of those bathing belles. Which one? – Donald doesn't care.

This lechery of Donald's was picked up and castigated in the *New Yorker*:

... a somewhat physical romance between a two-foot duck and a full-sized woman, although one happens to be a cartoon and the other pleasantly rounded and certainly mortal, is one of those things that might disconcert less squeamish authorities than the Hays office. ... It might even be said that a sequence involving the duck, the young lady, and a long alley of animated cactus plants would probably be considered suggestive in a less innocent medium.

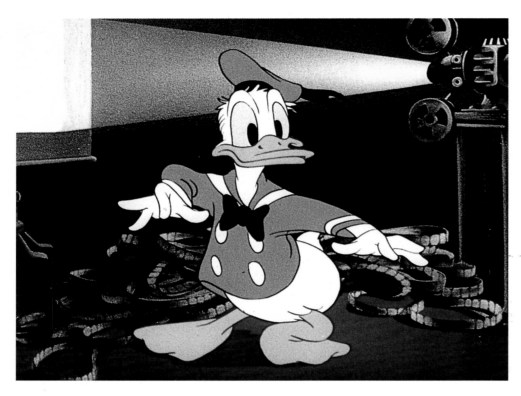

Donald Duck, beginning to enjoy his birthday presents in *The Three Caballeros*.

The *New Yorker* was probably going a little too far here – one has a schoolboy fantasy that they got a lot of letters from irate two-foot ducks – but certainly the intrusion of would-be promiscuity into Donald's life was no real success. Notably, it was not carried over into Donald's many later performances.

Much more fun, if we are to be honest, is the glorious piece of tomfoolery after a flattened Donald has been pulled from the heavy covers of the pop-up book by his pal José and told that he has further birthday presents to unwrap. Donald "deflattens" himself successfully, but realizes that he is still in the miniaturized form he had to adopt to take part in the pop-up book's scenes: how can he grow back to normal size in order to have a chance of tackling the parcels successfully? The answer, José suggests, is to stop up your mouth with your finger and blow very hard, so that you

Don enjoying the . . . er . . . scenery in *The Three Caballeros*.

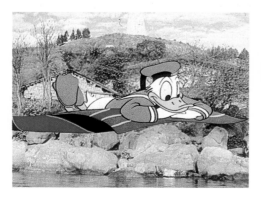

inflate yourself to huge proportions. Donald, ever perverse, uses a thumb instead of a finger, and his hand blows up like a balloon – which would not be too bad except that the air then shifts to his bottom and various other parts of his body, so that he is forced into a succession of ever more bizarre configurations: he finally deflates like a leaky balloon. Only when José points

out to him the correct finger to use does the trick finally work.

A pity for Donald that it does: out of the package concerned springs Panchito . . .

Pablo

All of the penguins in the Antarctic love the cold except poor Pablo, the cold-blooded penguin. In his igloo (possibly the only igloo in the Antarctic) he sits huddled beside a black and lethal-looking stove, "Smokey Joe"; Pablo is never happy without his scarf, his gloves and his nightcap-style hat. His favourite pictures are tourist posters for hot – *hot!* – countries.

He decides to leave for milder climes, and the other penguins in the colony give him a great send-off. However, he gets only so far before he freezes solid and, like a snowball, rolls all the way back to crash into his own igloo. He tries again on skis with Smokey Joe strapped to his back for warmth, but this time he slides back right through the village to end up trapped upside-down in a crevasse. His third attempt is with hot-water bottles strapped to every available extremity: all that happens is that he melts a hole in the ice, and has to be brought back home by the other penguins encased in a solid block.

Then inspiration strikes: a boat! He cuts out of the ice surrounding his igloo a boat shape and sails off northwards up the western coast of South America for day after day. After a lovely gag with a cloud of fog – it is so thick that he has to cut through it with a knife – he reaches the equator. This is like a huge elastic band, and seems set to

Pablo, all kitted out and ready to face the rigours of the warmer lands up north.

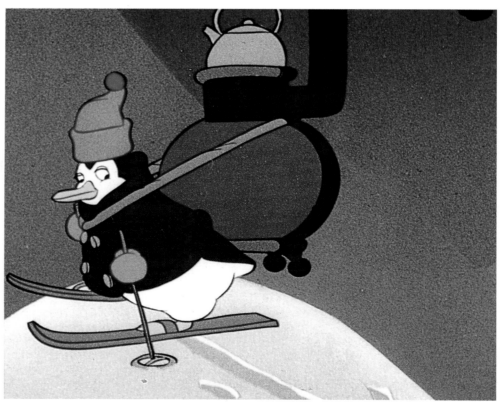

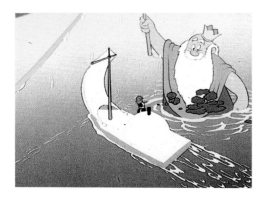

Father Neptune, who helped Pablo "cross the line" in a less than orthodox fashion.

cause Pablo problems should he try to cross it, but fortunately King **Neptune**, who looks very much like his counterpart in the shorts (►51), intervenes to hold the equator up with his trident so that Pablo can sail underneath it.

The cold-blooded penguin sails along parallel to the equator but then disaster strikes: his igloo melts and almost immediately afterwards his boat does likewise. He leaps urgently into his bath-tub, but the plug pops out and soon this makeshift vessel begins to sink as the water fountains out of the plughole. Quick-wittedly Pablo jams the shower attachment into the plughole so that the whole ensemble acts like a rocket-boat, and soon he makes his way to the scorching tropical island of his dreams.

We next see him some while later lying suntanned in a hammock and musing wistfully about the pictures on the wall … pictures of penguins having fun in all the blissful frigidity of the Antarctic.

The Gauchito and his Burrito

The Flying Gauchito is a charming short, and very much in the Disney tradition; there were plans to revive its characters for other

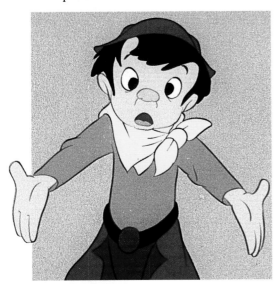

The Gauchito, finding the Burrito something of a problem.

movies but these came to naught. The story here is narrated to us by (ostensibly) the Gauchito himself, reminiscing about his foolish youth.

One day our hero goes out to hunt the condor. He proves not to be completely competent in the necessary skills, but he spots, high up in the Andes, what he assumes to be the nest of a condor. In fact it proves to be the nest of a cheeky young **Burrito** – a very special animal, because it has wings and can fly. The Burrito, which is cuddly and brown and features a foolish grin and two prominent front teeth, amiably flies up to nuzzle the little Gauchito, but the boy's response is to cast his bolas, entangling the Burrito's feet; fortunately it shakes the weapon off. A second time it comes around to nuzzle the boy in a friendly fashion, and this time he lunges at it … and topples over the edge of the cliff. Just as he is about to be dashed on the rocks below the Burrito swoops from the skies to rescue him.

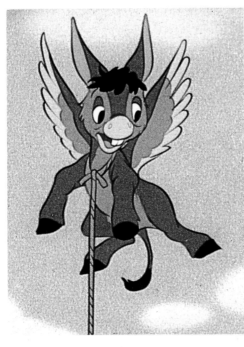

The Burrito. Who could blame him for having won the race?

Rather ungratefully the Gauchito proceeds to try to capture the Burrito, and a sensational bucking-bronco act all over the sky ensues. At the end of it the Burrito is indeed "broken", and seems to fall in love with the boy, for we next see him floating in the sky but tethered to the boy's campsite, eagerly doing tricks in exchange for a sip of the Gauchito's glass of maté.

Next day at the fiesta the boy and the Burrito determine to take part in the horse-race to try to win the Grand Prize – 1,000 pesos. The boy ties up the Burrito's wings so that they will be hidden under his saddle-blanket. There is much ribaldry from the full-size gauchos on their full-size horses as they see the little Gauchito on his little Burrito.

At first the Burrito refuses to start; when he finally moves it is to trot primly along miles behind the rest. Finally, though, the boy cuts loose the Burrito's wings and he rockets along to win the race – and the adulatory plaudits of the once-jeering crowd. All is well until, attracted by the singing of a little bird on the top of a signpost, the Burrito flies up to join it, pulling the Gauchito upward by its tether. The crowd turns ugly when they see that the Gauchito has been cheating, and he and the Burrito wisely decide not to return to earth but instead to fly off into the sunset. As the narrator – i.e., the grown-up Gauchito – concludes: "Neither him nor me was ever seen again as long as we lived."

José (Joe) Carioca

Like Donald, José appeared in both of Disney's South American features; they were the only two characters to do so.

José is still the same old resourceful character as in the earlier movie, and he is as pleased as ever to introduce Donald to the exuberances of South American life, but he has also developed a somewhat sadistic streak that, while there before, was far from pronounced. It seems to develop in him in response to Panchito, who really *is* a sadistic character, and the Aracuan Bird, who is a destructive, practical-joking madcap. Certainly José reacts with convulsive laughter every time one of their merry pranks results in Donald seriously injuring himself. A typical example is when Donald is trying to smash open his *piñata*: Panchito lassoes it away a first time and Donald does a vertiginous corkscrew; the rooster repeats the trick and this time Donald batters himself severely with a floorboard. On both occasions the rooster and the parrot find this utterly hilarious (to be fair, so might Don were it to be happening to someone else!), yet the earlier José might have had a little more compassion.

José, we discover from this movie, is capable of some superhuman feats. During one of his songs he shows himself able to split up into four identical replicas of himself, then "reunite", then split up once more but this time into four female versions of himself doing the samba, and then finally transmute into four *malandros* (male dancers) – and all this while keeping on singing! José is also able to change his size at will – not having to call upon Donald's desperate technique of blowing on his finger.

José was to appear once more in a Disney feature, along with Donald Duck and the Aracuan Bird, in the *Blame it on the Samba* section of *Melody Time* (1948).

Panchito

Panchito was a major character, created especially for this movie: he made no further screen appearances. Mexican born and bred, he creates in a viewer the first

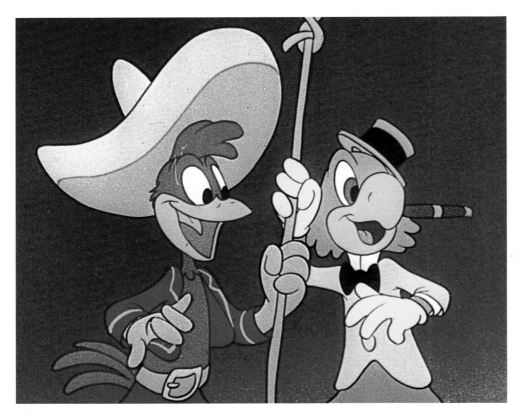

Panchito (*left*) with José Carioca. Panchito dominated *The Three Caballeros* not just in terms of screen time but in terms of general noise level.

impression of intensely bright purple-redness: he is so bright that, until one gets used to him, it almost hurts the eyes to watch him. The effect is enhanced by his frenetic activeness and his noisiness: it seems as if every syllable he utters is punctuated by crashing reports from his two ever-ready revolvers – and, if he happens not to be saying anything, well, he simply fires them anyway. Aside from his gun belt, trousers and waistcoat, he wears a vast grey-white sombrero. His eyes are lit with a maniacal zeal. Animated by Ward Kimball, he appears constantly to threaten to burst right out of the cinema screen and land in the laps of the audience – which, bearing in mind some of the astounding special effects in *The Three Caballeros*, seems to be not beyond the bounds of technological possibility.

The September 1944 issue of *Popular Science Monthly* carried a report of the various problems encountered in the creation of this new Disney star. It began

with the conception of his character. Then came his visualization in the studio, checking up on his background, and – a most important consideration – his color scheme. Panchito must not clash with the blue, white, and yellow of Donald Duck, nor the green, cream, yellow, and vermilion of Joe Carioca. He must be individual and also look well against the many backgrounds. The studio settled the matter by giving Panchito a yellow beak and feet, red comb, gray hat, and purple outfit. After this, it was a good deal of a chore to find a voice that would make Panchito suitably articulate on the screen. From more than 100 actors tested, they selected Joaquin Garay.

It is impossible to be neutral about Panchito: individual viewers find him either delightfully flamboyant or intensely rebarbative, with very little middle-ground in between. His wild humour is extremely sadistic – it is highly surprising that Donald survives Panchito's merry little japes until the end of the movie – and some people have found it distastefully so: James Agee declared bitterly that the "streak of cruelty which I have for years noticed in Walt Disney's productions is now certifiable" (although, to be fair, Agee had clearly loathed everything Disney had ever produced, and was always eager to cast the first stone). Whatever the rights and wrongs of the matter, the critics who complained of the movie's sadistic streak were directing their blasts at the character of Panchito, and it may be for this reason that he never appeared on screen again.

Maybe, though, people like cruelty for, despite the critics, the film was a definite box-office success.

Aracuan Bird

Another significant character to be introduced in *The Three Caballeros* was the zany Aracuan Bird; unlike Panchito, he made two further screen appearances, in the 1947 short *Clown of the Jungle* and in the *Blame it on the Samba* section of *Melody Time* (1948).

Panchito's sense of humour is actively malicious; the Aracuan Bird's can be as violent in its outcome but yet it is the product of a totally irresponsible character. The bird, like a small child, does not realize

that it is dangerous to play with matches, as in *Blame it on the Samba* (➤**228**); he has no conception of the days of work that have gone into the construction of the nest of the *Marrequito* bird, and so merely finds it intriguing when the twig he supplies causes the whole edifice to fall to pieces. Just as with a baby, it is hard to be cross with the Aracuan Bird for his follies.

We first meet him when he crawls out of Donald's home movie and up the projector's beam of light to shake hands with the Duck. Thanks to his bright red mop of hair (one cannot see it as a comb) and the fact that he is dressed in what seems to be an old-fashioned bathing suit striped in green and yellow, one suspects that perhaps he is not going to be a very bland character. And one's suspicions soon prove correct. Immediately after he returns to the picture on Donald's movie screen he sings a crazy little song and performs the curious trick of appearing here, there and everywhere on screen without apparently taking any time at all to travel from one position to the other.

His other major part in *The Three Caballeros* is to disrupt the progress of the train on which Donald and José Carioca are attempting to ride to Baia. Moving with his usual fitful speed, the Aracuan Bird, spotting that the rails in front of the train look for all the world like crayon lines, pulls out a crayon and draws all over the screen a complicated network of "alternative routes" that the train might take. Bits of the train go every which way but the engine, fighting off an incipient nervous breakdown, finally gathers all the diverse pieces together and succeeds in delivering the train to Baia.

In the 1947 short *Clown of the Jungle* the Aracuan Bird played a significant part in frustrating Donald's initially calm efforts to photograph birds in their native habitats. It is hard not to sympathize with the Duck when he turns to a machine-gun in order to cope with the zany red-mopped creature which attempts to ruin his each and every photograph … and it is surprising that he did not succumb to the same temptation in *The Three Caballeros*. What patience!

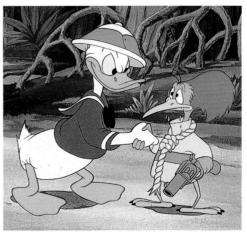

Don shakes hands with the Aracuan Bird.

MAKE MINE MUSIC

Characters:

The Martins and the Coys Section:
Grandpa Coy; Henry Coy; Grace Martin; Band-leader

Casey at the Bat Section:
Casey; The Mudville Nine; Manager; Umpire

Peter and the Wolf Section:
Peter; Wolf; Sasha (bird); Sonia (duck); Ivan (cat); Grandpa;
Hunters: Mischa; Yascha; Vladimir

Johnnie Fedora and Alice Bluebonnet Section:
Johnnie Fedora; Alice Bluebonnet

The Whale Who Wanted to Sing at the Met Section:
Willie the Whale; Professor Tetti Tatti; Isolde; Sailors; Whitey (seagull)

Credits:

Voices: Pinto Colvig (animal noises); Nelson Eddy (*The Whale Who Wanted to Sing at the Met*)

Narrators, Singers and Live Actors: Nelson Eddy; Dinah Shore; Benny Goodman; The Andrews Sisters; Jerry Colonna; Sterling Holloway; Andy Russell; Tania Riabouchinska; David Lichine; The Pied Pipers; The King's Men; The Ken Darby Chorus

Process Effects: Ub Iwerks

Sound Recordings: C. O. Slyfield; Robert O. Cook

Music Director: Charles Wolcott

Music Associates: Ken Darby; Oliver Wallace; Edward H. Plumb

Songs by: Ray Gilbert; Eliot Daniel; Allie Wrubel; Bobby Worth

Story: Homer Brightman; Dick Huemer; Dick Kinney; John Walbridge; Tom Oreb; Dick Shaw; Eric Gurney; Sylvia Holland; T. Hee; Ed Penner; Dick Kelsey; Jim Bodrero; Roy Williams; Cap Palmer; Jesse Marsh; Erwin Graham

Layout: Kendall O'Connor; Charles Philippi; Hugh Hennesy; Donald Da Gradi; Al Zinnen; Lance Nolley; Ed Benedict; Charles Payzant; John Niendorff

Colour Consultant: Mique Nelson

Backgrounds: Claude Coats; Ray Huffine; Art Riley; Al Dempster; Ralph Hulett; Thelma Witmer; Merle Cox; Jimi Trout

Art Supervision: Mary Blair; Elmer Plummer; John Hench

Animators: Les Clark; Ward Kimball; Eric Larson; John Lounsbery; Milt Kahl; Oliver M. Johnston, Jr.; John Sibley; Fred Moore; Hal King; Hugh Fraser; Judge Whitaker; Jack Campbell; Harvey Toombs; Cliff Nordberg; Tom Massey; Bill Justice; Phil Duncan; Al Bertino; Hal Ambro; John McManus; Ken O'Brien

Effects Animators: George Rowley; Andy Engman; Jack Boyd; Brad Case; Don Patterson

Directors: Jack Kinney; Clyde Geronimi; Hamilton Luske; Bob Cormack; Josh Meador

Production Supervisor: Joe Grant

Release Date: April 20, 1946

Running Time: 75 minutes

THE MOVIE

It was and is difficult for critics of *Make Mine Music* (and of 1948's *Melody Time* [➤225]) not to make disparaging comparisons between it and Disney's earlier pioneering work *Fantasia* (➤176). *Fantasia* was generally regarded as having many faults but being nevertheless a worthy experiment; *Make Mine Music* was widely regarded as a cheap imitation. One factor in some of the adverse criticism was sheer disappointment: the Disney wartime movies had been regarded as just that, and people were now expecting a return to the good old days of *Snow White* and *Pinocchio*. Otis L. Guernsey of the *Herald Tribune* judged that the movie "merely boils the pot without mixing in the ingredients of a masterpiece", although he added that even a Disney potboiler was better than most of the other films on offer. James Agee, who anyway loathed Disney movies on principle, was rather overstating things when he said that it had "enough genuine charm and imagination and humor … to make up perhaps one good average Disney short", but there is nevertheless an element of truth in the remark. However, other, less highbrow, critics found much to recommend the movie. The Los Angeles *Times* said it was

as diverting an excursion on the screen as has ever been contrived, one which brings delight to a throng of fans.

The New York *Post* agreed:

Make Mine Music is Walt Disney's latest and most fantastic cartoon-musical, a veritable vaudeville show, three-ring circus, and grand opera thrown together into one technicolor masterpiece.

Unfavourable reviewers pointed out, essentially, that such a pot-pourri could have been specially designed not to appeal to vaudeville, circus or opera fans – just to fans of all three types of entertainment.

In fact, it makes much more sense to regard *Make Mine Music* not as a feature but as a collection of ten shorts of varying standards and styles. Of these, one is utterly brilliant – *The Whale Who Wanted to Sing at the Met* – one is little short of that –

All the Cats Join In – and several are, in their different ways, very good: *Casey at the Bat, Peter and the Wolf, Johnnie Fedora and Alice Bluebonnet* and *After You've Gone*. Viewed in this light the movie is a very good anthology, and perhaps one should not ask more of it than that.

The truth was that the Disney studio, having survived early dire poverty, had gone from rags to riches but was now back in rags again. Roy Disney had succeeded in hammering some financial sense into Walt's head: it had been all very well to gamble with fortune when his company had been comparatively small, but now he had a host of employees and stockholders to consider. Walt champed at the bit, of course – he was, after all, a perfectionist by nature – but he had to see the force of his brother's argument. An insight into his state of mind is given by a reported exchange between two of the animators around this time. One remarked: "At last Walt's finally learned the value of a dollar." The other responded: "Yes, now he thinks it's worth only one dollar fifty."

Make Mine Music is the product of this sort of thinking: it seems to be constantly trying to break out of the straitjacket of its own cheapness – and often succeeds in doing so. *All the Cats Join In*, for example, uses limited animation to brilliant artistic effect. The trouble is that this level of brilliance could not be sustained, and the successes served merely to point up the failures.

Not all of the shorts contain distinguishable or named characters. The sections of the movie therefore omitted from the ensuing discussion are *Without You, All the Cats Join In, After You've Gone, Blue Bayou* and *Two Silhouettes*.

THE CHARACTERS

The Martins and the Coys Section

Living in shacks on the tops of adjacent hills, the Martins and the Coys are lovable hillbilly folk who just happen to enjoy shooting each other to pieces: any excuse will do. Like opposing armies, which is what on a small scale they are, the two families wear uniforms: the Martins are dressed in blue dungarees and red hats while the Coys wear red shirts with black hats and trousers.

The excuse for their latest bout of warfare is provided by **Grandpa Coy**. Having had just a bottle or three too many of mountain dew he creeps off while the rest of his family are sleeping (in a scene highly reminiscent of the Dwarfs snoozing in *Snow White*) on an errand of nefarious nature.

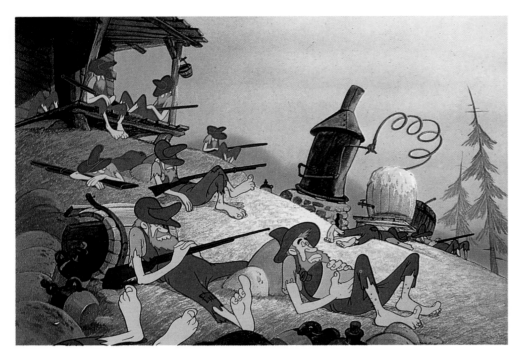

The Martins, looking typically belligerent.

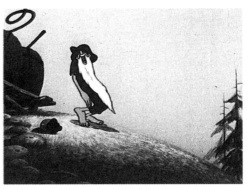

Grandpa Coy, inspired by some moonshine to go on a little raiding expedition.

King's Men assure us tunefully on the soundtrack, the young couple "fight worse than all the rest – they carry on the feud just like before". But we should not regard this as an entirely unhappy ending: the ghosts on the clouds overhead are convulsed with thigh-slapping delight. At least after death the Martins and the Coys have something on which they agree.

Casey at the Bat Section

It is 1902 and the **Mudville Nine** are in the process of not winning a baseball game, supervised by a somewhat slothful **Umpire**. However much their **Manager**, a small, active hectic little man with an aggressive moustache, harries them there is no substitute for real sporting talent, and that the Mudville Nine sadly do not possess – with the glaring exception of Casey, their brilliant star player.

The first man up to bat is pear-shaped with a similarly pear-shaped head: his playing skill is summed up in Jerry Colonna's "musical recitation" on the

Tripping and stumbling over his long white beard and filled with Dutch courage, this little wizened fellow has the temerity to steal a stack of eggs from the Martins' henhouse. Unfortunately for him, he loses all the eggs as the Martins awaken and send a hail of bullets after him.

There is no period of "uneasy truce": war is instant, and both sides suffer casualties, whose ghosts we see ascending to perch on the clouds above. Every Coy is sworn to kill every Martin, and *vice versa*.

Two of the combatants – the last survivors – are Henry Coy and Grace Martin. **Henry Coy** is tall, slender but manly, with a prominent blonde cowlick jutting out rigidly over his forehead; he looks as if he might have difficulty finding two brain-cells to rub together, but otherwise he is the answer to every maiden's prayer. **Grace Martin** is a blonde bombshell of intense feminine cuteness, covered in bows and wearing a skimpy top and a purple skirt slit up the side to dizzying heights. One day these two are out stalking each other with intent to kill; as

soon as they espy each other, however, the stalk takes on a different nature. It is love, and the ghosts on the clouds above are insane with rage.

There is a raucous wedding barn-dance with somewhat uneasy guests. A character of some note here is the **Band-leader**: dressed in a black suit and tie, with a moustache and a halo of white hair surrounding his bald pate, he is so small that he has to stand on a chair in order to supervise proceedings.

The wedding celebrations over, Grace and Henry settle down to domestic bliss. "Bliss"? – well, not exactly. Indeed, as the

Grace Martin and Henry Coy finding out about love.

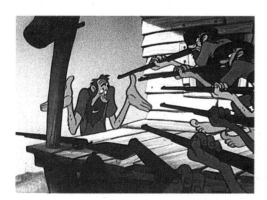

The Coys, threatening a Martin.

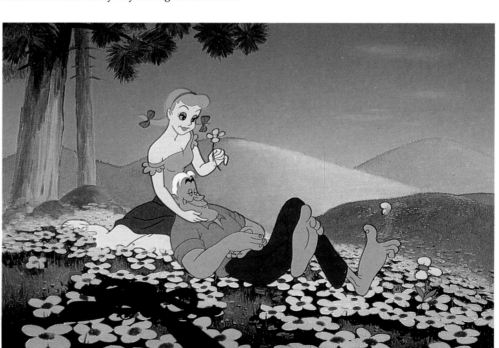

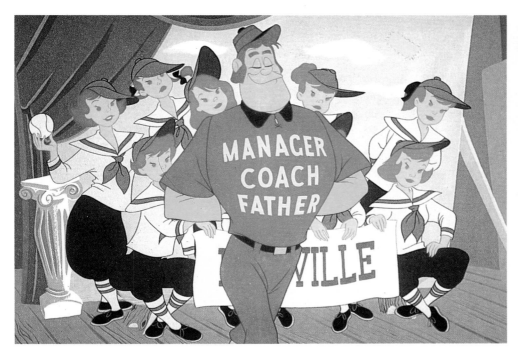

Casey sought glory as his daughters' manager in the 1954 short *Casey Bats Again*.

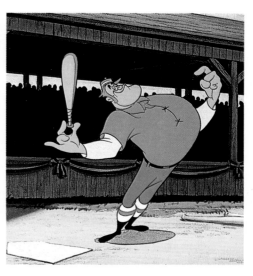

Casey, all ready to show how he can save the Mudville Nine, or, alternatively, not save them.

soundtrack by the remark that "all he had to offer was three hundred pounds of fat". The next man in has a match stuck in his shoe, and when the flame reaches his foot, just as the pitcher pitches, he leaps so energetically that he hits the cover right off the ball. That is his only athletic contribution to the contest.

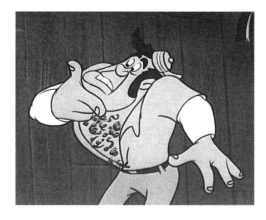

The Manager of the Mudville Nine had a difficult obstacle to hurdle – his team's lack of talent.

Still, still there is **Casey**. He has a chest like a barrel, shoulders like a rhinoceros, a chin like a boxer's practice-ball, and red hair. His gleaming array of white teeth is marred by a single yellow one. According to the commentary, he keeps his eye on the ball but "mostly the ladies", who regard him as the "Frank Sinatra of 1902". He does not seem to be too bright, but he is clearly a world expert in one field of academia: himself. The women in the audience tearfully cheer him and the pitcher is clearly terrified of him.

Casey needs to do well today, for the situation is parlous. However, he is not the

kind of guy to panic in circumstances like these – indeed, he contemptuously ignores the first ball, simply letting it whistle by, and as the second is pitched towards him he sits easily on his bat reading (with some difficulty, one assumes) a copy of the *Police Gazette*. He is waiting for his moment: the third and final pitch, which of course he is going to despatch to distant climes.

Except that he does not. He strikes out. We leave him, long after the match has been

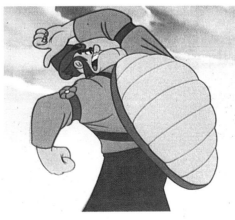

The Umpire in the *Casey at the Bat* section of *Make Mine Music*.

well and truly lost, still in the stadium but now in pouring rain, desperately, desperately trying to hit the ball *just once*.

Casey was to reappear in the 1954 short *Casey Bats Again*. Here, after his downfall and now married, he prays for a son who can make up in the diamond for his disgrace ... but all that happens is that he has nine daughters in a row. Then it is pointed out to him that the girls are all natural baseball players and that there is just the right number of them for a girls' team. Sure

enough, the girls progress to win the championship – despite their father's well meaning "help" – and the name of Casey is restored once more to baseball's Hall of Fame.

Peter and the Wolf Section

Sergei Prokofiev's famous 1936 composition for voice and orchestra was deemed by many to be one of those works that simply could not be interpreted on the cinema screen: the whole point of the piece, it was felt, is that it asks children to visualize *for themselves* what is happening, to allow the sounds of the instruments to conjure up mental pictures. In large part such people were proved correct by the Disney treatment: this version of *Peter and the Wolf* is not one for the purist, and significantly, while it was one of the pieces considered for inclusion in *Fantasia*, it had been omitted. Matters are not helped by the fact that the narration, here given by Sterling Holloway, has been largely rewritten: it is more like the commentary to a True-Life Adventure nature shorts than like the original.

Nevertheless, such carping is really rather irrelevant: what is important is whether or not the short works *as a short*, and it patently does. It may not be one of Disney's greatest, but it is by no means a dud movie.

At the start we are introduced to the principal characters. Of these the Wolf is the last to be introduced. According to a piece by Dick Huemer, the order in which the characters were to be introduced presented something of a problem. In the original work the Wolf is the first to appear, but it was felt that on screen this would destroy his potential dramatic impact. The order was therefore shuffled, and the Wolf is introduced by the words "And there was also a ... *wolf*!" (loud thunder of music and wide roar from the Wolf) immediately before we plunge into the story proper.

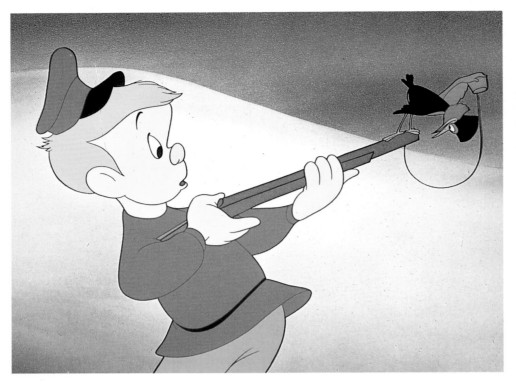

Peter, looking typically defiant in the *Peter and the Wolf* section of *Make Mine Music*.

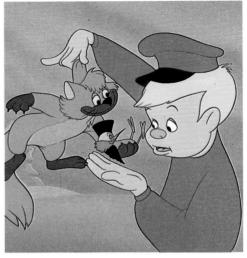

Could Ivan the cat contain a terrible secret? A still from the *Peter and the Wolf* section of *Make Mine Music*.

The neighbourhood, in the depths of winter, is being terrorized by the fierce Wolf. Young **Peter**, however, unlike the adults, is not in the slightest frightened; armed with his trusty popgun he determines to hunt the beast down. With his pale blond hair, his red cap and jacket, his pale trousers, his black boots and his generally rounded, little-boy appearance, he does not look the sort of hunter that will strike fear into the heart of the average carnivore, but of course he is not aware of this: he is off to kill the wicked Wolf.

His first foray is thwarted almost before it starts by **Grandpa**, who has a face very similar to that of *Snow White*'s Sleepy (►**165**). Peter is petulant over this, imagining himself as the proud hero of the community, returning from his hunt leading the Wolf by a chain around its neck, and so forth.

Soon enough Grandpa dozes off, and Peter takes the opportunity to trek away for a second time through the snow. After a

Sasha, the little bird, catching Peter off-guard.

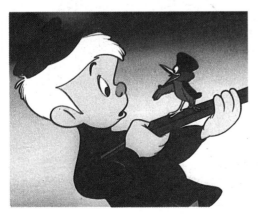

little while he is joined by **Sasha**, a little bird with tufty red hair surrounding his baldness, a purple belly, a black back and wings, a black cossack hat, and a streetwise expression on his face.

Not long afterwards the intrepid duo are petrified by the shadow on the snow of what they assume to be the Wolf – but it proves to be only **Sonia**, a pert little duck.

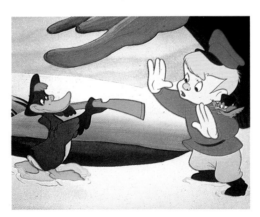

Sonia the duck was almost as reticent as a famous other Duck in *Peter and the Wolf*.

She is largely blue with a yellow beak and feet, a black cap and tail, and, like Sasha, red hair (she is startlingly unlike the most famous Duck of all). She has a repeat of Peter's dream of glory, but in this instance the Wolf turns and roars terrifyingly and Sonia – in real life as well as in the dream – turns and flees. Sasha runs after her, berates her, and brings her back to join the hunting party.

Out of the forest appears **Ivan**, a pale brown cat with a white tummy, who chases Sasha until the feisty little bird takes refuge

in Peter's hat. Peter is not amused by all this, and insists that Ivan should promise not to chase either of the birds again. Ivan, too, joins the hunting party.

The Wolf is finally located when Ivan nervously retreats under his huge form; the little cat's tail tickles the Wolf's belly. Ivan flees, in his flight knocking over the others like ninepins and, most seriously of all, stunning Sonia. Defenceless, she only narrowly escapes with her life when the Wolf comes upon her.

The **Wolf** is a pretty awesome creation – much more frightening than, say, the Big Bad Wolf (►**54**) and one of the most terrifying creatures in the Disney oeuvre. He froths at the mouth and his eyes are wild; his generally grey coat is divided by several black longitudinal stripes; and he has a forest of teeth surrounding his malevolently red tongue and throat.

Peter fires his popgun in defiance, but the cork merely bounces off the Wolf's nose. The Wolf chases Sonia onto a frozen pond, and there is a lovely piece of animation with the duck desperately swimming around below the ice and the Wolf skidding around on top. Finally, however, the Wolf apparently catches and consumes poor Sonia: we see her passing through the Pearly Gates, complete with obligatory halo.

Sasha, determined to avenge his friend, has a plucky fist-fight with the Wolf; at one point he even ends up inside its toothy mouth. Luckily he escapes (although he has to pop back in for a moment to salvage his hat) and continues the fight; *un*luckily, though, he then flies into a tree-trunk and knocks himself unconscious. The monster is just about to eat him when Peter and Ivan tie a rope around the Wolf's tail and drag him backwards. Peter, Ivan and the Wolf in due course find themselves with the rope slung over a horizontal branch: Peter and Ivan are dangling on one end while the Wolf hangs from the other, snapping at them.

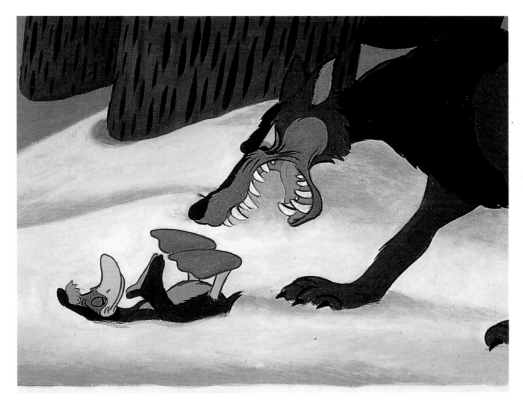

The Wolf in *Peter and the Wolf* was one of the scariest monsters Disney ever produced.

local hero – as are Ivan and Sasha. But the latter is bitterly unhappy because he grieves over poor dead Sonia. Do not worry: a happy ending is on its way. It proves that Sonia is not dead at all. What happened was that, when she realized that the Wolf was on the verge of capturing her, she hid in a hollow tree-trunk. So, in the end, the only unhappy one is the Wolf.

Johnnie Fedora and Alice Bluebonnet Section

The Andrews Sisters sing this touching tale of two hats suffering the vicissitudes of lost love before finally being reunited. While the names of the two protagonists are more usually spelled "Johnny Fedora" and "Alice Blue Bonnet", here we follow the spelling as given on the short's introductory card.

Alice Bluebonnet – a blue sunhat decorated with red roses, frills around her edges and pink and red frilly ties – first encounters the handsome **Johnnie Fedora** – grey with a brown ribbon – in the display window of the Bonton department store, New York. It is a case of love at first sight. Johnnie is heartbroken when Alice is sold, but then he too is sold.

Over succeeding weeks, as he is carried atop his owner all around town, he scrutinizes every street hoping to catch just a glimpse of his beloved. At last he catches sight of her, away in the distance, but before he can make contact he is blown off his owner's head and into the street, where he is almost run down, is fought over by dogs, and so on. He is eventually found and claimed by a hoodlum, and narrowly escapes with his life from a shoot-out. He hides, and then as the seasons turn by he lives the life of a vagrant, scouring the streets and haunting the Bonton window.

Despair is close at hand – as is drowning in a flooded gutter – when he is saved by an

Things are not going too well for our friends when the hunters arrive. Animated by Ward Kimball, these three stouthearted gentlemen are **Vladimir**, who is very tiny and has a yellow beard and hair; **Yascha**, who is tall and thin, with black beard and hair, a blue top and red trousers, and **Mischa**, who is of medium height but of improbable stoutness, wears a red top and blue trousers and, like Yascha, has a black beard and hair. Armed with antique and delapidated blunderbusses, bumbling along clumsily, they look collectively about as vicious as a puppy-dog. A now-recovered Sasha encounters the hunters and succeeds in persuading them to come to the rescue of Peter and Ivan.

At first all they can see of Peter are his hat and popgun lying piteously in the snow. Then, though, their attention is attracted upwards, and they see that he and Ivan have managed to truss the Wolf upside down to the branch. How did the two friends do this? We do not know, because we were not looking while they did it!

The hunters carry the Wolf back to the village and Peter is, just as he had dreamt, a

Alice Bluebonnet on the left and Johnnie Fedora on the right: the short in *Make Mine Music* described their romance.

The three hunters, Mischa, Yascha and Vladimir.

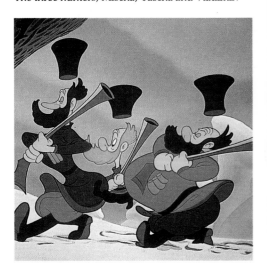

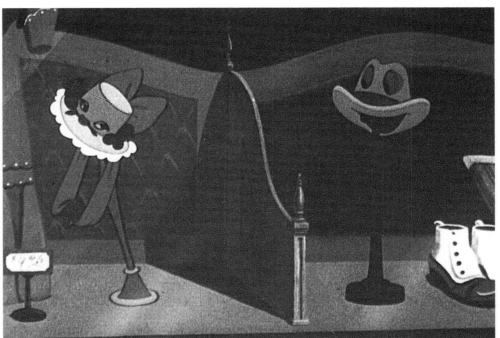

iceman, who punches a couple of holes in him and pops him on the head of one of his pair of horses. And there on the head of the other horse, to Johnnie's great delight, is none other than Alice, still true to him. The two hats live happily ever after.

The Whale Who Wanted to Sing at the Met Section

The highlight of the feature is this final short, featuring the voice of Nelson Eddy - in fact, his *voices*, for astonishingly he is responsible for every word spoken or sung during the short. This might not seem too amazing until you realize that part of his performance was as a 400-voice choir in a rendition of the *Ave Maria*. This was achieved by having Eddy multitrack a quartet of his own voice and then multiplying this up by multitracking the multitrack several times over (presumably there were in fact 512, rather than 400, voices in the choir, but no one was counting).

We are introduced to the story of Willie the Whale by a newspaper article:

MYSTERY VOICE SINGS AT SEA
A fantastic tale of a ghostly opera-singing voice heard in mid-Atlantic was brought here by disembarking passengers today. Some trick of the radio air waves is the explanation most generally accepted. The voice, it was claimed, rendered operatic airs in a most professional manner.

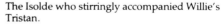

Willie the Whale, suitably costumed and made up for a resounding reception.

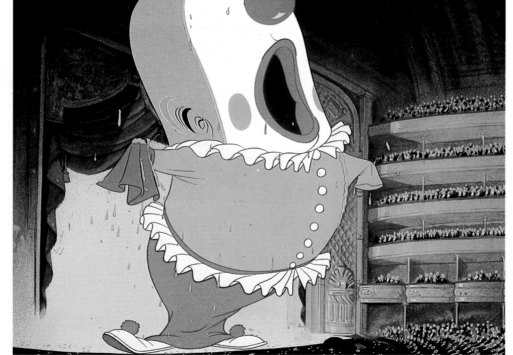

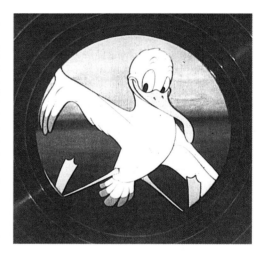

Tetti Tatti, on the lookout for poor Willie.

We see various other newspaper accounts until the story is summed up in a banner headline: WHALE SINGS!

The only person who is certain that he knows what is up is the impresario **Professor Tetti Tatti**. Plump with a pear-shaped head, bald except for a patch of white hair at the back, his face decorated with a black moustache and goatee and a monocle, Tetti Tatti explains in a thick Italian accent to several press conferences his theory: the whale has swallowed an opera singer. As he explains later in the movie, he has discovered opera stars in fish markets and in honky-tonks, so why not in a whale?

A discarded newspaper carrying a report of all this drifts out to sea, where it is spotted by a rather ragamuffinish seagull called **Whitey**. He picks it up in his beak and flies over the waves with it to where his singing friend Willie is performing "Short'nin' Bread" to an audience of enraptured gulls and seals. (Since this song

had been a smash hit for Eddy and is not notably operatic, clearly there was some in-joking going on.)

Willie the Whale is of a curious shape, more like a sofa-cushion than a whale – or perhaps it is simply that we see him almost exclusively vertically, and that he would look much more like a whale if viewed horizontally: students of the issue can be recognized by their stiff necks. Willie's back is very dark brown; his stomach and the underside of his fins are by contrast pinkish-mauve.

He is delighted by the news from Whitey, which he assumes means that Tetti Tatti is a talent scout come to recruit him for future operatic productions. He instantly sets off to

Whitey, the seagull who befriended Willie.

confront the impresario's expedition and render an extract from *Figaro*. Unfortunately he somewhat muffs his entrance, coming up under Tetti Tatti's ship and singing the first part of his piece with the vessel perched jauntily on his head. However, Whitey points out the mishap, and Willie completes the audition more normally.

The sailors aboard the vessel are rapt by the performance and refuse to act when Tetti Tatti tells them to harpoon Willie and so save the singer whom the whale has supposedly swallowed. When Willie moves to singing simultaneously in three different

The Isolde who stirringly accompanied Willie's Tristan.

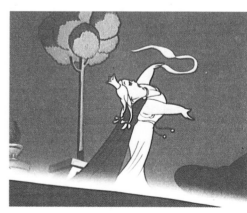

voices – tenor, baritone and bass – Tetti Tatti exclaims "He's swallowed a-*three* opera singers!" and himself heads for the harpoon-gun. While Whitey continues delightedly to conduct Willie's three separately vibrating uvulae, the sailors flatten Tetti Tatti and sit on him while they listen to Willie's rendition.

We are then treated to an extensive sequence of Willie's daydreams – daydreams of himself singing in various roles at the Met. One of these is as Tristan: his **Isolde** is a perceptive version of opera's standard "beautiful young maid" – plump to the point of bursting and certainly some decades past girlhood.

His other roles are as Mephistopheles and in *Pagliacci* (he is hilarious in clown's costume), but the visions end abruptly as

Tetti Tatti at last gets to the harpoon-gun and does the fatal deed. However, the narrator (Eddy) tells us:

Now Willie will never sing at the Met, but don't be too harsh on Tetti Tatti. He just didn't understand. You see, Willie's singing was a miracle, and people aren't used to miracles.

He reassures a distressed Whitey that "miracles never really die", and as if to confirm this we see, 'way up in the clouds, Willie singing in Heaven: on the Pearly Gates is a sign saying "SOLD OUT".

The short is a thumping success for several reasons. Oddly enough, one of these is not the drawing, which by Disney standards is adequate but nothing special (except in Willie's series of visions of himself performing at the Met, which is brilliantly

done). The animation is good, and the characterization superb. But the two elements which really make the short so good are, first of all, Nelson Eddy's virtuoso performance in all the vocal roles and, second, the *story*, which has to be one of Disney's best ever. Willie is like Dumbo (➤193), a bulky animal endowed with special talents; unlike Dumbo, however, he fails to survive his ordeal at the hands of humans. Unless, that is, you count his survival in Heaven. Most people – even children – do not count it, and so it is hardly surprising that the end of *Make Mine Music* sees many a damp eye. Willie is a divine mixture of fantasy and comedy, and for once the fantasy does not have a happy ending. Congratulations to Disney for having the courage to countenance that.

SONG OF THE SOUTH

Characters:

Brer Rabbit; Brer Fox; Brer Bear; Brer Possum; Brer Frog; Mr. Bluebird

Credits:

Animated sequences based on stories from *Uncle Remus* (1880) and *Nights with Uncle Remus* (1883) by Joel Chandler Harris

Live Actors: James Baskett; Ruth Warrick; Bobby Driscoll; Luana Patten; Lucile Watson; Hattie McDaniel; Erik Rolf; Glenn Leedy; Mary Field; Anita Brown; George Nokes; Gene Holland

Voices: Johnny Lee (Brer Rabbit); James Baskett (Brer Fox); Nicodemus Stewart (Brer Bear)

Special Processes: Ub Iwerks

Sound Director: C. O. Slyfield

Sound Recording: Fred Lau; Harold Steck

Film Editor: William M. Morgan

Music Director: Charles Wolcott

Photoplay Score: Daniele Amfitheatrof

Cartoon Score: Paul J. Smith

Vocal Director: Ken Darby

Songs by: Ray Gilbert; Sam Coslow; Allie Wrubel; Arthur Johnston; Johnny Lange; Hy Heath; Eliot Daniel; Robert MacGimsey; Foster Carling

Orchestration: Edward Plumb

Original Story: Dalton Reymond

Cartoon Story: Bill Peet; Ralph Wright; George Stallings

Screenplay: Dalton Reymond; Morton Grant; Maurice Rapf

Background and Colour Stylists: Claude Coats; Mary Blair

Backgrounds: Ralph Hulett; Brice Mack; Ray Huffine; Edgar Starr; Al Dempster

Cartoon Art Direction: Ken Anderson; Charles Philippi; Harold Doughty; Hugh Hennesy; Philip Barber

Art Treatment: Elmer Plummer

Art Director: Perry Ferguson

Photography: Gregg Toland

Technicolor Colour Director: Natalie Kalmus

Technicolor Colour Associate: Mitchell Kovaleski

Costume Designer: Mary Wills

Directing Animators: Milt Kahl; Eric Larson; Oliver M. Johnston, Jr.; Les Clark; Marc Davis; John Lounsbery

Animators: Don Lusk; Harvey Toombs; Tom Massey; Ken O'Brien; Murray McClellan; Al Coe; Jack Campbell; Hal Ambro; Hal King; Cliff Nordberg; Rudy Larriva

Effects Animators: Josh Meador; George Rowley; Blaine Gibson; Brad Case

Associate Producer: Perce Pearce

Cartoon Director: Wilfred Jackson

Photoplay Director: Harve Foster

Release Date: November 2, 1946

Running Time: 94 minutes

THE MOVIE

Song of the South represents an important transitional stage between the full-length animated films, which had made Disney's name in the realm of features, and the studio's popular live-action features which would become so significant in later years. Disney had experimented with a mixture of animation and live action before, of course, notably in 1945's *The Three Caballeros* (➤208), but in such earlier essays the animation had been the dominant element, with the live

action in a very secondary role. *Song of the South* is essentially a live-action movie, with interspersed animated sections. Walt, when asked on one occasion why he had opted for this course, responded:

In this case, a living cast was absolutely necessary to get the full emotional impact and the entertainment value of the legends.

This seems to have been something of a rationalization after the event, because the critics were almost unanimous in hailing the animation as among the best Disney had ever produced while regarding the live portions of the movie as unexceptional. (They also agreed that the song "Zip-A-Dee-Doo-Dah" by Allie Wrubel and Ray Gilbert was a major highlight; it won an Academy Award.) In terms of the animation the general consensus was relief and delight to discover that, in Adrian Bailey's words, "the old Mousetro hadn't lost his touch, he'd merely mislaid it".

It seems more likely that the reason for this experiment was financial. Some years earlier Walt had said that "We're through with caviar. From now on it's mashed potatoes and gravy." Hence the "anthology" features and hence the drift towards live action. Live action was cheaper than animation – so much so that Disney could easily afford the brilliant special effects (by Ub Iwerks) on the few occasions when the two genres were mixed on screen. What Disney was trying to do in movies like *Song of the South* and the later *So Dear to My Heart* (➤229) was to practice economy while maintaining the pursuit of excellence.

Whether they succeeded is a matter of some debate. A number of critics have complained that the movie's pathos is really bathos, and in more recent years some have objected to what they see as a patronizing racism in a number of the sequences. The latter criticism is somewhat nonsensical: the movie is set in the Old South, after all. Perhaps such critics would welcome a version of *Huckleberry Finn* in which Jim was not a runaway slave.

Song of the South is not one of the Disney "greats", but it makes pleasant viewing, and the animation and special effects are superb. The characterization is likewise excellent, and of course "Zip-A-Dee-Doo-Dah" remains as infectious as ever: it is one of those songs that, as soon as you think of its title, remains running around in your head for hours.

THE STORY

The overall story of the movie need concern us only insofar as the fables told to Johnny (Bobby Driscoll) by Uncle Remus (excellently portrayed by James Baskett), and represented on screen by animation, are each used to point up a moral relevant to the boy's problems.

Johnny's parents are separating temporarily because of his father's journalistic exploits and so he comes with his mother to live on his grandmother's plantation. The sole attraction of his life there is Uncle Remus, the old black teller of tales; but even his presence is not enough to stop Johnny setting off clandestinely to try to rejoin his father. Uncle Remus sees what is happening and, while pretending to join in his flight, tells him the tale of the time Brer Rabbit decided to run away from his home in the Briar Patch. Brer Rabbit had not got very far when he fell into a trap laid by Brer Fox. This forces him to hang upside-down from a tree-trunk, and as Brer Fox sharpened his axe to chop down the tree and up Brer Rabbit the latter's situation seemed terminal ... that is, until the bumbling Brer Bear came along and asked him what he was doing up there. The wily rabbit responded that he was "keepin' de crows outa de cornfield. I'se makin' a dollar a minute." It was the work of a moment to persuade Brer Bear that he, Brer Rabbit, had earned plenty for his needs of the moment: out of the goodness of his heart he would let the bear take over and start earning a dollar a minute as well. When Brer Fox arrived and discovered the substitution he was furious. The fox grabbed the rabbit and they fought, with the bear pitching in to help the fox; in the cloud of dust raised by the melee Brer Rabbit sneaked off, leaving the two allies blindly fighting each other. He left them to it and went laughingly home to the Briar Patch.

The moral of the tale, as Uncle Remus explains, is that "just like I tol' 'im in the fus' place, you can't run away from trouble. Dey ain't no place dat fur." Significantly, it is Johnny himself who decides to go home again, with Uncle Remus putting on a show of having to be persuaded to give up the venture.

The next fable is recounted by the old man to help Johnny in a dispute over the ownership of a puppy. This has been given to Johnny by little Ginny Favers (Luana Patten) to protect it from her two bullying brothers – which brothers later claim that he has stolen it. Ginny tells Johnny that her mother approves of the gift, knowing the reason for it. Uncle Remus supports Ginny and Johnny against the bullies, but tells Johnny that he is just as bad as Brer Rabbit for sticking his foot in it. Take the case of the Tar Baby.

One day Brer Rabbit was out for a stroll, greeting his various friends cheerfully, when he came across one individual who made no acknowledgement. This was the Tar Baby, an imitation creature constructed (out of tar, of course) by the wily Brer Fox in order to trap the rabbit. Brer Rabbit repeated his greeting to the "stranger" more than once, but still there was no response. Finally, profoundly irritated, the rabbit said: "Look, if you don't say 'Howdy' time I counts three, I's goin' bus' you wide open." On the count of three he punched the Tar Baby, and his paw was trapped; the more he struggled to escape the worse became his predicament.

An argument broke out while Brer Fox and Brer Bear were preparing for supper. Brer Bear had long had a hankering to knock the rabbit's head off, and this he determined to do, swinging a large club lustily. Brer Fox, by contrast, wanted to make the rabbit suffer for all his tricks of the past. The bear was astonished when Brer Rabbit anxiously encouraged him: "Go on, knock my head clean off," he said, "but please don't fling me in dat Briar Patch." Brer Fox continued to argue for hanging, say, or maybe skinning alive, to which Brer Rabbit responded: "Skin me if ya likes, Brer Fox, but ... bu-bu-bu-but there's one thing I don't wantcha to do ... wa-wa-wa-whatever you do, please, please Brer Fox, please don't fling me in dat Briar Patch." So, of course, he was flung into the Briar Patch, and once again his wits had saved him from a grisly end.

Johnny puts the tale to good use moments later when the two bullies threaten to tell his mother that he has stolen their puppy. He retorts that he does not mind that so much but that please, please, could they not tell *their* mother? Of course they do just that, and get a hiding for their pains.

The third fable appears when Ginny and Johnny are in misery after harsh physical treatment at the hands of the bullying brothers. Uncle Remus cheers them up by telling the tale of the Laughing Places.

One day Brer Rabbit was tied up securely in Brer Fox's cave, and the fox and the bear were preparing once more to have him for supper. As the rabbit was held over the flames, however, he began to laugh. Asked why, he explained that he had just been to his Laughing Place, and every time he

thought about it he just could not help giggling. Everyone had their own Laughing Place which had this effect on them. Brer Fox was suspicious, but Brer Bear insisted on untying the rabbit so that he could lead them to *their* Laughing Places. Roped around the neck, the rabbit led the two to a bees' hive, with which Brer Bear became intimately involved. When the fox laughed at him over this he lost his temper, and a fight broke out amid the angry swarm.

> *Brer Bear* (to the rabbit): Now look, you said dis was a Laughin' Place, an' I hain't laughin'!
> *Brer Rabbit*: I didn't say it was *yo'* Laughin' Place, I said it was *my* Laughin' Place, Brer Bear.

And sure enough it proved to be, as the two rogues vanished over the hills pursued by the viciously buzzing bees.

The final piece of animation occurs late in the movie, after Uncle Remus has narrowly escaped exile and Johnny death. Johnny, Ginny and their friend Toby (Glenn Leedy) are skipping down a lane singing when suddenly Brer Rabbit appears to join in their song. Uncle Remus, amazed actually to *see* his creation, soon becomes part of the band, as do many other of the characters from Joel Chandler Harris's fables. And so they all dance off happily over the horizon to (one assumes) live happily ever after.

THE CHARACTERS

Brer Rabbit

Different mediums have different capabilities and so, while the Disney versions of Harris's characters are much wilder and wackier than the originals, they do not have the same psychological depth. Nevertheless, in terms of the cartoon medium, two of them are surprisingly profound, the two being Brer Rabbit and

Brer Rabbit, who had an unfortunate habit of wrecking Brer Fox's plans.

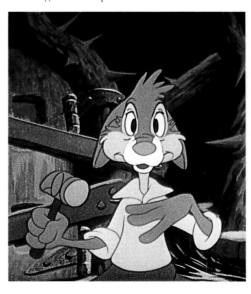

Brer Fox. Both are portrayed as wily, resourceful fellows, yet they are so in different ways. Brer Rabbit is certainly the more intelligent of the two (although perhaps not by much – he generally succeeds in outwitting the bear rather than the fox), but, as so often with extremely clever people, his intelligence is capable not just of getting him out of jams but also of getting him into them in the first place. For example, although Uncle Remus tells Johnny that it was sticking his nose into other people's business that landed Brer Rabbit in such trouble with the Tar Baby, it was really curiosity – the hallmark of intelligence.

Brer Rabbit is, obviously by design, much smaller and drawn to look more cuddlable than the other two main characters. With his big feet and his quick, merry eyes, he is every child's image of the ideal pet or soft toy. He has pricked-up alert ears and a red button of a nose, two goofy front teeth and an impertinent scut of white, blue trousers and a pink sweater. His habit of bouncing adds to his overall screen persona, as do his rapid movements and changes of facial expression. Another important point in this respect is that he is never the initial aggressor with the other two, and any physical punishment they receive by way of his revenge is brought upon them by themselves. He is the weak but clever little kid at school who succeeds in diverting the bullies to fighting among themselves.

And his laugh, of course – well, it is hard to stop oneself from joining in.

Brer Fox

Like Brer Rabbit, Brer Fox is intelligent . . . except, that is, in his choice of companion in arms. It is very easy to forget that Brer Fox outwits Brer Rabbit every time he tries to do so, whereas the rabbit succeeds in outwitting the fox only the once – and even then would not have been able to do so had it not been for the fact that Brer Bear was staggering around eagerly wielding a club. Brer Fox's only liability in terms of his cunning is that he has a streak of cruelty in him which he allows to take charge of his

Brer Fox, ready and eager as always.

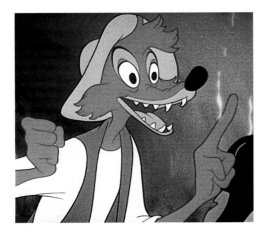

intelligence: his intended victim would be supper very early on if only the fox did not delay the execution to give himself time to relish the moment and threaten the rabbit with a terrible death. Indeed, on the one occasion when the rabbit *does* succeed in tricking the fox directly, it is for precisely this reason: allowing his sense to succumb to his cruelty, Brer Fox throws him into the Briar Patch and so to freedom.

Brer Fox is the zaniest of the three main characters in both behaviour and speech. Marc Davis, who worked on the fox, explained in an interview with A. Eisen published in 1975 that

> The fox in *Song of the South* spoke very rapidly; he had a tremendous scale of speaking levels, which gave an interpretation of movement to him.

In this respect he is probably the most successful of the Disney foxes, most of whom are anyway heroes rather than villians. (The only other fox "baddies" are Foxey Loxey (➤100) and J. Worthington Foulfellow [➤172]). Because his speech (produced by James Baskett, who starred as Uncle Remus in the live action) is so vivacious, rapid and flamboyant, his movements seem to be even more rapid than in fact they are – which is pretty rapid!

A further interesting point is that Brer Fox has, of course, a rust-brown body, which must have caused the animators something of a problem, because such a colour, in the subliminal code which they either consciously or unconsciously used (see discussion under *Snow White* (➤157), being an earth-color, signified warmth and general goodness. They therefore dressed him fully in greens, hiding as much of the rust-brown as possible. His bulb of a nose is not pink and friendly like Brer Rabbit's but a shiny black.

Yet he is never a villian of the same kind as, say, the Wolf in *Peter in the Wolf* (➤215); no child will come out of *Song of the South* and start having nightmares about Brer Fox. Indeed, it is hard not to have a touch of affection for him. Just *once*, one of his elaborate schemes ought to come off!

Brer Bear

Brer Rabbit and Brer Fox both have large, eager eyes, signifying their intelligence; Brer Bear's eyes are, by contrast, proportionately very small. In fact, even his best friend would not claim that Brer Bear is overendowed with intellect; this is especially true since his best friend appears to be Brer Fox, who has constant cause to curse the bear's dimwitted stupidity. In fact, everything about Brer Bear signals to the audience that he is very dim indeed: his shambling form, his hugeness, his dopey voice (supplied by Nicodemus Stewart), his huge honk-nose, the solitary tooth in his lower jaw . . .

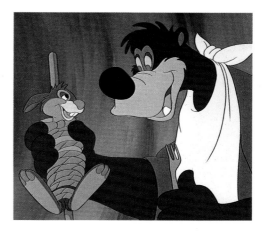

Brer Bear was always keen to assist Brer Fox, but the grey matter was sadly lacking.

Yet, unlike many other similar characters in Disney (Baloo in *The Jungle Book* [➤278]) is the closet obvious example) Brer Bear is by no means on the side of the angels: he is every bit as eager to eat Brer Rabbit as is Brer Fox, just rather less subtle in his approach. While the fox is cheerfully dreaming up lingering deaths for his old adversary, the bear is keen simply to knock his head right off. This is probably not because he is in any way more merciful than his ally, but simply because he has less imagination. Yet so attuned are we to the idea that the big bumbling fellow has really a heart of gold (and is probably not as stupid as he looks) that once again Brer Bear inspires our affection.

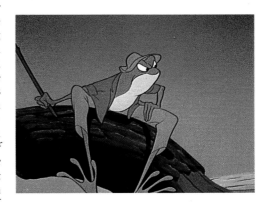

Brer Frog, who played only a small part in *Song of the South* – but can one see traces of the forthcoming Toad (➤231).

This effect is enhanced by the way in which his ally, the fox, treats him. Take the scene in which Brer Fox is preparing the Tar Baby:

> *Brer Fox:* It sho' gonna fool 'im. Yes Sir!
> *Brer Bear:* Oh, no it . . . it . . . hain't. It hain't gon' fool nobody. It hain't got no eyes!
> *Brer Fox:* Eyes! Oh yes indeed. Eyes! I'm glad I thought of that. [Pulls buttons off bear's coat. Bear looks down at torn coat.] . . . Now, ah, uh, lemme see. Oh, yes. A nose too . . . got to have a nose. Needs one of those very badly. Got to have a nose. This is sho' gonna do the trick. [Bear covers up his nose, but the fox grabs bowl of the bear's pipe, shoves stem of pipe

back into bear's mouth. Uses pipe-bowl as Tar Baby's nose.] This is lookin' mo' natural all de time!

Brer Bear: It hain't . . . it hain't . . . it hain't got no hair.

Brer Fox: Oh! Hair! [Fox looks at bear's hair. Bear pulls hat down over head and turns away from fox. Yells. We cut to find the fox putting on Tar Baby's head, now liberally covered with plucked-out hanks of bear's hair. Bear twists around to regard his own bare and throbbing bottom.] Now . . . hee . . . hum . . . arite. come on, he'p me 'long, he'p me 'long, come on. Us ain't got all day. Come on . . .

It is hard, in fact, to see why the fox and the bear remain allies, because neither seems to profit at all from the relationship. The fox sees all his schemes founder because of the bear's stupidity, and would certainly get along better on his own; the bear's reward for the "help" he provides is usually a

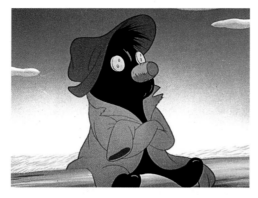

The Tar Baby, which *should* have spelled the end of Brer Rabbit, but fortunately didn't.

torrent of abuse or a rain of blows, and he too might be better off on his own. Yet allies they remain, and both are surprisingly likeable villains.

Minor Characters

There are a few minor named characters in the movie, a couple of whom have vocal roles. (It is not on record who provided these.) **Brer Frog**, **Brer Possum** and **Brer Fish** exchange pleasantries with Brer Rabbit on the morning on which he is to meet the Tar Baby, although the frog's greeting contains a few words of warning: "Mind out, Brer Rabbit, better mend yo' ways. You's headin' for trouble one o' these days." And, of course, he proves to be right. There is also **Mr. Bluebird**, a typical member of that Disney ilk, who plays a small part in both the live-action and the animated sequences and acts as a sort of link between them: significantly, he is the first of the animated characters to become visible to the children in the final sequence.

FUN AND FANCY FREE

Characters:

Jiminy Cricket

Bongo section: Bongo; Lulubelle; Lumpjaw

Mickey and the Beanstalk section: Willie the Giant; Singing Harp; Mickey Mouse; Donald Duck; Goofy; The Cow

Credits:

Bongo based on an original story by Sinclair Lewis

Live Actors: Edgar Bergen; Luana Patten

Dummies: Charlie McCarthy; Mortimer Snerd

Voices: Jim Macdonald (Lumpjaw, Mickey Mouse); Anita Gordon (Singing Harp); Cliff Edwards (Jiminy Cricket); Billy Gilbert (Willie the Giant); Clarence Nash (Donald Duck); Edgar Bergen (Narrator); Dinah Shore (Narrator); Pinto Colvig (Goofy); The King's Men; The Dinning Sisters; The Starlighters

Process Effects: Ub Iwerks

Sound Supervisor: C. O. Slyfield

Sound Recording: Harold J. Steck; Robert Cook

Film Editor: Jack Bachom

Technicolor Colour Director: Natalie Kalmus

Technicolor Colour Associate: Morgan Padelford

Music Director: Charles Wolcott

Score: Paul Smith; Oliver Wallace; Eliot Daniel

Songs: Ray Noble; Buddy Kaye; Bennie Benjamin; William Walsh; Bobby Worth; George Weiss; Arthur Quenzer

Story: Homer Brightman; Harry Reeves; Ted Sears; Lance Nolley; Eldon Dedini; Tom Oreb

Layout: Don Da Gradi; Al Zinnen; Ken O'Connor; Hugh Hennesy; John Hench; Glenn Scott

Backgrounds: Ed Starr; Claude Coats; Art Riley; Brice Mack; Ray Huffine; Ralph Hulett

Directing Animators: Ward Kimball; Les Clark; John Lounsbery; Fred Moore; Wolfgang Reitherman

Character Animators: Hugh Fraser; Phil Duncan; Judge Whitaker; Art Babbitt; John Sibley; Marc Davis; Harvey Toombs; Hal King; Ken O'Brien; Jack Campbell

Effects Animators: George Rowley; Jack Boyd

Live-action Photography: Charles P. Boyle

Live-action Director: William Morgan

Directors: Jack Kinney; Bill Roberts; Hamilton Luske

Production Supervision: Ben Sharpsteen

Release Date: September 27, 1947

Running Time: 73 minutes

THE MOVIE

Most of the feature movies produced by Disney during the 1940s were "mashed potatoes and gravy" ventures, and of these most were compilations. Two of them consisted of paired featurettes: one was *Fun and Fancy Free*, the other *The Adventures of Ichabod and Mr. Toad* (1949 [➤230]). Although the featurettes in the latter are rather more ambitious than those of the former, *Fun and Fancy Free* probably has the more charm.

Its two unassuming components – one of which stars Mickey and the gang – are both excellent. In addition, the link passages performed by Jiminy Cricket are genuinely funny in their own right and the special effects of mixed animation and live action, which Ub Iwerks had raised to great heights in *Song of the South* (➤219), are brilliant. One

would not talk about *Fun and Fancy Free* in the same breath as *Pinocchio*, but it is nevertheless a very watchable movie.

One surprise name in the credits is that of Art Babbitt. Babbitt had been one of the prime foci of the strike at the studio in the early 1940s, and the received story is that, although Walt had to reinstate Babbitt as part of the strike's settlement, he never spoke to him again, gave him merely futile make-work tasks to do, and forbade the mention of even his name. Unless there was an unlikely slip-up in the secretarial department this received story, to judge by *Fun and Fancy Free*'s credits, would seem to be incorrect. Clearly relations between the two men were bad – to the detriment of both – but equally clearly they were not quite as petulantly bitter as some of Walt's more hostile critics have suggested.

Fun and Fancy Free marked an interesting debut: that of Jim Macdonald as the voice of Mickey Mouse. Walt himself had voiced Mickey throughout his career, with occasional help from other members of the staff, notably Carl Stalling, better known as a composer for the Silly Symphonies. But now Walt, throughout his life a heavy cigarette-smoker, may have felt himself incapable of providing the right falsetto voice – or perhaps he was just too busy. It was time for someone else to take over, and so in this movie Walt shared the voice-work with Macdonald. Macdonald was to retain the role for many years.

Another interesting point about the feature was that it had a major role for Jiminy Cricket, first introduced in *Pinocchio* (1940), under which Jiminy's career is largely discussed (➤169). Very few of the characters introduced in the full-length features made further screen appearances – Figaro (➤171) is the major exception – and

Jiminy was the only one to have a major role in two features. (Donald Duck, of course, starred in several features, but he is essentially a shorts character.) In *Fun and Fancy Free* Jiminy was voiced, as before, by Cliff Edwards. His song "I'm a Happy-go-lucky Fellow" in this movie had originally been intended for *Pinocchio*.

Fun and Fancy Free has not to date been rereleased, although its two components have been seen separately on television and video and *Bongo* has been released as a theatrical featurette. This is a little surprising. As the critics of the time observed, Disney was rather "coasting" with the feature, but the average cinema audience could do a lot worse.

THE CHARACTERS

Bongo Section

Bongo was based on a story by Sinclair Lewis. One cannot help but reflect that, by the time of *Fun and Fancy Free*'s release in 1947, he and Walt were rather strange bedfellows. The story is narrated by Dinah Shore, who once again might seem not to be too devastatingly *simpatico* with Lewis's ideas.

Bongo, a little performing bear who has become a star of the circus, is tired of the life he leads. Looking rather more like a teddy-bear than a live one, he has red-and-yellow pillbox hat, a "smart" red jacket and a blue bow-tie, and he is adept at riding a unicycle. Despite his willingness to perform – "He would gracefully plunge 300 feet into a wet sponge," the narration tells us – he is poorly treated by his human masters: at night he is cast rudely into a too-small cage. Travelling miserably encaged on a circus train one day, he finds that the call of the wild – personified in an image of himself beckoning towards freedom – becomes too strong to resist. He shakes the bars of his cage until finally the lock breaks and he escapes on his unicycle.

Out in the forest he meets various other animals (including a pair of chipmunks who are extraordinarily like Chip an' Dale, although they squeak rather than "speak" [►**96**]). The wild animals are essentially friendly, although they cannot help themselves from laughing as he amiably tries to emulate their forest skills. He plays with them until nightfall, when they all retire to bed.

Bongo's night is a disturbed one. First a munching caterpillar, then a marching centipede, and then finally and most conclusively a thunderstorm serve to ensure that he has little sleep. Fleeing blindly from the thunder and lightning on his unicycle, he eventually finds somewhere to settle; it is only when he awakens in the morning that he discovers he has bedded down on the very edge of a clifftop. Terrified, he hops

onto his unicycle and pedals off, but a sudden sneeze blasts him backwards to teeter dangerously on the cliff-edge. Somehow he survives. Depression fills him. As the narration has it

> . . . he didn't even know how to *act* like a bear. This rough, rugged stuff wasn't for him – especially on an empty stomach.

His futile attempt to catch a fish ends in a drenching. He is all ready to give up and head back to the circus when he espies a female bear, **Lulubelle**, a somewhat paler brown than he is, with big eyes, exuberantly fluttering eyelashes and a pink flower in her hair. At first sight, love strikes them both with the subtlety of a pneumatic drill, and they engage in a balletic (on her part) and quasi-balletic (on his clumsier part) romantic chase through the forest. Finally she lets him catch her and they rub noses – their touching noses form a loveheart – while two little teddy-bear cupids hover around, providing assistance.

But all dreams come to an end, and after this one so, almost, does Bongo's life, for up charges the vast and villainous **Lumpjaw**, the biggest and most terrifying bear in the forest. Needless to say, he is prognathous in the extreme; he is also huge, of such a dark brown that he is almost black (it should be stressed that Disney used dark colouring in animals to suggest massiveness rather than for any other reason), and with an array of teeth that any gear-wheel would be proud of. He picks up our diminutive hero easily in one hand. He is unimpressed when the little fellow introduces himself in terms of his circus persona, "Bongo the Wonder Bear"; indeed, his response is to thrash Bongo mightily, until Lulubelle stops him. Then she too cuffs Bongo, and his heart shatters. Brought up in captivity, he has no idea that, as the soundtrack tells us, "a bear likes to say it with a slap" – in other words, by cuffing him Lulubelle is declaring her love. However, when she tries to do it again she accidentally smites Lumpjaw, who knows exactly what the gesture means and rejoicingly assumes the best.

Tearfully Bongo departs on his unicycle. As he looks back, however, he sees the betrothal jamboree of Lumpjaw and a less than thrilled Lulubelle, with crowds of celebrating bears (plus Dinah Shore) singing about how "a bear says it with a slap". Realizing his mistake he unicycles back, picks a fight with Lumpjaw, which he eventually wins using his many circus tricks, sees Lumpjaw swept away downriver, and generally acts like the usual Disney little guy winning out despite the odds against him. The last we see of the two lovers is their sitting atop adjacent trees, the two trees bending under their weight to form the outline of a loveheart as the two bears rub noses.

None of the characters in *Bongo* is portrayed with any great depth of insight,

but that hardly matters. The featurette has great charm and verve, as well as a certain fine feeling for fantasy which has always typified the best of the Disney *oeuvre*. It may not be great Disney but, by gosh, it is a lot of fun and very watchable.

Mickey and the Beanstalk Section

In *Brave Little Tailor* (1938) Mickey Mouse took on a giant and won (►**33**), and here he repeated the feat – but this time with the not always stalwart help of his pals Donald and Goofy.

The featurette is introduced by a live-action section, with ventriloquist Edgar Bergen proposing to tell Luana Patten and his dummies Charlie McCarthy and Mortimer Snerd (not to mention a gate-crashing Jiminy) a fairy story. Bergen then narrates the tale, during which there are occasional flips back into live action. The animation, in fact, starts off as a thought-bubble above Patten's head as she imagines the scene that Bergen is describing.

The tale is set in Happy Valley whose happiness, we discover, has been maintained by the presence in the local castle of the magical **Singing Harp**; we see this golden character, a sort of cross between Marilyn Monroe and a musical instrument, singing on the balcony of the castle, spreading joy throughout the valley. However, one day a dreadful shadow settles over the valley, and when it lifts the Singing Harp has gone. Soon drought and despair fill the neighbourhood.

Nowhere more so than on a rundown farm seemingly owned by **Mickey Mouse** and staffed by **Donald Duck** and **Goofy**. Their poverty is desperate – and Donald is in imminent danger of cracking completely. When Mickey cuts the loaf so thinly that the slices are transparent, Donald finally hits the roof. Telling the soothing narrator to "Shaddap!", he builds himself a sandwich out of the assembled plates and cutlery and eats much of it before the other two can stop him. Maniacally he spots the farmyard axe, seizes it, and is off to catch the **Cow** which, as Bergen has told us in the narration, "used to be a good milker but now . . . she's an udder failure". Once again, Mickey and Goofy have a hard time holding him down.

If slaughtering the cow is not acceptable, what can they do? Well, Mickey sets off to sell the cow for what the other two assume will be at least a small fortune, but on his return they find that he has exchanged it for nothing more than a handful of "magic" beans. On receipt of this news Donald is as equable as Hurricane Betsy: he throws the beans contemptuously away, and they fall through a knot-hole in the floor.

Night comes, and the light of the full Moon stimulates the beans into eager growth. The beanstalk soars upward and upward, carrying with it the farmhouse

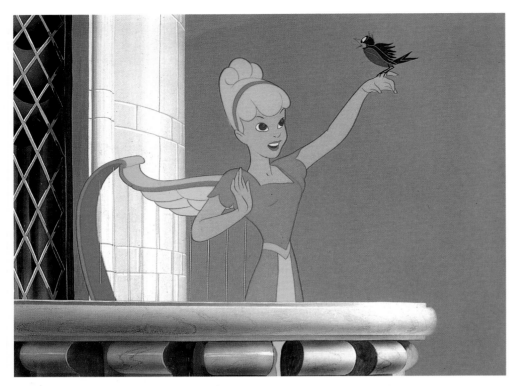

The Singing Harp, which sent the great trio of Mickey, Donald and Goofy off on a heroic quest.

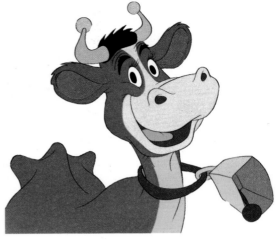

The cow on the trio's farm was at high risk until they set off to seek the Singing Harp.

(much of which drops off) and our sleeping pals, who survive numerous brushes with death. When dawn wakes them they find themselves in the grounds of a magic castle in the heavens. They go to explore, but are "buzzed" by a flight of military-style dragonflies; luckily the one that seems really anxious to catch them is gulped down by a cheerful fish, and they survive to reach the front of the castle. They climb its huge stone steps with some difficulty and in due course find themselves in a colossal banqueting hall. It is the work of only a few moments to shin up the helical legs of the table and start gorging on the food they find there.

After some gaggery with the gigantic helpings of food – Goofy, characteristically, comes second in a contest with a bowl of jelly – they are spotted by the Singing Harp, who has been captured by a giant (so *that* explains the great shadow in the valley!) and placed for safekeeping in a locked box. The pals peer incredulously at her through the box's keyhole.

Enter **Willie the Giant** – but he proves to be no ordinary giant. No, he can shrink himself to tiny proportions, dissipate into thin air and so forth because, as he tells himself while displaying these tricks to what he imagines is an empty hall, "I know the magic wordies". This Willie is by no means the kind of frightening character one might expect: he is positively lovable, with his bright red hair, his paucity of teeth (one at the front of the lower jaw and a scanty few at the sides), his pear-shaped evening-shadowed face, his bright red "parp" nose and a voice which suggests that he is perhaps as clever as Goofy . . . or maybe not. His eyes are very like those of Dopey (➤162), despite the vast disparity in size.

Willie reckons he can smell food – but, no, it is not the blood of an Englishman; instead it is a chocolate pot-roast. He attacks the food on the table. Mickey, who has hidden in a wedge of cheese – emmenthal, at a guess – indulges in a great piece of gaggery as Willie cuts himself a slice: although the Goof escapes from the cheese, the Mouse is caught up in the slice and incorporated by Willie into a gargantuan cheese sandwich. Luckily the giant peppers this, and Mickey sneezes with such force that he blasts the sandwich to pieces. He flees, but Willie catches him.

Mickey has his wits about him. Clutched in the giant's hand he simulates an expert palmist, and pretends to "read" that the giant can change himself into anything. Willie, not realizing that the Mouse has witnessed his virtuoso display, is staggered by this percipience, and proceeds to show off. Mickey, spotting a nearby flyswatter,

cunningly suggests that Willie turns himself into a fly but Willie, despite currently being a cute pink rabbit, deduces what the pals are up to, transmutes himself back into giant form, catches the pals, and pops them into the locked box in place of the Singing Harp. As the lid closes Mickey manages nimbly to escape.

It is now Willie's desire that the Singing Harp should sing to him, which she does. He drops the key to the box into his pocket and settles back to enjoy her dulcet tones . . . and he slowly nods off to sleep. (A very similar scene, with similar animation, was later used in one of the Gummi Bears' TV shorts, with Sunni as the captive and the evil Duke Igthorn [➤137] as the captor.)

Abseiling on a thread down from the high shelf where Willie has put the box, Mickey, after some terrifyingly sneezy adventures with the giant's snuffbox, succeeds in swiping the key to the locked box and releasing his pals. As they all escape – with the Singing Harp – Mickey oversteps the mark a little by knotting Willie's shoelaces together in order to buy time; all this manoeuvre succeeds in doing is to wake the giant. A great chase ensues through the castle grounds and down the beanstalk, with the pals eventually ensuring

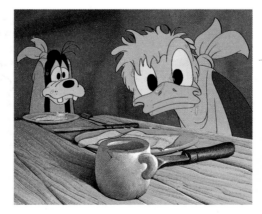

Goofy and Donald in the *Mickey and the Beanstalk* section of *Fun and Fancy Free*. Note the generosity of the slices of bread on the plate.

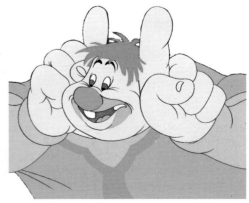

Willie the Giant, ready to frighten *anybody*! Well, except the dynamic trio.

that Willie (as per the fairy tale) falls to his death. Thanks to the demise of the giant and the restoration of the Singing Harp, happiness returns to Happy Valley.

We return to the live action to find Edgar Bergen's dummy Mortimer Snerd weeping because he liked the giant (as, to be frank, do we all) and is sad that he has been killed. Bergen reassures him that the giant was not real, just a figment of the imagination. Just at that moment, however, the roof of the house is raised and Willie peers politely in to ask: "Say, has anyone seen any signs of a teensy-weensy little mouse?" Bergen's reaction is a dead faint, and the others fare little better. Shrugging, the genial giant, trailed by Jiminy, heads off down through Hollywood, peering here and there into the houses he passes, borrows for a hat a café rooftop flashing in neon the message that it is the famous "Brown Derby", and, thus clad, disappears into the fadeout that signals the end of the movie.

Willie reappeared years later as the Ghost of Christmas Present in *Mickey's Christmas Carol* (1983 [►130]), in which his genial – if less than intellectual – characteristics were stressed. It is rather hard to establish whether he was resuscitated at the end of *Fun and Fancy Free* because he was such a friendly-seeming chap or whether, conversely, he was designed as such in order to permit the final twist. Either way, he is one of the few Disney giants – if not the only one – to elicit from the audience a true sense of compassion and friendship. He just happened to be on the wrong side of the argument – which is not a good place to be when the person on the other side is a certain Mouse.

MELODY TIME

Characters:

Once Upon a Wintertime section:
Jenny; Joe

Bumble Boogie section:
The Bee

Johnny Appleseed section:
Johnny Appleseed; Johnny's Angel

Little Toot section:
Little Toot; Big Toot

Blame it on the Samba section:
Donald Duck; José (Joe) Carioca; Aracuan Bird

Pecos Bill section:
Pecos Bill; Widowmaker; Slue Foot Sue

Credits:

Live Actors/Musicians: Ethel Smith; Luana Patten; Bobby Driscoll; Roy Rogers; Trigger; Bob Nolan and the Sons of the Pioneers

Voices/Musicians: Pinto Colvig (Aracuan Bird); Buddy Clark (Master of Ceremonies); Frances Langford; Freddy Martin and his Orchestra; Dennis Day; The Andrews Sisters; Roy Rogers; Bob Nolan and the Sons of the Pioneers; Fred Waring and his Pennsylvanians

Special Processes: Ub Iwerks

Sound Director: C. O. Slyfield

Sound Recording: Robert O. Cook; Harold J. Steck

Film Editors: Donald Halliday; Thomas Scott

Musical Direction: Eliot Daniel; Ken Darby

Musical Associate: Paul Smith

Special Arrangements: Vic Schoen; Al Sack

Songs: Kim Gannon; Walter Kent; Ray Gilbert; Johnny Lange; Allie Wrubel; Bobby Worth; Benny Benjamin; George Weiss

Story: Winston Hibler; Erdman Penner; Harry Reeves; Homer Brightman; Ken Anderson; Ted Sears; Joe Rinaldi; Bill Cottrell; Art Scott; Jesse Marsh; Bob Moore; John Walbridge; Hardie Gramatky (*Little Toot*)

Folklore Consultant: Carl Carmer

Layout: Hugh Hennesy; Mac Stewart; Ken O'Connor; Lance Nolley; Al Zinnen; Bob Cormack; Don Griffith; Thor Putnam; Don Da Gradi

Colour and Styling: Mary Blair; Claude Coats; Dick Kelsey

Technicolor Colour Director: Natalie Kalmus

Technicolor Colour Associates: Morgan Padelford; Robert Brower

Live-action Photography: Winton C. Hoch

Backgrounds: Art Riley; Brice Mack; Ralph Hulett; Ray Huffine; Merle Cox; Dick Anthony

Directing Animators: Eric Larson; Ward Kimball; Milt Kahl; Oliver M. Johnston, Jr.; John Lounsbery; Les Clark

Character Animators: Harvey Toombs; Marvin Woodward; Ed Aardal; Hal King; Cliff Nordberg; Don Lusk; John Sibley; Rudy Larriva; Ken O'Brien; Bob Cannon; Judge Whitaker; Hal Ambro

Effects Animators: George Rowley; Josh Meador; Jack Boyd; Dan MacManus

Cartoon Directors: Clyde Geronimi; Wilfred Jackson; Hamilton Luske; Jack Kinney

Release Date: May 27, 1948

Running Time: 75 minutes

THE MOVIE

Melody Time was the last of the Disney anthologies (with the exception of the 1949 double-featurette *The Adventures of Ichabod and Mr. Toad*) and it is difficult not to describe it as the least distinguished. Unlike *Make Mine Music* it has no especially strong short – no *The Whale Who Wanted to Sing at the Met* – and unlike *Fantasia* much of the music is workaday stuff. However, the movie as a whole is genial, and it does have its highlights: the surreal animation of *Bumble Boogie*, possibly an indirect result of the abortive attempt by Salvador Dali and Disney to produce a short, *Destino*, together; and the special effects in *Blame it on the Samba*, which have to be seen to be believed – Iwerks was up to his new tricks again. *Little Toot* is a very good short by anyone's standards, although not among Disney's very best. One cannot help but feel that somewhere along the line Disney realized that this feature was no masterpiece, and was likely to receive a critical and box-office pounding, for the introduction of a live-action Roy Rogers and Trigger towards the end seems like a somewhat artificial attempt to ensure that the film could boast big-drawing names on its posters.

On the other hand, *Melody Time* is very pleasant to watch, albeit rather bland. None of the shorts is actually *bad* – in fact all of them are quite good and a couple of them – *Bumble Boogie* and *Blame it on the Samba* – are spectacular as sequences (quite a different thing from being spectacular shorts). In those two cases one feels that Disney was aiming at excellence; for the other shorts one feels that Disney was aiming at being good enough to pass muster. It is as if the studio was holding its collective breath, waiting for the glories of *Cinderella* in two years' time.

The ultimate critical judgement of *Melody Time* must be what *modern* critics have to say about it. Every other Disney feature attracts modern critical comment, generally favourable but occasionally very hostile. About *Melody Time*, however, none of the modern critics have anything to say. Perhaps they have not seen it (this author had to view its shorts individually rather than watch the movie as a whole), but more likely it is merely that *Melody Time* is one of those movies to which nobody can take exception – which means that nobody is ecstatic about it, either.

A "best of" feature called *Music Land* was released in 1955 containing five shorts from *Melody Time* and four from *Make Mine Music*.

The short *Trees* which appears in *Melody Time* contains no true characters, and is therefore omitted from the ensuing discussion.

THE CHARACTERS

Once Upon a Wintertime Section

The story of *Once Upon a Wintertime* is one of lovers falling apart and then being reunited. In terms of animation and parts of the story it has a lot in common with the 1935 short *On Ice* (➤46). That it is set at some indeterminate period in the long-ago is evidenced by the yellow hooped dress and old-fashioned bonnet of **Jenny** and the cut of the red jacket and black trousers of **Joe** – not to mention that they drive out for a skating excursion in a horse-drawn sleigh. In particular, the short is introduced by shots of framed photographs of a middle-aged couple, obviously Jenny and Joe in later life.

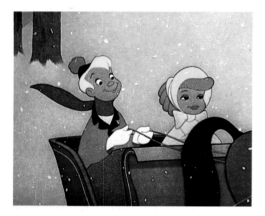

Joe and Jenny, the two young lovers in *Melody Time*'s *Once Upon a Wintertime* section.

In fact, Jenny and Joe are not the only pair of lovers in the short: there are pairs of rabbits, horses, squirrels and bluebirds as well. The rabbits in particular go through very much the same sort of lovers' tiff as the humans.

Jenny and Joe ride out in their sleigh to skate on a frozen lake; they little realize that two rabbits have hitched a ride. The males of both species show off their prowess on the ice, which means that Jenny gets covered in ice-spray and the female rabbit gets dumped in a snowdrift – male attempts to impress females often go awry. After Jenny, by this time less than pleased, has fallen on her bottom a few times to the amusement of Joe, she stalks off in a temper; the doe does likewise. What neither of them realizes is that they are heading for thin ice, and they are both too mad to pay attention when the buck rabbit tries to point this out to them by waving the THIN ICE sign. He, thereby infuriated, stabs the sign back into the ice and so starts a monumental crack-up: the females find themselves moving swiftly on an ice-floe towards a waterfall. Joe does his best to rescue Jenny by holding down a hand as she passes under a bridge, but all he succeeds in

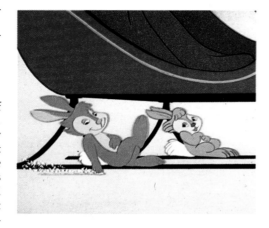

The two rabbits reflected the emotions of Joe and Jenny.

catching is a thread of her dress: a lot of unravelling goes on. Jenny faints, doubtless from the sudden cold, and the doe does likewise. Joe and the buck rabbit daringly chase their females along the bank in the sleigh, but at a corner they both fall off and are submerged in snowdrifts and frozen solid. It is up to the squirrels, the bluebirds and the horses to rescue Jenny and the doe, which they ingeniously do. Indeed, both females end up in the laps of their respective males, who therefore thaw out rather suddenly.

As Jenny and Joe ride home in their sleigh, approved by the courting pairs of animals, they pass into an area of deep shadow and, when they emerge, we see that Joe has acquired a vast red lipstick kiss on his cheek: Jenny clearly believes that she owes him her life. And then we are back to the photographs of a middle-aged couple once more ...

Bumble Boogie Section

The short *Bumble Boogie* is largely a surreal endeavour, an attempt (very successful) to show images on screen that match the wildly clashing, swirling soundtrack.

Its sole character, **The Bee**, is either a paranoiac or the Universe really *is* out to get him. He is in fact not so much a character as an "experiencing object" – for example, he

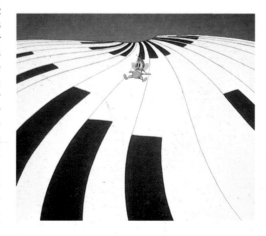

The bee flees from a marauding keyboard in *Bumble Boogie*.

changes colour according to the mood of the music and background. He first appears in sections, "painted in" by an animated paintbrush.

Life is a genuine nightmare for him. Wherever he flies he is assaulted from one side or the other - or all sides at once – by seemingly hostile flowers, musical instruments, musical symbo'· or even just plain lines. His experience is much like waking up, hungover, three feet away from the loudest boogie band in history. However, the audience is not really interested in the fate of the character: what is stunning is the artistry of the short, which takes one's breath away. Indeed, it does so to such an extent that it is difficult to spot that some of its illusions are in fact *double* illusions. To take just a single example, at one point The Bee is threatened by the bells of some flowers, which pounce at him like the bells of predatory trombones, blasting him with raw sound. The illusion works well ... even though, if one thinks about it, it is the *slides* of trombones which move backward and forward, not the bells. Yet those flowers are very definitely acting like trombones.

As noted above, many people believe that *Bumble Boogie* owes an indirect debt to *Destino*, the surrealist short which Salvador Dali and Disney attempted unsuccessfully to produce together. This is not to say that *Bumble Boogie* is anything like *Destino* would have been – the two are totally different. However, what Dali's influence did make the animators realize was that they could experiment with surrealism without producing something pretentious or, even worse, something that would alienate the traditional Disney audience.

Johnny Appleseed Section

Johnny Appleseed tells a much fantasized version of the life of the folk hero John Chapman (1774-1845), who wandered around the Ohio River region for some 40 years planting and tending apple orchards and preaching religion: the fantasy is legitimate, because Johnny Appleseed's adventures have indeed been coloured by the oral tradition – coloured deep purple, in fact.

The **Johnny Appleseed** of the short is portrayed as a rather skinny, pigtailed simpleton – or perhaps "ignoramus" would be a better word, for he is not particularly stupid, just a little narrow-minded: he knows nuthin' about nuthin' except apple-trees. He is inspired one day by a vision of himself accompanying a pioneer wagon-train out West, but tells himself that that rugged life is not for him: he is far too puny. **Johnny's Angel**, who looks much like him but is older and dressed in buckskins and a coonskin cap, appears and tells him not to be so faint-hearted. Think of all the good things that can be made from apples – and

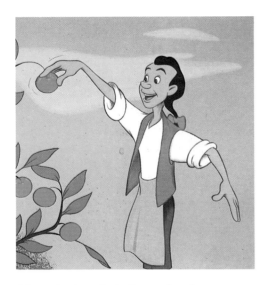

Johnny Appleseed, planting apples wherever he can.

Finally we see him as an old man, sitting under an apple-tree. His Angel reappears, telling him that he is needed in Heaven, where they have virtually everything except apples. Leaving his body behind, Johnny sets off with his Angel for that Kingdom in the Sky.

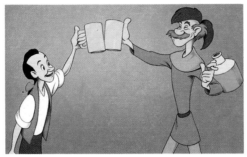

Johnny's Angel – on the right – told Johnny that the work he was doing was good.

right now there are no apple-trees out there in the wilderness.

And so we follow Johnny as for 40 years, through flood and cold and tempest, surrounded by a faithful band of animal friends, he roams the great unknown, planting appleseeds wherever he goes. His efforts are not in vain, for in one scene he sees a group of pioneers having a tremendous celebration based entirely on the products of the apple-trees he has planted – apple tarts, cider and so on. As Dennis Day, the narrator, tells us, "you'll find he left his blessings three – love and faith and the apple tree".

Little Toot Section

As the Andrews Sisters tunefully tell us,

Little Toot was just a tugboat,
A happy harbour tug.
He came from a line of tugboats fine and brave.
But it seems that Little Toot
Simply didn't give a hoot:
Though he tried to be good he never could behave.

In other words, like many another small Disney hero, **Little Toot**, a New York Harbor tug, is the "naughty one". Indeed, he is an extremely mischievous little boat.

We see him indulging in all sorts of minor misdemeanours before one day he goes too far, peppering the portholes of a liner with blasts of dense smoke. After this excursion he is lucky not to be caught by the prowling police boats, which are grim-faced and blue and strongly resemble, in a boatish sort of a way, Butch (➤91).

Little Toot resolves in future to be good and to help his father, **Big Toot**. His first attempt ends in disaster: a vast liner ends up spinning uncontrollably to land in the streets of New York, surrounded by bent and shattered skyscrapers. Little Toot is escorted out to sea – past the 12-mile limit – by the police boats and left there to the mercy of whatever Fate might have in store for him.

A storm blows up. As the sky thunders and the waves crash, a chorus of huge, red, shark-jawed buoys verbally chastises him: "Shame! Shame! Too bad! Too Bad!" Little Toot is such a reject that even the circling beam of a nearby lighthouse detours around him. This is bad enough, but then the storm really hits. The poor little tug is having difficulty just staying afloat when a rocket flare lights up the sky: a liner is in distress out by the dreaded rocks. Little Toot promptly sends back an SOS to the New York tugs and they immediately set out on a rescue expedition, but he is by far the nearest to the liner and so it is really up to him.

Hooked up to the liner, he strains to pull it clear but to no avail ... until a bolt of lightning hits his stern. The effect is electrifying in both senses of the word, and in no time Little Toot has saved the liner and the day. He returns to a hero's welcome, and at last – and for the first time – his father, Big Toot, has cause to be proud of him.

Stills of Little Toot do not do him justice: he is not the flat, neutral character he appears to be in them. The drawing of him is simple, yet somehow it conveys the fact that he is essentially a naughty child – infuriating much of the time, but nevertheless very lovable. His father, Big Toot, comes across as a gritty workin' man, gruff and reserved yet with a heart of gold.

The grim police boats ran Little Toot out of the harbour.

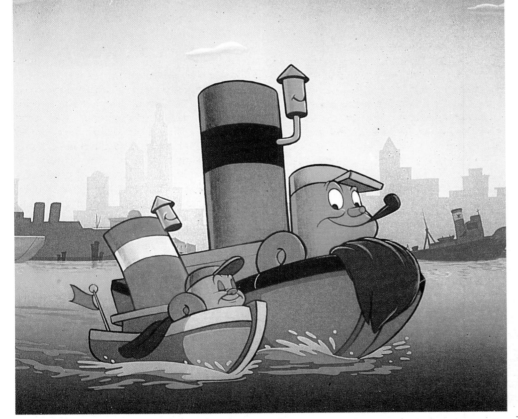

Little Toot, sailing proudly alongside his father, Big Toot.

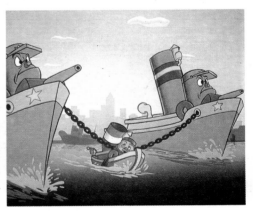

Quite how the Disney animators achieved such depths of characterization is impossible to tell: perhaps they did not know themselves, but did it all by instinct.

Blame it on the Samba Section

The three animated protagonists of *Blame it on the Samba* are **Donald Duck**, **José (Joe) Carioca** and the **Aracuan Bird**, all of whom had appeared in features before, while Donald, of course, was by this time *the* Disney shorts star (➤61). In *Blame it on the Samba* the Aracuan Bird is as irresponsibly destructive as in *The Three Caballeros* (➤212), José is much more his flamboyant but friendly self as in *Saludos Amigos* (➤205) than his rather crueller version of *The Three Caballeros* (➤211), while Donald Duck is Donald Duck. Otherwise, like The Bee in *Bumble Boogie*, they are in this feature really less like characters and more like "experiencing objects", battered around by the whims of the turbulent, pulsing music.

While the short is not especially interesting from the point of view of the characters, it is absorbing in every other way. The music, supplied by Ethel Smith and the Dinning Sisters, is excellent, and the surrealism of much of the animation echoes *Bumble Boogie*. But the special effects are what really mark it out. The highlight occurs when the Aracuan Bird, having already put a lighted match under the foot of the organ-playing (live-action) Ethel Smith – the rhythm "hots up", obviously! – now decides to repeat the trick with a stick of dynamite. The (live-action) organ explodes, sending our pals flying, but in an amazing piece of special-effects work Ethel Smith continues to play the *bits* of the organ as they tumble around the screen and then finally fall together again to form a normal (live-action) organ. The effect would be stunning if achieved in 1988: *Melody Time* was released in 1948.

Many people have criticized Ub Iwerks as an animator and gagsmith, but his special effects have rarely, if ever, been matched. And even Iwerks' own in *Mary Poppins* (1964 [➤274]) pale by comparison with what he achieved here.

Pecos Bill Section

Like *Johnny Appleseed*, *Pecos Bill* is set 'way back in that period of American folklore when men were men and ... Unlike *Johnny Appleseed*, the *Pecos Bill* section of this feature incorporates a certain amount of live action, with Bobby Driscoll and Luana Patten – the young stars of 1946's *Song of the South* (➤219) – being entertained by Roy Rogers, Trigger (who does not sing) and Bob Nolan and the Sons of the Pioneers.

Long ago, as the covered wagons head West, the pioneers come across the Pecos River and discover it to be frighteningly alkaline. As one group of pioneers passes

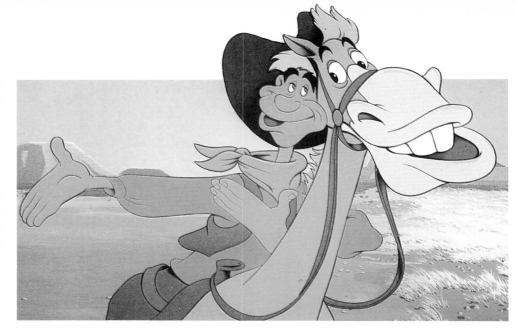

Pecos Bill with his horse, Widowmaker.

by, a little baby blonde boy falls out of their wagon and into the river. Unknowing, the pioneers press on without him.

Fortunately, the little foundling, who will grow up to be the famed **Pecos Bill**, finds succour in a litter of coyotes, and as he grows up with his "brothers" and "sisters" he becomes the toughest "coyote" of the whole family: as Roy Rogers' sung narration tells us, he "outloped the antelope, outjumped the jack-rabbit".

Bill grows up to become a typical Disney blonde lunk: big of chin, big of frame, apparently small of brain. One day, however, he saves the life of a horse that has been pursued across the desert by vultures, and a beautiful friendship ensues. This horse is the famed **Widowmaker**, his boon companion throughout his later adventures.

And what adventures they are! A "rootin' tootin' cowboy", Pecos Bill becomes so tough that he can roll a cigarette while riding atop a cyclone. When there is a drought in his native Texas he uses his lasso to haul in a raincloud from as far away as California ("that's the way we got the Gulf of Mexico," says the sung narration). When again short of water, Pecos Bill digs out the

Rio Grande. And one night, when he has nothing else to do, he shoots out all the stars except one – which is why Texas is the Lone Star State.

All of these adventures would have been fine except that one day, riding down the river on the back of a giant fish, Pecos Bill spots the red-headed, blue-eyed, scantily clad **Slue Foot Sue**. It is love at first sight, and Bill accordingly courts her – to the great distress of Widowmaker, who feels slighted. Sue agrees to marry Bill, but wants also to ride his old pal Widowmaker. This she does in bronc-busting style for a while, but then she is thrown and, thanks to her springy nuptial bustle, bounces higher and progressively higher until she finally impacts on the Moon.

Bill, thwarted in love, goes back to join the coyotes. Whenever the Moon is up he howls at it, and soon the other coyotes learn to follow his example.

Make Mine Music ended on a highpoint – *The Whale Who Wanted to Sing at the Met*. *Melody Time* by contrast finishes with a somewhat lacklustre short (by Disney standards). More than anything else, this is probably why one movie has received so much more attention than the other.

Slue Foot Sue and Pecos Bill had their subtle ways of declaring their romantic interest in each other.

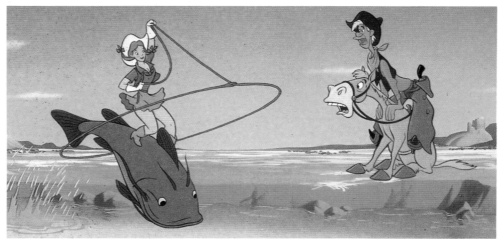

SO DEAR TO MY HEART

Characters:

Danny; Wise Old Owl; Christopher Columbus; Robert the Bruce / Robert Bruce; David; Goliath; Joshua

Credits:

Based on *Midnight and Jeremiah* (1943) by Sterling North

Live Actors: Burl Ives; Beulah Bondi; Bobby Driscoll; Luana Patten; Harry Carey; Raymond Bond; Walter Soderling; Mat Willis; Spelman B. Collins

Voices: Burl Ives; John Beal; Ken Carson; Bob Stanton; The Rhythmaires

Special Processes: Ub Iwerks

Sound Director: C. O. Slyfield

Sound Recording: Max Hutchinson; Robert O. Cook

Film Editors: Thomas Scott; Lloyd L. Richardson

Music Editor: Al Teeter

Score: Paul Smith

Vocal Director: Ken Darby

Orchestration: Edward H. Plumb

Songs: Ticker Freeman; Irving Taylor; Eliot Daniel; Larry Morey; Don Raye; Gene DePaul; Robert Wells; Mel Torme

Story (cartoons): Marc Davis; Ken Anderson; Bill Peet

Screenplay (live action): John Tucker Battle

Photoplay Art Director: John Ewing

Photoplay Set Director: Mac Alper

Director of Photography: Winton C. Hoch

Cartoon Art Treatment: John Hench; Mary Blair; Dick Kelsey

Layout: A. Kendall O'Connor; Hugh Hennesy; Don Griffith; Thor Putnam

Technicolor Colour Director: Natalie Kalmus

Technicolor Colour Associate: Morgan Padelford

Backgrounds: Art Riley; Ralph Hulett; Jimi Trout; Dick Anthony; Brice Mack; Ray Huffine

Animators: Eric Larson; John Lounsbery; Hal King; Milt Kahl; Les Clark; Don Lusk; Marvin Woodward

Effects Animators: George Rowley; Josh Meador; Dan MacManus

Technical Director: Larry Lansburgh

Associate Producer: Perce Pearce

Cartoon Director: Hamilton Luske

Director: Harold Schuster

Release Date: January 19, 1949

Running Time: 82 minutes

THE MOVIE

So Dear to My Heart was one of Walt's own favourites of all the movies that Disney made, because he felt that it genuinely portrayed the ambience of his own childhood. It comes as something of a surprise, therefore, to discover that he played much less of a part in its production than usual: he hired the director whom he thought was right for the job, Harold Schuster, and to a large extent simply let him get on with it – for once, his suggestions were nothing more than that.

Animation plays only a small part in the film. *Song of the South*, the movie with which *So Dear to My Heart* is inevitably compared, received critical acclaim largely because of its animated sections; *So Dear to My Heart* received praise almost despite them. In both cases, however, the animated sequences are used as a means of giving the youthful hero (played by Bobby Driscoll) a sort of moral guidance in the predicaments in which he finds himself. In this movie the animation springs from the boy's scrapbook, and is much more obviously moralistic in nature: the titles of the songs "Stick-to-it-ivity" and "It's Whatcha Do With Whatcha Got", both sung by the Wise Old Owl, betray as much.

Despite the fact that it was a favourite of Walt's, *So Dear to My Heart* is largely forgotten today, probably because it is not so much an A-movie as a B-movie which people prefer to the A-movie with which it shares the billing. Modern critics, if they mention it at all, tend to be dismissive about it – which only goes to show that reviewers of films aimed at children (which *So Dear to My Heart* very definitely is) should take children with them and see how *they* react.

So Dear to My Heart has some importance in that it persuaded Walt that there was a future in making live-action family features. The inclusion of the animated sequences here can be seen as a reluctance to take the risky step of making movies entirely without the element that had made the Disney studio famous. Encouraged by the results of the experiment, Disney went on to make completely live-action features, starting with 1950's *Treasure Island*.

THE STORY

In terms of the animated characters, the story need concern us little. Young Jeremiah (Bobby Driscoll), having "adopted" a newborn black lamb and naming it Danny after the racehorse Dan Patch (also black; Dan Patch makes a fleeting animated appearance), determines to exhibit the mischievous animal at the county fair. There the lamb wins a special-merit award,

given by the judges only when a beast of outstanding qualities emerges.

The animated sequences have no story as such, being essentially moral examples.

THE CHARACTERS

The primary animated character is **Wise Old Owl**, the deliverer of the moral lectures. The first of these is to an animated version of **Danny** the black lamb who, being the only black lamb in a litter of white ones, is feeling somewhat persecuted. "It's whatcha do with whatcha got that counts," sings the Owl, and he illustrates the point

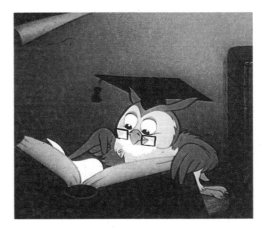

The Wise Old Owl, who gave good counsel to young Jeremiah (played by Bobby Driscoll).

with some animated sequences of **David** killing **Goliath** with nothing more than a stone and **Joshua** tumbling down the walls of Jericho using only a horn. The lamb misunderstands the message and, in live action, proceeds to destroy everything in sight.

The next moral lecture is delivered by Wise Old Owl to Jeremiah; its burden is that the boy should encourage a little "Stick-to-it-ivity" in himself, and not just give up when things seem to be going badly. The song/ lecture is illustrated with the tales of **Christopher Columbus** forging on when all

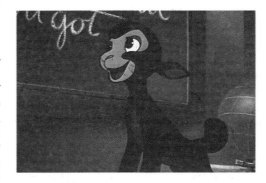

Jeremiah named his real-life lamb Danny, after the racehorse Dan Patch. Danny appeared also in the animated sequences of the movie.

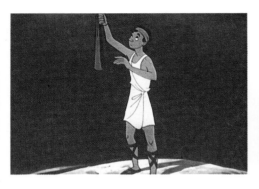

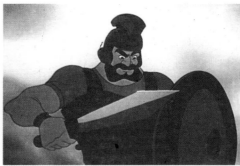

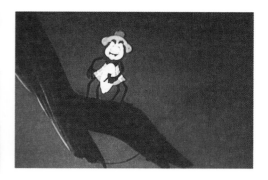

Jeremiah drew an object lesson from the victory of David *(left)* over Goliath *(right)*.

seemed lost and **Robert the Bruce** (referred to in the movie as **Robert Bruce**) being told by the spider to try, try and try again: both men displayed "stick-to-it-ivity" and won out in the end. (Around this time Walt was saying that the studio ought to get back into full-length animated features and the cautious Roy was reluctant, because of the huge expense. Roy lost the argument, and at one point remarked: "I'm afraid if I'd been running this place we would have stopped several times *en route* because of the problems. Walt has the stick-to-it-iveness.")

Robert the Bruce learned some "stick-to-it-ivity" from this little spider.

The third animated sequence serves merely as an introduction to the (live-action) county fair, and the final one is merely the movie's finale. Both feature Wise Old Owl, who is the only animated character of note in the film. He is one of a distinguished line of Disney owls: Friend Owl in *Bambi* (➤200), the pedagogue Professor Owl (➤118), Owl in the Winnie the Pooh shorts (➤128) ... There are a number of them, and all have the same characteristic of wisdom mixed with zaniness. Here the owl has to rely on his "Wisdom Book" to serve up his anodyne proverbs; otherwise he has much in common with the others.

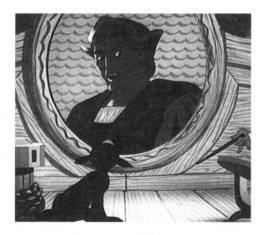

Christopher Columbus, one of the historical characters of whose experiences Jeremiah was reminded.

THE ADVENTURES OF ICHABOD AND MR. TOAD

Characters:

Mr. Toad section:
J. Thaddeus Toad; Rat; Mole; Angus MacBadger; Cyril Proudbottom; Winkie; Prosecutor; Judge; Doctor; Court Clerk

The Legend of Sleepy Hollow section:
Ichabod Crane; Katrina Van Tassel; Baltus Van Tassel; Brom Bones / Headless Horseman; Tilda; Gunpowder

Credits:

Based on *The Wind in the Willows* (1908) by Kenneth Grahame and *The Legend of Sleepy Hollow* from *The Sketch Book* (1819-20) by Washington Irving

Voices: Basil Rathbone (narrator of *Mr. Toad*); Bing Crosby (narrator of *The Legend of Sleepy Hollow*); Eric Blore (Mr. Toad); Colin Campbell (Mole); Claude Allister (Rat); Campbell Grant (Angus MacBadger); J. Pat O'Malley (Cyril Proudbottom and minor parts); John McLeish ([as John Ployardt] Prosecutor); Alec Harford (Winkie); Leslie Dennison (Judge, first weasel); Edmond Stevens (second weasel); The Rhythmaires

Special Processes: Ub Iwerks

Sound Supervision: C. O. Slyfield

Sound Recording: Robert O. Cook

Film Editor: John O. Young

Music: Oliver Wallace

Vocal Arrangements: Ken Darby

Orchestration: Joseph Dubin

Ichabod Songs: Don Raye; Gene dePaul

Music Editor: Al Teeter

Story: Erdman Penner; Ted Sears; Joe Rinaldi; Homer Brightman; Winston Hibler; Harry Reeves

Layout: Tom Codrick; Thor Putnam; Al Zinnen; Charles Philippi; Lance Nolley; Hugh Hennesy

Colour and Styling: Mary Blair; Don Da Gradi; Claude Coats; John Hench

Backgrounds: Art Riley; Ray Huffine; Brice Mack; Merle Cox; Dick Anthony

Directing Animators: Frank Thomas; Ollie Johnston; John Lounsbery; Wolfgang Reitherman; Milt Kahl; Ward Kimball

Character Animators: Marc Davis; Hugh Fraser; Don Lusk; Fred Moore; Harvey Toombs; John Sibley; Hal King; Hal Ambro

Effects Animators: George Rowley; Jack Boyd

Directors: Jack Kinney; Clyde Geronimi; James Algar

Production Supervisor: Ben Sharpsteen

Release Date: October 5, 1949

Running Time: 68 minutes

THE MOVIE

The Adventures of Ichabod and Mr. Toad was the last of the Disney features to be an animated anthology. Like *Fun and Fancy Free* a couple of years earlier, it is a double-featurette. In this case, however, the two featurettes are much more ambitious – one of them is the Disney version of Kenneth Grahame's *The Wind in the Willows*, no less – but this is not to say that it is a more successful feature than *Fun and Fancy Free*. If anything, indeed, the reverse is true: both of the featurettes could have done with a more prolonged treatment (especially *Mr. Toad*), and so one leaves the cinema slightly frustrated. The featurettes in *Fun and Fancy Free*, on the other hand, are superbly designed to fit their lengths.

The two featurettes in *The Adventures of Ichabod and Mr. Toad* have no real relation to each other, although a somewhat desperate and half-hearted attempt is made to make them seem so: both Toad and Ichabod Crane, the narration explains, are great classic characters of literature, and so it makes sense to talk of them together. Like Fanny Hill and Huckleberry Finn, perhaps?

The critics at the time were delighted, because at last Disney was getting back to what it did best: extended animated treatments of great tales. *Cinderella* – although presumably the reviewers did not know this – was just around the corner, and finally Disney was pulling itself out of the "mashed potatoes and gravy" phase.

That said, one cannot help but feel that Disney could have done better by *The Wind in the Willows*. To be sure, it is one of Disney's best attempts at a British children's classic, but it still omits much of the power of Kenneth Grahame's original. Even the names of the characters are changed, to no apparent advantage: generations of children know all about Badger, so who is this "Angus MacBadger" fellow? Still, *Mr. Toad* is a very good featurette, if viewed on its own terms rather than as an animated representation of Grahame's book. *The Legend of Sleepy Hollow* is perhaps more satisfying, probably because it is based on a short story rather than a full-length book: one is less aware of the omissions. Another point of difference is that *Mr. Toad* has characters with voices, although Basil Rathbone's narration supplements these; *The Legend of Sleepy Hollow*, by contrast, is merely narrated (by Bing Crosby).

THE CHARACTERS

Mr. Toad Section
Basil Rathbone, in an introductory section, tells us that for his money Toad is the most fabulous character in English literature (the feature had originally been titled *Two Fabulous Characters*).

We first encounter **Rat** (who habitually wears a Sherlock Holmes deerstalker – an

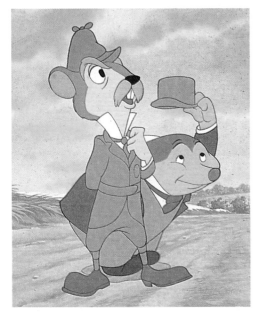
Rat and Mole, polite as ever.

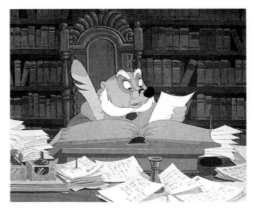
Angus MacBadger, desperately trying to keep control of Toad's accounts.

in-joke about Rathbone's narration?) and **Mole** as they are at tea. This ceremony is disrupted by an urgent message from **Angus MacBadger**, who has taken over the accounts at Toad Hall because Toad has, through his folly, run things grievously down. Angus is nearly a nervous wreck because this time Toad has gone "too far": he has taken to going around the country in "a canary-yellow gypsy cart with a horse named Cyril".

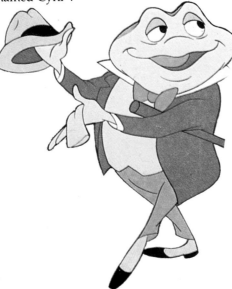
J. Thaddeus Toad. The term "animated character" could have been invented for him.

We shift to find Toad and **Cyril Proudbottom**, his horse, singing a duet about the joys of being out on the open road. Cyril is a very irresponsible character – every bit as bad as Toad – with a voice which, while supplied by J. Pat O'Malley, sounds much like that of the great British music-hall star George Formby. He wears a little orange hat. On being confronted by Rat and Mole, who have come to save Toad from himself, he announces that he is "a bit of a trotter, a bit of a rotter", which is a fair description.

Toad's response to the verbal chastisement from Mole and Rat is periodically to put his hands over his ears – an action which has the amusing effect of

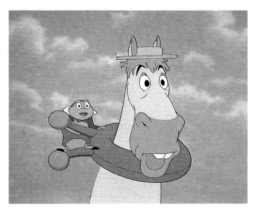
Cyril Proudbottom was a little more responsible than Toad – but only a little.

muting the entire soundtrack. Finally he whips Cyril into a gallop and leaves the two friends with a cry of "You'll never get me to give this up!". Just around the corner, however, he and Cyril see a motor-car, and the eyes of both of them become fascinated spirals: "Gad!" says Toad. "What *have* I been missing?" It takes little imagination to realize that he is one of those faddy characters who are never satisfied unless they have some new obsession to dominate their minds.

A car – that is what Toad *must* have. Rat and Mole lock him for "safekeeping" in his chambers – to give him time "until the poison worked out of his system", we are told – but of course this measure does not work: Toad ties some sheets together and climbs out through the window. We next see him arrested for dangerous driving and for apparently having stolen a car – although he claims to have bought it – and there follows the celebrated trial scene. Rat and Mole as witnesses agree reluctantly that

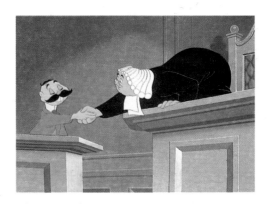
The Judge congratulating Winkie on his testimony: it's nice to know who your friends are.

they had locked Toad up in an attempt to stop him getting a car, but most damaging is MacBadger's admission that he had frozen Toad's funds: how could Toad have bought a car without any money? Proceedings are enlivened by the excellent portrayals of a number of minor characters: the **Judge**, the **Prosecutor**, a **Doctor** and the **Court Clerk** among them.

Toad acts as his own lawyer, calling Cyril as his first witness. The horse tells, in flashback, how the two of them had been on the road after Toad's escape when Toad had spotted and fallen in love with a flashy car driven by a group of weasels (dressed like Prohibition gangsters). They had followed the weasels into a bar run by a certain **Winkie** (Winkey or Winky – spellings differ in various versions), where Toad had offered them Toad Hall in exchange for the car. The sale agreed, a contract had been drawn up and witnessed by Winkie. The Prosecutor, with some justi-

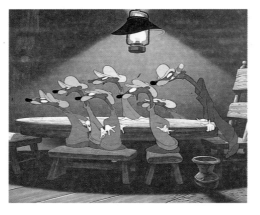

A representative sampling of the villainous weasels.

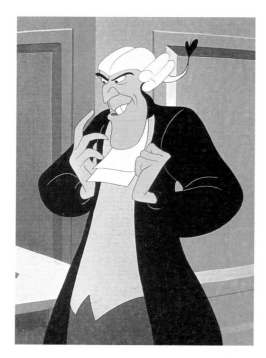

The Prosecutor gave Rat and Mole a hard time of it.

fication, refuses to believe anybody could be so stupid as Cyril claims Toad to be.

Winkie, who has a moustache like Hercule Poirot, slick black hair and a pudgy expression, is Toad's next witness – but he tells a completely different story. What *really* happened, he says, is that Toad tried to sell him a stolen car. Toad is immediately found guilty and sentenced by the Judge to prison.

Christmas finds Toad in the Tower of London, ruing his many sins: he vows to himself never again to hurt his friends or let himself indulge in one of his foolish fads. However, his jailer explains that, since it is the festive season, he is allowed one visitor, his Grandma – who proves to be Cyril in a most improbable disguise. He has brought a pink frock and a blue smock cap with which Toad likewise can disguise himself. They escape, and soon the whole of London is alive to the manhunt ... or, rather, toadhunt.   The fact that Toad is still wearing a ball-and-chain slightly mars his disguise. Pursued by the police, he steals a train – the police chase after him in another, guns ablaze. At last, going over a bridge, Toad heaves the heavy ball – and hence

himself – into the waters below. He is proud of his escape ... until he remembers the little matter of breathing. Finally he frees himself from the ball.

Rat and Mole are sadly having Christmas dinner when Toad arrives exhausted. Rat in particular is aghast: he believes Toad guilty and thinks he should pay his debt to society. But then Angus MacBadger appears with the news that the weasels have taken over Toad Hall and that their leader is none other than – Winkie. So Toad was innocent all the time!

MacBadger says that the only way of reclaiming Toad Hall is to recover the bill of sale from Winkie. In a thrilling sequence the four friends invade Toad Hall from beneath and, at no little danger to life and limb, finally succeed in thwarting both the weasels and Toad's repeated stupidities to achieve their objective. Toad can prove his innocence and Winkie's guilt, and can now regain Toad Hall. It seems, too, that he has become a reformed character ... until, that is, to the horror of his friends he appears with Cyril aboard a 1900s-style biplane. Yes, he has a new fad, and if anything it is the most dangerous to date.

Basil Rathbone posits in his closing comments that all of us Rats, Badgers and Moles dream sometimes of having wild adventures like Toad's, and that it is because of such dreams that he (Rathbone) thinks Toad to be the most fabulous character in English literature.

A number of the characters from *Mr. Toad* appeared in the 1983 featurette *Mickey's Christmas Carol* (►**130**): Cyril, Toad (as Scrooge's first employer), Rat and Mole (as collectors for the poor) and two of the weasels (as gravediggers).

The Legend of Sleepy Hollow Section

As noted, at an early stage the feature had been titled *Two Fabulous Characters* before somebody wisely decided that this was hardly likely to have audiences flocking to the cinema. Moreover, it would have been rather confusing, because while Rathbone uses the word "fabulous" in its modern

sense to describe Toad, the voice that takes over from his (Bing Crosby's) is using it of Ichabod Crane in its original sense: he is a creature of fable.

It is late Autumn and Tarrytown's neighbour Sleepy Hollow has a new arrival, an itinerant schoolmaster named **Ichabod Crane**. We first see not him but his huge, inverted shadow; the narration describes him evocatively as he himself comes into view, shambling along on his knock-kneed horse:

The worthy pedagogue was ... a most unusual man. To see him striding along, one might well mistake him for some scarecrow eloped from a cornfield. He was tall, and exceedingly lank. His head was small and flat on top with a long snipe nose, so that it looked like a weathercock perched upon his spindle neck. Altogether he was such an apparition as is seldom to be seen in broad daylight.

He has huge ears, too, and wispy red hair plaited tightly back into a pigtail, but none of these attributes seem to be failings in the eyes of the local womenfolk, for Ichabod,

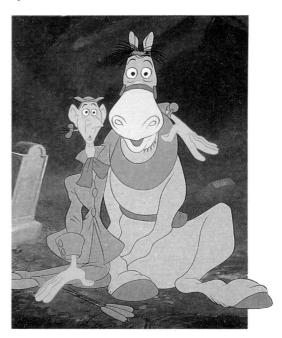

Ichabod and his horse consoled themselves that they had been scared over nothing – but that was before the Headless Horseman appeared.

largely animated by Frank Thomas, proves to be quite a ladies' man.

This does not endear him to **Brom Bones**, self-appointed leader of the "Sleepy Hollow Boys", a band of young drunks and bovine ne'er-do-wells who terrorize the neighbourhood. "There was no malice in his mischief," says the narration of this "burly roistering blade, always ready for a fight", adding that he was "quite the hero of all the country round", a judgement which seems to be flattering in the extreme. Tall, beefy and black-haired, with a prevalent expression of doltish good humour, he is a natural bully and petty thief. As we are later told: "It was inevitable that such a man as

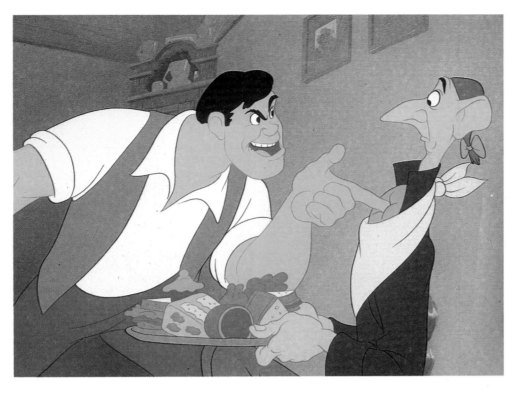

Brom Bones making it clear to Ichabod that might is right.

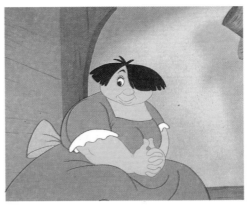

Tilda might not have been able to compete in the glamour stakes, but she possessed plenty of determination.

Ichabod should become an object of ridicule to Brom Bones and his gang."

Ichabod, too, proves to be a less than perfect personality. Indeed, aside from being an amateur Lothario he is something of a glutton. In school he tempers justice with mercy – if, that is, the child's mother is a good cook. We see him stealing a pie from a passing tray and, most revolting of all, lying on his bed scoffing turkey drumsticks he pulls out of his coat pocket. Even when eating he usually has his nose deep in a book.

The local love goddess is **Katrina Van Tassel**, big, blonde and bland, the daughter of the richest farmer in the area, **Baltus Van Tassel**. She is "a blooming lass, plump as a partridge … and rosy-cheeked", and she wears Dutch costume including the traditional triangular-flapped cap. Her father, red-haired and -nosed, sucks on a poisonous-looking pipe; small and wide, he is only about half the height of his lissom

daughter. She, indeed, proves to be something of a coquette. When we first see her she blows a kiss at random into the air and is instantly, to her delight, surrounded by every eligible male in town, not to mention a few of the ineligible ones.

Ichabod is much smitten by the sight of Baltus Van Tassel's ostentatious wealth – sorry, of Katrina's beauty – so much so that he absentmindedly puts a chicken on his head and eats his hat. Unfortunately, Brom too has set his sights on the farmer's daughter, although his attentions "both piqued and provoked the fair Katrina, and she often wished that some champion would appear and for once take the field open". Ichabod is an eager volunteer, throwing down his cape, Walter-Raleigh-style, for her to step on to save her fair feet from a puddle. Brom's response is to gallop over the cape, drenching Ichabod, and to scoop up Katrina onto the back of his huge snorting horse, **Gunpowder**. She gigglingly casts Ichabod a handkerchief. We are told that in the ensuing weeks his star is very much in the ascendant with her.

Hallowe'en arrives, and with it invitations to both Ichabod and Brom to the Van Tassels' Hallowe'en party. Ichabod's has a note attached to it – "PS: Please come – Katrina" – and one suspects from her general behaviour in such matters that Brom's invitation is similarly embellished.

At the party Ichabod proves to be a top-notch dancer, and, to Brom's fury, he has it all his own way with Katrina. Brom cunningly substitutes the plump, eager and toothless cook **Tilda** in Ichabod's arms, but Ichabod, equally cunningly, reverses the switch – the process is repeated several

times, to hilarious effect. Nevertheless, "There was no doubt that Ichabod was the man of the hour. Brom knew that he must concede his rival still another victory."

However, Ichabod proves to have an Achilles' heel: he is very superstitious and mightily afraid of ghosts. Leering happily, Brom Bones proceeds to tell the story of the Headless Horseman, who haunts these parts looking for a head to "borrow". He gives Ichabod an evilly significant stare, and the scrawny schoolmaster pales and perspires.

After the party, Ichabod is terrified as he makes his way home on his horse. An owl's hoot petrifies him; a frog's croak chills him. Then ahead he sees a ghost standing with arms upraised and eyes ablaze … but it proves to be nothing more than a hollow tree with fireflies lurking in its recesses. Ichabod has the good grace to laugh at his own fears, and carries on a little more confidently towards the bridge that, according to the legend, marks the far boundary of the Headless Horseman's evil realm.

But then, from behind him, he hears the clatter of galloping hooves and a loud shout of wicked laughter. He turns to see a spine-freezing apparition: the **Headless Horseman**, a huge black figure with a long red scarf tied around where his neck would be – if he had one. Waving his sword and

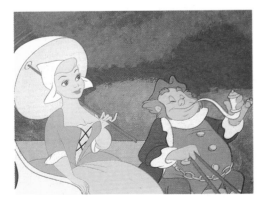

The pulchritudinous and flirtatious Katrina Van Tassel with her ovoid father Baltus.

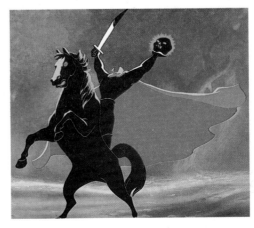

The Headless Horseman, astride a spectral steed that bears a remarkable resemblance to Gunpowder, Brom Bones' horse.

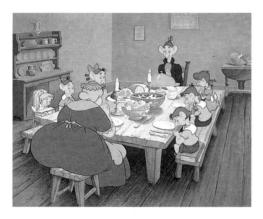

A cosy domestic scene with Ichabod, Mrs. Crane, and their offspring.

booming with laughter, he chases Ichabod on his vast black horse (which bears a strong resemblance to Gunpowder, aside from its fiercely bared teeth and glowing red eyes). Through the hostile forest they pound, and at last Ichabod reaches and crosses the bridge. As he pulls up he turns to see the Horseman pull out a fiery "head" and hurl it at him; the picture fades in an explosive flash.

All the villagers ever find of Ichabod in the morning is his hat, with a shattered pumpkin lying beside it. They *know* that he has been spirited away to the Headless Horseman's den of evil – although in due course rumours arise that the schoolmaster has been seen in the next county, where he has married a widow and "inherited" six children (all of whom look surprisingly like him), not to mention a fair amount of money.

In due course, Katrina succumbs to Brom's oafish blandishments, and permits herself to be taken to the altar. As for the Headless Horseman? Well, Brom has good reason to believe that he will never be seen in these parts again . . .

The Legend of Sleepy Hollow seems to have a curious moral. In most Disney movies bullying is not the way to win the hand of a fair lady (although Katrina is such a heartless coquette that one wonders if marriage really does constitute a happy ending for Brom). None of the main characters is depicted as especially likeable; nevertheless, Ichabod played fair, Brom did not, and yet Brom's suit is the successful one. Is the moral that skinny, bookish men should not set their sights on beautiful women? Is it that might is right? Of course, Disney was following Washington Irving's original, and so one should not read too much into this apparent moral. Nevertheless, it is a flaw – albeit a minor one – in what is otherwise an excellent and highly enjoyable featurette.

CINDERELLA

Characters:

Cinderella; Prince Charming
Mice: Gus; Jaq; Suzy; Perla; Blossom; Luke; Mert; Bert
Lucifer; Lady Tremaine; Anastasia (Ugly Sister); Drizella (Ugly Sister); Fairy Godmother; King; Grand Duke; Bruno (dog)/ Footman; Major (horse)/Coachman

Credits:

Based on the traditional story as recounted by Charles Perrault in *Histoires ou Contes du temps passé* (1697)

Voices: Ilene Woods (Cinderella); Eleanor Audley (Lady Tremaine); Verna Felton (Fairy Godmother); Luis Van Rooten (King, Grand Duke); Rhoda Williams (Drizella); James Macdonald (Gus and Jaq, Bruno); June Foray (Lucifer); William Phipps (Prince Charming); Lucille Bliss (Anastasia); Betty Lou Gerson (Narrator); Helen Seibert; Lucille Williams; June Sullivan; Clint McCauley (mice)

Special Processes: Ub Iwerks

Sound Director: C. O. Slyfield

Sound Recording: Harold J. Steck; Robert O. Cook

Film Editor: Donald Halliday

Music Editor: Al Teeter

Musical Direction: Oliver Wallace; Paul Smith

Songs: Mack David; Jerry Livingston; Al Hoffman

Orchestration: Joseph Dubin

Story: Bill Peet; Ted Sears; Homer Brightman; Kenneth Anderson; Erdman Penner; Winston Hibler; Harry Reeves; Joe Rinaldi

Layout: Mac Stewart; Tom Codrick; Lance Nolley; Don Griffith; A. Kendall O'Connor; Hugh Hennesy; Charles Philippi; Thor Putnam

Colour Styling: Mary Blair; Claude Coats; John Hench; Don DaGradi

Backgrounds: Brice Mack; Ralph Hulett; Dick Anthony; Art Riley; Ray Huffine; Merle Cox; Thelma Witmer

Directing Animators: Eric Larson; Milt Kahl; Frank Thomas; John Lounsbery; Wolfgang Reitherman; Ward Kimball; Ollie Johnston; Marc Davis; Les Clark; Norm Ferguson

Character Animators: Don Lusk; Hugh Fraser; Fred Moore; Judge Whitaker; Marvin Woodward; George Nicholas; Phil Duncan; Hal King; Harvey Toombs; Cliff Nordberg; Hal Ambro; Ken O'Brien

Effects Animators: George Rowley; Josh Meador; Jack Boyd

Directors: Wilfred Jackson; Hamilton Luske; Clyde Geronimi

Production Supervision: Ben Sharpsteen

Release Date: February 15, 1950

Running Time: 74 minutes

THE MOVIE

The general attitude of the critics to the release of *Cinderella* can be summed up in two words: DISNEY'S BACK. And back with a vengeance. His first full-length animated feature since 1942's *Bambi* (➤**197**) returned to the territory he had made very much his own: the children's classic fantasy. Not everyone loved the movie – Richard Schickel in his *The Disney Version* characteristically finds a few contemporary brickbats – but generally critics were enthusiastic and the public voted in its favour overwhelmingly with their hard-earned dollars: on its first release the movie's "take" surpassed even that of *Snow White and the Seven Dwarfs*.

The reasons for the movie's success are not hard to establish. (a) It was a retelling of what is perhaps *the* most famous fairy-tale of all time. Disney's version of another classic fairy-tale, *Snow White*, had been brilliant, and so *Cinderella* could be expected to be, too. (b) *Cinderella* is indeed a very good movie. (c) Finally, Walt's "formula"; as Walt himself put it, "My formula – people always like to root for Cinderella and the Prince." In other words, *Cinderella* is a tale of goodies *versus* baddies, and the goodies win to the delight of the average audience.

In an interview with A. Eisen in *Crimmer's* in 1975 John Hench, who worked on the movie, discussed this aspect in a little more detail:

. . . fairytales . . . all fall into a pattern, often a Biblical pattern. In the case of Cinderella, she was very high born. Through some set of circumstances, she was reduced to a kitchen maid. This is clearly Man being kicked out of Eden. Along comes a redeemer, a prince, and there's always a gimmick, a key, a talisman. In *Sleeping Beauty* it's a kiss, in *Cinderella* it's a glass slipper. And the person is returned to the former state.

One understands Hench's point, although one cannot help wondering why kitchen-maids of high birth should be returned to luxury while all the *other* kitchen-maids should just have to lump never having any luxury at all!

In fact, the feature did not represent Disney's first stab at the story of *Cinderella*. Long ago in the Laugh-O-gram days Walt had released in 1922 a greatly distorted version of the fairy-tale. The Laugh-O-gram short is distinguished primarily by the characterizations of the two Ugly Sisters, one of whom is fat and seen lying in a hammock reading a book called *Eat and*

Grow Thin (she eats, all right, but it does not seem to work for her) and the other of whom is skinny and seen poring over a book called *Beauty Secrets*. Otherwise the short is primitive – as all animated shorts were in those days.

Nobody could say that the feature version of *Cinderella* is primitive, however. Although the animation does not possess the detail of that seen in earlier works such as *Snow White*, *Pinocchio* and *Bambi*, it is brilliantly effected. The characters are excellently depicted, and the voices (notably those of Eleanor Audley as Lady Tremaine, June Foray as Lucifer and Jim Macdonald as Gus and Jaq) are superb. The song "Bibbidi Bobbidi Boo", sung by the Fairy Godmother, was designed to be – and was – a smash hit. Overall, the movie was made with great integrity: critics could claim that some of the earlier anthology features were somewhat cynically produced, merely cashing in on the Disney reputation, but it is untenable to maintain this of *Cinderella*. As Leonard Maltin remarks in his *The Disney Films*, "It is easy to dismiss *Cinderella* as an unremarkable Disney product, but those who do so obviously haven't seen it recently." Indeed, it is one of Disney's all-time greats, and decades later still makes extremely fine viewing.

THE STORY

Once upon a time there was a good widower who decided to remarry so that his little daughter Cinderella might enjoy a mother's love. His second wife, herself of noble birth, brought two daughters of her own, Anastasia and Drizella, to the marriage. In due course the widower died, and that was the signal for Cinderella's stepmother to reduce her to the rank of a tormented kitchen-maid. However, while Cinderella might be despised and oppressed by Lady ("that's stretching a point") Tremaine and the two ugly, vain stepsisters, she is befriended by many animals, notably a troop of mice led by Gus and Jaq, some bluebirds, Major the horse and Bruno the dog; indeed, the only animal in the movie to be hostile to her is Lucifer, the overfed, pampered cat.

Cinderella's daily routine is one of drudging servitude. She has to rise before everyone else, feed all the animals, take up breakfast trays to her stepmother and her stepsisters (universally known as the Ugly Sisters), be upbraided for imagined imperfections, receive a long list of impossible tasks to perform ... It is all very much in the tradition of Perrault's fairy-tale.

However, unknown to her, salvation is at hand. The King is disturbed because his son seems to show no interest in the women of the palace. How will the royal line be continued? He instructs his Grand Duke to organize a ball to which shall be invited every eligible maiden in the land. The Ugly Sisters are delighted when the invitation arrives, less so when Cinderella points out that she too is eligible (and she, like them, is palpably a maiden, although perhaps for rather different reasons). Lady Tremaine rather surprisingly agrees that Cinderella may attend the ball – assuming, that is, that she finds "something presentable to wear" and "gets all her work done". This is easier said than done, because as soon as Cinderella starts to patch up one of her own mother's old dresses she is summoned and given the standard impossible list of chores. However, her animal friends complete the dress for her, using scraps of finery discarded by the Ugly Sisters.

These borrowed trimmings are Cinderella's downfall, for as soon as she appears in her magnificent dress the stepmother spots where they have come from and the Ugly Sisters use this as an excuse to shred the dress. Weeping, Cinderella rushes out into the garden and, as the rest of the family depart for the ball, she tells her animal friends that she no longer has any faith in dreams of better times to come. But ... but what is this? A mysterious light appears, and from it materializes a dumpy, scatterbrained woman who announces that she is Cinderella's Fairy Godmother. With a wave of her wand and the singing of a magic spell, she transforms a nearby pumpkin into a coach, the mice into horses, the dog into a footman, the horse into a coachman, and, most important of all, the tatters of Cinderella's dress into a gorgeous gown. However, the Fairy Godmother warns, on the last stroke of midnight the spell will expire and all will be restored to the way it was before.

At the ball Prince Charming is transfixed by the beautiful Cinderella, and dances the night away with her. He is about to propose to her when the first stroke of midnight sounds. She flees, but one of her glass slippers comes off and he finds and treasures this trophy. On the way home the spell expires and Cinderella is once more in rags, her horses mice, her coach a pumpkin, and so forth. However, thanks to a special dispensation on the part of the Fairy Godmother, she is allowed to retain the mate of the slipper she has lost – as a souvenir.

Prince Charming is heartbroken: he insists that he will marry no woman other than the owner of the glass slipper. The King instructs the Grand Duke to scour the countryside and find the maiden whose foot fits the slipper. When the expedition reaches Lady Tremaine's establishment she suddenly realizes that Cinderella was the beautiful woman dancing with the Prince, and Cinderella for the first time realizes who it was with whom she was dancing. Lady Tremaine promptly locks Cinderella into her tower room, in the hope that one of the Ugly Sisters will be able to fit her foot into the slipper.

Gus and Jaq steal Lady Tremaine's key and desperately attempt to carry it up the stairs to Cinderella – a task made more difficult by Lucifer attacking them. Eventually, however, thanks to the intervention of Bruno, they succeed. Just as the Grand Duke is preparing disappointedly to leave Cinderella appears. Lady Tremaine smashes the glass slipper, but Cinderella produces its mate and slips that on instead.

The finale of the film is a vast wedding celebration. Lady Tremaine and the Ugly Sisters get nothing; Cinderella and Prince Charming get each other; the King gets a well received kiss from his new daughter-

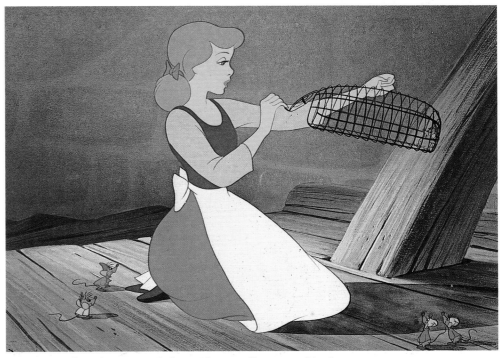

Sweet Cinderella, in her serving clothes, with some of her mouse friends.

in-law; the populace get a blow-out; and Cinderella's animal friends get the prospect of living as happily ever after as Cinderella and the Prince. The audience gets the feeling of having watched a thoroughly good movie, so on all counts it really *is* a happy ending.

THE CHARACTERS

Cinderella

The character of Cinderella was posed in live action by Helene Stanley who, to judge by stills of her performance, was even more beautiful than the screen Cinderella – although she was brunette rather than blonde. In a 1982 interview with Kurt Wiley, Marc Davis, largely responsible for animating Cinderella, compared the character with another of his "creations", Cruella De Vil:

> ... I think that Cinderella would have to be the more difficult because she has to be the substance that carries the story all the way through. She *has* to be believable, she *has* to be real, and she has to be [someone] that you can feel sympathy for. Storytelling characters like these are rather thankless characters to do because ... they don't get *laughs*! When you do something in animation and the whole audience laughs at one time at something you've done, it is a tremendous thrill.

Many of the central characters in Disney's features are essentially cyphers – things happen to them, instead of their making things happen – but Cinderella is an exception. She is by no means a weak-willed character content to let events flow on around her: on the contrary, when the invitation to the ball arrives she uses everything short of physical force to persuade her stepmother and stepsisters that she has every right to attend. Snow White (➤159) would never have had the strength of character to stick up for herself in this way, but Cinderella does. It is for this reason perhaps more than any other that she is the most memorable of the Disney heroines.

Prince Charming

By contrast with Cinderella, Prince Charming is a rather anonymous character – much like the Prince in *Snow White*, for example (➤160). His role is purely to be a handsome and high-born spouse, marriage to whom will raise Cinderella from her life of unjust drudgery. Even his insistence that he will marry no other than the beautiful girl with whom he danced at the ball is rendered to us at second hand, in a hilarious interview between the King and the Grand Duke. It was not until much later, in 1959's *Sleeping Beauty*, that Disney was able to bring us a handsome fairy-tale prince capable of being more than a symbol.

The Mice

Disney introduced a number of brand-new characters to the age-old story of *Cinderella*, and of these the most notable are the animals – none more so than the mice, the most significant of whom are **Gus** and **Jaq**. The mice were largely the responsibility of Ward Kimball. *Newsweek* commented at the time that

> ... in Gus, the mouse commando, and his pawky pal Jaq, Disney has a pair of heroes the like of which has not been seen since the reign of Mickey. Most memorable scene of the whole movie is the breathless climax in which Gus and Jaq filch a monumental key from the stepmother's pocket and try and huff and hoist it up to the room in which Cinderella has been hidden from the prince's heralds.

Walt was in no doubt about the value of the addition of these characters. In a 1953 article called "Ways of Telling the World's Great Stories" he remarked:

> To some [timeless] stories a film version can give wider scope and even add characters without damage to the original tale. In *Cinderella* ... there was every proof that audiences enjoyed our addition of the mice characters, Gus and Jaq, and the valiant, fun-loving little band of Cinderella's helpers.

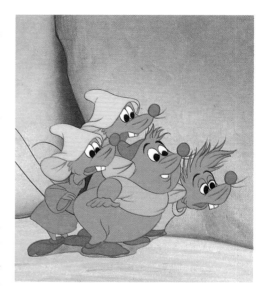

The mice were the major support actors in *Cinderella*.

The full list of the named mice can be seen above (➤234); the only two important ones are Gus and Jaq. Gus, a tubby, chubby little fellow is not too terribly bright, but he has a good heart and is Cinderella's most devoted admirer, with the possible exception of Prince Charming. Jaq is much wirier and certainly a more "streetwise" character; he is the cunning brain of the pair. The famous scene in the movie in which the two mice do their best to struggle up the stairs with the gargantuan (in their terms) key was largely the work of Wolfgang Reitherman. The scene encompasses so much emotion – panic, conquest of panic, difficulty, frustration, and so on – that it is difficult to credit that it can have been produced using merely moving drawings. Very few live actors could have conveyed this spectrum of emotions successfully; it was one of Disney's triumphs that they were able to make two animated mice do so.

Lucifer

The character of the cat Lucifer was largely inspired by Ward Kimball, who used his own cat as a model. The *Newsweek* review of *Cinderella* singled out Lucifer as one of the movie's highlights, describing him as a "fat

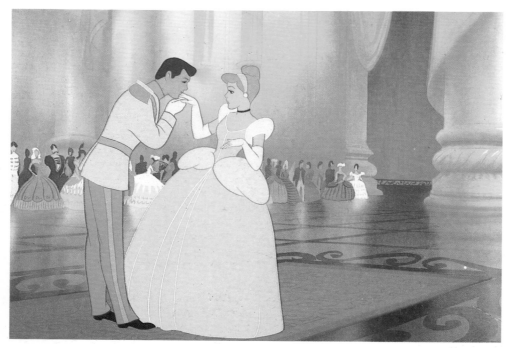

Cinderella receives the adoration of Prince Charming.

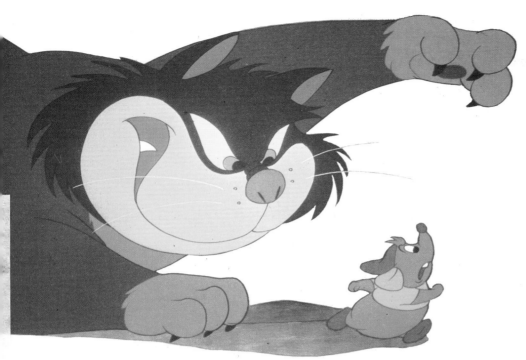

Gus, finding the mean cat Lucifer a little too much to handle.

and unutterably smug house cat whom Disney has dreamed up as a wonderful villain to set against the resident mice". In a long and fascinating 1978 article, however, Thomas A. Nelson sees Lucifer rather differently: he views him as helping to tone down the stepmother's malevolence, as a comic-relief villain rather than as an inspirer of nightmares:

> A marvellous Disney creation, Lucifer parallels in the animal world of the film the wicked stepmother's thoroughly humanized evil and contributes to the softening of her impact. Lucifer is petulant, loutish, and vicious enough, except throughout we realize his domesticity makes him a comic-villainous foil for the film's enlarged household animal action. In truth, the action developing the conflict between Lucifer and the mice almost steals the show. Lucifer's overweight and bumbling evil sufficiently characterizes him so that we view his villainy as belonging to an overstuffed house pet spoiled by too much milk and easy, upperclass living. Lucifer's animal cunning, therefore, has been corrupted by a human vanity and sloth familiar to manners comedy. Naturally, we cheer for the proletariat mice and the fairy-tale aspirations of Cinderella, representing as they do that special society known as Disney democracy.

The technique of using a bumbling assistant villain (or villains) as a way of ameliorating the terror of the arch-villain was used many times in the Disney features; one thinks, for example, of Horace and Jasper Badun in *One Hundred and One Dalmatians* and even of Creeper in *The Black Cauldron*. However, even though Lucifer may not have the spiteful malignancy of Lady Tremaine, he is quite certainly a villain, and the scene in which he attacks the mice on the stairs is quite as frightening as virtually anything

produced by Disney. Partly this is achieved through the animation – there are some marvellous effects of scale, contrasting the tiny mice with the relatively huge cat – and partly through the character of Lucifer himself, for the cat has no *need* to be malevolent: he has a comfortable enough life, and the mice are generally prepared to leave him alone.

Lady Tremaine

Although she possesses no known magical powers, it is hard not to see Cinderella's wicked stepmother, Lady Tremaine as anything other than a witch, the counterpart of the evil stepmother in *Snow White* (➤160) – indeed, she even has a familiar, in the shape of the cat Lucifer. Curiously, she was principally animated by Frank Thomas, much better known for his

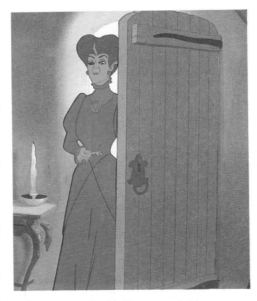

Lady Tremaine, Cinderella's unspeakable stepmother.

soft and sentimental scenes and characters (although he was responsible for Hook in *Peter Pan* [➤251], too). Certainly she is a denizen of the evil realm, as Thomas A. Nelson points out:

> The stepmother, in herself, appears to be a substantial villain in Disney's [version of the tale, as opposed to Perrault's]. Her glowing, slanted eyes and mocking smile, animated with a fuller realism than either [*Snow White*'s] Wicked Queen or [*Pinocchio*'s] Stromboli, make her a chilling presence. An early scene, for instance, shows her inhabiting a world of darkness, her fierce eyes peering at Cinderella from an inner sanctum.

Like Lucifer, Lady Tremaine is quite gratuitously malicious: her sole reason for persecuting Cinderella is that she prefers to assist the fortunes of her own appalling daughters – also, of course, that it is useful to have cheap labour on the premises. Indeed, Cinderella is not just cheap labour: she is a slave, and a badly treated one at that.

Lady Tremaine enjoys the power she holds over her stepdaughter. Take, for example, the scene in which Cinderella appears, ready for the ball, clad in the dress which the animals have rigged up for her using some of the Ugly Sisters' cast-offs. Lady Tremaine had agreed that Cinderella could go to the ball if only she were dressed in something suitable, and, to her fury, the girl is exactly that. So:

> *Lady Tremaine*: … we did make a bargain, didn't we, Cinderella? And I never go back on my word.
>   Hmmmm … How very clever, these beads. They give it just the right touch. Don't you think so, Drizella?
> *Drizella*: No, I don't. I think she's … oh, why, you little thief! They're *my* beads! Give them here!

And the two loathsome sisters proceed to tear their "belongings" from Cinderella's trembling form. Lady Tremaine, in other words, has succeeded in humiliating the girl, but without taking any physical part in the act herself. She has succeeded in increasing the hurt, in deepening the humiliation, yet she is able to say that she is keeping her word: Cinderella cannot go to the ball because Cinderella no longer has something suitable to wear – just as the terms of their bargain went. And it is not Lady Tremaine herself who is directly responsible for Cinderella's disqualification – she cannot even be said to have overtly encouraged the Ugly Sisters.

She is a cunning villain, this one, rather than a mere brute, and that makes her all the more frightening.

Anastasia and Drizella

Anastasia and Drizella are the epitome of spoilt children – the worst type of spoilt children, in fact: those who stay that way right through into adulthood. Their voices

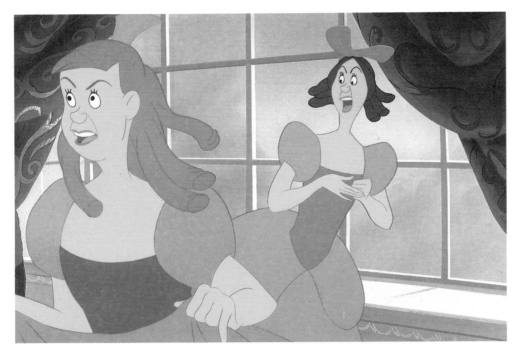

Anastasia (in the foreground) and Drizella, Cinderella's two revolting stepsisters.

The King and the Grand Duke

The King and the Grand Duke, both voiced by Luis Van Rooten, are richly comic characters. It is fitting that they are voiced by the same actor, because in a curious way there is little to choose between them – while one is irascible and the other eager to please, the broad comedy that inspires them both is identical.

Their characters are best summed up in the exchange that takes place between them once the Grand Duke has discovered that the beautiful woman who has captured the Prince's heart has fled. Somehow he has to break this news to the King:

> *Duke* (alone, rehearsing his speech to the King): Your Majesty, I see no point in beating about the bush. I regret to inform you, Sire, that the young lady has disappeared, leaving behind only this glass slipper. [Turns to knock on the King's door.] Yes ... yes, I'll do it. [Holds his hand back] No, I can't! I just *can't*!

But he must. When he interrupts his sovereign the King is asleep in bed, dreaming merrily about the grandchildren he assumes he soon will have. Two of them ride piggy-back upon him, and he is finally woken by one of them beating him over the head with a stick in time to the Grand Duke's knocks.

> *Duke*: Your Majesty ...
> *King*: So – he's proposed already! Tell me all about it. Who is she? Where does she live?
> *Duke*: Well, I didn't get a chance ...
> *King*: Eh? No matter. We've more important things to discuss. Arrangements for the wedding, invitations, national holiday, all that sort of thing.
> *Duke*: But that's ...
> *King*: Here, have a cigar. [Jams one into Duke's mouth and fills his pocket with more.] Well, take a few more. Got to practise passing these out.
> *Duke*: But, but, if you'd only listen ...
> *King*: And for you, my friend ...
> *Duke*: Bu ... bu ... your Majesty ... bu ... bu ... please ... [He drops to his knees. The King misunderstands; produces a sword and touches him on the shoulder with it.]

are raucous and grating; their singing is dire; their faces are milk-curdling; their dancing is little short of terrifying ... but all of these things might be forgiven them, and they might succeed in finding their own Prince Charmings, were it not for the fact that their innate selfishness shines through in their every word and deed. In fact, they could be as beautiful as Cinderella and yet still be repellent for exactly this reason: a marvellous part of the Disney characterization of them is that they are *not* physically too revoltingly ugly.

In terms of personality there is little to choose between them (Drizella is the one with the dark hair), but this in no way diminishes the cleverness of their characterization. Moreover, they provide a welcome burst of slapstick humour among the movie's baddies, because they are in truth such buffoons. That said, they are not the kind of stepsisters that you or I might wish to have: comedians or not, they make poor Cinders' life a daily hell.

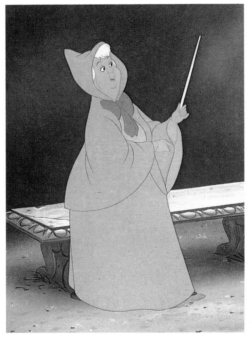

The Fairy Godmother listened sympathetically to Cinderella's tale of woe after the girl's dress had been shredded by the stepsisters.

Fairy Godmother

The absentminded Fairy Godmother – she even mislays her magic wand from time to time – was not universally approved: some critics found her too saccharine. Thomas A. Nelson, who has written one of the best overall critiques of the movie and its characters, remarks that her "jovial and absent-minded good nature comes off as a bit too sticky, that extra helping of the cute and charming which irritates rather than entertains". Most audiences found her dumpy good humour and eccentricity great fun – she would have been far less effective had she been cast as a fairy like *Pinocchio*'s pristine and ethereally beautiful Blue Fairy (➤176), for example.

With her hooded cloak, her dimpled face and her shock of white hair, the Fairy Godmother is everybody's idea of their favourite grandmother, and her absentmindedness adds to this impression – as does her voice, brilliantly supplied by Verna Felton, whose only earlier work for Disney had been as one of the elephants in Dumbo. Certainly she is Cinderella's dream grandmother, if viewed through the eyes of a child: grandparents can always do the things that parents cannot, and the Fairy Godmother is no exception.

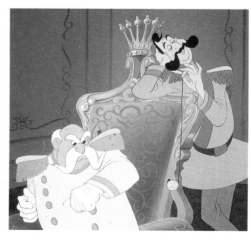

The King, seated, and the Grand Duke, preening.

King: . . . a knighthood! I hereby dub you Sir . . . uh . . . hmmmm . . . Oh, by the way, what title would you like?
Duke: Sire, she got away.
King: "She Got Away"? A peculiar title, but if that's what you . . . She *what*? Why you – you *traitor*!

Moments later the King is endeavouring to use the sword for purposes other than giving the Grand Duke a knighthood. The role of a Grand Duke in this movie seems to be much like that of a Grand Vizier in the *1,001 Nights*, and similarly dangerous.

Bruno and Major

Bruno the dog and Major the horse are comparatively minor members of Cinderella's entourage of animal friends, but both are rather likeable and worth individual mention.

Bruno is easy-going to the point of sloth – he has to be forcefully encouraged by the mice to help fight off Lucifer so that the key to Cinderella's tower room can be delivered. However, his heart is in the right place, and when circumstances demand it he is prepared to stand up and be counted. Like Gus and Jaq he was voiced by Jim Macdonald, who by now was of course also the "official" voice of Mickey. Thanks to the Fairy Godmother's spell, he is transmuted into a slightly officious footman.

Major's role is even smaller, and primarily consists of his being transformed into, for once, a coachman, driving horses (the transformed mice) rather than being a horse. As the Fairy Godmother puts it,

But tonight for a change
You'll handle the reins
And sit in the driver's seat, too,
For instead of a horse
You're the coachman, of course,
Bibbidi Bobbidi Boo.

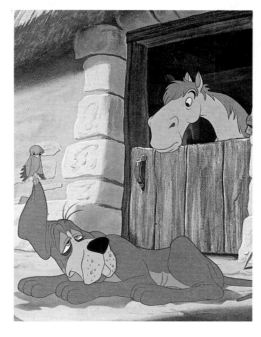

Bruno the dog and Major the horse – not to mention a representative of the bluebirds.

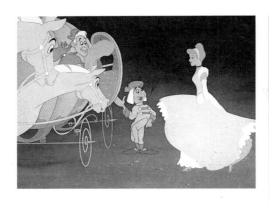

Bruno (on the ground) and Major, temporarily transformed into footman and coachman, respectively, welcome Cinderella into what used to be a pumpkin.

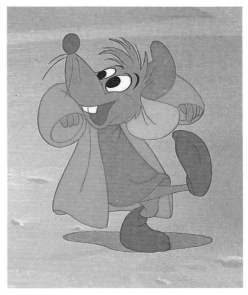

Jaq, one of the engaging little mice to appear in the movie.

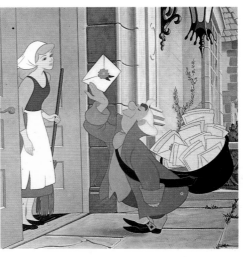

Cinderella's invitation to the ball, delivered by one of the royal lackeys.

ALICE IN WONDERLAND

Characters:

Alice; White Rabbit; Alice's Sister; Mad Hatter; March Hare; Dormouse; Walrus; Carpenter; Queen of Hearts; King of Hearts; Tweedledum; Tweedledee; Cheshire Cat; Door Knob; Caterpillar/Butterfly; Dodo; Bill; Dinah; Nesting Mother Bird

Minor Characters:

Oysters; Red Rose; Live Flowers; Playing Cards; Roses; Mome-raths; Rocking-horse Fly; Hedgehogs; Flamingoes; Mirror Bird; Glasses Bird; Bulb-horn Bird; Umbrella Birds; Shovel Bird; Bird-cage Bird; Hammer Birds; Pencil Birds; Drum Frog; Bread-and-butterflies; Fish; Lobsters; Starfish; Pelicans; Toucan; Eaglet; Brush-dog; Owl; and others too many to count

Credits:

Based on *Alice's Adventures in Wonderland* (1865) and *Through the Looking Glass* (1872) by Lewis Carroll

Voices: Kathryn Beaumont (Alice); Ed Wynn (Mad Hatter); Richard Haydn (Caterpillar); Sterling Holloway (Cheshire Cat); Jerry Colonna (March Hare); Verna Felton (Queen of Hearts); J. Pat O'Malley (Walrus, Carpenter, Tweedledum, Tweedledee); Bill Thompson (White Rabbit, Dodo); Heather Angel (Alice's Sister); Joseph Kearns (Door Knob); Larry Grey (Bill, card painter); Queenie Leonard (Nesting Mother Bird); Dink Trout (King of Hearts); Jim Macdonald (Dormouse); Doris Lloyd (Rose); Pinto Colvig (Flamingoes); The Mellomen (card painters); Ken Beaumont (card painter); Lucille Bliss

Special Processes: Ub Iwerks

Sound Director: C. O. Slyfield

Sound Recording: Robert O. Cook; Harold J. Steck

Film Editor: Lloyd Richardson

Music Editor: Al Teeter

Music: Oliver Wallace

Songs by: Bob Hilliard; Don Raye; Mack David; Sammy Fain; Gene dePaul; Jerry Livingston; Al Hoffman

Orchestration: Joseph Dubin

Vocal Arrangements: Jud Conlon

Story: Winston Hibler; Bill Peet; Joe Rinaldi; Bill Cottrell; Joe Grant; Del Connell; Ted Sears;

Erdman Penner; Milt Banta; Dick Kelsey; Dick Huemer; Tom Oreb; John Walbridge

Layout: McLaren Stewart; Tom Codrick; Charles Philippi; A. Kendall O'Connor; Hugh Hennesy; Don Griffith; Thor Putnam; Lance Nolley

Colour Styling: Mary Blair; John Hench; Ken Anderson; Claude Coats; Don DaGradi

Backgrounds: Ray Huffine; Art Riley; Dick Anthony; Ralph Hulett; Brice Mack; Thelma Witmer

Directing Animators: Milt Kahl; Ward Kimball; Frank Thomas; Eric Larson; John Lounsbery; Ollie Johnston; Wolfgang Reitherman; Marc Davis; Les Clark; Norm Ferguson

Character Animators: Hal King; Judge Whitaker; Hal Ambro; Bill Justice; Phil Duncan; Bob Carlson; Don Lusk; Cliff Nordberg; Harvey Toombs; Fred Moore; Marvin Woodward; Hugh Fraser; Charles Nichols

Effects Animators: Josh Meador; Don MacManus; George Rowley; Blaine Gibson

Directors: Clyde Geronimi; Hamilton Luske; Wilfred Jackson

Production Supervision: Ben Sharpsteen

Release Date: July 28, 1951

Running Time: 75 minutes

THE MOVIE

'Way back in 1923 Walt had made a short called *Alice's Wonderland* (►**13**), which introduced a little (live-action) girl to the "wonderland" of animation. Years later, in 1936, Disney produced an excellent Mickey Mouse short called *Thru the Mirror* (►**29**). In 1959 Donald Duck was to play the role of Alice in a short called *Donald in Mathmagic Land* (► **68**). Clearly Walt felt some kind of an affinity for Lewis Carroll's great double masterpiece, and so it was hardly surprising that he decided to make a full-length feature version of *Alice in Wonderland*. Afterwards he claimed that he himself did not much like the movie, because he felt the characters were unsuitable:

The picture was filled with weird characters you couldn't get with. Even Alice wasn't very sympathetic. I wanted to make the White Knight a romantic figure and have him always popping up through the story ... Alice could have tried to help him out. But I was talked out of it.

The real problems with *Alice* were, first, that there really isn't room in the story for two creative geniuses of fantasy, second, that Carroll's original simply could not be packed into a mere 75 minutes, and, third, that Carroll's *Alice in Wonderland* relies to a great extent on the fantasy-images created by the reader him- or herself: crystallizing those images on screen was bound to be an unsuccessful venture because it subverted the very reason for the books' great popularity. Another difficulty was that, according to Walt's own count, the book contains some 80 different characters, which amounts to just over one per minute of screen-time: it would have been difficult in terms of both finances and audience-recognition to have introduced all of them. Some weeding had to be done, and this led to some notable absenteeism. Walt himself explained:

... the sad and weepy Mock Turtle and Gryphon were without other compensating interest. Humpty Dumpty was not used because he was too talky. Moreover, he wasn't even a Carroll creation ... [Humpty Dumpty's "Unbirthday" verses of the book are in the Disney version spoken by the Mad Hatter and March Hare.] We combined the four Queens and the Duchess into the one figure, the raucous Queen of Hearts, who keeps demanding more decapitations. ... We created one new character. He is the personified Doorknob, who guards the precincts of Wonderland. He was invented in order to avoid a long explanatory monologue at the beginning of the story and to give Alice a foil to talk to. The Doorknob [*sic*] has been approved, incidentally, by some of the strictest of *Alice* purists in England.

Another notable absentee, although like the White Knight it comes from Carroll's *Through the Looking Glass* rather than *Alice in Wonderland*, is the Jabberwock. Its absence is glaring because for reasons unknown the Cheshire Cat in the Disney version recites to us the first verse of *Jabberwocky*.

Disney had acquired the movie rights to Sir John Tenniel's *Alice* illustrations as long before as 1933 but, while it was possible for the animators to use Tenniel's work as a basis, it was financially impossible merely to turn them into "moving drawings": Tenniel used too many lines, and animating them all would have taken forever. (For exactly this reason there are, for example, many Disney lions but very few Disney tigers.) Walt added that

... they had to be seen round, not flat. They had to be made mobile by the illusory processes of animation. They had to be seen in a life-like flow of action from various angles. For the cartoon medium the characters had to be virtually born anew, since their behavior would have to be conveyed in movement rather than with words and pen-and-ink drawings. And yet, I think we have managed to follow Tenniel in such close detail that no one can say our delineations distort the images Carroll and Tenniel worked out together. ...

The features of our Alice are somewhat more youthful than those of the Victorian maid depicted by the great cartoonist of *Punch* [this is debatable]. We have made her figure less stubby. Her hair is more kempt in our portrait. Though her costume is little changed, the stockings on our Alice are plain instead of striped, in order to save time devoted to drawing and for reasons related to Technicolor. We are somewhat less realistic than Tenniel in portraying some of the animal characters. We have made the features of the Walrus more human, for example. Our March Hare is more humanesque, and so is our White Rabbit.

The Disney version of *Alice* was neither the first nor the last. In 1933 Norman McLeod had directed a version with an all-star cast headed by W. C. Fields and including, intriguingly, Sterling Holloway; despite some interesting special effects the movie is insufferably tedious. More to the point was that in 1950 a version was released, directed by Dallas Bower, which had Carole Marsh as Alice supported largely by Lou Bunin's puppets; it was premiered in Paris in 1949. An enterprising distributor decided to release it in the USA at the same time as the Disney version – a move that Disney claimed was a deliberate attempt to mislead the public into going to the "wrong" movie! Pointing out that it had registered the title with the Motion Picture Association of America as long ago as 1938, the Disney studio went to the courts in an attempt to have showings of the Bower/Bunin movie banned during the 18 months following its own release. In this it was unsuccessful – which one cannot help but feel was a fair decision on the part of the courts: the whole episode is one of the few unsavoury ones in Disney's history. In fact, no one was confused and the Bower/Bunin movie received mixed (to put it politely) reviews and vanished from the scene pretty swiftly.

Incidentally, one of the actors who provided voices for this version, Peter Bull, later appeared in the 1972 UK attempt, *Alice's Adventures in Wonderland*, a live-action movie produced by Josef Shaftel and directed by William Sterling.

The other version of *Alice* worth noting was an animated movie produced as a television special in 1966 by Hanna-Barbera: it was called *The New Alice in Wonderland, or What's a Nice Girl Like You Doing in a Place Like This?* The Cheshire Cat was voiced by Sammy Davis Jr. and so tended to dominate the movie, which according to most critics was an appalling travesty.

Mind you, some critics have maintained that *any* screen version of *Alice* is bound to be an appalling travesty, for the reasons noted above: it is largely impossible to translate Carroll's fantasy onto the screen, they maintain. Moreover, it is a very *British* fantasy, and long before the Disney version was even made the British critics had their pens sharpened to slash it to pieces. One of their quite legitimate concerns was the voice of Alice, and their worries were intensified when Walt replied to a question on the subject that "I am going to try to find someone with what I would call a good international accent". In the end he had the good sense to opt for a British actress, the 13-year-old Kathryn Beaumont (she also modelled the part), who had come to the USA *via* Canada and had already appeared in the MGM movie *On an Island with You* (1948), largely notable for the amount of screen-time its beautiful star, Esther Williams, spends clad only in a bathing-suit.

However, the Disney *Alice in Wonderland* was surprisingly well received in the UK. In a 1957 article the UK critic and film-maker Jonathan Routh summed up the general attitude when he said that

> One thing that always worried Dodgson during his lifetime ... was that the pantomime and stage productions of *Alice* were never sufficiently unreal, never quite as he had imagined them and Tenniel drawn them. Disney's film, if he could have seen it, would have settled his doubts and satisfied him completely. As it will yours if ever you had any.

It is noticeable that this comment was (a) British and (b) came six or so years after the movie's release, for one of the reasons why *Alice in Wonderland* was coolly received was that in many places it was unashamedly surreal – possibly as a result of the abortive Dali/Disney proposed collaboration *Destino*, which had opened up new horizons to the animators. (The same can be said of *Melody Time*'s section *Bumble Boogie*, and the Living Flowers in *Alice* share much in common with the threatening plants in that short [►226].) US popular audiences, who persisted – and largely still persist – in thinking of Disney's animated features as designed for children long after adults in the UK have cheerfully started regarding them as fit fare for the grown-ups too, were simply not prepared for such an outrageous departure from strict realism – in terms of the art, that is.

In fact, the critics attacked Disney from both sides, because they complained also about the definiteness with which some of the characters were depicted. The *New Yorker* stated that the movie showed "a blind incapacity to understand that a literary masterwork cannot be improved by the introduction of shiny little tunes, and touches more suited to a flea circus than to a major imaginative effort", while Richard Schickel much later complained that "the fact is that by this time the studio style was so inflexibly realistic, so harsh and so obviously the product of a factory system, that it was incapable of catching more than the broad outlines" of *Alice* and *Peter Pan* – a criticism that is quite incredible in the context of *Alice* (and fairly untenable in terms of *Peter Pan*, too).

For whatever reason, no one much liked *Alice* at the time of its release, although many people praised its high points. Walt said that he was unsatisfied with it, and Ward Kimball, who worked on it, concurred: he blamed the fact that the movie's five sequence directors were each trying to top the other for general zaniness. Critics panned it, for one reason or another, and audiences largely stayed away. However, during the 1960s and 1970s the movie underwent a sudden swell in popularity, probably because its surrealism matched well with the hippy culture of psychedelia. Indeed, Disney was slow to rerelease the movie to accord with the popular demand precisely because they felt that the hookah-smoking Caterpillar, while he appealed to the hippies, might give the wrong image of Disney! This is particularly ironic for two reasons: first, Carroll portrays the Caterpillar as being very much "under the influence"; second, one of the consultants called in by Disney in the early stages was none other than the UK writer Aldous Huxley, renowned for his experiments with hallucinogens. (In the end, Huxley's contributions to the movie were nonexistent.)

Viewed today, *Alice in Wonderland* is a fine piece of work and, most important, it has a considerable *integrity*: Disney really tried hard to do Carroll's masterpiece justice.

THE STORY

Recounting the story of *Alice in Wonderland* would take many pages of this book: it is composed of innumerable episodes, each of which creates a whole new world of its own. What follows is, therefore, the baldest of summaries.

Alice's sister is giving a history lesson in the garden, and the younger girl's attention wanders. She sees the White Rabbit and follows it, tumbling down the rabbit-hole into a world of fantastic illogic. She has a long and floating fall, landing in a bizarre room. It has a door, and through its keyhole she spies the great outdoors. The Door Knob tells her that by drinking from the "Drink Me" bottle she can shrink her size enough to pass through that keyhole. She has various misadventures in trying to change her size, and bursts into frustrated tears; these become a sea through which she floats willy-nilly. She meets the Dodo, who takes her to the Caucus Race over which it officiates; this consists of running madly around a rock in the middle of the sea, and being periodically submerged in the waves.

Alice finally escapes and starts again to pursue the White Rabbit. She meets Tweedledum and Tweedledee, who tell her the famous story of the Walrus and the Carpenter (not forgetting the oysters) and sing her a version of "You Are Old, Father William". After leaving them, she finds and enters the White Rabbit's house where she makes the mistake of eating another size-changing delicacy; she grows huge, filling the house. The Dodo and the White Rabbit persuade Bill the lizard to go down the chimney to investigate, but his passage generates a cloud of soot, Alice sneezes, and he is shot back up out of the chimney like a bullet from a gun. Alice succeeds in reducing her size once more and flees.

Soon she is in a garden full of talking flowers who finally decide that she is a weed and drive her out. Her next encounter is with the Caterpillar, who baffles her with his *non sequiturs*. However, before turning into a butterfly, he tips her off as to the size-changing properties of the toadstool on which he sits. Her first nibble makes her grow to a vast size, right up to the treetops, where a Nesting Mother Bird accuses her of being a serpent out to steal her eggs. Eating a piece of the toadstool's *other* side, however, reduces Alice to normal proportions once more.

As she continues to seek the White Rabbit she meets the Cheshire Cat, who suggests that the Mad Hatter might help her. He, when she finds him, is having the famous tea party with the Dormouse and the March Hare. She gets little sense from them, but at last the White Rabbit turns up and she pursues him from the tea party into the Tulgey Woods. Here, in the most surreal sequences of the movie, she meets countless bizarre minor characters and her dream turns into an anxious nightmare: she wants to go home. The Cheshire Cat suddenly reappears, however, and tells her that there is no way for her to go home because "all ways here, you see, are the Queen's ways". He opens a door and ushers her through it into the realm of the Queen of Hearts.

Alice finds some cards painting roses red – they had accidentally planted white ones whereas the Queen prefers them red. Alice helps them in their task. But then the Queen appears, together with her diminutive husband the King. She objects to the whole endeavour and orders various executions. Alice, however, she regards as a useful new opponent to be beaten at croquet. There follows the famous croquet match with flamingoes as mallets, a hedgehog as the ball and cards as hoops. The Queen does not play fair. The Cheshire Cat appears to Alice, although to no one else, and despite Alice's protests hooks the Queen's flamingo onto her (the Queen's) dress in such a way that the Queen's next shot sends her tumbling in a display of brightly coloured bloomers.

The Queen blames her ignominy on Alice and gives a typical cry of "Off with her head!" However, the King intercedes and suggests it would be fun to have a trial first. This is of course a farce, the result predetermined. The White Rabbit is the Clerk of the Court. Alice, however, finds she still has some pieces of the toadstool; she eats them and grows to a huge size. Confidently, she tells the Queen the truism that she is a fat, pompous old tyrant – an unwise move, because the effect of the toadstool swiftly wears off. However, Alice escapes from the army of cards and flees through a nightmare sequence of her earlier adventures in reverse before emerging from the rabbit-hole and her dream into the safety of the English country garden where the whole adventure began.

THE CHARACTERS

Alice in Wonderland contains more characters than any other Disney animated feature, but the vast majority of them appear on screen for only scant seconds. The subsequent discussion will therefore deal only with the more major ones; the reader is referred to the list above (➤**239**) for the names of the countless minor characters.

Alice

Over the many years since 1933 during which Disney had been dickering with the *Alice* project it had gone through some transformations. It could have been a live-action feature or, more probably, a mixture of live action and animation. A number of actresses had been interviewed at different times as candidates for the role of Alice herself. Luana Patten was an obvious possibility; others interviewed included Mary Pickford, who was prepared to give the project some financial backing, and even Ginger Rogers. Kathryn Beaumont, the child star chosen to both voice and model the character, could consider herself lucky.

In fact, her voice is not entirely successful, coming across as over-affectedly English much of the time, and on occasion lapsing into what is for all the world like an upper-class Scots accent. Clearly, though, she had a very difficult task: unlike characters such as Snow White and Cinderella, Alice is no romantic heroine but instead a slightly prissy young Victorian schoolgirl. Beaumont (and the animators who directed the voicing) could either aim to give this impression or they could try somehow to transform the part. Wisely they chose the former course.

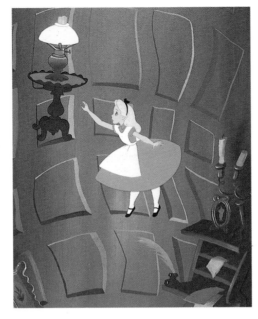

The distorted shapes of incongruous objects drifted by as Alice fell into Wonderland.

This coldness on the part of Alice was not well received in all quarters. Nonetheless Judith Martin commented:

Disney's Alice in Wonderland is distinguishable from his Snow White only because Alice is a blonde and wears Mary Jane shoes with white stockings, while Snow White has dark hair and what appear to be Dr. Scholl shoes. Both – like all Disney heroines – have china doll faces topped by ribbons tied in bows centered in their bouffant hair.

This is first-rate criticism except, perhaps, for the fact that Alice differs from Snow White not only in every conceivable aspect of her physical appearance but also in her character (Snow White is a romantic heroine) and even her function in the film (Alice, perhaps paradoxically, is an active, "doing" character rather than a passive one). Perhaps Martin was thinking of Cinderella (➤**236**).

Walt himself disliked the character of Alice because he thought she was prissy and off-putting. More recent critics often suggest that, instead, Alice was a little too sophisticated in the Disney version; much of the humour in the Carroll books derives from the fact that a naïve Alice gravely reproduces wisdom picked up from adults, the trait of an eight- or ten-year-old rather than an apparent thirteen-year-old.

It is tempting but futile to compare this movie's animated Alice with the live ones of the Alice Comedies (➤**13**). Apart from the age gap, the Alice of those old shorts was coping not with Wonderland but with Walt's and Ub Iwerks' animated clownery; furthermore, she was designed to sustain shorts, not a full-length feature.

White Rabbit

Perhaps more than any other in the movie, the character of the White Rabbit reflects accurately the one created by Carroll and Tenniel. This is because in many ways he is something of a non-character in both versions: he is the chimera that Alice, for no real reason, finds herself pursuing. His perpetual worry about being late is his only notable characteristic, although, as a sort of adjunct to this, he is capable of fretting about other things, too – as when Alice grows to fill up his house. His sole good lines in the movie are when he is acting as Clerk of the Court during the kangaroo trial:

Rabbit: The prisoner at the bar is charged with enticing Her Majesty, the Queen of Hearts, into a game of croquet, thereby wilfully, and with malice aforethought, teasing, tormenting and otherwise annoying our beloved and ...
Queen: Never mind all that! Get to the part where I lose my temper!
Rabbit: ... thereby causing the Queen to lose her temper!

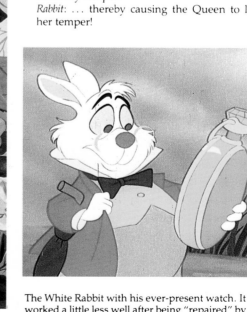

The White Rabbit with his ever-present watch. It worked a little less well after being "repaired" by the Mad Hatter and the March Hare.

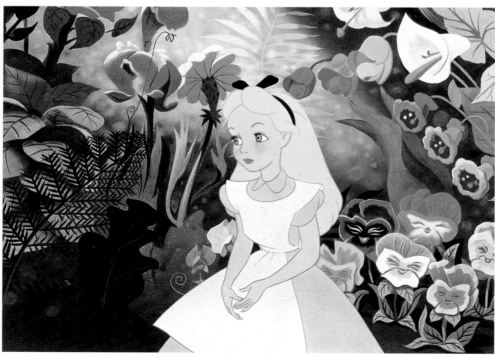

A very young-looking Alice, surrounded by the talking flowers.

Alice's Sister

Alice's elder, dark-haired sister appears only briefly, in the two sections at front and rear of the film which frame the dream-sequence. Nevertheless, her character is well depicted – she is a slightly strict yet by no means heartless young woman – and this is largely achieved by the excellent vocal part supplied by Heather Angel. The sister's cameo role is a highpoint of the movie.

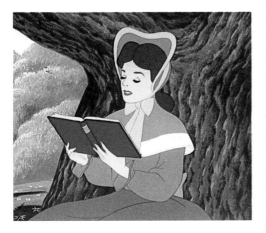

Alice's elder and rather severe sister played only a small part in the movie.

Mad Hatter, March Hare and Dormouse

The tea party, one of the great moments of Carroll's original, was translated into pure Disney knockabout farce. One might have expected that this would draw "justified critical attack", but in fact the converse is the case: it drew "justified critical praise", probably because here for once there was no clash between the two very different masters of fantasy. The tea party is an out-and-out triumph.

The characters of the Mad Hatter and the March Hare were, for the first time in Disney history, modelled largely around their voices (Ed Wynn and Jerry Colonna, respectively): the match is superb. In fact, things went further, as Ward Kimball, who did most of the animation in this sequence, recalled years later in an interview with Ross B. Care:

After the script had been written, and we had what we thought was a good prerecorded dialogue track, we decided to shoot a rough black-and-white live-action version to serve only as an inspiration for my animation, and from which I could select any bits and business that I might choose to re-work into animation. For this live-action test we decided to use Ed Wynn who had provided the voice of the Mad Hatter. The problem was, Ed had trouble following the playback that had been recorded by himself. It drove him crazy. Sitting there with his big hat among all those knives, forks, and teacups, he said, "I can't do it. Why don't you just turn that darn voice-track thing off, and I'll remember roughly what I said." We agreed by saying, "OK, we'll just use one little mike with no attempt at fidelity to pick up

what you say so that Ward can later identify the action."

Well, the nonsense stuff that Ed ad-libbed on that sound-stage was a lot funnier than some of the recorded stuff that we had carefully written out for him. When Walt saw the black-and-white test he said, "Let's use *that* soundtrack! That's great!" The sound department hit the fan, complaining, "We can't use that test-track; there's too much background noise!" To which Walt simply replied, "That's your problem!" and walked out of the room.

Walt was right, in this instance. Unfortunately the example of this success was to encourage the studio in later years to model animated characters a little too closely on the personalities of the actors who had voiced them.

Wynn's vocal rendition, though, is superb. He gives the Mad Hatter a dopey voice and a pronounced lithp. Thith lithp works to best effect when, during the tea party, the White Rabbit turns up and worries about the time. The assembled company suggests that this is because his watch is wrong, and proceeds to "mend" it by pouring into it virtually the entire contents of the table. Finally, though, the Mad Hatter is passed the mustard and, just before loading it into the unfortunate

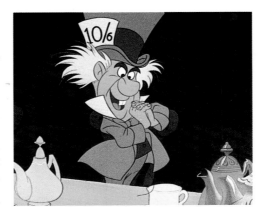

The Mad Hatter represented a hilarious piece of voicing – matched by hilarious animation.

timepiece, does a quick take, stops, and says reprovingly: *"Muthtard!?* Don't let'th be *thilly!"*

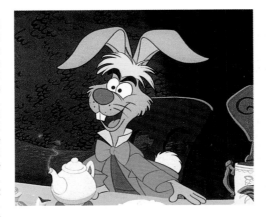

The March Hare was almost as much of a zany as the Mad Hatter.

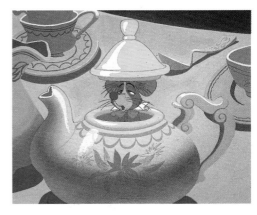

The dozy little Dormouse, the third of the three irrepressible characters at the tea party.

He slams shut the watch and it goes berserk. The March Hare, a character only slightly less zany than the Mad Hatter, flattens it with a mallet, explaining meaningfully: "There's only one way to deal with a mad watch!"

Alice might have chosen less reliable allies than these two ... but she would have found some difficulty. The two are as bad as each other, although the Hatter is the more strongly depicted.

The Dormouse plays a very muted role, by contrast, his love for being incarcerated in teapots being his primary characteristic. At one point, when he has been blown sky-high because the Hatter's unbirthday cake has exploded, he drifts downwards under an opened umbrella reciting part of "Twinkle, Twinkle Little Bat", but aside from that his lines are few and his character self-effacing. He does, however, require occasional pacification, effected through the application of jam to his nose. This occurs not only at the tea party but also later, during the trial, when much of the jam ends up not on the Dormouse's nose but on the Queen of Hearts. The effect, of course, is that Alice's chances of the death penalty go up from 100 to 110 per cent.

The Walrus and the Carpenter

The blimpish Walrus and the skinnily eager Carpenter make their appearance in the famous tale told – or rather sung – by Tweedledum and Tweedledee. We encounter them strolling along the beach and discover that there is a certain difference in attitude to the work-ethic between them: says the Carpenter of the sand, "We'll sweep this clear in half a year if you don't mind the work", but at the mention of the word "work" the Walrus almost chokes on his cigar smoke. He changes the subject to such matters as "cabbages and kings". Indeed, he treats the Carpenter quite ferociously, and it is when he has thrown him into the sea that the Carpenter spots the innocent young oysters. The Carpenter, the dimwitted one of the pair, is all for attacking them then and

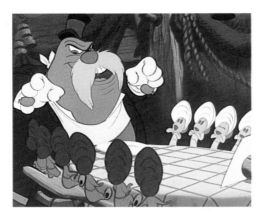

The young oysters waiting in adoring fashion to become the Walrus's lunch.

there, but the subtler Walrus instead invites them for a walk – the Carpenter adding "helpfully" that "Yes, and should we get hungry on the way, we'll stop and . . . uh . . . have a bite". The little oysters foolishly take up the invitation, although

> . . . Mother Oyster winked her eye and shook her heavy head.
> She knew too well this was no time to leave her oyster bed.

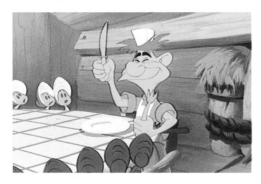

The oysters might have become the Carpenter's lunch had the Walrus not, shall we say, protected them from that dire fate.

The Walrus deals with her by flicking cigar-ash into her shell and smashing it shut with his walking-stick. All eager for the forthcoming "treat" the little oysters, clothed in blue bonnets and pink dresses, follow the villainous pair. The Carpenter goes ahead and swiftly erects a shack in which the pair may dine. On either side of the long table sit the oysters expectantly; at the table's head sits the Walrus, and the Carpenter would be sitting at its foot except that the Walrus keeps encouraging him to fetch further condiments from the kitchen. And then comes the moment of truth:

> *Walrus*: Oh yes, uh, the time has come, my little friends,
> To talk of food and things . . .
> *Carpenter*: Of peppercorn and mustardseed
> And other seasonings.
> We'll mix them all together in a sauce that's fit for kings;
> Calloo, callay, we'll eat today like cabbages and kings.

Great verse it is not, and neither is the Carpenter's meal, for when he returns from the kitchen after yet another foray he discovers the Walrus looking bloated and weeping crocodile tears and the oysters, of course, all gone. We leave the pair of them as the Carpenter, armed with his flailing hammer, chases the Walrus furiously down the beach and out of sight.

The Queen and King of Hearts

If one believes that the Disney *Alice in Wonderland* is a failure – and by no means everybody does – a possible reason might be that there is no real, identifiable villain: there is no out-and-out baddie dogging Alice's footsteps and attempting to thwart her at every turn. The only real villain in the movie is the brutish Queen of Hearts, whose raucous voice (supplied by Verna Felton) and lethal temper provide some of the movie's most nightmarish moments. But she appears only towards the end, and anyway her malignancy is directed not purely at Alice but at every denizen of her unhappy realm who should happen to cross her path.

Moreover, she is not nearly so subtly depicted a character as the average Disney villain: think of the seductive wiles of the witches in *Snow White* and *Sleeping Beauty*, or the apparent bonhomie of *Pinocchio*'s Stromboli, for example. By contrast, the Queen of Hearts is a brute – nothing more than the "fat, pompous, bad-tempered old tyrant" Alice (rather unwisely) describes her as. She has no ingratiating or ameliorating characteristics at all, and is thereby a less than successful villain.

Disney clearly did not know quite how to handle the Queen of Hearts, and this inability reached a nadir in the scene during the croquet match when the Queen sends herself sprawling. As Brian Sibley put it in a 1974 lecture to the Lewis Carroll Society,

> . . . the Queen of Hearts' performance, otherwise the very embodiment of the uncontrollable fury Carroll envisaged, is brought to absurdity by the indecorous display of her heart-embroidered XOS [extra-large] bloomers.

Can you imagine *Sleeping Beauty*'s Maleficent even wearing bloomers, let alone displaying them? No. She is a real villainess, whereas the Queen of Hearts, for this and other reasons, is only an ersatz one.

The Queen's dapper little husband, the King, is entirely in her thrall: he is as much afraid of her as anybody else. Only rarely does he cross her, as when he suggests that Alice should be tried before execution and then later that there should be something by way of evidence and witnesses before the verdict is handed down and the sentence decreed. Most of the time, though, he does exactly what he is told. One wonders (a)

why he married the Queen of Hearts, (b) why she married him, and (c) why he married anyone at all, for in modern

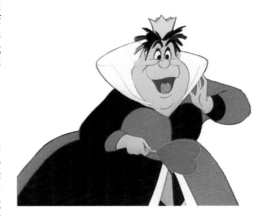

The Queen of Hearts, widely regarded as being too abrasive and insufficiently evil to be a great Disney villainess.

parlance he is very camp. He provides, however, an excellent comic counterpoint to his massive spouse's loud-mouthed bloodlust.

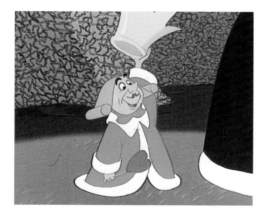

The diminutive King of Hearts, utterly dominated by his mountainous wife.

Tweedledum and Tweedledee

Tweedledee and the lisping Tweedledum were both voiced by J. Pat O'Malley, by now on his way to becoming a Disney veteran; in this movie he voiced also the

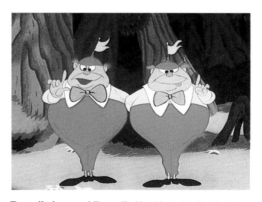

Tweedledum and Tweedledee. If you're finding it hard to tell them apart, Tweedledum is the one with a lisp.

Walrus and the Carpenter. The two of them are primarily distinguishable by the fact that they have their names on their collars and by Tweedledum's lisp; otherwise they are alike. Both are pneumatic and obnoxious, insisting that Alice is *gauche* and that they are the only true arbiters of proper manners. After a largely futile lesson in decorum they find an excuse to sing her the tale about the Walrus and the Carpenter. In an interesting piece of animation, Tweedledee's face becomes the Sun and Tweedledum's the Moon at the start of this tale, and the Sun and Moon transmute back into the two faces at its end.

Cheshire Cat

In his 1974 lecture Brian Sibley stated that

the Cheshire Cat is one of Disney's finest creations; his violet stripes rolling up like bandages as he disappears, and his lingering grin masquerading as the crescent moon. The Cat owes much of its success to its voice talent, Sterling Holloway, whose sibilant tones are as admirably suited to the Cat's purr-sonality as is the English pedantry of Richard Haydn's [voicing of the] Caterpillar.

Viewed conversely, the Cheshire Cat is one of the least satisfactory characters in the movie. Divorced from his original context, he is a sort of *deus ex machina* wheeled on whenever the directors' imaginations were flagging: say, what do we need to brighten up the croquet match? - bring on the Cheshire Cat to perform some mischief. It is all a little "formula". The Cat, clearly intended to be a major character holding the whole movie together, emerges as a rather rebarbative character who appears generally to no good purpose. His charm, both vocally and visually, is spurious: he cares

not whether Alice is beheaded for a crime which he committed, for example. He could have been a great character; instead he is merely a nuisance.

The general feeling around the Disney Studio was that the Cheshire Cat stole the show. Animator Ward Kimball explained this viewpoint:

... because all of the other sequences in the show tried to be "mad," the result was that the only really "mad" thing in the picture, in my opinion, turned out to be the Cheshire Cat! Why? Because compared to the constant, all-out, wild gyrations of the other characters, he played it real cool. ...

Door Knob

Disney introduced one new character to *Alice* and that was the Door Knob. The introduction was a startling success – unlike, for example, that of the Gopher to the Pooh saga (►127). One is almost led to wonder why Carroll omitted the character,

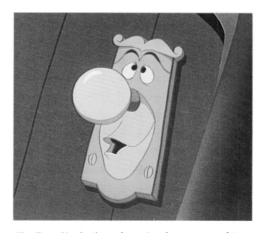

The Door Knob, the only major character not drawn from Carroll's books, is one of the movie's great successes.

so successful is he. In large part this is attributable to the animation (mostly by Frank Thomas) and the voice (supplied by Joseph Kearns), but an additional factor is certainly the script. Here, for example, is the dialogue when Alice first gives the Door Knob an exploratory twist:

Door Knob: Ouch!
Alice: Oh, I do beg your pardon.
Door Knob: It's quite all right. But you did give me quite a turn.
Alice: You see, I was following . . .
Door Knob: Rather good, what? "Door Knob" – "turn"! Ha ha!
Alice: Please sir . . .
Door Knob: Well, one good turn deserves another. What can I do for you?

The dreadfulness of the puns and the Door Knob's incorrigible good humour meld perfectly; if only he could have walked he would probably have done so like Goofy. Moreover, among so many hostile or callous characters, he represents a joyous breath of friendliness: to a great extent he takes Alice under his wing. Mind you, he is not overly concerned by the disastrous results (for her) of the size-changing experiments in which he has persuaded her to participate, but in this movie that would be too much to expect.

Caterpillar/Butterfly

The fey Caterpillar, voiced by Richard Haydn, is a delight. He is capable of producing with his hookah's smoke not just smoke-rings but also smoke-consonants and smoke-vowels. These he uses to conduct much of his conversation: the question "why?" is rendered in smoke by either "Y" or "?", depending upon whim. He can even produce smoke-illustrations, as he demonstrates during his recitation of "How Doth the Little Crocodile?" In

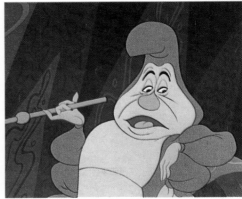

The world-weary caterpillar – three inches tall and proud of every inch of it.

conversation it emerges that both he and Alice are exactly three inches high; but when she complains that this is not her ideal height he says contemptuously – almost spits – that it is a very good height

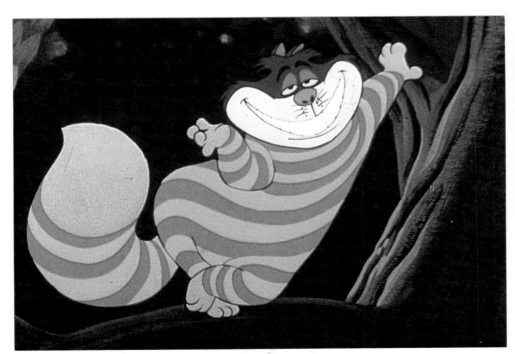

The Cheshire Cat – you either love him or hate him.

indeed. There are a lot of gags about the fact that he has three pairs of arms and three pairs of legs; for example, there is a lovely moment when he crawls onto his toadstool but his final pair of legs fails to make it, so that he has to haul his bottom on by embarrassed hand. When Alice finally shouts at him – "You needn't SHOUT!" – she blows away the covering cloud of smoke that he has puffed to leave only his feet, hands, hookah and outer skin ... and he transforms into a huge butterfly (initially blue, then red). It is in his butterfly form

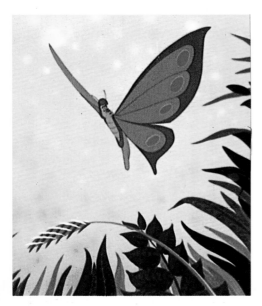

Just after his conversation with Alice, the Caterpillar had an unusual experience.

that he tells her the toadstool way to size-change.

Dodo

The Dodo, first encountered by Alice as he rides through the sea of her tears on a toucan, is by his own proclamation a sea-faring man:

A sailor's life is the life for me.
How I love to sail o'er the bounding sea.
And I never, never ever
Do a thing about the weather,
For the weather never ever does a thing for me.

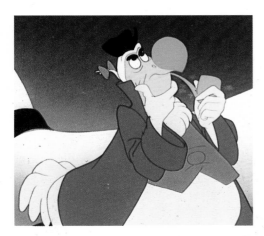

The Dodo – livelier than the average dodo.

He is the Master of Ceremonies of the great Caucus Race, and he is also the advisor to the White Rabbit when Alice has swollen to fill up the latter's home. However, he is a curiously forgettable character; one gains the impression that the animators put him in solely because they had to.

Bill

Bill the lizard has a small but heroic part: he is the poor fellow drafted in to clear the gigantic Alice from the White Rabbit's house. The White Rabbit does his best to effect a smooth recruitment but it is the Dodo who succeeds:

> *Rabbit*: We need a lazard with a lizard ... a liddered ...
> *Dodo*: Bill, m'lad, have you ever been down a chimney?
> *Bill*: Guvnor, I've been down more chimneys ...
> *Dodo*: Excellent, excellent! You just pop down that chimney and send that monster out of there!

Bill balks when he sees Alice's huge eye through a window, but eventually the Dodo forces him up his ladder and down the chimney. Bill's ventures create a cloud of

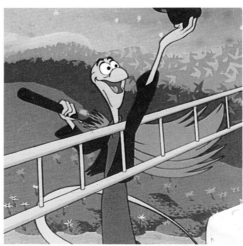

Bill the lizard, cheerfully ignorant of what is just about to happen to him.

soot which causes Alice to sneeze, so that the poor little lizard is shot heavenwards like a bullet from a gun.

Dinah

Dinah, Alice's kitten, imported to *Alice in Wonderland* from *Through the Looking Glass*, plays the very minor part of Alice's companion before and after her nightmare trip into Wonderland. The kitten is built much along the lines of Figaro (➤**171**), although colored brown-red, as opposed to black-and-white, and without the tufty ears.

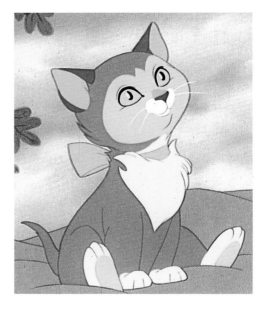

Dinah, Alice's little kitchen and real-life companion.

Nesting Mother Bird

The part of the Nesting Mother Bird (a pigeon in the book) is only a cameo one, yet it represents the Disney animators at their wacky best. She has the bad luck to be brooding over her eggs in a treetop when Alice does one of her more dramatic size-changes, turning from a small child into a bizarre beast taller even than the trees. Her swiftly rising head misses the bird's nest by inches, at most, and creates an instant panic: anything this long and thin *must* be a serpent, out to steal eggs from the bird's nest. Fussing rather more than, say, Donald Duck might have, the Nesting Mother Bird gathers her eggs and departs even as Alice is reducing herself to normal proportions again.

The Nesting Mother Bird had only a cameo role, but made the most of it.

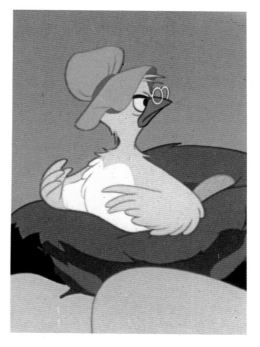

PETER PAN

Characters:

Peter Pan; Crocodile; Tinker Bell
Lost Boys: Foxy; Rabbit; Raccoon Twins;
Cubby; Skunk
Tiger Lily; Indian Chief; John; Michael
Pirates: Captain Hook; Mr. Smee; Turk; Black
Murphy; Mullins; Starkey; Skylights; Bill
Jukes; Wendy; George Darling; Mary Darling;
Nana

Credits:

Based on Sir James Barrie's play *Peter Pan*
(1904) and his subsequent book versions

Voices: Bobby Driscoll (Peter Pan); Kathryn
Beaumont (Wendy); Hans Conried (Hook,
Mr. Darling); Bill Thompson (Smee and other
pirates); Heather Angel (Mrs. Darling); Paul
Collins (John); Tommy Luske (Michael);
Margaret Kerry (Michael and mermaids);
Candy Candido (Indian Chief); Tom Conway
(Narrator); Stuffy Singer; Johnny McGovern;
Robert Ellis; Jeffery Silvers; Karen Kester;
Carol Coombs; Norma Jean Nilsson; Anne
Whitfield; The Mitchell Choirboys

Special Processes: Ub Iwerks

Sound Director: C. O. Slyfield

Sound Recording: Harold J. Steck; Robert O.
Cook

Film Editor: Donald Halliday

Music Editor: Al Teeter

Score: Oliver Wallace

Songs: Sammy Fain; Sammy Cahn; Oliver
Wallace; Frank Churchill; Erdman Penner;
Winston Hibler; Ted Sears

Orchestration: Edward Plumb

Vocal Arrangements: Jud Conlon

Story: Ted Sears; Erdman Penner; Bill Peet;
Winston Hibler; Joe Rinaldi; Milt Banta; Ralph
Wright; Bill Cottrell

Layout: Charles Philippi; McLaren Stewart;
Tom Codrick; A. Kendall O'Connor; Hugh
Hennesy; Ken Anderson; Don Griffith; Al
Zinnen; Thor Putnam; Lance Nolley

Colour Styling: Mary Blair; John Hench;
Claude Coats; Don Da Gradi

Backgrounds: Ralph Hulett; Ray Huffine; Art
Riley; Thelma Witmer; Al Dempster; Dick
Anthony; Eyvind Earle; Brice Mack; Art
Landy

Directing Animators: Milt Kahl; Frank
Thomas; Wolfgang Reitherman; Ward
Kimball; Ollie Johnston, Jr.; Marc Davis; Eric
Larson; John Lounsbery; Les Clark; Norman
Ferguson

Character Animators: Hal King; Cliff
Nordberg; Fred Moore; Bob Carlson; Hal
Ambro; Harvey Toombs; Ken O'Brien; Don
Lusk; Bill Justice; Judge Whitaker; Marvin
Woodward; Jerry Hathcock; Hugh Fraser; Art
Stevens; Eric Cleworth; Clair Weeks

Effects Animators: George Rowley; Joshua
Meador; Dan MacManus; Blaine Gibson

Directors: Hamilton Luske; Clyde Geronimi;
Wilfred Jackson

Special Credit: "With gratitude to the Hospital
for Sick Children, Great Ormond Street,
London" (owners of the copyright in J. M.
Barrie's *Peter Pan*)

Release Date: February 5, 1953

Running Time: 77 minutes

THE MOVIE

In 1951 Disney produced *Alice in Wonderland*
and in 1953 *Peter Pan*, both based on
modern classics of British children's
literature, yet two more different movies
could hardly be imagined. Of the former,
after it had flopped in the box-office, Walt
remarked: "We had a classic we couldn't
tamper with; I resolved never to do another
one." It might have been thought that *Peter
Pan* was another example of "a classic we
couldn't tamper with", but Walt elsewhere
made the cogent point that, as the original
had been a stage play, none of the
characters had a physical appearance
already stamped in the public's mind – in
Alice, of course, the converse was true,
thanks to Tenniel's illustrations. Disney
could therefore build up the *Peter Pan*
characters more or less from scratch,
retaining their essential characteristics but
otherwise developing them freely.
However, Disney did not do this arbitrarily;
Walt added that

> Barrie's own play notations and stage
> directions, scribbled during rehearsals, were
> extremely helpful to us. His concepts of the
> characters and their reactions to magical events
> and strange circumstances gave us more
> insight into what he had in mind than the
> actual dialogue and scene description.

The Disney version of *Peter Pan* is a delight,
retaining all the magic of the play and
Barrie's novelizations of it, yet being much
more than merely a filmed rendition of the
originals. Viewing it is a satisfying
experience for adults and children alike.
Walt put his finger on the reason why this is
so in yet another article on the movie:

> All the characters in *Peter Pan* are in some way
> touched with magic, even the villainous
> Captain Hook and the clownish Smee. The
> little fairy Tinker Bell glows like a firefly and
> leaves a trail of pixie dust behind her as she flits
> about with the speed of a hummingbird. No
> crocodile that ever prowled a river bank would
> even nod to the grotesque reptile that terrifies
> Hook. The Indians in their camp, the Lost Boys
> – who don't even know what a mother is –
> beloved Wendy and her brothers – all are
> creatures of enchantment. They exist only in
> the land of fable and can be brought to life in
> pictures only through the arts of animation.

For example, Walt adds, "We could detach

Peter from his elusive shadow with the
stroke of an animator's pencil" – an effect
much harder to achieve in the theatre.

In fact, Walt was defending himself
against some severe critical attacks when he
said this, for many people were claiming
that he had mangled *Peter Pan* in bringing it
to the screen – that the movie was not so
much a screen version of Barrie's play as an
exercise in vampirism, Disney sucking out
all the best bits and putting them into a
context of his own. Such critics are
nowadays very quiet, because it has been
generally realized that *Peter Pan* is
something of a masterpiece. Generations of
children have loved *Peter Pan* during its
various reissues, and their parents have
been only too eager to take them to the
cinema to watch it.

THE STORY

Wendy has been telling fantastical bedtime
stories in the nursery to her two younger
brothers, John and Michael, about Peter
Pan, the little boy who never grows up. Her
father, Mr. Darling, feels that such fantasies
are corrupting the boys' minds; although he
and Mrs. Darling are going out to a party
that night, and so cannot immediately do
anything about it, in the morning, he
promises, Wendy will be moved out of the
nursery – as will Nana, the faithful dog who
has been the children's nanny. Indeed,
Nana's exodus will happen this very night;
he takes the dog and ties it up outside.

Mr. Darling is convinced that Peter Pan
does not exist, but Wendy knows that he
does, because the other night she found
that he had left his shadow behind, and
locked it up for safe-keeping. The Darling
parents leave, and Peter and Tinker Bell
creep in to try to find his shadow; they
make enough noise to wake the children.
After some high jinks, Wendy agrees to
Peter's idea that she should travel home
with him to Never Land, there to be mother
to his troop of Lost Boys; her brothers,
obviously, want to join in this great
adventure. (The spelling "Neverland"
appears in some Disney documents and
publications, but the "official" version is
"Never Land".) Using Tinker Bell's "pixie
dust" as an aid, Peter teaches them to fly,
and they all set off to fly to Never Land
along the traditional route – "second star to
the right and straight on 'til morning."

Never Land is no Utopia, as the children
discover even before their arrival. The
wicked pirate Captain Hook, whose hand
Peter long ago amputated and tossed to the
Crocodile, is eager for vengeance; spotting
that there is a flight of children led by Peter
flying in towards the island, he orders his
cannon to open fire on them. Peter bravely
determines to draw the fire, and instructs

Tinker Bell to lead the other children to safety. She, however, poutingly jealous of the growing friendship between Peter and Wendy, flies ahead to warn the Lost Boys that a "terrible Wendy bird" is on its way, and that Peter wants them to shoot it down. Peter arrives in time to save Wendy's life and, learning of Tinker Bell's wickedness, banishes her.

The next few days are ones of adventure for all concerned. The Lost Boys take Michael and John out on an Indian hunt, with the result that they are captured by the Indians, whose Chief accuses them of having abducted his daughter Tiger Lily. In fact, as Peter and Wendy discover on an expedition of their own, she has been captured by Hook and Smee, who are rowing out to Skull Rock, where they will tie her until either she tells them the location of Peter's hideout or she drowns in the incoming tide. Peter duels with Hook, who narrowly escapes with his life, chased by the Crocodile, who liked Hook's hand so much, all those years ago, that he would rather like to eat the rest of him too.

Peter, having saved Tiger Lily, is the Indians' hero, but Hook has further plans. Learning that Peter has banished Tinker Bell, he realizes quite how useful the disgruntled fairy could be to his cause, and sends Smee out to capture her. Simultaneously, Wendy is recognizing that she really does not *like* the vain and arrogant Peter very much: she thinks it is time for herself and her brothers to think of going home.

Hook persuades Tinker Bell that he has decided to concede defeat at Peter's hands, and plans to leave the island; however, being generous of spirit, he would like to take Wendy with him, so that Peter and Tinker Bell may be happy together once more. Only, er, where is Wendy hiding? Tinker Bell, foolishly believing his promises not to lay either "a hand or a hook" on her much loved Peter, tells him – and is promptly imprisoned in the ship's lantern.

Meanwhile, back in the Lost Boys' subterranean hideout, Wendy has persuaded John and Michael that it is indeed time to go home; and the other Lost Boys are showing interest too, keen to discover what a "real mother" actually looks like. Peter points out to all of them that, should they leave, they will never be able to return to Never Land, but they all decide the risk is worth it. Unfortunately, as they emerge from their hideout they are seized by the pirates. Only Peter remains safe below ground, but Hook and Smee lower to him a bomb disguised as a present from Wendy.

Back on Hook's ship (referred to in the Disney copyright synopsis as the *Jolly Roger*), Hook tries to persuade his captives to become pirates; all of them are tempted except Wendy, who maintains that Peter Pan will save them. This causes Hook and Smee great mirth, and Hook explains about the bomb. Tinker Bell overhears, breaks out of her prison, flies to Peter and saves him from the explosion, almost at the cost of her own life; she revives only when he convinces her that she is the most important person in his world. They return to Hook's ship to save the life of Wendy as she walks the plank. The Lost Boys stirringly defeat the pirates, and Peter duels with Hook successfully; the rascally captain ends up in the water, swimming for dear life from the eagerly snapping jaws of the Crocodile. Thanks to Tinker Bell's "pixie dust" Hook's ship is raised into the sky and sets sail through the air for London and the Darlings' home.

Back home, the Darling parents return from their party to find Wendy's bed unslept-in, but the girl herself is there. She tells all about the children's adventures with Peter Pan, and points out to her mother and father the silhouette of Hook's ship against the Moon. Convinced of Peter Pan's reality at last, Mr. Darling reluctantly confesses that many years ago, when he too was young, he saw such a flying ship ...

The dénouement of the Disney version of *Peter Pan* is therefore rather different from that of the original, but it seems a perfectly reasonable substitution.

THE CHARACTERS

Peter Pan

Walt claimed that Peter was a character with whom he had particular cause to feel closely associated. In an article dated *c*.1951 he explained that his first experience of Barrie's work had come when he and Roy were children on the family farm near Marceline:

... one morning as we walked to school we found entrancing new posters on the barns and fences along the road. A road company was coming ... and the play they were presenting was *Peter Pan* with Maude Adams.

Roy and Walt had to rob their piggy banks to get enough money to go to the play, but they reckoned it was worth it:

I took many memories away from the theater with me, but the most thrilling of all was the vision of Peter flying through the air.

Not long afterwards Walt had the exciting privilege of himself playing the part of Peter Pan – in the school play:

No actor ever identified himself with the part he was playing more than I – and I was more realistic than Maude Adams in at least one particular: I actually flew through the air! Roy was using a block and tackle to hoist me. It gave way, and I flew right into the faces of the surprised audience.

Walt also outlined elsewhere his own idea of Peter:

[He] is a boy who can do very strange things. He flies without wings. His shadow leads a merry life of its own. Face to face with the terrible Captain Hook, Peter dispatches that pirate with jaunty ease. Peter is at home with mermaids and understands their language. He is twelve years old forever simply because he refuses to grow up beyond that comfortable age. Most remarkable of all, he knows just where Neverland [*sic*] is and how to get there.

There were a number of differences between the stage and the screen Peter Pan, not the least of which was that Disney decided to dispense with the old tradition (born from pantomime) that Peter should be played by a girl – or, rather, young woman.

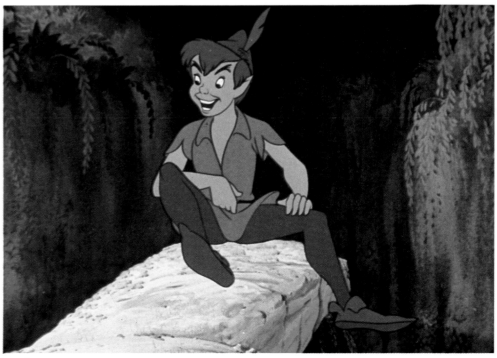

Peter Pan. Disney captured brilliantly the amoral nature of Barrie's hero.

Peter in the movie was voiced by the Disney stalwart Bobby Driscoll – and very well too. His visual image is not that of a young woman but that of a little boy. Nevertheless, Walt – who, being on the defensive, wrote extensively about the movie – claimed that "his" Peter and the stage one were identical in spirit:

[Peter is] able to do a lot of things, besides flying, that he could never do on the stage. But he's the same Peter and it's the same Neverland [sic] and the same Tinker Bell and the same Darling family that we have always loved.

Not everyone agreed. The UK critic Brian Sibley has written that "Disney's Peter has charm and bravado but lacks the self-sacrificing heroism of the original". This seems a fairly untenable viewpoint. The original Peter was a fey and, very importantly, an *amoral* character: he was brave when it suited his vanity to be so, and self-sacrificing never. This personality is exactly reproduced in the Disney movie – a matter for which Disney should be loudly congratulated, because it would have been only too easy to turn him into a stereotyped hero.

Peter is then, as depicted in this movie, a genuine member of the "little people", friendly or hostile according to whim, obeying moral rules totally divorced from those of Western culture, totally egocentric and totally uncaring about others' anguish (for example, he cares nothing about the possible suffering of the Darling parents). In short, he is very much like a ... well, like a little boy.

Crocodile

A long time ago Peter gleefully threw one of Captain Hook's hands to the Crocodile, and it liked what it tasted; ever since, it has been pursuing Hook around the seven seas hoping to mop up the rest of him. Fortunately for Hook, it has swallowed also an alarm clock, the loud ticking of which gives him warning whenever the Crocodile is in the vicinity.

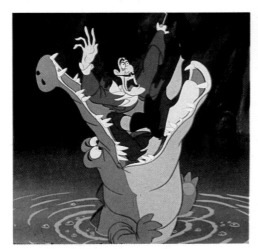

The Crocodile, here shown having a heated discussion with Hook.

Disney chose to give a visual rendition of the Crocodile – in the play he is usually present only as an off-stage ticking – and this decision may or may not have been wise. On the one hand, the invisible but eternally ominous monster gains terror from its very invisibility; on the other, the Disney version of it is excellent. It is in essence a friendly beast, with a perpetual grin on its face – although the grin changes its nature when the Crocodile has Hook in its sights.

Tinker Bell

Tinker Bell is the sole controversial character in the movie. In the play she is of course nothing more than a darting spot of light, but Disney saw fit to render her as a visible fairy, complete with a gorgeous figure; she is still in vogue as the introductory image of many Disney television shows. A very feminine young lady she is, and persistent rumours went round that she was based on Marilyn Monroe. This was not in fact true: she was modelled by the actress Margaret Kerry, pains being taken by the Disney publicists to point out that Ms Kerry had a totally different personality from the pouting, spiteful, jealous Tinker Bell.

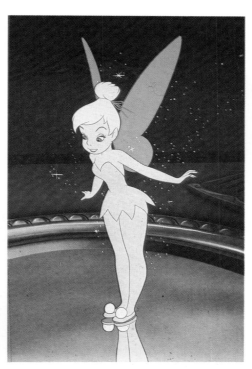

Tinker Bell, Disney had to part with tradition and show the tiny fairy as more than a moving point of light.

Walt, enthused with the marvels of animation as demonstrated in *Peter Pan*, eulogized the fact that

We could make the little sprite ... glow like a firefly as she darts through space and have her speak with the sound of bells

but some years later the critic Frances Clarke Sayers was to use less flattering language:

Look at that wretched sprite with the wand and the over-sized buttocks which announces every Disney program on TV. She is a vulgar little thing, who has been too long at the sugar bowls.

This seems a little unfair on poor Tinker Bell – whose buttocks, according to the average adolescent male (as personified by the present writer), are in fact exactly the right size. What Sayers was really objecting to, whether she knew it or not, was the fact that Tink had been *personalized*: she had been turned (by Marc Davis) from a spiteful but invisible little entity into an all-too-visible coquette. In fact, this transformation works very well in the context of the movie, but it does come as something of a shock to those familiar with the play.

Since the "Disneyland" TV shows in 1954, Tinker Bell has been identified with Disneyland's castle, darting about its towers to set off fireworks with a wave of her wand. In 1961 that image became real, as a live Tinker Bell began a nightly summertime flight above the castle, heralding the fireworks show.

The Lost Boys

The Lost Boys each play a surprisingly small part in the movie, being content to follow the leadership of Peter, or perhaps Michael, or even John. There are six of them: Foxy, Rabbit, Skunk, the Raccoon Twins and

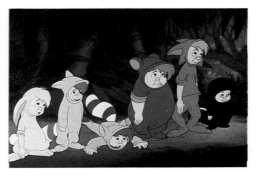

The Lost Boys, looking recalcitrant, Wendy brought many changes into their lives – not all, they temporarily thought, for the better.

Cubby, and it takes little imagination to work out what kind of furs each is dressed in. Moreover, their forms reflect their furs: Rabbit has two prominent buck teeth, Skunk is small and complacent, and so forth. If the group have a leader at all it is certainly Cubby, a plump and forceful, if not terribly clever, member of the gang. (As an irrelevance, we can notice that a major member of the television Mouseketeers was a little boy called Cubby, and one of the prominent members of the Gummi Bears is Cubbi [➤138]; obviously it has been a popular name on the Disney lot!)

The Lost Boys are devoted fans of Peter, whom they regard as their lord and master. Although much tempted by the prospect of travelling back with Wendy and her brothers to find out what it is like to have a "real mother" (Wendy cheerfully offers to share hers: "I'm sure Mother would be glad to have you"), they eventually opt to stay having rollicking adventures with Peter in Never Land – a decision assisted, of course, by the lure of everlasting youth.

Tiger Lily and the Indian Chief

The Indians on the island of Never Land have a good working relationship with the Lost Boys, as we discover when the boys are captured by the Indians:

> *Chief*: For many moons red man fight paleface Lost Boys.
> *Boys*: Ugh! Ugh! Ugh!
> *Chief*: Sometime you win, sometime we win.
> *Cubby*: OK, Chief. Uh, you win this time. Now turn us loose.
> *John*: Turn us loose? You mean this is only a game?
> *Foxy*: Sure. When we win we turn them loose.
> *First Twin*: When they win, they turn us loose.
> *Second Twin*: They turn us loose.
> *Chief*: This time no turn 'em loose.
> *Boys*: Huh?
> *Foxy*: The chief's a great spoofer.

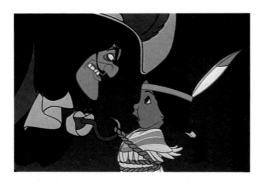

Tiger Lily, threatened by Hook.

Of course, on this occasion the Chief is not being "a great spoofer": someone has kidnapped his beautiful little daughter Tiger Lily, and he believes the Lost Boys may be responsible. Unless Tiger Lily is restored by sundown the boys will be burned at the stake for presumed malfeasance. Of course, Peter saves Tiger Lily and harmony is restored.

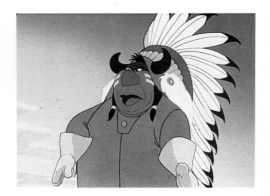

The Indian Chief, Tiger Lily's father, spent much of his time looking forbidding.

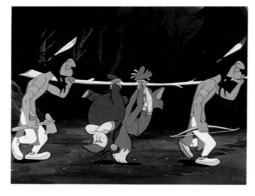

Two of the Red Indians escort Foxy and Cubby back to camp.

The Indian Chief is vast – whatever the dimension you measure. Tall, broad and wide, with an imposingly huge feathered headdress and a brick-red face – and a nose that somehow manages to be even redder! – he is a thoroughly appealing character. The same is true of his little daughter Tiger Lily – much younger in the movie than she is usually depicted on stage. However, her youthfulness and apparent placidity do not conceal the fact that she is also extremely courageous, as she demonstrates when, tied up on Skull Rock by Hook and Smee, she elects to drown rather than give away Peter's hiding-place.

John and Michael

Wendy's two brothers are "supporting actors" – and John, the elder, really ought to have been nominated for an Oscar for "Best Supporting Actor", because he is brilliantly realized. Possibly the finest part of his characterization is his rather stuffy voice, supplied by Paul Collins, but this on its own would not be enough to "carry" the character: the voice is so successful because it melds perfectly with John's screen image. With his top hat and his circular, thin-rimmed spectacles, not to mention his carefully furled umbrella, he is the epitome of a little boy trying to be a grown-up long before his time; and, unfortunately for his pretensions, his behaviour keeps giving away his youthfulness.

This is most obvious when he is leading the Lost Boys on their hunt for Indians, having told Peter, who has appointed him leader of the expedition, that "I shall try to be worthy of my post". He takes his responsibility seriously – except, that is, when he forgets to. A joyous sequence sees him hopping light-heartedly over a river, from stepping-stone to stepping-stone, obviously without a memory of even the word "responsibility" in his mind!

Michael is much smaller and has a much smaller part. Never to be separated from his faithful teddy-bear and throughout the movie clad in his pink baby sleepsuit, he follows where others will lead him, rarely instigating anything on his own behalf. He is so young and so easily led that at one point he even shares the Lost Boys' confusion by asking: "Aren't *you* our mother, Wendy?" So soon after leaving home he has forgotten.

Michael was voiced by Tommy Luske. It is widely reported that Luske's voice unfortunately broke during the movie's long gestation period, so that Margaret Kerry had to supply some of the additional lines. However, the Disney archivists have been unable to prove whether or not this story is true.

The Pirates

The pirates are largely indistinguishable from each other with the notable exceptions of **Captain Hook** and **Mr. Smee**. At least eight other pirates appear, although only six are named: Turk, Black Murphy, Mullins, Starkey, Skylights and Bill Jukes.

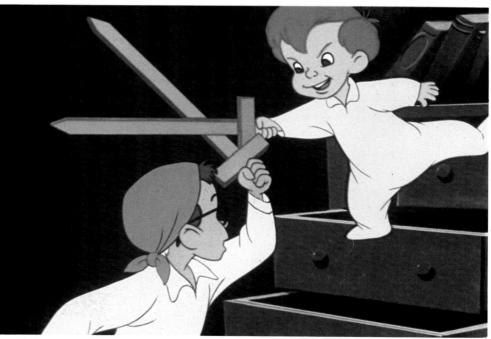

John indulging in a little swordplay with his younger brother Michael.

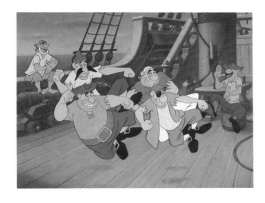

Hook's villainous crew celebrate the capture of the Lost Boys.

The two noteworthy pirates are, however, splendid creations. No stage can ever have seen a Hook quite so flamboyantly disreputable as Disney's, animated by Frank Thomas; and for generations of children the Disney version of Smee, animated by Ollie Johnston, simply *is* Smee: no substitutes acceptable!

An interesting point about Hook is that he took on something of the character not of the actor who modelled him (this often happened), but of the animator who worked on him, Frank Thomas. (The same happened in the case of Ollie Johnston and *The Rescuers'* Rufus [➤297].) Of course, this is not to say that Hook is merely a self-caricature of Thomas, but the resemblances are definitely there. Some critics have felt that the consequent introduction of Thomas's much attested *niceness* into the character of Hook was a mistake, Brian Sibley, for example, remarking in a 1980 article for the partwork *The Movie* that "the whimpering buffoonery of ... Captain Hook has nothing of the genuine malevolence of J. M. Barrie's

black-hearted old Etonian". Margaret J. King, however, in a 1972 thesis, sees Hook as definitely malevolent and also as one of a more widespread "type" among the Disney characters:

Disney productions abound with ... images of the highbrow intellectual as an eccentric, usually as a malign force in the plot. Captain Hook ... is perhaps the best known example. His dress, manners, and language are a parody of the English gentleman, and for most Americans the parody is indistinguishable from the real item. For Disney, Englishness is the core of highbrow character, and this definitional confusion is so overwhelming that it becomes difficult for those in the Disnification process to conceive of aristocrats in other cultures (contemporary) or to picture highbrow attitudes as having a non-English embodiment.

In terms of Hook, there is a fair amount in what King says: it would be impossible even to think of him as anything other than English. A similar very English villian who comes to mind in the animated features is of course Prince John in *Robin Hood* (➤293); but aside from him and one or two others, her hypothesis works better for the live-action features than for the animated ones.

Hook may have his moments of charm, but in fact these make him even more of a villain – for the mask of civilization all too swiftly slips when he is thwarted, and, as he spends at least 90 per cent of his screen-time being just that ... well, the result can be imagined. He is also more treacherous than a schizoid rattlesnake, as he shows during his exciting final duel with Peter. As soon as Hook demands a temporary truce and Peter has agreed, the pirate attacks the boy, and it is only through some moments of greatly athletic bravery

that Peter survives. Peter's vengeance is vicious:

Hook: You wouldn't do old Hook in, now would you, lad? I'll go away forever. I'll do anything you say.
Peter: Well, all right. If you say you're a codfish!
Hook (softly and hesitantly): I'm ... a codfish.
Peter: Louder!
Hook: I'm a codfish!

And then, of course, Hook has to take his chance with the Crocodile. He lives, however, to perpetrate other dirty deeds on distant shores.

The oleaginous, unctuous Smee, who shaves Hook each morning and obeys his every whim, whether stated or merely anticipated, is a villain of a quite different type. Astonishingly, Disney saw fit to portray him in a form which, in the normal way, would have instantly set him on the side of the angels: he is small and with all the outward appurtenances of scatter-brainedness: with ridiculous little spectacles (which he never seems to need), long pale tufty sideburns, and a dilapidated red nightcap which one suspects covers baldness. His voice, too, supplied by Bill Thompson, would in other movies set him apart as a goodie, but in many ways he is every bit as black-hearted as his captain. Or perhaps not: Hook is intelligent enough to know that he is doing evil and that the consequences of his actions may be very cruel, but one senses that Smee simply does not have the imagination to realize quite how bad he is being. He is only following orders – and if those orders should include staking out a Red Indian child to drown, well, who is he to question them? So one comes away from the movie thinking of Smee as a lovable old bumblewit, and it is only later that one begins to think about some of the atrocities the pirate is prepared cheerfully to abet.

If anything, for this reason, Smee is even more of a sinister villain than Hook!

Wendy

It must have seemed to Disney at the outset that it had a choice of which character to give the starring role: the movie could star Peter alone, or Wendy alone, or both of them in tandem (as, essentially, does the play). Whether by conscious decision or not, Disney opted to have Peter as a solo star, which means that Wendy's role is a decidedly "laid-back" one. Her character is scarcely allowed to develop, presumably for fear that, if it did, it might accidentally be permitted to outshine Peter's.

Wendy is much more of a child than most of the other Disney animated heroines – despite the fact that she willingly adopts pseudo-maternity towards the Lost Boys. Unlike the case in the play, one never feels that she is a wiser and older sister to such irresponsible characters as Peter and her own genuine brothers. She is acting the role of motherliness, rather than living it.

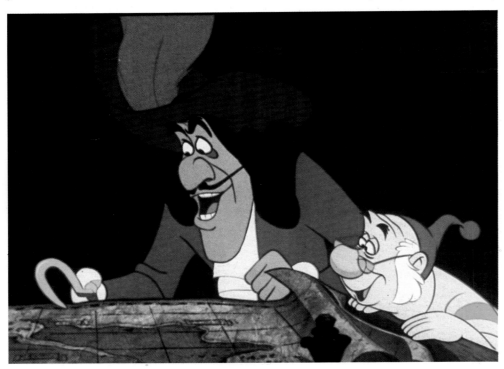

Hook and Smee, planning villainy as usual. Believe it or not, Smee is looking unusually intelligent here.

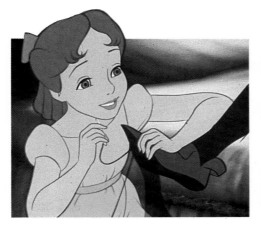

Wendy sewed Peter's shadow back on for him.

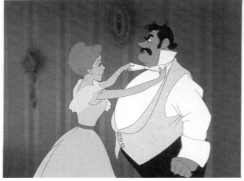

George Darling looking as appreciative as most husbands when their wives adjust their ties.

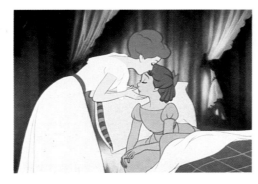

Wendy, receiving a goodnight kiss from Mrs. Darling.

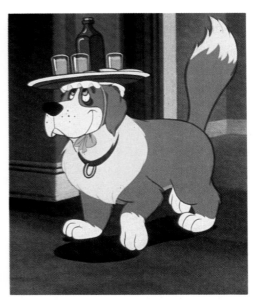

Nana was always willing to please.

It might seem curious to state that she is somewhat boring but that this is a good thing. However, the statement is not as paradoxical as it might seem. Wendy's very ordinariness is a brilliant way of offsetting and thereby pointing up the fantastic nature of Peter's personality and the bizarre nature of the adventures they all share. Every now and then, just as the viewer is forgetting that the ways of the Never Land are not the norm in the "real world", Wendy suddenly brings him or her to earth by remarking that it really is bedtime, or some such. In this way, her apparently neutral character is used very effectively in the movie, and is, in terms of the plot and the general ambience of the film, extremely important.

George and Mary Darling and Nana

These three characters have very minor roles to play – if anything, even more minor than in Barrie's original. The portly, mustachioed George Darling is a typical Victorian father (rather like the one in *Mary Poppins* [➤274]) who pretends to himself – and certainly in front of his children – that

he never really had a childhood of his own. Mary Darling, who is slenderly pretty in a slightly strait-laced sort of a way, rather like a grown-up version of Wendy, knows him a little better than this of course: she recognizes the little boy lurking within him. As he, too, does at the end, when confronted by the sight of the ship sailing away through the skies towards the second star from the right: he confesses that

> You know, I have the strangest feeling that I've seen that ship before. A long time ago, when I was very young.

The other member of the Darling household is of course Nana, the good-natured dog who acts as the children's nanny and who knows far better than the adult Darlings what is going on. On screen she is a perfect amalgam of the stage original and the "Disnification process". Often enough such blendings work to the detriment of either the original or the Disney version, so that one factor completely outweighs the other (which is not necessarily to say that the resulting character is a poor one), but in Nana *both* traditions are melded perfectly. She is a somewhat goofy dog of indeterminate breed, rather than the English sheepdog we are used to seeing on stage, but her essential character is exactly as in the Barrie original. Indeed Barrie, had he lived to see the movie, would have been proud of her.

LADY AND THE TRAMP

Characters:

Lady; Tramp; Jock; Trusty
Siamese cats: Si; Am
Tony; Joe; Jim Dear; Darling; Aunt Sarah; Peg; Boris; Toughy; Nutsy; Pedro; Bull; Dachsie; Beaver; Scamp; Pet-store Clerk; Policeman; Professor; Dog Catcher; Bill

Credits:

Based on a story by Ward Greene

Voices: Peggy Lee (Darling, Si, Am, Peg); Barbara Luddy (Lady); Larry Roberts (Tramp); Bill Baucom (Trusty); Verna Felton (Aunt Sarah); George Givot (Tony); Lee Millar (Jim Dear, Dog Catcher); Bill Thompson (Bull, Dachsie, Jock, Joe); Stan Freberg (Beaver, Pet-store Clerk); Alan Reed (Boris); Dallas McKennon (Toughy, Professor, Pedro); The Mello Men (dogs in pound)

Special Processes: Ub Iwerks

Sound Director: C. O. Slyfield

Sound Recording: Harold J. Steck; Robert O. Cook

Film Editor: Don Halliday

Music Editor: Evelyn Kennedy

Musical Score: Oliver Wallace

Songs by: Peggy Lee; Sonny Burke

Orchestration: Edward Plumb; Sidney Fine

Vocal Arrangements: John Rarig

Story: Erdman Penner; Joe Rinaldi; Ralph Wright; Don DaGradi

Layout: Ken Anderson; Tom Codrick; Al Zinnen; A. Kendall O'Connor; Hugh Hennesy; Lance Nolley; Jacques Rupp;

McLaren Stewart; Don Griffith; Thor Putnam; Collin Campbell; Victor Haboush; Bill Bosché

Backgrounds: Claude Coats; Dick Anthony; Ralph Hulett; Al Dempster; Thelma Witmer; Eyvind Earle; Jimi Trout; Ray Huffine; Brice Mack

Directing Animators: Milt Kahl; Frank Thomas; Ollie Johnston

John Lounsbery; Wolfgang Reitherman; Eric Larson; Hal King; Les Clark

Character Animators: George Nicholas; Hal Ambro; Ken O'Brien; Jerry Hathcock; Eric Cleworth; Marvin Woodward; Ed Aardal; John Sibley; Harvey Toombs; Cliff Nordberg; Don Lusk; George Kreisl; Hugh Fraser; John Freeman; Jack Campbell; Bob Carlson

Effects Animators: George Rowley; Dan MacManus

Associate Producer: Erdman Penner

Directors: Hamilton Luske; Clyde Geronimi; Wilfred Jackson

Release Date: June 16, 1955

Running Time: 76 minutes

THE MOVIE

Lady and the Tramp marked a departure from the Disney pattern in two respects. It was the first animated feature to be made in CinemaScope, and it was the first of the full-length animated features not to be based on a published novel or story. This latter point gave it considerable appeal for Walt, still stinging from the critical lashing he had received over the two previous animated features, *Alice in Wonderland* and *Peter Pan*, whose characters and story-lines had not accorded with people's preconceptions of them. Walt felt also that it gave his animators much more freedom to take a character, play with it, change it, develop it and so forth without the constant feeling that the critics were preparing to dislike it.

The film was a long time in the making, with various versions of it being under consideration as early, according to one source, as 1936. In an article in *Theater and Cinema* dating from around the time of the movie's release Walt explained that, after those early experiments, "we were not satisfied, so the project was put on the shelf".

It stayed there a long time. It was not until the latter part of the 1940s that there was significant progress, as a result of a series of meetings between Walt and writer Ward Greene. Walt considered a story by Greene, "Happy Dan, the Whistling Dog, and Miss Patsy, the Beautiful Spaniel", liked it, but felt that somehow it was not quite right. He asked Greene to try again, and in due course the story "Lady and the Tramp" emerged. Even then, several years elapsed before the movie's release.

Lady and the Tramp is generally regarded as one of Disney's most charming features (although contemporary critics were generally less than kind about it), and certainly it is one of the most tightly controlled in an emotional sense. A story of lovable doggies, executions in the dog-pound, and so forth could easily have become little more than a sloshing bucket of sentimentality, but by dint of careful self-editing Disney was able to produce a film that is genuinely moving in all the right places. The humour, too, is restrained: certainly many incidents make one smile or chuckle, but there is very little of the out-and-out clowning so often found in sections of the other features. This was a wise move: some stories can be enhanced by high humorous relief but *Lady and the Tramp* is not one of them.

The use of CinemaScope had an effect on the movie. Ward Kimball (cited by Leonard Maltin in his *The Disney Films*) recollects a major discovery by the animators: because of the much wider screen, it was the characters who moved around rather than the backgrounds. In other words, the character could move around very much more without, as it were, running off the edge of the picture. Also, more characters could move *in relation to each other* without encountering the same danger; and for the same reason fewer cuts backwards and forwards between characters were required. This was of course very useful in many ways, but it did have the drawback that the film was rather more realistic than might otherwise have been the case. As adverse critics put it, surely the whole point of the animated cartoon is that it allows the film-maker (and the audience) to escape from realism.

Such criticisms are perhaps rather beside the issue. *Lady and the Tramp* is a good story, stylishly and well told. To decry it because it is not, say, *Snow White and the Seven Dwarfs* is to complain that Jane Austen is not Leo Tolstoy. Just because Disney had more or less single-handedly invented the fantasy animated feature did not mean that they should be forever confined to a single genre. Viewed on its own terms, this is a splendid movie.

THE STORY

The year is 1910 and the place is somewhere in the Eastern USA. One day Jim Dear gives his newish wife Darling a present – a six-month-old spaniel puppy, which she elects to call Lady. Soon Lady is settled in, sleeping on their bed and waking them at six every morning, burying bones in the garden and bringing in the newspaper, and all the other things you expect a growing dog to do.

When she is six months old she receives her licence and a new collar to display it, and she goes around proudly to show it to her two close friends Jock, a Scottie-dog, and Trusty, a bloodhound who has unfortunately lost his sense of smell. Some days later, Lady spots that Jim Dear is on his way home. She runs, as is her habit, to race with him back to the front door, but tonight he is not interested in playing with her: he seems preoccupied, and Darling, too, is acting strangely. In due course Jock and Trusty, er, explain to Lady that Darling is, er, expecting a baby. At that moment the mongrel Tramp arrives, having been chased across town by the Dog Catcher. Tramp is much more cynical about babies than the other two; before Jock chases him off the premises he has time to tell Lady that "a human heart has only so much room for love and affection. When a baby moves in, the dog moves out."

This proves not to be quite the case, but certainly the baby spells bad news for Lady. Jim Dear and Darling are keen for the two to be friends, and indeed Lady falls instantly in love with the new member of the family; but not long afterwards Jim Dear and Darling have to go out of town for a while, and the baby and Lady are left in the charge of elderly Aunt Sarah ... who brings with her her two malicious and mischievous cats Si and Am. When these plot to steal the baby's milk Lady intervenes; Aunt Sarah assumes that she has attacked the two cats gratuitously, and has Lady muzzled.

Lady flees, and is soon being chased by some vicious street-dogs. Tramp spots her, however, and chases off her pursuers. He reckons that the best way to get rid of her muzzle is to take her to the zoo to find an animal with teeth sharp enough to cope with the task. The zoo's entrance, however, has a big notice saying "NO DOGS ALLOWED" and is guarded by a policeman. Tramp is equal to this problem – one senses that he is equal to most problems – and he manages to confuse the policeman into thinking that he (Tramp) is the pet of a visiting eccentric professor. While the two humans are busily arguing Tramp and Lady slip unnoticed into the zoo. There they find the Beaver, whom Tramp tricks into removing Lady's muzzle.

The night is young and so are they. Tramp takes Lady to Tony's Italian Restaurant, one of his regular ports of call, and there the good-natured Tony treats both Tramp and his new girlfriend to "two spaghetti *especialle* – heavy on the meats-a ball". He and his cook Joe even entertain the two dogs with a rousing rendition of the song "Bella Notte". Afterwards Tramp takes Lady for a romantic stroll in the park.

In the morning, though, Lady insists on going home to look after the baby. Tramp agrees reluctantly to escort her – he has been extolling the joys of life on the run – but on the way home he talks her into raiding a chicken-coop. Alas, Lady is caught during this adventure, and taken to the pound by the Dog Catcher. There she meets a number of great characters – Bull the bulldog, Dachsie the dachshund, Boris the Russian wolfhound, Pedro the chihuahua and most notably Peg, a somewhat delapidated ex-showgirl dog with a heart of gold and indubitably A Past. She it is who explains to Lady that Tramp has a reputation for womanizing.

Unlike the unlicensed dogs, which face execution, Lady is eventually returned home, but she is chained in disgrace to an outdoor kennel. Trusty and Jock both offer to marry her to save her good name, but she miserably declines. When Tramp happens by, though, fury conquers misery: she shouts at him for having deserted her at the chicken-coop and for his womanizing career, and soon he goes on his way.

Just then, however, a rat that has been haunting the area sees that Lady is chained up, and takes the opportunity to sneak up to the baby's nursery. Lady strains against her chain and barks furiously. Tramp, hearing the commotion, comes rushing back, and chases after the rat up to the nursery, where he kills it. Lady, who has at last succeeded in breaking her chain, joins him.

Aunt Sarah, who has been awoken by the noise, dashes in to find the two dogs, who she assumes have been attacking the baby. Lady is locked in the cellar while Tramp is taken off to the pound by the Dog Catcher. Jim Dear and Darling arrive home, are told Aunt Sarah's version of the story, and then, when Lady leads them to the dead rat, realize the truth. They call the pound but get no answer. Jock and Trusty set off to attempt a rescue, and for once Trusty's sense of smell is sufficient for him to pick up the scent of the Dog Catcher's wagon and so enable them to find the pound. They succeed in intercepting the wagon, but their frenzied barking frightens the horses and the wagon is overturned. Just then a taxi arrives with Jim Dear, Darling and Lady – who are delighted to find that Tramp is alive and well.

But all is not well for Trusty. When the wagon overturned it landed on him, and we leave them mourning over his corpse.

Well, not his corpse, in fact, because he survives. We next see the dogs at Christmas-time in the home of Jim Dear and Darling. Trusty has a cast on his leg, Tramp has a licence on his collar, and Tramp and Lady have a litter of naughty puppies – one of whom, Scamp, almost steals the show. We leave them happily celebrating together.

THE CHARACTERS

Lady

The opening sequence in the movie, when Darling opens up a hatbox to discover that the gift which Jim Dear has given her for Christmas is a puppy, Lady, had its origins in an incident in Walt's own life. Many years before he had forgotten about a dinner date with his wife, and some sort of gift by way of a peace-offering was definitely called for – something really special. His solution was to give her a

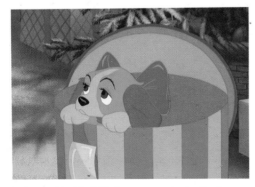
Lady was the ideal Christmas present for Darling.

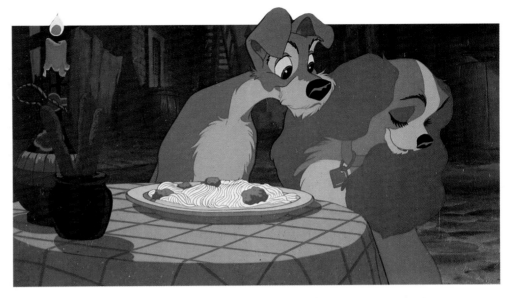
It's amazing how a plateful of spaghetti goes to a lady's head.

puppy in a hatbox. It worked: she forgave him. It was an event which Walt knew he could someday put to good use in a cartoon.

The model for Lady was a cocker spaniel called Lady which belonged to the animator Hamilton Luske. In reality, however, there are two "Ladies" in the movie – the newborn puppy and the young female dog. Both are evidently the same animal, but the older version has quite definite female characteristics while the puppy is, like all puppies, essentially sexless. However, the underlying character – loving, basically trusting, good-spirited – is much the same.

Although Lady is not such a strong character as Tramp, she is by no means the useful cipher that so many of the Disney central characters are: romantic she may be, often terrified and confused she may be, but there is also a deal of steel in there, as we discover during the consecutive sequences when she first tells Tramp to go away and leave her and, second, attempts to break her chain (she is finally successful) in order to chase and fight the rat and thereby save the baby. Barbara Luddy voiced these two aspects of Lady's character excellently, being by turns romantic and stern; she also managed to convey Lady's fundamental decency – the voice alone tells you that Lady is the sort of dog you would ideally like to own and let your children grow up with.

Lady is decent, but she is no naïve innocent. Without really skirting around the issue, Disney managed to get over the idea that dogs do in fact mate, even before "marriage", yet in no way is this at all offensive. That, for the studio, was a minor and generally ignored triumph.

One trivial point of interest: Lady has a blue collar while both Jock and (in due course) Tramp have pinkish-red ones. No "blue for a boy, pink for a girl" here!

Tramp

Tramp, the dog not so much from the other side of the rails as from sixty leagues

beyond them, is a magnificent cartoon creation. As with Lady, his character is superbly conveyed by his voice, supplied by Larry Roberts: it is the type of voice (and dialogue) that all the best Philip Marlowes have. Both words and voice show him as a rather cynical realist; for example, while Jock and Trusty – and for a long time Lady – regard human beings as essentially faultless demigods, Tramp sees them as the flawed mixture they really are.

He is also extremely wily, a point no better proved than in the sequence where he convinces the Beaver in the zoo to bite off Lady's muzzle (earlier an alligator had offered to oblige, but Tramp realized in the nick of time that its intentions were not entirely honest):

Tramp: Pardon me, friend. I wonder if you'd do us a little …
Beaver: Busy, sonny, busy. Can't stop to gossip now. Gotta slide this sycamore to the swamp.
Tramp: Yeah. Well, this'll only take a second of your time.
Beaver: Only a second? Listen – listen sonny. Do you realize every second seventy centimetres of water is wasted over that spillway?
Tramp: Yeah, but …

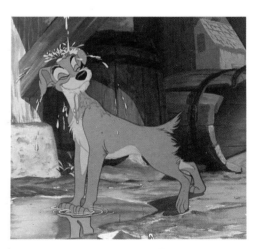
Tramp having a shower – and enjoying every moment of it.

Beaver: Gotta get this log movin', sonny. Gotta get it movin'. 'Tain't the cuttin' takes the time, it's the doggone haulin'.

Tramp: The haulin' – exactly! Now what you need is . . .

Beaver: Hmm, better bisect this section here.

Tramp: Whatcha need is a log puller. I said, *a log puller!*

Beaver: I ain't deef [*sic*], sonny. There's no need to . . . did you say "log puller"?

Tramp: Ha ha! And by a lucky coincidence you see before you, modelled by the lovely little lady, the new improved patented handy-dandy never-fail little-giant log puller! The busy beaver's friend!

Beaver: Ya don't say?

Tramp: Guaranteed not to wear, tear, tip or ravel. Turn around, sister, and show the customer the merchandise. And it cuts log-hauling time sixty-six per cent.

Beaver: Sixty-six per cent, eh? Heh, heh, heh, think of that. Well, howzit work?

Tramp: Why, it's no work at all. You merely slip this ring over the limb, like this, and haul it off.

Beaver: Uh, say, you mind if I slip it on for size?

Tramp: Help yourself, friend, help yourself!

Beaver (struggling with the muzzle): OK, heh, heh. Don't mind if I do. [Struggles] How do you get the consarned thing off, sonny?

Tramp: Glad you brought that up, friend. Glad you brought that up. To remove it, simply place this strap between your teeth.

Beaver: Like this?

Tramp: Keerect, friend. Now – bite hard! You see?

Lady: It's off!

Beaver: Say, that *is* simple.

Tramp: Well, friend, ha ha, we'll be on our way now so . . .

Beaver: Ah ah ah. Not so fast now, sonny. Heh heh, I'll have to make certain it's satisfactory before we settle on a price.

Tramp: Ah, no, it's all yours friend. You can keep it.

Beaver: I can, eh? I can?

Lady: Uh-huh. It's a free sample.

Beaver: Well, thanks a lot. Thanks ever . . .

On the basis of this conversation, you might decide against buying a used – or even a new – car from Tramp, but certainly you would respect his wits.

An important point of the movie is that Tramp lives in constant fear of execution in the dog-pound, yet clearly he is a very fine dog – just look at the way Tony, the restauranteur, and his cook Joe welcome him. Disney did not in general give dog catchers a very good press – look at the one played by Pete (►15) – and usually assumed that nice dogs were being dragged off by evil catchers to be instantly exterminated. In this movie we find both Lady and Tramp threatened with death in the pound, not to mention the other lovable characters incarcerated there, yet the gang of mongrels that chases Lady is made up of very unpleasant characters indeed. The message is a little confused.

The model for Tramp lived out the rest of his days happily at Disneyland's pony farm.

Jock

Over the years Disney has been criticized for some of the voices it has given its characters, yet *Lady and the Tramp* is brilliantly voiced, and nowhere more so than in Bill Thompson's rendition of Jock, the Scots terrier. (Thompson voiced also Bull and Dachsie.) The great triumph of Thompson's voicing is that he sounds genuinely Scottish, rather than the curious amalgam of American Scots so prevalent in the movies of the day.

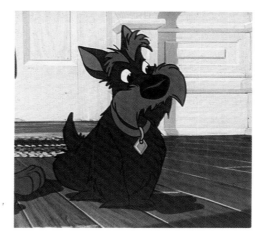

Jock, the plucky little terrier who proved to be such a good friend to Lady.

Jock is depicted well not only verbally but visually. He is the epitome of the Scots terrier in every sense, from his stubby physique all the way through to his slightly gruff personality, which is tempered by his essential good nature. He it is who constantly stops Trusty from repeating the saws of his grandfather, Old Reliable; but he it is also who plays a main part in concealing from the unfortunate bloodhound the painful fact that he has lost his sense of smell. Similarly, although Jock is not particularly enamoured of Tramp, he does his best to save him from annihilation.

During the movie Jock gives his *real* name as the imposing Heather Lad o' Glencairn. Presumably he answers to the name of Jock only in order to please his owners – and Lady. Of all the dogs in the movie, Lady is the one most "bonded" to human beings, so it is fitting that she, too, should call the gritty terrier "Jock".

Trusty

Poor old Trusty, a bloodhound with a distinguished past, has lost his sense of smell – but nobody likes to tell him this, so he spends his life in happy oblivion, remembering the golden days when he and his grandfather, Old Reliable, used to stalk criminals all over the land. In fact, Old Reliable seems to have been not only a first-rate tracker but also a source of wise *bon mots*, for Trusty's standard line is "As my grandpappy, Old Reliable, used to say . . .

don't recollect if I've ever mentioned Old Reliable before, though". Of course, he *has* mentioned Old Reliable before, and Jock is constantly keen to cut the reminiscence short, having apparently heard it many times before. Right at the end of the movie, Tramp and the puppies finally give Trusty an opportunity to recall what it is that Old Reliable used to say, and Trusty embarrassedly confesses: "Uh, er . . . hmmm . . . doggone, heh heh! You know, I clean forgot what it was he used to say."

Trusty is a generally doleful character, yet a faithful one. Like Jock he reluctantly offers his paw in marriage to Lady when she feels herself in the pits of degradation: it is the least he can offer to do for a friend. He is prepared to risk his life (and almost loses it) rescuing Tramp, whom he usually has regarded as a foe – although whether this is because of his benevolence toward Tramp or his friendship for Lady is never made clear.

Trusty, again like Jock, is by no means a major character in the Disney canon, or even a major supporting one, but he is well rounded and completely satisfying. He is an example of that great Disney quality: strength of characterization all the way down the cast-list (although in this movie the humans were deliberately treated differently – see below).

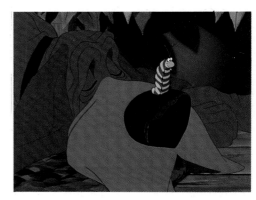

A striped caterpillar perched on Trusty's nose while he dreamed of the old days, when he was chasing convicts through the swamps.

Si and Am

The two Siamese cats belonging to Aunt Sarah were both voiced by the great Peggy Lee; neglecting for a moment her customary raunchy style, she gave them thin voices and produced a classic piece of work in the "Siamese Cat Song", better known "We are Siamese if You Please" – surely among the catchiest of all Disney songs.

Aside from the song, the two cats have little by way of distinct characters. They are not so much mischievous as wantonly destructive, going for the canary and then the goldfish with a blissful disregard for any untoward consequences: the birdcage is upended and the goldfish's bowl knocked over. Lady tries to stop their vandalism – especially when they head for the baby's nursery. But then, of course, she falls foul of the fact that Aunt Sarah believes her cats to be innocent little darlings.

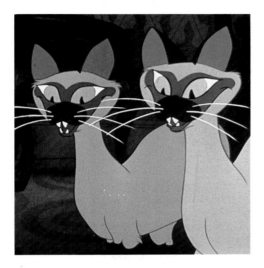

Si and Am, whose arrival was distinctly bad news for Lady. The pair sang one of Disney's most popular songs of all time.

Having served their purpose in the plot – getting Lady into hot water – the two Siamese cats vanish from the scene.

Tony and Joe

Tony and Joe, respectively proprietor and chef of the Italian restaurant to which Tramp takes Lady on their inaugural night out, are delicious cameo parts. Tony is large

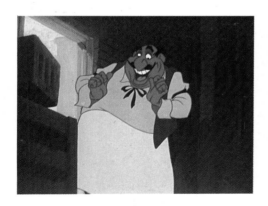

Tony (*above*) and Joe (*below*) give Lady and Tramp a meal to remember.

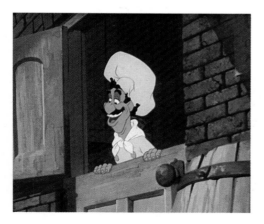

– both tall and wide – and equally large in presence: his broad face and his expansive toothy grin (although those teeth do not bear too close an examination) are the pointers to his generous personality. His ensemble is completed by a would-be natty black moustache that seems to have filtered the vapours from a thousand minestrones, mobile, forest-thick black eyebrows, rolling eyes and a bald head. One senses that every customer is given vastly generous meals – and all of them "heavy on the meats-a ball".

Joe, his chef, is about half the size of Tony but is equally big in spirit. Dressed in full chef's outfit, including the tall hat, he too has an intensely mobile face and a black moustache, although his is more in the style of Groucho Marx. His eyes are filled with a certain impish glee as he plays a virtuoso part on his mandolin during Tony's rendition of "Bella Notte". Incidentally, his mandolin-playing actually features on the soundtrack, whereas Tony's accordion succeeds in imitating a full-scale string orchestra!

Jim Dear and Darling

The stars of *Lady and the Tramp* are dogs, and when they converse among each other they speak English. When they are trying to communicate with the humans in the

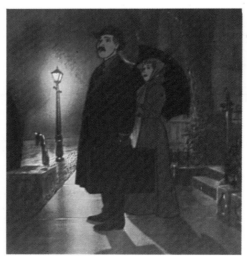

Jim Dear and Darling.

movie, however, they do so using barks. This is a type-symptom of the way in which the humans, for the purposes of this film, are outsiders, belonging to a different world. Thus, while participants such as Jim Dear, Darling and Aunt Sarah may play fairly major roles in terms of both screen-time and influence on events, they are not deeply etched characters. We are shown about as much of their personalities as the dogs around them understand – that is to say, we see what they do and, like the dogs, we have a fair idea of why they do it, but we have no cognizance of their inward motivations.

Jim Dear and Darling are a young and very definitely middle-class couple. Darling, the lesser of the two parts, has well kempt brown hair and is always dressed demurely; her habitual facial expression, too, is demure. Although the movie is set in 1910, she is really the epitome of the ideal American housewife of the 1950s as seen through the eyes of television advertisers. She knits and sews and keeps the house in trim – and, of course, she looks after her husband well. Jim Dear, for his part, is obviously in business – something in finance, we guess, because on his return from work he is usually dressed in a sober brown three-piece suit and a matching bowler hat. His moustache is small and well groomed. Perhaps belying this image, he has a great sense of fun and play, as he demonstrates each evening when he is greeted by Lady.

Aunt Sarah

Few of the Disney villains are male – indeed, from Snow White's stepmother to Cruella De Vil to Madame Medusa, the vast

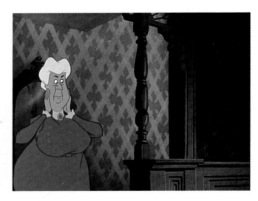

Aunt Sarah. She refused to believe that her little darlings, Si and Am, could do any wrong.

majority of them are female. Aunt Sarah, a rotund elderly matron, is cast in the role of villainess in *Lady and the Tramp*, yet her villainy is not born from genuine malice: she likes cats, and she simply does not understand dogs – she assumes that they are all full of germs and antisocial instincts, unlike cats and, for that matter, people. Otherwise, she is in many ways a sympathetic character – she does, after all, offer to look after the baby while Jim Dear and Darling are away – and, although she is all too ready to believe the worst of Lady (and any other dog), she is not motivated by any active malevolence.

The Dogs in the Pound

When Lady arrives in the pound she finds a chorus of assorted dogs giving a moving rendition of "Home Sweet Home". The irony is obvious – these dogs are doomed and their final surroundings grim. We smile, but a little uneasily.

The four songsters (voiced when singing by the Mello Men) prove to be **Toughy**, an

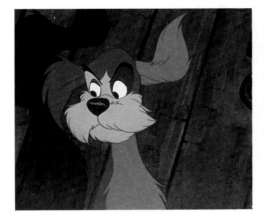

Toughy.

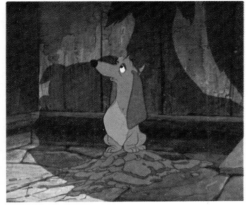

Dachsie.

Siamese cats were for a while called Nip and Tuck.)

Peg has that traditional heart of gold. When the other dogs look to be bullying the terrified Lady, it is Peg who steps in with a cry of "All right, all right, you guys. Lay off, will ya!" and she adds: "Oh, can'tcha see the poor kid's scared enough already?" She it is, along with Toughy, who gently breaks it to Lady that dogs without licences are doomed: we watch as poor flea-ridden **Nutsy** is led away "through da one-way door", as Toughy puts it. Peg it also is who, as a dog who has been around and seen it all, explains to Lady about Tramp's exotic past and his loose ways with females. It should be noted that she does this more as an older sister might offer words of wisdom to a younger than as a gossip; she has clearly taken Lady, at least temporarily, under her wing.

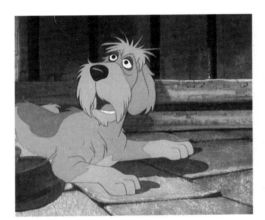

A doomed dog in the pound.

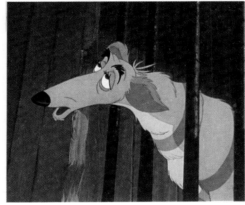

Boris.

American mongrel; **Boris**, a Russian wolfhound; **Pedro**, a Mexican chihuahua; and **Bull**, an English bulldog. Their singing, however, we discover as the camera pans around the pound to where a dachshund called **Dachsie** is eagerly attempting to dig a tunnel under the wall, is not a celebration of their situation but a sonic camouflage. As Dachsie puts it a Teutonic whisper, "Chust vun more chorus und ve're out." As it happens, just then Lady is put into the cell and Dachsie has swiftly to fill in his hole to avoid detection by the guard. All of these dogs speak with their respective national accents; the multi-talented Bill Thompson, who also voiced Jock, was both Bull and Dachsie, and Toughy and Pedro (as well as the Professor and a hyena in the zoo) were voiced by Dallas McKennon; Alan Reed played Boris.

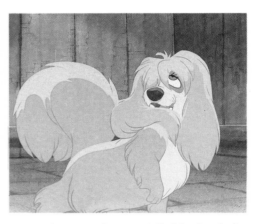

Peg was the outstanding star of all of the dogs in the pound. She was – surprise, surprise – based on the inimitable Peggy Lee.

Beaver

The backwoods Beaver in the zoo deserves a little notice; with his wonderful whistling lisp, he is a caricature of the traditional rustic simpleton conned by the smart-talking city twister. He is a friendly enough fellow, his sole personality defect being monomania: he can think of nothing but chewing down logs, hauling them to the river and there building dams with them. Tramp slyly twists his request for help in removing Lady's muzzle around to fit in with the Beaver's monomania, and all is

The Beaver, who was persuaded by Tramp to do Lady such a good turn.

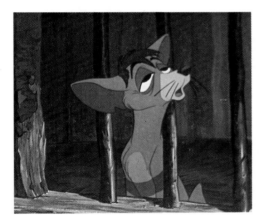

Pedro.

The star of the pound, however, is the broken-down old showgirl of a dog, **Peg**, whose provocative walk was based on the stage-prowl of Peggy Lee (who co-wrote the songs in the movie). In fact, it had originally been decided that Peg be called Mame, but it was suddenly felt that this might cause offence to First Lady Mamie Eisenhower. Miss Lee, who voiced the part and was proud of her ability to swing her hips, was only too glad to permit the dog to be named after herself. (During work on the movie, Tramp had at different times been called Homer, Rags and Bozo, while the two

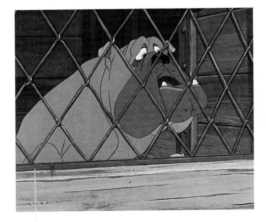

Bull.

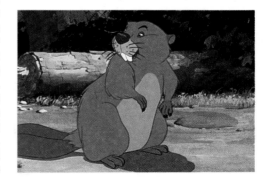

well. The fact that the "log puller" proves actually to work is, of course, a surprise to Tramp and to the audience – but not to the trusting Beaver.

Scamp

The litter of puppies produced by Lady and Tramp contains three little angels who take after their mother and one little non-angel who definitely takes after his father. Frequently – especially in the shorts – Disney used the "naughty one" as a focus for humour and sympathy, and in *Lady and the Tramp* Scamp is cast in the role of the "naughty one". His screen-time is brief and his role very minor – he grabs hold of an end of wool from Jock's red jersey and pulls doughtily, unravelling the garment – but this cameo part caught the attention of cinema audiences and Disney employees alike, and so Scamp went on to have a long and still-continuing career in the comics.

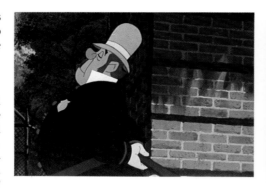
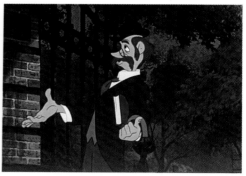

The Policeman (*left*) and the Professor (*right*). Tramp induced the two of them to fight so that he could slip Lady into the zoo.

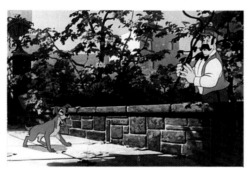

The movie's *real* symbol of evil – the Dog Catcher – ready to seize Tramp.

Minor Characters

A few minor characters deserve mention, if little else. These include the **Pet-store Clerk** who sells Aunt Sarah the muzzle for Lady; and the **Policeman** and the **Professor** whom the resourceful Tramp inveigles into a fight so that he and Lady can slip into the zoo. A slightly more major part in the movie is played by the **Dog Catcher**, although he is really more of a ubiquitous threat than a character as such. Finally there is the guard in the pound, **Bill**, who rather strangely in the context of his job shows the trembling Lady at least some momentary kindness as he gently puts her in her cell.

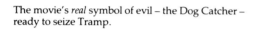

SLEEPING BEAUTY

Characters:

Princess Aurora/Briar Rose; Prince Phillip; Samson; King Stefan; Queen; King Hubert
Good fairies: Fauna; Flora; Merryweather
Maleficent/Dragon; Raven; Lackey

Credits:

Based on the traditional story as recounted by Charles Perrault (1628-1703) in *Histoires ou Contes du temps passé* (1697)

Voices: Mary Costa (Princess Aurora/Briar Rose); Eleanor Audley (Maleficent); Barbara Luddy (Merryweather); Taylor Holmes (King Stefan); Bill Shirley (Prince Phillip); Verna Felton (Flora); Barbara Jo Allen (Fauna); Bill Thompson (King Hubert); Candy Candido, Pinto Colvig, Bob Amsberry (Maleficent's Goons); Dallas McKennon (Owl); Marvin Miller (Narrator)

Special Processes: Ub Iwerks; Eustace Lycett

Sound Supervisor: Robert O. Cook

Film Editors: Roy M. Brewer, Jr.; Donald Halliday

Music Editor: Evelyn Kennedy

Music Adaptation (from Tchaikowsky): George Bruns

Songs by: George Bruns; Tom Adair; Winston Hibler; Ted Sears; Erdman Penner; Sammy Fain; Jack Lawrence

Choral Arrangements: John Rarig

Story: Erdman Penner

Additional Story: Joe Rinaldi; Winston Hibler; Bill Peet; Ted Sears; Ralph Wright; Milt Banta

Production Design: Don DaGradi; Ken Anderson

Layout: McLaren Stewart; Don Griffith; Basil Davidovich; Joe Hale; Jack Huber; Tom Codrick; Erni Nordli; Victor Haboush; Homer Jonas; Ray Aragon

Colour Styling: Eyvind Earle

Character Styling: Tom Oreb

Backgrounds: Frank Armitage; Al Dempster; Bill Layne; Dick Anthony; Richard H. Thomas; Thelma Witmer; Walt Peregoy; Ralph Hulett; Fil Mottola; Anthony Rizzo

Directing Animators: Milt Kahl; Frank Thomas; Marc Davis; Ollie Johnston; John Lounsbery

Character Animators: Hal King; Blaine Gibson; Ken Hultgren; George Nicholas; Henry Tanous; Hal Ambro; John Sibley; Harvey Toombs; Bob Youngquist; John Kennedy; Don Lusk; Bob Carlson; Fred Kopietz; Eric Cleworth; Ken O'Brien

Effects Animators: Dan MacManus; Jack Boyd; Joshua Meador; Jack Buckley

Sequence Directors: Eric Larson; Wolfgang Reitherman; Les Clark

Supervising Director: Clyde Geronimi

Production Supervision: Ken Peterson

Release Date: January 29, 1959

Running Time: 75 minutes

THE MOVIE

Sleeping Beauty was in production for about a decade and cost $6 million – the most ever spent on an animated cartoon up to that time. It was the last of the great classic fairy-tales to be filmed by Disney, and is invariably compared with *Cinderella* and more especially *Snow White and the Seven Dwarfs*. It grossed only $7.7 million (netting less than its cost), even though high admission charges were levied, and was the target of critical vilification. Today it seems hard to understand why the reviewers should have hated it so much (although a few still do): to the average modern eye *Sleeping Beauty* seems arguably the finest thing that Disney has ever done. The pre-release publicity claimed it to be the ultimate animated movie, and it probably is – and may forever remain so.

It is worth looking, however, at one or two of the adverse criticisms. Some writers on the movie have not so much loathed it as been left cold by it – indeed the comment that it was somehow soulless was a frequent one. Thomas A. Nelson, writing in *Film Literature Quarterly* in 1978, summed up this viewpoint – and in so doing he had some interesting things to say about the movie's major character:

Maleficent … and her bevy of animalized grotesqueries provide an extremely dark and menacing presence. Although the force of her evil lessens through the bunglings of her caricaturized goons, Maleficent would seem to recall the Wicked Queen of *Snow White*, especially during that episode when she transforms herself into a huge, fire-breathing dragon. Whatever intensity Maleficent's cadaverous darkness creates finds some relief in the comic protection afforded Sleeping Beauty by the three good fairies ... This domesticated supernatural trinity merely duplicates thrice the fairy godmother from *Cinderella. Sleeping Beauty*, moreover, lacks the elaborate subplot business supplied by the animals in *Cinderella*, which should intensify the terror of Maleficent's dark powers. Yet, strangely, *Sleeping Beauty* turns out to be much less frightening than *Snow White, Pinocchio* or *Alice in Wonderland*.

In light of Nelson's last point – frequently enountered in writings on the movie – one cannot help wondering how many terrified kids of, say, 10 watched *Snow White* in 1937 but were sophisticated theatre critics of 32 when they saw *Sleeping Beauty* in 1959.

Adrian Bailey, in his *Walt Disney's World of Fantasy* (1982) was more concerned with the artistic style of the movie:

> The soft Thirties and early Forties style of artwork had given way to a stronger, less sensitive graphic style. Disney animators were influenced by – and in turn influenced – the art and illustration styles of the period, a style that would be excellent for *The Jungle Book, 101 Dalmatians*, and the animated sequences in *Mary Poppins*, but it lacked the magical quality essential to a classic fairy story.

Although one concedes that this may be a matter of opinion, one cannot help wryly noting that the several stills from *Sleeping Beauty* contained in Bailey's book would seem to be fine examples of the cartoon-makers' art working brilliantly with the "feel" of the classic fairy story.

Both of these writers are in effect damning the movie with faint praise, but other critics have been less kind. C. A. LeJeune, writing in the London *Observer* at the time of the film's release, was one: she compared the movie with what he called its "sister", *Snow White*.

> The two films have a great deal in common, apart from the marked family resemblance between the heroines, and the question naturally arises, has Disney's work developed from that time to this time? So far as techniques are concerned, yes, undoubtedly. In all that affects the imagination, regrettably but definitely no.

There are, it is true, strong resemblances between the two movies – but these resemblances in general come directly from the original fairy-tales (the only obvious exception is that both villainesses have tame ravens as their familiars). The two heroines are in similar situations, and both wed handsome princes, but there the "family resemblances" end: their appearances and characters are quite different. The artwork

of *Sleeping Beauty* actually *is* on its own a great imaginative leap forward from that of *Snow White*, and there are many other elements of the film which display impressive imaginative flair – Maleficent's Goons, for example, are brilliant creations.

The school of critical thought epitomized by LeJeune was, however, temperate in its remarks. Others were not. Most of the cruellest reviews have been rendered obsolete by time and a change in our overall critical perspectives. However, what was probably the most cutting comment of all was that by Paul Beckley in the *Herald Tribune*, that *Sleeping Beauty* was merely "Disney imitating Disney". He saw in it every Disney stereotype carried to the *n*th degree without any creation of the emotional impact one had come to hope for from the makers of *Snow White*.

Summing all of these up, we discover that *Sleeping Beauty* was a poor movie because it was too like *Snow White* and because it was not like *Snow White*. The latter is possibly the truer point. The reviewers and public had been hoping for a rehash of the other movie, and instead Disney gave them something different. That this "something different" might be even better than *Snow White* (although it is really rather futile to say that either is better than the other; their styles are so different) did not trouble the hostile critics. They attacked *Sleeping Beauty* and hence Disney because the movie did not accord with what they had expected.

Curiously, those who see *Sleeping Beauty* first and *Snow White* second are often disappointed in *Snow White* – because it does not accord with *their* expectations!

THE STORY

Once upon a time in the 14th century King Stefan and his Queen have a baby daughter, whom they christen Aurora, after the dawn, because she brings sunshine to their lives. They hold a great celebratory party, to which they invite King Hubert and his son Prince Phillip, who is to be betrothed that very day to the infant Princess so that in the due course of years the two kingdoms will become united. Also present are three good fairies, Flora, dressed in green, Fauna, dressed primarily in pink (with some orange), and Merryweather, dressed in blue; the first two give the babe the gifts of beauty and of song, and Merryweather is just about to give her a third gift when the wicked fairy Maleficent arrives. Furious that she has not been invited, she invokes a curse:

> I too shall bestow a gift on the child. Listen well, all of you. The Princess shall indeed grow in grace and beauty, beloved by all who know her. But, before the sun sets on her sixteenth birthday, she shall prick her finger on the spindle of a spinning-wheel and die.

After she has gone, Merryweather explains that her own magic is not powerful enough to counteract Maleficent's, but that as her gift to the baby she can at least ameliorate the curse, so that the prick of the spinning-wheel will merely send Aurora into a deep sleep until awoken by the kiss of true love.

King Stefan orders every spinning-wheel in the kingdom to be burnt as a precaution. The three good fairies realize that Maleficent will easily get around that, and so Flora convinces the other two that they should disguise themselves as peasant women living in the forest and raise the princess as a foundling child; as an additional precaution, they will forgo the use of magic for the necessary sixteen years. With the permission of Stefan and his Queen they put their plan into effect.

Many sad and lonely years pass in the kingdom, but the time of Princess Aurora's sixteenth birthday draws nigh and hearts begin to lighten, for Maleficent's domain, the Forbidden Mountains, still thunders with her wrath, showing that she has yet to fulfil her evil curse. We see her upbraiding her Goons, who say that they have searched every cradle in the land: she blasts them with lightning for their stupidity, and instead sends out the Raven, her familiar, to "search for a maid of sixteen with hair of sunshine gold and lips red as the rose".

Meanwhile, in the cottage, it is the girl's birthday and the three fairies are planning a special surprise. They get Aurora (now called Briar Rose by way of disguise) out of the house on the pretext that they need *lots* of berries – "And don't speak to strangers," adds Flora – and settle down to prepare her a "real birthday party" with "a real birthday cake" and "a dress a princess can be proud of". Sixteen years, however, have not taught them much about how non-magical mortals do things: the cake is a disaster and Flora's ideas of dressmaking can be gathered from the fact that first of all she cuts a hole in the centre of the cloth "for the feet to go through".

Out on her walk Briar Rose is singing to her animal and bird friends, including a personable little owl. Prince Phillip, riding through the woods on his mighty steed Samson, hears the song and makes towards it, but unfortunately falls off and lands in a stream. He hangs up his cloak on the trees to dry out, and takes his boots off.

Strolling through the forest Briar Rose has been telling the animals that, while she is aggrieved that the three "peasant women" will never let her meet anyone, nevertheless she has succeeded in meeting a handsome stranger – in her dreams. She has met him so often, she says, that she is convinced that one day they will meet in real life and wed. The birds and animals come upon Phillip's clothes and by hook or by crook assemble them to provide Briar Rose with a dancing partner; as she dances she sings the best song of the movie, "Once Upon a Dream", by Sammy Fain and Jack Lawrence, with a little help from P. I. Tchaikowsky. In due course she bumps into the Prince, who recognizes her from his dreams, and together they continue the song. However, when at the end of the song he asks her name, she turns to flee from him. (Interestingly, it is tradition in many cultures that one should not give one's name to strangers, for it contains part of one's soul.) She does, however, make a date to meet him at the cottage that evening.

At home, the full disaster of their domestic efforts is becoming evident to the fairies. Merryweather is the first to crack, and fetches the wands. They plug up the doors and the windows as a safeguard against any of the magic leaking out and alerting Maleficent and then set to work remaking the cake and dress and cleaning up the cottage. (To do this last Merryweather activates bucket, mop and broom – shades of *The Sorcerer's Apprentice* [➤181]!) An argument about the color of the dress develops between the pink-clad Fauna, on the one hand, and Merryweather, dressed in blue, on the aggressive other. A fierce battle of colour-changing ensues. And, unfortunately, because they have forgotten to block up the fireplace, the whole forest is lit up by the various blasts of pink and blue magic erupting from the cottage chimney. By rotten luck, this phenomenon is spotted by the searching Raven.

Ending their foolishness, the three fairies have everything ready for Briar Rose's return. She is delighted by dress and cake, and says that "This is the happiest day of my life. Why, everything's so wonderful. Just wait 'til you meet him." When they realize that she has met a stranger and fallen in love with him the fairies are horrified. They explain to her that she "must never see that young man again", despite her date, and that she is really a princess and already betrothed to a certain Prince Phillip. This somewhat mutes her birthday celebrations. Exit Briar Rose, weeping.

At King Stefan's castle, he and King Hubert are having a feast, in which wine is playing a major part. (It is playing a major part also in the duties of a Lackey, who is downing at least as much as the two kings.) That very evening they are expecting the arrival of the Princess Aurora, who at midnight that night will have outlived Maleficent's curse; soon their two children will marry and unite the kingdoms. However, Hubert is much more eager than Stefan for things to proceed immediately – Stefan is concerned that Aurora ought at least to be consulted in the matter (even if her opinions will then be overruled) – and a drunken brawl breaks out between them. However, they soon come to see sense, and make it up.

The revelry is disrupted when Phillip arrives to announce that he has met the girl he loves and is going to marry; "A ... a

peasant girl, I suppose," he fails to reassure his father on being asked who she is. He departs to make his tryst at the cottage.

The three good fairies, all this time, have been bringing Aurora to the castle to prepare her for the great moment when she will be reintroduced to princess-hood. They take her to a secret room and deck her out in finery. When she begins to weep they decide to leave her alone for a few moments to compose herself – a fatal mistake, for in the fireplace a smoky cloud of Maleficent's green-yellow light appears. Aurora, hypnotized, unquestioningly follows the light into the fireplace, the back of which fades away to show a winding staircase, up which she climbs.

Outside, the fairies have decided that, if she really loves the stranger, she shall have him. They come in but sense Maleficent's vile presence. They chase up the staircase, but too late: Maleficent persuades Aurora to touch the spindle of her spinning-wheel, and the girl falls into a deep sleep. (Here is an interesting difference from the original story, in which the old woman in the turret was an innocent crone who just happened to have the last surviving spinning-wheel in the land.)

Maleficent having departed, the good fairies lay Aurora out in state and decide that they cannot face telling the two kings what has happened. They therefore determine to put the entire castle to sleep until – if ever – Aurora should wake. But, as they are flying around spreading sleep wherever they go, Flora overhears Hubert telling Stefan something about the young girl Phillip has met "once upon a dream". Recognizing the expression from Briar Rose's account of the man she met, Flora realizes that the "stranger" and Phillip are one and the same. Drawing the other two around her, she heads for the cottage, where Phillip must even now be waiting.

Alas, 'he has been and gone, for Maleficent and her Goons were lying in wait for him, and have carried him and Samson (his horse) off to her stronghold in the Forbidden Mountains; all that is left is his hat. The good fairies, having inferred what must have happened, daringly go to Maleficent's castle and follow the wicked witch down into Phillip's dungeon, where Maleficent taunts him with the fact that his "peasant girl" is actually the Princess. She torments him with a vision of himself as an old, old man, set free to ride *slowly* to wake Aurora with "love's first kiss". After Maleficent has left, the three fairies release the Prince and present him with the Shield of Virtue and the Sword of Truth. As they escape they are spotted by the Raven, and Merryweather prettily turns it to stone – but not before it has alerted the Goons. As the Prince flees on Samson the Goons throw everything at him, but the good fairies counter the onslaught effectively – turning an avalanche of boulders into an avalanche of bubbles, and so on. Maleficent, aroused

by the racket, appears and despairingly hurls a bolt of lightning at the fleeing Prince; but she is too late.

Thwarted, she casts another evil spell, surrounding Stefan's castle with a forest of thorns which she plans as a trap for Phillip:

A forest of thorns shall be his tomb,
Borne through the skies on a fog of doom.
Now go with a curse and serve me well:
Round Stefan's castle cast my spell!

When Phillip reaches the castle he begins to hack his way through the seemingly impenetrable barrier of thorns, to Maleficent's laughing glee. However, her mirth changes to fury as he succeeds in gaining a passage through the forest, and she is forced to take recourse in desperate measures. "Now you shall deal with me, oh Prince, and all the powers of Hell!" she screams as she transforms herself into a vast Dragon, breathing flame.

A terrible battle between the two ensues. All seems lost for Phillip when Flora waves her wand at his sword and incants:

Now Sword of Truth fly swift and sure
That evil die and good endure.

With a last desperate effort he hurls the sword, which impales itself in the Dragon's breast.

The Dragon is dead, and with it Maleficent and all her evil. Phillip makes his way into the castle and to the room where Aurora lies sleeping. He kisses her and she awakes. Soon the whole castle is awake, and the festivities carry on as if they had never paused.

There is a final piece of comedy as Aurora and Phillip dance together. The battle resumes among the good fairies as to whether her dress should be pink or blue, and as the movie ends and the two young lovers waltz together to "Once Upon a Dream" we see Aurora's dress becoming pink, then blue, then pink, then blue, then ...

THE CHARACTERS

Princess Aurora/Briar Rose

Although she is the central character of the movie, the part of Princess Aurora/Briar Rose is in fact a very small one – smaller, for example, than that of Prince Phillip (in marked contrast with *Snow White and the Seven Dwarfs*, whose Prince hardly made an appearance, but whose heroine occupied a fair deal of screen-time). In fact, her functions in the movie are three: (a) to be cursed; (b) to meet and fall in love with Phillip; and (c) to prick her finger and fall into a death-like sleep. Over (a) and (c) she has no control whatsoever, and over (b) her control is as limited as that of anyone falling

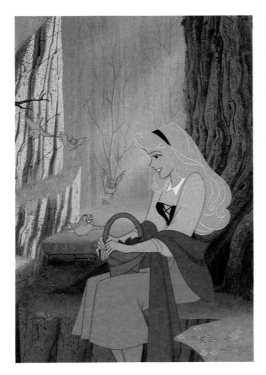

Like so many Disney heroines, Briar Rose was in empathic contact with the creatures of the countryside.

in love. Yet these three elements constitute the vital catalyst without which none of the rest of the action in the movie could occur.

Largely animated by Marc Davis, the doyen of Disney animators of women (he was responsible also for Cinderella and Cruella De Vil), Aurora is physically and temperamentally much more mature than Snow White; she is less cute, much more pretty. However, like Snow White she has a special affinity with the animals of the forest, who replace all the human friends of her own age that in normal circumstances she would have had. Indeed, it is hardly surprising that she falls in love with Phillip on sight: he is the first person of roughly her own age, and the first man, whom she has ever met – unlike the case with Snow White (or so we can safely assume, Snow White having been brought up in a castle). One assumes that she has been able to obey the command not to talk to strangers because there have never been any strangers to talk to; as soon as one does appear she disobeys orders – as, of course, in a way does Phillip, who is on his way to his betrothal to, as he thinks, a different woman.

The smallness of Aurora's role does not imply that Disney in any way skimped on her. In an interview with A. Eisen, Marc Davis commented:

> Sleeping Beauty is a milestone of a certain type of film that we never did again. We did a lot more design with the characters than we had ever done before. Sleeping Beauty herself was more designed in a two-dimensional way [i.e., visually] than any other character we've done.

It is because of that that she is a successful heroine. Snow White seemed rather too young to be in the business of falling romantically in love, but Aurora, albeit she is not quite sixteen years old, seems exactly the right age. She is a sleeping beauty in every sense, for her womanhood is about to awaken.

Prince Phillip

The handsome Prince in *Snow White* was nothing more than a cipher – it was not thought necessary even to name him. Prince Charming in *Cinderella* was more than just a plot device, but nevertheless still had only a minor part. For the third in their trio of great fairy stories, however, Disney gave the handsome Prince a far meatier role, and consequently his character had to be portrayed in more detail.

Phillip is gentle, good-natured, well spoken, courteous, romantic and above all courageous – just as you would expect him to be – but what is interesting is that these characteristics are all well blended together to create a convincing, fully rounded personality. When he fights his way through the forest of thorns or battles the Dragon, this behaviour is perfectly consonant with the gentleness he displayed towards Aurora as well as with his determination of mind when he tells his father that he is going to marry the peasant girl he loves rather than the intended Princess. It is in the course of this argument, by the way, that he comes out with one of the best gags in the movie:

> *Hubert*: No, you can't do this to me! Give up the throne, the kingdom, for some ... some nobody! By Harry, I won't have it! You're a Prince and you're going to marry a Princess!
> *Phillip*: Now, father, you're living in the past. This is the fourteenth century ...

It is astonishing that so many critics have condemned Phillip as "cardboard" or "two-dimensional", because he is much more than that: one suspects that they saw what they expected to see – a revamped version of Snow White's true love – and not what was actually there.

Phillip also enjoys an intriguing relationship with his horse **Samson**, which like himself effects the transformation from good-natured jolliness to intrepid courage without any of the seams showing. When first we encounter Samson he seems to be nothing more than an incidental comic character, put in to create some light relief, but it is on his back that Phillip undergoes the terrifying escape from Maleficent's fortress and then the even more terrifying duel with the Dragon. When Samson needs to be he is a doughty steed, but otherwise he is ever so slightly a clown, more concerned with where his next bag of oats is coming from than with making sure he is an efficient warhorse. Nevertheless, it is obvious from the start that he and his master share a tremendous amount of

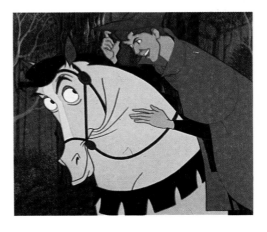

Prince Phillip and a somewhat sceptical-looking Samson.

Prince Phillip with the Princess Aurora. To think, she used to be plain old Briar Rose!

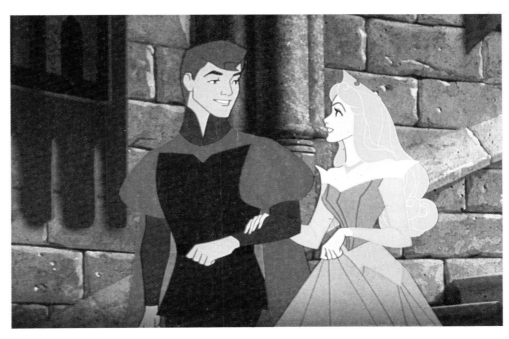

mutual trust and understanding – invaluable, of course, when it comes to such serious matters as killing dragons.

King Stefan, King Hubert and the Queen

The two kings are brilliantly comic characters, and for the most part their screen appearances are played definitely for laughs – even if this means adding gratuitous scenes to the script. The prime example of this is during the revelry as they wait for the arrivals of Aurora and Phillip preparatory to the formalization of their betrothal. Tall, cadaverous **Stefan** and tubby, somewhat smaller **Hubert** have perhaps been toasting the joyous day a little too enthusiastically, and when Hubert springs on Stefan the news that he has built the young couple a castle as a present Stefan is not well pleased:

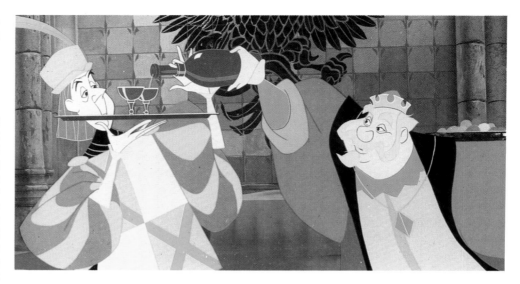

King Hubert, pouring a toast. The drunken Lackey, here shown holding the tray, proved to be one of the stars of the show.

> *Hubert*: Nothing elaborate, of course. Forty bedrooms, dining-hall ... honeymoon cottage, really.
> *Stefan*: You, you mean you're building it already?
> *Hubert*: Built, man. Finished! Lovebirds can move in tomorrow.
> *Stefan*: Tomorrow! But Hubert, they're not even married yet!
> *Hubert*: Ha ha, take care of that tonight. To the wedding! [Toasts.]
> *Stefan*: Hold on, Hubert. I haven't even seen my daughter yet and you're taking her away from me.
> *Hubert*: Getting my Phillip, aren't you?
> *Stefan*: Yes, but ...
> *Hubert*: Want to see our grandchildren, don't we?
> *Stefan*: Of course, but ...
> *Hubert*: Then, no time to lose. Getting on in years, ha ha ha. To the wedding! [Toasts.]

King Stefan and his elegant Queen, awakened from their long slumber, greet their daughter.

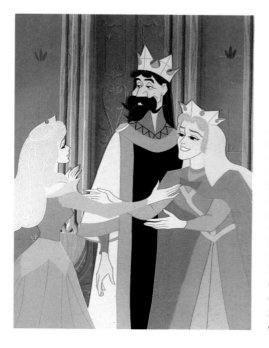

> *Stefan*: Now be reasonable, Hubert. After all, Aurora knows nothing about all this.
> *Hubert*: Well?
> *Stefan*: Well, it ... it may come as quite a shock.
> *Hubert*: "Shock"? My Phillip a shock? What's wrong with my Phillip?
> *Stefan*: Nothing, Hubert, I only meant ...
> *Hubert*: Why doesn't your daughter like my son?
> *Stefan*: Now ...
> *Hubert*: I'm not so sure my son likes your daughter.
> *Stefan*: Now see here!
> *Hubert*: I'm not so sure my grandchildren want you for a grandfather.
> *Stefan*: Why, you ... you unreasonable, pompous, blustering old windbag!
> *Hubert*: "Unreasonable"? "Pompous"? On guard, sir! [Seizes fish from nearby table and advances with it as if it were a sword. Attempts to hit Stefan over head with it, but Stefan uses platter as a shield. Hubert stops, looks at floppy fish.]
> *Stefan*: I warn you, Hubert. This means war!
> *Hubert* (losing confidence): Forward! For honour! For country! For ... for ... [Both he and Stefan look at limp fish and start to laugh.] What's this all about, anyway?
> *Stefan*: Nothing, Hubert. Absolutely nothing.
> *Hubert*: Children bound to fall in love with each other.
> *Stefan*: Precisely. And, as for grandchildren, I'll have the royal wood-carvers start work on the cradle tomorrow.

And the two kings are the best of friends again. It is interesting to note from this exchange that, despite the superb visual gag of the fish, there is a lot of humour in the script itself. This is not typical of Disney, most of whose humour derives from characterization and visual effect (for example, Donald Duck is the funniest Disney creation, yet you cannot even understand most of what he says). It was, however, typical of *Sleeping Beauty*, which contains more than its fair share (as it were) of excellent verbal jokes – curiously, this may have been another reason why many critics disliked it.

Stefan's graceful **Queen** has the tiniest named role in the film (indeed, she does not even have a given name). Her presence is necessary purely because, of course, Aurora must have a mother.

The Good Fairies

The three good fairies – **Flora**, **Fauna** and **Merryweather** serve not only as Aurora's guardians while she lives as Briar Rose in the forest but also as a constant source of comic relief.

Flora is their leader, without a doubt. Fauna is prepared to tag along, hardly ever questioning Flora's decisions. Merryweather, the smallest fairy clad in blue, if not the brains of the trio, at least believes herself to be so, and consequently rebels from time to time against Flora's decrees. She is also the most pugnacious:

> *Merryweather*: Ohhh – I'd like to turn [Maleficent] into a fat ole hoptoad!
> *Fauna*: Now, dear! That *isn't* a very nice thing to say.
> *Flora*: Besides, we can't. You know our magic doesn't work that way.
> *Fauna*: It can only do good, dear – to bring joy and happiness.
> *Merryweather*: Well, that would make *me* happy!

In a Harvard honours paper from 1975 Ada M. Fan has described the three good fairies as

a trinity of Mother Nature ... visually ideal, the perfect archetype of the Anglo-American godmother. Elderly spinsters, they are plump, stately, and irrepressibly cheerful. From their persons emanates a mythological aura. They may be considered the three Fates, spinning out destiny's thread. ... The gifts of Flora and Fauna [to the infant Princess] are beauty and song, fitting gifts for a woman – who should be seen and only heard in lullabies and songs sung to accompany housework. Coincidentally, the gifts are aspects with which

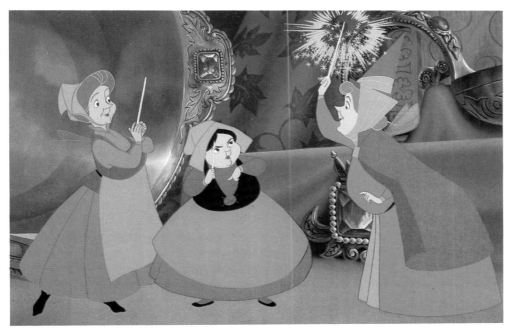

The good fairies – from right, Fauna, Merryweather and Flora.

Aurora's beauty is to be the beauty of the sunlight and the rose, realizing both her given name and the name she grows up with, Briar Rose ... It is appropriately Flora who bestows this gift. Fauna, governess of animals, presents the infant with song and likens Aurora to the nightingale, a metaphor quite within her province.

The names of Flora and Fauna – and, just, Merryweather – are clear indications that the three good fairies are nature spirits.

Walt's instructions to his animators on *Sleeping Beauty* had included that they should aim for the ultimate in realism, and this they certainly did for characters such as Phillip and Aurora. For the three fairies, however, they used a much more stylized technique, apparently aiming to convey their goodness through what is almost caricature – caricature done with an economy of line. Curiously enough, though, the stylized figures of the three fairies in no way clash with the other, much more human characters in the film.

The sense of their goodness thus conveyed was, incidentally, by no means universally admired by the critics. Paul V. Beckley, whom we have already noted as a hostile critic, said that in *Sleeping Beauty* "goodness gets itself defined as a form of bumbling innocence with a perky tail-twitching, simpering quality". This seems a little untenable – although his further comments about the stereotyping of the villainous characters are of some interest. No, the fairies' goodness is better epitomized by their actions – which are indeed often coloured by "bumbling innocence" but which, ignoring that, show them to be truly benevolent. Consider their plan to outwit Maleficent by hiding Aurora as a peasant foundling:

Merryweather: ... Well, what won't [Maleficent] expect? She knows everything.
Fauna: Oh, but she doesn't, dear. Maleficent doesn't know anything about love, or kindness, or the joy of helping others. You know, sometimes I don't think she's really very happy.
Flora: That's it! Of course! It's the only thing she can't understand and won't expect! Ohh-o-ho-ho-ho. Now, now, now, we'll have to plan it carefully ...

Of course, here the movie is making stark the difference between the goodies and the baddies, but this is in keeping with its fairy-tale context. It is hard to think of a traditional fairy tale in which the villain(ess) has some ameliorating traits! And good fairies are always just that: good. Flora, Fauna and Merryweather are part of the great tradition.

Maleficent

Of all the characters in *Sleeping Beauty*, the one that everyone remembers, even decades later, is the wicked fairy Maleficent. She is one of the finest creations ever to come out of the Disney studio – and the brilliant transformation of her into the Dragon to fight Phillip merely adds to the strength of the characterization. Even her name – a wonderful combination of "malice" and "malevolent" – testifies to her pure evil. People who thought that the wicked Queen in *Snow White* (➤169) might frighten their children were presumably petrified themselves when they took their grandchildren to see Maleficent. To an extent this is achieved because she is a much more rounded character than her earlier counterpart – she has something of the dashing style of Cruella De Vil in *One Hundred and One Dalmatians* (➤267) – which is hardly surprising, because Marc Davis

did much of the work on both of them. In his interview with A. Eisen, Davis described the experience:

I had nothing to do with the dragon [that was Ken Anderson's province] but it was based on Maleficent. ... there was a consistency; this wasn't just a dragon that she turned into, this was her own particular dragon. Maleficent was a very difficult character, because she always raised her arms and gave a speech. This is a very difficult thing to make come off. When one character is working with another character, you get the contact, you feel the reaction. ... Once you have two characters that work together, then they come to life.

Despite these difficulties, Disney succeeded in making Maleficent come to life in both her forms. Tall and thin with a black horned headdress and a capacious, swirling cloak, with a contemptuous face and highly arched eyebrows, with a long neck that seems to be nothing more than thinly covered vertebrae, she is a terrifying figure even in her rare moments of repose. Her driving emotion is hatred – hatred of all things good – and as a result she incidentally hates fairies, human beings, animals ... anything capable of displaying the gentler emotions. Her reason for cursing the newborn infant is a trivial one – she was slighted by the failure to send her an invitation to the festivities – and its triviality is emphasized by the fact that she is so superior in terms of power and influence to anyone else in the movie that one would not expect her to notice, one way or the other, whether or not she received an invitation at all. No, her "reason" for setting the curse is not that at all: it is merely an excuse for her to exercise her all-consuming malevolence and hatred.

The Dragon into which she transforms herself has physical similarities to her, but the animators also managed to endow it with the same bitterness and maliciousness. In its every movement we see that it is intent upon the destruction not only of Phillip, the immediate problem, but also of the forces of good in general. No greater contrast could be found than between this monster and Ken Anderson's other famous dragon creation, Elliot in the much later *Pete's Dragon* (➤304).

Maleficent is a frightening character even for adult audiences, let alone children. However, the screen force of her evil is diluted to non-toxic strengths by her companions, the incompetent Goons – dimwitted travesties of various animal forms – and the rather more competent but nevertheless not especially scaring **Raven**. This familiar of hers has a far bigger role than its equivalent in *Snow White*, and not only its personality but also its physical appearance are given to us in much more detail. Clearly it worships Maleficent – or, at least, is too terrified of her to show any other attitude – but at the same time it has a certain likeable goofiness. The only time

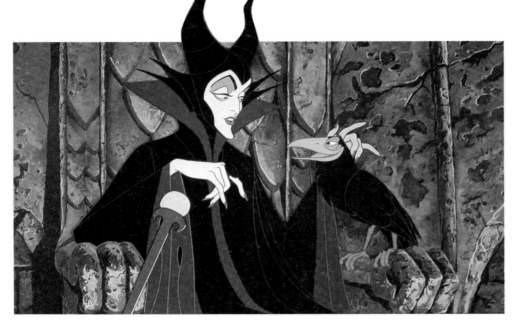

Maleficent with the Raven; she has been one of Disney's most scaring villainesses, and it has been one of the studio's most endearingly villainous sidekicks.

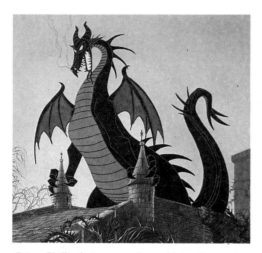

Prince Phillip facing up to the terrifying Dragon into which Maleficent transformed herself.

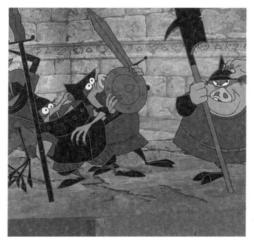

Maleficent's repulsive goons in the process of discovering why all the rest of us don't take jobs from wicked fairies.

that it seems to be really evil is when the three fairies are inadvertently lighting up the skies with their varicoloured blasts of escaping magic; then the Raven's appearance and its manifest realization that it has succeeded in carrying out its mistress's assignment do strike a definite chill to the heart. However, this effect is as much created by the music as by the character itself. More than one child in the average cinema audience will shed a secret tear when Merryweather turns the Raven to stone.

Lackey

Mention should also be made of the Lackey, who is supposed to be serving Hubert and Stefan with wine while they await the arrivals of Phillip and Aurora. In fact, they do get some of the wine – but not all of it, or even most of it, for the Lackey is adroit at intercepting and downing any that they might conceivably overlook. In particular, he is an expert at catching copious quantities of the nectar in his lute, to be swigged at a more convenient moment. Finally he is discovered by the two kings sleeping under the table, his face in his lute, producing elegant musical snores as the strings vibrate. The sudden arrival of Phillip saves him from any wrath at his pilferage which the kings might display.

He makes an amusing although extremely brief appearance a little later, when the good fairies are spreading their magic sleep-dust all over the castle. Merryweather thinks she has completed her task in the banqueting hall, but the deeply slumbering Lackey chooses this moment to wake up. Realizing her mistake, the little fairy zaps him with a dose of sleep-dust – just in time.

ONE HUNDRED AND ONE DALMATIANS

Characters:

Pongo; Perdita; Roger Radcliff; Anita Radcliff; Nanny; Cruella De Vil; Jasper Badun; Horace Badun
Puppies: Rolly; Patch; Penny; Lucky; Freckles; Pepper
The Captain; The Colonel; Sergeant Tibs; Danny; Prissy; Coco; Lucy; Towser; Labrador; Collie
Cows: Queenie; Princess; Duchess
TV Characters

Credits:

Based on *The Hundred and One Dalmatians* (1956) by Dodie Smith

Voices: Rod Taylor (Pongo); Lisa Daniels (Perdita); Cate Bauer (Perdita); Ben Wright (Roger Radcliff); Lisa Davis (Anita Radcliff); Martha Wentworth (Nanny, Queenie, Lucy); J. Pat O'Malley (The Colonel, Jasper Badun, etc.); Fred Worlock (Horace Badun, Inspector Craven); Betty Lou Gerson (Cruella De Vil, Miss Birdwell); Tudor Owen (Towser); Tom Conway (Quizmaster, Collie); George Pelling (Danny); Thurl Ravenscroft (The Captain); Dave Frankham (Sergeant Tibs); Ramsay Hill (Television Announcer, Labrador); Queenie Leonard (Princess); Marjorie Bennett (Duchess); Barbara Beaird (Rolly); Micky Maga (Patch); Sandra Abbott (Penny); Mimi Gibson (Lucky); Barbara Luddy (Rover); Paul Frees (Dirty Dawson); Bob Stevens; Max Smith; Sylvia Marriott; Dallas McKennon; Rickie Sorensen; Basil Ruysdael; Lucille Bliss (singer of TV commercial)

Special Processes: Ub Iwerks; Eustace Lycett

Sound Supervisor: Robert O. Cook

Film Editors: Donald Halliday; Roy M. Brewer Jr.

Music Editor: Evelyn Kennedy

Music: George Bruns

Songs: Mel Leven

Orchestration: Franklyn Marks

Story: Bill Peet

Art Direction and Production Design: Ken Anderson

Layout Styling: Don Griffith; Collin Campbell; Erni Nordli

Layout: Basil Davidovich; Joe Hale; Dick Ung; McLaren Stewart; Dale Barnhart; Homer Jonas; Vance Gerry; Ray Aragon; Al Zinnen; Sammie June Lanham; Victor Haboush

Colour Styling: Walt Peregoy

Backgrounds: Al Dempster; Ralph Hulett; Anthony Rizzo; Bill Layne

Directing Animators: Milt Kahl; Frank Thomas; Marc Davis; John Lounsbery; Ollie Johnston; Eric Larson

Character Styling: Bill Peet; Tom Oreb

Character Animators: Hal King; Les Clark; Cliff Nordberg; Blaine Gibson; Eric Cleworth; John Sibley; Art Stevens; Julius Svendsen; Hal Ambro; Ted Berman; Bill Keil; Don Lusk; Dick Lucas; Amby Paliwoda

Effects Animators: Jack Boyd; Dan MacManus; Ed Parks; Jack Buckley

Directors: Wolfgang Reitherman; Hamilton Luske; Clyde Geronomi

Production Supervision: Ken Peterson

Release Date: January 25, 1961

Running Time: 79 minutes

THE MOVIE

It is obviously foolish ever to try to decide which is "The Best" of the Disney animated features, because one is not really comparing like with like, but *One Hundred and One Dalmatians* is certainly one of the best. The first of Disney's features to be set contemporarily, it is a wonderful blend of fantasy, humour, sentiment, adventure and suspense – the kind of mixture, in fact, at which Disney has always been *the* world leader – and it features one of the best, if not the best, of all of the Disney villains, Cruella De Vil. Satire, not usually a weapon in the armoury of the Disney features, is wielded effectively in the parodies of television programmes. The film appeals to audiences of all ages, and its songs, of which there are only four (surprisingly few for a Disney animated feature), are good ones. It is hard to find a single complaint against the movie, which is presumably why Richard Schickel fails even to mention it in his *The Disney Version* (1968). Of course, there are other Disney films that can be described as bland precisely because one cannot find a complaint, but bland *One Hundred and One Dalmatians* most certainly is not.

All told, 6,469,952 animated Dalmatian-spots appear during the movie – a figure this author takes on trust. (For completists, Pongo has 72 spots, Perdita 68 and each of the 99 puppies 32.) In the old days this would have been impossible – there is a dearth of tigers in Disney movies because of the difficulties of animating stripes, a simpler task than keeping track of 3,308 spots. That Disney was able to cope with this was thanks to the technical genius of Ub Iwerks, who adapted the Xerox process to create "Xerography", a technique that not only made it possible to contemplate making a movie with 101 spotty dogs, at a time when other studios avoided even *one*

spotty dog because of the technical difficulties, but also reduced the number of steps in transferring the animators' drawings to the finished film, thereby retaining much more of the vigour of their original work. The use of the technique shows also in the style of the film: moving away from the realism that had come to be so much criticized, Disney produced animated caricatures, genuine cartoon creations rather than animated attempts to reproduce live action. In the case of this particular film the result is terrific – which is not to denigrate the realism of, say, *Sleeping Beauty*, which would have been disastrous if done in this style.

The critics of the time unanimously loved *One Hundred and One Dalmatians*, and writers ever since have clearly held it in a position of special affection. This was reflected in the box office: the movie cost something over $4 million dollars to make – much less than *Sleeping Beauty*, even despite inflation – and made a healthy profit on first release. Its subsequent reissues have, if anything, been even more successful.

THE STORY

Pongo, a Dalmatian, lives in London with his pet Roger Radcliff, a hard-working but not-too-well-off songwriter. It is Spring, a time of boredom for all bachelors, and Pongo decides to do something about it. Looking out from the window one day, he spots a woman, Anita, walking a beautiful female Dalmatian, Perdita; although Pongo is a little uncertain as to Anita's qualifications to be Roger's mate, he is quite sure about Perdita's to be his own. He drags Roger out of the house and engineers a fairly boisterous meeting in the park. Roger and Anita both end up toppling into a pond, a suitable prelude to true love. In due course they are married, and so too are Pongo and Perdita.

Soon Perdita, with the Radcliff's servant, Nanny, as midwife, produces a litter of pups – no fewer than 15, although one is still-born. However, even this one survives, thanks to Roger's valiant resuscitative efforts, in a scene that practically sets the cockles of your heart on fire. But the horizon is not unclouded, for Anita's old school "chum", the wealthy and spoilt Cruella De Vil, wants to buy the puppies and has great difficulty in taking "no" for an answer. When Roger refuses to sell, she sends in professional crooks Jasper and Horace Badun, to steal the puppies.

The Radcliffs, Pongo and Perdita are desolated by the loss, and the press is full of the "dognapping" story. Roger is sure that Cruella is behind it. However, there seems little the police can do and so, as a last resort, Pongo and Perdita make use of the "Twilight Bark", a sort of canine telegraph system whereby news traverses the country

swiftly from dog to dog. The news comes that the puppies are in Hell Hall, the old De Vil place near Withermarsh in Suffolk. Pongo and Perdita ₁scape from the house and set off on the long quest.

At Hell Hall three of the local animals – a cat named Sergeant Tibs, a horse named the Captain and an Old English sheepdog named the Colonel – were responsible for locating the puppies and 84 other Dalmatian pups. Tibs is in Hell Hall when he overhears a conversation between Cruella and the Baduns: the police are swarming everywhere and so Cruella wants the two crooks to kill all of the puppies and skin them that very night. It proves that she has been planning to rear all 99 to adulthood and then use their fur to make marketable coats; now, however, she wants to cut her losses and make as many coats as possible out of the puppies' hides. Tibs takes immediate action, and escorts all of the puppies out of Hell Hall – helped in the later stages by the Colonel and the Captain and by Pongo and Perdita, who have just arrived from London.

There follows a desperate journey home through the winds and blizzards of a nightmare winter. Fortunately the convoy has allies in the form of a Collie and especially a Labrador who belongs to the grocer in Dinsford. The Labrador has noticed that a furniture van destined for London has broken down in the village; there is plenty of room in it for the dogs if only they can all climb aboard before the repairs are complete. This is not easy, because Cruella and the Baduns are prowling the village. Pongo has an idea, however: if all the Dalmatians cover themselves in soot they will look like black Labradors, and thereby escape detection. The plan almost succeeds, and most of the pups are aboard the van before one of them, inappropriately named Lucky, is splashed by melting snow so that some of the soot is washed off. Cruella immediately tumbles to what has been going on and, although Pongo and Perdita do succeed in herding all of the puppies aboard just before the van starts, she in her car and the Baduns in their truck are in hot pursuit.

Cruella is a woman possessed. She drives like the maniac she is, trying to force the furniture van off the road – to the bewilderment of its driver. In due course, however, the efforts of the Baduns to help her succeed only in creating a huge smash-up between their truck and her car, so that the three crooks end up sitting in vast snowdrifts surrounded by a litter of debris rather than a litter of puppies.

Back home, Roger, Anita and Nanny are mourning the loss not only of the puppies but now also of the two adult Dalmatians. Even the fact that Roger's song "Cruella De Vil" has become a major money-earning hit cannot console them. But then, oh joy, there is the sound of barking from without. Pongo, Perdita and 99 puppies burst into

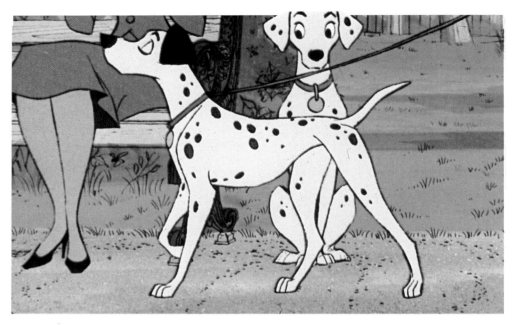

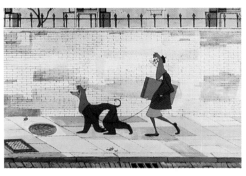

The way-out artist who resembles her equally way-out Afghan.

Pongo demonstrates how to impress the girls – just ignore 'em. Perdita is all too clearly aware of his presence.

the room, and a delighted pair of Radcliffs determine to keep all of them. The mind boggles at the scale of this undertaking, but the Radcliffs and Nanny are convinced that this constitutes a happy ending – and so, of course, are 101 very contented Dalmatians.

So, too, are millions of delighted viewers all over the world.

THE CHARACTERS

Pongo and Perdita

Pongo is the theoretical star of the show – obviously the *real* star is Cruella – and he acts also as narrator during the opening sequences, during which the knots are tied between Anita and Roger and between the cultured Perdita and himself. He is a very civilized dog in every way, possessing a suave wisdom in both voice and behaviour that belies his years. He is very paternal towards his pet, Roger Radcliff, yet at the same time as looking out for his interests he has no hesitation at all in using him for his own ends: it is fortunate that Roger and Anita prove to get along so well, but the black-eared Pongo is really interested in furthering their romance only as a way of furthering his own with Perdita.

Cultured Pongo and Perdita may be, but they are also tough and courageous when the need arises. Their growlingly savage arrival at Hell Hall to confront the Baduns, who are intent on murdering the pups, strikes terror into the hearts not only of the crooks but also, initially, of many a youthful member of the audience. And they are both intelligent, a fact which Cruella dimly realizes but which Horace and especially Jasper fail to – to their repeated cost. Pongo's brainwave about the Dalmatians

covering themselves in soot to escape detection is truly inspired.

Perdita, although superficially the cooler character of the two, in fact displays greater depths of emotion. Much of the work on her was done by Ollie Johnston, who has always been good at such things. Years later Frank Thomas recalled in an interview that two of Perdita's scenes which Johnston was charged with tackling seemed so emotionally packed that he (Thomas) at the time thought they were impossible to bring off successfully: they "seemed to me beyond the realm of cartoon". In fact, the Disney animators had for years been proving that there was very little "beyond the realm of cartoon", so perhaps Thomas should have known better. The two scenes in question were (a) where Cruella has arrived to try to claim the as yet unborn puppies, and Perdita is hiding anguished under the stove while Pongo tries to reassure her, and (b) where she displays maternal grief on discovering the theft of the puppies.

Pongo and Perdita are very lovable heroes – in two ways. They are not only everyone's ideal dogs, they are also appealing in human terms: through voices, dialogue and actions they give the impression that they are everyone's ideal human friends, too.

Roger and Anita Radcliff

When Pongo is looking out for mates for both himself and Roger, there is a joyous sequence in which a succession of owners who resemble their dogs appear – a way-out artist with her equally way-out Afghan hound (who we later discover is called Prissy), for example. This joke is carried right through to Roger and Anita, who both resemble their Dalmatians. In Roger's case

this is effected through vague facial similarities: he has a long chin and a prognathous jaw, a feature emphasized by his habitual puffing of his pipe. In Anita's case it is more that the dog is drawn to imitate the woman, for she has no noticeable physical resemblances to Perdita yet the dog has very much the *manner* of her mistress. Both Anita and Perdita are cool, cultivated, almost prim personalities who are nevertheless capable of great emotion.

Roger gives the impression of scruffy tweediness, whether or not he happens to be wearing tweeds; a generation ago his neighbours would have said of him that he needed "a woman to look after him". In this judgement Pongo patently agrees. As a romantic Roger leaves much to be desired being, as Pongo remarks, "married to his work". Roger is, however, both impetuous and generous of spirit, and like his dog can be courageous when forced to it: his refusal of Cruella's peremptory demand that he sell her the puppies obviously causes him great inner striving – he is one of those people who are normally so polite and compliant – yet he goes through with it and stands up to the devil woman. When need be he can conquer his shyness.

The sweetly competent Anita is an ideal complement to the scatterbrained Roger. She is in the great tradition of Disney

Roger and Anita introducing each other.

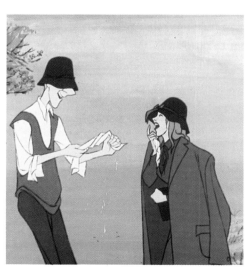

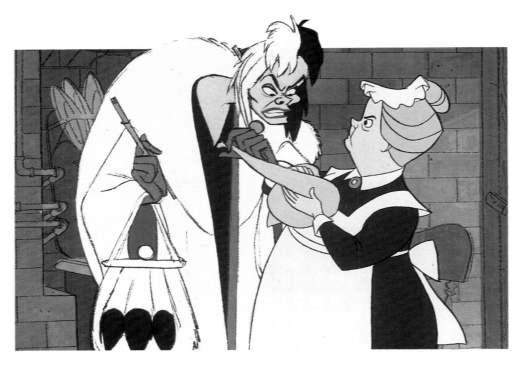

Cruella did her best to dominate Nanny, but Nanny wasn't having it . . .

animated (and, for that matter, live-action) heroines: extremely pretty without being overtly sensual. If Pongo and Perdita are everyone's ideal dogs and friends, Anita is every man's ideal girl next door. Although Roger may be the creative genius of the family, Anita possesses the more analytical mind. Without her he might struggle along, but with her he is bound to succeed.

In many ways Anita is the most attractive of the (human) Disney animated heroines, in that she is a woman rather than – like most of the rest of them – a girl. Also, while the characters of many of the other (human) heroines have been based to a great extent on their prettiness, Anita's is based on her intelligence and "personality" – as, come to that, is Perdita's.

Nanny

Nanny – sometimes referred to in the Disney literature as Nanny Cook – is a round little dumpling of a woman with a Cockney voice and a heart of gold. The housekeeper to the Radcliffs, she proves also to be a skilled midwife when it comes to organizing the delivery of Perdita's 15 puppies. And, like the Radcliffs, she is crazy about dogs: if anything, she is even more distraught than the Radcliffs are when the puppies are stolen. She is a lovely down-to-earth character with a touch of romanticism and a little more than a touch of bravery – her resistance to the forcible incursion of the dognapping Baduns is admirable.

At first sight it is surprising that Disney did not develop Nanny as a comic diversion – certainly she would have been a prime candidate for this treatment in many others of the features – but in fact, in the context of this movie, it is sensible that she be kept fairly low-key.

Cruella De Vil

What can you say about Cruella De Vil, probably the finest Disney villain of them all? Well, over the years, people have said quite a lot about her, most notably Marc Davis, whose screen creation she was. The reviewers and the public agreed, for once, on a Disney character. As one critic put it:

The real triumph of the film is Cruella De Vil ... She is the most sophisticated of the Disney bad guys.

She is also one of the most evil, especially since, unlike the witches in *Snow White* and *Sleeping Beauty*, she is very much a monster of today, unendowed with magical powers and all the other trappings of that golden past which never in fact existed. She was born from the imaginations of not only Marc Davis but also, of course, Dodie Smith – a fact that Disney-buffs are prone to forget, although Davis himself did not:

There are two or three people who I would say are patterns for her: an actress that we had run through the part, because we wanted a comic villainess; there was a little Tallulah Bankhead;

An enraged Cruella, pursuing "her" Dalmatian puppies.

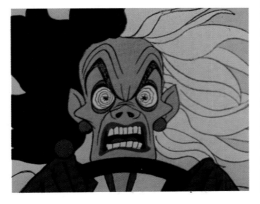

and there was a little of a fashion designer that I happened to know who was extremely volatile – she could react quickly in any direction. While Cruella was a marvelous villainess, she was still entertaining. Her black and white hair, her coat came with her from the book. It was a matter of bringing together a character that could perform a certain role but always be consistent.

Davis was responsible also for two others of the "great" Disney women, Cinderella (➤**236**) and Maleficent (➤**263**), and has often been asked to compare Cruella with those two. Comparing her with Cinderella in an interview with Kurt Wiley he said that characters like Cinderella were unsatisfying for an animator because

... they don't get *laughs*! When you do something in animation and the whole audience laughs at one time at something you've done, it is a tremendous thrill!
That's why I loved doing a Cruella de Ville [*sic*], because she was erratic, eccentric and violent. You didn't have any restrictions of trying to keep her innocent and believable because she was an action character! She'd come in and go out and leave havoc wherever she went! She was a funny villainess and I think people enjoyed her even though she was a monster and wanted to make fur coats out of those puppies.

In an interview with A. Eisen, Davis complained of Maleficent that the difficulties in animating her included that she always acted on her own. Not so with Cruella:

Cruella was comparatively simple. She was always working *with* somebody – slapping them around or whatever. Being able to draw a little better than any of the other men, I sometimes got sidetracked on[to] the more difficult-to-draw characters, which are not always the most fun.

(In this latter comment Davis is not being boastful: he is talking of *drawing* rather than animation.)

Cruella is a fabulous caricature. Her desperately thin body is a physiological impossibility, yet is perfectly attuned to her character, so that no viewer worries about this. Her cheek-bones, were they any higher, would brush her temples. Her voluminous fur coat dominates the screen. Her ubiquitous cigarette-holder is probably best measured in parsecs and her presence is marked by the clouds of evilly swirling cigarette-smoke which surround her. Her public-school English voice, supplied by Betty Lou Gerson, is utterly perfect because, unlike the screen image, it is not overstated: this dichotomy between the two treatments is brilliant, and adds immeasurably to the power of Cruella's portrayal. In fact, on the basis of the voice and dialogue alone, one can meet a Cruella at virtually any uppercrust gathering in the British Isles (and probably in any other country): totally egocentric, totally ruthless, totally impervious to any outside ideas, totally prepared to override any objections to her behaviour. It is because every member of every audience has encountered – to their regret! – someone like Cruella that her character works so well.

Cruella is also one of those people whose fault it never is. She is the epitome, although female, of the type of human being whom A. E. Van Vogt described as the "Right Man" (Colin Wilson has expanded on this idea). When her insane driving results in a pile-up with the truck driven by the Baduns it never crosses her mind that she might be remotely to blame: "You idiots ... you ... you fools! Oh, you imbeciles!" she cries, and audiences cheer when Jasper, who like his brother has been subjected to this sort of stuff throughout the movie, for once turns round and responds: "Aw, shaddap!" Once again, it is the *realism* of her character that makes her so believable and hence so scarifying: we all know "Right Men", either male or female, just like Cruella.

She has, however, been the subject of one major criticism: Cruella was the first of a long line of comic villains in Disney animated features. And were comic villains a good thing?

Of course, it could be argued that the studio was rather repeating the formula by making *all* the villains comic, but to criticize Cruella as a creation on these grounds is really verging on the ridiculous!

Jasper and Horace Badun

As soon as this duo of hired dunderheads comes on screen you know that even their most cunning machinations will come to naught. Especially their most cunning machinations, in fact. It is not that they lack brain – between them they probably have one – but that the wrong man is in charge. Jasper reckons that he is definitely the intellect of the pair, and Horace is happy to accept this, which is his big mistake. In fact, every time plump and shambling Horace succeeds in completing a brilliant deduction, the lanky, doleful Jasper

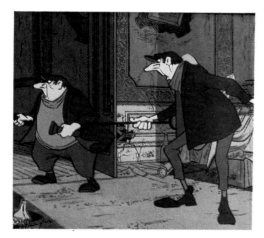

Jasper and Horace Badun preparing to seek out the escaping puppies.

promptly overrules him. For example, when the Dalmatians have rolled in soot to make themselves look like labradors:

> *Horace*: Look, Jasper. Do you suppose they've disguised themselves?
> *Jasper* (sarcastically): Say, now, Horace, that's just what they did. Dogs is *always* paintin' themselves black. *You idiot!*

Earlier on, during the dogs' trek across the countryside:

> *Horace*: What if they went down the froze-up creek so's not to leave their tracks?
> *Jasper*: Aw, Horace, you idiot. Dogs ain't that smart.

And so the dogs continue unmolested on their way down the "froze-up creek".

Both of the crooks have wit enough to know, however, that crime does not pay – at least, if it is crime involved with the lunatic Cruella. They know that they are in dire risk of being caught, because of her ostentatious way of ignoring the possibility that the forces of law and order just might take an interest in her activities. And they know, too, that if the police catch them criminally engaged just the one more time the keys will simply be thrown away. Yet it is for this very reason that Cruella has them entrapped: at the slightest sign of rebellion she simply threatens to call the police. Instant quelling of Badun revolt.

Most of the Disney villains have comic accomplices, from *Snow White*'s Raven (➤**166**) right through to *The Great Mouse Detective*'s Fidget (➤**324**). These accomplices are designed to make sure that the villains are not *too* terrifying. Paradoxically, although the Baduns are among the funniest of such characters, they are unable to lessen the "evilness" of Cruella. Probably no comic character could.

The Puppies

The Seven Dwarfs were a triumph because they each had definite personalities. Giving 99 puppies separate identities would have been a fairly tall order, but nevertheless seven of them can be picked out.

Six of these are among Perdita's litter of 15, the seventh, Rover, being not really a named character: he or she is the puppy first approached by Sergeant Tibs in Hell Hall, and who explains to him the situation. Tibs initially attracts the pup's attention by hissing: "Rover! Spotty!"

The six noteworthy offspring of Perdita are **Rolly**, **Patch**, **Penny**, **Lucky**, **Freckles** and **Pepper**. Rolly is ... well, roly-poly. He is always "mentioning" that he is hungry – even at the most inopportune times, as when the dogs are trekking through the snows. When the puppies are being fed by the three cows Rolly is furious not to be first at the udder. **Lucky** has a habit of not being – he is the one on whom the meltwater falls to wash away the soot – but his most notable feature is his addiction to television:

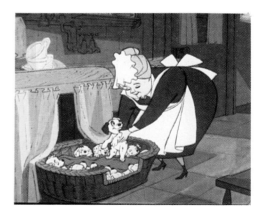

Nanny loved the puppies almost as much as their parents did.

both at the Radcliffs' home and in Hell Hall he persists in putting himself between the screen and whoever else happens to be trying to watch. **Patch** is likewise keen on television – although, as with the other puppies, he is not as addicted as Lucky. We notice him primarily because of his vivid way of describing the niceties of thespianism:

> *Patch*: That dirty old Dawson, the yellow-livered old skunk, I'd like to tear his gizzard out.
> *Perdita*: Why, Patch! Where did you ever hear such talk? Certainly not from your mother.

The Captain, the Colonel, and Sergeant Tibs

These three stalwarts mastermind the escape of the puppies from Hell Hall – at least, Tibs and the Captain do and the Colonel thinks he does.

The Captain is a rather efficient horse, who doubles as transport for the other two. He is also useful as a weapon of offence, something that Jasper and Horace discover to their agony when they attempt to set the barn on fire in order to smoke out the puppies. "Detonated" by Tibs pulling on his ears, with two neat blows from his rear hooves the Captain despatches the crooked brothers with such force that they land not so much against as *in* the barn wall.

The Colonel is a magnificently blimpish Old English sheepdog with a startling lack of organizational ability; were it not for the Captain and especially Sergeant Tibs he would be lost, but of course he does not realize this. His first interpretation of the message from the Twilight Bark is that 15 spotted puddles have disappeared; it is only at Tibs's prompting that he checks to find that it is 15 spotted *puppies*. Even his grasp of military strategy is dubious:

> *Colonel*: Blast 'em, Tibs. Go on, give 'em what for!
> *Tibs*: No, Colonel. Retreat. Retreat.
> *Colonel*: Retreat? Yes, oh, yes. Of course Retreat.

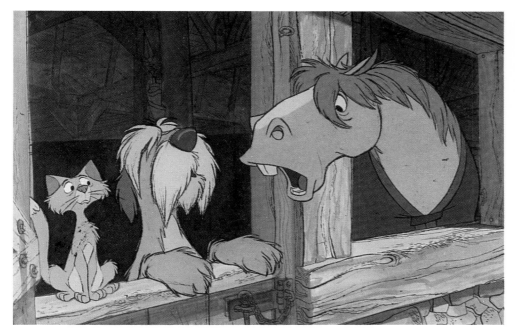

From left to right, Sergeant Tibs, the Colonel and the Captain. These three – especially Tibs – were largely responsible for saving the puppies' skins.

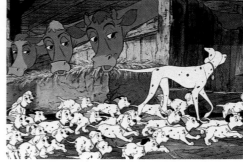

The three cows – Queenie, Princess and Duchess – provided the puppies with a little liquid substance.

The most significant member of the three, although the Colonel is the most strongly portrayed *character* of them, is **Sergeant Tibs**, the feisty barnyard cat. His English accent slipping only occasionally, he first reconnoitres Hell Hall to discover the puppies and their dire circumstances, and then carries out the much more demanding task of ushering them out into the night. In so doing he displays considerable courage: there is one terrifying moment when Jasper and Horace, bent on violence, advance relentlessly towards a huddle of 99 puppies with only Tibs standing defiantly in the way. Fortunately the arrival of a snarling Pongo and Perdita saves him having to forfeit his life, but one knows he would have willingly done so – and all for puppies, beasts of a different genus, whom he had barely met before. Although his part is lesser than, say, that of Pongo, Tibs must be isolated as the real hero of the movie.

Members of the Twilight Bark

Pongo and Perdita use the Twilight Bark in order to locate the puppies, and its members act rather like a resistance group in order to guide them to Hell Hall and back. Several of these members are on screen for moments only, but a number have more significant roles.

Danny, the Great Dane at Hampstead, is the one who gets the ball rolling, he being the nearest member of the chain to Pongo and Perdita. He is in cahoots with a little terrier, and it is the latter's barking that finally activates the others. The first links in the chain are the dogs seen earlier in the movie when Pongo was prospecting for mates for himself and Roger: they include **Prissy**, an Afghan hound who much resembles her art-student owner, and **Coco**,

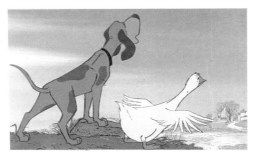

Towser and Lucy aided the Twilight Bark.

a fancified poodle who reflects her fancified owner's fancified lifestyle.

Other significant links in the chain are the dog **Towser** and his friend, the goose **Lucy**. The role of Lucy is essentially to interpret for the audience the barked and howled messages of the dogs in the Twilight Bark. These two are closest to the Colonel's patch, and therefore play a vital part in relaying the fact that the puppies have been located.

More significant are the **Labrador** and the **Collie**, who actively assist the Dalmatians in their cross-country trek. The Collie is the dog who offers them shelter in the dairy where the puppies are all fed on warm milk by the three cows (see below), and who stands guard while Pongo and Perdita catch up on some much-needed sleep. The Labrador, whose pet is the Dinsford grocer, not only has fixed up their "lift" back to London but indirectly inspires Pongo's brainwave about covering the puppies in soot so that they look like labradors. Both are exceptionally well voiced, by Tom Conway and Ramsay Hill respectively.

Queenie, Princess and Duchess

These three cows are the stalwarts of the dairy to which the Collie introduces 101 weary Dalmatians. They instantly fall in love with the myriad pups. *En masse*, the three cows are very reminiscent of the elephants in *Dumbo* (➤**195**), but although gossipy they are very much more generous of spirit. Generous of milk, too: when they learn that the puppies are starving they volunteer to feed all 99 of them, straight from the, um, horse's mouth. They find the blessings mixed:

> *Duchess*: Don't worry, kids, there's plenty for all. *Ouch!* The little darlings.

Television Personalities

A great delight in *One Hundred and One Dalmatians* is that there are two hilarious parodies of television programs.

The first of these concerns the superhero collie **Thunderbolt** and his (one gathers) perennial foe **Dirty Dawson**; the former is, of course, idolized by the puppies, the latter equally loathed by them. The second program is the favorite of the Baduns, "What's My Crime?". It features a pushy **Quizmaster** (Paul Wexler did live-action modeling for this part – most studios would not have gone to the trouble) as well as a panel of hopeful questioners, **Miss Birdwell**, **Mr. Simpkins** and **Inspector Craven**. But the real star is the crook who is put in the hot seat and has to face their penetrating questions, a certain **Percival Fauncewater**. If this name should sound distinguished, all of Percival's pretensions to grandeur are destroyed before us, for the Baduns know him well, and not as Percival. "Yes. Hey," cackles Jasper, "whatta ya know? Old Meathead Fauncewater."

SPINOFFS

Disney has produced a live-action remake (1997), and is preparing to launch (September 1997) an animated television series based on the central characters. It is impressively ambitious that a team of television animators should embark on a project involving scores of spotted dogs.

THE SWORD IN THE STONE

Characters:

Arthur/Wart; Merlin; Madam Mim; Sir Ector; Sir Kay; Archimedes; Sir Pelinore; Bullfrog; Pike; Girl Squirrel; Granny Squirrel; Hawk; Wolf
Dogs: Tiger; Talbot
Scullery Maid; Black Bart

Credits:

Based on *The Sword in the Stone* (1939) by T. H. White

Voices: Sebastian Cabot (Sir Ector, Narrator); Karl Swenson (Merlin); Rickie Sorensen (Wart); Richard Reitherman (Wart); Robert Reitherman (Wart); Ginny Tyler (Girl Squirrel); Norman Alden (Sir Kay); Junius C. Matthews (Archimedes); Martha Wentworth (Madam Mim, Granny Squirrel, Scullery Maid); Alan Napier (Sir Pelinore); Barbara Jo Allen (Scullery Maid); Thurl Ravenscroft; Jim Macdonald; Tudor Owen

Sound Supervisor: Robert O. Cook

Film Editor: Donald Halliday

Music Editor: Evelyn Kennedy

Music: George Bruns

Songs by: Richard M. Sherman; Robert B. Sherman

Orchestration: Franklyn Marks

Story: Bill Peet

Layout: Don Griffith; Basil Davidovich; Vance Gerry; Sylvia Cobb; Dale Barnhart; Homer Jonas

Art Direction: Ken Anderson

Backgrounds: Walt Peregoy; Bill Layne; Al Dempster; Anthony Rizzo; Ralph Hulett; Fil Mottola

Directing Animators: Frank Thomas; Milt Kahl; Ollie Johnston; John Lounsbery

Character Animators: Hal King; Eric Cleworth; Cliff Nordberg; Eric Larson; John Sibley; Hal Ambro; Dick Lucas

Effects Animators: Dan MacManus; Jack Boyd; Jack Buckley

Director: Wolfgang Reitherman

Production Supervision: Ken Peterson

Release Date: December 25, 1963

Running Time: 79 minutes

THE MOVIE

For some reason, few people actively like *The Sword in the Stone* very much. That said, few people actively *dislike* it. It certainly is a bit of a let-down from T. H. White's cerebral classic, but in its own terms it is not a bad movie: it is a thoroughly enjoyable viewing experience, but like so many other enjoyable movies – and unlike most Disney animated features - is utterly forgettable. The voices were largely responsible for this: aside from (debatably) Archimedes there was not a good one among them, and the thoroughly Americanized Wart/Arthur (voiced by three boys, two of them Wolfgang Reitherman's sons) was offensive to many ears, even in the USA. The *New Republic*'s Stanley Kauffmann was among the most extreme critics when he wrote that the movie was a

> huge coast-to-coast malted milk made of pasteurized Arthurian ingredients. Every element in it, pictorial and musical, is derivative of earlier and better Disney pictures, and the whole has a factory-line feeling devoid of joy.

Adrian Bailey has remarked that the movie "failed on all levels except the animation"; Leonard Maltin has described it as a "pat, unexceptional film with little of the Disney 'magic' to recommend it"; Richard Schickel justly called it "the least well known of Disney's animated films".

So, what went wrong? Probably the problem is that "Arthurianism" has attained the status of a pseudo-religion, so that attempts to imprint the Disney treatment on it were doomed to failure. The voices, as noted, certainly did not help. The occasional attempts to introduce contemporary notes – Merlin at one point turns up dressed in 20th-century Bermuda shorts fresh from a water-skiing holiday – were a disaster (even the friendliest of the movie's critics would admit this). The character of Wart/Arthur was inadequate. Overriding all of these criticisms, however, is the fact that people expect the Arthurian legend to be treated *reverentially*, and this the movie (and one come to that the T. H. White books) did not do. Many years later, in *The Black Cauldron*, Disney achieved the right "feel" for the Arthurian legend; in this movie it failed to do so.

THE STORY

One day during the Dark Ages – infuriatingly referred to by Merlin throughout the movie as "medieval" – the orphan Wart/Arthur is out helping his older foster-brother Kay to hunt. Thanks to one of Wart's little "assistances" Kay's arrow flies off at random into the forest. Despite Kay's warning that the forest is full of wolves, Wart sets off to find it, instead dropping in on the wizard Merlin and his familiar Archimedes, a generally uncooperative owl. Merlin, who has been expecting the visit, says that what Wart needs is education, and this he sets out to give him.

First the boy must learn to be like a fish, and so the wizard transforms both of them – with the result that Wart narrowly escapes being eaten by a Pike. Next Merlin transforms them both into squirrels, and this time love is the predator, with a Girl Squirrel and a Granny Squirrel falling for the mismatched pair. Merlin's third effort, transforming Wart into a sparrow, is equally disastrous, since he is pursued by a Hawk and escapes only by plunging down the chimney of the witch Madam Mim. This evil lady fights a spectacular duel with Merlin, during which the two of them change shapes frequently, becoming a succession of different animals. Merlin eventually defeats Madam Mim by turning into a germ and infecting her.

Wart has been told by his adoptive father, Sir Ector, that he will not be permitted to act as Kay's squire in the great tourney in London, the victor of which will be acclaimed as the new King of England. However, at the last moment Kay's squire-designate Hobs (who never appears on screen) catches mumps – Merlin looks very innocent – and so Wart is taken after all. However, once they are there, he makes the great mistake of leaving Kay's sword at their inn, and in desperation hefts out one he finds embedded in an anvil on a stone in a nearby cemetery. The person who can draw the sword from the stone, it has been decreed, will be the future King of England, and so Wart, despite initial reluctance, is elevated from his lowly position to the highest in the land.

THE CHARACTERS

Arthur/Wart

Like many of the other Disney protagonists, Wart is by design rather anonymous. Skinny, and dressed in a skimpy brown tunic, he has scruffy blond hair and is generally willing to please. This is possibly his trouble: he is prepared to obey the gruff Sir Ector when that worthy is around, but intuitively turns to obeying Merlin should the wizard be in closer proximity. During the initial hunting scene and at the tournament he treats Kay as his born master. It would be refreshing if, just *once*, he turned around and told one of these masters to get lost. Instead, Wart just carries on being subservient.

He is also very much the underdog in his excursions in the animal world. In the water he is pursued by the Pike; on the land he is pursued by the Girl Squirrel; in the air he is pursued by the Hawk. In each case he is saved only by the intervention of Merlin or Archimedes: he seems to have no self-preserving powers of his own. Of course, all this makes his elevation to the throne even more ironic – which is the precise purpose of the lack of characterization.

Wart was voiced by three different boys. The principal voice-artist was Rickie Sorensen, but additional lines were supplied by two sons of director Wolfgang Reitherman. All three boys had aggressively American accents, a fact which offended Arthurian enthusiasts and T. H. White purists.

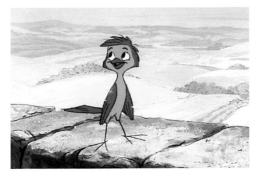

Wart went through many transformations during the movie. He was in turn a fish, a squirrel and – *above* – a sparrow.

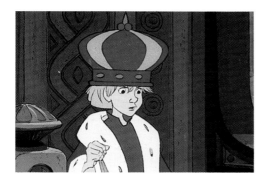

But perhaps the most astonishing change came at the end of the movie, when he turned into a fully-fledged king – Arthur.

Merlin

Possessed of supernatural powers, the long-bearded Merlin is an antique who quite literally loses track of time – he constantly forgets which era he happens to be in. Mind you, he has a habit of constantly forgetting everything else, too. In his genius he is the most absent-minded character in the entire Disney canon, with the possible exception of *The Jungle Book*'s Colonel Hathi (➤281). He is certainly the most time-hopping, disappearing at one stage for a holiday in 20th-century Bermuda. He constantly refers to things that have yet to be invented, such as aircraft – and in fact wears such an anachronism on his face, in the form of a pair of spectacles. At one point he even says:

Oh, big news, eh? Huh. Can't wait for the London *Times*. First edition won't be out for at least twelve hundred years. Ha!

Much humour is gained from the other characters' inability to grasp even the first essentials of 20th-century knowledge – for example:

Merlin: Now, first of all, lad, we've got to get all these medieval ideas out of your head.

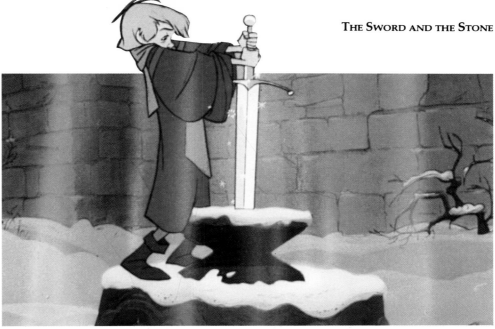

Wart pulling the sword from the stone.

Clear the way for new ideas. Knowledge of Man's fabulous discoveries in the centuries ahead. Now that would be a great advantage, boy.

Archimedes: "Advantage", indeed! Huh! If the boy goes around saying the world is round, they'll take him for a lunatic.

Wart: The world is round?

Merlin: Yes, yes, that's right. And it also … ah … goes around.

Wart: You mean it'll be round someday?

Merlin: No, no, no. It's round now. Man will discover this in centuries to come, and he will also find that the world is merely a tiny speck in the Universe.

Wart: "Universe"?

Archimedes: Ah, you're only confusing the boy. Before you're through he'll be so mixed up he'll … he'll be wearing his shoes on his head. Man has always learned from the past. After all, you can't learn history in reverse. It's … it's confusing enough, for Heaven's sakes.

Merlin: All right, all right. Have it your own way, Archimedes. …

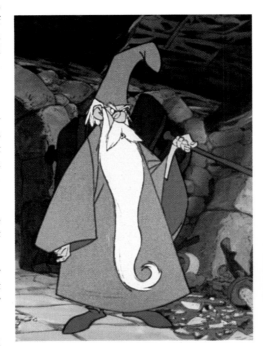

Merlin mustering as much dignity as he can.

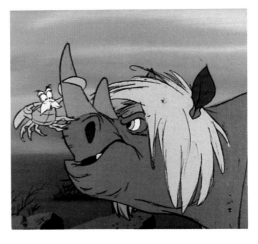

Merlin, transmuted into a crab, doing battle with Madam Mim, who has decided she looks nice in rhino-hide.

Merlin's voice is highish, slightly petulant and certainly aged: his "esses" come across as "eshesh". His robe is blue, and he retains this colour even when he indulges in the shape-changing battle with Madam Mim – a vital help to the audience in keeping track of which of the plethora of animals is which magician! He has a magical way with housework: he simply gets all of the castle dishes to wash themselves, the brooms to sweep the floor (reminiscent of *The Sorcerer's Apprentice* [➤181]), and so forth. Packing is similarly child's play to a wizard such as Merlin: he just tells all the contents of his

Madam Mim in the form of a crocodile; Merlin clearly finds her unappealing.

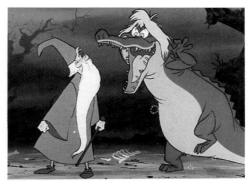

house, including the statutory thousands of wizened tomes, to scramble into his small suitcase.

In his various animal guises he remains "Merlinish" throughout. The only time he really drops out of character is when he returns from his holiday in 20th-century Bermuda: it really is hard to reconcile this sunglasses-toting apparition with *any* version of Merlin, Disney's included.

Madam Mim

Plump and piggy, grey hair astraggle, clad in a purplish-and-pinkish shapeless but tacky dress, her eyes filled with craziness, Madam Mim serves no function in this movie except to be a memorable animated character. Indeed, her career has continued in the Disney comics, where she has aided and abetted her good friend Magica de Spell in the systematic persecution of poor (?) Scrooge McDuck.

Her duel with Merlin, while totally irrelevant to the overall plot, is *the* highlight of *The Sword in the Stone*. It is a feast of animationary pyrotechnics, the two sorcerers changing themselves at will from one animal into another. The rules are explicitly set out by Madam Mim before the contest:

> *Mim*: Ah, rule one, no mineral or vegetable: only animal. Rule two, no make-believe things like, ah, oh, pink dragons and stuff. Now, rule three, no disappearing.
> *Merlin*: Ah, rule four, no cheating.

Naturally Madam Mim, who can be trusted rather less far than the average skunk can

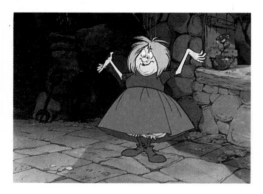

The appearance of Madam Mim as herself (*above*) perhaps explains why she was so keen to adopt various animal forms – like the cat *below*.

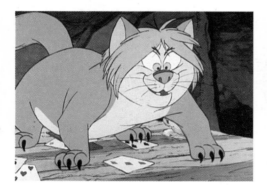

throw her, is soon transforming herself into a pink dragon. *En route*, she is a crocodile, fox, hen, elephant, tiger, rattlesnake and rhinoceros, in response to Merlin's adoption of the roles of turtle, rabbit, caterpillar, walrus, mouse, crab and billy-goat. Finally Merlin bests her by transmuting himself into a germ, which infects her swiftly so that she has to be confined to her bed. In so doing Merlin underlines his repeated theme to Wart that it is brain, rather than brawn, which will always win the day.

Possessing medical knowledge a millennium and a half before its time is helpful too, of course . . .

Sir Ector and Sir Kay

Wart's adoptive family leave more than a little to be desired.

His foster-father, **Sir Ector**, Master of the Castle of the Forest Sauvage, is big and boorish, with red moustache and hair, but is basically good at heart: it is just that his heart is submerged beneath acres of unkind fat. Quite why he took in Wart in the first place is uncertain: he treats him like a slave, but slavery seems not to have been his initial motive. Indeed, by his own lights Sir Ector is fair and benevolent – just a trifle strict. In his case, strictness necessitates awarding Wart "demerits" for every conceivable offence, real or imagined. A "demerit", of course, renders poor Wart obliged to perform yet another household duty.

Ector is passionately devoted to the cause of his doltish son Kay, believing him to have the makings of kingship in him. However, to give him his due, the grizzled knight is one of the first to recognize Wart's new status after the boy has shown that he is indeed capable of drawing the sword from the stone.

Ector (kneeling and kissing Wart's hand): Oh, forgive me, son, forgive me.
Wart: Oh, please don't, sir.
Ector: Kay, bow down to your King.

Ector has also the unfortunate habit of addressing Merlin as "Marvin", a practice which does not go down too well with the good wizard.

One quite likes Sir Ector, even though he is one of the banes of young Wart's life, but the same cannot be said of the oafish, bullying **Sir Kay**, a walking justification for the abolition of the aristocracy. He has little care for the welfare of his young foster-brother – when Ector verbally chastises him for allowing the boy to wander off into the wolf-infested forest Kay's only concern is to make it plain that It Is Not His Fault – and appreciates Wart only as a useful slave. Kay is, moreover, convinced that he should be King (as is his doting father), and takes it hard when it proves to be Wart who can pull the sword from the stone.

> *Kay*: Now wait a minute. Anyone can pull it once it's been pulled. [Shoves Wart to one side and sets to.]
> *Ector*: Go to it, Kay! Give it all you've got! Put your back into it!

Of course, Kay gets nowhere.

Sir Pelinore

Sir Pelinore is portrayed as a skinny, scrawny knight with a vast Adam's apple – much like the White Knight who failed to appear in the Disney *Alice in Wonderland*, in fact. He has a bushy grey moustache, a long nose, a grey-edged bald head and a sort of "dash it all" English accent. His role is not extensive: he arrives at the Castle of the Forest Sauvage to tell Ector and Kay (and

A bibulous Sir Pelinore, a lunkish Sir Kay, and, on the right, a bibulous and lunkish Sir Ector.

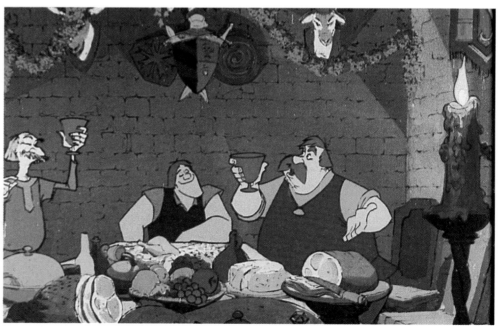

incidentally Arthur) of the forthcoming tournament, he gives Kay a little tuition in the art of jousting, and he accompanies the party on the journey to London. He is one of the first to notice that Wart has the miraculous sword, and is the first, along with Black Bart, to insist that the boy be given a chance to show that he really *can* pull the sword from the stone at will. Good old Sir Pelinore is an honest knight: one could pay him, in his own terms, no higher compliment.

Archimedes

Merlin is eccentric to the point of scatterwittedness, but fortunately he has his sane, analytic owl Archimedes to keep him on course: otherwise, one senses, he would not last five minutes in the violence of the Dark Ages.

Archimedes has a superficial zaniness that belies both the logic of his nature and his down-to-earthness: not for him all the marvels from ages yet to come which Merlin keeps describing:

> *Merlin*: Archimedes, have you seen that, ah, flying-machine model?
> *Archimedes*: I have nothing to do with your futuristic fiddle-faddle, you know that.
> *Wart*: What's that thing up there?
> *Merlin*: Hum? Oh, oh, yes, of course. Here we are.
> *Wart*: You mean Man will fly one of those someday?
> *Archimedes*: If Man were meant to fly he'd have been born with wings.

Because of his level-headedness Archimedes is the object of much mirth on the part of the youthful Wart and the youthfully irresponsible Merlin:

> *Merlin*: Archimedes, wha … wha … what *is* that "fish" formula?
> *Archimedes*: Huh? Oh, huh? Huh? Who? Who? What?
> *Merlin*: You know, that … that Latin business.
> *Archimedes*: Huh? Fish? Latin? Oh, ah, ah, ah: "Aquarius, Aquaticus, Aqualitis." And … and … now if you don't mind, I say "good day" to the both of you, if you please.
> *Merlin* (to Wart): When he stays out all night, he's always grumpy the next morning.

Archimedes, who was constantly disapproving of Merlin's antics.

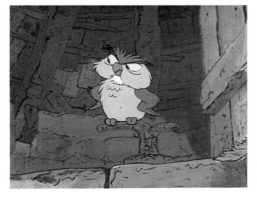

Wart: Ha! Then he must stay out *every* night!
Merlin: Yes, yes, yes, yes, oh, ah, ho, ho, yes, oh, I say, that's very good, boy, very …

Although he would never admit it, Archimedes's affection for the boy who suddenly intrudes on his life is deep. It is the owl who, for example, saves Wart's life when Wart, as a fish, is in severe danger of being eaten by the Pike, Merlin being powerless – or, at least, preferring to treat the whole affair as a perhaps terminal lesson for Wart in using brains rather than brawn. Afterwards, transformed back to the shape of a boy, Wart is effusive about Archimedes's bravery, but the owl shrugs it all off. A colossal understatement from him: "I did nothing of the sort. Ahem! I intended to eat him. Young perch is my favourite dish. You know that."

Minor Characters

There are a number of minor characters – mainly animals – in *The Sword in the Stone*.

Five of these are encountered by Wart and/or Merlin during their sojourns as animals. The **Bullfrog** is the first notable the two of them meet during their excursion in piscine form. Wart gratuitously insults it – "Oh, you big bug-eyed bully, you!" – and is promptly scolded by Merlin for his rudeness:

> Oh. Here, here, here, here, boy. No sense going 'round insulting bullfrogs. A fish has plenty of other problems without that. The water world has its forests and its jungles, too. So it has its tigers and its wolves. …

The truth of this proposition is proved moments afterwards when Wart finds himself enthusiastically pursued by the **Pike**, a vast green monster of a fish with more teeth in its capacious jaws than one would wish to count. Certainly Wart does not stop to, having the good sense to forsake academic enquiry and instead flee for his life.

In the world of land animals Wart and Merlin, as squirrels, meet the **Girl Squirrel** and the **Granny Squirrel**, both of whom (animated by Frank Thomas) fall instantly in love with what they assume are attractive male squirrels of the appropriate age. While the scene between Merlin and the Granny Squirrel is very much played for laughs, that between Wart and the Girl Squirrel is really rather touching and pathetic, especially since, as Merlin puts it: "When a girl squirrel chooses a mate it's for life." On Wart's sudden transformation back into a boy, with the Girl Squirrel still cuddling him affectionately, her grief is piteous to behold.

While flying as a sparrow Wart narrowly escapes being slaughtered by the **Hawk**. Interestingly, in this sequence Merlin does not transmute himself into a bird along with Wart – probably because a merlin is a type of small falcon.

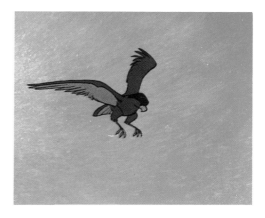

The Hawk, which menaced Wart when he was in his guise as a sparrow.

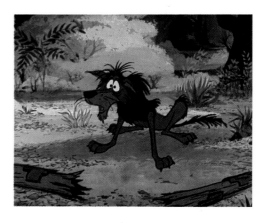

The Wolf, whose frustrated pursuit of human fodder provided a major running gag.

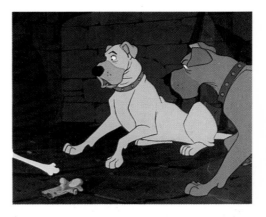

Sir Ector's two dogs, Tiger and Talbot, were friends to Wart.

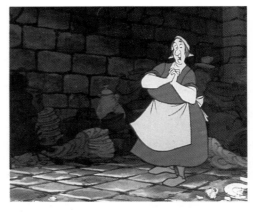

The Scullery Maid.

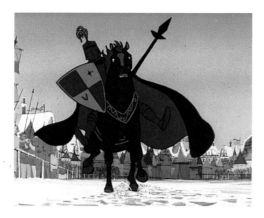

Black Bart, in full cry at the tourney.

One of the running gags of the movie is the **Wolf**, which has its eyes on Wart as a likely future meal. It first notices this walking delicacy when Wart, right at the start of the film, goes in search of Kay's arrow. Thereafter, on several occasions, it stalks him with such glorious stealth that he is never even aware of its existence. More than once it narrowly fails to snatch a mouthful of boy-meat as Wart passes unconsciously by. It is interesting that, when Wart is in animal guise, the predators eager to catch him are very obvious to him, but when he is simply a boy he never realizes that there is a large and very dangerous predator on his trail.

Sir Ector's two huge hounds, **Tiger** and **Talbot** appear briefly to prove that they have better taste than their master, being madly affectionate towards Wart; one gains the impression that Wart is what makes the dogs' life worth living.

Of the minor human characters two are of note. First, there is the **Scullery Maid**, whose function it is to shriek how terrible it all is when Merlin is engaging in magic:

> *Scullery Maid*: Oh, the kitchen! It's under an evil spell! . . . It's bewitched! Oh!
> *Ector*: I bet it's that old goat Marvin. Come on, son. I knew he'd give us trouble.

Ector and Kay then engage in an unsuccessful duel with the various free-moving items of kitchen equipment, which, under Merlin's orders, are cleaning themselves up.

The other human character with a minor role is **Black Bart**, a knight taking part in the tournament in London. (Hands up anyone who can't help wondering if "Bart" is short for "Baronet"!) He is a decent fellow and, like Sir Pelinore, sides with Wart when everyone else is refusing to let him even have a try at repeating his feat of drawing the sword from the stone.

MARY POPPINS

Characters:

no named characters

Credits:

Based on the series of books by P.L. Travers starting with *Mary Poppins* (1934)

Live Actors: Julie Andrews; Dick Van Dyke; David Tomlinson; Hermione Baddeley; Glynis Johns; Ed Wynn; Karen Dotrice; Matthew Garber; Arthur Treacher; Elsa Lanchester; Reginald Owen; Arthur Malet; Reta Shaw; Jane Darwell; Cyril Delevanti; Lester Matthews; Don Barclay; Clive L. Halliday; Marjorie Bennett; Alma Lawton; Marjorie Eaton

Voices include: J. Pat O'Malley; Jim Macdonald

Special Effects: Peter Ellenshaw; Eustace Lycett; Robert A. Mattey

Film Editor: Cotton Warburton

Sound Supervision: Robert O. Cook

Sound Mixer: Dean Thomas

Music Editor: Evelyn Kennedy

Choreographers: Marc Breaux; Dee Dee Wood

Dance Accompanist: Nat Farber

Music Supervisor, Arranger and Conductor: Irwin Kostal

Conductor's Assistant: Jim Macdonald

Songs by: Richard M. Sherman; Robert B. Sherman

Screenplay: Bill Walsh; Don DaGradi

Story Consultant: P. L. Travers

Hair Stylist: La Rue Matheron

Make-up: Pat McNalley

Costumes Executed by: Bill Thomas

Costumers: Chuck Keehne; Gertrude Casey

Costume and Design Consultant: Tony Walton

Nursery Sequence Design: Bill Justice; Xavier Atencio

Art Directors: Carroll Clark; William H. Tuntke

Set Decorations: Emile Kuri; Hal Gausman

Photography: Edward Colman

Backgrounds: Al Dempster; Don Griffith; Art Riley; Bill Layne

Animation Director: Hamilton S. Luske

Animation Art Director: McLaren Stewart

Animators: Milt Kahl; Ollie Johnston; John Lounsbery; Hal Ambro; Frank Thomas; Ward Kimball; Eric Larson; Cliff Nordberg; Jack Boyd

Live-action Second Unit Director: Arthur J. Vitarelli

Assistant Directors: Joseph L. McEveety; Paul Feiner

Director: Robert Stevenson

Co-producer: Bill Walsh

Release Date: August 29, 1964

Running Time: 139 minutes

THE MOVIE

It is hard to find something new to say about *Mary Poppins*. The movie broke all box-office records, it was acclaimed by the critics, it was almost certainly Julie Andrews' finest hour, it was immeasurably better than the books upon which it was based, its songs linger infuriatingly on the lips, its section mixing live action with animation is brilliant – and every child ever taken to see it loves it dearly. It is some movie. Even Richard Schickel, in his *The Disney Version*, a book which hesitates little before kicking Disney below the belt, decided to disagree with Frances Clarke Sayers when she stated that "The acerbity of Mary Poppins, unpredictable, full of wonder and mystery, becomes, with Mr. Disney's treatment, one great, marshmallow covered cream puff". The truth is that the "acerbity" of Mary Poppins in the books is a straightforward irritant; the slightly waspish version portrayed in the movie is, by contrast, a delight.

The story of the Disney version of *Mary Poppins* goes back a long way – probably some 20 years before the movie was made. One night in the early 1950s, or even earlier, Walt picked up a book lying by his daughter Diane's bedside and asked her if it were any good; she said that, yes, it was very, very good, and urged him to buy the movie rights so that he could make a cartoon version of it. He tried, but discovered that everyone else in Hollywood was after those rights; that they remained unsold was because Mrs. Travers was "difficult". Not until 1960 was Walt able to persuade her to sell the movie rights – and even then it was under condition that (a) she be allowed to vet the script and (b) it be a live-action movie rather than a cartoon.

Walt decided that his ideal Mary Poppins was Julie Andrews, who had starred on stage in *My Fair Lady* and *Camelot*. She dithered when offered the part, though, because she was pregnant and because Warner Brothers, who were to make the screen version of *My Fair Lady*, were worried whether her recognized stage talents would transfer successfully to the cinema. They thought, indeed, that Audrey Hepburn would be much better in the part of Eliza Doolittle than would Julie Andrews. In the end, Andrews became Mary, Hepburn Eliza. Andrews, in many ways, could hardly have been better tailored as a Disney heroine: her earlier roles in pantomime had included Little Red Riding Hood, Cinderella and Snow White!

The Sherman brothers excelled themselves in the songs for this movie, several of which have become perennial classics – notably "Chim-Chim-Cheree", "A Spoonful of Sugar" and of course the immortal "Supercalifragilisticexpialidocious". Of this last the Shermans told how they had initially heard the word when they were both children, but had forgotten about it until one day Walt had told them to invent a word (and the song to go with it) expressing the super-superlative. Suddenly the word came back to them. The song has been recorded by artists as disparate as the Cheltenham Orchestra and Chorus and Duke Ellington.

THE STORY

The story of *Mary Poppins* need not concern us much: the animated sequence is isolated among the live-action ones.

Jane and Michael are so naughty that their parents find difficulty in keeping a nanny. After the last one has left in a huff the children's father determines to write an advertisement for a new one. The children write their own version:

WANTED
A nanny for two adorable children. If you want this choice position, have a cheery disposition, rosy cheeks, no warts, play games (all sorts) . . .

and so forth. Father thinks this ridiculous, rips it up and throws it into the fireplace. The fragments of paper, wafted up the chimney, reach Mary Poppins (Julie Andrews), who devastatingly removes all the other applicants for the job: they are all blown away by a hurricane.

Mary is strict – and, according to her own description, "practically perfect" – but she is also a lot of fun, especially when she acts in conjunction with her old friend Bert, a pavement artist (Dick Van Dyke). They and the children have a series of exciting and sometimes hilarious adventures. It is into one of Bert's coloured drawings that the main cast-members leap for the animated "Jolly Holiday" sequence. This has no real story, but sees Mary, Bert and the children making their way across country to a teashop, then on to a merry-go-round, then on their merry-go-round horses to join a hunt, then into a flat-race (which Mary wins, having politely requested the other jockeys to let her pass them) and then finally, thanks to the rain beginning to wash

out Bert's pavement art, back into the real world.

There is, in fact, a second piece of animation in the movie, but you have to know that it is there or you are unlikely to spot it. This is the sequence when the song "Feed the Birds (Tuppence a Bag)" is sung, and the children have a vision of the old lady who sells passers-by birdseed outside Saint Paul's Cathedral. The animated section is very short, and essentially shows pigeons swirling around the dome of Saint Paul's.

The sequence is introduced by use of one of those liquid-filled "snowstorm" paperweights. The original was discovered some years ago by the Disney Archivist, David R. Smith, on the discard heap during an office clearance, and is now lovingly preserved in the Disney Archives.

The movie ends with Mary Poppins leaving the children, temporarily sadder but permanently wiser, to return whence she came.

THE CHARACTERS

There are no named animated characters in *Mary Poppins*, and those that can be identified generally appear only fleetingly – as for example the pair of **turtles** which Mary and Bert use as, as it were, swimming stepping-stones in order to cross a stream. However, there are a few animated characters of note in the movie.

Certainly worth attention are the four **penguins** who serve as waiters in the tea-shop. They are hyper-busy, always hurry-scurrying and beetling about, but they are prepared to slow down just a little in order to serve someone as magical as Mary Poppins. "Order what you will – there'll be no bill – it's complimentary," they sing, making one wonder why there are no other customers in the teashop. They do a wacky tap-cum-formation dance with Bert, at the end of which one of them plucks up enough courage to give Mary a kiss.

Much later, after the release in 1981 of *The Fox and the Hound*, animator Frank Thomas remarked:

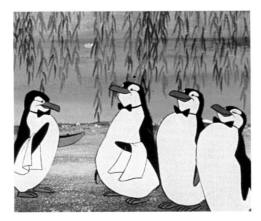

Four cheerful penguins served as waiters when Mary, Bert and the children paused for refreshment.

There's a delicacy to the skeleton of a fox, and once you see that, the drawings begin to look like a fox. When I was working on the penguins for *Mary Poppins*, I discovered there are 26 varieties. What we wanted was what most people think a penguin is.

The penguins in this movie are indeed of indeterminate species, but they are very definitely "penguinish". Thomas had done his structural homework well.

Also of note is the **guard** on the merry-go-round. He is plump and smiling with a red uniform and cap and a grey moustache and hair. On Mary's instructions he pulls the control-lever hard over so that the merry-go-round horses on which she, Bert and the children are riding can "break loose" and gallop off across the countryside. As they do so the guard starts to speak like a racing commentator – "They're off!" is the least frenetic of his remarks.

The five members of the **Pearly Band**, who provide the backing when Mary sings "Supercalifragilisticexpialidocious" after she has won her prize in the race are dressed in deep-blue coats which have pearl buttons and are otherwise studded with pearls wherever a pearl can be made to go; the two female members are additionally adorned each with three colossal pink plumes on their hats. Of the word "supercalifragilisticexpialidocious" Mary at one point sings " . . . bétter use it carefully or it could change your life". To this the smallest male in the Pearly Band sings: "For example . . . One night I said it to me girl and now me girl's me wife!" Moments later his head is driven down almost to groin level by a thundering blow from the tambourine of the largest, and incidentally female, member of the band, and he adds with choked difficulty: "And a lovely thing she is too."

The real star among the animated characters is the **fox** pursued by the hunt. This creature Bert determines to save – loud cheers from the average audience – but he little realizes quite how feisty is the little fellow he has taken on. This is no decorous fox like Tod (➤307) or Robin Hood (➤292) – he is a disreputable, scuffy little fellow. He has a powerful Irish

The fox was the major star of the animated sequence of *Mary Poppins*.

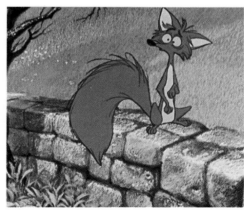

accent–supplied by Dallas McKennon – to add humour as he makes various acerbic comments. "Faith and begorrah! – 'tis dem redcoats again!" he remarks of the pursuing huntsmen when first he sights them. Once scooped up by Bert onto his horse he is momentarily defiant, sitting on the horse's rump and delivering rude remarks, gestures and in one instance a blow to the hounds. However, he soon thinks better of this and scuttles

nervously to the horse's head beauty, where he encourages it: "Faster, me beauty! Faster!"

Later he is part of the little group – including also Bert and the children – cheering Mary as she receives her trophy for winning the flat-race.

Of minor note is the small band of **reporters** who pester Mary after her victory. They are very much products of old movies rather than of real-life journalism –

homburgs, long coats, overt notebooks and all the other trappings. It is when one of them gives her the clichéd leading question "There probably aren't words to describe your emotions?" that Mary replies "On the contrary, there's a very good word" and starts to sing that song. Well, what better word *could* there possibly be than "supercalifragilisticexpialidocious" to describe both her emotions and the movie?

THE JUNGLE BOOK

Characters:

Mowgli; Bagheera; King Louie; Baloo; Kaa; Shere Khan
Vultures: Ziggy; Buzzie; Flaps; Dizzy
Wolves: Rama; Akela
Elephants: Colonel Hathi; Winifred; Baby Elephant; Bugler; Slob Elephant; Lieutenant Elephant
The Girl

Credits:

Based on: *The Jungle Book* (1894) by Rudyard Kipling

Voices: Phil Harris (Baloo); Sebastian Cabot (Bagheera); Louis Prima (King Louie); George Sanders (Shere Khan); Sterling Holloway (Kaa); J. Pat O'Malley (Colonel Hathi, Buzzie); Bruce Reitherman (Mowgli); Verna Felton and Clint Howard (elephants); John Abbott (Akela); Ben Wright (Rama); Chad Stuart (Flaps); Digby Wolfe (Ziggy); Lord Tim Hudson (Dizzy); Darleen Carr (The Girl); Hal Smith; Pete Henderson; Leo de Lyon; Bill Skiles

Sound: Robert O. Cook

Film Editors: Tom Acosta; Norman Carlisle

Music Editor: Evelyn Kennedy

Music: George Bruns

Songs by: Robert B. Sherman; Richard M. Sherman; Terry Gilkyson

Orchestration: Walter Sheets

Story: Larry Clemmons; Ralph Wright; Ken Anderson; Vance Gerry

Layout: Don Griffith; Basil Davidovich; Dale Barnhart; Tom Codrick; Sylvia Roemer

Background Styling: Al Dempster

Backgrounds: Bill Layne; Art Riley; Ralph Hulett; Thelma Witmer; Frank Armitage

Character Animators: Hal King; Eric Larson; Walt Stanchfield; Eric Cleworth; Fred Hellmich; John Ewing; Dick Lucas

Directing Animators: Milt Kahl; Ollie Johnston, Jr.; Frank Thomas; John Lounsbery

Director: Wolfgang Reitherman

Production Manager: Don Duckwall

Release Date: October 18, 1967

Running Time: 78 minutes

THE MOVIE

The Jungle Book, the last animated movie to be supervised by Walt himself – he died just before it was finished – is a curious mixture. It is certainly no movie for Kipling enthusiasts, having little to do with the original book aside from the coincidence of names and having nothing of the same "feel" as Kipling's work. It is very much jazz hitting the jungle. Walt himself set the scene when, after he had finally succeeded in purchasing the rights to Kipling's book (in 1963) he told storyman Larry Clemmons: "Here is the original by Rudyard Kipling. The first thing I want you to do is not to read it."

This was the first of the Disney animated features in which the major characters were based solidly on the personas of the voice-artists – a technique much used by other studios whose animation was less sophisticated. Shere Khan the tiger *is* George Sanders, Baloo the bear *is* Phil Harris, and King Louie *is* Louis Prima. Wolfgang Reitherman, the movie's director, explained: "In *The Jungle Book* we tried to incorporate the personalities of the actors that do the voices into the cartoon characters, and we came up with something totally different [from the characterization of earlier Disney features]." Some critics have been less flattering about the results, describing this form of characterization, which requires less creative input from the animators, as laziness – and worse. Whatever the rights and wrongs of the matter, *The Jungle Book* was enormously successful, and so the practice continued in several further Disney features. Mike Barrier, in *Funnyworld # 18*, has remarked bitterly of it that

In some cases, the use of star voices has resulted in rich and satisfying characterizations (as with Sanders' tiger [Shere Khan]), but more often, the result has been an unfortunate resemblance between the Disney features and the TV situation comedies from which most of their voice artists are now drawn.

This is perhaps overstating things, and is anyway irrelevant in those parts of the

world not subjected to the various sitcoms involved, but it is noticeable that the most recent Disney features have reverted to the earlier mode of characterization (with some exceptions, as in the use of Vincent Price for Ratigan in *The Great Mouse Detective* [➤318]).

The animation of *The Jungle Book* is, undebatably, otherwise superb – as is its art in general: many of the jungle backgrounds are literally breathtaking. The movie's only really weak point – astonishing when one considers Walt's close involvement – is its story line, which meanders a little aimlessly; one keeps waiting for something really boggling to happen, but it never quite does. Instead, in many places, the story seems to exist solely for the purpose of linking the song-and-dance items, which are tremendous – notably "The Bare Necessities".

All that said, the critics loved the movie and so did the public, and it has become one of the most popular Disney features of all time.

THE STORY

Once upon a time the wise old panther Bagheera hears a strange noise in the jungle. It proves to be the wailing of an abandoned mancub. Thinking quickly, the panther soon has the babe adopted by a family of wolves and Rama becomes Mowgli's new "father". All goes well for a few years, until Shere Khan, the tiger who loathes mankind, returns to that part of the forest: the wolf-pack, led by Akela, convenes and decides that the only safe course for Mowgli is that he be returned to humanity. Bagheera volunteers to escort the little boy to a man-village he has located, but of course Mowgli, a child of the jungle, does not want to go.

On the first night of their trip they bed down on a lofty tree-branch, where Mowgli has a close brush with death. The hypnotic and hypochondriac snake Kaa, a constrictor of prodigious length and evil, attempts to capture him, and is beaten off only when Bagheera awakens and creates enough of a diversion for Mowgli to awaken from his hypnotic trance and belabour the treacherous serpent. Unfortunately, this episode convinces the boy that he is capable of looking after himself in the jungle.

His next adventure is with a herd of elephants led by the would-be dignified militarist Colonel Hathi and including his wife Winifred and his baby son. Mowgli joins in the parade of the elephants to the fury, when he finally notices the intruder, of Hathi. However, Bagheera succeeds in pacifying the rage of the jingoistic jumbo.

Mowgli is still rebellious and Bagheera has generally had enough; he tells the boy that, if that is the way of it, he must "go it alone". Off stalks Mowgli in one direction and off stalks Bagheera in the other. Shortly afterward, however, Mowgli bumps into the friendly bear Baloo – regarded by Bagheera as a "jungle bum" – and the two very swiftly become firm friends. Soon, though, Mowgli is captured by a troop of mixed apes and monkeys, and is rudely escorted to the ruined temple in the jungle where King Louie, a portly orang-utan, holds his court. Louie is convinced that, if only he can learn the secret of fire, he will be a man, and he tells Mowgli that if he will tell him the secret he can become an honourary ape and stay in the jungle. Mowgli explains that he does not know the trick, either, but soon the apes and monkeys are cavorting to a scat-jazz song, "I Wan'na Be Like You". Baloo and Bagheera do their best to filch Mowgli away from the company during this song, Baloo disguising himself as an ape, but their plans come adrift as Baloo's disguise does likewise, and a mad chase ensues, during which Louie's already crumbling palace is effectively razed.

While Mowgli sleeps that night Bagheera persuades Baloo that the boy really *must* be taken to the man-village, and the following morning Baloo explains things to his little friend. Mowgli, however, runs away, saying that Baloo is betraying their friendship.

A lost mancub with Shere Khan in the district – the situation simply does not bear thinking about. Baloo and Bagheera go off in search, encountering Hathi and his herd. With some difficulty Bagheera persuades him to send out his troops to reconnoitre for the boy. Sadly, Shere Khan has been eavesdropping on the conversation, with many an anticipatory lick of the lips. He too sets out to look for Mowgli.

The boy, however, is in the throes of a further meeting with Kaa, who is intent on both a meal of and vengeance on the person who so humiliatingly worsted him the last time around. Mowgli is in grave danger, but luckily Shere Khan appears and asks a terrified Kaa if he has seen anything of the wandering mancub. This diversion is sufficient to distract Kaa and so Mowgli makes an escape.

Everyone seems to have betrayed Mowgli, and he is weeping when four beatnik vultures discover him. They too offer him eternal friendship, but just then

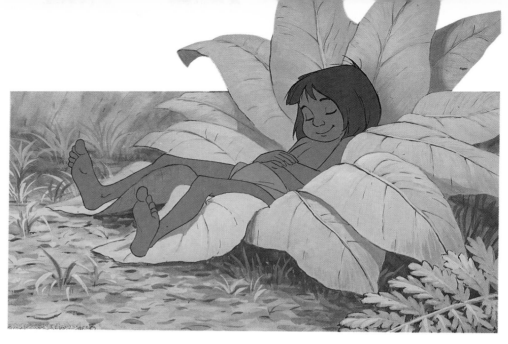

Mowgli beds down for the night – justifiably exhausted.

Shere Khan appears and their valour falters. The tiger tells Mowgli that he will give him a count-of-ten start, and is unimpressed when the boy uses the time to beat him over the head with a club. On the cry of "ten!" Shere Khan is off, but Baloo just succeeds in grabbing his tail. The two animals fight furiously, with Shere Khan in the end apparently slaying the big bear with a violent swipe.

Mowgli is now sheltering in the vultures' tree while a thunderstorm rages all around. Suddenly lightning strikes the tree, which catches fire. The vultures have an idea: fire is the one thing that Shere Khan fears over all others. While they harass the tiger Mowgli sneaks up and ties a burning branch to his tail. Shere Khan flees from that part of the jungle for, one assumes, ever.

There is a tearful sequence in which everyone mourns Baloo's death, Bagheera delivering a stirring funeral oration. However, it proves that the bear was merely knocked unconscious, and has been listening appreciatively to Bagheera's words ever since coming round. Mowgli, delighted, hugs his pal and swears eternal friendship – but just then his attention is attracted by a strange animal that he has never seen before. This proves to be a female mancub from the nearby village ... and, despite Baloo's cajolings, Mowgli is very soon lost to his animal friends forever.

Bagheera, now reconciled to the big bear, even allows himself to join in a rousing chorus of "The Bare Necessities" as the movie ends.

THE CHARACTERS

Mowgli
Many of the Disney central child characters are two-dimensional – reactors rather than doers – but the same cannot be said of Mowgli, although his role does rather tend to get overlooked because of the strength of the characterizations of the company he keeps. He is a determined and determinedly difficult little fellow. He also has a minor identity problem: to which genus of the animal kingdom does he belong? During this movie he is, by turns, a wolf, an elephant, a bear, an ape and a vulture – all of these identities being strictly honorary, of course. Thanks to the heinously hypnotic attempts of Kaa, Mowgli is very nearly an honorary (albeit dead) snake, too.

He was largely animated by Ollie Johnston, which is probably why he engages our emotions so much. Indeed, he is the epitome of all of us at that age in our fantasy worlds, the little boy at home in the jungle, able to speak with his animal friends. When one thinks about the ferocity of the animals involved – a panther, a bear, a pack of wolves – it becomes obvious that this is a fantasy-world: cute little bunnies and the like have no place in it.

For all his youth, Mowgli is advanced in some ways. His reactions on sighting the Girl are those of the late adolescent rather than the prepubescent: instant fascination and, who knows?, love. But this is at the end of the movie. His dominating characteristic earlier is his dogged determination. He is certain that he can survive on his own in the jungle, and is willing to stake his life on the proof of this point. He is determined, indeed, to tackle any task that comes his way – as when Bagheera encourages him to climb a tree: claws Mowgli may not have, but he does his level best to claw his way up the unyielding trunk. Whether this is all determination or just plain stubbornness is of course debatable.

Certainly he would be incapable of surviving alone in the jungle, primarily because of his gullibility: anyone who says that they will be his friend is instantly adopted as a bosom pal. In fact, Mowgli is lucky in the assortment of beasts he befriends – only Kaa is lethal, and anyway Mowgli does not like him much – but he could so easily have come to grief right at the start. Of course, had Mowgli tried to make friends with a certain tiger, first off, there would not have been a story to tell ...

Bagheera

The civilized, sophisticated panther is really the central character of the movie, being on screen much of the time and acting as the story's narrator/introducer. He is predominantly a sort of purple-black, and is definitely a member of the Old School – although his accent is American. Also, he is brilliantly animated. Mike Barrier, in his *Funnyworld* review of the movie, which is generally unfavourable except when it comes to the animation, remarks:

> Bagheera moves marvellously, like a real panther, but since there is nothing in the story itself that requires him to look like a panther (the fact that he's a specific kind of animal doesn't make much difference) his feline movements look too much like academic exercises.

This, of course, cuts both ways: if it does not matter what type of animal Bagheera should be, then why should he not be a panther? In that case, it seems rather petty that Disney should be criticized for making him look like one.

Bagheera is the staunchest of all of Mowgli's jungle friends – much more so even than Baloo, who funks when given the difficult task of explaining to the boy that he must return to humanity. Bagheera, by contrast, is prepared to bite the bullet and conquer his own emotions and reticences in order to do what is right for the boy. His part is very stereotype-British, despite his accent. Only once does he seem to desert the lad, when Mowgli has been (indirectly) responsible for Bagheera receiving a ducking and a bang on the head; but even then the panther keeps a weather-ear open for news of his protégé, and rushes to rescue him when he is captured by the monkeys and apes. He, too, despite his

affection for the boy, encourages him to follow the girl back into human society when Baloo is all for restraining him. Bagheera's friendship is totally unselfish.

King Louie

If Bagheera's part is "veddy British" King Louie's is utterly American. His less than prepossessing face surmounts a red pot belly of overgenerous proportions; his general expression would persuade even the most assiduous of neurologists that there was little for them here. His chief ambition is to become a human being, something which he believes can be effected if only he can master the secret of creating and controlling mankind's "red flower", fire. It is for this reason that, believing Mowgli, as a real human, knows the secret,

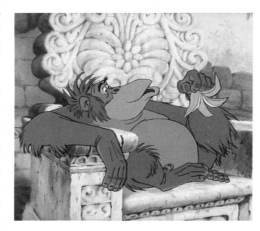

All King Louie wanted was to be a human being.

he has his army of guerrilla monkeys bring the boy in. His other dominating characteristic is his speech, much of which is scat, the form of jazz vocalization in which it *sounds* as though words are being used but one just cannot pin them down. In fact, his scat, supplied by Louis Prima, is brilliant, turning the song "I Wan'na Be Like You" from mere acceptability into a front-line number.

If King Louie were a human being, as he so much desires, he would be one of those people who constantly hands out cigars as a way of buying superficial friendships. Cigars are in short supply, so King Louie has to make do with bananas – but he makes up in quantity for any perceived lack. Like human cigar-donors, he overdoes this, so that at one point poor Mowgli has two of the things shot simultaneously into his mouth at about Mach 3.

Despite his monomania and the hazard which he represents to Mowgli, King Louie is in no way a real villain. Indeed, as some critics have remarked, the movie as a whole suffers from a significant lack of true villains: Kaa is evil, but like King Louie suffers from the fact that he is also a bit of a buffoon; and Shere Khan is hardly deeply enough characterized to qualify.

Others of the monkeys have distinctive personalities. None are named on screen but the attendant carrying a palm frond has become generally known as **Flunkey Monkey**.

Louie features in TV's *TaleSpin* (➤143).

Baloo

It had been originally planned that Baloo should have no more than a cameo role, but

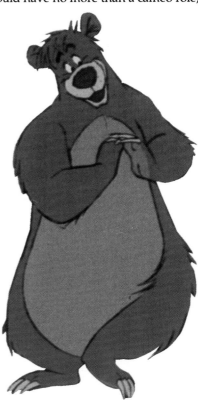

Baloo was Mowgli's pal almost from the very start.

the animators (Ollie Johnston was largely responsible for him) found Phil Harris's vocalization fascinating to work with and so in due course Baloo became one of the movie's major stars. Indeed, in terms of popularity and screen presence, he is *the* main star of *The Jungle Book*, eclipsing even Bagheera, whose role is much more fundamental to the story.

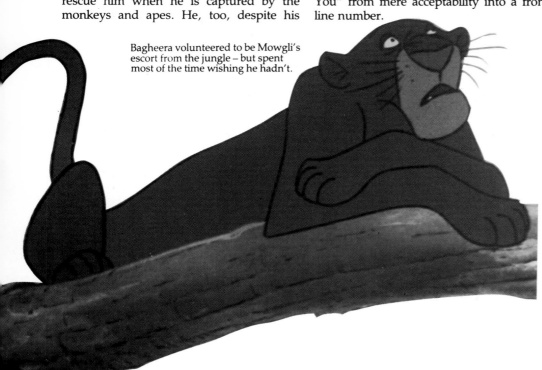

Bagheera volunteered to be Mowgli's escort from the jungle – but spent most of the time wishing he hadn't.

A big, blue-grey burly character, Baloo has adopted easy-goingness as the keystone of his life. According to Bagheera, who calls him a "jungle bum" and various worse names, Baloo has taken this to excess, and the panther is worried that Mowgli will follow in Baloo's path and become a disreputable pest of the jungle. The panther is probably right, but Baloo, despite his general fecklessness, proves to be a true friend to the little boy. His decisions may not always be admirable, and his friendship is not always selfless – he is largely impervious to Bagheera's powerful arguments that Mowgli should be returned to the company of mankind, preferring to try to keep his new-found pal with him, rollicking through the jungle – but at the same time he cheerfully risks his life saving Mowgli from the vengeance of Shere Khan. This courage is, in fact, totally in keeping with his overall geniality and *laissez-faire* attitude; Baloo's character, like his physical appearance, is a well rounded one.

His most brilliant scene is undoubtedly his first, when he – joined in due course by Mowgli – sings "The Bare Necessities". Events seem to prove Baloo's principal ethic of life – that if you take things as they come the bare necessities of life will always come your way – as bananas fall from the trees into his coincidentally upraised hand, pawpaws come readily to the paw, and so forth. There is a gaiety and spontaneity in this sequence rarely matched anywhere else in animated movies. The fact that it is totally ancillary to the main plot of the movie – such as it is – is quite irrelevant to the audience: the sequence is simply a joy to watch. A similar effect is attempted when Baloo joins in the jazz-dance of the monkeys and apes, to the tune of "I Wan'na Be Like You", but it proves impossible to achieve the same thing twice in the same movie.

Perhaps it could have been managed had the two sequences not followed in such quick succession.

As noted above, there was at the time of the movie's release and has been more especially since a fair deal of criticism of the fact that Baloo is so much an animated version of Phil Harris's voice and mannerisms; the storm was really to break when very much the same character appeared a few years later in the guise of *Robin Hood*'s Little John (➤**292**). Such criticisms seem to miss the point. Question: Is Baloo a great screen creation, his presence a delight? Answer: Yes. End of criticism – it does not matter how that effect was created. Whether Baloo were modelled on Phil Harris or a bowl of maggots, the end-product is what counts, and the end-product is a marvel. You'd better believe it.

A rather more urbanized version of Baloo has become popular in the television series *TaleSpin* (➤**143**).

Kaa

Sterling Holloway surpassed himself in the vocalization of the sinister, hypnotic hypochondriac python – *Python reticulatus*, to judge by Kaa's length. It was a masterpiece of casting to give Holloway, for once, the role of a villain: all traces of that occasionally over-honeyed almost-unctuousness have gone, and instead we have a voice to send shivers up even the doughtiest of spines. Vincent Price would have a voice to send shivers up even the doughtiest of spines. Vincent Price would have been proud of it.

The screen persona of Kaa is rather less frightening than his voice, since he is rather accident-prone. When Mowgli first deals with him the unfortunate python ends up with a knot in his tail, and this knot is still present when next the serpent meets up with the boy. In this latter encounter Kaa once more receives a fairly comprehensive buffeting. In both cases Mowgli copes with Kaa by the simple expedient of shoving his extensive coils off a high branch, so that the serpent's head is dragged downward with them, being battered against other branches as he falls. In a huff, the second time this happens, Kaa sums up his emotions in a deliciously peeved tone of voice:

> If I never see that skinny little shrimp again it will be too soon. Oh, my sacroiliac.

But Kaa's usual hypochondriacal complaint is about his sinuses. One has a vague feeling that someone on the Disney lot at the time must have taken to complaining about his or her sacroiliac.

A marvellous piece of action occurs when Shere Khan pops by to ask if Kaa has seen the lost mancub. Mowgli is at the time reclining in a trance in the midst of Kaa's coils, but the serpent, while abjectly terrified of the tiger, is not about to reveal this.

Kaa: Yes, yes, who is it?
Shere Khan: It's me, Shere Khan. I'd like a word with you, if you don't mind.
Kaa: Shere Khan, what a surprise.
Shere Khan: Yes, isn't it? I just dropped by. Ah, forgive me if I've interrupted anything.
Kaa: Oh, no, nothing at all.
Shere Khan: Ah, I thought perhaps you were entertaining someone up there in your coils.
Kaa: Coils? Someone? Oh, no: I was just curling up for my siesta.
Shere Khan: But you were singing to someone. Who is it, Kaa?
Kaa: Oh, I was just singing to myself.
Shere Khan: Indeed?
Kaa: Yes. Yes, you see I have [gulp] trouble with my sinuses.
Shere Khan: What a pity.
Kaa: Oh, you have no idea. It's simply terrible. I can't eat, I can't sleep, so I sing myself to sleep. You know, self-hypnosis. Let me show you how it works. [Sings:] Ah, trust in me . . .
Shere Khan: Ah, now I can't be bothered with that. I have no time for that sort of nonsense.
Kaa: Some other time perhaps?
Shere Khan: Perhaps. But at the moment I'm searching for a mancub.
Kaa: Mancub? What mancub?
Shere Khan: The one who's lost. Now where do you suppose he could be?
Kaa: Search me.
Shere Khan: That's an excellent idea. I'm sure you wouldn't mind showing me your coils, would you, Kaa?
Kaa (showing first tail, then head): Oh, certainly not. Nothing in here, and nothing in here.
Mowgli: [Snores.]
Kaa (in panicky imitation): Oh, my sinuses!
Shere Khan: Hmmm. Indeed. And now, how about the middle?
Kaa: The middle? Oh – the middle. [Carefully he unwraps his middle from the slumbering Mowgli and loops it down to show Shere Khan.] Absolutely nothing in the middle.
Shere Khan (with lingering doubt): Hmmm . . .

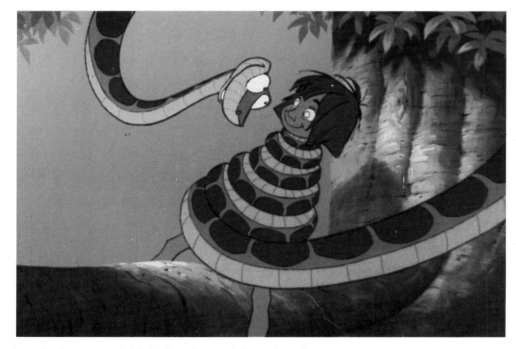

The role of Kaa was probably Sterling Holloway's finest piece of voicing.

really. Well, if you do just happen to see the
mancub, you will inform me first.
Understand?

Kaa: I get the point. Cross my heart, hope to
die.

Shere Khan: Good show. And now I must
continue my search for the helpless little
lad. [Moves off.]

Kaa: Oh, who does he think he's fooling?
"Helpless little lad." Oh, he gives me the
shivers . . .

Moments later, Kaa has been clobbered by
Mowgli once again. Poor Kaa!

Shere Khan

The personality of Shere Khan is based
primarily on the suavity of George Sanders'
stage and screen personality – as can be
gathered from reading the script extract
reproduced above. In a way, this is a great
weakness in the characterization, for
instead of being an evil, menacing villain,
cold and implacably bent on vengeance
against the whole tribe of humanity, Shere
Khan seems much too civilized a fellow to
indulge in any such emotion-governed
activity: he is a Lord Peter Wimsey
suspected by the clodhopping local
constabulary of having committed a
country-house murder; you *know* he has not
done it.

Everyone in the jungle fears Shere Khan,
however. The wolves are convinced that
even the whole pack of them could not
stand against him. The very mention of his
name strikes panic into the heart of the
average jungle denizen. Only two
characters – aside from Mowgli – display
any degree of equanimity at the prospect of
encountering him: Colonel Hathi, who is
convinced that nothing and no one could
prevail against his well drilled herd and his
own tactical genius; and Baloo, who just as
with Hathi is really a little too stupid or
unaware to realize what he might be up
against. Baloo, of course, is the one who
must finally take Shere Khan on, and this
he does with courage and very little
hesitation. Shere Khan naturally has the
better of their battle, but only just.

It is difficult to understand why Disney
did not make Shere Khan much more of an
out-and-out villain than he is. Probably the
studio was simply overwhelmed by the
glories of Sanders's voice. Nevertheless, in
technical terms the animation of the tiger is
excellent, as Mike Barrier pointed out in his
Funnyworld review:

> . . . the dryness of the animation in *The Jungle
> Book* is used to advantage to enhance the
> elegance of Shere Khan the tiger. Milt Kahl's
> animation of the tiger would be even more
> impressive if *The Jungle Book* were a different
> kind of movie, and the tiger more of a menace,
> but at least the gap between substance and
> technique was closed.

Barrier is here referring to a discrepancy
which he perceives in the preceding few
Disney animated features between

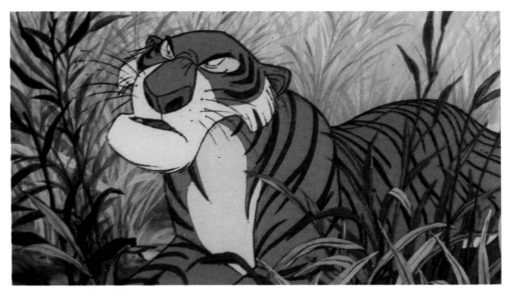

Shere Khan was the movie's only true villain, but his role was astonishingly minor.

animated pyrotechnics and emotional
impact. In *The Jungle Book*, while the
standard of animation is almost
unbelievably high, there are no animated
pyrotechnics of the type that embellished,
say, *Sleeping Beauty* and hence the lack of
emotional impact is not so glaringly
obvious. It should be noted that, while not
all critics agree that *Sleeping Beauty* lacks
emotional impact, the general point still
stands.

In the TV series *TaleSpin* (►143), Shere
Khan is adapted to a different jungle – that
of organized crime.

The Vultures

It is hard not to compare *The Jungle Book*'s
vultures with *Dumbo*'s crows. Aside from
the fact that both types are carrion birds
with a somewhat unsavoury reputation,
both groups appear late in the movie,
smart-talk among themselves, are dialect-
oriented and, after initially raucously
mocking our hero(es), become genuine and
wholehearted friends. The crows are
disreputable in a very American way, the
vultures in a very British way, although
they are more of a mixture than the crows.
It is hard to determine exactly where within

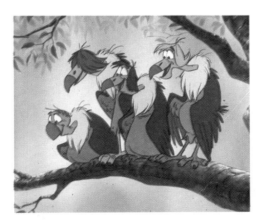

The four vultures – definitely not to be confused
with the Beatles.

the British Isles they all come from,
although **Buzzie** is definitely a Londoner
and **Dizzy** is so much the internationally
exported Liverpudlian paradigm that it
comes as a shock to discover that he is
voiced by Lord Tim Hudson rather than by
Ringo Starr. Indeed, the quartet is very
reminiscent of the Beatles in many ways,
although when they finally do put their
heads together for a song they render it
more like a barber-shop quartet than the Fab
Four.

Their dialogue, too, reminds one of the
Beatles' movies, especially in their initial
portrayal of boredom:

Buzzie: Hey, Flaps, what we gonna do?

Flaps: I don't know. What you wanna do?

Ziggy: I've got it. Let's flap over the east side of
the jungle. They've always got a bit of
action, a bit of a swingin' scene. All right?

Buzzie: Ah, come off it. Things are right dead all
over.

Ziggy: You mean, you wish they were.
[Laughter.]

Dizzy: Very funny.

Buzzie: OK, so what we gonna do?

Flaps: I don't know. What you wanna do?

Buzzie: Look, Flaps, First I say, "What we
gonna do?", then you say, "I don't know,
what you wanna do?" Then I say, "What
we gonna do?" You say, "What you wanna
do? What we gonna do? What you want
. . ." Let's *do* something.

Flaps: OK. What you wanna do?

Buzzie: Oh, blimey. There you go again. . . .

It is the sort of conversation repeated a
million times each night by the unmarried
students of the world.

Ziggy and **Flaps** are less ostentatiously
characterized than the other two but, as can
be seen from the dialogue above, they have
their moments – Flaps especially. All four,
however, contribute to what is in essence a
single character: the group of them. Like
Dumbo's crows, they cannot be considered
in isolation from each other, since no single
one of them would function as a character

on his own. This gestalt, then, can be typified as: generally hooliganish and scruffy; willing to form friendships; and initially cowardly in the face of threat but thereafter staunch in the protection of their friends. You can meet youths like this on every street corner but generally they are characterized as undesirables and so you do not stop to talk to them.

The Wolves

Although Mowgli is raised in a family of wolves, they play little part in his ensuing story. The members of his immediate "family" are portrayed as lovable doggies – especially the young cubs. This is only to be expected: the persistent legends about various children raised in the wild by wolves, from Romulus and Remus onward, would have little credence if the much maligned wolf were as vicious a creature as tradition maintains. (The North American wolf is a much more timid character than its Old World counterpart, which helps the Disney characterization.)

The only two named wolves are **Rama**, Mowgli's adoptive father, and **Akela**, the leader of the pack, a wise old beast whose counsel is generally accepted by the rest. Both of the parts are minor, but Rama's is notable because of the convincing way in which a truly vulpine wolf is made to appear downright paternal on screen.

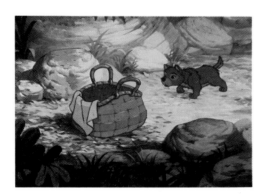

Rama's son suspiciously approaches the package left by the family home.

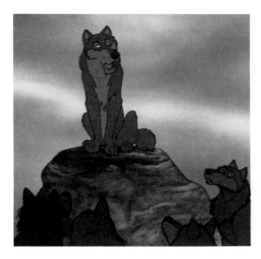

Akela, splendidly silhouetted against the skyline.

The Elephants

The leader of the elephant herd is **Colonel Hathi**, a *quondam* member of Her Majesty's Fifth Pachyderm Brigade. He is wonderfully British Empire, and totally convinced that "an elephant never forgets" – despite the fact that he does, frequently. Most of his herd are unwilling recruits, including his

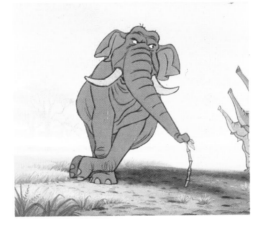

Colonel Hathi, who believed in discipline above all else.

own wife **Winifred**, who is slapped around by his military cane if anything even more than the other pachyderms. Vocalized by Verna Felton, who had supplied one of the voices for the rather different elephants in *Dumbo*, she is the voice of his conscience when it comes to searching for Mowgli:

> *Bagheera*: Wait a minute. HALT!
> *Hathi* (as herd piles into him): Who said "Halt"? I give the commands around here. Well, speak up! Who was it?
> *Bagheera*: Oh, it was me, Colonel.
> *Hathi*: What do you mean, sir, taking over my command? Highly irregular, you know.
> *Bagheera*: Oh Colonel, I'm sorry, but … but I need your help.
> *Hathi*: Absolutely impossible. We're on a cross-country march.
> *Bagheera*: But it's an emergency, Colonel. The mancub must be found.
> *Hathi*: Mancub? What mancub?

Winifred, Hathi's wife, was the only elephant who held any sway over him . . .

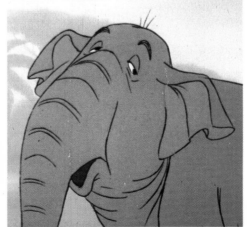

> *Bagheera*: The one I was taking to the man-village.
> *Hathi*: Good. That's where he belongs. And now, sir, if you don't mind, we'd like to get on with the march.
> *Bagheera*: No, no, you don't understand. He is lost. He ran away.
> *Hathi*: Well, serves the young whippersnapper right.
> *Bagheera*: But … but Shere Khan, the tiger – he's sure to pick up the mancub's trail.
> *Hathi*: Ah, Shere Khan … Nonsense, old boy. Shere Khan isn't within miles of here. Oh, sorry, Bagheera, the fortunes of war and all that sort of thing, you know?
> *Winifred*: This has gone far enough. Far enough. [To Hathi:] Now just a minute, you pompous old windbag.
> *Hathi*: Winifred! What are you doing out of ranks?
> *Winifred*: Never mind. How would you like to have *our* boy lost and alone in the jungle?
> *Hathi*: Our son? Alone? Ah … but Winifred, old girl, that's an entirely different matter.
> *Winifred*: Ha!
> *Hathi*: Different, entirely.
> *Winifred*: That little boy is no different than our own son. Now, you help find him, or I'm taking over command.
> *Hathi*: What!? A female leading my herd? Utterly preposterous!
> *Baby Elephant*: Pop, the mancub and I are friends. He'll get hurt if we don't find him. Please, pop, sir, please.
> *Hathi*: Now don't you worry, son. Your father had a plan in mind all the time.
> *Winifred*: Ha! Sure you did!

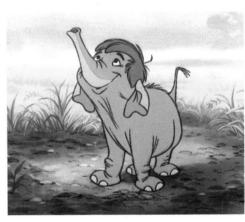

. . . except Baby Elephant, who became Mowgli's firm friend.

Colonel Hathi, it will be noted, is crazy about his son, **Baby Elephant**, and will give way to almost his every whim. This infant, whose voice is much like that of *Bambi*'s Thumper (➤201), although supplied by Clint Howard rather than by Peter Behn (who was in his later thirties by now!), befriends Mowgli early on, when the little boy joins in the elephants' parade. It must have been very tempting for the Disney animators simply to reproduce Dumbo (➤194), but they wisely decided against falling into the trap and instead created an entirely new character. The little elephant is a joy to behold; when he grows up he wants to be a military colonel, just like daddy.

Of the other elephants, three are of note. **Bugler** is capable of trumpeting so loudly that the very jungle shakes. **Slob Elephant** is not only the scruffiest member of the herd but also the greediest: any pause in the action sees this rapscallion contentedly eating away. **Lieutenant Elephant** initially has a contemporary haircut until Colonel Hathi shears it down to size: "Lieutenant," remarks Hathi as all this goes on, "that haircut is not regulation. Rather on the gaudy side, don't you think?"

The Girl

The little lass with a red spot on her forehead who comes down from the man-village to captivate Mowgli is full of eastern

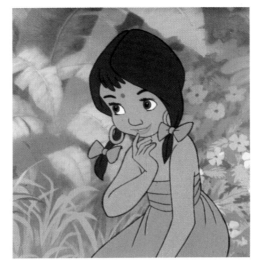

promise. Although it will be a decade or so before the promise turns into anything else, she nevertheless enchants Mowgli as she fetches water from the river and sings the song "My Own Home", yet another fine piece of work from the Sherman Brothers. She has little by way of character except her basic allure, which weaves a more powerful spell upon Mowgli than even Kaa's hypnotic attempts. Baloo advises the boy when he sees a female human for the first time: "Forget about those – they ain't nothin' but trouble!"

Mowgli, though youthful, has more sense.

Mowgli did not want to become part of humanity . . . until, that is, he saw the Girl.

THE ARISTOCATS

Characters:

Duchess; Thomas O'Malley; Roquefort; Edgar; Madame Adelaide Bonfamille; Scat Cat; Chinese Cat; English Cat; Italian Cat; Russian Cat
Kittens: Berlioz; Marie; Toulouse
Abigail Gabble; Amelia Gabble; Uncle Waldo; Frou-Frou; Napoleon; Lafayette; Georges Hautecourt; French Milkman

Credits:

Based on a story by Tom McGowan and Tom Rowe

Voices: Phil Harris (Thomas O'Malley); Eva Gabor (Duchess); Sterling Holloway (Roquefort); Scatman Crothers (Scat Cat); Paul Winchell (Chinese Cat); Lord Tim Hudson (English Cat); Vito Scotti (Italian Cat); Thurl Ravenscroft (Russian Cat); Dean Clark (Berlioz); Liz English (Marie); Gary Dubin (Toulouse); Nancy Kulp (Frou-Frou); Charles Lane (Georges Hautecourt); Hermione Baddeley (Madame Adelaide Bonfamille); Roddy Maude-Roxby (Edgar); Bill Thompson (Uncle Waldo); George Lindsey (Lafayette); Pat Buttram (Napoleon); Monica Evans (Abigail Gabble); Carole Shelley (Amelia Gabble); Pete Renoudet (French Milkman)

Sound: Robert O. Cook

Film Editor: Tom Acosta

Music Editor: Evelyn Kennedy

Music: George Bruns

Songs by: Richard M. Sherman; Robert B. Sherman; Terry Gilkyson; Floyd Huddleston; Al Rinker

Orchestration: Walter Sheets

Story: Larry Clemmons; Vance Gerry; Frank Thomas; Julius Svendsen; Ken Anderson; Eric Cleworth; Ralph Wright

Layout: Don Griffith; Basil Davidovich; Sylvia Roemer

Backgrounds: Al Dempster; Bill Layne; Ralph Hulett

Directing Animators: Milt Kahl; Oliver M. Johnston, Jr.; Frank Thomas; John Lounsbery

Character Animators: Hal King; Eric Cleworth; Fred Hellmich; Eric Larson; Julius Svendsen; Walt Stanchfield; Dave Michener

Effects Animators: Dan MacManus; Dick Lucas

Assistant Directors: Ed Hansen; Dan Alguire

Director: Wolfgang Reitherman

Production Design: Ken Anderson

Producers: Wolfgang Reitherman; Winston Hibler

Release Date: December 24, 1970

Running Time: 78 minutes

THE MOVIE

The Aristocats was originally planned as a live-action two-part "special" for TV's *Wonderful World of Color*, and scripted as such by Tom McGowan, Tom Rowe and Harry Tytle. However, the project was shelved because Walt preferred it as an animated feature, and Disney was at the time devoting its attentions to *The Jungle Book*. It became the first animated feature to be made by Disney after Walt's death.

The movie's title song was sung by Maurice Chevalier. This represented something of a coup for Disney, because Chevalier had officially retired a couple of years before at the age of 80 – and when Chevalier said "retired" he meant it. Studio executive Bill Anderson appealed to him, however, to record "The Aristocats", and to his astonishment – and everyone else's – the old French *chanteur* agreed promptly, and the song was recorded in Paris. In fact, it had been Walt himself who had persuaded Chevalier to make his very last movie, *Monkeys, Go Home!*, in 1967. Later Chevalier wrote of *The Aristocats*:

I would not have done it for anybody else and for any kind of money, except the honour of showing my love and admiration for the one and only Walt.

Curiously, the Chevalier version is missing from the Disney record based on the movie.

The film was a thundering success, although the critics in general proclaimed themselves a trifle underwhelmed by it. For one thing, they felt it was merely a feline version of *101 Dalmatians*, an attempt to take all the ingredients that had made that movie a success, mix them up and serve reheated as if they were a freshly cooked dish – but without any of the culinary brilliance of the original. This criticism is probably technically true – the movie *was* in part an attempt by Disney to profit from its earlier-discovered successful formula – but it is also slightly irrelevant. There is little point in *comparing* different Disney features: each should be looked at as a unique entity. *The Aristocats* is a very good movie by anybody's standards, and it is not the film's fault that *101 Dalmatians* just happens to be one of the all-time greats of animated-movie history.

The second main criticism of *The Aristocats* was that it continued the practice, started in *The Jungle Book*, of basing the animated characters on the vocal personas of contributing stars. The offence was made yet more heinous by the fact that one of those stars was Phil Harris, and indeed Thomas O'Malley, the alley cat, is as near as one could possibly hope to find to a feline impersonation of Baloo the bear (➤278). The other main star involved was Eva Gabor, as Duchess, the well bred lady cat. Wolfgang Reitherman has defended the practice, saying (as reported in *International Photographer*) that it was with *The Jungle Book* that, for Disney,

voices became more significant. For our female lead of Duchess we have Eva Gabor, who is probably the freshest femme voice we've ever had in a cartoon. Her voice was integral in Duchess' personality, a real lady.

The hero is Phil Harris, but this character is much different from Baloo, the bear in *The Jungle Book*. [This is, shall we say, debatable!] O'Malley is considerably sharper and more like Clark Gable than Wallace Beery, who was partly the model for Baloo.

However, the criticisms of the practice, widely regarded as demeaning to the Disney studio, are fair . . . except for the fact that, if a cartoon character is a great success in every way, it surely hardly matters how he or she attained that success. The result may be unsatisfying to an animation purist, but if the audience finds the character rewarding should the purists complain?

The Aristocats was a huge success on its first release, and has remained so during further releases. Its success may be gathered from the fact that in the first edition of David Duff's serious biographical study *Albert and Victoria* one chapter is titled "Albert and the Aristocats". In fact, this was a printer's error for "Aristocrats". The only person who noticed the mistake at proof stage was the author's wife, who assumed it was a topical quip by Duff and so did not draw it to anyone's attention!

Decades earlier, incidentally, Warner Brothers had produced an animated short called *The Aristo-Cat*. Despite the coincidence of names it is entirely different from the Disney feature, and there is no suggestion that Disney had "lifted" the title.

THE STORY

Once upon an unspecified time (but at a guess in the 1930s) the rich Madame Adelaide Bonfamille has a cat called Duchess and her three kittens called Toulouse, Berlioz and Marie. These cats are the light of her life, and so she calls in her lawyer, M. Georges Hautecourt, to change her will: in the event of her death her money will all go to the cats, although after they have died the estate will pass to Edgar, her butler. Edgar, an impatient fellow, decides that the sooner the cats' claim is over the better, and so he drugs their food with sleeping pills – accidentally, he also dopes their friend, the house-mouse Roquefort. Edgar puts the drugged cats in the sidecar of his motorbike and sets off to dump them in the country, but his plans are spoiled by two militaristic farm-dogs, Napoleon and Lafayette, who see their mission in life as the mangling of passers-by. They attack Edgar and his motorbike, and he loses the basket of sleeping cats as well as his hat, sidecar and umbrella.

When Duchess and her kittens awake they are very frightened, especially since a thunderstorm is ripping the night apart. In the morning, though, there comes along Thomas O'Malley, an alley cat who immediately falls in love with Duchess and

offers to help the family get back to Paris. He terrifies the driver of a passing milk-truck into stopping, and soon Duchess and her kittens, plus O'Malley, are on their way home aboard the truck.

Back at home, Roquefort, encouraged by the horse Frou-Frou, has spent the night prowling in search of his feline friends. With the morning, Edgar comes to feed Frou-Frou and, assuming that she is dumb, boasts to her about his "perfect crime". Mid-boast, however, he realizes that his umbrella, sidecar and hat are still lost out there with the cats, and so he nervously determines to go back and fetch them that very night.

O'Malley and the aristocats have been ejected from the milk-truck, whose driver has spotted them drinking his cream for breakfast. They continue on foot, but as they cross a railway bridge they are almost mown down by an express; they survive by clinging on to the sleepers, but Marie tumbles off into the waters below. O'Malley dives in and saves the kitten, but then finds himself in difficulties.

Luckily two very English geese, Abigail and Amelia Gabble, on a walking-tour of France, happen by and, although at first they think he is learning to swim and therefore nearly drown him by "helping", in due course save his life. As it proves, Amelia and Abigail are likewise going to Paris – where they plan to meet their Uncle Waldo – and so they join the party.

Edgar's foray to rescue his hat, umbrella and sidecar is rendered fairly chaotic by the two dogs, Napoleon and Lafayette, but he succeeds in recovering his lost property.

The cats and the geese arrive in Paris and meet up with Uncle Waldo; he is rather the worse for wear, having been marinated in white wine by a restaurant chef. Abigail and Amelia elect to leave the cats in order to escort their tipsy uncle home.

It is by now too late at night for the cats to reach the house of Madame Bonfamille, and so they put up at O'Malley's Paris "pad", where they are entertained musically – the song is "Ev'rybody Wants to Be a Cat" – by a jazz band consisting of Scat Cat, the Chinese Cat, the English Cat, the Italian Cat and the Russian Cat. After the band has left Duchess puts the kittens to bed and then strolls the rooftops with O'Malley, who proposes marriage. However, although she explains that she loves him, she says also that her first duty is to Madame Bonfamille.

Next morning, Edgar is whooping it up with a bottle of Madame's best champagne when he hears the approaching cats miaowing. Roquefort tries to warn them to keep out, but without effect: the moment they step into the house they are thrown into a sack by Edgar, who then persuades his mistress that the miaowing she thought she heard was only an aural illusion. This time Edgar's wheeze is to put the cats into a trunk which he has carefully marked for delivery to Timbuktoo.

Roquefort, aware of all this chicanery, chases after O'Malley to seek his help. The tough alley cat says that he will go back to Madame Bonfamille's house to see what he can do, and that Roquefort should hurry to fetch Scat Cat and his friends. This the mouse reluctantly does, remembering only in the instants before certain death at their hands the name "O'Malley" as his reference. As soon as Roquefort comes out with it, though, they hurry to help the cats.

Edgar has the aristocats in the trunk, but the attack of the scat cats is too much for him; while he endeavours to fight them off, Roquefort picks the trunk's padlock with his tail. Frou-Frou willingly kicks Edgar into the open trunk, and before anyone can stop it he has been picked up by the baggage-men and sent on his way to Timbuktoo.

Madame Bonfamille is delighted by the return of her little darlings and welcomes O'Malley as a member of her family. She invites Georges Hautecourt to change her will, excising the name of Edgar and inserting a provision for Duchess's "future little ones". Also, she announces, she has decided to turn her home into a foundation for all the alley cats of Paris.

And then she, her lawyer, our heroes and ourselves join Scat Cat and his band in a pounding reprise of "Ev'rybody Wants to Be a Cat".

THE CHARACTERS

Duchess

Duchess, the mother cat, is based on the voice of Eva Gabor – "a real lady", as Wolfgang Reitherman observed. She is a slender, slinky, well kempt white cat with white trimmings and a gold-yellow collar; she has a surprisingly bushy tail, almost like a squirrel's. Gabor's voice renders every other initial "w" as a "v", which is appropriately European, if not exactly French.

Duchess is very well aware of her aristocratic stock, and is eager to instill some recognition of their good blood into her three kittens:

Duchess: Marie, darling, Marie, you must stop that. This . . . this is really not lady-like. And Berlioz, but such behaviour is most unbecoming to a lovely gentleman.
Berlioz: Well, she started it!
Marie: Ladies do not start fights, but they can finish them.
Duchess: Berlioz, now, don't be rude.
Berlioz: We were just practising biting and clawing.
Duchess: Aristocats do not practise biting and clawing and things like that. That's just horrible.

Largely this works, except in the case of Toulouse – to the delight of O'Malley when he encounters the family.

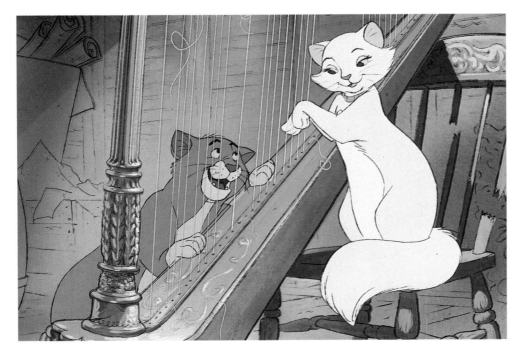

Duchess harped on, but O'Malley enjoyed every moment of it.

Duchess is also very pretty (as is Ms. Gabor, on whom she is modelled), with her blue eyes and her consistently elegant facial expression. It is one of the repeated triumphs of the Disney animators that they can give to an animated animal so many human characteristics and at the same time retain the essential "animalness" of the character.

Thomas O'Malley

Abraham de Lacy Giuseppe Casey Thomas O'Malley, to give him his full name, is the hero of the movie, a rather tattered knight in shining white armour who comes to the rescue of Duchess and, initially rather reluctantly, her three kittens. As he puts it himself, with characteristic *brio*, "Helping beautiful dames . . . ah . . . ah . . . damsels in distress is my specialty." A major subplot of the movie is his transformation from a devil-may-care, don't-give-a-damn free-wheeler of an alley cat into a caring, brave, loving foster-parent. In fact, despite that early reluctance to take the kittens on board, by the end of the movie one feels that if anything he is more attracted to his new and elevated lifestyle by them than even by Duchess herself.

It is his love for her which inspires his three great acts of courage, however: the dangerous stopping of a milk-truck by jumping out in its path, his saving of Marie from the river although he himself cannot swim, and of course his final battle, initially solo, with Edgar in the garage.

In terms of his character development – from irresponsibility to responsibility, and the display of courage when necessary – he is indeed extremely like *The Jungle Book*'s Baloo (➤278). His "normal" persona, joking and happy-go-lucky is largley Baloo's, and

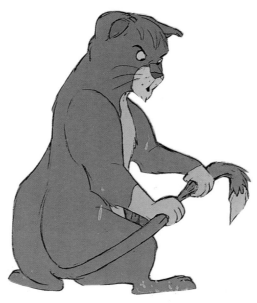

O'Malley wringing out his tail after his immersion in the river.

there are even similarities in physical appearance, for O'Malley is a big, stocky, chunky cat. Finally, of course, his voice is virtually identical and is supplied by the same actor, Phil Harris. This recycling of the same character in slightly different guises was what so offended the critics of the day and is still decried by many historians of the animated movie. The public did not mind, however: they loved O'Malley, and cared little about similarities to the Baloo whom they had also loved.

Although "J." is not one of the initials in his imposing string of Christian names, he announces himself on occasion as "J. Thomas O' Malley". Could this perhaps be a tribute to the veteran Disney voice-man J. Pat O'Malley, whose last Disney performance was as Otto in *Robin Hood*?

Roquefort

The punctiliously polite and very civilized house-mouse Roquefort, voiced by Disney regular Sterling Holloway, is an engaging little fellow. Resourceful and brave, and utterly loyal in his friendship with the cats, he is at other times, despite or perhaps because of his shabby-genteel appearance, almost cumbersome in his gentlemanly courtesy:

Roquefort (clearing throat shyly): Good evening, Duchess. Hello, kittens.
Marie: Hello, Roquefort.
Toulouse: Hi, Roquefort.
Duchess: Good evening, M'sieu Roquefort.
Roquefort: Umm. Something smells awfully good. What *is* that appetizing smell?
Marie: It's *Crème de la Crème à la Edgar*.
Duchess: Oh, won't you join us, M'sieu Roquefort?
Roquefort: Well, yes . . . I . . . I mean, well, I don't mean . . . ah . . . but . . . it so happens I have a cracker with me.

And so, protesting politely, he joins them in eating the delicious but doped meal – in fact, it proves that he has another cracker lurking in his mousehole, which he runs to fetch just before sleep overtakes him.

His bravery is intense. Although he mutters a little with worry, he obeys O'Malley's instructions to run and fetch the scat cats to help do battle with Edgar in the

Little Roquefort was, surprisingly, a friend of the cats.

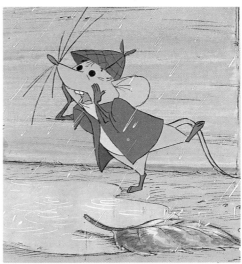

garage. He is right to worry, as it proves, because when in his terror he forgets O'Malley's name they are on the verge of slaughtering him on principle. (His last-moment salvation comes when he snaps in frustration to himself: "Oh, *why* did I listen to that O'Malley cat?") His bravery is coupled with his resourcefulness: when the aristocats are in the trunk ready for shipment to Timbuktoo he succeeds in unpicking the padlock with his tail.

Despite all of his admirable qualities he has, as implied above, a slight overinterest in food. Indeed, when Madame Bonfamille during the closing celebrations starts to take photographs of the cats we find the following:

> *Madame*: Now, don't move. Smile. Say "cheese".
> *Roquefort* (eagerly): Did somebody say "cheese"?

Years later Roquefort, who fancies himself as something of a Sherlock Holmes, at one point appearing in the requisite garb, would find an echo in the character of Basil (➤320).

Edgar

The scheming butler Edgar is of course the bumbling villain of the piece, although in a way one sees his point! What sense is there in leaving all that money to a bunch of pampered cats? His major crime is impatience, which as we all know is a sin: if only he were prepared to wait a few years the money would in the end be his anyway, and in the mean time he would no doubt be comfortably "employed" by the wealthy aristocrats. Moreover, even if he had succeeded in despatching the cats to distant parts, there would always have been the risk that Madame Bonfamille might take on another family of cats and change her will again, and he could hardly expect to get away with the same trick twice.

Edgar is a very British villain, and in his claret-coloured tailed jacket and grey-blue trousers, with a little bowler on his head, is really quite genteel. He was voiced by Roddy Maude-Roxby, described by Reitherman at the time of the movie's release as "that snobbish sort of Englishman who was on *Laugh-In* two years ago". (Maude-Roxby also voiced the few words spoken by the removal men who come to collect the trunk and who are far from snobbish sorts of anything.) Moreover, Edgar is not a totally evil fellow. If he could lace the cats' meal with sleeping powder he could equally well have used a more lethal ingredient. Similarly, although it is by no

means a benevolent action to send the cats to Timbuktoo he could almost certainly have escaped detection had he simply annihilated them, for by this time Madame Bonfamille has virtually given them up for lost.

In some ways, then, our sympathies lie with Edgar. The fact that he is not an out-and-out baddie in the Disney tradition may have been one of the reasons why some critics complained that the movie was a blander version of *101 Dalmatians*: Edgar is not a patch on Cruella De Vil!

Madame Bonfamille

Madame Adelaide Bonfamille, the rich eccentric old lady, was voiced by yet another star with a wide reputation, Hermione Baddeley. Reitherman described

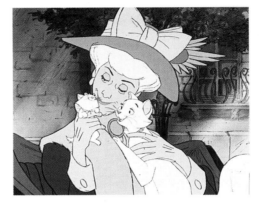

Madame Adelaide Bonfamille loved Duchess.

her as the actress "who did that tremendous characterization of the maid in *Happiest Millionaire*", which, while it is fairly

understandable in terms of the Disney connection, is a statement that seems to ignore quite a lot of thespian history!

Madame Bonfamille's role in the movie is in fact a very small one, although of course it is fundamentally important to the plot: without her money and her eccentric disposition of it Edgar would have had no stimulus to turn to crime and, one senses, might have lived out his days as a perfectly happy butler. The most striking thing about her screen presence is her utterly aristocratic, elegant grace, a quality directly reflected in Duchess. Like master, like dog was the rule in *101 Dalmatians*; here it is like mistress, like cat.

The Scat Cats

Scat Cat's merry band of jazzcats are among the more appealing of the supporting players in the Disney animated features. Only **Scat Cat** himself has a significant identity. It had originally been intended that his part should be voiced by Louis Armstrong, which would have been a tremendous coup (think of it – Chevalier and Armstrong singing in the same movie!), but Satchmo, who died not long after the film's release, was unavailable and so Scatman Crothers played the part instead. He did so superbly, making it very much his own.

While Scat Cat and his friends are very much on the side of the angels, they have not lost their cattishness (in the way that Duchess, O'Malley and the kittens for obvious plot reasons have to). When Roquefort is attempting to enlist their aid in the fight against Edgar, the dialogue is a verbal rendition of a cat playing with a

Edgar having a contretemps with Berlioz.

The Scat Cats – doing their best, as always, to make life noisy.

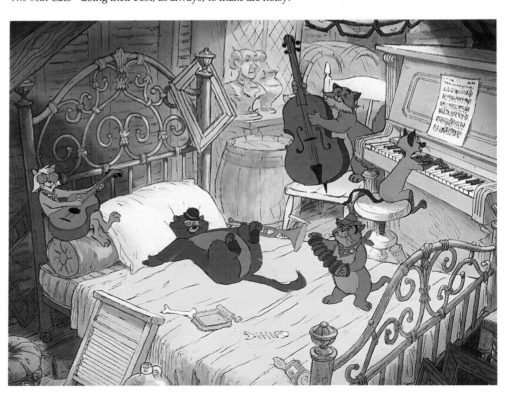

mouse before the kill – as in fact they simultaneously play with him.

> Scat Cat: What's a little swinger like you doin' on our side of town?
> Roquefort: Oh, please ... ah, I was sent here for help by a cat.
> Scat Cat: Why, this is outrageous. Crazy.
> Roquefort: Oh, but, but, but, honest. He told me just to mention his name.
> Russian Cat: So, start mentioning names, rodent.
> Roquefort: Oh, now, wait a minute, fellows ... D ... Don't rush me. His name is O'Tool ...
> Scat Cat: I don't dig him. Strike one.
> Roquefort: Oh ... oh ... O'Brien.
> Scat Cat: Strike two.
> Roquefort: Oh, boy. You believe me, don't you?
> English Cat: Keep talkin', mousey.
> Roquefort: How about O'Grady? Huh?
> Scat Cat: Mousey, you just struck out. Any last words?

The other four jazz-players – the **Chinese Cat**, the **English Cat**, the **Italian Cat** and the **Russian Cat** are essentially identifiable only by their accents, none of them displaying any clear national differences otherwise – apart from the Chinese Cat, which has slanted eyes and (rather tastelessly) two prominent buck teeth. Collectively, however, they form a sort of composite character which is very much in keeping with the high spirits of the music they play.

The Kittens

Two of the three little kittens have quite pronounced personalities, the third, **Berlioz**, being more two-dimensional – more of a typical cute cartoon kitten as animated by most studios other than Disney, in fact.

Marie is very much the little lady, the sort of small girl which most small boys dread being forced to play with, and remember with a shudder for the rest of their lives. White, with a pink bow daintily tied in her topknot, she is something of a mummy's girl, although her virtue is somewhat feigned – as when she lands her brothers in hot water for participating in a fight which she has largely been responsible for starting.

> Toulouse: Why should you be first?
> Marie: Because I'm a lady, that's why.
> Toulouse: Oh, you're not a lady.
> Berlioz: You're nothin' but a sister!
> Marie: Oh! I'll show you if I'm a lady or not.

A great rampage ensues, during which Toulouse observes sourly, "Females never fight fair." It is ended when a candle falls on Marie's head and she begins to cry: "Mama. Mama." And, as her mother berates the boys, Marie observes primly: "Ladies do not start fights, but they can finish them." Liz English's voicing of this part is a highlight of the movie.

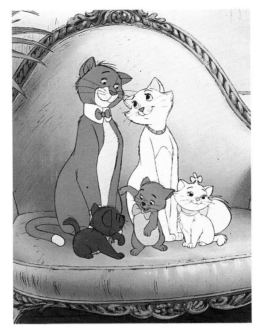

After all those adventures, the family could settle down – Duchess, O'Malley, Berlioz, Toulouse and Marie.

Toulouse is the pugnacious member of the trio, ready to take on anyone or anything – even the comparatively huge Thomas O'Malley, a characteristic which immediately endears him to the latter. (One's mind is drawn inevitably to the scene in which Mowgli attracts the friendship of Baloo for exactly the same reasons [➤279].) Swinging his paws like a heavyweight boxer in miniature, giving the sound-effect *fft! fft! fft!* as he does so, he is a hilarious example of minuscule aggression. Mama wants him to grow up to be a painter, however, rather than a pugilist. His approach to painting, though, has the same quality of aggression as his approach to just about everything else, and the results are messy. A charitable art-critic might take the view that his style displays energy; a less charitable one might recommend Duchess to let him seek a career in the ring.

The Geese

The two giggling English spinster geese, **Amelia Gabble** and her sister **Abigail Gabble**, are perfectly cast. Their voices are exquisitely rendered by Carole Shelley and Monica Evans, respectively: they both alternate between a sort of crisp English glaciality, as taught at all the *best* schools, and, immediately afterwards, fits of shared uncontrollable laughter.

They are somewhat straitlaced, and shocked to find that O'Malley, whom they assume at first to be Duchess's husband, is not in fact married to her. Of course, this state of affairs is all O'Malley's fault:

> Amelia: It's scandalous.
> Abigail: Nothing but a cad.
> Amelia: Absolutely impossible. A reprobate. And his eyes are too ...
> Abigail: A roué.
> Amelia: ... close together.
> Abigail: Shifty, too, and look at his crooked smile.
> Amelia: And his chin is weak, too.
> Abigail: Obviously a philanderer who trifles with unsuspecting women's hearts.

Although their characters are extremely well depicted, their joint role in the plot is somewhat formless. They appear in the nick of time to rescue a struggling O'Malley from the turbulent river, and rescue him they do – although, assuming that he is trying to learn to swim, they virtually drown him in the process. They then, having explained that they are on a walking (partly swimming) tour of France, agree to help the party on their way back to Paris, where the sisters are planning to meet their Uncle Waldo. They form the party up into a V-shape formation, as per geese in flight, and set off. In Paris they meet their uncle, who is somewhat the worse for wear, and then they just waddle off out of the plot.

Uncle Waldo is a deliciously portrayed character. When the party arrives at Le Petit

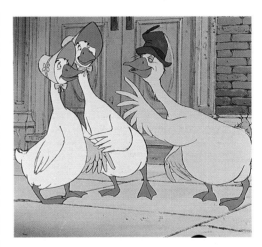

Amelia and Abigail Gabble having a minor discussion with Uncle Waldo.

Café, the appointed rendezvous, they discover that Uncle Waldo's presence there is not exactly as they had assumed: "Prime Country Goose *á la Provençale*," says the sign, "Stuffed in Chestnuts and Basted in White Wine." Uncle Waldo himself is the process of being forcibly ejected by the chef, whose thumb he has just bitten – but who, to be fair, has been plucking Waldo's tail-feathers. Unfortunately – or fortunately? – he did the basting in white wine first, and Waldo is definitely weaving about the pavement. The elderly goose laments: "Dreadful! Being British, I would have preferred sherry." How tastes in Britain have changed!

Minor Characters

The friendly mare **Frou-Frou**, warmly voiced by Nancy Kulp as a sort of middle-aged lady living in diminished circumstances, is the only one of our group

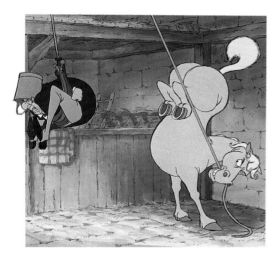

Edgar having another contretemps – this time with Frou Frou.

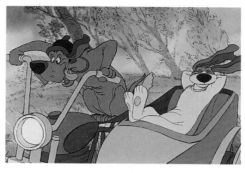

Napoleon and Lafayette, two eagerly militaristic dogs.

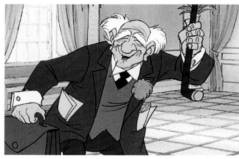

Georges Hautecourt, the elderly lawyer in charge of Madame Bonfamille's estate.

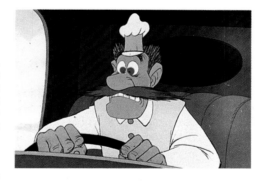

The French Milkman, who was terrorized by O'Malley.

of assorted animal friends to be physically big enough to be able effectively to tackle Edgar, and this she does in the final stages of the fight, kicking out viciously and accurately to send him sailing into the awaiting trunk. Earlier she acts as a source of comfort to the disconsolate Roquefort as they commiserate over the loss of their feline friends; immediately thereafter she receives a revealing confession from Edgar, who assumes she is merely a dumb animal:

> *Edgar*: 'Morning, Frou-Frou, my pretty steed. Can you keep a secret, huh? Of course you can. I've some news straight from the horse's mouth – if you'll pardon the expression, of course. Look, Frou-Frou, I've made the headlines: "Mysterious Catnapper Abducts Family of Cats." Aren't you proud of me?

The two rough farm-dogs **Napoleon** and **Lafayette**, with their militaristic belief that all "invaders" must be repelled with the maximum of force, are fine cameo roles. Voiced in deep, ill-educated American tones they come across well as deep, ill-educated French rustics. Napoleon is the self-appointed leader – rather like the Colonel in *101 Dalmatians*:

> *Napoleon*: Listen. Wheels approaching.
> *Lafayette*: Oh, Napoleon, we done bit six tires today, chased four motor cars, and a bicycle, and a scooter.
> *Napoleon*: Hush your mouth. It's a motorcycle. Two cylinders, chain drive, one squeaky wheel – on the front, it sounds like. Now, you go for the tires and I'll go right for the seat of the problem.
> *Lafayette*: How come you always grab the tender part for yourself?
> *Napoleon*: 'Cause I outrank you, that's why. Now, stop beatin' your gums and sound the attack.

Later Napoleon chides Lafayette: "Wait a minute. I'm the leader. I'm the one that says when we go. Here we go."

The elderly lawyer **Georges Hautecourt** – described by Reitherman in the *International Photographer* interview as "the oldest lawyer in the world" – seems to be as devoted to cats as Madame Bonfamille herself, because he appears to take positive delight in drawing up her wills in the cats' favour. Stooping and elderly, bald with white eyebrows and tufts of remaining hair at the sides, he is everybody's favourite grandpa.

Among other very minor characters – the chef at Le Petit Café and the two removal men who call to collect the trunk – the only significant one is the generously moustachioed **French Milkman** whose truck O'Malley hijacks to help the party on the first stage of their journey back to Paris. His only two words of French appear to be "*Sapriste*!" and "*Sacrebleu*!", but he communicates his emotions ably using them whenever need be. Otherwise he speaks English in a "French" accent.

BEDKNOBS AND BROOMSTICKS

Characters:

King Leonidas; Mr. Codfish; Fisherman Bear; Secretary Bird
Soccer players: Ostrich; Cheetah; Kangaroo; Hippopotamus; Elephant; Rhinoceros; Crocodile; Hyena; Warthog; Gorilla
Mouse; Vultures; Octopus

Credits:

Based on *The Magic Bedknob* (1945) and *Bonfires and Broomsticks* (1947) by Mary Norton

Live Actors: Angela Lansbury; David Tomlinson; Roddy McDowall; Sam Jaffe; John Ericson; Bruce Forsyth; Tessie O'Shea; Arthur E. Gould-Porter; Ben Wrigley; Reginald Owen; Cyril Delevanti; Rich Traeger; Manfred Lating; John Orchard; Ian Weighill; Roy Snart; Cindy O'Callaghan

Voices: Lennie Weinrib (King Leonidas, Secretary Bird); Robert Holt (Mr. Codfish); Dallas McKennon (Fisherman Bear); Jim Macdonald

Director of Photography: Frank Phillips

Art Directors: John B. Mansbridge; Peter Ellenshaw

Film Editor: Cotton Warburton

Music Editor: Evelyn Kennedy

Screenplay: Bill Walsh; Don DaGradi

Set Decorators: Emile Kuri; Hal Gausman

Costume Designer: Bill Thomas

Assistant to Designer: Shelby Anderson

Title Design: David Jonas

Sound Supervisor: Robert O. Cook

Sound Mixer: Dean Thomas

Costumes: Chuck Keehne; Emily Sundby

Make-up: Robert J. Schiffer

Hair Stylist: La Rue Matheron

Assistant Director: Christopher Hibler

Script Supervisor: Lois Thurman

Assistant to the Conductor: James Macdonald

Dance Accompanist: Albert Mello

Choreography: Donald McKayle

Assistant Choreographer: Carolyn Dyer

Second Unit Director: Arthur J. Vitarelli

Technical Consultants: Manfred Lating; Milt Larsen; James McInnes; Bob Baker; Spungbuggy Works

Animation Director: Ward Kimball

Animation Film Editor: James W. Swain

Musical Direction: Irwin Kostal

Songs by: Richard M. Sherman; Robert B. Sherman

Backgrounds: Al Dempster; Bill Layne; Dick Kelsey; Ralph Hulett

Animation: Milt Kahl; John Lounsbery; Eric Larson; Fred Hellmich; Art Stevens; Julius Svendsen; Hal King; Jack Buckley; Jack Boyd

Animation Story: Ralph Wright; Ted Berman

Layout: Don Griffith; Joe Hale

Animation/Live Action Design: McLaren Stewart

Special Effects: Alan Maley; Eustace Lycett; Danny Lee

Director: Robert Stevenson

Producer: Bill Walsh

Release Date: October 7, 1971

Running Time: 139 minutes

THE MOVIE

Bedknobs and Broomsticks is generally compared critically with *Mary Poppins*, and usually the comparison is unfavourable. This is unfair to the later movie, although it is obvious why the parallels are drawn: both films have the same director, Robert Stevenson, and in both of them David Tomlinson plays a starring role. Both, moreover, have a fairly extensive central section in which live action and animation are blended. In fact, the association between the two movies is even deeper, because Walt bought the movie rights in Mary Norton's stories around the same time as he bought those in the P. L. Travers ones and, when Travers proved justifiably fussy about the version of her books which the studio was producing, considered switching production to *Bedknobs and Broomsticks*; he even felt that the songs already written for *Mary Poppins* by the Sherman brothers could be transplanted *in toto* into the putative movie. As it turned out, of course, production went ahead on *Mary Poppins*, and *Bedknobs and Broomsticks* entered a sort of limbo for several years – the movie was finally released almost five years after Walt's death.

Despite all these close associations, however, unfavourable comparisons of *Bedknobs and Broomsticks* with *Mary Poppins* are particularly odious because the two movies are actually very different; it is as if one were comparing the animated *Robin Hood* (1973) with the live-action *The Story of Robin Hood* (1952). *Mary Poppins* is targeted at a very much younger audience and is episodic in structure; otherwise it would not have held the attention of its audience for its full 140 minutes. *Bedknobs and Broomsticks*, despite occasional excursions outside the plot (such as the animated section), is essentially a single story which has to carry its audience for 117 minutes. (It is, like *Mary Poppins*, a long film, although a 1979 reissue sheared some 20 minutes off its length.) It is more of an adventure story than is *Mary Poppins*. It never flirts with bathos, which *Mary Poppins* most certainly does. It . . . but one could fill pages itemizing the differences between the two movies.

Viewed in isolation, *Bedknobs and Broomsticks* is an excellent movie. The pace never flags, the story is a good one, and the acting performances are excellent. The special effects cannot be faulted, and of the mixed animation/live-action section all one needs to say is that it is better than its equivalent in *Mary Poppins*; the animation itself is among Disney's very best.

THE STORY

It is 1940 and Carrie, Paul and Charlie are evacuated from London to Pepperinge Eye, where they are billeted with a middle-aged spinster, Eglantine Price (Angela Lansbury), who, they discover, is an apprentice witch. In order to keep them quiet about this, she enchants one of the knobs on Paul's bedstead so that, if you say where you want to go while twisting the knob, the bed magically takes you there.

Eglantine wants to use the spell of "substitutiary locomotion" to end the war. However, finding out what the spell *is* proves difficult, especially since the correspondence course she has been taking stops mid-stream, just before describing substitutiary locomotion. Using the bed, our heroes track down the organizer of the correspondence course, Professor Emelius Browne (David Tomlinson), who proves to be a conman. He has been copying all his spells out of the *Book of Astaroth* (not Ashtaroth, for reasons known only to Disney), but as he has only half the book, which has been ripped apart, he has had to pretend that it is the war that has curtailed his course.

Paul, the youngest child and the titular owner of the bedknob, in the course of all this comes across a children's book which features the "Lost Isle of Naboombu". He wants to take the bed there, but everyone tells him not to be silly – it is just a fantasy island. However, when our heroes find the other half of the *Book of Astaroth* it directs them towards Naboombu. It seems that the animals, 'way back in the hazy past, rebelled against Astaroth and sailed off to Naboombu, taking with them the pendant upon which are inscribed the words of the substitutiary locomotion spell. So, using the bed, off our heroes go to this fabled island.

They are entering a different world, and this is symbolized by the use of animation to depict everything except our heroes. They meet Mr. Codfish as the bed travels through the waters of the lagoon which the island surrounds; they find themselves in an underwater ballroom, where Eglantine and Emelius win a dancing trophy; and finally they are hooked ashore by Fisherman Bear. He wants to throw them back – not because he doesn't like them but because it is against Naboombu law to catch people. Still, they persuade him to take them to see King Leonidas. This worthy, a forceful lion who wears the coveted pendant around his neck, is convinced that he is the world's finest soccer player, but is furious that the Royal Cup Match cannot be held today owing to the lack of a referee. Emelius volunteers to fill the vacancy, and a hilarious soccer match ensues. Finally Emelius is able to snitch the pendant from around the King's neck, and the humans escape just in time.

Back in the real (live-action) world, Eglantine and Emelius decide to experiment with the substitutiary locomotion spell written on the pendant, but it has vanished – proving that you cannot take artefacts from one world to another. It turns out that little Paul knew the spell all along, because it was printed quite clearly in that children's book. They try it – TREGUNA MEKOIDES TRECORUM SATIS DEE – and it works. This is useful, because an advance guard of German submariners are invading England *via* the coastal town of Pepperinge Eye. Eglantine animates the suits of armour in the local museum to fight off the Germans – successfully. (The special effects here are brilliant.)

Of course, details of the battle are never publicly known: this is an unsung episode of World War II. The children decide that they love Eglantine; she decides that she loves them; Emelius decides that he loves her and can put up with the children but nevertheless joins the army. As the movie ends one instinctively knows that he will return unscathed from the war and that everyone will live happily ever after.

THE CHARACTERS

Aside from the ones discussed in more detail below, the animated characters in *Bedknobs and Broomsticks* are all soccer players with the exception of the Mouse, the Vultures and the Octopus. The **Mouse** is produced during the soccer match by the Crocodile in order to terrify the Elephant, who is keeping goal. The **Vultures** are particularly assiduous stretchermen, rushing on to carry off the various casualties in the match, of whom there are many – including the referee, Emelius.

The **Octopus** features in the earlier part of the animated section of the movie, when the bed is sailing underwater in the lagoon. We first encounter him when he is playing cards with a flounder and a cod; as the bed passes above it knocks off his hat to reveal that he has been hiding three aces in it.

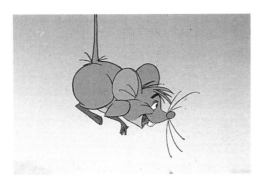

The Mouse, produced during the soccer match in order to terrify the Elephant.

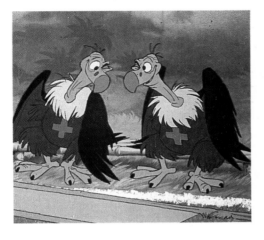

The two Vultures were always eager to carry off the soccer players.

Later he – or his twin brother – is the drummer of the band, The Briny Boys, playing in the ballroom where Eglantine and Emelius win their prize.

The two soccer teams have the following line-ups:

Yellows	Blues
King Leonidas	Ostrich
Rhinoceros	Cheetah
Crocodile	Kangaroo
Hyena	Hippopotamus
Warthog	Elephant
Gorilla	

Not only does the King's team have an extra player but the animals involved are, on average, a little more carnivorous than those playing for the Blues. No wonder the King's team won – even if he did have to cheat.

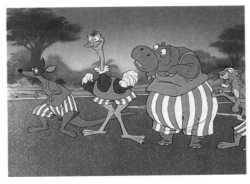

The Blues' forwards line up: from left to right, they are the Kangaroo, Ostrich, Hippo and Cheetah.

King Leonidas

The important elements of Leonidas's character – aside from his loud-mouthed bullying nature – are that he likes neither (a) people nor (b) losing, and that he is an impassioned devotee of soccer. This last element is capable of conquering at least (a), for he accepts his human visitors when Emelius announces that he will gladly play the part of referee so that the great soccer match can go on.

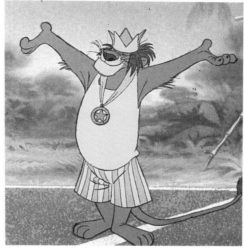

King Leonidas – not so much just a bad soccer player, more a bully.

We first encounter not the King but his voice: the very blast of it is enough to hurl the unfortunate Secretary Bird out of his regal tent. When we do see His Royal Highness in person we discover him to be a rather petty-minded-looking lion, full of his own importance. He wears a red robe with ermine trimmings; on his head is an undersized gold crown, and around his neck, on a chain, is the green pentagram of Astaroth. His attitude to soccer is simple: he *must* win, because otherwise his self-image as the world's finest soccer player would be destroyed. During the incredibly foul-packed soccer match the following exchange betrays the King's attitude to the game:

> *Charlie:* Don't they have no rules?
> *Paul:* Course they do. The King makes them up as he goes along.

His voice is a powerful weapon. After the human heroes have stolen the pendant and fled, Leonidas' furious roar of discovery is so potent that it blasts off all of his Secretary Bird's clothes with the exception of his neat British tie.

Mr. Codfish

The urbane Mr. Codfish is first encountered in the waters of the lagoon. Reminiscent in a curious way of Mr. Toad (➤**231**), he is green with a small reddish homburg, a pale-brown sports jacket, a pale-colored shirt and a reddish bow-tie. His voice (supplied

by Robert Holt) is fittingly that of a rurally retired English army colonel. When asked where Naboombu is he responds with a discouraging tone: "You mean the land part? Oh, that. Straight up. You can't miss it. None of my business, of course, but I shouldn't go there. Having troubles, they are." The "troubles" are, of course, largely encapsulated in King Leonidas.

Later, in the ballroom, Mr. Codfish presents Eglantine and Emelius with the dancing trophy. "Bravo, bravo. Most exciting, most exciting," he says. "You've won the ruddy cup." Robert Holt should perhaps have studied British slang a little more carefully before agreeing to speak that last sentence.

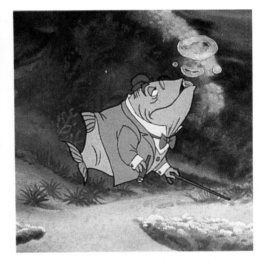

Mr. Codfish, one of the first animated characters to appear in the movie.

Fisherman Bear

The Fisherman Bear is none too delighted when his catch proves to be a metal bedstead with five people aboard – does it not say on the sign "NO PEOPLING ALLOWED – By Order of the King"? He is all ready to throw them back, but Paul dissuades him by showing him the children's book, which says that *anyone* on

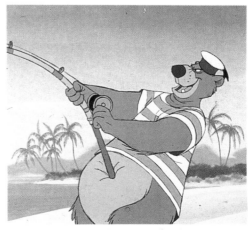

Fisherman Bear, whose misfortune it was to haul our friends ashore.

the island of Naboombu is allowed to see the King.

Two of the characters in *Bedknobs and Broomsticks* can be viewed as "warm-ups" for those in *Robin Hood*. Although the voices are different, King Leonidas is much like the later movie's Prince John. The Fisherman Bear, although again differently voiced (by Lennie Weinrib) is strongly reminiscent of the later movie's Little John as well as of Baloo in the earlier *The Jungle Book* (both voiced by Phil Harris).

Secretary Bird

The Secretary Bird, who has the unfortunate task of being chief adviser to King Leonidas, is a caricature of the English

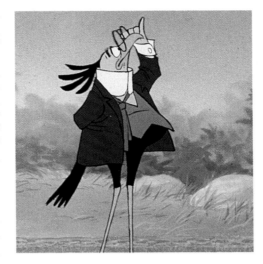

The Secretary Bird had the job of bearing the full brunt of King Leonidas' fury – over and over again.

civil servant. His exaggeratedly posh voice is matched by his lorgnette, grey waistcoat, high stiff white collar, black coat and so forth. Although he is ungainly he is not nearly so much of a fool as he looks: he is the first to (apoplectically) spot that the pentagram of Astaroth has been stolen from around the King's neck. It takes him a little while to communicate the lack to the King, who then roars: "Why didn't you *say* so?" The roar is so powerful that the poor Secretary Bird is left clad in only his tie.

ROBIN HOOD

Characters:

Robin Hood; Maid Marian; Little John; Prince John; King Richard; Sir Hiss; Lady Kluck; Friar Tuck; Allan-a-Dale; Sheriff of Nottingham; Trigger; Nutsy; Church Mouse (Sexton); Mother Rabbit; Skippy Bunny; Tagalong; Sis; Toby Turtle; Mr. Turtle; Mother Mouse; Grandma and Grandpa Owl; Otto; Crocodile; Country Dog (archer); Sheep Dog (archer)

Credits:

Based on character and story conceptions by Ken Anderson

Voices: Roger Miller (Allan-a-Dale); Peter Ustinov (Prince John, King Richard); Terry-Thomas (Sir Hiss); Brian Bedford (Robin Hood); Monica Evans (Maid Marian); Phil Harris (Little John); Andy Devine (Friar Tuck); Carole Shelley (Lady Kluck); Pat Buttram (Sheriff of Nottingham); George Lindsey (Trigger); Ken Curtis (Nutsy); Billy Whitaker (Skippy); Dana Laurita (Sis); Dora Whitaker (Tagalong); Richie Sanders (Toby Turtle); J. Pat O'Malley (Otto); Candy Candido (Crocodile); Barbara Luddy (Mother Rabbit); John Fiedler (Church Mouse)

Sound: Herb Taylor

Film Editors: Tom Acosta; Jim Melton

Music Editor: Evelyn Kennedy

Music: George Bruns

Songs by: Roger Miller; Floyd Huddleston; George Bruns; Johnny Mercer

Orchestration: Walter Sheets

Story: Larry Clemmons

Story Sequences: Ken Anderson; Frank Thomas; Julius Svendsen; Vance Gerry; Eric Cleworth; Dave Michener

Layout: Basil Davidovich; Sylvia Roemer; Joe Hale; Ed Templer, Jr.

Colour Styling: Al Dempster

Backgrounds: Bill Layne; Ralph Hulett; Ann Guenther

Directing Animators: Milt Kahl; Frank Thomas; Oliver M. Johnston, Jr.; John Lounsbery

Character Animators: Hal King; Art Stevens; Cliff Nordberg; Burny Mattinson; Eric Larson; Don Bluth; Dale Baer; Fred Hellmich

Effects Animators: Dan MacManus; Jack Buckley

Key Assistant Animators: Dale Oliver; Bob McCrea; Chuck Williams; Stan Green

Assistant Directors: Ed Hansen; Dan Alguire; Jeff Patch

Art Director: Don Griffith

Production Manager: Don Duckwall

Produced and Directed by: Wolfgang Reitherman

Release Date: November 8, 1973

Running Time: 83 minutes

THE MOVIE

The most striking thing about *Robin Hood* is that all of the parts are played by animals. In this tale of human history – or pseudo-history – not a single human being appears. The decision was made by Ken Anderson, who explained in an article in the *Official Bulletin of IATSE* for Winter 1973-4 that Disney "decided to do what we do best: use animals for the characters". Anderson continued:

As director of story and character conception, I knew right off that sly Robin Hood must be a fox. From there it was logical that Maid Marian should be a pretty vixen. Little John, legendarily known for his size, was easily a big overgrown bear.

Friar Tuck is great as a badger, but he was also great as a pig, as I had originally planned. Then I thought the symbol of a pig might be offensive to the Church, so we changed him. Richard the Lion-hearted, of course, had to be a regal, proud, strong lion; and his pathetic

cousin [historically, and in the movie, his brother] Prince John, the weak villain, also had to be a lion, but we made him scrawny and childish. I originally thought of a snake as a member of the poor townspeople but one of the other men here suggested that a snake would be perfect as a slithering consort [Sir Hiss] to mean Prince John.

In fact, the conception of the animal-starring *Robin Hood* can be traced back a very long way indeed – right back to the 1930s. Around the time of *Snow White* Walt became interested in the possibilities of basing an animated feature on the twelfth-century legend (as revamped by Goethe and numerous others) of Reynard the Fox. In the tale, the kingdom of the beasts is ruled over by an avaricious and spiteful lion. One day Reynard fails to attend court, and the King furiously sends messengers for him. The first of these, Bruin the Bear, finds Reynard but is tricked by him into trying to raid a hive. Badly stung, he gives up. The second messenger, Tibert the Cat, fares worse – Reynard's trick loses him an eye. Finally another fox succeeds in bring Reynard to book.

On the scaffold, Reynard begins to talk of a secret treasure-trove. The avaricious King eagerly pardons him and sends him off with the Ram and the Hare to fetch the treasure. Once they are some distance from court, Reynard kills the Hare, puts its head in a bag and gives this to the Ram, telling him that it is the treasure. The Ram hurries to the King with it, and the sovereign is less than pleased when he discovers the ruse.

Once again, Reynard faces execution, and once again he avoids it by talking of a treasure-trove. This time, however, the Wolf, keen for justice, challenges him to a duel. Through cheating, Reynard wins the duel, killing the Wolf, and as a reward for his cunning is appointed the King's chief adviser.

From the Disney point of view there were

obvious problems with this story. As Walt himself put it, "I see some swell possibilities in Reynard, but is it smart to make it?" and "The whole central character is a crook. That's what I'm afraid of." Nonetheless, the project seems to have niggled away at the backs of the minds of all the Disney creative team – including Walt. Over the years a number of story treatments were prepared and various attempts at concept-sketches made. Most significantly, Walt seriously considered putting into *Treasure Island* (1950) three animated sections, each one of the Reynard tales, to be told by Silver to Jim as moral fables at apposite moments. In the end, of course, it was decided that Disney should take the plunge and make *Treasure Island* its first exclusively live-action feature.

Ken Anderson was the one who kept the Reynard project alive after that. He did some storyboard sketches in 1956 and in 1960 prepared a script based loosely on the legend – with Reynard portrayed not as the hero but as the villain. Still, though, nothing came of it.

However, all those years of research finally bore fruit in the animated version of *Robin Hood*. In the movie we find all kinds of elements taken from the earlier attempts to "tie down" the Reynard legend. The fox's prime adversaries are the spiteful and greedy King – or would-be King – and the rather stupid wolf, in the form of the Sheriff of Nottingham, both of whom he defeats by cunning. There are some more detailed parallels. In early Disney treatments Reynard was a master of disguise, appearing as a woman and as a blind beggar, and in at least one instance he used the opportunity of kissing the King's hand to steal the rings from his fingers.

One wishes one could say that the product of all those years of research was worth it, but one cannot. *Robin Hood* is the weakest of the Disney animated features. It has no proper plot: it is just a collection of sequences, some of them superb, cobbled together any which way. Watching it, one has the feeling that Disney was planning a much more major treatment but then baulked at the cost and swiftly tacked together the already-animated sequences. (This was not in fact the case, one gathers, but that is how it seems.) None of the characters except Little John appeals very much – although Prince John and Sir Hiss are a lot of fun (and are excellently voiced, by Peter Ustinov and Terry-Thomas, respectively). The quality of the animation is patchy – one piece, Maid Marian's dance at the forest party, having been lifted directly from *Snow White and the Seven Dwarfs*.

Reviewers at the time and ever since have put these points, and many more, but this has not affected the box office: *Robin Hood* has been startlingly successful in that respect. Quite how pleasing a prospect this is in the long term is uncertain: *Robin Hood* is the only Disney feature to have bored this author's (then) seven-year-old daughter.

THE STORY

The scene is set in the traditional Disney style, with the pages of a book:

Long ago, good King Richard of England departed for the Holy Land on a great crusade. During his absence Prince John, his greedy and treacherous brother, usurped the crown. Robin Hood was the people's only hope. He robbed from the rich to feed the poor. He was beloved by all the people of England. Robin and his Merry Men hid in Sherwood Forest to elude the Sheriff of Nottingham …

The rooster Allan-a-Dale appears to tell us that this is all very well, but that there is another version to the story:

Ya know, there's been a heap of legends and tall tales about Robin Hood. All different, too … Well, we folks in the animal kingdom have our own version. It's the story of what really happened in Sherwood Forest …

And so we are introduced to the "real version". First we see Robin and Little John narrowly escaping death in one of the Sheriff's ambushes. Then they spot Prince John's entourage moving slowly along the road and propose to rob it. Inside one of the wagons Prince John and Sir Hiss are playing with a mountain of gold coins and gloating over the ease with which money can be extracted from the poor in the form of taxes. Robin and Little John appear disguised as female fortune-tellers. Prince John stops his convoy and permits Robin and Little John to kiss his hands, during which process large quantities of finger-jewellery disappear. (Sir Hiss spots this, but his protests are silenced by the "phony King".) After a little jiggery-pokery with a faked crystal ball, so do all the bags of the King's gold and even his robes and the gold hubcaps from his coach. Then Robin and Little John do likewise.

Rewards are posted for the capture of the thieves, but of course the pair remain free.

Next we see the vulpine Sheriff of Nottingham gaily extorting taxes from the poor – particularly Otto, the hound-dog blacksmith with a broken leg, and the poverty-stricken family of the widowed Mother Rabbit, who are celebrating the birthday of one of the children, Skippy: his birthday present, a "whole farthing" is appropriated by the Sheriff as tax. When a blind beggar appears at the latter home, begging for alms, the Sheriff swipes his meagre collection, too. However, after the Sheriff's departure, the "beggar" reveals himself as Robin Hood, and gives Skippy a bow-and-arrow and a Robin Hood hat for his birthday, and Mother Rabbit a pouchful of money on general principles.

The next set-piece sees a bunch of the kids, including Skippy, Toby Turtle, Skippy's sister Sis and his baby sister Tagalong, setting off to play with the bow-and-arrow. Skippy fires the arrow, and it lands in the grounds of Nottingham

Castle. Despite the dire warnings of the other kids, Skippy determines to fetch it back. In the grounds he finds Maid Marian and Lady Kluck playing badminton; they welcome Skippy and in due course the other children. It emerges that Marian is Robin's sweetheart, but is prevented from joining him by Prince John. After much clowning, in which Lady Kluck mimics Prince John, Skippy mimics Robin Hood and Maid Marian mimics herself, the last gives Skippy an ear-splittingly romantic kiss, to the mirth of the other kids.

In a couple of shortish scenes we discover first that Marian truly is yearning for Robin and that he, too, is yearning for her; moreover, there is to be a big archery tournament in Nottingham on the morrow, one of the prizes being a kiss from Maid Marian.

Of course, it is a plot: Prince John knows that Robin will be unable to resist taking part, and plans to capture him. Robin, instinctively wise to this, turns up disguised as a stork; Little John arrives in the guise of a dissipated aristocrat – Sir Reginald, Duke of Chutney – and sucks up to the Prince (whom he nicknames, to that worthy's delight, "PJ"). He ends up ensconced in the royal box.

Hiss is intent on catching Robin. He buys himself a balloon and floats skyward attached to it. In due course, while Robin is busy winning the tournament, Friar Tuck shoots Hiss out of the skies by firing an arrow from a mandolin-string and stuffs him into a beer-barrel.

The finale of the tournament is between the Sheriff of Nottingham and a certain spindle-shanked stork. The Sheriff shoots first and, thanks to the fact that he has his acolyte, the vulture Nutsy, ready to adjust the target to meet the arrow's flight, he appears to win. Just to make sure, he jerks Robin's bow just as the latter is about to fire, but the quick-thinking outlaw shoots off a second arrow which deflects the first so that it hits the bull, knocking the Sheriff's arrow from its place.

However, the prize-giving ceremony is not all it should be. Prince John's rhinoceros soldiers seize Robin and things look bleak until Little John, by dexterous pressure of a dagger on the Prince's spine, ensures that Robin is temporarily reprieved. Once the Sheriff discovers Little John's ploy, however, the game is up, and a vast fight ensues, Lady Kluck playing a major part in defeating the forces of evil. In the midst of it all Robin and Marian hastily plight their troth.

After the battle there is a romantic party in Sherwood Forest. Among the guests are Friar Tuck, Church Mouse, Mother Mouse, Otto, the Rabbit family, Lady Kluck, Little John, Allan-a-Dale, Toby Turtle and dozens of other miscellaneous animals. There is also a puppet show parodying Prince John and Hiss, and Little John sings the movie's main song, "The Phony King of England":

... Too late to be known as John the First,
He's sure to be known as John the Worst.
A pox on the Phony King of England ...

and so on.

Next we find ourselves in the interior of Nottingham Castle, where the Sheriff is happily if foolishly singing the hit song of the day, "The Phony King of England"; Sir Hiss joins in, but the two are almost brained by a wrathful Prince John. The latter's response to the news that the whole town is singing the song is to double the taxes.

If you cannot pay your taxes you end up in jail – and that is exactly where most of the population of Nottingham does end up. Exceptions are Friar Tuck, Church Mouse and Mother Mouse, who are trying to hold a church service despite the fact that all the congregation is imprisoned. When the trio resist the Sheriff's raiding of the poor-box, they too are carted off to prison.

Prince John, though, despite the cheering fullness of his jails, is depressed because the prisoner he really wants is Robin Hood, still on the loose. He determines to hang Friar Tuck, on the basis that Robin will turn up to try to rescue him, and thus be captured. While the scaffold is being built by Nutsy and Trigger (a crossbow-toting fellow-vulture), Robin turns up in his blind-beggar outfit and discovers the plot. During the night, he and Little John not only release all the prisoners from the jail but also "liberate" Prince John's gold.

John, Hiss, the Sheriff and the two vultures finally find themselves in a penal rock-breaking quarry. Meanwhile, Robin and Marian are being married, to the delight of the returned King Richard and most of the other characters in the movie.

As Allan-a-Dale says in conclusion: "Well, folks, that's the way it really happened." Perhaps it did. The Disney version is no more historically inaccurate than any of the others.

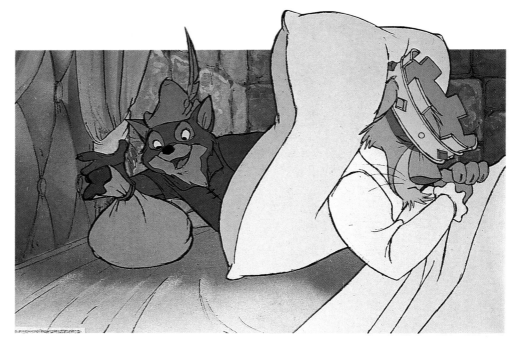

Robin found stealing loot from a slumbering Prince John as easy as taking candy from a baby.

THE CHARACTERS

Robin Hood

Robin is a master of disguise. In his "natural state", though, he wears the traditional outfit of Lincoln green and a yellow hat with an ostentatious red plume. For his disguise as a fortune-teller he wears a blue dress, a red headscarf with white polka-dots, big hoop-like gold earrings and brunette gypsy-style wig. His disguise as a blind alms-collecter, used both when he is delivering money to the rabbit family and when he is picking up the datum that Friar Tuck is to be executed, is more convincing, primarily because so much of him is covered up by his dark glasses and long coat that it is impossible to tell who he is – or even that he is a fox!

Robin, as we have noted, has much in common with the unscreened character Reynard. Of course, he is not too much like

the murderous crook Reynard, but he is also not much like the Robin Hood we have all read about – or even seen, played by Richard Todd, in Disney's own live-action feature *The Story of Robin Hood* (1952). For one thing there are no Merry Men. This was because there was a feeling around the studio that he and Little John should be, as it were, animated versions of Butch Cassidy and the Sundance Kid; a band of Merry Men would have been impossible to reconcile with this.

Robin has been described as the least interesting character in the movie (e.g., by Leonard Maltin in his *The Disney Films*), which might tend to suggest that his personality is totally two-dimensional – that he is a cypher. This is not in fact the case. The trouble is that his irresponsible personality – he is in the business of outlawry for the hell of it, and cares not for life nor limb – does not really adapt or react in any way to the events of the movie. In one way this is fair enough – some real people are actually like this – but it does make it difficult for the audience to identify with him. One cannot imagine Robin experiencing anguish, or fury, or even love (his declarations to Maid Marian lack conviction) – the deeper emotions are beyond his personality.

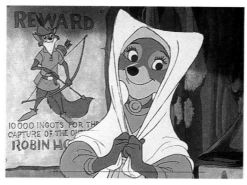

Maid Marian, looking as enticing as a vixen can do.

Maid Marian

Maid Marian, niece to King Richard, plays a very small role in the movie, and after she and Robin have plighted their troth she seems to be largely forgotten about. Her function is essentially to provide a motive for Robin to attend the archery tournament and thereby set things up for one of the movie's major sequences. What is intriguing, however, is that the animators have succeeded in making a vixen have the screen presence of an attractive woman. In part this must be due to her voice, supplied by Monica Evans, but this cannot be a total explanation. One must simply applaud the skill of the Disney animators.

Little John

The lumbering bear Little John, voiced by Phil Harris, by now a Disney stalwart, is a different kettle of fish: he certainly has a personality. The only complaint might be that this is the same personality as Baloo of *The Jungle Book* (➤278) – in other words, that the character has been moulded entirely to Phil Harris's voice, rather than being a genuine cartoon creation. (It comes as something of a shock to discover that Harris is not fat and lumbering in real life!) But this is a petty criticism: Little John is great fun to watch, listen to, and even identify with.

Where Robin is totally irresponsible, Little John has the occasional qualm about the dangers and the ethics of their lifestyle. In the opening sequences of the movie, for example, while he and Robin are hiding in a tree from the Sheriff's men, the two have a conversation in which the big bear expresses some doubts:

Little John: You know somethin', Robin? You're takin' too many chances.
Robin: Chances? You must be joking. That was just a bit of a lark, Little John.
Little John: Yeah? Take a look at your hat. [Robin finds it has been impaled by an arrow.] That's not a candle on a cake.
Robin: Hello. This one almost had my name on it, didn't it? They're getting better, you

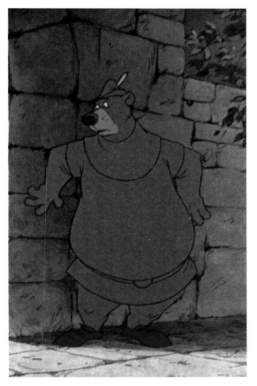

Little John was intent on springing the prisoners.

know. You've got to admit it, they are getting better.

Little John: Uh, yeah. The next time that Sheriff'll probably have a rope around our necks. Ugh! Pretty hard to laugh hangin' there, Rob.

Robin: Ha! The Sheriff and his whole posse couldn't lift you off the ground! ... Oh, come along. You worry too much, old boy.

Little John: You know somethin', Robin? I was just wonderin', are we good guys or bad guys? You know, I mean, out robbin' the rich to feed the poor.

Robin: "Rob"? Tsk, tsk, tsk, tsk, that's a naughty word. We never rob. We just sort of borrow a bit from those who can afford it.

Little John: "Borrow"? Ha! Boy, are we in debt.

Moments later Robin is disguising himself as a fortune-teller in order to rob the royal entourage and, although Little John joins him in this enterprise, he does so not without mild initial demur: "The Prince! Wait a minute, there's a law against robbin' royalty."

In many ways he is Robin's superior in the disguise stakes. This is particularly noticeable in the sequence at the tournament. While Robin's disguise – as a stork – is ostentatious, Little John's rendition of a slightly disreputable passing aristocrat, a disguise requiring little by way of "props", is in fact the more effective, because it is a disguise of the *personality* rather than merely of the appearance.

Interestingly, while most of the characters speak with English accents, Little John's voice is unashamedly American, and yet it clashes in no way with the others. In fact, his character – humorous, carefree, thoughtful and courageous by turns – could probably not have been convincingly voiced by an Englishman. It is a fine piece of work.

Prince John

Prince John is the other major character in the movie, which records him as the traditional mean, avaricious and cowardly figure imagined by schoolchildren. He is contrasted with the fine upstanding figure of his brother, Richard Coeur de Lion. The fact that Richard was one of the worst monarchs in English history, neglecting his sovereign duties to the extent that he probably spent less than a year of his entire life in the country and, it is thought, could not even speak English, seems always to be forgotten. It is no wonder that John attempted to usurp the throne: his elder brother was expecting him to do the job without having the title. And those brutal taxes were in part caused by the fact that Richard's crusades did not come cheap.

Of course, recognition of all this would deprive the legend and the movie of its principal villain! Voiced by Peter Ustinov, John is depicted as an absurdly pathetic, vain and childish figure; the slightest reverse sends him off into a sort of trance, sucking his thumb and pleading for his mummy. (Somehow one cannot really imagine anyone feeling that way about Eleanor of Aquitaine!) He has the cruelty and cold-bloodedness of a child rather than of an adult villain, and generally speaking he takes it out on the sycophantic Sir Hiss, whom he delights in pummelling, knotting, and so forth. At one stage one of John's punches fails to make contact:

John: Hiss, you deliberately ducked!
Hiss: But ... but ... Sire, please!
John: Stop snivelling and hold still. [Wallops Hiss over the head.]
Hiss: Thank you, Sire.

John's cowardice is epitomized when he has sentenced Robin to death at the tournament and Little John has decided to intervene – by the simple process of sticking a knife to the Prince's back and telling him to change his mind in a hurry. In fact, it is difficult to know what one would do oneself in the Prince's position other than obey orders, but his instant panic and his pathetic flailing

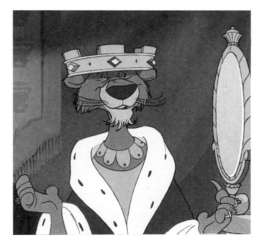

Prince John found his best flatterer was his mirror.

are used for a good deal of humorous mileage. He is treacherous, too: as soon as it is safe to do so he rescinds his pardon.

While the criticism has been levelled at Little John that he is just an animated version of Phil Harris's voice, the same cannot be said of the Prince – although it must have been very tempting for the animators simply to model the character on such a prestigious actor as Ustinov. Partly, of course, precisely because he is such a skilled actor, he was able to depict in his vocalization a character quite different from his customary persona, and it was the character he vocally created, rather than Ustinov himself, which the animators portrayed; however, clearly there was more to it than that. Little John was designed to be Phil Harris, while Prince John was designed to be Prince John.

One line of the Prince's deserves special mention: "This crown gives me a feeling of *power*! POWER! (Forgive me a cruel chuckle.)"

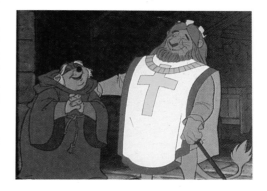

King Richard played as small a part in the movie as he did in English history. Here he congratulates Friar Tuck.

The Prince's brother, **King Richard**, makes only the most fleeting of appearances in the movie – a fairly accurate representation of his historical practice. He turns up to bless the bride and groom at Robin's wedding to Marian. He has a good one-liner as his sole piece of dialogue: "Ah, Friar Tuck, it appears that I now have an outlaw for an inlaw. Not bad."

Sir Hiss

In contrast with Prince John, the snivelling snake Sir Hiss is very closely modelled on his voice, Terry-Thomas. Of course, he is physically somewhat different, but his movements and his facial expressions are powerfully reminiscent of the British actor and he even has two front teeth with a gap between them.

In a way, Sir Hiss deserves much better than he gets from Prince John, because despite all the maltreatment and abuse he is fiendishly loyal to the "phony King". He may be slimy, underhanded and disingenuous, but he strives hard to further John's interests, even in the face of physical punishment. At the tournament he alone gets truly stuck into the task of trying to find

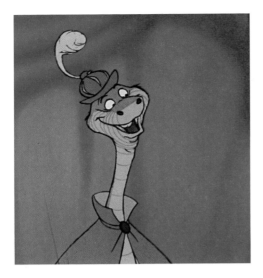

Sir Hiss, who bore an astonishing resemblance to Kaa (➤279).

Robin Hood, soaring aloft on a balloon in order to scrutinize the crowd from above. The fact that he is shot down by Friar Tuck and Allan-a-Dale, and then stuffed into a vat of ale with the result that he gets uproariously drunk, is not his fault, and even in the full throes of his drunkenness he works to inform his master of the terrible truth. His fidelity is the one favourable characteristic in an otherwise fairly repellent personality.

While Little John has been widely criticized as being merely a repetition of *The Jungle Book*'s Baloo, Sir Hiss has frequently been likened to that movie's Kaa (➤279). In fact, the similarity is not an especially strong one, apart from the fact that both of them are snakes. Both, too, have hypnotic powers. Although we are not treated to a great display of these in the case of Sir Hiss, we are informed that it was because of his hypnotic intervention that Richard went off on his crusade, thereby leaving John to fiscally plunder the poor of England.

Lady Kluck

Maid Marian's lady-in-waiting is a hen of that age best described as indeterminate. She is buxom and grey and is dressed in a sort of shapeless blue *thing*. She has prominent red dewlaps – wattles, to be precise – and upon her head perches a blue pillbox hat. Her most prominent feature, however, is her broad Scots accent, excellently supplied by Carole Shelley. Her laughter, like her humour, is raucous, and she is not averse to throwing her weight around, either for the sake of merriment, as when she produces her hilarious imitation of the Prince for the benefit of the children, or in fighting for the forces of good, as in the fiasco with which the tournament ends, during which she acts like an American-football player to scatter the Sheriff's soldiers like ninepins.

One cannot help liking Lady Kluck; she is the female equivalent of the lovable Little John. One must idly wonder, however, how it could be that a hen could survive for so long in such close proximity to a vixen . . .

Friar Tuck

The role of the badger Friar Tuck is very low-key. He first makes an impact on our consciousness when he is out giving some of Robin's takings to the poor – in this case to Otto the blacksmith. Unfortunately, he is pursued by the Sheriff, who promptly extorts the cash from Otto as taxes. Tuck tries to persuade the Sheriff to go easy on the old broken-legged hound, but his arguments are like water off a duck's back.

Tuck thereafter is shown as, really, the only other Merry Man in the movie aside from Little John (and Allan-a-Dale, but this latter is not really a part of the main action of the movie). His sole other major scene is when he and the two church mice are hoping against hope that a congregation will turn up for the evening service. When the Sheriff appears instead, and steals the last mite from the poor-box, it is all too much for Tuck, who loses his temper and beats the Sheriff with a stick. He is immediately arrested and dumped in Nottingham Prison. It is the possibility of his execution – a threat used by the baddies in an attempt to entrap Robin – that sets up the whole climactic sequence of the movie, with Robin and Little John releasing all the prisoners and, into the bargain, relieving Prince John of his hard-extorted gold.

It is surprising that more was not made of the character of Friar Tuck, who is, after all, a fairly major figure in the legends.

Allan-a-Dale

The red rooster Allan-a-Dale, voiced by Roger Miller (who also wrote three of the movie's five songs), is a good character but in a curious way cannot be thought of as a character *in the movie*: he is the narrator, and his role in the movie is restricted to lending his mandolin to Friar Tuck as an improvised bow with which to shoot down Sir Hiss, who is engaged on aerial reconnaissance at the tournament. The rooster is also one of the prisoners sprung from jail by Robin and Little John.

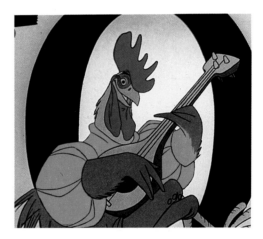

Allan-a-Dale, who narrated the movie as well as playing a small part in the on-screen action.

Allan's animated persona is fairly appealing, but it is his voice which "carries" him and indeed, debatably, the whole movie. This is true not just of his speaking voice but also of his singing voice, and of his songs themselves. The song "Not in Nottingham", while very short, is one of the most melodic and least contrived in the entire Disney canon; because of its simpleness, it can be hummed months after even a single viewing of the movie.

The Sheriff of Nottingham

Where Sir Hiss is a somewhat sinister villain and Prince John a rather psychopathic one, the Sheriff of Nottingham is almost a likeable fellow; he is rather like Little John, being big and lumbering, but just happens to be on the wrong side. He is not overloaded with intellect, but he has a certain lackwitted genial charm. He is, of course, a wolf, as are his soldiers (with the exception of the vultures Trigger and Nutsy). His hat – round, striped red and white, and with a blue-white plume – is much like Sir Hiss's. He has a US sheriff's

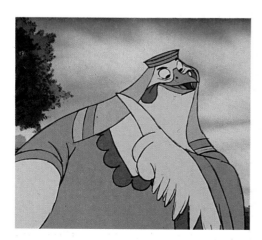

Lady Kluck, the movie's star comedy character.

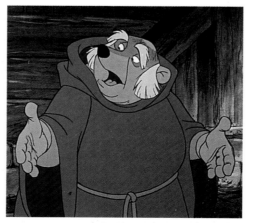

Friar Tuck found himself protesting his innocence.

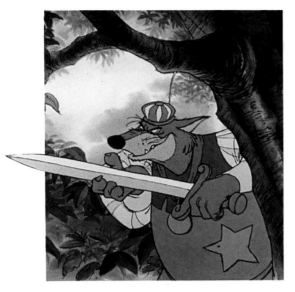

The Sheriff of Nottingham, looking vulpine in all directions. He seemed much too nice to be a villain.

star pinned to his belly – a witty little anachronism.

"Do de do do do," he hums to himself as he is out on his tax-collecting rounds. He is not actively malicious about his extortionate activities: so far as he is concerned it is all in a day's work, and he is really quite polite – although at the same time utterly ruthless – as he extracts cash from the needy:

Otto: Oh, oh, take it easy on me, Sheriff. What with this busted leg and all, you know, I'm way behind in me work, Sheriff.
Sheriff: I know, Otto, but you're way behind with your taxes, too.

And:

Sheriff: Well now, sonny, that box is done up right pretty, ain't it?
Skippy: Well, Mister Sheriff, s-sir, it's my birthday present, sir.
Sheriff: It sure is. Why don't you open it?
Skippy: Oh boy! One whole farthing!
Mother Rabbit: Have you no heart? We all scrimped and saved to give it to him.
Sheriff: Now that's mighty thoughty of ya, widder-woman. The family that saves together, pays together.

Moments later, when what he assumes to be a beggar (in fact, Robin) enters the house, he does the clever trick of tossing one coin into the beggar's cup with a sufficient flick that it and the other two coins there bounce out. The Sheriff pockets all three and goes on his way with a merry laugh.

The Sheriff's stupidity and general characteristic of indolent doltishness prove his downfall, of course. He falls asleep while he is supposed to be guarding Nottingham Jail, which allows Robin and Little John to clear out the prison as well as Prince John's coffers. Like the Prince and Sir Hiss, the Sheriff ends the movie and presumably his days slaving as a rock-breaker in the nearby quarry.

Trigger and Nutsy

These two vultures are personal guards/soldiers of the Sheriff of Nottingham, and they are about as safe and reliable as a Molotov cocktail. Nutsy's is very much a supporting role, but **Trigger** has a quite developed personality as a sort of militaristic psychopath eager to put a crossbow-bolt through someone – anyone – on the basis that, as a soldier, he is "allowed" to. In fact, because he has the nasty habit of keeping his crossbow, "Old Betsy", on a hair-trigger, his murderous efforts never come to much because he looses his bolt long before the appropriate moment, usually creating

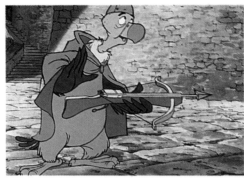

Trigger, ever ready.

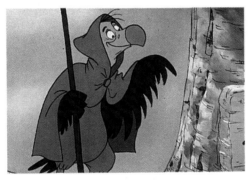

Nutsy was a rather more simpatico vulture than Trigger, for some indefinable reason.

havoc among the members of his own side as it ricochets hither and thither.

Nutsy's chief feature is his stupidity, as revealed in a lovely exchange when the three are guarding the jail:

Nutsy: One o'clock and all's well!
Sheriff (seeing that clock says it is three): Nutsy, you'd better set your brains ahead a couple of hours.
Nutsy: Yes, sir. Ah . . . does that mean addin' or er . . . subtractin'?
Sheriff: Oh, let's forget it.
Nutsy: Yes, sir, Sheriff, sir.

The Rabbit Family

There are four noteworthy members of the rabbit family – **Mother Rabbit**, **Sis** (a daughter rabbit), **Tagalong** (a small toddler daughter) and especially **Skippy** (the son of the house).

Mother Rabbit is a widow, and desperately poor, but generous with what little she has – she willingly welcomes to the house a blind beggar (who proves, of course, to be Robin) and she scrimps and saves so that Skippy will have a farthing for his birthday. She wears spectacles and a red head-shawl, and clearly cannot have been widowed for more than a few years, for Tagalong is very young indeed. Her voice is a sort of Deep South drawl, which is odd – why not have given her an English accent? – but in fact it does not seem out of place.

Sis and Tagalong are really there only to bump up the number of the little group of children, but Skippy, physically and temperamentally reminiscent of *Bambi*'s Thumper (➤201), is a charater of some note. "Seven years old, goin' on eight," he clearly is fixated on Robin, with whom he identifies strongly, so that his birthday gift of a Robin Hood hat and a bow-and-arrow could hardly have been better tailored.

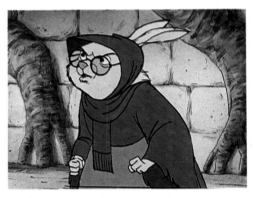

Mother Rabbit, angry at the Sherriff for appropriating her son Skippy's birthday money.

From that point onward he attempts to emulate his hero at every turn. During the final battle in the prison courtyard he is at work with his bow, as is Robin; every time the latter carries off some incredible feat of archery, however, it is Skippy who gives himself the credit. Well, since he has little idea where his own arrows are going, for all he knows those other ones could indeed be his!

Toby Turtle

Toby is a friend of Skippy and his sisters, and forms part of the quartet of children who travel around town adding their comments to the general activity. He is rather like Toby Tortoise (➤73) but even more like the little tortoise who plays such a hilarious role in *Snow White* (➤166).

Toby is rather shy. He has thick-rimmed spectacles behind which his terrified eyes blink nervously as he views with horror the recklessness of his friends, especially Skippy. At moments of high panic he withdraws his head into his shell, from which one can hear his voice echoing its remonstrances and reproaches. Clearly the others do not entirely trust his courage:

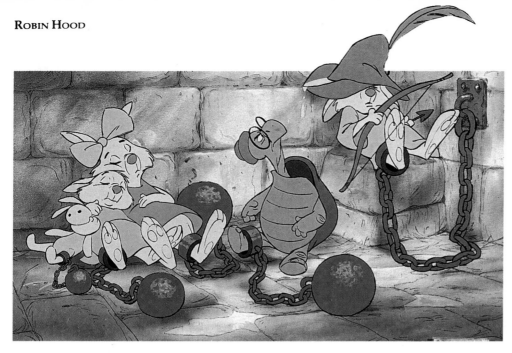

Toby Turtle showing how much he enjoys prison; Skippy Bunny is on the right and Sister Bunny and Tagalong are on the left.

Sis: Wait a minute. Toby might tattle on you.
Skippy: Yeah, Toby, you gotta take the oath.
Toby: An oath?
Tagalong: Put your hand on your heart and cross your eyes.
Skippy: Spiders, snakes and a lizard's head . . .
Toby: Spiders, snakes and a lizard's head . . .
Skippy: If I tattle-tale I'll die till I'm dead.
Toby: If I tattle-tale I'll die till I'm dead.

His father, **Mr. Turtle**, makes a brief appearance as one of the competitors in the archery contest – which, of course, rather divides Toby's loyalties.

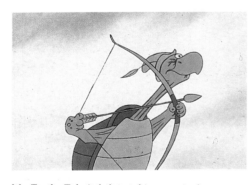

Mr. Turtle, Toby's father, taking part in the great archery contest.

Mother Mouse and the Church Mouse

These two characters make a brief appearance at the forest party – Mother Mouse jumps up and down on Tuck's head to Little John's rendition of "The Phony King of England" – but their important role is in the scene where Friar Tuck is tolling the church-bell and hoping that a congregation might appear.

The **Church Mouse** (also known as the **Sexton Mouse**) plays the organ, which is no mean feat, it being rather a big organ and he being rather a small mouse. **Mother Mouse** is house-proud – we see her sweeping the "Welcome" mat in front of their mousehole

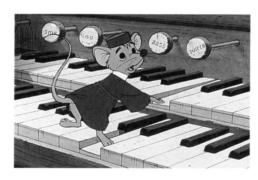

The Church Mouse made the foolish mistake of defying the Sheriff of Nottingham.

– and, while as impoverished as most of the rest of the population of Nottingham, is like Mother Rabbit generous with what little she has. When Friar Tuck discovers that the poor-box is, like his church, totally empty she hesitates hardly a moment before running to the mice's bed, lifting up the mattress, and producing the solitary farthing they have been able to put by. As Friar Tuck puts it: "Your last farthing? Ahhhhh, little sister, no one can give more than that. Bless you both."

Both of the mice are as bellicose as Friar Tuck when the Sheriff drops by promptly to remove the farthing as Prince John's due. Unfortunately, being small, they can do little to manifest their bellicosity; even more unfortunately, despite their impotence,

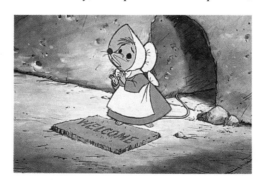

The Mother Mouse.

they share the good Friar's fate, being in due course hauled off to jail.

Otto

Otto is a rather versatile but lugubrious hound-dog. He features first as the broken-legged blacksmith (assuming the leg really *is* broken) whose donation from Robin Hood is speedily appropriated by the Sheriff, who cunningly recognizes that the plastercast on Otto's leg is a useful repository for hidden coins. Later Otto keeps popping up in minor parts, notably as the balloon-seller

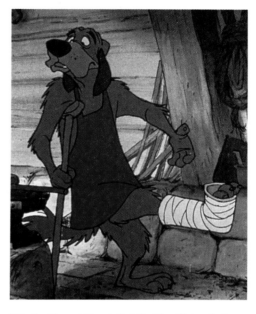

Otto the Hound Dog defied the Sheriff, too, but with rather less style.

at the archery tournament. Perhaps surprisingly, he even consents to sell Sir Hiss a balloon, with which that unworthy proceeds to conduct his aerial survey of the crowds, hunting for a sight of Robin.

Minor Characters

For a minor feature *Robin Hood* has an astonishing number of characters. In addition to the ones mentioned above there are several other distinct characters with

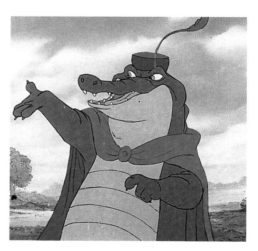

The Crocodile, announcer at the archery contest.

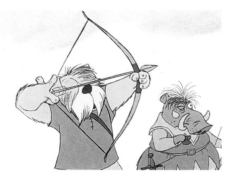

The Sheep Dog was one of the contestants at the archery contest.

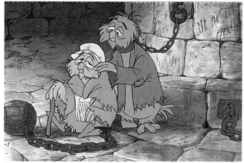

Grandma and Grandpa Owl, two of the prisoners whom Robin and Little John released.

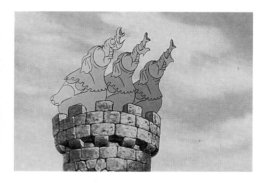

Three of the elephants who served as Prince John's trumpeters.

minuscule roles. These include the **Crocodile** who acts as the announcer at the archery tournament; the **Country Dog** and the **Sheep Dog**, who are contestants in the tournament; and **Grandma and Grandpa Owl**, who are among the prisoners released from jail by Robin and Little John. Also, there is a plethora of unnamed animals: the rhinoceroses who act as guards, the wolves who are the Sheriff's soldiers, and the elephants who appear as trumpeters to produce apposite fanfares.

THE RESCUERS

Characters:

Penny; Bianca; Bernard; Rufus; Madame Medusa; Mr. Snoops; Nero; Brutus; Orville; Evinrude; Luke; Ellie Mae; Deacon; Deadeye; Digger; Gramps; Chairman; Doorman; Mouse delegates; Human delegates; Mouse Scouts; T.V. Interviewer; Adoptive mother; Adoptive father; Orphans; Bats; Beachcomber mice

Credits:

Based on *The Rescuers* (1959) and *Miss Bianca* (1962) by Margery Sharp

Voices: Bob Newhart (Bernard); Eva Gabor (Bianca); Geraldine Page (Madame Medusa); Joe Flynn (Mr. Snoops); Jeanette Nolan (Ellie Mae); Pat Buttram (Luke); Jim Jordan (Orville); John McIntire (Rufus); Michelle Stacy (Penny); Bernard Fox (Chairman); Larry Clemmons (Gramps); James Macdonald (Evinrude); George Lindsey (Deadeye); Bill McMillan (TV Announcer); Dub Taylor (Digger); John Fiedler (Deacon)

Sound: Herb Taylor

Music Score Composed and Conducted by: Artie Butler

Music Editor: Evelyn Kennedy

Songs by: Carol Connors; Ayn Robbins; Sammy Fain; Robert Crawford

Story: Larry Clemmons; Ken Anderson; Frank Thomas; Vance Gerry; David Michener; Ted Berman; Fred Lucky; Burny Mattinson; Dick Sebast

Art Director: Don Griffith

Backgrounds: Jim Coleman; Ann Guenther; Daniela Bielecka

Layout: Joe Hale; Guy Deel; Tom Lay; Sylvia Roemer

Colour Styling: Al Dempster

Titles: Melvin Shaw; Eric Larson; Burny Mattinson

Directing Animators: Ollie Johnston; Milt Kahl; Frank Thomas; Don Bluth

Character Animation: John Pomeroy; Cliff Nordberg; Andy Gaskill; Gary Goldman; Art Stevens; Dale Baer; Chuck Harvey; Ron Clements; Bob McCrea; Bill Hajee; Glen Keane

Effects Animation: Jack Buckley; Ted Kierscey; Dorse A. Lanpher; James L. George; Dick Lucas

Key Assistant Animators: Stan Green; Dale Oliver; Chuck Williams; Harry Hester; Walt Stanchfield; Dave Suding; Leroy Cross

Production Manager: Don Duckwall

Editors: James Melton; Jim Koford

Assistant Directors: Jeff Patch; Richard Rich

Directors: Wolfgang Reitherman; John Lounsbery; Art Stevens

Executive Producer: Ron Miller

Producer: Wolfgang Reitherman

Release Date: June 22, 1977

Running Time: 77 minutes

THE MOVIE

The Rescuers is a transitional movie; it marks the transition between the old school of Disney animators and the new. While several of the Nine Old Men played important roles in the movie's genesis, the list of animation credits reflects the great influx of new talent which the Disney studio had first discovered and then nurtured. Shortly after the movie's completion, Frank Thomas, Ollie Johnston and Milt Kahl retired; Wolfgang Reitherman retired in 1980, three years later; and John Lounsbery died in 1976, a few months before *The Rescuers* was released. Many of the new generation of Disney animators,

trained under the direct supervision of Eric Larson, made their debuts in *The Rescuers* and went on to take charge of later features.

It would be wrong to describe *The Rescuers* as more than a modest feature. Probably for exactly this reason, it was received warmly by the critics (and did brisk business at the box office): Disney had set itself modest objectives, and these it had triumphantly achieved. Sadly, it seems that reviewers generally prefer the safe and successful to the adventurous but flawed. There was almost certainly another reason for the plaudits. Since *One Hundred and One Dalmatians* (1961) the Disney full-length animated features had not maintained a very distinguished run by the company's own standards. *The Sword in the Stone* (1963) had been regarded universally as a "flat" viewing experience; *The Jungle Book* (1967) had had its charms, but was somewhat lightweight and poorly constructed; and *Robin Hood* (1973) had been probably the least satisfactory of all Disney full-length animated features. Only *The Aristocats* (1970) stood out (in the opinion of this writer), and even that had been panned in many quarters as being too much like a feline rehash of *One Hundred and One Dalmatians*. (Strangely, *The Rescuers*, which has just as many similarities with *One Hundred and One Dalmatians*, largely avoided this criticism.) In such a context, *The Rescuers* was a welcome reassurance that the Disney magic was still there.

No one loses their temper over this movie. No one hates it bitterly; no one adores it above all others. It is quiet and noncontroversial. In this respect, as with the "changing of the guard" of the animators, it can be regarded as a turning-point. Disney *had* to do something to change direction: there was no future in churning out more *Robin Hood*s and hoping for the best. But before such a branching-out could take place there needed to be a time of consolidation, and this *The Rescuers* represented. It is a competent, well crafted movie which provides a lot of fun for all the family. If we expect anything more of it we will be disappointed. Gone is the practice of basing animated characters exclusively on the personae of the actors who voiced them (with the possible exception of Bianca – see below); gone are the intrusive songs which disrupted the main action of *The Jungle Book* and *Robin Hood*. In their place are strong, freshly created characters and a well plotted script (the story-men, led by Larry Clemmons, took over a year to carve the script from Margery Sharp's two popular children's books).

This matter of the characters is important. It will be gathered from the brief synopsis of the movie given below that, while the plotting is tight, the story is not the most important element of *The Rescuers*. However, while one is watching the movie, this deficiency goes largely unnoticed. This is because *The Rescuers* contains a generous helping of some of the best and brightest animated characters to have appeared in a Disney movie for some while. Walt himself might have strengthened the story-line, but he would have been more than content with the characterization. Moreover, after *The Rescuers* this trend was to be continued: the three Disney full-length animated features released so far during the 1980s (*The Fox and the Hound*, *The Black Cauldron* and *The Great Mouse Detective*) have all featured excellent and memorable characters. For that we have to thank a humble, unambitious little movie: *The Rescuers*.

THE STORY

Once upon a time a bottle bearing an urgent message floats into New York Harbor, where it is discovered by two beachcomber mice, who pass it to the International Rescue Aid Society. They take it to the basement of the UN Building, where an assembly of mice from all around the world is meeting. The note reads: "To Morningside Orphanage, New York. I am in terrible, terrible trouble. Hurry. Help! – Penny." A little girl in trouble? – time for the Disney treatment.

An adventurous, albeit chic, little mouse called Bianca volunteers to follow up the case, and she selects Bernard, a shy janitor, to be her partner in sleuthery. Shy he may be, but he is capable of feigning sufficient bravery to lead Bianca to the orphanage, where the pair of them search for clues. They come upon a box containing Penny's meagre possessions.

They also meet Rufus, a philosophical old cat, who says that Penny was upset because no one wanted to adopt her. He suspects that she has run away, but adds that an evil woman who runs a pawnshop tried to give Penny a ride in her car just before the girl's disappearance. Armed with this clue, the two mice scurry round to Madame Medusa's Pawn Shop Boutique, where they find one of Penny's schoolbooks and overhear Madame Medusa herself on the telephone talking about the girl, and raging over the fact that Penny has found the chance to send messages in bottles. Medusa refers also to a place called Devil's Bayou. When Medusa drives off through New York in a frenzy, heading for the airport to catch a plane for Devil's Bayou, Bernard is hiding inside her suitcase and Bianca is desperately clutching a dangling garter-belt on its outside; she has just about reached the safety of the suitcase with Bernard when it is thrown from the car as Medusa lurches on her reckless way.

The two mice pause to pack a few bits and pieces and look for their own transportation. It is Albatross Air Charter Service to the rescue – in the shape of its proprietor, pilot, and indeed sole aircraft, Orville, a large, superficially grumpy but fundamentally genial albatross. Bianca and Bernard climb aboard an empty sardine can strapped to his back, and soon they are aloft and bound for Devil's Bayou.

They arrive at this malodorous spot at dawn. However, Penny has escaped from her evil captors, who are using flares in their attempts to recapture her. One of these singes Orville's tail ("Suffering sassafras! My rudder's on fire! ... Mayday! Mayday!") and the two mice are forced to bail out on an umbrella, leaving the unfortunate bird to crash-land.

Down at ground-level, Bianca and Bernard are helped by two muskrats, Ellie Mae and Luke. Orville departs skywards, having first come off worst in an encounter with the exhaust of Madame Medusa's flame-spitting "swampmobile" (a vehicle that is distinctly less hi-tech than it sounds). The two mice, plus Ellie Mae and Luke, can do no more than watch as Madame Medusa's two pet crocodiles, Nero and Brutus, seize the fugitive orphan and her beloved teddy-bear and carry them back to their wicked mistress's lair, an old grounded riverboat. Bianca and Bernard, in quivering pursuit, hitch a ride on a leaf-boat propelled across the swamp by a dragonfly called Evinrude.

When they reach Madame Medusa's hideout, having survived stormy waters generated by the thrashing of the crocodiles' tails, they hear her and her bumbling accomplice, Mr. Snoops, discussing how they can force Penny to recover a fabulous diamond called the Devil's Eye from a nearby cave where it was long ago stashed by a pirate. Only a person as small as Penny would be able to get in through the cave's narrow opening to retrieve the gem.

After being chased around the houseboat by the crocs (who are attracted by Bianca's perfume), and then by Medusa and Mr. Snoops, the two intrepid mice despatch Evinrude to seek reinforcements among the swamp animals. Then Bianca and Bernard sneak into Penny's room, introduce themselves and tell her of their plan to effect her escape. In order to remove the crocodiles from the scene, Bernard will lure them into the elevator using sensual wafts of Bianca's perfume, and then ... but just then Madame Medusa charges out of her room and informs Mr. Snoops that they will carry the girl to the cave at once in order to take advantage of the low tide. The escape plan has to be abandoned for the while.

Bianca and Bernard slip into Penny's pocket and the three of them are lowered in a bucket into the cave. Once inside, they frantically search for the diamond as the tide begins to rise at a terrifying rate. At the last possible moment the gleaming diamond is found – embedded in a skull. Penny prises it from its socket using a rusty old sword she has found. She and the mice scamper back to the bucket and are hauled up just in the nick of time, as water floods the cave.

Exultant with greed, Madame Medusa clutches the Devil's Eye to herself, allowing even Mr. Snoops only the briefest of glimpses at it. She makes it plain to him that it would be almost blasphemy to divide a gem of this calibre into two parts, and so, since only one of the two conspirators may have it ... A fierce argument breaks out.

Evinrude, having survived a scarifying pursuit by some hungry bats, has made his way to the home of Luke and Ellie Mae. Here he finds a gathering of swamp creatures, who determine to attack Madame Medusa's boat. However, during the assault, Madame Medusa holds Penny and Mr. Snoops at gunpoint and prepares to flee, with the diamond concealed inside Penny's teddy-bear. However, Bernard and Bianca trip her up using a piece of string stretched across a doorway.

Almost needless to say, chaos ensues. Mr. Snoops' flares light the night sky and his explosives rip the eardrums of animated characters and cinema audiences alike: not since the Fall of the House of Usher, etc. Penny grabs her teddy-bear, complete with hidden contents, under cover of the distractions of exploding gunpowder and attacking river creatures, and she, the mice, and the swamp creatures make their escape aboard Madame Medusa's jet-powered swampmobile. Behind them the tormented riverboat cracks apart and settles into the mud of Devil's Bayou.

The stage is set for a happy ending and the tantalizing hint of a sequel, and these are exactly what the audience receives.

Back at the UN Building, the assembled mice watch a (human) television newscast in which Penny receives warm plaudits for having found the world's largest diamond and for her generosity in having decided to donate it to a museum. The happy little girl has been adopted by loving "parents". During the interview she makes a point of thanking her mice friends for having made it all possible – much to the puzzlement of the TV reporter and of millions of viewers.

As the newscast ends, Evinrude the dragonfly suddenly appears among the mice in the basement: someone else needs help, fast! Before Bernard can escape, Bianca has offered his services and her own. After the customarily chaotic attempt at takeoff by Orville the albatross, the two mice and the insect, aboard the bird, fly off to seek further adventures in pastures new.

THE CHARACTERS

Penny

The later Disney canon is full of examples of boys who, while in theory the lead character of a feature, are in fact depicted as a sort of "everyboy" personality: Wart and Taran are the obvious examples. Clearly Disney has discovered the effectiveness of having comparatively bland central characters as a sort of counterpoint to the zaniness of the more minor ones. In *The Rescuers* the same principle is applied, although there are some differences. First, Penny is a girl rather than a boy and, while it is unfortunate that this should be the case, the Western psyche is such that we find it less surprising that a girl should require assistance, in terms both of plot and of character, than that a boy should. (In *The Black Cauldron*, a few years later, Eilonwy was deliciously – and characteristically – to turn the tables in this respect.) Second, and rather more important, Penny is *not* the lead character: hers is a supporting role. She is the *raison d'être* of the entire plot, its lynchpin, but aside from that she contributes virtually nothing to it.

Penny is an attractive child, although perhaps a little too cute (especially in her voice). She has light brown hair, and her blue eyes are matched by her blue-grey tunic and light blue blouse. Her blondish hair is tied in a short bunch at the back. She

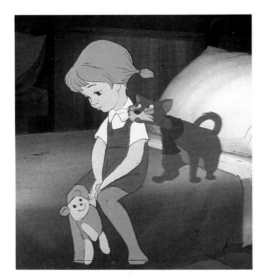

Penny, moping about her unhappy lot with her teddy and her chum, Rufus.

clutches a battered teddy-bear as a symbol of the friendship she lacks. Yet, like so many attractive people, she is convinced of her own unattractiveness. Take the flashback scene which Rufus the cat describes to Bianca and Bernard:

Rufus: What's wrong, Penny, honey?
Penny: Nothing.
Rufus: Oh, come on, now. Come on, no secrets. You tell old Rufus. Huh?
Penny: Well, it was adoption day at the orphanage.
Rufus: What, what happened?
Penny: A man and a lady came and looked at me, but they chose [*sic*] a little red-headed girl. She was prettier than me.
Rufus: Oh, she couldn't be. You just listen to me, darlin' ... you're somethin' extra special.
Penny: No, I'm not.

In due course Rufus manages to inspire some optimism in her (see below), but much later Madame Medusa deliberately plays upon, and reinforces, Penny's lack of self-esteem:

Medusa: Penny, don't you like it here? A big, beautiful boat all to yourself.
Penny: But if I don't get back to the orphanage, I'll never get 'dopted.
Medusa: Adopted? What makes you think anyone would want a homely little girl like you?

Penny's attachment to her teddy-bear is so powerful that it almost enters the field of clinical psychiatry – although, in the circumstances, perhaps it is understandable. When she is being put by Medusa and Mr. Snoops into the "black hole" leading to the treasure cave, Medusa claims the teddy and viciously refuses to allow Penny to take it with her. Mr. Snoops says to Medusa, "Boss, you've really got a way with kids," and the audience laughs. But of course Medusa really *does* understand the psychology of this particular child: Penny will do anything to save her stuffed toy, her only long-time friend.

Of course, it is this attachment to the teddy that proves Medusa's downfall, for when Penny escapes with the others she naturally takes her teddy, within the stuffing of which the villainess has hidden the Devil's Eye.

Bianca and Bernard

Whenever a Disney feature stars mice one looks for similarities between these new characters and a certain earlier Mouse. Always, of course, one looks in vain – and nowhere more so than in the figures of Bianca and Bernard. Frank Thomas summed this up when he said that

they are different from any mice we've done before. They have a different relationship, new personalities. One is Bob Newhart, and Eva Gabor is the other.

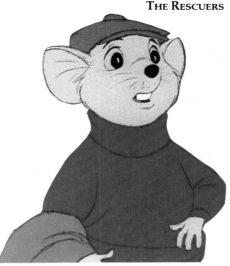

Bernard, who, though despite being reticent, proved to be a courageous rescuer.

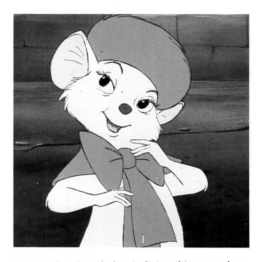

Bianca, who, though despite being chic, proved to be a courageous rescuer.

When Thomas said that the two mice were Eva Gabor and Bob Newhart, he was of course referring to the two voice actors who played the parts. However, in the case of Bianca, the Mata Hari of the mouse world, we can go further than that: she *is* Eva Gabor – or, to be more accurate, she is Gabor's screen persona. Her country of origin is not specified in the movie, her accent being a sort of all-purpose European one; but her fashion consciousness and general elegant chic are frequently stressed. For example, when the two heroes have climbed into the sardine can on top of Orville's back, ready for flight, Bernard says of her seatbelt: "Ah, Miss Bianca, be sure it's fastened good and tight." Gabor's – sorry, Bianca's – response is: "I *can't*. It'll wrinkle my dress!"

One aspect of her well groomed beauty plays an important part in the plot: her no doubt extremely expensive perfume. We do not know if this magical stuff works wonders on lounge lizards, but it has a potent effect on bayou lizards, in the shape of the two crocs. Medusa's toothy pets first locate the mice aboard the houseboat because of Bianca's perfume; later, while plotting Penny's escape, the mice plan to lure the crocs away from the action by enticing them into an elevator with the scent; and finally, during the battle on the houseboat, this plan is put into effect – and works.

Yet, for all her airs and graces, Bianca is unafraid of danger. Whether this is due to straightforward courage is a matter open to some doubt: it seems more likely that Bianca is one of those individuals who simply *assume* that, no matter how parlous the situation, they will emerge unscathed and all will be well.

This is a fine philosophy – until the first time it fails – but it does not make it easy to be Bianca's companion-in-arms, as Bernard soon discovers. For Bernard, the janitor of the mouse version of the UN, is very definitely Burns' "wee, sleekit, cow'rin', tim'rous beastie". He makes no pretence to be a professional agent like Bianca – indeed, he steadfastly retains his janitor's cap throughout – and it is only *in extremis* that his otherwise hidden reserves of courage bubble to the surface.

Bernard is very superstitious – at least insofar as the number 13 is concerned. When the mice decide to extract Penny's note from the bottle, early on in the film, it is the shy janitor, Bernard, who is deputed to perform the task. In order to climb up to the bottle's neck, he uses a battered old comb as a ladder. His reluctance is obvious: "Sir, ah, there's thirteen steps on this ladder." Later, at the airport, as he and Bianca prepare to fly aboard Orville to Devil's Bayou, we have:

> *Speaker Voice*: Albatross Flight Thirteen to tower. Albatross ...
> *Bianca*: Now, what did I tell you? We are lucky, Mr. Bernard.
> *Bernard*: Lucky? Flight Thirteen?

A few minutes later, after Orville has executed the most spectacularly bad landing of all time, preparatory to taking the two mice aboard, Bernard discovers to his horror that there are 13 steps on the boarding ladder. Bianca's response to his panic-stricken triskaidekaphobia is heartless: she laughs and says, "Why don't you jump the last one?" It is useless for Bernard to protest that that *wouldn't be the same*. Of course, whatever our views on superstition, we have to sympathize with Bernard's fears: that landing of Orville's really *was* dramatically bad. As they move uncertainly across the sky, Bernard speaks for all of us when he says: "Sure wish we'd a-taken the train."

Both Bianca and Bernard are white; and both are curiously "unmouselike". They have the full complement of tail, whiskers, snout, mouse-ears and so forth, yet they act like human beings in all ways. In the case of Bianca this is obviously because her character is so imbued with that of Eva Gabor; but Bob Newhart's voicing does not "take over" Bernard in the same way (perhaps because Newhart is capable of a wider variety of roles on screen). Clearly Disney could have opted for two mouselike mice or two humanlike mice, but not one of each. It seems likely that the character of Bianca, moulded on Gabor, was so appealing that the studio adopted the anthropomorphic approach. In this Disney was almost certainly right.

Rufus

Rufus, the elderly cat encountered by Bianca and Bernard at the orphanage, is a brilliant creation. His is only a minor part, yet it is memorable one – and he steals the movie's "pathos" scene. His role is rather like that of a Blue Fairy (➤176) or a Fairy Godmother (➤238), but without any of the magical abilities to make things come right – indeed, without any powers to alter the course of events at all. His only function within the plot is to give the two mouse

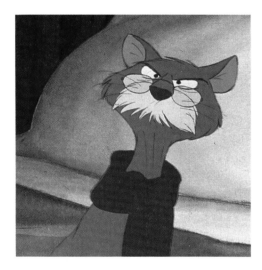

Rufus, the elderly cat who put Bianca and Bernard on Penny's trail.

detectives the clue about Madame Medusa and the sleazy pawn shop; his flashback scene with Penny is quite gratuitous. But it works – partly because of the animation, by Ollie Johnston, and certainly because of the voicing, by John McIntire. But we should not forget the script ...

> *Rufus*: Why, some day a mama and a papa will come to the orphanage, a-lookin' for a pretty little girl just like you.
> *Penny*: Honest?
> *Rufus*: I'll bet my whiskers on it. But you got to believe ... keep the faith, sweetheart. You see that bluebird?
> *Penny* Yes, I do.
> *Rufus*: Well, faith is a bluebird you see from afar. It's for real and as sure as the first evening star. You can't touch it or buy it or wrap it up tight, but it's there just the same, making things turn out right.
> *Penny*: "Can't touch it or buy it or wrap it up tight, but it's there just the same, making things turn out right." ... But whoever adopts me has to adopt Teddy, too!
> *Rufus*: Oh, they'll love him. He doesn't eat much, does he?

And then Penny produces some gingersnaps for her elderly friend. If there is a dry eye left in the house, well, it is not the fault of Larry Clemmons and his team.

Rufus, like the mice, is a human in animal disguise. He wears a red scarf around his long brown neck, and a pair of thin-rimmed spectacles on the end of his nose. To cap it all, he has a generously bushy white moustache. A couple more human traits and he'd be allowed to vote – he's certainly old enough.

Madame Medusa

Inevitably, *The Rescuers* was compared with *One Hundred and One Dalmatians*, and, equally inevitably, Madame Medusa (animated by Milt Kahl) was compared with Cruella De Vil ([➤267] animated by Marc Davis). At the time, these comparisons were generally favorable ones, but now that a little time has passed it is difficult to be so sure. It would be irrelevant to play the two movies off against each other here; but it is certainly relevant to compare the two villainesses.

Both are sophisticated types: you have met – or dodged – both of them at countless cocktail parties. They have aristocratic voices and overbearing personalities; and are always convinced of their own *rightness*. Everything they do is by definition right; everything done by anyone else on their behalf is by definition wrong. This latter half of the equation is usually borne out, of course, because both have dimwitted, bumbling sidekicks (Jasper and Horace for Cruella, Mr. Snoops for Medusa). Both plan

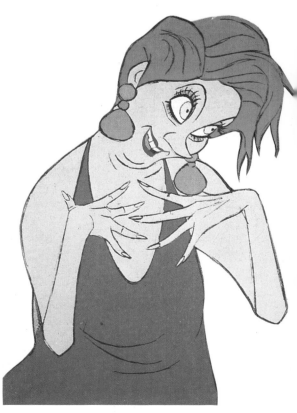

Madame Medusa, looking as lovable as ever.

to be cruel to the young, whether it be puppies or a little girl; and both are monomaniacal and thoroughly avaricious. Note, though, that in both cases this greed is not for money but for *objects* (fur coats or a diamond). Both fly into fanatical rages when thwarted. Finally, although the list of comparisons could be continued, both of them wear their evil on their sleeves: they *look* the part.

Yet ... yet Cruella is much the *more* evil of the two. Her flamboyantly malevolent presence is enough to chill the spine of anyone with a shred of sensitivity, whereas Madame Medusa is as likely to inspire a giggle as a shudder. Moreover, Medusa's planned cruelty is not as ruthless as Cruella's. To be sure, Medusa shows little concern as to Penny's survival (except insofar as it would cause difficulties were Penny to perish before retrieving the diamond), but this is not active malice – and is certainly not cruelty on the scale of skinning 99 puppies. Even though Medusa is prepared to blast Mr. Snoops and Penny (and Penny's teddy!) with her automatic shotgun, she is still not especially scarifying. No child wakes up with nightmares after watching *The Rescuers*.

But she does have her chilling moments. The critic John Culhane, who was more intimately involved in the movie than one might expect (see below), recorded one of these in his excellent article on *The Rescuers*:

> ... the scene in which Mme Medusa takes off her makeup while plotting child abuse. The way that Milt Kahl accents Geraldine Page's [the voice artist's] fruity, cruel voice by making her tug extra hard at her false eyelash until her eyelid snaps back like a rubber band is like a drawing from Daumier's *Sketches of Expression* series – but in movement!

This sort of highlight is, of course, a product of Kahl's genius at animation. But there was a limit to what he could do with the character and image of Medusa with which he had to work. In terms of appearance alone, Madame Medusa looks more like someone dressed up as a villainess than like the genuine, 24-carat article. She has eye-stingingly bright red lipstick and a coif of thick hair of similar hue, green eyes surrounded by a quart or two of blue eye-liner, a pointed retroussé nose, and vast greenish baubles as earrings. She is spiteful towards everyone and everything around her except her two crocodiles, Nero and Brutus (who, if the truth be told, display rather more of the human virtues than she does). In particular, she is spiteful towards Penny: even though on occasion she attempts to coax the child with synthetic kindness, she is never able to keep the act up for long. An exchange with Mr. Snoops outlines her attitude towards child-rearing:

> *Snoops*: She won't take orders.
> *Medusa*: You are too soft.

> *Snoops*: But the water was rising, and the tide was coming in, and all she did down there was fuss about her teddy-bear getting wet.
> *Medusa*: Snoops, you don't have a way with children. You must gain their confidence, *make* them like you.
> *Snoops*: Yeah? How do you do that?
> *Medusa*: You *force* them to like you, idiot!

Her monomania is as self-pervading as it is irrational: she wants that big diamond and she wants it totally – as Penny explains to Bianca and Bernard as they explore the treasure-cave, little diamonds have just been left where they lie because Madame Medusa isn't interested in them. Nothing but the Devil's Eye will do. In the end, of course, like so many monomaniacs who will never settle for anything less than the object of their desires, Madame Medusa ends up with nothing.

Mr. Snoops

Leonard Maltin, in his definitive book on the Disney movies, has said in praise of the animal characters in *The Rescuers* that so many of them "are *pure cartoon creations*, not mere imitations of live actors on screen" (his italics). This is very true. However, one of the *human* characters in the movie is very definitely based on a live human being, although not an actor. That character is the dimwitted Mr. Snoops, Medusa's luckless sidekick, and the person upon whom he was based was the critic John Culhane. According to Culhane's account in the *New York Times* in August 1976, he was visiting the Disney lot when he realized that the animators were taking a more than usual interest in him. The end result, as he proudly stated, was the character of Mr. Snoops. A glance at a photograph of Culhane would seem to confirm the story!

Why Culhane should be so proud of this, though, is anyone's guess, for Mr. Snoops is no Adonis. He has untidy red-brown hair that looks more as if it has been deposited on his head than grown there; he has large, round, thin-rimmed glasses and an equally large, round girth. His clothes are baggy and rumpled, which is probably just as well because that way they disguise his figure.

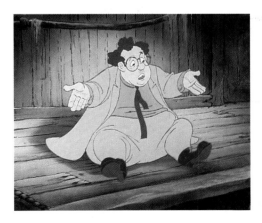

Mr. Snoops was Madame Medusa's accomplice and her downfall.

Mr. Snoops may be a dimwit, but he is also a sort of low-order technocrat. He places much reliance on his arsenal of flares and fireworks – on gadgetry, in fact. These contribute to the downfall of himself and Madame Medusa, as the houseboat is disrupted by countless explosions towards the end of the movie. (If Disney intended to draw a moral here, it is lost in the movie's overall geniality. However, it is interesting to note that the villains employ analogues of the two most sinister types of weapons possessed by the world's powers today. Mr. Snoops employs missiles, in the form of rockets, while Medusa opts for biological agents, in the form of Nero and Brutus.)

We suspect that Mr. Snoops has a heart of gold – he would hardly fit the stereotype for a Disney villain's sidekick if he had not – but there is little evidence of it in the movie. Superficially he has some concern for the welfare of Penny, and certainly he displays no iron-willed ruthlessness *à la* Madame Medusa. Yet in a curious way he is worse: he essentially *forgets* about Penny's misery and/or peril when it is not manifest there in front of him. This is a very childish trait, of course – a child will cosset a pet adoringly, and then forget about it for a fortnight so that it starves to death – but for all that it is an unpleasant one. And, let us make no mistake about it, Mr. Snoops is as much of an out-and-out crook as is Madame Medusa. Consider their "discussion" of the Devil's Eye:

> *Snoops*: All yours? Why, half of it is mine, you double-crossing crook! [Moments later:] Double-crosser!
> *Medusa*: Cheap pickpocket!
> *Snoops*: Chiseler!
> *Medusa*: Oh, cheap crook!

Meanwhile, Penny is struggling not to fall back down into the black waters of the pirates' cave – but Mr. Snoops has forgotten her completely.

Nero and Brutus

Madame Medusa's two pet crocodiles are largely indistinguishable from each other: they are massive, and solid, and the watcher just *knows* they are heavy. Neither is the type of crocodile you want to meet up a dark alley, yet Nero and Brutus are not especially terrifying. Indeed, their viciousness is kept under very strict control. For example, when they retrieve Penny and her teddy-bear from the swamp, they carry the two back to the houseboat in their mouths, yet there is never the slightest feeling that one or other of the crocs might, well, accidentally have an early supper.

And they are not brainless, either. When Bianca and Bernard have boarded the houseboat, and Bianca's scent has betrayed her presence to the crocodiles, there is a marvellous sequence in which the two mice take shelter in a pipe-organ. One of the crocs plays thunderous chords on the

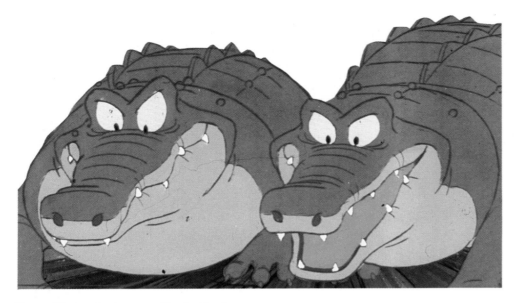

Nero and Brutus, the two crocodiles, looking for supper.

keyboard, and this has the effect of blasting the two mice – singly or together – into the air above the pipes, where the other croc makes futile attempts to snap them up. Each shave is closer than the last for Bianca and Bernard, and surely they would fail to survive were it not for the fact that Madame Medusa becomes fed up with the noise and crossly forces her pets to desist.

Orville

Ollie Johnston was the primary animator for Orville the albatross, the grumpy proprietor and total flying strength of the Albatross Air Charter Service. Like Rufus, also the responsibility of Johnston, Orville plays only a supporting role, yet his performance is a memorable one: it is significant that virtually every still one sees reproduced from the movie features this accident-prone aviator.

Orville's performance is divided into two separate sections: first, and more important, the sequences during which he conveys an eager Bianca and a distinctly unwilling Bernard to Devil's Bayou; and, second, the sequence in the closing moments of the movie when he takes the two colleagues

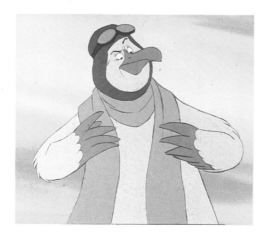

Orville, of Albatross Air Charter Service: proprietor, pilot and craft.

plus Evinrude off into the skies towards a further, and unspecified, adventure.

As noted above (➤300) Bernard is terrified of the prospect of flying aboard Orville. In this he is justified. Leaving aside the little janitor's superstition (it is Flight 13, and there are 13 steps on Orville's boarding ramp), there is the small matter of Bernard's – and our – first experience of Orville's aviationary abilities. This is when the two mice see Orville coming in to land. There is an old light-aircraft saying that any landing is a good one so long as you can walk away from it, and clearly Orville subscribes to this view: he impacts on the runway face-first, bounces about, and then brakes to a halt using his face once more. Bernard rushes up to the albatross, who is humming "Wild Blue Yonder" while brushing himself off.

> *Bernard*: I, ah … are you … are you hurt, sir?
> *Orville*: Nope. One of my better landings, bud.
> *Bernard*: Oh, great. Come on, we're gonna take the train. Play it safe.

Bianca, however, overrides Bernard's qualms and the mice climb on. Orville then requires Bernard to read out the pre-takeoff checklist. The little mouse is far from reassured when he finds that the final item on the list is "If at first you don't succeed, try, try again"!

After Orville has crash-landed at Devil's Bayou, his tail-feathers singed by one of Mr. Snoops' flares (it is worth noting that Bernard, despite his natural timidity, courageously makes his way to Orville's stern and battles against the fire), the albatross flies out of the movie, returning only at the very end. Here his passengers include not only Bianca and Bernard but also Evinrude, the plucky little dragonfly from Devil's Bayou. In fact, Evinrude proves in the early stages of this final flight to be less of a passenger, more of an auxiliary engine. For Orville has some

difficulty taking off from the roof of what we must assume is the UN Building thanks to snow and high wind. Blown from the roof, he plummets towards the street below, being brought out of his uncontrolled dive only by Evinrude manipulating his tail-feathers and adding an iota of upward thrust.

Although, as noted, Orville was largely animated by Ollie Johnston, Johnston was assisted by a newcomer to the Disney fold, Chuck Harvey. Harvey studied Johnston's work, and then set about devising a gait for the bird. This gait, he determined, should not only blend in with the character's existing personality but also extend and enhance it. The measure of Harvey's success is that, on seeing the movie, you *do not notice* Orville's gait: it is simply a part of his overall persona. (Of course, as soon as you start looking out for the gait, you notice it all right!)

Rufus the cat is a minor character who "makes good" in large part because of his voice. It should be noted that Orville is successful almost *despite* his voice. From Orville's visual image one might expect tones more of the Goofy type, but in fact his voice (supplied by Jim Jordan) is a curious mixture of crisp youth and genial oldster: it is youthful when touchily reacting to Bernard's implied criticisms of his abilities, and more elderly when responding ("Aw, shucks, just call me Orville, little lady") to Bianca's emollient flattery. This may, of course, have been an attempt to portray vocally yet further depth of character, but if so it is less than totally successful. However, the strength of Orville's animation – and his script – is such that the vocal discrepancy goes largely unnoticed.

Swamp Animals

Of the "swamp critters" in the movie, three are of especial note: Evinrude the dragonfly and the two muskrats, husband and wife Luke and Ellie Mae.

Evinrude is quite a strong character, which is in a way surprising: he does not utter a word (although he coughs and pants

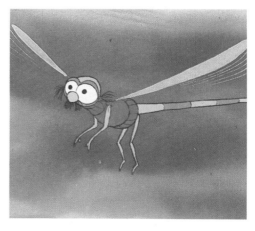

Evinrude, who was probably more responsible than anyone else for Penny's release.

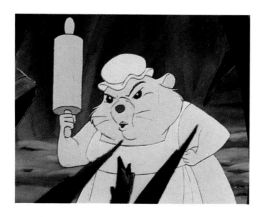

Ellie Mae, who did her best to keep Luke in order.

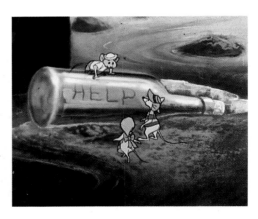

The beachcomber mice who found Penny's bottle.

exhaustedly from time to time), and anyway it is not at all easy to imbue a dragonfly with personality. The fact that Disney succeeded in doing so is probably a result of the terrifying scene in which Evinrude is pursued by hungry bats. These creatures are terrifying of aspect, with glowing red eyes and a general appearance of mindless malevolence: their faces are almost as hideous as those of real bats, in fact. They are, too, much bigger than Evinrude, and this means that we identify strongly with him as he flies in fear of his life from their voracious, snapping jaws. Even once he has found sanctuary in an empty bottle the bats fly menacingly around it, thwarted by the barrier of glass but reluctant to give up the chase. Finally they settle patiently to wait for his inevitable emergence from the bottle. He is able to reach the safety of the muskrats' cottage only after a further hair-raising pursuit.

Of the two muskrats, Ellie Mae is the dominant one in terms of action while Luke is the dominant one in terms of comic relief. **Ellie Mae** is, indeed, the force behind the swamp animals' final rebellion against the presence of Madame Medusa and Mr. Snoops, and one senses that she is in general the prime mover among the little creatures of the bayou. It is ironic, then, that she should be clad in all the trappings of the housewife: she wears a blue mobcap and a pink apron, and her principal offensive

weapon is a rolling-pin – even during the final cataclysmic battle. In terms of forcefulness of personality and of decisiveness she could hardly provide a greater contrast to her husband, **Luke**, who accords to the stereotype of the drunken hillbilly: most of his life seems to be spent sleeping it off, and the remaining fraction is devoted to drinking it on again. His barrel of firewater travels everywhere with him, even into battle – where no doubt it might prove useful for strictly medicinal purposes. Firewater the stuff most certainly is: when the animals are trying to revive Evinrude after his flight from the bats, a single drop of Luke's hooch not only achieves the desired resuscitation but also makes the dragonfly's breath burst into flames. Luke's personality is rounded off by his habitual costume – a battered hat and a nightshirt of dubious hygiene.

None of the other swamp creatures plays more than a bit part. **Gramps**, an elderly turtle, is of interest not only because he is one of the long and distinguished line of Disney tortoises/turtles that can be traced right back to Toby (➤ 73) but also because his voice part is supplied by Larry Clemmons, who headed the story-writing team on the movie. **Deacon**, likewise, continues a tradition: he is the movie's wise old owl. However, he does not play the sort of pivotal role given to, for example, Big Mama in *The Fox and the Hound* (➤308); his part is strictly one of swelling out the numbers. The same is generally true of **Deadeye** the rabbit and **Digger** the mole. During the final battle all of these four characters do their individual bits – for example, Deacon and Deadeye are primarily responsible for detonating Mr. Snoops' cache of fireworks – but in essence the four of them are "extras".

Minor Characters

The Rescuers has a plethora of minor characters. Aside from the two **beachcomber mice**, who appear on screen for a few seconds at the end of the opening credits – they discover Penny's bottle and react to the word "help" which they read through the glass – and the bats that chase Evinrude, these minor characters fall into two main groups: (a) the humans and mice present in or under the UN Building, and (b) characters viewed on TV during the movie's happy ending.

Of the characters under the UN, by far the most notable is the **Chairmouse** of the International Rescue Aid Society. He is a somewhat pompous mouse, clearly aware of his position and responsibilities, and of course his chief function in the movie is to provide comedy by having his pomposity deflated. This occurs when Bernard, commanded to climb into Penny's bottle to retrieve the note, is staggering around under the weight of a gap-toothed comb

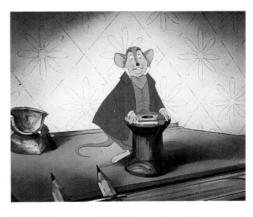

The Chairmouse of the International Rescue Aid Society.

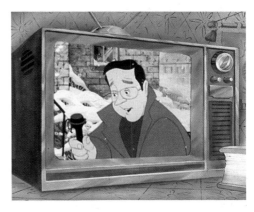

The TV interviewer whose broadcast brought the Rescuers the glad news of Penny's adoption.

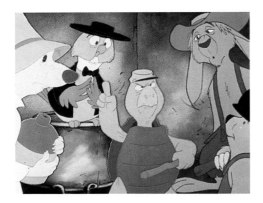

The swamp animals who helped in the struggle to achieve Penny's release. From left to right, Luke, Deacon, Gramps, Deadeye and Digger.

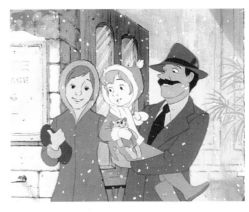

Penny with her adoptive parents – somehow you knew there was a happy ending on the way.

which he will use as a ladder. The comb swings dangerously over the heads of the assembled mice, and then narrowly misses the Chairman himself – indeed, it is only because he drops swiftly to his knees that he escapes injury. This manoeuvre is greeted with mirth by the other mice, and the Chairman responds testily, pounding his gavel and crying: "Delegates, this is no time for levity! Serious business, you know. Serious business."

A number of human delegates to the UN appear very briefly, and to each of these there is a corresponding mouse delegate to the International Rescue Aid Society. Quite how the mice beat the US customs check is unexplained: presumably they hid inside diplomatic bags. Among the humans one can distinguish an Indian, an Austrian and a Scottish delegate (recognition of an independent Scotland at the UN?), and these have their mouse counterparts. Other nations represented among the mice are China, Korea, France, Germany, the Netherlands and an unspecified African nation. The UN **Doorman** is also fleetingly on screen.

After the main adventure the mouse delegates watch a report of the events on TV. Penny is talking with a **TV interviewer**, who patronizes her when she claims to have been assisted by a pair of mice: well, if your children made the same claim, you would patronize them, too. To the delight of a chorus of merry orphans, Penny is united with her new-found **adoptive father** and **adoptive mother**. Clearly these are going to be the finest mummy and daddy in the history of parenthood – or, at least, Penny clearly thinks so and we are given the same impression. The pair are extremely middle-class – obviously of comfortable means yet not actually rich. She is demure and blonde; he has dark hair and moustache, and is dressed in tasteful browns. Penny has kept the faith, as Rufus proposed, and sure enough things have turned out right.

PETE'S DRAGON

Character:

Elliott

Credits:

Based on a story by Seton I. Miller and S. S. Field

Live Actors: Helen Reddy; Jim Dale; Mickey Rooney; Red Buttons; Shelley Winters; Sean Marshall; Jane Kean; Jim Backus; Charles Tyner; Gary Morgan; Jeff Conaway; Cal Bartlett

Voice: Charlie Callas (Elliott)

Special Effects: Eustace Lycett; Art Cruickshank; Danny Lee

Sound Supervisor: Herb Taylor

Sound Mixer: Frank C. Regula

Sound Editor: Raymond Craddock

Film Editor: Gordon D. Brenner

Music Editor: Evelyn Kennedy

Music Supervised, Arranged and Conducted by Irwin Kostal

Songs: Al Kasha; Joel Hirschhorn

Choreography: Onna White

Associate Choreographer: Martin Allen

Dance Arrangements: David Baker

Screenplay: Malcolm Marmorstein

Stunt Coordinator: John Moio

Costumes: Chuck Keehne; Emily Sundby

Hair Stylist: La Rue Matheron

Make-up: Robert J. Schiffer

Costume Designer: Bill Thomas

Set Decorator: Lucien M. Hafley

Layout: Joe Hale

Director of Photography: Frank Phillips

Matte Artist: Peter Ellenshaw

Art Directors: John B. Mansbridge; Jack Martin Smith

Animation Editor: James Melton

Animation Art Director: Ken Anderson

Elliott created by Ken Anderson

Animation Director: Don Bluth

Assistant Animator Supervision: Chuck Williams

Character Animators: John Pomeroy; Ron Clements; Gary Goldman; Bill Hajee; Chuck Harvey; Randy Cartwright; Cliff Nordberg; Glen Keane

Effects Animator: Dorse A. Lanpher

Assistant Director: Ronald R. Grow

Second Assistant Director: John M. Poer

Director: Don Chaffey

Unit Production Manager: Christopher Seiter

Production Manager: John Bloss

Producers: Ron Miller; Jerome Courtland

Release Date: November 3, 1977

Running Time: 129 minutes

THE MOVIE

The major criticism of *Pete's Dragon* on its release was that, to mix several metaphors, it tried to hit all bases at once and succeeded only in falling between every possible stool. One critic described it as "the erector-set type of corporate movie". There was a general cry that it was a failed attempt to repeat the successful formula of *Mary Poppins* – a curious cry, because the movies could not be more dissimilar. A more realistic criticism was that the musical score was a trifle lacklustre. *Pete's Dragon* is, despite the score, a first-rate piece of family entertainment; in fact, viewing it today, one wonders if those hostile critics saw the same movie.

Pete's Dragon is noteworthy as the first Disney feature involving animation in which none of the Nine Old Men played a part; however, a top nominee for the post of "tenth old man", Ken Anderson, was intimately involved: he was the man who created and designed Elliott, the movie's sole animated character. Another link with the past was the presence as cinematographer of Frank Phillips: his links with Disney went back so far that he was one of the local children hired to play a bit part in the Alice Comedies!

The special effects in the movie are astonishing. For them, both sodiumlight photography and blue-screen photography were used extensively. (In the seastorm sequence miniatures were also used.) In blue-screen photography nothing that is coloured blue is recorded by the camera – this "mask of invisibility" enabled, for example, Pete apparently to slide down Elliott's belly when in fact he was filmed sliding down a blue-painted chute. Sodium-light photography, by contrast, involves the use of a lens system that splits the incoming light into two beams: one is used to expose a normal colour film and the other to make a black-and-white film which can be used as a template. In this process, shooting is done on a sodium-lit stage: the principle is that the back of the stage is a yellow-painted cloth screen front-lit by sodium-vapour lights to which the colour film is "blind" because a dichroic sodium-line filter is placed in the camera as a barrier to light of this wavelength. Conversely the black-and-white film records a black background where it "sees" the screen; the action in the foreground is a moving silhouette against this. It is therefore comparatively (!) simple to slot in backgrounds to match with the live action.

Another technique used in *Pete's Dragon* was "compositing", whereby up to three scenes might be composited together – for example, there might be a live foreground and a live background but an animated middleground in which Elliott was doing his stuff, so that things could be seen happening both in front of and behind him.

Some of the special-effects scenes in the movie caused especial difficulty. Among them were the ones in which Pete throws apples up for Elliott to catch in his mouth (the Disney people had to use strategically placed targets for Sean Marshall to aim at) and in which Elliott becomes invisible in parts – where the problem was getting Sean Marshall to look in the right direction at the right time. These technical difficulties were solved superbly: there is a moment in *Pete's Dragon* where Elliott scoops up a tear from Pete's eye that is possibly one of the finest pieces of special effects in the history of the cinema.

THE STORY

Young Pete (Sean Marshall) has been sold into virtual slavery to a family of vicious Maine backwoodsmen, the Gogans. But now he is on the run, helped by his friend Elliott, a good-natured dragon who can be visible or invisible at will. They arrive in Passamaquoddy, where they meet up with the lighthouse-keeper Lampie (Mickey Rooney) and his daughter Nora (Helen Reddy), who take Pete into their home, Elliott being housed in a cave on the beach. Because Elliott stays invisible most of the time, few people believe in his existence, and consequently Pete gets blamed for all of the little mishaps caused by the dragon's clumsiness.

One person who does believe in Elliott, though, is Dr. Terminus (Jim Dale), an itinerant conman and quack, who sets out with his buffoonish sidekick Hoagy (Red Buttons) to capture the dragon in order to cut him up and sell the pieces for use as potions. They link up with the Gogans on the basis that both parties want to separate the boy and the dragon. However, their attempts end in failure.

Lovely Nora has been grieving over her boyfriend Paul, who has been missing at sea for some while and is now believed dead. One stormy night, however, his ship nears the port of Passamaquoddy – and just as it does so the seas crash into the lighthouse, extinguishing the lamp and drenching the wicks. Try as they might, Lampie and Nora just cannot get the thing relit, and Paul's ship is heading for the rocks! Enter Elliott who, with some difficulty, produces a fierce burst of flame to light the lamp once more. The ship is saved, and Nora is reunited with the lover whom she had thought lost forever.

Now that Pete is settled with a new family who love him dearly, Elliott tells him that he must go – that there is another little boy in trouble who needs the help of a dragon. He flies off into the skies, and we leave our friends walking along the beach and singing "Brazzle Dazzle Day".

This very artificial ending – the song has nothing to do with the rest of the movie, and the sequence "feels" as if it had just been tacked on – seems to have been the product of someone's bright idea that the movie just *had* to end with a song, for in the version first screened the "Brazzle Dazzle Day" sequence fell just after Nora and Lampie had invited Pete to live with them, in which position it makes a lot more sense. However, the feebleness of the ending is the only blemish on what is otherwise a most enjoyable piece of scripting.

THE CHARACTER

Elliott is green with darker blotches. He has pink hair on his head and pink fins running all the way down his spine to a pink three-stranded tuft on the end of his tail. The "whites" of his eyes are in fact blue, surrounding black irises. He has cavernous nostrils and long ears that stick out at the side. His customary expression is an eager-to-please grin. His "talk" is a mixture of curious grunts, slurps, high-pitched cackles, boom-boom-da-boom-booms, etc. His overall construction is on the same simple basis as those of Smee, the Seven Dwarfs and even Donald and Mickey: he is almost entirely made up of circles and pear-shapes. He could hardly be more different from that other famous dragon created by Ken Anderson – the Maleficent-dragon in *Sleeping Beauty* (➤263)!

Originally it had been planned that Elliott should remain invisible throughout the movie except for one short sequence – later scrapped – in which Dr. Terminus tried to hack him up into marketable portions (even just a bit of a dragon would be a great sideshow attraction!). However, Ken Anderson felt that this constant invisibility was a bad plan: the characters spent much of their time explaining for the benefit of the audience what the invisible character was actually doing. Hence his decision to make Elliott a full-blown animated dragon who was invisible in only a few scenes. He opted for the oriental rather than the occidental type of dragon because oriental dragons are normally associated with good, whereas occidental dragons, of course, have a pretty unsavoury reputation. His first "thought-model" for the character was Wallace Beery. (Beery had in fact been directly caricatured in the 1933 Disney short *Mickey's Gala Premiere* [➤433].)

In a 1977 interview with David Hammond published in *American Cinematographer* Anderson went on to explain his thinking on Elliott:

> He had to blend, not pop out. This took very precise planning and care. For example, every shadow had to fall exactly right. Whenever we drew an animated sequence we had to know exactly where the light was falling in the

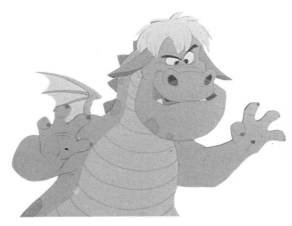

Elliott doing his best to look frightening.

live-action scene. Also, human skin tones change along with the quality of light as they move from one area to another and at different times of day. Elliott's coloring had to be adjusted accordingly.

The matter of Elliott's colouring – and indeed all the details of his appearance – was a problem in more ways than one. Some 80-90 people were involved in animating him, including 42 animators and in-betweeners, and so there was an incredibly high chance of noticeable inconsistencies in his appearance creeping in. In fact, if one looks very carefully, one can spot the occasional fluctuation of colour that seems not to be deliberate – but of course this may simply be a result of the printing of the film.

Elliott is overwhelmingly genial: although he is big and powerful and can breathe flames (albeit not too often), he is gentle, and it takes a lot to rouse his ire. Mind you, he gets a lot, thanks to the brutishness of the Gogans and the machinations of Dr. Terminus and finally, in a scene of (literally) dazzling pyrotechnics, he explodes into violence. (It is for this reason that, shortly afterwards, he has difficulty summoning sufficient flame to light the lighthouse's lamp.) People seeking to harm his orphan pal Pete can make him react angrily, too; in an earlier scene of more minor violence he walks right through the walls of the schoolhouse to try to save Pete from an undeserved beating.

Strong alcohol is not to Elliott's taste. When Lampie and Hoagy, both terrified, visit his cave so that Lampie can prove to his new-found boozing buddy that Elliott really exists, Hoagy tries to appease the "monster" by giving him a stiff belt from his hipflask. At first Elliott likes the sensation, but almost at once he realizes the stuff tastes horrible and tries to spit it out. The result is a most impressive burst of flames and fireworks. It is odd that Lampie did not remember this trick when trying to get Elliott to light the wick of the lamp!

Earlier in the sequence in the cave, Hoagy comes out with the movie's finest line of unconscious (or conscious?) irony. Of the "monster" he tremblingly says: "Them eyes ... l-lookin' right through us ..."

THE FOX AND THE HOUND

Characters:

Tod; Copper; Big Mama; Amos Slade; Vixey; Widow Tweed; Chief; Dinky; Boomer; Squeeks; Bear; Badger; Abigail

Credits:

Based on *The Fox and the Hound* (1967) by Daniel P. Mannix

Voices: Pearl Bailey (Big Mama); Dick Bakalyan (Dinky); Paul Winchell (Boomer); Jeanette Nolan (Widow Tweed); Mickey Rooney (Tod); Jack Albertson (Amos Slade); Kurt Russell (Copper); Pat Buttram (Chief); Sandy Duncan (Vixey); John Fiedler (Porcupine); John McIntire (Badger); Keith Mitchell (Young Tod); Corey Feldman (Young Copper)

Sound: Herb Taylor

Music Editors: Evelyn Kennedy; Jack Wadsworth

Musical Score Composed and Conducted by: Buddy Baker

Songs by: Richard O. Johnston; Stan Fidel; Jim Stafford; Richard Rich; Jeffrey Patch

Orchestration: Walter Sheets

Story: Larry Clemmons; Ted Berman; David Michener; Peter Young; Burny Mattinson; Steve Hulett; Earl Kress; Vance Gerry

Art Director: Don Griffith

Layout: Dan Hansen; Glenn V. Vilppu; Sylvia Roemer; Guy Vasilovich; Michael Peraza, Jr.; Joe Hale

Colour Styling: Jim Coleman

Backgrounds: Daniela Bielecka; Brian Sebern; Kathleen Swain

Supervising Animators: Randy Cartwright; Glen Keane; Cliff Nordberg; Ron Clements; Frank Thomas; Ollie Johnston

Character Animators: Ed Gombert; John Musker; Dale Oliver; Jerry Rees; Ron Husband; Dick N. Lucas; David Block; Jeffrey J. Varab; Chris Buck; Chuck Harvey; Hendel S. Butoy; Phil Nibbelink; Darrel Van Citters; Michael Cedeno; Phillip Young

Effects Animation: Ted Kierscey; Jack Boyd; Don C. Paul

Coordinating Animators: Walt Stanchfield; Leroy Cross; Dave Suding; Chuck Williams

Key Assistants: Tom Ferriter; Sylvia Mattinson

Assistant Directors: Don Hahn; Mark A. Hester; Terry L. Noss

Directors: Art Stevens; Ted Berman; Richard Rich

Editors: James Melton; Jim Koford

Production Managers: Edward Hansen; Don A. Duckwall

Creative Assistant to the Producers: Melvin Shaw

Coproducers: Wolfgang Reitherman; Art Stevens

Executive Producer: Ron Miller

Release Date: July 10, 1981

Running Time: 83 minutes

THE MOVIE

Precise figures are not available, but it is thought that *The Fox and the Hound* grossed a staggering $50 million – and it all came about because of a father's nostalgia. Wolfgang Reitherman was the Disney person who read Daniel P. Mannix's novel about a puppy and a foxcub becoming friends, and he found it particularly touching because it reminded him of the pet fox one of his sons had owned years before. He decided that the story could make a good animated feature, and so it came to pass. This story of the movie's genesis is reminiscent of how things came about in Walt's day.

The main characters were developed by Frank Thomas and Ollie Johnston, but the animation itself was done by the "new breed" of Disney animators – the young men specifically brought in and trained to take over from the old guard, who were by now reaching retirement age with increasing frequency. There was therefore considerable excitement among animation buffs as the release date drew near: what would be different? In fact, as it turned out, very little. Although rather lower-key and less ambitious than most of the other features, the movie is on the surface typical Disney fare – which means, of course, that it is very good, but it was not the innovatory vehicle which the critics had been expecting. (A few years later *The Black Cauldron* was pummelled for being innovatory: it seems you can't win it either way.) However, some of the reviewers were perceptive enough to notice that there were indeed some differences from what had gone before. The issues with which the movie deals are rather more intellectually mature than, say, whether or not a raucous villainess will succeed in her plan to make fur coats out of Dalmatian skins. The disruptions of childhood friendships as people grow older and their characters change are a worthy subject of many a serious literary novel. That same theme of the movie had also obvious parallels in the sphere of racial tension: children do not inherit racism, but have its poison injected into them by their elders, so that childhood playmates may in reality end up on opposite sides of the barricade. (It would be very easy to remake the movie substituting black and white children for the animals.) The movie also raises questions about the morality of the annual exercise in indiscriminate slaughter known as the hunting season.

Richard Corliss, in his review in *Time*, was one who noticed this new, more "adult" approach – and he was wise enough to welcome it:

As Tod and Copper learn more about themselves and each other while on the run, so the young Disney artists making their feature-film debut here realize the emotive and kinetic power of animation in the chase sequences. They are as finely shaped and paced as the desert drive in *Raiders of the Lost Ark* – and almost as violent. More important, they suggest a dimension of conflict within as well as between the antagonists. Will Tod escape not only the surly Chief but his old friend, now a deadly nemesis? Will Tod defend Slade, who has sworn to kill him, against the attack of a huge ferocious bear? Will Tod and Copper ever be friends again?

This mental dynamic, in addition to the purely physical one, was a genuine innovation in a Disney feature (although some less well known animated features by others, e.g., Martin Rosen's 1978 movie *Watership Down*, had already displayed a cerebral approach). In a way the "new breed" were forcing the 1960s- and 1970s-style Disney feature to come of age for the 1980s.

The links with the past were still strongly there, however – and sometimes in unexpected ways. One curious one was that, since for one reason or another it was thought a bad idea to bring in live animals for the animators to observe and sketch, they instead made extensive use of live-action footage – the same footage, according to one report, that had been used by the animators on *Bambi*! In fact, the references used were more recent Disney nature films; for example, *King of the Grizzlies* (1970) helped the animators with the spectacular fight with the bear.

THE STORY

One day, out in the backwoods, Big Mama, a plump owl, sees a vixen fleeing with a bundle in her mouth from a hunter and his baying dog. The vixen drops her bundle in some long grass and hurries on. Moments later shots ring out, and Big Mama knows the vixen is dead.

She swoops down to examine the long grass and finds there a tiny foxcub – clearly now an orphan. With the help of Dinky the sparrow and Boomer the woodpecker she fetches the cub to the doorstep of kindly Widow Tweed. Boomer knocks and sure enough, moments later, the cub has a new home. The widow calls him Tod, because he is hardly more than a toddler. (As it happens, the word "tod" is used in much of Britain to mean "fox", so her choice of name was a good one!)

In the neighbouring cabin foul-tempered hunter Amos Slade lives with his equally grouchy dog Chief, as well as now a new puppy which Amos has just bought called Copper. One day Copper picks up a strange scent which he follows into the forest, where he meets Tod. The two little creatures have a rollicking game of hide-and-seek, at the end of which:

> *Tod*: You're my very best friend.
> *Copper*: And you're mine, too, Tod.
> *Tod*: And we'll always be friends, forever, won't we?
> *Copper*: Yeah! Forever.

Copper is bawled out by Slade for having run off and the following day is tied up to his barrel. When he fails to appear in the forest, Tod goes to find him. Tod is amazed by the size and ferocity of the snoring Chief – but then the big dog awakens and, dragging his barrel behind him, gives snarling chase. Tod runs in terror into the chicken yard, and all the squawking and barking rouse the hunter, who joins in the chase. The cub leaps aboard Widow Tweed's fortuitously passing truck just in time to avoid being blasted with shotgun pellets.

A huge row develops between the widow and the hunter, during which he tells her flat that, if he ever sees Tod again he is going to be one dead fox. From then on the widow keeps Tod in.

Late in the autumn Slade packs up his dogs and his guns and sets off for a winter-long hunting trip, and Tod's life becomes rather less restricted. When the hunter returns both Tod and Copper have reached young adulthood – but Copper has changed in another way, too: "Those days are over," he says. "I'm a huntin' dog now."

Suddenly Chief, who has been snoozing nearby, awakens, and once more he, Slade and this time Copper pursue the fox. Copper indeed succeeds in tracking him but tells Tod that, for the sake of old times, just this once he will let him escape; the hound draws Slade away in the wrong direction. But Chief is still on Tod's trail, and the two meet on a high railway bridge. Tod turns to flee, but a train is coming. The fox is just small enough to cower down between the railroad ties, but Chief is hit a glancing blow and knocked into the ravine below. As Tod flees, Copper, assuming Tod to have done the deed deliberately, stands over his badly injured colleague and swears vengeance.

Slade goes to Widow Tweed's home and murderously demands entrance, which she declines. However, she has come to realize that the only safe place for Tod is far from here. The next day she drives Tod to a game preserve and with many a tear leaves him there.

Tod has a foul night in the forest, but in the morning Big Mama appears to comfort him, and the world looks a much brighter place altogether when he meets and falls in love with a beautiful vixen called Vixey.

Slade is intent on vengeance, however, and so takes Copper and his guns to exterminate the fox. Ignoring the "No Hunting" signs he sets traps in all the places which Copper's keen nose tell him are frequent haunts of Tod. In fact, Tod very nearly succumbs to a group of these, and the noise of his flight sets Slade and Copper on his trail. The racket they create, however, and the smoke from the fire which Amos lights in hopes of smoking Tod and Vixey out of a burrow where they have hidden, attract the attention of a vast bear. As it advances upon Slade, knocking his gun from his hand, he steps into one of his own traps. Copper bravely leaps between the two but the bear swats him to one side, injuring him.

All seems lost for Slade and Copper, but Tod hears Copper howling and rushes back to try to help his old friend. The bear starts to chase him instead. It pursues him onto a log jutting out from the side of a deep gorge, but its weight sends them both tumbling into the swirling rapids below.

Half-drowned, Tod pulls himself to shore – only to find that Slade has released himself from his trap and is standing there with his gun. No matter that Tod has just saved his life: the man is intent on murder. But then Copper limps into the line of fire and refuses to budge. Slowly it at last begins to dawn in Slade's brain that there are perhaps more things to life than the mindless massacre of wild animals just because they are foxes – that friendship is a more powerful force than killing – and he puts up his gun and leaves, Copper limping along behind him. As he goes the dog looks back over his shoulder and his smile tells the fox that they are indeed friends forever, just as they promised long ago.

THE CHARACTERS

Tod

There are really two characters called Tod in the movie, a foxcub and a grown fox, for the two are totally different – by design, of course, for one of the movie's themes concerns the differences between the young and the adults they become. The infant Tod (who is excellently voiced by Keith Mitchell) is as cuddly as any puppy, and behaves very much like one: it is hardly surprising that Big Mama and then Widow Tweed adopt him, each in their different ways.

He is very much the instigator of the oaths of bosom friendship which the two pals make in their youth: if one looks at the four lines of dialogue cited above one notices that Tod's two lines are assertive; Copper merely agrees with him – albeit

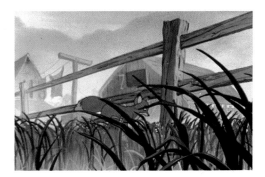

Tod's mother, who had to leave her cub and hope for the best.

enthusiastically. This same pattern is maintained in their adulthood: Tod is keen to maintain the friendship but Copper tells him that things have changed, that now he is a hunting-dog he must regard Tod as his natural enemy. Moreover, when the chips are down and Copper faces death at the paws of the bear, it is Tod who risks his life to save him: one very much doubts if Copper would have done the same had things been the other way around ... although in the end Copper does stand between Tod and Amos Slade's gun.

The adult Tod, voiced by Mickey Rooney (who had earlier served as a live-action star in *Pete's Dragon*), is a fairly streetwise fellow, although with the obligatory heart of gold. At least, he is streetwise in his sharpness and perception: he is barely fit to survive when the moment comes that he must learn to live on his own in the wild, and it is lucky that Vixey takes him under her wing. (Bongo [➤223] found himself in a very similar situation).

Overriding any other characteristic is the fact that Tod is a very affectionate, gentle little creature – to the extent that one wonders what he and Vixey are going to eat in the wild. He is tender with Widow Tweed, with even the grown-up and unfriendly Copper, with Big Mama ... in

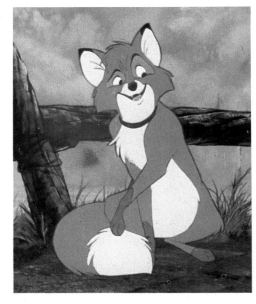

Tod, looking characteristically devil-may-care.

short, with anyone who comes his way. He even regrets the injury to Chief when that implacable foe is batted by the train.

Significantly, at the end of the film it is Tod who hears in the air those four lines of dialogue sealing friendship; we are not shown Copper having the same experience. To be fair, Copper did stop Slade shooting Tod; but Tod is the true friend – the friend all of us hope to have.

Copper

Copper is obedient, first as a puppy to the more forceful Tod when they forge their friendship, and later as a full-grown dog to the hunter Amos Slade and the old hound Chief. This makes him a fickle friend so far as poor Tod is concerned. His claim, on the return from the winter hunting trip, that he and Tod can no longer be friends is arrant nonsense: there is absolutely no reason why the friendship may not continue (if clandestinely, thanks to the bigotry of Chief and Slade). What is being gently satirized here is the myth, fostered by the military and, to be fair, by the nonmilitary that the donning of a uniform somehow "changes things". Or perhaps it is that kids of different races, when they grow up, should abandon their old friendships because it "has to be that way".

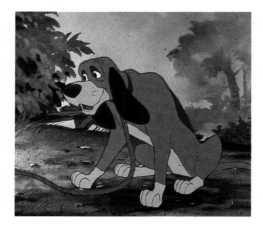

Copper: in adulthood he had to try to relinquish his friendship for the fox.

As a puppy Copper is far less wholehearted about the friendship between himself and Tod than is the little foxcub: as noted above, it is Tod who does all the running. Clearly Copper does not take their promise of friendship too seriously. All this is cunningly reflected in the fact that, while Tod is very confidently and accurately voiced, Copper is much less so: the fact that his voice is less well acted means that his promises sound far less sincere – they are more rote – and this precisely reflects his attitude to them. (In other sections of Copper's dialogue Disney had to accept as a price for this that the voicing was less than convincing.)

As an adult Copper is much less devoted to the friendship than is Tod – in fact, he

tolerates the fox's presence, but that is about all. The short scene in which Copper discovers the hiding Tod while Slade and Chief are searching the countryside for him is revealing, especially in terms of one of Copper's lines: "Tod, I ... I don't want to see you get killed. I'll let you go this one time." How kind! With friends like this ...

Soon afterwards, Copper is only too ready to believe that Tod has deliberately maimed Chief, and swears revenge upon the fox – his "lifetime friend" – even though he does not even *like* the old dog.

In the end, of course, after Tod has saved his life at the very obvious risk of his own, Copper comes good, as it were: he suddenly realizes that the promised friendship is a two-way thing, and that he too ought to start doing something about it – to wit, saving Tod's life, although at little risk to his own (Slade is not about to shoot his best hound). Copper, one trusts, has become a reformed character: certainly his personality was deficient in earlier stages, when he happily helped Slade set up the cruel traps for Tod. During the movie he moves from youth to that infuriating state of adolescence which regards itself as adult, and then finally, right at the end, he achieves genuine adulthood. The pity is, as the movie strongly implies, that so many human beings fail to progress beyond the second stage – a fact which is something of a tragedy for the rest of us.

Big Mama

The Disney team, having flirted with the scheme of basing their animation on the personalities of the voice artists, were by now returning to their old and critically more acceptable tradition of creating animated characters from scratch. However, in the case of Big Mama they made an exception, and for once it was a wise one: they based the affectionate owl on the fabulous Pearl Bailey. They decided early on that Big Mama should be more of a village do-gooder than the traditional Disney sage owl (however scatterbrained, Disney owls have usually had the rudiments of wisdom), and when Pearl Bailey agreed to be the voice they had their hearts' desire – especially when she produced several fabulous singing performances (notably "Appreciate the Lady").

Big Mama, of course, is not much like a real owl in terms of behaviour: right at the beginning, when she swoops down to find out what the mother fox has dumped in the tall grass, she nurtures the infant fox rather than eating him. (Much the same sort of circumstance prevailed with *Bambi*'s Friend Owl [▶**200**], who held paternal conversations with young members of his natural prey.)

Big Mama is Tod's spiritual mother, and she comforts him in times of distress – for

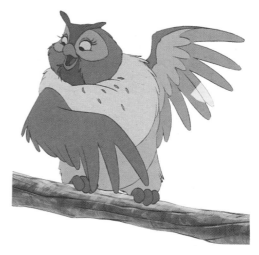

Big Mama – the movie's major comic character.

example, when he has just had an awful first night in the wild:

> *Big Mama*: Mornin', Tod.
> *Tod*: Oh, hello, Big Mama.
> *Big Mama*: Last night was pretty miserable for you, wasn't it, honey?
> *Tod*: Just terrible.
> *Big Mama*: Cheer up and look around. The forest is beautiful this morning.
> *Tod*: After last night, nothing looks beautiful. Wow! Who ... who ... is ... is ... that?

Big Mama's job – and for that matter her role in the movie – is over: Tod has spotted Vixey. He is a big boy now, and has no need of a fostermother.

Amos Slade

Art Stevens, *The Fox and the Hound*'s supervising director, said that of all the characters the most problematic in all sorts of ways was Amos Slade, the vicious old hunter who believes that the only good fox is a dead one:

> Basically, [he] has a permanent scowl, and sometimes an animator would have him raise an eyebrow and I'd say, "No, get him back into character."

In fact, the only time that Slade allows himself to give birth to anything more friendly than a frown is when he and his two dogs are returning from their hunting trip aboard a truck heavily laden with the skins of the animals they have been slaughtering. Then – to the anguish of Chief – he bursts into so-called song, explaining to the world at large and the audience in particular the ethos of his life:

> I ain't got no job.
> I'm a huntin' man
> And I'd rather have a dog than a dollar ...

Slade looks the part. Clad in a leather fur-lined jacket and vast leather boots, with a wide-brimmed hat jammed at an aggressive angle on the back of his head, he has thick hair and a belligerently bushy moustache. His eyes vary between anger and hatred. But it is his chin which is the principal indicator of his character: it spends most of its time jutting forwards with all the power of a battering ram.

For approximately 80 of the movie's 83 minutes it seems that Slade is utterly incorrigible, that he will continue forever on his bullying, foul-tempered way, harassing his neighbours – when there are no neighbours on hand he even bullies his ancient pick-up truck – and massacring the wildlife. However, in the closing moments Copper's late-discovered loyalty to his childhood friend opens Slade's mind to the higher emotions. One hopes that he will continue on his newly discovered course.

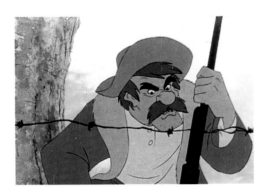

Amos Slade, whose blind hatred of all foxes led him to hunt down Tod.

Vixey

Vixey, ideally voiced by Sandy Duncan, is a very feminine, very beautiful, and very knowing fox. It is interesting to observe how the Disney artists have managed to capture her femininity. In the scenes where she and Tod appear together we can compare the two directly. First, there is a slightly greater softness of line about her portrayal (for example, she is outlined in pink-orange rather than black), and this is enhanced by the fact that her colour has been subtly altered – it is slightly less orange than Tod's, with a little pink blended in – so that she stands out less prominently against any background. Second, and possible more importantly, she moves in a different way: her walk is slightly feline, whereas Tod's is if anything slightly canine. Such techniques of artistry may not conform to reality, but they do conform to sexual stereotypes which are fairly deeply ingrained in each of us and so, unconsciously, we register her as a graceful female. An interesting further piece of stereotyping occurs when she is the first to sense danger from the path where Slade has laid his traps, with Tod picking up the "vibes" later: that is *feminine intuition*!

Another difference in her character from Tod's arises because she has not been raised in domesticity: she is a child of the forest, and so is a much better survivor than he is. Notably, when Tod is turning to go back to try to rescue his friend from the bear, Vixey

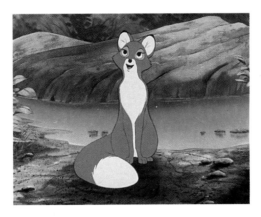

Vixey, who befriended Tod in the wild and saved his life.

– quite rightly, in forest terms – tells him not to be such an idiot (although not quite in those words). Her loyalty is to her new-found mate: he has to be quite forceful in instructing her to seek safety. Tender at appropriate times, she is much tougher-minded when danger threatens.

Widow Tweed

Kindly Widow Tweed, the old farm woman who adopts Tod, is a character designed to warm the cockles of every heart. With her grey hair tied in a bun at the back, her expressive dumpling of a face, her plump matronly figure, her thin-rimmed circular spectacles, and the soft greys and maroons of her clothing, you just *know* that she will offer you a helping of apple pie should you ever happen to knock at her door. If there were any doubt about it, you just have to look at her pale purple hat for confirmation.

Her voice, supplied by Jeanette Nolan, is in keeping with her character: kindly and middle-aged, it is the voice of a Good Woman. One suspects this must have caused the animators some problems when it came to her having to sing a song: Widow Tweed just is not the sort of person to burst into either a jazz number or a La Scala aria. The problem is solved by having her speak, rather than sing, "Goodbye May Seem Forever", which she does as she takes Tod to the game preserve. The result is a very pretty song.

The Widow Tweed with her obliging cow Abigail.

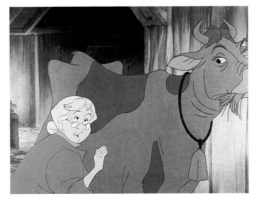

Chief

Chief is his master's dog. There are quite strong physical resemblances – both have distinctive bushy eyebrows, and the coloration of both is largely from the same tonal range – but more significant are the similarities of character. Chief is a humourless old sourpuss with a world-view identical to Slade's: if it moves, and it isn't a dog or a human, kill it – and humans had better be careful, too. He is not even especially kindly disposed towards Copper, particularly when the latter is a puppy: Chief regards him as an unwanted intruder, and agrees to help in his training only with the greatest reluctance.

In a way, Chief is even worse than Slade. Perhaps it was felt that, since he was an animal rather than a human, Disney could safely take even further the vicious satire of the kind of intolerant, bigoted, ignorant rednecks who make life such a misery for all the rest of us. For while Chief is enthusiastic about everyone else getting hurt – and an eager volunteer to do the hurting – he is self-pitying when he himself is the one to sustain injury, and milks the sympathies of those around him for all the situation is worth.

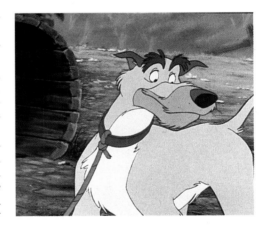

Chief, whose character matched that of Amos Slade: both of them hated foxes – except dead foxes.

When he is not preparing to hunt or actually hunting, Chief spends most of his time asleep – dreaming of hunting, as the two young animals discover when they hear him talking in his sleep:

> *Chief:* I'm gainin' on him now. He won't get away now!
> *Copper:* He's wakin' up! Get out, Tod!
> *Tod:* No, he's havin' a dream. He's chasin' somethin'.
> *Chief:* I've got him cornered now! It's ... well, it's a ... it's a big old badger.
> *Tod:* Copper, he's chasin' a badger.
> *Chief:* No, no. It ain't a badger. It's a ... it's a ... it's a ... fox! A FOX!

And then of course he is awake and madly chasing the tiny foxcub, heedless of any destruction he wreaks around him as he single-mindedly pursues his prey.

Dinky and Boomer

Dinky the sparrow and Boomer the woodpecker are also obsessive hunters, and a minor subplot centres on their devoted efforts to catch a smug little caterpillar called **Squeeks**. Green and surprisingly fast-moving when the occasion arises, Squeeks is a humorous wide-eyed zany in the best Disney tradition.

Boomer, voiced by Paul Winchell of Tigger fame (➤125), is another zany: it is pleasing to note that the voice is designed to match the character, not the other way around. We first meet him when Big Mama recruits his help in finding a home with Widow Tweed for the foxcub. With his wildly disarrayed crest trembling with the importance of the task, Boomer clings to her doorknob and batters on her door a few times. Unfortunately he is unprepared when she throws her door wide open and flattens him against the wall. Blithely oblivious to his suffering – "Well, I was *sure* I heard someone knocking" – she stoops to take up the squirming bundle.

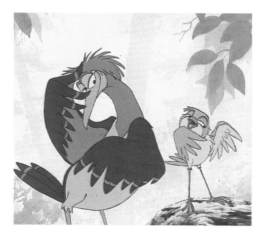

Dinky, on the left, and Boomer provided moments of comic relief.

Dinky, the little yellow sparrow, is in appearance not nearly such a broad caricature as Boomer, but his voice, supplied by Dick Bakalyan, most certainly is – in fact, it is a slightly higher-pitched version of Phil Harris's rendition of Thomas O'Malley (➤284). He is somewhat more decisive than his chum, being the first to respond to Big Mama's appeal for assistance as well as the character to devise Boomer's novel technique of door-knocking.

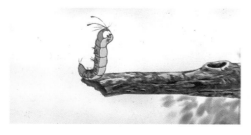

Squeeks the caterpillar, the target of a constant quest by Dinky and Boomer.

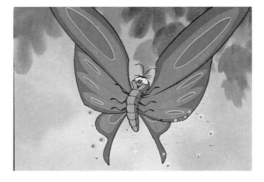

Squeeks foiled the two birds' attempts to gobble him up by turning into a butterfly.

The climax of the two birds' single-minded pursuit of Squeeks comes with winter. The fat little caterpillar has succeeded in crawling through a keyhole into Widow Tweed's house, and the two birds watch impotently through the cold glass of her window as Squeeks, a grin plastered right across his face, ecstatically warms his rear end by the fireplace. At last the two birds give up the chase and migrate south.

Minor Characters

There are a number of minor characters in the movie, the most notable being the Bear and the Badger.

The **Bear** is important in terms of the plot, but has no distinct personality outside its ferocity. It is a gigantic monster, standing perhaps eight or ten feet at the shoulder, and its mouth has more teeth in it than a clockwork motor. Its eyes are like glowing embers.

The scene with the bear is the most dramatic moment of the film, and is powerfully rendered by Glen Keane. While the other animators used live-action footage and ball-and-socket models in order to help them capture the motions of the various animals in the movie, Keane went so far as to have a scale model of a bear's skeleton standing by his easel! His attention to detail was worth it.

The **Badger** is of note because he is such a lot of fun: it's surprising his part was not expanded. Tod meets him when the drenched fox finds what he thinks is a nice, warm and unoccupied den.

Badger: Hold it, sonny! Back off! Consarn it, where ... where do you think you're going?
Tod: Oh, oh, excuse me. I-I-I was, I was just trying to ...
Badger: You barge in on somebody's house like you own it!
Tod: I honestly didn't know anybody lived here and I ...
Badger: Now get off my property. Go on, beat it!

There are a number of other animals encountered by Tod in the forest, including a porcupine, a butterfly, a rabbit and, most amusingly, a fish which, in order to impress the newly met Vixey, he tries but fails to catch. She is impressed, all right – by what a fool he is making of himself.

Finally, Widow Tweed's elderly cow **Abigail** makes a brief appearance. Widow Tweed tries to milk poor Abigail despite the fact that Tod is pestering them both: finally the widow responds by squirting Tod a powerful stream of milk. Disney cows from as long ago as *Steamboat Willie* (1928) had done much the same to their tormentors.

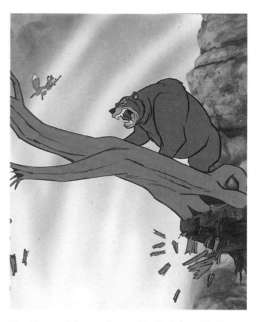

The climax of the movie was Tod's fight with the Bear. The Bear was the runner-up, as expected.

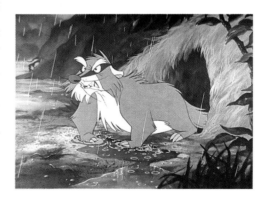

The Badger was one of the testy animals which Tod met when he first encountered the wild.

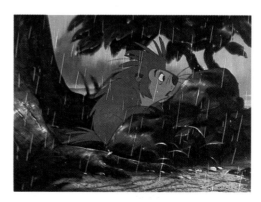

The Porcupine was rather more friendly than the Badger – but not a lot.

THE BLACK CAULDRON

Characters:

Taran; Eilonwy; Gurgi; Fflewddur Fflam; Dallben; The Horned King; Creeper; King Eidilleg; Doli; Orgoch; Orddu; Orwen; Hen Wen

Credits:

Based on Lloyd Alexander's five *Chronicles of Prydain* books (1964-68)

Voices: Grant Bardsley (Taran); Susan Sheridan (Eilonwy); Freddie Jones (Dallben); Nigel Hawthorne (Fflewddur Fflam); Arthur Malet (King Eidilleg); John Byner (Gurgi, Doli); Eda Reiss Merin (Orddu); Adele Malia-Morey (Orwen); Billie Hayes (Orgoch); John Hurt (The Horned King); Phil Fondacaro (Creeper, henchman); John Huston (Narrator); Lindsay Rich, Brandon Call, Gregory, Levinson (Fairfolk); Peter Renaday, James Almanzar, Wayne Allwine, Steve Hale, Phil Nibbelink, Jack Laing (henchmen)

Picture and Sound Effects Editors: James Melton; Jim Koford; Armetta Jackson

Sound Effects Designer: Mike McDonough

Sound Effects: Paul Holzborn; Wayne Allwine

Re-recording Mixers: Richard Portman; Nick Alphin; Frank C. Regula

Music Scoring Mixer: Shawn Murphy

Re-recorded at: International Recording

Sound Supervisor: Bob Hathaway

Music Editor: Kathy Durning

Music Supervisor: Jay Lawton

Supervising Music Editor: Jack Wadsworth

Music Preparation: Norman Corey

Music Contractor: Regnal Hall

Music: Elmer Bernstein

Orchestration: Peter Bernstein

Special Photographic Effects: Phillip Meador; Ron Osenbaugh; Bill Kilduff

Story: David Jonas; Vance Gerry; Al Wilson; Roy Morita; Ted Berman; Peter Young; Richard Rich; Art Stevens; Joe Hale

Additional Story Contributions: Tony Marino; Steve Hulett; Mel Shaw; Burny Mattinson; John Musker; Ron Clements; Doug Lefler

Additional Dialogue: Rosemary Anne Sisson; Roy Edward Disney

Colour Styling: James Coleman

Layout Styling: Mike Hodgson

Layout: Don Griffith; Guy Vasilovich; Dan Hansen; Glenn Vilppu; William Frake III

Assistant Layout: David Dunnet; Karen Keller; Greg Martin; Kurt Anderson; Carol Holman Grosvenor; Frank Frezzo

Backgrounds: Donald Towns; Brian Sebern; Tia Kratter; John Emerson; Lisa Keene; Andrew Phillipson

Key Coordinating Animator: Walt Stanchfield

Animators: Andreas Deja; Phil Nibbelink; Hendel Butoy; Steven Gordon; Dale Baer; Doug Krohn; Ron Husband; Shawn Keller; Jay Jackson; Mike Gabriel; Barry Temple; Phillip Young; Tom Ferriter; Jesse Cosio; Ruben Aquino; Ruben Procopio; Cyndee Whitney; Vicki Anderson; George Scribner; David Block; Mark Henn; Charlie Downs; Terry Harrison; Sandra Borgmeyer; David Pacheco

Assistant Animators: Tony Anselmo; Jane Baer; Dorothea Baker; Philo Barnhart; Bill Berg; Ben Burgess; Reed Cardwell; Brian Clift; Jesus Cortes; Rick Farmiloe; June Fujimoto; Terrey Hamada; Ray Harris; Jeffrey Lynch; Mauro Maressa; Michael McKinney; Jim Mitchell; Brett Newton; Gilda Palinginis; Phil Phillipson; David Pruiksma; Natasha Selfridge; Toby Shelton; David Stephan; Russ Stoll; George Sukara; Larry White

Additional Animation: Kathy Zielinsky; Sue Diciccio; Jill Colbert; Richard Hoppe; Kevin Wurzer; Dave Brain; Sylvia Mattinson; Maurice Hunt

Effects Animators: Don Paul; Barry Cook; Mark Dindal; Ted Kierscey; Jeff Howard; Kelvin Yasuda; Patricia Peraza; Bruce Woodside; Scott Santoro; Kimberly Knowlton; Glenn Chaika; Allen Gonzales

Assistants Effects Animators: Gail Finkelde; Tom Hush; Joe Lanzisero; Ronaldo Mercado; Steve Starr; John Tucker

Breakdown Artists: Sue Adnopoz; Anthony DeRosa; Barbara DeRosa; Denise Ford; Edward Coral; Tina Grusd; Christine Liffers; Elyse Pastel; Kaaren Spooner; Louis Tate; Peggy Tonkonogy; Jane Tucker; Maria Ramocki-Rosetti; Stephen Zupkas

Effects Breakdown Artists: Ed Coffey; Peter Gullerud; Christine Harding

Animation Consultant: Eric Larson

Character Design: Andreas Deja; Mike Ploog; Phil Nibbelink; Al Wilson; David Jonas

Key Cleanup Artists: Retta Davidson; Tom Ferriter; Dave Suding; Fujiko Miller; Chuck Williams; Isis Thompson; M. Flores Nichols; Lureline Weatherly; Martin Korth; Wesley Chun

Assistant Directors: Mark Hester; Terry Noss; Randy Paton

Directors: Ted Berman; Richard Rich

Produced in Association with: Silver Screen Partners II

Producer: Joe Hale

Executive in Charge of Production: Edward Hansen

Production Manager: Don Hahn

Production Coordinators: Joseph Morris; Dennis Edwards; Ronald Rocha

Executive Producer: Ron Miller

Release Date: July 24, 1985

Running Time: 80 minutes

THE MOVIE

The publicity brouhaha in the months and even years leading up to the release of *The Black Cauldron* was extensive and clamorous, so that it was inevitable that the movie itself should be met with general critical dissatisfaction. $25 million – a world-record sum for an animated feature – had been expended on it, and it had been widely described as the *Snow White* of the "new breed" of Disney animators, those recruited raw from art colleges and so forth and trained up in a programme headed by Eric Larson, a Disney veteran of over 45 years' standing. The speculation that it would contain the first ever movie hologram – a deathless warrior coming straight out of the screen and over the heads of the audience – increased the excitement. Another "first" was that the movie featured animated backgrounds, a technique used even as early as some of the Mickey shorts but never before in a feature. The fact that it was based on a prestigious and prize-winning series of children's fantasy novels, Lloyd Alexander's intermittently excellent "Chronicles of Prydain", was another bonus – although Disney assured the agog public that the movie would be aimed at a more adult audience than the books.

This proved to be a mistake. In the USA especially, animated features are widely regarded as children's fodder, and the movie was generally too frightening and horrific for younger children. (In fact, it is not nearly so visually shocking as 1982's Frank Oz/Jim Henson venture in animated puppetry, *The Dark Crystal*, during the titles of which the average small child asks if it would be possible to go home.) *The Black Cauldron* treats adult issues of good and evil in a fairly adult fashion – which is not to the taste of many long-time Disney followers. It mixes traditional Disney fare with a large measure of the type of action and stylization of evil characteristic of movies like *Star Wars* – itself a sort of hi-tech fairy-tale.

In fact, the major tenable criticism of *The Black Cauldron* – aside from the fact that its happy ending is hopelessly contrived – is that it is in every respect a mixture, notably of animation styles. Some find this very refreshing, especially since the more experimental sequences are probably the best pieces of animation ever created, but to others it jars. On the one hand you have the realistic characters, such as Taran and Eilonwy, and on the other you have the purely cartoon creations, such as Creeper, Gurgi and Fflewddur Fflam, while floating somewhere in the middle are characters such as Dallben and Hen Wen. The superbly surreal moments when the Cauldron Born emerge from the Black

Cauldron are light-years away from some of the straightforwardly comic sequences. (There is also the fact that several times in the opening few minutes, for the first time from Disney since the "shimmering" Prince at the end of *Snow White* [➤160], there is some downright sloppy animation.)

Obviously such things are a matter of opinion, but it is worth asking the question: why *should* an animated feature use only a single style of animation? It seems legitimate to use different styles for different scenes, depending on their content, much as a novelist – examples range from Wilkie Collins to John Fowles - may choose to use several different "voices" to tell a single tale. Some of the sequences in *The Black Cauldron* are artistically staggering, others are more concerned with advancing the plot, but this is surely fair enough.

It was genuinely disappointing that the holographic scene came to naught – it was dropped for the very simple reason that it proved technologically impossible. The movie suffered also some cuts, and these were less justifiable. These occur most notably in the episode where the Cauldron Born creep out from their immobile death intent on the conquest of the world – in fact, the cuts are actually noticeable here, because the sequence seems "too short" and also slightly irrelevant (it just sort of unexpectedly peters out). Some of the cuts were instituted because it was felt that various moments were too frightening – for example, a moment when one of the Horned King's human guards inadvertently gets in the way of one of the Cauldron Born and in consequence is promptly strangled, the life sucked out of him, thereby conveying to the audience the invincibility, ruthlessness and soullessness of the Cauldron Born. The cutting of such scenes was in response to some adverse critical reaction to Disney's (very) recently released *Return to Oz* (1985), which had some frightening scenes. The other reason for cutting was that the movie was too long – a view which seems astonishing when one considers that Disney's greatest hit of all time, *Mary Poppins*, ran for almost twice as long, a cool two hours and 19 minutes.

Animation of *The Black Cauldron* actually started in May 1981; the result was not released until 1985. It was the first Disney animated feature to be filmed in 70mm since *Sleeping Beauty*.

Several screen treatments prepared by Lloyd Alexander were summarily rejected over the years; ironically, a number of critics criticized the movie on grounds of inadequacy of story. Yet a further reason for critical hostility was a perceived overabundance of characters – strange, because in reality *The Black Cauldron* has far fewer characters than, say, *The Rescuers* (compare the list above with that on page 276). Perhaps what the critics had latched onto was that the movie contains very few *minor* characters – i.e., that it has an unwontedly extensive list of major ones. This, it was felt, was a mistake. Brian Sibley, in a 1986 review in *The Animator*, summed this issue up:

> The complicated storyline may have seemed to require all these characters to advance the plot, but it allows little or no time for most of them to be adequately established, let alone fully developed. The inability to resolve this problem is a major weakness in *The Black Cauldron* (just as it was in Bakshi's *The Lord of the Rings* and the recent live-action fantasy *The Never-Ending Story*). It results in an almost total lack of involvement [by the audience] with the characters and, therefore, with the purpose of their quest. Nowhere is this more clearly seen than when the hitherto cowardly Gurgi throws himself into the Cauldron to break its power and save his friends. What should be a moment of great drama and emotion leaves one, instead, unmoved and unconcerned.

This is reasonable criticism – although Sibley may not have had to comfort a weeping seven-year-old during the sequence he cites – but it seems to ignore quite a lot, especially the evil of the Horned King, which is so powerfully depicted that in fact one *does* become involved in the heroes' quest simply because one wishes to see the (inevitable) downfall of this malevolent grotesque.

Another *Snow White The Black Cauldron* probably is not. Nonetheless it is almost certainly the finest animated feature of the 1980s (to the time of writing) and, taken overall, is a magnificent feat. In this light, to carp seems trivial.

THE STORY

> Whosoever uses the Black Cauldron for evil will be all-powerful, for my blood will flow with his, and together we will either rule the world or destroy it.
> The curse of the Black Cauldron

Many centuries ago in a kingdom of Wales that never in fact existed, Prydain, there was a king so evil that even the gods feared him. He was thrown alive into a crucible of molten iron, where his demonic spirit was captured in the form of a great black cauldron. For centuries thereafter the cauldron lay hidden, although it was much sought-after by evil people, for whoever possessed it would possess also the power to create from it an army of deathless warriors – the Cauldron Born – who, unkillable, would enable their master to rule the world.

Now – still centuries ago – there lives in Caer Dallben with the old wizard Dallben a young boy called Taran, whose official position is Assistant Pig-Keeper; his duties are to tend a dainty little pig called Hen Wen. He is restless, however: surely he is of the age where he ought to be fighting for the freedom of Prydain against the evil Horned King? However, Dallben tells him that looking after Hen Wen is more important than he can know.

One day, as Taran is bathing the pig, she begins to struggle. Dallben, hearing the commotion, appears on the scene and tells Taran that Hen Wen is a magical oracular pig, and that she is creating a fuss because she has something to tell him. Cautioning Taran to silence, he fills another tub with water and places candles about it; as Hen Wen puts her snout to it the surface of the water shows images . . . The Horned King is seeking the Black Cauldron, and he knows of the existence of Hen Wen, whose powers are such that, if the evil monarch ever laid hands on her, she would reveal its location. Immediately Dallben provides Taran with food and tells him to take Hen Wen off into hiding in "the hidden cottage at the edge of the Forbidden Forest". The pair set off.

In a short but very dramatic scene – the use of colours in this movie is exceptional, and in this scene it is particularly outstanding – we see the Horned King in his private chamber, a vast and gloomy hall littered with crumbling skeletons. Over these the Horned King evilly gloats for, with the help of the Black Cauldron which he is confident of finding, he will be able to turn them into the Cauldron Born.

On the way to the hidden cottage Taran and Hen Wen pause by a stream, and Taran goes into a daydream of himself as a great warrior. When he awakens from it he discovers that Hen Wen is gone. As he searches for her he hears a scrabbling in the undergrowth and, assuming that this is the pig, he profers an apple – which is promptly snatched by a curious hairy creature, who swiftly chomps most of it while intermittently muttering about the joys of "munchings and crunchings". Gurgi proves to be eager to please, and swiftly responds when Taran asks if he has seen Hen Wen – yes, she went thattaway. But by the time Taran arrives on the scene the oracular pig is being chased by the Horned King's gwythaints – creatures featuring all the worst aspects of both vultures and pterodactyls – and before the lad can save her she is seized and transported off to the Horned King's louring castle.

Despite warnings from Gurgi that his plans are imprudent, Taran makes for the castle, and succeeds in climbing in through an open window. From his hiding-place he watches Creeper, a bizarre little *thing*, introduce the newly captured Hen Wen to the Horned King. Threatening the pig with red-hot tongs Creeper pushes her towards a bowl of water and attempts to persuade her to reveal the location of the Black Cauldron. Taran shouts out in protest and is immediately captured. The Horned King instructs him to tell Hen Wen to reveal the whereabouts of the cauldron, but Taran refuses – until, that is, Creeper places the pig on a chopping-block and the executioner's axe is raised. Then Taran submits, saying:

Hen Wen, from you I do beseech
Knowledge that lies beyond my reach.

As before, images form in the water, sufficient to convince the Horned King that the Black Cauldron is indeed still in existence, but then Taran stumbles into the water, sending splashes agonizingly into the Horned King's redly glowing eyes. In the confusion Taran grabs Hen Wen and runs from the room. From a high parapet he hurls the pig into the moat, far below, and is just about to follow himself when he is seized by a troop of goons led by Creeper; soon after he is in a dungeon beneath the castle.

As he sits there dejectedly one of the paving-stones of the floor is raised and through the hole thereby revealed come first a ball of magic golden light and then a beautiful young girl, who proves to be the princess and apprentice enchantress Eilonwy. She is disappointed that he is not a famous warrior, but the two soon discover they have much in common: both are prisoners and both have been seized because the Horned King believes their magical companions – in Eilonwy's case the golden bauble, in Taran's the pig – will help lead him to the Cauldron.

They go off seeking a means of escape beneath even the lowly level of their own dungeons and come across a burial chamber, where lie many treasures surrounding the cobwebbed body of a long-dead noble who had inhabited the castle in the years before the Horned King did. On the chest of this corpse is a beautiful sword, which Taran impulsively takes.

Their attention is attracted by a nearby scream. They follow the sound and spy on one of the Horned King's goons tying a scrawny minstrel to a raised beam. This proves to be Fflewddur Fflam. After the goon has gone they release the bard and, as the alarm is sounded among the Horned King's followers, the trio flee. During a dramatic battle which results in their escape, Taran discovers that the sword he has picked up is capable of shattering any weapon wielded against it and even of cutting through the iron chains of the castle drawbridge.

Creeper, accustomed to being violently manhandled whenever he has to report a reverse to the Horned King, is delighted when his sovereign is postively pleased that Taran has escaped. After all, the monarch points out, who better to lead his ever-watchful gwythaints to the oracular pig than the Assistant Pig-Keeper himself?

In a clearing near the castle our heroes rest – for a few moments, before Taran and Eilonwy quarrel over who was *really* responsible for their escape. They stalk off in opposite directions, leaving Fflewddur Fflam on his own. Abruptly Gurgi springs from the undergrowth onto the bard, knocking him flat and preparing to rob him of all of his worldly goods. Fflam's cries bring Taran and Eilonwy running, and their is a joyous reunion between the boy and the hairy creature – who announces, *en passant*, that he has recently seen tracks of Hen Wen. He leads the party to where the pig's tracks can be seen on stepping-stones across a small pond; but as they follow the trail the stones begin to sink and the pond to turn into a maelstrom. Our friends are sucked down below the surface … into the subterranean realm of the Fair Folk.

King Eidilleg of the Fair Folk and his sidekick, the irascible Doli, happen along and find the party doing their best to recover consciousness. It immediately emerges that Hen Wen, too, has fallen into this underground kingdom. After a touching reunion between Hen Wen and her assistant keeper, Eidilleg discloses that the Black Cauldron is in the Marshes of Morva, and details Doli to help our friends get there – Hen Wen being left with the Fair Folk for eventual transportation back to Caer Dallben.

Doli sprinkles the others with fairy dust and they are soon among the marshes, amid which stands the creepy cottage of the Witches of Morva – Orgoch, Orddu and Orwen. Our friends break into the cottage, which appears to be empty. As they search the cottage they release a myriad of frogs, the transmuted bodies of people who have in the past offended the Witches. However, Gurgi ignores Eilonwy's shrieks and locates the Cauldron – or, at least, a whole roomful of cauldrons.

Just then the Witches arrive: they are furious. The intruders have "stolen" their nice collection of frogs. As punishment, the companions will themselves be turned into frogs … and eaten. However, Orwen – a buxom lady with more X chromosomes than the average female Disney character, finds Fflewddur Fflam very fetching. The bard appears to think digested-froghood preferable to Orwen's endearments – something which he is able to test when Orwen immediately turns him back into a man. As a result of this byplay Taran has time to announce defiantly that the companions are there to fetch the Black Cauldron – the first time the Witches have been asked for it in two millennia.

The response of the beldames is magically to hurl a succession of other cooking implements at Taran, whose sword takes on a life of its own and shatters the pans, pots, etc. The performance of the sword is easily enough to attract the attention of the Witches, notably Orddu, and they determine to swap the sword for the Cauldron – although the deal is not strictly fair:

Orwen: But what can they *do* with the Cauldron, Orddu?
Orddu: Nothing. That's the point. Don't you see? We'll end up with both!

As soon as the deal is finalized the Witches disappear with the sword and the Cauldron appears from the bowels of the Earth. Our friends do their best to destroy the Cauldron, but as they do so the Witches, perched on a nearby cloud, inform them that it is in fact indestructible – the only way that even its evil powers can be destroyed is if a sentient being voluntarily climbs into it; that being will be sacrificing his or her life in so doing.

As the witches disappear and our friends debate whether Taran is an incompetent (Taran) or a hero (Eilonwy), suddenly there burst upon the scene the Horned King's gwythaints and then, shortly after, a bunch of his goons. Soon after Taran, Eilonwy and Fflewddur Fflam (minus Gurgi, who has sensibly fled) are tied up in the castle of the Horned King, who proceeds to show them how the vicious Cauldron Born can be created simply by tossing skeletons into the Cauldron. Even the evil monarch's goons run in terror.

The Horned King and Creeper go up onto one of the castle's parapets to watch with glee the hideous warriors setting forth to slaughter every living thing. Suddenly Gurgi reappears; he has determined to follow the path of courage. He unties our friends but then, as Taran prepares to throw himself into the Cauldron and thereby negate its evil, insists on doing so himself on the basis that "Taran has many friends, Gurgi has no friends" (except, of course, Taran). Gurgi's sacrifice results in the sudden disintegration of the army of the Cauldron Born, as they collapse back into musty skeletons.

The Horned King and Creeper are quite naturally a little displeased. They climb down from their parapet to find Taran doing his best not to get sucked into the voracious Black Cauldron, which is creating a powerful inrush of wind toward itself. In trying to ensure that Taran becomes a new victim of the Cauldron, the Horned King dramatically becomes one himself, dying in a fountain of light. All sorts of aftereffects are felt, notably the collapse of the castle, from which our heroes are lucky to escape.

Using a convenient boat they soon find themselves on a foreign shore; the Horned King's castle has sunk beneath the waters; the Black Cauldron is bobbing cheerfully on the waves. Suddenly the Witches of Morva appear among the clouds: they want the Black Cauldron back – for free. Fflewddur Fflam and Taran bargain with them, and eventually it is agreed that the companions will trade the Cauldron for the return of Gurgi.

This is effected, but Gurgi, on his magical reappearance at the foot of a whirlpool of light, seems to be dead … until suddenly, for no explained reason, he proves to be alive.

The last scene has been viewed by the wizard Dallben, thanks to Hen Wen's miraculous ability to conjure up distant scenes in bowls of water. As the old man watches, the countryside around regenerates itself, becoming green and blooming where before it was rotting. The evil influence of the Horned King on the land of Prydain is at an end.

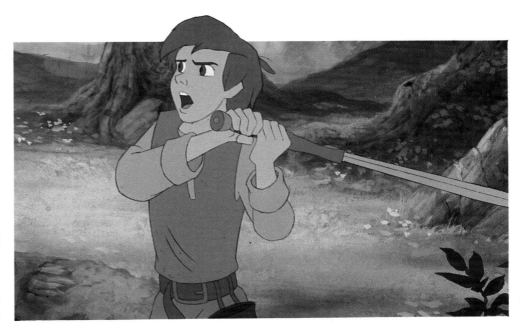

Taran was defiant – especially before he had to do battle with the Horned King and his evil cohorts.

THE CHARACTERS

Taran

Taran, the Assistant Pig-Keeper who wants to make good by becoming a great warrior, is a member of that great fraternity of Disney central protagonists who are rather indefinitely characterized. To say that they are nonentities – as some critics have done – is to be a little harsh, because they are not; but they are definitely, and quite deliberately, painted in pastel colours so that the more ostentatiously bizarre characters around them may shine. The "new breed" of Disney animators saw fit to make Taran an amalgam between the (approximate) appearance of Wart (➤270) and the personality of Mowgli (➤277). This was probably a wise decision, since, *The Black Cauldron* is, debatably, overloaded with strong principal characters, and so a powerfully portrayed Taran would simply have eclipsed such delightful creations as Fflewddur Fflam, Gurgi and Doli.

Voiced by the 14-year-old Grant Bardsley, Taran is a typical 14-year-old boy, with ambitions 'way above his abilities: his desire to be a great warrior is ridiculous in terms of his own scrawny youth. His face is unpocked by a 14-year-old's acne, but he has most of the personality defects of a typical young adolescent – for example, his ability at the very wrong moment to fall into a daydream about his own glorification, so that Hen Wen is lost. Yet, when courage is called for and his life depends upon it, courage he is able to display. He is helped, of course, by the magic sword (a Freudian could have a lot of fun here), but nevertheless he still displays true bravery after the Witches have deprived him of the sword. He is even willing to surrender his life to aid the forces of good – although in the event Gurgi beats him to it.

Taran may not be a strongly depicted character but he is nevertheless a satisfying one – in a way that, say, Wart never was. (Wart was ideal for his role in what was anyway a very different movie, but he hardly inspired affection.) While some critics anathematized Taran as being just a sort of puppet hero, it should be noted that the Taran of Lloyd Alexander's novels is exactly the same character. In both cases, of course, the aim was to produce a character just "real" enough to be convincing but at the same time loosely defined enough so that little boys everywhere could identify with it. Thus Taran in the movie has hair that is neither red nor brown nor black; he has eyes which are dark but whose colour is otherwise indeterminate (sometimes they look dark brown, sometimes almost black, sometimes dark grey-blue); he has a face which is not distinctive; and so on. Even his English voice is of that timbre which could be upper-, middle- or lower-class.

If he has any fault it is that his tunic mysteriously changes colour between scenes – from brown-green to straight green – but then this was a movie worked on over a period of years by countless hands, and anyway most audiences never notice.

Eilonwy

Eilonwy has been widely accused of being the typical Disney saccharine heroine, an accusation which is untenable in two different ways. First, when you start examining the so-called saccharine heroines – such as Cinderella (➤236) and Aurora, the "sleeping beauty" (➤260) – you find that they are anything but saccharine. Second, Eilonwy, despite her physical resemblance to uncounted Disney heroines, is in fact a very strongly portrayed character indeed. In part this comes about because of her voice, supplied by Susan Sheridan (astonishingly aged 34 at the time the soundtrack was made); in yet larger part it comes about because of the character of Eilonwy as rendered in Lloyd Alexander's books. There she is an underage minx and shrew, ever ready to slap Taran down whenever he does something foolish, such as save her life; she is also almost unpleasantly class-conscious, deriding him for the fact that he is nothing more than an Assistant Pig-Keeper. In the last pages of the fifth volume we discover, as we suspected from early on in the first, that all of this is merely a façade, erected by her to conceal the fact that she has been passionately in love with him from approximately the moment that she first set eyes on him. A fair deal of all this spills over into the movie. Not all of it, though: Disney realized that Eilonwy's shrewishness, which verges on the rebarbative in the books, would be intolerably irritating on screen. Still, we have the lines in her introductory meeting with Taran:

Eilonwy: ... I'm Princess Eilonwy. Are you a lord ... or a warrior?
Taran: Er, no, I'm, uh, an assistant pig-keeper.
Eilonwy: Oh, what a *pity*. I was so hoping for someone who could help me escape! Oh well, if you want to come with me you may.
...

As in the books, Eilonwy has a golden bauble which flits around being magical in all directions but serving very little other useful function. Alexander presumably created it because it served to show that Eilonwy was not just any young princess but also a trainee enchantress, and the device worked over a sequence of five

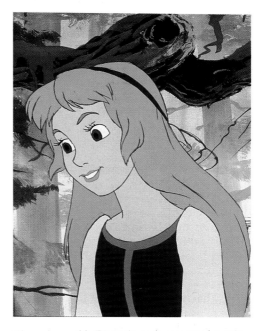

Eilonwy, possibly Disney's most engaging heroine of all time.

novels in which Eilonwy did indeed demonstrate the occasional miraculous ability. In the movie, where she does not, the bauble is a puzzling distraction.

Despite her waspishness, the Disney Eilonwy – blue-eyed, blonde, beautiful and like Taran definitely immediately prepubescent – is a very lovable character. Much of her attractiveness was achieved by the animators but, it should be stressed, much of it was a result of Susan Sheridan's excellent vocalization of the part.

Gurgi

There are two major comic-fantasy creations among the characters in *The Black Cauldron*, one among the goodies and one among the baddies. Gurgi is the one on the side of the angels. He is an indescribable creature: about the most that one can say about his zoological status is that he is definitely mammalian, with his furriness and general cuddliness. With big blue eyes and a white mop of hair and bushy moustache to match, standing perhaps a foot or eighteen inches high. he is very different in physical appearance from the Gurgi of Lloyd Alexander's books, who is bulky and covered in matted hair and smells powerfully. In terms of personality, however, the Disney Gurgi is close to the original, with his talk of "munchings and crunchings" – i.e., food – and his fear of receiving "whackings and smackings". His mixture of cowardice and courage – he is prepared to make the ultimate sacrifice on behalf of his friends – is likewise straight from the book, as is his general tendency to abase himself whenever there is a gap in the dialogue.

His voice, provided by John Byner, is like no other voice you have ever heard – with a single exception. Although one could never mistake Donald Duck's distinctive tones for those of Gurgi there is a definite aural resemblance. It is hard to put one's finger on exactly where that resemblance lies – especially since the two characters are so very different (one cannot imagine Gurgi flying into a rage *à la* Donald) – but it is definitely there. It is as if Byner had started out to try to imitate Clarence Nash and accidentally stumbled over a quite new and independent vocalization.

As well as being one of the major comic characters in the movie, Gurgi can also be considered in many ways its hero. It is who saves the world from conquest by the soulless warriors by diving into the Cauldron, thereby forfeiting his own life. The fact that through a rather clumsy *deus ex machina* he will be resurrected at the end of the movie in no way belittles his self-sacrifice: at the time of his great deed he thinks that he is due for the real, permanent death.

Loopy, loving and lovable, Gurgi is a gift to the soft-toys manufacturers of the world.

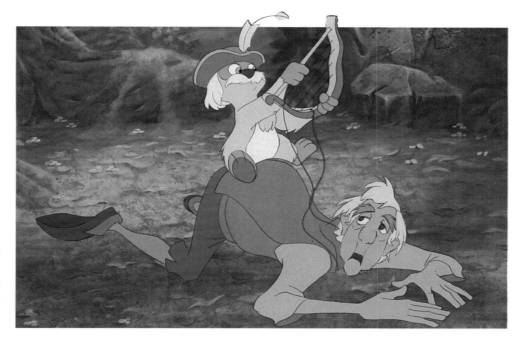

Gurgi, seen here astride Fflam, was a sometimes unhelpful member of the band of heroes.

Fflewddur Fflam

The wandering minstrel Fflewddur Fflam – "minstrel of minstrels", as he modestly describes himself, "balladeer to the grandest courts in all the land" – is a zany, a deliciously overdrawn caricature of the coward who believes himself brave, a numbskull who believes himself touched with genius. His primitive harp (its number of strings varies from time to time during the movie but is never more than about six) knows him better than he does, for at every lie, exaggeration or prevarication from Fflewddur Fflam it breaks a string – a characteristic which it inherits from the books.

The minstrel is no hunk; indeed, there is a vague morphological similarity between him and Ichabod Crane (➤232), as if two different artists had had the same person described loosely to them and had then made independent drawings. With a neck far too thin and scrawny to support his obviously intelligent head, he is, even in repose, quite obviously something of an absent-minded eccentric. He has white hair, grey eyelashes and a hat that was obviously meant to be jaunty by whoever made it but succeeds in sitting on Fflam's head with all the virile confidence of a "Wife and Seven Children to Support" sign. His knees are inclined to knock and his toes to turn in; and at the prospect of any reverse he is the first to announce, with a sort of doleful satisfaction, that the companions are doomed – or at least that he is, which, in his manifest opinion, is even worse.

His is not a very active role in terms of shaping the plot: Taran, Eilonwy and of course Gurgi are the three goodies who do that. Fflewddur Fflam is merely the fourth of the companions – and a good companion he proves to be. Mercifully he has more

sense than his spiritual relation Cacophonix, of Asterix fame, and does not burst out into some doubtless dire ditty. Indeed, this lack of songs from Fflewddur Fflam or anyone else in the movie is something that marks out the "new breed" of animators from the old. (There is not even a theme song to go with the credits. There is, however, a super score by Elmer Bernstein.)

Poor old Fflewddur Fflam. Some are born mediocre, some achieve mediocrity, and some have mediocrity thrust upon them. Fflewddur Fflam, one suspects, surpasses mediocrity only in having attained all three of these options. This is, of course, talking about the depicted human being: as a cartoon creation Fflewddur Fflam is tremendous fun and very convincing.

Dallben

The role of the wizard Dallben, Taran's mentor and, presumably, foster-father, is a very minor one and must be something of a mystery to those viewers who have never read Lloyd Alexander's books: just who *is* this old fellow?

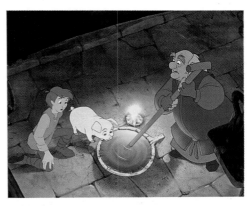

The wizard Dallben used Hen Wen's magical powers to foretell the future.

He is in fact more of a sage than a wizard: he seems not to have the power independently to perform magic, but is able to perceive magical properties in others – i.e., Hen Wen. He draws arcane wisdom from *The Book of Three*, a mystic tome which only he may touch; in that he is privy to its secrets, which are clearly beyond the current knowledge of Prydain, he is of course in a sense a magician after all – according to Arthur C. Clarke's law that any technology significantly advanced beyond your own is indistinguishable from magic.

He is the head of what seems to be little more than a croft with an acre or two but is distinguished by the name of Caer Dallben. He has his servant Taran and a few animals, including some hens and a cheerfully pugnacious goat as well as the oracular pig. Facially Dallben has some similarities with Fflewddur Fflam: like the minstrel he has white hair yet grey bushy eyebrows, but most interesting of all is that they both seem to share the same bulky nose. Otherwise, in character as well as physique, the two could hardly be more different. Dallben wears his scholarship lightly, but it is clear that he is both intelligent and wise, neither of which qualities instantly spring to mind when one thinks of Fflewddur Fflam. Physically Dallben is big and solid, whereas the minstrel, despite a protuberant pot-belly, is overall scrawny. Moreover, Dallben is selfless, willing to risk all, even the life of the lad he so clearly loves, for the sake of the folk of Prydain.

It would have been easy to build up his role to resemble that of Gandalf in Tolkien's rather more extensive, but similar, set of fantasy adventures. Wisely Disney chose not to do this, preferring not to poach on someone else's territory. Still, Dallben is such an appealing character that one leaves the cinema wishing one had seen more of him – which, in terms of the craft of movie-making, is exactly right.

The Horned King

In Lloyd Alexander's pentalogy the Horned King met a grisly end in volume one, *The Book of Three*, and so did not take part in the dispute over the ownership of the Black Cauldron. Disney, however, saw him as an ideal arch-villain, as Joe Hale, the producer of *The Black Cauldron*, explained:

> We thought he would make a good animation character mainly because he had horns sticking out of his head.

This is the artist's habitual false modesty: the Horned King makes a brilliant animated villain because Lloyd Alexander could not have created a better one if he had tried. However, it has to be said that the Horned King bears an embarrassing resemblance to *Star Wars*'s Darth Vader: both lurk mysteriously behind grotesque masks; both are implacably evil; both have voices notable

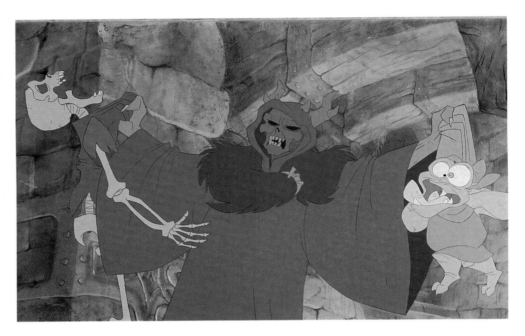

The Horned King demonstrates his unhappiness to one of the Cauldron Born and to Creeper (on the right).

for profound accompanying aspiration. One could take all this much further, comparing their long robes and so forth, but this would be unfair.

The mask of the Horned King is a skull – but the species of the original artiodactyl is dubious: although horned, the skull has much in common with that of a human being. He is the epitome of evil; his every movement and vocal inflection (the latter supplied perfectly by John Hurt) betray this. Even if one met him without his mask at somebody's party, swapping jokes (although it is hard to imagine the Horned King doing this) one would know that he was a villain of the vilest kind. Some critics have disagreed with this judgement of the Horned King. Brian Sibley again:

> The Horned King himself is a particularly unpleasant piece of work, although he lacks the dignity and calculating malice of either the Queen in *Snow White* or Maleficent in *Sleeping Beauty*, and only possesses a fraction of the elemental pagan power which Disney's animators [Tytla] bestowed on the demon of Bald Mountain in *Fantasia* [➤186].

In fact, because he is better *drawn* than either of those two villainesses (ignoring questions of animation, and likewise the dragon-transformation of Maleficent), the Horned King is probably the most frightening of the three, although he lacks the power to transmute himself. Also, he has no redeeming characteristics whatsoever – unlike many other Disney villains. He wants to rule the world and ensure that the future of humanity is, in George Orwell's words, "a boot stamping on a human face – for ever". In this sense he is the worst of *all* of the Disney villains, whose aim has generally been the extermination of the occasional stepdaughter, princess, family of cats or few-score Dalmatians: the

Horned King wants to persecute the entire *world*.

Of course, his efforts come to nothing: he is thwarted first by the courage of Gurgi, who stops the Cauldron Born in their tracks almost before they have started to make them, and second by the implacable vengeance of the Cauldron itself – this second thwarting being terminal. Nonetheless, he is a major Disney villain, and it is interesting to note that often the same critics who compared him unfavourably with Maleficent were, two and half decades earlier, saying that Maleficent herself wasn't up to much. On the next rerelease of *The Black Cauldron* the Horned King can expect a good press.

Creeper

Many people saw Creeper as the star of the show; interestingly, he was the sole character in the movie to be created entirely by Disney, having no parallel whatsoever in Lloyd Alexander's "Chronicles". The goodies had their great comic creation in the form of Gurgi; so it was only fair that the baddies had theirs in the form of Creeper.

As with Gurgi, working out genus and species for Creeper is somewhat difficult; one is not even given a clue, as in the rather similar Fidget (➤324), by a general aura of battishness. Certainly there is something reptilian about Creeper (by contrast with Gurgi's mammalian appearance); equally certainly there is something human about him: more than that one cannot say. Perhaps all such taxonomic guesses are wrong and he is really the offspring of the Horned King and a piranha fish – who knows?

Wonderfully voiced by Phil Fondacaro, Creeper is the equivalent of all those comic villains who have, in Disney features, diluted the pure malicious evil of the main villians: the most obvious example in the canon is provided by the goons in *Sleeping Beauty* (➤264). Creeper is the picture of incompetence: how he ever got his job as chief sleuth and torturer is a major mystery. Although incompetent, although humorous, he is no saint: he is prepared to have Hen Wen barbarously executed in order to elicit the whereabouts of the Black Cauldron, and he displays a gleeful affection for the art of torture which might have been frowned upon had *The Black Cauldron* been a live-action movie.

Like Sir Hiss in *Robin Hood* (➤293) he is poorly treated by the master whom he serves so faithfully: the average response of the Horned King to any reverse, whoever's fault it might be, is to take it out on Creeper. Hence Creeper's abject delight when he discovers that, far from being subjected to grievous bodily harm because of the escape of Taran, he is actually congratulated; and hence his positive ecstasy when he discovers that the Horned King is genuinely dead – and unable to punish him, whether it was Creeper's fault or not!

Creeper has been described widely as the star of *The Black Cauldron*, and his virtual duplication in the form of Fidget would seem to suggest that Disney took such views seriously. Of course, he is nothing of the kind: he is one of the sequence of brilliant supporting actors that Disney has created over the years . . . in fact, he is one of the best of them. But in no way is he a star like the Horned King.

Eidilleg and Doli

The accidental excursion of the companions into the land of the Fair Folk seems to serve little plot purpose other than to introduce to

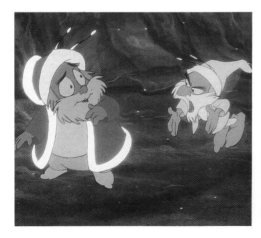

King Eidilleg, on the left, persuading Doli that he really *does* want to help Taran and his friends.

the tale **Doli**, a hot-tempered little flying fellow with the power of invisibility who leads them to the Marshes of Morva. Readers of the "Chronicles" will know that in them Doli is a major character, one of the regular members of the companions, and presumably it was thought by Disney that it

would be wrong to leave him out completely. Alexander's Fair Folk are rather smaller than humans, but Disney's are tiny and brightly coloured, and possess the power of flight. (Among the Fair Folk we see a brief cameo of Tinker Bell [➤249].) Doli himself, when visible, is dressed in bright yellow with a traditional-pattern elfin cap on his head. His features are sharp – even his white beard has jagged edges – and he *looks* constantly irascible, an impression borne out by his vexed dialogue and especially his superb voice, supplied by John Byner, doubling up on Gurgi.

King Eidilleg has an even smaller part, welcoming the travellers to his realm, discovering the nature of their quest, and ordering Doli to accompany them on the next stage of their journey. He is a rather Santa Claus-like figure: plump, bearded, and dressed in a red jacket with trimmings of white fur and with a hat to match. Eager to please everyone, he is obviously no argumentative match for the sharp-witted Doli.

The Witches of Morva

The three witches of Morva, with their obsessive penchant for turning passing strangers into frogs, are caricatures in the great Disney tradition. Although two of them – Orgoch and Orddu – are as grotesque as *Snow White*'s evil Queen in her guise as hag (➤160), and their faces show many similarities with hers (Orwen is likewise grotesque, but in a different way), curiously they are not in any way frightening. This is a good thing in terms of *The Black Cauldron*'s construction – the Horned King is quite enough villain for one movie – but nevertheless seems odd: after all, turning people into frogs on whim is a fairly evil activity, and they are perfectly prepared to swindle the companions out of their lives.

Orddu is the biggest of the three, and acts as their leader. Her fascination with Taran's magic sword leads her to propose the dishonest exchange. She has a long, warty, pointed nose, a cacklingly toothless grin,

and the torso of a tall plump matron to which are attached scrawny, bony limbs. She may be evil, but she certainly does have some charm in her manner. The same can hardly be said for **Orgoch**, the most evilly vindictive of the three, who is keen to counter any suggestion by the other two that the companions should not suffer an amphibian doom. Her facial features have much in common with those of Orddu but succeed in being even sharper. She is roughly half the height of the bigger witch, and is crabbed with extreme age.

Orwen is built on a totally different model. While the other two have straggly red hair, Orwen's is not so much red as fluorescent orange, and her appearance is quite the opposite of pointy or skinny: one does not like to say this of a lady, but Orwen is out-and-out fat. One can say this because, as it proves, Orwen is no lady – at least in the conventional sense. She clearly regards herself as a sumptuous sexpot, and gaily indulges in the suggestions of her rampaging hormones. Heavily made-up in tones which match her hair for eye-puncturing brilliance, she has a button-bow mouth, a snub nose, and eyes which brightly peer out for any signs of a prospective mate. Fflewddur Fflam has the misfortune to be caught in those twin searchlights and although Orwen's desire for him saves him from ending his days as a frog – Orgoch magically zaps him, but Orwen zaps him back again – it seems likely that he will suffer an even worse fate. During his short experience of being a frog he has some agonizing moments – and a horrifying preview of the prospects in store for him - as he struggles trapped between Orwen's voluminous breasts. (The scene has raised a few eyebrows on various scores.) A desirable mate Orwen may not be, but in her own plump, over-the-top way she is certainly likeable.

Strangely, at the end of the movie, the witches go out of their way to aid the grieving companions, returning Gurgi to them and then reversing the spell of the Cauldron to bring him back to life. Earlier in the movie their magic was apparently not

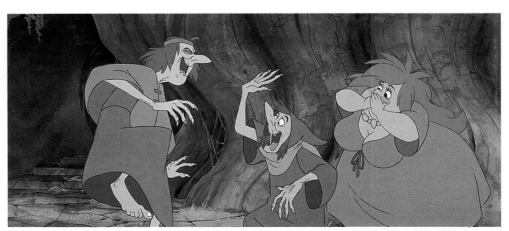

The three witches of Morva – from left to right, Orddu, Orgoch and Orwen.

strong enough to control its power, so the episode seems inconsistent. It seems even more inconsistent in a psychological sense, because when we meet them in the cottage all three witches, in their different ways, are governed entirely by selfishness.

Hen Wen

Although the oracular pig is of pivotal importance in the plot and occupies a fair deal of screen-time, she is hardly a character at all. She is small and cute, with bright blue human-like eyes equipped with a full complement of dainty eyelashes and eyebrows. (The Hen Wen of the books is a rather more substantial beast.) Giddy-headed and unreliable, she essentially disappears from the story after Taran has freed her from the Horned King's castle.

Minor Characters

There are very few minor characters in *The Black Cauldron*; rather, there are three "group characters" of note (four, if one counts the Fair Folk). There are the Horned King's heavy-jowled, lumbering, brutish henchmen, who seem to possess not a braincell between them. Although their commander is the incompetent Creeper, one senses that they would be even more incapable without him. One of them, Moose, was named in some advance trailers, but failed to appear in the final movie.

In an early scene a rather sexy dancing-girl appears: her role is to entertain the troops.

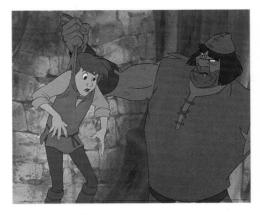

Taran discovering that life is not without its little problems.

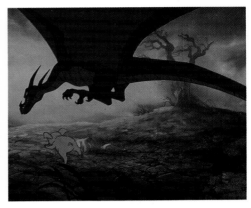

Taran tried to protect Hen Wen from the attack of the gwythaints.

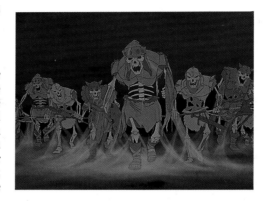

The Cauldron Born.

The spine-chilling gwythaints, huge reptilian equivalents of birds of prey, are as powerfully depicted as any anonymous villains in Disney. In a way they are terrifying because they are not actually evil, just mindless and implacable, dedicatedly carrying out the orders of their master.

Equally petrifying are the ranks of the Cauldron Born, animated in an impressionistic, semi-abstract style quite different from anything seen in a Disney feature before. Moving with slow inexorability, they seem to leave behind them after-images of themselves, and long tresses of not-quite-discernible, phosphorescent-green gossamer trail from their fleshless limbs. The short sequence in which they are released from the Cauldron and engulf and overwhelm anything or anybody that stands in their way is simultaneously one of the most harrowing and one of the most beautiful pieces of animation ever produced.

THE GREAT MOUSE DETECTIVE

Characters:

Basil; Dr. Dawson; Olivia Flaversham; Hiram Flaversham; Ratigan; Toby; Felicia; Fidget; Queen Moustoria; Mrs. Judson; Bartholomew; Thugs; Dancing Girl; Bar Maid; Bartender; Pianist; Juggling Octopus; Lady Mouse

Credits:

Based on *Basil of Baker Street* by Eve Titus (1974)

Voices: Vincent Price (Ratigan); Barrie Ingham (Basil, Bartholomew); Val Bettin (Dr. Dawson, thug, guard); Candy Candido (Fidget); Alan Young (Hiram Flaversham); Susanne Pollatschek (Olivia) ; Diana Chesney (Mrs. Judson); Eve Brenner (Queen Moustoria); Basil Rathbone (Sherlock Holmes); Laurie Main (Dr. Watson); Ellen FitzHugh (Bar Maid); Shani Wallis (Lady Mouse); Walker Edmiston, Wayne Allwine, Tony Anselmo (thug, guards)

Music: Henry Mancini

Music Editor: Jack Wadsworth

Songs by: Henry Mancini; Larry Grossman; Ellen Fitzhugh; Melissa Manchester

Story Adaptation: Pete Young; Vance Gerry; Steve Hulett; Ron Clements; John Musker; Bruce M. Morris; Matthew O'Callaghan; Burny Mattinson; Dave Michener; Melvin Shaw

Art Director: Guy Vasilovich

Backgrounds: Donald A. Towns; Lisa L. Keene; John Emerson; Brian Sebern; Michael Humphries; Tia Kratter; Andrew Phillipson; Philip Phillipson

Layout: Dan Hansen; David A. Dunnet; Karen A. Keller; Gil Dicicco; Michael A. Peraza, Jr.; Edward L. Ghertner

Colour Styling: Jim Coleman

Supervising Animators: Mark Henn; Glen Keane; Robert Minkoff; Hendel Butoy

Coordinating Animators: Tom Ferriter; Dave Suding; Chuck Williams; Walt Stanchfield; Bill Berg

Character Animators: Matthew O'Callaghan; Mike Gabriel; Ruben A. Aquino; Jay Jackson; Kathy Zielinski; Doug Krohn; Phil Nibbelink;

Andreas Deja; Phil Young; Shawn Keller; Ron Husband; Joseph Lanzisero; Rick Farmiloe; David Pruiksma; Sandra Borgmeyer; Cyndee Whitney; Barry Temple; David Block; Ed Gombert; Steven E. Gordon

Effects Animators: Ted C. Kierscey; Kelvin Yasuda; Dave Bossert; Patricia Peraza; Mark Dindal

Computer-generated Graphics: Tad A. Gielow

Animation Consultant: Eric Larson

Animation Camera: Ed Austin

Editors: Roy M. Brewer, Jr.; James Melton

Assistant Directors: Timothy J. O'Donnell; Mark A. Hester

Directors: John Musker; Ron Clements; Dave Michener; Burny Mattinson

Producer: Burny Mattinson

Release Date: July 2, 1986

Running Time: 74 minutes

THE MOVIE

One's opinion of *The Great Mouse Detective* (confusingly released in the UK under the slightly different title of *Basil – The Great Mouse Detective*) depends upon what one wants from a movie. If you are seeking a great Disney classic – a *Snow White* for the 1980s – then *The Great Mouse Detective* is not for you. If, by contrast, you simply want to see a movie that provides virtually nonstop rollicking fun, then you would find difficulty in making a better selection than *The Great Mouse Detective*. It is very definitely a movie for those who prefer *Star Wars* to *2001* and *Sleeper* to *Annie Hall*. It has no deep psychological undertones, but nor does it lapse into bathetic excess. It is not a "Disney classic" in the sense that, perhaps, *Bambi* and *Pinocchio* are; but there is a good case to be made for its being a classic nevertheless, for it is one of a kind: it sets out to be nothing more than a hilarious and breathtaking romp, and in this it succeeds magnificently. It is hard to think of a Disney animated feature which is more plain, straightforward *fun*. It passes one particular test with flying colours: in any audience watching *The Great Mouse Detective*, the adults and the children *laugh at the same jokes*. At a more mundane level, the movie grossed $18 million in the United States in the first month after its release – an astonishing feat by any standards.

Needless to say, the reviewers were divided over the movie. Their reactions ranged from the frankly hostile …

The supporting cast includes more mice, and three of the film's four directors have surnames beginning with M, which suggests to my suspicious mind that they might be mice too. Certainly they have created a film with somewhat tiny comic appeal and nothing at all of the pictorial splendour of old Disney.

Financial Times

… through the "mixed" …

… the best full-length animated film the Disney boys have produced since the Master's death. Yet only in the odd frame do we find that magical spark that set the great Disney classics of the late 1930s and '40s ablaze.

Observer, London

… to the wildly enthusiastic:

Basil is intelligent fun, with enough bite to delight. Do go and enjoy. It is a film the children can safely take grown-ups to in the confidence that they will not be bored.

Daily Telegraph

… a highly recommended picture … should not be missed under any circumstances.

Richard Holliss, *Starburst*

David Hancock chose a most inopportune journal in which to be patronizing about the movie:

Sherlock Holmes is given the spoof treatment and the little ones will enjoy it.

The Sun, London

And at least one reviewer used the movie as an excuse for an exercise in advanced postmodernistic incomprehensibility:

Disney cartoons, with their oozy tumescent contours and their naively filled-in colour, their histrionic shrieks and gestures … and their cast of goodies (pale, middle class) and baddies (swarthy, poor), pretend to wholesomeness and rectitude while extracting, as in *Basil*, maximum entertainment from the underlying horror.

The Independent, London

"Yes," one aches to ask, "but did you enjoy the movie?"

It is difficult to list the full strengths of the movie, but there are a few which should certainly be mentioned.

First, the script. Not only is this exquisitely plotted, fast-paced and dramatic, it is also exceptionally funny. Whether the gags are verbal or visual, they all share a genuine ingenuity, a love of lateral thinking and skew-logic for their own sake. A prime example occurs when Dawson and Basil have been roped to a mousetrap. A record is being played. The ending of the record will release a ball down a chute, and this will (a) set off the mousetrap, (b) fire a revolver at them, (c) release a crossbow-bolt at them, (d) cause an axe to chop them in half, (e) let a vast cast-iron anvil drop on top of them, and (f) cause a camera to take a photograph of their gory demise so that the vile Ratigan can gloat over it in the years to come. Basil, however, after feverish calculation realizes that, if he and Dawson set off the mousetrap at exactly the right time, the ball will stop the bar of the trap inches above their necks. But there is more! The pin flies out of the trap, knocking the gun off target so that its bullet deflects the crossbow, whose bolt in turn deflects the axe, which falls to cut the ropes and mousetrap so that the two mice are well clear when the anvil plummets. Complicated enough … but there is yet more. Moments later, Basil has posed himself, Dawson and Olivia in seaside-snap postures just in time for the camera to click and so preserve forever his proud grin.

This entire complicated sequence takes up only a few seconds of screen time, yet is meticulously crafted in terms of both animation and timing. Yet it is the ingenuity of the sequence of events which makes the audience burst into applause.

A second major strength of the movie is its characterization. In most Disney animated features one expects to find two or three of the "supporting major" characters powerfully depicted, plus a gaggle of minor zanies to produce comic relief. In *The Great Mouse Detective*, however, *all* of the characters are strong ones – even Queen Moustoria, who might have been expected to have been a symbol rather than a fully developed personality, is given a well rounded character of her own. (A well rounded physique, too, but that is by the by.) If one has to identify a weak link in the chain, it is probably Mrs. Judson, Basil's housekeeper, but she seems to be two-dimensional only by contrast with those around her: in most other movies she would register as a fully fledged supporting actor.

A third of the movie's strengths one mentions almost reluctantly: the animation. The climactic scenes of the chase inside the workings of Big Ben (strictly speaking, the clock of which Big Ben is the bell) were executed with the assistance of computers – humans did the figures, computers the clock's gears and cogs – and they are stunning. As the *Sunday Times* summed it up, this sequence "couldn't have easily been done in the old days and must rank as one of the high spots in film animation". The point, of course, is that Disney used the computers to *assist* the human animators, not to replace them – for the animation of Basil, Ratigan and Olivia in the sequence is magnificent. *Has* to be magnificent, in fact, because otherwise it would have looked appalling when matched to the precision of the computer work.

The reason for the reluctance to praise the animation too highly has nothing to do with the use of computers, however. It is that, in some parts of the movie, the animation is not good; and in other parts the use of static background figures mars some excellent work in the foreground. An example of the former flaw occurs early in *The Great Mouse Detective*, when Dawson hops down to the pavement from the step of a hansom cab. The movement is all wrong, and the "illusion of life" is momentarily destroyed. Examples of the latter defect occur when Basil and Dawson are in the seedy riverside pub: behind their animated figures we see a flat, motionless backdrop of other customers – who are more sketched than fully painted. To add insult to injury, an attempt is made to give some life to this background by superimposing upon it the occasional waft of pungent tobacco smoke.

Still, one has to bear in mind the facts of modern economics – if facts they are – and, anyway, the quality of the rest of the film is so high that such blemishes are forgotten almost as soon as noticed (to be fair, some viewers never notice them in the first place). This latter fact reflects the time taken for the two major ingredients involved in the making of *The Great Mouse Detective*: the planning of the movie took four years; the actual making of it took only one.

It is this equation which determines the status of *The Great Mouse Detective* as a classic of a different sort from the other Disney classics. One can pick away at minor technical blemishes, but this cannot alter the overall effect of the movie – which is to provide the best entertainment that there's been in town for many a long year. The

Daily Telegraph, as cited above, recorded the only sensible critical reaction to *The Great Mouse Detective*: "Do go and enjoy."

THE STORY

It is the eve of Queen Moustoria's Diamond Jubilee and, more importantly, the birthday of young Olivia Flaversham. Her father, a toymaker, gives her a clockwork dancing-girl as a present; but almost immediately afterwards he is kidnapped by Fidget, a one-legged bat who is chief assistant to the crime baron Ratigan.

Dr. David Q. Dawson has returned to London after some years spent in Afghanistan. He is seeking lodgings when he hears sobbing from within a discarded Wellington boot. There he finds Olivia, who has set out in search of Basil, the famous detective, who lives in the basement of 221B Baker Street. Dawson does not know Basil, but he does know where Baker Street is, and so he leads the little child to Basil's home. Basil is not at home, but his housekeeper/landlady Mrs. Judson lets the two in out of the rain.

When Basil returns he immediately recognizes Fidget from Olivia's description. Clearly this case involves Basil's arch-enemy, Ratigan – and we cut to a song-and-dance scene with Ratigan and his cronies, during which we learn that Ratigan plots to overthrow Queen Moustoria and set himself up as King Ratigan I. He has kidnapped Flaversham in order to force him to build a robot replica of the Queen. Back to Basil's flat, and moments later Fidget appears at the window. He escapes before our friends can catch him, but Basil determines to follow him, assisted by a puppyish bloodhound called Toby.

Fidget's trail leads to a toyshop, where the hideous little bat is purloining items on a "shopping list" which Ratigan has given to him: these include toy soldiers' uniforms, clockwork springs and, most notably, Olivia. Fidget has had time to gather all the items except Olivia when Basil arrives with the girl herself and Dr. Dawson. After some minor sleuthing, Basil and Dawson become separated from Olivia, who goes wandering off to look at the toys and is captured by Fidget. Basil gives chase, but eventually Fidget escapes. (One of the toys in the shop is a bubble-blowing wooden model of Dumbo [➤194].)

However, Fidget has accidentally left behind his "shopping list", and this is found by Dawson. Basil subjects the paper to chemical analysis, and discovers incontrovertible evidence that it must have emanated from a riverside pub near where a sewer disgorges itself into the Thames: the only possible candidate is a pub called "The Rat Trap", and thither Basil and Dawson make their way, disguised as rough sailors.

They are recognized for what they are by the bar maid and bartender, and their pints of ale are spiked with soporifics. Basil is not to be caught out so simply, but before he has time to tell Dawson not to drink his beer the good doctor has downed it. Its effect on Dawson is to encourage his lechery, and soon he is dancing on stage with a troupe of sexy chorus-mice. At the end of their song-and-dance number, an enormous fight breaks out among the pub's patrons. Basil and Dawson escape unscathed, and follow Fidget, who has made a brief appearance.

In pursuit of the bat they make their way through a maze of sewage pipes, finally to emerge at Ratigan's lair. However, the whole thing has been a trap: they are captured, Basil is humiliated, and the two friends are tied tightly into a mousetrap: at the end of the playing of a gramophone record the trap will spring – and, simultaneously, they will be shot by a gun, impaled by a crossbow bolt, chopped in half by an axe, and flattened by a falling anvil. Oh, yes, and photographed for Ratigan's later delectation. The arch-criminal sets off for a grand mousehole at Buckingham Palace.

Basil and Dawson escape, of course, and release Olivia, too, but already Ratigan has captured the Queen and set in her place his clockwork robot. This pseudo-Moustoria announces that she has decided to marry Ratigan, and he instantly proceeds to read out the new laws that he plans to put into effect forthwith – taxing the poor and crippled, etc. But then Basil and Dawson arrive, seize the robot's controls, and show Ratigan up as the imposter he is.

Ratigan and Fidget, with a recaptured Olivia, flee in their pedal-powered dirigible. Basil swiftly concocts an airship out of balloons, string, a Union flag and a matchbox, and he, Dawson and Flaversham give chase. Eventually Ratigan's dirigible crashes through the face of the clock atop the Houses of Parliament. He and Basil do battle among the cogs within, Fidget having been cast by Ratigan into the Thames some while back in order to lighten the dirigible's load. Basil and Ratigan finally fall all the long distance into the fog-enshrouded Thames, and it seems that our hero has lost his life, *à la* Reichenbach Falls, in putting an end to his foe. However, moments later Basil reappears, pedalling furiously on the remains of Ratigan's dirigible, and the day is saved.

Inevitably, there is a happy-sad ending. Olivia and her father must leave (sob), and so too must Dawson (sob) ... except that just then there is a caller, a veiled lovely with a problem that can be solved only by the acumen of Basil, the great mouse detective. And Basil introduces Dawson to her as his permanent assistant. The audience cheers lustily, the titles begin to run, and an eminently satisfying movie concludes.

THE CHARACTERS

Basil

The received wisdom is that Basil was given his name as a small memorial to Basil Rathbone, the actor who was *the* screen Sherlock Holmes. The truth of this assertion is hard to establish since, of course, the name "Basil" comes from Eve Titus' 1974 book, and there is no especial reason why a book character should be named for a movie actor. That said, Disney was obviously aware of the coincidence of names, for in one scene we see the shadows of Rathbone and his Watson, Laurie Main (who took over from the one and only Nigel Bruce), cast against Holmes' study wall, and hear a

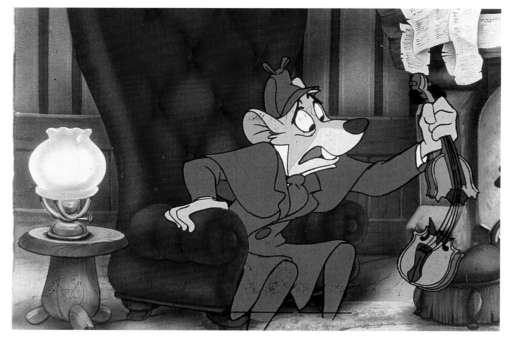
Basil discovering how much fun it is to have kids around.

snatch of conversation between them drawn from the soundtrack of one of those old movies. (Interestingly, when we elsewhere see Holmes silhouetted against his window, playing the inevitable violin, the image is not especially Rathbone-ish.)

Clearly Basil himself is portrayed along the lines of the popular conception of Holmes, but to say this is to simplify – for Basil is much more than Holmes in mouse's clothing. It would be wrong to go so far as the reviewer in *Today* who said that "Basil is a more lovable mouse than that dreadful Mickey", but the fact remains that Basil is more of a *mouse* than Mickey. To understand Basil's personality we have to recognize that he is a mouse with many of the attributes of the great detective whom he emulates, rather than being Holmes in fancy dress.

He is luminously intelligent, and like so many intelligent individuals he displays a sort of psychological neoteny: he has never quite grown up so that, despite his adult form, his mind still exhibits a childlike sense of wonder. He is entranced by his own cleverness (as when he uses a complex chemical experiment in order to show that Fidget's "shopping list" is saturated with sodium chloride), and can be thrown into the pits of depression when that cleverness, so much relied upon, fails to produce the required results (as when, early in the movie, he discovers from forensic comparison of two bullets that he has tracked down the wrong gun). These are characteristics of a precocious child. When he and Dr. Dawson face death, having been outwitted by Ratigan, Basil falls headfirst into a slough of despond from which it is almost impossible for his more mature assistant to extract him. This again is a feature of the youthful mind. However, while immature personalities may have their drawbacks, they have too their advantages over their more "grown-up" counterparts, and these advantages Basil has in full measure. The quickness of his movements reflects the equal quickness of his thinking; and he is capable of following logical processes that simply would not occur to people more set in their ways. In the sequence in which he releases Dawson and himself from Ratigan's "overkill" execution set-up, for example, Basil – once stimulated by Dawson into mental activity – realizes that their sole hope of escape is to start out by taking what is apparently the most dangerous possible course of action: springing the mousetrap. He shows no fear whatsoever about doing this once he has decided that it is necessary. On the one hand this represents the childish beliefs (a) that everything will be all right no matter how dangerous actions may seem and (b) that one's own cleverness can be relied upon 100 per cent; one could add a (c), that Basil is so fascinated by the ingenuity of the plan that, childishly, he completely forgets about the dire consequences should it fail.

But on the other hand his lack of fear shows the recognition by the intelligent individual that, if there is indeed only one possible course of action, then it is silly to be frightened. It is notable that Dawson, who has been up until then trying to put a brave face on things, who has been playing the adult to Basil's child, trembles with uncontrollable terror when it comes to actually *doing* something about their predicament.

There are some similarities to be observed between Basil and the Disney version of Robin Hood (➤292). Both are depicted as quick-witted, fearless in adversity, pitted against much more powerful enemies, and so forth. However, the character of Basil has been much more carefully thought through. One critic had it, perhaps a little unfairly, that Robin was the most boring character in *Robin Hood*, despite his gleeful childish cleverness; but one certainly could not say the same of Basil, who would be an outstanding character in any movie. For Basil is more than just a collection of behaviour patterns: one leaves the cinema feeling that one knows him as a personality. Every characteristic rings true. When, for example, Ratigan escapes from the palace in his bat-powered dirigible, we may be surprised at the nature of the Heath Robinsonish vehicle which Basil devises for the purposes of giving chase, but *we are not surprised that Basil should have been capable of inventing it.* This is not simply because we are confident, as ever, that the goodies will triumph over the baddies' fellest manoeuvres; it is because the invention is exactly the type of gadget which we expect Basil – or any other child! – to produce.

Basil's characterization has many strengths in itself, but it has in addition an

Basil and Dr. Dawson, sveltely disguised.

extra one which originates in the relationship between him and his audience. This is that, adult or child, we *identify* with him. If we are not like Basil we would like to be, and for an hour and a quarter we believe that we are. This is something of a departure for the Disney features of the last couple of decades: many of them have a central character whose personality is two-dimensional. It is this character with whom we are intended to identify, and the two-dimensionality is deliberately created so that we can graft onto the character sufficient of our *own* attributes for the identification to be successful. In *The Rescuers* Penny is "everygirl"; in *The Sword in the Stone* Wart is "everyboy". In *The Great Mouse Detective*, however, the character who might have been expected to take on this role, Olivia, is far from two-dimensional, and it is Basil with whom we are intended to – and do – identify.

As a final note, it should be added that the voicing of Basil, performed by Barrie Ingham, could not be bettered. It complements and enhances Basil's screen personality perfectly. If one heard it on the radio one would conjure up in one's mind's eye a figure very much like the screen Basil. There were rumours before the release of *The Great Mouse Detective* that Disney, scared by the poor reception given a few months earlier to Steven Spielberg's *The Young Sherlock Holmes*, had plans to dub American voices onto the soundtrack for the movie's North American release. Fortunately these were rumours, and Ingham's marvellous performance has been preserved.

Dr. Dawson

If Basil is *himself*, rather than a mouse version of any human actor, Dr. David Q. Dawson, late of Her Majesty's 66th Regiment in Afghanistan, is modelled to a

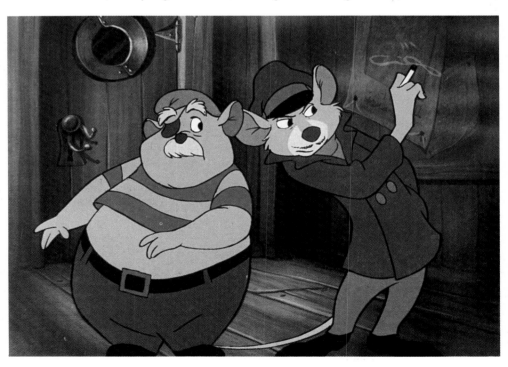

great extent on that doyen of screen Watsons, Nigel Bruce. Indeed, were it not for his ears and tail, Dawson would display none of the attributes of a mouse at all.

It is argued above that Basil is essentially a childlike character: while possessed of great intelligence, he has a multitude of childlike traits. Dawson, by contrast, represents the voice of adulthood, common sense, sensibleness ... which all means that he is of little use in the mental duel against an intellectual criminal such as Ratigan. Indeed, it is hard to think of any reason why Basil should be so keen, at the end of the movie, to enlist Dawson's assistance in future cases – except, perhaps, that Basil may have been finding life as a solo operator a trifle lonely. Dawson's only contribution to the fight against evil in this adventure is to keep *talking* to Basil after the latter's humiliation by Ratigan: left to himself, Basil would have perished on the mousetrap.

Like Nigel Bruce's version of Watson, Dawson cannot be relied upon: he is a well meaning blunderer. When the companions are in the toyshop, Basil entrusts Olivia to Dawson's care; yet the good doctor succeeds in losing the little girl almost at once. Similarly, in the seedy riverside pub, "The Rat Trap", Dawson forgets his freshly adopted persona sufficiently to try to order a dry sherry; while Basil nips this notion in the bud, he is not swift enough to stop Dawson from swilling down his pint of drugged ale post haste. Thereafter, in a scene reminiscent of the gently parodic movie *The Private Life of Sherlock Holmes*, Dawson allows the temptations of the flesh to lure him into an intimate dance with the pub's seductive chorus girls. All of these

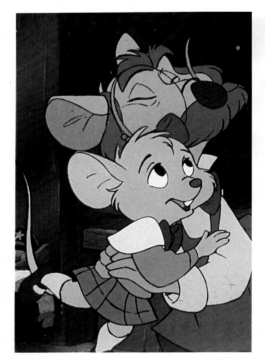

Olivia Flaversham and her father, Hiram. All was well until Ratigan intervened.

faux pas not only embarrass Basil, they hinder his chase after Ratigan.

It is perhaps a pity that Dawson should be modelled on the Nigel Bruce representation. In Conan Doyle's books Watson was by no means a buffoon; the same is true of Eve Titus' Dawson in *Basil of Baker Street*. Still, an intelligent Dawson might have drawn one's attention away from Basil, which would have been a bad thing in terms of the overall structure.

On the positive side, it would be unfair not to mention Dawson's essential *goodness*. Not only does he good-heartedly take Olivia from her dank misery in the gumboot to the sanctuary of Basil's flat, he also perseveres in pressing her case when Basil is all too keen to forget about her. In this respect, Dawson is like one's favourite uncle: always ready to help out in times of trouble, but not the ideal person upon whom to rely, or with whom to discuss theoretical physics.

Olivia Flaversham

In many other Disney features the "token child lead" is not really a character at all, merely a symbol of "everychild". Delightfully, in *The Great Mouse Detective* the lead child is a fully rounded personality. Olivia Flaversham, the toymaker's daughter, is definitely no cypher. Also, she does not fall into the other possible trap – that of being nauseatingly cute. Although somewhat mouselike in appearance, she is a very realistic little girl.

The Scots accent helps, of course. This was supplied by eight-year-old Glaswegian Susanne Pollatschek: it is comparatively rare for a US movie-maker to use a genuine Scot to provide a Scots voice but, to judge by this performance, US movie-makers ought to do it more often.

Olivia is a stubborn wee girl: she usually gets her way. Consider the dialogue we hear when she suggests to Basil that she ought to accompany himself and Dawson on the perilous journey to the toyshop:

> *Olivia*: Wait for me ... I'm coming too!
> *Basil*: What! Certainly not! This is no business for children!
> *Olivia*: Are we going to take a cab?
> *Basil*: My dear, I don't think you understand. It will be quite dangerous. [Distractedly sits on his violin, smashing it. Continues angrily:] Young lady! You are most definitely not accompanying us, and that is final.

The next shot we see is of Olivia accompanying Basil ...

It is one of Basil's little failings that he is not good with children. Throughout most of the movie he regards Olivia as little more than an unavoidable pest – which, in many respects, she is. However, she has a great many good qualities, notably her courage in adversity (she struggles stoutly to escape

from the bottle in which she has been imprisoned, hoping to release Basil and Dawson from Ratigan's trap), and by the end of *The Great Mouse Detective* even Basil's ascetic heart has warmed to her – to the extent that he is almost tearful when she and her father say farewell. Even then, however, he proves incapable of getting Olivia's name right – a running gag throughout the film. His final attempt at "Flaversham" is his most ornate:

> *Olivia*: Goodbye, Basil, I'll never forget you.
> *Basil*: Nor I you, Miss ... Miss ... Flangerhanger.

It is to be hoped that future Disney animated features will continue the practice of *The Great Mouse Detective* and have strong, *realistic* children in the leading roles.

Hiram Flaversham

Olivia's father, the kind old toymaker, is a pleasing character voiced in Scots tones by Alan Young, who did such a fine job as Scrooge in the featurette *Mickey's Christmas Carol* (►130). His part in *The Great Mouse Detective* is not a major one, yet his personality has been carefully created. On the one hand he is every child's favourite grandfather, mild, gentle, fond of the little ones; but on the other he has a certain steel concealed beneath the soft exterior. He is prepared to die rather than assist Ratigan's diabolical scheme, and it is only when the "large mouse" threatens instead to torment Olivia that Hiram concedes defeat.

Ratigan

Chris Peachment, writing in *Time Out*, put into words what many audiences must have felt on watching *The Great Mouse Detective*:

> As usual with film noir, however, it is the villain who steals the heart. Who could resist a crime baron in a top hat, and crimson-lined cape, who speaks in a voice which emanates from somewhere at the back of Ligeia's tomb? In the final breathtaking showdown, high up in the cogs and ratchets of Big Ben, which looks like one of Piranesi's prisons, I know who I was rooting for. The final splashdown in the Thames leaves the way open for a possible sequel, and I'll be at that one too, shouting "Let's hear it for Ratigan".

Well, we all know what Piranesi's prisons look like, don't we?

In voicing the arch-villain Vincent Price plays the part of Vincent Price with gusto, and it is to the animators' credit that they did not simply model the character on the actor. To be sure, Ratigan has some of the pretensions to culture displayed by Price's usual screen persona – represented physically by a three-piece suit, a foot-long cigarette-holder, etc. – but aside from these (and Price's eyebrows) he is a new creation, modelled on no one but himself – and Conan Doyle's Moriarty.

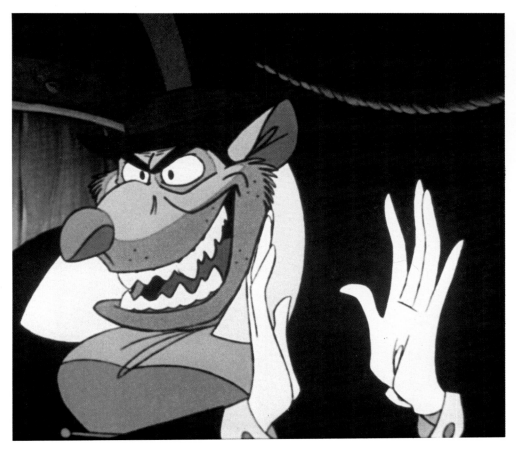

Ratigan: would *you* buy a used car from this rat . . . er, mouse?

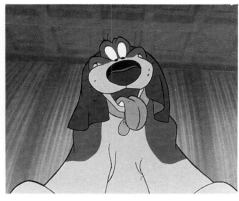

Toby, the (relatively) vast hound who helped Basil and Dawson on their quest.

It has to be said: Ratigan is a sewer rat. However, it should not be said whenever he is within earshot, because he is ashamed of his species: you may remark upon the fact that he is exceptionally large for a mouse, but to go any further is to invite doom at the jaws of Ratigan's voracious cat Felicia. It is, in fact, essential that Ratigan be generally accepted as a mouse, for one suspects that he would not cut much of a figure among other rats: he has opted to be a big guy among small ones.

He is, of course, the Moriarty to Basil's Holmes; and like Moriarty he is not simply some numbskulled crook: he is as much of a genius as Basil. That his genius has concentrated on crime is another item of fidelity to Doyle's original creation, as is his somewhat gratuitous cruelty. His flamboyant personality is matched only by the grandiosity of his plans – this, like his pleasure in bullying, is a very childlike characteristic, and indeed all the arguments in favour of Basil being essentially a child work equally well when considering Ratigan. One can take this much further (although perhaps not as far as some Sherlockian scholars, who claim that Moriarty actually *is* Holmes in disguise) by noting the many similarities between the personalities of Basil and Ratigan. For example, both have the same love of ingenuity for its own sake – overingenuity, even. While we applaud Basil for the complexity of his escape from the fiendish

set of death-dealing gadgets, we must remember that it was Ratigan's mind which originally assembled the collection. And, like Basil, Ratigan is vain; he likes nothing better than to surround himself with cronies eagerly (and literally) singing his praises. Finally, he shares with Basil the quality of courage: although it could be argued that his fearlessness during the fight in and on Big Ben is a result of his hatred having taken him over, nonetheless such fearlessness does not spring from nowhere. Somewhere deep inside him Ratigan must have a strong strain of the genuine article.

Ratigan's presumed demise, plunging into the Thames, is very reminiscent of Moriarty's at the Reichenbach Falls. Both Basil and Holmes survive the escapades. However, Doyle never resurrected Moriarty. Perhaps, though, Disney will bring Ratigan back to the screen – although this seems, at the time of writing, to be unlikely.

Toby

Whose dog *is* Toby? Basil seems to imply that he is Toby's owner, but this seems a little improbable – although certainly Basil has trained the dog for his own purposes. Actually, as we discover, Toby is really Holmes' dog. Well, mostly...

In fact, Toby is really not so much a dog as a puppy. The Disney animators seem to have incorporated into his physical appearance and his behaviour every puppyish characteristic they could think of: eager, panting, lolling tongue, soft yet mischievous eyes, general rotundity of

form ... and clumsiness. Indeed, the finest strictly visual gag in the movie comes when Basil commands the hound to set off on Fidget's trail. From the top of the screen descends a vast, brown and very determined puppy-paw to flatten the little detective.

Toby obeys Basil, much of the time. For some reason he detests Dawson, and greets him with a growl on all occasions. Olivia, however, is another matter. From the instant that she meets him and gives him a cheese crumpet, he is her slave. For example, when he is being left outside the toyshop, we have the following:

> *Basil*: Now, Toby, sit! [Toby fails to sit.]
> Toby, *sit!* [No reaction.]
> *Olivia*: Sit, Toby! [Toby sits instantly.]
> *Basil*: Good boy.

Felicia

Ratigan may be Basil's criminal *alter ego*, but the parallels are not carried as far as the two characters' pet animals, for Felicia is nothing at all like Toby. She is a huge, fat, spoiled, cowardly pink cat, whose main contribution to Ratigan's schemes is to gobble up those of his cronies who have hurt his feelings. Summoned by his little bell, she lurches plumply into his presence and devours whatever miserable offender he places before her; afterwards she licks her lips with a loathsomely smug little smile of self-satisfaction. But she is a coward. She is content to consume small animals that go unprotestingly to their doom, but should

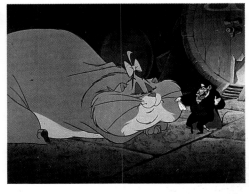

Felicia, Ratigan's repulsive feline friend and executioner.

one of them fight back – as Fidget does, most determinedly – she has no comprehension of how to respond. She would be an idle lap-cat if only Ratigan's lap were large enough. Similarly, towards the end of the movie, she is enthusiastic about the prospect of devouring a defenceless Queen Moustoria, but as soon as Toby – who is more her size – appears on the scene she is off like a shot.

This chase culminates in a superb gag. Felicia comes to a high wall and leaps up on top of it, leaving a thwarted Toby down at ground level. Mockingly Felicia shimmies her ample bottom at the yapping puppy, and then she calmly jumps down on the far side of the wall. After a minuscule pause, all hell breaks loose. We discover why when the camera pans slowly across to reveal the sign: ROYAL GUARD DOGS.

Fidget

If you feel that you've met Fidget somewhere before, then this is probably because you've seen *The Black Cauldron*, whose character Creeper (➤316) is astonishingly similar. The likeness extends even to the voice, although in fact two different voice-actors played the two parts (Creeper was Phil Fondacaro, Fidget Candy Candido).

Fidget – whose name is given in some Disney documents as "Fidgit" – is a peg-legged bat of evil countenance. He is the most recent representative of a long line of dimwitted, bumbling assistant villains; indeed, it is hard to see why such an intellectual criminal as Ratigan should have chosen him as sidekick. Mind you, Fidget is not quite such a lamebrain as Ratigan makes him out to be: the bat's sole error is to leave behind him in the toyshop his "shopping

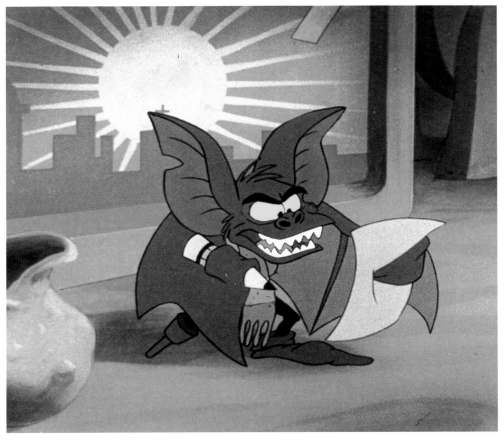

Fidget, Ratigan's "enforcement officer".

list" of items to be appropriated to help Ratigan's scheme. This is something that anyone might have done. Ratigan, of course, does not see things quite this way, and Fidget is destined for death at the teeth of Felicia before Ratigan suddenly realizes that he still has a use for the small incompetent.

Fidget is designed to be two apparently contradictory things simultaneously: first he must be funny, and second he must be scary. Funny he most certainly is, but Disney had to devote a little more effort to making him frightening. The usual solution is to introduce his repulsive face very suddenly onto the screen, to the accompaniment of appropriate music. This effect is slightly corny, but it works well.

Fidget is one of Disney's best comic sidekick-villains. As with several others of them, one cannot help but wonder why on earth Fidget sticks with Ratigan: he is bullied and abused, and goes in constant fear of being fed to Felicia. He seems to gain nothing from the liaison. Surely he could fly off to pastures new?

Queen Moustoria

The queen of the mice is obviously based on Queen Victoria, her human counterpart. She is rounded and small, with pear-shaped pendulous cheeks and a double chin. Cosmetics have painted two stark pink blush-ellipses on her cheek, and on her head perches an undersized crown.

Her role in the movie is a very minor one, yet she is given some of the best lines. For example, in conversation with Fidget, who is disguised as one of her guards but remains as revolting as ever: "Have you been with us long?" The movie is set at the time of her Diamond Jubilee – an anniversary about which she is delighted: "Oh, I just *love* jubilees!"

The clockwork model of her produced by Hiram Flaversham bears many of her physical characteristics. However, it fails to

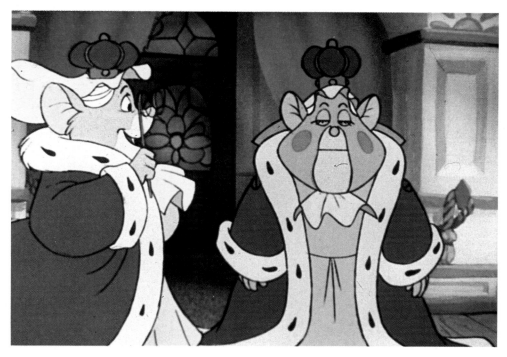

Queen Moustoria initially thought the robot version of herself was rather fun. Fortunately, she wasn't around later, when things fell apart.

move with her regal grace (a sort of upperclass waddle): instead, it jumps and jerks uncontrollably. It is astonishing that Moustoria's loving subjects are fooled by it for a moment.

Mrs. Judson

Basil's landlady, based on Holmes's Mrs. Hudson, plays much the same sort of part in *The Great Mouse Detective* as Mrs. Hudson played in Doyle's books: basically, she is just part of the scenery. She is keen to preserve the tidiness of the house, Basil's privacy, and a dimple in her chin; but she is at the same time kind-hearted: at first she refuses ingress to Dawson and Olivia but then, as soon as she sees the little girl's damp clothing and drowned-rat expression (no joke intended), she transforms herself into a fussing maternal figure, eager to dry clothes and supply cheese crumpets. In short, she is much the same as Mrs. Hudson.

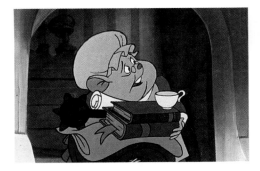

Mrs. Judson, Basil's landlady – not to be confused with Mrs. Hudson in the flat upstairs.

Bartholomew

A delightful little cameo part is played by a drunken mouse called Bartholomew. While the other thugs are singing of "Ratigan – the world's greatest criminal mind", Bartholomew unfortunately forgets himself so far as to sing of "Ratigan – the world's greatest rat". Fortunately Bartholomew is too intoxicated to know what is going on when Ratigan rings his little bell to summon Felicia to polish off the perpetrator of such a howler.

Bartholomew, incidentally, shared Barrie Ingham's voice with Basil.

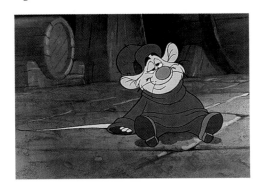

Bartholomew. This little mouse made an error of judgement – and paid for it with his life.

Minor Characters

Among the noteworthy minor characters are the individuals found in the seedy waterside pub where Basil and Dawson seek clues as to Olivia's whereabouts. These include a very sexy **Dancing Girl** mouse, whose act provokes Dawson into the most ungentlemanlike behaviour; the **Bar Maid** and **Bar Tender** who, clearly in cahoots with Ratigan, spike the drinks of our heroes; the **Pianist** whose attempt to retaliate against an

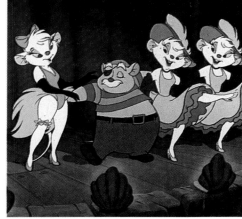

Dawson having a whale of a time with the dancing girls – the one on the left being the singer. Blame it on the beer.

intrusive Dawson starts the gigantic fight; and a **Juggling Octopus**, whose sad performance has to be seen to be believed.

Elsewhere, a number of Ratigan's **thugs** have speaking parts. Of interest is a thug who does not look like a mouse at all. He is bog-green, and has a face less like a mouse's than like that of Bill the lizard (➤246) or of

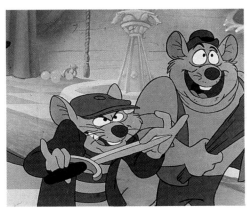

The principals among Ratigan's gang of thugs.

one of the little tortoises/turtles – e.g., Toby Turtle (➤295) - to be found in so many Disney movies. Why this should be the case is something of a mystery. Fidget one can accept as part of the crew, he being a "flying mouse," after all; but mice and tortoises are not known to crossbreed.

And, of course, right at the end there is the beautiful **Lady Mouse** who persuades Basil and Dawson to take on their next case.

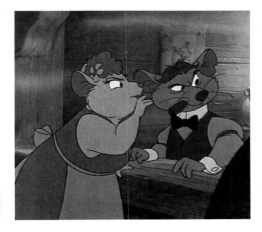

The Bar Maid and Bar Tender.

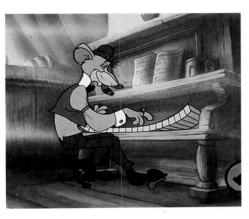

The Pianist in the waterside pub where Basil and Dawson look for clues.

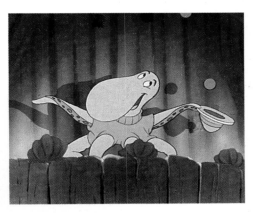

The hopelessly merry Juggling Octopus.

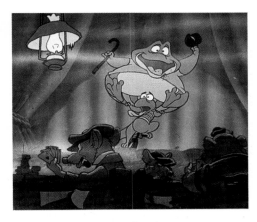

Another act in the waterside pub.

WHO FRAMED ROGER RABBIT

Characters:

Roger Rabbit; Jessica Rabbit; Benny the Cab; Baby Herman; Mrs. Herman; Bongo (Gorilla), Hippo; Smart Ass; Greasy; Psycho; Stupid; Wheezy; Droopy Dog; Lena Hyena; Bullets; Singing Sword; Octopus Bartender; Blonde Starlet *and* Babe, the Blue Ox (➤122); Bambi (➤198); Bashful (➤164); Ben Buzzard (➤95); Betty Boop; Big Bad Wolf (➤54); Bill the Lizard (➤246); Brer Bear (➤221); Brooms (from *Fantasia* [➤181]); Bugs Bunny; Cheshire Cat (➤245); Chicken Little (➤100); Clarabelle Cow (➤36); Clara Cluck (➤71); Cupids (from *Fantasia* [➤185]); Cyril Proudbottom (➤231); Daffy Duck; Daisy Duck (➤80); Danny (from *So Dear to My Heart* [➤229]); Doc (➤164); Donald Duck (➤61); Dopey (➤163); Dumbo (➤194); Elmer Elephant (➤78); Elmer Fudd; Emotion (➤99); Ferdinand the Bull (➤88); Fiddler Pig (➤56); Fifer Pig (➤56); Flowers and Trees (➤51); Foghorn Leghorn; Girl bunnies (from *Tortoise and the Hare* [➤74]); Gnomes; Goofy (➤44); Goons (from *Sleeping Beauty* [➤259]); Grumpy (➤164); Happy (➤164); Horace Horsecollar (➤37); Hyacinth Hippo (➤186); Jenny Wren (➤75); Jiminy Cricket (➤169); Joe Giraffe (➤78); José Carioca (➤205); Lampwick (on poster only [➤174]); Mlle. Upanova (➤185); Marc Anthony; Marvin Martian; Merry Dwarfs (from *The Merry Dwarfs*); Mickey Mouse (➤23); Mickey's Orphans (➤28); Minnie Mouse (➤32); Mrs. Jumbo (➤195); Mr. Toad (➤231); Mushrooms (from *Fantasia* [➤178]); Pedro the Plane (➤203); Pegasus (from *Fantasia* [➤182]); Pelican; Penguin Waiters (from *Mary Poppins* [➤269]); Pete (➤15); Peter (➤216); Peter Pig (➤63); Pinocchio (➤169); Pluto (➤38); Porky Pig; Practical Pig (➤56); Red Riding Hood (➤54); Reluctant Dragon (➤190); Road Runner; Sam Sheepdog; Singing Harp (➤223); Sir Giles (➤192); Sleepy (➤165); Sneezy (➤165); Snow White (➤159); Speedy Gonzales; Sylvester; Tar Baby (➤221); Tinker Bell (➤249); Toby Tortoise (➤73); Tweedledum (➤244); Tweety Bird; Unicorn (from *Fantasia* [➤182]); Water Babies (from *Water Babies*); Wile E. Coyote; Witch (from *Snow White and the Seven Dwarfs* [➤160]); Woody Woodpecker; Yosemite Sam

Credits:

Based on *Who Censored Roger Rabbit?* (1981) by Gary K. Wolf

Live Actors: Bob Hoskins; Christopher Lloyd; Joanna Cassidy; Stubby Kaye; Alan Tilvern; Richard Le Parmentier; Joel Silver; Morgan Deare; Laura Frances

Voices: Charles Fleischer (Roger, Benny the Cab, Greasy, Psycho); Lou Hirsch (Baby Herman); April Winchell (Mrs. Herman); Morgan Deare (Bongo the Gorilla); Mae Questel (Betty Boop); Mel Blanc (Daffy Duck, Tweety Bird, Bugs Bunny, Sylvester,

Porky Pig); Tony Anselmo (Donald Duck); Mary T. Radford (Hippo); Joe Alaskey (Yosemite Sam); David Lander (Smart Ass); Fred Newman (Stupid); June Foray (Wheezy, Lena Hyena); Russi Taylor (Minnie Mouse, Birds); Les Perkins (Toad); Richard Williams (Droopy Dog); Wayne Allwine (Mickey Mouse); Pat Buttram, Jim Cummings, Jim Gallant (Bullets); Frank Sinatra (Singing Sword); Tony Pope (Goofy, Wolf); Peter Westy (Pinocchio); Cherry Davis (Woody Woodpecker); Kathleen Turner (Jessica Rabbit speaking—uncredited); Amy Irving (Jessica Rabbit singing)

Supervising Sound Editors: Charles L. Campbell; Louis L. Edemann

Sound Editors: Larry Carow; Paul Timothy Carden; Richard C. Franklin, Jr.; Chuck Neely; Colin C. Mouat; Paul Bruce Richard-son

Music: Alan Silvestri

Orchestration: James B. Campbell

Music Editor: Kenneth Karman

Music Performed by London Symphony Orchestra

Songs by: Joe McCoy; Cliff Friend; Dave Franklin; Jack Meskill; Charles O'Flynn; Max Rich; Coleman & Leigh

Singers: Amy Irving; Frank Sinitra

Screenplay: Jeffrey Price; Peter S. Seaman

Director of Photography: Dean Cundey

Film Editor: Arthur Schmidt

Visual Effects Supervisor: Ken Ralston

Mechanical Effect Supervisor: George Gibbs

Production Designer: Elliot Scott; Roger Cain

Costume Designer: Joanna Johnston

Director of Animation: Richard Williams

Supervising Animators: Andreas Deja; Russell Hall; Phil Nibbelink; Simon Wells

Layout: Roy Naisbitt

Storysketch: Hans Bacher; Mark Kausler; Joe Ranft; Harald Siepermann

Animated Effects Supervisor: Christopher Knott

Animated Production Manager: Patsy de Lord

Animation Editor: Nick Fletcher

Animators: James Baxter; David Byers-Brown; Roger Chiasson; Alain Costa; Caron Creed; Alvaro Gaivoto; Chuck Gammage; Raul Garcia; Marc Gordon-Bates; Joe Haidar; Alyson Hamilton; Brigitte Hartley; Greg Manwaring; Gary Mudd; Jacques Muller; Brent Odell; Nik Ranieri; Alan Simpson; Tom Sito; Dave Spafford; Rob Stevenhagen; Mike Swindall; Peter Western; Colin White

Assistant Animators: Margot Allen; Sue Baker; Rej Bourdages; Neil Boyle; Bella Bremner; Paul Chung; Christopher Clarke; Irene Couloufis; Annie Dubois; Helga Egilson; James Farrington; Gary French-Powell; Martyn Jones; Helen Kincaid; Elaine Koo; Vera Lanpher; Calvin Le Duc; John McCartney; Brenda Chat-McKie; Denise Meara-Hahn; Robert Newman; Andrew Painter; Isabel Radage; Phillippe Rejaudry; Phillip Scarrold; Glen Sylvester, Nicolette Van Gendt; Roger Way; Boguslaw; Wilk Alexander Williams; Hugh Workman

Inbetweeners: Richard Bazley; Stella Benson; Graham Binding; David Bowers; Clare Bramwell; Malcolm Clarke; Anthony Ealey; Matthew Freeth; Peter Gambier; Manjit Jhita; Siobhan Larkin; Debbie Jane Lilly; Adrian Marler; Roman Ostir; Howard Parkins; Silvia Pompei, Emma Tornero; Simon Turner; Anne Whitford

Effects Animators: Dave Bossert; Jon Brooks; Andrew Browlow; Kevin Davies; Christopher Jenkins; Dorse Lanpher; Les Pace

Effects Assistants: Graham Burt; Lily Dell; Fraser MacLean; Tim Sanpher; David Sigrist; Micheal Patrick Smith; Amanda J. Talbot

Effects Inbetweeners: Lisette Coates; Marc Ellis; Christopher Kingsley-Smith III; Derek Robert Mason; Mike Pfeil; Dave Pritchard; Barney Russell; Derek Wood

Backgrounds/Renderings: Nick Harris; Shelley Page; Jill Tudor

Animation Camera Supervisor: John Leatherbarrow

Animation Camera: Graham Chenery, Martin Elvin; Stuart Holloway; Nic Jayne; Brian Riley; Pete Wood

Chief Executive and Supervising Animator (additional animation): Dale L. Baer

Animated Effects Supervisor (additional animation): Don Paul

Additional Animation Production Manager: Ron Rocha

Additional Animation Editor: Scot Scalise

Animators (additional animation): Mark Kausler; Matthew O'Callaghan; Dave Pacheco; Bruce W. Smith; Barry Temple; Frans Vischer

Effects Animators (additional animation): Glenn Chaika; Randy Fullmer; Scott Santoro

Special Visual Effects: Industrial Light & Magic (A Division of Lucasfilm Ltd)

Animation Supervisor (special visual effects): Wes Takahashi

Chief Visual Effects Editor (special visual effects): Bill Kimberlin

Animation Coordinator (special visual effect): Paul Lucas

Animators (special visual effects): Gordon Baker; Tim Berglund; Chris Green; Nick Stern; Sean Turner

Stop-Motion Animator (special visual effects): Tom St. Amand

Puppet Construction (special visual effects): Sheila Duignan; Paula Luchesi; John Reed

Production Manager (UK): Patricia Carr

Directors (UK second unit): Frank Marshall; Ian Sharp

Unit Production Manager/Assistant Director (ILM Production): Ian Bryce

Unit Production Manager (US): Jack Frost Sanders

Director (US second unit): Max Kleven

Director: Robert Zemeckis

Post-Production Supervisor: Martin Cohen

Associate Producers: Don Hahn; Steve Starkey

Executive Producers: Kathleen Kennedy; Steven Spielberg

Producers: Frank Marshall; Robert Watts

Release Date: Premiered at Radio City Music Hall June 21, 1988; general release June 22, 1988

Running Time: 103 minutes

THE MOVIE

In attempting any description of *Who Framed Roger Rabbit* it is difficult not to find oneself running out of superlatives. From the moment that the ''Maroon Cartoon'' logo, with its heads of Roger Rabbit and Baby Herman, explodes onto the screen, the audience are aboard a rollercoaster from which there will be no release either granted or requested for 103 minutes of sensory overload. In part this feeling of exhilaration derives from a plot that mimics and is a homage to the hard-boiled detective yarns of Raymond Chandler, Leigh Brackett, Ross Macdonald, James M. Cain and others; in part from the movie's fundamental premise, that Toon characters are not ink-and-paint two-dimensional creations but lead full, independent existences in the real world; in part from fine performances by the human participants in the romp, notably Joanna Cassidy, Bob Hoskins and Christopher Lloyd; in part from the brilliant animation technology, which pitches live actors into a Toon world so adroitly that it is impossible to ''see the joins''; but most of all from the sheer zest, inventiveness and exuberance of the production as a whole. Virtually every frame is packed with extraneous detail, with small delights of animation and/or invention, and, while the sheer amount of work that went into such an elaborate creation is obviously staggering, the final result never seems in any way laboured—on the contrary, the whole

''feel'' of the movie is one of spontaneity, of effortlessness.

The screenplay is based on the novel *Who Censored Roger Rabbit?* (1981) by the US SF/fantasy writer Gary K. Wolf. While the novel is intended primarily to entertain, it would be wrong to ignore its underlying satirical thrust. In *Who Censored Roger Rabbit?*—and also in the movie —the satire concerns the status of Toons in a society run by humans. The real reason why Roger, hunted for the murder of the human Marvin Acme (Stubby Kaye), so desperately requires the aid of the down-at-heel human private eye Eddie Valiant (Bob Hoskins) is not because the circumstantial case against Roger is particularly strong—it isn't—but because human beings hold the reins of power, Toons are regarded as subhuman, and no human being really cares enough about the life of an individual Toon to worry whether or not the human agent of legal retribution, Judge Doom (Christopher Lloyd), is correct or even honest to proclaim that Roger is guilty. Roger is guilty because a member of the socially dominant race—in this instance, humans—says he is, and for no other reason. This is the root of Roger's helplessness; it is also the pivot on which the whole plot turns. The analogy with the status of blacks—or members of any other visibly different minority—in unenlightened societies is emphasized further in the movie by the depiction of Toontown as a ghetto and of the staff and artistes of the Ink & Paint Club as members of a subculture, earning their livings by ''performing'' for a human audience, and patronized (in both senses of that word) by people whom they are forced to regard as their superiors.

Another significant element of the plot carries a similar burden. Many of the shenanigans involved are motivated by the desire to further a corrupt business plan, the realization of which will involve the obliteration of Toontown. Yet this is not regarded by the perpetrators as being a very severe obstacle: after all, the only ones who will kick up a fuss about this annihilation will be the inhabitants of Toontown themselves—and, by definition, the opinions of Toons don't matter. The attitude portrayed is quite consciously representative of the kind of mental imperialism that defaces most human societies.

As noted, it is admirable that those involved in the creation of the film should have declined to let this more serious message be lost in the joyous welter of gay inventiveness—which is not to say that the satirical import is ever permitted to obtrude into the freshness and lightness of the presentation. Even so, it is startling that some of the critics seem to have missed this subtext entirely. On the subject of its success as an entertainment the critics—although seemingly not the public—were again divided. Julie Salamon in *The Wall Street Journal* probably summed

up the public attitude in distinctly non-*WSJ* terms: ''This one you simply must see for yourself. Zowie.'' Yet a summation by Jeannie Williams in *USA Today* could hardly have been more different:

> If you go to movies to be wowed by technical feats, fine. Some may prefer a film featuring real stories and relationships with depth. *Roger Rabbit* is really one long Hollywood-insider-California-freeway joke.

In *Newsweek* David Ansen picked up on Williams's essential point but came to a quite different conclusion:

> Given the level of expectation this unprecedented collision of movie myths raises, there are bound to be disappointments. . . . Backseat driving aside, let us be grateful for a summer movie like no other. Stuffed with marvels, ''Roger Rabbit'' is a hare for all seasons.

Favourable or disparaging, the critics were unanimous about the movie's technical brilliance, both as a masterpiece of animation and as a triumphant demonstration of the marriage of live action with animation. In both of these linked respects, the movie was state-of-the-art stuff.

It may seem slightly artificial to discuss the animation in isolation for a few moments, but the exercise can be justified on a number of grounds—not least the fact that the movie could have been made (albeit not very well) without the live action, whereas the converse, a *Roger* with live action and no animation, would have been impossible. Indeed, one could go further than this—as the movie's director, Robert Zemeckis, has in effect done—and say that without the participation of one man the movie would not have been worth making. That man was the London-based Canadian animator Richard Williams, whose work had been attracting attention for years but, despite a 1973 Oscar for his short *A Christmas Carol*, almost always for marginal or ephemeral projects. These projects he has regarded, in fact, as mere money-making diversions from his main enterprise, his idée fixe, the painfully slow creation of a feature-length animated movie whose projected title periodically varies but is often *The Thief and the Cobbler*; Williams has predicted that *The Thief* will be ''the greatest animated film ever made'', and it probably will be—when and if it is finished.

Although Williams had in childhood yearned to become a Disney animator, he did not immediately leap at the chance of working on *Roger*. The background is rather more complicated than that. The movie rights for Wolf's novel had been purchased some years earlier by Disney. The project had been put on the shelf, although an approach had been made to Robert Zemeckis, who was highly impressed by the draft screenplay shown to him but privately assumed that the then

327

Disney management lacked the vigour ever to realize the project. Zemeckis went off and did things like make *Back to the Future*, and it was some years before he mentioned "that project" to Steven Spielberg, and discovered that Spielberg had likewise been approached by Disney on the matter, and that both he and Disney were by now seriously interested in the project. Once convinced that a suitably vast budget would be available for the movie not just to be made but to be made well, Zemeckis counted himself in.

The difficulty then was to find an animator with the imagination and perception to see how the live-action and animated components of the movie could contribute to each other rather than fight for prominence with each other. The aim was not just to produce an artwork at which people might marvel—such as the animated/live section of *Mary Poppins* (➤274)—but a movie in which the interactions between humans and cartoon characters would be such that the audience would be able to believe in the concrete reality of the whole. This is by no means easy. When we watch a piece of full animation we suspend our disbelief in order to make the portrayed scenes more realistic than in fact they are. This is perhaps best observed among children, who will see even the flattest and crudest of TV cartoon characters as fully rounded, three-dimensional personages; even when the animation is of a very high calibre indeed, this same process of self-deception—of acceptance of the medium's conventions—is required from the audience. When animation and live action are combined, it is hard for the viewer simultaneously to suspend disbelief for part of the image and accept the other part as a straightforward depiction of reality.

Might it be that no one had ever succeeded in creating a proper marriage of the two media because such a marriage was impossible? Zemeckis was on the verge of accepting this when Richard Williams's short completed section of *The Thief* entered his life. The "animator's animator" Milt Kahl, one of Walt's Nine Old Men and Williams's lifelong hero, was dying. Williams came to California to show Kahl the fifteen minutes or so of animation that he'd completed—in 23 years!—of *The Thief*, and word of the brilliance of this short section reached Spielberg and Zemeckis, who decided to take a look. They were bowled over. But would Williams be similarly bowled over by the prospect of working with them on *Who Framed Roger Rabbit*?

The immediate answer was no. For reasons akin to those outlined above, Williams thought that animation/live-action mixtures were dreary and doomed to failure. Before Williams could be persuaded to take the job on (and we shouldn't lose sight of the fact that he regarded it as a money-making enterprise

which would help underwrite *The Thief*) he wanted to establish that Zemeckis was to dictate exactly what he wanted from the movie, and it was to be up to Williams to supply it. As has been widely quoted, he said to Zemeckis: "I'm your pencil."

Williams was given a budget of $100,000 to produce the animation for a single minute's worth of film, one in which he had to solve a whole host of technical problems in order to blend Toons with a live Eddie Valiant (played by a stand-in—the part hadn't yet been cast). The result was sensational and, after it had been checked with Disney that the company was indeed truly aware of the size of the budget that would be required and had the funds to foot it, the show was on the road.

It was a very slow vehicle. From the outset it had been plain to Williams that there could be no shortcuts in the production of 82,080 frames, each done by hand on a photostatic blow-up of a single frame of live action. The animation crew numbered 326—254 directly under Williams in London, 72 others in California. Also in California was the special-effects company Industrial Light & Magic (ILM), which painstakingly used a combination of high tech and low cunning to add additional "elements" to the animation—shadows, skin tones, even the flashing sequins on Jessica's skintight performance costume (done by scraping a plastic bag with steel wool and then shining light through it). A further handicap to speed was the use throughout the film, for the sake of verisimilitude of the animation/live-actors interaction, of moving (rather than fixed) cameras—customary in live-action filming but heretical in animation.

Thanks to round-the-clock work by all concerned, the final deadlines were missed by only a few weeks. The movie itself was outrageously successful in commercial terms, and also generated significant revenues through merchandising; it received four Academy Awards, all for technical achievements, including a much deserved Special Award to Williams for "outstanding achievement in animation direction". At the time of writing (1992) development is under way for a further feature, a prequel, provisionally called *Who Discovered Roger Rabbit* and with a possible release date in 1994.

Some have seen in *Who Framed Roger Rabbit* a last glorious fling of outmoded styles of animation: the vast costs involved in labour-intensive handwork must surely preclude its use on anything even half as ambitious as this in the future, the painstaking efforts of craftsman-animators being superseded by the rapid and cost-effective manipulations of the computer artists. The movie supplied Disney with a legion of new animating talents to deploy on its challenging new programme of animated features, but was the recruitment a wise one? After all, these were artists who had discovered, through *Roger*, the obso-

lete ways of doing things—not the new, high-tech ones. Or so the reasoning runs.

Yet this reasoning, despite or perhaps even because of its unassailable logic, is false. Very similar arguments were applied way back in the late 1930s to "Disney's folly", an enterprise that was widely viewed as being an expensive exercise in art for art's sake, *Snow White and the Seven Dwarfs* (➤157). Over half a century later, that movie is seen not only as an artistic but also as a commercial triumph, with each of its periodic reissues awakening a whole new audience to its magic. One can predict with some confidence that in decades to come *Who Framed Roger Rabbit* will achieve similar classic status, and for exactly the same reason.

It is just too overwhelmingly good not to.

THE STORY

The movie opens with a colour cartoon short, *Somethin's Cookin'*, featuring Roger Rabbit and Baby Herman; it is, we're told, "A Maroon Cartoon" dating from 1947. It is also one of the fastest-moving, most inventive slam-bang animated shorts of all time, with enough action for about six Donald Duck or Tom & Jerry cartoons rolled into one. It is in its final stages, with a clunked Roger surrounded by cutesy tweeting birds, when an off-screen director's voice suddenly yells: "Cut! Cut! Cut!" It is at this point that we begin to see the feature's magical blend of live action and animation, for a living director appears to slap Roger around the head and berate him for having fouled up the take: "Roger, read the script! Look what it says. It says: 'Rabbit gets clunked. Rabbit sees stars.' Not birds, stars!"

The truth is that Roger Rabbit, one of the megastars of the rather down-at-heel Maroon Cartoons, is losing his mind with worry over the fact that his wife, Jessica, is seeing too much by half of Marvin Acme (Stubby Kaye), the king of gags and the owner of Toontown. Maroon's own boss, R. K. Maroon (Alan Tilvern), calls in depressed, booze-swilling private eye Eddie Valiant (Bob Hoskins) to trail Jessica with the aim of obtaining incriminating photographs that will shock Roger back into doing his best work. Valiant is reluctant: he hates Toons because, as it soon emerges, one of them killed his brother Teddy by dropping a piano on his head. Nevertheless, he agrees to go to the Ink & Paint Club, a sleazy nightclub where Jessica sings. Here he is admitted by Bongo the Gorilla on giving the password "Walt sent me", and finds himself a seat as penguin waiters (from *Mary Poppins* [➤274]) move among the audience and, on stage, Daffy Duck and Donald Duck (➤333) perform a raucous piano duet. Valiant is seated near Marvin Acme, who as a prank squirts his shirt with "disappearing ink". Betty Boop, selling cigarettes, pauses to chat with Valiant and thus touchingly juxtapose her outmoded form of sexuality with that of the star of the next stage act, Jessica Rabbit. After her sultry song Jessica departs and Acme (followed by Valiant) rushes to her dressing room, bouquet in hand. Thrown out as a peeping Tom by Bongo, Valiant photographs the pair through the dressing-room window: they are (shock horror!) playing patty-cake.

Roger is graphically distraught on being presented with the evidence of his wife's perfidy; on being given a "calming" shot of whisky he literally hits the roof, destroying much of R. K. Maroon's office. Back in his own office, Valiant drinks himself to sleep. He is awoken by Police Lieutenant Santino (Richard Le Parmentier), who tells him that Marvin Acme has been slain—a safe has been dropped on his head—and that Roger is presumed the killer (although of course the m.o. is familiar to Valiant). They go to the Acme Gag Factory; Jessica arrives to slap Valiant's face for taking the photographs. More significantly, law officer Judge Doom (Christopher Lloyd) appears, telling Valiant that Roger is clearly guilty; soon afterwards follows the paddy wagon bearing the judge's five idiot weasel henchmen—Smart Ass (their leader), Greasy, Psycho, Stupid and Wheezy. Judge Doom demonstrates that he has found a way to kill Toons—a noxious chemical mixture called Dip, which he demonstrates by murdering a Toon shoe.

Baby Herman tells Valiant that Acme had made a will leaving Toontown to the Toons, which is why he was killed; the will (which no one has actually seen) is missing, but if suppressing it was indeed the motive then clearly Roger is innocent. Valiant, having little patience with Herman, examines a newspaper photograph and sees a will poking out of Acme's pocket; he also finds hiding in his office, Roger, who tells him how he wrote Jessica a love letter on a sheet of paper he found at the Ink & Paint Club; taking it home to read it to her, Roger found the weasels in wait and fled here. Valiant wants to get rid of Roger but the two become accidentally handcuffed to each other. The weasels arrive to search the premises, but Valiant conceals Roger by holding him under the water while pretending to be washing his laundry.

We shift to the Terminal Bar, where Valiant's longtime on-and-off girlfriend Dolores (Joanna Cassidy) works. Valiant arrives with Roger hidden inside his trenchcoat and explains his predicament to Dolores; she takes them to the secret Rot Gut Room off the bar, where Valiant sets to work with a hacksaw. Roger easily slips out of his side of the handcuffs, to Valiant's fury. Then Valiant explains his theory: R. K. Maroon and Jessica were together plotting, using Jessica as bait, to

get hold of Acme's will, but obviously failed because they're still looking for it even after having murdered him. Leaving Roger with Dolores, Valiant goes back to his office, where this time Jessica is waiting to see him. She tells him that she's a pure-hearted gal; Valiant was set up by Maroon to take the photographs of her with Acme, whom Maroon wanted to blackmail—she'd been forced to take part by the threat that otherwise Roger would never work in Toontown again. Dolores arrives to find the pair in a seemingly compromising position. After Jessica goes, Dolores tells Valiant that it's not Maroon but Cloverleaf Industries, a company that's buying up everything, which is the real threat to Toontown: unless Acme's will is found before midnight, they'll become the town's new owners.

Valiant and Dolores arrive at the Terminal Bar to find Roger has blown his cover and is entertaining the patrons; outside, Smart Ass, Psycho and Greasy have heard his act and set off to fetch Judge Doom. Valiant angrily slings Roger back into the Rot Gut Room; they hide there as Judge Doom arrives. Doom eventually lures Roger out of hiding. Roger is about to be immersed in Dip when Judge Doom, at Valiant's insistence, grants him a last request: a shot of liquor. This has the same explosive effect as in Maroon's office, and Roger and Valiant escape.

They plan to hijack the weasels' paddy wagon but find in its rear Benny the Cab; they release him and in him make their getaway. After a chase, Benny drops them at a movie theatre, where they watch part of the Goofy (►44) cartoon *Goofy Gymnastics* (1949—an anachronism) while Valiant explains to Roger his hatred of Toons. Dolores arrives. On the cinema screen, a newscast tells how Cloverleaf Industries has just bought not only the Pacific Red Car Trolley Line but also Maroon Cartoon Studios. "That's it!" says Valiant. "That's the connection!"

Valiant goes to raid Maroon Cartoons, leaving Roger outside with the car (borrowed from Dolores). Almost immediately Roger is sapped from the shadows. Inside, Valiant finds Maroon and, pretending Roger's love letter is Acme's will, uses violence to get Maroon to tell all. Maroon admits blackmail, not murder, but before he can say more is killed by a shot from the window. The gunman then turns on Valiant, but unsuccessfully. Valiant sees Jessica fleeing the scene and discovers that Roger has gone. Leaping into the car, Valiant gives chase to Jessica, who drives to Toontown. Pausing before following her into the town, Valiant forswears booze and fetches out his trusty Toon revolver (a gift from Yosemite Sam), whose six Toon bullets engage in some byplay with him. Then it's into Toontown and a colourful, tuneful welcome from a bewildering host of Toons including baby Mickey Mouses, mushrooms and cupids

from *Fantasia* (►179), the Three Little Pigs (►55), the Reluctant Dragon (►190) and Jiminy Cricket (►169). No sooner has Valiant parked Dolores's car by Jessica's than a fire engine bearing Mr. Toad (►231) high on its ladder speeds by. Looking up at a nearby building, Valiant sees what seems to be Jessica's silhouette at a window. He rushes up in the elevator (manned by Droopy Dog); in the background the Road Runner and Coyote scoot along the various floors of the building. However, the figure glimpsed at the window proves to have been not Jessica but Lena Hyena, who chases Valiant lustfully. He flees, finishing outside the building, many storeys up; he does a typical Toon double take before falling. He grabs a flagpole, but Tweety Bird appears and unpicks his grasping fingers, remorselessly reciting "This Little Piggy". Falling again, he encounters Mickey Mouse (►23) and Bugs Bunny, both with unopened parachutes on their backs; Bugs gives him what purports to be a spare parachute but which proves to be, on opening, a "spare" rubber tyre marked ACME.

On and on Valiant falls, to land with a thump at street level in Lena Hyena's arms. He runs. She chases. He escapes. Soon he comes across Jessica, her gun out; she is aiming not at Valiant but behind him at Judge Doom. She shoots the gun from Doom's hand. Jessica explains that she followed Doom to the Maroon studio and saw all. Valiant fires at a fleeing Doom but the Toon bullets miss their target. Jessica explains also that she felled Roger to keep him out of trouble. Benny the Cab screeches up to Valiant and Jessica and they climb aboard to be driven back out of Toontown. More explanation from Jessica: Acme had told her he was giving her his will, but when she looked at it there was just a blank sheet of paper. Then Benny skids on a pool of Dip spread over the road, and crashes. Judge Doom and the weasels catch up with Valiant and Jessica and take them to the Acme Gag Factory. Meanwhile Roger encounters a groaning Benny and learns what's up.

At the Acme Gag Factory, Doom reveals himself as the sole owner of Cloverleaf Industries, and that he proposes to obliterate Toontown using a vast, steamroller-mounted squirting tank of Dip, so that he may develop the site to take advantage of a proposed new freeway. Roger suddenly appears, pistol in hand, but soon he and Jessica are bound to a large hook at the target point of the tank's jet. Valiant uses a Toon routine to persuade the weasels to laugh at him so much they die—except for Smart Ass, who ends up in the Dip. Valiant and Doom have a colossal fight using various Toon props (including those seen earlier), at the end of which Doom is under the steamroller.

But even then the villain survives, revealing himself to have been a Toon disguised as a human all this time—and "Not just any Toon! Remember me, Eddie? When I killed your brother I talked just like this!" Again Doom and Valiant battle. Valiant wins and Doom is dissolved in his own Dip. Valiant frees Roger and Jessica, who smooch as the police, accompanied by Benny the Cab and Dolores, arrive. The mystery is explained to Lt. Santino and countless Toon characters spill into the scene, among them the Road Runner, Bambi (➤198), Betty Boop, Bugs Bunny, Mickey Mouse, Minnie Mouse (➤32), Daffy Duck, Donald Duck, Pinocchio, Baby Herman, Goofy, the Big Bad Wolf (➤54), Woody Woodpecker and Sylvester. Moreover, on the back of Roger's love letter, which Valiant still has, writing begins to appear: it is Acme's will, written in disappearing ink. Toontown belongs to the Toons, and all is well. Police appear to usher away the cast; they are helped by Porky Pig, who gives us the "That's all, folks!" message before Tinker Bell makes him disappear with a wave of her wand.

THE CHARACTERS

Roger Rabbit

It is noted below that really there are two Baby Hermans in the movie—his screen persona for *Somethin's Cookin'* and his actuality as a middle-aged sourpuss. There is, however, only one Roger: the zany, flapping, wobble-eared, wide-eyed crazy in the introductory short changes not one whit on his emergence into the "real-"world. He is a Toon through and through; there is no attempt on the part of the moviemakers to make him in the slightest credible, and that, paradoxically,

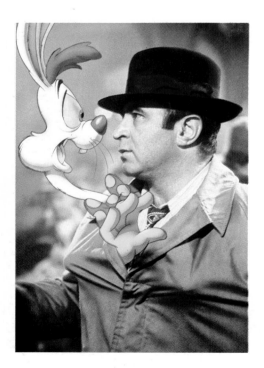

Eddie Valiant (Bob Hoskins) clearly wishing that he'd never consented to coat-share.

is what gives Roger his considerable screen credibility.

He is a somewhat un-Disney type of Toon: one searches fruitlessly for any rabbit or behavioural precursors in the Disney canon. Yet, even though his rapid, ungainly movements and his staccato speech remind us more of other studios, there is a certain elusive Disney quality about him. It may possibly be simply his three-dimensional appearance, because the classic Disney shorts characters have generally been depicted in a more rounded way than those of their competitor studios—it is rare for them to "take advantage" of the fact that they are two-dimensional creations. Roger, however, has no qualms about his own artificiality—indeed, it is one of the proofs he cites of his innocence of the murder:

> This whole thing's a setup! A scam! A frame-job! (Ouch!) Eddie, I could never hurt anybody! (Ow!) My whole purpose in life is to m-make peopl-l-l-le laugh!

Not long afterwards, during what has become one of the most famous scenes in the movie, Valiant is desperately trying to get the handcuffs off the pair of them with a hacksaw. The crate on which Valiant is working wobbles. "Hold still, will you?" he says crossly to Roger, who promptly slips his hand out of the handcuff and moves to hold the crate steady:

> *Roger*: Does this help?
> *Valiant*: Yeah. Thanks. (*double take*) Do you mean to tell me that you could have taken your hand out of that cuff at any time?
> *Roger*: No, not at any time. Only when it was funny.

This is one of the many behavioural laws—as seemingly rigid as the laws of physics—which Toons must obey.

One of the fundamental mysteries of the movie is why a clown like Roger should come to be married to a high-voltage woman like Jessica. It is obviously in the forefront of Valiant's mind from the moment he sets his popping eyes on her —"*That*'s Jessica Rabbit?" he says incredulously. For long tracts of the movie he is unable to conceive of Roger being anything more than a husband of convenience to her, and he therefore assumes, despite her claims to the contrary, that she plays pretty fast and loose. Even once she's straightened him out on that little item, he is still fascinated by the conundrum. Her response to one of his queries is clearly designed to bring hope to the hearts of many a male who, like Roger, doesn't look like much and is forever bumbling. They are gazing at the evidence of a clumsily appropriated car:

> *Jessica*: It looks like it was Roger. He was never very good behind the wheel.
> *Valiant*: Better lover than a driver?
> *Jessica (drawling)*: You'd better believe it.

This little exchange may give us a pointer to Roger's appeal and credibility as a character. In many ways, some of the greatest of all the animated characters appeal to us precisely because they act out, in grossly exaggerated fashion, a single unpraiseworthy aspect of ourselves—Donald Duck and Goofy, for example, epitomize our mindless rages and our clumsiness. Roger is a distillation of all the madcap animated antiheroes we can imagine, plus a few; it is therefore hardly surprising that, in his feverish and almost rebarbative way, he displays a whole gamut of the cues that make us identify with the Donalds and the Goofies. He is also dealing life a few strong counterblows on behalf of all the little guys—which, in one way or another, means almost all of us.

Jessica Rabbit

Jessica Rabbit represents one of the most significant animated achievements of all time. It is likely that no other animated character, not even Betty Boop (see below), has so perfectly encapsulated female sexuality on the screen—and, moreover, conveyed its full force to the audience. In most contexts Valiant's facial reaction when he first sees her coming onto the stage of the Ink & Paint Club would seem stereotyped, clichéd and distinctly unfunny: in Jessica's case, however, his reaction seems perfectly reasonable, because it is being mirrored by most of the males in the audience.

She is more a caricature of a desirable woman than any pretence of an accurate depiction of one. Her voice, marvelously husked by Kathleen Turner (uncredited) for speech and Amy Irving for the song, certainly helps, as does her dialogue. "I'm not bad. I'm just *drawn* that way" must be *the* line of the film. Yet she has a very definite and overwhelmingly sensuous *presence*; when she squeezes Marvin Acme's cheeks, her lips nearly touching his, we

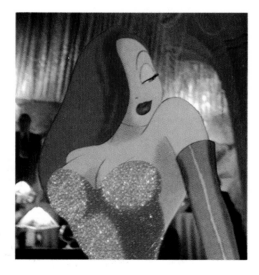

Jessica Rabbit, almost certainly the sexiest animated character ever to scorch the big screen.

can almost feel her breath. This is more than just a matter of good special effects!

Naturally her participation in the movie inspires quite a number of sex-oriented jokes, perhaps rather too many for all of them to be funny. The best is possibly when Greasy, given the task of frisking her, plunges his arm lasciviously into her cleavage only to have his hand agonizingly clamped by a massive Toon bear trap.

Benny the Cab

The Toon taxicab is a marvellous characterization: it never occurs to us for a moment that, in the context of the movie, a cab should be anything *but* a Toon.

We first encounter him when Roger and Valiant are seeking to use the weasels' paddy wagon as their vehicle of escape from Judge Doom and the weasels themselves. Initially they don't realize that the wagon already has a passenger: Benny, locked into the rear compartment. On his release, he offers them (and us) a few words of explanation: "Whoo! Ah, that's better! I can't believe they locked me up for drivin' on the sidewalk. . . . It was just a couple of miles."

Soon we're being led to wonder why Benny should have had to drive on the sidewalk at all. A fantastic chase ensues, in a form that would be an archetype of thriller-movie chases were it not for Benny's revealed abilities. He starts off in typical New York cabby movie style, insulting the pedestrians, talking tediously and cutting off the rest of the traffic, ignoring Roger's screams of panic. The humour of all this is compounded by the fact that Benny's physical appearance is so chubby and friendly-seeming: he looks like the sort of cab you might expect to find in a toddler's

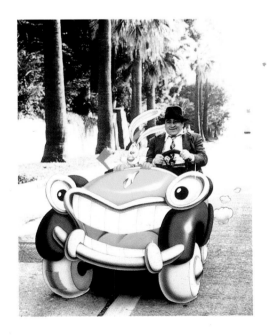

Eddie and Roger aboard Benny the Cab. For the moment, all is good cheer.

toy box. New York cabdrivers have been known to spring similar surprises when they start to speak.

However, as soon as Benny realizes that the weasels are pursuing in the paddy wagon and then that a couple of motorcycle cops have joined in, he becomes a different little vehicle completely. In terms of personality, he shifts from grump to staunch buddy; in terms of his physical demeanour . . . well. His first antic is the high-speed reverse:

> *Roger*: Benny! There's cops right behind us!
> *Benny*: Not for long, Roger! *(vrrroom!)* Now they're right in front of us!

Moments later he expands his chassis to carry his passengers over the heads of their pursuers.

Benny later reappears in, once again, the nick of time, when Jessica and Valiant, in Toontown, have just spotted that the paddy wagon, weasel-packed, is racing towards them: "So, Valiant, you call a cab or what?" In fact, Valiant has done no such thing: his total acceptance of Benny's abrupt arrival is one of the indications that he is becoming adapted to the bizarre logic of Toontown.

Soon after, Benny runs into a pool of Dip spread over the road by Judge Doom; skidding and yelling wildly, he smashes into a lamppost, which clamps down over him like a paper clip. He is left behind when Valiant and Jessica are driven off but, for some reason which is never properly explained, does not die, despite his partial immersion in Dip: all he suffers is a degree of tyre-melting. Thereafter Benny's role is confined to dropping off Roger at the Acme Gag Factory and fetching the cops.

Baby Herman

Although billed as if he were a costar with Roger, and although obviously a great hit with the public, Baby Herman in fact plays a very minor role in the movie. In essence, there are two Baby Hermans. One is the character portrayed in the short *Somethin's Cookin'*, who gurgles and coos (thanks to April Winchell) his way through a succession of graver and graver potential disasters, to the distress and discomfort of Roger. In his other persona, he is a gravelvoiced (Lou Hirsch), foul-mouthed, stogie-smoking, ill-tempered lecher, a fifty-year-old man locked up inside the body of a toddler—a dilemma which he himself describes somewhat less tastefully but rather more graphically: "My problem is, I got a fifty-year-old lust and a three-year-old dinkie."

This horrendous juxtaposition is the sole source of the "adult" Baby Herman's comic appeal, and the moviemakers wisely milk it for what it is worth, but no more; were he to be given any greater a role the joke would be stretched too thin. Its introduction comes as a brilliant shock.

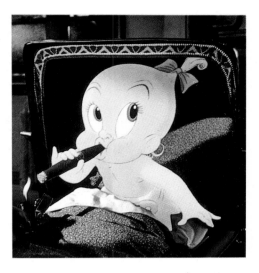

Baby Herman. Butter wouldn't so much melt as catch fire in his mouth.

Just as we have become accustomed to Baby Herman as a cutesy little baby, *Somethin's Cookin'* abruptly comes to its premature end. We have no sooner adjusted ourselves to that than we are, equally abruptly, presented with the baby's *alter ego*: "What the hell was wrong with that take?" he bellows hoarsely before storming off to his star's trailer, shoving up a script girl's skirt as he stomps beneath her.

Yet great pains are taken to show that underneath that fairly repulsive exterior Baby Herman still has what it takes: heart (perhaps with a capital *H*). Although he is less than charitable towards Roger when the latter fails to produce stars on being clunked—"That rabbit can't do anything right! I am so sick of this! That stupid damn' rabbit!"—he is later, on explaining to Valiant the reason for his coming to the office, really rather sentimental about his costar: "He's not a murderer. I should know. He's a dear friend of mine."

Mrs. Herman

Baby Herman's mother features briefly in the short prefacing the main movie, *Somethin's Cookin'*, as well as in the two further Maroon Cartoons that have appeared since (see below). In all instances, in the tradition of, for example, the Tom & Jerry cartoons, we see only the lower part of her legs. Her voice is April Winchell, who also supplies the baby voice of Baby Herman.

Bongo

Bongo is the vast-jawed, vast-muscled and vast-bodied gorilla doorman and bouncer at the Ink & Paint Club; he is aptly voiced by Morgan Deare. He has no direct predecessor in the Disney portfolio (with the possible exception of the Movie Gorilla [►33]), but characters like him—human rather than gorilla—have appeared in virtually every live-action hard-boiled-detective movie ever made; he is a very faithful rendition of the type. He grumbles and mutters throughout most of his two brief appearances—one when he admits Valiant to the club, the other when he flings him out of it—and his responses are uniformly surly.

Smart Ass, Greasy, Psycho, Wheezy and Stupid (The Toon Patrol)

Of Judge Doom's five slimy hench-weasels, by far the most important in terms of the size of his role is Smart Ass. He is their leader, and the only one to show more than a modicum of intelligence—and, even then, not much more. Dressed in his flashy suit, like as not with a revolver in his hand, he uses his stridently grating nasal twang to perform gratuitous acts of mutilation on the English language: almost his first line is "We got deformants all over the city", and if anything his misuse of vocabulary goes downhill from there. Greasy is as flashy but his vocalization is much more muted, conjuring up instead thoughts of dark alleys, low-level Mafia men armed with stilettos and, indeed, greasy cafés. Wheezy's presence is marked by his perpetual wheezing and by clouds of smoke from his omnipresent cigarette; he is somewhat larger than the others, and totes a machine-gun. Psycho has a punkish, serrated hairstyle, popping eyes and needle-thin teeth; his whole head looks as if it has been drawn schematically rather than with any attempt at "realism". And finally there is Stupid, whose name amply sums up his character. On his head he wears an idiotic little propeller-beanie; at the front of his jaw there is a very protuberant single tooth which would make him look conventionally goofy were it not for its sharpness.

Smart Ass is the only one of the five who has any control over his laughter: the rest are likely to collapse in piercing hysterics at the slightest provocation. Smart Ass at one point yells: "You know what happens when you can't stop laughing! One of these days you're gonna *die* laughing!"

And this is exactly what happens. Late in the movie, in the buildup to the final showdown between Valiant and Judge Doom, in desperation Valiant goes into a bizarre and quite incredible (high marks to the special-effects team) Toon-style comedy routine, and one by one the four raucously hysterical weasels either collapse or inadvertently kill themselves, their still-grinning wraithlike souls ascending from their bodies heavenwards. (This is a *very* Disney touch.) Only Smart Ass is able to resist the mirth; Valiant has to deal with him by kicking him in a part of the body that doesn't rhyme with "nose", the force of the impact sending the weasel soaring into the vat of Dip.

Droopy Dog

Droopy Dog plays the role of the elevator attendant in the apartment block where Lena Hyena lives. The Tex Avery creation (for MGM) Droopy Dog is a figure from the classic cartoons, and would accordingly be dealt with in our section on cameo appearances were it not for two facts: first, his voice part was supplied by Richard Williams, the movie's Director of Animation; second, his part in this movie seems to have signified a wholesale revival of the character, since he appears also in the two subsequent Maroon Cartoons (see below).

Lena Hyena

After Valiant has pursued Jessica into Toontown, he looks up at the apartment block outside which she has parked her Packard and, in a high window, sees a silhouette which looks exactly like that of Jessica; he is helped to this false conclusion by the soundtrack. On opening the door of the relevant apartment, however, he receives a dreadful shock: the woman whose silhouette he has seen moving in such sultry fashion is not Jessica at all but a nymphomaniacal caricature of female loathsomeness, Lena Hyena. She takes one look at him and dashes forward, lips and arms outstretched. At the end of a longish chase he darts through a men's-room door, not noticing its OUT OF ORDER sign, and finds himself poised in midair many storeys up. Lena reappears some time later, somehow having managed to get all the way down to street level during the time it has taken him to fall that far; she breaks his fall and the chase briefly resumes. He finally gets rid of her once she has started pursuing him down the white central dividing line of one of the streets; he lifts up a loose end of the line and diverts it towards a wall, into which she runs headlong.

It does not, perhaps, profit us to contemplate too long the implications of the deliberate contrast between Lena (revoltingly ugly, sex crazy) and Jessica (devastatingly beautiful, virtuous).

Bullets

When Valiant, prior to driving into Toontown, pulls his trusty Toon revolver from its case, it's only to be expected that there should be a half-dozen Toon bullets to go with it. All six of them take the form of traditional Wild Western stalwarts: four are cowpokes with a distinctly saddle-hardened appearance about them, the fifth would appear to be a Mexican (his face is invisible under his hat) and the sixth is a Native American. It is the last of these whom Valiant uses to test fire the revolver, tossing his emptied booze bottle high in the air as a target: the bullet catches up with it like a smart bomb, produces a tomahawk several times his own size, and smashes the bottle to smithereens.

Valiant fires three of the cowpokes after Judge Doom when the latter is fleeing from his unsuccessful showdown with Jessica. The three come to a corner:

> *Bullet #1*: Which way did he go?
> *Bullet #2*: Well, I don't know. Well, he went thataway.
> *Bullet #1*: Then let's *go*!

And off they head in the wrong direction. Valiant throws the Toon revolver away with a snarl: "Dum-dums!"

Singing Sword

After Valiant has managed to dupe the weasels to their deaths, his next chore is to try to disable the steamroller that is relentlessly advancing towards the suspended Roger and Jessica. Hoping that it will be of use to him, he grabs up the gleaming, golden Singing Sword. Immediately its blade distorts to produce a semblance of the face of Frank Sinatra, crooning the Coleman & Leigh song "Witchcraft". Valiant throws the sword aside as useless before we have the chance to realize that it really *is* Sinatra who's singing the part.

Octopus Bartender

The bartender of the Ink & Paint Club is a minor character who, although he (one assumes it's a he) has no lines, catches the eye. With his enormously long tentacles he is able to mix several drinks simultaneously while lighting a customer's cigarette, taking payment, etc.

Toon Doom

Although Judge Doom is played throughout the vast majority of the movie as a live-action figure (a fine performance from Christopher Lloyd), he reveals himself in the final minutes to have been a Toon all along. His abandonment of his human disguise comes at an appropriate moment for him: he has just been flattened under a steamroller—nothing more than a painful nuisance for a Toon. The transformation scene is like something out of a horror movie—the part where the vile monster, having been (as we think) well and truly annihilated, proves to be not just still somehow alive but even more hideously menacing than before. Here the parallel is quite consciously done: in a nice little macabre touch, we see Doom's glass eyes drop out onto the floor. The Toon face he then suddenly reveals to us is shocking enough to make even the grown-ups yelp. The eyes are its dominant feature: they bulge repulsively, showing hypnotically spinning patterns.

Doom's reversion to Toon form gives him some distinct advantages in his continuation of his battle with Valiant: a hand can become a massive anvil, for example, or a lethally whizzing chainsaw. How-

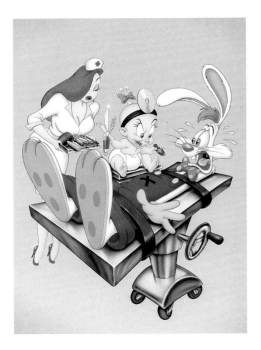

It's pretty obvious who's suffering from *Tummy Trouble* in the Maroon Cartoon. Jessica is the dream nurse, Baby Herman the nightmare surgeon.

ever, it also brings with it the colossal disbenefit that he is now vulnerable to Dip, and it is that weakness which brings about his eventual demise.

Guest Cameos

Who Framed Roger Rabbit is marked by the huge number of old Disney and Warner Bros. characters who appear in small cameo roles, often merely as members of a crowd; their profusion is such that it is virtually impossible to identify them all. There are a few notable absences, however: the moviemakers were unable to get copyright clearance for Popeye, Tom & Jerry and Felix the Cat, for example. A complete listing of those sighted is given at the start of the list of credits (➤326), and many are also mentioned in the story summary; others of interest are **Brer Bear** (➤221), the *Fantasia* **Brooms** (➤181) along with **Mlle. Upanova** and **Hyacinth Hippo** from the same movie, **Dumbo** (➤180), a **Pelican** mailman who looks much like Monte (➤101) and some animated **Gnomes**, all of whom appear to be among the job lot of antiquated Toons that R. K. Maroon has brought to bump up his studio staff. The most significant role among these is played by Dumbo. Maroon explains: "I got him on loan from Disney. Him and half the cast of *Fantasia*. The best part is—they work for peanuts!"

Hyacinth Hippo bumps into Valiant as he is leaving the Maroon Cartoons studios; she has obviously not long beforehand flattened the bicycle of the Pelican, who gathers up the mail he has spilled and cycles off as best he can on the wreck-

age of his machine, a toad peeping from his cap.

Yosemite Sam, aside from having been the donor of Valiant's Toon revolver, turns up in the movie just as Santino and Valiant are arriving for the first time at the Acme Gag Factory.

When Valiant enters the Ink & Paint Club the act on stage is a piano duet performed by the two great cartoon Ducks, Daffy and Donald. With two such volatile tempers in such close juxtaposition, it's hardly any wonder that very soon sparks begin to fly, and the most volcanic duel breaks out between them while each, amazingly, makes at least a token attempt to keep on playing.

A little group of the characters stand around Judge Doom's remains at the end of the movie, among them the Big Bad Wolf (appropriately dressed in sheep's clothing):

Mickey: Gosh, uh, I wonder who he really was.
Bugs: I tell you one thing, Doc. He weren't no rabbit.
Daffy: Or a duck!
Goofy: Or a dog!
Pinocchio: Or a little wooden boy!
Big Bad Wolf: Or a . . . a sheep!
Woody: Or a woodpecker!
Sylvester: Or a pussy!
Woody: Ha-ha-ha-ha-ha . . .

Of the remainder, the one who leaves with us the most lasting impression is certainly Betty Boop. She is working as a cigarette-girl in the Ink & Paint Club and recognizes Eddie from the old days—that they were indeed the old days is stressed by the fact that she is depicted in black-and-white. The meeting as a whole is very touching; not only are we driven to

compare Betty's faded glamour with flamboyant, full color curves of Jessica that will in a moment burst onto the screen, the nostalgic chat between them serves also as a sort of wistful memorial to the *really* old cartoons:

Betty: Long time no see.
Valiant: What are you doing here?
Betty: Work's been kinda slow since cartoons went to color. But I still got it, Eddie. (*shimmies*) Boop boop be-boop, boop!
Valiant: Yeah . . . you still got it.

The Maroon Cartoons

Following the success of *Who Framed Roger Rabbit* and the praise heaped on the knockabout comic short shown in its opening minutes, there have been three further "Maroon Cartoons": *Tummy Trouble* (1989), Roller Coaster Rabbit (1990), and *Trail Mix-Up* (1993). The first represented Disney's first foray into animated short (as opposed to featurette) production since *Goofy's Freeway Trouble* (➤48) in 1965. In *Tummy Trouble*, as in *Somethin' Cookin'*, Roger is left to babysit for Baby Herman. There is a foolish prediction: "And everything's going to be fine. Not like last time." Baby starts to yell as soon as his mother has departed; in order to silence him Roger gives him a rattle, which the brat promptly swallows. Roger dials for Casualty, and he and Baby are rushed to Casualty at St. Nowhere Hospital. There is a witty moment as Roger, in despair, briefly hits the bottle . . . the bottle in question being Baby's baby bottle. In due course Baby expels the bottle and Roger swallows it, thus facing surgery himself. There are some crudely inventive gags—various of them involving the radioactives found in hospitals,

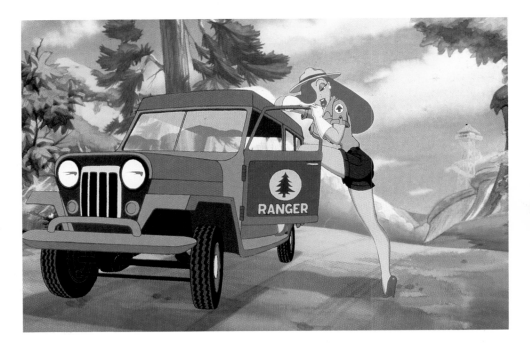

Jessica Rabbit plays a park ranger in *Trail Mix-Up*.

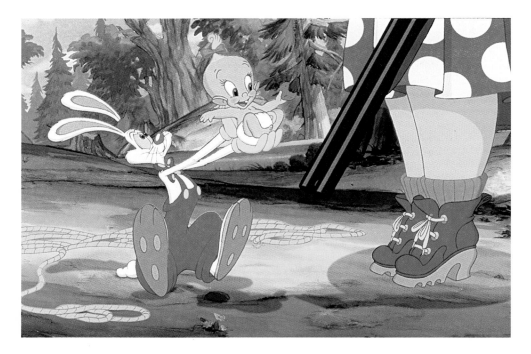

Roger Rabbit, Baby Herman, and Mrs. Herman from *Trail Mix-Up*.

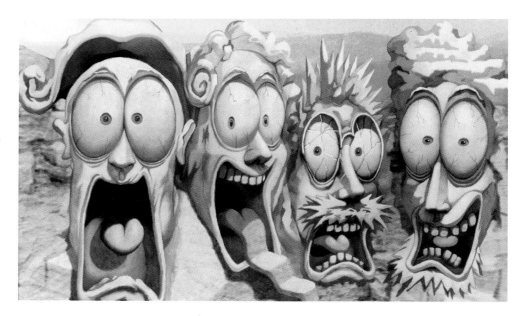

A much-changed Mount Rushmore.

"adult" Baby; Corey Burton is an aggressive **Orderly** and Richard Williams is Droopy Dog. *Roller Coaster Rabbit* again has Kennedy, Marshall, and Spielberg as executive producers and the animation again directed by Minkoff, with producer this time Donald W. Ernst.

Mrs. Herman takes Roger and Baby to a carnival and soon decides to have her future foretold by a psychic. Baby loses his balloon and starts to scream; Roger goes to fetch a replacement but by the time he returns Baby is trying to gain a balloon that is one of the targets in a darts stall. A shooting gallery and the cogwheels of a Ferris wheel soon follow, each time Baby surviving miraculously unscathed while Roger suffers great damage. The next course is the pen of a giant **Bull**—visually rather like a vicious version of Ferdinand (➤88)—where Roger is thoroughly doused in what cannot be described as other than bull excrement before he and Baby are hurled by the bull into a terrifying roller-coaster ride. Partway along this ride they encounter Jessica tied to the line; as their roller-coaster car skips over her, a dapper Droopy Dog (this time voiced by Corey Burton) remarks laconically: "Curses, foiled again." A final nightmare voyage through the Terror Tunnel sees both characters shot right out of the animated short into the studio.

With the same team of executive producers as before and directed by Barry Cook, *Trail Mix-Up* sees Roger dumped with Baby in Yellowstain National Park while Mrs. Herman (her legs significantly fatter than before, for some reason) goes off hunting; Jessica appears as a Ranger. Burton is again Droopy Dog, and Frank Welker voices the **Beaver** and the **Bear** who share some of their adventures—notably a nightmare journey through a sawmill, a typically exaggerated scene whereby our pals go over the lip of an enormously high waterfall, and the destruction of Mount Rushmore. At the end Roger inadvertently destroys the world.

The three *Maroon Cartoon* shorts have their moments, but none has the same verve or is as funny as *Somethin's Cookin'*. Perhaps that was one of a kind and attempts to reprise it were misguided.

here taking missile form—before the rattle is freed and Roger is presented with the medical bill.

The animation is directed by Rob Minkoff and the live action by Frank Marshall; the producer is Don Hahn, with executive producers Kathleen Kennedy, Frank Marshall, and Steven Spielberg. Charles Fleischer voices Roger and Kathleen Turner (this time credited) voices Jessica; April Winchell is Mom and the young Baby; Lou Hirsch is the

OLIVER & COMPANY

Characters:

Oliver; Dodger, Tito; Einstein; Francis; Rita; Fagin; Sykes; Roscoe; DeSoto; Jenny Foxworth; Winston; Georgette; Louie; Pekingese

Credits:

Inspired by: *Oliver Twist* (1837-1838) by Charles Dickens

Voices: Joey Lawrence (Oliver); Billy Joel (Dodger); Cheech Marin (Tito); Richard Mulligan; (Einstein); Roscoe Lee Browne (Francis); Sheryl Lee Ralph (Rita); Dom DeLuise (Fagin); Taurean Blacque (Roscoe); Carl Weintraub (DeSoto); Robert Loggia (Sykes); Natalie Gregory (Jenny); William Glover (Winston); Bette Midler (Georgette)

Sound Design and Supervision: Sandy Berman

Sound Editors: Randle Akerson; Mark Papas; Beth Sterner: Marvin Walowitz

Score: J. A. C. Redford

Orchestration: Thomas Pasatieri

Music Supervisor: Carole Childs

Supervising Music Editor: Kathleen Bernett

Songs by: Howard Ashman, Barry Mann; Dan Hartman; Charlie Midnight; Dean Pitchford; Barry Manilow; Jack Feldman; Bruce Sussman; Rob Minkoff; Ron Rocha; "Buscando Guayaba" by and performed by Ruben Blades; "Fast Lane" by and performed by Rocky Pedilla, Michael Eckhart and Jon St. James

Singers: Huey Lewis; Billy Joel; Ruth Pointer; Bette Midler; Myhanh Tran

Screenplay: Jim Cox; Timothy J. Disney; James Mangold

Story: Roger Allers; Chris Bailey; Michael Cedeno; Mike Gabriel; Vance Gerry; Leon Joosen; Kevin Lima; Dave Michener; Jim Mitchell; Joe Ranft; Gary Trousdale; Kirk Wise; Pete Young

Additional Story Material: Gerrit Graham; Samuel Graham; Chris Hubbell; Steve Hubett; Danny Mann

Editors: Mark Hester; Jim Melton

Supervising Animators: Ruben A. Acquino; Hendel Butoy; Mike Gabriel; Mark Henn; Glen Keane; Doug Krohn

Layout: Rasoul Azadani; James Beihold; Marc Christiansen; Fred Cline; Fred Craig; Karen Keller; Dan McHugh; Alex Mann; Bill Perkins; Phil Phillipson; Bob Smith

Art Director: Dan Hansen

Production Manager: Kathleen Gavin

Character Animators: Viki Anderson; Chris Bailey; David Cutler; Anthony DeRosea; Russ Edmonds; Rick Farmiloe; Will Finn; Tony Fucile; Ron Husband; Jay Jackson; Dan Jeup; Leon Joosen; Shawn Keller; Jorgen Klubien; Kevin Lima; Jeffrey Lynch; Dave Pruiksma; David P. Stephan; Barry Temple; Kevin Wurzer; Phil Young; Kathy Zielinski

Coordinating Animators: Bill Berg; Tom Ferriter; June M. Fujimoto; Marty Korth; Dave Suding; Chuck Williams

Computer Animation: Michael Cedeno; Tina Price

Animating Assistants: Tony Anselmo; Carole Holliday; Broose Johnson; Steve Markowski; Kirk Wise; Ellen Woodbury

Character Design: Andreas Deja; Mike Gabriel; Glen Keane

Inbetweeners: Sue Adnopoz; Scott Anderson; Matthew Bates; Carl Bell; Jerry Brice; Lee Dunkman; James Fujii; Mike Genz; Peter Gullerud; Karen Hardenbergh; Kevin Harkey; Marcia Kimura; Nancy Kniep; Brian McKim; Theresa Martin; Terry Naughton; Eric Pigors; Brian Pimental; Mike Polvani; Michael Show; Alan Smart; Juliet Stroud; Chris Wahl; Cathy Zar

Effects Animators: Dave Bossert; Glenn Chaika; Barry Cook; Mark Dindal; Randy Fullmer; Jeff Howard; Ted Kierscey; Dorse A. Lanpher; Mark Myer; Eusebio Torres; Kelvin Yasuda

Backgrounds: Steve Butz; Jim Coleman; John Emerson; Lisa L. Keene; Tia Kratter; Andy Phillipson; Phil Phillipson; Brian Sebern; Bob Stanton

Animation Camera: John Aadal; Errol Aubry; Ed Austin; John Cunningham; Roncie Hantke; Brandy Hill; Ron Jackson; Dan Larsen; Dave Link; Jim Pickel; Lindsay Rogers; Dean Teves; Chuck Warren

Director: George Scribner

Assistant Director: Tim O'Donnell

Release Date: November 18, 1988

Running Time: 72 minutes

THE MOVIE

Dickens it ain't. Any attempt to analyse *Oliver & Company* in terms of Charles Dickens's popular novel is doomed to failure; it is much better to regard the two stories as sharing a few basic themes and a good number of character-names but being otherwise unconnected. Fortunately for Disney this is exactly what most of the critics did.

Oliver & Company marked the start of a new flood of feature-animation productivity by Disney, which had set itself the target of releasing one new full-length animated feature per year. This pattern of annual release had been a dream of Walt's since the time of *Snow White and the Seven Dwarfs* (➤157); it is a pity that it wasn't realized until over two decades after his death.

The movie marked a significant step forward in the use of computer animation; indeed, it was the first film to have its own department set up expressly for the purpose of generating this form of animation. Of course, computer animation had earlier played a part in *The Great Mouse Detective* (➤318), but with *Oliver & Company* it began to come into its own, with just under 11 minutes of computer-assisted imagery used in combination with traditional hand-drawn character animation. The list of objects created and animated on computer includes cars of all shapes and sizes, cabs, buses, Sykes's limo, Fagin's trike, a cement mixer, a sewage pipe, a piano, subway tunnels and trains, sunglasses, cityscapes and the Brooklyn Bridge. In terms of complexity, the most difficult object on the list was Fagin's trike: this odd-looking motorized vehicle (part scooter, part shopping cart) is composed of 18 separate moving parts, each of which is subject to 15 different motion controls.

It is perhaps in terms of motion against complicated backgrounds that the computer really comes into its own, for it can create a setting that is in effect in the full three dimensions, rather than only the two available to the hand-animator. Tad Gielow, the movie's head computer-graphics engineer, summed the matter up thus:

> Animating with a computer is like building a set. It may take a day or a week to compose a single frame or model, depending on its complexity. But once it's built, you can change the camera angle or revise the scene in no time at all.

This facility of changing the aspect of a setting permitted the animators to include scenes that, for reasons of time and cost, would almost certainly otherwise have been omitted. For example, the scene in which Dodger sings "Why Should I Worry?" inside a section of piping and we are able to follow him as the pipe is carried by a crane through a construction site, a sequence involving all sorts of complex perspective shots, would have been achievable using traditional animation techniques but in practice would almost certainly not have been done.

The most spectacular sequences extensively involving the computer were the climactic car chase and the subsequent confrontation between Sykes and Fagin's gang. In the subway scenes, the tunnel was created as a three-dimensional setting and the cars likewise were three-dimensionally generated. This allowed the directors almost limitless opportunities to throw everything they wanted—every weird camera angle, every piece of extraneous action—into the chase. Again, the sequence in which Sykes faces the gang was given much of its impact through the creation within the computer of a database of the Brooklyn Bridge, so that the animators were provided with almost an embarrassment of choice in the way they treated each aspect of the scene.

There was a further, partly related reason for the use of so much computer animation. Here one can almost hear the ghost of Walt prompting director George Scribner:

> Because the city itself is in some respects another character in the picture, we wanted it to be realistic with lots of movement and traffic; not just static backgrounds. The computer has enabled us to generate the rhythm and action that goes with an urban center and then animate our characters on top of it.

There was a slight downside to this. Although the aim of computer animation (at least in this context) is to create an effect such that it never crosses our minds that a computer has played any part in the creation, on occasion the results can be, as it were, *too* good—too pat, if you like—so that we become aware that we're watching something that only a machine could have realized. The chances are that we won't notice anything at all; but, like an itch, as soon as we've once become aware of this overrightness we begin to see it everywhere. As Charles Solomon—otherwise bowled over by the movie—pointed out in his review of it in the *Los Angeles Times*, "a fleet of New York taxis without a single dent is difficult to accept."

One further computer advance should be noted. In previous exercises—notably *The Great Mouse Detective*—the animators, in order to realize their drawings, had to work through a computer-graphics engineer. In *Oliver & Company*, this process was short-circuited because the movie's two specially trained computer animators, Tina Price and Mike Cedeno, could work directly with the machine.

Of course, in the end result it is the message that is important, not the medium: what really matters to us is the experience of watching *Oliver & Company*, not the artistry or technology utilized to bring it to the screen.

THE STORY

The story starts with a rainy New York and a cardboard box, labeled KITTIES NEED HOME, abandoned on the sidewalk. The other kittens are adopted, one by one, leaving only Oliver, who that night finally departs the waterlogged box in search of his fortune. He comes across Louie, a hot-dog seller, who rudely rebuffs his hungry approaches. But Oliver meets Dodger, a brown spotted mutt, who shows him how it's done: he chases Oliver into Louie's shirt and, the man thus distracted, scampers off with the franks. Oliver follows, expecting his fair share, but Dodger tells him that, on the New York streets, "fairs are for tourists, kid!" and decamps. Oliver trails him to a decrepit canal barge, where Dodger begins to share out his haul of franks with a mangy gang of other dogs—Tito, Francis, Einstein and Rita—telling them the while of the awesome adversary with whom he has duelled in order to get the food . . . until a terrified Oliver quite literally drops into the scene. The other dogs are still ragging Dodger about the disparity between Oliver and the "psychotic monster, with razor-sharp claws, dripping fangs . . . eyes burning" when their human master, the disreputable Fagin, arrives on the scene to inspect the loot the dogs have gathered. The haul is not good, which is ill news for Fagin because he is expecting at any moment the arrival of the villainous Sykes (not Sikes), a money-lender seeking repayment. A car draws up outside and Sykes's two heavies, Dobermans called DeSoto and Roscoe, invade the barge. Fargin goes out to Sykes's car and has the screws put on him in no certain fashion while, inside, the Dobermans try to intimidate the motley crew. DeSoto attempts to chomp Oliver but gets a clawed nose for his pains; he gathers Roscoe and they advance for the kill. But Dodger steps in and faces them down. At the honking of their master's car they retreat, snarling of dire vengeance.

The next morning Fagin takes the dogs out for their daily thievery: "I don't want to put any undue pressure on you, hee, hee, but as you march off to do your duty I want ya ta keep one thing in mind: dead men do not buy dog food!" Dodger is deputed to show Oliver the ropes. Inside the limo they plan to rob is Jenny Foxworth, a rich little girl whose parents are forever away on business; she is chauffeured by kindly Winston. Francis and Einstein between them pull a fake-accident stunt; as Jenny and Winson hop out of the limo to look at the "injured" dog, Tito and Oliver hop in to steal whatever they can. Tito nearly electrocutes himself, and in the chaos Jenny finds Oliver still in the limo, instantly adopts him, and off they drive.

Inside Jenny's home we are introduced to the beautiful but vain poodle Georgette, who of herself remarks in song that inter alia,

Jaws drop, hearts stop,
So classic and classy—
We're not talkin' Lassie . . .

She is understandably less than delighted to find Oliver eating from her bowl and ensconced in her mistress's affections. Nevertheless, Oliver rapidly adapts to the good life.

However, the gang has tracked him down. Waiting until Jenny is out at school, they invade the house and with Georgette's enthusiastic collaboration abduct Oliver; it is only on getting back to the barge that they realize Oliver didn't want to be abducted. Dodger, furious at Oliver's presumed snobbery, casts the kitten out; but Fagin rescues Oliver and, realizing that the kitten has been adopted by someone from the snooty part of Fifth Avenue, sends a ransom note. He and Dodger also take the plan to Sykes, but, before he can explain it, the two Dobermans beat Dodger up.

Later, at a deserted pier, Jenny, following Fagin's map, turns up with her piggy bank and Georgette to make the rendezvous; of course, Fagin doesn't recognize in the sobbing little girl the plutocratic cat-owner he'd expected. Once he has made the connection, he realizes how rotten he's been and, even though Sykes is watching from the limo, "finds" Oliver behind some trash and hands him over to Jenny. Sykes's response to all this is to kidnap Jenny, driving off with her in his limo. The gang—including Georgette and a now reconciled Dodger—resolve to rescue her from the dastard's clutches.

They get into Sykes's warehouse and succeed in tangling up the two Dobermans in a net (although Sykes soon releases them). Fagin crashes onto the scene in his motorized trike. All of our pals pile aboard this vehicle and make off, but

Sykes gives chase. On an inspiration, Fagin steers his trike down into a subway station, assuming that Sykes won't be able to follow in the car—but the rage-maddened Sykes, caring not a fig for his suspension, does so. The chase continues right into one of the tunnels. Sykes succeeds in grabbing Jenny from the trike; Oliver follows, bites Sykes so that Jenny is freed, and is himself tossed into the back of the limo, where the Dobermans prepare to do their worst . . . but Dodger bravely follows and takes them on. There is a fracas, and Roscoe and then DeSoto fall from Sykes's car to their deaths on the electrified track.

Both vehicles exit the tunnel onto Brooklyn Bridge—and into the path of an oncoming train. Fagin and Sykes have something of a tug o' war, with Jenny as rope, between the car and the trike; finally Fagin wins, but now the train is very close. Thanks to Tito's and Fagin's dexterous steering, the trike escapes the collision but Sykes's car and presumably Sykes are smashed to smithereens. But Dodger and Oliver were still in the car! Not to worry: they jumped clear at the last moment and are safe.

After a celebration of their triumph which coincides with Jenny's eighth-birthday party, our pals go their separate ways—Oliver, Jenny and Georgette to live happily ever after in the Fifth Avenue house while the gang returns to the slums.

THE CHARACTERS

Oliver

It is not always the case that juvenile parts in Disney cartoons are actually played by juveniles, but for the pretty and very young Oliver a child actor was indeed used. This was Joey Lawrence, aged twelve and a half; he was able—just—to avoid the overcuteness that must certainly have been a danger.

The animators likewise neatly avoided that hazard—indeed, in a way they exploited it, for in the early scenes of the movie the impression is deliberately created that Oliver, clambering out of the rain-sodden box in which he has been dumped, is going to be just another lovable wide-eyed fur ball. This image is preserved for only a few minutes, until the argument between Oliver and Dodger over the proprietorship of the stolen franks. Thereafter a balance is quite carefully maintained between cuteness and cattishness, so that Oliver's slashing response to DeSoto's menace (he rakes the big Doberman across the nose) seems perfectly consistent with his youthful timorousness only moments before. And, in the frenetic scenes during the chase through the subway, his ability to attack viciously if need be comes as no surprise. In this respect his portrayal might be compared to that of Figaro (➤90), who likewise—albeit to humorous rather than adventurous effect—is capable of this perfectly acceptable switch, between one frame and the next, from charm to claws. Supervising animator Mike Gabriel summed up:

> . . . the original concept was to make him a little older, more of a gangly teenager. But we quickly discovered that an innocent waif on the street was more sympathetic and vulnerable if he was played younger. By studying some of the classic Disney characters like Thumper [➤201] in *Bambi*, we learned that young characters didn't have to be cloying or just a cute ball of fur. They worked because they were sincere and genuine. That's what we wanted for Oliver.

Another distinctly cattish feature of Oliver's depiction is his adaptability. Just like many a real cat (but not all), he is equally at home with a ragamuffin existence on

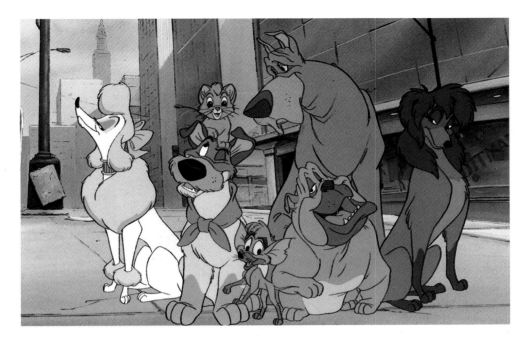

Georgette clearly regards herself as too good to be associated with rest of the gang. Clockwise from her: Oliver, Einstein, Rita, Francis, Tito and Dodger.

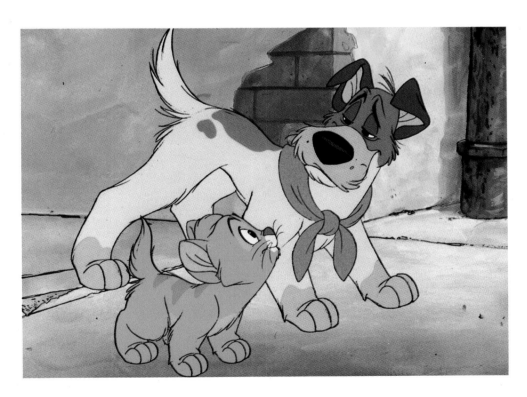

Dodger looking distinctly bored by Oliver's fresh-faced enthusiasm.

the streets as with a life of luxury as a lazing lap-kitten. And, although we see no graphic representation of it on screen, he is clearly able to cope with Georgette's initial hostility to his presence in the Foxworth home.

In terms of this dual persona of the kitten, the relationship between him and Dodger is of especial interest. On their first encounter, Dodger responds to Oliver's cuddliness and total unthreateningness in two quite separate ways: initially

it inspires the mutt to charitability—he offers him a form of ephemeral friendship—and then, the franks having been seized, it permits the dog to dismiss Oliver and Oliver's wishes as beneath notice. Here the behavior is perhaps less typical of animals than of children. It is only later, after Oliver has shown that he has some spirit of his own, that any proper relationship begins to develop between himself and Dodger—and it is this progressive deepening of that relation-

ship that serves as the movie's emotional dynamic. In a curious way, even Dodger's wrath and rejection of Oliver after it becomes evident that the whole abduction effort has been a waste represents a considerable compliment paid by dog to kitten: in Dodger's subliminal perceptions Oliver has graduated from being a little bundle of fun to become an individual whose personality is strong enough to have a strong emotional effect on the mutt. And by the end Dodger recognizes Oliver as in many ways his equal.

Oddly, some of the critics described Oliver as insipid, yet we can see that the plot of the movie holds together only and precisely because Oliver is *not* insipid.

Dodger

Despite the title, Dodger is the most important character in *Oliver & Company*. Somewhat daringly, since he had had no relevant experience whatsoever, rock star Billy Joel was cast as the mongrel's voice; the experiment proved to be an astonishing success—"absitively, posolutely", as Dodger himself might remark. It is to Joel that we owe Dodger's other catchphrase, "Chill out, man" (to which some of the fainter-hearted reviewers objected).

One need hardly add that the casting of Joel made Dodger's song "Why Should I Worry?" something special: while many movie songs earn the description "suitable for all ages" simply because they work in context and don't repel anyone too much, this is a good, gusty rendition that could easily have made it as a successful single in it own right.

Supervising animator Andreas Deja

noted in connection with the scruffy yet charismatic mutt that

> In designing the character of Dodger there was a natural tendency in the beginning to model him after Tramp (➤254) since both are happy-go-lucky street dogs. But we wanted Dodger to have a unique look, so we gave him a rougher and scroungier appearance that seemed to fit in with the city setting.

As noted in the discussion of Oliver, the relationship between Dodger and the kitten provides the movie's essential emotional dynamic, without which the rest of the action would be largely irrelevant. Also of note are the relationships between Oliver, on the one hand, and the gang members and (separately) Fagin, on the other; but equally interesting is that between Dodger and the rest of the gang, generally including Fagin. Merely to say that Dodger is their leader would be oversimplistic: as the most affirmative personality among them, he is also their *focus*. It is only when Dodger arrives with the stolen franks that the personalities of the other dogs begin to take on their three-dimensional quality: they seem to exist as personalities only insofar as they are reflections of Dodger's own. This is less true of Fagin; however, because the emotional dependence of Fagin on Dodger is so strongly depicted (and explicitly when Dodger has been beaten unconscious by Sykes's Dobermans), we again have this sense that it would be hard to imagine what Fagin would be like—what he would be thinking, what he would be doing—were we to encounter him in Dodger's absence.

It is likewise difficult to imagine what the real Dodger would be like on his own, for a great part of his character is the easy way that he shifts from one surface persona to another, so that, even though he dominates the other characters around him, the personality he presents is nevertheless to a large extent governed by them. We see this most clearly in the early sequence of the film, before· he encounters Louie and Oliver, when he is in a setting that would for most people imply urban solitude: the crowded, bustling streets of New York City. But Dodger is *not* alone here: he is in a constant state of *reaction* to those around him, drawing their attention to himself through acts of extroversion that are, as it were, in themselves preemptive reactions. He dons and doffs his various personas in what we can describe as a continuous process of social camouflage, even though its purpose seems to be the opposite of concealment. Moreover, he seems to be perfectly conscious of the fact that this is what he is doing—and even of the mental immaturity behind it—as we see slightly later,

when he has brought the franks to the gang and is acting the part of brave and resourceful warrior-leader:

> *Rita*: So how'dya do it this time, Dodgie baby?
> *Dodger*: Let me tell you, Rita, it was tough. Only I could have done it.
> *Tito*: Hey, wha' happened, wha' happened? I mean, did you have to fight, huh, huh, did you fight, how many were there?
> *Dodger*: Picture the city. Eighth and Broadway, the crowd's bustlin', the traffic's roaring, the hot dogs are sizzling.
> *Einstein*: I love a story with food in it.
> *Dodger*: Enter Dodger, one cool puppy, not just out for himself but community-minded—but he's not the only one out there. Enter the opposition—a greedy, ugly psychotic monster with razor-sharp claws, dripping fangs. He comes at me, eyes burning. I knew my time had come. Suddenly . . .

And then, of course, Oliver falls in through the roof of the barge. Although the gang members (Rita excepted—her response is rather different, more like that of a tolerant fellow-parent) have been sufficiently swept into the atmospherics of Dodger's story that their initial reaction to this sudden incursion is panic, it is interesting to notice that none of them really believes the yarn—and Dodger doesn't really intend them to.

The trouble with such assertive superficiality—to which Dodger's flip speech-modes contribute—is that it may become so dominant that the true personality becomes submerged to the point of extinction. The scriptwriters and animators of *Oliver & Company* must have been very well aware of this pitfall, for it was crucial to the entire enterprise that, at the end, the true Dodger should be dignified in his acceptance of the fact that his pal (now!) Oliver is going to stay uptown while he and the rest of the gang are voluntarily returning to the slums. The solution that the scriptwriters used was to retain rather than discard Dodger's veneer while at the same time supply sufficient clues to the audience so that we *knew* what was going on under Dodger's self-created surface layer. This was quite a sophisticated treatment of the issue, and required great subtlety in building up our appreciation of Dodger's personality right through the movie—largely through those transformations of his attitude towards and relationship with Oliver.

At the end of the movie we're left with the wonderfully warm feeling that, somewhere out there in the streets of New York City, Dodger is still playing his way through life, surrounded by, if not the gang of followers we've come to know, then another one very like it. In a curious way, we sense that somehow Dodger will never die.

Tito

Many of the Disney animated features boast a show-stealing zany, usually in the role of the villain's sidekick. In the more recent movies most of these characters have fallen into one of two categories: there are the reptilian clowns like Sir Hiss (➤293) and Joanna (➤362) and the funny-little-monster ones like Creeper (➤316) and Fidget (➤324). Tito—or, to give him his full name, Ignacio Alonzo Julio Federico de Tito—comes into the latter classification, yet interestingly he breaks with tradition by being not a villainous sidekick but one of the (relatively) good guys.

The frenetic little Chihuahua was one of those Disney characters who just grew and grew from the moment that recording started of his vocal part. This is hardly surprising, given that the voice actor playing the role was Cheech Marin—the Cheech of Cheech and Chong—although Marin later claimed that he read about 75 percent of the lines given to him just as they were (and that the moviemakers declined his urgings to give Tito a song). As often occurs, the animators sketched Marin's grimaces and gesticulations during the recording sessions for references and sometimes straightforward copying; around the time of the movie's release Marin remarked that not only could he see himself in the character as rendered on the screen but that (more tellingly, perhaps) his nine-year-old daughter recognized him immediately. Nevertheless, Tito's supervising animator Hendel Butoy remarked in an interview with Charles Solomon for the *Los Angeles Times* that

> Cheech was very animated while he was recording—Tito's expressions and body language were all there. But if I hadn't seen him his voice would have been enough. The energy and spontaneity and entertainment value he put into his readings were very inspirational.

Butoy also observed:

> George [Scribner] described Tito as having one paw in the light socket all the time—energy just flowing through his body. But you still had to believe he had something going on in his head. The challenge was to keep the thought process in an energetic performance.

The notion of Tito "having one paw in a light socket all the time" goes beyond metaphor, for his primary role in the gang's nefarious activities is to deal with the electrics—specifically the chore of hot-wiring them. To judge by the first of his efforts, when he trying to extract the dashboard radio from the Foxworth family car, he is accustomed to a lack of success that is as eruptive as his own personality. As he later grumbles, "Man, I always get the fuzzy end of the lollipop."

He is a classic example of the little guy who thinks of himself as a big guy, whether it be in doing battle with giants—"You guys don't scare me. C'mon, I'll kill you both man. C'mon, let me at 'em, I'll kill 'em, I'll kill 'em, grrrr!" he pipes enthusiastically at DeSoto and Roscoe—or in his perceptions of himself in his dealings with the fairer sex.

Tito proved to be a smash hit not only inside the studio—advance publicity seemed almost to suggest that he was not so much the movie's star as its supernova—but also with audiences everywhere. Around the time of the release of *Oliver & Company* there were rumors that he was to make further appearances in further movies, either in forthcoming features or, less probably, as a new shorts star. Ever since the brilliant success of Dopey (➤163), such rumors have circulated about the great zanies of the Disney features but—with the exception of Roger Rabbit (➤330), who anyway comes in a rather different category—these expectations have never come to anything. However, in the case of Tito, it is too early to dismiss them.

The Other Gang Members

The number of dogs in the gang is rather difficult to establish, since in visual terms Tito isn't really a dog and in psychological terms a good case could be made for counting Fagin, despite his human appearance, as one among others. Looking at things conventionally, however, the gang is five dogs strong, the three aside from Dodger and Tito being Einstein, Francis and Rita.

Only a handful of the Disney animating crew of over 100 had worked on *The Fox and the Hound* (➤306), and so for the vast majority of them the animation of dogs and cats—creatures that walk on four legs rather than two—was a new and difficult assignment. In order to prepare for the challenge, regular classes in dog anatomy were held at the studio. They were lucky to have as one of their Supervising Animators Glen Keane, who had worked on *The Fox and the Hound* under the master animator Ollie Johnston: with characteristic generosity of spirit Johnston had passed on to Keane much of what he knew of the animation of creatures like dogs. Another major source of reference was the recruitment of countless dogs of every shape and size to be brought to the studio each week and given free run while animators sat around observing and scribbling away feverishly in their sketchbooks. Extensive videos were made of the dogs in action, and often a video printer was used to provide the animators with a sequence of still images

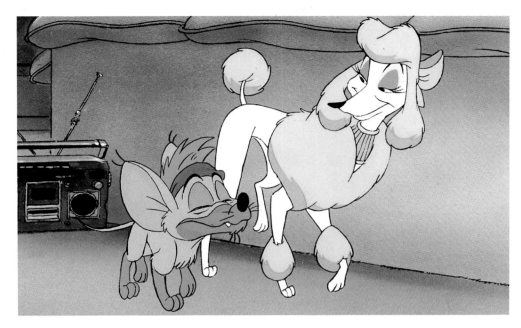

The well-coiffed Georgette with pipsqueak Tito.

for frame-by-frame action analysis. The results of this attention to realism are of course observable in the treatments given to all the feline and canine actors in the movie, but in a way they are most important in connection with Einstein, Francis, Rita, DeSoto and Roscoe—realism is less important for the stars, whose personalities are potent enough and whose roles are large enough that they would transcend the phyisical form in which they were depicted.

Einstein, voice by Richard Mulligan, is a slow-moving, -speaking and -thinking Great Dane whose main function within the movie seems to be to act as a foil to the darting, explosive, chattering Tito and, to a lesser extent, to the equally swift-thinking Dodger. He is useful in the gang's criminal excursions for his innate ability to act the part of a dumb lunk who doesn't mind too much being hurt. He also provides an amusing contrast to the pompus, more-British-than-the-British bulldog **Francis** (and *not* Frankie, as Tito infuriatingly loves to address him). Voiced by Roscoe Lee Browne, Francis, who never uses one word where a multiplicity of polysyllables would adequately substitute, has a carefully cultivated veneer of intelligence and culture—so that it comes as quite a surprise when we discover that indeed he *is* intelligent and cultured. This occurs when the gang invades the Foxworth establishment with the aim of freeing Oliver: as he admires the pictures on the walls, we find him murmuring appreciatively and sincerely, "Chagall, Matisse . . . these are all masterpieces."

The most interesting of the three is undoubtedly **Rita**, her dialogue voiced in rapid, brittle New Yorkese by Sheryl Lee Ralph. This Afghan Hound, whom one imagines to be a not-quite-strumpet with a heart of gold, has a certain sensuality which seems to be born more from the animator's line and probably also Ralph's voicing than from any of her actions or dialogue. She is at the same time both the most hardheaded and the most sympathetic of the gang when Oliver arrives precipitously in their midst; it's an odd and pleasurably disconcerting mixture. She supplies an illuminating contrast to the overcoiffured, spoiled, prize-winning minx Georgette: it is a nicely subtle aspect of the depth of characterization of Tito that his fundamental immaturity renders him instantly passionate about the titivated, brassy poodle while seemingly unable to recognize even that Rita is female. This is in contrast to her relationship with Dodger. The two of them are obviously good companions and have a great deal of mutual respect: we suspect that it is perhaps to her sense of humor that his tall tale of the "psychotic monster" is primarily designed to appeal—her response to the story is quite different and distinctly more adult than those of the other three.

Rita's song, "Streets of Gold", is one of the musical highlights of the movie. But then you'd expect that: her singing voice was supplied by Ruth Pointer of the Pointer Sisters.

Fagin

One is almost tempted to treat Fagin as one of the dog characters, because in many ways, although he is their titular master, he is really just a member of the thieving gang—and, at that, lower in the pecking order than Dodger. His curious position in the scheme of things may have come about because the moviemakers were facing the same problem as Charles Dickens had to when creating Fagin in the novel *Oliver Twist*: that of presenting a criminal and an exploiter of children as a sympathetic character. In the Disney case the solution seems to have been to portray him as a man completely in love with his charges, so that, even when he is terrified at the prospects of Sykes's imminent arrival (as he is during his initial appearance in the movie, while on the barge), he can still be immediately reduced to merry, affectionate laughter by the dogs' attentions. The corollary of this is that he can be taken as more than a little spineless and certainly as less of a leader than is Dodger. The only firm, clear mercenary decision that we are permitted to see him take is when he grabs the opportunity of Oliver having been "rescued" from the Foxworth house in order to indulge in a little extortion—and even then there is no actual malice in the act . . . which is very soon anyway nullified by his immediate sentimental response on being confronted by a weeping Jenny. To be fair, there is a certain amount of courage—or could it just be fecklessness?—in this change of heart, for he is consciously running the very probable risk that Sykes will punish him with physical violence and likely worse. But, unlike any of the other changes of heart in the movie, his impulse to pursue Sykes and attempt to rescue Jenny comes as something of a surprise to us—indeed, were Fagin a more sharply delineated character, we would probably recoil in disbelief at this point; as it is, we are left with a vague worry. It seems similarly curious that Fagin is so unaffected by the shock of Sykes's ostentatious death: it is one thing that he should be relieved that the burden of debt has been lifted from his shoulders (though only, one suspects, until the next Sykes comes along), but quite another that he displays no sign of trauma whatsoever at having witnessed another human being quite literally pulverized. Of course, some people are so feebleminded that they're incapable of this sort of empathic response, but Fagin doesn't seem to be quite *that* retarded.

Leaving aside the success of the character in terms of his function in the plot, what we can note is how well Fagin is portrayed for what he is. His weakness of personality is visible in his movements and in every line of his body, most especially in his face: his feeble chin, his perpetual five o'clock shadow, his ragged nondescriptly carrot-red hair, his disreputable old hat, his disembodied eyebrows, his overlarge and almost triangular eyes, and his curiously vulnerable-looking Adam's apple. This ineffectual physical presence is brilliantly complemented by his vocal part, for which credit must go both to the scriptwriters and to Dom DeLuise, who gave Fagin his voice. His silly giggles and his odd ditherings help depict the character so effectively that we feel almost as if we could have drawn a picture of the character even if we had sat through the movie with our eyes shut.

This overall depiction is carried further by the portrayal of Fagin's trike, a bizarre vehicle which has obviously been constructed by cannibalizing the parts of both a motor scooter and a shopping cart; because of its push-me-pull-you appearance and its complexity unreliable, diffident-seeming motion one would expect that, if it were given a voice, it would sound very much like Fagin does himself.

There is one interesting aspect of Fagin's role in the plot which seems to have been left undeveloped by the animators. At the end of the movie, after the celebratory/birthday party, no very clear reason is offered why the gang members (Fagin included) should opt to return to the streets. In terms of logic, however, there *is* a very clear reason why they must do so; while it would be plausible (just) for Jenny to be able to adopt all the canine gang members so that they could enjoy the life of ease that awaits Oliver, there would be no room in that expanded household for Fagin. He has no choice but to return to his old ways. And gang loyalty dictates that the dogs must do so too.

Sykes

From the outset the animators wanted to make the movie's villian something rather out of the ordinary. They needed to portray someone who could be brutally threatening and yet not just a thug, sinister and yet very powerfully physical—neither a sly Ratigan (➤322) nor a brute McLeach (➤361) but possessing some characteristics of both of them. The supervising animator Glen Keane summarized the resulting character very well:

> We wanted him to be a solid, powerful guy who is seen mostly in shadow. He is personified by his car. We found it was much more intimidating if we didn't show him in light all the time. Also suggesting a sense of power are his hands, which are big, meaty mitts with bratwurstlike fingers—yet they are very dexterous and delicate. In fact, his hobby is building miniature models of his car.

A good perspective on Sykes's persona can be derived from a glance at the screen career of Robert Loggia, the actor who supplied the villian's voice. It is odd, perhaps, that we should find ourselves noting as a curiosity the fact that Disney chose a professional screen heavy to voice the part of an animated heavy.

Roscoe and DeSoto

The two huge Doberman pinschers employed by Sykes as his thugs are in many ways not much more than that: thugs. Any character differences between the two of them are slight (DeSoto seems keener on cat-killing than does his colleague)—although the other characters in the movie are clearly able to tell them apart, as witness Fagin's recognition by

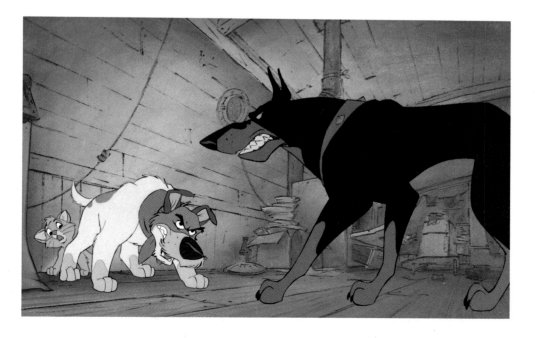

Dodger bravely facing down one of Sykes's two Doberman thugs, while Oliver cowers behind.

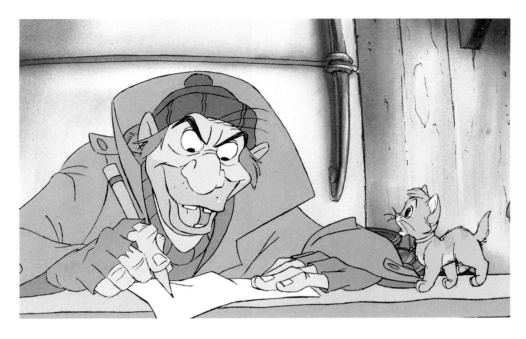

Fagin, the prospect of money setting his eyes alight, pens the ransom note as Oliver looks on.

name of the fact that it is DeSoto, not Roscoe, who has had his nose slashed by Oliver during the two dogs' invasion of the barge.

In fact, the almost completely characterless nature of the Dobermans' thuggishness serves the very useful function of pointing up more effectively the personalities of the members of the gang and of Oliver. This is done through the different ways in which the gang members express their personal courage against the anonymous and much more powerful aggressors. Tito is of course all tiny flying fists and pipsqueak threats of mayhem. Francis risks physical harm by using intellectual pretension like a blunt instrument: "Isn't it rather dangerous," he sneers in response to an insult from Roscoe, "to use all of one's vocabulary in a single sentence?" Einstein relies on straightforward physical bravery—he is closest in size to the intruders. Dodger, as one might expect, uses a mixture of boldness with a very large measure of quick-wittedness. Rita retains an aloofness until the two Dobermans are retreating, when she jabs Roscoe in the ribs and, as it were, twists the jab with: "Run along, Roscoe, your master's callin'."

Because they are cyphers, we are little affected—by either triumph or regret—when first Roscoe and then DeSoto falls to his death on the electrified rail of the subway.

Jenny Foxworth

The poor little rich kid, left extensively on her own with the servant Winston by her jet-setting parents, bears some physical resemblance to Penny (➤299) of *The Rescuers*; however, she is much more vigorously portrayed (voice by thirteen-year-old Natalie Gregory) than Penny, as befits the very differing styles of the two movies.

She is the only major character in the movie to be treated as a completely realistic human being. Certainly some of the critics found her irritatingly shallow, if not wimpish. This was to miss the point. The focus of the movie is on its animal stars plus the caricatured Fagin (honorary dog) and the dramatically treated Sykes. Jenny's role is that of a symbol: she represents the life of ease, prosperity and tranquillity to which we would all like to become accustomed. Sweet Jenny, sympathetic in her sadnesses and quietly in-fectious in her buoyancies, is perfectly tailored for the function her role demands.

Winston

The part of Winston, the Foxworth chauffeur, is a small one. He is required in the movie because, however egocentric Jenny's parents might be, it would be stretching plausibility too far to suggest that they might leave her on her own: he thus represents the army of retainers that would in reality been left with her. He was voiced by William Glover.

Georgette

Georgette is one of those characters, common in the Disney features, who have no real plot function but who, despite this status as an add-on, turn in such a blistering performance that it would be hard, now, to imagine the movie without them. A large measure of the blister of Georgette's performance is supplied by her voice-actor, Bette Midler, who has the old-fashioned Hollywood star ability to turn any performance into an occasion; but this shouldn't make us forget the efforts of the animators, the scriptwriters and perhaps most especially, the songwriters. Not since Peggy Lee, as Peg (➤257), belted out "He's a Tramp" in *Lady and the Tramp* has a Disney dog been permitted to give us quite such a character-analysis-in-song as Georgette's "Perfect Isn't Easy", a catalogue of self-adoring bitchery sung by Midler with vigour and a faint redolence of Tom Lehrer—and perhaps also Lassie. The song was written by lyricists Jack Feldman and Bruce Sussman, with Barry Manilow supplying the music.

The moviemakers made considerable

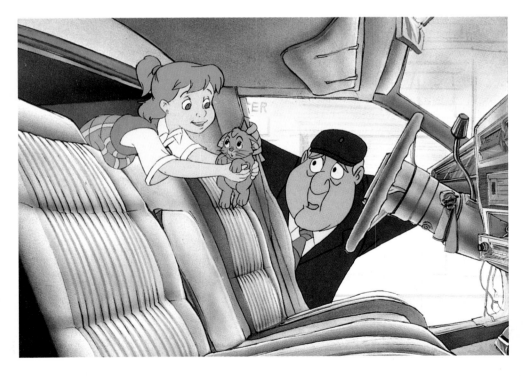

The chauffeur Winston is clearly not pleased to discover Jenny's delight on finding Oliver.

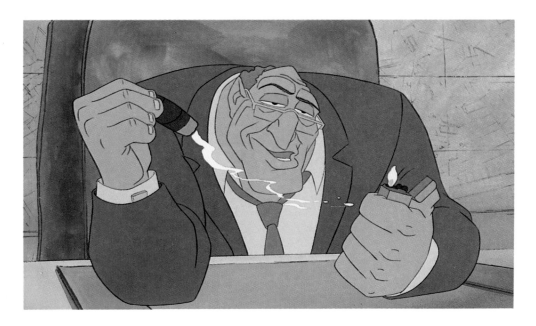

Sykes, in whose figure we can detect a representation not only of organized crime but also of the heartlessness of big business confronted by weak individuals.

course, stifled as soon as Tito realizes that the attainment of his heart's desire will require bathing—a variation on the soap-opera theme—and we are left with the feeling that his flight from the minor hell has saved him from a major one.

Her willingness to take an active role in rescuing Jenny seems rather curious—until we realize that, of course, Jenny is Georgette's meal ticket.

Louie

The big, fat, unshaven, cigar-smoking Louie is the hot-dog seller we encounter during the movie's opening sequences. We are obviously meant to look on him as ill tempered—"a well known enemy of the four-legged world", as Dodger puts it—and he is depicted accordingly. He serves also as a symbol of the downside of New Yorkers—the callous indifferences to the fate of others that can be regarded as typical of the city. By extension, then, he is an expression of Oliver's solitude and vulnerability.

Pekingese

Personable and somewhat hoity-toity, Pekingese is the reluctant recipient of Dodger's quasi-amorous and very public attention.

comic play with Georgette's changing attitude towards Tito; one feels that, in their depiction of her easy modulation from initial snobbish revulsion to what is, although concealed by mannerly cosmetics, essentially upper-crust lust, they were having fun parodying every upstairs-downstairs soap opera we would care to name. The burgeoning affaire is, of

---

THE LITTLE MERMAID

Characters:

Ariel; Eric; Sebastian; Flounder; Triton; Ursula; Vanessa; Flotsam and Jetsam; Scuttle; Seahorse; Ariel's sisters (Aquata, Andrina, Arista, Attina, Adella, Alana); Shark; Grimsby; Louis; Max; Carlotta; Minister; Seadog; Laundrywoman

Credits:

Based on ''The Little Mermaid'' by Hans Christian Andersen

Voices: Jodi Benson (Ariel); Christopher Daniel Barnes (Eric); Samuel E. Wright (Sebastian); Ben Wright (Grimsby); René Auberjonois (Louis); Pat Carroll (Ursula); Kenneth Mars (Triton); Buddy Hackett (Scuttle); Jason Marin (Flounder); Paddi Edwards (Flotsam and Jetsam); Edie McClurg (Carlotta); Will Ryan (Seahorse)

Supervising Sound Editors: Louis L. Edemann; Richard C. Franklin, Jr.

Sound Editors: Charles L. Campbell; Leonard T. Geschke; J. Chris Jargo; Nils C. Jensen; G. C. ''Chuck'' Neely; P. Bruce Richardson

Original Score: Alan Menken

Orchestration: Thomas Pasatieri

Supervising Music Editor: Kathleen Bennett

Songs by: Howard Ashman; Alan Menken

Screenplay: John Musker; Ron Clements

Visual Effects Supervisor: Mark Dindal

Art Direction: Michael A. Peraza, Jr.; Donald A. Towns

Directing Animators: Ruben Aquino; Andreas Deja; Mark Henn; Glen Keane; Duncan Marjoribanks; Matthew O'Callaghan

Character Animators: Tony Anselmo; Chris Bailey; James Baxter; Michael Cedeno; David Cutler; Anthony DeRosa; Russ Edmonds; Rick Farmiloe; Will Finn; Tony Fucile; Chuck Harvey; Ron Husband; Jay Jackson; Dan Jeup; Leon Joosen; Shawn E. Keller; Jorgen Klubien; Doug Krohn; Rob Minkoff; David A. Pacheco; David Pruiksma; Nik Ranieri; Tom Sito; Dave Spafford; David P. Stephan; Barry Temple; Chris Wahl; Ellen Woodbury; Phil Young; Kathy Zielinski

Layout Supervisor: David A. Dunnet

Layout: Rasoul Azadani; James Beihold; Fred Cline; Lorenzo E. Martinez; Bill Perkins; Daniel St. Pierre

Production Manager: Maureen Donley

Editor: Mark Hester

Computer Animation: Tina Price; Andrew Schmidt

Animating Assistants: Arland Barron; Gee-Fwee Boedoe; Carole Holliday; Humberto DeLaFuente, Jr.

Breakdown/Inbetweeners: Francesca Allen; Scott Anderson; Dorris Bergstrom; Jerry Lee Brice; Sheila Brown; Merry Kanawyer Clingen; Lee Crowe; James A. Davis; Eileen Dunn; Tom Ellery, Jr.; Mark Fisher; James Fujii; Daniel A. Gracey; Peter A. Gullerud; Karen Hardenbergh; Tim Ingersoll; Patrick Joens; Jason Lethcoe; Teresa Martin; Tom Mazzocco; Cynthia Overman; Don Parmele; Ginny Parmele; Eric Pigors; Brian Pimental; Mike Polvani; William Recinos; Stan Somers; Bruce Strock; Juliet Stroud; Michael Swofford; Marianne Tucker; Tuck Tucker; Jim van der Keyl; Dave Woodman; Susan M. Zytka

Effects Animators: Dave Bossert; Glenn Chaika; Barry Cook; Randall Fullmer; Christine Harding; Jeff Howard; Chris Jenkins; Ted C. Kierscey; Dorse A. Lanpher; Mark Myer; Don Paul; Eusebio Torres; Kelvin Yasuda

Backgrounds Supervisor: Donald A. Towns

Backgrounds: Kathy Altieri; Doug Ball; Jim Coleman; Greg Drolette; Dennis Durrell; Dean Gordon; Lisa L. Keene; Tia Kratter; Cristy Maltese; Andrew Richard Phillipson; Philip Phillipson; Craig Robertson; Brian Sebern; Robert Edward StantonDirectors: John Musker; Ron Clements

Associate Producer: Maureen Donley

Producers: Howard Ashman; John Musker

Release Date: November 17, 1989 (with advance release in Los Angeles and New York on November 15, 1989)

Running Time: 82 minutes

THE MOVIE

This project was born in 1985 when Ron Clements, who was just finishing work on *The Great Mouse Detective* (➤318), was casting around for something new for Disney animation. Hans Christian Andersen's story seemed to him to provide an ideal basis, especially since he was intrigued by the possibilities of animating an underwater setting. After substantial revision of the story to remove its downbeat ending and to give it a strong villain (the seawitch is unnamed and less prominent in the original), serious development work got under way and in 1986, it having been decided that the movie should be a musical, Howard Ashman and Alan Menken were brought in not only as songwriters but also as cocreators of the project as a whole—a practice which was reminiscent of Disney's early days, when often the music was written before animation began. The final result makes extensive use of songs and underscoring to accentuate and advance plot points, story action and the personalities of the characters. Moreover, Ashman and Menken brought to the movie a theatrical approach and style; this is especially evident in the way that some of the songs are presented, notably "Daughters of Triton" and "Under the Sea".

To create a distinctive design and fitting color style, the directors looked to various sources for inspiration. Among these were cartoonist Rowland B. Wilson, the renowned children's book illustrator (and author) Chris Van Allsburg and veteran Disney layout man Ken O'Connor. Also helpful during the planning stages were some evocative pastel drawings by Kay Nielsen unearthed in the Walt Disney Archives. Nielsen is best known in our context for the work he did on the *Night on Bald Mountain* sequence (➤186) of *Fantasia*. In the early 1940s he had created storyboard art for two proposed features based on Andersen stories, and it was some of this that the Archives supplied.

Starting from here, art directors Michael Peraza and Donald Towns began to experiment with colour and backgrounds to see how these elements could strengthen the telling of the story. Their palette for the underwater scenes was most certainly not limited to shades of blue: because this was an animated rather than a live-action movie, they could draw on a whole host of other colours to help convey mood and emotion, to enhance the theatrics of the musical numbers, and, very importantly, to convey a feeling of warmth in the movie despite the fact that the setting is in real life so obviously chilly. So that there would be a consistent style and flow of colour throughout, Towns created a sort of visual outline for the movie, a board on which small squares of colour represented the various scenes. By looking at this he was able to assess the impact of the changing colours over the movie as a whole.

The use of special effects in the movie is likewise interesting: almost 80 percent of *The Little Mermaid* required some kind of effects work—according to Mark Dindal, the effects animation supervisor, that figure represented "more effects than probably any film since *Fantasia*". The scenes in which we are most aware of the effects are the two storms at sea—one leading to Eric's shipwreck and the other when the giant Ursula emerges from the waves. For research and inspiration for these, Dindal and his team studied the relevant scenes in *Pinocchio* involving Monstro (➤175)—and the results are certainly reminiscent of the whale's great chase after Pinocchio and Geppetto.

In fact, although the standard of the animation is incredibly high in the film, and although there are parts of it which represent Disney at its very best, a few clumsinesses were, astonishingly, permitted to remain. As one might expect, none of these occur in scenes of any importance and none of them last for more than a few seconds, so they are hardly noticeable in the overall scheme of things, but it still comes as a surprise to find them. One recalls noticing similar trivial lapses in the opening scenes of both *The Black Cauldron* and *The Great Mouse Detective*.

Such minor carps aside, the movie is a brilliant achievement—and for once the reviewers seemed virtually unanimous in agreeing with that assessment. What a number of the critics did point up, however, was that this was far from just a movie for children. To my knowledge none of them quite dared to go the whole hog and mention the fact that its primary subject is, through analogy, sexual awakening, a theme emphasized early in the movie when Triton (father) is berating his daughter for going to the surface:

> Triton: You went up to the surface again, didn't you?
> Ariel (*smiling and shrugging*): Nothing happened.
> Triton: Oh, Ariel! How many times must we go through this? You could have been seen by one of those barbarians—by, by one of those humans!
> Ariel: Daddy, they're not barbarians! They're . . .
> Triton: They're dangerous! Do you think I want to see my youngest daughter snared by some fish-eater's hook?
> Ariel: I'm *sixteen years old*! I'm not a child any more!
> Triton: Don't you take that tone of voice with me, young lady. . . .

And so it goes, echoing precisely the kind of argument billions of fathers have had with their daughters after the latter have been out too late and with "unsuitable company". Later underscorings of the theme are the song "Part of Your World" and Triton's final surrender of Ariel to Eric.

That said, *The Little Mermaid* is a gloriously enjoyable musical fantasy—and there is no reason why we shouldn't appreciate it on that basis alone. The fact that it is a more profound movie—that it gives us something extra to think about—is the mark not just of a good but of an excellent entertainment.

THE STORY

The movie starts remarkably quietly, with swirling sea gulls. We are taken to the deck of a sailing vessel, where sailors sing a very short song, "Fathoms Below", and we are introduced not just to Eric, Grimsby and Eric's dog Max but also to the notion of the submarine kingdom of the merpeople and of Triton, who controls the elements. Next, after the titles, we go to a great underwater cavern where the Court Composer, Sebastian, is about to present a musical extravaganza for the benefit of King Triton, starring Triton's daughters, notably the youngest of them, Ariel. The show starts with considerable razzmatazz, but Ariel is found to be missing. We discover her exploring an old wreck in search of human artefacts for her collection, in the company of her sidekick, a fat, youthful little fish called Flounder. They are chased off by an enormous shark and go to the surface where they chat with Scuttle, a zany sea gull who explains to them—with extravagant inaccuracy—the functions of a couple of the artefacts Ariel has brought with her.

Suddenly she remembers where she should be. She and Flounder dash off homewards, little knowing that they are being observed not only by the great seawitch's two repulsive hench-eels, Flotsam and Jetsam, but also, through their eyes, by the sea-witch herself, Ursula. We briefly see Ursula gloating at the prospect of gaining vengeance (although we're not quite certain for what) against Triton through the foibles of his youngest daughter, and then we cut to the king himself, who is in the process of giving Ariel a blistering row, assisted vigorously by a sycophantic Sebastian. Flounder speaks up for her, but accidentally lets slip that the two of them have been to the surface, and the dispute gets even more severe; its culmination is the appointment of Sebastian as Ariel's trustee to keep her out of trouble in future (we are irresistibly reminded of the role of Jiminy Cricket [➤169] as Pinocchio's guardian).

Sebastian comes across Flounder and Ariel in the latter's secret grotto where she keeps her considerable collection of salvaged human artefacts. She sings "Part of Your World", expressing her yearning to be out of the water and mixing among humans. At the end of the song Sebastian remonstrates with her, but they're both distracted by the sight of a ship's hull overhead, and she and Flounder swim up to investigate with Sebastian in hot pursuit. It is of course Eric's ship. It is his birthday, and as part of the festivities Grimsby presents him with a life-size statue of himself (Eric) in battle gear—the implication being that Eric should in real life more often be so clad. Ariel climbs up the side to spy droolingly on him as he talks with Grimsby of how he yearns one day to find his ideal woman. Suddenly a tempest breaks and the ship founders; all the humans escape but the dog Max is left behind; heroically Eric saves him but is too late to save himself when the ship's arsenal explodes; equally heroically Ariel saves Eric and hauls him to shore where she tends him and reprises "Part of Your World" as he recovers consciousness. Just then Grimsby and Max turn up and she flees, leaving Eric with only a vague memory of her face but an obsessive one of her singing voice.

Once again we briefly see Ursula gloating. She shows us her garden of mersouls—poor, etiolated, mourning little polyps—and explains that Ariel's love for Eric will enable her to capture Triton's soul to add to her collection.

Ariel is clearly in love. Triton is delighted, assuming that at last she's found the right merman. Sebastian is keen that the king remain as long as possible in this misconception, but Ariel dreams only of ways she could realize her dream of wedding the prince. Sebastian persuasively sings the excellent and very catchy calypso-style song "Under the Sea", assisted by a bewildering variety of fishy musicians and singers—the sea-snails who serve as his doo-wop backing singers are brilliant and brilliantly funny, a fluke resembling Duke Ellington plays on a saxophone-shaped shell, and so on—but at song's end Sebastian finds that Ariel has gone: "Somebody's got to nail dat girl's fins to de floor!"

Triton's Seahorse-page summons Sebastian to the kingly presence, where the truth of Ariel's love emerges. Meanwhile, Ariel is showing Flounder her latest acquisition: the life-size statue of Eric, sunk with the ship; she canoodles dreamily with it. But Triton arrives to destroy her idyll; the stern father, he zaps her collection of artefacts—including the statue—with his trident (which functions much like a laser-blaster in a *Star Wars*–type movie) in the hope of simultaneously shattering her infatuation with humanity. His draconian action has exactly the opposite effect, so that she is ripe for temptation when Flotsam and Jetsam appear and lure her to Ursula's sanctum with promises that the sea-witch will help her realize her dreams. Indeed, Ursula emphatically repeats those claims, raunchily delivering the burlesque-style song "Poor Unfortunate Souls" and drawing up a contract whereby Ariel can be a human for three days: should Eric give her true love's kiss before the sunset of the third day she will remain human, otherwise she will revert to mermaidhood and then become one of the polyps in Ursula's soul-garden; the price for this "service" will be Ariel's voice—anyway, as Ursula sings, "The men up there don't like a lot of blabber". The transaction complete, Ariel goes ashore in human form, mute.

Eric has been combing the land for the girl whose voice so captivated him. He comes upon Ariel (who has been dressed "idiosyncratically" by Scuttle); Max recognizes her, but of course Eric does not. Nevertheless, he takes her back to his palace, where she is looked after by his housekeeper Carlotta, who gets her ready for lunch with the prince and Grimsby. Sebastian, who has tagged along, goes wandering in the palace and has a hilarious slapstick encounter with the chef Louis, who sings "Les Poissons" while attempting to add Sebastian to the menu.

The next day Eric takes Ariel on a tour of his (very small) country; they are trailed by Sebastian (aboard their coach), Flounder (along rivers) and Scuttle (aloft), all three eagerly hoping for That Kiss. But it never quite happens. Finally the two humans go out in a rowing boat together, and Sebastian wearily musters another collection of faunal musicians to sing encouragingly the smoochy "Kiss the Girl"—which Eric is at last on the verge of doing when Flotsam and Jetsam overturn the rowing boat.

Ursula, hearing of the narrow escape, resolves to take human form herself, and the next morning Ariel awakes to find the palace abuzz with the news that Eric has not only become engaged but has determined to wed this very day. As Ariel soon discovers, the object of Eric's affections is a woman called Vanessa, who much resembles Ariel except for her coloration and her rather sly facial expressions, and who also possesses Ariel's own lost voice (which is why Eric assumes that she is the girl of his dreams). Ariel, forgotten, is left behind as the wedding ship sails off into the sunset.

But Scuttle comes across the ship at sea and, spying through a porthole, realizes that Vanessa is in fact Ursula in human guise. He rushes back to tell his pals the news. Ariel climbs aboard a floating barrel and is towed off to sea by Flounder while Sebastian rushes to tell Triton what's a-fin; just before he goes he instructs Scuttle to stall the wedding—somehow.

Scuttle gathers various marine and avian friends and the service, already under way, is satisfactorily disrupted. In the process, Ariel's voice is knocked free from the neck of Vanessa (who has been wearing it as a pendant) and rolls to the feet of the just-arrived Ariel herself; it suffuses up into Ariel's body, and at last Eric realizes that she is indeed the one with whom he fell in love. But as he leans to kiss her the sun sets: it is too late. Ursula spectacularly discards her human form in time to confront Triton as he hurries to the scene; he submits to her demand that he should give up his soul (and hence his crown) to her in exchange for Ariel's.

Now Ursula becomes truly gigantic—yet Eric and Ariel are prepared to do battle with her as she stirs up a vast vortex and blasts at both of them with the trident she has inherited along with Triton's kingdom. A blast meant for Eric is, thanks to Ariel's intervention, diverted to incinerate Flotsam and Jetsam. Eric climbs aboard a wreck raised from the deep and heroically steers it around through the clashing waves until its splintered bowsprit stabs Ursula fatally in the belly. The souls are released from her macabre garden, once more becoming living merpeople. Ariel, Triton, Eric and all the other humans and friendly creatures are saved. Triton concedes that he must at last give his daughter her liberty, and she touchingly tells him that she loves him but.

There is a joyous wedding of our two protagonists, Louis and Sebastian have another fight (which Sebastian wins), and the credits roll to a reprise of "Under the Sea".

THE CHARACTERS

Ariel

Tawny-haired Ariel was one of the most immediately popular animated heroines to emerge from the Disney stable for a very long time—indeed, it's hard to remember any at all that might match her in this respect. It is easy enough to explain away this phenomenal success in terms of sexual allure, of which she has plenty, yet that doesn't really get to the heart of the matter, for in many ways she is also a very childlike character.

Ariel is a girl who is in the process of becoming a sexually attractive woman; thus our responses to her, while linked to her sexuality, are nostalgic rather than prurient. This is particularly evident in the scenes when Ariel has just come ashore in human form and has discovered that she's got legs. Despite the obvious sexual overtones in the fact that she is now bifurcate, where she really appeals to us is in her wonder at finding these marvellous new appendages joined onto her. We're al-

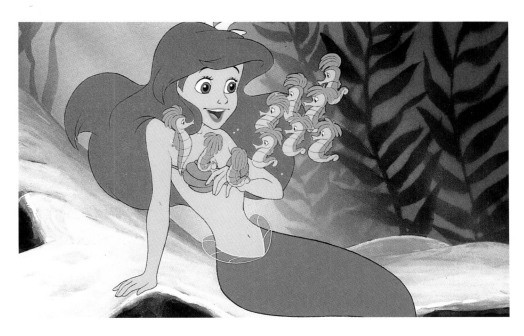

Ariel, whose independence and modernity marked her as the first of a new breed of Disney-feature heroines.

ready smiling in resonance with her when she tries to stand up on these odd limbs; when they wibble-wobble uncontrollably beneath her, like the legs of a child trying roller skates for the first time, our smiles turn to laughter—but it's empathetic laughter.

Ariel was voiced for both speech and song by Jodi Benson, an actress whose previous credits had been largely on the stage. The movie's codirector, Ron Clements, remarked:

> Because the songs are structured almost as extensions of the dialogue, we felt it was really important to have the same person doing the singing and speaking voice. Jodi had a sweetness and purity to her singing voice and a youthfulness to her speaking voice that was very unique [*sic*]. We felt she best captured the innocent and vulnerable quality we were looking for.

The latter part of that remark is confusing, because Ariel's innocence is that of a teenager, and, except in her moments of greatest distress, we don't hear much by way of vulnerability from her: one of her great attractions is that she is for the most part—except when expressing her foolish besottedness with the lacklustre Eric—very definite about what she is doing and very confident in her own ability to successfully accomplish exactly what she plans. Of course, a good deal of that confidence is ill placed—that is surely the hallmark of the teenager—but, whatever its origins or its wisdom, it can hardly be described as vulnerability. Nevertheless, Ms. Benson voices the part captivatingly enough aside from her irritatin' habit when singin' of self-consciously missin' out the letter *g*.

An interesting technical point concerned Ariel's coloration. For all of the characters great care had to be taken to compensate skin tones and hair colour in changing environments and light sources, some of which were in the water and some outside it. For Ariel alone the animators used no fewer than thirty-two colour models—and then of course there were the costume changes, from mermaid fin to rag improvisation to bridal dress. The blue-green of her fin was a hue specially mixed by the experts in the Disney paint lab: as you might expect, they called this "new" colour Ariel in the mermaid's honour.

Eric

It is a recurring theme of this book that Disney's glamorous princes tend on the whole to be cyphers, and Eric (voiced by Christopher Daniel Barnes, then the US national teenage spokesperson for the environmental organization Greenpeace) is no exception. The habit of using purely symbolic characters in the princely role is not normally a particularly noticeable one in the other features; it is only later that we realize that, whereas we have the feeling we've *met* the other principal characters, the one in the role of prince has never been more than a sort of blur to us. In the case of *The Little Mermaid*, however, probably because Ariel was so much designed to be the movie's dominant character, the fact that Eric doesn't have much going for him except his rock-jawed good looks becomes particularly obvious. Oddly, though, a better excuse can be made for *The Little Mermaid* requiring a cypherlike prince than for most of the other Disney features: just as Triton is (in part) a symbol of paternal authority and possessiveness, and therefore needs no deep character portrayal, so Eric is not so much any particular man as an embodiment of the type of relationship with males that Ariel so devoutly yearns to explore. In a way, then, one could argue that to give Eric any specific personality would be a mistake, that it is important to the thematic structure of the movie that he has none. Yet these arguments don't wash: Eric's lack of any real presence is a hole at the heart of the movie. What they do mean is that at least the hole is a small one.

As a prince, Eric is simply not bothering to do the job properly. Grimsby serves as the voice of his conscience, but Eric has the habit of brushing off as irrelevant anything that Grimsby says which doesn't happen to fit in with Eric's own selfish inclinations. It is important for the king-

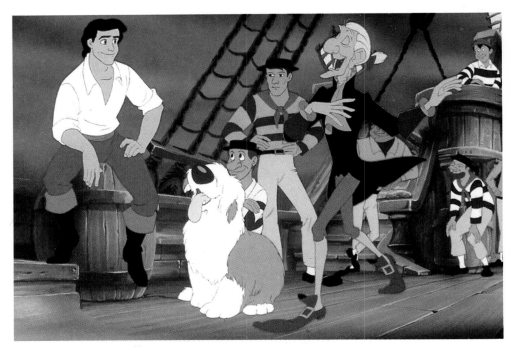

The scene aboard Eric's ship, as witnessed by a hidden Ariel. Grimsby, Eric's general factotum, is in full flight. Max watches.

dom that Eric find himself a suitable spouse with whom to start breeding heirs, yet Eric still wants to cling onto the irresponsible ways of his youth.

It is thus as an adolescent infatuation that we must regard (as Grimsby does) Eric's quest for the voice of his dreams. Although one might be tempted to depict his idée fixe romantically, in fact it is the exact opposite of romantic: he isn't seeking a human being at all but a self-indulgent fantasy which has much more to do with himself than with anyone else, dream girl or not. Thus, even when Ariel herself is right there in front of him, a real live young woman who has a vivacious, exceptionally attractive personality and is almost literally begging to be kissed, and even when Eric himself has clearly fallen for her hook, line and sinker, he *still* lets his infatuation with the dream voice of his memories get in the way.

In any sensible discussion of Vanessa we come up against the question of why she wants to marry Eric. That's a matter of plot. In terms of character, however, we confront the same question: what on earth has possessed Ariel that *she* would want to marry Eric? Of course, he was the first eligible bachelor that she clapped eyes on (his human-ness adding to his charms for her), but other than that it's hard to find a good motive that might drive such an intelligent and independent young woman to prostrate herself humbly before such an essentially uninteresting, egocentric and callow youth.

Until near the end of the movie, that is. Corny it may be, but it seems natural enough that being thrust suddenly out of his warm cocoon of self-regard and into the tumultuous danger of the great sea battle with Ursula forces Eric to allow his personality to take shape. Yes, his new-found expression of determination as he tussles through the waves is something of a caricature, but now at last it is a caricature that rings true.

Sebastian

With the exception of Ariel—and possibly not even with that exception—the star of the whole show is Sebastian, or (to be fittingly pedantic) Horatio Felonious Ignacious Crustaceous Sebastian, the little crab who is Triton's Court Composer and then Ariel's reluctantly conscripted Jiminy Cricket (➤169). The animation of Sebastian is a delight, and that surrounding him during the performance of his two brilliant songs—the calypso/reggae "Under the Sea" and the smoothly crooned "Kiss the Girl"—is devastatingly good, but the foundation of the character and the reason for its overwhelming success in the film is undoubtedly the outstanding vocal performance turned in by the actor Samuel E. Wright. Originally it had been planned that Sebastian be English, but the movie's songwriters, Howard Ashman and Alan

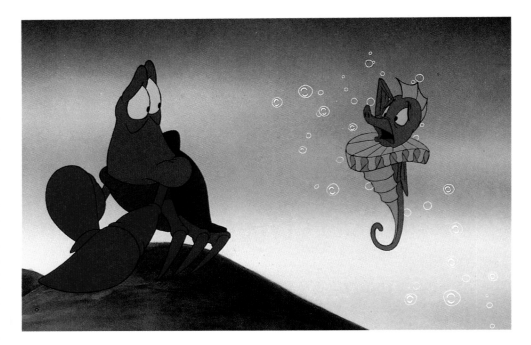

The Seahorse delivering Triton's summons to Sebastian.

Menken, were looking for something a bit more upbeat and foot-tapping from the music and so it was decided to give Sebastian's two numbers West Indian rhythms; from there to the adoption of a West Indian Sebastian was of course a very short step.

Both ourselves and the moviemakers were lucky to find Wright. Ashman and Menken scoured Hollywood for actors who might fit the part, but rather surprisingly found not a single one who would do. They therefore shifted the search to a somewhat unpromising venue in New York, near to the Port Authority Bus Terminal. To an outsider the whole exercise must have seemed a bit half-hearted, and it was in a mood of "why not?" that Wright bothered to go along. It was in a similar mood that, once there, he decided not just to demonstrate his vocal abilities but also to put on a complete physical performance, as if he were auditioning for a new stage musical rather than for a voice part in an animated movie. His act electrified Ashman and Menken—and soon afterwards had the same effect on the movie's codirector, Ron Clements, who later made a videotape of a repeat performance in order to inspire the animators.

But what can one say about that voice? David Denby, in *New York Magazine*, described it as "a haughty Jamaican accent whose formal contours and suave modulations caress the words", which is apt enough, although Wright himself says that he derived it not from Jamaicans but from a couple of Trinidadian college-friends. Whatever its origins, the voice bubbles and bumbles much like Sebastian himself—except when it breaks into song, a medium in which the character is totally confident in his own abilities.

The development of Sebastian through

the movie is, in an odd sort of way, a parallel to the process of maturation through which we might expect Eric to go. In Eric's case, of course, this would be the traditional story of the progression from adolescence into adulthood via the implicit rite-of-passage of the shouldering of responsibility. With Sebastian that age-related development doesn't occur—he's already of a respectable vintage when we first encounter him—but something rather like it does. In the early parts of the movie Sebastian seems less like a three-dimensional personality than like someone hiding behind a shield he has constructed out of his own pretensions. This is made clear in the pomposity with which he makes his fanfared entrance to the great cavern where his composition "Daughters of Triton" is to be performed; his bladder of dignity is rapidly punctured, of course, and we briefly see him for the fallible—but infinitely more likeable—creature he really is. Similarly, in the early stages he deems it fitting that he should opt for respectability through siding with the voice of convention, which is of course Triton's voice: Sebastian's sycophantic contributions to the browbeating the mer-king delivers to Ariel are quite repellent. Then, once he has been saddled with the responsibility of acting as Ariel's conscience and things have almost immediately gone wrong, Sebastian goes through a transitional phase, revealing himself as something of a craven: his chief concern is not to put matters right but to paper them over just enough that Triton won't find out. Later still, once the action has really got under way, Sebastian comes to the final stage in the growth of his personality: for all his huffing and puffing protests, he is firmly in Ariel's camp and supports her staunchly in all her efforts as

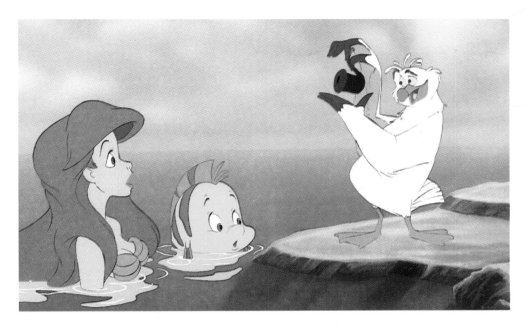

Everything's crystalline clear—to Scuttle. It's a pity that Ariel and Flounder are being so *obtuse* today.

she fights not just for her life but for her soul.

This serious undercurrent to Sebastian's role in the movie might seem at odds with the brilliance of his creation as a comic character, but in fact it is a major contribution to it. We not only laugh at Sebastian, we love him while we're doing so—which makes us laugh that much harder and more genuinely. Were he to be just a cute comic cut—a cardboard figure of fun—we could never be brought to those wonderful moments of pure, innocent, joyous hilarity which his portrayal inspires.

Flounder

Flounder, Ariel's rotund little companion, is certainly not an example of the species from which he takes his name: he is less a flatfish than a fatfish.

The most prominent feature of his personality is his youthfulness. In every important respect his face is not that of a fish but that of a little boy; in terms of his facial mannerisms there is much about him of the young Thumper (➤201) in *Bambi.* (To United Kingdom audiences there is also some resemblance to the character Arthur the Caterpillar in the non-Disney children's animated TV series *Will o' the Wisp.*) His voice, too, is a young boy's—Jason Marin's, in fact.

To describe Flounder as Ariel's sidekick would be to misrepresent their relationship: his position is much more that of a favoured dog (like Eric's dog Max), although Flounder has been gifted with speech. Although he may on occasion voice some protest over whatever it might be that Ariel next plans to do, he nevertheless invariably tags along with her. This is the case particularly during the scene that provides Flounder with his

most significant slice of screen time. It happens quite early in the movie. Ariel, who should really be taking part in the grand performance of "Daughters of Triton", is anxious to explore a sinister newly discovered shipwreck in search of further artefacts. Flounder, as ever, is wriggling along behind her, constantly voicing his doubts yet reluctant not to be with her. With great difficulty because of his plumpness, he squeezes himself in through a porthole after her. (Curiously, despite her greater overall size and generous curves, Ariel has insinuated herself through this aperture with graceful ease. But we don't think about that at the time.) Now he adopts the studied casualness of

the real cool dude—or, like a small child, attempts to:

> *Flounder*: Do you really think there might be sharks around here?
> *Ariel*: Flounder, don't be such a guppy.
> *Flounder*: I'm not a guppy. This is great. I mean, I really, uh, love this excitement . . . adventure . . . danger lurking around every corn—

He comes suddenly face-to-face with a skeleton and screams; his fins stand up on end in instant terror. He bolts in panic, walloping Ariel firmly in the belly. This time it's a false alarm, of course. But a couple of minutes later it's for real, as the monstrous shark (➤349) comes on the scene. At the start of their flight Flounder again rams Ariel in the stomach in almost identical fashion—presumably reusing the same piece of animation, which seems an odd economy. We're given little chance to register this, though, because then the frenetic chase is on.

Flounder's subsequent moments in the movie are perhaps more important in terms of the plot, but somehow he never again seems to be anywhere close to centre stage.

Triton

The character of Triton is in many ways rather nondescript, for the mer-king's role in both the plot and the emotional subtext of the movie is as a symbol—and, at that, a symbol of two different things. First, he is the symbol of constitutional authority, convention and staidness: he is the establishment against which Ariel is rebelling, the past which she wishes to leave behind. Second, he symbolizes parental authority; in this respect, the fact that he is a mighty king (and she a princess) is irrelevant.

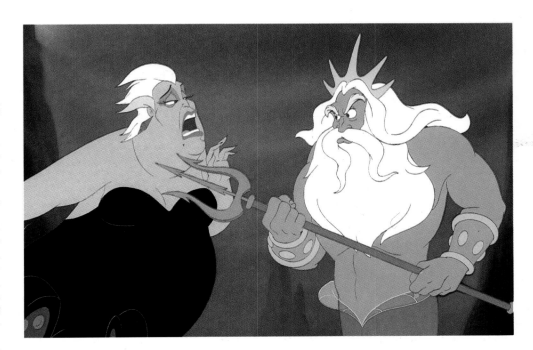

A moment of truth for Triton as Ursula explains a few blunt realities to him.

347

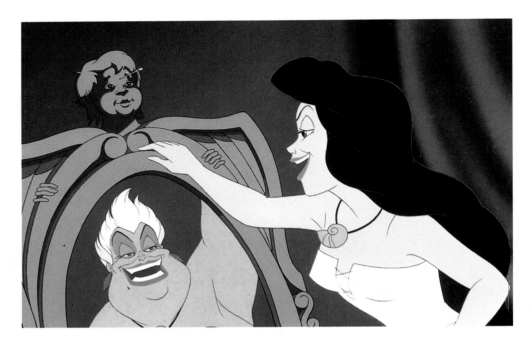

Vanessa—she looks so like Ariel, and yet the smile and the reflection give it all away.

What is relevant is that he is her father: like most young women, she must go through the process of switching her allegiance (by which term we don't mean subservience) to a male outside the family. This process is frequently painful for both participants but is necessary, as we see exemplified close to the movie's end, when Triton and Ariel embrace just before her wedding to Eric: it is the first moment in which we see genuine love expressed between them, yet there is also a great deal of sorrow involved. It is also, with one fleeting exception, the only moment in the film in which we see Triton's personality depicted in any depth.

Ursula

The Emmy-winning Pat Carroll, who voiced the part of the sea-witch (spelt with a *b*), is a very experienced actress on both stage and screen. Carroll envisioned the role as "part Shakespearean actress, with all the flair, flamboyance and theatricality, and part used-car salesman with a touch of con artist". She deliberately deepened her own voice, especially for the singing (she's naturally a contralto); in an interview with Lou Cedrone she added: "I'm not really a singer, and I would rather have talked-sang the role, but they wanted me to sing it, so I did. . . . The producers sharpened and heightened all of it, particularly the singing." The first stanza or so of "Poor Unfortunate Souls", before she hits her triumphant stride, shows the necessity of this.

Ursula is a marvellous villainess, one of the Disney classics of her malicious genre. She has the gross oleaginous unsubtlety of *The Great Mouse Detective's* villain Ratigan (➤**322**) but substantially more brio. Although facially somewhat similar to *The*

Rescuer's Madame Medusa (➤**300**), her screen impact dwarfs that of her predecessor. Bejewelled and lip-pouting like an overweight, overrich, overpampered, over-the-top society hostess from whose ghastly parties we've all fled at one time or another, her human upper part squats with loathsome bulk on top of her octopoid nether regions—it is a measure of the success of her animators that those nether regions seem positively humane by comparison with the rest of her. Except when her wrath—the only genuine emotion she seems capable of expressing—bursts through, her every movement is a deceitful artifice, so that even her evilly chuckling gloating seems mannered, as if performed for an audience. Her vile hobby of collecting souls so that they can suffer humiliation in her repellent garden is utterly in keeping with her society-hostess persona —for the kind of person of whom Ursula is a caricature is nothing if not a collector of and would-be destroyer of souls.

As noted, though, anger brings out true emotion in Ursula, and the effects are quite staggering when it does. We are treated to our first real dose of it when Ursula is still in her human guise as Vanessa (for discussion of which see the separate entry below) and Scuttle and his friends have successfully disrupted Vanessa's marriage to Eric. Knocked away from her, Ariel's quasi-licitly pilfered voice rolls across the deck of the ship and to the quondam mermaid's feet. As the voice psychically osmoses up and into Ariel, Vanessa/Ursula sees that this aspect of the game is up. Her look of stark hatred, even while her face is still human, must certainly have brought some small children in the audiences awake with a start on subsequent nights.

Then, of course, there is almost imme-

diately the eruptive transformation back to her natural shape. As if that were not enough, soon afterwards she adopts a genuinely giant form, towering up through the waves and above the puny mortals—Ariel and Eric—who would dare still to thwart her. The feeling of bulk, of mass, conveyed by the animators in this rendition of her embodied fury is quite breathtaking—and, oddly, it gives her a certain degree of repugnant grandeur. For the first time we begin to see that she would indeed be capable of occupying Triton's abandoned throne. We may loathe her, seeing in her the embodiment of Evil, but we have to concede that it is not solely in the physical sense that she has attained a new stature. Earlier we might have found ourselves chuckling at her villainy; there's no chuckling now.

This makes her eventual deflation, on being stabbed by the bowsprit of the wreck that Eric has commandeered, all the more affecting. For just a moment, as her broad face turns in a mixture of incredulity and something like grief, we actually feel sorry for her. The moment doesn't last, of course, but it's very impressive that the moviemakers managed to create it at all: they succeeded in making Ursula, for all the breadth of the strokes with which her character was caricatured, in some way come across to us as a real personality.

Vanessa

When Ursula adopts human guise in order to ensnare Eric romantically (with the aid of Ariel's hostage voice), she takes for herself the name Vanessa. Vanessa so strongly resembles Ariel that it is easier to note the differences than the similarities. Some are superficial—the hair colour, for example—and others much more fundamental. A curious feature of Vanessa is that, even though Ariel is in theory still a little uncertain on her legs, Vanessa is actually a much clumsier mover—something that is particularly noticeable in the scene where, witnessed through the porthole by Scuttle, Vanessa climbs up on her dressing table to admire herself in the mirror. (Her reflection, of course, shows her true self: we see the gloating, malicious, adipose face of Ursula's habitual form.)

The primary difference between the two beautiful young women is in their facial language. Vanessa's is full of sly grins and malevolent glances; Ariel's has a general sweetness of expression. Even in anger Ariel looks feistily, childishly cross, whereas Vanessa's anger transforms her visage into a look of genuine spite, as when she ruthlessly kicks a snarling Max's face during the introduction to the wedding ceremony. This use of contrast is so reminiscent of the difference between Maria and her robot counterpart in Fritz Lang's *Metropolis* that we must surely dismiss the possibility of coincidence.

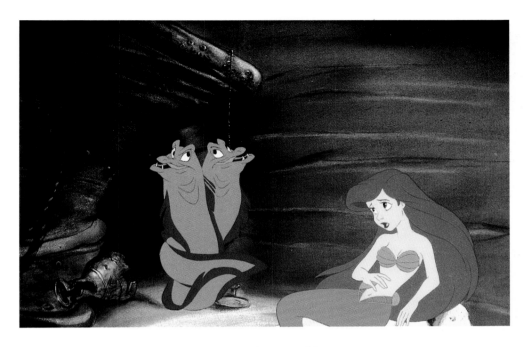

Ariel, shrinking from Ursula's two hench-eels, Flotsam and Jetsam.

Flotsam and Jetsam

Ursula's two hench-eels are certainly villainous-looking creatures: seen head-on they resemble not so much eels as gnarled old alligators, with their skewed eyes, crumpled-looking jaws and haphazard teeth. Their eyes glow luminously in the dark—indeed, they do more than that, for Ursula, gazing into a large air bubble that looks astonishingly like a crystal ball, is able to look through those eyes in order to spy on distant events. (This business of scrying—far-seeing—has become very popular in recent Disney animated features: it plays an important part in the plot of *Beauty and the Beast* as well [➤364]).

The two eels (indistinguishable except for their eye colors) play a significant part in one of the movie's most effective minor pieces of animation. As Ursula is building up in the first few lines of her song "Poor Unfortunate Souls" they swim sinuously around her, reflecting the curves of her ample body, seeming to trail like the long scarves of an exotic dancer. The effect lasts for only a few seconds, but is very striking.

Although Flotsam and Jetsam have been clearly cast in the role of heavies, in truth they don't have very much "heavying" to do until the closing scenes of the movie and Ursula's titanic battle with Ariel and Eric. They meet their end when Ursula is preparing to incinerate Eric with her trident and Ariel attacks her, pulling her aim wild so that instead the bolt fries the two eels, whose ashes trickle downwards and into the witch's vast hands. Oddly, for a moment we are persuaded that Ursula was actually fond of them, for she mourns: "Babies! My poor little poopsies!" But the grief passes rapidly and she wades back into the action.

The voices of Flotsam and Jetsam, sup-plied by Paddi Edwards, were electronically processed for additional effect. Presumably the implication is that they're electronic eels.

Scuttle

Buddy Hackett, who voiced Scuttle, was a genuine veteran, with more than forty years of nightclub, television, movie and stage work behind him. As so often happens, much of the Scuttle we see on screen owes his persona to the actor responsible for his voice. According to animator Dave Stephan, whose responsibility Scuttle primarily was, "We tried to put Buddy's sort of cross-eyed look and side-of-the-mouth delivery into the character. His readings were just so funny it gave us a real handle on the character . . ."

Our initial encounter with Scuttle provides us with most of the essential keys to his personality. Ariel, with Flounder in tow, has come to him to show off her latest trove of human artefacts and to ask for his help in identifying the objects; of course, having lived underwater all her life, she has no way of knowing that Scuttle's "encyclopedic" knowledge of such matters is just so much hogwash.

> *Scuttle*: Hey, lemme see. (*takes bent fork*) Look at this. Wow! This is special. This is very, very unusual.
> *Ariel*: What? What is it?
> *Scuttle*: It's a dingelhopper. Humans use these little babies to straighten their hair out. See (*working the fork spaghetti-fashion*), just a little twirl here and a yank there and voila! You got an aesthetically pleasing configuration of hair that humans go nuts over.

And so the garbaged explication goes on. Later, of course, when she is in her human form Ariel finds embarrassment in her belief in Scuttle's veracity. Carlotta is to say the least bemused when her new charge insists on combing her hair with a fork.

Later, once Scuttle has spied on Vanessa and found out her secret, and once he has mutilated several sections of the English language conveying the news to Sebastian, Flounder and Ariel, he is charged with the very difficult military task of stalling the wedding, which he chooses to do by mustering a host of as yet unsuspecting sea creatures in order to create a riot. This is a considerable logistical proposition and, bearing in mind all that we have seen of him so far, we naturally expect the results to be disastrous. Yet he not only has the idea, he successfully carries it through to fruition. Oddly enough, this achievement does not seem to us as audience in any way to represent an inconsistency of personality: instead, because his entire mentality is so hit-or-miss, we accept it quite happily on the principle that, well, lightning has to strike somewhere after all. That said, we would not expect it to strike in the same place ever again . . .

Seahorse

A minor role is played by the little Seahorse who acts as the announcer/master-of-ceremonies during the abortive presentation of the production number "Daughters of Triton". He has a prominent ruff around his neck, and both his face and his voice proclaim that he is very youthful—more, perhaps, of a pageboy than a full-blown Court Announcer. This impression is confirmed later when he is employed as a messenger boy to summon Sebastian to Triton's performance.

Ariel's Sisters

Groups of Ariel's six elder sisters appear briefly from time to time during the movie—notably when Ariel's extended toilette is seen as symptomatic of the fact that she has fallen in love—but their big moment is undoubtedly early on, during the grand production number ("Daughters of Triton") to which Ariel forgets to turn up. Before the song's sudden end the sisters give us their names: Aquata, Andrina, Arista, Attina, Adella and Alana. However, even though they have different hairstyles, etc., it's very hard to tell them apart—presumably deliberately, for it is part of the performance that they should display as much fixedly grinning individuality as a troupe of synchronized swimmers. Their artificiality is starkly contrasted with Ariel's naturalness.

Shark

One of the early action highlights of the movie occurs when Ariel and Flounder are exploring a wrecked ship on the ocean bottom. As Ariel potters about looking for

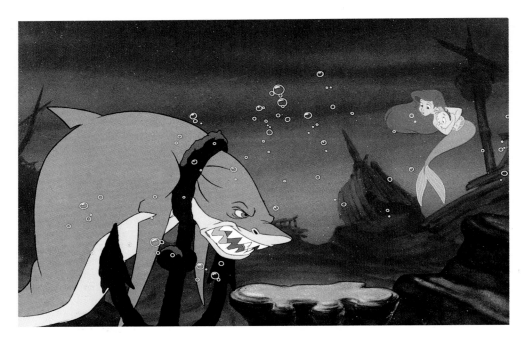

The end of the chase for the shark that has been terrifying Ariel and Flounder.

human artifacts, Flounder tremulously hovers nearby, clearly terrified. A couple of lines of dialogue that could have been plucked from any melodrama inform us that Flounder's fears are justified:

> Flounder: W-what was that? Did you hear something?
> Ariel (musingly to herself): I wonder what this one is . . . (then, offhandedly): Flounder, relax. Nothing is going to happen . . .

Sure enough, behind Flounder we see looming up the jawed face of a Shark larger than any in your worst nightmares. Flounder slowly senses the bulk and the malevolence close behind him, reluctantly turns and . . . the action explodes as the beast chases them, moving with impossible speed, smashing or chomping its way through anything—even parts of the hull—that might stand between it and its intended prey. Its progress seems utterly inexorable; its huge, rapidly snapping teeth remorseless. Our friends would be certainly doomed were it not for the fact that, of course, there's still quite a lot of the movie to go.

Grimsby

The story behind the voicing of Grimsby, Eric's sophisticated elderly adviser and general factotum, is interesting. Ben Wright—a stage, radio, television and movie actor, a RADA graduate—was in his 70s and in semiretirement when he auditioned for and got the part. In itself that wouldn't be particularly noteworthy, except for the fact that, unknown at the time to the moviemakers, he had in the past narrated several Disney movies and, more pertinently, had twice played voice parts in Disney animated features. One of these had been comparatively minor—the wolf

Rama (➤281), Mowgli's adoptive father in *The Jungle Book*—but, for many of today's adults, his other Disney voice-role must form an intimate part of hazy childhood recollections of rowdy cinemas and tussles over sticky sweets: Roger Radcliff (➤264) in *One Hundred and One Dalmatians*. Sadly Wright died in July 1989, just before the release of *The Little Mermaid*.

Grimsby's status in Eric's small and unnamed nation is nowhere clearly defined: he seems to be part valet, part prime minister and part advisor in loco parentis. With his distinguished, well-modulated tones and his smilingly craggy features, he puts us much in mind of the elderly Sir John Gielgud. His task is to persuade Eric to don maturity in his fulfilment of the role of prince. When he unveils the great statue that he has commissioned of Eric in regal pose, he broadly hints as much, and continues:

> Of course, I had hoped it would be a wedding present but, eh . . .
> Eric: Oh, come on, Grim, don't start. Look, you're not still sore because I didn't fall for the Princess of Glowerhaven, are you?
> Grimsby: Oh, Eric, it isn't me alone. The entire kingdom wants to see you happily settled down with the right girl.

What Grimsby is saying has, of course, nothing to do with romance: it is Eric's *duty* to find a suitable woman who can share his throne, and Eric, although his embarrassment indicates that at heart he recognizes the fact, is too immature to face up to it. Later, once Ariel has become ensconced in the palace and it is clear to Grimsby's experienced eye not only that Ariel (whom he obviously adores) is in love with Eric but that Eric, if only he would forget about the wraith-woman, would discover that he has complementa-

rily fallen in love with Ariel, the old man returns to the subject: "If I may say, far better than any dream girl is one of flesh and blood". Grimsby doesn't in fact care *which* woman Eric weds so long as it's someone presentable. Thus, even though he makes it clear in minor nuances of expression that he personally doesn't much care for Vanessa, he is among the first to shower his relieved blessings on the proposed union.

We miss, therefore, the most important part of Grimsby's personality if we fail to recognize that, behind his genial exterior and despite the fact that he's obviously a very kindly old man, his primary motivation insofar as the movie is concerned is pragmatic. Which is as it should be for a trusted adviser.

Louis

The fat, frenetic chef in the kitchens of Eric's palace, voice by René Auberjonois, really has only a bit part but he makes the most of it. His moustache would be a crisp pair of tapering horizontal lines were it not for their broken ends; his nose is an eagle's beak, much like a caricature of Triton's. Clearly he is self-inflatingly proud of his abilities in preparing a seafood cuisine—when Sebastian (who has just had a nasty encounter with the corpse of a fellow crab laid out in lettuce leaves) comes across him, Louis is singing a triumphant song while zestfully slashing, chopping, mutilating and eviscerating a whole host of marine creatures. Sebastian, watching, cowers and retches. Soon after, Louis catches sight of him, assumes him to be an overlooked part of the menu, and strikes. After a noisy and highly destructive chase (its energy and panache would seem to owe much to the opening minutes of *Who Framed Roger Rabbit* [➤326]) Sebastian is finally secured on the plate; and not long after that the plate is in front of Grimsby on the dinner table. Fortunately Sebastian is able to scuttle across to Ariel's plate and safety.

During the wedding celebrations in the closing moments of the movie—and quite irrelevantly—Louis once more spots Sebastian and the chase resumes. This time, though, Sebastian triumphs.

Max

Max is Eric's big, shaggy, ebullient, floppy-eared Old English Sheepdog; as a member of that species he obviously bears quite a strong physical resemblance to the Colonel (➤268) in *One Hundred and One Dalmatians*, but Max has no pretensions to military competence: he is everybody's fun-loving, bouncy darling.

Well, not everybody's. He alone of the land-based characters immediately recognizes Vanessa as a wrong'un, and snarls at her as ferociously as his roly-poly appearance will permit. Naturally—having adored Ariel on sight—he joins in soon

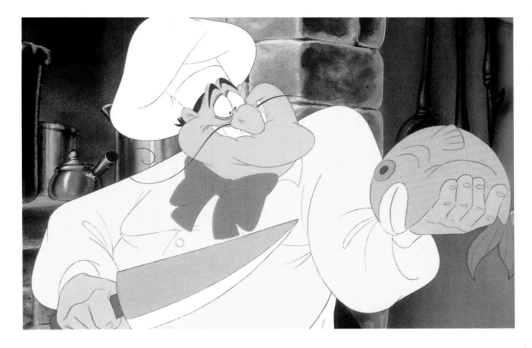

Louis, the fat French chef—and would-be nemesis of Sebastian.

Minister

A very small cameo role is played by a character called the Minister in the cutting continuity (script) although to all appearances and in all logic he should be at the very least a bishop. He is of slight stature; above his scrawny, uncertain-looking neck and his wrinkled face perches an outsize mitre which surprisingly never quite falls off. The querulosities of his voice are amusingly matched by the tremulous bobbings of his head.

Seadog

In the opening scenes of the movie, during the sailors' singing of the introductory song "Fathoms Below" and as we are first encountering Eric aboard ship, he chats briefly with a gnarled sailor who briefly tells him (and, more importantly, us) about the merpeople and about Triton, their king.

Laundrywoman

After Eric has brought Ariel to his palace, and while she is being attended to by Carlotta, Sebastian comes across three laundrywomen hard at work with their washtubs. Their spokeswoman prattles on entertainingly about the girl who has shown up in rags and doesn't speak. Sebastian departs, leaving them giggling.

afterwards with the efforts of the marine animals to disrupt the marriage ceremony.

Carlotta

Carlotta is the broad, curvaceously buxom housekeeper of Eric's palace. She is clearly amiably disposed towards the beautiful but speechless young waif whom Eric has brought back from the shore, and seems also to have an especial soft spot for Grimsby. Voiced by Edie McClurg, Carlotta has more of a part on screen than in fact she does in the plot; she is really only a symbol of the retinue of servants that Prince Eric's palace might be expected to support.

DUCKTALES: THE MOVIE—TREASURE OF THE LOST LAMP

Characters:

Scrooge McDuck; Huey, Dewey and Louie; Webbigail Vanderquack; Mrs. Beakley; Duckworth; Launchpad McQuack; Merlock; Dijon; Genie; Mrs. Featherby; Baby Elephant; Waitress; Master of Ceremonies

Credits:

Voices: Alan Young (Scrooge McDuck); Russi Taylor (Huey, Dewey, Louie, Webbigail Vanderquack); Christopher Lloyd (Merlock); Richard Libertini (Dijon); Rip Taylor (Genie); Joan Gerber (Mrs. Beakley); Chuck McCann (Duckworth); June Foray (Mrs. Featherby); Terence McGovern (Launchpad McQuack)

Additional Voices: Charlie Adler; Jack Angel; Steve Bulen; Sherry Lynn; Mickie T. McGowan; Patrick Pinney; Frank Welker

Voice Direction: Bob Hathcock; Andrea Romano; David Wiemers

Supervising Sound Editors: Louis L. Edemann; Howard Neiman

Sound Editors: Leonard Geschke; Nils C. Jensen; Colin C. Mouat; Chuck Neely; Bob O'Brien; Dave Pettijohn

Music: David Newman

Supervising Music Editor: Craig Pettigrew

Music Editing: Segue Music

DuckTales Theme: Music and lyrics by Mark Mueller, performed by Jeff Pescetto

Animation Screenplay: Alan Burnett

Film Editor: Charles King

London Film Editor: Keith Holden

Processed Effects: Alan Howarth, Mel Neiman

Production Designer: Skip Morgan

Prop Design: Terry Hudson

Animators: Gary Andrews; James Baker; Javier Gutierrez Blas; Eric Bouillette; Moran Caouissin; Caron Creed; Caroline Cruikshank; Roberto Curilli; Sylvain Deboissy; Joe Ekers; Mark Eoche-Duval; Pierre Fassel; Al Gaivoto; Manolo Galiana; Bruno Gaumetou; Dina Gellert-Nielsen; Arnold Gransac; Teddy Hall; Peter Hausner; Francisco Alaminos Hodar; Daniel Jeannette; Bob McKnight; Nicholas Marlet; Ramon Modiano; Sean Newton; Brent Odell; Catherine Poulain; Jean-Christophe Roger; Pascal Ropars; Stephane Sainte-Foi; Alberto Conejo Sanz; Anna Saunders; Ventura R. Vallejo; Jan Van Buyton; Duncan Varley; Simon Ward-Horner; Johnny Zeuten

Computer Animation: Kelly Day; Mike Peraza; Patricia Peraza

Assistant Animators: Laurence Adam; Jose Sanchez Alonso; Luis Amor; Phillipe Balmosiere; Philippe Beziat; Carlos Blanco; Bolhem Bouchiba; Claire Bourdin; Valerie

Braun-Paricio; Juan Jose Bravo; Patricia Brizzi; Rafael Diaz Canales; Didier Cassegrain; Thierry Chaffoin; Jon Collier; Patrick Delage; Gwen Delande-Roche; Rene Dieu; Helga Egilson; James Farrington; Sylvia Fitzpatrick; Jerry Forder; Pierre Girault; Maria del Carmen Gonzalez Gomez; Charo Moronta Gonzales; Manuel Sirgo Gonzales; Miguel Angel Alaminos Hodar; Martyn Jones; Isabelle Lelubre; Javier Pozo Luchena; Gizella Maros; Dominique Monfery; Florence Montceau; Rosario Moronta; Belinda Murphy; Rob Newman; Tom Newman; Gilles Noll; Andrew Painter; Sylvie Penege; Odile Perrin; Manuel Javier Garcia Pozo; Isabel Radage; Sophie Riviere; Steve Roberts; Maria Vincenta Rodriguez; Larry Ruppel; Mireille Sarault; Marivi Rodriguez Serrano; Jeffrey Short; Christian Simon; Karen Stephenson; Pierre Sucaud; Juan Antonio Torres; Christophe Villez; Bob Wilk; Karel Zilliacus

Key Layout: Joe Pearson; Carol Kieffer Police

Layout Directors: Douglas Kirk; Jean-Christophe Poulain

Layout: Jean Duval; Dave Elvin; Pierre Fassel; Neil Graham; Clive Hutchings; Zoltan Maros; Vincent Massy; Sean Newton; Simon O'Leary; Das Petrou; Pascal Pinon

Layout Assistant: Andrew Awbrey

Inbetweeners: Javier Espinosa Banuelos; Sabina Suarez Basanta; Isabelle Bourelly; Corinne Bretel; Monica Brown; Marie Cabo; Veerle Calcoen; Carmen Nunez Calogne; Antonio Campiglio; Miguel Canosa; Martin Chatfield; Paul Chorley; Mary Coombes; Tony Cope; Anne Daniels; Jean-Pierre Delisse; Belen Dominguez; Michael Douaud; Angela Iturriza Friere; Morton Fullerton; Jody Gannon; Juan Antonio Torres Garcia; Bernard Georges; Maximo Diaz Gerveno; Thierry Goulard; Arturo Lopez Iriarte; Ana Carmona Jiminez; Ivan Kassabov; Pierre Lecomte; Bill Lee; Marie-Ange Lelong; Ludovic Letrun; Pierre Lyphoudt; John McCartney; Jenni McCosker; Dave McFall; Colas Mermet; Christopher Morley; Jean-François Panayotopoulos; Steve Perry; Vittorio Pirajno; Maria Soledad Garcia Pozo; Alain Remy; Wolf Rudiger-Bloss; Daniela Tigano; Emma Tornero; Juan de Dios Pozublo Valverde; Xavier Villez; Denis Viougeas; Stephanie Walker

Effects Animators: Andrew Brownlow; Glenn Chaika; Hock-Lian Law; Henry Neville

Effects Inbetweeners: Norma Greenaway; Simon Swales

Key Background: Fred Warter

Backgrounds: Oliver Adam; Errol Bryant; Nicholas de Crecy; Thierry Fournier; Helene Godefroy; Mike Hirsh; Walter Kossler; Andrew McNab; Pierre Pavloff; Michel Pisson; Brigitte Reboux; Colin Stimpson

Colour Key Stylists: Robin Draper; Marta Skwara

Art Coordinator: Karen Silva

Ink/Paint and Camera: Pacific Rim Productions Inc.

Project Supervisor: Ellen Xu

Project Coordinator: Hilary Leung

Additional Final Checking Supervisor: Russel Murch

Special Effects and Camera Coordinator: Serge Conchonnet

Sequence Directors: Gaetan Brizzi; Paul Brizzi; Clive Pallant; Mattias Marcos Rodric; Vincent Woodcock

Slugging and Timing Directors: Robert Alvarez; Vonnie Batson; Dave Brain; Leslie Gorin; Terence Harrison; Jeff Hall; Marsh Lamore; Rick Leon; Mircea Mantta; Jamie Mitchell; Mitch Rochon; Ernie Schmidt; Bob Shellhorn; Mike Svayko; Robert Taylor; Richard Trueblood; James Walker; Neal Warner

International Production Supervisor: Marlene Robinson May

Production Supervisor: Dale Case

Production Coordinators: Stephanie Elliott; Nigel Matheson

Supervisor of Archives: Krista A. Bunn

Manager of Post Production: Sara Duran

Coproducers: Jean-Pierre Quenet; Robert Taylor

Associate Producer: Liza-Ann Warren

Produced and Directed by: Bob Hathcock

Release Date: August 3, 1990

Running Time: 74 minutes

THE MOVIE

To say that the critics were unanimous in their condemnation of *DuckTales: The Movie* would be inaccurate, but only just. Reactions varied from the tepid to the outraged. Unfortunately, there is no space here to give a representative sample: eager students of vituperation should consult the Bibliography (➤**435**). Outside the USA, however, the critics were generally kinder, and a few were genuinely enthusiatic; it is perhaps slightly embarassing that one such enthusiast is the author of this book.

A recurring criticism of *DuckTales: The Movie* is that it is a rip-off of the modern Spielbergian adventure romp, à la Indiana Jones, and by extension a betrayal of the brilliant Carl Barks comics which gave the movie its genesis. Yet the Indiana Jones movies, and others of their ilk, are continuations of a tradition that can be traced back to the boys' fiction of the nineteenth century, most notably to the dime novel. Simply by changing the protagonists' names and a few background details, one could convert an Indiana Jones adventure into a Frank Reade, Jr., adventure, and vice versa. The Carl Barks stories, like the Indiana Jones movies, were part of that same tradition—and hence so is *DuckTales: The Movie*. The only sensible interpretation of the affectionate parody of an Indiana Jones movie (it is also a self-parody) contained in the opening scenes of *Duck-*

Tales: The Movie is surely that it is an acknowledgment of this joint inheritance.

Xenophobia was an omnipresent attitude in the original dime novels, not as a result, most of the time, of active racism (although some of it, sickeningly, was) but more because the function of characters of non-WASP backgrounds in the stories was exactly analogous to that performed in pulp science fiction a few decades later by aliens (a characteristic perpetuated in the SF cinema to this day); the exotic foreign locales, the lost valleys and all the rest were in essence distant planets, and their natives were *alien*, which often meant that they were hostile and certainly meant that their cultural priorities were different from those of the average wholesome, narrowly educated, overpatriotic boy who both starred in and read the dime novels. Since alien cultural values, by definition, were inferior to those of the home society, the heroes need have no compunction about violating them.

DuckTales: The Movie retains this stereotyping but shows it for the stupidity it is by conscious self-parody. This is actually done very firmly right at the outset. The plane carrying Scrooge and his entourage and piloted hazardously by Launchpad McQuack demolishes a magnificent, many-pillared ancient artefact and, with it, thousands of years of history. The rational attitude—voiced by Scrooge, for once—is contrasted with that of the philistine:

> *Scrooge (incensed by the vandalism)*: Launchpad! Look what you've done to these ancient ruins!
> *Launchpad (shrugging lunkishly)*: Well, it could have been worse—it could have been something *new*.

The satire of philistine cultural imperialism encapsulated in this remark is surprisingly savage, especially in the context—for we, the audience are just as shocked and dismayed by the destruction as are Scrooge and the Arabs (presumably Egyptians) who have been excavating the site. We are, unless dead to irony, jolted into the realization that, while lip service is being paid to the old endemic dime-novel prejudice, it is that prejudice itself, rather than its targets, which is the butt of our derision.

All of this is not to say that *DuckTales: The Movie* is flawless—far from it. It is not the sort of movie that will inspire us to engage in profound philosophical discussions after seeing it, but then that is hardly its purpose. Some of the scenes once the lamp has been taken to Duckburg and the Genie has been set loose are unashamedly fillers, and must indeed seem tedious and pointless to those who aren't too busy grinning at them to be bothered with analytical judgement. The cast is a limited one—as will be seen by the numerical paucity of the character-discussions below.

The animation lacks the attention to detail that we have come to expect from the Disney animated features: this is a stripped-down version of the full-blooded Disney treatment (and no bad thing, either: the customary richness would clash horrendously with the whole tenor of the movie). But what the movie triumphantly succeeds in being is what it was intended to be: a rollickingly good piece of entertainment that can be enjoyed by all the family. In its rapid-fire action and gaggery, in its wonderful adherence to the qualities of the old cartoon shorts of not only Disney but notably Warner Bros. (an aspect dismissed by some critics as cheapskatery—which in part it probably was), in the way it revels in silliness and in so many of its other attributes, this is a great little movie.

DuckTales: The Movie was the first film to be presented from a new Disney venture, marked by a new label: Disney Movietoons. This label was created, according to the press briefs,

> to revive a wackier, more irreverent cartoon-like style most closely associated with the Disney animated shorts and comic books of the 1930s and 1940s. "Disney Movietoons" takes a slapstick-oriented, more verbal and decidedly more off-the-wall approach to provide a different kind of animated experience.

Reading between the lines, one senses also that Disney Movietoons was created at least in part to respond to the nontraditional Disney audience that had been discovered a couple of years earlier with the release of *Who Framed Roger Rabbit* (➤326).[1] As with that movie, the animation was done in Europe; a number of the animators were veterans of *Roger*. In this instance the seat of animation operations was a new facility in a suburb of Paris, Walt Disney Animation France, where animators and technical staff from France, the United Kingdom, Denmark, Hungary, Spain, Ireland and Australia were gathered to work on the film. A futher team worked at Walt Disney Animation United Kingdom to create the complex opening and closing sequences, in which computer techniques were used—notably, in the opening sequence, both to animate the plane and to help plot out the intricate twists and turns of viewpoint required as the plane crazily weaves around and between a score of obstacles. Just to add to the international flavor, the movie was written, storyboarded, laid out and color keyed in California; all the cels were painted in Schen Zen, China; and most of the camerawork (apart from some especially complicated special-effects-oriented scenes, photographed in London) was likewise done in China.

[1] Another motive was to show that the movie was outside the main sequence of Disney "classic" animated films.

THE STORY

The movie opens with Scrooge McDuck's small private airplane, piloted by Launchpad McQuack, following a jagged course across the sky and between the buttes and mesas of a desert somewhere in Arab lands:

> *Scrooge*: Is this a stunt you learnt in flight school?
> *Launchpad*: "Flight school"?
> *Scrooge*: You mean, you never took flying lessons?
> *Launchpad*: Well, I took a crash course.

In between the squeals of the terrified passengers—Scrooge, the Nephews and Webbigail Vanderquack—we learn that Scrooge is here for the final stages of the search for the long-lost treasure chamber of Collie Baba and his Forty Thieves. After a chaotic landing they are welcomed by a team of native workers—weasels—who have succeeding in locating the buried treasure chest of Collie Baba, which they are right now raising to the surface. The contents of the chest prove disappointing—"Nothing but old robes. Forty years of searching and I end up with Collie Baba's dirty laundry," Scrooge summarizes—but then, in a coat pocket, they find a treasure map. As Scrooge cons it one of the Arab workers, an especially disreputable weasel called Dijon, looks over his shoulder and sees that it is indeed the genuine article. Dijon turns to look upwards; we follow his gaze to see, high atop a butte, an imposing figure whom we will soon discover to be the evil sorcerer Merlock. Soon Dijon is reporting to Merlock, who seeks not the treasure per se but the magic lamp it contains. Wrathful on discovering that Dijon has failed to steal the map, Merlock instructs the weasel to ensure that he gets the job of guide on Scrooge's trek out into the desert to where the treasure is buried. Then Merlock transforms into an eagle and flaps off.

In the desert Dijon leads a camel-mounted caravan of our pals. They sight the mountain near which, according to the map, the treasure should be, but otherwise the desert seems bare . . . until Launchpad's camel trips over what seems at first to be a miniature pyramid. The gang dig down through the sands and soon reveal a colossal stepped pyramid which, with Merlock in eagle form watching, they enter. They survive a series of booby traps—here there is overt parody of the Indiana Jones movies—before falling through a door in the floor and discovering the treasure chamber. The treasure is cradled in a huge turtle shell on a platform atop a tall column in the cavern's centre; the only way to reach the treasure from the entrance is across a rope bridge; at the base of the column snarl what Launchpad vividly describes as "Sumo-wrestling scor-

pions". The party negotiates the bridge to wallow in the treasure, and Dijon spots the lamp. Before he can purloin it, however, he is sent by Scrooge to fetch sacks; in his absence, Webby takes a fancy to the lamp, deciding it would go well with her dolls' tea set, and, since he regards it as worthless junk, Scrooge "generously" tells her she can have it.

The sacks are loaded and transported across the bridge. As Dijon staggers precariously over with the last of them, the winged Merlock suddenly appears and transports him and the sack the rest of the way. Reverting to human form, he sets fire to the bridge, leaving our pals stranded on top of the column. Merlock pushes a nearby lever and the column slowly retracts into the ground, bearing the ducks inexorably down towards the vicious scorpions. After some skirmishing with these beasts, they flip over the now empty turtle shell and scuttle away under it until they reach an underground river; here the shell is pressed into service as a boat, and after a scarifying voyage the crew reach the open air and safety. One of the Nephews remarks, "I wouldn't mind doing it again—now I know that you could *live* through it," and Scrooge shudders expressively.

Merlock and Dijon have meanwhile discovered that the lamp is missing from the treasure and that the ducks have vanished. After initially accusing Dijon of having stolen it, Merlock then reckons that Scrooge's party must have rubbed the lamp and forced its attendant genie to liberate them.

Two days later our pals are at home in Duckburg where, unknown to Scrooge, Webby is polishing up her "teapot" for the dolls' party. The lamp starts to leap around and then, a few moments later, it releases the Genie, who swears allegiance to Webby and the Nephews as his new masters. After some foolery with household appliances, he heads for the library, where he swiftly reads an encyclopedia and is then persuaded by Webby to grant her first wish (of the statutory three owed to each of the youngsters): a baby elephant. Mrs. Beakley arrives on the scene and has hysterics; she rushes off to fetch Scrooge, whose limo has just pulled up outside. Before the two adults can reach the library, one of the Nephews says: "I wish Webby never made her stupid wish." All trace of the elephant—including breakages, etc.—promptly vanishes, and the kids scarper with the lamp and their newfound pal. Suspicious, Scrooge follows them to their bedroom. They pass off the Genie as an old friend who has come to spend the night.

Soon the youngsters are having a whale of a time wasting their wishes; the most ostentatious is the world's largest ice-cream sundae, which falls from the skies and is—impossibly!—devoured by the five. As the youngsters later settle down for the night they realize that they are rapidly running out of allotted wishes. The shadow of a bird of prey passes across the Genie's bunk; he panics, believing it to be Merlock, and miniaturizes himself. On being reassured by the Nephews that it was only an old owl that regularly comes by, he tells them that Merlock is immortal and is allowed unlimited wishes from the lamp because of the talisman he wears around his neck. The Genie also confesses to some of the vile deeds he committed in Merlock's name the last time the sorcerer owned the lamp.

The next day Merlock, as an eagle, arrives with Dijon in his talons. After some byplay, Merlock transforms himself into a large rat and sneaks into the house, where Webby has lured the Genie away from a game of cops and robbers to join her dolls' tea party. Mrs. Beakley spots the "rat" and gives chase with a broom: although Merlock stumbles upon Webby's party he cannot stop for long because Mrs. Beakley is still in grim pursuit—"If there's anything I hate more than elephants in the house it's rats!" Webby demands, with the last of her three wishes, that the Genie bring all her toys to life; as soon as he has done so they roughhouse him and erupt out into the rest of the house. (One of them proves to be a little fairy who looks and behaves like a somewhat stylized version of Tinker Bell [➤249].) A stuffed tiger, now living, catches the "rat" and gobbles it up. Soon after, however, one of the Nephews uses up his own last wish to reverse Webby's and, while this redeems the chaos, it also permits Merlock's survival.

Scrooge has discovered the Genie's existence and, while Launchpad waits outside with the helicopter to take him to the annual Archaeological Society Ball, the miser conjures up grandiloquent notions of how he might best use his three wishes. One he puts into practice immediately: the return of Collie Baba's treasure. This pops into existence in midair, directly above where the rat-Merlock is hauling himself free of the stuffed tiger; the mountain of wealth plummets to the ground, flattening him. Then Scrooge, bearing the lamp with the Genie inside it, is off to the ball. Dijon slips into the house and Merlock returns to human form, erupting out of the mound of gold and jewellery. Pausing only to transmute himself next into a giant eagle, he seizes Dijon in his claws and flies off in pursuit of Launchpad and Scrooge.

At the ball, Scrooge lets the Genie out of the lamp on condition he stays no larger than a mouse. Hidden in a potted plant, the Genie enjoys some refreshment. He grabs the cloak of a passing guest to wipe his lips, looks up, and sees to his horror that the "guest" is Merlock. Scrooge has begun his address to the assemblage, but the now life-size Genie drags him offstage as Merlock rushes forward through the throng in pursuit. Scrooge and the Genie

flee upstairs and into a bedroom. Merlock, in the form of a giant bear, breaks in through the door, but by then the lamp is hidden inside a light fixture and, in turn, Scrooge and the Genie are hidden, miniaturized, inside the lamp. Dijon arrives, his baggy pants slipping from his waist because of the weight of all the stolen cutlery he has stowed away in them; reverting to his eagle shape, Merlock leaves, telling Dijon to search for the elusive pair. This Dijon proceeds half-heartedly to do.

As soon as he has gone from the room, Scrooge and the Genie restore themselves to their regular size; then Scrooge commands the Genie back to the lamp and tiptoes off, not realizing that Dijon is behind him. Scrooge trips over a cluttered tea cart in the corridor, and drops the lamp, inadvertently picking up a gravy boat in its stead. Dijon, following, comes across the fallen lamp and rubs it to make sure it's the genuine article. He plans to give it to Merlock, but the Genie eloquently persuades him that there's no reason why he, Dijon, shouldn't keep the lamp for himself and enjoy all the consequent power, riches, and so on.

Scrooge and Launchpad, with Merlock in hot pursuit as first a panther and then yet again an eagle, take the helicopter back to the Money Bin, where Launchpad drops off his boss. But Dijon (with the Genie) is now ensconced in Scrooge's place: even the great dollar sign ($) on the building's front has been altered so that the S has become a D, for "Dijon". The weasel has the police haul a protesting Scrooge off to jail.

Soon the Nephews, Webby, Mrs. Beakley, Launchpad and Duckworth arrive to tell him that they've raised bail (the youngsters have even scraped out their piggy banks) but that Dijon has now taken over not just the Money Bin but *everything*—"Even your spat collection, sir," adds Duckworth suavely. They hatch a plot to break into the Money Bin, despite the fact that it is guarded by so many booby-trapped alarms:

> *Scrooge*: Aye, hundreds. And 14,657 ways to trigger them.
> *Nephew*: And you know each and every one, don't you, Uncle Scrooge?

Back at the Money Bin, Dijon is enjoying his newfound riches. Merlock arrives and adopts the form of a locust. The Nephews and Webby, dressed in commando gear, comprise the ground assault; the four code letters they have to use to unlock the main entrance are, of course, *C, A, S* and *H!* Scrooge parachutes down onto the roof and, via walkie-talkie, endeavours to talk the ground forces through the Money Bin's defences. Scrooge himself then enters the building and breaks into the elevator shaft, little knowing that the locust-Merlock is battering himself against the "start" button of the compartment itself.

Later Scrooge unwittingly treads on the tiny Merlock . . . with a very pleasing *splat!!* He filches the lamp from Dijon, but Merlock restores himself to his full grandeur and grabs it, then forces the Genie to turn Dijon into a squalling hog, which lumbers off with pathetically lopsided speed.

Merlock then commands the Genie to transform the Money Bin into the great fortress that he (Merlock) long ago enjoyed; further, the Genie must transport the whole vast, clawed edifice back to the old country. (The transformation scene, which includes the struggles of the Nephews and Webby inside the mutating building, provides the opportunity for some spectacularly exciting animation. Simplified it may have been, but it nevertheless stands alongside Disney's finest of this type.) Once they are aloft, Merlock demands that the Genie throw Scrooge magically overboard so that he must undoubtedly perish. Somehow, though, Scrooge succeeds in hanging on to the flying fortress's edge. A Nephew knocks the lamp from Merlock's hand, grabs it and hurls it towards Scrooge—but both lamp and Scrooge now plummet down through the clouds. Merlock shifts his shape to that of a griffin and gives chase, not realizing that the Genie is clinging to his tail. Merlock and Scrooge have a midair fight, and then Merlock drops his talisman; almost immediately he lapses into human form and plummets to his doom. Scrooge catches hold of the lamp.

> *Genie*: This time you *have* to make a wish.
> *Scrooge*: Aye—I wish me and my family and the Bin were back in Duckburg—right now!

And so it happens. Scrooge's third and final wish from the lamp is that the Genie should become a "real boy". This effected, the lamp crumbles to dust, and Dijon, who has been lurking in the bin as a hog, becomes a weasel once more. He fills his pants with money and attempts to steal away, but naturally Scrooge gives highly voluble chase through the streets of Duckburg.

THE CHARACTERS

The Gang from *DuckTales*

Eight of the characters in *DuckTales: The Movie*—**Scrooge McDuck**, the three **Nephews**, **Webbigail Vanderquack**, **Mrs. Beakley**, **Duckworth** and **Launchpad McQuack**—are regulars in the *DuckTales* television series. Their roles in the movie are outlined in the plot synopsis above; more general discussion of their personalities, relationships and other roles are contained within the section on the series as a whole (➤139-140).

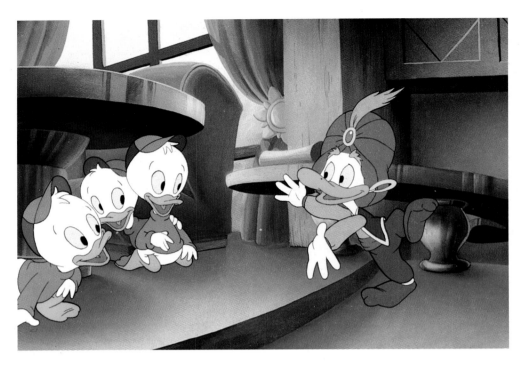

Genie with the Nephews—the stars of *DuckTales*.

Merlock

The villainous sorcerer Merlock (voiced by Christopher Lloyd) seems to have been something of a hit even among those audiences who otherwise disliked the movie. He has the ability to metamorphose, appearing as a bear one moment and a leonine human being (to use the term loosely) the next; shapeshifters are classic figures of dread in folklore (it is only more recently that fantasists have allowed shape-shifters to be predominantly on the side of Good), so it is not surprising that Merlock should spark off uncomfortable resonances in us. Also, his "natural" form is pretty impressive in its own right. He is somewhat reminiscent of Pete (►15) but lacking the various exaggerated elements that make Pete a villain of fun and with the addition of a sort of ominous potency— epitomized by the leonine qualities of the face—that informs us that Merlock is not a threat to be lightly dismissed. The addition to his broad features of an evilly pointed moustache may be a somewhat clichéd device, but in combination with the rest of Merlock's physical ensemble it works quite effectively. Even in those scenes where Merlock has to act the part of a comic buffoon—as in his early squabbles with Dijon—we are never permitted to forget his fundamental evil, especially when he is in other than human form.

This disconcerting mixture of humour and evil extends to other aspects of Merlock's characterization. It is interesting to note that this is confusing enough that, although the bird-Merlock is clearly a predator (here described as an eagle, although precise identification must obviously be tentative), some audiences see it as a vulture—traditionally a figure of some fun for Disney, however unsavoury vultures' real-life connotations might be. If we ignore such forgivable aberrations, we are still left with the seeming paradox that while the eagle is normally taken as a symbol of nobility, the eagle-Merlock most certainly cannot be. Once more we find the dichotomy in the Genie's recollections of Merlock's past brutalities: Atlantis, we learn, was everybody's favourite tourist resort until the time that Merlock was unable to get reservations, and so sank the continent in a fit of pique. A good joke, of course, but at the same time we're sublim-

inally reminded that real-life despots have committed similar acts of genocide under equally "laughable" provocation.

Merlock's source of power is the green gem that hangs at his neck. This talisman not only permits him an infinite number of wishes, rather than the statutory three, when it is used in conjunction with the lamp, it also enables him to shapeshift—a point that is made explicit only at the end of the movie, when the loss of the talisman causes him to revert from griffin to human form and thus deprives him of the power of flight. He plummets to his distant doom—*or so we assume*: we do not see that doom. Recalling that he was able to survive being flattened (as the locust-Merlock) by Scrooge's heavy foot, it is legitimate for us to wonder if perhaps Disney has plans for his return.

Dijon

Listing all of Dijon's attributes—he is devious, slimily servile, dishonest, untrustworthy, cowardly and much else besides— somehow might give the impression that he is not altogether lovable. However, this is far from the case. Dijon comes across to us as really rather likeable: we sympathize with his misfortunes and even with his temporary vanities in a way that we never quite do with the characters who have parallel roles in many of the other features. This difference probably comes about because, with so few principal characters in the movie, there was the scope for Dijon (voiced lovingly by Richard Libertini) to emerge as a fully rounded personality.

As we might expect, he is treated abominably by Merlock and yet, for no apparent logical reason, keeps coming back for more; interestingly, during the short pe-

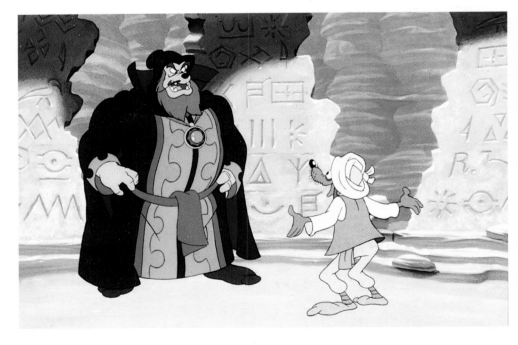

Merlock is wrathful but, as always, Dijon has a perfectly good explanation. Well, perhaps "perfectly good" is the wrong term—"perfectly convoluted" might be better.

riod of the movie when he is at least the-oretically under Scrooge's command, he is still not particularly well treated but nev-ertheless, despite many a terrified yell, acts with a certain measure of loyalty.

He is a compulsive thief, of course, stowing away any nearby valuables in his capacious baggy pants. Curiously, this doesn't offend us too much: Dijon has such a rotten time of things in general that there seems to be some justice in it when he tries to claw a little of his own back. His kleptomania can usually be relied on to lead to his undoing—and most certainly to the undoing of his pants belt, which is incapable of resisting the colossal strains his pilfering puts on it.

As noted, it is easy to forgive Dijon his kleptomaniacal tendencies; likewise, once he has used the power of the lamp to gain for himself all of Scrooge's fortune, it is hard to grudge him his (inevitably short-lived) time of richness. Sniffing delight-edly the food that he is preparing, he observes to a glum Genie: "Everything smells more delicious when you are rich." Then he checks his armpit and adds, with a purity of joy that almost brings a tear to the eye: "Even *me!*" There is a touch of pa-thos in his good cheer. When he says of Merlock, "He would not dare to confront the great and powerful Dijon. Why, I don't think he knows about me yet", our hearts sink at this none-too-subtle signal that Merlock surely would and surely does.

And so, in a rather guilty fashion, we are left at the end of the movie—as Dijon clankingly flees Scrooge's wrath—with the furtive hope that he does indeed manage to escape with that vast collection of "loose change".

Genie

The Genie, voiced by Rip Taylor, is an en-gaging enough individual but does not emerge as a particularly defined, affecting personality. Perhaps this is just as well, as he is surrounded by characters like Mer-lock, Dijon and Scrooge himself: too many more such screen-dominating roles and the movie as a whole might have become overpowering. In appearance he is cer-tainly duckish, and in his natural presen-tation he is of about the same stature as Webby and the Nephews; he has large ear-rings and a squashy turban of size similar to his head as a whole, and his face is dis-tinguished by bushy, prominent eyebrows which give it a look of maturity that oth-erwise it might not have. Some physical recognition of his age is certainly called for, as we discover from his first line on being released from the lamp: "Who are you? Where's Collie Baba? Did Rome fall yet?" A little later, on its being explained to him what the globe in the library represents, he expresses surprise that the Earth isn't flat. Despite this and various other historical references, however, he is at heart a child —he plays with the youngsters as an equal.

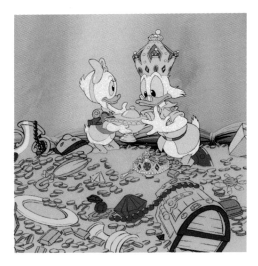

In the midst of all Collie Baba's treasure, what use would Scrooge McDuck have for an undistinguished-looking old lamp? Of course Webbigail Vanderquack may have it for her dolls' tea parties . . .

Despite all the seeming gaiety he fre-quently displays, the Genie is in fact mis-erable with his lot, forced to carry out the wishes of whoever should chance to be his master—especially when that master is Merlock, whose wishes are truly foul. What the Genie really envies, we discover, is the sort of life that Webby and the Nephews enjoy: the life of a mortal boy (or, to be more pedantic than the script is, duckling). When Scrooge uses his third and final wish to convert the Genie, Pinocchio-style (➤166), into a real boy, the Genie is naturally delighted with his new status, although a little confused:

Now I can do all the things real boys do— run through fields, play catch, roll over . . . Wait! That's a dog.

And then he rushes off to play cops and robbers with the Nephews.

Mrs. Featherby

Voiced by the veteran artiste June Foray— who in the television series (➤139) speaks also for Magica de Spell and Ma Beagle— Mrs. Featherby is Scrooge's secretary. An elderly duck with grey hair swept back into a bun, spectacles perched as if glued onto her beak, she tries to give him a lunch tray once he has returned to his Duckburg office. She also informs him that the *Duck-burg Daily News* is on the line with ques-tions about Collie Baba's treasure (he tells them to mind their own business and slams the receiver down) and, fatally, at-tempts to cheer him up by showing him his invitation to the Archaeological Soci-ety Ball.

> *Scrooge:* Ugh—I can't face those old fossils again! Every year I tell them I'll find Collie Baba's treasure, and every year I come back empty-handed.
> *Featherby:* But you did have it for a *little* while. . . .

After the ensuing demonstration of grief, Scrooge storms from the room.

> *Featherby:* But what about your lunch?
> *Scrooge:* Sell it!

Minor Characters

In keeping with its general air of econ-omy, *DuckTales: The Movie* has very few subsidiary characters. We see a number of weasels clad in desert garments who act as native labourers on Scrooge's desert ar-chaeological dig, perhaps a score or so of guests at the annual ball of the Archaeo-logical Society, and fleeting glimpses of a few residents of Duckburg. In addition,

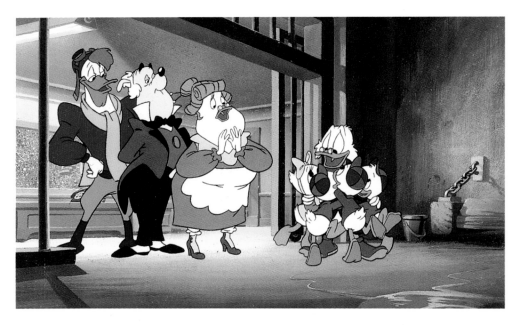

The *DuckTales* gang—Scrooge McDuck, Launchpad McQuack and the Nephews—engaged in one of their most typical activities: preparing to discover treasure. Actually *discovering* it is, of course, another matter.

there are the toys brought to life by dint of Webbigail's third and final wish: significant among these are the tiger that gobbles up the rat-Merlock and the "Tinker Bell" (➤249) fairy who appears briefly and taps Scrooge on the shoulder with her magic wand. Two policemen answer Dijon's summons to eject Scrooge from the Money Bin and incarcerate him at HQ; to judge by Scrooge's threats to stop their Christmas bonuses, etc, these officers of the law do not exactly live up to the reputation of Duckburg's Finest.

Three characters have roles just a little more major than this. The first wish that the Genie grants at Webby's behest is to bring into existence a **Baby Elephant**. Even though indeed a baby, this creature is obviously pretty huge (certainly by duck standards), and yet it is also very cute and cuddlesome: were it not for the ears it could easily be mistaken for Dumbo (➤192).

Two individuals present at the Archaeological Society Ball have speaking parts. A slender, shabby-elegant **Waitress** of avain heritage—possibly goose—offers Scrooge a soda, and a **Master of Ceremonies**, a portly fellow of blimpish aspect, introduces Scrooge as a speaker on the subject of Collie Baba's treasure.

THE RESCUERS DOWN UNDER

Characters:

Bernard; Miss Bianca; Wilbur; Jake; Cody; Percival McLeach; Joanna; Frank; Krebbs; Polly; Red; Kookie; Snake; Marahute; Chairmouse; Dowager; Milktoast; François; Cricket Cook; Doctor; Telegraph mice; Baitmouse; Faloo; Nelson; Sparky; Twister; Razorback hog; Cody's Mother; Ranger

Credits:

Suggested by characters created by Margery Sharp

Voices: Bob Newhart (Bernard); Eva Gabor (Miss Bianca); John Candy (Wilbur); Tristan Rogers (Jake); Adam Ryen (Cody); George C. Scott (McLeach); Wayne Robson (Frank); Douglas Seale (Krebbs); Frank Welker (various animal noises including those mouthed by Joanna); Bernard Fox (Chairmouse, Doctor); Peter Firth (Red); Billy Barty (Baitmouse); Ed Gilbert (François); Carla Meyer (Faloo, Mother); Russi Taylor (Nurse Mouse)

Supervising Sound Editors: Paul Timothy Carden; Louis Edemann

Sound Editors: Leonard Geschke; Doug Jackson; Nils Jensen; Fred Judkins; Suhail Kafity; Robert O'Brien

Music by: Bruce Broughton

Orchestration: Mark McKenzie; Don Nemitz

Supervising Music Editor: Kathleen Bennett

Songs by: Joe Bennett; Jimmy Denton; A. B. Paterson; Marie Cowan

Singers: Joe Bennett and The Sparkletones

Story Supervisor: Joe Ranft

Screenplay: Jim Cox; Karey Kirkpatrick; Joe Ranft; Byron Simpson

Art Director: Maurice Hunt

Supervising Animators: Ruben A. Aquino; David Cutler; Anthony DeRosa; Russ Edmonds; Ed Gombert; Mark Henn; Glen Keane; Duncan Marjoribanks; Nik Ranieri; Kathy Zielinski

Character Animators: Chris Bailey; James Baxter; GeeFwee Boedoe; Rejean Bourdages; David Burgess; Mike Cedeno; Roger Chiasson; Ken Duncan; Rick Farmiloe; Will Finn; Joe Haidar; Brigitte Hartley; Ron Husband; Leon Joosen; Jorgen Klubien; Doug Krohn; Alexander S. Kupershmidt; Jacques Muller; Dave Pruiksma; Tom Roth; David P. Stephan; Barry Temple; Chris Wahl; Larry White; Ellen Woodbury; Phil Young

Character Design/Visual Development: Kelly Asbury; Chris Buck; Kevin Donoghue; Gil Hung; Glen Keane; Gay Lawrence-Ventura; Valerio Lawrence-Ventura; Kevin Lima; Duncan Marjoribanks; Christopher Sanders; Bruce Zick

Computer Animation: Tina Price; Andrew Schmidt

Layout Supervisor: Dan Hansen

Key Layouts: Rasoul Azadani; Bill Perkins

Layout: Karen Keller; Robert Walker

Production Manager: Sarah McArthur

Editor: Michael Kelly

Animating Assistants: Tony Bancroft; Aaron Blaise; Dan Boulos; Bob Bryan; Broose Johnson; Brad Kuha; Mike Nguyen; Cynthia Overman; Michael Show

Inbetweens/Breakdowns: Beverly Adams; Hee Rhan Bae; Noreen Beasley; Gordon Bellamy; Philip S. Boyd; Inna Chon; Robert D. Corley; Tony Craig; Vincent DeFrances; Wendie Fischer; James Fujii; Susan Gal; Richard H. Green; Peter Gullerud; Edward Gutierrez; Michael Hazy; Grant Hiestand; Ken Hettig; Todd Hoff; Allison Hollen; Mark Kennedy; Christine Lawrence; Laura Nichols; Matt Novak; Ed Olson; Gary Payne; Karen Rosenfield; Martin Schwartz; Donald Selders; Kevin Smith; Bryan M. Sommer; Michael Swofford; David Teague; Bill Thinnes; Jane Vytiskova; Elizabeth Watasin; Daniel Wawrzaszek; Wendy Werner

Effects Supervisor: Randy Fullmer

Effects Animators: Dave Bossert; Glenn Chaika; Barry Cook; Mark Dindal; Christine Harding; Ted Kierscey; Mark Myer; Eusebio Torres; Kelvin Yasuda

Effects Inbetweens/Breakdowns: Kennard Betts; Peter DeMund; Cynthia Neill-Knizek; Masa Oshiro; Tony West

Background Supervisor: Lisa L. Keene

Backgrounds: Douglas Ball; Jim Coleman; Dean Gordon; Michael Humphries; Tia Kratter; Cristy Maltese; Phil Phillipson; Robert E. Stanton; Donald Towns; Diana Wakeman; Tom Woodington

Animation Camera Supervisor: John Cunningham

Animation Camera: John Aardal; Chris Beck; Mary E. Lescher; Gary W. Smith; Chuck Warren

Directors: Hendel Butoy; Mike Gabriel

Technical Director: Edward Kummer

Associate Producer: Kathleen Gavin

Producer: Thomas Schumacher

Release Date: November 16, 1990

Running Time: 74 minutes

THE MOVIE

At first glance it difficult to understand why *The Rescuers Down Under* has been such a successful movie. Traditionally, sequels never perform as well as their originals, and one would have expected this fall-off to have been exacerbated by the interval since the release of that original, *The Rescuers* (➤297) in 1977, especially since both are children's movies: thirteen years, half a generation, is too long for the same children to be going back to see the "second installment," but not long enough for the original audience to have grown up and borne moviegoing children of their own. Second, *The Rescuers Down Under* is, at least superficially, one of Disney's more modest animated features: it is based upon neither an established children's book (although using characters from an established series) nor a classic tale, and it does not pretend to the flamboyance of other Disney features of the era, such as *Who Framed Roger Rabbit* and *Beauty and the Beast*. Third, it has no obvious "hook" characters to support its publicity and marketing: indeed, of its two principals, one, Bernard, is by defintion a retiring, shy personage, hardly suited to the razzmatazz typically desired by the publicists. As a final point, the movie is set in Australia, a land which is neither wholly familiar to the average child viewer outside Oceania nor yet intriguingly exotic to that same viewer: Australia seems to occupy a sort of halfway stage in the consciousness.

And yet *The Rescuers Down Under*, despite all these factors, received favourable critical coverage and, more importantly, drew large audiences. A trite explanation would be that this came about because it is a very good movie, but there were lots of good movies around at the time that received nothing like the response gained by this one. What seems more likely is that some of its theoretical disadvantages proved in reality to be strengths.

First, although it was widely bruited on its release as a sequel, in fact it isn't. Although it shares two characters (or three, if one counts Wilbur) with *The Rescuers*, as well as the basic premise that there is an organization composed of mice and called the International Rescue Aid Society, and although there is a basic plot similarity (Bernard and Bianca rescue a kidnapped child), the two movies are otherwise separate entities: there is no feeling while watching the second that somehow one is missing out on part of the fun because one failed to see the first. Indeed, it may be a mistake to view the two of them too close together, because their styles and their ways of treating their slightly similar themes are very different. Moreover, the assumption that the only major audience for children's movies is children is a false one: a significant slice of the audience for *The Rescuers Down Under* almost certainly consisted of adults in their twenties, eager to see more of something fondly remembered from their childhood.

Next, the movie's very modesty may have been a prime reason for its attraction. One can tenably argue that *The Rescuers* itself has been so perennially successful because of its unassuming, wholesome quality. To say that a movie is undemanding—at least for its audience, if not for its creators!—need not imply any criticism.

Third, the characters are in their own usually quiet way very satisfying ones. Leaving aside for the moment Bernard, Bianca and Wilbur, we have a good strong villain in Percival McLeach; an appealing character in the Jiminy Cricket role, Jake; and, perhaps most significantly, one of the best and most credible of all the Disney animated children, Cody: one could make the analogy that, like Pinocchio, he makes the transition from artificial construct (albeit in this case a product of the animator's rather than the marionette maker's art) to "real boy". This depth of characterization, as opposed to a more instant floridity, was a strength of *The Rescuers* and is likewise a strength of its "sort-of sequel".

Finally, the setting in Australia seems in fact to have marked the movie out in the perceptions of its intended audience. It was refreshing that Disney was sticking its neck out in this way rather than keeping to the safe, well tested territories of the USA, UK or some nation so little known to its audience that it was Shangri-La in all but name. Moreover, the fact that the movie's creators were determined to exploit rather than defend their choice of setting was evident from the opening of *The Rescuers Down Under*—an exhilaratingly rapid journey, close to ground level, across fields and prairie, past Ayers Rock and finally to the shack where Cody lives—is one of the most spectacular, breathtaking starts to grace any movie.

This inspired treatment of the setting is continued throughout most of those sequences of the movie that are set in Australia. Aside from the obvious resources of printed materials, the animators could also draw upon the products of a 2½-week, 4,000-mile expedition around the Australian interior undertaken by five of the movie's key personnel: producer Thomas Schumacher, codirectors Hendel Butoy and Mike Gabriel, art director Maurice Hunt and story supervisor Joe Ranft. These five returned with countless photographs and, importantly, countless sketches; they were also able to capture in their own minds some of the beauty, desolation and vastness of the continent— as no photograph could ever do.

To ensure realistic observation of the animal characters, the animators resorted to the practices of their predecessors throughout Disney's animation history. San Diego Zoo was a popular haunt, while a number of animals were brought to the studio for short or long visits: a three-foot monitor lizard called Little Dude became a special favourite.

A further and far less commonplace facet of realism relied on less traditional procedures, being brought about by the use of techniques more typical of a live-action than an animated movie. Disney's advance publicity for *The Rescuers Down Under* claimed it as the "first-ever animated action-adventure film"—a claim that is debatable—yet one can understand what the publicists were trying to get at. For, outside those scenes set in New York, the movie as a whole has more the texture of a Spielbergian action movie—*Raiders of the Lost Ark* (1981), perhaps—than any form of animated adventure that we have been used to. Much of this is achieved through the use of a constantly varying camera angle, and was probably a direct consequence of the stimulating experiences that many of the new breed of Disney animators had had with moving cameras during the making of *Who Framed Roger Rabbit*.

We seem to have come a long way from that modest little movie we were talking about. And yet, as noted, it is in such terms that most viewers—including the critics—regard *The Rescuers Down Under*. A paradox? Or is it merely a sign of success? After all, it is the aim of any good adventure-fiction writer to "make the words disappear", so that they do not stand between the reader and the story. Perhaps something analogous accounts for this movie's undoubted achievement.

THE STORY

Poachers in the Australian Outback are capturing rare wild animals, to the considerable distress of a young boy, Cody, who is a friend of the beasts to the extent that he can talk with some of them. Called from his home shack near Mugwomp Flats by a kangaroo named Faloo, Cody is told that Marahute, the great golden eagle, has been caught in a poacher's trap high on a ridge. He goes to cut her free; as a reward for his help, the bird takes him to her nest, shows him her recently laid eggs, and gives him one of her feathers. On his way home on foot, Cody finds a trap baited with a mouse; in releasing the mouse he falls into the trap himself. The poacher Percival McLeach arrives in a bushwacker with his slimy sidekick Joanna, a six-foot goanna lizard, and spots the feather given to Cody by Marahute. Confessing that he has already abducted Marahute's mate, he tries to browbeat Cody into telling him where Marahute herself and, most importantly, her eggs can be found. Cody refuses and runs, but is caught by the edge of a croc-infested river. Throwing Cody's backpack into the water so that the crocs will scatter its contents (leaving the illusion that Cody has fallen in and been devoured), McLeach carries off the struggling boy—eventually to imprisonment in his compound at some remote and desolate opal mines. However, the Baitmouse runs with the news to the nearest mousish telegraph office, and a distress signal is sent to New York and the HQ of the International Rescue Aid Society (RAS).

The message goes more or less directly to a plenary meeting of the RAS, where the Chairmouse explains that this must be a task for none but the best—Bernard and Miss Bianca. These two, however, are playing hooky in a posh restaurant, where Bernard is plucking up his courage to propose. After some byplay and slapstick during which the proposal fails to be made, Bernard discovers that Bianca has accepted on behalf of both of them the mission to Australia. Not long after, they are on the building's snowbound roof, arranging for a flight via Albatross Air, in the shape of a bopping albatross called Wilbur (who has taken over from his very similar-looking brother Orville of *The Rescuers*). After a predictably nightmarish launch and early flight, Wilbur stows them all in the undercarriage of an intercontinental jumbo jet.

And so to Australia where, after a hair-raising landing at Mugwomp Flats, Bernard and Bianca meet a bouncy kangaroo mouse called Jake, while Wilbur is trundled off for slapstick treatment of the back he has injured during the landing. Jake knows at once why Bernard and Bianca are here, and paints a horrifying picture of the perils in store for them while simultaneously mesmerizing Bianca with his jaunty macho charm. They set off to try to find Cody, who—we discover in a vignette—is being tormented by McLeach in pursuit of Marahute's whereabouts; the plucky little fellow is refusing to tell. Jake captures a vast snake, Twister, for the trio to ride on. Back at the compound, McLeach slings Cody into a subterranean prison containing a scattering of captured animals, including Red, Krebbs, Kookie and notably Frank, a twittish frill-neck lizard who shares Cody's cage. McLeach hears on the radio that the search for Cody has been called off, the boy being presumed a victim of the crocodiles. McLeach and Joanna perform some byplay with eggs, and this gives him an idea as to how he can extract the required information from Cody. Meanwhile Wilbur has violently discharged himself from medical care and is on the search for his pals.

Bernard, Bianca and Jake arrive at the compound in time to witness McLeach lying to Cody that Marahute is dead and kicking the boy out of the compound, while dropping heavy hints that the eggs will go unhatched without their mother. Naturally Cody makes a beeline towards the nest; McLeach and Joanna pursue him covertly in their bushwacker, with the mouse trio as stowaways. Cody reaches the cliff and begins to climb down to Marahute's nest; the mouse trio follow and introduce themselves. Marahute arrives; McLeach fires a net at her and catches her, hauling her and the net aloft with his bushwacker's hoist; Cody grabs the net; Jake lassoes Cody's leg and he and Bianca are swept off into the skies, leaving Bernard. The "net party" safely locked into the rear of the bushwacker, McLeach sends Joanna down the cliff, slurping at the prospect of the eggs she will find in the nest. On arrival, she makes the tooth-shattering discovery that the eggs have been replaced by ovoid rocks.

With the help of a ride on a timorous Razorback Hog, Bernard finds McLeach lowering Cody from his bushwacker's hoist into the croc-infested river: this time the disappearance is going to be for real. Bernard stalls the hoist's engine; he steals the keys to his pals' prison and, after some skirmishing with Joanna, delivers them to the cage. McLeach attempts to shoot through the rope supporting Cody; he is partly successful, so that the rope begins to fray. Bernard heroically manoeuvres Joanna so that she knocks both McLeach and herself off the cliff's edge and into the river; the crocs pursue them downstream, leaving Cody. But the rope finally breaks,

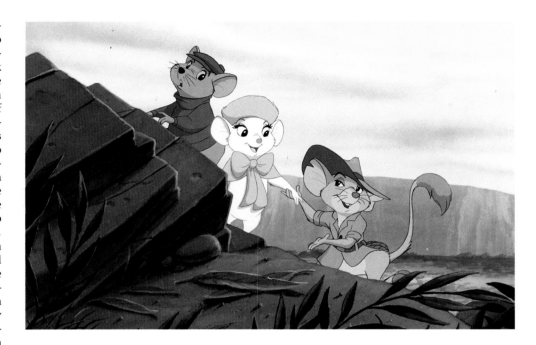

Bernard watches worriedly as Jake subjects a seemingly receptive Bianca to a Force-9 gust of blandishment.

and Cody is plunged into the water. Joanna reaches shore but McLeach goes over a vastly high cataract to, presumably, his doom. Jake and Bianca finally free themselves and, on Marahute's back, head for the action. Cody and Bernard (who has been valorously attempting to save him) go over the falls, but Marahute plunges after them into the spray and soon (in terms of dramatic timing, *too* soon: a similar climax was considerably better timed in *The Great Mouse Detective* [➤318]) emerges with all our pals on her back. There is a happy ending for all the good guys except Wilbur, who is left struggling with the rapidly hatching eggs—to which, for some unexplained reason, Marachute has not rushed back.

THE CHARACTERS

Bernard and Miss Bianca

The characters of the two heroic little mice from the RAS have been discussed at some length in the context of *The Rescuers* (➤297), so there is little further to add here. As before, their voices were supplied by Bob Newhart and Eva Gabor, both of whom brought a sense of greater ease to their characterizations than in the earlier movie, as if after a gap of 13 years they had gone beyond simply portraying the mice to actually being them.

This easy familiarity in the roles, this sense of years-born rapport between Newhart and Gabor, adds a certain depth to the relationship between them that transcends the dictates of the script. In the scenes where Bernard is plucking up his courage to propose marriage the relationship that comes across through the voices is fondness between two companiable old friends. This is perhaps not quite the relationship that was anticipated when the screenplay was first drafted, but it is a curiously affecting and very real one: from the moment that Bernard starts fishing unsuccessfully for the ring, we know that his suit will in the end be successful, and that the same will be true of the ensuing marriage. This seems all at odds with some of the movie's other moments, of course, when Bernard displays thwarted resentment as Jake seems to be dazzling Bianca with his macho charms, yet there is a certain consistency there, too. We sense that Jake is all too well aware of the closeness between the two visiting mice, and knows that there is no chance of his being able to turn Bianca's head in any but the most ephemeral of ways—she may seem to flirt with him, but only because she genuinely enjoys his company.

Wilbur

The part of Wilbur, the great albatross who serves as both staff and vehicle of Albatross Air Charter Service, was an especially challenging one to portray. In *The Rescuers* the role was played by the grumpy, dour Orville (➤302), voiced by Jim Jordan, and one assumes that Orville would have served the same function in the new movie had it not been for the fact that in the interim Jordan had died. In fact, there are many similarities of appearance between Orville and his replacement and brother, Wilbur; the differences are behavioral.

Wilbur's character is a far cry from that of the grouchy, crotchety Orville; instead, voiced by the popular comedian John

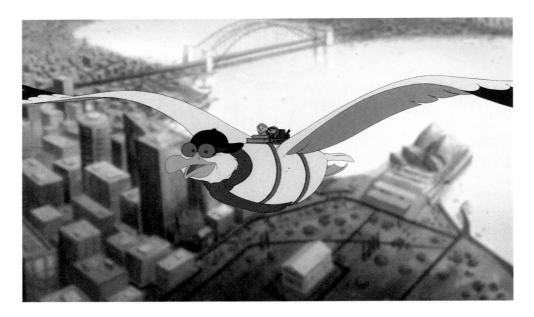

Far above the city Wilbur soars, the two adventurers aboard him every bit as nervous as they were when they took a similar flight with his brother, Orville.

from the animal on which Jake is based, the kangaroo mouse (or, more correctly, kangaroo rat). Jake's toughness stems—of necessity—from his strength of personality rather than from his physique. This must have made him an extremely interesting character for all concerned to work with, and certainly makes him enormously appealing to the audience as a pivotal contributor to the story. For, in a way analogous to his method of coping with obstacles, his performance derives its strength not from raucous extroversion nor even from a vast amount of screen time but instead from a much more subtle, nuance-filled behaviour. If it is valid to describe a personality as wiry, then that is what his is.

Jake's personality also provides a perfect foil for Bernard's, which is likewise that of the determined little guy who gets things done—although never, except in extremis, with the same confident precision as Jake would. A major difference, of course, is that Bernard wears his depths on the surface. With Jake, by contrast, the depths are very well hidden: it is as if his superficial smart-aleck veneer had been applied over a wood of the same grain, so that only a very determined appraiser would discover that, beneath even the solid wood, there is a core of some quite different material which is the true personality of Jake.

This is in no way to say that the face Jake presents to the world is in anyway unlikeable or undeserving of our respect—Bianca clearly doesn't think so! Far from it: one can imagine oneself meeting Jake and, like her, being instantly captivated by him. However, whereas plenty of people have this ability in real life, many of them have little of interest under that fascinating surface: Jake, by contrast, is a resourceful good guy through and through.

Candy (whose body language apparently contributed greatly to the final character as seen on screen), he is an ebullient, loud, gauche figure—a buffoon with a heart of gold, much like the version of *The Jungle Book*'s Baloo who appears in *TaleSpin* (➤142)—whose heart initially seems to be more in pop music than in flying. His antics are certainly great fun—but in saying that we are pointing up one of the other great difficulties with which Candy and the animators of Wilbur were presented: although Wilbur was obviously going to be, by intention, presented as one of the strongest characters in the movie, his clowning cannot disguise the fact that his role in the plot is as a filler—a welcome supplier of (sometimes very) comic relief, but of nothing that is integral to the main story except the transportation of Bernard and Bianca to Australia.

This should not detract from the many good things about Wilbur's performance. His deliberately unsubtle humour is very entertaining and on occasion hilarious, and Candy's voice artistry cannot be denigrated: it is his triumph, and the animators', that after only the first few seconds following the initial disappointment at the absence of an old friend, we're already regarding Wilbur as a fully fledged character in his own right rather than as a sort of substitute Orville. And Wilbur's immense popularity with audiences, especially young ones, cannot be denied. Yet the very fact that a number of reviewers picked up on the point that Wilbur's role is essentially extraneous to the main action must imply that in this case the great, time-tested Disney ploy of turning a minor character into a major one and letting the character's powerful extroverted appeal do the rest—a ploy used in almost all of the animated features, and responsible

for some of Disney's most enduring favourites—didn't quite work out.

Jake

The character of the Australian Mr. Competent, Jake, has a very difficult role to perform: he must be simultaneously an adventure hero and a comical figure; moreover, he mustn't be Crocodile Dundee. This last point the animators seem to have taken very much to heart for, although Jake's persona has many of the macho, tough-guy attributes of that hero and countless other Australian stereotypes, the core of the characterization has the same sort of rapid-moving, energetic, flighty grace that one might expect

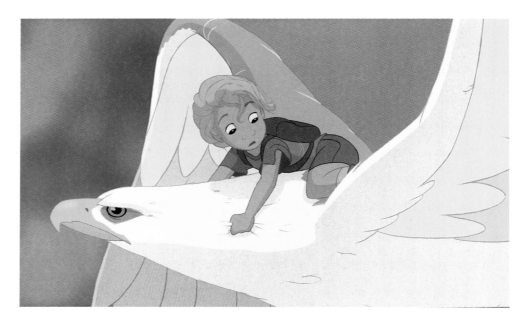

Paralleling bumpy rides aboard Wilbur are Cody's majestic flights with the great golden eagle, Marahute. These scenes are among the greatest triumphs of *The Rescuers Down Under.*

A practical difficulty in bringing Jake to the screen was that his dialogue had both to ring true to watching Australians and to be intelligible to US audiences. Disney hasn't always been wholly successful in such matters (one cringingly recalls Dick Van Dyke's "Cockney" accent in *Mary Poppins* [➤**274**]) but here they seem to have got it about right—by the simple means of using an Australian actor (Tristan Rogers) in the part.

Cody

If one were seeking to draw parallels between this movie and *The Rescuers*—and many reviewers found the temptation irresistible—one would immediately dismiss Cody as merely filling the role played by Penny (➤**299**). In fact, nothing could be further from the truth. At some time during those thirteen years Disney had abandoned the (often highly successful) practice of inevitably giving the central role to an essentially bland, passive child character—a sort of Everychild—in the aim of inducing a high measure of viewer identification among the young audience. It is a much more difficult task for the animator—or indeed for any creator of fiction—to present a character whose attributes are such that we recognize in that figure people whom we know well: we care about the character's fate because she or he is an amalgam of the diverse personal characteristics of those whom we like or love.

In order for this illusion to work, the fictional character has to be very firmly rooted in reality, and it is in this respect that Cody is such a brilliant accomplishment. Time and again, adult viewers remarked that the most striking thing about *The Rescuers Down Under* was that Cody was "a *real* boy" (except for a single shot, very close to the end, when the sunlight catches his teeth as he gives the camera an all too toothpaste-advertisement grin). Although it would be wrong to say that Disney supplied us with a warts-and-all portrait of the Outback lad—we see him commit no youthful sin—nevertheless we are offered numerous visual clues to the more rounded personality that we would know were we to encounter Cody outside the confines of the story.

In terms of his function in the plot, too, Cody is a significant figure. Where Penny might be regarded as something of a symbol—Good ensnared by Evil—and thus as a motivator rather than a doer, Cody becomes, and stays, thoroughly embroiled in the action. Indeed, he has intruded himself into the dynamics of the plot long before Bernard and Bianca even make their first appearance: rather than simply wait around for the figure of Evil, McLeach, to come along and kidnap him, Cody actually courts such a risk of his own free will by freeing Marahute and, soon after, the Baitmouse, and also through ar-

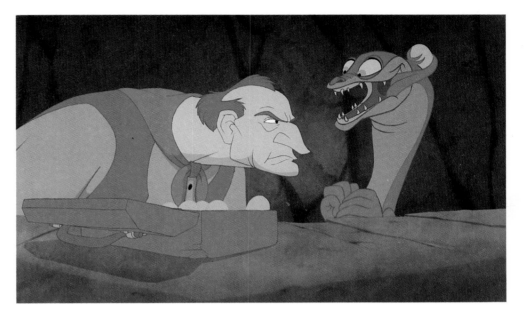

McLeach and Joanna in the midst of their hilarious "business" with the eggs.

guing with McLeach rather than simply skedaddling. After capture he actively resists the torments to which he is subjected by McLeach, takes a vehement role in the imprisoned animals' attempts to free themselves from bondage, and refuses to betray the bird which he regards as his friend. Close to the end, however, when McLeach is dangling him over the croc-infested river, Cody does slip into an unwonted passivity; but this complaisant mask rapidly slips when the plot once more requires him to play a more vigourous role.

Cody was voiced by Adam Ryen, a ten-year-old (Cody is eight) of Norwegian birth who came to the USA only in 1985. It may be that the slight Scandinavian cadence in his normal speaking voice assisted him in voicing the part of an Australian youth with such conviction. At no time does one have that dreaded feeling that somehow sound and image are two separate components.

Particularly enjoyable to children of all ages are the scenes in which Cody is riding atop the great eagle, Marahute: these are animated very convincingly, and thus represent the nearest we are likely to get to the full-scale realization of this particular childhood fantasy.

Percival McLeach

The rangy poacher is not one of Disney's more subtle villains—he has none of the leering, joyful, almost likable evil of, say, a Ratigan (➤**322**), a Cruella De Vil (➤**267**) or for that matter a Madame Medusa (➤**300**). Instead, he falls into the category of those Disney villains whom, like Amos Slade (➤**308**) or the religious or political bigot of your choice, it would be senseless to try to engage in any logical argument;

such brute, ruthless stupidity is one of the more chilling forms of Evil.

And evil McLeach most certainly is: all the knucklehead jokes at his expense in the script cannot conceal this. In some instances, when the villain gets his fatal comeuppance at the close of a Disney animated feature, we suddenly feel a sense of disappointment that it had to end thus. By contrast, when McLeach vanishes into the mists of the waterfall, presumably doomed to death by drowning, we feel no such quasi-sympathy; instead we feel vaguely pleased that he's out of the way.

McLeach's aim in poaching rare examples of the Australian fauna is to "recycle" their skins as handbags, belts, luggage, etc.—a motive that echoes Cruella's in *One Hundred and One Dalmatians*. However, where her menace is all mannerisms and flamboyance and gleefully animated artificialities, McLeach's is born from his realism: we've all met and been repelled by people exactly like him. This numbskulled ruthlessness is excellently conveyed not only through the animation but also by the well-executed voice-acting of McLeach's part, done by George C. Scott.

Only once during the movie does McLeach show himself to be capable of any measure of creative thought. This occurs after some extended clowning between himself and his sidekick—McLeach tries to prepare an egg supper for himself while Joanna ingeniously snitches the eggs right out from under his nose. This sequence, important to the plot in that it sets up McLeach's brainwave, is rather laboriously introduced by McLeach's announcing, out of nowhere: "I still gotta get that boy to talk. I'm hungry . . . can't think on an empty stomach . . . gotta have protein . . . gotta have *eggs*!" However, once under way, the clowning provides some of the movie's most hilarious moments—thanks to Joanna—and it seems reasonable that, at its end, McLeach's brain should lurch to the realization that, if he plays on Cody's fears for the fate of the eagle eggs, the boy might lead him to the nest.

McLeach, it will be clear, is by no means a deep, layered character. Nevertheless, he makes a good, satisfying villain and excellently counterbalances the good guys in the emotional dynamics of the plot. Moreover, since the good guys are animals plus one small boy, McLeach's role reinforces a Disney message that was brought to us as long ago as 1942 in *Bambi* (➤197), when the young deer asks why distress and destruction have been brought into the forest idyll and receives from his mother that brief but complete explanation: "Man was in the forest."

McLeach's bushwacker is almost an animated character in its own right, and was so treated—with the aid of computers.

Joanna

If you feel that you've encountered McLeach's sidekick Joanna before, then you're in good company. Although she is of a different species from them—she's a blue, slithery, six-feet-long goanna lizard—it cannot be denied that she is a reincarnation of the two earlier Disney villainous sidekicks, *The Jungle Book*'s Kaa (➤279) and *Robin Hood*'s Sir Hiss (➤293), more especially of the latter. A quality not possessed by either of her predecessors is her femininty: although her wide-eyed looks of pseudo-innocent quasi-bashfulness and her distinctly unfrightening grimaces of sternness mimic children of either sex, she registers as definitely female.

Her evil cannot be—clearly was not meant to be—taken seriously. Where our laughter at McLeach's stupidities is somewhat uneasy, Joanna's mere entrance on screen is enough to set the corners of our mouths a-twitch. And our mirth at her buffooneries is not altogether mocking, either: we become quite fond of her, not just because she's an innately humourous creation but also because of her disarming childishness and the way in which, through her pursuit of as many of the Seven Deadly Sins as she can count up to (notably gluttony), her private interests frequently come into conflict with those of her master, a difference of motivation which of course she is too fawning ever to confess. Some of our affection for her is based on the illogical proposition that our enemy's enemy must be in part our friend.

This must have made her character a tricky one for the moviemakers to handle at those points in the film where she must definitely be seen to represent the forces of darkness. The most notable of these occur when the captured animals are endeavouring to obtain the keys that will enable them to escape their imprison-

ment. These two occasions are very similar; however, from the second of them there develops immediately a madcap sequence of clowning, and the transition of her role from symbol-of-evil to object-of-affectionate-mirth is interesting both in its rapidity and in the fact that the audience senses no dislocation of character.

Joanna manages to be every bit as satisfying a sidekick as, say, Sir Hiss without the benefit of any dialogue at all; the only sounds that she can make are snarls, whimpers, yelps and the like. (These were supplied by Frank Welker.) Another point of note is that the two visually very different adversaries in the titanic struggle for possession of the keys were in fact largely based on different animators' observations of a single animal, a three-foot-long monitor lizard called Little Dude, who spent some while on the lot being watched by animators David Cutler (for Joanna) and Kathy Zielinski (for Frank). And, like so many other slimy Disney sidekicks, Joanna is roundly abused by her master at every turn (indeed, on one occasion only a quirk of events saves her from being blasted to bits by him); as soon as we give their relationship anything more than a cursory glance, it is hard to think of the reason that binds her to him.

Frank

The dimwitted little frill-necked lizard who shares Cody's cage in McLeach's animal prison, and who twice so despairingly tries to enable his own and his companions' (but primarily his own) escape, is a distinguished member of a long tradition of Disney zanies.

His is a cameo role. We see him only during those scenes in which Cody is imprisoned by McLeach along with various

animals whose futures are intended by the poacher to be as belts or handbags, a fate that is accepted phlegmatically by many of them but not—most emphatically not—by Frank. The very thought of being turned into a purse is enough to make his ruff stand out in all its lurid glory.

Frank's brainlessness makes him an easy butt for the rather sadistic humour of the other incarcerated animals, most notably Krebbs. It also sends him into instant panic whenever he is expected to do anything, no matter how simple: the very desperation of his wish to escape renders him incapable of putting two sensible actions in the right order so as to facilitate that escape.

Frank's virtuoso vocal performance was supplied by Wayne Robson. He was spotted in an episode of *The Twilight Zone* by some sharp-eared member of the Disney team, and the part was his.

The Captured Animals

Frank is, of course, not the only animal to share Cody's incarceration in McLeach's compound. Not all of the others are named, serving almost as mere elements of the background, but singled out in approximate decreasing order of significance are Krebbs, Red, Polly, Snake and Kookie.

Krebbs is a large, plump, rounded Koala bear—he looks like the sort of furry stuffed toy that an infant would love. This cuddly appearance is belied by his behaviour and more especially by his dialogue, which is acid and occasionally verges on the sadistic. He is clearly the dominant character among the animals: inevitably we are reminded of all those stolid officers in POW-escape movies whose nihilistic acceptance betrays their men. Chained as he is by the ankle inside a barrel, his attitude

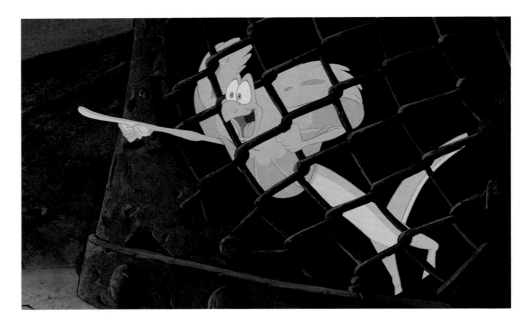

The scatterbrained Frank, the frill-necked lizard whose antics were designed to steal the show—and almost did.

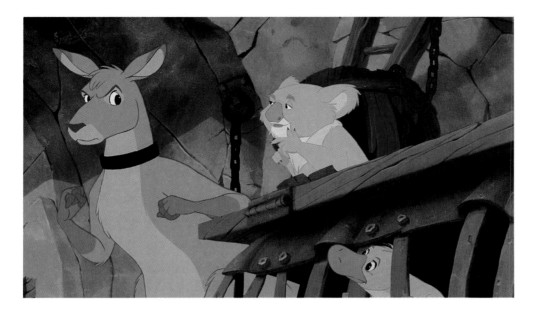

A selection of the animals who have been captured by McLeach. From left: Red, Krebbs and Polly.

towards freedom is fatalistic—he is unimaginatively resigned to the fact that he is destined to become a coat adorning some rich person's back. Although he gives practical and vocal assistance to the attempts to gain freedom, his general attitude towards them is one of world-weary professional scepticism. Moreover, he is one of those individuals who defend themselves from the gloomy prospect of their own futures, or lack thereof, by relishing the fact that others are doomed to an equally dire fate.

The other animals all have much more minor parts. **Red** is a kangaroo of obvious coloration who acts as Krebbs's second-in-command. He is much more amenable than is his senior to the escape plans voiced by Frank and, more seriously, Cody; it is his decision to participate in them that seems to swing Krebbs around to support them. **Snake** assists at a crucial moment when Cody and Frank are desperately seeking something with which they can lash together their Heath-Robinson construction of sticks and poles; he reaches out his long tail and draws forth a dilapidated boot whose lace is promptly appropriated. **Polly** is a somewhat stoical platypus, and **Kookie**, tied in a tire, is a brightly coloured bird; she swings her tire to knock over some wooden slats so that they are brought within the reach of the creatures who are trying to construct the long pole.

We assume that, after McLeach's death, Cody and the others flew to release the captured animals.

Marahute

By popular acclaim, the huge golden eagle Marahute—with a wingspan of seemingly forty feet or more—is one of the great success stories of the movie. Although she can mouth no words, only screeches and

cries supplied by the versatile Frank Welker, she nevertheless comes across as having a distinct character—and one that is natural rather than anthropomorphic. This is most evident when she first brings Cody to her aerie. Through the use of curiously angled shots as well as acute observation, the animators—supervised for Marahute by Glen Keane—manage to create between Cody and the eagle a conversation (albeit wordless on her part) which simultaneously seems delightfully intimate while nevertheless always acknowledging the species barrier: at no time do we get the impression that Marahute is really just a human being locked inside the form of an eagle.

Surprisingly, Marahute was the character in the movie whose appearance benefited the most from computer animation both in terms of her muscled movements and, far more importantly, for her dramatic flights with Cody astride her back.

The key to first-rate animation of animals is of course observation of them in life. Naturally, with a golden eagle, this presented something of a problem. Glen Keane and his team were able to borrow from the Los Angeles Museum of Natural History a stuffed specimen which they could examine in close-up in order to gain a clear understanding of the bird's mass distribution, overt musculature, and so on. In addition they took extended trips to observe live birds in their natural environment at the Peregrine Fund near Boise, Idaho, a centre for the breeding of and research into hawks, falcons and other birds of prey, including eagles. And then, finally, there was the imaginative contribution to the final result, as Keane explained:

> The more I can relate to the eagle and understand the way it moves, the more I can feel like it's me flying in the air. And once I

can feel like it's *me* flying and I'm not just doing a drawing, then it takes the animation to the next level up, and the audience believes it because the artist believed it.

This could almost be taken as an animator's manifesto.

Minor Characters

The Rescuers Down Under deploys a significant number of minor named characters. These can be discussed in various main groups.

In New York we have the **Chairmouse** (➤**303**) of the RAS from *The Rescuers*, as well as brief glimpses of a number of that organization's delegates. In the mouse restaurant housed in a chandelier over a human restaurant near RAS headquarters there are various diners, including notably two characters, named in the cutting continuity as the **Dowager** and the **Milktoast**, under whose table Bernard dives in pursuit of the engagement ring that he's dropped. Groping for the ring, Bernard inadvertently fondles the Dowager's foot; she glares at her companion who, mistaking the look for one of admiration, simpers in return—just in time to receive her doughty outraged slap. Three of the restaurant's staff also make their presence known. One is **François**, a deliciously bow-tied, pompous cockroach maître d' with a slippery grasp of French. Another is a forager cockroach, whose task is to grab fallen food detritus from the floor of the human restaurant beneath and send it up for the culinary use of the **Cricket Cook**.

The next group is of the various medical mice involved in treating Wilbur's damaged back. Most prominent among these is the smug **Doctor,** a mouse who clearly relishes his surgical tasks rather more than perhaps a benevolent physician should. There are also various nurse mice, one of whom has a speaking part.

Various **Telegraph mice** are seen transmitting the emergency message halfway round the globe to New York from Australia; the operator at the Australian end receives the information directly from the seemingly pusillanimous **Baitmouse,** who has just escaped with Cody's help from McLeach's trap and, hiding in the bushes, has seen Cody abducted. The Baitmouse is quite an endearing little character, and it's mildly surprising that he wasn't reintroduced to the story later on in some slightly more major role. Cody is first apprised of Marahute's entrapment by a kangaroo called **Faloo,** who sounds the alarm to the Outback animals by blowing into the hollow limb of a fallen tree; on his way to question Faloo, Cody hops over a prickly echidna called **Nelson,** who follows him and various other animals to seek the news. At Mugwomp Towers, the local airport for Mugwomp Flats, we encounter Jake's assistant, a fly called **Sparky.** It is thanks to Sparky's help there

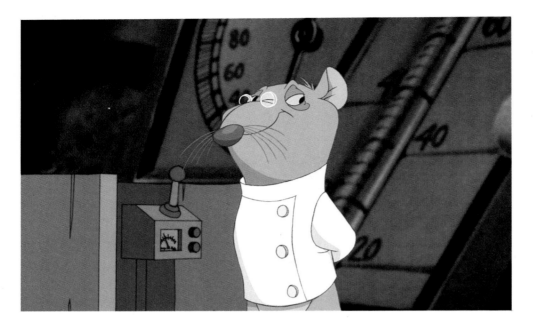

The seemingly sadistic mouse Doctor, contemplating his next tortu . . . er, treatment.

that Wilbur's landing isn't even more catastrophic than it is. Later, out in the bush, Jake lassoes a huge snake called **Twister** whom he employs as one of several bestial vehicles to transport himself, Bianca and Bernard in pursuit of McLeach and Cody; the expression on Twister's face as he finds himself submitting to the tiny kangaroo mouse's will is comic in the extreme. Very much later, similarly devoid of transport, Bernard shanghais a (relatively) vast **Razorback hog** in precisely the same way, using very similar words; the expression on the hog's face is a hilarious visual echo of Twister's.

Finally there are two further human characters. **Cody's Mother** is heard offscreen in the opening moments of the movie, instructing Cody to be home in time for supper. In a short, poignant later scene she opens the door to a **Ranger,** who has brought her her son's abandoned backpack. There is no need for either of them to say anything, for in the background the radio is announcing:

In other news, authorities in Mugwomp Flats have called off the search for the missing boy. His backpack was found near Crocodile Falls, and local rangers believe he was yet another victim of crocodile attack.

BEAUTY AND THE BEAST

Characters:

Belle; Beast/Prince; Maurice; Gaston; Le Fou; Philippe; Monsieur D'Arque; Wolves; Birds; Baker; Marie; Butcher; Mother; Chimneysweep; Prisoner; Driver; Large Man; Three Young Guys; Bimbettes; Blacksmith; Basketweaver; Matronly Woman; Hat-shop Owner; Hat Buyer; Fruit Shopper; Cheese Merchant; Cheese Buyer; Fabric Buyer; Baker's Customer; Fishmonger; Fishmonger's Customer; Fat Crony; Tall Crony; Big Crony; Bartender; Bookseller; Mrs. Potts; Chip; Lumiere; Cogsworth; Wardrobe; Featherduster; Footstool; Hat Rack; Stove; Palanquin; Creamer; Dresser; Sugarbowl; Globe; Brush and Comb; Beer Steins

Credits:

Voices: Paige O'Hara (Belle); Robby Benson (Beast); Rex Everhart (Maurice); Richard White (Gaston); Jesse Corti (Le Fou); Angela Lansbury (Mrs. Potts); Jerry Orbach (Lumiere); David Ogden Stiers (Cogsworth, Narrator); Bradley Michael Pierce (Chip); Hal Smith (Philippe); Jo Anne Worley (Wardrobe); Mary Kay Bergman (Bimbette); Kath Soucie (Bimbette); Brian Cummings (Stove); Alvin Epstein (Bookseller); Tony Jay (Monsieur D'Arque); Alec Murphy (Baker); Kimmy Robertson (Featherduster); Frank Welker (Footstool and special vocal effects)

Live-Action Reference: Peter Hastings; Dan McCoy; Sherri Stoner

Dance Sequence Models: Mary Anderson; Duane May

Sound Editors: J. H. Arrufat; Ron Bartlett; Michael Benavente; Julia Evershade; Jessica Gallavan

Sound Effects: Mark Mangini; Dave Stone

Original Score: Alan Menken

Orchestration: Danny Troob

Music Editor: Segue Music

Songs: Howard Ashman; Alan Menken

Screenplay: Linda Woolverton

Story Supervisor: Roger Allers

Story: Kelly Asbury; Brenda Chapman; Tom Ellery; Kevin Harkey; Robert Lence; Burny Mattinson; Brian Pimental; Joe Ranft; Christopher Sanders; Bruce Woodside

Preproduction Script Development: Jim Cox; Dennis Edwards; Tim Hauser; Rob Minkoff; Rebecca Rees; Darrell Rooney

Layout Supervisor: Ed Ghertner

Layout Supervisor (Florida Unit): Robert Walker

Visual Effects Supervisor: Randy Fullmer

Art Director: Brian McEntee

Supervising Character Animators: Ruben A. Aquino; James Baxter; Andreas Deja; Russ Edmonds; Will Finn; Mark Henn; Glen Keane; Dave Pruiksma; Nik Ranieri; Chris Wahl

Character Animators: Tim Allen; Tony Anselmo; Tony Bancroft; Aaron Blaise; Geefwee Boedoe; Dan Boulos; Rejean Bourdages; David Burgess; Randy Cartwright; Michael Cedeno; Lorna Cook; Anthony DeRosa; Ken Duncan; Rick Farmiloe; Lennie Graves; Joe Haidar; Ron Husband; Broose Johnson; Mark Kausler; Doug Krohn; Brad Kuha; Alexander S. Kupershmidt; Mike Nguyen; Cynthia Overman; Michael Show; Tom Sito; David P. Stephan; Barry Temple; Larry White; Ellen Woodbury; Phil Young

Animating Assistants: Tom Bancroft; Arland Barron; Bob Bryan; Brian Ferguson; Michael Gerard; Mark Kennedy; Michael Surrey

Character Sculptures: Ruben Procopio; Kenny Thompkins

Cleanup Supervisor: Vera Lanpher

Cleanup Supervisor (Florida Unit): Ruben Procopio

Supervising Character Leads: Bill Berg;

Brian Clift; Renee Holt; Richard Hoppe; Nancy Kniep; Marty Korth; Vera Lanpher

Character Leads: Debra Armstrong; Emily Jiuliano; Dave Suding; Alex Topete; Stephan Zupkas

Inbetweeners: Travis Blaise; Elliot M. Bour; Lillian Chapman; Anthony Cipriano; Vincent DeFrances; Laurey Foulkes; Ken Hettig; Grant Hiestand; Ken Kinoshita; Dylan Kohler; Tom LaBaff; Paul McDonald; Jane Misek; Maurilio Morales; Marsha Park; Mary-Jean Repchuk; Jacqueline M. Sanchez; Kevin Smith; Michael Swofford; Charles R. Vollmer; Daniel A. Wawrzaszek

Breakdown: Beverly Adams; Hee Rhan Bae; Noreen Beasley; Inna Chon; Robert O. Corley; Wendie Fischer; James Fujii; Edward Gutierrez; Kris Heller; Allison Hollen; James Y. Jackson; Kellie Deron Lewis; Tamara Lusher; Anthony Wayne Michaels; Cheryl Polakow; Norma Rivera; Martin Schwartz; Bryan M. Sommer; Bill Thinnes; Elizabeth Watasin; Wendy Werner; Ron Westlund; Dave Woodman

Supervising Effects Animators: Dave Bossert; Ted Kierscey; Dorse Lanpher; Mark Myer

Effects Animators: Ed Coffey; Christine Harding; Chris Jenkins; Eusebio Torres; Kelvin Yasuda

Effects Breakdown/Inbetweeners: Kennard Betts; Kristine Brown; Peter DeMund; Sandra Groeneveld; Paul Lewis; Dan Lund; Masa Oshiro; Lisa Ann Reinert; Tony West

Effects Graphics: Bernie Gagliano

Backgrounds Supervisor: Lisa Keene

Backgrounds Supervisor (Florida Unit): Richard John Sluiter

Backgrounds: Doug Ball; Jim Coleman; Gregory Alexander Drolette; John Emerson; Dean Gordon; Tia Kratter; Cristy Maltese; Phil Phillipson; Robert E. Stanton; Donald Towns; Diana Wakeman; Tom Woodington

Visual Development: Kelly Asbury; Michael Cedeno; Joe Grant; Jean Gillmore; Kevin Lima; Dave Molina; Sue C. Nichols; Christopher Sanders; Terry Shakespeare

Production Consultants/Visual Development: Hans Bacher; Mel Shaw

Animation Camera Supervisor: John Cunningham

Animation Camera: John Aardal; Mary Lescher; Gary W. Smith

Visual Effects Supervisor: Randy Fullmer

Visual Effects Supervisor (Florida Unit): Barry Cook

Computer Graphics Images Supervisor: Jim Hillin

Production Manager: Baker Bloodworth

Production Manager (Florida Unit): Tim O'Donnell

Editor: John Carnochan

Associate Editor: Gregory Perler

Assistant Editors: Deirdre Hepburn; Pamela G. Kimber; Jim Melton

Florida Editorial Staff: Beth Ann Collins; Chuck Williams

Directors: Gary Trousdale; Kirk Wise

Associate Producer: Sarah McArthur

Executive Producer: Howard Ashman

Producer: Don Hahn

Release Date: November 22, 1991 (Prerelease engagements began November 13 in New York and November 15 in Los Angeles.)

Running Time: 84 minutes

THE MOVIE

Beauty and the Beast is the thirty-eighth Disney feature to be discussed in this book. It comes as something of a surprise that it is only the fifth to be based on a classic fairy tale.

The origins of this movie can be traced back at least forty years to initial discussions between Walt and the rest of his pioneering team about the possibility of adapting the story for such treatment. However, no satisfactory way could be found of dealing with the tale's claustrophobic second half, when Beauty (la Belle) is imprisoned in the Beast's castle, and so the project was put on the shelf. There it remained until the middle of 1989, when producer Don Hahn led a small group of artists and animators—including Glen Keane and Andreas Deja—to London for a ten-week period of development and preproduction work. There they worked on the story and experimented with character design while soaking up the flavour and atmosphere of the movie's European setting; they also made an excursion to the Loire Valley. The result of all this effort was, however, a serious drama with very little humour and no real scope for music; in short, they had run into the same problem that had persuaded Walt to stay his hand several decades earlier.

It was decided to start all over again. Kirk Wise (who had worked as an animator on *The Great Mouse Detective* and *Oliver & Company* and as a storyman on *The Rescuers Down Under*, *The Prince and the Pauper* and others) and Gary Trousdale (who had worked on story development for *Oliver & Company*, *The Little Mermaid* and *The Rescuers Down Under*) were appointed directors in place of the original director, Richard Purdum (who had come to the conclusion that the revised movie was not one he wanted to direct and had therefore resigned), and were given the task of further redeveloping the project. Screenwriter Linda Woolverton (who has since scripted the remake of the 1963 Disney live-action classic *The Incredible Journey*) was sent to work for over a month with Howard Ashman (producer and lyricist for *The Little Mermaid*; sadly, he died during *Beauty and the Beast*'s production, in March 1991) on the general structure of the movie and, more particularly, on the placement of songs within the new script.

Among his other contributions, Ashman came up with an important new notion. Linda Woolverton:

> Before Howard came onto the project, the enchanted objects were not really leading characters. They just sort of floated around magically and didn't speak at all. Howard really needed the objects for the music, and his greatest contribution was in bringing them in, giving them personalities and making them an important part of the story.

In fact, such developments would not seem to be out of keeping with the mood of the original fairy tale, which goes back as far as history. The best known version of it was the one adapted by Madame le Prince de Beaumont from the *Contes marins* (1740–1741) of Madame Gabrielle de Villeneuve, in which Beauty is the youngest and favourite daughter of a merchant who has fallen upon hard times. He sets off to try to drum up some business, and tells his daughters that he will bring them back gifts from afar; all respond with greedy demands except Beauty, who asks only that he bring her a rose. As he returns from what has proved to be a flop of a business trip, he comes across an apparently deserted castle in whose garden he plucks a rose. At once the Beast emerges; it is his castle and he will exact the death penalty for the theft of the flower unless the merchant offers him instead his youngest daughter. The merchant returns home and breaks the news to the others; the virtuous Beauty willingly agrees to sacrifice herself, and goes to live in the Beast's castle. Over the years she becomes fonder and fonder of the monster, recognizing that the qualities of his soul are more important than the defects of his appearance. Learning through scrying into a mirror that her father is seriously ill, she begs to be allowed to go to him. The Beast agrees, but tells her that he will die if she is gone for more than a week. Her unpleasant sisters delay her return, and when she arrives back at the castle she finds that the Beast is on the verge of death. She tells him that she has fallen in love with him and wishes to marry him. At that moment he is transformed into a handsome prince; long ago a spell had been cast upon him such that he was turned into a monster and would remain in that guise until he succeeded in winning the hand of a beautiful virgin.

Naturally Disney made some changes to this basic plot, the most fundamental of which concerned the characterization of Beauty. Don Hahn made this point:

> We felt we needed to energize the story by creating more dramatic scenarios and making our heroine move things forward by valiantly going to the castle on her own to fight for her father's release.

The other big change was in terms of central viewpoint. The original tale is really about Beauty: she is a virtuous maid whose self-sacrifice is rewarded; her reward is in fact something of a deus ex machina. For Disney it seemed more interesting to turn the tale around so that it became the Beast's story: he has landed himself in a dire predicament because of an "accident" in his earlier life, and he has to solve various problems in order to get out of it.

A very important aspect of the visual presentation of the tale was the use of color. The moviemakers wanted to come up with a rich colorful style suggestive of the film's European setting but which would also have the quality of the classic Disney animated features. Brian McEntee, the movie's art director, studied the works of the great French Romantic painters like Jean Honoré Fragonard and François Boucher as well as the result of that field trip to the Loire Valley. In addition he closely analysed the beautifully understated simplicity of the long-ago movie *Bambi* (➤197), and tried to incorporate the realistic yet stylized approach which the Disney animators had used on that film nearly half a century earlier. McEntee worked with the directors and with the background artistic supervisor Lisa Keene to develop a unique color theory which was extended throughout the movie. Sometimes this was used quite overtly, as for Belle: she is the only person in her village to be dressed in blue, which means that she is visually set apart from the others—an almost subliminal way of conveying to the audience that she doesn't really fit in with the rest. (It is also, of course, isolates her as one of the movie's stars.) Don Hahn described the more general—and usually more subtle—play with color that affected the movie as a whole:

We tried to tell the story as much with colours as with shapes. The seasons became a metaphor for our story and they change along with the moods and action of the film. We start out with very October colours, pumpkins and falling leaves. When Maurice gets lost in the woods, we get a real chill in the air and things begin to turn very cool. By the time Belle arrives at the castle, a cold winter climate becomes evident. The first snows of winter appear when Belle attempts to escape, but by the time she and the Beast start getting closer and fall in love, the snows begin to melt and the blossoms are on the trees. Gaston leads the mob attack on the Beast's castle during a spring thunderstorm. At the end of the film, as the spell is lifted and Belle and the Prince are reunited, spring is in full bloom and there is a full release of colour. The palette reflects all these seasonal changes and adds to the dramatic impact of the story.

Also used to improve the colour range of the movie was a technologically advanced post-production system which allowed the artists an almost unlimited palette: several of the main characters were treated to as many as seventeen paint colours and

seven different colours of ink outline. This was the sort of detail that hadn't been used in animation since the "Golden Age", decades before. A sophisticated new blending technique, pioneered in the making of *Beauty and the Beast*, was used to give the effect of rouged cheeks on Belle and Mrs. Potts.

Will future generations regard *Beauty and the Beast* as one of the classic Disney features? It is perhaps too soon to judge. Readers interested in a much more detailed discussion of the movie are recommended to Bob Thomas's book *Disney's Art of Animation: From Mickey Mouse to Beauty and the Beast* (1991), about half of which is devoted to a highly illustrated account of the making of the movie.

THE STORY

Beauty and the Beast starts with a prologue that echoes the classic fairy-tale features, with a succession of stained-glass windows in place of the traditional turning pages of a book. The Narrator (David Ogden Stiers) tells us what happened all those years ago:

Once upon a time, in a faraway land, a young prince lived in a shining castle. Although he had everything his heart desired, the prince was spoiled, selfish and unkind. But then, one winter's night, an old beggar-woman came to the castle and offered him a single rose in return for shelter from the bitter cold. Repulsed by her haggard appearance, the prince sneered at the gift, and turned the old woman away. But she warned him not to be deceived by appearances, for beauty is found within. And, when he dismissed her again, the old woman's ugliness melted away to reveal a beautiful enchantress. The prince tried to apologize—but it was too late, for she had seen that there was no love in his heart, and as punishment she transformed him into a hideous beast, and placed a powerful spell on the castle and all who lived there. Ashamed of his monstrous form, the Beast concealed himself inside his castle, with a magic mirror as his only window to the outside world. The rose she had offered was truly an enchanted rose, which would bloom until his twenty-first year. If he could learn to love another, and earn her love in return by the time the last petal fell, then the spell would be broken. If not, he would be doomed to remain a beast for all time.

As the years passed he fell into despair and lost all hope. For who could ever learn to love a beast?

The fairy-tale ambience is picked up almost immediately in the next scene, in which we encounter Belle and her fellow villagers: she remarks that "I just finished [reading] a wonderful story about a beanstalk and an ogre and. . . ." We also meet Gaston, who is shooting geese, and his chief sycophant Le Fou, who is acting essentially as a retriever dog; Gaston states his intention of marrying Belle, mean-

while being admired by three swooning Bimbettes. After Gaston unsubtly attempts to chat Belle up, she goes on her way—just in time to see a great explosion erupt from her home: the latest invention which her father, Maurice, is trying to finish in time for the morrow's fair has failed yet again. She and Maurice get the device (a log-chopping machine) working and load it on a wagon drawn by the horse Phillipe, and Maurice sets off for the fair.

We next meet Maurice and Philippe lost in the night, the horse panicking because of nearby wolf howls, fluttering bats, and so on. Finally Philippe runs off. Maurice, attacked by wolves, manages to reach the safety of the enchanted castle. He enters it and finds it seemingly empty, although we as audience are aware that he is being observed by some of the (apparently) inanimate objects around him—particularly Lumiere (a three-branched candle-holder) and Cogsworth (a mantle clock), who finally introduce themselves to an understandably incredulous Maurice. Lumiere leads the shivering man to the fireside, Cogsworth protesting vociferously in case "the Master" should find him there, especially when Maurice usurps "the Master's" very own chair. The other objects are less retiring: the doglike Footstool rushes in to sit on Maurice's lap, the Hat Rack drapes a blanket over him, and Mrs. Potts (teapot) and Chip (cup) hurry in on a trolley to serve him with tea.

The party is brought to an abrupt halt by the dramatic entrance of the Beast; the household objects run for cover. The Beast comes across the intruder, erupts, and drags Maurice off dungeonwards.

Meanwhile, back in the village, Belle is suffering Gaston-trouble. He has gathered a wedding party and calls on her to tell her she is about to marry him; to his surprise, she rejects and ejects him. Just as she's celebrating her escape Philippe arrives, and Belle naturally fears for her father. Leaping onto the horse, she makes him guide her back to the enchanted castle. After running a long time through its bleak and echoing corridors, observed by various domestic objects, she finally locates her father in the dungeon. The Beast appears out of the shadows and Belle, despite Maurice's protests, insists on taking her father's place.

Without further ado the Beast drags Maurice off, throws him into the Palanquin, and tells it to take the man back to his village. Advised on matters of protocol by Lumiere, the suddenly bashful Beast leads Belle to her room, telling her she can have the run of the castle except—and surely there should have been an ominous rumble of drums here!—the West Wing.

That evening, the Beast awaits her at the dinner table with snarling impatience. Mrs. Potts and Lumiere try to persuade him to moderate his brutish tones. They also insist the Beast learn to control his temper—a lesson whose effect lasts just as long as it takes him to discover that Belle is disobeying his command to join him for dinner: despite their attempts to calm him he bellows through her bedroom door that if she won't eat with him he won't eat at all. In defiance of his wishes, the domestic artefacts prepare Belle for dinner to the accompaniment of music in the shape of the movie's big presentation number, "Be Our Guest", sung by Lumiere (Jerry Orbach) with the assistance of Mrs. Potts, Cogsworth and a chorus of dancing plates, silverware and other objects.

Gaston, like the Beast, is feeling rejected by Belle and is cheering himself up by leading a raucous tavern song listing his many manly virtues—right down to "I'm especially good at expectorating"—when Maurice arrives gasping on the scene. He begs for help to rescue Belle, but is treated offensively by Gaston and his cronies; yet Gaston swiftly evolves a plot to exploit the situation so as to force Belle to marry him. As we soon discover, his notion is to bribe Monsieur D'Arque, who runs the local lunatic asylum, to threaten to lock up the "insane" Maurice unless Belle agrees to the match.

Meanwhile, Lumiere and Cogsworth have been taking Belle on a guided tour of the castle. She shows an insatiable curiosity concerning the taboo West Wing. She stumbles into the Beast's lair and, poking about in it, is just about to pick the rose from its bell jar when the Beast himself appears. He erupts, and she flees— "Promise or no promise, I can't stay here another minute!"—not only from the West Wing but right out of the castle, riding off on Philippe into the forest, where they are attacked in the snow by hungry wolves. All seems lost until the Beast appears, but he is savaged while fighting the beasts off. After toying with the notion of fleeing even from her rescuer, Belle relents, and she and Philippe help him back to the castle, where she tends his wounds. Some while later, following Lumiere's advice, the Beast romantically gives Belle the run of his library. The two are clearly becoming more at ease with each other, a familiarity which has become positively slushy by the following breakfast time, when they go feeding the birds and playing peek-a-boo and snowballs in the garden.

That night the Beast steels himself to propose. But first he lets Belle see her father using the magic mirror and—horror of horrors!—she sees the mess Maurice is in. Nobly the Beast gives her her unconditional freedom so that she can go to her father; he also gives her the magic mirror so that "you'll always have a way to look back . . . and remember me". Cogsworth is frantic on learning of all this—will the spell forever remain unbroken?—but the Beast explains that he had to let her go, because he loves the girl.

Belle finds Maurice in the snow and takes him home. Le Fou runs off to tell Gaston. From Belle's bag springs Chip—a

stowaway. D'Arque arrives to take away Maurice, who is taunted by Le Fou in front of the crowd as he is led from the house, convincing the onlookers of his madness as he tells them about the huge Beast. Gaston none too subtly puts it to Belle that he'd be willing to "clear up this little misunderstanding" should she accept his proposal; she declines with less tact than before, and holds up the magic mirror so that all can see the Beast and know her father is not talking madness. She also, on being quizzed by Gaston about her feelings for the Beast, quite explicitly spells out a primary theme of the movie: "He's no monster, Gaston—*you* are!"

Gaston whips up the villagers until they are a bloodthirsty lynch-mob, and his cronies fling Belle and Maurice into a cellar before they all set off to besiege the castle. When they reach it they batter down the doors and a frantic battle ensues between the rioters and the household objects. There is more door-battering going on in the village, where Chip has got Maurice's log-chopping device working and is using it to pulverize the cellar door. At the castle, even though the Beast shows no interest in joining the fray, the household objects succeed in repelling the mob.

But Gaston is still inside. He enters the Beast's lair and attacks him with bow, arrow and sadistic glee. They end up fighting on the roof, the Beast still showing no enthusiasm, barely retaliating—until he hears Belle's distant but approaching voice, at which point strength roisters into his every sinew. Soon after, he is dangling a despairing Gaston over the edge of the roof, and seems about to give way to impulse before he comes to his senses and puts the lout down safely. Belle and the Beast have a tearful reunion, interrupted when Gaston, recovered, stabs the Beast from behind. The Beast flails in pain, causing Gaston to lose his grip and fall.

The Beast is dying. The last petal is about to drop from the rose. The Beast actually dies. The petal drops. Belle announces, tearfully and a bit tardily, that she loves the Beast. This is followed by a spectacular transformation scene and, of course, a lack of dry eyes in the house.

THE CHARACTERS

Belle

It was decided early that the movie's heroine should display a lot more spirit than the somewhat passive virtue of the character in the original fairy tale. The live-action performance for the animators' reference was supplied by Sherri Stoner, the actress who had not long before served the same function so very excellently for *The Little Mermaid*'s Ariel (➤344), another feisty female part. Belle's part was spoken and sung by Paige O'Hara, a talented and strong actress who could be re-

lied upon to give the role both depth and variety: she was able to provide the right lightness of touch for the comic scenes and the dramatic strength required for the serious ones. Belle was also given a very prominent role in terms of appearance time: she is on screen for just under half an hour, which is about twice as long as any of the other characters. Her animators, under the supervision of the young James Baxter (who used an early sketch by storyman Roger Allers as a main reference), let her spirit be emphasized as much through her facial expressions as through her movements or her dialogue. Although she has the large eyes typical of many a more passive Disney heroine, they have a slightly exotic shape, and they are certainly very expressive (they also have something of Bambi's [➤198] about them). Her mouth, too, with its quite full lips, is extremely mobile; in tandem with her dialogue, it conveys the impression of a young woman from whose tongue a rapid retort is never far.

Belle needed to be a strong character if the balance of the movie were to be right: she had, after all, to act as a counterweight to the Beast. She also had to hold her own against the brutish Gaston, and it might have been this that gave the moviemakers the key to her final personality: what holds her together, what gives her her strength, is the fact that she is a thinking, intellectual young woman placed in an era in which women were supposed neither to think nor to be interested in matters of the mind—as exemplified by book reading.

In terms of capturing our sympathy for Belle, the moviemakers chose to walk something of a tightrope for, while we can understand her wish to escape from her very conservative and tedious (however lovely) surroundings, it would be easy enough to read her aspirations as something not far from snobbery. Throughout her introductory song she has expressed her rejection of the narrowness of "this provincial life" (much as Ariel [➤344] expressed her yearning for the human world through her song "Part of Your World" in *The Little Mermaid*); this could be interpreted as an example of the kind of facile dismissiveness with which spoiled children decide they're far too good for their home backgrounds. We are given another of these slightly mixed messages about her personality as she leads into a brief reprise of that song:

> Is he gone? Can you imagine . . . he asked me to marry him! Me! The wife of that boorish, brainless . . . Madame Gaston! Can't you just see it? Madame Gaston . . . his "little wife"! No sir! Not me! I guarantee it!
> *I want much more than this provincial life.*
> *I want adventure in the great wide somewhere—*
> *I want it more than I can tell—*
> *And for once it might be grand*
> *To have someone understand*
> *I want so much more than they've got planned . . .*

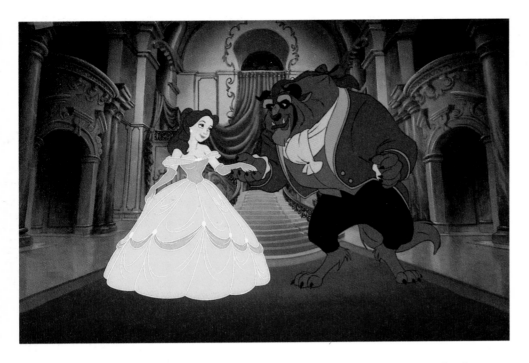

The Beast does his ponderous best to look like a suave escort—and perhaps that is exactly what Belle sees him as.

Then Philippe staggers into view, sans Maurice, the main action of the movie is underway, and from then on we recognize Belle for the sterling character she is. This "real" Belle is particularly to the fore when she scries her father's plight and begs immediately to leave what has become something of an idyll in the castle in order to rescue the old man. And, of course, once we have become properly acquainted with this "real" Belle, we no longer in any way begrudge her the happiness she finds.

The Beast/Prince

In discussing the movie, producer Don Hahn at one point remarked:

> It's not about a young girl who wants her man and has to sacrifice things to get there like Ariel in *The Little Mermaid*. It's about a guy with a very serious problem . . .

Well, yes, that's one way of putting it. Hahn continued:

> . . . He has to redeem himself through a series of events. For him, the meter's ticking and he has to find somebody to love him before the flag tips over.

This sense of time running out is more than adequately conveyed through the screenplay and especially through the animation of the character, which was done by a team of six character animators working under the supervision of Disney veteran Glen Keane. He had previously worked on *The Great Mouse Detective's* Ratigan (➤322), *The Little Mermaid's* Ariel (➤344), *The Rescuers Down Under's* Marahute (➤363) and, perhaps most signifi-

cantly, the climatic bear fight in *The Fox and the Hound* (➤306).

For the physical form of the Beast, he created a hybrid of features drawn from various animals: the mane of a lion, the beard and head structure of a buffalo, the tusks and nose bridge of a wild boar, the heavily muscled brow of a gorilla, the legs and tail of a wolf and the big and bulky body of a bear—as Keane described it, "an evolutionary mess". All of the animals from which he borrowed these attributes are big, powerful, and very animalistic, exactly the impression he wanted to give in his depiction of the Beast. We can suggest that his success in so doing was that he cor-

rectly identified which of the characteristics of the individual creatures most convey to the human unconscious the vitality and strength of that particular species of animal. The Beast can thus be regarded as a distillation of animalistic qualities tempered by, but in no way diluted by, the kind of sincerity which Keane describes: the solution, the retention of humanlike eyes rather than the use of those from yet another powerful creature, was an obvious one, but none the worse for that.

One of the problems that Keane must have faced in presenting the tragic aspects of the Beast is that for large parts of the movie he is set up not just as a comedic creature but as a richly comic one. In his inability to control his temper, even when it is vital that he should do so—and even though we know that the primary reason for the failing, the long years of solitude during which frustration must have built up to intolerable levels as the rose petals marked the passing of the days, is exactly the opposite of funny—there is a great deal of the child suffering from temper tantrums: seeing such behaviour in a (fictional) adult, and perhaps even more especially in a monster, is something which inevitably makes us grin, and the screenplay very effectively converts those grins into out-and-out laughter. Of course, even as we laugh, we know that we're skirting very close to the edges of disaster—rather as if we were giggling at an infant playing grown-up soldiers.

This dichotomy is nowhere more evident than in the matter of the Beast's "invitation" to Belle for dinner. From the outset we're chuckling over the Beast's gaucheries: even under persuasion from Lumiere that he might best win the girl's friendship if he were just a little bit *nice* towards her, the best the Beast can man-

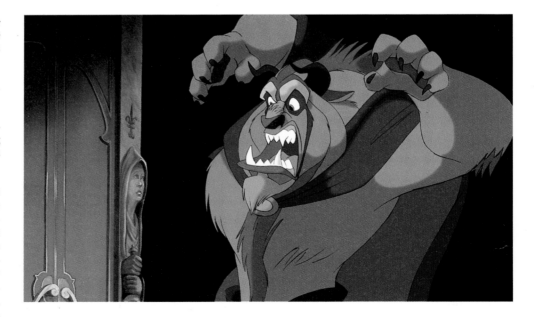

The Beast in spectacular wrath, his primary emotion until Belle elicits his underlying tenderness.

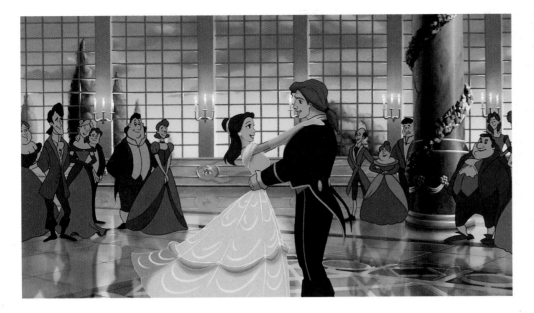

What fairy tale would be complete without its happy ending? The Prince has shed his Beastly form, and has reverted to being a handsome young man. Yet this barely affects Belle's love for him, for she was perceptive enough to see the soul behind the monstrous facade. The servants who were enchanted along with the Prince have likewise returned to their human forms, and look on approvingly as the comely couple dance.

age is "You will join me for dinner. That's not a request." The effect is reminiscent of a child forced to apologize. Then, when Cogsworth has broken it to the Beast that Belle will not, after all, be joining him, still the wrath is infantile and at first risible: the Beast's response is to rush to her quarters and start beating furiously on her door:

Beast (hammer, hammer, hammer): I thought I told you to come down to dinner!
Belle (through door): I'm not hungry.
Beast: You come out or I'll . . . I'll break down the door!
Lumiere (coaching soothingly): Master, I could be wrong but . . . ah . . . that may not be the best way to win the girl's affections.
Cogsworth: Please. Attempt to be a gentleman.
Beast: But she is being so *difficult*!
Mrs. Potts (urging): Gently . . . gently.
Beast (tries again): Will you come down to dinner?
Belle: No!
Beast: Hmmph!
Cogsworth: Ah . . . ah . . . ah . . . suave . . . genteel . . .
Beast: It would give me great pleasure if you would join me for dinner.
Cogsworth (sotto voce): Ah . . . um . . . we say "please"?
Beast: Please.
Belle: No. Thank you.

And then, after all this mirthful flirtation with danger, we suddenly trip over the rim:

Beast (yelling): You can't stay in there forever!
Belle: Yes I can!
Beast: Fine! Then go ahead and starve! If she doesn't eat with me—then she doesn't eat at all!

Suddenly there's a chill—because we know that, if past performance is anything to go by, the Beast is only too well capable of carrying out his threat, so that Belle will indeed starve.

Belle, too, in this exchange is acting the part of a truculent child. The dialogue is funny so long as both the antagonists are in juvenile roles. But in the last few lines the Beast suddenly adopts the language of a parent driven to ultimate frustration. So the Beast's threat actually strikes at us at a fairly deep psychological level: he epitomizes the parent whose threat is for once not empty.

Continuing for a moment to cast Belle as a child and the Beast as an adult in some parts of their early relationship, we see that "parent" is not his only adult role. When first she arrives he is much like a grumpy bachelor uncle or aunt who's had a niece dumped on him/her for the weekend. The Beast doesn't actually detest the girl as an individual, but girls as a species are not something he's ever had to cope with before, and he doesn't much relish changing his ways now.

The adult-child roles are completely reversed, of course, when the Beast has been injured by the wolves and Belle is tending his wounds. The scene is reminiscent of countless Hollywood thriller movies, television serials, novels and, on occasion, real life: the female, who has in true sexist fashion hitherto been regarded as subservient to the tough guy, is now suddenly the competent member of their partnership—the mother tending a child.

It is not only for comic reasons that the Beast's essential childishness is exploited; the same reading can be taken of those very poignant moments when we are ex-

posed to the true tragedy of his predicament. For example, when he first comes across the intruding Maurice he brushes away the man's flustered explanation of his trespass with "What are you staring at? . . . So you've come to stare at the Beast, have you?" which is an intensely infantile response—but nevertheless a tragic one. Likewise, after he has furiously threatened Belle with starvation and is spying on her via the magic mirror, he sees how much she loathes him and tears begin to ooze from his eyes, his pain especially bitter because he recognizes that her detestation of him is his own fault.

His other great moment of (seeming) tragedy is expressed in much more adult terms; this is also the moment at which he reveals the depths of his true humanity. Even though he believes that his decision will lead to his own death, he permits Belle to leave the castle in order to go to her father's rescue.

When we see the Beast in his human form after the spell has been lifted, he is of course a handsome but somewhat anonymous prince. We have no real opportunity to see him as anything more than a symbol. We assume that he has learnt the error of his ways, but we have no real evidence of this—and a lot of evidence to the contrary, for the Beast's conversion from petulance and temper has occurred only minutes before: for all we know, Belle might find herself stuck with the same spoiled brat depicted at the movie's outset.

The Beast's dual nature—ogre and Prince Charming—is the movie's main theme, being expressed not only through the Beast but also in Gaston's personality, which shows exactly the same duality but in reverse. It might seem trite to point out that we identify much more with the Beast than with Gaston, but the reasons for our doing so go much deeper than the obvious one (we identify with the good guys): the real point is that the Beast is *each one of us*. Underneath our substantially less-than-perfect exteriors, lurking behind all our tetchinesses and other character faults, each of us knows there is a heart of gold—if only other people could see it. In short, when we are watching the Beast we are watching *ourselves*.

Which may be the reason why the Beast is one of the richest and most interesting characters ever to have emerged from Disney.

Maurice

Animated under the supervision of Ruben Aquino and voiced by the veteran stage actor Rex Everhart, Maurice is an archetypal lovable eccentric: we understand exactly why Lumiere and the other enchanted objects should so readily welcome him out of the storm, and why Belle should be so steadfastly loyal to him. Were we to look for parallels to his char-

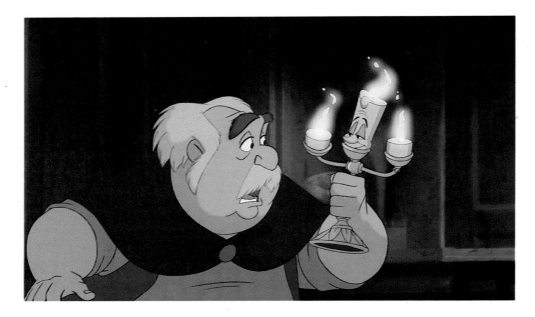

A complacent Lumiere and an apprehensive Maurice.

resistible: it is natural law, according to his observations, that women always seek out the most handsome men, the natures of those men being irrelevant because, after all, women have no power of rational thought and hence lack the ability to consider such matters.

It is this narrowness which renders him incapable of understanding not only why Belle should not be bowled over with delight at the prospect of being permitted to marry him but also why she might find the Beast remotely appealing, why it should not be permissible for Gaston to mount the attack on the castle, and even why it should not be a perfectly valid act for him to stab the Beast in the back, even though the latter has just spared his life. For Gaston is unable to conceive that anything except the welfare of Gaston is remotely important—a typical sign of the sociopath. It is alarming that, as Deja and White both pointed out, there are so many Gastons around.

acter (not his appearance) in earlier Disney movies, we might find one in Merlin (➤271), although there are also some quirks which could remind us of Hiram Flaversham (➤322)—who shares with him also the requirement that the actions of a feisty daughter should rescue him from a pitiful captivity—and even, in terms of personality, Ludwig Von Drake (➤124).

We must not regard Maurice solely as a nutty inventor and forget his personal bravery. After his attempt to rally support among Gaston and his sycophants has failed, Maurice sets off on his own with the intention of sacrificing his life, if need be, in order to secure her delivery. Misguided, foolhardy and suicidal such a decision might be, but nevertheless it shows admirable devotion and very considerable courage.

Gaston

Where the Beast is ugly on the outside but proves to be beautiful within, Gaston is the exact reverse: his devastatingly handsome exterior conceals a vile interior. His supervising animator, Andreas Deja, has recounted how at first he had some difficulty getting to grips with this: his natural inclination was to give Gaston something more of the looks of a villain. Then it was put to him that it was crucial for the movie that Gaston be every bit as good-looking as the Beast is repulsive, and suddenly the character took life: "When I saw the first test reels, I thought, 'God, I know such people. Los Angeles is full of them.'" But Deja was also concerned that Gaston's external persona shouldn't be merely a caricature of the type we all know and loathe: "I wanted Gaston to be a dimensional character that the audience would feel they could reach out and grab." A further inspiration was supplied to Deja by Rich-

ard White, who was Gaston's voice. White is an actor and singer, and as soon as Deja heard some of his early tapes he recognized that, as he put it, "it sounds like he never stops singing". Deja decided to make this a part of Gaston's personality—the feeling that he's so pleased with himself and confident that everyone adores him that he can't stop singing about himself, which indeed he does quite devastatingly in his string of self-congratulations during the tavern scene.

In fact, Gaston's most distinguishing characteristic is not his self-adoration or his awareness of his own good looks or even his inner evil, but instead something that is central to all of these character defects: his narrowness of mind. We see this not only in his quite genuine belief that Belle should find his offer of marriage ir-

Le Fou

There is no straightforward "villain" role in *Beauty in the Beast*, since Gaston is no more than incidental to the main thrust of the plot—he is not a prime mover in it. Yet he is the nearest the movie has to such a figure, and thus it is fitting that Disney should supply him with, among all the other sycophants around him, a character in the role of sycophant-in-chief. Thus individual is Le Fou; and although he is human rather than reptilian or monstrous in form, he is very much in the tradition of other Disney villainous sidekicks such as Sir Hiss (➤293) or Fidget (➤324)—that is to say, he is of rather feebler wit than he realizes. Also—and this is a quite significant part of the tradition—he has no particular reason for subjugating himself to his master, who frequently mistreats him.

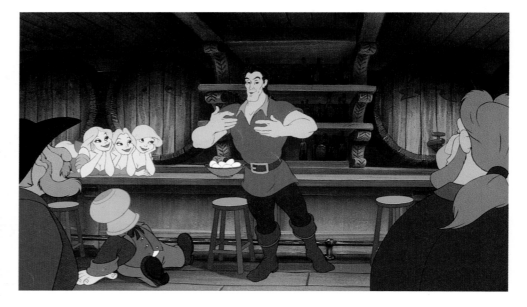

Gaston impressing the customers in the tavern, the swooning Bimbettes, a spittoon-topped Le Fou and, most important of all, himself.

Philippe

It would be wrong to claim that Philippe is one of the great Disney horses: he is certainly no Cyril Proudbottom (➤231). One gains the feeling—perhaps quite falsely—that at one time it was thought to give Philippe a rather stronger role in the movie than eventually he came to play Certainly we get no particularly firm impression of his personality beyond the fact that he is both intelligent and steadfast: he swiftly grasps the idea when Belle desires him to retrace his steps from the village back to the enchanted castle, and he remains dutifully outside the castle gates waiting for Belle when she has rushed away in anger and confronts the wolves.

Monsieur D'Arque

The proprietor of the local lunatic asylum, voiced by Tony Jay, plays a very small role in the movie, and yet we are given just enough of him that he becomes, as it were, a complex character in miniature. He is prepared to fall in with Gaston's plan to "frame" Maurice because he is eager for the money that Gaston offers him; that is, D'Arque is corrupt. Yet he seeks to defend Maurice from the charge of being genuinely insane, declaring him to be quite harmless; in other words, D'Arque is not so corrupt after all. Yet, when the plan is explained fully to him, his response is "Oh, that's despicable! I love it!"—which tells us that D'Arque is not only corrupt but sadistic. It is hard to reconcile the three messages that we're given about his character, all within a few scant seconds of screen time, yet oddly his character does seem to hang together realistically.

Villagers

The cast of *Beauty and the Beast* contains a huge number of minor characters—a number that is swelled yet further by the fact that the characters who are household objects in the enchanted castle throughout most of the movie are transmuted into human beings right at the end. There are also the marauding **Wolves** that attack Maurice and later Belle, and which tussle violently with the Beast; and the cute little **Birds** that surround Belle and the Beast, Disney-fashion, during their brief sojourn in the castle garden.

In the introductory scene in the village, during Belle's singing of her song, "Belle", she encounters a veritable slew of villagers, most of whom have no more to say than a word or two interpolated into the song—indeed one of them, **Marie**, neither appears on screen nor speaks a word: she is merely yelled to by her husband the **Baker**. Other villagers briefly met are the **Butcher**, a **Mother**, a **Chimneysweep**, a **Prisoner**, the **Driver** of a wagon, a **Large Man**, the village **Blacksmith**, a **Basketweaver**, a **Matronly Woman**, the **Hatshop Owner** and a **Hat Buyer**, a **Fruit**

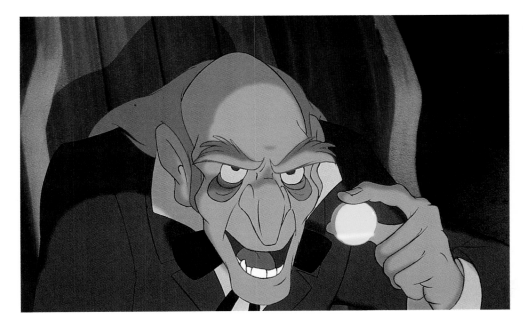

Monsieur D'Arque, who runs the local institution for the insane, is only too pleased to help out when Gaston approaches him with his plan to incarcerate Maurice.

Shopper, a **Cheese Merchant** and a **Cheese Buyer**, a **Fabric Buyer**, one of the **Baker's Customers**, and the **Fishmonger** and one of the **Fishmonger's Customers**. Then there are **Three Young Guys** who eye Belle appreciatively through the bookshop window, clearly affected by her beauty and, by way of afterthought, her mind. These are matched by the three **Bimbettes**, who during Gaston's exhibitionist demonstration of his goose-shooting prowess and again later, during his self-adulatory song in the tavern and his abortive attempt to propose to Belle, squirmingly and gigglingly convince us that they would give their right arms and much more besides for the merest flicker ·

of a lustful Gastonic glance in their direction.

Also featured in the tavern scene are various loutish sycophants of Gaston's—notably those described in the cutting continuity (script) as the **Fat Crony**, the **Tall Crony** and the **Big Crony**—as well as a **Bartender**.

However, one of the villagers has a slightly more significant part than the others. This is the kindly **Bookseller**, in whose shop Belle is permitted to exchange one book for another; indeed, because the next book she wants to reread is clearly a great favourite of hers, he disarmingly tells her that she may have it as a present from him. Aside from her father, the

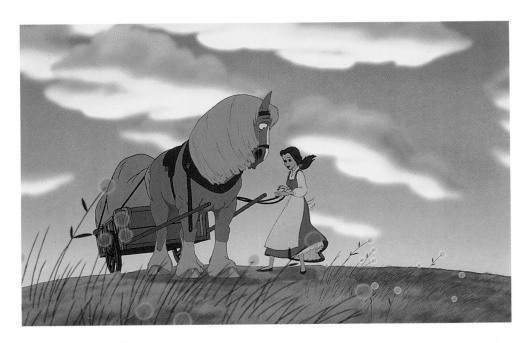

Belle and the less than doughty family horse Philippe.

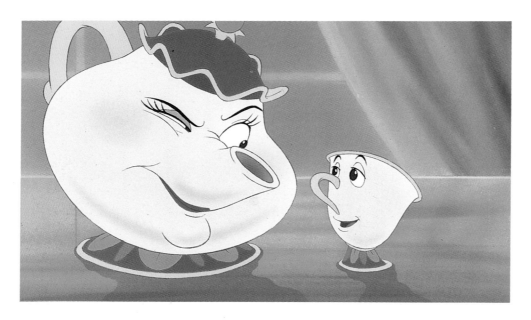

Mrs. Potts and her son Chip. It's interesting to see how much of the two personalities the animators were able to put into the simplified features of these enchanted objects.

Bookseller seems to be the sole villager with whom Belle has any common ground at all: in effect they are two castaways, both interested in the magic of the written word but surrounded by others whose attitude towards books is summed up by a remark from the illiterate Gaston: "It's not right for a woman to read. Soon she starts getting ideas—and *thinking!*"

Mrs. Potts and Chip

Mrs. Potts and Chip—the teapot and one of its enchanted cups—are mother and son both in their enchanted versions and after transmutation into human form at the movie's end, when Mrs. Potts proves to be the castle's housekeeper. She was voice-acted by Angela Lansbury, who also sang the movie's title song.

We are more used to seeing Lansbury in spinster-aunty roles—for example, Eglantine Price in *Bedknobs and Broomsticks* (➤287) and of course Jessica Fletcher in the long-running TV series *Murder, She Wrote*—rather than maternal ones. The subtle vocal adjustment for the part of Mrs. Potts is remarkably skilled. Dave Pruiksma, the supervising animator for both Mrs. Potts and Chip, testified to the influence Lansbury had on the teapot's final screened character:

She has a very distinctive way of acting and is very subtle. She's also very contained in her movements and accentuates her dialogue with a lot of little head tilts. I tried to incorporate some of those mannerisms into Mrs. Potts.

Animating a teapot and a cup took some getting used to. I envisioned the teapot as a large woman shuffling around. She takes real short steps or hops and kind of wobbles from one side of her pedestal to another. It also helps when she's moving along to have her lip pop on and off to accent the action.

Bradley Michael Pierce supplied the voice for her cute young son Chip, whose puzzled enquiries as to the reasons for some of the action, and the embarrassed responses from his mother, provide several humorous moments in the film.

Remarkably, Pierce was only nine at the time the movie was made (although by then he'd already been a professional actor for three years); even more remarkably for a child so young, he proved to be so excellent in the part that the moviemakers immediately began adding significantly to the role's importance in order to give greater scope for the exploitation of his talent. His main function in the plot, apart from humorous byplay, is in the rescue of Belle and Maurice when they have been

imprisoned in the cellar by Gaston's henchmen.

Lumiere and Cogsworth

The three-branched candle-holder who, when not chasing the housemaidly Featherduster with a zest or advising the Beast in romantic stratagems and a caricatured French accent, acts the part of the butler in the enchanted castle—and later proves, on transformation, indeed to be a butler—was voiced by the veteran actor Jerry Orbach and animated under the supervision of Nik Ranieri. According to Ranieri, the character was an ideal one for him to work on, both because of his preference for broadly humorous characters and because "I had a lot of freedom in animating the character because no one really knows how an enchanted object moves".

Even so, at first sight a mobile candle-holder doesn't seem to offer a great deal of scope for the animator. Ranieri found that, as he warmed up to the character, he was able to make the design more animatable by continuing the rim around the head, giving the nose a bit more structure and accentuating the chest area. Perhaps most importantly, he was able to use the arms of the object to help Lumiere gesticulate Gallically and thus be more expressive.

With Lumiere being the butler and Cogsworth being the castle's majordomo, it is hardly surprising that many of the appearances of both characters are in tandem. The moviemakers therefore went to some lengths to ensure their personalities were very distinct from each other. Both characters are mutually compatible solutions to the problem of supplying the castle with a head servant: either could do the job perfectly adequately on his own, but the two complement each other (when permitted to do so) as exactly as a pair of

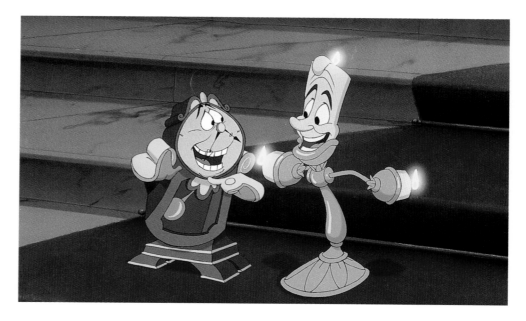

Cogsworth and Lumiere, the best of friends despite their many differences of temperament.

cogs so that, together, they do it that much better. Thus Lumiere's quick-wittedness—which is barely disguised by his flashy charm, overt warmheartedness, impetuosity, verbal flair and propensity for the ladies (his slavering over Belle on first meeting her is acute)—adroitly matches Cogsworth's levelheadedness (physically signified by his status as a sturdy carriage clock), sense of decorum, unremitting stressedness (everything always seems to be on the verge of becoming too much for him), indecision and, to be frank, slowness of mind. The contrast between and complementarity of their natures are probably best seen quite early on in the movie, when Maurice has staggered into the castle as a refuge from the blizzard. Cogsworth's reaction is sensible; Lumiere's is natural: both together would constitute a correct, measured reaction to the situation. In this instance Lumiere's hospitable instincts triumph over Cogsworth's recognition that the enchanted objects are heading for disaster if they carry on this way. Cogsworth proves right, of course—although it is Maurice who suffers the disaster when the Beast arrives—yet Lumiere and the others were *also* right, and Cogsworth wrong, in their immediate realization that Maurice couldn't simply be cast back out into the cold. A wise combination of both approaches, rather than a play of one extreme against the other, might have resulted in a better decision (taking Maurice off to the depths of the servants' quarters and regaling him there, perhaps)—but then, of course, the movie's plot would have been truncated before it had properly got under way. In other instances, of course, they get the blend right, notably when they're leading the fight against Gaston's besieging mob.

Cogsworth and Lumiere are quite rare among comic partnerships in that they are each capable of being extremely funny on their own. Their idiosyncrasies and failings are forgivable rather than irritating—and are anyway partly shared by most of us—in the light of the two characters' integral good-heartedness.

Enchanted Objects

Beauty and the Beast was not the first Disney feature to be marked by a profusion of inanimate objects given life and personality: its obvious predecessor in this respect was *Alice in Wonderland*, especially the Door Knob (➤245). Aside from the ones we've discussed above—Mrs. Potts, Chip,

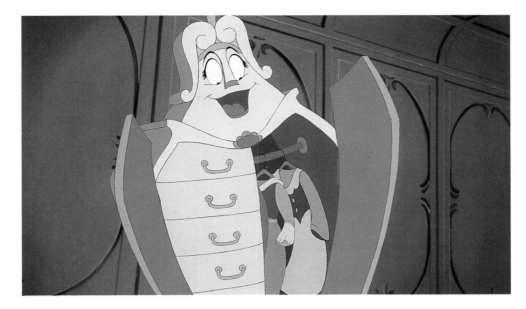

The Wardrobe taking time out for joy, even though trapped in its enchanted form.

Lumiere and Cogsworth—several others have roles of more than trivial significance.

The **Wardrobe**, voiced by Jo Anne Worley, plays a genial supporting part, giving the impression of an older and very loyal friend—someone, perhaps, half a generation older than Belle, and therefore able to offer mature friendship yet not to be seen by the girl as a part of her parent's generation. She has a sort of spinster girlishness, as in her embarrassment when she is offering clothes for Belle to dress in for dinner and moths suddenly flutter up as she opens her drawer. And, in the invasion of the castle, she gives us great if mischievous pleasure when she copes with one of the attackers by simply dropping on top of him and squashing him flat.

The **Featherduster**, voiced by Kimmy Robertson, plays a rather more minor supporting role, not quite large enough to establish a personality beyond our mental image of her as a rather flighty young girl (and not wholly immune to Lumiere's Gallic charm)—although our hearts bleed, late in the movie, when we come across one of the lynch-thirsty villagers sadistically plucking out her feathers one by one and cackling as she screams. It's hard to stifle a cheer when Lumiere rushes up and treats the villager's vast bottom to a burst of flame. The **Footstool**, scampering around and barking, has all the attributes of a dog—obviously—but, more than that,

registers in our minds as a lovable and *much loved* dog, as when he makes a fuss over Maurice, newly arrived in the castle, and finally settles in the old man's lap in front of the fire. The Footstool's vocal utterances were supplied by Frank Welker, who was responsible for most of the movie's other special voice effects. The **Hat Rack** appears hither and thither throughout—it plays the violin during the dining-room/ballroom sequence—but is perhaps at its most distinguished when dealing with the invading villagers in pugilistic fashion. The **Stove**, on hearing of Belle's rejection of the Beast's dinner "invitation", gives voice (courtesy Brian Cummings) to the grouse of cooks the world over: "I work and slave all day long—and for what? A culinary masterpiece gone to waste."

Even smaller roles are played by the **Palanquin** commanded by the Beast to take Maurice back to the village after the latter's expulsion from the castle, the **Creamer**, the **Dresser**, the **Sugarbowl**, a **Globe**, the **Brush and Comb**—who, in the battle for the castle, leap out from the Wardrobe with a ruthless expression to grab one of Gaston's cronies and drag him to a fate unknown (and probably best left so)—and the **Beer Steins** who cheer us up by splattering the invading villagers with rotten tomatoes.

ALADDIN

Characters:

Aladdin; Abu; Jasmine; Rajah; Genie; Sultan; Magic Carpet; Jafar; Iago; Peddler; Tiger's Head; Gazeem; Razoul; Prince Achmed; Fruit Vendor; Fire-Eater; Street Waifs

Credits:

Voices: Jonathan Freeman (Jafar); Gilbert Gottfried (Iago); Brad Kane (Aladdin singing); Linda Larkin (Jasmine speaking); Lea Salonga (Jasmine singing); Douglas Seale (Sultan); Scott Weinger (Aladdin speaking); Frank Welker (Abu); Robin Williams (Peddler; Genie)

Additional Voices: Charlie Adler, Jack Angel, Corey Burton, Philip Clarke, Jim Cummings, Jennifer Darling, Debi Derryberry, Bruce Gooch, Jerry Houser, Vera Lockwood, Sherry Lynn, Mickie McGowan, Patrick Pinney, Phil Proctor

Sound Editors: Ron Bartlett; Clayton Collins; Teresa Eckton; Donald Flick; Mary Ruth Smith

Music: Alan Menken

Songs by: Howard Ashman and Alan Menken; Tim Rice and Alan Menken

Animation Screenplay: Ron Clements and John Musker; Ted Elliott and Terry Rossio

Story Supervisor: Ed Gombert

Film Editors: H. Lee Peterson; Chuck Williams

Supervising Animators: Randy Cartwright (Magic Carpet); Andreas Deja (Jafar); Will Finn (Iago); Eric Goldberg (Genie); Mark Henn (Jasmine); Glen Keane (Aladdin); Duncan Marjoribanks (Abu); Dave Pruiksma (The Sultan)

Animators: Tim Allen; Tom Bancroft; Tony Bancroft; Aaron Blaise; Rejean Bourdages; Bob Bryan; David Burgess; Michael Cedeno; Lou Dellarosa; Anthony DeRosa; Ken Duncan; Russ Edmonds; Rick Farmiloe; Brian Ferguson; Tony Fucile; Raul Garcia; Joe Haidar; Ken Hettig; T. Daniel Hofstedt; Ron Husband; Broose Johnson; Doug Krohn; Brad Kuha; Alex Kuperschmidt; Teresa Martin; Cynthia Overman; Gilda Palinginis; Tina Price; Nik Ranieri; William Recinos; Michael Show; Tom Sito; David P. Stephan; Michael Surrey; Mike Swofford; Barry Temple; Chris Wahl; Dan M. Wawrzaszek; Larry White; Ellen Woodbury; Phil Young; Kathy Zielinski

CGI Supervisors: Steve Goldberg; Dan Philips

Layout Supervisors: Rasoul Adzani; Robert Walker

Visual Effects Supervisor: Don Paul

Clean-up Supervisor: Vera Lanpher

Background Supervisors: Kathy Altieri; Richard Sluiter; Robert E. Stanton

Visual Effects Supervisors: Barry Cook; Jeff Dutton

Art Director: Bill Perkins

Artistic Coordinator: Dan Hansen

Production Designer: Richard Vander Wende

Production Managers: Baker Bloodworth (Florida); Alice Dewey (Burbank)

Coproducers: Donald W. Ernst, Amy Pell

Producers: Ron Clements, John Musker

Directors: Ron Clements, John Musker

Release Date: November 11, 1992; general release November 25, 1992

Running Time: 90 minutes

THE MOVIE

Owing something in terms of its plotting to the Douglas Fairbanks version of *The Thief of Bagdad* (1924)—Aladdin the street urchin pretends to be a prince in order to win the hand of a fair princess who refuses the hands of all her lordly suitors—and a very great deal to the remake, *The Thief of Baghdad* (1940), this is one of the best animated Disney features to have appeared in recent years. Often abandoning realism in favor of surrealism, the animators really let their imaginations soar. While, as in any animated feature, there are times when the visuals are merely mundane (because otherwise the story would never get told), there are others when the jaw drops at the audacity—indeed, beauty—of the visual display. And the observation that many of the plot elements can be traced to earlier Arabian-fantasy movies is no particular criticism; all of the live-action movies in this curious subgenre, including notably the *Kismet* remakes, have fed liberally from each other.

Although in theory the tale is based on the traditional story "Aladdin" in *The Thousand and One Nights*, it has little to do with it. To say, as numerous critics have, that it is set not in any historical Arabia but in "Hollywood Arabia," is to state no more than the truth; but then the same sort of charge can be leveled at *The Thousand and One Nights* itself, because the collection was largely fabricated in the West. "Aladdin" may be a story invented by the French writer Antoine Galland, who produced the first version of the collection, *Les Mille et Une Nuits*, between 1704 and 1717; no known Arabian manuscript version of the story predates Galland's "retelling." Most English-language versions of the collection are derived from Galland. *The Arabian Nights: A Companion* (1994) by Robert Irwin gives much information about this entire saga of literary history.

Gina Ingoglia, in her *Disney's Treasury of Children's Classics* (1996), makes an interesting point about the making of the movie—that from the very first it was a cooperative job, involving not just the animators but also the other main members of the creative team. Her analysis is worth quoting:

> The integrated design process permitted the artists to create a world in which the backgrounds make as strong a statement about the personality of a character as the animation itself. Jasmine's room resembles a birdcage, reflecting her trapped situation. The egg motif in the columns, throne, and oil lamps in the Sultan's throne room mirror his rounded shape and soft-boiled character. When Jafar takes over as Sultan, the shapes in the throne room are reorganized to echo the far more angular silhouette of the elegant and sinister villain.

This sort of subliminal effect is very clever; it is only on repeated viewing that one notices what the moviemakers are up to, yet the emotional impact is certain.

There were problems when the movie was initially released: Islamic groups found some of the lines of the song lyrics offensive, and these were changed for later releases—a wise move, because those lines were indeed ill judged. This was not the first time that Disney had been criticized for a general insensitivity in the animated features toward the people of the Middle East: *DuckTales: The Movie—Treasure of the Lost Lamp* (➤351) attracted similar complaints. In the case of *DuckTales* there was a misunderstanding: the movie constantly parodies the attitudes of 1930s adventure books and flicks, and the attitude toward Arabs is just a part of this. In the case of *Aladdin*, however, there was definitely a misjudgment, and it was good to see that it was corrected.

THE STORY

We are introduced to the story by the Peddler: he shows us the Magic Lamp and tells us that all the events we are about to hear of happened a long time ago in the enchanted city of Agrabah.

The Sultan of Agrabah has a daughter, Jasmine, who will not obey the idiotic law that she should choose a fiancé from aristocratic stock by the time she is sixteen; she wants to marry for love, and so—as in the legend of Perseus and Andromeda—sends suitor after suitor packing. The Sultan also has a treacherous Grand Vizier, Jafar, who seeks to usurp the throne. The mechanics are never explained, but Jafar knows of the existence of the Magic Lamp and that it is hidden in the Cave of Wonders, but he does not know where the Cave of Wonders is located; he also knows that he himself cannot be the one to retrieve the Lamp, and that if he can only obtain the other half of a golden scarab-shaped ornament he will be able to find the Cave of Wonders. He enlists the aid of a thief and cutthroat, Gazeem, to recover the other half of the scarab, then sends him into the Cave of Wonders, whose opening rears from the desert sands in the form of a tiger's head. Gazeem is instantly "eaten" by the tiger, which tells Jafar that only a "diamond in the rough" can claim the Lamp. So Jafar starts to seek out a suitable individual.

This he does by magical means, hypnotizing the Sultan in order to borrow the diamond ring he wears and pair it with an hourglass in order to conjure up an image of Aladdin. Aladdin is at this stage merely a street rat who lives by stealing food from the stalls in the *souk*.

Jasmine, meantime, has decided she can no longer be confined forever within the walls of her father's significantly empty palace. She makes a break for it, and wanders through the *souk* marveling at what she sees. When she sees a hungry child, she picks an apple from the nearest stall, little realizing that she should pay for it. Aladdin saves her from the vengeance of the Fruit Vendor, but very soon they are caught by the palace guards, sent by Jafar in search of the "diamond in the rough."

Back at the palace, Jafar lies to her that Aladdin has been beheaded; in fact the lad has been imprisoned in a dungeon. He is not alone there, he soon finds: there is also an old beggar (in fact, a disguised Jafar). The "beggar" tells him of the Cave of Wonders, and enables both of them to escape. They go to the cave, where the Tiger's Head instructs Aladdin he must touch none of the other treasures, only the Lamp. Unfortunately, Aladdin's pet monkey Abu tries to filch a huge jewel from the hands of an idol, and the mouth of the cave seals shut as punishment. But the pair still have the Lamp, and Aladdin's rubbing of it brings a Genie into the action; the Genie gets them out of the cave, along with a Magic Carpet that has picked them up along the way.

The Genie has to grant Aladdin three wishes. His first is that he become a prince, so that he may woo Jasmine; he is transformed into Prince Ali Ababwa. By this time Jafar, on the suggestion of his pet parrot Iago, has produced spurious legalistic nonsense to persuade the Sultan that he ought to be the one who marries Jasmine and thus gain the sultanate (his plan is to thereafter murder both his wife and his father-in-law, so that he will have ultimate power). Jasmine declines to marry either Jafar or the apparent newcomer, Prince Ali. Very soon she realizes that Ali is the person who saved her in the *souk*, but he lies to her that he is really a prince who, like herself, wanted to mingle with the commoners for a while.

Jafar orders the palace guards to murder Ali/Aladdin; they throw him into the sea, and his second wish to the Genie proves to be that he is rescued from drowning. Jafar, meantime, hypnotizes the Sultan into agreeing that he must be the one to marry Jasmine. The reappearance of Aladdin, who destroys Jafar's magical hypnotic stick, stuns the villain, who flees. The Genie asks for the third wish—his own freedom—to be granted, but Aladdin at first hesitates, claiming that he must have the wish of remaining a prince as otherwise he will never be able to marry Jasmine. Iago steals the Lamp for Jafar. Aladdin realizes he must tell Jasmine the truth, but before he can do so he is presented to the populace of Agrabah as her successful suitor, Prince Ali.

Jafar is now the Genie's master. He gains the sultanate, and, as a second wish, makes the Genie turn him into the most powerful sorcerer in the world. Magically, he casts Aladdin and Abu to a snowbound waste at the far corner of the world, but fortunately the Magic Carpet is with them and they return. Aladdin tells Jafar he is a snake, and the vizier becomes a huge cobra. As he is about to squeeze Aladdin to death, Aladdin persuades him that he should go for one higher than being a major sorcerer: he ought to wish to be a genie. This Jafar duly does, and promptly Aladdin confines him in a Magic Lamp. The Sultan changes the law about his daughter's wedding requirements, and at once she and Aladdin become betrothed.

THE CHARACTERS

Aladdin

As is very often the case in the Disney animated features, the story of Aladdin as a character is that of growth from self-underestimation to the realization that the individual has worth and can achieve a particular aim, which is generally living happily ever after with the mate of his choice. The difference here is that Aladdin tries to cheat—he makes the Genie turn him into a prince so that he can woo Jasmine, and it is a time before the Genie gets it through to him that he should simply be himself and take his chances. We know from the first that Aladdin is going to succeed—we'd hardly have gone to the movie otherwise—but the point is firmly made in the early stages when the baggy-panted street rat Aladdin, accompanied by his tiny pet

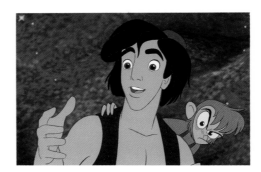

Aladdin and his mischievous friend, Abu.

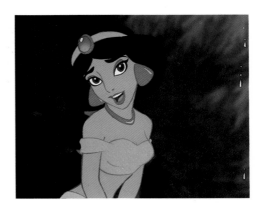

The beautiful Princess Jasmine.

monkey Abu, steals a loaf of bread (a crime) but then gives it to a couple of street waifs who are so desperately hungry that they are searching through an anachronistic garbage can for food. The waifs are then insulted by the pompous Prince Achmed, and Aladdin stands up for them. His rescue of Jasmine from the vengeful Fruit Vendor becomes little more than the icing on the cake. Yes, we know where the plot is going to go.

There are, of course, many twists and turns along the way, as outlined in the story synopsis above. And Aladdin must learn some further moral truths about himself. When he first releases the Genie from the Magic Lamp he promises that, as his final wish, he will give the Genie freedom. When it comes to the point, however, he is much more selfish:

Genie: Psst. Your line is, "I'm going to free the Genie." Any time.
Aladdin: Genie, I can't.
Genie: Sure ya can. You just go, "Genie, I wish you free."
Aladdin: I'm serious! Look, I'm sorry. I really am. But they want to make me sultan. No, they want to make *Prince Ali* sultan. Without you, I'm just Aladdin.
Genie: Al, you won.
Aladdin: Because of you. The only reason anyone thinks I'm worth anything is because of you. What if they find out I'm not really a prince? What if Jasmine finds

out? I'd lose her. Genie, I can't keep this up on my own. I, I can't wish you free.
Genie: Fine. I understand. After all, you've lied to everyone else. Hey, I was beginning to feel left out. Now, if you'll excuse me, Master . . .

The Genie vanishes back into the Lamp, and Aladdin spitefully hides it under a cushion. Moments later Iago, imitating Jasmine's voice, lures him away and then steals the Lamp—and thus the Genie—for Jafar. Aladdin's punishment fits his crime: he has betrayed a friend. This he acknowledges in due course, once he and Abu have been hurtled into the icy wastes by Jafar:

> *Aladdin*: Abu! Oh, this is all my fault. I, I shoulda freed the Genie when I had the chance. Abu! Are you okay?
> *Abu*: Uh-huh.
> *Aladdin*: I'm sorry, Abu. I made a mess of everything. Somehow I gotta go back and set things right.

The Magic Carpet rescues them and they do indeed get back to Agrabah and set things right, but only because Aladdin is now acting as *himself*—the trickster street rat rather than the prince who is poshly dressed but might have difficulty finding two brain-cells to rub together. He saves both the Sultan and, most important, Jasmine from Jafar's scant mercies, and thus is recognized by both of them as a prince because of what he is rather than for any genealogical inheritance.

Aladdin is not one of the more complexly created Disney heroes, of whom there have been very few: ever since *Snow White and the Seven Dwarfs* the more general pattern has been to make the central character a heroine and the handsome prince (or equivalent) something of a cypher rather than a doer of deeds; the Prince in *Sleeping Beauty* (➤261) is an obvious exception. Nevertheless, Aladdin appeals to us—as is apparent by the success of the television series and the two direct-to-video movies describing his further exploits.

Jasmine

Mark Henn, who created the look of Jasmine for the movie, had various inspirations. One was a theme-park guest at Disney World in Florida, whose long thick mane of black hair sparked off an idea. The most important, however, was his sister Beth—although an actress called Robina Ritchie did live-action modeling to help the animation. Linda Larkin, who gave Jasmine her speaking voice, and Lea Salonga, who sang for her, look not in the slightest like the screen version of Jasmine.

Continuing their practice in several previous movies, the Disney creators made Jasmine an independent-minded young woman; she is not going to be married off to any old lout, no matter how blue his blood, but is instead determined to marry for love. She is, moreover, impatient with her father's dictum that she should be confined within the palace (much of this movie's theme concerns confinement) and eventually escapes to discover what the outer world is like. There her naïveté lands her almost immediately in trouble, and Aladdin rescues her from a nasty fate.

Her antipathy to Jafar is evident early on. Her father believes that the vizier is his loyal adviser, but Jasmine can see right through him, and her solitary incentive to get married is made plain:

> At least some good will come from my being forced to marry. When I am queen, I will have the power to get rid of *you*.

This of course gives Jafar an extra motive, when Iago suggests the idea, to make Jasmine marry him: as her husband and thus the new sultan, he could not be ousted.

The best description of Jasmine comes from the script itself:

> *Genie*: So how about it? What is it you want most?
> *Aladdin*: Well, there's this girl . . .
> *Genie*: Wrong! I can't make anybody fall in love, remember?
> *Aladdin*: Ah, but, but, Genie, she's smart and, and, fun and . . .
> *Genie*: Pretty?
> *Aladdin*: Beautiful! She's got these eyes that just . . . And this hair. Wow, and her smile . . .
> *Genie*: *Ami, c'est l'amour.*
> *Aladdin*: But she's the princess. To even have a chance I'd have to be . . . Hey! Can you make me a prince?

Jasmine also has a marked lack of clothing. In order to disguise herself so that she can explore the outside world she puts on an enfolding hooded cloak, but otherwise, in her life in the palace, she wears the skimpiest of two-piece outfits. Clothes play a fair part in the plot of this movie, in fact, for it takes a little while for her to realize that the visiting "Prince Ali" is in fact the same person as the street rat Aladdin who saved her from doom only hours before. The improbability—we recognize each other by our faces, not our clothing—is skillfuly glossed over.

Jasmine and Aladdin are betrothed by the end and do eventually marry, but not in this movie: the joyous event has to await until the second of the direct-to-video movies, *Aladdin and the King of Thieves* (see below).

Abu

Frank Welker has done excellent bits of voicing work for Disney more times than one could count, but this is probably his best effort. Clarence Nash, in voicing Donald Duck (➤62), had the knack of conveying to the audience exactly what Donald was talking about even though no one could understand a single word. Welker has achieved this before and since *Aladdin*, but here his touch is magical. Probably the finest moment is when Aladdin tells his little monkey chum that they must give their stolen loaf of bread to a couple of street urchins. All we can normally hear from Abu are squeals and squawks, but—and the effect is assisted by the animation of his face—we know precisely what he is saying.

Abu is a glorious trickster character; if it's there to steal he steals it. Much of this thievery is done off-screen, as when he initially snaffles the Magic Lamp from both the Cave of Wonders and Jafar. A tiny figure in his normal form, he is given by the Genie what is presumably regarded as a wish-fulfillment gift when he is magically transformed into an elephant so that "Prince Ali" can ride this magnificent beast into Agrabah when he comes to woo Jasmine. That the "elephant" should assist in this romantic endeavour seems improbable, since from the first Abu has been jealous of the effect Jasmine has on his old buddy—her intrusion might break up their friendship—but Elephant/Abu goes through with it, and is thereafter loyal.

There is a funny bit of comedy from Abu when Aladdin first claps eyes on Jasmine in the *souk* and falls instantly in lust with her. Aladdin's eyes glaze in the way that male eyes do, at least in animated movies (the scene is almost exactly replayed in *The Hunchback of Notre Dame* when Phoebus first sees Esmeralda in the Paris streets). "Uh-oh," cries Abu. "Hello! Hello!" In the meantime he is waving his tiny paw up and down in front of those glazed eyes, which see it not at all. His biggest act of folly—and the monkey produces several for us–comes when he and Aladdin are in the Cave of Wonders. Both know it is essential for their survival that they touch nothing but the lamp; nonetheless, Abu's thieving instincts dominate, and he attempts to steal a huge gem. At that point the Cave begins to swallow the two chums, and they are lucky to escape with their lives—which they wouldn't do were it not for the Genie and the Magic Carpet.

To continue with the theme of *Aladdin* as a descendant of some of the earlier classic Arabian-fantasy movies, it should be noted that the eponymous character in the 1940 Alexander Korda version of *The Thief of Baghdad*, played by Sabu and indeed a lowly market thief to begin with, is called Abu.

Rajah

The characterization of Rajah is one of the most pleasing in the movie; although the role is not a major one, the effect is neatly executed. Before Jasmine makes her escape to the *souk*, Rajah is the only true companion she has—her father, while loving, has no comprehension of her at all. This vast tiger, cleverly animated to give the full impression not just of size but of sheer *weight*—his shoulders bulge and his movements are ponderous—becomes like a kitten when he is in the presence of Jasmine: she hugs him as if he were a domestic cat in her times of sorrow. Even though a real tiger would probably opt to have her for lunch, the scenes between her and Rajah are completely convincing, most likely because of the depiction of his eyes: there is an empathy there of the type we all hope for (and probably we entirely misinterpret the expression) from our own pets. This is most evident when Jasmine tells the tiger that she must explore the world outside the palace, and then climbs over the wall into her temporary freedom: the big cat is sorrowful (he believes he is going to lose his best friend forever) but at the same time he understands the misery she has been suffering.

Rajah's kittenishness is underlined toward the end of the movie, when the Genie has been forced to grant Jafar his wish of being the most powerful sorcerer in the world. With a bolt of light from his fingertips, Jafar turns the mighty tiger into a pathetic little tabby kitten, who gives a desperately plaintive meow.

Genie

Clearly the central story of this movie is about the romance between the urchin Aladdin and the aristocratic Jasmine, but there can be little doubt about who stole the show: the Genie. Released inadver-

tently by Aladdin from the Magic Lamp in which he has been trapped for ten thousand years, this character is, in his normal form, a huge, blue, grinning individual with a trail of "smoke" rather than legs. However, it is not all that often that he is in that normal form: inspired by the wild voice-acting and improvization of Robin Williams, the animators have the Genie shapeshifting in every possible direction, so that at one point he can be tiny, at another there can be several of him dancing around together, and at yet others he can be a submarine, or a man in a Goofy hat, a fruit machine, or even—very briefly—a mimic of the Disney version of Pinocchio (➤166). This constant shapeshifting is an especially impressive feat on the part of the creators in that we are never unaware of the identity of the character on the screen, whatever he looks like at that particular moment. An easy conclusion might be that this is a consequence of the continuity of voice, which definitely plays a large part in the construction of the continuously shapeshifting character, but very much is also owing to the skill of the animators.

The Genie is released into the movie by accident when Aladdin, in the Cave of Wonders, rubs the lamp. Aladdin says:

> Looks like such a worthless, beat-up piece of junk. Hey, I think there's something written here. But it's, it's, it's hard to make out.

Then Aladdin brushes away the dust that is covering the writing he is trying to read, and suddenly the Genie emerges as a whirlwind that includes various wild animals, then instantly bursts into a set of vocal and visual impersonations, including Arnold Schwarzenegger and Ed Sullivan, and others:

> *Genie*: So, what'll it be, Master?
> *Aladdin*: You're gonna grant me any three wishes I want, right?
> *Genie as William F. Buckley*: Uh, almost. There are a few provisos. A, a couple of quid pro quos.
> *Aladdin*: Like?

> *Genie*: Uh, rule number one: I can't kill anybody. So don't ask. Uh, rule number two: I can't make anybody fall in love with anybody. . . . [*as Peter Lorre*] Rule number three: I can't bring people back from the dead. It's not a pretty picture. I don't like doing it! Other than that, you got it.
> *Aladdin*: Provisos. You mean limitations? On wishes? Some all-powerful genie. Can't even bring people back from the dead. I don't know, Abu. He probably can't even get us out of this cave. Looks like we're gonna have to find a way out of here.
> *Genie as Robert DeNiro*: Excuse me. Are you lookin' at me? Did you rub my lamp? Did you wake me up? Did you bring me here and all of a sudden you're walkin' out on me? I don't think so. Not right now. You're gettin' your wishes, so sit down!

Aladdin duly states (rather than wishes, so that he gets a freebie) that he and Abu—plus the Magic Carpet and the Genie, as it turns out—should be released from the cave. The first explicitly stated wish is to be a prince, so that he can woo Jasmine. The next occurs when, heavily weighted, he has been thrown into a lake by Jafar's men on the assumption that, Mafia-style, he will be drowned. Underwater and stunned, Aladdin for obvious reasons has some difficulty making this wish:

> Oh, you can't cheat on this one! I can't help you unless you make a wish! You have to say, "Genie, I want you to save my life." Got it? Okay! Come on, Aladdin!

Aladdin's head slumps forward, and the Genie cries delightedly, "I'll take that as a yes." He transforms himself into a submarine (which speaks Mittel European) as he hoists Aladdin from the water. After the rescue he says, "I'm gettin' kinda fond of you kid." Then he adds: "Not that I wanna pick out curtains or anything." Aladdin's third wish will be to set the Genie free, but before that Iago, on Jafar's behalf, steals the Lamp, so that the Genie becomes the slave of the vizier. Jafar's greed for power proves his downfall as he makes one wish too many, desiring to be a genie and thus being enslaved in a Magic Lamp.

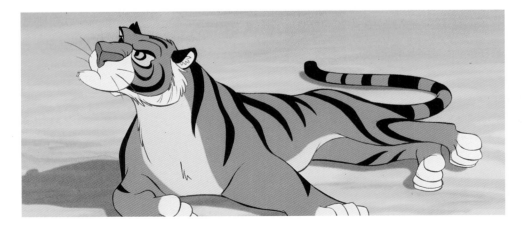

Rajah.

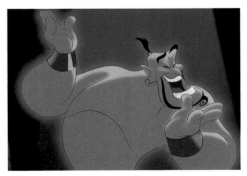

The incomparable Genie.

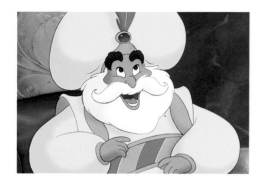

The Sultan.

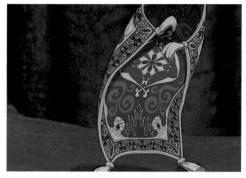

The Magic Carpet, who is always ready to help Aladdin.

Sultan

Portly and chubby-faced, with a large turban and a small stature, the Sultan hardly conforms to one's image of the average despot, yet he is a despot toward his daughter: confined within the palace walls, she must choose a suitor of noble blood by the time she is sixteen, because that is the law. It does not occur to the Sultan until very late in the movie that, although he did not originate the law, it is within his power to change it if he wants to, and it never seems to cross his mind that it is an unjust law—a stupid and bigoted tradition. Yet it is also very clear that he loves his daughter more than anything in the world: it is simply that he cannot understand what seems to him to be her perversity, her demand for independence.

The Sultan is slow on the uptake about most things. It takes him a very long while indeed to realize that he has unwittingly passed the rule of Agrabah over to his vizier, Jafar, who can control him hypnotically by use of his magical cobra-headed staff. When finally the truth is made plain to him—Aladdin smashes the cobra head, thus lifting the mesmeric spell—he is clearly astonished that his power has been usurped.

Aside from Jasmine, his other passion is collecting toys—another echo of the 1940 version of *The Thief of Baghdad*, whose Sultan has a similar hobby.

Magic Carpet

For a sequence of Disney features during the 1990s it has been a practice to concentrate a considerable amount on objects that would be, in the real world, regarded as inanimate: in *Oliver & Company* (➤335) there is Fagin's trike; in *The Rescuers Down Under* (➤357) there is the amazingly articulated bushwacker driven by Percival McLeach; in *Beauty and the Beast* there are the enchanted objects; in *The Hunchback of Notre Dame* (➤421) there are of course the bouncing Gargoyles. In *Aladdin* the focus is on the Magic Carpet, and here the "animated inanimate" is again given a personality of its own. When it first meets Aladdin in

the Cave of Wonders it is a coy creature, slipping quickly out of sight whenever it believes either Aladdin or Abu might have seen it. Later, assuming that the two have been largely instrumental in freeing it from the Cave—although in fact the truth is really the converse—it becomes their strong ally. Mainly blue, but with gold tassels at each corner, the Magic Carpet could be described as the furnishing equivalent of Marilyn Monroe.

Jafar

The evil vizier is represented as a caricature villain—he has a long thin face, a curly black wisp of beard, two great spikes of *something* sticking out from the shoulders of his customary garb, an unpleasant habit of hypnotizing people, a sinister voice, and very much more. However, the exaggeration works: the characterization is such that we early become fully aware of his evil, and we cheer when he gets his deserved comeuppance. Much of this is, of course, a result of his deeds: we discover that he abuses power, both political and financial. He shows no compunction at all, having discovered the Cave of Wonders and cognizant that the Magic Lamp is contained within, in sacrificing the life of the criminal Gazeem in an ill-fated attempt to steal

the Lamp. He lies cruelly to Jasmine in telling her that the street rat (Aladdin) who saved her from having her hand chopped off has been beheaded for the crime of kidnapping her (an obvious miscarriage of justice); the measure of his general cruelty is that she believes him. He employs every tricky means he can—notably hypnosis using his cobra-headed stick—in order to gain complete control over the sultanate of Agrabah. When Aladdin delivers the Magic Lamp to him (or so they both think—Abu has filched it) he tries to kill the "diamond in the rough" whom he has exploited. And, when Aladdin is in his guise as Prince Ali, Jafar does his best to humiliate him by constantly getting his name wrong—calling him Prince Abooboo—a petty trick known to playground bullies worldwide. The list of sins is a long one.

Like the Genie, although certainly not to the same extent, he is a shapeshifter. When Aladdin has been clapped in jail for the crime of theft, there is an old beggar sharing his cell: he has a long beard, a crutch, rotten teeth . . . and is overall a character to be pitied. It is this person who persuades Aladdin that they must retrieve the Magic Lamp, and who engineers their escape from prison. The beggar proves to be Jafar, disguised within this different form. Interestingly, the animators chose—once Aladdin's task within the Cave of Wonders had apparently been performed—to show the "beggar" stripping off his costume to reveal himself as the vizier, but this is a bluff on their part that does not work: the two individuals are so differently constructed, physically, that it is impossible that Jafar could have merely dressed himself up.

Ambition is what drives Jafar, and it is this ambition that proves his downfall. He wants to usurp the Sultan. He wants to marry the luscious Jasmine in order to cement that usurpation. He wants to become the most powerful sorcerer in the world, a wish that the Genie is forced to grant. With his new magic he makes him-

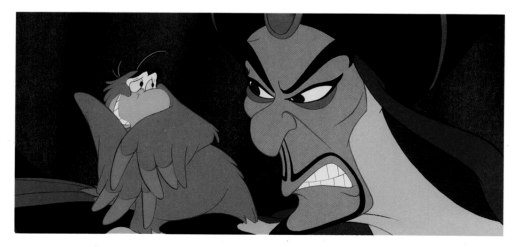

The scheming vizier Jafar with his constant companion Iago.

self into a giant serpent so that he can squeeze the life out of Aladdin . . . except that finally Aladdin tricks him into a further desire than that: the vizier wants to become an all-powerful genie himself. What he doesn't realize, until too late, is that genies are not in fact all-powerful: they can be confined in Magic Lamps, and this is exactly what Aladdin does to the transformed vizier.

The imprisonment proved not to be permanent, as we discovered in *The Return of Jafar* (see below).

Iago

Jafar's sidekick is an irascible parrot, who—unusually for birds—has teeth, and a lot of them at that. Hilariously voiced by Gilbert Gottfried at a general level of about one hundred decibels, Iago is as malicious as his master (although his character changed for *The Return of Jafar*—see below). As is customary in the animated features, he is constantly being subjected to indignities by the one he serves—at one memorable stage he is deliberately trapped by Jafar in a sliding door—yet in this instance the slave is wiser than the master, for it is Iago who has the idea that Jafar's tactic to attain the sultanate should be through marrying Jasmine.

Peddler

The Peddler is the one who introduces us, in song, to the story. With a huge turban and a chubby face, he makes it clear through his dialogue that here is someone nobody should trust—his story is almost certainly going to be a lie—and certainly someone from whom nobody should buy. He addresses the audience directly, and thus is really a narrator rather than a character in his own right. But he is very entertaining in his short part in the movie:

> Welcome to Agrabah, city of mystery, of enchantment . . . and the finest merchandise this side of the River Jordan. On sale today! Come on down. Look at this. Yes, combination hookah and coffeemaker, also makes julienne fries. Will not break.

Promptly, as he demonstrates its supposed toughness, it breaks. But he carries on with his hucksterism, still addressed to the viewers:

> Look at this. I have never seen one of these intact before. This is the famous Dead Sea Tupperware. Listen. [*He opens the lid of what looks like a plastic box, meanwhile imitating the sound of an airtight seal being broken.*] Ah, still good.

By this time, of course, we have realized him for the fraud he is, but then he pro-

duces the Magic Lamp to drag us into the tale of the "diamond in the rough." A very pretty effect is that from the spout emerge onto the Peddler's hand a multitude of white lights; these he throws into the night sky, where they become the stars. The symbolism is, obviously, that we have now entered the realm of magic. From here on, anything is possible.

Tiger's Head

The Tiger's Head is both the face of the Cave of Wonders and its voice. The Cave has been (we guess) unknown for many generations, yet Jafar knows that the Magic Lamp is somewhere within it. The logic of the plot is not particularly strong here, so that viewers have to take on trust what is being offered to them; the visuals and the imagery, however, are breathtaking. Jafar has hired the bandit Gazeem to find the second half of a gold scarab that will enable him to find the Cave. Those two molded pieces of gold, hurled into the desert sands, become the glowing eyes of the monstrous head—whose mouth is the Cave's entrance—which rears up to confront the would-be insurgents with the question, spoken in deep tones, "Who disturbs my slumber?" The first to do so at Jafar's behest is Gazeem (see below), and he gets chomped in short shrift. The Tiger's Head, with a shiningly golden throat between its impressive teeth, demands a "diamond in the rough" as a person who might enter its mouth—the phrase has already been overused in the movie—and finally Jafar tracks down Aladdin as a candidate.

What is exciting about the animation of the Tiger's Head, aside from the beauty of the depiction, is the sense of sheer *mass* that is conveyed through the artwork. Even when one looks at a still of the character one is immediately aware one is looking at a structure that is *big*.

Minor Characters

Gazeem is a general crook whom Jafar recruits to send into the Cave of Wonders in search of the Magic Lamp; he is small, plump, and exudes a redolence of sleaze, and therefore he doesn't last very long after his trepiditous entry into the Cave. **Razoul** is the Chief Guard in Agrabah—or, at least, the leader of the bunch of guards who chase the miscreant Aladdin on several occasions and who are generally, and treacherously, beholden to Jafar rather than the Sultan. As Razoul puts it himself to Aladdin, "We just keep running into each other, don't we, street rat?" He is a very clumsy would-be nemesis, and naturally gets his comeuppance. **Prince Achmed** is the sole aristocratic suitor of Jasmine's that we see; he is representative of all the others we have been

told have come to try to win her hand. Dialogue gives the key to his arrogant personality as, on horseback in the midst of a seemingly triumphal parade, he comes across the couple of street waifs whom Aladdin and Abu have just fed from their meager (and stolen) resources:

> *Achmed*: Out of my way, you filthy brats! [*He raises a whip at them, but Aladdin snatches it out of his grasp.*]
> *Aladdin*: Hey! If I were as rich as you I could afford some manners.
> *Achmed*: I'll teach you some manners! [*He charges down on Aladdin and kicks him into a puddle.*]
> *Aladdin*: Look at that, Abu. It's not every day you see a horse with two rear ends.
> *Achmed*: Ha! You are a worthless street rat. You were born a street rat. You'll die a street rat, and only your fleas will mourn you.
> *Aladdin*: I'm not worthless. And I don't have fleas!

The message—that riches are less important than the person—could not be hammered into us more heavily, so it comes as no surprise when, moments later, our last view of Achmed is of him having been thrown out on his ear by Jasmine, who has accurately perceived him as the arrogant fool he is.

Various merchants are encountered by Aladdin and then Jasmine in the *souk*; they are all just bit parts except the **Fruit Vendor** from whose stall Jasmine, in her ignorance, takes an apple to give to an urchin, not realizing that such a matter as payment is important. The vendor is preparing to chop off Jasmine's hand by way of punishment when Aladdin steps in to save her. Also in the *souk* is a skinny, scantily clad **Fire-Eater**, whose highly dramatic act is ignored by all around him. And there are, of course, those two **Street Waifs**, obviously orphans thrown out to starve; the acts of Jasmine, Aladdin, and a somewhat reluctant Abu in offering them food give us a clear indication, from the outset, of who the good guys are going to be. **Sebastian** (➤346) the crab from *The Little Mermaid*, makes a very brief appearance, being plucked from a book of recipes by the Genie.

SPINOFFS

Aside from the television series (➤146) derived from the movie, there have been two direct-to-video sequels.

The first was *The Return of Jafar* (1994), which was directed by Toby Shelton, Tad Stones, and Alan Zaslove. Most of the voices were as before, the only important change being the substitution of Dan Castellaneta (a courageous man!) for Robin Williams as the Genie.

The plot is not complicated. Iago

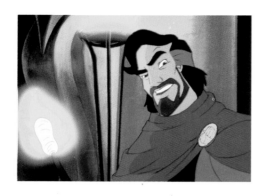

The legendary Cassim, leader of the Forty Thieves, and Aladdin's long-lost father, in the spin-off film *Aladdin and the King of Thieves*.

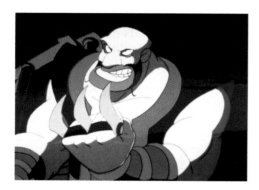

The evil Salouk, the bad guy in *Aladdin and the King of Thieves*.

switches sides and ingratiates himself with Aladdin, who has yet formally to be betrothed to Jasmine. **Abi Smal**, a thief whose enmity Aladdin has earned, discovers the Lamp and releases Jafar who,

although still bound by the Lamp's restrictions, seeks revenge on Aladdin. He fails and is destroyed. Aladdin rejects the Grand Viziership offered to him by the Sultan and, with Jasmine and the rest, decides to seek adventure in the wide world—thereby setting things up for the succeeding television series. Some spectacular visuals are involved in the shapeshifting activities of both Jafar and the Genie, and the whole production has the same joyous flamboyance as its big-screen precursor. Direct-to-video movies usually have a half-heartedness about them. This is an exception.

Aladdin and the King of Thieves (1996) has many charms, including a quick cameo turn from Tinker Bell (➤249) and a short representation of Jasmine as Snow White (➤159). Less attractive, among the Genie's many acts of shapeshifting, are his performances as Woody Allen, Mrs. Doubtfire, Bob Hope, Bing Crosby, Albert Einstein, Pumbaa (➤393), Pluto (➤38), Elvis Presley, and even as Mickey Mouse in *Steamboat Willie* (➤24); it is tiresome of the moviemakers to have thought that such stale tricks would make us automatically laugh. Most kids watching the movie wouldn't know who was being parodied; most adults probably feel patronized. This is cheap humor.

Screenplay was by Mark McCorckle and Robert Schooley; production and direction were by Tad Stones. A lot of the animation was done in Japan, and quite often this shows; some of the scenes have the stripped-back feeling of animé. The cast are much as usual, except that Williams has returned to voice the Genie.

Jasmine and Aladdin are about to be married when the legendary **Cassim** and the Forty Thieves raid the Palace of Agrabah in search of loot. It proves that Cassim is not quite the villain he seems; moreover, he is Aladdin's long-lost father. However, Cassim's lieutenant, **Salouk**—who has three golden claws on one hand where his fingers should be—has plans to do away with the leader of the Thieves.

Assisted by an **Oracle**—a spectral female robed figure who habitually occupies much of the night sky—Aladdin, Jasmine, Iago, Abu, and the Magic Carpet track down the Thieves to their hidden cave, which is on an isolated peak of land, which one can reach only by crying "Open Sesame," at which point the sea splits (as per Moses) and the cave door opens. What Cassim and Salouk seek most of all is a legendary treasure, the long-lost Hand of Midas, which turns everything to gold. With Aladdin's help, Cassim finds it in the Vanishing Isle, which appears only occasionally, being borne on the back of a giant turtle. Salouk has followed; he foolishly catches the Hand of Midas when Aladdin throws it to him, and thus is himself turned to gold.

Cassim realizes the real treasure he has discovered is not the magic hand but his son, whose marriage to Jasmine he covertly watches before riding off with Iago to commit, one assumes, further thievery.

The world is full of animated movies far worse than *Aladdin and the King of Thieves*; however, it is pleasing that the series came to an end before there was yet another sequel.

TIM BURTON'S THE NIGHTMARE BEFORE CHRISTMAS

Characters:

Jack Skellington; Sally; Evil Scientist; Mayor; Zero; Lock; Shock; Barrel; Oogie Boogie; Santa Claus; Shadow Chorus; Ghost Chorus; Creature Under the Bed; Man Under the Stairs; Vampires; Big Witch; Small Witch; Cat; Harlequin Demon; Wolfman; Melting Man; Hanging Tree; Skeletons; Clown with the Tearaway Face; Ghouls; Corpse Kid; Corpse Mom; Corpse Dad; Withered Winged Demon; Behemoth; Mr. Hyde; Cyclops; Undersea Gal; Sax Player; Bass Player; Man in the Bass; Accordion Player; Devil; Igor; Bathtub; Easter Bunny; Mrs. Claus; Timmie; Wanda; Ronnie; Howie; Granny; Police Sergeant; Radio Announcer

Credits:

Voices: Sherwood Ball (Mummy; Vampire); Randy Crenshaw (Mr. Hyde; Behemoth; Vampire); Debi Durst (Corpse Kid; Corpse Mom; Small Witch); Danny Elfman (Jack Skellington singing; Barrel; Clown with the Tearaway Face); William Hickey (Evil Scientist); Ed Ivory (Santa Claus); Kerry Katz (Man Under the Stairs; Vampire; Corpse Dad); Susan McBride (Big Witch; Withered Winged Demon); Catherine O'Hara (Sally; Shock); Ken Page (Oogie Boogie); Gregory Proops (Harlequin Demon; Devil; Sax Player); Chris Sarandon (Jack Skellington speaking); Glenn Shadix (Mayor); Carmen Twillie (Undersea Gal; Man Under the Stairs); Glenn Walters (Wolfman)

Additional Voices: Mia Brown; L. Peter Callender; Judy Durand; Ann Fraser; Doris Hess; Daamen Krall; Jennifer Levey; David McCharen; Jesse McClurg; Christina MacGregor; John Morris; Robert Olague; Bobbi Page; Elena Praskin; Gary Raff; David Randolph; Gary Schwartz; Trampas Warman

Supervising Sound Editor: Richard L. Anderson

Special Sound Effects: John Pospisil

Sound Effects Editors: Michael Chock; James Christopher

Music: Danny Elfman

Songs by: Danny Elfman

Story and Characters: Tim Burton

Animation Screenplay: Caroline Thompson, based on adaptation by Michael McDowell

Storyboard Supervisor: Joe Ranft

Editor: Stan Webb

Production Manager: Philip Lofaro

Animation Supervisor: Eric Leighton

Animators: Michael Belzer; Paul Berry; Kim Blanchette; Stephen A. Buckley; Joel

Fletcher; Angie Glocka; Timothy Hittle; Owen Klatte; Justin Kohn; Eric Leighton; Loyd Price; Anthony Scott; Trey Thomas; Richard C. Zimmerman

Effects Animators: Gordon Baker; Miguel Domingo Cachuela; Chris Green

Art Director: Deane Taylor

Director of Photography: Pete Kozachik

Coproducer: Kathleen Gavin

Associate Producers: Danny Elfman; Jill Jacobs; Philip Lofaro; Diane Minter

Producers: Tim Burton; Denise DiNovi

Director: Henry Selick

Release Date: October 13, 1993; general release October 22, 1993

Running Time: 76 minutes

THE MOVIE

Described in *Samhain* by that magazine's editor, John Gullidge, as "the best movie ever made, without exception," this is hardly likely to disappoint even those who would not wholeheartedly endorse Gullidge's opinion. *The Encyclopedia of Fantasy* (edited by John Clute and John Grant, 1997), while generally approving, is a little more critical:

The Nightmare Before Christmas is a visually riveting movie; it is improbable that any other stop-motion animated movie equals it for technical proficiency. The script, largely in verse and much of it narrated or sung, has a mesmeric, driving quality that is somehow light rather than oppressive; the underlying fantasy premise is fascinating. The voice acting and characterization are superb. And yet, as so often with Burton's work, one comes away with the feeling that it could have been better: for much of its duration it promises as climax something truly spectacular, but then it fails to deliver, as if Burton, nearing the end, were suddenly in a hurry to get the whole thing wrapped up and over with. Nevertheless, viewed as an artwork rather than as a story, *The Nightmare Before Christmas* is magnificent.

As it was the present author who wrote that paragraph, there is, as you might expect, no critical dissent with it in *this* book.

According to Frank Thompson's book *Tim Burton's Nightmare Before Christmas* (1993)—which discusses the genesis and making of the movie at some length—the idea for the movie came to Burton while he was still working as an animator at Disney in the 1980s. The studio wasn't ready for his ideas at the time, and in the end he left to direct a succession of hit fantasy movies—*Beetlejuice* (1988), *Batman* (1989), and *Edward Scissorhands*

(1990). In most of these he displayed a deliberately somewhat circumscribed directorial vision of the world, maintaining everything within what John Clute has described as a "polder": the action of *Batman* never ventures outside Gotham City, while that of *Edward Scissorhands* is placed in a commuter dormitory whose artificiality is relentlessly stressed and which is utterly separated from the real world, as if Burton were trying to tell us that the little town is a variant of the place where fairy tales come from (which for the purposes of that movie indeed it is). Another common factor shared by his various movies is the theme of the misfit as hero. This is overt in *Edward Scissorhands* , but it is also very evident in Burton's two Batman movies—the other being *Batman Returns* (1992). The villains of these two movies are also misfits, but Burton gives them, too, some frisson of heroism.

By the early 1990s, then, Burton had a fair amount of commercial clout: no studio that he approached with an idea for a movie was *not* going to take him seriously. Although to a lesser extent, his name on the posters had the same magic touch as Steven Spielberg's: people flocked to a Burton movie. (This is undoubtedly why the full name of the movie is *Tim Burton's The Nightmare Before Christmas*, although it is generally referred to as just *The Nightmare Before Christmas*.) A revived Disney—more accurately, Touchstone—was only too eager to accept the idea that the company had earlier rejected. Yet Burton chose not to direct the movie himself, instead giving that role to Henry Selick, who had worked with him at Disney and who had shared his dream of making *The Nightmare Before Christmas*. Selick's contribution to the movie was enormous. Despite the full title, *The Nightmare Before Christmas* was very much a joint effort between the two men, and although it is clearly a Burton movie, it is visibly a Selick movie as well.

One element of the movie is distinctly Disney: the moral that you should not try to be who you are not. This is slightly disappointing, because if one rephrases that message it is saying that one should not have ambitions or aspirations.

The Nightmare Before Christmas caused a sensation on its release. Willis H. O'Brien and then Ray Harryhausen had used stop-motion extensively in creating their special effects for various monster (and other) movies. Will Vinton had made, using his "Claymation," a stop-motion animated feature a few years earlier, *The Adventures of Mark Twain* (1985), but this had not been a hit. The Czech director and animator Jan Svankmajer had made a stop-motion feature not long before— *Alice* (1988)—and would make another feature partly using stop-motion—*Faust*

(1994)—but both of these, though excellent, were regarded as "difficult" and hence more or less restricted to the arthouse circuit. Stop-motion has been used for numerous children's television shows, and by Nick Park in his Oscar-winning *Wallace and Gromit* shorts. Burton and Selick, however, created a stop-motion movie (there are moments of orthodox animation) that was both populist *and* designed not just for kids but for adults as well. Through their characters they were able to convey a warmth of emotion that Svankmajer's movies lack (deliberately, because his objectives are entirely different). Highly successful on theatrical release, and certain to be revived frequently at the obvious season of the year, *The Nightmare Before Christmas* had lines forming when it was issued on video. And it deserved those lines.

THE STORY

The story of *The Nightmare Before Christmas* is comparatively simple but is based on a delicious fantasy premise. Around a glade stands a circle of trees, each having in its bark an appropriately painted and shaped door that serves as a portal to one of the "holiday towns"— Christmas Town, Halloween Town, and so forth. In these towns dwell the various creatures whose activities make up the character of each holiday. Of course, such individuals are in real life merely mental creations—unless the reader still believes in Santa Claus—but for the purposes of this fiction they are regarded as having genuine physical form and entering our world once a year in order to strut their stuff.

In Halloween Town—which is of course the one we are primarily interested in—the populace are returning from what they feel has been their best and most frightening Halloween ever, the star of the show having been, as always, Jack Skellington, the Pumpkin King. Yet Jack himself is bored with the whole affair— he has been "doing" Halloween too long. Strolling in the forest with his ghostly dog, Zero, he discovers the glade with its ring of trees and, prying, falls into Christmas Town. He is delighted by what he discovers, and determines that he will, this coming Christmas, take over the role of Santa Claus and *do Christmas better*. Many of the assorted ghosts, ghouls, vampires, and so forth, of Halloween Town have their doubts—notably the rag doll Sally, who loves Jack deeply and silently but has the gumption to tell him that the whole effort is going to be a disaster—but they fall in with his plans because, after all, he is the Pumpkin King. Jack sends Lock, Shock, and Barrel, three noxious little trick-or-treaters to kidnap Santa Claus while the whole town prepares presents and stockings and all the usual paraphernalia of Christmas.

Sally was right: Jack's attempt to be Santa *is* a disaster. The folk of Halloween Town wildly misjudge the nature of the toys children expect at Christmas: a shrunken head, a vast and voracious boa constrictor that swallows an unfortunate family's Christmas tree—these are not gifts generally associated with Santa's cries of "ho, ho, ho." Yet Jack, oblivious of the terror he is causing, believes he is spreading joy wherever he goes . . . until the people of the real world shoot down his sleigh, with its team of fleshless reindeer. He returns to Halloween Town a sadder but wiser skeleton, determined to release Santa Claus in hopes that the situation can be remedied. What he discovers is that Lock, Shock, and Barrel—always untrustworthy—have handed Santa to Halloween Town's one truly evil citizen, Oogie Boogie, the bogey man. Oogie Boogie proposes to kill and eat Santa—and also Sally, who has mounted a rescue attempt but has been caught by the monster. Jack arrives, destroys the creature, and saves the day. There is still time for Santa to travel the world giving all the children their *real* presents, and after he has departed Jack and Sally acknowledge their love.

THE CHARACTERS

Jack Skellington

In every respect, Jack is the most important character in the movie. Not only does the story center almost exclusively on his activities, so that he is on screen for the majority of the time, but it is his misguided inspiration that drives the plot; furthermore, the image of him standing against the backdrop of a full moon has become instantly recognizable and represents the movie as a whole. These days one could advertise *The Nightmare Before Christmas* without having to put the title on the poster. Aside from Jack, only Sally and perhaps Oogie Boogie can really be regarded as major characters, and even their roles are almost trivial by comparison with his.

He appears briefly in the opening sequences, but we first properly encounter him as the Halloween Town citizens are returning after their night of fright in the human world. Jack, star of this year's show (as always), arrives to a great accolade and performs an act of fire-eating and then what can best be described as a cartwheel of flame. He plunges into a well to quench the blaze that is himself, then rises from the water, an arm outstretched, in a sequence that

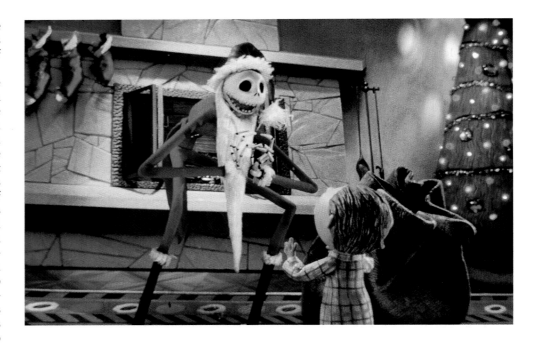
Jack Skellington, dressed as Santa Claus, is about to make one youngster very unhappy.

seems deliberately to echo the Ascension of Christ—a very clever touch, and one that is quite devoid of any blasphemy. But all is not what it seems; although he accepts the plaudits of his peers, he is sick at heart. Collecting his loyal ghost-dog Zero from the animal's plot in the cemetery, he sings to the night sky of his boredom:

I, Jack, the Pumpkin King,
Have grown so tired of the same old thing.

(This is a very good song, full of pathos rather than bathos: Jack is someone who seems to have everything except happiness. Indeed, the songs in this movie are generally excellent. Danny Elfman, who wrote them, also sings Jack's part—Chris Sarandon speaks it.)

Jack doesn't know it, but shy rag doll Sally has followed and is observing; it is immediately obvious to us that she loves the Pumpkin King but dare not say so. Jack, with Zero floating through the air nearby, walks off into the forest and discovers Christmas Town. There is a sweet moment of humor en route when he throws the demandingly barking Zero a bone—one of Jack's own ribs.

Zero doesn't follow him as the Pumpkin King stumbles into Christmas Town; there Jack's glee on discovering a land of happy children, toys, and toiling elves is childlike, as is his covetousness, because he decides he wants all this for himself. And so the plot is hatched and the rest of the story occurs. Throughout the movie this childish aspect of Jack is emphasized—especially when, in his naïve guise as Santa Claus, he is delivering hideous gifts to the world's children with no realization at all of the devasta-

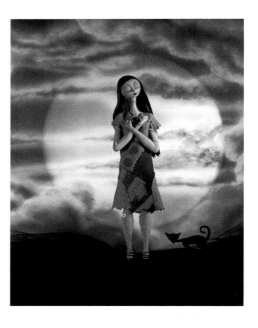
The rag doll, Sally, who secretly loves Jack.

tion he is causing—until the moment comes when he must abruptly grow up. His sleigh is shot down by soldiers, and he falls into the Halloween Town cemetery, landing with a crash on the open stone book held by a statuary angel. Thereafter the juvenility has been knocked out of him; he must become an adult, accepting the adult responsibilities of trying to set matters aright, dueling with Oogie Boogie to free Sally and Santa, realizing that he must occupy his rightful place in the scheme of things, and recognizing Sally's love for him. Perhaps the childishness of Jack's attempt to take over Christmas has been a one-off aberration, or perhaps he may attempt something similar again: we are not told. But, at least for a time, his experiences have made him a more mature individual.

One could hardly have predicted that a character whose limbs are spaghetti-thin and whose face is a simplified skull would be so appealing, but that is what Jack is. He is also fascinating, with his nimbleness and his delight in discovery. He is also *a* Jack—by which one refers to the oft-appearing personality in myth and legend, the Jack (who under this or any other name) can be a giant-killer or Puck or Robin Hood. At an early point in the movie he displays the jacklike ability to perfection when he plucks his skull from his neck and it continues to sing:

> *And since I am dead*
> *I can take off my head*
> *To recite Shakespearean quotations . . .*

The reference to "Alas, poor Yorick" is a sublime jest on the part of the moviemakers, but there is more to this moment than that. Jack figures are what we would like to be—they are, in part, Everyman—but they can do things that we could never do, and so we admire and identify with them. This is certainly the case with Jack Skellington, even at the height of his folly he is a hero. *Our* hero.

Sally

Jack is certainly the mainspring of the movie, but perhaps its most sympathetic character is Sally. She is a big-eyed, reticent rag doll who loves Jack from afar, but she is more than that. Like Jack she is a monster whom one comes to love (although she has been designed to offer a more instant attraction, with her wide eyes, her flowing brown hair, and her demureness of movement), but she is the analogue of a *specific* monster: the one created by Baron Frankenstein. In the novel in which Mary Shelley created that character, *Frankenstein, or The Modern Prometheus* (1818), there is no suggestion that the creature was stitched together, but that has become something of a convention in the dozens of movies based on or extending Shelley's tale, and it is the one followed here. She has been rather crudely sewn together by the Evil Scientist during his creation of her, and this gives her the advantage, at crucial moments, of being able to quickly unpick the stitches that have been holding a limb or a part of a limb in place. Furthermore, she is then capable of operating that part of her body as if it were still joined onto her; for example, when she is attempting to rescue Santa Claus from Oogie Boogie's lair, she detaches a leg with which to distract the beast with a sexy enticement, plus her hands, which scurry to untie the knots that bind Santa.

There is a further connection with Baron Frankenstein's monster: She hates her creator. He's easy enough to hate, in that he treats her as his slave—on the principle that she owes her existence to him—and is anyway repellent. During the course of the movie she attempts with various herbs such as Deadly Nightshade to poison him and put an end to her servitude. At last she is released by Jack's love and because the Evil Scientist builds a female replica of himself—a rather more murky analogue of the bride the original Frankenstein constructed for his monster.

Jack has an impish innocence. Sally has an almost childlike one (Jack's is childlike too, but in a different way), a point underlined in various ways, as in her inability to declare her love to the Pumpkin King and in her inferiority complex (she is easily the prettiest and kindest resident of Halloween Town, yet assumes the opposite) but most especially in the nature of her singing voice, which could easily be that of a child.

> *And does he notice my feelings for him?*
> *And will he see how much he means to me?*
> *I think it's not to be.*
> *. . .*
> *And will we ever end up together?*
> *No, I think not. It's never to become,*
> *For I am not the one . . .*

As she sings in her half-broken voice about Jack, she brings together all three of the elements that indicate her childlike innocence. Yet there's a big difference between innocence and foolishness, as Sally demonstrates. Jack's folly in trying to take over Christmas occurs because in so many ways he is an innocent, a naïf—

he is too carried away by his rash scheme ever to think there might be something wrong with it, or to listen to doubting voices—but Sally, with the clarity of a child's mental vision, can see right through it to its underlying foolishness. Moreover, timid and childish or not, it is she who first penetrates Oogie Boogie's lair to try to save Santa—an act of considerable courage. The experience transforms her, in parallel with the transformation of Jack, into a full-scale adult: In the very final scenes of the movie there is no question but that she is now a woman.

Perhaps the most revealing line she utters is very early in the movie, when she has overheard Jack singing of his boredom with the status quo, of his *angst*. "Jack," she says, "I know how you feel." This very simple line might seem at first to be expressing nothing more than her love and sympathy for him, but it is doing more than that. The structure of Halloween Town and its annual activities have been the same for far too long, and both of them have recognized this in personal terms—she rather more clearly than he. He tries to change affairs in an extroverted and ultimately madcap fashion—clearly he's an alpha male. She, despite her attempts to poison her creator, takes a more rational, quiet approach.

Evil Scientist

Named as Dr. Finklestein in Thompson's book about the movie though not in the movie itself, nor in the script—it may have been a name bandied about in the animation studios—this character is, as noted above, an analogue of Mary Shelley's Baron Frankenstein. But, where-

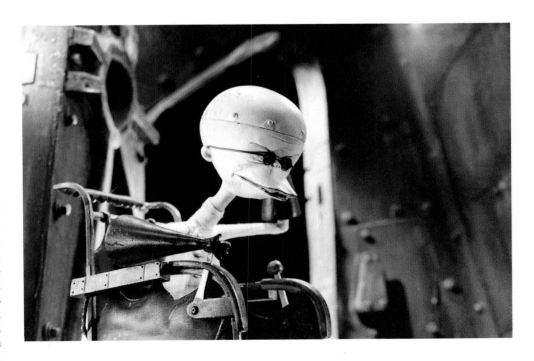

Sally's wheelchair-bound creator and tormentor, the Evil Scientist.

as Frankenstein was a misguided quester after scientific truth, this version is decidedly evil. His face is somewhat like that of a duck, although with teeth inside the bill, and his voice is like that of a spoiled child grown old. He believes that Sally, as his creation, is also his possession: she must be his housekeeper and who knows what else because she owes everything to him. In his worldview, it is impossible for him to understand that she might legitimately desire independence from him—hence her frequent attempts to poison him and gain her freedom. When she is "bad" he locks her in an attic equivalent of a cellar.

Physically he is no beauty. Aside from the characteristics already mentioned, he has the ability to tip back the top of his skull and quite literally scratch his brain. He travels around in a powered wheelchair (many have expressed dubiety about this seeming connection between disability and evil, though it is something one thinks about on the way home from the movies rather than while watching the film). But physique really has nothing to do with his portrayal as a nasty; what conveys that is his behavior toward Sally.

His house looks from the outside rather like a plumped-up radio telescope. Inside, it pays homage to the mill in which the Baron Frankenstein of James Whale's movie *Frankenstein* (1931) created his home and laboratory, with a helical path to the upper floors just like the helical staircase in Whale's version. The lab itself is full of predictable bubbling retorts and even an eyeball held between the jaws of a clamp.

Although she hates him and often tries to kill him, Sally also regularly encourages him to construct someone else who would be happier with him, and in the end the Evil Scientist does so—a creature in his own mold, but female.

A brief appearance is made by his one-eyed assistant, Igor, who looks just like one of the many Igors who have appeared in the *Frankenstein* movies over the years.

Mayor

The Mayor of Halloween Town, although only a subsidiary character (despite his having a fair amount of screen time), is an interesting fantasy creation. The main part of his body is perfectly conical, with tiny feet waddling beneath and arms sticking out from no perceptible shoulders; even his head, on top of which perches precariously a ridiculously tall stovepipe hat, follows the line of the cone. He wears a spider as a bow tie. It is the head itself that is such an inspiration on the part of the creators, for the Mayor has two faces.

That bald statement might give the impression that he is a Janus figure, but certainly he is no god ("I'm just an elected official")—indeed, he seems to have no power at all within Halloween Town. In the movie's script the Mayor's two faces are described as Optimistic Face and Pessimistic Face; in order to show one or the other, the Mayor swivels his head a full 180 degrees—although he can also swivel his body while leaving his head in the same position. The Optimistic Face is that of any basically useless small-town politician: tanned and elaborately healthy, it rarely bears anything other than a falsely confident smile (expressed also in the eyes) as the mouth booms the glad news that everything is well within the community. At the slightest reversal, however, the Mayor's head rotates to present the bleak and anguished Pessimistic Face; this face may be angry but is more usually in despair, revealing the weakness of the politician.

Using the term "two-faced" about politicians is not uncommon. To see it taken literally causes a smile.

Zero

Jack's loyal pup is a wraith who "lives" in a grave in Halloween Town's cemetery, but can come out of the ground whenever called. Clearly devoted to his master, behind and around whom he drifts through the air rather than walks, the semitransparent Zero appears to be orthodoxly animated rather than rendered by stop-motion. Apparently this was not the case. As with the other characters, Zero was modeled, and thereafter the solidity was removed from his image to convey his ghostliness.

That Zero is a dog one can tell mainly by his barking and by his behavior; his physique is not particularly doggish, aside from his floppy ears. The very tip of his nose is a glowing red blob, and this plays a significant part in the plot. Sally, knowing that Jack is about to make the biggest mistake of his life by trying to be a substitute Santa Claus, tries to arrest his venture by pouring "Fog Juice" into the Halloween Town well. This makes the atmosphere so murky that there is no possibility of Jack launching his sleigh, and therefore her ploy seems successful. However, Jack then suddenly realizes that Zero's glowing nose can guide the reindeer through the gloom—and so the party sets off, just like Santa would have done with Rudolph the Red-Nosed Reindeer.

Lock, Shock, and Barrel

Most adults do their best to go out to a restaurant on the night of October 31, although wary that the trick-or-treaters, frustrated by the lack of gifts or money,

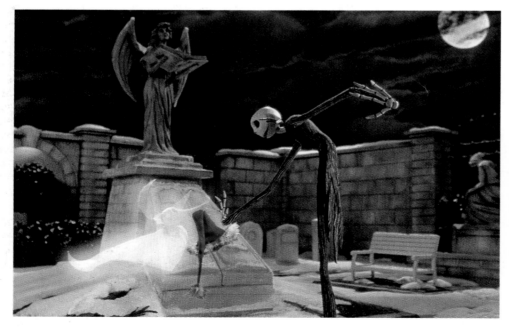

Zero, Jack's faithful ghost-dog, with his master.

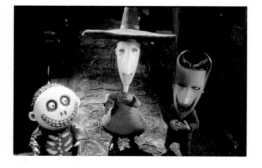

Lock, Shock, and Barrel, three malicious children who help Oogie Boogie carry out his evil plans. You wouldn't want to find them outside your doorstep on Halloween.

might well break in and steal the video recorder instead. This particular trio would almost certainly do a lot worse, whether the house was occupied or not. They represent a joyous parody of what the average grown-up actually thinks of the sweet little children who ring the doorbell repeatedly at Halloween demanding goodies. All three wear masks: Lock has the mask of a devil, Shock has the mask of a witch (and also a witch's hat), and Barrel has the mask of a grinning ghoul. A visual joke is that, when they cast off their masks, the faces beneath are almost identical.

Normally the three malicious children work in partnership with Oogie Boogie, helping him carry out his vile plans. It is an act of stupidity for Jack to enlist them to aid his own. He sends them out to kidnap Santa Claus from Christmas Town, and off they go in a walking **Bathtub**—their usual method of transportation, essentially a character in its own right, and one of the most bizarre ideas in the movie. Their first attempt is a failure—they return with a terrified **Easter Bunny** (pink and plump and suitably aquiver)—but they get it right second time. Then, although enjoined by Jack to keep Santa safe, they decide it would be fun to feed him to their regular master, who is only too keen to partake. Their desolated discovery, late in the movie, that Jack has not after all died after his sleigh has been shot down, is excellently depicted—it is one of those moments when the entire movie audience lets loose a little cheer. These kids are going to get the trouble they deserve.

And kids they are. For all their malice—essentially, they try to commit a murder—they are so irresponsible that it is hard to dislike them. Except, of course, if they turn up on your doorstep on October 31.

Oogie Boogie

Oogie Boogie is the ogre of Halloween Town. Ghoulies and ghosties the rest of the major characters in *The Nightmare Before Christmas* may be, but almost all of them are basically kindly—except Lock, Shock, and Barrel, of course, but their malice is a product of their childishness. Oogie Boogie, by contrast, is into Evil in a big way—a very big way, because he dwarfs all the other characters. To look at him you would think of him as a stuffed sack, and that proves to be exactly what he is when Jack Skellington, in saving Sally and Santa, destroys him by pulling out the stitching of the sack: the inside of Oogie Boogie, as we had already been led to expect, is a mass of insects, maggots, and other creepy-crawlies. His tongue is a serpent that flicks intimidatingly as he confronts his victims.

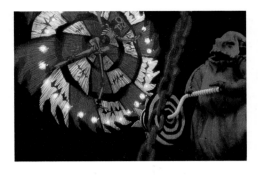

The evil Oogie Boogie, a stitched sack of insects, maggots, and other creepy crawlies gambling others' lives away in his ultraviolet lair.

The character is reminiscent of the later manifestation of Audrey II, the by now huge carnivorous plant in the 1986 remake of *The Little Shop of Horrors*, and it is difficult to believe that this was other than a conscious homage: that musical was written and scored by the Ashman/Menken team who did so much for Disney over the years. Just like Audrey II, Oogie Boogie is interested first in one thing: eating people. Unlike Audrey II, however, he has another interest, which is gambling—assuming, always, that he wins. His lair, in which the light is ultraviolet, has every manner of gambling-oriented appurtenance: a string of one-armed bandits (who are literally one-armed bandits rather than mere fruit machines, and are capable of shooting at people), a giant roulette wheel, and an Iron Maiden accoutred as the Queen of Spades. What he likes to do best, however, is cast dice in front of his victims so that they can find out whether or not he is going to eat them; the answer is always "yes," even if that involves cheating. It is a form of psychological torment used by torturers the world over. As he sings to Santa Claus:

The sound of rollin' dice to me is music in the air
'Cause I'm a gamblin' boogie man, although I don't play fair
It's much more fun, I must confess, when lives are on the line.
Not mine, of course, but yours, old boy. Now that'd be just fine.

Frank Thompson, in his book about the making of the movie, has written that originally Oogie Boogie was "a villain without a cause," and that Caroline Thompson—who wrote the screenplay—had to rely on Elfman's song to give the monster a character. In fact, Oogie Boogie *remains* that villain without a cause; his presence in Halloween Town is an anomaly. There is nothing wrong with the character—indeed, he is splendidly conceived and reified—but there is the sense that he has been put into the movie only so that the dramatic final battle with

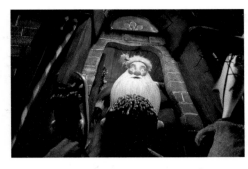

Santa Claus surprised to see Lock, Shock, and Barrel on his doorstep in Christmas Town.

Jack can be set up. And it's a great song he sings.

Santa Claus

It is when Jack Skellington is in Christmas Town that he first encounters this figure—only in the most remote of fashions—and he mishears the name, believing the character to be called "Sandy Claws". When the two first meet—Lock, Shock, and Barrel having kidnapped the elderly gentleman to Halloween Town—Jack says in astonishment: "Why, you have hands. You don't have claws at all." It is an indication of Jack's Halloween-oriented naïveté that this should be such a surprise to him.

Santa, in this movie, is very much as one would expect him to be: he has the requisite long white beard and round body. His peppery disposition owes a lot to Edmund Gwenn's performance as Kris Kringle in the 1947 movie *Miracle on 34th Street*. This particular Santa, the Santa of *The Nightmare Before Christmas*, has many more reasons to be irate, of course—it is not often that a mental construct is kidnapped, usurped, and nearly eaten—but the spikiness is as easily recognized as the essential good-heartedness.

The character is here represented as a rather passive one; although he gives the folk of Halloween Town the gift of a fall of snow as he leaves them to perform his Christmas acts, he is otherwise a mere plaything in the hands of other characters—he is kidnapped by the three trick-or-treaters, he is threatened by Oogie Boogie, he is almost rescued by Sally, and then *is* rescued by Jack. In all of these important turns of the plot he is almost what on the stage would be called a prop, or in fiction/film a McGuffin—he is a reason for the plot to happen rather than a character in his own right. Even at the end of the movie, as he reassumes his allotted place, we hardly think of him as a personality.

Santa Claus serves also as the narrator of the opening sequence that lays down the fantastical underpinning of the story—that each of the festivals has its own town.

Minor Characters

The Nightmare Before Christmas is stuffed with minor characters, many of whom are named in the cutting continuity but not mentioned in the screenplay. Trying to catch all of them would be something only a fool would do, so here goes.

Many occur in the pretitle sequences. The **Shadow Chorus** sings part of the introductory song, "This is Halloween"; all we see of these three is their shadows on gravestones, but those shadows are enough to tell us that the singers are monstrous in form. The **Ghost Chorus** is a trio of ghosts that are rendered in full animation; they are simple creations who take up the song from the Shadow Chorus. The **Creature Under the Bed** is the next singer to take over, and its words are a self-portrait:

I am the one hiding under your bed,
Teeth ground sharp and eyes glowing red.

The **Man Under the Stairs** similarly describes himself:

I am the one hiding under your stairs,
Fingers like snakes and spiders in my hair.

From here on the various characters who join in the song will also play trivial parts in the movie proper. There is a quartet of **Vampires**, one of whom is small and round, the others being more like a Christopher Lee representation of Dracula. Two witches, the **Big Witch** and the **Small Witch**, pop up from time to time: the Small Witch really *is* small, to the extent that one would have to take care not to tread on her, while the Big Witch's portrayal is dominated by the hugeness of her nose, which is roughly the length of a forearm. Later in the movie the witches encourage Jack in his folly, especially the Small Witch. A little gray **Cat** walks along an alley and jumps onto the lid of a trash can, which bursts open to reveal the **Harlequin Demon** (which has three chubby antennae and more teeth than would be good for most of us); then the ground erupts as first a **Wolfman** and then a **Melting Man** join the song. The **Hanging Tree** has a couple of long, horizontal branches from which dangle **Skeletons**; tree and skeletons join in for a line or two of the song, as do the **Clown with the Tearaway Face** (when he tears it away he looks rather like a television set to whom someone has given a body and legs; his head is topped by a propeller beanie; he rides around on a monocycle), various **Ghouls** and the **Corpse Kid**, who will turn up from time to time during the movie with his **Corpse Mom** and **Corpse Dad**. He is a fat little guy who looks as if he has just been let out of prison.

And then the opening sequence is over. **Behemoth** turns up quite frequently during the movie; he is a big, bulky creature with a hatchet firmly implanted in his head, but nevertheless gives all the signs of having a gentle nature . . . which is more than most of us would aspire to if someone had stuck a hatchet in our heads. He and the Clown with the Tearaway Face bump stomachs and then turn to offer phatic congratulation to the Wolfman, Mr. Hyde, and the Cyclops. **Mr. Hyde**—an odd figure for Halloween, surely—has an intendedly Victorian-style top hat and eyes that seem to be white jelly; later on we discover there is a smaller version of him inside *that* hat . . . and an even tinier version inside that version's hat. The **Cyclops**, as one might expect from the name, has one eye fewer than Mr. Hyde. It is a most curious creature, being about the size of a jackdaw but rather less lovable. **The Undersea Gal** is another fan of Jack's, and appears briefly to tell him how fine his perfor-

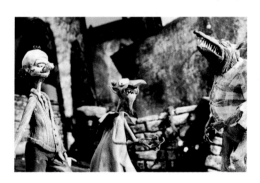

Minor characters Wolfman, Devil, and Corpse Dad.

mance has been this Halloween; she looks a little like The Creature from the Black Lagoon, and has little fins sprouting from her neck.

Of more note are **The Band**. This trio of street performers (no connection with the legendary rock group) is described in the cutting continuity as The Skeleton Band, but none of them is a skeleton. The single word that characterizes them is *Muppets*. The most important of the three is the **Sax Player**, much smaller and more Muppet-like than the rest; he has a protruding chin and a habit of offering bad advice at bad moments. The **Bass Player** is probably the least-realized character in the movie: he is hardly more than a lump who sits behind his double-bass, stroking the strings. Inside the front of his instrument there is the **Man in the Bass**; although we only ever see his face, he has a cheery personality of his own. The **Accordion Player** is a huge hulk; it is amusing that he can create such a dismal, depressing music from an instrument like the accordion. The dismal version of "Jingle Bells" The Band produces is quite funny.

A **Devil** appears during Jack's presentation to the other Halloween Townies of the idea of Christmas and occasionally thereafter; he mishears a line from the Harlequin Demon and assumes that a gift is placed in a pox, rather than a box. Further figures involved in this sequence are a skinny **Mummy** and the **Withered Winged Demon**—the latter, another recurring character, resembles a large but bodiless bat.

In Christmas Town there are numerous elves and children, and we have a quick sight of **Mrs. Claus**; she is a female version of Santa himself. In the real world there are children called **Timmie**, **Wanda**,

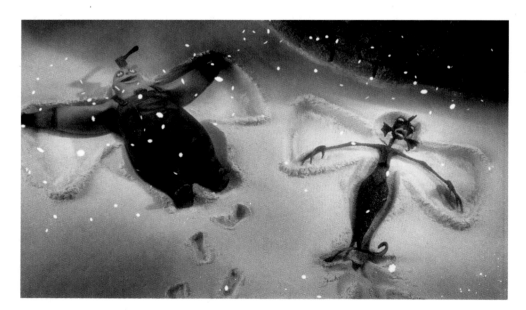

The Behemoth and Undersea Gal making snow angels after Santa Claus gives the residents of Halloween Town the gift of snowfall.

Ronnie, and **Howie,** all of whom are the soon-screaming recipients of Jack's gifts. An elderly woman, **Granny,** receives a Christmas wreath that has a homicidal mind of its own. Finally, although we do not see their faces, a **Police Sergeant** (male) and a **Radio Announcer** (female) play a part in stopping Jack's progress around the globe.

VINCENT

During his time at Disney, Burton made, with Rick Heinrichs, a stop-motion short called *Vincent*; Burton is quoted in Thompson's book as saying:

> It was a weird time at Disney, and some things slipped through the cracks. I think *Vincent* was just something they let slide.

The short went largely unnoticed on its first release in 1982, but it attracted a great deal of attention when it was re-released in 1993 as a companion to *The Nightmare Before Christmas*. Done almost entirely in drab colors, it tells of a little boy—the **Vincent** of the title—who has become obsessed by horror stories and, one night, in his imagination begins to

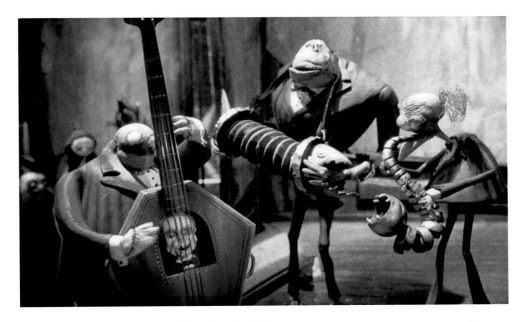

A ghoulish band plays for an equally ghoulish audience.

live them out. The movie is interesting in its use of Escheresque angles and displacements of perspective. The character himself is also of interest in that he is a far from typical boy protagonist for an animated movie. His face is approximately triangular (vertex downward), and seems pinched and hollow; we are given the impression that he is a deprived child, if not even an abused one. One gets the eerie feeling that the horrors he experiences reflect not just his chosen literature but the reality of his life. Beautifully made, the movie is narrated by Vincent Price.

THE LION KING

Characters:

Mufasa; Simba; Scar; Zazu; Nala; Rafiki; Timon; Pumbaa; Shenzi; Banzai; Ed; Sarabi; Sarafina; Mole

Credits:

Voices: Rowan Atkinson (Zazu); Matthew Broderick (Simba); Niketa Calame (Young Nala); Jim Cummings (Ed); Whoopi Goldberg (Shenzi); Robert Guillaume (Rafiki); Jeremy Irons (Scar); James Earl Jones (Mufasa); Moira Kelly (Nala); Nathan Lane (Timon); Zoe Leader (Sarafina); Cheech Marin (Banzai); Ernie Sabella (Pumbaa); Madge Sinclair (Sarabi); Jonathan Taylor Thomas (Young Simba)

Music: Hans Zimmer

Songs: Elton John and Tim Rice

Additional Songs: Hugo Peretti, George Weiss and Luigi Creatore; Fred Heatherton; Robert and Richard Sherman; Johnny Noble and Leleiohaku

Supervising Music Editor: Adam Milo Smalley

African Vocal Solos and Improvisations: Lebo M.

Animation Screenplay: Irene Mecchi; Jonathan Roberts; Linda Wolverton

Story: Jim Capobianco; Lorna Cook; Thom Enriquez; Andy Gaskill; Francis Glebas; Ed Gombert; Kevin Harkey; Barry Johnson;

Mark Kausler; Jorgen Klubien; Larry Leker; Rick Maki; Burny Mattinson; Joe Ranft; Chris Sanders; Tom Sito; Gary Trousdale

Supervising Editors: John Carnochan; Tom Finan

Production Design: Chris Sanders

Supervising Animators: Ruben Aquino (Simba); Tony Bancroft (Pumbaa); James Baxter (Rafiki); Aaron Blaise (Young Nala); David Burgess (Hyenas); Niketa Calame (Young Nala); Andreas Deja (Scar); Anthony Derosa (Nala); Russ Edmonds (Sarabi); Tony Fucile (Mufasa); Mark Henn (Young Simba); Alex Kuperschmidt (Hyenas); Michael Surrey (Timon); Ellen Woodbury (Zazu)

Animators: Tim Allen; Dale Baer; Tom Bancroft; Rejean Bourdages; Ken Boyer; Bob Bryan; Randy Cartwright; Michael Cedeno; Lorna Cook; Lou Dellarosa; Joe Ekers; Brian Ferguson; Doug Frankel; Randy Haycock; T. Daniel Hofstedt; Ron Husband; Broose Johnson; Mark Koetsier; Brad Kuha; James Lopez; Greg S. Manwaring; Jean Morel; Gilda Palinginis; Dave Pruiksma; Mike Show; Michael Swofford; Barry Temple; Chris Wahl; Danny Wawrzaszek; Larry White; Alex Williams; Phil Young

Computer Animation for Wildebeest Stampede: Linda Bel; Gregory Griffith

Computer Software: Kiran Bhakti Joshi; Mary Jane Turner

Key Layout: Mitchell Bernal; Jennifer Chiao-Lin Yuan; Fred Craig; Guy Deel; Jeff Dickson; Ed Ghertner; Tom Humber; Lorenzo Martinez; Tom Shannon; Allen Tam; Tanya Wilson

Effects Animators: Christine Blum; Allen Blyth; Dave Bossert; Ed Coffey; Tom Hush; Chris Jenkins; Ted C. Kierscey; Dorse Lanpher; Mauro Maressa; Joey Mildenberger; Steve Moore; Eusebio Torres; Marlon West; Garrett Wren

Art Direction: Andy Gaskill

Artistic Supervisors: Doug Ball; Brenda Chapman; Scott F. Johnston; Vera Lanpher; Dan St. Pierre; Scott Santoro

Character Design/Visual Development: Hans Bacher; Jean Gillmore; Joe Grant; Michael Hodgson; Lisa Keene; Sue C. Nichols; Mel Shaw; Bob Smith; Bruce Zick

Production Manager: Dana Axelrod

Associate Producer: Alice Dewey

Executive Producers: Sara McArthur; Thomas Schumacher

Producer: Don Hahn

Directors: Roger Allers; Rob Minkoff

Release Date: June 15, 1994; general release June 24, 1994; rereleased (there was a gap during the school term) November 18, 1994

Running Time: 88 minutes

THE MOVIE

Most of the Disney animated features, whether based on an existing story or developed by one or more of the creative team, have a fairly well worked-out plot in the first place—even though that plot will certainly be changed frequently along the route, with minor amendments being made right up until as little as a fortnight before release. The Lion King, however, seems very much more to have been made up by the team as it went along. Initially it was just a glimmer of an idea—it was to be a rite-of-passage tale set among African animals, almost certainly lions—and its working title for a long time was King of the Jungle.

Perhaps the pivotal moment was the recruitment of Tim Rice and Elton John to provide the songs, because their early offering "The Circle of Life" not only became the movie's theme song but supplied one of its primary themes. Setting a movie intended for (among others) children in the African wild presents, obviously, a major problem: Some of those cuddly animals are being eaten by others of those cuddly animals, so it becomes hard for a child to know where her/his loyalties lie. The song gave a way out of this impasse, essentially by explaining honestly the way that nature works: while it seems cruel that there is such a thing as the food chain, the descendants of the lowliest organisms on it eventually eat the carcasses of the topmost. In fact, the creators distorted this message somewhat: the only creatures we see being eaten by good characters (Simba, Timon, Pumbaa) are creepy-crawlies, for whom we should presumably feel no sympathy; Scar's offering of a chunk of zebra to ravenous hyenas is an indicator of his evil. That Simba should *not* be eating creepy-crawlies but be fulfilling his role as a predator is a message that is distinctly and subtly played.

As noted below, the story of The Lion King in the end came to have many parallels with that of Bambi (➤197): the young heir loses a parent, goes through various adversities, then discovers how to inherit his rightful position as king. As with Bambi, one of the problems facing the animators was that of giving a sense of realism to wild animals, particularly in terms of their movement; however, as much of a caricature as the physical form of an animal character might be, if it moves unconvincingly it loses all credence in the eyes of the viewer. So, again as with Bambi (and various other of the animated features), wild animals were brought to the animators in Burbank so that they could study them; behavioral lectures were given by Jim Fowler and anatomical ones by Stuart Sumida. The result of this exercise was astonishingly effective: We are never in any doubt that, for example, Simba is an artists' creation, yet at the same time we accept him as a lion. A further bit of research that gives the movie credibility was that a group of the creators was sent to East Africa to get the *feel* of the place; this experience, passed on to the rest of the team in the form of sketches, and so on, and just straightforward discussion, gives the movie the quality that we perceive it as being played out against a real backdrop rather than just some fantasyland. The story thus be-comes much *truer*, and our emotions much more involved, which may be why *The Lion King* was such a phenomenal commercial success. One could name plenty of other Disney features whose animation has more inventiveness, but this movie's art has very considerable conviction.

As has become standard Disney practice, some of the animation was done with the aid of computers—notably the sequence in which we see a vast herd of stampeding wildebeest: apparently about 1,000 animals are depicted here, so animating by hand would have been impossible.

Not everyone liked The Lion King, and some critics objected to it strongly. Writing in *Attitude*, Taral Wayne commented:

> . . . We come to the core of The Lion King, and why it is arguably the vilest filmed [in North America] since *Mission in Moscow*—in 1943. . . . It was no surprise that the story was about monarchy. When you itemize Disney animated films, the majority turn out to be about kings and kingdoms, one way or another. I would have been surprised if monarchy had been shown in a poor light. I knew in advance that the story would be the usual folderol about the rightful heir regaining his throne, hip hip hurray. What I was not prepared for was the offensively sucky and fundamentally religious love affair the film had for the divine right of kings. . . . The writers of *The Lion King* have forsaken the 20th century and reached back into the past, into the era in which monarchy was a living idea, and brought back the rotten corpse of the "Golden Chain of Being."

Wayne continues in this vein for some while, even if at the same time disagreeing profoundly. Most monarchs of the past have indeed used their "divine right" to exploit, execute, or torment their subjects or to go off to other countries and perform a few massacres—he validly uses the example of Richard the Lionheart. Yet he misses the point of the story of *The Lion King*, which is not about kingship as a right. In this tale kingship is a *responsibility*, and the crux of the story is that Simba for a long time ducks out of that responsibility. One's approval or otherwise of a monarchical political system is irrelevant—a classic theme of traditional tales, and indeed of modern genre fantasy, is that the rightful heir has been ousted or otherwise dispossessed, but in one way or another regains the throne. Disney was not so much worshiping kingship as continuing a tradition. Where the movie's theme is considerably less sure-footed is in its implication that Scar, the usurper, *cannot* be a good ruler; to continue with the example of Richard the Lionheart, his brother John was despite popular mythology the better and more dutiful monarch, albeit himself a nasty piece of work.

In an interesting work called *Coming of Age in Fantasyland: The Self-Parenting Child in Walt Disney Animated Films* Lynne Lundquist and Gary Westfahl point out how frequently the main characters in Disney's animated features are either orphaned or part orphaned: they have usually one parent, if any at all. Simba is somewhat different, in that he at least starts off with two parents, but then of course his father is murdered—while his mother's role in the movie is only a small one. Lundquist and Westfahl go further, noting that a very frequent theme is that the orphan is first parented by individuals he or she comes across by chance but then in effect becomes the parent of: *Snow White and the Seven Dwarfs* (➤149) is a paradigm, with Snow White being taken in by the Dwarfs (earlier she has been "mothered" by forest animals) but very soon making herself their parent, telling them to wash behind their ears. *The Lion King* exemplifies the same general pattern, in that the cub Simba is adopted by Timon and Pumbaa and taught in their ways, then recovers his natural place within the Pride Lands, thus becoming effectively their parent—or, at the very least, their patron in that he stops the other lions from using his friends for a quick snack.

The Lion King is not the most intriguing of the animated features, but it has enjoyable and emotive characters and, as noted, was a colossal commercial success. Its opening sequences are beautifully executed, and bear repeated watching; the scene, depicted from above, of a flock of birds flying above the African terrain is particularly striking.

The Art of The Lion King (1994) by Christopher Finch has a lot of pretty artwork, including both early sketches and stills from the movie, and a highly informative afterword; unfortunately, the book is unindexed. There are short but informative essays in Gina Ingoglia's *Disney's Treasury of Children's Classics* (1996) and the third edition of Bob Thomas's *Disney's Art of Animation* (1997).

THE STORY

Mufasa, the Lion King of the region called the Pride Lands, and his mate, Sarabi, have produced their first son, Simba. All the animals gather to watch as Rafiki, a bent baboon who occupies the position of shaman among them, presents the heir apparent from atop Pride Rock. But all is not well among the royal family, because Mufasa's disloyal younger brother Scar covets the kingship. Mufasa tells Simba that he will one day be ruler of all he surveys, but that he must never venture into the "shadowy place." This place, Scar reveals to the youthful Simba in such a way as to encourage him to go there, is an Elephant Graveyard. Simba and his pal Nala do indeed explore the area, despite the efforts of Mufasa's chief of staff—a zany bird, Zazu—to stop them. Three hyenas—Shenzi, Banzai, and Ed—have been sent there by Scar to kill the vagrant cubs. But Simba and Nala are rescued by Mufasa, to Scar's fury.

Scar recruits all the local hyenas to his cause, the three named being his most loyal disciples. Under his instruction they start a stampede of wildebeest that is designed to kill Simba and Mufasa. Mufasa saves Simba, again, but is thrown under the feet of the terrified beasts by Scar, who then tells Simba that the king's death has been all his fault and that the only option left open to the cub is to leave the Pride Lands forever, in shame. In fact, Scar commands the three hyenas to kill the cub, but they fail. Scar assumes the kingship and proclaims "the dawning of a new era, in which lion and hyena come together." The result is the devastation of the land. Since at least the time of the Arthurian legends it has been a recurring image in fairy tales that if the rightful king is ailing or absent, the land suffers too. Here the devastation is represented by an overall graying of the scenery. The land grows empty of food and the hyenas gradually become rebellious.

Meanwhile Simba, far from home, makes friends with the meerkat Timon and the warthog Pumbaa and grows up in their company (becoming an insectivore in the process, which is a further violation of the natural law that he is supposed to obey) to become a visual replica of his father. One day a lioness attacks Pumbaa with intent to devour; Simba fights her off and discovers she is his childhood friend Nala—and obviously love ensues. She persuades him that it is his responsibility to return to the Pride Lands and regain the kingship; while he is still battling with his conscience, Rafiki arrives to make the final persuasion, assisted by what is in effect the ghost of Mufasa. Simba, Nala, Timon, and Pumbaa return to the Pride Lands, where, after Scar has publicly confessed to murdering Mufasa, there is a final climactic battle between lions and hyenas—but most notably a fight between Simba and Scar, which Simba of course wins (although Scar in fact meets his death at the jaws of the hyenas).

Simba assumes his kingship. At the very last there is a scene that is a conscious part repetition of the opening; now, the land recovered, it is the cub of Simba and Nala that Rafiki is presenting to the massed animals.

THE CHARACTERS

Mufasa

With his great orange mane and his powerful physique, the first of the movie's two Lion Kings, Simba's father appears much as we might expect him to, and he is voiced appropriately in the deep tones of James Earl Jones. In a way, after the initial scene when Rafiki is presenting the new cub to the massed animals, we see Mufasa only from the viewpoint of the young Simba; he is not so much large as huge, and we have the feeling that he is the ruler not just of the Pride Lands but of the world. This feeling is reinforced by a

section of dialogue in which Mufasa tries to give his young son some idea of the responsibilities of kingship:

Mufasa: Look, Simba. Everything the light touches is our kingdom.
Simba: Wow.
Mufasa: A king's time as ruler rises and falls like the sun. One day, Simba, the sun will set on my time here and will rise with you as the new king.
Simba: And this will all be mine?
Mufasa: Everything.
Simba: Everything the light touches.

"Everything the light touches" would seem to imply the entire world, but immediately we are informed by Mufasa that all kingdoms have their boundaries:

Simba: What about that shadowy place?
Mufasa: That's beyond our borders. You must never go there, Simba.
Simba: But I thought a king can do whatever he wants.
Mufasa: Oh, there's more to being king than getting your way all the time.
Simba: There's *more*?
Mufasa: Simba, everything you see exists together in a delicate balance. As king, you need to understand that balance, and respect all the creatures, from the crawling ant to the leaping antelope.

Thus are set out the three major themes of the movie. First, obviously, that with power comes duty: kingship is not something that can merely be enjoyed as a privilege but carries a burden of responsibility with it. Second, that any monarchy is confined to its own proper region. And, third, that there is a "circle of life" to which all of the animals belong, from those (like the lions) who are at the top of the food chain to the humblest of creatures. Mufasa expands:

Simba: But, Dad, don't we eat the antelope?
Mufasa: Yes, Simba, but let me explain. When we die, our bodies become the grass and the antelope eat the grass. And so we are all connected in the great circle of life.

This is a point that is hammered home on several occasions throughout the movie, although Disney may have received the occasional letter from an angry antelope.

There is another moral lesson that Mufasa teaches Simba—although it will be a long time later, and only after the intervention of Nala and Rafiki, before the lesson makes itself heard. Mufasa has just rescued the two cubs, Simba and Nala, from the hyenas in the Elephant Graveyard and has led Simba away for a strict paternal talking to:

Mufasa: You deliberately disobeyed me. And, what's worse, you put Nala in danger.

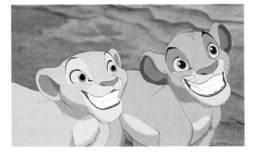

As cubs, Simba and Nala are compatriots, joint troublemakers, and, of course, the best of friends.

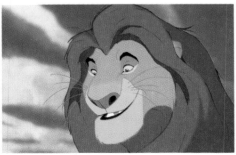

The regal Musafa, given life by the booming voice of James Earl Jones.

Simba: I was just trying to be brave like you.
Mufasa: I'm only brave when I have to be. Simba, being brave doesn't mean you go looking for trouble.
Simba: But you're not scared of anything.
Mufasa: I was today.
Simba: You were?
Mufasa: Yes. I thought I might lose you.
Simba: Oh. I guess even kings get scared, huh?

Just before this sequence, which becomes one that shows Mufasa is not as strait-laced as his customary majesterial bearing might suggest—rather than continuing to be severe with the cub he ends up romping around with him in a mock fight—there is one particularly effective visual. Simba, following in the trail of his father and expecting Real Trouble, puts his own paw into one of Mufasa's pawprints. The difference in size is spectacular. What is conveyed to us is not just the obvious physical disparity but that Simba, who has earlier been cheerfully boasting about his inheritance, has a long way to go yet before he *learns* to be a true heir.

But after the play there is more somberness. Mufasa has something to teach his son, and it is the greatest piece of myth-making in the movie's screenplay. This has been taught to Mufasa by his father (and, it is implied, has been passed down over many generations): the great Lion Kings of the past "look down on us" from the stars in the night sky.

In terms of straightforward action, Mufasa's peak is his rescuing of the young Simba from a herd of stampeding wildebeest, followed immediately afterward by his own murder at the paws of Scar, but there is a much more significant episode later on. Rafiki, having uncovered the grown Simba in the country beyond the Pride Lands, is trying to per-

suade him that it is his obligation to take up his kingship. The baboon tells the younger lion that his father is still alive, and makes him look into still water by way of demonstration: Mufasa is still alive in that he lives on in Simba. Simba rejects the moral, but then—in a twisted form of scenes in Shakespeare's *Hamlet*—is visited by an apparition of his father.

Mufasa: Simba.
Simba: Father?
Mufasa: Simba, you have forgotten me.
Simba: No. How could I?
Mufasa: You have forgotten who you are, and so forgotten me. Look inside yourself, Simba. You are more than what you have become. You must take your place in the circle of life.
Simba: How can I go back? I'm not who I used to be.
Mufasa: Remember who you are. You are my son and the one true king. Remember who you are. . . .

The short sequence packs a punch, and it is only on the way home from the movies that one begins to think that if Simba is no longer worthy of kingship, why is he "the one true king"?

Simba

The story of Simba is the story of the movie: Born to kingship, he is tricked into abandoning it and then deliberately turns his back on it until persuaded by others to assume his responsibilities. Stripped down like that, the story seems a very simple one, but that is not the *real* story. The *real* story is of the transformation of Simba's character through several pronouncedly different stages.

As a baby and then a cub he is what Bill Cotter has described as "warm and fuzzy"—what used to be a typical Disney

animal, in fact. As a cub he is as cocksure as the average preteen, and as gullible. It could not be made more patent that "Uncle Scar" is a stinker from root to branch, yet the young Simba swallows everything he says. The characterization is such as to evoke great sympathy—we have all been through that stage ourselves.

It is more difficult to sympathize with the adult Simba—at least, before he takes on his responsibilities. We see little of Simba's maturation—within a second or two he develops from cub to full-grown adult. As an adult, and under the influence of Timon and Pumbaa, he still has the mentality of a child: all that's important in life is to have fun, and the overall philosophy should be *hakuna matata* ("no worries") about the past or the future. Adults who persist in childish ways are always either irritating or depressing, and this version of Simba is no different. By the time that Nala comes across him she is a fully matured lioness but he, while physically at least as powerful as her, is infantile in terms of personality; even his loyalty to Timon and Pumbaa, as he fights with her to save them from her, has a feeling of playground loyalty.

Physically, by this time, Simba looks very much like his father, Mufasa, although his features are rather more gentle. When Rafiki tells him to look into the water at his reflection and see his father there, we do indeed see Simba's face transmogrify into Mufasa's, but the difference is not considerable—it is little more than a change in facial expression. There is a difference in deportment, however: Mufasa always moves in a way that suggests ponderousness (even when romping with his young son), whereas at this stage in his life, Simba appears to lack that physical mass. He seems to be an adolescent—possessed of the stature while still needing to fill out the bulk. Nala, we are led to understand, reacts to him also as a woman might react to a man who was still innately adolescent: after the joys of physical attraction she effectively tells him to shove off until he gets his act together.

All this changes, of course, once the guiles of Nala, the sophistry of—and, more forthrightly, a thump over the head from—Rafiki, not to mention a visitation from the wraith of his father, have persuaded Simba that he must depose the usurper Scar for the sake of the well-being of the Pride Lands and all the animals who dwell therein. Now the resemblance to Mufasa is profound in every way—to the extent that on first seeing him Scar assumes he *is* Mufasa, and even Simba's own mother, Sarabi, seems to have a moment of confusion.

Simba cannot be said to be one of the more complex of the major characters in

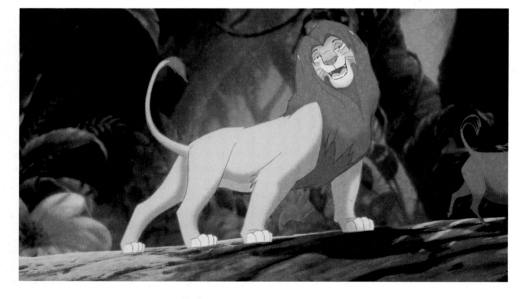

Simba as an adult, voiced by Matthew Broderick.

Disney's recent animated features; indeed, one can go back a lot further than "recent," for his tale has many parallels with that of *Bambi* (➤197), whose personality was explored in much greater depth. Nevertheless, Simba has proved an enduringly popular character, possibly because the movie as a whole was aimed at a younger audience than some of the other Disney features of the 1990s.

Scar

Villains should look like villains—that seems certainly to have been the policy in *The Lion King*. He is much skinnier than the two other adult male lions and moves in a slinkier fashion; his eyes are a cruel green; and (this is a little worrying to think about) he is distinctly browner than either Mufasa or Simba and has a black rather than a golden mane. At some stage he has been slashed across his left eye, for the line of a scar still remains on the flesh above and below it. And he is voiced by an Englishman (Jeremy Irons), in whose tones one has come to recognize in Hollywood movies as designating "cad" and "scoundrel." Of course, Scar certainly is a cad and a scoundrel—and a murderer and usurper to boot—but it's hard not to feel that this younger brother of a Lion King was handed a pretty raw deal. And then, of course, Mufasa and Sarabi had a child, so that Scar could no longer even contemplate inheriting the throne.

Scar is thus depicted as a beta male, and irredeemably unworthy of kingship. During his time with Timon and Pumbaa, Simba is persuaded by them—or, really, persuades himself—that he too is a beta male, and all through this same period Scar is telling himself that he is the alpha male, which he is not. The reflection between their careers is carried further, because once Simba recognizes himself as an alpha male, Scar begins, although too late for him, to realize what he is, or could have been: a follower rather than a leader.

Although there is the difference that they are siblings, the relationship between Scar and Mufasa is rather like that between Iago and Othello, as is stated more or less outrightly by Scar at a very early stage, when Mufasa has rescued Zazu from not just Scar's appetite but his actual mouth. Zazu encourages Mufasa to have a fight with his brother, but Mufasa refuses—as does Scar:

> Well, as far as brains go, I got the lion's share. But when it comes to brute strength I'm afraid I'm at the shallow end of the gene pool.

As with Iago, so with Scar: he is a clever fool in that he cannot realize before or after that to allow the hyenas to

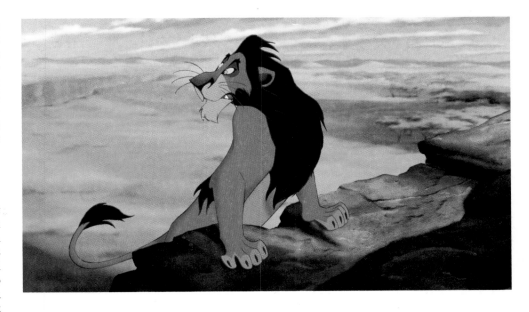

Simba's villianous Uncle Scar, who wants nothing more than to see Simba and Musafa dead and himself on the throne.

become his army will compromise the land. There is a moment somewhat later on when we see him watching an army of hyenas virtually goosestepping in fascist fashion; a clever trick of the animators is that Scar's shadow hereabouts is grossly enlarged, because he sees himself as much greater than he is.

Yet, although a fool, he *is* clever—certainly in the art of manipulating others. He persuades Simba to go and play in the Elephant Graveyard by the tactic of telling him not to. Parents all over the world know that the sure way of getting children to do something stupid is to tell them that, while exciting, it is forbidden. Then Scar expertly maneuvers Simba into the path of the wildebeest stampede initiated by his allies, the three zany hyenas:

> *Scar*: Now, you wait here. Your father has a marvelous surprise for you.
> *Simba*: Oooh. What is it?
> *Scar*: If I told you it wouldn't be a surprise, now would it?
> *Simba*: If you tell me, I'll still act surprised.
> Scar: Ho, ho, ho. You are such a naughty boy.
> *Simba*: Come on, Uncle Scar.
> *Scar*: No, no, no, no, no, no, no. This is just for you and your Daddy. You know, a sort of father-son thing. Well, I better go get him.
> *Simba*: I'll go with you.
> *Scar*: No!

At about this point even the less intelligent of lion cubs might have begun to think there was something fishy going on, but not Simba: he has cast himself into the belief that his uncle is his friend. That Scar manifestly is not is a matter that, in plotting terms, it takes Simba rather too long to recognize. Then, the

stampede having failed to kill the cub because Mufasa has saved him, Scar kills the father instead and manipulates Simba into believing that he is responsible for the Lion King's death and so must flee from the Pride Lands. The cub—for which read "child"—trustingly takes his uncle's word for it and goes.

The king and the heir gone, the land becomes a waste. Scar is unconscious that his usurpation is the cause—that he has brought in the hyenas is almost secondary. Although it is not made explicit, it is implied that he takes Sarabi, Mufasa's "widow," to be his own mate. Certainly she heads the pack of lionesses whose charge it is to find food for the pride.

It is Scar's own duplicitousness that does him in in the end. Threatened by Simba, he yet again does his best to talk himself out of the situation:

> *Simba*: You don't deserve to live.
> *Scar*: But . . . Simba . . . I am, uhhh, family. It's the hyenas who are the real enemy. It was their fault. It was their idea.
> *Simba*: Why should I believe you? Everything you ever told me was a lie.
> *Scar*: What are you going to do? You wouldn't kill your old uncle?
> *Simba*: No, Scar. I'm not like you.
> *Scar*: Oh, Simba, thank you. You are truly noble. I'll make it up to you, I promise. And how can I, uh, prove myself to you? Tell me. Any . . . anything.
> *Simba*: Run. Run away, Scar, and never return.
> *Scar*: Of course. As you wish, Your Majesty.

True to form, Scar waits until Simba's back is turned and then jumps ferociously at him. Simba wins the fight and throws Scar over the edge of a cliff, a deed that should have killed the villain—

but Scar is lucky, or so he thinks. He escapes into a cave where the three hyenas whom he has regarded as his most loyal subjects—Shenzi, Banzai, and Ed—who have overheard his conversation with Simba, literally tear him to pieces.

Zazu

More than with any other character in the movie, the personality of Zazu is governed by the voicing, done by the British comic actor Rowan Atkinson. The hornbill, the Pride Lands' chief of protocol, has been put in charge of the education of the young Simba much as Jiminy Cricket found himself acting toward Pinocchio (➤169), and being just as ineffective as *The Little Mermaid*'s Sebastian (➤346) was in his attempts to persuade a young person to behave sensibly. As with Sebastian, Zazu encounters numerous pratfalls: at one point, while issuing moral instructions, he flies straight into the back of a rhino, his consequent concussion allowing Simba and Nala the freedom to continue toward the for-bidden territory that is the Elephant Graveyard.

Zazu is one of the classic Disney zanies. His pomposity is immense, his cowardice fairly understandable (he is living among carnivores, after all, and would have been eaten by Scar had not Mufasa intervened just as the last of Zazu was disappearing into Scar's mouth), his

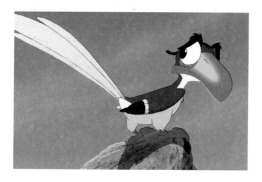

Musafa's chief of protocol, Zazu, who is glad to give advice and orders, though no one ever listens.

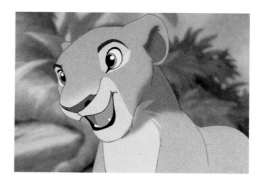

The spunky and courageous Nala, who eventually succeeds in persuading Simba to return to the Pride Lands.

recommendations to the cub Simba generally useless. Although he feels free to utter orders and advice, few pay particular attention to him. He has a difficult job because his boss Mufasa offers him little support.

His opinion of Scar is made clear just after Scar has tried to make a meal of him: "He'd make a very handsome throw rug. . . . And, just think, whenever he gets dirty you could take him out and beat him." Much later, once Scar has established himself as usurper king, Zazu is imprisoned within a skeletal ribcage and must entertain his master with a song. He tries *Nobody Knows the Trouble I've Seen* and is immediately told by Scar to opt for something more cheery. Next comes *It's a Small World*, which offends Scar because by this time he is thinking of himself as Master of the Universe. Finally poor Zazu settles on *I've Got a Lovely Bunch of Coconuts*, and his dismal voice tells us all.

He is still in his cage when Simba and the rest arrive to save the Pride Lands from the reign of Scar. The three main hyenas pursue Timon into the cave where the cage is sited, and the meerkat rushes toward the protection of Zazu's jail:

> *Zazu*: Get me out! Let me out!
> *Timon*: Let me in! Let me in!

One of Zazu's joke lines from the earlier part of the movie is reprised later on by Pumbaa. The hornbill is trying to dissuade Simba and Nala from exploring outside the Pride Lands; Simba, being young and foolish, mocks his mentor:

> *Simba*: Look, Banana-Beak is scared.
> *Zazu*: It's Mister Banana-Beak to you, Fuzzy.

Zazu is a finely created character, although of course his role is only a supporting one. Naturally, since he is benign, the plot ensures that he becomes an integral part of the new kingdom that Simba establishes.

Nala

Childhood friend of Simba, Nala in later life becomes his mate and gives birth to his cub—as one might have predicted. Both as a cub and as an adult lioness she is a very attractive character, largely because of the voicing (by Niketa Calame and then Moira Kelly for the adult Nala) and the script but also because of the animation, which shows her as a lovable child/cub and then as an equally lovable adult/lioness. The cleverest trick of all is that, in the transition of Nala from child to adult, we are never in any doubt about who she is; since she has been off-screen for a long time when she reappears as an adult, this is good work.

The relationship between the young

Simba and the young Nala is much as one might expect in a Disney animated feature: they are pals, and the matter of gender is not important.

> *Zazu*: One day you two are going to be married.
> *Simba*: Yuck!
> *Nala*: Ewww!
> *Simba*: I can't marry her. She's my best friend.
> *Nala*: Yeah, it'd be too weird.

As cubs, they romp around having mock fights, and it is implied that Nala normally wins these—perhaps with Simba's consent. Later on, when they are adults and after they have fought with each other not knowing who they are, then discovered they are old friends, Simba is the one who wins the fight, and one suspects Nala lets him do so, certainly the expression on her face indicates that this is the case. (There are various "adult" moments in the more recent Disney animated features. This is one of them.)

The full-grown Nala is an impressive character. After she and Simba have rolled around in the joy of rediscovering each other, she begins to explain to him some of the issues he has been avoiding:

> *Nala*: You're our only hope.
> *Simba*: Sorry.
> *Nala*: What's happened to you? You're not the Simba I remember.
> *Simba*: You're right. I'm not. Now are you satisfied?
> *Nala*: No. Just disappointed.
> *Simba*: You know, you're starting to sound like my father.
> *Nala*: Good. At least one of us does.

She then, not inexplicably, dumps her newly remet friend, and does not return her loyalty to him until she discovers from Timon and Pumbaa that he has at last resolved to risk his life in order to save the Pride Lands. Suddenly she becomes his staunchest defender, effectively facing down Scar; she has become the leader of the lionesses, in place of Sarabi—a transition over which Sarabi is apparently quite happy. The animation and voicing of this particular section are excellent: Nala's movements are determined and her words equally so. She is the girlfriend who tells her boyfriend to get his act together and does so very effectively; thereafter she backs him to the hilt. And, of course, her accession to power matches Simba's: this is a movie full of such reflections.

Rafiki

Crooked and bent with age—he is so at the start and remains very much the same at the end—the baboon Rafiki acts as shaman to the animals of the Pride Lands. It is he who has the task of holding aloft each new lion heir so that the infant can be admired and knelt to by the assembled wildlife. In such moments Rafiki has great dignity; elsewhere he has a cackling whimsicality that, oddly enough, in no way detracts from his dignity. In short, he is the holder of wisdom. It is up to him how he expresses his wisdom, and if frolics and jokes are the Tao then none of the animals will respect him the less for that.

After the birth of Simba, Rafiki paints on a cave wall a caricature of the new Lion King. Later, assuming Simba dead, he smears it over, in grief. Later still, on catching leaves and pods that have been wafted away from the world outside the Pride Lands and thus discovering (somehow) that Simba is still alive, he reinstates the picture, paintings on adult mane around Simba's head. The plot logic is rather hard to follow—how could the leaves and pods have made their way to him, and how could he have told from them that Simba was alive?—but in a curious way it seems, as one watches the movie, to make sense. That's a shaman's job, after all. Even more improbable is that Rafiki is then able immediately to track Simba down. The tracking down done, Rafiki persuades Simba—with a forceful swipe of the stick he always carries—that he must return to the Pride Lands and save them. As Simba himself puts it:

> I finally got some sense knocked into me. And I've got the bump to prove it.

It is about three-quarters of the way into the movie that Rafiki really comes into his own as a character. He uses various techniques to tell Simba that his place is back in the Pride Lands. One of them is the enunciation of nonsense:

> *Rafiki*: Asante Sana, squash banana, we we nugi, mi miapana.
> *Simba*: Enough already! What is that supposed to mean anyway?
> *Rafiki*: It means you are a baboon. And I'm not.
> *Simba*: I think you're a little confused.
> *Rafiki*: I'm not the one who's confused. *You* don't even know who you are.

A little afterward Rafiki shows Simba that he is really Mufasa—or at least that Mufasa still lives, because he lives within Simba—by forcing him to look at his own reflection in a pool. And finally, again the wise joker, he cracks Simba over the head with his stick. The dialogue here is particularly good:

> *Simba*: I know what I have to do, but . . . going back means I'll have to face my past. I've been running from it for so long.

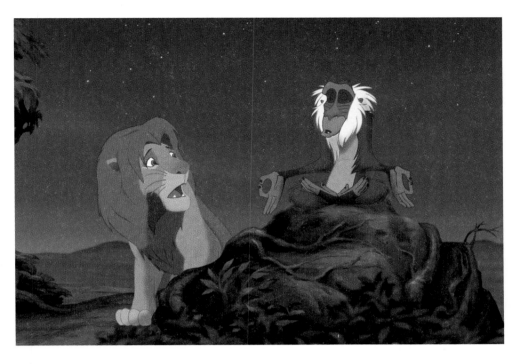

Simba meets up with a yoga-practing Rafiki.

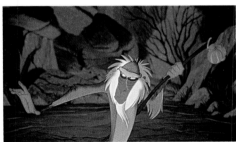

The shaman baboon Rafiki, a marvelous character of great wisdom and humor.

> *Rafiki hits him.*
> *Simba*: Ow! Geez, what was that for?
> *Rafiki*: It doesn't matter. It's in the past.
> *Simba*: Yeah, but it still hurts.
> *Rafiki*: Oh, yes, the past can hurt. But, the way I see it, you can either run from it or learn from it.

Certainly, whether consciously or unconsciously, the moviemakers derived much of Rafiki's character from the trickster figure of Chinese legend, Monkey. (A Japanese television series based on Monkey's exploits was broadcast 1979–1981.) Of course, Monkey is but one representative of an archetype in the world's collective legends—the Trickster, the individual who seems to be a fool, but who through jest and trickery conveys wisdom to others—but that Rafiki is a baboon seems no coincidence.

Timon and Pumbaa

These two characters are the movie's essential comics. It might seem an unlikely partnership—a diminutive meerkat and a warthog with a propensity for flatulence—but clearly the two are the very best of friends, and for a good part of the movie Simba makes the duo into a trio. Timon, the meerkat, has a rapid-fire mode of speech, filled with wisecracks, and clearly believes himself cleverer than he probably is. Pumbaa seems to be much slower-witted and frequently comes out with malapropisms ("You gotta put your behind in your past"), yet one has the impression that, in some sort of way, he is actually the more intelligent—that he has come to assume himself a fool because every time he goes near another animal (besides Timon and then Simba), it reacts to his pervasive odor by heading for the hills.

The pair have the philosophy—which they inculcate in Simba—of *hakuna matata*, as they expound almost immediately on meeting the doleful young Simba:

> *Timon*: Look, kid, bad things happen and you can't do anything about it, right?
> *Simba*: Right.
> *Timon*: Wrong! When the world turns its back on you, you can turn your back on the world.
> *Simba*: Well, that's not what I was taught.
> *Timon*: Then maybe you need a new lesson. Repeat after me: *"hakuna matata."*
> *Simba*: What?
> *Timon*: *"Hakuna matata."* It means "no worries."

There is an extended song on this theme, and by the end of it Simba not only has grown into adulthood but is joining in with the cheerful chorus. The trouble is, of course, that the philosophy is exactly wrong for *him*: he, as Lion King, cannot turn his back on the world and cannot merely forget about the past, but must do his best to amend whatever has gone before.

The pair act well together—they later starred in a cinematic short called *Disney's Timon and Pumbaa in Stand by Me* (1995), a rendition of the famous song whose hilarious effect cannot adequately be described in cold print (the effort would be like trying to explain why a particular Jacques Tati movie was funny, because one could describe the events but not the lunacy of the whole affair), and a television series, *The Lion King's Timon and Pumbaa* (➤149). Within *The Lion King*, because of Pumbaa's flatulence, some of their lines become distinctly near to the knuckle for a Disney animated feature. An early example occurs in a song they share:

Pumbaa: And it hurt
That my friends never stood downwind.
And, oh the shame . . .
Timon: He was ashamed!
Pumbaa: Thought of changin' my name . . .
Timon: Oh, what's in a name?
Pumbaa: And I got downhearted . . .
Timon: How did ya feel?
Pumbaa: Every time that I—
Timon [slapping his hand over Pumbaa's mouth and looking towards camera: Hey, Pumbaa! Not in front of the kids!

Much later they do another excellent piece of clowning together as they help Simba and Nala sneak past the hyenas to confront Scar. Simba has suggested that the way to divert the hyenas' attention is to use "live bait," and he looks meaning-

fully at Timon. The result is that Timon performs a crazy hula dance, in drag, while Pumbaa lies enticingly in medieval-banquet fashion, complete with an apple in his mouth.

Naturally the pair prove tough thereafter, Pumbaa beating the stuffing out of the three central hyena characters as he reprises Zazu's earlier line: this time it's "They call me *Mister* Pig." During this episode Timon, being so small, can provide little more than vocal encouragement (as does Zazu), but *what* vocal encouragement.

There are further beautiful bits of work on behalf of both of them. At one stage Pumbaa stalks a little blue beetle as if he were a wolfish predator; the humor of this is nicely contrasted with his terror, seconds later, on finding himself confronted by Nala—who wants to kill him and take the meat back to the Pride Lands. Pumbaa runs, but gets trapped under a log. Timon makes a move to defend. There is not much he can do, of course, but the loyalty is fine to see.

By far the funniest bit of dialogue between this madcap pair occurs one night when they and Simba have just enjoyed a good meal and are lying around looking at the star-spangled heavens.

Pumbaa: Timon?
Timon: Yeah?
Pumbaa: Ever wonder what those sparkly dots are up there?
Timon: Pumbaa, I don't wonder. I *know*.
Pumbaa: Oh, what are they?
Timon: They're fireflies. Fireflies that, eh, got stuck up in that big bluish-black thing.
Pumbaa: Oh. Gee. I always thought they were balls of gas burning billions of miles away.
Timon: With you it's aways gas.

Shenzi, Banzai, and Ed

Scar imports hundreds of hyenas to the Pride Lands, but his main allies are these three—none of the others are given individual personalities. In physical appearance there is not a lot to choose among the trio, although Ed has a facial expression of idiocy that the others do not share; they are into malevolence but are not very good at it. Shenzi, superbly voiced by Whoopi Goldberg, is the female; Banzai is the prime male; Ed is the secondary male and fool—at one point Ed suddenly discovers that the meat he is eating is his own leg.

Shenzi is the ambitious one: she is the first to realize that if it weren't for the lions, the hyenas could take over the Pride Lands. She seems the most eager to follow Scar's orders to start the stampede of wildebeest. Yet Banzai, otherwise a rather bland character, is the first to say that, under Scar's regime, there is something rotten in the state of the Pride Lands. Toward the end of the movie the trio find themselves significantly beaten up by Pumbaa.

Minor Characters

Sarabi is Mufasa's mate and Simba's mother; in physical appearance and indeed in voicing she is very much like an older version of the adult Nala: her coat is a little darker, her voice a little firmer and she is slightly larger, but otherwise there is not much difference between the two. She is certainly the boss lioness of the herd and, as such—at least, this is the implication—becomes Scar's mate after the death of Mufasa. She even, for a short time after Simba's return to the Pride Lands, believes that her son was

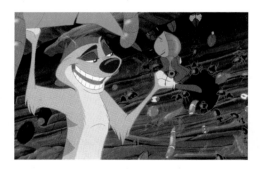
Wise-cracking meerkat Timon, voiced by Nathan Lane, enjoying a typical good meal of insects, grubs, and other creepy-crawlies.

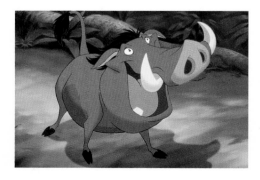
Good-natured warthog Pumbaa, who means well, but doesn't seem to get it.

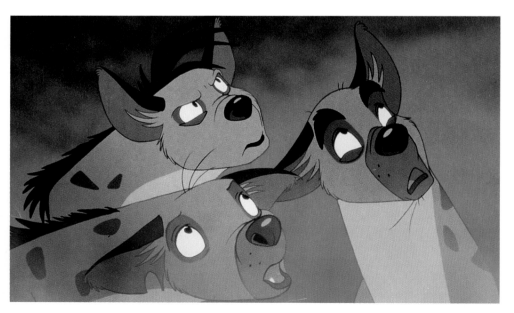
Shenzi, Banzai, and Ed, a trio of hyenas, who provide more than their share of laughs, as well as trouble, in the film.

responsible for his father's death. Finally, however, she gives her blessing to the union of Simba and Nala.

Of slight interest is **Sarafina**, who is Nala's mother: she is almost indistinguishable from Sarabi and plays a very small part in the movie. Playing an even smaller part, although a very arresting one, is a **Mole**: at an early stage he suddenly pops up out of the earth—"Zazu? . . . Sir, news from the underground"—to inform the bird that hyenas are entering the Pride Lands. He has an air about him of a World War I British Army sapper. One has the suspicion that initially he was destined for a slightly larger bit part, but that for one reason or another it never quite happened.

A GOOFY MOVIE

Characters:

Goofy; Max; Pete; P.J.; Roxanne; Principal Mazur; Stacey; Powerline; Treeny; The Bigfoot; Roxanne's Father; Security Guard; Waitress; Miss Maples; Prisoner; Wendell; Mickey Mouse; Donald Duck; Dowager; Piano Player; Cowgirls; Truck Driver; Nuns; Bride; Groom; Corpse; Hillbilly Emcee; Lester Robot; Beuford; Beulah; Mordachai; Lester Character; Little Girl; Photographer; Tourist Boy; Elvis Impersonator; Chad; Lisa

Credits:

Voices: Wayne Allwine (Mickey Mouse); Klée Bragger (Tourist Boy); Pat Butrum (Hillbilly Emcee); Jim Cummings (Pete); Bill Farmer (Goofy); Kevin Lima (Lesters); Jason Marsden (Max); Kellie Martin (Roxanne); Rob Paulsen (P.J.); Wallace Shawn (Principal Mazur); Herschel Sparber (Security Guard); Florence Stanley (Waitress); Jenna von Oy (Stacey); Frank Welker (The Bigfoot); Jo Anne Worley (Miss Maples)

Additional Voices: Dante Basco; Sheryl Bernstein; Julie Brown; Corey Burton; Pat Carroll; E. G. Daily; Carol Holliday; Joey Lawrence; Steve Moore; Brian Pimental; Robyn Richards; Brittany Alyse Smith; Jason Willinger

Voice Direction: Jamie Thomason

Supervising Sound Editor: David E. Stone

Music: Carter Burwell

Songs: Sammy Cahn and James Van Heusen; Patrick DeRemer and Roy Freeland; Barry, Robin, and Maurice Gibb; Randy Petersen and Kevin Quinn; Tom Snow and Jack Feldman

Animation Screenplay: Jymm Magon; Chris Matheson; Brian Pimental; additional material by Curtis Armstrong and John Doolittle

Story: Jymm Magon

Film Editors: Gregory Perler (United States); Catherine Rascon (Paris)

Production Designer: Fred Warter

Animation Supervisors: Nancy Beiman; Matias Marcos; Dominique Monfery; Stéphanie Sainte-Foi

Animators: Jean-Luc Ballester; Michael Benet; Eric Bergeron; Arnaud Berthier; David Berthier; Wolf-Rudiger Bloss; Bolhem Bouchiba; Sylvain Deboissy; Patrick Delage; Eric Delbecq; Marc Eoche-Duval; Bruce Ferriz; Thierry Goulard; Carole Holliday; Holger Leihe; Philippe le Brun; Sergio Pablos; Catherine Poulain; Jean-François Rey; Ventura Rodriguez; Yoshimichi Tamura; Andreas Wessel

Layout Supervisor: J. Michael Spooner

Background Supervisor: Christophe Vacher

Inbetween Supervisors: Peter Brown (Toronto); Mickie Cassidy (Sydney); Pierre Girault (Paris)

Clean-up Supervisors: Claire Bourdin (Paris); Janey Dunn (Sydney); James McCrimmon (Toronto); Brett Newton (Burbank)

Effects Animation Supervisors: John Collins (Toronto); Jean-Christophe Poulain (Paris); Alexis Stadermann (Sydney)

Art Direction: Lawrence Leker; Wendell Luebbe

Paris Chiefs: Gaëtan Brizzi; Paul Brizzi

Associate Producer: Patrick Reagan

Producer: Dan Rounds

Director: Kevin Lima

Release Date: April 7, 1995

Running Time: 77½ minutes

THE MOVIE

This can best be seen as extension of the television series *Goof Troop* (➤**145**), in the same way that *DuckTales: The Movie—Treasure of the Lost Lamp* (➤**351**) is an extension of the television series *DuckTales* (➤**139**). It features various of the television characters, most notably Goofy, Max, and Pete, but it is a far less ambitious movie than what one might call its spiritual predecessor, although there are some delightful moments, the entire movie seems more like an extended television episode—or a conflation of several episodes—than an independently conceived experience.

Character design, art direction and storyboarding were done at Burbank, but most of the animation was done at Disney's new French studio. On initial release the movie had only limited success; in the United States it was very swiftly issued on video, although viewers in the United Kingdom had to wait nearly two years for the video.

THE STORY

Goofy's son Max is much entranced by the high school beauty Roxanne and eventually plucks up the courage to ask her to a party to be held by their friend Stacey. Roxanne accepts, but Goofy has other ideas. Told by Max's principal, Mazur—a fool of the Puritan kind—that the lad is headed for a life of crime, Goofy feels he should spend more quality time with his son, so he drags the unfortunate adolescent much of the way across North America so that they can have "fun" fishing together, just like Goofy and his father did in the old days. Needless to say, this is initially a recipe for disaster. In order to help his cause with Roxanne, Max has impersonated famous rock star Powerline at a school concert, and then claimed he will be on television with the star in Beverly Hills at the end of his horrible trip with his father—he says, was once in a band with Powerline.

The trip is as bad as Max's expectations, most of the jokes are based on the difficulty adolescents have in relating to their parents, with both Goofy and Max getting things wrong with each other time after time. There are other jokes concerning fishing, a pastime that Goofy professes he and his own father repeatedly enjoyed together. An early extravaganza, as their much-overloaded auto teeters along the freeway, is a song ("Open Road") shared not only by Goofy and Max (who can hardly be said to share it, since Max's lines are growls of adolescent revulsion) but by many of the minor characters in the movie.

Almost a character in *A Goofy Movie* is the roadmap used by Goofy: on it is traced out the route that he and his father used when they went off on fishing trips. He is determined that he and his son will pursue the same trail, still marked there in pencil. In due course Max alters the annotation so that they will finally reach Beverly Hills rather than the remote Lake

Mystic, assuming (correctly) that Goofy will be too thick to notice the difference. But, before that, Max has to endure a lot. There is a visit to Lester's Possum Park, a kid-oriented diner/camping park of the type all kids hate. There is an encounter with Pete (➤15) which Max finds humiliating because of Pete's evident opulence. There is a long period during which Goofy and Max are terrorized by a Bigfoot; at least their collective fright begins a bonding process, as signified by Max forming the statement "Hi Dad" out of the last letters of a tin of Alphabet Soup.

But thereafter Pete, having eavesdropped on a conversation between Max and P.J., "helpfully" tells Goofy about the forging of the map, so temporarily wrecking the relationship. The bonding begins again when Goofy and Max have to save each other's lives as they career into a racing river and over the predictable waterfall. Max confesses the lie he told to Roxanne about going to be on stage with Powerline; Goofy, suddenly beginning to understand his son's priorities, determines to ensure that the promise can be kept. He takes Max to Los Angeles and to the Powerline concert, managing (more by accident than cleverness) to get both of them onstage for the vital television show.

Back home, Max—now totally reconciled with his father—at Goofy's instigation confesses the truth to Roxanne, who forgives him for the lie; it was unnecessary, she says, because she liked him quite enough anyway. Elements of this touching romance are to be found in a *Goof Troop* episode called "Puppy Love."

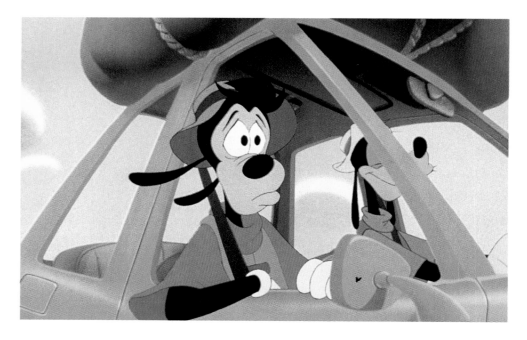
Max and father Goofy in the car.

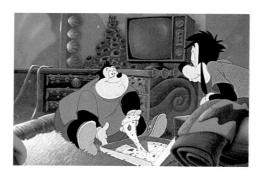
Pete's son P.J. and Max sharing pizza.

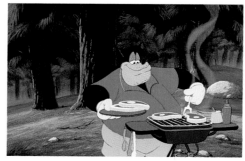
The boorish, egocentric Pete, Goofy's neighbor and business partner, grilling steaks.

THE CHARACTERS

The Gang from Goof Troop

Once upon a time **Goofy** was a regular adornment of our cinema screens, starring in countless shorts. Then he was in effect reincarnated as a television character for the purposes of *Goof Troop* (➤145). The two characters are not the same, and so it is strange to see the *television* version of Goofy on the big screen, as if someone had usurped the role of an old friend. As noted, Scrooge McDuck (➤139) made a better transition to the cinema in *DuckTales: The Movie—Treasure of the Lost Lamp* (➤351). The Goofy of the shorts (➤44) was always a bumbling clown, but in a curious way there was something subtle about the unsubtlety of his clowning: the effect is difficult to describe, but is probably best exemplified in his performance as Marley's ghost in *Mickey's Christmas Carol* (➤49). Perhaps, too, the clowning is better suited to the shorts, in

which anything goes—they are fantasies, whereas in this movie, as in the television series, there is some pretence to realism. Goofy is a father having problems over his relationship with his adolescent son, and in such a context his tomfoolery is not nearly so funny. His dancing scene with Powerline, toward the end of the movie, is particularly painful; one has the feeling that the moviemakers were desperately trying to drag into the late twentieth century a character whose main appeal is his antiquity, and thereby the performance induces the same uneasy feeling one might have if one saw Fred Astaire forced, because he needed the money, to dance at a Spice Girls concert.

Max works much better on the big screen. Stuck with a dad he quite rightly regards as a numbskull, he is the perfect image of the rebellious adolescent: oppressed by the goofiness of his father, most of the time he is also incapable of realizing that his father is acting in Max's best interests—or trying to. Max is also suffering from a torrent of teenage hormones, especially regarding Roxanne

(Max seems here a bit older than in the television incarnation). The dream sequence that starts the movie, in which Roxanne proffers a kiss to him, is one of the funniest and most successful parts of *A Goofy Movie*. The symbol of Max's teenage angst is "the perfect cast"—an angling maneuver that his father incessantly tries to teach him during their long trip across the United States. Of course, Max would much rather watch a Powerline video or, even better, date Roxanne at the same time as watching the Powerline video, but his pop is trying to give him angling instructions. Poor Max.

Pete, far less evil than in most of his earlier screen incarnations (➤15), is certainly a boor; it is just about possible, although difficult, to believe that he might be a well-meaning boor. He and Goofy, as well as being neighbors, share a photographic business; it is clear that the Goof is regarded as the junior partner. This version of Pete has very fixed ideas about the way parents should deal with their teenage children. They should be firm:

Goofy: You know, maybe Max isn't all the things that you think a son should be, but he loves me.
Pete: Hey. My son respects me.

Of course, Pete's son, P.J., doesn't respect him in the slightest, but this is something Pete will never realize, because he is utterly egocentric. This egocentricity is used to brilliant comic effect when Goofy, trying to demonstrate to Max "the perfect cast," accidentally hooks out from under Pete's nose the steak he has been barbecuing, Pete's incredulity that fate could play such a nasty trick is a wonder to behold.

Pete does not hide his wealth under a bushel: a couple of times during the movie he turns up in his camper, which is large enough to contain a Jacuzzi, a bowling alley, a swimming pool . . . Max, a friend of P.J.'s, has difficulty accepting that P.J.'s father is so much richer than his own, who drives a rickety old car overburdened with luggage.

The nastiest thing Pete does during the movie is when he has overheard Max and P.J. talking about how Max has altered the map, and tells Goofy:

> *Pete:* So, um, tch, you and your son seem to be, uh . . . gettin' along just hunky-dory, uh?
> *Goofy:* Yeah, it's been great. You know, it's funny, but none of your techniques worked for me. Harder I tried, the worse it got. Once I eased up, things just clicked.
> *Pete:* Oh, that's swell. So there's no problems then, uh?
> *Goofy:* Not a one.
> *Pete:* Oh, nuts. Oh, I just hate to be the bearer of bad news, but, uh . . .
> *Goofy:* What is it, Pete?
> *Pete:* Your kid's dupin' you.

The reason that Pete comes so badly out of this sequence (apart from his recent leap into a bath when he splashed most of the water out of it, such is his bulk) is that he takes very visible pleasure in alerting Goofy to Max's duplicity.

P.J., Pete's unfortunate son, is rather like a junior version of Pete but, as with Max, rebellious against his father—although to a lesser degree. Often called "Peej," P.J. is prepared to help Max in the pseudo-Powerline concert staged for

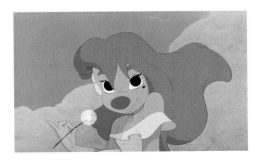

Roxanne, the object of Max's affections, in one of his dream sequences.

Roxanne's benefit at the high school and is most obviously a good friend. He does his best to persuade Max that altering the map was a foolish idea. ("Whatever made you think your dad would fall for a stupid idea like that?" asks P.J. To which Max responds: "It wasn't stupid.") In any event, P.J. is proved right, but by then the emotional argument is between Goofy and Max alone, with no others being involved. P.J.'s relationship to Max in this movie might be compared to the role Stacey plays against Roxanne, but Stacey is by far the more interesting character.

Roxanne

When we first come across Roxanne she isn't really there: she is merely a figment of Max's adolescent dream, which is in itself a parody of countless dream sequences in nonanimated movies where young lovers waltz among the wonders of the empty countryside and eventually share a kiss. Few cheeks in the audience can be dry as Max, just as Roxanne is about to kiss him, is rudely awakened by his father; it is time to get up and go to school. Much later in the movie Max looks up at a cloud and it miraculously takes on the form of Roxanne. Even the ripples in lake water can represent her image. In short, wherever he looks he sees her.

The reality of the relationship seems rather different: Roxanne is no distant untouchable. The day after the dream Max makes a public fool of himself on the football field, eventually falling flat on his face. While other kids stand around making derisive remarks, Roxanne is the one who helps him to his feet. Even from this early moment it is clear to us, as outside observers, that Max and Roxanne are interested in each other, but of course this is something they cannot confess, being teenagers. Stacey almost has to physically bang their heads together. That the high school dreamboat should be intrigued by someone like Max is never properly explained.

There is something of Minnie Mouse (➤32) about Roxanne, and also a hint of Chip 'n Dale (➤141). It is difficult to determine to what mammalian species she belongs, but certainly it is one that allows for a turbulent mop of strawberry-blond hair. The word *cute* could have been invented for her. Oddly, though, she has little influence on the plot beyond, through her beauty and their mutual attraction, forcing Max to come out with his foolish lie that he will be onstage with Powerline. Her best pal Stacey believes that Max will be able to pull this off; Roxanne's faith crumbles rather earlier, thus making her the less interesting character.

In the final scenes of the movie it is amusing to discover how much under Roxanne's thumb her father is. Also, when Goofy makes a fool of himself for the final time, it is a witty note that Roxanne simply assumes that this is how fathers always are—idiotic and embarrassing.

Principal Mazur

The master of a high school, Principal Mazur appears to regard himself as, instead, the master of all he surveys. Tall and icy—it would come as a shock if any smile other than a sadistic one broke out on his face—he is the epitome of those people whose attitudes, which are usually uncharitable, become rigidly fixed with astonishing rapidity. It is he who kick-starts the main linking strand of the movie's plot: having discovered Max performing in the illicit Powerline concert, he predicts to Goofy that the lad is destined for the electric chair. Despite Max's crime being so obviously a trivial one, it is Mazur's prediction that convinces Goofy that, if his son is ever to be saved from a life of heinous crime, they must spend some quality time together—and so off they go for the fishing trip.

Stacey

Roxanne's best friend, Stacey is one of the most appealing of the secondary characters. Every school knows such duos. Where Roxanne is the pretty, vivacious one of this pair, Stacey is the steady-minded companion, always seeming to play second fiddle yet perhaps in fact the dominant member of the friendship . . . as seems to be the case in the first sequence in which Stacey plays an important role. The girls have seen Max's Powerline impersonation. The subject of their conversation is Stacey's forthcoming party, at which the assembled kids will watch the Powerline concert on television:

> *Stacey:* . . . And then my parents' air-conditioning went on the fritz, so I figured with all those kids in my house the place would be like a sauna, so I'm all freaked out, but then I thought, like, use it! So my theme's gonna be "Powerline Goes Rainforest." Too much? [*Roxanne is distracted at the sight of the disconsolate Max*] Roxanne, are you listening? Ahhh . . .
> *Roxanne:* Stacey, no! I don't wanna . . .
> *Stacey:* Talk to him.
> *Roxanne (to Max):* A-ahem . . . A-a-ahem! . . . Hm . . .
> *Stacey:* Tap him.

The result of the tap is that Max leaps from his fit of depression with such surprise that he knocks some of the books and papers out of Roxanne's arms. From here on, thanks to Stacey's influence, the ancillary mainspring of the plot is initiated:

Max: Oh, gosh, I'm sorry.
Roxanne: It's Okay. Really . . . Umm, I — I liked your dance.
Max: Yeah. Eh . . . yeah? Uh, yeah? . . . It's from Powerline's new video.
Roxanne: I know. He's totally a genius.
Max: Y-y-yeah, he's, uh, he's doin' a concert next week in L.A.
Roxanne: Oh, yeah! Stacey's showing it at her party.
Max: Yeah.
Roxanne: Yeah.
Max: Um, uh . . . Roxanne, I was, uh . . . sorta kinda thinkin' that maybe I'd, um . . . ask you to go with me, that is, to the party. Of course, if you don't want to I'd completely understand.
Roxanne: Well, I was sorta thinkin' that . . . I'd love to.

There is a very interesting little tangle of emotions at play here—an unusually complex one in a movie that rarely aims for emotional depth. (The theme of the restitution of the relationship between Goofy and Max, father and teenage son, is one that has been used in thousands of movies, books, and other forms of fiction over the centuries.) The superficial emotional event in the scene is that Roxanne and Max manage, with typical teenage clumsiness, to stagger toward a mutual admission that they are attracted to each other. But there is a deeper level in the sequence than this. Bear in mind that Stacey was the person who engineered the whole occasion, and bear in mind further that Stacey—as we later discover—is, even more than Roxanne, the person who keeps the faith that Max will indeed keep his promise to appear onstage at Powerline's televised concert. It would therefore seem that in a way Stacey's love for the boy who has not long before been jeered at as "the Goof Kid" is actually more profound than Roxanne's; yet of

course she loves her prettier best friend as well. And so she throws the two of them at each other.

Stacey wears glasses and her hair has been cropped into a disciplined shape—quite unlike Roxanne's provocative mop. She is plain and seemingly studious to the point where for occasional fleeting moments of her performance on-screen she seems in effect middle-aged—certainly mentally but also physically. It comes almost as a relief when in the final few moments of the movie, as she and Bobby begin to be drawn together, she gives a broad smile and we see the sparkle of her braces.

One gets the impression that someone at Burbank put a lot of effort into making Stacey the intriguing, attractive, and profound character she is.

Bobby

A relatively minor character, Bobby (more formally, Robert Zimuruski) is a fellow student of Max's and Roxanne's. He has a prominent forelock of brown hair, blue sunglasses, and an appetite for processed cheddar cheese—a spray can of which Max and P.J. have to give him as fee for the loan of audiovideo equipment for Max's pseudo-Powerline act. His speech is a mess of neologisms.

In short, Bobby is the epitome of the teenage computer nerd, but clearly he regards himself as something of a high school lothario and assumes he will have no difficulty in turning Roxanne's head. He seems to regard Max as not even a distant rival for her affections. When, toward the end of the movie, a bunch of the students are watching the Powerline concert on television and Max does not immediately appear alongside the rock idol, it is Bobby who is the first—with the

inevitable sneer—to point out the absence to Roxanne. Naturally, when Max does appear it is the ultimate put-down for Bobby, and he realizes his chances with Roxanne are doomed. Moments later, however, he is making moves toward Stacey instead—and she, astonishingly, seems to respond in encouraging fashion. One would have thought she had better taste in teenage heartthrobs.

Powerline

In effect there are two Powerlines in the movie: the impersonation by Max of the man he regards as the greatest rock star in the universe, and the rock star himself. The latter looks like a cross between Michael Jackson and Goofy, with more than a touch of Ronald Reagan thrown in for good measure. His songs include lines like:

We'll set the world in motion
By reaching out for each other's hand

In other words, the songs are of the sort that teenagers might think profound while still teenagers, then wince at five years later.

Powerline seems more genial than the average rock star. First Goofy is launched onto his stage, then Max. Rather than have them both pitched out by the bouncers, he welcomes them—especially when, on Max's instructions, Goofy begins to perform the requisite bodily contortions required for "the perfect cast." Powerline assumes this is some new dance step and starts to copy Goofy, adapting the movement to the song.

Powerline is less important on-screen than he is off it. As idol of the high school students, he inspires Max into lying to Roxanne, were it not for this lie the rest of the plot would fall apart, leaving the movie exposed as merely a series of humorous sequences.

Treeny

Treeny is Powerline's main backup singer, but she appears long before the climactic concert. We first encounter her during the singing of the song "Open Road" as Goofy and Max are motoring along the freeway. Alongside her diminutive husband Wendell, she is in a convertible. Although she occupies the passenger seat, it is fairly obvious who does the couple's driving. Somewhat surprisingly, after we've seen a few other motorists, she reappears, this time dancing on top of the convertible.

Her much more significant role in the plot comes later. That Powerline should have a backing singer who looks rather like *The Little Mermaid*'s Ursula (➤348), albeit with redder hair, is astonishing enough. That Goofy should stumble into

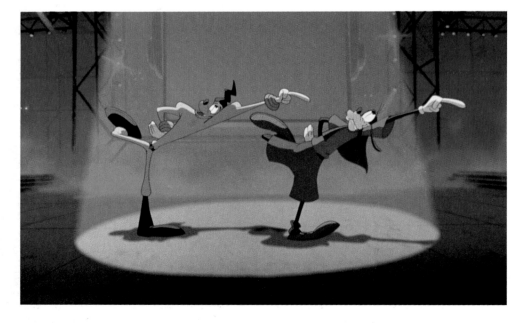

Rock star Powerline, copying Goofy's ridiculous dance movements onstage.

her dressing room when she is (let us be decorous here) less than completely dressed causes one to suck in one's breath—although Esmeralda (➤424) is likewise embarrassed in *The Hunchback of Notre Dame*. Treeny's response to Goofy's intrusion is to deliver him a forceful punch, so that he staggers into one of Powerline's hi-tech stage props—and, groggily still lying on it, is elevated to the stage, where he is decanted amid an explosion of sparks. This sets things up, of course, for Max being able to fulfill the promise he gave to Roxanne.

The Bigfoot

The giant brown gorilla that assails Goofy and Max can hardly be described as a fully developed character, although some of its antics are inspired—notably its first appearance. This occurs as a consequence of Goofy trying to demonstrate "the perfect cast" to Max. Nearby, Pete is cooking a steak on a grill. The flying hook snatches the steak from under a bemused Pete's nose and then whips it through the air so that it lands directly in front of the Bigfoot. The Bigfoot's initial response is disinterest; instead it starts chewing a log. But this is no declaration of vegetarianism. As soon as the next part of Goofy's "perfect cast" begins and the steak begins to twitch away from the Bigfoot, the monstrous animal becomes voraciously interested and gives chase.

Thereafter the animal persecutes Max and Goofy, eventually besieging them in their car. Despite their terror, Goofy is delighted to have managed, during the pell-mell action, to film the only clear video to show definitive proof of the existence of Bigfoot. Unfortunately, the animal gets hold of the tape and eats it.

Roxanne's Father

Although really only a minor character, Roxanne's father is one of the most delightful comic creations in the movie: he is a caricature of the father every adolescent boy would least like his sweetheart to have. He appears only on a couple of brief occasions. When Max arrives at Roxanne's house to plead his cause, Roxanne's father answers the door—filling the doorway as if he were a truck somebody had tried to drive through it and makes no response to Max except to growl repeatedly, like a rottweiler that would rather shred the cat than ask questions. There is indeed something doggish about his appearance: one is vaguely reminded of Butch (➤91) and indeed of Pete.

When Max calls after the return from California, however, and the father repeats the performance, Roxanne appears almost immediately and it is easily apparent that he is completely under her thumb. The diminutive girl dismisses her

gigantic parent from the scene as if he were an errant schoolchild.

Minor Characters

This movie contains a huge number of named minor characters, most of whom are on-screen for mere seconds—although some are of more significance. Many of the former appear as Goofy persuades Max to sing the song "Open Road" with him as they drive down the freeway. They are either other drivers or other passengers, and they each fill in a line or two in the song: a **Piano Player** sitting in the back of a truck; three **Cowgirls,** who emerge from the top of his piano and are of such beauty that Goofy nearly swerves off the road; the **Truck Driver,** a huge and stubble-chinned individual, topped by a red cap, who gestures wrathfully at the swerving Goofy; a **Prisoner,** clearly being driven to the penitentiary, who looks rather like one of the weasels in the "Mr. Toad" section of *The Adventures of Ichabod and Mr. Toad* (➤230); **Wendell,** the tiny husband of Treeny (see above); a plump and elderly **Dowager,** who is incongruously driving a sports car (the first line she contributes to the song is equally incongruous: "Look out, you dirtbags, eat my dust!"); four **Nuns** in a station wagon; a **Bride** whose **Groom** parachutes down to join her in the convertible in which she is being driven; a **Corpse** who heaves himself up out of the coffin in the hearse in which he is being driven; plus **Donald Duck** (➤61) and **Mickey Mouse** (➤23), who are briefly seen at the side of the freeway trying to hitch a lift. The penultimate line of the song is "I'm feelin' fancy free," which may be an unconscious reference to the anthology feature *Fun and Fancy Free* (➤222). The song sequence must have been more fun to make than it is to watch.

A further plethora of characters appears once Goofy and Max come off the freeway to arrive at a sleazy theme park: Lester's Possum Park. "Garwsh, it's even better than I remembered," remarks Goofy to a disbelieving Max. Max's obvious opinion is borne out by the plaint of a **Little Girl** who is being dragged into the place by yet another parent who assumes she is spending "quality time" with her child: "No, Mommy, I don't wanna go." Once Goofy has managed to persuade Max to follow him through that same doorway, Max is mortified as a **Hillbilly Emcee** introduces the floor show, which involves four **Lester Robots:** these are rather nasty pseudo-possums whose obvious teeth and evident artificiality make not only Max but the viewer cringe—this is stuff for Saturday-morning television (if even for that), not for a feature movie. The first Lester Robot

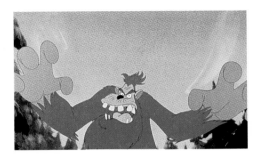

The Bigfoot, a giant brown gorilla, who eats Goofy's videotape—the only evidence of his existence.

introduces the other three as **Beuford, Beulah,** and **Mordachai,** and the four perform a hillbilly song. Shortly afterward, as Max is escaping from this, he and Goofy encounter a **Lester Character** —i.e., a man dressed in a possum suit— who treats him like an infant ("I know! You need a big hug from Lester! . . . See? Now you feel all *good* inside!"). One's heart lifts when Max hits him. Immediately afterward Goofy buys a couple of possum hats and tries to insist that he and Max should pose for the theme park's **Photographer** while wearing them. Max refuses, but Goofy himself does some clowning for the camera—with the usual disastrous results—and Max's mood is not improved by the mockery of a Tourist Boy: "It's Dork and Dork Junior!"

Later Goofy and Max stop at a wayside diner. Here they are served by a **Waitress** who yet again could hardly be further from Max's ideal: she is plump and vaguely doglike and wears half-moon glasses . . . and calls him "cutie." Among the other patrons in the diner is an **Elvis Impersonator** who has acquired a belly just as large as the King himself did. Since Max has been a Powerline impersonator earlier in the movie, this seems a subtle further allusion to the intergenerational gap.

Two of Max's fellow students, aside from those who play a significant part in the plot, are given names: **Lisa** and **Chad** are first encountered sneaking a quick kiss in the precincts of the high school.

Of slightly more importance are **Miss Maples** and, at the Powerline concert, a **Security Guard.** Miss Maples is Principal Mazur's secretary. Middle-aged and tweedy, bearing a mantle of respectability, she is subjected to some of the consequences of the movie's early clowning. She is rather like *The Great Mouse Detective*'s Mrs Judson (➤325). The Security Guard—a hulking figure in a suitably imposing uniform—appears much later on, he does his very best to stop Max getting to the stage with Powerline. Some idea of his scale can be gathered when Max, escaping from his officiousness, is able to dive between his legs.

POCAHONTAS

Characters:

Pocahontas; John Smith; Governor Ratcliffe; Meeko; Flit; Powhatan; Thomas; Percy; Grandmother Willow; Wiggins; Ben; Lon; Roy; Nakoma; Kocoum; Kekata; Namontack

Credits:

Based on an idea by Mike Gabriel

Voices: Joe Baker (Lon); Christian Bale (Thomas); Irene Bedard (Pocahontas speaking); Billy Connolly (Ben); James Apaumut Fall (Kocoum); Mel Gibson (John Smith); Linda Hunt (Grandmother Willow); John Kassir (Meeko); Judy Kuhn (Pocahontas singing); Danny Mann (Percy); Russell Means (Powhatan); Michelle St. John (Nakoma); David Ogden Stiers (Governor Ratcliffe; Wiggins); Gordon Tootoosis (Kekata); Frank Welker (Flit)

Additional Voices: Travis Blaise; Sasha Dorogov; Branko Mihanovic; D. Anthony Wawrzaszek

Sound Effects Editors: Scott Martin Gershin; Peter J. Lehman; Brian McPherson; Anthony J. Miceli; Rick Morris; Joseph Phillips; Alan Rankin

Music: Alan Menken

Songs: Alan Menken; Stephen Schwartz

Animation Screenplay: Carl Binder; Susannah Grant; Philip LaZebnik

Story: Tom Sito; plus Chris Buck; Robert Gibbs; Francis Glebas; Ed Gombert; Joe Grant; Kaan Kalyon; Glen Keane; Todd Kurosawa; Duncan Marjoribanks; Burny Mattinson; Bruce Morris; Ralph Zondag

Film Editor: H. Lee Peterson

Visual Effects Supervisor: Don Paul

Supervising Animators: Ruben A. Aquino (Powhatan); Chris Buck (Percy; Wiggins; Grandmother Willow); Michael Cedeno (Kocoum); Anthony DeRosa (Nakoma); Ken Duncan (Thomas); T. Daniel Hofstedt (Ben; Lon); Glen Keane (Pocahontas); Duncan Marjoribanks (Governor Ratcliffe); John Pomeroy (John Smith); Dave Pruiksma (Flit; Forest Animals); Nik Ranieri (Meeko)

Animators: Tim Allen, Tom Bancroft; Richard Bazley; Aaron Blaise; Rejean Bourdages; Ken Boyer; Bob Bryan; David Burgess; Brian Ferguson; Trey Finney; Doug Frankel; Raul Garcia; Tom Gately; Steven P. Gordon; Joe Haidar; Kent Hammerstrom; Randy Haycock; Mark Henn; Ken Hettig; Ron Husband; James Young Jackson; Broose Johnson; Mark Koetsier; Doug Krohn; Brad Kuha; Dave Kuhn; Dave Kupczyk; James Lopez; Gregory S. Manwaring; Craig R. Maras; Teresa Martin; Anthony Wayne Michaels; Jean Morel; Philip Morris; Gilda Palinginis; Ralf Palmer; Gary J. Perkovac; William Recinos; John Ripa; Pres Antonio

Romanillos; Chris Sauve; Michael Show; Michael Swofford; Barry Temple; Chris Wahl; Bill Waldman; Eric Walls; Larry White; Ellen Woodbury; David A. Zaboski

Computer Graphics Imagery: Steve Goldberg

Layout Supervisor: Rasoul Azadani

Effects Animators: Allen Blyth; Ed Coffey; Jazno Francoeur; Troy A. Gustafson; Kathleen Quiafe Hodge; Tom Hush; Ted C. Kierscey; Dorse Lanpher; James De V. Mansfield; Stephen B. Moore; Marlon West; Garrett Wren

Background Supervisor: Cristy Maltese

Art Director: Michael Giaimo

Artistic Coordinator: Don Hansen

Production Manager: Traci Tolman Mars

Associate Producer: Baker Bloodworth

Producer: James Pentecost

Director of Technology: Paul Yanover

Directors: Mike Gabriel; Eric Goldberg

Release Date: outdoor one-shot premiere in Central Park, New York, June 10, 1995; limited release June 16, 1995; general release June 23, 1995

Running Time: 81 minutes

THE MOVIE

Pocahontas is certainly one of the most emotionally moving Disney animated features since *Bambi* (➤197), and possibly of all time. There are various reasons for this, not least among them the song "Colors of the Wind," which Menken and Schwartz composed early on during the movie's creation and which deeply influenced much of the rest—animation, characterization, atmosphere, and more. Indeed, the songs in this movie—most of them concentrated in its earlier parts—are generally impressive. Also poignant is "Savages," later on in the proceedings, alternate verses of which are chanted by the Native Americans and the would-be Colonists as they prepare for war: each side regards the people of the other as nothing more than savages and, in their own worldviews, both are right . . . and, as this strongly antiracist movie stresses, wrong.

But there are other reasons why *Pocahontas* is moving. One is our knowledge of the true history of John Smith and the Native American princess who was called by that name. Matoaka (1595–1617), as she was originally known, seems indeed to have saved the British adventurer John Smith

(1580–1631) from death at the hands of her tribe at least once if not twice. At the time she seems to have been about thirteen; there is no real evidence of an amorous liaison between the two. She was lured to Jamestown, Virginia, in 1612—by which time Smith had several years earlier left for home (although he would return to the New World in 1614). In Jamestown she was converted to Christianity and renamed Rebecca; in 1613 she married a different Englishman, John Rolfe (1585–1622), and with him she came in 1616 to Britain, where she was much feted by the chattering classes, who seem to have regarded her as an interesting curio. In 1617 she and her husband decided to return to Virginia, but she died (of smallpox) en route. What there is of romance in her tragically brief biography has been added by retellings. Of which this is one.

The project was the brainchild of Mike Gabriel, who came up with it at a 1991 Disney brainstorming meeting. In retrospect, it is surprising that his colleagues didn't turn it down flat: The company was enjoying astonishing success with a string of animated features that deployed the traditional Disney qualities of comedy and imagination, so why should anyone think of taking on a quasi-historical drama? For whatever reason, Gabriel was given the go-ahead to develop the idea, and the result was a landmark in the history of animated moviemaking—one of those rare animated movies that one would happily watch several times in a row, and, as noted, one of the few that genuinely brings a lump to the throat.

Music and history contribute to the emotional intensity of *Pocahontas* in more ways than one. It seems evident that those involved in the making of the movie became *driven* by the story and by the character of Pocahontas herself; more than one has commented that it wasn't so much a question of creating a character as of finding one that was already there. (This is echoed at several points in the movie: Pocahontas's mother is dead, but her spirit, according to Pocahontas's father, is still everywhere; both Pocahontas and Smith, on different occasions, explain that their spirits will always be together.) Other factors drove the moviemakers, notably the way that the tale could be manipulated in order to proclaim a message of tolerance between different peoples. It soon became clear to them that this was not just another on the production line of Disney smash-hit animated features but a movie that could *say* something, a movie whose theme was important.

And such a theme deserved the very best they could give it. If nothing else singled out the experience of watching *Pocahontas*, then the loving care devoted to virtually every frame would. The comedic element is cut to a level far below that of the normal Disney animated feature, and does not detract from the drama; in fact, some of the comedy, especially that involving the vile Governor Ratcliffe, contributes to it, being very dark indeed. Most of the human characters are depicted realistically—a difficult task for the artists—and are treated with respect. Even minor characters like Nakoma (Pocahontas's best chum) was given a fully developed personality. But realism is not allowed to dictate everything; in some of the movie's finest moments we are treated to symbolic imagery whose use of light and pattern is breathtaking.

A useful comparison can be made with the FAI/Youngheart production *Fern-Gully: The Last Rainforest* (1992). This too is an animated feature that conveys an important message relevant to our times (here concerning the preservation of our natural world) at the same time as it entertains. Any attempt to decide which is the better or more effective of the two would be invidious. What is interesting, though, is the way in which they ration comedy and drama to almost exactly the same extent, so that in neither instance does one ever feel oppressed by the weight of the theme, while at the same time the theme is not trivialized. In Stephen Rebello's *The Art of Pocahontas* (1995) there is cited a quote by Mike Gabriel that perhaps sums it all up:

> Ignorance and bigotry are taught. If this song, this movie, makes one child begin to question anyone who teaches hatred and fosters misunderstanding, that will be a wonderful thing.

THE STORY

The ship *Susan Constant* sets sail from London with settlers for the New World; in practice their leader is John Smith although the titular head of the expedition is the greedy Governor Ratcliffe. The settlers have heard that the New World is full of gold; in order to get it they will happily slaughter any Native Americans ("Red Indians") who might choose to stand in their way—with Smith regarded as the chief potential Indian killer. Soon the ship runs into a heavy storm, which gives Smith and the young settler Thomas an opportunity to prove their valor, especially Smith, who in due course saves Thomas from the waves.

We cut to the Indian village, where Powhatan has just returned from con-quering the Massawomecks; his daughter is the headstrong Pocahontas. Bravest among the warriors has been Kocoum, to whom Pocahontas is betrothed against her will. But she has been having a pre-cognitive dream and knows that her life-course is directing her otherwise—a view confirmed by Grandmother Willow, a tree spirit, who tells her to listen with her heart to the message of the wind. Pocahontas is told to see what she can see—which proves to be the sails of the *Susan Constant*.

Smith, Ben, Lon, and Thomas go ashore, observed by Pocahontas; she is almost seen by Smith as the others pull the *Susan Constant* in to moor. The Indians are mystified by the invaders; the shaman Kekata uses divination by fire to predict that the strangers are like ravening wolves, and Kocoum proposes to attack them at once—a proposition vetoed by Powhatan, even after the settlers have begun to ruin the land, which Ratcliffe has declared as Jamestown, in their quest for gold.

Smith eventually discovers Pocahontas, and his first impulse is to shoot her on sight—an impulse he conquers only on realizing she is beautiful. She learns English immediately, thanks (one assumes) to the voice of the wind, and it is clear that she and Smith have fallen instantly in love. A little later, after he has explained to her the benefits "civilization" will bring to her people, she gets through to him that she is no savage but has a knowledge greater than, though different from, his own.

In the meantime Ratcliffe's party find they are being observed by a group of Indians and open fire at once, one Indian being wounded. Powhatan decides to call all the neighboring tribes for assistance to repel the invaders. The settlers build a stockade but Smith creeps out to meet Pocahontas; she introduces him to Grandmother Willow, who identifies him as the one whom her dream was referring to. The young lovers, in their own ways, try to persuade their respective leaders that war is unnecessary, but are singularly unsuccessful: Powhatan believes battle is sad but inevitable, while Ratcliffe merely wants to exterminate the "savages." The lovers agree that Smith will speak to Powhatan in an attempt to avert war, but as they kiss to seal this pact they are spied upon by Kocoum and Thomas. Kocoum attacks Smith and Thomas shoots and kills Kocoum. For this apparent murder Smith is sentenced to death by Powhatan. At the last moment Pocahontas prevents the execution and, in so doing, persuades her father to prevent the outbreak of war. Ratcliffe nevertheless shoots at Powhatan but Smith saves the Indian Chief, being wounded as he does so. Ratcliffe is thrown into chains by the settlers, who at last realize how he has manipulated them. Smith must be taken home to Britain for medical attention; Pocahontas, deciding that her people need her, declines to go with him. Still entirely in love, the lovers part.

THE CHARACTERS

Pocahontas

A recurrent characteristic of the Disney animated features over the past few years—at least since 1989's *The Little Mermaid* (➤342)—has been the presence of a strong female character in a central

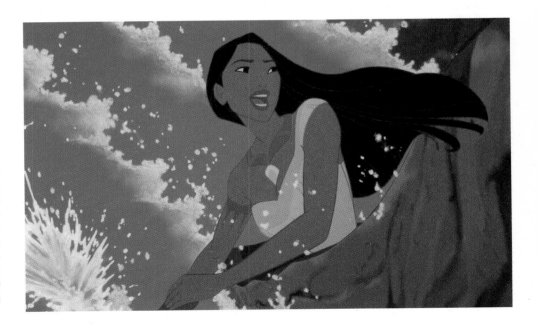
The young heroine in her canoe.

role. Belle (➤367), Jasmine (➤376), and Esmeralda (➤424) are other examples. None of these, however, can compare with the figure of Pocahontas: She *is* the movie, to the extent that, when everything else might be forgotten, her image persists in the memory. The reasons for this phenomenon are multiple, involving not only her conceptualization and animation (Glen Keane was the supervising animator) but also her voicing (Irene Bedard for Pocahontas speaking and Judy Kuhn for Pocahontas singing), her dialogue, her way of moving, and perhaps above all, her hair, which moves in the wind in such a way as to express a freedom no longer available to us. She is not some chic beauty thrust at us as a politically correct image of the Native American; she is exotic and beautiful and as wild as any of the animals the settlers might have come across in the New World.

Perhaps her way of moving, especially in the first half of the movie, is the key to her appeal. Where all the other human characters move as humans do, she slinks with the stealth and subtlety of a four-legged animal. It comes as no surprise when, early on, Smith, having set off to look for Indians, walks right past her: She is so much a creature of the forest that she is barely distinguishable from the bark and leaves. When she is revealed, to us rather earlier than to Smith, we discover that her flowing hair conveys the same wildness. She symbolizes the element of human existence that Westernized humanity has lost: no primitive, no "savage" (as Governor Ratcliffe and far too many bigots ever since would find it convenient to believe), she is instead someone totally in touch with her world.

This point is made by the moviemakers particularly acutely when Smith interrogates her about the gold that the settlers supposed would be lying around all over the territory, just waiting to be picked up. He asks her if her tribe knows of this valuable yellow stuff that comes out of the ground; she answers that of course they do, and shows him a head of corn as an example—because to her people mere metal has no value.

Pocahontas has dreamed of the arrival of Smith and the other settlers. The image in her recurring dream is of a spinning arrow, which is interpreted by Grandmother Willow as an indication that Pocahontas should choose her own path into the future rather than governed by conventional wisdom. Pocahontas takes this advice during her developing relationship with Smith. It is only later that she discovers there was a more literal truth in the image, when she is given by Meeko—who earlier stole it—Smith's compass, which sure enough displays the spinning arrow of her dreams.

There is a major difference between Pocahontas and most of the other Disney strong female leads of recent years (Esmeralda [➤424] is another exception). Those others tend to be on the cusp between girlhood and womanhood, but there is no doubt that Pocahontas is a full-fledged adult, which adds great strength to the movie as a whole.

John Smith

Like Pocahontas, Smith is a genuine historical character. He started his career as a mercenary, fighting first under the French and then in Hungary against the Turks; the latter captured and enslaved him, but he eventually escaped to join the expedition that would found Jamestown. In the New World he was twice, he claimed in his somewhat unreliable autobiography, captured by the tribe led by Powhatan and twice spared thanks to the intercession of Powhatan's daughter Pocahontas. In 1608, because of his skill in negotiating with the Native Americans, he was elected Virginia's president; however, the following year he returned to Britain. He came back to the New World in 1614 to explore the coast of New England. That his initially murderous ways were changed by the influence of Pocahontas is at least a matter for debate.

Disney has made much of the importance of Smith being voiced by Mel Gibson—claiming that the actor significantly affected the animated part. This is an argument hard to sustain: The Smith we see on screen is blond-haired and blue-eyed, and his body language is quite different from Gibson's. Yet there is a certain laid-backness that is very much Gibson's.

When we first meet Smith he is a racist bigot:

> That's right. I'm not about to let you have all the fun.

The fun in question being the slaughter of the Native Americans. A very short while later there is an ugly moment of discussion:

> *Thomas*: This New World's gonna be great. I'll get a pile of gold, build a big house, and if an Indian tries to stop me I'll blast him.
> *Smith*: You just worry about your fortune. Leave the savages to me.
> *Lon*: Will they give us much trouble?
> *Ben*: Not as much trouble as Smith will give them.
> *Settlers* (*singing*): We'll kill ourselves an Injun
> Or maybe two or three.
> We're stalwart men and bold
> Of the Virginia Company . . .

Smith's initial encounter with Pocahontas takes all such thoughts out of his

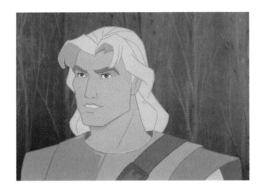

Captain John smith, voiced by Mel Gibson.

head; he has suddenly discovered that the Native Americans are not only people, and that their slaughter would be murder, but that they know more about the land than he does.

Thereafter he becomes a fairly stereotypical Disney hero: He is the male support to Pocahontas's lead. There is an interesting moment later, however, when he is finally able to see Grandmother Willow:

> *Smith*: What was that?
> *Pocahontas*: Did you see something?
> *Smith*: No. I just, uh . . . I didn't see anything. Did I?
> *Pocahontas*: Look again.
> *Grandmother Willow*: Let it break upon you, like a wave upon the sand . . . Hello, John Smith.
> *Smith*: Pocahontas, that tree is talking to me.
> *Pocahontas*: Then you should talk back.
> *Grandmother Willow*: Do not be afraid, young man. My bark is worse than my bite.
> *Pocahontas*: Say something.
> *Smith*: What do you say to a tree?
> *Pocahontas*: Anything you want.

It is a profound time of recognition: Smith discovers that he is living in a different land, where the rules are different, so that talking to a tree is not the nonsense it would have been back in Britain. He learns more as the movie progresses, even though his personality never develops much. As he awaits execution Pocahontas comes to visit him:

> *Pocahontas*: I'm so sorry.
> *Smith*: For what? This? I've been in worse scrapes before. Can't think of any now, but . . .
> *Pocahontas*: We should never have met. None of this would have happened.
> *Smith*: Pocahontas, look at me. I'd rather die tomorrow than live a hundred years without knowing you.
> *Pocahontas*: I can't leave you.
> *Smith*: You never will. No matter what happens to me, I'll always be with you. Forever.

This is a moment of great poignancy, and it is directly mirrored later when

Pocahontas must say farewell for the last time to Smith as he is being shipped off home to receive medical attention for his wound—a piece of improbability, since the voyage home would have taken several weeks. It is a measure of Smith's portrayal that, when the couple must part, our sympathies are entirely with Pocahontas: We sense that Smith will find other women in other ports. He is a shallow character alongside her.

Governor Ratcliffe

Fat and toothy, corrupt from the top of his head to the soles of his feet, eager not just for the supposed riches of the New World but for advancement at the court of King James, Ratcliffe has no real interest in life except his own betterment; were he not such a vilely depicted character it would be easy to feel sympathy for his sterile loneliness. As it is, the only two living creatures in any way close to him are his flunky, Wiggins, whom he rather overtly despises and from whom he can thus expect not respect but toadying servility, and his pet dog Percy, from whom he is sufficiently distanced that it is Wiggins's chore to see that the beast is pampered.

Various none-too-subtle symbols are used to delineate Ratcliffe's alienation from those around him and, more important, the land that is the New World. As he struts up the gangplank to board the Susan Constant we see, in the foreground, a rat scuttling in parallel up a mooring rope. Where the land is portrayed in natural, muted colors—and the settlers come to be more and more so as well—Ratcliffe is rigged out in visually painful flamboyant reds. His voice is supplied (excellently) by David Ogden Stiers, the epitome,

so far as television audiences are concerned, of misplaced snobbery.

Ratcliffe has no care for what he might have to do in order to further his own greed for riches and aristocratic preferment—indeed, his character takes things a step further than that, for he is positively eager to murder a few Native Americans, as if that would somehow add to his own glory. This is not what he says when he first arrives in the New World:

> I hereby claim this land and all its riches in the name of King James the First, and do so name this settlement "Jamestown."

But very soon afterward his tune changes:

> *Ratcliffe*: Don't forget what the Spanish found in the New World. Gold. Mountains of it. For years, they've been ravaging the New World of its most precious resources, but now it's our turn.
> *The gold of Cortez*
> *The jewels of Pizarro*
> *Will seem like mere trinkets*
> *By this time tomorrow*
> *The gold we find here*
> *Will dwarf them by far*
> *With all you got in ya, boys*
> *Dig up Virginia, boys*
> *Mine, boys*
> *Mine every mountain*
> *And dig, boys*
> *Dig till you drop*
> *Grab a pick, boys*
> *Quick, boys*
> *Shove in a shovel*
> *Uncover those lovely pebbles that sparkle and shine*
> *It's gold and it's mine*
> *Mine*
> *Mine!*

There is no doubt that the last line of this song sequence is not an instruction but a

proclamation of possession. During the singing of this song we are treated to various of Ratcliffe's wish-fulfillment fantasies, certain of them including the attentions of beautiful women.

Ratcliffe's worst act—and there are many that could qualify—is his attempted murder of Powhatan, late in the movie. Pocahontas has stopped her father from executing Smith, and it dawns on the settlers, watching this, that perhaps the Native Americans are civilized beings after all. Alone among them Ratcliffe, knowing that he is safe because the Native Americans have likewise downed their bows, lifts his musket in an attempt to kill Powhatan. Thanks to Smith the attempt fails, although Smith is wounded by the shot. It is this event that turns the settlers against Ratcliffe, so that they truss him in chains for shipping home in disgrace; it is a wonder why it has not happened before.

Meeko

Lovably gluttonous, eager for any mischief that might bring a reward of food, the raccoon Meeko shares with Flit the traditional Disney role of wacky sidekick to the central character. At least at first; although his personality does not go through any significant evolution, his function in the plot and in the development of one of the movie's major themes does. He thus becomes a more important character than Flit.

When we first come across Meeko he is only a clown: seeing Pocahontas dive into the river from a great height he decides to emulate her, only halfway down realizing quite how long the drop is and clutching at Flit for support. But very soon afterward Meeko is making friends with Smith, who seems to offer an unceasing supply of biscuits, and enemies with Percy, whose food can be easily stolen. Meeko and Percy squabble and fight, much as do their human counterparts although to much more comedic effect, until Grandmother Willow calls them to order and they do what has been in the cards all along—become friends

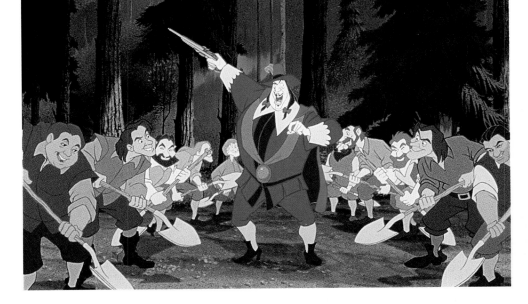

The vile Governor Ratcliffe egging his men on.

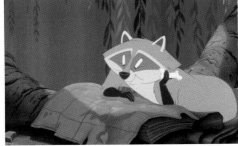

Pocahontas's amusing and food-loving raccoon sidekick, Meeko.

with each other. By the end of the movie they are inseparable. In this they mirror what is happening in the rest of the plot, by the conclusion the Native Americans and the settlers have discovered they have more in common than they thought.

Nik Ranieri, the supervising animator on Meeko, contrasted the raccoon with Flit, describing the former as "the more fun-loving, grab-the-gusto type." Ranieri added:

> I worked to give Meeko a really simple shape and a somewhat ethnic look, closer to the native designs in the film.

This is not a unique example of an animator underestimating the character he has created or developed. Meeko may be knockabout at a superficial level, but he is fundamental to the evolution of *Pocahontas*'s plot.

Flit

The little hummingbird sidekick of Pocahontas could be the angel sitting on her shoulder, with Meeko representing the devil on the other. In fact, that comparison does neither of the characters justice: Flit is hardly an angel and Meeko is certainly no devil. Each is as mischievous as the other, but Flit is far more concerned with the retention of the native ways than is his fellow sidekick; he takes an instant dislike to Smith and to everything that might upset the *status quo*. Dave Pruiksma, the character's supervising animator, expressed this rather differently:

> Flit and Meeko share a role that was played by the mice in *Cinderella* or Jiminy Cricket in *Pinocchio*. We established a kind of sibling rivalry between them. Flit epitomizes what Pocahontas should feel, as if he's telling her, "You should marry Kocoum, that's the path you should take," where Meeko seems to say, "Go on, follow your heart."

At first this seriousness of intent is not evident. Flit seems to be just one more in the long line of Disney zany sidekicks. It is only as the movie progresses that we begin to appreciate his contribution to the underlying themes. As far as Flit is concerned (as with many other characters), the "New World" is in fact the world as it has always been, and he is instinctively resistant to anything that might change what he views as the natural order.

Powhatan

The Native American tribal chief is presented to us as a respected figure, a man revered by all his tribe—even the high-spirited Pocahontas behaves deferentially in his presence—so that it is a real

shock when she defies him to save Smith's life, putting herself between Smith and her father's upraised club. Powhatan is of indeterminate age, although his graying hair and his widowerhood would suggest that he is older than one might think Pocahontas's father would be. In order to add to the sense of ancestral wisdom, his diction is deliberately crafted as somewhat stilted, and this is particularly obvious in some of his conversations with Pocahontas, as, early in the movie, when he she is welcoming him home from the war with the Massawomecks:

> *Powhatan*: My daughter.
> *Pocahontas*: *Wing-gap-o* ["welcome"], Father.
> *Powhatan*: Seeing you gives me great joy.
> Pocahontas: I'm so glad you've come home safely.
> *Powhatan*: Come with me. We have much to talk about. I want to hear everything you've been doing.
> *Pocahontas*: Father, for many nights I've been having a strange dream. I think it means something exciting's going to happen.
> *Powhatan*: Something exciting *is* about to happen.
> *Pocahontas*: Really? What?

The "something exciting" is that Kocoum wants to marry her, a piece of news that Pocahontas receives with less than enthusiasm. It is indicative of Powhatan's character that he cannot understand why his daughter should find the idea of wedding the finest warrior of all the tribe so repulsive. It would, after all, make a good and sensible match. It takes all the tangles of a complex plot to make Powhatan recognize that his daughter, too, is sensible, although her sensibility differs from his.

Thomas

A callow youth, Thomas epitomizes the changing mood of the settlers. When we first see him he is kissing his mother goodbye on the dock in London—they may never see each other again. Within an instant, however, he is enthusiatic about the challenge of the voyage and by the prospect of serving with the great "savage" slayer John Smith. Later Smith saves his life as, during the storm at sea, Thomas very courageously attempts to save a cannon from being washed overboard. But Thomas, despite his valor, is no master of the martial arts; derided on occasion by Ratcliffe, he is nevertheless sent by him into the forest in pursuit of Smith, and it comes as a surprise—to Thomas and us when he shoots dead the murderous Kocoum, for beforehand Thomas has done nothing much with his musket except miss whatever target he has aimed at. Smith sends him back with

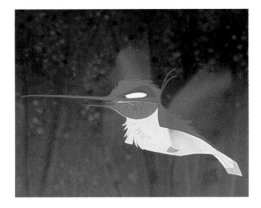

Flit, the hummingbird.

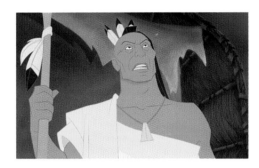

Powhatan, Pocahontas's father.

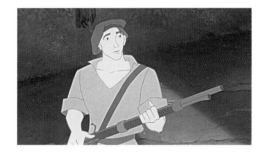

Expedition member Thomas.

his tail between his legs to the stockade, and for the first time, it seems, Thomas begins to realize his error in accepting the racist wisdom of the other settlers. Thereafter he is among the first of the whites to recognize the humanity of the Native Americans.

Percy

Governor Ratcliffe's pet is a spoiled white pug, Percy. We first see him being carried on a velvet cushion; later he is being treated by Wiggins to a bubble bath so that he will be nice and clean for his first arrival in the New World. In between he twice has his head tousled by an absentminded Smith and growlingly resents the disruption of his coiffure. The bane of his life becomes the ever-hungry Meeko, who takes particular joy in stealing Percy's food.

A character beyond redemption, one might think, and certainly Pocahontas

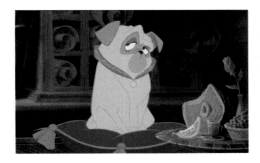

The spoiled Percy.

does as raccoon and dog show signs of a never-to-be-ended mutual hostility. Their last and most spectacular fight ends with Percy being seemingly irremovably jammed into one end of a hollow branch; as he lurches around inside it he becomes a "New World monster" capable of giving even the most stout-hearted of the settlers the creeps. Yet once he has escaped this prison he and Meeko—thanks in large part to the mediation of Grandmother Willow—become fast friends; at the end of the movie Percy, happy to have his head tousled and dressed in a travesty of Native American garb, clearly plans to spend the rest of his life in the New World with his pal Meeko. He has learned the better of his earlier ways, and in so doing he encapsulates in microcosm the major theme of the movie: Enemies can become friends. Thus while Percy seems on a first viewing to be merely a character tossed into the mix for the sake of comic relief, the development of his personality is an analogue of the message of the movie.

Wiggins

Visually and behaviorally reminiscent of the Lackey (➤256) in *Sleeping Beauty*, Wiggins is the campy faithful flunky of

Governor Ratcliffe. When Ratcliffe is boss the ascendant Wiggins is the ever-eager toady; as soon as Ratcliffe's downfall is apparent, Wiggins's allegiances change. Early in the movie Ratcliffe, exasperated by some new attempt by Wiggins to curry favor, says to the camera: "And he came so highly recommended." Near to the movie's end, as Ratcliffe is hauled off in chains, Wiggins echoes this sentiment in a sigh: "And he came so highly recommended." In both instances it is hard to know which of the two more deserves our sympathy.

Wiggins is effete to an extreme, an exaggeration of a view of sixteenth-century English aristocracy that probably owes more to moviemakers, primarily U.S. moviemakers, than to any factual base; at the court of King James, a place where life expectancy might not be long, Wiggins would probably have lasted less than a year before some lord or other found an excuse to have him executed or just murdered. Nevertheless, his portrayal is fun in the traditional Disney manner: As the other Englishmen are digging up the ground and felling mighty trees, Wiggins spends his time creating fancy topiary.

It is worth comparing Wiggins's character development during the course of the movie with that of Percy. Both start out as spoiled acolytes of the seemingly all-powerful Ratcliffe, but Percy learns better while Wiggins does not.

Ben, Lon, and Roy

Aside from Thomas, three of the settlers are given individual personalities. The two most important are Ben and Lon. Ben is a stubble-chinned, dark-haired Scot. Lon has a flowing red beard and flowing red hair and seems to be somewhat older than Ben although also junior to him in

the settlers' hierarchy. He and Ben pop up from time to time during the movie, most notably when the pair are sent into the forest to track down Smith, who is having a tryst with Pocahontas, and when they are among the first to realize that Powhatan is genuinely talking peace and that Ratcliffe is the warmonger, their conversion at this moment is swift.

Roy barely has a part, being seen in the foreground briefly during the scene where the *Susan Constant* is struggling with the elements during the sea storm the settlers survive early in the movie.

Nakoma

Pocahontas's best friend, Nakoma is something of a character in search of a personality; in their pairing, Pocahontas is certainly the dominant one and certainly the brighter. Nakoma represents, in a subtler way than Kocoum, the reluctance of most of the Native Americans to embrace change, and thus contrasts completely with Pocahontas, who is a wild, free spirit enthusiastic to find adventure in each new moment. Their physical appearances reflect this: Pocahontas has a genuine Native American face and untamed hair that is almost a character in itself; Nakoma, by contrast, has an almost Asiatic face that is surrounded by neatly trimmed hair. Only once in the movie does she really let herself go—when she and Pocahontas indulge in a splashing match in the river.

Otherwise Nakoma thinks and does what is right—at least in her view, which may not be entirely consistent. She covers for Pocahontas once when the latter sneaks off for a rendezvous with Smith but is not prepared to do so a second time; this failure, of course, causes great tragedy, with Kocoum being killed and Smith being sentenced to death, but Nakoma seems not to realize the implications of what she has done—especially since Pocahontas generously grants forgiveness.

Nakoma would make an excellent partner to Kocoum, whom she obviously desires—like him she is sensible and

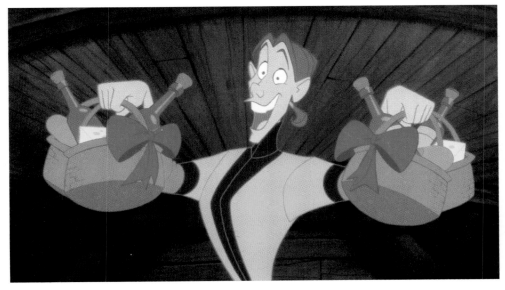

Governor Ratcliffe's overeager servant, Wiggins.

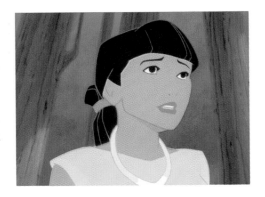

Pocohontas's best friend, Nakoma.

dutiful. That she rather than Pocahontas is thrown at the warrior by Powhatan is among the first signals we are given that this plot is destined for a tragic rather than a saccharine ending.

Kocoum

The bravest of all the Native American warriors, Kocoum is affianced by Powhatan to Pocahontas much against her will; when Nakoma gasps at Kocoum's rugged handsomeness Pocahontas replies with sarcasm: "Hm. I especially love the smile." For that is Kocoum's dominant personality trait—he is incapable of smiling, either at himself or at anything else. Despite his courage—he is much honored among his tribe and especially by Powhatan—and his physical good looks, he lacks any spark of the imagination that could make him appealing to Pocahontas. Always he is somber and, above all, dutiful. It is he who carries the wounded Namontack back to the village; it is he who is sent out by Powhatan to ensure Pocahontas's safety, a task that he performs sternly rather than with flair. The only time he shows much emotion is when he comes across Pocahontas, his intended mate, in a passionate embrace with Smith: Then his fury knows no bounds, and he would certainly kill the white man were it not that Thomas kills Kocoum first. In this respect Kocoum is the most Westernized of the Native American characters depicted in the movie: A more likely response would be either that he accepted the situation or that he killed Pocahontas (perhaps after some form of ritual trial).

Like Pocahontas, watchers of the movie find it hard to empathize with Kocoum, and yet he is a person of some merit. He has courage, dignity, and loyalty. Although he does not have the sensitivity of Pocahontas, he shares with her a profound belief in and respect for the traditional ways of the Native Americans. He, too, although rather differently, is in touch with the land. When he is shot by the callow Thomas it is not just the death of a human being we witness but a harbinger of the coming destruction of that land.

Kekata

The elderly shaman is interestingly animated. Whereas the other human characters in the movie are depicted either realistically or at least with clean, sharp delineation (the visual portrayals of Ratcliffe and Wiggins cannot be described as realistic), Kekata is shown in a much more impressionistic fashion,

conveying something of the magic that he has at his command. Significantly, the palette of colors used in his depiction, while not identical to that employed for Grandmother Willow, is certainly reminiscent. Kekata is a healer and also a diviner; he casts herbs or charcoal upon fire to create, through the smoke, prophetic images that he and the rest of the tribe can see. The most powerful of these images are seen when he is asked by Powhatan to probe the inner natures of the white intruders. He sees them as ravening wolves set to lay waste to all before them, the villagers included. Kekata proves to be not just a prophet of war but an advocate of it; the bitter irony is that, now that history has given us the benefit of hindsight, Powhatan should probably have listened more to Kekata's advice than to his daughter's.

Grandmother Willow

In many ways Grandmother Willow is the most interesting of all the characters in *Pocahontas* in that it is made clear that people can see her and communicate with her only when their minds are sufficiently attuned to the spirits of nature. When she first speaks to Smith his conscious mind overrules his perception, because after all it is "impossible" that a tree might speak. Only a little later is he capable of making the conceptual shift required to converse with her.

Her face in repose is merely a gap where the bark of the tree has wilted away to expose the gnarled wood beneath. When she is speaking, however, this area of wood comes alive to show eyes, nose, and lips, although still without losing the woody texture and colors—largely dark green and gray-brown. She utters sage guidance—more advisory than dictatorial—in a grandmotherly voice (supplied by Linda Hunt), which seems suitable, although the diction owes little to any Native American speech pattern. She is, in effect, the shaman of *Pocahontas*, although one is given the impression that others consult her as well—and certainly Smith learns to, as do Meeko and Percy. Although she seems not to have the power of locomotion—unlike, say, the Ents, the sentient trees in J. R. R. Tolkien's *The Lord of the Rings* (1954–1995)—she is capable of moving her extremities; Ben and Lon discover this when they come in search of Smith and are deftly tripped by a suddenly elevated root, then whipped by a branch. She is also very much the dominant personality in her patch of the forest: when she calls for silence among the forest animals there is immediate silence (except

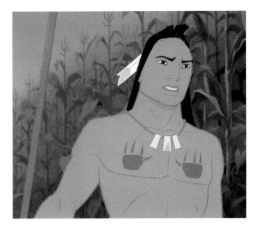

Pocahontas's betrothed, the fierce warrior Kocoum.

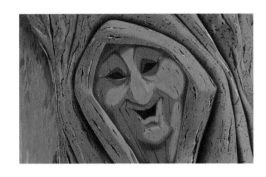

Grandmother Willow, the talking tree, dispenses advice.

from a small frog, whose inadvertent croak incurs a steely glare from her and an expression of terror from him).

Her animation and coloration are reminiscent of those used for Kekata: Gone are the clean lines and firm colors with which the other characters are depicted, and in their place are muted natural colors and a somewhat impressionistic use of line. She has the appearance and aura of the way one tends to remember one's favorite grandmother—kindly, yet capable of exercising discipline when need be.

Namontack

It is the shooting of Namontack by Ratcliffe that starts what seems to be an inevitable progress toward war between the Native Americans and the settlers. In fact, Namontack is merely hit in the leg, so presumably he survives—although Kekata, attempting to heal his wound, seems dubious: "This wound is strange to me." The scene of Ratcliffe shooting Namontack is reflected toward the end of the movie when once again the governor triumphantly raises his musket to an exposed Native American, this time Powhatan.

TOY STORY

Characters:

Andy Davis; Molly Davis; Woody; Buzz Lightyear; Mr. Potato Head; Slinky Dog; Rex; Hamm; Bo Peep; Sid Phillips; Mrs. Davis; Sergeant; Hannah Phillips

Credits:

Voices: Tim Allen (Buzz Lightyear); R. Lee Ermy (Sergeant); Sarah Freeman (Hannah Phillips); Tom Hanks (Woody); Laurie Metcalf (Mrs. Davis); John Morris (Andy Davis); Annie Potts (Bo Peep); John Ratzenberger (Hamm); Don Rickles (Mr. Potato Head); Wallace Shawn (Rex); Jim Varney (Slinky Dog); Erik von Detten (Sid Phillips)

Additional Voices: Jack Angel; Spencer Aste; Greg Berg; Lisa Bradley; Kendall Cunningham; Debi Derryberry; Cody Dorkin; Bill Farmer; Craig Good; Gregory Grudt; Danielle Judovits; Sam Lasseter; Brittany Levenbrown; Sherry Lynn; Scott McAfee; Mickie McGowan; Ryan O'Donohue; Jeff Pidgeon; Patrick Pinney; Phil Proctor; Jan Rabson; Joe Ranft; Andrew Stanton; Shane Sweet

Supervising Sound Editor: Tim Holland

Sound Design: Gary Rydstrom

Music/Songs: Randy Newman, plus a fragment of "Hakuna Matata" by Tim Rice and Elton John

Executive Music Producer: Chris Montan

Screenplay: Joel Cohen and Alec Sokolow; Andrew Stanton; Joss Whedon

Story Supervisors: Robert Lence; Joe Ranft

Story Coordinator: Susan E. Levin

Film Editors: Robert Gordon; Lee Unkrich

Supervising Animator: Pete Docter

Directing Animators: Ash Brannon; Rich Quade

Animation Managers: Bz Petroff; Triva von Klark

Animation Coordinator: Maureen E. Wylie

Computer Animation: Michael Berenstein; Kim Blanchette; Colin Brady; Davey Crockett Felten; Angie Glocka; Rex Grignon; Tom K. Gurney; Jimmy Hayward; Hal T. Hickel; Karen Kiser; Shawn P. Krause; Anthony B. Lamolinara; Guionne Leroy; Bud Luckey; Matt Luhn; Les Major; Glenn McQueen; Mark Oftedal; Bob Peterson; Jeff Pidgeon; Jeff Pratt; Steve Rabatich; Roger Rose; Andrew Schmidt; Steve Segal; Dog Sheppeck; Alan Sperling; Doug Sweetland; David Tart; Ken Willard

Computer Systems Manager: David H. Ching

Character Design: William Cone; Jean Gillmore; Dan Haskett; Tom Holloway; Steve Johnson; Bud Luckey; Bob Pauley; Andrew Stanton

Layout Manager: Bz Petroff

Supervising Layout Artist: Craig Good

Art Director: Ralph Eggleston

Supervising Technical Director: William Reeves

Production Supervisor: Karen Robert Jackson

Executive Producers: Edwin Catmull; Steve Jobs

Producers: Bonnie Arnold; Ralph Guggenheim

Director: John Lasseter

Release Date: November 22, 1995

Running Time: 80½ minutes

THE MOVIE

The first ever movie to be made using entirely computer-animation techniques, *Toy Story* might have been expected to be little more than an orgy in special effects, a self-indulgent wallow in the new technology. It proved to be anything but. Director John Lasseter and his colleagues at Pixar—co-producers with Disney of this movie—were determined from the outset to match the storytelling standards and visual brio of the classic Disney features, and they succeeded triumphantly. Far from being the lightweight movie that audiences might have accepted because of its novelty, *Toy Story* confronts what are basically adult themes and does so with creative responsibility—an insistence on perfection in every respect—that is often lacking from the live-action movies that tackle those themes.

Toy Story is often described, even by its creators, as a variation on the buddy movie: two central characters, thrust together for one reason or another, start off by either detesting or despising each other but, through their joint experiences of various life-threatening escapades that necessitate their mutual cooperation, eventually become best friends. Certainly *Toy Story* is that in part—the axis of its plot is the relationship between Woody and Buzz—but its primary theme is much more interesting. John Clute, in *The Encyclopedia of Fantasy* (co-edited with John Grant; 1977), coined the term "wainscot society" to describe those communities, frequently found in fantasy, which co-exist with us but are unseen by us; figuratively, they live behind the wainscots of our existences. Margery Sharp's series of books about the Rescuers, partly adapted by Disney as *The Rescuers* (➤**297**), offer a prime example of the theme, as do Eve Titus's *Basil of Baker Street* (1974), adapted by Disney as *The Great Mouse Detective* (➤**318**), and Mary Norton's *The Borrowers* (1952). Numerous science-fiction tales—especially Zenna Henderson's extensive *The People* series—have picked up the theme by imagining humanoid aliens peacefully, and very covertly, living among us. But the originality of *Toy Story* is its conception that a wainscot society dwells within the bedroom of every child, everywhere. The toys are not invisible but, like Henderson's aliens, though on clear view they are far from what they seem. The toys have a prime directive: whenever they are likely to be seen by a human being they must become immobile objects, capable of being inspired into "life" only by the imagination of the child who plays with them. In reality, however, they are sentient creatures, equipped with the full gamut of human emotions, aspirations, and vulnerabilities: They feel pain even when they cannot show it.

A further subtheme in the movie concerns cooperation. Human beings are, once reaching adulthood, all very much of the same shape and size: some may be stronger or more clever than others—and some may suffer disabilities—but overall the differences are, when considered on other scales, very slight. When humans are required to or desire to cooperate on some venture, they do so from a common base: Individuals may have specialist contributions to make, but all share what one might call the same intellectual underpinning. This is not the case among the toys who star in *Toy Story*. Their physical capabilities are widely divergent, from those of a tough plastic space ranger to those of a pair of wind-up binoculars able to do nothing except help others see at a distance. In between are such characters as a dog with a long Slinky spring as a body—and then there are the grotesque mutant toys created by the movie's archvillain, Sid. When all of these toys find themselves in the position where they must function as a team, they cannot, as humans would, cooperate on the basis that, despite any specialisms, they largely share the same spectrum of abilities. The toys must draw on all their disparate abilities as the time demands. Thus, when acting in cooperation, they form not so much a team as a gestalt. In the early part of the movie most of the toys are basically aware of this but it takes most of them a very long time to come to fully understand it.

Toy Story has, of course, a history that is of technical interest. The central figure is its director, John Lasseter. He spent a few years with Disney as a conventional animator before becoming more interested in what could be done with computers and joining a division of LucasFilms. In 1986 he and various colleagues left LucasFilms to found Pixar, which devoted itself to computer animation—and showed the importance of the genre by almost immediately receiving an Oscar nomination for the short *Luxo Jr.* (1986) and an Oscar for the short *Tin Toy* (1988). All this time Walt Disney Feature Animation, while continuing to produce conventional animation as its mainstay, had been experimenting with new techniques, partnering Tim Burton's team for the stop-motion of *The Nightmare Before Christmas* (➤380) and introducing computer effects animation into many of its feature movies to a greater or lesser extent. When Disney set its heart on a full-length computer-animated feature it was hardly surprising that it formed a partnership with Lasseter and his colleagues at Pixar in order to do so.

Pixar had the technological expertise and the creativity required to make a computer-animated movie, but no experience of the art of creating a full-length feature that could keep an audience glued to its seats for over an hour. Storytelling was one aspect of the development. By analogy, writing a novel requires no more skill than writing a short story, but it is *different*. The development of characters that would sustain interest for a long period was another hurdle. The Disney Feature Animation team spent as much editorial and advisorial time on *Toy Story* as they would have for any of their own features, cooperating with the people at Pixar the same as they would have their own animation department. At the same time, Pixar had to build up just such an animation department: it takes comparatively few animators to produce a short but a feature-length movie is another matter. (Even so, about one-seventh as many animators were required for *Toy Story* as for, say, *The Lion King*.) On the basis that what distinguishes good animators is not knowledge of technology but the ability to imagine and visualize, Pixar recruited people from Disney and elsewhere and educated them to understand what this unfamiliar medium could do. This animator-oriented approach was a triumphant success: *Toy Story* is above all a movie with warmth—a far cry from what might have appeared had those involved merely been entranced by the possibilities of computer animation. It also very clearly bears the Disney stamp: the concentration on the relationships among characters could have emerged from few other studios.

A useful book is *Toy Story: The Art and Making of the Animated Film* (1995) by John Lasseter and Steve Daly.

THE STORY

Among the piles of presents young Andy Davis receives for his birthday is Buzz Lightyear, a space-age action figure that is the trendiest toy around. Buzz promptly takes over as Andy's favorite toy, a position formely held by Woody, a ragdoll Western sheriff. A rivalry develops—largely on the part of Woody, for Buzz believes himself not a plaything but a genuine space ranger—for the position of top toy in Andy's estimation. It is a contest which Buzz apparently wins with consummate ease. But there is a threat to all the toys, though Andy doesn't realize it, and they must learn how to cooperate—most especially Woody and Buzz—if they are to survive. The threat is the boy Sid who lives in the house next door. Assisted by his vile dog Scud, he takes delight in sadistically destroying toys or, perhaps worse, in cobbling bits from one onto bits of another to create a flock of grotesque mutants. Andy's toys anticipate eagerly the day, not far distant, when Andy and his mother move to a new home.

One night Andy's mother takes Andy and his younger sister Molly out to the local Pizza Planet, telling him he may bring only one toy. Woody, realizing Buzz is likely to be the choice, tries to shove him into the darkness down the back of the bed but inadvertently knocks him out of the window and, conceivably, into Sid's yard. He is promptly denounced by the other toys—notably the irascible Mr. Potato Head—as having attempted if not succeeded in commiting murder. Before they can carry out summary justice, Andy, unable to find Buzz, takes Woody out for the evening instead.

But Buzz has not fallen into Sid's yard. Seeing the Davises departing for the pizza joint with Woody he climbs aboard the rear of their car and eventually, when the family stops at a gas station, confronts him. As the two scrap, the Davises drive off. Luckily a Pizza Planet delivery truck has likewise paused at the gas station; Buzz is transfixed by the spaceship logo on top of the delivery truck. The two hitch a ride on the truck to Pizza Planet, a sort of superfuturistic multimedia fast food joint offering not only pizzas but also brightly flashing games and activities for kids. For the first time Woody and Buzz begin to realize the benefits of cooperation, although they can hardly yet be said to be friends.

But Sid, too, is at Pizza Planet. Buzz gets inside a crane game to greet a host of little green three-eyed "aliens." Woody follows to rescue him, but Sid manages to capture not just Buzz but Woody too, plus Alien #4, one of the little gossipy toys. Sid, once home, tosses Alien #4 to Scud, then performs "brain surgery" on his little sister Hannah's doll Janie, giving it the head of another toy, a plastic pterodactyl. It is now that Woody and Buzz encounter the mutant toys, whom they assume to be hostile cannibals.

The following morning, as the pair attempt to escape Sid's house despite being chased by a snarling Scud, Buzz watches a television ad for Buzz Lightyear action figures and finally realizes that he is indeed no more than a toy. He shakes off the news at first, but when he attempts to fly with his wings he plunges down the stairwell and one of his arms falls off. When next we see him he sharing a doll's tea party with Hannah and is in a fit of profound depression. Woody tries to get help from Andy's other toys by calling to them, but when they discover Buzz's arm has been broken off they assume Woody has committed further atrocities and refuse to help him. Then Sid's mutant toys repair Buzz's arm.

A new toy arrives for Sid: a powerful rocket that will, at the height of its arc, blow up. He tapes Buzz to it, but a fortuitous rainstorm means launch date will have to be postponed until the next day. This gives Buzz time to recover from his depression and, after many diversions, Woody to conspire with the mutants in a rescue mission—which concludes with the massed toys confronting Sid and telling him to be nice to his toys, thus terrorizing him into a change of attitude.

But all seems too late: the Davises are about to leave for their new home. There ensues a frenetic chase scene, as Scud pursues the two friends who are in turn pursuing the Davises. At length it is through use of the rocket strapped to Buzz's back that the two buddy toys are able to drop not into the moving truck but in fact directly into the box sitting beside Andy in the back of the family car.

In their new home, all the toys are reconciled with one another. Christmas comes, and the toys are sure that their status will be unthreatened. But—horror of horrors!—Andy has been given one extra present: a puppy.

THE CHARACTERS

Andy Davis

The young boy who owns Woody, Buzz, and the rest is a passive character rather than a central one: his function is largely

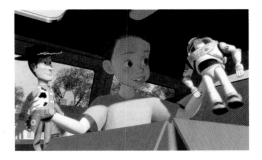

Andy with his two favorite toys.

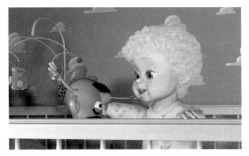

Andy's little sister, Molly, in her crib.

to be inconsolable when his favorite toys keep inexplicably disappearing. It is interesting to note that his preoccupations in play are much the same as those of Sid, but without the sadistic destructiveness: adventure games largely influenced by the clichés of Saturday-morning science-fiction television for kids. Thus in an opening piece of play Andy thrusts Woody into his obvious role as the brave sheriff confronting a bank robber, then the robber (Mr. Potato Head as "One-Eyed Bart") brings into the action his "attack dog with built-in force field" (Slinky Dog); Woody—in Andy's game—retaliates by bringing on his own sidekick, a dinosar (Rex).

Molly Davis

Andy's young sister Molly has almost the smallest named part in the movie; her age is a little uncertain, but she is still small enough to sleep in a crib that serves as the jailhouse into which Bart is thrown at the denouement of Andy's Western scene described above. Certainly she is under three years old, as we discover when Mr. Potato Head grumbles:

> Ages three and up. It's on my box. I shouldn't be baby-sitting Princess Drool.

It is a terrifying prospect for any toy to be confined with a toddler this age and, sure enough, with an expression of glee on her face she immediately begins to batter Mr. Potato Head against the bars of her crib.

Woody

There can be no question that Woody is the central character of the movie: It is he whose emotional development is at the heart of the story as he changes from a complacent, potentially malicious, somewhat overweening top toy into a courageous, inventive character, along the way discovering the power of friendship and his own innate ability to exercise that power—a far more valuable one than the governing power he exercised over the rest of Andy's toys before the arrival of Buzz.

Yet it would not be correct to describe Woody's developing character as an especially complex one. As so often in animated features, the character depicted on screen owes much to the interpretation the voice actor gives to the role. In this instance it is almost impossible to separate Woody from the performance given by Tom Hanks: the facial and physical resemblances are striking, and much of the body language is strongly reminis-

cent of the live-action Hanks in one of his more broadly clowning roles. Thus, while one might have expected the development of Woody to act as a more mercurial, introspective foil for the stolid evolution of Buzz's character, this never quite happens. Woody's cavortings rarely cease to entertain us, but his exaggerated facial expressions and his tangling limbs as each new crisis strikes him are much according to the method. This must certainly have been intentional, of course; it is perhaps a pity that the character was not allowed more depth and thus a greater ability to involve our sympathies.

Woody is a toy born of a more old-fashioned time. Except for the string-pull in his back—whereby, in a crackling artificial voice, he is able to "speak" a limited repertoire of appropriately clichéd phrases—he lacks all the various whirring appendages and facilities that seem to be so much a part of modern toys. Although there are clean edges to his plastic face, otherwise he seems almost infinitely floppy and flexible; for this reason, when all the toys have to throw themselves into immobility on the imminent approach of any human being, Woody is the one who seems to have the least potential for life. He looks exactly as he is, from the perspective of the humans in the movie: a toy dropped by a childish hand to fall where and as it will.

Although Woody demonstrates a fair degree of resolve and commanderly skills while organizing the campaign to free Buzz from blast-off and sure death, the one time a true seriousness enters his personality is almost immediately after the rescue. Woody and Buzz run for the Davises' departing car through a hole in Sid's garden fence—at least, Woody makes it but Buzz, still encumbered by the rocket, gets stuck. By the time Woody realizes this he has safely climbed onto the car's rear bumper. Buzz exhorts him to escape while the going is good. Woody is momentarily indecisive, but then we see an expression of utter resolution come into his face and he hops back down again to come to the assistance of his comrade.

Buzz Lightyear

In order to create a toy that would convincingly topple Woody from his perch, the moviemakers decided to think back to their own childhoods and study what modern kids were going for, and to pack every special feature they reasonably could into a single toy. "And that of course had to involve outer space," remarked director John Lasseter. Flight was another must—hence the wings—as were flashing lights, flexible limbs, bits for the child to push and prod. They succeeded beyond their wildest dreams, for

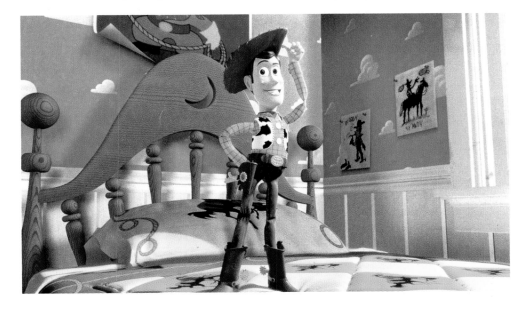

Woody the cowboy, voiced by Tom Hanks.

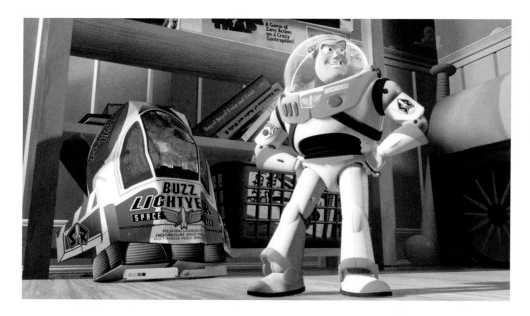

Woody's new rival Buzz, given life by Tim Allen.

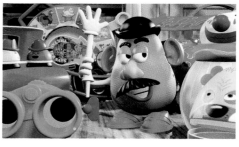

The acid-tongued Mr. Potato Head, voiced by Don Rickles.

the manufactured Buzz Lightyear action figure became throughout much of the world the most sensationally popular children's toy in the year of the movie's release.

They tried various concepts concerning how his personality could be conveyed by his physical presence, initially thinking of him as some kind of intergalactic superman figure, but in the end realized this was all wrong—it would certainly not have showed much creative originality. Instead Buzz, for all his inflated impressions of his importance to the future of the universe, comes across much more as one of the troopers—not a foot soldier, of course, but still quite low in the hierarchy. For the most part he goes from one place to another without any excess fussiness of movement, a bodily characteristic that reflects the unfussiness of his thought processes. He is a dreamer, but his dreams operate within fairly limited boundaries—zapping with lasers and flying the spaceways:

Actually, I'm stationed up in the Gamma quadrant of sector four, Universe Protection Unit of the Space Ranger Corps. I protect the galaxy from the threat of invasion from the Evil Emperor Zurg, enemy of the Galactic Alliance!

These may seem to represent fairly far-reaching ambitions, but of course they do not. Buzz's mind-set apparently entertains few visions outside this tersely described arena; for example, we cannot imagine him harboring dreams about displacing Woody in Bo Peep's affections.

Nor—and this is a governing part of his personality—does he have sufficient imagination to conceive of the possibility that he is anything other than what he thinks himself to be—that is, a genuine

space ranger rather than a mere toy. His resulting smugness is an aspect that fuels Woody's detestation of him: brute, unreasoning, supercilious certainty in the truth of one's beliefs, in the teeth of all the evidence, is an exceptionally infuriating trait.

When he catches sight of the television ad, he assumes at first that this is confirmation of what he has been saying all along—that Star Command has at last got in touch with him:

TV announcer: Calling Buzz Lightyear. Come in. This is Star Command.
Buzz [to himself]: "Star Command."
Boy's voice from TV: Buzz Lightyear responding. I read you.
TV announcer: Buzz, planet Earth needs your help.
Boy's voice: On the way!
Chorus: Buzz Lightyear!
TV announcer: The world's greatest superhero, now the world's greatest toy! Buzz has it all! Locking wrist communicator. Karate chop action! Pulsing laser light! Multiphase voice simulator!
Buzz's voice on TV: There's a secret mission in uncharted space. There's a secret mission in uncharted space.
Second TV announcer: And, best of all, high-pressure space wings!
Buzz's voice on TV: To infinity and beyond.
TV announcer: Not a flying toy.
Caption/disclaimer on TV: NOT A FLYING TOY.
TV announcer: Get your Buzz Lightyear and save a galaxy near you!
Chorus: Buzz Lightyear.
Third TV announcer: Available at all Al's Toy Barn outlets in the tri-county area.

There can be little underestimating the pathos of the scene as Buzz, his worldview and his confidence shattered, opens his wrist panel to discover these stamped words: MADE IN TAIWAN

But Buzz's self-belief is resilient. Taunted by Woody, he slowly persuades himself that, whatever the television might have said, he can indeed fly. He turns his attention to an open window high above the stairwell, extends his wings, and leaps into empty air . . . with the predictable result that he crashes to the floor far beneath. His further humiliation comes when, his arm broken by the fall, he is found by Hannah, who puts a flowery blue hat on top of his space helmet and treats him to a dolls' tea party. From here on Buzz is not just physically shattered but psychologically so until Woody by both example and impassioned argument persuades him that his true position in the order of things is far more significant than his imagined one:

Buzz: You were right. I'm not a space ranger. I'm just a toy. A stupid little insignificant toy.
Woody: Wait a minute! Being a toy is a lot better than being a space ranger.
Buzz: Yeah, right . . .
Woody: It is. Next door is a kid who thinks you're great—and not because you're a space ranger, because you're a toy. You're his toy!
Buzz: Why would Andy want me?
Woody: Why would Andy want you? Look at you! You're a Buzz Lightyear! Any toy would give up his moving parts to be you. You have wings! You glow in the dark! You talk! Your helmet does that, that "whoosh" thing! You're a cool toy!

Henceforth Buzz shows all the courage and no little of the ingenuity one would expect of a real space ranger—and, of course his relationship with Woody blossoms into a powerful friendship.

Mr. Potato Head

This toy is markedly the least willing of all in Andy's bedroom to give Woody the benefit of the doubt at any stage in the proceedings. One could regard his behavior and dialogue as refreshingly caustic, but in fact far too often it goes right over the edge into mean-spiritedness—a rather dangerous mean-spiritedness, indeed, for Mr. Potato Head is of the put-to-death-first-find-out-the-facts-later school. At several stages in the plot Woody could well lose his life because of this; it is only by luck and fortitude that he does not. One would like to think that Mr. Potato Head has, by the end of all the adventures, learned better—but one doubts it.

A running gag with Mr. Potato Head is that his parts are removable. Early in the movie, after he has been knocked about by Molly so that he has eyes where his ears should be, and so forth, he addresses Hamm, the piggy bank:

> *Mr. Potato Head*: Hamm, look—I'm a Picasso!
> *Hamm*: I don't get it.
> *Mr. Potato Head*: You uncultured swine.

Later, when the radio-controlled car smashes in the back of the moving van, it is hard to resist a mild cheer as every single part of Mr. Potato Head goes flying—although his detached voice still manages to utter condemnations of Woody. In the final sequence, as the gang are listening to the news of the influx of Christmas toys, they discover that one is to be a Mrs. Potato Head. "Gee, I better shave," he says, and simply plucks off his plastic moustache.

Slinky Dog

With a floppy-eared wooden head at one end of a seemingly almost infinitely extendable spring and pert hindquarters at the other, Slinky Dog is—there can be no question about it—very definitely *Woody's* dog. He is loyal to his master, being the last of all the toys—except possibly Bo Peep—to become convinced that Woody is, after all, guilty of crimes against Buzz. This occurs when Woody is shouting to the assembled toys across the street from Sid's window, trying to persuade them that Buzz is alive and well. In fact, at the time Buzz is almost comatose from depression and refuses to show himself at the window, so Woody is forced to mime the ranger's presence

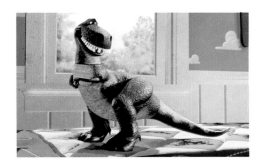

Andy's neurotic dinosaur Rex.

using his disembodied arm around the window-frame. When it becomes obvious that the arm is indeed detached, however, the toys turn away from their window with varying cries that they hope Woody gets what's coming to him. Slinky Dog's reaction is, however, one less of anger than of anguished betrayal; as he slowly pulls down the venetian blind, one senses he is doing so as much to hide his own tears as to give a physical symbol to the expulsion of Woody from the "family." And Woody, for his part, clearly likewise feels grief.

Slinky Dog has his moment of heroism later on when, astride the radio-controlled car, Woody and Buzz are chasing the moving van. The dog acts as a "living" tow-rope for as long as possible, clearly in great pain, his spring stretching beyond its limit of elasticity. When finally he rebounds back into the interior of the van it is hard to know how he will ever function as a Slinky again.

Rex

Although the green dinosaur has been designed by his manufacturers to represent a *Tyrannosaurus rex*, at the same time care has been taken to ensure that he will not terrify small children: his contours are rounded to indicate amiability. His personality very much meshes with his physical presence: it is the opposite of ferocious despite his claim that he would like it if a herbivorous dinosaur toy could be brought into the home so that he could have a spell of being the dominant predator.

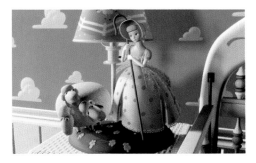

Bo Peep tending her flock.

As with Hamm, it can be difficult to understand quite what role Rex is intended to take in the overall structure of the team, whose members otherwise each have a distinctive contribution to make. Rex and Hamm, by contrast, seem merely there to make up the numbers and perhaps also to emphasize the "family" nature of the group of toys.

Hamm

The pink piggy bank is the least complicated of all the characters in the central gang in terms of both personality and physical makeup—although it should be stressed that despite this seeming simplicity of form, *none* of the characters in *Toy Story* was easy to animate. Hamm's body is essentially made of two approximate ovoids, one extended to form a snout with a pair of dimples as representations of nostrils and adorned by almost equally rudimentary eyes, ears, and mouth. His legs are stubby stumps. As with Rex, it is hard to establish what his contribution is in the overall personality matrix of the team: to mix usages, he neither moves nor shakes, being just one of the good guys. Slow-moving and slow-thinking he may be much of the time, but it would be a misperception to dismiss him as a simpleton: he defeats Mr. Potato Head with seeming ease in a game of Battleship.

Bo Peep

Despite her cute, maidenly appearance, the Bo Peep doll seems, to put it mildly, prepared to be adventurous. Near the start of the movie it is made clear that she has been having a long-term romantic liaison with Woody, in which relationship it is explicit that she has been playing the dominant hand—it is she who invites him back to her place. The love affair falls into something of an abeyance as Woody begins to appear more and more certainly guilty of vengeful crimes against Buzz but, unlike the other principal toys, she never quite seems to give up on his innocence. Definitely she is little short of aggressive in her expression of passion in the aftermath of the adventures: as the

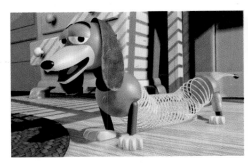

Slinky Dog.

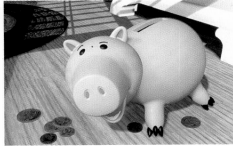

The piggy bank, Hamm.

toys prepare for Christmas she hooks the sheriff around the neck with her crook, gets him under the mistletoe, and plunges her face down upon his with a ferocity such that it is a good thing whatever ensues occurs off-screen.

Of all the characters in *Toy Story*, Bo Peep could have been the most difficult to convincingly animate; her exterior form is extremely complex—with her petite, graceful face and the intricacies of her costume—and this could have led to impossible complications as the animators tried to make the play of light across her seem natural. Instead, they chose to give her qualities such that she seems somehow a little divorced physically from the rough and tumble of the real world. This points up exquisitely the difference between the seeming purity of her appearance and the occasional raunchiness of her dialogue and behavior.

Sid Phillips

The boy next door can lay claim to occupancy of one of the highest ranks in the pantheon of Disney animated villains. He combines all of the worst elements of the kids at school who tormented us with their bullying and abrasiveness. It might seem strange to think of Sid as in the same league as Maleficent (➤263) or Cruella De Vil (➤267), but that is to look at him from an adult's perspective: he terrorizes those around him, including his younger sister Hannah, but most especially, toys, which, while sentient and mobile in the absence of human beings, must play dead in their presense—and are thus absolutely defenseless when assaulted or dismembered by this malicious little tyrant. And that, even in their inanimate modes, the toys do suffer pain is hardly in doubt: at one stage

Sid burns Woody's forehead with a magnifying glass and the moment he departs so that the sheriff can react, it is clear that the agony has been profound.

Sid seems to have no redeeming qualities whatsoever. His grating voice (this is an excellent piece of work by voice actor Erik von Detten), lingers lasciviously on the details of each new act of brutality he plans to commit. He seems voraciously greedy in everything he does. His face is a pliant mask of delighted spite, the movements of his eyes, cheeks, and mouth serving to accentuate the vileness of his proposed and actual behavior. Even his teeth form a gray wall studded by the sharp protrusions of braces.

We first encounter him engaged in a typical activity: he has attached a firecracker to a toy soldier and—despite Buzz's attempt to intervene—blows the little figure to pieces.

Sid: Yes! He's gone! He's history!

We next seem him strutting through Pizza Planet, selecting the most violent games: his sole reason for picking the crane game seems to be to seize a cute little alien in order to feed it to Scud, although of course he picks up Buzz and Woody as well—which is where the adventures properly begin. After he gets home we see him making his younger sister's life a misery:

Sid (*in mock concern*): Oh, no, Hannah. Look! Janie (*Hannah's doll*)—she's sick!
Hannah: No, she's not!
Sid: I'll have to perform one of my operations.

Grabbing the doll, he runs off with it to his room.

Sid: We have a sick patient here, nurse. Prepare the OR—stat! (*He puts the doll in a*

vice and tightens.) Patient is prepped. No one has ever attempted a double-bypass brain transplant before . . .

A little later he shows the girl the result of his effort: he has replaced her doll's head with that of a pterodactyl. She runs off screaming for her mother, followed by Sid yelling that whatever Hannah says he's done she's lying. It is then that it is revealed to us, through the eyes of Buzz and Woody, the enormity of the barbarities that Sid has inflicted on his toys, for from the shadows creeps first the spiderish Babyface. Further horrors appear: Legs, which has the lower half of a doll and a body made from a toy fishing rod; a Jack-in-the-box with a hand replacing the Jack; and many others, some of whom have an important part to play later.

Sid tortures Woody by singeing his forehead with his magnifying glass and plans to blow him apart by taping him to a powerful rocket that will explode high in the air; Sid reads from the rocket's packaging:

Extremely dangerous. Keep out of reach of children. Cool . . . What am I going to blow? Man. Where's that wimpy cowboy doll?

In fact, of course, it is Buzz he eventually picks on: a more suitable payload for his rocket.

But the catalogue of Sid's cruelties is still far from over. Once Woody has launched the final attempt by the mutant toys to save Buzz, with Sid's match just about to touch the rocket's fuse, the boy spots the sheriff on the ground nearby:

Hey, how did you get out here? Oh, well. You and I can have a cookout later.

He tosses Woody onto the barbecue and tucks a match into his holster. It is all too obvious just who or what is going to be grilled. Sid turns back to the pressing business of igniting the rocket, but he is brought up short as Woody's creaky voice box rasps into action:

Reach for the sky. This town ain't big enough for the two of us. Someone's poisoned the water hole.

Sid's terror grows as, from all sides of the yard, mutant toys begin to advance toward him. For the sake of winning this battle, the toys have briefly relaxed the prime dictate that they must never move of their own accord when within the eyeshot of human beings. Sid's screams mount; as with all tyrants, at his core is cowardice, and now for the first time it dawns on him that his victims may be able to fight back. Woody presses home the advantage:

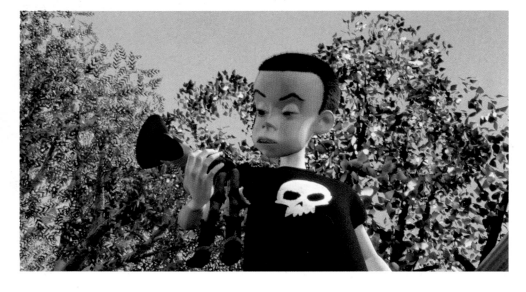
The movie's villain and torturer of toys, Sid.

From now on, you must take good care of your toys. Because, if you don't we'll find out, Sid. We toys can see . . . everything. So—*play nice*!

Running into the house Sid comes across Hannah clutching a dolly, and even sight of that lifeless toy is enough to send him into screaming flight. It is clear his reign of destruction is over.

Yes, it is true that the villainous character of Sid is exaggerated far beyond (we hope) any child we could hope not to meet, but he nevertheless—through the combination of so many true-life personality traits—does touch a chord in all of us. He is the monster of our collective childhood.

Hannah Phillips

Sid's younger sister has a minor but quite important role. Her character is utterly dissimilar from that of her elder brother: she is neatly turned out and seems well-mannered and well-behaved. Although she may bring misery briefly to Buzz's life by bringing him to her dolls' tea party—where he must act the role of middle-aged "Mrs. Nesbitt"—it is certainly not within her motives to harm him in any way: She is acting out of, at worst, innocence and, at best, a form of childly kindness.

Her principal importance in the advancement of the plot is when the final expedition to save Buzz is being mounted by Woody and the mutant toys. Legs and Ducky between them succeed in ringing the doorbell and Hannah, like a helpful child, goes to answer it. As she opens the door a clockwork frog scoots between her legs followed by a ferociously yapping Scud. The frog is hoisted aloft by Ducky and Legs, and Hannah shuts the door leaving Scud outside. This gives Woody and the rest the chance to escape at the back through the dogflap.

Scud

It is only to be expected that the destructive, sadistic Sid should have a dog reflecting his personality. Scud—it is no coincidence that the name is shared by a particular type of military missile—is a ball of solid, venomous muscle wrapped up behind a bear trap of teeth and jaws. This is the sort of dog you dread meeting in a dark alley—even more so if you are merely toy-size. Like his master, Scud delights in the willful destruction of toys; the most vicious such destruction we see is that of Alien #4, fed to the dog by Sid.

It is significant that Scud is the only individual smaller than himself whom Sid does not, given the opportunity, attempt to terrorize. Their relationship

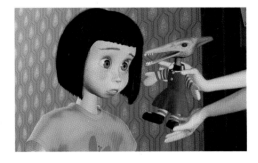

Sid's helpless sister, Hannah, receiving the result of Sid's surgical procedure.

could have been made in . . . well, in this instance, Hell.

Mrs. Davis

Andy's mother in fact plays only a very small part, often merely as a voice off-screen. There is no questioning her general love for her children—she is in her own terms always kind to them, never raising her voice—but she is at the same time distanced from them, particularly from Andy. (Molly plays too little part in the proceedings for us to be able to guess at her relationship with her mother.) Whatever Andy's concerns might be, and almost all of them that we see in the movie relate to the periodic loss of his two favorite toys, she glosses them over with calmly reassuring words, not realizing the trauma the boy is suffering. Perhaps this is simply a question of her having forgotten what things were like in her own childhood, but it is more tempting to believe that scriptwriters and animators alike were going for a greater depth of characterization than that: We suspect that she has recently undergone a divorce, and she is subject to all the very

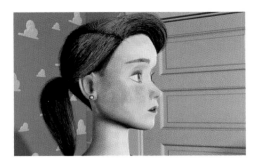

Andy's mom.

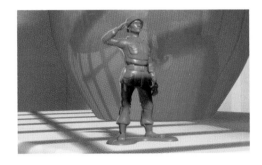

Sergeant rallies the troops.

adult strains of the impending house move (strains which Andy, as a child, can hardly be expected to understand), so it is hardly surprising that his troubles seem to her to be of only the remotest interest.

Sergeant

The Sergeant is the officer in charge of Andy's troop of Green Army Men, and he is suitably military, ever ready with a salute and a stand to attention. He is also heroic, as when he rescues one of his men who has been accidentally trampled underfoot by Mrs. Davis. He and his sol-

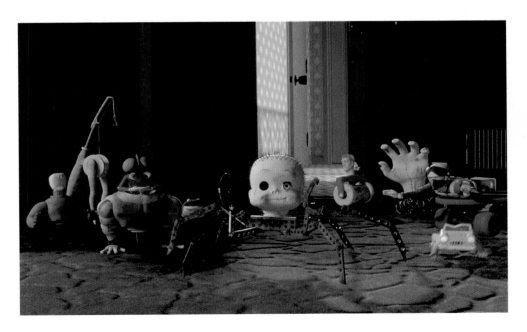

Sid's gruesome collection of mutant toys.

413

diers jump rather than walk from place to place—their plastic bases impede their movement. Their main task within the movie is to mount exploratory missions at Andy's birthday and later at Christmas to report back to the existing toys in the bedroom on the new toys that are arriving downstairs. They do this by smuggling one half of Molly's baby monitor into the drawing room and using it as a walkie-talkie. The scenes of the Sergeant and his men in operation are neither profound nor, in terms of the plot, important, but they are among the most memorable.

The Mutant Toys

Not all of the toys that Sid has hideously cobbled together from bits of other toys are named, and many are just part of the background crowd.

Some, however, are significant characters in their own right, most especially **Babyface**, constructed using a doll's head, its hair plucked to make the head look like that of a baby, mounted on a complicated system of struts and hinges so that the toy moves forward like a spider. The psychological contrast between the upper and lower parts of this silently moving amalgamation gives it an almost unbearably sinister aura; it is little wonder that Woody and Buzz initially assume the various mutant toys are cannibals rather than healers. As in many other Disney animated movies—*James and the Giant Peach* (➤414) is another—we are reminded in due course that superficial appearances are no guide to the true nature of the personality. This notion has, quite fairly, been pulled from the common stockpot of fantasy and science fiction, in which can be found countless examples of hideously ugly and sinister-seeming mutants/aliens who prove to be

benign. Babyface is the leader of the mutant toys; once Woody has established a positive relationship—indeed, a friendship—with Babyface, the course is open to them both to mount the rescue mission to save Buzz.

Also of significance are **Legs** (a toy fishing rod mounted on doll legs) and **Ducky** (a duck head mounted on a baby's torso with a suction-disc base). Legs has a noticeable fraction of the sinisterness of Babyface, but an extra part of her/his character is efficiency: the accurate, almost militaristic stride of the plastic legs matches the concept that fishing rods are precision-built instruments. Ducky, by contrast, seems a happy-go-lucky sort of fellow; at one point he gives us a brief burst of incomprehensible Donald Duck–speak.

RollerBob has a skateboard as base; on top of it is a toy soldier's head and torso. **The Frog** is a red wind-up toy that seems singularly unmutated: perhaps its turn was next. **Pump Boy** has the head of a youth with a pump as its base. **The Jack-in-the-Box** has a hand where the Jack should be; using this spring-supported hand it is able to haul itself around.

Other Toys

There are a few further named toys among the "family" in Andy's bedroom. Among them are **Lenny**, a pair of wind-up toy binoculars through which other toys occasionally survey distant action—as when Buzz is given his first sight of Scud and Sid—and **Rocky**, whose main role occurs near the end of the movie during the great chase scene: a hulky weightlifter doll, he is the only toy strong enough to lower the ramp of the moving van. Also there is **RC**, the acronym standing for Radio-Controlled Car. RC squeals

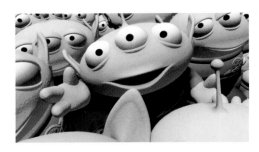

The aliens in the vending machine at Pizza Planet.

on Woody after Buzz falls out of the window. Then the character is used by Woody during the chase to help retrieve Buzz from the hazards of the road and the jaws of Scud. All seems doomed when RC's batteries run out at a crucial moment. It is then that Woody succeeds in igniting Buzz's rocket (using Buzz's helmet and the sun to light the match), and the trio hurtle toward the open rear of the moving van. As Woody and Buzz head for the skies, RC zooms into the group of toys in the van to perform a satisfying demolition job on Mr. Potato Head.

Hannah's doll **Janie** and the **Pterodactyl** whose head Sid grafts onto her are worth mention, but by far the most interesting among the other toys are the little three-eyed **aliens** who are the prey in the arcade crane game at Pizza Planet. Chattering in a consciously cute way, this pile of cuddly creatures eventually explain to the immersed Woody and Buzz about their religion. The claw that periodically descends from on high to seize one or other of the aliens is really the arm of their god; those taken away by it from the rest of the gaggle are indeed fortunate, for they have been chosen for better things.

JAMES AND THE GIANT PEACH

Animated Characters:

James Henry Trotter; Aunt Spiker; Aunt Sponge; Mr. Grasshopper; Commodore Centipede; Mrs. Ladybug; Miss Spider; Earthworm; Glowworm; Rhino; Shark; The Pirates

Credits:

Based on: James and the Giant Peach (1961) by Roald Dahl (1916–1990)

Live Actors: Steven Culp (Father); Joanna Lumley (Aunt Spiker); Miriam Margolyes (Aunt Sponge); Pete Postlethwaite (Old Man); Mike Starr (Beat Cop); Paul Terry (James Henry Trotter); Susan Turner-Cray (Mother)

Voices: Simon Callow (Mr. Grasshopper); Richard Dreyfuss (Commodore Centi-

pede); Jane Leeves (Mrs. Ladybug); Joanna Lumley (animated Aunt Spiker); Miriam Margolyes (animated Aunt Sponge; Glowworm); Pete Postlethwaite (Narrator); Susan Sarandon (Miss Spider); Paul Terry (James Henry Trotter); David Thewlis (Earthworm)

Music/Songs: Randy Newman; lyrics to "Eating the Peach" by Roald Dahl

Screenplay: Karey Kirkpatrick; Jonathan Roberts; Steve Bloom

Editor: Stan Webb

Storyboard Supervisors: Kelly Asbury; Joe Ranft

Conceptual Designer: Lane Smith

Production Designer: Harley Jessup

Animation Supervisor: Paul Berry

Animation Coordinator: Jane Hartwell

Animators: Michael Belzer; Paul Berry; Steven A. Buckley; Kent Burton; Webster Colcord; Chuck Duke; Christopher Gilligan; Timothy Hittle; Josephine T. Huang; Michael W. Johnson; Justin Kohn; Guionne Leroy; Daniel K. Mason; Tom St. Amand; Anthony Scott; Trey Thomas; Richard C. Zimmerman

Directors of Photography: Pete Kozachik; Hiro Narita

Computer Animation Supervisors: Jerome Chen; Harry Walton

Computer Animation: Louis Cetorelli; Allen Edwards; Arnaud Hervas; Alex Sokoloff; David Vallone; Peter Warner

Art Directors: Bill Boes; Kendal Cronkhite

Visual Effects Supervisors: Pete Kozachik; (for Rhino) Gary Platek

Visual Effects Producer: Nancy St. John

Visual Effects Coordinator: Amy Hollywood Wixson

Special Effects Coordinators: Craig Mohagen; Steven Riley; Thomas F. Sindicich

Production Manager: Richard Quan

Coproducers: Brian Rosen; Henry Selick

Executive Producer: Jake Eberts

Producers: Tim Burton; Denise DiNovi

Director: Henry Selick

Release Date: April 12, 1996

Running Time: 79 minutes

THE MOVIE

Produced in association with Allied Filmmakers, this production is a very fine recreation of Roald Dahl's much-loved children's novella for the screen. As a tale, it bears the usual stamp of the obsessions to which Dahl gave vent in his children's work, primary among them being the evil to which adults subject children. This theme has been extensively exploited in earlier movies based on Dahl's work: in *Willy Wonka and the Chocolate Factory* (1971), based on the author's *Charlie and the Chocolate Factory* (1964), there is no such thing as a sympathetic adult with even Mr. Wonka himself, who bequeaths his magical chocolate factory to young Charlie, being an untrustworthy, somewhat chilling trickster figure; in *The Witches* (1989), based on Dahl's *The Witches* (1983), although there are benign adults in the form of Grandma and Miss Irvine, the central foci are the middle-aged female witches, led by Eva Ernst, who plot to change the children of the world into mice by feeding them doctored candies. This bleakness of vision of adult behavior toward children is very much Dahl's; it is also, if exaggerated, very much the way that children can regard their position in society's pecking order; which is why, despite shrill adult cries of disgust, Dahl's children's books are so popular among their chosen audience . . . and among enlightened grownups who can remember only too well the hell that childhood could all too often be.

In *James and the Giant Peach* Dahl tackled a serious problem: child abuse. The young protagonists of *Charlie and the Chocolate Factory* and *The Witches* have, respectively, to put up with slobbish and (in Mr. Wonka's case) steely adults and adults who are positively malicious yet are clearly the products of fantasy. In *James and the Giant Peach*, however, the

two tyrannical aunts are all too credible. To them James is not a child, or even a fellow human being, but a *thing* to be exploited, much as is the Giant Peach of the title. It is difficult to read the book or to watch the movie without a tear; far too many children in this world are treated as objects, whether psychologically, sexually, violently, or in terms of cheap labor. That Dahl chose to set his examination of this theme—in this and in other stories—in a superficially civilized, middle-class milieu may have drawn some of the sting from the message he was trying to impart, but not much.

The second notable influence on the overall vision of this movie is that of Tim Burton. Burton is not as fine a moviemaker as his box-office receipts might suggest. He has the knack, like Steven Spielberg, of spotting popular themes at exactly the right moment, but always there is the sense, as one leaves the theater, that the resultant movie might have been, somehow, a bit better. Yet, despite these caveats, he has, like Dahl, an ability to identify and accurately represent the paranoia of childhood, as especially in his stop-motion short *Vincent* (1982); indeed, the character of Vincent could be regarded as a precursor of the cinematic James Henry Trotter. The darkness of Burton's vision superbly complements that of Dahl's in *James and the Giant Peach*. If one were to indulge oneself in one of those fantasies about movies that were never made, one could do worse than start with a Dahl-scripted *The Nightmare Before Christmas*.

Although there are a few short moments of traditional animation in *James and the Giant Peach*, by far the bulk of the action involves stop-motion animation; there is also a sizable amount of footage shot as live action with animated interventions—as when Aunt Spiker, early on, swats an animated butterfly with the classically antilife statement:

Eaugh. Wouldn't want one of those nesting in your knickers.

Indeed, the only important characters in the movie to be shot almost exclusively in live action (they have brief animated appearances; James himself, acted by Paul Terry, has longer periods of live action but is primarily of interest as an animated character) are the two aunts, and this introduces an intriguing dichotomy because they are presented as being in all respects antilife, unlike the central animated characters, who are almost uniformly prolife, and thus more human—in a certain sense—than the aunts themselves are. This argument can be extended. The aunts, who are alive, pathologically detest both insects and James with the same detestation—it is

clear that to them, children, and anyone who is not one of the aunts themselves, occupy the same status as bugs. By contrast, and as a psychological result, James is fond of bugs and regards them as his equals, because that is how he has been educated to regard himself by his aunts. In *Who Framed Roger Rabbit* (➤**326**) there was a certain amount of discussion of the theme whereby fantasy creatures (in its case toons) may be much more lovable and admirable than living human beings, but then the arch-villain, Judge Doom, proves to be a toon, so muddling the message; in *James and the Giant Peach* there is no such muddling. Those creatures we as children create in our own worlds of fantasy are indeed better than the people we find surrounding us in reality. In this movie, also, the animation is more distanced from the live action: James crosses the boundary between live action and animation, and the aunts very briefly do, but the integration of both modes, so much a part of *Who Framed Roger Rabbit*, is absent. That said, this was Disney's first attempt at mixing stop-motion animation with live action.

Like Dahl's other children's fantasies, *James and the Giant Peach* is concerned with wish fulfillment, the powerless conquering the powerful; even in the nonfantastic *Danny, The Champion of the World* (1975), whose hero is in at least one sense entirely amoral, it is hard to withhold our support from the child who cheats the local landlord of his gamebirds even though the gamebirds pay with their lives, in effect, for the child's victory. *Fantastic Mr. Fox* (1970) likewise cheers for the underdog—or, in this instance, underfox—against a hostile human, adult world.

It is curious that Walt Disney himself never quite understood the appeal that Dahl's work had for both children and "adult children." The two men discussed the possibility of an animated feature based on a short story Dahl had written about gremlins (➤**206**). Dahl thought Walt Disney was more interested in the project than he actually was, and thereafter relations between the two men were not entirely cordial. It was only after the death of both of them that the movie *James and the Giant Peach* could come into existence. Perhaps this was a good thing. The movie exemplifies the best of Walt and the best of Dahl. If either or both had been personally involved it might not have been the case.

Lucy Dahl, daughter of Roald, has written an extremely short account from her viewpoint (as a child) of the book her father wrote and (as an adult) of the movie Disney made: *James and the Giant Peach: The Book and Movie Scrapbook* (1996). Her two children make a very brief appearance in the movie.

THE STORY

Young James lives an idyllic life on the coast with his loving parents, but one day a rhinoceros charges out of the clouds and kills them, so that he is forced to live with his vile aunts Sponge and Spiker, who use him as their slave. Both of the aunts are revolted by the local population of insects and arachnids, who consequently become James's friends. He dreams of escaping from his misery to go from England to New York, the city where his parents planned to emigrate, assuming its streets were paved if not with gold then at least with opportunity.

One night, while rescuing a spider from the aunts, James encounters an Old Man—perhaps a tramp—who gives him a bagful of glowing green magic crocodile tongues and tells him that they will make his dreams come true; however, should he let them escape, they will make true the dreams of whomever they first encounter:

> *Old Man*: There's more magic in them things than in all the rest of the world put together.
> *James*: But what are they?
> *Old Man*: Crocodile tongues.
> *James*: Tongues?
> *Old Man*: One thousand long, slimy crocodile tongues boiled in the skull of a dead witch for twenty days and twenty nights. And the fingers of a young monkey, the gizzard of a pig, the beak of a parrot and three spoonfuls of sugar. Stew for a week and then let the Moon do the rest.
> Have 'em, and marvelous things will happen. Things even you never dreamt of.
> *James*: Like what?
> *Old Man*: Well, like, you'll never be miserable again. And you *are* miserable, aren't you, James? You weren't meant to be, you know. And that place you're dreamin' of, it's not as far away as you think.
> *James*: New York City.
> *Old Man*: And it'll be that much closer once you take the first step.

The Old Man thus serves, very briefly, as a sort of Merlin to James's Arthur in what is perhaps the pivotal scene of the movie. Needless to say, James loses the worms almost at once, and they infest his aunts' barren peach tree—which for the first time in memory bears a peach. The peach grows until it is as large as a house and even beyond; the aunts make a small fortune out of charging visitors an admission fee to see this prodigy, while James goes as underloved and underfed as ever. Driven by starvation, he eventually helps himself to a handful of the fruit's flesh; the hole he makes opens a portal into the peach's interior. He climbs in and, as he does so, becomes a stop-motion animated character rather than a live-action boy actor.

Within the peach he discovers a colony of roughly boy-size bugs who are as keen to escape from the tyrannical presence of Sponge and Spiker as he is. They know the aunts will sooner or later destroy them with pesticide. The aunts do indeed come to search for James, but Commodore Centipede bravely gnaws the peach free of its tree so that it rolls down the hill and floats away out to sea. James rediscovers, magically, a travel brochure about New York, which he and his parents had adored but which Aunt Sponge had destroyed; the brochure now shows the peach en route to the fabled city.

Yet all is not to be easy for the comrades. They are attacked by a mechanical shark, which is capable of firing metal, sharp-toothed missiles at them. They are able to escape through capturing a flock of seagulls in a ropework made from Miss Spider's web, thereafter being able to travel by air. For navigation they rely upon the Commodore Centipede's skills, which prove illusory; he redeems himself—and James and Miss Spider are likewise heroes—when recovering from the depths the compass of a sunken pirate ship, fighting off skeletal pirates in the process.

The peach reaches New York in due course, impaling itself on the Empire State Building's spire. From there it is fetched down by a massive crane to street level, where the aunts suddenly (and, in plotting terms, rather artificially) appear, having seemingly driven by car over the bottom of the Atlantic Ocean in order to reclaim James as their legal ward and thus slave. But James, through his adventures having rediscovered his own sense of identity, has the courage to denounce the two grown-ups publicly and, with the help of the bugs, wraps them up with the web of Miss Spider. His remaining days are spent with his many friends in New York City, in whose Central Park he and the bug gang dwell within the pit of the peach, now converted into a comfy house.

Before the closing credits a series of magazine and newspaper articles appears reporting the mighty achievements of the central gang; one example is headlined "DR. LADYBUG DELIVERS 1,000TH BABY" and goes on to tell us how New Yorkers love to have the presumably now graduated Mrs. Ladybug on hand at the vital moment of childbirth. The idea for the sequence seems to have been lifted wholesale from *Bill & Ted's Bogus Journey* (1991), but the execution is much less witty. This is a great pity: *James and the Giant Peach* is in many ways a highly original piece of moviemaking, but the viewer's appreciation of its originality is marred by this apparent ripoff.

In a very brief final sequence, which occurs after the credits and therefore would have been missed by many, a child (James, we must assume) plays an old-fashioned carnival game called "Spike the Aunts." This involves the player controlling a mechanical rhinoceros in order to commit abuses on two dolls representing Aunts Sponge and Spiker. The effect of this sequence is to throw yet another layer of meaning onto what has come before; of course, we knew that what we were watching was a fantasy, but now it seems possible that everything was an escapist dream couched within a realistic hell. That the movie offers us no way of deciding which of these options is the truth is one of its great strengths as a work of fantasy.

THE CHARACTERS

James Henry Trotter

Unusual in a modern Disney animated feature, the central character is both male and something of a cypher: James captures our sympathies during his sequences in live action (where he is excellently portrayed by Paul Terry) but, as an animated character, he is someone who reacts to events rather than someone who causes events to happen. On occasion he displays inventiveness and even heroism—as when he plunges into icy Arctic waters in order to retrieve both Commodore Centipede and the pirates' compass—but more usually he is a tool of those around them, doing their bidding and agreeing with any assessment they make of him.

This is no accident; nor does it represent any sloppiness of characterization. It is established very early in the movie that one of the vilest of the tortures perpetrated by the aunts on the young James is their attempt to destroy any sense he might have of his own identity; at one point in the opening few minutes of *James and the Giant Peach* he sings to himself, as he must have done countless times before, a touching little song that has the effect of reminding him of his own name, the sole thing he any longer can cling to. The understory of the movie is, above all else, that of James discovering that he is more than a named abstraction, more than a slave. Here there is a very strong echo of the way in which various political regimes throughout the world have persuaded their subjects to commit acts of genocide by indoctrinating into them the idea that their victims are not really human beings but animals whose slaughter is no cause for concern. In this sense *James and the Giant Peach*, both movie and book, is highly political, for very few of today's advanced nations can proclaim their histories free of such depersonalization of foreigners. James, persuaded by the aunts that he is not a person at all but merely a thing that works until it drops from exhaustion, is a symbol of all those sufferers. The parallel is carried further in the several sequences—notably that at the end where the aunts try to reclaim him in New York—in which it is made quite plain that tyrants cannot exist without the acquiescence of those they tyrannize.

Watching the animated James is not an unalloyed pleasure: he is far too reminiscent of the kid we all knew in childhood who drew victimization upon herself or himself. He is emotionally disturbing because we have come across children like him. That he triumphs in the end is a triumph in which we can all share . . . although whether we deserve to is another matter.

James partakes in a dramatic moment of what might be regarded as animation within animation. Toward the end of the sequence in which he and the bugs sing the song "Family"—which describes their love for each other but especially the esteem in which the bugs hold James—we see the peach drifting into a night sky that eventually becomes an mobile, with the peach as the major component of this solar system model. Then James's hand reaches into view to pluck the peach from the mobile, and finally the field of view moves back to show James still clutching the peach but at the same time standing on the giant flying peach. The overlayered perception shifts involved in this sequence—which lasts only a few seconds—are superbly controlled.

There is a separate animated James. During an extended dream sequence he is (in conventional animation) a James-headed caterpillar gnawing on a large, if not giant, peach and being threatened by the aunts. He is equated with the bugs the aunts used to take such delight in slaughtering in the bleak garden of their home, and the spray Aunt Sponge puffs at him becomes, in his dreaming vision, the rhinoceros that killed his parents.

Aunt Spiker and Aunt Sponge

These two characters appear hardly at all in animation: their sole depictions are briefly in a nightmare of James's and as a double figurehead on the sunken pirate ship. The latter appearance is really just a joke, but the former bears a greater weight: James sees them as near-stick figures, their personalities being conveyed by their voices, their primitive body language, and especially by the accentuation of their gross physical characteristics—in this latter respect Spiker (played in live action by Joanna Lumley) is of special note, being depicted as essentially a pelvis with sticks deployed above and

below. The image is striking, as is its nightmarishness: It is made very clear to us that, at this stage in the tale, with the peach halfway across the Atlantic, James has still not lost his terror of the two tyrants.

Commodore Centipede

With his greasy flat cap, his omnipresent cigar, and his working-class Brooklyn accent, the Centipede is presented as a character who aspires to a status he does not deserve. His braggart claims to have sailed the seven seas are in due course exposed, largely by the snobbish, upper-class English Mr. Grasshopper—for reasons of class his arch-enemy through the early parts of the movie—as nonsense: Commodore Centipede's exposure to the world has been temporary residence within a copy of *National Geographic* magazine. His claims to be able to navigate, because of his nonexistent naval history, lead the gang aboard the flying peach into mortal danger when they find themselves far off course in the chill of the Arctic; yet he more than redeems himself by being the first to plunge, apparently suicidally, into the frozen waters to retrieve the compass from a sunken pirate ship. He has already displayed a great deal of courage during the battle with the mechanical Shark—"Teach you to mess with me, you overgrown sardine! I'm from Brooklyn!"—but this has not been generally recognized by the gang, especially not by Mr. Grasshopper.

Commodore Centipede is voiced excellently by Richard Dreyfuss. His performance is not only extremely funny but also affecting. Like James and (to a lesser extent) Mr. Grasshopper, the character of Commodore Centipede is appealing because through the movie he evolves into someone worthy of our admiration rather than our pity.

This character has some of the funniest lines, mostly self-mocking, in the movie. While being stretched on the rack by the spectral pirates he comes out with:

> Listen, fellas, I got a long history of back problems and I don't need it to get any longer.

Moments later, while beating up the pirates, he comes out with an excruciating pun:

> I got a good one for ya. Why don't skeletons play music in church? 'Cause they got no organs.

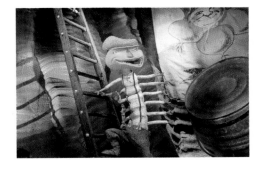

The fast-talking Centipede, voiced by Richard Dreyfuss.

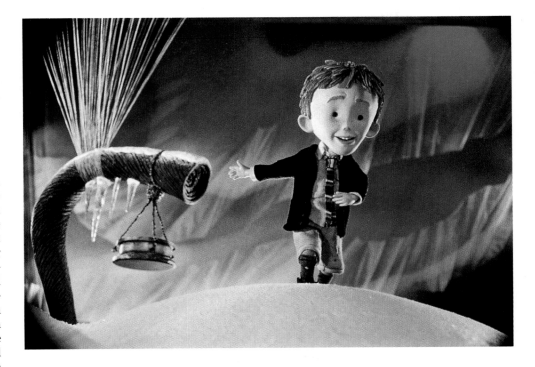

Young James in animated form.

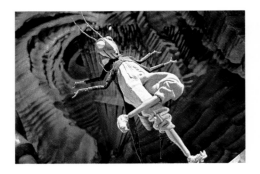

The cultivated and cultured Mr. Grasshopper.

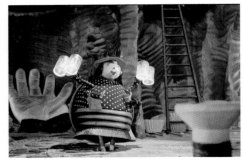

Gentle Mrs. Ladybug.

Earlier, when urged by Mr. Grasshopper to hurry while various members of the gang are ensnaring the flock of seagulls that will carry them across the ocean, he retorts:

> Keep your pants on! I've only got twelve hands!

Mr. Grasshopper

In complete contrast to Commodore Centipede, Mr. Grasshopper is an English aristocratic snob of the sort portrayed on the screen by such luminaries as Noel Coward and Basil Rathbone—the comparison with Rathbone is accentuated when Mr. Grasshopper produces his violin, à la Sherlock Holmes, and proceeds to play. Tall—he is certainly the tallest of the animated characters—and angularly skinny, he clearly feels himself also a moral cut above the others until he lapses into what even he clearly recognizes as an attack of childishness when, in a fit of hunger, he fights with Commodore Centipede over the chunk of soda bread that Mrs. Ladybug had produced from her handbag—with the result that the piece of bread is lost to both of them, tumbling away through the clouds to fall, one assumes, into the ocean. A more profound moment of reconciliation occurs after James, Miss Spider, and Commodore Centipede have stolen the compass from the sunken pirate ship. Now Mr. Grasshopper has no option but to recognize Commodore Centipede's heroism, whatever the difference between their social classes:

> Grasshopper: I'm so sorry.
> Centipede: Hey, I'm sorry.
> Grasshopper: My sincere apologies.
> Centipede: I just, I just wanna apolo—
> Grasshopper: I just wanted to say—
> Centipede: —gize. What I'm tryin' to say . . .
> Earthworm: That's enough chitchat. I'm freezin'.

Monocled and wearing a top hat, Mr. Grasshopper is every inch an aristocrat. Even his suit, which has seen better days but nevertheless speaks "quality" from every crease, adds to his dominating image. His sharp-edged face, with its double mouth, seems to be made rather from bronze than from anything organic. It would be easy to regard him as an unsympathetic character—in real life he would almost certainly be one—but it is hard not to like him, even at his most snobbish.

Mr. Grasshopper's prowess with the violin reflects, in Disney animation, that of Basil (➤320), the hero of *The Great Mouse Detective*; both, obviously, owe their talent to Sir Arthur Conan Doyle's Sherlock Holmes. But Mr. Grasshopper has a further debt in the scene in which James comes across him fiddling: he is also a dead ringer, for these few moments, for Jack Skellington in *The Nightmare Before Christmas* (➤382), striking very similar postures against the night sky and deploying very similar stick-figure body language. "Music," says Mr. Grasshopper, "should be the voice of the soul." And he proceeds to demonstrate this idea with a merry tune (poorly animated, for once in this movie) and a doleful one.

This makes his final acceptance of and avowals of friendship with James and Commodore Centipede all the more moving. One comes away from the movie *liking* Mr. Grasshopper, for all his evident faults.

Mrs. Ladybug

Like all of the bugs except Commodore Centipede, Mrs. Ladybug is very English. Despite her green face, she has the stringent accent of a northern Englander and the red hat and white-on-black spotted dress to match. At the same time she has much of the bulky sensibleness of Agatha Christie's Miss Marple, especially as portrayed on screen by Margaret Rutherford. Like Rutherford in that role, she has something of the appearance of a Russian nesting doll, as if one might be able to open her up and discover ever-smaller versions of Mrs. Ladybug nestling within. Her wings normally rest as a red-with-white-spots carapace on her back, but on a couple of occasions she exercises them and then her personality changes: the stolid, weighty possessor of great common sense suddenly becomes a creature of light and grace.

Above all, Mrs. Ladybug is *decent*. There is no spite in her, and one is convinced that there are no guilty secrets in her past. Her moral code is based on decorum: When the peach is being attacked by the projectile sharks she courageously swats away a couple of them with her handbag on the basis that:

> Well, they were being very rude. I can't abide rudeness.

That they were threatening to deal out death to her and the rest of the gang seems not have occurred to her.

Miss Spider

Miss Spider makes her first appearance in *James and the Giant Peach* as a live-action character, if that's what this individual can be called. James discovers a spider and its web in the broken window of his miserable bedroom in the aunts' house. He brings the arachnid into his room for a while, telling it that he is its friend; later the same night, when the aunts discover the creature and wish to kill it (or have James do so), he rushes out into the darkness and ushers the spider into what he assumes is the safety of an old brick wall. Much later he recognizes the bug he saved as the one who has become his friend aboard the peach.

The first thing that must be observed about the animated Miss Spider is that she is extremely sexy—no analysis of her character would be complete otherwise. Voiced by Susan Sarandon in husky French-accented tones, she wears a beret and what appears to be a Japanese Noh–style mask, while moving with the calculated seductiveness of a professional supermodel on the catwalk. She is also vaguely threatening (an aspect assisted visually by her eyes, each of which contains two eyeballs which adds to her alure and her vampirelike teeth). Alone among the bugs aboard the peach, she offers a benignity that cannot be entirely counted upon—as when Commodore Centipede triumphantly returns from the raid on the pirate ship. He has, through his delayed escape, caused everyone's heart to miss at least a few beats (no character in a Dahl story is guaranteed survival in such circumstances). Miss Spider holds a sword to his throat and says:

> Centipede, I do not know whether to kill you or . . . kiss you.

In fact, she kisses him, but for that crucial second or so we—and he, and one suspects Miss Spider herself—cannot be *sure* what she will do. It is a moment of great

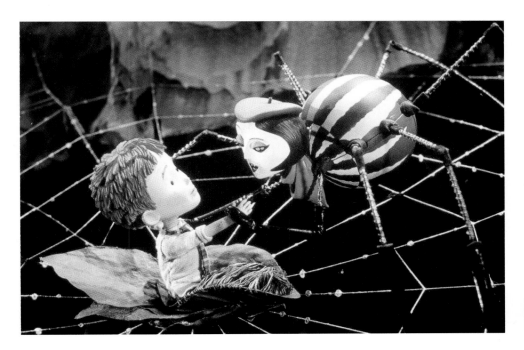

Femme fatale Miss Spider, voiced by Susan Sarandon.

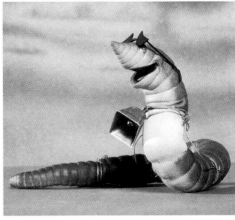

Earthworm.

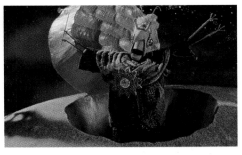

Glowworm.

tension: She is more frightening than the deathly homicidal pirates whom she, James, and Commodore Centipede have only just earlier been fighting. Perhaps it is wrong to admire a character who is potentially a psychopath, as Miss Spider most certainly is, but at the same time it is hard not to feel her tremendous appeal as the latest in the recent line of strong Disney female animated characters. If this is a male-dominated world, no one has yet informed Miss Spider of it; the result is a joy to watch. It is entirely fitting that, as we discover in the mock newspaper headlines near the end of the movie, her chosen career in New York is to open a fashionable if somewhat questionable nightclub.

Yet, femme fatale or no, she is not without a sort of older-woman kindness—to call it maternal would be to mislead. James is visibly baffled by the sexuality he can sense emanating from her—baffled, attracted, and frightened all at the same time—as exemplified in a curious little scene about halfway through the movie, when he sits in the middle of the web she is weaving:

James: You keep to yourself, don't you?
Miss Spider: I prefer to be alone.
James: I was alone for a long time once. I think it's much nicer to have friends, don't you?
Miss Spider: I would not know.
James: They would be your friends, too. The others, I mean. If you'd just let them.
Miss Spider: No, it is in their nature to have fear of me. This I cannot change.
James: You're very kind to me.
Miss Spider: Maybe this is because you are kind to me first.
James: You were the spider in my window!
Miss Spider: Um-hm.

James: You were my first friend. I mean, since I went to live with my aunts. They hated me.
Miss Spider: Shhh. Do not think of them now.
James: But what if they find us? What if we don't make it to New York? I'll die if I have to go back to the way I was. They can't make me.
Miss Spider: Nobody can make you do anything, James, if you do not let them. You are a brave boy. [kisses him] Now, to sleep.

Her relationship with James is probably the most interesting in the movie—the other bugs are generally happy-go-lucky souls who have offered him their instant camaraderie—but Miss Spider's is the most valuable friendship of all in that he has had to earn it.

Earthworm

Wearing would-be fashionable shades, Earthworm is something of a caricature of the English working-class depressive, always ready to speak of his assumption that death and doom are imminent. He has a large mouth, which he is not unready to put to extensive use in the enunciation of his gloomy sarcasm, much of which is superficially self-mocking but seems in fact designed to make it clear to the rest of the gang how rotten they are always being to him. To be fair, there is some truth in this. Because he so often depicts himself as their doormat they tend on occasion to treat him like one, most notably when he is used as living bait by the others in order to attract the seagulls to the peach so that they can be snared. At first he is merely popped out through the hole at the peach's top and forced to wriggle enticingly by being tickled by Commodore Centipede, safely

secluded below; in a second attempt Commodore Centipede abandons subtlety and swings Earthworm around his head with a loud cry of "Come and get it!"

Earthworm's natural fatalism is amusingly on display early in the movie when James has not long entered the peach and the two aunts are hunting him. Commodore Centipede ("the Yank") is busy gnawing through the peach's stalk to set the fruit free.

Mrs. Ladybug: Oh, please, don't let them spray us!
Earthworm: Spray us? They'll see the Yank up there and come after us with a shovel! It happened to my brother.
James: How awful.
Earthworm: Split him right down the middle. Now I have two half-brothers.

Glowworm

The Glowworm is the least of the central band of friends. She is largely confined to a glass case, rather like a stuffed bird might be in an old-fashioned museum; this case hangs from the "ceiling" of the peach's interior, so that she is able to supply lighting much as in a conventional room. Her dialogue is minimal, most of it being confined to the song "Family," which the gang sings as New York comes into view.

She is the most grotesque of the bugs, being made up of yellow-green and

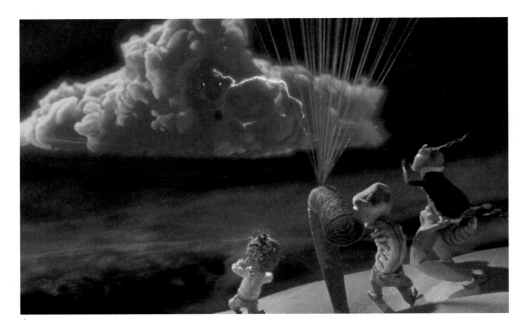

The Rhino approaches the peach in James's recurring nightmare.

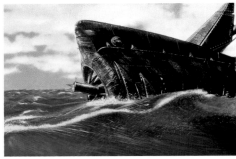

The terrifying mechanical Shark chases the peach.

angular shapes and very little else except the impression that she is an elderly middle-class widow of somewhat muddled views and a distinct hardness of hearing. It comes as rather a surprise when, in "Family," she declares her love for James and the rest: it has not been much evident before.

Rhino

The rhinoceros that charges out of the clouds to gobble up James's parents and later to threaten, at the aunts' behest, James himself (either in reality or in his dreamworld—the ambiguity is exquisite) is reminiscent of Bill Tytla's Chernabog (➤186) in *Fantasia*. Here is a beast of immense power; it is also a beast unbound by the laws of nature (in real life, you know, rhinoceroses rarely charge from the skies to eat people), just as are gods and devils. Every aspect of the animation reinforces this: the rhinoceros is huge as it charges, its eyes alight, directly toward the viewer. There is no question that it is a threat, not only to James but also to us. In this respect it is a primary driver of the movie's fantasy content.

The rhinoceros's final appearance is as the peach approaches nighttime New York; dredged from the depths of James's earliest fears—the aunts did a good job of persuading him that he would never be able to achieve anything he tried—it charges from the thunderous clouds toward the peach and our heroes, determined to destroy all. James, like a fool,

challenges it in a fight conducted through insults alone but, though he wins the battle, loses everything else. The rhinoceros zaps the peach with a bolt of lightning, and all seems as much lost as it was for James's parents. Luckily movies have happier endings than that.

Shark

The Shark is no shark; it is instead a metal mechanism, bolted and plated together, capable of dealing out death. Its first appearance is from a maelstrom observed by the passengers of the floating peach; as an expression of its intentions (and of the multiple levels of fantasized perception at work here) it spits out a series of dishes on which are fish heads, echoing the revolting meals of fish heads that James's aunts attempted to feed him. The metallic shark does its best to bring about the downfall of the peach as it is hoisted aloft by the flock of seagulls—the machine fires from its mouth salvoes of robotic flying creatures called hammerhead sharks (they are rather like sentient harpoons), which have sharp jaws capable of cutting right through the gossamer strands linking the peach to the seagulls—but in the end it is defeated. The first sign of the hammerheads' demise comes when Mrs. Ladybug swats a couple of them on the nose with her handbag, all the while berating them. Finally one hammerhead shark, thumped free from the peach by a determined Miss Spider, plunges back into the Shark's

mouth, destroying its whirling metal teeth, and the two explode dramatically.

Like the Rhinoceros, the Shark is a villain whose destruction is necessary if James and his pals are ever going to make it to New York and survive there. Unlike Rhino, however, the Shark is not essential to the plot; its sequence is there merely to add excitement when the action might otherwise have slowed down. Nevertheless it is a fine creation—an excellent bit part.

The Pirates

The Pirates play a small part in the movie. As with the Shark, their role is to provide a hindrance and an extra adventure for our friends. Commodore Centipede is the first to dive into the icy Arctic waters in search of a compass for the peach. He soon discovers the dead **Captain**, whom he describes as Captain Skellington—a joke on the name of The Nightmare Before Christmas's Jack Skellington (➤382). Believing he was escaping scot-free with the dead Captain's compass, Commodore Centipede discovers that the pirates are still alive—in a sense. His suspenders are seized by the Captain, and his exit is halted in dramatic fashion. While the Captain himself is of little visual inventiveness—he is a skeleton wearing a naval hat on his skull—some of the other pirates are interesting. The hulky **Eskimo Pirate** and a much smaller colleague called Pegleg (not at all like **Pegleg Pete** (➤15) have the fun of stretching Commodore Centipede on the rack; the **Viking Pirate** is about to cut Commodore Centipede in half when James intervenes to save his friend's life; a further pirate, **Duckman**, has the faintest of resemblance to a vastly elongated Donald Duck. In a final mass fight between the pirates and our heroes, the Captain's skeletal **Parrot** also plays a part, albeit a small one.

THE HUNCHBACK OF NOTRE DAME

Characters:

Quasimodo; Esmeralda; Judge Claude Frollo; Captain Phoebus; Clopin; The Gargoyles (Hugo, Victor, and Laverne); Djali; Archdeacon; Achilles; Brutish Guard; Oafish Guard; Boatman; Quasimodo's Father; Baby Quasimodo; Quasimodo's Mother; Gypsy Boy; Whipsman; Old Heretic; Miller; Little Girl; Baby Bird

Credits:

Based on: Notre Dame de Paris (*The Hunchback of Notre Dame*) (1831) by Victor Hugo

Voices: Jason Alexander (Hugo); Mary Kay Bergman (Quasimodo's Mother); Corey Burton (Brutish Guard); Jim Cummings (Guards and Gypsies); Bill Fagerbakke (Oafish Guard); Tom Hulce (Quasimodo); Tony Jay (Frollo); Paul Kandel (Clopin); Charles Kimbrough (Victor); Kevin Kline (Captain Phoebus); Heidi Mollenhauer (Esmeralda singing); Demi Moore (Esmeralda speaking); Patrick Pinney (Guards and Gypsies); David Ogden Stiers (Archdeacon); Gary Trousdale (Old Heretic); Frank Welker (Baby Bird); Mary Wickes (Laverne); Jane Withers (additional Laverne dialogue)

Additional Voices: Jack Angel; Joan Barber; Scott Barnes; Bob Bergen; Mary Kay Bergman; Susan Blu; Maureen Brennan; Rodger Bumpass; Corey Burton; Victoria Clark; Philip Clarke; Jennifer Darling; Debi Derryberry; Jonathan Dokuchitz; Bill Farmer; Laurie Faso; Merwin Foard; Dana Hill; Judy Kaye; Eddie Korbich; Alix Korey; Michael Lindsay; Sherry Lynn; Howard McGillin; Mickey McGowan; Anna McNeely; Mona Marshall; Bruce Moore; Denise Pickering; Patrick Pinney; Phil Proctor; Jan Rabson; Peter Samuel; Kath Soucie; Gordon Stanley; Mary Stout; Marcelo Tubert

Music: Alan Menken

Songs by: Alan Menken and Stephen Schwartz; Herbert Stothart, George Bassman and George Stoll

Orchestration: Michael Starobin

Vocal Arrangements: David Friedman

Animation Story: Tab Murphy

Animation Screenplay: Irene Mecchi; Tab Murphy; Jonathan Roberts; Bob Tzudiker and Noni White

Story Supervisor: Will Finn

Story: Christine Blum; Gee Fwee Boedoe; Gaëtan Brizzi; Paul Brizzi; Jim Capobianco; Brenda Chapman; Will Finn; James Fujii; Francis Glebas; Edward Gombert; Kirk Hanson; Kevin Harkey; Burny Mattinson; Sue C. Nichols; Floyd Norman; Denis Rich; John Sanford; Jeff Snow; Kelly Wightman

Editor: Ellen Keneshea

Supervising Animators: James Baxter (Quasimodo); David Burgess (Archdeacon); Russ Edmonds (Captain Phoebus); Will Finn (Laverne); Tony Fucile (Esmeralda); Ron Husband (Djali); David Pruiksma (Hugo, Victor); Michael Surrey (Clopin); Kathy Zielinski (Frollo)

Animators: Anne-Marie Bardwell; Jared Beckstrand; Travis Blaise; Bolhem Bouchiba; Réjean Bourdages; Christopher Bradley; David Brewster; Robert Bryan; Michael Cedeno; Roger Chiasson; Sylvain Deboissy; Patrick Delage; Robert Espanto Domingo; Sasha Dorogov; Marc Eoche Duval; Trey Finney; Doug Frankel; Danny Galieote; Raul Garcia; Tom Gately; Steven Pierre Gordon; Kent Hammerstrom; David Hancock; T. Daniel Hofstedt; Shawn E. Keller; Mark Koetsier; Gilda Kouros; Doug Krohn; Bradley Kuha; Dave Kupczyk; Teresa Martin; Dominique Monfery; Jean Morel; Jamie Oliff; Daniel O'Sullivan; Sergio Pablos; Ralf Palmer; Catherine Poulain; Mark Pudleiner; William Recinos; John Ripa; Stéphanie Sainte-Foi; Christopher Suave; Yoshimichi Tamura; Chris Wahl; Bill Waldman; Eric Walls; Larry White; Anthony Ho Wong; Phil Young; David A. Zaboski

Computer Animation: Gregory Griffith; Mike "Moe" Merell

Director of Technology: Paul Yanover

Key Layout: Scott Caple; Fred Craig; Lorenzo Martinez; Samuel Michlap; Tom Shannon

Layout Supervisor: Ed Ghertner

Background Supervisor: Lisa Keene

Cleanup Supervisor: Vera Lanpher Pacheco

Visual Effects: Christopher Jenkins

Supervising Visual Effects Animators: Tom Hush; Dorse Lanpher; Brice Mallier

Computer Graphics Imagery: Kiran Bhakta Joshi

Backgrounds: Jennifer Ando; Allison Belliveau-Proulx; Olivier Besson; Justin Brandstater; Brooks Campbell; Dominick R. Domingo; Gregory Alexander Drolette; Debbie Du Bois; Jean-Paul Fernandez; Brad Hicks; Michael Humphries; Mi Kyung Joung-Raynis; William Lorencz; David McCamley; Serge Michaels; Patricia Millereau; Don Moore; Joaquim Royo Morales; Patricia Palmer-Phillipson; Pierre Pavloff; Colin Stimpson; George Taylor; Maryann Thomas; Christopher Vacher; Tom Woodington

Art Director: David Goetz

Artistic Coordinator: Randy Fullmer

Sequence Directors: Gaëtan Brizzi; Paul Brizzi

Production Manager: Patricia Hicks

Production Coordinators: Catherine Alexander; Onil Alfredo Chibás; Kara Lord; Maryann McLeod; Christian Schmidt

Coproducer: Roy Conli

Associate Producer: Phil Lofaro

Producer: Don Hahn

Directors: Gary Trousdale; Kirk Wise

Release Date: Premiered June 19, 1996; general release June 21, 1996

Running Time: 91 minutes

THE MOVIE

Once upon a time Disney made animated movies about ugly ducklings but would never have had the courage to make the central character of a feature movie a person so ugly that a main part of the plot was that few people could bear to look at him. In 1996 they tried it with this movie, and succeeded with what it is hard not to call triumph. The movie is also a very adult one. No physical scenes are explicitly depicted, of course, but it is very clear that a principal character (Frollo) is mainly inspired by physical lust for one of the others (Esmeralda). Two further adult themes treated in *The Hunchback of Notre Dame* are sadism and racism. One expects directors of animated movies like Ralph Bakshi to take on adult themes—indeed, it is rare for Bakshi to do anything other—but it is strange to find Disney doing it. One hopes the company will do so again. The idea that animated movies are only for kids is surely one that has outlived its usefulness.

Of course, Victor Hugo's novel has been filmed before—although always in live action: in 1923 (directed by Wallace Worsley, starring Lon Chaney), 1939 (directed by William Dieterle, starring Charles Laughton—this is the most admired live-action version, with Laughton in splendid form), 1956 (directed by Jean Delannoy, starring Anthony Quinn), and 1982 (directed by Michael Tuchner, starring Anthony Hopkins—although made for television, this is another highly admired movie). The idea of turning the novel into not just an animated movie but an animated musical — it is packed with songs to the extent that, although almost all of them are good songs, sometimes one wishes they would stop for a while (Gary Westfahl has suggested that the moviemakers had in mind the undoubtedly forthcoming stage version)—was an unusual one, to say the least. The movie was apparently the brainchild of David Stainton, Disney's Creative Affairs Vice President. He thought of the idea in 1993, remembering how much he had enjoyed reading the story when he was a child in its adaptation as a *Classics Illustrated* comic, then later when he read the novel proper. The directors Gary Trousdale and Kirk Wise were given the task of developing Stainton's dream. They naturally enough called upon the services of Disney's Paris studio for part of the work and spent some time in Paris themselves—as did various of the animators—in order to capture the "character" of the cathedral itself as well as that of the city. It was decided to use computer animation to generate some of the crowd scenes—the movie must have a cast of literally thousands—but, oddly enough, in places one is irresistibly reminded, as the camera pans down over the rooftops of historical Paris, of the effect achieved as long ago as 1940, using the multiplane camera, in the opening sequence of *Pinocchio* (➤166).

Various characterizations were changed profoundly from those in Hugo's novel. Two of these are important. Quasimodo—in fact almost a minor character in the book, despite his pivotal role in the plot—became central and turned from a creature little above ape level into a giftedly creative man. Esmeralda, originally a naïf who was rather more molded by circumstances than able to mold them, became one of Disney's strongest heroines—perhaps even stronger than Pocahontas (➤401).

However unlikely the subject matter of *The Hunchback of Notre Dame* might have seemed to be, the result is a highly creditable movie—and one that on occasion is very moving, because one *cares* about a couple of the characters—Quasimodo and Esmeralda. The movie was also commercially successful, but then this has been true of every Disney classic animated feature since *The Little Mermaid*.

A useful reference is *The Art of The Hunchback of Notre Dame* (1996) by Stephen Rebello.

THE STORY

The movie begins with a very extended flashback, extremely and cleverly melded with a song sequence in which various different characters take up lines of the song. The gypsy puppeteer Clopin starts things off, singing to eagerly attentive children about how Once Upon A Time . . .

Once upon that time Judge Frollo comes across a group of gypsies. He has seemingly infinite power within Paris and, as he loathes gypsies, orders them to be arrested on sight. One of the handful of gypsies is a young mother who is carrying her newborn baby. She flees through a snowscape, the baby in her arms, with Frollo in hot pursuit; as he is

on horseback, it is inevitable that he catches her, but not before she has pounded on the doors of Notre Dame Cathedral, begging for sanctuary. Through clumsiness he kills the mother on the steps of the cathedral; through malice, having discovered how hideous her infant is, he prepares to drop the child into a well when he is stopped by the cathedral's Archdeacon. They make a compromise: both of them, in different ways, will be responsible for the child, the Archdeacon for housing him in the cathedral's belltower and Frollo for what one has to describe, albeit reluctantly, as his moral education. Almost at the end of the song, as for the first time we see the adult Quasimodo, we are asked: "Who is the monster and who is the man?" It takes little time to answer the question.

All of this happens before *The Hunchback of Notre Dame*'s title comes up. This must be one of Disney's most ambitious opening sequences.

One day the adult Quasimodo looks out from the belltower to discover that the Feast of Fools is taking place in the square below. This is one of those topsyturvy festivals in which the person judged by the mob to be the greatest fool is crowned as king for the day. Encouraged by his sole friends—three living gargoyles—he decides that for once, despite Frollo's prohibition of him ever venturing into the outside world, he will attend the festival and have some fun. Crowned as king, he is then pelted with rotten fruit and vegetables by the mob, and his humiliation is heightened when a furious Frollo sends him back to the belltower as if he were a naughty schoolchild playing truant.

Meanwhile, there has been a subplot. Captain Phoebus, newly back from remote lands on instructions to serve under Frollo, spots a gypsy woman, Esmeralda, in the street and falls immediately in love with her. When she is bullied by two army guards he strikes out at them in her defense. On arriving at the Palace of Justice, Phoebus is instructed by Frollo that the city must be ethnically cleansed of its gypsies.

Frollo and Phoebus, like Quasimodo, attend the Feast of Fools, where Esmeralda dances; just as Phoebus did, Frollo falls at once for her sensual charms—although his reaction differs from Phoebus's: Frollo, one might say, shows little interest in her mind. Frollo, too, is perfectly happy to watch Quasimodo's humiliation—it is the hunchback's just punishment for having disobeyed orders—but Esmeralda stops the torment, in the process displaying magical powers. Phoebus and his guards, obeying Frollo's orders—although Phoebus shows reluctance—attempt to arrest her, but are thwarted by her spunk-

iness and agility. She, in disguise with her pet goat Djali, find their way into the cathedral; Phoebus pursues but persuades her to claim sanctuary—despite Frollo's anger.

She befriends Quasimodo in the belltower but cannot stand the prospect of being, in effect, imprisoned in the cathedral forever. In a dizzyingly vertiginous descent, Quasimodo helps her escape, and in return she gives him a locket, which is—although he doesn't know it yet—a crude map that will enable him to find the Paris gypsies' secret hideout, the Court of Miracles.

Frollo promptly begins a freshly increased persecution of the gypsies, while also trying to bribe any that are discovered in the chance that they will reveal Esmeralda's whereabouts; his lust for her has now been made more than patent. Phoebus turns against Frollo when the latter tries to burn a family alive; although shot by an arrow by one of Frollo's guards, Phoebus is saved by Esmeralda. Frollo's lust reaches the stage where he orders that large parts of Paris be burnted down in order to find the woman.

Esmeralda brings Phoebus to Notre Dame, begging Quasimodo that he give shelter to the wounded soldier. Frollo arrives and declares that he knows where the Court of Miracles is and that he will destroy it next morning. Between them, Quasimodo and Phoebus decipher the map/locket and make their way to the Court of Miracles, which is in Paris's Catacombs. There they are almost hanged by the gypsies, led by Clopin, but the execution is halted by Esmeralda. What the pair haven't realized is that Frollo did not in fact know where the Court of Miracles was located; he and his guards have simply followed them through the nighttime Parisian streets.

By the next morning, Quasimodo is chained in the belltower, Phoebus is publicly caged, and Esmeralda is to be burned at the stake as a witch. Frollo, waving the torch that will consign her to the flames, makes his worst proposition to her yet: she can die or give herself to him. She rejects him, but before the fire can claim her Quasimodo escapes from his chains and rescues her. Phoebus, too, escapes, and leads a popular revolution against the tyranny of Frollo. Frollo, trying to kill Quasimodo and Esmeralda, himself falls to his death from the parapet of Notre Dame. In the final burst of action, Quasimodo saves Esmeralda's life, Esmeralda saves Quasimodo's life, and Phoebus saves Quasimodo's life: quite a lot of lifesaving, but in the context of the movie it works nicely. Phoebus and Esmeralda are initially hailed as the heroes who have liberated Paris, but Esmeralda insists that the crowd recognize Quasimodo as the true hero.

THE CHARACTERS

Quasimodo

In a way, why Esmeralda should choose Phoebus as her lover rather than Quasimodo is something of a mystery. One is left with a slight puzzlement at the end of the movie, as if suddenly discovering that the romantic heroine whose adventures one has followed entranced throughout a long novel actually has lousy taste in men. There is also a feeling of confused morality, since the primary theme of the movie—as expressed more than once in song as "who is the monster and who is the man?"—is that outward appearances are not what are important, yet Esmeralda opts for the man with the better outward appearance.

This is not to suggest, of course, that Quasimodo is much of a looker. Quite the contrary: he is almost certainly the ugliest hero ever to have starred in an animated feature. His face is quite hideously distorted: when Esmeralda first encounters him she assumes he is wearing a deliberately grotesque mask. He has huge orange-red eyes that are of different sizes, his left eyebrow is a misshapen lump, his mouth is a twisted line and his nose is a blob—and all of this is topped by a most unappealing mass of carrot-red hair. The enormity of the face is exaggerated in the movie because often we are looking at it not straight on but from a downward angle: because of his hump, this is how most of the other characters see it. Quasimodo's arms are ungracious appendages: in shape they look more like legs of mutton than like human arms, and one would expect them to have all the subtlety of legs of mutton.

One would be wrong. Certainly those arms have colossal strength, because using them Quasimodo hauls himself around the belltower with all the agility of a chimpanzee, and on various occasions he uses them to great effect against his foes—as when he throws Frollo across the room in a late scene in the movie. Yet they are indeed capable of great subtlety—or at least the hands at the end of them are. Quasimodo's hobby, in his loneliness, is what can only be described as art. Central among his creations is a carved model of what he can see from the belltower, with miniature figures, exquisitely executed, of the people most often to be observed crossing the square in front of Notre Dame. (The model also includes an accurate representation of the cathedral itself, which is a little puzzling. If Quasimodo has never been outside the cathedral, how could he know what it looks like? But that is by the by.) Others of his artefacts have been equally delicately rendered, notably a mobile con-

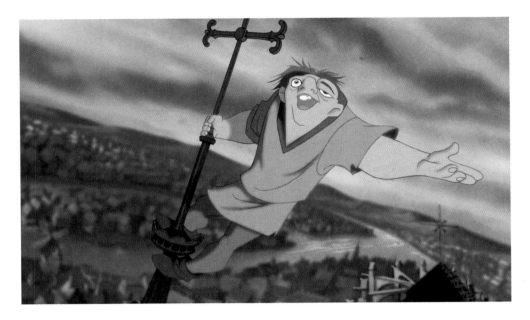

Quasimodo sings atop the cathedral as the city of Paris lies before him.

structed from what appear to be shards of variously colored glass—this mobile is what first fascinates Esmeralda when she comes to the belltower. Quasimodo's aestheticism extends beyond just creation, he is also able to perceive. Soon after Esmeralda has arrived in the belltower he shows her the vista of Paris he has looked out on since childhood; this is fittingly shown on screen as if it were a classical painting, so that we know how Quasimodo sees and appreciates it.

Quasimodo is also, despite his impressive strength, most of the time exceptionally gentle and kind. This is demonstrated to us very early in the movie. A pigeon has nested in the mouth of one of the three gargoyles who are at the time Quasimodo's sole friends. Still remaining in the nest is a final chick. Although Quasimodo clearly loves the chick, it is time for the bird to learn the art of flying—to join the rest of its own kind. The tenderness with which he helps it to launch itself into the air for the first time is very touching.

The story of the movie is not that of Quasimodo's love for Esmeralda; it is the story of Quasimodo slowly beginning to realize that the man he has always regarded as a surrogate father—as his "master," in fact ("I'm sorry, master. I will never disobey you again")—is a man not to be loved or respected or even trusted but is a villain of the darkest stripe: someone to be rejected. Frollo, who would have murdered the baby Quasimodo had it not been for the intervention of the cathedral's Archdeacon, has totally indoctrinated our hero, who has even accepted the name Frollo has given him, "Quasimodo," meaning "the half-formed one." Everything Frollo says, Quasimodo has been brainwashed into believing,

must necessarily be true: since he has had no real contact with anyone else, it is easy to understand how the bell ringer could have come to accept Frollo's word. It is only when he meets and falls in love with Esmeralda that he begins to have doubts. Frollo hates gypsies and believes they should be exterminated, yet Esmeralda has saved Quasimodo from a horrific humiliation. Early lines of dialogue between the two characters go thus:

Quasimodo: But you're not like other gypsies. They're evil.
Esmeralda: Who told you that?
Quasimodo: My master. Frollo. He raised me.
Esmeralda: How can such a cruel man have raised someone like you?
Quasimodo: Cruel? Oh no. He saved my life. He took me in when no one else would. I am a monster, you know.
Esmeralda: He told you that?
Quasimodo: Look at me.
Esmeralda: Give me your hand.
Quasimodo: Why?
Esmeralda: Just let me see it. Hmm . . . a long life line. Oh, and this one means you're shy. Hmm . . . hmm-hmm-hmm . . . Well, that's funny.
Quasimodo: What?
Esmeralda: I don't see any . . .
Quasimodo: Any what?
Esmeralda: . . . "monster" lines. Not a single one. Now you
Quasimodo: No! No, no. You are kind and good, and, and . . .
Esmeralda: And a gypsy. And maybe Frollo's wrong about the both of us.

It is the beginning of Quasimodo's faith in himself and in his own opinions. Nevertheless, it takes him a long time to build up that faith to the extent that he can defy Frollo's instructions on any matter of importance—his prohibited visit to the Feast of Fools, early in the movie, he regards as a minor impertinence that Frollo may never discover. Only when he makes a sudden decision to help Phoebus find the Court of Miracles and warn the gypsies that a renewed persecution is about to start does he finally realize the heinousness of his "master's" crimes. But still, after what is in effect Frollo's betrayal of him, he is not quite able to recognize the tyrant as anything other than his "master"; he is still a slave, still—in his own view—the "half-formed one."

One of the most heinous of all Frollo's crimes, of course, was the gratuitous murder of Quasimodo's mother. All through the movie until very close to the end, Frollo has claimed that Quasimodo is alone because his mother cast him off at birth. It is only when Frollo confesses the lie that Quasimodo's resentment and self-faith become complete. Although he does his best to save Frollo's life while they are both dangling on the frontage of Notre Dame (another indication of the innate gentleness of his character), there is little evidence of regret after Frollo falls to his doom.

Quasimodo is—as who wouldn't be—mightily depressed in the later stages of the movie when he discovers that Esmeralda's affections are directed toward Phoebus rather than him, the gargoyles having persuaded him that the opposite might be the case. Yet in the conclusion he gently places her hand in Phoebus's, thereby symbolically giving his seal of approval to the love-match. It is yet another touching moment.

Disney wrung as much emotion as it could out of this facially hideous character. The result could have been schmaltz. Instead, the animators succeeded in creating one of their most appealing characters of all time.

Esmeralda

If Quasimodo is Disney's ugliest hero, Esmeralda is indubitably the company's sexiest—apart from Jessica Rabbit (►330). Esmeralda, the gypsy dancer who performs in the street in order to earn coppers to feed herself and her pet goat Djali, has a huge mane of black hair, turquoise eyes that flash whenever her ire is roused, a risqué sense of humor, and an approach to life that is underlined by an attitude of steel. She is also clearly intelligent. It is little wonder that Quasimodo and Phoebus fall in love with her, and that Frollo finds his lust inflamed by her.

It is not immediately obvious (except to those who have read the original novel) that she is going to be the movie's central female star: we see glimpses of her as

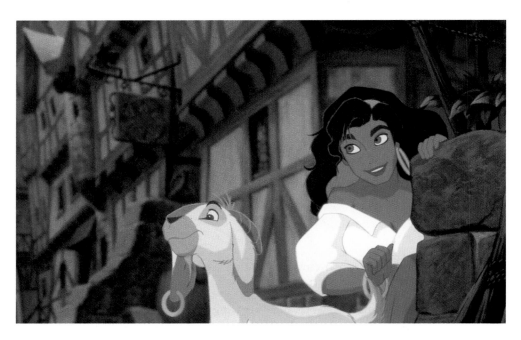

The beautiful gypsy dancer Esmeralda (voiced by Demi Moore) and her pet goat Djali, roaming the streets of Paris.

part of the Parisian cityscape, but then there are other street characters whom we see from time to time. It is only when Phoebus, returned from the wars to take up office under Frollo, first sets eyes on her that we begin to realize the central role she is going to occupy in the movie. The suspicion isn't really confirmed until we discover her at the Feast of Fools, not so much while she is dancing—she might be just (in plot terms) a representative of Paris's gypsy population—but when Quasimodo accidentally stumbles into her tent and discovers her underclad. Shortly afterward she courageously saves Quasimodo from the humiliation the mob is inflicting on him, and then we know how important she is going to be in his life.

A little before all this, we see her dance for the Feast of Fools. It is this dance that entrances Frollo, who has come with Phoebus to watch the festival only to act as a moral arbiter—or at least that is his claim. Clearly transfixed by sexual longing while watching the dance, Frollo says: "Look at that disgusting display." Phoebus, also watching the dance, reacts with a healthier: "Yes, sir!" Esmeralda proceeds to wrap her silk scarf around Frollo's neck, flirtingly, then teasingly pushes his hat down over his eyes. He is utterly ensnared by her charms.

The sequence in which she frees Quasimodo from the abuse of the mob is where we see Frollo try to reify his lust as hatred for her. Already enraged that Quasimodo has disobeyed orders by leaving the belltower to enjoy himself at the festival, Frollo is more than content to see the humiliation continue. The relationship between Frollo and Esmeralda is again established:

Frollo: Gypsy girl, get down at once!
Esmeralda: Yes, Your Honor. Just as soon as I free this poor creature.
Frollo: I forbid it!

Esmeralda nevertheless, despite orders, cuts Quasimodo free from the ropes that have been used to tie him in place so that he will be an easier target for the crowd, which is pelting him with fruit and vegetables. The dialogue between Frollo and Esmeralda continues:

Frollo: How dare you defy me?
Esmeralda: You mistreat this poor boy the same way you mistreat my people! You speak of justice, yet you are cruel to those most in need of your help!
Frollo: Silence!
Esmeralda: Justice!

And moments later there is the following exchange:

Frollo: Mark my words, gypsy, you will pay for this insolence.
Esmeralda: Then it appears we've crowned the wrong fool. The only fool I see is you!

Frollo instructs his soldiers to arrest her for her insolence, but:

Esmeralda: Well, let's see. One, two, three, four, five, six, seven, eight, nine . . . So, there's ten of you and one of me. What's a poor girl to do?

The mock pathos is perfectly voiced (by Demi Moore) and perfectly animated. Esmeralda pulls a handkerchief from her dress, sneezes into it, and vanishes in a puff of colored smoke. (That she has magical abilities is suggested here and elsewhere, but is not followed up as an element of the plot. If she can perform tricks like this, why does she later get into such difficulties?) Of course, this infuriates Frollo yet further, and it is only because she is able, disguised, to claim sanctuary within the cathedral of Notre Dame that she is able to escape with her life.

She is a mistress of disguise—at least, when aided by Djali. Several times during the movie she appears as a cowled beggar smoking a pipe: in fact it is Djali who, sitting on her head, has the pipe between his teeth. Phoebus, who has seen her do the trick as he entered Paris, recognizes the "beggar" sneaking into the cathedral and follows. Her initial reaction is, of course, that Frollo's captain intends to arrest her, and here again she responds with the kind of fire we have by now come to expect, snatching his sword and then, when he regains it, seizing a candelabrum with which to fight him:

> *Esmeralda:* You sneaky son of a—
> *Phoebus:* Watch it. You're in a church.
> *Esmeralda:* Are you always this charming, or am I just lucky?
> *Phoebus:* Candlelight, privacy, music— what better place for hand-to-hand combat? You fight almost as well as a man.
> *Esmeralda:* I was going to say the same thing about you.
> *Phoebus:* That's hitting a little below the belt, don't you think?
> *Esmeralda:* No, this is . . .

She proceeds to do her best to hit him "a little below the belt." Even so, Phoebus claims sanctuary on her behalf when Frollo demands that she be dragged from the hallowed ground.

Shortly afterward she discovers the delicate artifacts that Quasimodo has made for himself—the portrayal of her here is as of one who has come upon an enchanted place (which is what, in a way, she has). But, more important, she discovers Quasimodo—that he is a man and not a monster. They could have shared a perfect life together except that she, as a gypsy, cannot bear the prospect of being imprisoned by walls of stone.

Thereafter her characterization subtly changes. Until now she has been a character who does rather than one to whom things are done. The focus of the plot, so far as she is concerned, shifts, we become more aware of the motivations of the three principal men than we do of hers. Although she saves Phoebus's life after he has been pierced by an arrow and fallen into the Seine, one still has the feeling that she is reacting rather than molding the course of events: my buddy needs help so I'll help him. Very briefly, she makes a stand to save Clopin from hanging Quasimodo and Phoebus in the Court of Miracles; this is a much briefer reprise of the stand she made to save Quasimodo

during the Feast of Fools. Only much later, toward the end of the movie as Frollo is preparing to burn her at the stake as a witch, does the earlier spunkiness reemerge. When he tries to blackmail her by giving her the choice between death by the flames or a life as his mistress, she spits in his face.

Good for her.

Judge Claude Frollo

Of all the villains created for Disney animated features, Frollo is perhaps the most interesting in the complexity of his motivations; he completes an unusual triumvirate, for Quasimodo is the most difficult lead character to make sympathetic and Esmeralda is (quite deliberately) the sexiest heroine. Physically and vocally owing much to the actor Christopher Lee, Frollo is not just the embodiment of evil within the movie, he is also a hypocrite— but a self-deceiving hypocrite, in that he does not know his own hypocrisy. As far as he is concerned everything he does is perfectly virtuous. This sort of psychological character was dubbed by the science fiction writer A. E. van Vogt the "Right Man," and the author and philosopher Colin Wilson has picked up that term and explored it in greater depth. It never occurs to Frollo that anything he does could conceivably be wrong—he is the moral scourge of Paris, and it cannot cross his mind that the cruelty he inflicts on others is in any way reprehensible. Even in the very powerful song sequence in which he confesses—at least to himself and to the flames he perceives around him—that he lusts for Esmeralda, he blames the lust he is experiencing on *her* for her beauty and flirtatiousness; she must clearly be a child of the Devil, for how otherwise could she have so ensnared him?

He is also a racist, the object of his racism being the gypsies of Paris. He is determined to destroy them. Frollo is not the first racist villain to appear in a Disney animated feature—in *Pocahontas* there is another, Governor Ratcliffe (➤403)—but he is certainly the vilest because, while Ratcliffe is simply a fool who thinks of Native Americans as mere animals, Frollo is an intelligent man who should know better and has used the deviousness of his intelligence to persuade himself that racially based persecution can be justified. As a nasty piece of work, he has few parallels in animated movies. As a model of characterization within animated movies, and as a display of fine animation, he is by contrast a very nice piece of work.

We encounter him right at the start of the movie, when he personally leads a clump of his guards to perform an atrocity. A few gypsies are surreptitiously

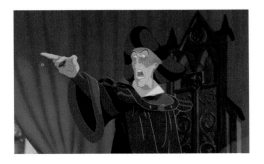

The evil Judge Claude Frollo. one of Disney's most complex villians ever.

creeping by boat into Paris when they are discovered. One of them is a young woman bearing a blanketed package. Frollo, with his bigotry toward gypsies, assumes this must be "stolen goods." As he tries to seize the package the woman flees, and he pursues her on his horse. She tries to claim sanctuary at the cathedral of Notre Dame, but before anyone opens the doors Frollo knocks her down on the steps, killing her. This he does not regard as an act of murder, and neither does he regard as an act of murder his subsequent plan to throw the contents of the package—the baby Quasimodo— down a nearby well. The cathedral's Archdeacon stops him, even though Frollo claims:

> This is an unholy demon. I'm sending it back to Hell, where it belongs. . . . I am guiltless. She ran, I pursued. My conscience is clear.

This is our first real clue about the self-deceiving hypocrisy that is at the heart of Frollo's character.

The Archdeacon of course prevails, insisting that Quasimodo must be given the sanctuary of the cathedral and that Frollo must hereafter act as a surrogate father, feeding the lad and educating him in the belltower. This Frollo does exceptionally badly, providing the food but giving neither fatherhood nor any real education, almost the only thing that Quasimodo is taught is that he is loathsome.

The most graphic display of Frollo's racism comes later in the movie, when he is describing to the newly arrived Phoebus how it must be his job to help exterminate the gypsies. The two are high up on the architecture of the Palace of Justice as Frollo explains why Phoebus has been brought to the city. Frollo then demonstrates physically his hatred of Romany, and his intention to wipe out the gypsies entirely:

> For twenty years I have been taking care of the gypsies . . . one . . . by . . . one.

With each of these words he squashes, with calculated deliberation, an ant down against the stone of the parapet beside which he and Phoebus are standing.

> And yet, for all my success, they have thrived.

Frollo lifts up a stone of the parapet to reveal a populous ant colony.

> I believe they have a safe haven within the walls of this very city. A—a nest, if you will. They call it the Court of Miracles.

He then jams down the stone to kill all of the ants who had previously—and harmlessly—been thriving beneath it. The image is very strong; this is not someone who has much room in his heart for compassion.

Frollo is also a sadist. The pleasure he displays at the moment he believes he is personally about to burn Esmeralda alive, presaged by his attempt to consign a miller and his family to flame, is first rehearsed when he introduces Phoebus to the torture chambers of Frollo's dreaded Palace of Justice. Phoebus, a humble soldier, is clearly not pleased by what he can hear going on, but Frollo is smug; people are suffering at his behest, which means that he has power over them. To make sure that the audience gets the message, a Whipsman briefly appears in the gloomy corridor in front of Frollo and Phoebus:

> *Frollo*: Ease up. Wait between lashes. Otherwise the old sting will dull him to the new.
> *Whipsman*: Yes, sir.

Moments afterward there is the following bit of dialogue:

> *Frollo [to Phoebus]*: I expect nothing but the best from a war hero of your caliber.
> *Phoebus*: And you shall have it, sir. I guarantee it.
> *Frollo*: Ye-e-s. You know, my last Captain of the Guard was, um, a bit of a disappointment to me.
> *Voice off*: Scream.
> *Frollo*: Well, no matter. I'm sure you'll whip my men into shape.

Much after this there is a surrealistic song sequence in which Frollo admits in great detail—at least to himself—his physical longing for Esmeralda. Still it is her fault, if she were someone other than herself he wouldn't be tempted. This is one of the great Disney song sequences. Drawing inspiration from the fire in the grate one assumes is at an end of Frollo's ascetic study, the animators show us the hypocrite, as he sings, surrounded by mountainous walls of flame. The flames have been given mouths, but this is not just so that they can join in the song; we are being told that Frollo perceives himself as

being surrounded by the demons of Hell. At the same time he can see a motile image of Esmeralda in those very same flames; what he wants is (to this God-fearing man) a sin, but sin is what he wants. Flames play an important part in his worldview; elsewhere he picks up the effigy Quasimodo has carved of Esmeralda and sets it afire.

The lyrics of the song also give an insight into the duality of his character—indeed, they are crucially important to any understanding of the twisted character Frollo has been from the start:

> *Beata Maria*
> *You know I am a righteous man*
> *Of my virtue I am justly proud*
> *You know I'm so much purer than*
> *The common, vulgar, weak licentious crowd.*
> *Then tell me, Maria,*
> *Why I see her dancing there,*
> *Why her smoldering eyes still scorch my soul.*
> *I feel her, I see her,*
> *The sun caught in her raven hair*
> *Is blazing in me out of all control . . .*
> *It's not my fault—*
> *I'm not to blame—*
> *It's the gypsy girl,*
> *The witch who set this flame.*
> *It's not my fault*
> *If in God's plan*
> *He made the Devil so much stronger than a man . . .*

There is yet more fascination for fire within Frollo's obsession. Despite Phoebus's furious objections he attempts to destroy a miller and his family by fire simply because he suspects they might have been illicitly harboring gypsies. In order that the escaped Esmeralda—she does a lot of escaping—be unearthed, he orders at one point that his guards should burn Paris to the ground if that is necessary. (Much of Paris is indeed put to the torch.) And, of course, near the end of the movie he attempts to have her burned at the stake. In his monologue in this scene occurs his most blatant act of hypocrisy throughout the entire movie:

> The time has come, gypsy. You stand upon the brink of the abyss. Yet even now it is not too late. I can save you from the flames of this world and the next.
> Choose me or the fire.

Torquemada, who got his kicks out of torturing people to death so that they would be better disciples of Christ, could hardly have put it better.

Captain Phoebus

Superficially, the story of *The Hunchback of Notre Dame* has four principal characters, but with three of them—Quasimodo, Esmeralda, and Frollo—being each so noteworthy in his or her own way, it

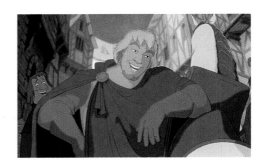

Tall, fair-haired, dashing Captain Phoebus, the love interest of Esmeralda, and an "action-hero" in the film.

would have been impossible for the movie to have supported a fourth. One of the four had to take a somewhat subordinate role. This is not to say that Phoebus is in any way a minor character (he is, after all, on screen much of the time and plays a great part in the action), more that he is, in effect, the "love interest."

We initially meet him as he returns to Paris to take up a new post as Frollo's Captain of the Guards. Tall, fair-haired, and clad in a suit of golden armor, the first thing he does is protect Esmeralda from the bullying of a brace of the guards he is soon to command. This he does with the assistance of his white stallion **Achilles,** who sits firmly on one of them. (The visual joke is repeated toward the end of the movie, but otherwise Achilles' role is far smaller than one might expect.)

Reaching the gloomy Palace of Justice and being shown around it by the equally gloomy Frollo, Phoebus very rapidly becomes unhappy about his new appointment, wincing at the noises he hears from the torture chambers and incredulous when Frollo explains his primary task is to round up gypsies:

> I was summoned from the wars to capture fortune-tellers and palm readers?

Still, it is a soldier's job to follow orders, and follow them he does (although he subverts them once, when pretending that Esmeralda has claimed sanctuary) for much of the movie, although with visibly increasing reluctance. Finally, although it will mean his death, he flatly refuses to incinerate the miller's family and, when Frollo sets the place alight, courageously rescues the people. Thereafter he is Esmeralda's knight in shining armor, helping her and Quasimodo defeat Frollo and save the citizens of Paris. It is Phoebus who arouses the Parisian mob to counter the guards during Frollo's assault on Notre Dame.

There is a certain amount of rivalry between him and Quasimodo, which very occasionally becomes overt; they both love the same woman, after all. This adds an emotional dynamic to Phoebus's role, but nothing very much is ever made of it. As is right, our concentration is directed to the bell ringer's emotions rather than Phoebus's.

Clopin

This character seems to play several roles rather than just one. When we first meet him he's a puppeteer—his puppet is comically a miniature of himself— but more significantly he's a story-teller, ostensibly to a group of childœren watching his performance in the Paris streets but in fact to us. The story he tells is that of the orphaned Quasimodo's incarceration in Notre Dame. Thus the first of Clopin's roles is as the movie's narrator.

His second role occurs when he reappears as the Master of Ceremonies at the Feast of Fools. Now he is no longer a mere street puppeteer. Although earlier he asked us, "Who is the monster and who is the man?"—referring to Frollo's inhumane treatment of Quasimodo—so that we assumed his nature was kindly, here he has become rather more mean-spirited. Performing flamboyant antics, he is prepared to do anything, no matter how cruel, for the sake of the display— for "fun." It is he who initiates the humiliation of the very person for whom he was earlier asking our sympathies.

And his third role emerges when Phoebus and Quasimodo have penetrated the Court of Miracles to warn the gypsies of Frollo's evil intentions. Now he seems to have become the King of the Gypsies, and his cruelty is distinctly more menacing: he orders the two to be prepared for hanging without trial, and intends to act as their executioner, teasing them most unpleasantly as he readies himself to pull the lever. How many other innocents has he murdered in this fashion?

In this incarnation he is also a shapeshifter, going through a bewildering series of rapid-fire guises. One of them is an impersonation of Frollo, and we cannot help but make the obvious comparison.

The Gargoyles

The three mobile gargoyles are the prime source of comic relief. They are Quasimodo's sole companions in the belltower. They have no legs, instead generally getting around by bending their bodies and jumping.

Hugo is an excitable, pot-bellied zany. His face has a long, piggish snout, but his porcine nature is contradicted by his two horns. In one instance, when the gargoyles are dancing all over the belltower, these horns offer a good visual gag. Hugo jumps vertically into the air and the horns thwock directly into a beam, so that he dangles there helplessly while the others merrily continue cavorting around him.

One particular running joke concerns Hugo. When Esmeralda and Djali first come together to the belltower, the three gargoyles give a chorus of whoops of the "What a beauty!" variety—and Hugo adds, "Yeah, and the girl ain't bad either." Later, in order to cheer up a despondent Quasimodo, the trio draw romantic pictures for him: the other two draw Esmeralda, but Hugo draws Djali.

Victor is much taller and more slender, and has about him an aura of what he would presumably call dignity but which should really be termed pomposity, because it breaks down quite often. When Quasimodo is crowned the King of Fools, Victor is the member of the watching trio of gargoyles who is most ridiculously demonstrative in his enthusiasm, repeatedly blowing a long party squealer. We first meet his self-importance early on. Hugo, immobilized into stone because there is a living creature other than Quasimodo present, has a birds' nest in his mouth. Once the bellringer has removed the nest's final occupant and encouraged it to learn how to fly, Hugo comes back to life and spits out the nest:

Hugo: Man! I thought he'd never leave. I'll be spittin' feathers for a week.
Victor [disdainfully]: Well, that's what you get for sleeping with your mouth open.
Hugo: Go scare a nun.

Perhaps the best joke concerning his "dignity" is during Frollo's attack on Notre Dame. The other two gargoyles are merrily dropping anything heavy they can think of onto the guards who are assaulting the cathedral's doors below. Victor, looking ashamed, by contrast drops a single brick. When the brick smashes into the head of some unfortunate guard, Victor says a disconsolate: "Sorry."

Victor is in a way visually reminiscent of a sort of demonized angel: he is equipped with all the standard equipment you would expect an angel to have, notably the wings, but there's a touch of the devil in his depiction.

It is a curiosity that the third gargoyle, **Laverne,** should not have been called Marie—the original author's full name was, after all, Victor Marie Hugo, and Marie can just as easily be a female's name as a male's. One of life's little puzzles. Laverne has the voice and mannerisms of an irascible elderly woman—irascible but with a heart of gold. She behaves toward Quasimodo much as if he were her favorite grandson. Very clearly she has taken him under her wing. The principal running gag concerning her is that she is constantly being plagued by distracting pigeons, which she fights off with cries of fury. The last line of dialogue in the movie is from her: throwing off yet another flock, she cries in exasperation, "Don't you ever *migrate?*"

The genesis of the mobile gargoyles is of interest. In the original novel, Quasimodo had a habit of chatting to the gargoyles as if they were alive—after all,

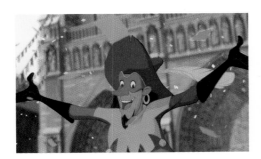

Clopin, the King of the Gypsies and Master of Ceremonies at the Feast of Fools.

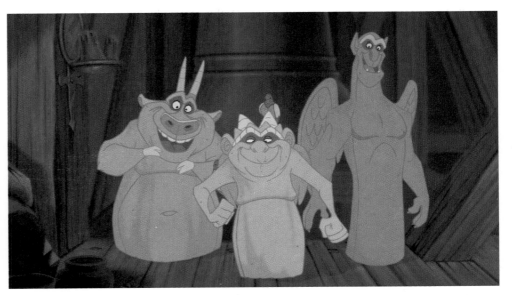

Quasimodo's three gargoyle companions Hugo, Laverne, and Victor.

he had no one else to chat to. The animators thought this was a touching idea, and decided to literalize it. Of course, in the movie depiction the three must become stone again whenever anyone else arrives on the scene (in this they remind us of the toys in *Toy Story* [➤407]), although at one stage Djali catches just a hint of movement. For obvious reasons no visitor to the belltower ever thinks it odd that three gargoyles should be in positions different from those they occupied the last time the person called: animators' license!

The three gargoyles between them serve not only as the movie's zanies, they are also Quasimodo's advisers. The trouble is that, though well-motivated, the advice they give him is almost always bad, because they are as isolated from the realities of the outside world as he is. The cruelty of giving friends advice on matters about which they know nothing is something that doesn't occur to them—and cruelty it is. Were it not for their encouragement, Quasimodo would never have gone to the Feast of Fools and been subjected to public humiliation. Worse still, they build up his confidence and expectations concerning Esmeralda to such an extent that his realization that he can never win her is indescribably more painful than it would have been otherwise. Of course, all turns out well in the end, but the conclusion of the story is decidedly bittersweet.

Djali

Esmeralda's pet goat possesses human intelligence and a fierce loyalty to his owner. When she is persecuted by the two guards in the early street sequence, it is Djali—before Phoebus intervenes—who initially almost sees them off, butting them with determined ferocity, even though he is a very small goat. He helps in other ways, most notably by assisting her in her oft-used disguise as a cowled male figure—he sits on her head with a pipe clutched between his teeth. A nice visual touch is that, just like Esmeralda, he has a large golden ring through one ear.

Like any other goat, he has an appetite for the strangest things—at one stage devouring most of the carved figurines dotted around Quasimodo's miniature model of Paris. Unlike any other goat (well, one assumes so), he is the target of the passions of a gargoyle.

Archdeacon

The Archdeacon of Notre Dame makes a few appearances during the movie, the most important of which is the first. Frollo, having pursued Quasimodo's mother to the doors of Notre Dame, kills her through callous disregard for her

safety; it is, in reality, a murder. He is just about to drop the infant "monster" down a well when the plump and hooded figure of the Archdeacon emerges from the cathedral doors against which Quasimodo's mother piteously knocked in her attempt to gain sanctuary for herself and her child. "Stop!" yells the Archdeacon. His next lines of dialogue are largely sung—we are still in the extended opening song sequence—but they comprise a fairly strident denunciation of everything that Frollo stands for:

Archdeacon: See there the innocent blood you have spilt
On the steps of Notre Dame.
Frollo: I am guiltless. She ran, I pursued.
Archdeacon: Now you would add this child's blood to your guilt
On the steps of Notre Dame.
Frollo: My conscience is clear.
Archdeacon: You can lie to yourself and your minions,
You can claim that you haven't a qualm,
But you never can run from
Nor hide what you've done from
The eyes,
The very eyes of Notre Dame.
Clopin [narrating]: And for one time in his life
Of power and control
Frollo felt a twinge of fear
For his immortal soul.
Frollo: What must I do?
Archdeacon: Care for the child and raise it as your own.
Frollo: What? I'm to be saddled with this misshapen . . .
Very well, but let him live with you in your church.
Archdeacon: Live here? Where?
Frollo: Anywhere.
[Back into song:] Just so he's kept locked away
Where no one else can see.
[Back into speech:] The belltower, perhaps. And who knows? Our Lord works in mysterious ways.
[Back into song:] Even this foul creature
May yet prove one day to be of use to me.

The Archdeacon is an attractive character. Stern when sternness is required, he can also be amiable and kindly. He is the only figure in the movie to whom Frollo will concede any higher authority, as when he insists that Esmeralda's apparent request for sanctuary be respected despite Frollo's demands that she be dragged back out of the cathedral so that she might be arrested outside its precincts. Of course, this respect finally breaks down during Frollo's final insanity; when the judge enters the cathedral determined to exact his wrath in the belltower the Archdeacon tries to stop him, but is hurled ruthlessly to the ground.

Minor Characters

Most villains in Disneny animated features have comic sidekicks who are equally wicked in intent but somehow forgivable because the are zanies. Frollo is an exception, since much of his characterization is that he is icy: to give him any kind of comopanion would seem incongruous. Instead two guards who feature here and there during the movie in effect fulfill, between them, The plot function of the clownish sidekick. They are described in the credits as **British Guard** and **Oafish Guard**. For those attempting to distinguish which is which, the British Guard is the taller of the two. He is firmly sat upon by Phoebus's horse Achilles in a couple of instances, and he has a generaous moustache—part of which is sheared off by Phoebus's sword early on but seems miraculously to have regrown by the end of the same day. The Oafish Guard is much fatter and speaks in a way that can only be described as "kinda dumb."

Having tried to persecute Esmeralda, they later begin pelting Quasimodo with fruit and vegetables during his public humiliation at the Feast of Fools. Later on, they are the pair ordered by Frollo to execute Phoebus for his crime of having saved the lives of the miller's family. And, in the finale, the British Guard is the one who heads the assault on Notre Dame while the Oafish Guard is put out of action by Phoebus with a powerful downward punch on the head.

Several minor charcters play a part in the extended prologue: the **Boatman**, **Quasimodo's Father**, **Baby Quasimodo** (whom we never in fact see) and, most important, **Quasimodo's Mother**. Blonde and pretty, in her anguished flight from Frollo as she tries to protect her baby from him, she arouses our very considerable sympathies. As an aside, her way of running is much like that of Pocahontas. In the street where the guards have attempted to rob Esmerald, a small **Gypsy Boy** taunts them from the top of a wall. He moves with the nimbleness of a monkey. In the torture block of the Palace of Justice there is a brief appearance by a toadying **Whipsman**: he seems almost to be a hunchback himself. A comic character who arrives brielfy on screen twice is the **Old Heretic**: the first time, he is bounced out of his cage, and cries, "I'm free! I'm free!" He then promptly trips on a bar of his cage and falls into a set of stocks: "Dang it!" Near the end of the movie the stocks are banged open and he staggers away in rejoicing . . . only to fall into a sewer. (This character was voiced by the movie's co-director, Gary Trousdale.)

Phoebus saves from incineration a **Miller** and his family. Plump and bearded, the miller's sole "crime"—which he confesses to Frollo in a voice quavering with equal mixtures of humility and fear—is that he provides a night's lodging to any weary traveler who might pass his way, and thus could well have briefly harbored gypies.

Once Paris has been relieved of Frollo's despotic rule, Esmeralda and Phoebus emerge from the cathedral to receive the accolade of the crowd. But Esmeralda determinedly turns back and, her hand in Quasimodo's, brings him out to join them. There is a horrified silence when the assembled throng see Quasimodo's ugliness but then a **Little Girl** climbs the steps to give the hero of the hour a hug and a kiss, unlike the adults, she can see the goodness that lies behind the ugliness.

One final character should be mentioned, if only for the sake of auctorial self-indulgence. Almost our first sight of Quasimodo is as he is encouraging a **Baby Bird**—who has been residing in Hugo's mouth—to go through the rite of passage of learning to fly and thus be able to share the freedom of the other birds. Of course, this symbolizes the freedom that Quasimodo himself is not permitted to enjoy. The fledgling is beautifully animated and beautifully voiced (by Frank Welker), so that we are both amused and touched: a delight.

HERCULES

At the time of this writing the Disney team was still hard at work on their newest animated feature, *Hercules*, scheduled for release on June 27, 1997. .

Characters:

Hercules; Hades; Pain; Panic; Philoctetes; Megara; Pegasus; Hydra; The Cyclops; Apollo; Athena; Zeus; Hera; Hephaestus; Hermes; Muses; Fates; Titans; Alcmene; Amphitryon; Nessus

Credits:

Voices: Barbara Barrie (Alcmene); Roger Bart (young Hercules singing); Corey Burton (Rock Titan, Tornado Titan); Mary Kay Bergman (Athena); Jim Cummings (Lava Titan, Nessus); Keith David (Apollo); Danny DeVito (Philoctetes); Tate Donovan (Hercules); Paddi Edwards (Atropos); Susan Egan (Megara); Samantha Eggar (Hera); Cheryl Freeman (Melpomene); Matt Frewer (Panic); Bobcat Goldthwait (Pain); Bug Hall (Child Panic); Kellen Hathaway (Child Pain); Charlton Heston (Narrator); Hal Holbrook (Amphitryon); Josh Keaton (young Hercules speaking); LaChanze (Terpsichore); Patrick Pinney (Cyclops, Hephaestus, Ice Titan, Rock Titan); Amanda Plummer (Clotho); Roz Ryan (Thalia); Paul Shaffer (Hermes); Vanesse Thomas (Clio); Carole Shelley (Lachesis); Rip Torn (Zeus); Lillias White (Calliope); James Woods (Hades)

Additional Voices: Mary Kay Bergman; Corey Burton; Jim Cummings; Eric von Detten; Kathleen Freeman; Wayne Knight; Scott McAfee; Aaron Michael Metchik; Patrick Pinney; Riley Steiner

Music: Alan Menken

Songs by: Alan Menken and David Zippel

Head of Story: Barry Johnson

Editor: Tom Finan

Production Stylist: Sue Nichols

Supervising Animators: Chris Bailey (Nessus); Richard Bazley (Alcmene, Amphitryon); Nancy Beiman (Fates, Thebans); Andreas Deja (Hercules); Anthony DeRosa (Hera, Zeus); Ken Duncan (Megara); Brian Ferguson (Panic); Eric Goldberg (Philoctetes); Randy Haycock (Hercules); James Lopez (Pain); Nik

Ranieri (Hades); Mike Show (Muses); Ellen Woodbury (Pegasus)

Head of Layout: Rasoul Azadani

Head of Effects: Mauro Maressa

Head of Backgrounds: Tom Cardone

Head of Computer Animation: Roger Gould

Art Director: Andy Gaskill

Production Designer: Gerald Scarfe

Producers: Alice Dewey; Ron Clements; John Musker

Directors: Ron Clements; John Musker

Release Date: June 27, 1997

THE MOVIE

The person to dream up the idea for *Hercules* was the Disney artist Joe Haidar, although after the very preliminary stages of development, his involvement with the project ceased. It was taken up by the veteran Disney writer-director team Ron Clements and John Musker, who altered the story of the myth of Hercules very considerably—indeed, aside from the nature of the central character it is virtually unrecognizable.

The most astonishing aspect concerning the movie's evolution, however, is the involvement of Gerald Scarfe as production designer. Scarfe had worked in animation before, notably on the 1982 album *Pink Floyd The Wall* and his own television movie *A Long Drawn-Out Trip* (1972)—the latter quite violently parodying American manners and mores—but is best known for his savage political caricatures, which have appeared in numerous British magazines. For a long time he was connected with the magazine *Private Eye*, which, depending on your taste, may be described either as satirical or as scurrilous and scabrous; it is certainly about as far from Disney as one could get. Several issues were banned by the news agency chains because of his

vicious caricatures on their covers, starting with one that depicted the then Prime Minister, Harold Macmillan. Further controversy arose when the broadsheet newspaper *The Sunday Times* commissioned from him a drawing of the late Winston Churchill, then refused to publish it. He has also worked for such U. S. magazines as *Esquire* and *Life*. Taken all in all, to find him in a list of Disney credits comes as quite a shock.

The choice was an inspired one, however. There are quite a number of examples of Scarfe's work in Stephen Rebello's *The Art of Hercules: The Chaos of Creation* (1997), and it is easy to see how radical was Scarfe's injection into the work of the creative team—and how surprisingly often the animators adhered very closely to his conceptualizations. Further examples of his work appear in the extended discussion of the movie in *Disney's Art of Animation: From Mickey Mouse to Hercules* (1997) by Bob Thomas.

THE STORY

On Mount Olympus, Zeus and Hera throw a party to celebrate the birth of their son Hercules, whose birth gift is the baby wingèd horse Pegasus. One guest who doesn't much join in the fun is the god Hades, who is tired of being stuck in the Underworld and has plans to usurp Zeus's throne. The Fates tell him that in eighteen years' time the planetary alignments will favor his usurpation, but that "should Hercules fight, you will fail." Hades sends his dimwitted sidekicks Pain and Panic to abduct the infant and feed him a potion that will render him mortal, so that he can be promptly killed. They bungle this mission, so Hercules, while becoming mortal, nevertheless retains godlike strength. Hercules—like Superman before him (or after him, depending on the way you think about it)—is raised by a mortal couple, Amphitryon and Alcmene.

Now a teenager, Hercules is aware that he is not like the other kids on the block. He goes to the Temple of Zeus in search of answers; a statue of Zeus comes to life and at last father and son are reunited. Zeus tells Hercules that the only way he can return to Mount Olympus is to prove himself a true hero on Earth and recommends a professional hero trainer, the satyr Philoctetes. After suitable bouts of training, the pair head for Thebes, stopping off en route so that Hercules can rescue—or so he believes—a beautiful woman named Megara from a malicious centaur, Nessus. In fact, Megara is a servant of Hades and a reluctant rescuee. Hades, on hearing from her that Hercules is still alive, plots afresh to kill him.

Megara comes to Thebes with Pain and Panic, the latter shapeshifting into the forms of two small boys who require rescuing. Lured, Hercules finds himself battling with the Hydra and then with a slew of other monsters Hades sends against him, defeating all and becoming a publicly lauded hero. He goes back to the Temple of Zeus to tell Dad that he's performed the task, but Zeus tells him that being famous isn't the quality that is required, he must look into his own heart for the secret of being a true hero.

Hades, meanwhile, has realized that Hercules's sole weakness is the lovely Megara; what he doesn't quite realize is that Hercules is *Megara's* weakness. Hades persuades Hercules to give up his strength for twenty-four hours as a price for the granting of Megara's safety and freedom. Needless to say, the twenty-four hours just happen to coincide with that planetary alignment. At the opportune moment, Hades releases the Titans—his foot-soldiers, as it were, for the conquest

of Mount Olympus—and sets the Cyclops on the weakened and dispirited Hercules. It is in this condition that Hercules fights back, learns what heroism is really all about, saves the day, and discovers that he would rather stay mortal and live happily ever after with Megara.

A rather different version of the Hercules legend can be found in many standard reference books.

THE CHARACTERS

Hercules

As so often with Disney animated features, it's true to say that there is more than one character sharing a name. The figure at the forefront of the movie is of course the adult Hercules (voiced by Tate Donovan)—somewhat revoltingly called "Herc" much of the time — a rock-jawed hero with a jockish sense of humor and thighs that bulge in places where other people don't even realize they *have* thighs. Fight a monster? Save a distressed damsel? Nothing to it so far as Hercules is concerned. It takes him the course of the movie, however, to learn the art of being a hero.

The other two characters called Hercules are himself as a baby and then as an adolescent (voiced by Joshua Keaton for speech, Roger Bart for singing).

Hades

A wonderful villain, showing perhaps more clearly than any other character in the movie—except maybe Philoctetes—

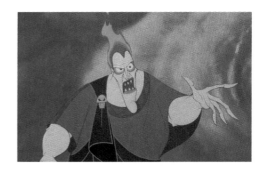

One of Disney's most wonderful villains, Hades, Lord of the Underworld, is voiced by James Woods and has a gas-blue flame for hair.

the distinctive style of Scarfe, Hades (voiced by James Woods) is the Lord of the Underworld. Gray of skin and with what appears to be flame in place of hair, he has a voice that can chill the dead. He is tired of ruling the Underworld—the job is hell—and plans to conquer Mount Olympus and take over Zeus's role.

Pain and Panic

Most of the Disney villains have zany sidekicks, and Hades—one almost feels sorry for him—is stuck with two. Pain (voiced by Bobcat Goldthwait) and Panic (voiced by Matt Frewer) are as carelessly accident prone as any of the other Disney zanies, even though they are capable of shapeshifting, which one might have expected would give them the advantage over Hades' foes. One transformation is into a female winged horse, in hopes of tempting Pegasus. When they are in their "normal" forms, Pain is a tubby little pink demon who could almost be described as cute, and Panic is quite the opposite—a small-winged green beanpole topped with a big-eyed head, almost as if he would have liked to have been Road Runner in an earlier incarnation, enjoying that character's imbecilic self-confidence rather than wallowing in his own neuroses.

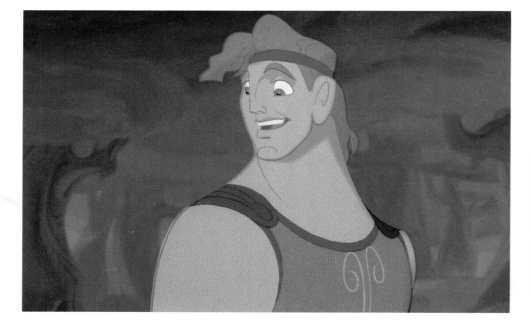

The square-jawed hero of the film, half-mortal half-god Hercules, voiced by Tate Donovan.

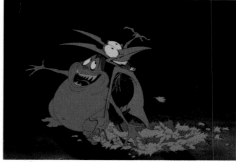

Hades' two accident-prone sidekicks, Pain and Panic.

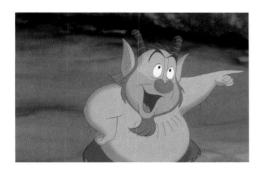

Voiced by Danny DeVito, the satyr Philoctetes, frequently dubbed "Phil," trains Hercules for stardom.

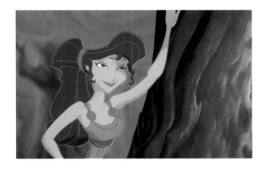

The smart and sassy, as well as lovely, Megara, "Meg" to her friends. In the end, the love between her and Hercules triumphs.

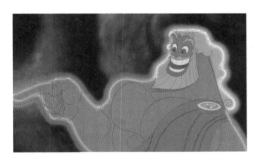

Hercules' father Zeus, ruler of Mount Olympus and the gods.

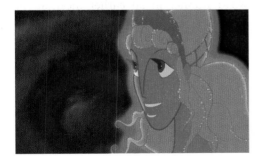

Hera, Hercules' mother and wife of Zeus.

Philoctetes

A rough idea of the characterization of the satyr Philoctetes, frequently dubbed "Phil," can be inferred from the actor who voices his part, Danny DeVito. It is Philoctetes who trains Hercules for

herodom. He has done it before, after all, with a chronologically confused miscellany including Odysseus, Perseus, Theseus, and Achilles. Some of those heroes didn't work out too well, so Philoctetes puts a lot of effort into Hercules—and the effort pays off.

Megara

With her mass of red-brown hair and her expressive eyes, Megara (voiced by Susan Egan) is a woman whom one senses has a past she would rather forget. Although she is immediately attracted to Hercules, at the same time she distrusts him because he is a man, and she has been betrayed by so many men before. Her soul, unfortunately, is the property of Hades, so that she must do what he commands rather than what her emotions begin to tell her—that she should ally herself with Hercules. Finally, of course, love wins all.

Zeus and Hera

Voiced by Rip Torn, Zeus is big and bearded in a somewhat formal fashion. His wrath is mighty to behold but so also is his mirth, he is much more gentle-hearted than the myths would have him — in general, Leda is pretty safe from this domesticated version of the ruler of the gods. Although he is in theory the master of all he surveys, he is incapable of dispensing with the rulebook in order to bring his own much-loved son, Hercules, back to Mount Olympus. All he can do is, in the form of a living statue, advise the lad on the way to go about *earning* his passage home.

Hera (voiced by Samantha Eggar), Zeus' wife and Hercules' mother, is portrayed in both personality and physical appearance as a somewhat ethereal character—her hair and her garments are ever rippling and flowing. She is more feminine than any mortal could hope to be and yet at the same time possessed of a certain vagueness that is all too mortal.

Minor Characters

The flying horse **Pegasus** (whinnied by Danny Mann) is fiercely loyal to Hercules and is in effect the hero's sidekick, ever ready to play with him rather than concentrate on the job at hand. The **Hydra**, regenerates three heads each time one is chopped off, is perhaps the most terrifying of Hercules' physical foes. The **Cyclops** (voiced by Patrick Pinney), sent by Hades to dispose of the mortal Hercules, is rather less frightening.

Among the various gods who make small appearances are **Apollo** (voiced by Keith David), **Athena** (voiced by Mary

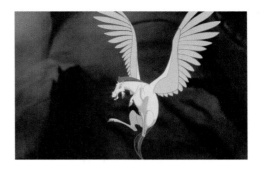

Hercules' lifelong companion Pegasus, the flying horse of myth.

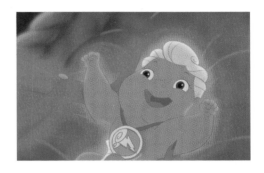

Baby Hercules, covered with the golden light characteristic of the gods.

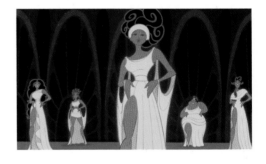

The gospel-singing Muses.

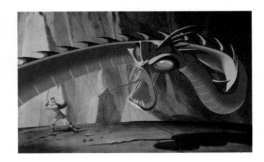

The terrifying Hydra, who regenerates three heads for every one that is cut off, is a brilliant piece of computer imaging.

Kay Bergman), **Hephaestus** (voiced by Patrick Pinney), and **Hermes** (voiced by Paul Schaffer). The Muses are **Calliope** (voiced by Lillias White), **Clio** (voiced by Vanesse Thomas), **Melpomene** (voiced by Cheryl Freeman), **Terpsichore** (voiced by LaChanze) and **Thalia** (voiced by Roz

Ryan). The Fates are **Atropos** (voiced by Paddi Edwards), **Clotho** (voiced by Amanda Plummer), and **Lachesis** (voiced by Carole Shelley). The four Titans whom Hades releases from imprisonment in his attempt to conquer Mount Olympus are the **Ice Titan** (voiced by Patrick Pinney), the **Lava Titan** (voiced by Jim Cummings), the **Rock Titan** (voiced by Corey Burton and, again, Pinney) and the **Tornado Titan** (voiced by Burton). The egocentric centaur **Nessus,** from whom Hercules comparatively early on in the movie "rescues" Megara, is voiced by Jim Cummings.

Not to be forgotten are Hercules' adoptive parents, the down-to-Earth mortals **Alcmene** (voiced by Barbara Barrie) and **Amphitryon** (voiced by Hal Holbrook). There is obviously some pathos when they realize they have to break it to the lad that he is not a mortal as others are and release him so that he can find his destiny.

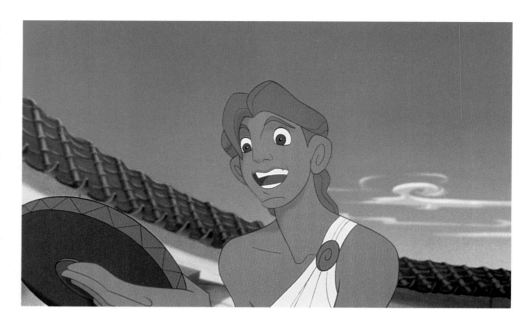

Hercules as a gawky teenager trying to fit in.

APPENDIX I

Historical Personages in the Disney Shorts

The first appearance of a "real person" in a Disney short that has so far been traced is not so much a caricature as a puppet. In the 1932 Christmas short *Santa's Workshop* (►51) one of the toys is a marching doll of comedian Charlie Chaplin.

Aside from such sports as that, the appearances of historical personages caricatured in Disney animated shorts fall into two main categories: (a) the several movies in which Walt attempted to "cash in" on the fame of Hollywood celebrities, presumably in the belief that audiences would find it irresistible to see their screen idols behave in unexpectedly zany ways (curious reasoning: Walt's own name was by this time as big a crowd-puller as many); and (b) the movies produced during wartime, in which Axis leaders were depicted bilefully and other historical characters occasionally. In addition, there are a few other shorts in which "real people" appear in various guises.

The plots of the "Hollywood shorts" are reasonably uninteresting. In *Mother Goose Goes Hollywood* (1938) the various Mother Goose characters appear as caricatures of famous film stars. There was a fair amount of integrity involved in the animation; years later I. Klein, who animated Laurel and Hardy in the roles of Simple Simon and the Pieman, recalled:

> The studio on my request obtained several Laurel and Hardy comedy shorts which were screened for me one afternoon, to brush me up on the mannerisms of those two great comics.

The running gag in *Mother Goose Goes Hollywood* is that Bo-Peep (Katharine Hepburn) is constantly seeking her sheep. At the end of the short the punchline occurs when Joe E. Brown steals a kiss from Martha Raye: he lets out a yowl of delight, and as we zoom in on his vast mouth we see Hepburn emerging with, at last, one of her sheep.

The Autograph Hound (1939) has possibly the most amusing plot of these "Hollywood shorts". The autograph-hunter himself is a certain Mr. D. Duck, who has a habit of making plots amusing. He is hanging around one of the Hollywood studios, hoping to meet the famous. Greta Garbo arrives in a car that looks just like her: droopy eyelids over the headlamps, a sulky scarlet mudguard, and so forth. Donald steals into the studio behind her, and is soon in conversation with Mickey Rooney, who swaps conjuring tricks with him. One of Rooney's tricks results in Don receiving a broken egg on his head: in a nice touch, as the world's favourite Duck begins to . . . er . . . feel marginally irritated, the egg neatly fries.

Other stars feature in this short. Sonja Henie signs her autograph on the ice using

her skates but, alas, as Donald tries to carry it away it melts. Shirley Temple collides with him on the stairs while practising her tap-dancing and they tumble down together. She is delighted to meet the famous Donald Duck, and the two ask for each other's autographs simultaneously. One might think that Temple were getting much the better of the bargain except that she dots the "i" of "Shirley" with a heart-shaped rosebud kiss.

The guard at the studio is preparing to throw the intruder, Donald, out, but Temple stops him, stressing: "That's *Donald Duck!*" Word runs round like wildfire and out of the woodwork pop more Hollywood stars than the eye can readily follow, all eager for the Duck's autograph. Even the guard joins in the fray, but Donald vindictively squirts him with his ink-filled fountain pen; the words "Donald Duck" form as if by magic on the guard's chest.

There is a curious myth attached to *The Autograph Hound*. According to it the popular comedy trio the Ritz Brothers were originally scheduled to appear but, thanks to a rather tasteless radio parody of Disney's *Snow White and the Seven Dwarfs* which they broadcast during the short's production, Walt personally banned them. (I. Klein recalled: "I thought that skit was nastier than funny.") In fact, the Ritz Brothers *do* appear in *The Autograph Hound*, giving Donald their autograph. They sign it on his bottom.

The 1935 Christmas short *Broken Toys* likewise features a number of showbiz stars. We discover a heap of damaged toys – Hollywood personalities in disguise – lying on the city dump. Ned Sparks stars as an optimistic sailor doll: whereas the others are despondent, he has had a great idea as to how they could give pleasure to others this Christmas. Exhorting the rest not to "give up the ship", he shows them by example how to restore themselves to "newness". After many a gag the troop of toys marches from the dump over the snowy fields to the iron gates of an orphanage.

Most of the caricatured stars in the "Hollywood shorts" appear for moments only – sometimes less than moments – so the following lists may be incomplete.

Mickey's Gala Premiere (1933): Marie Dressler, Wallace Beery, Jimmy Durante, Will Hays, Eddie Cantor, Greta Garbo, Ed Wynn, Laurel and Hardy, Boris Karloff, Bela Lugosi, Frederic March, Joe E. Brown, Buster Keaton, Douglas Fairbanks, Will Rogers, Bert Wheeler, Robert Woolsey

Broken Toys (1935): W. C. Fields, Zasu Pitts, Ned Sparks, Stepin Fetchit (also Zasu Pitts doing an impersonation of Mae West)

Mickey's Polo Team (1936): Jack Holt, Shirley Temple, Harpo Marx, Clark Gable, Laurel and Hardy, Edna May Oliver, W. C. Fields, Charlie Chaplin

Mother Goose Goes Hollywood (1938): Cab Calloway, Charles Laughton, Charlie McCarthy (features also "live" in *Fun and Fancy Free* [►222]), Edward G. Robinson, Fats Waller, Fred Astaire, Freddie Bartholomew, George Arliss, Joe E. Brown, Joe Penner, Katharine Hepburn, Martha Raye, the Marx Brothers, Spencer Tracy, Stepin Fetchit, Laurel and Hardy, Greta Garbo, Wallace Beery, Clark Gable, W. C. Fields, Hugh Herbert, Ned Sparks, Eddie Cantor

The Autograph Hound (1939): Armetta, Bette Davis, Charles Boyer, Edward Arnold, Groucho and Harpo Marx, Hugh Herbert, Irvin S. Cobb, Joan Crawford, Lionel Barrymore, Mickey Rooney, Mischa Auer, the Ritz Brothers, Roland Young, Slim Summerville, Sonja Henie, Greta Garbo, Shirley Temple, Clark Gable, Charlie McCarthy, Stepin Fetchit, Joe E. Brown, Martha Raye, Katharine Hepburn, Eddie Cantor

The personage possibly most prolifically caricatured in the Disney canon made his appearances for very different reasons. He was Adolf Hitler, and he was treated with a pleasing lack of respect in 1943's *Der Fuehrer's Face* (►64) and the same year's *Education for Death* (►95). In the former movie both Mussolini and the Emperor Hirohito also made an appearance. (Interestingly, although Hitler could not stand Mickey Mouse, Mussolini loved him – as did their great foe F. D. Roosevelt.) Hitler appears also in the prologue to the 1942 wartime educational short *Stop That Tank!* (also known less excitingly as *Boys' Anti-Tank Rifle*). Here he gives a hysterical peptalk to his troops and then comes under fire. His tank, badly crippled, zooms all over the battlefield and finally (loud cheers) over a cliff. Hitler tumbles all the way down to Hell, where he is welcomed by Satan. Hitler is furious – he can do much more evil "upstairs" than ever one could find in Hell – and goes into yet another froth-lipped rant. As Satan makes smart-aleck asides to the audience, Hitler weeps impotently and the short ends.

On a rather different scale was the wartime feature *Victory Through Air Power* (►206). This featured a number of historical aviators: Orville and Wilbur Wright, Alberto Santos-Dumont, Eugene Ely, Calbraith P. Rodgers, Sir John Alcock and Arthur Brown, and Charles Lindbergh.

The 1953 short *Ben and Me* featured historical personages in a less controversial framework. Benjamin Franklin and Thomas Jefferson had fairly noteworthy parts in the movie (►120); also in the short were Dr. Palmer and Governor Sir William Keith. In the 1969 short *It's Tough to be a Bird* (►131) two great navigators are seen using birds as navigational aids: they are Christopher Columbus and Leif Ericsson. In this short also Edgar Allan Poe makes the briefest of appearances – the connection, of course, being "The Raven".

Several historical characters appear in the 1957 featurette *The Truth About Mother Goose*, which tells the tales behind two nursery rhymes and a nursery song.

A number of Biblical characters have appeared in the Disney shorts, as have a number whose historicity is dubious (e.g., Robin Hood). Also of note are such characters as Prince John and King Richard, who both appear, although distorted out of all recognition, in the 1973 feature *Robin Hood* (➤290).

Finally, mention must be made of those Disney staff who have been caricatured in one short or another. A complete list is probably impossible – the animators enjoy their little games – but it is worth noting the presence of Walt and others in the 1938 short *Ferdinand the Bull* (➤88) and that of the great animators Fred Moore and Ward Kimball in the 1941 short *The Nifty Nineties* (➤34).

APPENDIX II

Nursery Characters in the Disney Shorts

Nursery characters feature widely in the Disney shorts, their stories being told (albeit frequently in much altered form) in such movies as the Laugh-O-grams (➤12), *The Pied Piper* (➤57), *Lullaby Land* (Mr. Sandman [➤58]) and *The Big Bad Wolf* (Little Red Riding Hood [➤54]).

Nursery characters made "mass appearances" in two Disney shorts, *Mother Goose Melodies* and *Old King Cole*, Old King Cole being a character common to both of them. He is a great big bulky fellow with a red nose much like the bulb of an old-fashioned motor-horn, heavy black eyelashes, and a little gold crown that is far too small for the expansive bald pate upon which it sits. In his latter movie each nursery character, or group of nursery characters, emerges in a cheerful rush from a separate pop-up book – a clever effect.

It is infernally hard to spot every nursery character in these two movies – most are on-screen only moments – so the following lists may be incomplete:

Mother Goose Melodies (1931): Old King Cole, Miss Muffet, Jack and Jill, Simple Simon, Jack Horner, Little Boy Blue, Bo-Peep, Mother Goose, Humpty Dumpty, Three Blind Mice, the Cat with the Fiddle, the Little Dog (who laughed), the Cow (who jumped over the Moon)

Old King Cole (1933): Old King Cole, Mother Hubbard, Pied Piper, Old Woman Who Lived in a Shoe, Red Riding Hood (and Big Bad Wolf), Cat with the Fiddle, Mary Mary Quite Contrary, Peter Pumpkin-Eater, Mr. and Mrs. Jack Spratt, Goosie Gander, Little Boy Blue, the Crooked Man (who walked a crooked mile), Three Little Kittens, Three Blind Mice, Ten Little Indians, Bo-Peep

In a rather different vein, the three sections of the excellent 1957 featurette *The Truth About Mother Goose* told the stories behind two nursery characters and a popular nursery song, "London Bridge is Falling Down". Jack Horner is identified with a servant sent by a prominent official with a gift to Henry VIII; as was fashionable, the gift is encased in a pie. Horner steals the gift – the deeds to a valuable estate. Mary Mary Quite Contrary is identified with Mary Queen of Scots, of course.

In a vein so different that it probably belongs to the person standing next to you, the 1938 short *Mother Goose Goes Hollywood* has various showbiz stars of the day playing the roles of nursery characters (➤433).

BIBLIOGRAPHY

Books

Bailey, Adrian: *Walt Disney's World of Fantasy*, London, Paper Tiger, n.d. but *c.* 1982; New York, Everest House, 1982

Bain, David, and Harris, Bruce (eds.): *Mickey Mouse: Fifty Happy Years*, New York, Harmony, 1977

Bettelheim, Bruno: *The Uses of Enchantment*, New York, Knopf, 1976

Blitz, Marcia: *Donald Duck*, New York, Harmony, 1979

Culhane, John: *Fantasia*, New York, Harry N. Abrams, 1983

Eyles, Allen: *Walt Disney's "Three Little Pigs"*, New York, Simon and Schuster, 1986; London, Collins, 1986

Fawcett, John: *The Drawings of John Fawcett*, St Louis, privately published, 1969

Feild, Robert D.: *The Art of Walt Disney*, New York, Macmillan, 1942; London, Collins, 1943

Finch, Christopher: *The Art of Walt Disney*, New York, Harry N. Abrams, 1973

Gunther, John: *Taken at the Flood*, New York, Harper, 1960

Holliss, Richard, and Sibley, Brian: *Walt Disney's Mickey Mouse – His Life and Times*, New York, Harper & Row, 1986; London, Fleetway Books, 1986

Maltin, Leonard: *Of Mice and Magic: A History of American Animated Cartoons*, New York, McGraw-Hill, 1980

Maltin, Leonard: *The Disney Films*, New York, Crown, 1984 (1st edn. published 1973)

Miller, Diane Disney, and Martin, Pete: *The Story of Walt Disney*, New York, Holt, 1957

Mosley, Leonard: *Disney's World*, New York, Stein & Day, 1985; London, Grafton, 1986 (as *The Real Walt Disney*)

O'Brien, Flora: *Walt Disney's Donald Duck – 50 Years of Happy Frustration*, London, Three Duck Editions, 1984; Tucson, HP Books, 1984

O'Brien, Flora: *Walt Disney's Goofy – The Good Sport*, London, Ebury Press, 1985; Tucson, HP Books, 1985

Peary, Danny, and Peary, Gerald (eds.): *The American Animated Cartoon: A Critical Anthology*, New York, E. P. Dutton, 1980

Schickel, Richard: *The Disney Version* (revised edn.), London, Pavilion Books, 1986 (1st edn. published 1968 New York, Simon & Schuster). [Note: revised edn. published in paperback only in US in 1985 by Touchstone; original edn. published in England in 1968 as *Walt Disney* by Weidenfeld & Nicholson.]

Stravinsky, Igor, and Craft, Robert: *Expositions and Developments*, Garden City, New York, Doubleday, 1962

Thomas, Bob: *The Art of Animation*, New York, Simon & Schuster, 1958

Thomas, Bob: *Walt Disney: An American Original*, New York, Simon & Schuster,
1976; London, New English Library, 1977 (as *The Walt Disney Biography*).

Thomas, Frank, and Johnston, Ollie: *Disney Animation: The Illusion of Life*, New York, Abbeville Press, 1981

Thompson, Stith: *The Folktale*, Berkeley, University of California Press, 1977

Weber, Msgr. Francis: *Mickey's Golden Jubilee*, Los Angeles, Junipero Serra Press, 1979

Writers' Congress (Proceedings of a Conference held in October 1943 under the sponsorship of the Hollywood Writers' Mobilization and the University of California), Berkeley, University of California Press, 1944

Articles, Reviews, Essays, Theses, Papers, Pamphlets

Adamakos, Peter: "Ub Iwerks", *Mindrot*, June 15, 1977

Adamson, Joe: "With Disney on Olympus: An Interview with Dick Huemer" *Funnyworld*, Fall 1977

Adamson, Joe: "What's Cooking in the Black Cauldron", *American Cinematographer*, July 1985

Adler, Stephen: "Snow White for the Defense: Why Disney Doesn't Lose", *The American Lawyer*, March 1983

Algar, James: "The Animated Film: Fantasy and Fact", *The Pacific Spectator*, Winter 1950

Allan, Robin: "Alice in Disneyland", *Sight & Sound*, Spring 1985

Anderson, Ken: "*Robin Hood*", *Official Bulletin of IATSE*, Winter 1973-4

Andrews, Peter: "The Mightiest Mouse", *Signature*, November 1978

Ansen, David, and McGuire, Stryker: "Disney's New Cauldron", *Newsweek*, November 20, 1978

Apple, Max: "Uncle Walt", *Esquire*, December 1983

Art Digest: "*Pinocchio*", February 15, 1940

Bancroft, Mary: "Of Mouse and Man", *Psychological Perspectives*, Fall 1978

Barkley, Richard: "A Game of Rat and Mouse", *Sunday Express*, October 12, 1986

Barrier, Mike, Webb, Graham, and Ware, Hames: "The Moving Drawing Speaks", *Funnyworld*, No. 18, Summer 1978

Barrier, Mike: "'Building a Better Mouse': Fifty Years of Disney Animation", *Funnyworld*, No. 20, Summer 1979

Barrier, Mike: "Screenwriter for a Duck: Carl Barks at the Disney Studio", *Funnyworld*, No. 21, Fall 1979

Baskette, Kirtley: "The Amazing Inside Story of How They Made *Snow White*", *Photoplay*, April 1938

Bayer, Ann: "Happy 40th, Mickey", *Life*, October 25, 1968

Beard, Henry, and Bramley, Peter: "Disney
Rejects", *National Lampoon*, November 1970

Belmont, I.J.: "Painter of Music Criticizes *Fantasia*", *Art Digest*, December 15, 1940

Benson, John: "FW Interview: Mickey Mouse", *Funnyworld*, No. 11, May 1969

Best, Katharine: "Cosmic Relief", *Stage*, September 1935

Black, Ed: "Behind the Scenes at Walt Disney's", *Cartoonist Profiles*, June 1978

Blair, Preston: "The Animation of *Fantasia*", *Cartoonist Profiles*, No. 49, March 1981

Blake, Larry: "Re-recording and Post-Production for Disney's *Fantasia*", *Recording Engineer/Producer*, October 1982

Boone, Andrew R.: "When Mickey Mouse Speaks", *Scientific American*, March 1933

Boone, Andrew R.: "*Snow White and the Seven Dwarfs*", *Popular Science Monthly*, January 1938

Boone, Andrew R.: "Mickey Mouse Goes Classical", *Popular Science Monthly*, January 1941

Bowen, Neil: "*Fantasia*", honours essay for School of Graphic Design, Leicester Polytechnic, 1979

Bragdon, Claude: "Mickey Mouse and What He Means", *Scribner's Magazine*, July 1934

Brewster, Todd A.: "Happy Birthday Dear Mickey Mouse", *Americana*, November/December 1978

Calvert, Fred: "The Disney Myth", *Hollywood Reporter*, November 30, 1971

Canemaker, John: "Sincerely Yours, Frank Thomas", *Millimeter*, January 1975

Canemaker, John: "Grim Natwick", *Film Comment*, January/February 1975

Canemaker, John: "Art Babbitt, the Animator as Firebrand", *Millimeter*, September 1975

Canemaker, John: "Vladimir William Tytla (1904-1968), Animation's Michelangelo", *Cinéfantastique*, Winter 1976

Canemaker, John: "Disney Without Walt", *Print*, November/December 1978

Canemaker, John: "Disney Design 1928-1979: How the Disney Studio Changed the Look of the Animated Cartoon", *Millimeter*, February 1979

Canemaker, John: "Art Babbitt", *Cartoonist Profiles*, No. 44, December 1979

Canemaker, John: "David Hilberman", *Cartoonist Profiles*, No. 48, December 1980

Care, Ross B.: "Ward Kimball: Animated Versatility", *Millimeter*, July/August 1976

Care, Ross B.: "Threads of Melody: The Evolution of a Major Film Score – Walt Disney's *Bambi*", *Quarterly Journal of the Library of Congress*, Spring 1983

Carr, Harry: "The Only Unpaid Movie Star", *American Magazine*, March 1931

Catsos, Gregory J.M.: "Clarence 'Ducky' Nash, the Voice Behind Donald Duck", *Video Times*, July 1985

Cauduro, John: "*Fantasia* ... Science and Art Make Music the Master", *The Quadrant*,

University of Portland Engineers' Club, Summer 1941

Cawley, John: "Disney Out-foxed: The Tale of Reynard at the Disney Studio", *American Classic Screen*, July/August 1979

Cawley, John: "Walt Disney and 'The Gremlins', an Unfinished Story", *American Classic Screen*, Spring 1980

Chalker, Jack L.: "An Informal Biography of $crooge McDuck", *Markings*, July 1971

Chemical and Engineering News: "D. D. Wades Into Science", May 11, 1959

Churchill, Douglas: "Now Mickey Mouse Enters Art's Temple", *New York Times Magazine*, June 3, 1934

Cinemeditor: "Bag of Tricks is Emptied for *Mary Poppins*", Summer 1964

City Limits: review of *Basil – The Great Mouse Detective*, October 9, 1986

Cocks, Jay: "The Duck with the Bucks", *Time*, May 17, 1982

Collier, Richard: "Wish Upon a Star: The Magical Kingdoms of Walt Disney", *Reader's Digest*, October 1971

Collier's Magazine: review of *Saludos Amigos*, December 19, 1942

Conniff, James C.G.: "Man or Mouse?", *The Marianist*, December 1949

Corliss, Richard: "The New Generation Comes of Age", *Time*, July 20, 1981

Cruse, Howard: "Abduction of a Mouse", *Comics Scene*, November 1982

Culhane, John: "The Old Disney Magic", *New York Times Magazine*, August 1, 1976

Culhane, John: "The Last of the Nine Old Men", *American Film*, June 1977

Culhane, John: "A Mouse for All Seasons", *Saturday Review*, November 11, 1978

Daily Express (London): "Mouse Piece!", October 10, 1986

Daily Mail (London): "On the Tail of an Underworld Rat", October 10, 1986

Daily Mirror (London): "Basil's Battle Royal", October 10, 1986

Daily Telegraph (London): review of *Basil – The Great Mouse Detective*, October 10, 1986

Daugherty, Frank: "Mickey Mouse Comes of Age", *Christian Science Monitor Weekly*, February 2, 1938

Daugherty, Frank: "Disney's Back Again!", *Christian Science Monitor Magazine*, November 10, 1945

D'au Vin, Constance: "Mickey is 50 and Living off Residuals", *Valley*, November 1978

Davenport, Marcia: "Not So Silly", *Stage*, July 1936

Davidson, Bill: "The Fantastic Walt Disney", *Saturday Evening Post*, November 7, 1964

Davies, Russell: "Disney's World: 'Dreams are Always in Bad Taste'", *The Listener*, February 16, 1984

Disney, Walt: "Mickey Mouse is 5 Years Old", *Film Pictorial*, September 30, 1933

Disney, Walt: "Mickey as Professor", *Public Opinion Quarterly*, Summer 1945

Disney, Walt: "How We Do It", *Sunday Times Magazine* (Manila), August 15, 1948

Disney, Walt: "How I Cartooned *Alice*; Its Logical Nonsense Needed a Logical Sequence", *Films in Review*, May 1951

Disney, Walt: "Why I Made *Peter Pan*", source unidentified but *c.* 1953

Disney, Walt: "What Mickey Mouse Has Meant to Me", *Box Office*, December 20, 1952

Disney, Walt: "Ways of Telling the World's Great Stories", *Theater and Cinema*, 1953

Disney, Walt: "Animated Magic", *Theater and Cinema*, n.d. but *c.* 1955

Disney, Walt: "Humor – the World's Sixth Sense", *Wisdom*, May 1956

Eddy, Don: "The Amazing Secret of Walt Disney", *American Magazine*, August 1955

Eisen, A.: "Two Disney Artists", *Crimmer's: The Harvard Journal of Pictorial Fiction*, Winter 1975

Ellis, R.T.: "Behind the Scenes with Mickey Mouse", *DuPont Magazine*, February 1935

Fan, Ada M.: "Sleeping Beauty: A Rose to Dawn", unpublished honors paper, Harvard College, 1975

Ferguson, Otis: "Extra Added Attractions", *New Republic*, August 7, 1935

Financial Times: review of *Basil – The Great Mouse Detective*, October 10, 1986

Fisher, Bob: "Behind the Camera on *Pete's Dragon*", *American Cinematographer*, October 1977

Fitzgerald, John E.: "The Controversial Kingdom of Walt Disney", *US Catholic*, August 1964

Fleming, R.C.: "The Saga of Michael Rodent", *Compressed Air Magazine*, July 1934

FM and Fine Arts: "Walt Disney Accused: An Interview with Frances Clark Sayers conducted by Charles M. Weisenberg", August 1965

Forster, E. M.: "Mickey and Minnie", *The Spectator*, January 19, 1934

Fortune: "What? Color in the Movies Again?", October 1934

Fortune: "The Big, Bad Wolf, and Why It May Never Huff nor Puff at Walt Disney's Door", November 1934

Gardner, John: "Saint Walt: The Greatest Artist the World Has Ever Known", *New York*, November 12, 1973

Gordon, Stanley: "Julie Andrews Goes to Hollywood", *Look*, November 19, 1963

Gottfredson, Floyd: "Mickey Mouse and Me", *The Illustrator*, Fall 1976

Gould, Stephen Jay: "Mickey Mouse Meets Konrad Lorenz", *Natural History*, May 1979

Grant, Jack: "He's Mickey Mouse's Voice and Master", *Movie Classic*, November 1933

Guardian: review of *Basil – The Great Mouse Detective*, October 9, 1986

Guernsey, Otis L., Jr: "The Movie Cartoon is Coming of Age", *Film Music*, November/December 1953

Hamilton, Sara: "The True Life Story of Mickey Mouse", *Movie Mirror*, December 1931

Hammond, David: "Giving a Personality to an Animated Dragon", *American Cinematographer*, October 1977

Harris Museum and Art Gallery: "Walt Disney and his Animated Cartoons" (catalogue), 1935

Haver, Ronald: "Rescoring *Fantasia*", *Connoisseur*, July 1982

Henderson, Scott: "How Special Film Effects Brought Elliot [*sic*] to Life on the Screen", *American Cinematographer*, October 1977

Hiss, Tony, and McClelland, David: "The Quack and Disney", *New Yorker*, December 29, 1975

Holliday, Kate: "Donald Duck Goes to War", *Coronet*, September 1942

Holliss, Richard: "*Fantasia*", *Starburst*, No. 26, 1980

Holliss, Richard: "*Snow White and the Seven Dwarfs*", *Starburst*, No. 33, 1981

Holliss, Richard: "'When You Wish Upon a Star': The Walt Disney Story", *Starburst*, No. 65, 1983

Holliss, Richard: "*Basil – The Great Mouse Detective*", *Starburst*, No. 99, 1986

Hollister, Paul: "Walt Disney, Genius at Work", *Atlantic*, December 1940

Horn Book: "Walt Disney Accused", December 1965

Houseman, Jerry Paul: "A Study of Selected Walt Disney Screenplays and Films and the Stereotyping of the Role of the Female", unpublished EdD thesis, University of the Pacific, 1973

Hubley, John: "The Writer and the Cartoon", in *Writers' Congress*, Berkeley, University of California Press, 1944

Huemer, Dick: "Thumbnail Sketches", *Funnyworld*, No. 21, Fall 1979

Huemer, Dick: "The Battle of Washington", *Funnyworld*, No. 22, Spring 1981

Hughes, Robert: "Disney: Mousebrow to Highbrow", *Time*, October 15, 1973

Hulett, Ralph: "The Artist's Part in the Production of an Animated Cartoon", *American Artist*, May 1955

Hulett, Steve: "A Star is Drawn", *Film Comment*, January/February 1979

Independent: "Animation and the Uncanny", October 8, 1986

International Photographer: "One Hundred and One Dalmatians", March 1961

International Photographer: "Aristocats", November 1970

Isaacs, Hermine Rich: "New Horizons: *Fantasia* and Fantasound", *Theatre Arts*, January 1941

Jackson, Wilfred: letter in *Funnyworld*, No. 19, Fall 1978

Jungmeyer, Jack: "Baa! Baa! Black Sheep", *Mustang Roundup*, November 1946

Kent, George: "Snow White's Daddy", *The Family Circle*, June 24, 1938

Kilgore, Al: "The Disney Assault", *Film Fan Monthly*, September 1968

King, Margaret J.: "The Disney Sensibility", unpublished MA thesis, Graduate School of Bowling Green University, March 1972

Kinney, Jack: "Bambi and the Goof",

Funnyworld, Fall 1979

Klein, I.: "At the Walt Disney Studio in the 1930s", *Cartoonist Profiles*, September 1974

Klein, I.: "Some Close-up Shots of Walt Disney During the 'Golden Years' ", *Funnyworld*, No. 23, Spring 1983

Korkis, Jim: "Jack Hannah Interview", *Mindrot*, No. 11, July 24, 1978

Korkis, Jim: "A Brief Look at the Films of Donald Duck", *The Rocket's Blast/Comicollector*, September 1979

Korkis, Jim: "Jack Hannah: Another Interview", *Animania*, No. 23, March 5, 1982

Lacy, Lyn: "Happy Birthday Mickey!", *Teacher*, May/June 1978

Lanken, Dane: "The Old Master" (interview with Ward Kimball), *Take One*, November 1978

Leaf, Munro: "The Adventures of Snow White and the Seven Dwarfs", *Stage*, February 1938

Lenburg, Jeff: "Ub Iwerks", *Blackhawk Film Digest*, March and April 1979

Life: "*Snow White* Sets Record: Here is Her Model", April 4, 1938

Life: "Ferdinand the Bull Becomes a Movie Star", November 28, 1938

Life: "These are the Voices of *Pinocchio*", March 11, 1940

Life: "*The New Spirit*, Disney's Tax Film", March 16, 1942

Life: "*Make Mine Music*", March 11, 1946

Life: "Mickey's Children", November 1978

Literary Digest: "'Mickey Mouse' is Eight Years Old", October 3, 1936

Look: "Mickey Mouse Celebrates his Tenth Birthday ... By Capturing a Giant", September 27, 1938

Look: "The Three Little Pigs are in Trouble Again ... with a Wolf Disguised as a Mermaid", March 28, 1939

Lowry, Brian: "Animating *The Black Cauldron*", *Starlog*, August 1985

Lukas, J. Anthony: "The 'Alternative Lifestyle' of Playboys and Playmates", *New York Times Magazine*, June 11, 1972

McClure, Dudley L.: "The Real Lowdown on Mickey Mouse", *The New Movie Magazine*, February 1932

McEvoy, J. P.: "Mickey Mouse Squeals", *Country Gentleman*, March 1934

McKenney, J. Wilson: "Walt Disney, Showman and Educator, Remembers Daisy", *CTA Journal*, December 1955

Maltin, Leonard: "The Disney Studio Today", *Film Fan Monthly*, February 1970

Mano, D. Keith: "A Real Mickey Mouse Operation", *Playboy*, December 1973

Marlow, David: "Working for Mickey Mouse", *New York*, August 6, 1973

Martin, Judith: "Our World According to Walt Disney", *Houston Chronicle Magazine/Zest*, August 5, 1973

Martin, Quinn: "How Animated Cartoons are Made", *Sunday World Magazine*, September 28, 1930

Merritt, Karen: "Story and Character Development for *Snow White and the Seven Dwarfs*", unpublished film colloquium presented November 29, 1984, in the Department of Communications Arts, University of Wisconsin-Madison

Meyer, Larry L.: "A Film for Safety's Sake", *Westways*, May 1965

Modern Packaging: "Character Heroes", September 1955

Montoya, Sarah: "Disney Redefined: Expurgation, Censorship, and Transcription", *The Secretary*, April 1971

Morrow, James: "In Defense of Disney", *Media and Methods*, April 1978

Movie Spotlight: "Inside ... Walt Disney's Studio", April 1953

Murray, John: "Mickey Mouse: A Brief Psychohistory", *Television & Children*, Summer 1983

Murphy, Robert: "Disney Animator, Ollie Johnston", *Animator*, Spring 1985

Murphy, Robert: "The Voice of Donald Duck", *Animator*, Summer 1985

National Geographic World: "A Cartoon Star is Born!", November 1977

Natwick, Grim: "Animation", *Cartoonist Profiles*, No. 40, December 1978

Natwick, Grim: "3 Men, 3 Hobbies", *Cartoonist Profiles*, No. 43, September 1979

Nelson, Thomas A.: "Darkness in the Disney Look", *Film Literature Quarterly*, Spring 1978

Neumeyer, Kathleen: "Return from Neverland: Can Disney Do it Again?", *Los Angeles Magazine*, November 1977

Newsweek: "Benchley in Disneyland: Flesh-and-Blood Tour of Studio Bares Pen-and-Ink Technique", June 30, 1941

Newsweek: "Money from Mice", February 13, 1950

New York Sunday Mirror: "The Fabulous Disney's Latest Double Play", May 29, 1955

Observer (London): review of *Basil – The Great Mouse Detective*, October 12, 1986

Palmer, Charles: "Cartoon in the Classroom", *Hollywood Quarterly*, Fall 1947

Paul, William: "Art, Music, Nature, and Walt Disney", *Movie*, Summer 1977

Pic: "Hatching an Ugly Duckling", April 4, 1939

Peachment, Chris: review of *Basil – The Great Mouse Detective*, *Time Out*, October 9, 1986

Plant, Richard R.: "Movies – of Disney", *Decision*, July 1941

Popular Mechanics: "Color-Shooting in Fairyland: Building the Story of *Pinocchio*", January 1940

Popular Science Monthly: "Mickey Mouse and Donald Duck Work for Victory", September 1942

Popular Science Monthly: "How Disney Combines Living Actors with his Cartoon Characters", September 1944

Reid, Robert: "Who's Afraid of the Big Bad Wolf?", *Author and Composer*, n.d.

Routh, Jonathan: "Alice in Disneyland",

Everybody's, July 21, 1957

Saba, Arn: "Mickey Mouse", *Weekend Magazine*, November 5, 1977

SAM: "Walt Was Really a Ducky Guy", July 1980

Scapperotti, Dan: "*The Black Cauldron*", *Cinéfantastique*, June/July 1983

Schickel, Richard: "Bringing Forth the Mouse", *American Heritage*, April 1968

Schickel, Richard: "The Films: No Longer for the Jung at Heart", *Time*, July 30, 1973

Schickel, Richard: "The Great Era of Walt Disney", *Time*, July 20, 1981

Schneider, Steven: "The Animated Alternative", *Art in America*, December 1981

Seale, Jim: "*The Fox and the Hound*", *On Location*, October 1980

Sendak, Maurice: "Growing Up With Mickey", *TV Guide*, November 11, 1978

Shannon, Leonard: "When Disney Met Dali – the Result Was a Film that Was Never Finished", *Modern Maturity*, December 1978/January 1979

Sherie, Fenn: "Poetry in Celluloid", *Pearson's Magazine*, July 1933

Shine, Bernard C.: "The Mouse that Really Roared", *The Antique Trader*, July 23, 1980

Sibley, Brian: "A Californian Yankee at the Court of Queen Alice", *Jabberwocky*, Summer 1973

Sibley, Brian: "Microscopes and Megaloscopes, or Alice in Pictures-that-move and Pictures-that-stand-still", unpublished address to the Lewis Carroll Society, November 8, 1974

Sibley, Brian: "The Enchanted Realms of Walt Disney", *The Movie* (partwork), Chapter 33, 1980

Sibley, Brian: letter in *The Listener*, February 23, 1984

Sibley, Brian: "Animation Stew from *The Black Cauldron*", *Animator*, Spring 1986

Sibley, Brian: "Walt Disney's *Pinocchio*, Animation Masterwork", *Animator*, Summer 1986

Sibley, Brian: "Great Mouse – Great Movie", *Animator*, Autumn 1986

Sidwell, Robert T.: "Naming Disney's Dwarfs", *Children's Literature in Education*, Summer 1980

Smith, David R.: "Ub Iwerks, 1901-1971: A Quiet Man Who Left a Deep Mark on Animation", *Funnyworld*, No. 14, Spring 1972

Smith, David R.: "Ben Sharpsteen ... 33 Years with Disney", *Millimeter*, April 1975

Smith, David R.: "'The Sorcerer's Apprentice', Birthplace of *Fantasia*", *Millimeter*, February 1976

Smith, David R.: "Up to Date in Kansas City, but Walt Disney Had Not Yet Gone as Far as He Could Go", *Funnyworld*, No. 19, Fall 1978

Smith, David R.: "From the Archives: *Lady and the Tramp*", *Disney Times*, April 1980

Smith, David R.: "Singing about *Song of the South*", *Disney Newsreel*, December 5, 1980

Smith, David R.: "Return of *The Aristocats*", *Disney Newsreel*, December 26, 1980

Smith, David R.: "Donald Duck, 'This is Your Life'", *Starlog*, July 1984

Solomon, Charles: "Disney Today", *SightLines*, Winter 1985/86

Strzyz, Klaus: "Jack Bradbury, a Written Interview", *Duckburg Times*, No. 19, September 30, 1983

Stuart, Alexander: "Decay of an American Dream", *Films and Filming*, November 1973

Stull, William: "Three Hundred Men – and Walt Disney", *American Cinematographer*, February 1938

Summer, Edward: "*Pinocchio* – an Appreciation", *Starlog*, January 1985

Sunday Times (London): review of *Basil – The Great Mouse Detective*, October 12, 1986

'Teen: "Disney on Parade", March 1970

Tempo: "The Mouse Who Made Millions", September 7, 1953

Tennessen, Michael: "It All Started with a Mouse", *Rainbow*, Spring 1979

Theisen, Earl: "What Makes Mickey Mouse Move", *Modern Mechanix*, April 1934

Theisen, Earl: "Sound Tricks of Mickey Mouse", *Modern Mechanix*, January 1937

Thomas, Frank, and Johnston, Ollie: "The Illusion of Life", *Stanford Magazine*, Summer 1982

Thompson, Helen G.: "Wanna Fight?", *Stage*, July 1935

Thompson, Helen G.: "Madame Cluck – Prima Donna", *Stage*, May 1936

Time: "Regulated Rodent", February 16, 1931

Time: "Disney Family", September 16, 1935

Time: "Mouse and Man", December 27, 1937

Time: "The Mad Cocktail Party", December 2, 1946

Time: "Battle of Wonderland", July 16, 1951

Time: "Father Goose", December 27, 1954

Time: "The Disney Fetish", August 9, 1971

Times (London): review of *Basil – The Great Mouse Detective*, October 10, 1986

Today (London): review of *Basil – The Great Mouse Detective*, October 12, 1986

TV Fan: "This is Our Life, by Mickey Mouse", June 1955

Wagner, Dave: "Donald Duck: An Interview", *Radical America*, No. 7, 1973

Wallace, Irving: "Mickey Mouse and How He Grew", *Collier's*, April 9, 1949

Wasserman, Norman: "Special Projection Process Gives *Fantasia* New Look", *International Projectionist*, March 1956

Wells, John: "Mickey Mouse – the Rumours", *Punch*, December 16, 1970

Westwood, Peter: "Walt Disney: He Really Met Mickey Mouse", *The Outspan*, August 22, 1952

Whitcomb, Jon: "Girls Behind Disney's Characters", *Cosmopolitan*, May 1954

White, Robert P.: "Who's Afraid of the Big Bad –", *Redbook*, March 1950

Wiley, Kurt: "Marc Davis' Women", *Graffiti*, February 1982

Willett, Bob: "It All Started with Mickey", *New Liberty*, May 1953

Wolfe, Bernard: "Much Ado About Mickey Mouse", *Book World*, April 28, 1968

Wunderlich, Richard, and Morrissey, Thomas J.: "The Desecration of *Pinocchio* in the United States", paper presented at the Annual Conference of the Children's Literature Association, 1981

Zolotow, Maurice: "Unforgettable Donald Duck", *Reader's Digest*, May 1984

Most of the original books on which the animated features were based are available in divers editions and are easily obtainable. Also of interest in this context are some of Disney's own books based on the features; the Disney Family Classics series based on the features and published by Collins (London); and many of the "Storyteller" cassettes or records released by Disneyland/Buena Vista Records.

BIBLIOGRAPHY TO THE SECOND EDITION

Books

Canemaker, John: *The Animated Raggedy Ann & Andy*, New York, Bobbs-Merrill, 1977

Holliss, Richard, and Sibley, Brian: *The Disney Studio Story*, London, Octopus, 1988; New York, Crown, 1988

Holliss, Richard, and Sibley, Brian: *Walt Disney's "Snow White and the Seven Dwarfs" and the Making of the Classic Film*, New York, Simon & Schuster, 1987

Thomas, Bob: *Disney's Art of Animation: From Mickey Mouse to Beauty and the Beast*, New York, Hyperion, 1991

Articles, Reviews, Essays, Theses, Papers, Pamphlets

Anderson, Brad: " 'Oliver' Provides Good Holiday Fare", *Burbank Leader*, November 23, 1988

Ansen, David: "Cats and Dogs and Dinosaurs", *Newsweek*, November 28, 1988

Ansen, David: "A Hot Time in Toontown Tonight", *Newsweek*, June 27, 1988

Bleiler, Everett: "Dime-Novel SF", in Clute, John, and Nicholls, Peter (eds.), *The Encyclopedia of Science Fiction*, London, Little, Brown & Co. 1993

Byrge, Duane: " 'The Prince and the Pauper' ", *Hollywood Reporter*, November 16, 1990

Byrge, Duane: " 'The Rescuers Down Under' ", *Hollywood Reporter*, November 16, 1990

Byrge, Duane: " 'Who Framed Roger Rabbit' ", *Hollywood Reporter*, June 20, 1988

Cedrone, Lou: "TV Veteran's Voice Used in 'Mermaid' ", *Contra Costa Times*, December 8, 1989

Cleave, Alan: "Animator Extraordinary", *Movie Maker*, December 1975

Corliss, Richard: "Creatures of a Subhuman Species", *Time*, June 27, 1988

Corliss, Richard: "What the Dickens!", *Time*, November 28, 1988

Culhane, John: " 'Oliver & Company' Gives Dickens a Disney Twist", *New York Times*, November 13, 1988

Davis, Brian: "Animated Conversations", *Campaign*, June 18, 1976

Denby, David: "Sea of Love", *New York*, December 4, 1989

Ebert, Roger: "Jolly 'Little Mermaid' Will Delight Everyone", *Chicago Sun-Times*, November 17, 1989

Emerson, Jim: " 'I'm a Cartoon Character!' ", *Orange County Register*, November 17, 1989

Emerson, Jim: " 'Rescuers Down Under' Takes High Road Over the Top", *Orange County Register*, November 16, 1990

Eng, Monica: " 'DuckTales' Does Little for Disney Reputation", *Chicago Sun-Times*, August 3, 1990

Fleming, Charles: "Animation Is Disney's Heart and Soul", *Los Angeles Herald Examiner*, November 18, 1988

Foote, Donna: "Roger and Co.'s Master Draftsman", *Newsweek*, June 27, 1988

Garrett, Robert: " 'DuckTales' Isn't What It's Quacked Up to Be", *Boston Globe*, August 3, 1990

Givens, Bill: " 'The Rescuers Down Under' ", *Animation Magazine*, Fall 1990

Granville, Kari: "Without Him, Sebastian Would Be Speechless", *Los Angeles Times*, December 23, 1989

Grove, Martin A.: " 'Mermaid' Movie" (in "Hollywood Report" column), *Hollywood Reporter*, November 8, 1989

Harmetz, Aljean: "Behind Disney's Fairy-Tale Triumph", *New York Times*, December 11, 1989

Healy, Michael: "Despite a Few Bugs in 'Roger,' What's Up Is Ingenuity", *Los Angeles Daily News*, June 22, 1988

Hinman, Catherine: "Florida Animation Team Lends Hand to 'Rescuers' ", *Orlando Sentinel*, November 19, 1990

Holden, Stephen: "How 'Shop' Writers Scored 'Mermaid' ", *Chicago Tribune*, December 28, 1989

Klein, Andy: "Who Sketched Roger Rabbit", *Los Angeles Herald Examiner*, June 24, 1988

Laycock, John: "The Pen Is Mightier than the Camera", *Windsor Star*, May 31, 1975

Leydon, Joe: " 'DuckTales' Fun for Kids of All Ages", *Houston Post*, August 3, 1990

Maltin, Leonard: "Advancing Backward, with

Animation", *Print: America's Graphic Design Magazine*, March/April 1977

Masin, Janet: "Andersen's 'Mermaid', by Way of Disney", *New York Times*, November 15, 1989

Maslin, Janet: "In Today's Animation, It's Dog Eat Doggie", *New York Times*, November 27, 1988

Maslin, Janet: "Mickey's a Prince, and Rescuers Go Walkerabout", *New York Times*, November 16, 1990

Maslin, Janet: "Wacky Laws of Gravity and Humor in 'Rabbit' ", *New York Times*, June 22, 1988

Masion, Tony: "The 17-Year Quest that Has Haunted the World's Top Animator", *Campaign*, July 6, 1984

Meisler, Andy: "The Woman Behind the Little Mermaid", *Wall Street Journal*, November 19, 1990

Mills, Bart: "What the Dickens, *Marquee*, December 10, 1988

Pearson, Dan: " "DuckTales: The Movie' Lacks Staying Power', *Southtown Economist*, August 3, 1990

Richardson, John H.: "Actor Hoskins Was Left Seeing Co-Stars", *Los Angeles Daily News*, June 22, 1988

Reese, Micheal: "The Making of Roger Rabbit", *Newsweek*, June 27, 1988

Ridgeway, Karen: ". . . and That Beneath-the-Sea Voice", *USA Today*, November 30, 1989

Rouilard, Richard: " 'Rabbit' Bites the Big Apple", *Los Angeles Herald Examiner*, June 23, 1988

Salamon, Julie: "Ho-Ho-Hum's the Word", *Wall Street Journal*, November 23, 1988

Salamon, Julie: " 'Who Framed Roger Rabbit' ", *Wall Street Journal*, June 23, 1988

Sanz, Cynthia: "Those Faces! Those Voices!" *People*, December 11, 1989

Scheib, Ronnie: "Tex Arcana: The Cartoons of Tex Avery", in Peary, Danny, and Peary, Gerald (eds.): *The American Animated Cartoon: A Critical Anthology*, New York, Dutton 1980

Sheehan, Henry: "Computer Comes to the *Rescuers*", *Los Angeles Reader*, November 16, 1990

Sheehan, Henry: " 'The Little Mermaid' ", *Hollywood Reporter*, November 8, 1989

Sibley, Brian: "Fine Art Babbitt", *Animator*, October/December 1987

Solomon, Charles: "Cheech Marin As Animated Tito: Check It Out", *Los Angeles Times*, December 27, 1988

Solomond, Charles: "Fantasy, Animation Soar in 'Rescuers Down Under' ", *Los Angeles Times*, November 16, 1990

Solomon, Charles: "Live Action and Animation Join Forces with Human Genius and High Tech", *Los Angeles Times*, June 22, 1988

Solomon, Charles: " 'Oliver & Company' ", *Los Angeles Times*, November 18, 1988

Spillman, Susan: "Creating a 'Mermaid': The Body", *USA Today*, November 30, 1989

Spillman, Susan: ""Spielberg, Disney Work' Toon Magic", *USA Today*, June 20, 1988

Stark, Susan: " 'DuckTales': A Tiny Feather in Disney's Cap", *Detroit News*, August 3, 1990

Sterritt, David: "Disney Goes Back to Its Roots", *Christian Science Monitor*, September 27, 1989

Strauss, Bob: " 'DuckTales: The Movie' Xenophobic Waddle to Silliness", *Los Angeles Daily News*, August 3, 1990

Tucker, Ernest: " 'Oliver & Company' Launches New Goal for Disney Studios", *Chicago Sun-Times*, December 2, 1988

Updike, John: "Mickey Takes", *Observer Magazine*, February 16, 1992 (extracted from Yoe, Craig, and Morra-Yoe, Janet: *The Art of Mickey Mouse*, New York, Hyperion, 1991)

Van Gelder, Lawrence: "His Rabbit's Voice" (in "At the Movies" column), *New York Times*, June 24, 1988

Williams, Jeannie: "Jessica Rabbit's Frame", *USA Today*, June 23, 1988

Wilmington, Michael: " 'Little Mermaid' Makes a Splash", *Los Angeles Times*, November 15, 198

BIBLIOGRAPHY TO THE THIRD EDITION

Clute, John, and Grant, John (editors): *The Encyclopedia of Fantasy*, London, Orbit, 1997

Cotter, Bill: *The Wonderful World of Disney Television*, New York, Hyperion, 1997

Culhane, John: *Disney's Aladdin: The Making of an Animated Film*, New York, Hyperion, 1992

Finch, Christopher: *The Art of The Lion King*, New York, Hyperion, 1994

Jones, Diana Wynne: *The Tough Guide to Fantasyland*, London, Vista, 1996

Lasseter, John, and Daly, Steve: *Toy Story: The Art and Making of the Animated Film*, New York, Hyperion, 1995

Lenburg, Jeff: *The Encyclopedia of Animated Cartoons*, New York & Oxford, Facts on File, 1991

Linguist, Lynne, and Westfahl, Gary: "Coming of Age in Fantasyland: The Self-Parenting Child in Walt Disney Animated Films," 1997 (received in manuscript)

Rebello, Stephen: *The Art of Pocahontas*, New York, Hyperion, 1995

Rebello, Stephen: *The Art of Hunchback of Notre Dame*, New York, Hyperion, 1996

Rebello, Stephen: *The Art of Hercules: The Chaos of Creation*, New York, Hyperion, 1997

Smith, Dave: *Disney A to Z: The Official Encyclopedia*, New York, Hyperion, 1996

Smith, James Earl (III): *The Evolving Forms of Humor in the Donald Duck Cartoons* (thesis), Grand Forks, University of North Dakota, 1994

Taral: "The Lyin' King," *Attitude*, 1996

Thomas, Bob: *Disney's Art of Animation: From Mickey Mouse to Hercules* (revised edition of Thomas's earlier books), New York, Hyperion, 1997

Thompson, Frank: *Tim Burton's The Nightmare Before Christmas*, New York, Hyperion, 1993

ACKNOWLEDGMENTS – FIRST EDITION

This book could not have been brought into existence without the active and enthusiastic participation of the personnel of the Disney Archives at Burbank, who not only guided my footsteps in the research stages but also viewed my typescript and made numerous factual corrections as well as significant critical contributions. My most deeply felt thanks, therefore, to David R. Smith, Paula Sigman, Rose Motzko and Karen Brower.

Other members of the Walt Disney company have given sterling help. Brett Mattinson has been largely responsible for selecting the illustrations – not an easy job. David Cleghorn kindly sent me a stack of records and cassettes derived from the soundtracks of the features: these provided to be invaluable in stirring my recalcitrant memory.

Lydia Darbyshire, of the Justin Knowles Publishing Group, has significantly improved this book by dint of her editorial acumen – eagerly spotting *le mot injuste* – as well as through her constant encouragement during the long and not always easy process of the book's writing. Praise of her cannot be too high. Justin Knowles himself was likewise generous with encouragement, without which this book might never have got off the ground. My thanks also to Hazel Bell for compiling the index.

This book was developed by Charlotte Parry-Crooke. My thanks to her go without saying, but should be said anyway.

During my sojourn in Burbank, a number of people were generous with their friendship to a stranger in a strange land. Although its difficult to quantify the effects of such help, I am convinced that this book has benefited from that friendship. So sincere thanks to Lucille Appleman, Kanthi and David Barry, and John and Theresa of "The Dip".

This book was written on an Amstrad PCW8256 and typeset from the discs produced by that machine. The Index Film Titles was executed with the help of Ansible's AIX.COM program.

Finally, let me express my gratitude to Jane and Catherine Barnett, who have provided invaluable support. As always , this book is $4\pi+0$.

John Grant
Spring 1987

ACKNOWLEDGMENTS – SECOND EDITION

As before, this book could not have been written without the very considerable help of the personnel in the Walt Disney Archives: David R. Smith, Robert Tieman, Rose Motzko and Jennifer Henderickson. That they should be so unflaggingly helpful is one thing: they have also been consistently enthusiatic and friendly, and have thereby made what is perhaps an even greater contribution.

At Hyperion I've had the help and sympathetic ear of Martha Kaplan, my editor, who has exercised sterling patience in dealing with the waywardness of both her author and transatlantic telephone lines. Thanks, boss.

In the early stages of my work on this book I was given great help and encouragement by Justin Knowles, whose vision brought the first edition into being, and by Peter Wrigley, Sarah Stott, Ron Tiner and John Youé. My agent, Jane Judd, was a calming voice in times of stress, as were Kim Munro and Lydia Darbyshire.

I am especially grateful to those who spotted errors in and omissions from the first edition, and who took the time to communicate their knowledge to me: Rodolfo Otero, Russell Schroeder, William Silvester, James Smith III, Tony Specian and Norman Stewart. Three erudite Disney fans have been of invaluable help, especially for the television section, and have also generously given me large doses of their own unquenchable enthusiasm: Christopher Barat, Alberto Becattini and Joe Torcivia.

My acknowledgments would be incomplete were I not to express my considerable thanks for *being* to Jane Barnett, Catherine Barnett and Fionna O'Sullivan.

John Grant
Spring 1992

ACKNOWLEDGMENTS – THIRD EDITION

Various friendly editors at Hyperion have worked with me on this book, and my sincere thanks are due to them: Robin Friedman, Monique Peterson, and Sara Surrey. Bill Cotter was very helpful on the television front. Sue Langabeer of the Disneyana club Magical Moments & Memories (mmm@eclipse.co.uk) gave me invaluable assistance (and a much-prized Disneyland watch); the club's magazine is unfailingly useful. John Dallman of the magazine *Attitude* helped me on a tricky point; Taral Wayne allowed me to quote from his article in that magazine. Dave Smith of the Walt Disney Archives was as ever incredibly supportive: this book could not have been written without the generosity of Dave and his colleagues Rebecca Cline, Collette Espino, Adina Lerner, and Robert Tieman. Shelley Graham, Andrea Recendez, and Ed Squair of the Photo Library made a very obvious contribution. I also got help and good fellowship from George Kurten, Lynne Lundequist, Russell Schroeder, and Gary Westfahl. Daughters Jane and Fionna were their much-loved selves and supported my effort in divers ways. My wife Catherine must also be thanked—as always.

John Grant
Spring 1998

INDEX OF ANIMATED DISNEY FILMS
incorporating Filmography

General Index